Tuscany
& Umbria

THE ROUGH GUIDE

There are more than sixty Rough Guide titles covering
destinations from Amsterdam to Zimbabwe

Forthcoming titles include
Bali • Costa Rica • Mallorca • Rhodes • West Africa

Rough Guide Reference Series
Classical Music • World Music

Rough Guide Phrasebooks
Czech • French • German • Greek • Italian • Spanish

Rough Guide credits

Text editor:	Jonathan Buckley
Series editor:	Mark Ellingham
Editorial:	Martin Dunford, Samantha Cook, Jo Mead, Alison Cowan, Amanda Tomlin, Annie Shaw, Lemisse al-Hafidh, Catherine McHale
Production:	Susanne Hillen, Andy Hilliard, Melissa Flack, Alan Spicer, Judy Pang, Link Hall, Nicola Williamson
Finance:	John Fisher, Celia Crowley, Simon Carloss
Publicity:	Richard Trillo (UK) Jean-Marie Kelly & Jeff Kaye (US)

Thanks

The authors would like to thank Eliane Reggiori and Pierluigi, Marella Caracciolo, Andrew Gumble, Patrick Clare, Michael Sheridan, Jane Lambert, Fiona Norden, Natania Jansz, Barbara Ellingham, Giovanna Iannaco, Mark Thompson, Susan Madocks, Letizia and Jacopo Volpi. Thanks also to Matt Welton for work on the maps, to Sally Roy, Andy Hilliard and Margo Daly, and especially to **Justine Scott-McCarthy**, **Paul Gray** and **Brenda Keatley**.

This second edition published 1994 by Rough Guides Ltd, 1 Mercer Street, London WC2H 9QJ. Reprinted July 1994 and September 1995.
Distributed by The Penguin Group:

Penguin Books Ltd, 27 Wrights Lane, London W8 5TZ
Penguin Books USA Inc., 375 Hudson Street, New York 10014, USA
Penguin Books Australia Ltd, 487 Maroondah Highway, PO Box 257, Ringwood, Victoria 3134, Australia
Penguin Books Canada Ltd, 10 Alcorn Avenue, Toronto, Ontario, Canada M4V 1E4
Penguin Books (NZ) Ltd, 182–190 Wairau Road, Auckland 10, New Zealand

Previous edition published 1991 by Harrap Columbus Ltd.
Rough Guides were formerly published as Real Guides in the United States and Canada.

Typeset in Linotron Univers and Century Old Style to an original design by Andrew Oliver.
Printed in the UK by Cox & Wyman, Reading, Berks.

Illustrations in Part One and Part Four by Edward Briant
Basics and Contexts illustrations by Henry Iles.

608pp.
Includes index.

A catalogue record for this book is available from the British Library

ISBN 1-85828-091-5

Tuscany
& Umbria

THE ROUGH GUIDE

Written and researched by

Jonathan Buckley, Tim Jepson
and Mark Ellingham

THE ROUGH GUIDES

MAPS, PLANS & CHARTS

CONTENTS

Introduction viii

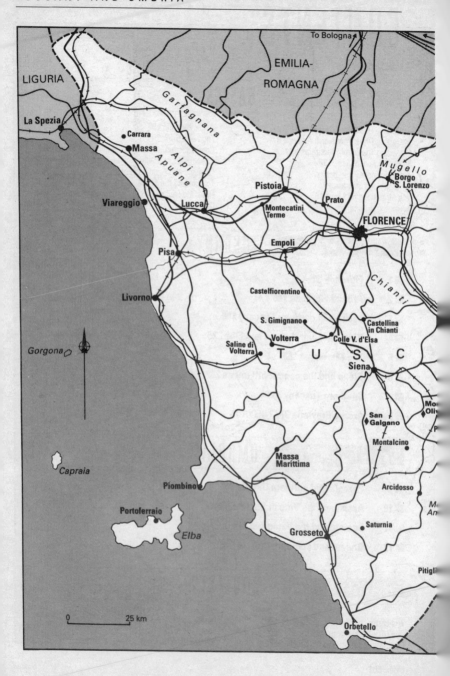

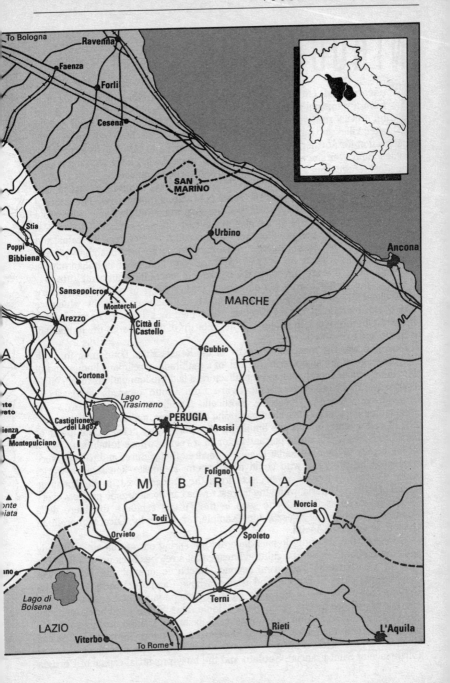

INTRODUCTION

Tuscany and Umbria harbour the classic landscapes of Italy, familiar from a thousand Renaissance paintings, with their backdrop of medieval hill towns, rows of cypress trees, vineyards and olive groves, and artfully sited villas and farmhouses. It's a stereotype that has long held an irresistible attraction for northern Europeans. Shelley referred to Tuscany as a "paradise of exiles", and ever since his time the English, in particular, have seen the region as an ideal refuge from a sun-starved and overcrowded homeland.

The expatriate's perspective may be distorted, but the central provinces – and especially Tuscany – are indeed the essence of Italy in many ways. The national language evolved from Tuscan dialect, a supremacy ensured by Dante, who wrote the *Divine Comedy* in the vernacular of his birthplace, Florence. Other great Tuscan writers of the period – Petrarch and Boccaccio – reinforced its status, and in the last century Manzoni came to Tuscany to purge his vocabulary of any impurities while working on *The Betrothed*, the most famous of all Italian novels. But what makes this area pivotal to the culture not just of Italy but of all Europe is of course the **Renaissance** period, whose masterpieces of painting, sculpture and architecture are an intrinsic part of any tour. The very name by which we refer to this extraordinarily creative era was coined by a Tuscan, Giorgio Vasari, who wrote in the sixteenth century of the "rebirth" of the arts with the humanism of Giotto and his successors.

Florence was the most active centre of the Renaissance, flourishing through the patronage of the all-powerful Medici, of a multitude of religious bodies and of the guilds, whose merchants and manufacturers laid the foundations of the city's prosperity. Every eminent artistic figure from Giotto onwards – Masaccio, Brunelleschi, Alberti, Donatello, Botticelli, Leonardo, Michelangelo – is represented here, in an unrivalled gathering of churches, galleries and museums.

If Florence tends to take the limelight, however, rivalry between the towns of both provinces – still an important factor in a region whose inhabitants feel a strong loyalty to their particular locality – ensured that pictures and palaces were sponsored by everyone who could afford them. Exquisite Renaissance works adorn almost every place of any size from the Tuscan coast to the Apennine slopes of eastern Umbria, while the largest towns can boast artistic projects every bit as ambitious as those to be seen in the Tuscan capital – the Piero della Francesca frescoes in **Arezzo**, for example, or those by Luca Signorelli in **Orvieto** or Giotto in **Assisi**.

Moreover, the art of the Renaissance did not spring out of thin air – Tuscany and Umbria both can boast a cultural lineage that stretches back unbroken to the time of Charlemagne and even beyond. **Lucca** is one of the handsomest Romanesque cities in Europe, and **Pisa** – whose Campo dei Miracoli, with its Leaning Tower, is one of Europe's most brilliant monumental ensembles – is another city whose heyday came in the Middle Ages. **Siena**'s red brick medieval cityscape, arranged around its fabulous scallop-shaped Campo, makes a refreshing contrast with the darker tones of Florence, while a tour through Umbria can seem like a procession of magnificent ancient hill towns. The attractions of **Assisi** (birthplace of Saint Francis), **Spoleto** and the busy provincial capital of **Perugia** are hardly secrets, but other Umbrian towns remain more obscure – such as **Gubbio** and the backwater delights of **Bevagna** and **Todi**. Many of the Umbrian towns retain a fair showing of their ancient past, too, with Etruscan and Roman walls and tombs to be seen on sites left undisturbed for centuries.

Even though the percentage of the population who make their living from the land has plummeted since the last war – in Umbria the figure fell from nearly sixty percent in 1950 to just over ten percent in 1980 – both Tuscany and Umbria are predominantly **rural** provinces. Just as the hill towns mould themselves to the summits, the terraces of vines follow the lower contours of the hills and open fields spread across the broader valleys, forming a distinctive balance between the natural and human world. The towns may have grown and industrial estates may have blocked in some of the outskirts, but great tracts of land still look much as they did half a millennium ago.

The variety of **landscape** within this comparatively small area is astounding. A short distance from central Florence spread the thickly wooded uplands of the **Mugello** and the **Casentino**, much of the latter still maintained by the monasteries to which the forests were entrusted hundreds of years ago. Lucca is a springboard for the **Alpi Apuane**, whose mountain quarries have supplied Europe's masons with pure white marble for centuries. Along the Tuscan shoreline the resorts are interspersed by some of Italy's best-kept wildlife reserves, including the fabulous **Monti Uccellina**, the last stretch of virgin coast in the whole country. Out in the **Tuscan archipelago**, the island of **Giglio** is unspoilt by the sort of tourist development that has infiltrated – though certainly not ruined – nearby **Elba**. The pastoral archetype is perhaps most strikingly subverted in the **deep south** of the province, where the agricultural hinterland of Siena soon gives way to the bleak *crete* and the sulphurous pools of Saturnia.

Landlocked Umbria may not be as varied as its neighbour, but the wild heights of the **Valnerina**, the **Piano Grande**'s prairie-like expanse and the savage peaks of the **Monti Sibillini** all contrast with the tranquil, soft-contoured hills with which the region is most often associated. In **Lago Trasimeno** the province has the largest body of water on the Italian peninsula, while in the south there's the **Cascate delle Marmore**, a spectacular if sporadic waterfall.

When to go

Midsummer in central Italy is not as pleasant an experience as you might imagine: the heat can be stifling, and from May to September you'll require luck to find accommodation in all but the most out-of-the-way spots. If at all possible, the month to **avoid** is **August**, when the great majority of Italians take their holidays. As a result many town restaurants and some hotels are closed for the entire month and the beaches are jammed solid. As the standard Italian idea of an enjoyable summer break is to spend a few weeks towel-to-towel on the sand, Umbria escapes the worst of the rush, but the problem of limited opening remains.

Florence throughout the summer is such a log jam of tour groups that the major attractions become a purgatorial experience – a two-hour queue for the Uffizi is not unusual. To enjoy a visit fully, go there shortly **before Easter** or in the **late autumn** – times of the year that are the best for Tuscany and Umbria as a whole, as the towns are quieter and the countryside is blossoming or taking on the tones of the harvest season. The Umbrian climate is slightly more extreme than Tuscany's, chiefly because of its distance from the sea; temperatures in summer are fractionally higher, while the hilltop locales of many towns can make them surprisingly windy and cool at other times. Winter is often quite rainy, but the absence of crowds makes this a good option for the cities on the major art trails. Bear in mind, however, that the high altitudes of much of the region means many roads are impassable in midwinter, and in places like the upper Casentino or the Sibillini the snow might not melt until March or even April.

Festivals

It's always worth checking when each town has its **festivals** or pilgrimages. Accommodation is always tricky during these mini peak seasons, but some of the festivities are enjoyable enough to merit planning a trip around. Many have been crucial to their town's image for centuries – the most celebrated of these being the Siena **Palio**, a hell-for-leather horse race round the central square. The frenzy of Gubbio's semi-pagan **Corsa dei Ceri** almost matches it, as does the passionate commitment of Florence's **Calcio Storico**, a football match in medieval attire with no holds barred. Costumed **jousts** and other martial displays are a feature of several festive calendars, notable examples being the jousts in Pistoia and Arezzo, and the twice-yearly **crossbow competitions** between Gubbio and Sansepolcro. **Holy days** and **saint's days** bring in the crowds in equal numbers, with Assisi leading the way as the most venerated site.

Among the innumerable **arts festivals**, the highest profiles are achieved by the contemporary arts extravaganza in Spoleto, the *Umbria Jazz* festival in Perugia and the *Maggio Musicale* in more conservative Florence – but as with the more folkloric events, even the smallest towns have their cultural *stagione*. Finally, there's scarcely a hamlet in Tuscany or Umbria that doesn't have a **food** or **wine** festival, the region seeming to find an excuse to celebrate almost every thing that breathes or grows. Appealing mainly to the local population and often lasting for just a day, these events place less stress on the hotels, though it might be a good idea to book a room if you're dropping by – fountains running with wine and other such excesses are pretty common.

AVERAGE TEMPERATURES AND RAINFALL					
		Florence	Livorno	Siena	Perugia
January	°C	6	9	5	5
	°F	42	47	40	40
	mm	62	70	70	70
	inches	3	3	3	3
April	°C	13	15	12	11
	°F	55	59	54	52
	mm	70	62	62	70
	inches	3	3	3	3
July	°C	25	24	25	24
	°F	77	75	77	75
	mm	23	6	20	30
	inches	1	0	1	1
October	°C	16	15	15	13
	°F	60	59	59	55
	mm	96	110	110	115
	inches	4	4	4	4

PART ONE

THE

BASICS

GETTING THERE FROM BRITAIN AND IRELAND

The easiest way to get to Tuscany and Umbria from Britain is to fly, and prices for charters compare well with those for the long rail journey. Fares inevitably fluctuate with the seasons – Easter and June to September are the peak times – but there are often special offers to be picked up at short notice at any time of year. The main destinations are Pisa and Bologna, though Florence's small Perètola airport is taking increasingly heavy traffic at competitive prices. There are plans to upgrade Perugia's tiny runway to accommodate international flights, too, but at the moment it receives only internal services from Milan.

BY PLANE FROM BRITAIN

The main airlines operating **scheduled flights** to central Italy are *British Airways* and *Alitalia*, who both fly direct from **London Heathrow to Pisa** (total of 2 flights daily), **Bologna** (2 daily) and **Rome** (6–7 daily). *British Airways* also fly from Heathrow to **Genoa** five times a week and from **Manchester to Rome** once a week. *Air UK* fly once daily from London **Stansted** and *Meridiana* fly once daily from Gatwick to the tiny Perètola airport on the outskirts of **Florence**, at the moment the only scheduled services from the UK to use this airstrip.

The cheapest *British Airways* or *Alitalia* ticket is an **Apex** return fare, which to Pisa costs £220 in low season and £280 at the midsummer peak; fares to the other central Italian cities should be

within £20 of this. The *Air UK/Meridiana* Apex fare to Florence costs from around £159, rising to £223 (*Meridiana*) and £253 (*Air UK*) in high season. Restrictions on Apex tickets are that you must book a minimum of fourteen days in advance, you must stay a Saturday night abroad, and there are no refunds.

Direct charter flights are a better bargain, though you'd be well advised to book some weeks in advance in peak season. *Sky Bus* and *Italy Sky Shuttle* (see below for addresses) offer frequent summer departures from London to the major central Italian destinations, with current prices working out at around £180 to Pisa during June, falling by about £20 off-season; you can cut their fares by about ten percent by booking at least three months in advance.

You can sometimes get flights even cheaper than this by going to a specialist **agent** – last summer's bargains were from about £100 return to Pisa. There are dozens of sources. Look in the classified sections in the Sunday newspapers – the *Sunday Times* especially – and, if you live in London, *Time Out* magazine and the *Evening Standard*. Or contact one of the big youth/student travel specialists like *STA Travel* or *Campus Travel*, good for cheap deals if you're under 26 or a student. There are also a number of specialist Italian agents (addresses below), who will normally have a range of fares.

Most agents offer **"open-jaw"** deals, whereby you can fly into one Italian city and back from another – a good idea if you want to make your way across the country, and generally no more expensive than a standard charter return. Consider also a **package deal** (see below), which takes care of flights and accommodation for an all-in price. Package operators can also be a source of cheap one-off flights.

AIRLINES IN BRITAIN

Air UK, Stansted Airport, Essex (☎0345/666 777).

Alitalia, 27 Piccadilly, London W1 (☎071/602 7111).

British Airways, 75 Regent St, London W1 (☎081/897 4000).

Meridiana, 15 Charles II Street, London SW1 (☎071/839 2222).

FLIGHT AGENTS IN BRITAIN

Campus Travel, 52 Grosvenor Gardens, London SW1 (☎071/730 3402). Also with branches in Bristol, Cambridge, Oxford and Edinburgh.

Council Travel, 28a Poland St, London W1 (☎071/287 3377).

CTS Travel, 44 Goodge St, London W1 (☎071/637 5601).

Flight File, 49 Tottenham Court Rd, London W1 (☎071/323 1515).

Italflights, 125 High Holborn, London WC1 (☎071/405 6771).

Italia nel Mondo, 6 Palace St, London SW1 (☎071/834 7651).

Italone, 200 Tottenham Court Rd, London W1 (☎071/637 1284).

Inter-Air, Liberty House, 222 Regent St, London W1 (☎071/439 6633).

Mundus Air Travel, 5 Peter St, London W1 (☎071/437 2272).

Nouvelles Frontières, 11 Blenheim St, London W1 (☎071/629 7772).

Orion, 320 Regent St, London W1 (☎071/580 8267).

Questultra, 243 Euston Rd, London NW1 (☎071/387 6122).

STA Travel, 86 Old Brompton Rd, London SW7; 117 Euston Rd, London NW1 (☎071/937 9921). Also with branches in Bristol, Cambridge, Oxford and Manchester.

CHARTER COMPANIES IN BRITAIN

Italy Skybus, 24 Earls Court Gardens, London SW5 (☎071/373 6055).

Italy Sky Shuttle, 227 Shepherds Bush Rd, London W6 (☎081/748 1333).

LAI, 185 Kings Cross Rd, London WC1 (☎071/837 8492).

BY TRAIN

Travelling by **train** to Italy won't save much money: an ordinary **return fare to Florence** on the route via Switzerland currently costs £207; the route via Paris, southern France and Pisa costs £174 and takes slightly longer. If you're **under 26**, you can get a slightly discounted *Explorer* ticket from *Eurotrain* (address below), or a *BIJ* ticket from student and youth agents and some high street travel agents; these tickets are valid for up to two months and give as many stop-overs as you like. The fare to Florence is currently £191 return via Switzerland, or £172 by the other route. You can also arrange connecting fares at a discount from outside London, or – if you prefer – qualify for reduced price tickets if you join the train at the Channel ports.

All in all, if you are planning a trip through Europe, and travelling around Italy once you're there, it might be a better idea to invest in an **InterRail** pass. If you're **under 26**, this costs £249 for one month's unlimited rail travel throughout Europe, and gives discounts on cross-Channel services and some ferry routes in Europe; the 15-day version costs £179. The pass for **over-26s** costs £269 for a month and £209 for 15 days. Once in Italy, the rail system is comprehensive and efficient, and much the best way of getting around the country (see p.17). *InterRail* passes are available from British Rail stations and youth/student travel agents; to qualify, you need to have been resident in Europe for at least six months.

Whichever method you plump for, it's well worth **reserving** a **seat** (currently £3) or **couchette bed** (around £10) for your trip to Italy – something you should do well in advance in season.

RAIL TICKET OFFICES

British Rail European Travel Centre, Victoria Station, London SW1 (☎071/834 2345).

Eurotrain, 52 Grosvenor Gardens, London SW1 (☎071/730 3402).

BY ROAD

It's difficult to see why anyone would want to travel to Italy by **coach**. But if you do have a phobia about trains and planes, there are direct services to Florence, taking a gruelling 32 hours and costing around £130, with small reductions for under-26s and students. Run by *National Express Eurolines* (☎071/730 0202), coaches leave once weekly in winter (Sat) and three times weekly in summer from London's Victoria Coach Station.

Drivers can make use of **ferry/hovercraft** links between Dover and Calais or Boulogne (with *Hoverspeed*, *P&O* or *Sealink*), Folkestone and Boulogne (*Sealink*) or Ramsgate and Dunkerque (*Sally Lines*). The fare structures are bewilderingly complex, with countless variations according to date of crossing, time of crossing, season and size of vehicle, but as an indication of cost, a one-way ticket for a small car with two passengers would cost £90–130, with a return ticket costing twice that.

Once across, you have a number of different route options. From northern France, the **Alpine route**, via Germany and Switzerland, is probably the shortest as the crow flies, but can be pretty arduous; most drivers hotfoot it **via the south of France** and then switch east into northern Italy. The former route is a preferable option for **hitchers** – getting rides south is notoriously difficult from the Channel ports and Paris. Members of the *RAC* or *AA* can obtain free advice on the quickest routes across the continent for any given week – the service is available to non-members for a small fee.

After numerous delays, the **Channel Tunnel** is scheduled to open in the early summer of 1994. Coaches, cars and motorbikes will be loaded onto a freight train known wittily as Le Shuttle, which will take 35 minutes to get between the loading terminals at Folkestone and Calais. Le Shuttle is planned to run every fifteen minutes at peak periods, hourly at the quietest times of the day, and each Shuttle will carry 180 cars or 120 cars plus twelve coaches. For foot passengers there will be frequent through trains between London and various major European cities, operated by British Rail and the French and Belgian rail companies. The tariffs are pretty well identical with those charged by the ferry companies – for information on fares, call ☎0303/271100.

PACKAGES AND ORGANIZED TOURS

Italy stands somewhat apart from other European package destinations: it's not especially cheap and is as much a venue for specialist interest and touring holidays as sun-sand-sea packages. Tuscany and, to a growing extent, Umbria, are prime destinations in most "specialist" Italian programmes, and – a definite plus – most of these holidays are sold by small, independently run travel companies. Holidays on the market mostly fall into one of the following categories:

● **Flight-plus-hotel**. These deals can be excellent value if you want to base yourself in one (or two) places, usually featuring a good three-star hotel. All-in prices for a week's bed and breakfast in Florence, for example, start at around £450 per person per week, rising by about £50 in high season. Prices are slightly lower for stays in some of the provincial towns, like Siena and Assisi.

● **Villas and farmhouses**. Numerous companies offer villa or farmhouse accommodation in rural Tuscany and Umbria; charter flights, ferry crossings or fly-drives are usually available as part of a package deal, but it's generally possible to book just the house if that's what you prefer. Always book well in advance for the summer season – this is one of the boom areas of Italian tourism. For the accomodation part, reckon on paying upwards of £150 per person per week – the shortest bookable period – for an average four-bedded Tuscan farmhouse, perhaps less in Umbria. Rental prices usually include insurance, water and electricity, and sometimes linen and maid service in the posher places. Be warned, though, that Italian villa companies are notorious for their added "extras", so read the small print. It's also worth checking that the swimmng pool attached to the villa is for your sole use – the "shared pool" scam is very common.

● **Specialist holidays**. Several operators offer walking tours, art and archaeology holidays, food and wine jaunts. Most of them don't come cheap: accommodation, food, local transport and the services of a guide are nearly always included, and a week's half-board holiday can cost anything up to £1000 per person.

CROSS-CHANNEL FERRIES

Hoverspeed, Maybrook House, Queens Gardens, Dover CT17 9UQ (☎0304/240202).

P&O European Ferries, Channel House, Channel View Rd, Dover CT17 9TJ (☎0304/203388); London (☎081/575 8555).

Sally Line, Argyle Centre, York St, Ramsgate, Kent CT11 9DS (☎0843/595522); 81 Piccadilly, London W1V 9HF (☎071/858 1127).

Stena Sealink, Charter House, Park St, Ashford, Kent TN24 8EX (☎0233/647047).

PACKAGE AND SPECIALIST OPERATORS

Alternative Travel Group, 69–71 Banbury Rd, Oxford OX2 6PE (☎0865/310399). All-inclusive walking holidays in Tuscany, Umbria, and Sicily. Costly, but very well organized. They also book holidays run by *Fresco Cycling*, a small company that arranges Tuscan cycling tours.

Citalia, 50–51 Conduit St, London W1 (☎071/686 5533). Hotel and villa packages all over Italy.

Cycling for Softies, 2–4 Birch Polygon, Manchester (☎061/248 5134). Easy-going cycle tours, with vans to transport your luggage from nice hotel to nice hotel.

Italian Escapades, 227 Shepherds Bush Rd, London W6 (☎081/748 2661). Package-tour arm of *Italy Sky Shuttle*, offering design-your-own tour deals.

Italiatours, 241 Euston Rd, London NW1 (☎071/383 3886). Package deals, city breaks, winter sun holidays and specialist Italian cuisine tours.The

Magic of Italy, 227 Shepherds Bush Green, London W12 (☎081/748 7575). Hotel and villa packages and city breaks.

Questultra, 243 Euston Rd, London NW1 (☎071/387 6122). Sea-and-sun packages, city breaks, fly-drive deals, and self-catering holidays in villas and apartments – even has an Umbrian castle on its books.

Sky Bus, 24a Earls Court Gardens, London SW5 (☎071/373 6055). Packages, self-catering holidays, short-stay city breaks and flights.

Sunvil Holidays, Sunvil House, 7–8 Upper Square, Old Isleworth, Middlesex TW7 7BJ (☎081/568 4499). Hotel and villa packages, city breaks and fly-drives.

Time Off, Chester Close, Chester St, London SW1 (☎071/235 8070). Short-break specialists.

VILLA AND FARMHOUSE HOLIDAYS

Allegro Holidays, 15a Church St, Reigate (☎0737/221323). Flats on Tuscan wine estates and properties all over Umbria.

Angel Travel, 34 High St, Borough Green, Tonbridge (☎0732/884109). All kinds of accommodation across Tuscany and Umbria.

Beach Villas, 8 Market Passage, Cambridge (☎0223/311113). Tuscan villas and country houses, including Elba.

La Bella Toscana, 119 Lynton Rd, Harrow, Middlesex (☎081/422 9218). Houses and flats around San Gimignano.

Bowhills Cottages, Swanmore, Southampton (☎0489/877627). Villas, farmhouses and even a watchtower; covers both Tuscany and Umbria.

Continental Villas, 3 Caxton Walk, London WC2H 8PW (☎071/497 0444). Villas and farmhouses all over both provinces.

CV Travel, 43 Cadogan St, London SW3 (☎071/581 0851). Expensive restored farmhouses in Chianti region.

Hoseasons, Sunway House, Lowestoft, Suffolk (☎0502/500555). All types of accommodation in both provinces.

Interhome, 383 Richmond Rd, Twickenham, Middlesex (☎081/891 1294). Accommodation only – no packages; both provinces.

International Chapters, 126 St John's Wood High St, London NW8 (☎071/586 9451). The

largest of the villa specialists, handling bookings for major Italian holiday home companies, including *Cuendet*. Good-value flights, too.

Lunigiana Holidays, 71 Busbridge Lane, Godalming, Surrey (☎04868/21218). Properties in the little-explored district in the very north of Tuscany.

SFV Holidays, Summer House, 68 Herne's Road, Oxford (☎0865/57738). Villas in various parts of Tuscany.

Traditional Tuscany, 108 Westcombe Park Rd, Blackheath, London SE3 (☎081/305 1380). Manor houses, farmhouses and cottages on working Tuscan farms.

Tuscany from Cottages to Castles, 54 Necton Rd, Wheathampstead, St Albans, Herts (☎058283/4333). Extensive lists of all types of Tuscan properties – several of them at the top end of the scale.

Vacanze in Italia, Dept 1086, Bignor, nr Pulborough, West Sussex (☎07987/421). Mainly upmarket properties in both provinces.

Villas Italia, 13 Hillgate St, London W8 (☎071/221 4432). Specializes in houses on the Tuscan coast, and around Florence, Pistoia, Siena, Perugia and Spoleto.

Westbury Travel, 1 Belmont, Lansdown Rd, Bath (☎0225/446328). Farmhouses, villas and flats in Tuscany and Umbria, including Elba.

● **Short-break deals**. Florence is a standby in major holiday companies' "Italian City Break" programmes; reckon on spending from about £250 per person for three nights, depending on season.

● **Fly-drive deals**. If you want to hire a car in Italy, it's well worth checking with tour operators before you leave as most deals work out a lot cheaper than hiring on the spot. *Italian Escapades* and *Citalia* have good prices (from £200 per week), and check out also *Questultra*, *Sunvil* and *Italiatours*, who all offer some kind of fly-drive deal. If you have bought your own flight through a regular agent, they can (or you can) book a car in advance through companies like *Holiday Autos* (see p.21).

● **Language courses**. An excellent way of learning Italian is to take a package, combining accommodation with tuition. There are a great many places where you can do this, usually offering courses of varying levels of intensity for between one and three months. Reckon on paying around £500 for a four-week course, including accommodation, which will normally be with an Italian family. For details, contact the *British Institute of Florence*, Palazzo Lanfredini, Lungarno Guicciardini 9, 50100 Florence, or *Università Italiana per Stranieri*, Palazzo Gallenga, Palazzo Fortebraccio 4, 06100 Perugia – both of which are long-established and run

regular courses. The *British Institute* also offers a combination of language and art history or painting courses.

No airline offers direct flights from Ireland to Tuscany or Umbria, but there are direct *Aer Lingus* and *Alitalia* flights to Milan from Cork and Dublin, with at least one flight daily between Ireland and Italy. The least expensive way of flying from Ireland to central Italy is to get to London and then catch a Pisa- or Florence-bound plane from there. There are numerous daily flights **from Dublin to London** operated by *Ryanair*, *Aer Lingus* and *British Midland* – the cheapest are *Ryanair*, which cost from around IR£60 for a return to Luton or Stansted, though the cost of the bus and underground journeys across London may make the total cost greater than *Aer Lingus* or *British Midland* fares to Heathrow. **From Belfast**, there are *British Airways* and *British Midland* flights to Heathrow, but the cheapest service is the *Britannia Airways* run to Luton, at around £70 return. From Dublin you can slightly undercut the plane's price by getting a **Eurotrain** ticket (IR£45 return), but from Belfast you'll save nothing by taking the train and ferry.

For the best youth/student deals from either city, go to *USIT* (see box below).

AIRLINES AND AGENCIES IN IRELAND

Aer Lingus, 42 Grafton St, Dublin 2 (☎01/794764); 46 Castle St, Belfast (☎0232/245151).

Alitalia, Norwich Union House, 60–63 Dawson St, Dublin 2 (☎01/775171).

Britannia Airways, no reservations office in Ireland – bookings from Luton Airport, Luton, Beds (☎0582/424155).

British Airways, 9 Fountain Centre, College St, Belfast (☎0232/240522); 60 Dawson St, Dublin 2 (☎01/610666).

British Midland, 54 Grafton St, Dublin 2 (☎01/798733); Suite 2, Fountain Centre, College St, Belfast (☎0232/225151).

Ryanair, College Park House, 20 Nassau St, Dublin 2 (☎01/797444 or ☎770444).

USIT, 19–21 Aston Quay, O'Connell Bridge, Dublin 2 (☎01/679 8833); Fountain Centre, College St, Belfast (☎0232/324073).

GETTING THERE FROM NORTH AMERICA

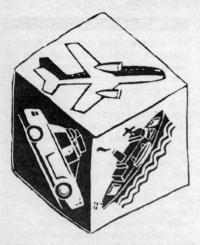

There are no direct flights from North America to Tuscany or Umbria, but you can fly to Rome (or less convenient Milan) from a number of US and Canadian cities, then move on by internal flight or by land. There are regular flights to Pisa and Florence from Milan and Rome, plus flights from Milan to Perugia, as well as a host of rail connections, including a twice-daily direct service between Florence and Rome's Fiumicino airport.

FLIGHTS

Flights to Italy from North America are so competitive that it is hard to generalize about fares: there are so many special deals, with prices depending on the level of restrictions, which day you travel and how long you decide to go for.

Regarding ordinary **scheduled** fares, there are a few general rules worth remembering. Firstly, it is during the low season – usually between the end of October and the end of March, excluding Christmas – that you will be able to take advantage of the most attractive offers, when airlines try and fill seats that might otherwise remain empty; fares increase somewhat in the so-called shoulder season – April and May, and September and October – while in the high season (June through to the end of August)

fares will be at their highest. Throughout the year it is more expensive to fly at weekends rather than during the week. On all the airlines the cheapest fares are usually Apex or SuperApex tickets, although these often come loaded with restrictions: you must book well in advance, normally at least three weeks; there is often some kind of minimum and maximum stay, usually a minimum of a week or so, and a maximum of 30 days; you often have to spend at least one Saturday night abroad; and the tickets are often non-changeable and non-refundable once you have booked them. One thing worth knowing is that the direct scheduled fares charged by each airline don't vary much, so you'll more often than not be basing your choice around things like flight timings, routes and gateway cities, ticket restrictions, and even the airline's reputation for comfort and service, as much as cost. It's a long flight, something like 9 hours from New York, Boston and the eastern Canadian cities, 12 hours from Chicago, and 15 hours from Los Angeles, so it's as well to be fairly comfortable and to arrive at a reasonably sociable hour.

Alitalia, the international airline of Italy, fly the widest choice of **routes between USA and Italy**. They fly direct every day from New York, Boston, Miami, Chicago and Los Angeles to Milan and Rome. As for American-based airlines, *Delta Airlines* fly daily from New York, Chicago and Los Angeles to Rome and Milan; *Trans World Airlines* fly daily from New York to Milan and Rome, and around four times a week from Los Angeles to Milan and Rome; *United Airlines* fly direct from Washington to Milan and Rome once daily.

The basic round-trip **fares**, with restrictions, do vary a little between airlines, although the only true variations start with the special offers that may be available, and even these often have a tendency to be mirrored from one carrier to another. At the time of writing, for the cheapest round-trip fare, travelling midweek in low season, you could expect to pay in the region of $650 from New York or Boston to Rome, rising to around $700 during the shoulder season, and to about $950 during the high summer months. Travelling on a weekend will normally cost you around $50 more, while you should also add on $20 or so for taxes. Flights from LA work out

AIRLINES IN NORTH AMERICA

Alitalia, 666 Fifth Ave, New York, NY 10103 (☎212/582 8900 or 800/223 5730); 2055 Peel St, Montréal, PQ H3A 1V8 (☎514/842 5201); 120 Adelaide St West, Toronto, ON M5H 2E1 (☎416/363 2001).

Delta Airlines, Hartsfield Atlanta International Airport, Atlanta, GA 30320 (☎404/765 5000 or 800/241 4141).

Trans World Airlines, 100 South Bedford Rd, Mount Kisco, NY 10549 (☎212/290 2141 or 800/892 4141).

United Airlines, PO Box 66100, O'Hare International Airport, Chicago, IL 60666 (☎312/952 4000 or 800/538 2929).

DISCOUNT FLIGHT AGENTS, TRAVEL CLUBS AND CONSOLIDATORS

Access International, 101 W 31st St, Suite 104, New York, NY 10001 (☎800/TAKE-OFF). Consolidator with good East Coast and central US deals.

Council Travel, 205 E 42nd St, New York, NY 10017 (☎212/661 1450). Head office of the nationwide US student travel organization. Branches in San Francisco, LA, Washington, New Orleans, Chicago, Seattle, Portland, Minneapolis, Boston, Atlanta and Dallas, to name only the larger ones.

Encore Short Notice, 4501 Forbes Blvd, Lanham, MD 20706 (☎301/459 8020 or 800/638 9278). East Coast travel club.

Interworld, 3400 Coral Way, Miami, FL 33145 (☎305/443 4929). Southeastern US consolidator.

Moment's Notice, 425 Madison Ave, New York, NY 10017 (☎212/486 0503). Travel club that's good for last-minute deals.

Nouvelles Frontières, 12 E 33rd St, New York, NY 10016 (☎212/779 0600); 800 bd de Maisonneuve Est, Montréal, PQ H2L 4L8 (☎514/288 9942). Main US and Canadian branches of the French discount travel outfit. Other branches in LA, San Francisco and Québec City.

STA Travel, 48 E 11th St, New York, NY 10003 (☎212/477 7166); 166 Geary St, Suite 702, San Francisco, CA 94108 (☎415/391 8407). Main US branches of the originally Australian and now worldwide specialist in independent and student travel. Other offices in Los Angeles, Boston and Honolulu.

Stand Buys, 311 W Superior St, Chicago, IL 60610 (☎800/331 0257). Good Midwestern travel club.

TFI Tours, 34 W 32nd St, New York, NY 10001 (☎212/736 1149 or 800/825 3834). The very best East Coast deals, especially worth looking into if you only want to fly one-way.

Travac, 1177 N Warson Rd, St Louis, MO 63132 (☎800/872 8800). Good central US consolidator.

Travel Avenue, 180 N Jefferson, Chicago, IL 60606 (☎312/876 1116 or 800/333 3335). Discount travel agent.

Travel Brokers, 50 Broad St, New York, NY 10004 (☎800/999 8748). New York travel club.

Travel Cuts, 187 College St, Toronto, ON M5T 1P7 (☎416/979 2406). Main office of the Canadian student travel organization. Many other offices nationwide.

Travelers Advantage, 49 Music Square, Nashville, TN 37203 (☎800/548 1116). Reliable travel club.

Unitravel, 1177 N Warson Rd, St Louis, MO 63132 (☎800/325 2027). Reliable consolidator.

Worldwide Discount Travel Club, 1674 Meridian Ave, Miami Beach, FL 33139 (☎305/534 2082).

about $200 on top of these round-trip fares; from Miami and Chicago, add on about $100.

You can, however, sometimes get **special deals** that start at around $400 round-trip from New York to Rome, flying midweek in low season, through around $650 during the shoulder season and rising to about $750 in the peak months, again adding on another $50 if you want to travel on a weekend, plus the usual taxes.

The only airline to fly direct to Italy **from Canada** is *Alitalia* who fly from Toronto and Montréal to Rome, with the usual connections to other cities in Italy. Their low-season one-month Apex **fare** costs CDN$899 midweek, rising to around CDN$1200 in high season. Bear in mind you'll always need to add on at least an extra CDN$40 in taxes. Fares from both cities are the same.

DISCOUNTED FARES

You can of course bypass the airlines altogether and go straight to a **travel agent**, who will at least guide you through the maze of fares even if they can't offer anything cheaper, and they will often be able to at least match any special deals the airlines are offering direct. Check the Sunday newspapers' travel sections, which are always advertising discounted fares, or consult one of the **youth and student specialists**, who often have excellent deals not just for students. Another option is to contact a **discount travel club** – organizations which specialize in selling off the unsold seats of travel agents for bargain rates, often at up to half the original price, though you usually have to be a member to get the best deals. You could also try a so-called airline ticket **consolidator**, who sells the unsold seats direct from airlines, though bear in mind that discounts are usually not as high as with travel clubs and you may not get the exact flight you want.

ORGANIZED TOURS

There are dozens of companies operating group travel and tours in Italy, ranging from full-blown luxury escorted tours to small groups sticking to specialized itineraries; if you're happy to stay in one (or two) places, you can also of course simply book a hotel-plus-flight deal, or, if you're keener to self-cater, rent a villa or a farmhouse for a week or two. Prices vary wildly, so check what you are getting for your money (many don't include the cost of the airfare). Reckon on paying at least $1500 for a ten-day touring vacation, up to as much as $3000 for a fourteen-day city package.

TRAVELLING VIA BRITAIN

It might be a good idea to transit **via Britain**, since there's a broad range of well-priced flights available to London from all North America, and there is a wide choice of options to Italy once there. **Flying** is the most straightforward way to get from Britain to Italy, and prices are competitive; see above for full details of flights and rail deals from Britain and Ireland.

If you're interested in seeing more of Europe en route to Italy, travelling **by train** from Britain may be more appealing, though be prepared for prices comparable to air fares if you're over 26, and a shortest possible journey time of at least 18 hours from London. If you're under 26, however, a range of youth fares is available, which have to be bought in Britain, or – the most attractive option – a **Eurail Youthpass**, which gives unlimited travel in seventeen countries and costs $578 for one month or $768 for two. It must be bought before leaving home (outlets are given below), as must the other kinds of *Eurail* pass. For over-26s there's the standard **Eurail pass**, giving 15 days' first-class travel for $498, 21 days for $648, 1 month for $798, 2 months for $1098, or 3 months for $1398. The **Eurail Flexipass** entitles you to a number of days' first-class travel within a two-month period: 5 days for $348; 10 days for $560; 15 days for $740; the under-26s' version of this card, the **Eurail Youth Flexipass**, costs $255, $398 and $540 respectively. If you're travelling in a group, it might be worth buying the **Eurail Saverpass**, which for $430 per person gives 15 days' first-class travel for 2 or more people travelling together – or 3 or more from April to September; the 21-day version costs $550 and the one-month $678. Finally, the **Eurail Drive Pass**, valid for any 7 days within a period of 2 months, gives you 4 days' first-class rail travel plus 3 days' car rental for around $320, with options for additional days at large discounts.

Australians and Canadians can also buy *Eurail* passes, though they must again be purchased before arrival in Europe.

RAIL ADDRESSES

CIE Tours International, 108 Ridgedale Ave, Morristown, NJ 07690 (☎201/292 3438 or 800/522 5258).

Italian State Railways, 666 Fifth Ave, New York, NY 10113 (☎212/697 2100).

Rail Europe, 226–230 Westchester Ave, White Plains, NY 10604 (☎914/682 2999 or 800/438 7245); and branches in Santa Monica, San Francisco, Fort Lauderdale, Chicago, Dallas, Vancouver and Montréal.

GETTING THERE FROM AUSTRALASIA

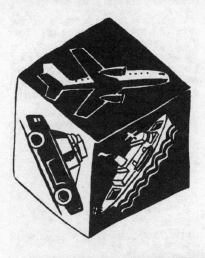

The only direct flights to Italy from Australia are to **Rome** from Melbourne, Sydney or Auckland. Two airlines fly these routes, *Qantas* and the Indonesian carrier *Garuda*, and their fares are pretty well the same, rising from about Aus$1700 in low season to Aus$2200 in high season, although you might be able to undercut these fares slightly by shopping around, scanning the ads in the *Melbourne Age* and *Sydney Morning Herald* or approaching an agent. From New Zealand, return flights to Rome with *Garuda* or *Thai* cost from around NZ$2300 in low season to a peak of NZ$2900. One of the best agents to try is the long-established *STA*, who operate out of several branches in both Australia and New Zealand – head office addresses below. Alternatively, from either country you can always pick up whatever deal you can get to **London** and take a cheap charter to Italy from there.

AUSTRALIAN DISCOUNT AGENTS

Anywhere Travel, 345 Anzac Parade, Kingsford, Sydney (☎02/663 0411).

Brisbane Discount Travel, 360 Queen St, Brisbane (☎07/229 9211).

Discount Travel Specialists, Shop 53, Forrest Chase, Perth (☎09/221 1400).

Flight Centres, Circular Quay, Sydney (☎02/241 2422); Bourke St, Melbourne (☎03/650 2899); plus other branches nationwide except the Northern Territory.

Passport Travel, 320b Glenferrie Rd, Malvern, Melbourne (☎03/824 7183).

STA Travel, 732 Harris St, Sydney (☎02/212 1255); 256 Flinders St, Melbourne (☎03/347 4711); other offices in Townsville and state capitals.

Topdeck Travel, 45 Grenfell St, Adelaide (☎08/410 1110).

Tymtro Travel, Suite G12, Wallaceway Shopping Centre, Chatswood, Sydney (☎02/411 1222).

NEW ZEALAND DISCOUNT AGENTS

Budget Travel, PO Box 505, Auckland (☎09/309 4313).

Flight Centres, National Bank Towers, 205–225 Queen St, Auckland (☎09/309 6171); Shop 1M, National Mutual Arcade, 152 Hereford St, Christchurch (☎09/379 7145); 50–52 Willis St, Wellington (☎04/472 8101); others countrywide.

STA Travel, Traveller's Centre, 10 High St, Auckland (☎09/309 9995); 233 Cuba St, Wellington (☎04/385 0561); 223 High St, Christchurch (☎03/379 9098); other offices in Dunedin, Palmerston North and Hamilton.

RED TAPE AND VISAS

British and other EU citizens can enter Italy, and stay as long as they like, simply on production of a valid passport. The temporary British Visitor's Passport, available over the counter at post offices, is valid for one year; full ten-year passports are available from passport offices, and you should allow around a month for delivery. Citizens of the United States, Canada, Australia and New Zealand need only a valid passport, too, but are limited to stays of three months. All other nationals should consult the relevant embassies about visa requirements.

Legally, you're required to register with the police within three days of entering Italy, though if you're staying at a hotel this will be done for you. Some policemen are more punctilious about this than ever, though others would be amazed and baffled by any attempt to register yourself down at the local police station while on holiday.

ITALIAN EMBASSIES AND CONSULATES

AUSTRALIA: 61–69 Macquarie St, Sydney 2000, NSW (☎02/2478 442); 509 St. Kilda Rd, Melbourne (☎03/867 5744).

CANADA: 136 Beverley St, Toronto (☎416/977 1566).

IRELAND: 63–65 Northumberland Rd, Dublin (☎01/601744); 7 Richmond Park, Belfast (☎0232/668854).

NEW ZEALAND: 34 Grant Rd, Wellington (☎04/7473 5339).

UK: 38 Eaton Place, London SW1 (☎071/235 9371); 6 Melville Crescent, Edinburgh 3 (☎031/226 3631); 111 Piccadilly, Manchester (☎061/228 7041).

USA: 690 Park Ave, New York (☎212/737 9100); 12400 Wilshire Blvd, Suite 300, Los Angeles (☎213/826 6207).

COSTS, MONEY AND BANKS

The days are long gone when Italy was a relatively inexpensive country to visit: the economic boom and the glut of visitors have conspired to make prices roughly on a par

with the UK, and in certain cases even more expensive – Florence is one of the three priciest Italian cities, with Milan and Venice. However, prices do vary a lot in Tuscany and Umbria, and even as popular a place as Siena is noticeably less costly than Florence.

AVERAGE COSTS

Most **basic things** are inexpensive compared with Britain: delicious picnic **meals** can be put together for under £5/$8, and a pizza or plate of pasta with a glass of wine will set you back around £7/$10 on average – though in some of the larger towns, Florence in particular, such budget places can be difficult to find. **Buses and trains** are comparatively cheap too, the rail journey from Florence to Siena, for instance, costing less than £15/$22 for a second-class return. Wine is cheap, but other **drinks** are not: soft drinks or coffee all cost around the same price, as in Britain, if not more, and a large glass of beer can cost £3/$5, even more if you decide to sit down.

Room rates start at a bottom line of £15/$22 for a double room in a one-star hotel, though again in Florence you won't find much under £30/$45. Overall, if you're really watching your budget – camping, hitching a little, buying food from shops and markets – you could get by on around £20/$35 per person per day; a more realistic **average minimum daily budget** for a couple staying in one-star hotels, taking trains and eating one modest-priced meal out a day, would be in the region of £40/$60 per person. If you want to allow yourself the occasional extravagance or an intensive bout of museum-visiting, then you'll need at least £50/$75 per day – and in view of the disproportionate cost of single hotel rooms, a person travelling alone should estimate an expenditure about 20 percent higher.

Time of year makes a big difference. During the height of summer, from Easter to September, hotel prices tend to escalate; outside the season, however, you can often negotiate lower rates in the smaller towns, and should find rooms in the cheapest hotels in the bigger places. State-owned museums offer **reductions** to people under 18 and for over-60s, but only a handful of other attractions accept ISIC cards, and buses and trains never do – though *Alitalia*'s domestic routes are subject to a 25 percent reduction if you're under 26 or a student.

MONEY AND BANKS

The Italian unit of **money** is the *Lira* (plural *Lire*), always abbreviated as L; for some time the rate has hovered around L2000 to the pound sterling, about L1500 to the US dollar. Banknotes come in denominations of L1000, L2000, L5000, L10,000, L50,000 and L100,000, and coins as L50, L100, L200 and L500. You might also be given a telephone token or *gettone* in change, which is worth L200.

The easiest and safest way to carry your money is as **travellers' cheques**, available for a small commission (1 percent of the amount ordered) from any major bank and some building societies, whether or not you have an account. You'll usually – though not always – pay a small commission, too, when you **exchange money** using travellers' cheques – again around 1

percent of the amount changed, although some banks will make a standard charge per cheque regardless of its denomination – usually L5000. It's worth knowing that *Thomas Cook* offices don't charge for cashing their own cheques, and *American Express* offices don't charge for cashing anyone's cheques. Alternatively, most banks in Britain can issue current account holders with a **Eurocheque card** and chequebook, with which you can get cash from the majority of banks in Italy (including from cash-dispensing machines, which can help to avoid the queues); you'll pay a few pounds service charge but usually no commission on transactions. Major **credit and charge cards** – *Visa, Access/Mastercard, American Express* and *Diner's Club* – are also accepted in many shops, and for cash advances in many banks. It's an idea to have at least some Italian money for when you first arrive, and you can buy *lire* in advance from nearly all banks, though you're not supposed to exceed L400,000 in cash.

In Italy, the best place to change money or travellers' cheques is at a **bank**. There are a few banking chains that you'll find nationwide, the *Banca Nazionale del Lavoro, Banca d'Italia* and *Cassa di Risparmio*, as well as regional chains like the *Banca di Roma, Banco di Napoli* or *Banco di Sicilia*. **Banking hours** are normally Monday to Friday mornings from 8.30am until 1pm, and for an hour in the afternoon (usually 3–4pm), though there are local variations on this. Outside these times, the larger hotels will change money or travellers' cheques, although if you're staying in a reasonably large city the rate is invariably better at those times at the railway station exchange bureaux – normally open evenings and weekends. You'll also find a growing number of "hole-in-the-wall" exchange machines in the larger towns, which automatically change notes from various currencies.

If you run out of money, or there is some kind of emergency, the quickest way to get **money sent out** is to contact your bank at home and have them wire the cash to the nearest bank. You can do the same thing through *Thomas Cook* or *American Express* if there is a branch nearby. You can also have cash sent out through *Western Union* (UK ☎0800/833833; North America ☎800/325 6000) to a nearby bank or post office – a process which takes 2–5 days; this is a last-ditch option, though, since commission rates are punitive.

HEALTH AND INSURANCE

EU nationals can take advantage of Italy's health services under the same terms as the residents of the country. You'll need form E111, which can be picked up at most major post offices. For ease of mind, travel insurance – covering health plus loss or theft of baggage – remains a good idea for EU nationals, and essential for travellers from other countries.

Before you purchase any insurance, check what you have already. North Americans, in particular, may find themselves covered for medical expenses and loss, and possibly loss of or damage to valuables, while abroad, as part of a family or student policy. Some credit cards, too, now offer insurance benefits if you use them to pay for your holiday tickets.

HEALTH PROBLEMS

If you need treatment, go to a **doctor** (*médico*); every town and village has one. If you're going to use your E111 to get free treatment and prescriptions for medicines at the local rate, there's a complicated process to go through first. You have to go to the local **Unita Sanitaria Locale** to exchange the E111 for a "certificate of entitlement" and a list of doctors and dentists that provide a service free of charge. The E111 will only get you immediate unconditional treatment if you're rushed into a hospital. If you're looking for repeat medication, take any empty bottles or

capsules with you to the doctors – the brand-names often differ.

An Italian **chemist** (*farmacia*) is well qualified to give advice on minor ailments, and to dispense prescriptions, and there's generally one open all night in the bigger towns and cities. They work on a rota system, and you should find the address of the one currently open on any *farmacia* door. If you are taken **seriously ill** or involved in an accident, hunt out the nearest hospital and go to the *Pronto Soccorso* (casualty) section; in a real emergency phone ☎113 and ask for *ospedale* or *ambulanza*. Major train stations and airports often have first-aid stations with qualified doctors on hand.

The inhabitants of the Chianti and Umbrian hills are quite neurotic about the danger of **vipers** (*viperi*), to the extent of keeping serum in their fridges. The chances of being bitten by a snake are negligible, but if you want to be prepared for every eventuality, serum is available from most local chemists. Should you be rummaging around in old farm buildings or collecting timber from a woodpile, keep an eye out for small **scorpions**, which can deliver nasty but not life-threatening bites. Low-lying zones on or near the coast, especially the once-swampy Maremma and Pisa areas, are plagued by mosquitoes (*zanzari*) and other insects from March till the end of the autumn. You can buy cheap little machines or sprays to zap them.

INSURANCE

In Britain, as well as those policies offered by travel agents, consider using a specialist, low-priced firm like *Endsleigh* (Cranfield House, 97–107 Southampton Row, London WC1; ☎071/436 4451), who offer two weeks' basic cover in Italy for around £20.

If transiting via Britain, **North Americans** might consider buying a policy from a British travel agent. British policies tend to be cheaper than American ones, and routinely cover thefts – which are often excluded from the more health-based American policies. (Most North American policies only cover property lost while in possession of an identifiable person – so you're OK if your partner misplaces your camera but not if a thief grabs it.) North Americans should in any case check carefully the insurance policies they already have before taking out a new one, since it may be that you're covered already for medical and other losses while abroad. Canadians especially are usually covered by their provincial health plans, and holders of ISIC cards are entitled (outside the USA and Canada) to be reimbursed for $3000 worth of accident coverage and 60 days of in-patient benefits (up to $100 a day) for the period the card is valid. Students may also find their health coverage extends to cover vacations, and many bank and charge accounts include some form of travel cover; insurance is also sometimes included if you pay for your trip with a credit card.

If you do want a specific travel insurance policy, there are numerous kinds to choose from:

short-term combination policies covering everything from baggage loss to broken legs are the best bet and cost around $25 per 10 days. Two companies you might try are *Travel Guard*, 110 Centrepoint Drive, Steven Point, WI 54480 (☎715/345 0505 or 800/826 1300), and *Access America International*, 600 Third Ave, New York, NY 10163 (☎212/949 5960 or 800/284 8300).

For **medical treatment and drugs**, keep all the bills and claim the money back later. If you **have anything stolen** (including money), register the loss immediately with the local police – without their report you won't be able to claim. This also applies to North American policies – ie, even if it's your best friend who has lost your prized possessions, you still have to report the loss to the police. The office to go to is the *Questura*, not the *carabinieri*.

INFORMATION AND MAPS

Before you leave, it's well worth dropping in at the *Italian State Tourist Office* (*ENIT*) or writing to them for a selection of their free maps and brochures, though don't go mad – much of what they have is available in Italy itself. Worth grabbing are any accommodation listings they may have for the area you're interested in, town plans and maps of the regions, and the annual *Travellers Handbook*, which can be an indispensable reference on all aspects of the country.

TOURIST OFFICES IN ITALY

Most Italian towns, main train stations and airports have a **local tourist office**: the Italian tourist system is reorganizing right now and you'll notice a number of acronyms – APT, AAT, IAT, AAST are just four – but all offer much the same mix of general advice, leaflets, free maps and accommodation lists, though rarely do they book rooms. In major towns you'll find an **EPT** (*Ente Provinciale Turismo*), which handles information on an entire province, while villages may have a tiny office known as a **Pro Loco**, which is often to be found in a shop. Most Tuscan and Umbrian

ITALIAN STATE TOURIST OFFICES ABROAD

UK: 1 Princes St, London W1 (☎071/408 1254); open Mon–Fri 9am–2.30pm.

IRELAND: 47 Merrion Square, Dublin 2 (☎01/766397).

US: 630 Fifth Ave, Suite 1565, New York, NY10111 (☎212/245 4822); 360 Post St, Suite 801, San Francisco, CA 94108 ☎(415/392 6206).

CANADA: 1 Place Ville Marie, Suite 1914, Montréal, Québec, H3B 3M9 (☎514/866 7667).

AUSTRALIA/NEW ZEALAND: c/o *Alitalia*, AGC House, 124 Phillip St, Sydney, NSW.

offices have someone who speaks English. Opening hours vary, but larger city offices are likely to be open Monday–Saturday 9am–1pm and 4–7pm, and sometimes for a short period on Sunday morning; smaller offices may open weekdays only, while Pro Loco times are notoriously erratic – sometimes they are open for only a couple of hours a day, even in summer.

A further source of information is the *Pagine Gialle Turismo*, a free supplement to the Yellow Pages (*Pagine Gialle*) aimed specifically at tourists. There are separate editions for Tuscany and Umbria and you'll find them in SIP or AAST public phone offices, in larger hotels and tourist offices.

MAPS

The **town plans** we've printed in this book should be fine for most purposes, and most tourist offices give out maps of their local area for free. But if you want an indexed town plan, *Studio FMB* cover the main towns, and *Falk* does a decent, fold-open plan of Florence. The best **road maps** are those published by the TCI (*Touring Club Italiano*); they have excellent 1:200,000 scale maps for both Tuscany and Umbria.

For **hiking**, the maps to go for are the ever-expanding *Kompass* 1:50,000 series. So far they produce two Tuscany maps (*Florence-Chianti* and

MAP OUTLETS

London
National Map Centre, 22–24 Caxton St, SW1 (☎071/222 4945);
Stanfords, 12–14 Long Acre, WC2 (☎071/836 1321);
The Travellers Bookshop, 25 Cecil Court, WC2 (☎071/836 9132).

Edinburgh
Thomas Nelson and Sons Ltd, 51 York Place, EH1 3JD (☎031/557 3011).

Glasgow
John Smith and Sons, 57–61 St Vincent St (☎041/221 7472).

Chicago
Rand McNally, 444 N Michigan Ave, IL 60611 (☎312/321 1751).

New York
British Travel Bookshop, 551 Fifth Ave, NY 10176 (☎800/448 3039 or 212/490 6688);
The Complete Traveler Bookstore, 199 Madison Ave, NY 10016 (☎212/685 9007);
Rand McNally, 150 East 52nd St, NY 10022 (☎212/758 7488);
Traveler's Bookstore, 22 West 52nd St, NY 10019 (☎212/664 0995).

San Francisco
The Complete Traveler Bookstore, 3207 Filmore St, CA 92123 (☎415/923 1511);
Rand McNally, 595 Market St, CA 94105 (☎415/777 3131).

Seattle
Elliot Bay Book Company, 101 South Main St, WA 98104 (☎206/624 6600).

Washington DC
Rand McNally, 1201 Connecticut Ave NW, Washington DC 20036 (☎202/223 6751)
Note that *Rand McNally* now have 24 stores across the US; phone ☎1-800/333 0136 (ext 2111) for the address of your nearest store, or for **direct mail** maps.

Toronto
Open Air Books and Maps, 25 Toronto St, M5R 2C1 (☎416/363 0719).

Vancouver
World Wide Books and Maps, 1247 Granville St.

Adelaide
The Map Shop, 16a Peel St, Adelaide, SA 5000 (☎08/231 2033).

Brisbane
Hema, 239 George St, Brisbane, QLD 4000 (☎07/221 4330).

Melbourne
Bowyangs, 372 Little Bourke St, Melbourne, VIC 3000 (☎03/670 4383).

Perth
Perth Map Centre, 891 Hay St, Perth, WA 6000 (☎09/322 5733).

Sydney
Travel Bookshop, 20 Bridge St, Sydney, NSW 2000 (☎02/241 3554).

Florence
Il Viaggio, Via Ghibellina 117r.

Perugia
Eliografica, Via delle Streghe.

Siena-Colline Senesi) and four in Umbria – *Perugia-Deruta, Assisi-Camerino, Gubbio-Fabriano* and *Monti Sibillini*. The Orecchiella and Apuan mountains north of Lucca are covered by the excellent 1:25,000 *Multigraphic-Wanderkarte* series. Even more detailed maps are beginning to

appear in recognised walking areas. These include the 1:16,000 sheet put out by the caving, climbing and walking club at Costacciaro in Umbria (northeast of Gubbio), and the 1:25,000 *Universo* map for the area around Norcia and the Sibillini. Both are available in local shops.

GETTING AROUND

If you want to travel extensively around Tuscany and Umbria, use of a car is a major advantage. By public transport, you can still get to all the major places, but away from main routes it can be a slow and sporadic business. In general, trains are most use for longer journeys, buses for local routes. We have detailed bus, train and ferry routes in the "Travel Details" section at the end of each chapter, with more specific information, where appropriate, in the main body of the guide.

TRAINS

Operated by Italian State Railways, *Ferrovie dello Stato* (*FS*), there are six types of train in Italy. At the top of the range is the **ETR 450 "Pendolino"**, an exclusively first-class inter-city service on which your ticket includes seat reservation, newspapers and a meal. **Eurocity** trains connect the major Italian cities with centres such as Paris, Vienna, Hamburg and Barcelona, while **Intercity** trains link the major Italian centres. **Espresso** trains are the common-or-garden long-distance expresses, calling only at larger stations; **Diretto** trains stop at most stations; lastly there are the **Locale** services, which seem to stop at every place with a population higher than zero.

In addition to the routes operated by *FS*, there are a number of **privately run lines**, often using

separate stations though charging similar fares; in cases where a private line uses an *FS* station, there will be a separate ticket counter. Where these lines are worth using, they're detailed in the text.

FARES, RAIL PASSES AND DISCOUNTS
Fares are simply calculated by the kilometre and a return fare (*andata e ritorno*) is exactly twice that of a single (*andata*), except for journeys of under 250km in total, for which you get a 15 percent reduction. For a return journey of less than 250km tickets you must travel the return leg within three days of the outward journey, so if you're coming back any later than that, you must buy two single tickets; every extra 200km of travelling adds a day to the period of validity, up to a maximum of six days.

Reservations are often obligatory on *Eurocity* and *Intercity* services, and a **supplement** in the region of 30 percent of the ordinary fare is always payable on these trains. (Make sure you pay your supplement before getting on board as the supplement is higher if you pay the ticket-collector– a *supplemento rápido* is what to ask for.) In summer it's often worth making a **seat reservation** on any main route. **Sleepers** are available on most long-distance services; expect to pay about an extra L15,000 on a journey of 500km.

Most stations have machines at the end of the platforms in which passengers should stamp their ticket immediately before embarking on the journey. If you fail to validate your ticket at a station where these machines have been fitted, you may be given a spot fine in the region of L40,000.

The Europe-wide **InterRail** and **Eurail passes** (see p.4 & p.10) give unlimited travel on the *FS* network, although you'll be liable for supplements on the faster trains. If you're travelling exclusively in Italy, however, you might want to invest in one of the many rail passes available on the *FS* system. Travellers from the UK have a choice of three **Euro-Domino** passes for the Italian network, giving 3 days' unlimited second-class rail travel for £100, 5 days' for £124, or 10 days' for £208. The under-26 equivalents of these passes cost £75, £94 and £156 respectively.

In addition, there are three Italian passes available at all the agencies listed below except *Eurotrain*, and at major city train stations. The **Biglietto Turistico Libera Circolazione** is valid for unlimited travel on all *FS* trains, except the Pendolino; for 8 days it costs £88/$140, for 15 days £110/$172, for 21 days £126/$198, and for 30 days £152/$240. The **Flexi-Card** is similarly valid for all trains except the Pendolino, and gives a certain number of days' travel within a specific period. For 4 days' travel in any 9-day period it costs £66/$105, for 8 days in 21 it costs £94/$150, and for 12 in 30 it costs £120/$190. The **Chilométrico** ticket, valid for up to five people, gives 3000km worth of travel on a maximum of twenty separate journeys; it costs £90/$150. However, you have to pay supplements on faster trains. With the last two cards, you must get the ticket office to validate the journey you're about to make before getting on the train.

There are two **discount cards** that come into their own if you're going to be spending a very long time in the country. For under-26s there's the **Carta Verde**, which is valid for one year, gives 20 percent discount on any fare, and costs L40,000; it's available from any main train station in Italy. Stations also issue the **Carta d'Argento**, for people over 60, which has the same validity and price, but gives 30 percent discount. Note that neither of these passes is vaild for the peri-

ods June 25–Aug 31 & Dec 24–31. Bear in mind, too, that **children** aged 4–12 qualify for 50 percent discount on all journeys.

TIMETABLES AND INFORMATION

Timings and route information are posted up at railway stations. In the larger stations, in addition to departure boards, there are video machines into which you can tap in your destination and desired arrival time to get a breakdown of the best services, routes and fares.

More conventional **timetables** are also available. *Rápido* and *espresso* routes are covered by a little national pocket book, *Principali Treni*, issued twice yearly by *FS* and free from most stations. You can purchase a full timetable detailing the nationwide *FS* network, also published twice yearly, from station tobacconists for around L8000; in addition, *FS* publish this in two volumes called *Sud Centro Italia* and *Nord Centro Italia* – the latter is the one you need for Tuscany and Umbria. *FS* timetables, however, are notorious for running out within a couple of weeks of being published. The smaller *Pozzorario*, also published bi-annually, is a better buy – it too covers the country in two volumes and is available from virtually every station and street kiosk in the country.

In all cases pay attention to the **timetable notes**, which may specify the dates between which some services run (*Si effetua dal . . . al . . .*), or whether a service is seasonal (*periodico*); *feriale* is the word for daily, *festivo* means a train only runs on Sundays and holidays.

TRAIN SERVICES IN TUSCANY

Not surprisingly, **Florence** is the centre of the Tuscan rail network. Two lines run westward from the city, one of them passing through **Prato**, **Pistoia**, **Montecatini** and **Lucca** on its way to the coast at **Viareggio**, the other going through **Empoli** and **Pisa** before reaching the sea at **Livorno**. A picturesque line runs through the Garfagnana from Lucca to **Aulla**, providing access to the Lunigiana region and connections to La Spezia and Milan. To the east, a line rises through the **Mugello** district and then loops out of Tuscany towards Faenza, roughly parallel to the route through the mountains to Bologna. South of Florence, the train follows the River Arno towards **Arezzo**, from where there's a private line up into the **Casentino** region, while the *FS* services continue south past Cortona to

Chiusi, Orvieto and Rome. Just beyond Cortona, at **Teróntola**, there's the junction for the branch line east to Perugia, the fulcrum of Umbria's network. A couple of trains go directly from Florence to Perugia each day.

Siena can also be reached directly from Florence – though you may occasionally have to change at Empoli. From Siena itself there's a choice of two main routes – southeast to Chiusi, or southwest to Grosseto.

A **coastal service** between Rome and the Ligurian town of La Spezia links the Tuscan coastal towns of **Orbetello**, **Follonica**, **Cécina**, **Livorno** and **Viareggio**, swerving inland to call at **Grosseto** in the south of the province and **Pisa** in the north. Above Pisa it serves the resorts of the Versilia coast, calling principally at **Massa** and **Carrara**. At Cécina there's a spur inland to **Volterra**, where the line abruptly ends.

TRAIN SERVICES IN UMBRIA

All Umbria's major towns, with the exception of Gubbio, are easily accessible by train. In the west, the **Rome–Florence** route is the main artery, with branch line connections throughout the region. Most of the high-speed services between the two cities stop at no Umbrian stations other than **Orvieto**; you will probably have to board a slower *diretto* to connect with the **Ancona line** at **Orte**, with the **Siena line** at **Chiusi**, or with the **Perugia and Foligno line** at **Teróntola**.

More useful for the heart of the region, especially if you're coming from Rome, is the **Rome–Ancona** line, which meets the Rome–Florence line at Orte. This line gives direct access to **Narni**, **Terni** (connections for Rieti, the Abruzzo and the *Ferrovie Centrale Umbra* – see below), **Spoleto**, **Foligno** (connections to Spello, Assisi, Perugia and Teróntola), **Nocera Umbra** and **Gualdo Tadino**.

Terni's *FS* station is shared with the **Ferrovie Centrale Umbra** (*FCU*), a private railway that fills some crucial gaps left by the state network. Using ramshackle, bone-crunching carriages, it runs through **Terni**, **Todi**, **Deruta**, **Perugia**, **Umbértide** and **Città di Castello** before reaching the terminus at **Sansepolcro**. Services are frequent, though trains are often replaced by buses over certain sections.

The line between **Foligno** and **Teróntola** (on the Rome–Florence route) goes by **Spello** and **Assisi** then intersects with the *FCU* line at

Perugia, continuing along the northern shore of Lago Trasimeno. In addition, there are a couple of direct trains daily between Perugia and both Rome and Florence.

BUSES

If you're limited to public transport and want to get know Tuscany and Umbria thoroughly, sooner or later you'll have to use **regional buses** (*autobus* or *pullman*). Almost everywhere is connected by some kind of bus service, but schedules can be sketchy, and are drastically reduced – sometimes non-existent – at weekends, something the timetable won't always make clear. Bear in mind also that in rural areas schedules are often designed with the working and/or school day in mind, meaning a frighteningly early start if you want to catch that day's one bus out of town, and occasionally no buses at all during school holidays.

There isn't a national **bus company**, though *Lazzi* and *SITA* – both of which have a major presence in Tuscany and Umbria – cover much of Italy and there are a few other companies that operate services beyond their own immediate area (see the box below). **Bus terminals** in larger towns are often next door to the railway station; in smaller towns and villages most buses pull in at the central piazza. We've detailed the whereabouts of all bus terminals in the text, but if you're not sure ask for directions to the *autostazione*.

Timetables are worth picking up if you can find one, from the local company's office, bus stations or on the bus. You generally buy **tickets** on the bus, though on longer hauls you should buy them from the bus company office, which will invariably be right by the stop; there are no seat reservations. On most routes it's usually possible to flag a bus down if you want a ride: the convention, when it stops, is to get on at the back, off at the front. If you want to get off, ask *posso scéndere?*; the next stop is *la próssima fermata*.

City buses are always cheap, usually a L800–1000 flat fare. Invariably you need a ticket **before** getting on. Buy them in *tabacchi* or from the kiosks at bus terminals and stops, and cancel in the machine inside the bus. The whole thing works on a basis of trust, though in most cities checks are regularly made, and hefty spot fines issued to offenders.

MAJOR BUS COMPANIES

GENERAL

Lazzi, Piazza Stazione 4, Florence (☎055/298.840).

SITA, Via Santa Caterina da Siena 15, Florence (Mon–Fri ☎055/ 483. 651, Sat & Sun ☎055/ 211.487).

TUSCANY

CAP, Via Nazionale 13, Florence (☎055/214.637). Northern Tuscany.

CAT, Via Fiume 2, Florence (☎055/283.400). Central and southern Tuscany.

CLAP, Piazza Stazione 15, Florence (☎055/ 283.734). Northern Tuscany.

COPIT, Piazza Santa Maria Novella 22, Florence (☎055/215.451). Northern Tuscany.

Nardini, Via Roma 7, Barga (☎0583/73.050). From Barga and around the Garfagnana.

RAMA, Via Topazio 12, Grosseto (☎0564/ 456.745). Around Grosseto and the Maremma.

TRA-IN, Piazza San Domenico, Siena (☎0577/ 221.221). Siena province.

UMBRIA

ACAP, Pian di Massiano, Perugia (☎075/74.641).

ACT, Piazza Europa 19, Terni (☎0744/59.541). From Terni through southern Umbria, Orvieto and the Valnerina.

ASP, Pian di Massiano, Perugia (☎075/751.145). Perugia, Assisi, Todi and northern Umbria.

SIT, Via Flaminia, Km 127, Spoleto (☎0743/ 48.347). Around Spoleto and the Valnerina.

DRIVING

Travelling **by car** in Italy is relatively painless. The roads are good, the motorway, or *autostrada*, network very comprehensive, and Italian drivers rather less erratic than their reputation suggests – though their regard for the rules of the road is sometimes lax. The secret, if driving, is to make it very clear what you're going to do, using your horn as much as possible, and then do it with great determination. Don't assume you're safe as a pedestrian, either, and *never* step off the pavement without looking first: Italian drivers aren't keen on stopping when they can simply swerve, and even on pedestrian crossings you can undergo some close calls.

Most motorways are toll-roads. Take a ticket as you come on and pay on exit; the amount due is flashed up on a screen in front of you. Rates aren't especially high but they can mount up on a long journey.

As regards **documentation**, if you're bringing your own car you need a valid driving licence and an international green card of insurance, available from your insurer (sometimes free, usually for a fee). You'll also need to get a translation of your licence from the state tourist board, unless you've got one of the new pink EU-style licences. It's compulsory to carry your car documents and passport while you're driving, and you may be required to present them if stopped by the police – not an uncommon occurrence. **Rules of the**

road are straightforward: drive on the right; at junctions, where there's any ambiguity, give precedence to vehicles coming from the right; observe the speed limits – 50kph in built-up areas, 110kph on country roads and on motorways during the week, 130kph on motorways at weekends; and *don't* drink and drive.

If you **break down**, dial ☎116 at the nearest phone and tell the operator where you are, the type of car and your registration number: the nearest office of the *Automobile Club d'Italia* (*ACI*), Via Marsala 8, 00185 Rome (☎06/ 499.8251), the Italian national motoring organization, will be informed and they'll send someone out to fix your car – although it's not a free service, and can work out very expensive if you need a tow. For peace of mind, you might prefer to join the *ACI* outright, and so qualify for their discounted repairs scheme. Any *ACI* office in Italy can tell you where to get **spare parts** for your particular car.

Italy is also one of the most expensive countries in Europe in which to buy **petrol**, though if you take your own car you're entitled to **petrol coupons** worth 15 percent off and concessions on the motorway tolls; information from the Italian State Tourist Office. For unleaded petrol, look for the sign, "Senza Piombo".

Never leave anything visible in the car when you're not using it, including the radio. If you're taking your own vehicle, consider installing a detachable car-radio, and always depress your aerial or else you might find it snapped off. Most cities and ports have **garages** where you can leave your car, a safe enough option. At least your car is unlikely to be stolen if it's got a right-hand drive and a foreign number-plate: they're too conspicuous to be of much use to thieves.

CAR RENTAL

Car hire in Italy is pricey, with costs for a Fiat Panda (the standard cheap car) currently around £200 per week with unlimited mileage. Italian and locally based firms are often a bit cheaper than the multinationals – there are plenty of companies with desks at Pisa airport, and other addresses are detailed in the relevant sections of the guide – but it usually works out cheaper to book in advance, before leaving. Most operators will only hire to drivers who have held a licence for over a year and are aged over 21.

In **Britain**, you can book with two Italian firms, *Maggiore* and *Italy by Car*, through agents: *Transhire*, Silver House, 31–35 Beak Street, London W1 (☎071/437 0951), *Questultra*, 243 Euston Road, London NW1 (☎071/387 6122), or *Italy Sky Shuttle*, 227 Shepherds Bush Road, London W6 (☎081/748 1333). Alternatively, contact *Holiday Autos*, 25 Savile Row, London W1 (☎071/491 1111); they arrange cars at the lowest prices around, through local agents. Some package companies also offer discounted cars as part of fly-drive holidays; see p.6.

In **North America** you'll proably get the best prices by arranging fly-drive deals through travel agencies, but it's always worth checking what's on offer from the major rental firms such as *Hertz* (☎800-654 3131), *Avis* (☎800-722 1333), *Budget* (☎800-527 0700), *National* (800-227 7368) or *Dollar* (☎800-421 6868). The North American car rental market is so competitive that even the biggest names might be amenable to haggling.

HITCHING

Getting around exclusively by **hitchhiking** (*autostop*) could be a frustrating experience, but for the odd short hop along a quiet country road, and long hauls between major towns, it's feasible enough. Note that it's illegal to hitch on motorways, and to do so would be to risk a spot fine; stand on a slip-road or at one of the service stations. Also, be aware that few women hitch alone in Italy, and not too many in all-women pairs; if you do it, always ask where the car is

headed (*Dovè diretto?*) before you commit yourself. If you want to get out, say *Mi fa scendere?*.

CYCLING AND MOTORCYCLING

Cycling is seen as more of a sport than a way of getting around in Italy – on a Sunday you'll see plenty of people out for a spin on their Campagnolo-equipped machines, but you'll not come across many luggage-laden tourers. Only in major towns will you find a shop stocking spares for non-racing bikes, so make sure you take a supply of inner tubes, spokes and whatever other bits you think might be handy. On the islands, in major resorts and in the larger cities it's usually possible to **rent** a bike, but generally facilities for this are few and far between and you may be better off bringing your own.

An alternative is to tour by **motorbike**, though again there are relatively few places to rent one. **Mopeds** and **scooters**, on the other hand, are relatively easy to find: everyone in Italy, from kids to grandmas, rides one of these, and, although they're not built for long-distance travel, for shooting around towns and islands they're ideal. We've detailed outlets in the text; roughly speaking you should expect to pay up to L100,000 a day for a machine. Crash helmets are compulsory.

FERRIES

In Tuscany there are three ports with **ferry** services:

● **Livorno** has services to Corsica (Bastia), and to the northern Tuscan island of Capraia.

● **Piombino** is the point of departure for Elba, connecting to Portoferraio, as well as the smaller ports of Cavo and Rio Marina. There are also ferries from Piombino for Corsica, and from Portoferraio for Capraia.

● **Porto Santo Stefano** on Monte Argentario has ferries to the island of Giglio.

Summer sailings from all ports are heavily subscribed, especially those to Elba, and **booking** is essential if you want to take a car across. In Britain you can book tickets on the *Navarma* Elba ferries through *Serena Holidays*, 40–42 Kenway Road, London SW5 (☎071/373 6548).

Journey **times and frequencies** are detailed in the relevant parts of the guide, along with addresses to contact for latest timetable and ticket information. Out of season, services are drastically reduced, and some stop altogether.

ACCOMMODATION

Accommodation is a major cost in Tuscany and Umbria. The hotels are more upmarket than in most Italian regions, with an increasing preponderance of two- and three-star places over one-stars, and a tendency for one-stars to price themselves ever closer to the plusher places; there are very few really inexpensive hotels, only a scattering of hostels, and even campsites are fairly pricey. On the plus side, however, both provinces have a lot of villas for rent, while a rapidly expanding aspect of the tourist industry is *agriturismo* – farmhouse rents, a little similar to the French *gîtes*.

HOTELS

Hotels are known either as ***alberghi*** or ***pensioni*** (there's no real difference between the two), and come rated on a system of one to five stars.

One-star places start on average at about L30,000 per night for a double room without private bath. In some out-of-the-way spot you may find something slightly cheaper, while in Florence you should assume that prices within each star category are at least L15,000 per night higher than anywhere else – it's difficult to find anything at all in Florence for under L60,000. **Two-star** hotels cost upwards of L50,000 for a double and facilities won't always be that much better; with **three-star** places you begin to notice a difference, though in them you'll be paying a minimum of L70,000.

In the more popular cities – again, Florence especially – it's not unusual for hotels to have a

minimum stay of three nights, and many proprietors will add the price of **breakfast** to your bill whether you want it or not; try to resist this – you can always eat more cheaply in a bar. Supplements for showers are also common in cheaper places. You can cut costs slightly by cramming three into a double room, but most hotels will charge you an extra 35 percent for this on average.

Note also that people **travelling alone** may be clobbered for the price of a double room even when taking a single.

Wherever you book in, establish the full price of your room before you accept it; out of season you may pay less than the advertised rate – if you ask first. In season, **booking ahead** is always a good idea, and essential through most of the region from June to August and in Florence for most of the year; we've given phone numbers throughout the guide for recommended hotels. The phrases at the end of the book should help you get over the language barrier, but in many places you should be able to find someone who speaks at least some English.

DAY HOTELS

One peculiar Italian institution is the *albergo diurno* or **day hotel** – not as sleazy as it sounds in fact, but an establishment providing bathrooms, showers, cleaning services, hairdressers and the like for a fixed rate, usually around L7000. You'll often find them at train stations and they're usually open daily 6am–midnight. Useful for a fast clean-up if you're on the move.

PRIVATE ROOMS

With the intense summer demands on hotel space, "**rooms for rent**" signs are becoming an increasingly common sight in both Tuscany and Umbria. Local tourist offices usually have lists of rooms on offer (though you'll invariably need to ask for these specially) and wandering around towns, or driving through the countryside, you'll see signs – often in English or German (*zimmer*), as well as Italian (*camere*). Most are in private houses, rather than the specially constructed blocks that seem to have taken over across the Adriatic in Greece.

YOUTH HOSTELS AND STUDENT ACCOMMODATION

Youth hostels cost an average of around L15,000 a night for a dormitory bed, which doesn't represent a massive saving on the cheapest double hotel room, especially if you have to take a bus out to their customarily peripheral locations. If you're travelling on your own, though, the savings are real, and many hostels have facilities – cheap restaurants, kitchens, etc – that enable you to cut costs further. In a few cases, too, the hostels are beautifully located.

Most of the hostels are members of the official International Youth Hostel Federation, and strictly speaking you need to be a member of that organization in order to use them. Many, however, allow you to join on the spot, or simply charge you extra. Whether or not you're a IYHF member, you'll need to book ahead at hostels in the summer months – and for major cities like Florence it's worth doing so at least fifteen days in advance. We've listed all the relevant hostels in the guide, but for the very latest information contact the Italian youth hostels association's travel section, *Associazione Italiana Alberghi per la Gioventù*, Palazzo della Civiltà del Lavoro, Quadrato della Concordia, 00144 EUR Roma (☎06/462.342).

Tuscany has just seven IYHF hostels, at Florence, Siena, Pisa, Volterra, San Gimignano, Lucolena and Tavarnelle (the last two in Chianti); Umbria has five, at Assisi, Foligno, San Venanzo, Sigillo and Trevi.

STUDENT ACCOMMODATION

In the university cities of Florence, Perugia, Siena and Pisa, it's possible to stay in **student accommodation** vacated by Italian students for the summer, or occasionally at other times. Accommodation is generally in individual rooms and can work out a lot cheaper than a straight hotel room; we've listed possible places in the text. In Florence, once again, contact locations as far ahead as possible to be sure of a room.

CAMPING

Camping is not especially popular in Tuscany, except on the island of Elba, and the sites that do exist are mostly on the upmarket side – well-equipped and expensive. Once you've added the cost of a tent and possibly a vehicle, they don't always work out any cheaper than staying in a hotel or hostel: prices range from about L5000 per person daily, plus L4000–7000 for each caravan or tent, plus around L4000 for each vehicle.

Useful sites are detailed in the text. If you're camping extensively it might be worth investing in the *TCI*'s *Campeggi e Villaggi Turistici*, available from the outlets listed on p.16, which gives full **details** of facilities. If you don't need something this detailed, you can obtain an abridged version free of charge from *Centro Internazionale Prenotazioni, Federcampeggio*, Casella Postale 23, 50041 Calenzano, Florence (☎055/882.391). This is also the place to **book places** on campsites in advance.

VILLAS AND AGRITURISMO

Travelling with a group of people, or even just in a pair, it's worth considering renting a **villa or farmhouse** for a week or two. These are not too expensive if you can split costs between, say, four people, are of a consistently high standard, and often enjoy marvellous locations. **British-**

YOUTH HOSTEL ASSOCIATIONS

Australia *Australian Youth Hostels Association*, Level 3, 10 Mallett St, Camperdown, New South Wales 2050 (☎02/565 1699).

Canada *Canadian Hostelling Association*, 400–405 Catherine St, Ottawa, Ontario, K2P 1C34 (☎613/237 7884).

England and Wales *Youth Hostel Association* (*YHA*), Trevelyan House, 8 St. Stephen's Hill, St. Alban's, Herts AL1 2DY (☎0727/55215). London shop and information office: 14 Southampton St, London WC2E 7HY (☎071/836 8542).

Ireland *An Oige*, 61 Mountjoy St, Dublin 7 (☎01/304555).

New Zealand *Youth Hostels Association of New Zealand*, PO Box 436, Christchurch 1 (☎03/799970).

Northern Ireland *Youth Hostel Association of Northern Ireland*, 56 Bradbury Place, Belfast, BT7 1RU (☎0232/324733).

Scotland *Scottish Youth Hostel Association*, 7 Glebe Crescent, Stirling, FK8 2JA (☎0786/51181).

USA *American Youth Hostels* (*AYH*), PO Box 37613, Washington, DC 200013 (☎202/783 6161).

based operators who rent villas, either on their own, or in conjunction with a flight or fly-drive package, are detailed on p.6.

If you want to book on the spot, once in Italy, your best bet is through the **Agriturismo** scheme, whereby farmers let out their unused buildings. Usually these have a self-contained flat or building to let, though a few places just rent rooms on a bed-and-breakfast basis. Costs are generally equivalent to one- or two-star hotel prices.

It is possible to call up *agriturismo* places directly, or even follow the signs and chance your luck. Most, however, require **advance booking** through the local *agriturismo* office (*Associazione Regionale Agriturist* — see box below for addresses). For a full **list of properties** all over Italy write to *Agriturist*, Corso V. Emanuele 101, Rome (☎06/651.2342).

A similar, though somewhat less centralized, organization to *Agriturismo* is **Turismo Verde**, who have outlets in a number of Tuscan towns. Most of the local branches arrange "*ospitalità*" —

again usually farm-based apartments — as well as promoting wine sales and the like.

MOUNTAIN RIFUGI

If you're planning on **hiking or climbing**, you may want to make use of the *rifugi* network of mountain huts. Most are owned by the *Club Alpino Italiano* who allow non-members to stay for around L12,000 a night, though a few are privately operated and charge around double this; most are open July–August only and winter weekends. *Rifugi* in general are fairly spartan, with bunks in unheated dorms, but their sites can be magnificent, and usually leave you well placed to continue your hike the next day.

All *CAI rifugi* are obliged to take you if you turn up on the off chance, but often it's better to book in advance, either through the local tourist office, the *Club Alpino Italiano*, Via Foscolo 3, Milan (☎02/8021.554), or direct with the *rifugi*. Addresses and phone numbers are given where relevant in the text of the guide.

REGIONAL AGRITURIST OFFICES

Florence: Piazza San Firenze 3, 50122 Firenze, (☎055/287.838).

Arezzo: Corso Italia 205, 52100 Arezzo (☎0575/22.280).

Grosseto: Via D. Chiesa 4, 58100 Grosseto (☎0564/21.020).

Livorno: Via G. Marrado 14, 57126 Livorno (☎0586/812.7445).

Lucca: Viale Barsanti e Matteucci, 55100 Lucca (☎0583/332.044).

Massa Carrara: Palazzo Standa, Via Marina Vecchia, Massa Carrara 54100 (☎0585/40.701).

Orvieto: Via di Piazza del Popolo 16, 05018 Orvieto (☎0763/42.820).

Perugia: Piazza B. Michelotti 1, 06100 Perugia (☎075/61.481).

Pisa: Via B. Croce 62, 56100 Pisa (☎050/262.212).

Pistoia: Via F. Pacini 45, 51100 Pistoia (☎0573/21.231).

Siena: Piazza G. Matteotti 3, 53100 Siena (☎0577/46.194).

Terni: Corso del Popolo 37, 05100 Terni (☎0744/43.448).

FOOD AND DRINK

The traditional dishes of Tuscany are Italy's most influential cuisine – the ingredients and culinary techniques of the region have made their mark not just on the menus of the rest of Italy but also abroad, even in France. Umbrian cooking may not be accorded quite the same degree of reverence, but the produce of Italy's only landlocked province is of the highest quality, with its truffles and ham being especially valued. And wine has always been central to the area's economy and way of life, with familiar names such as Chianti and Orvieto representing just a portion of the enormous output from the Tuscan and Umbrian vineyards.

BREAKFAST AND SNACKS

Most Italians start their day in a bar, their **breakfast** consisting of a coffee and the ubiquitous *cornetto* – a jam-, custard- or chocolate-filled croissant, which you usually help yourself to from the counter (unfilled croissants are occasionally ard to find; ask for *un cornetto semplice* or *normale*). Breakfast in a hotel (*prima colazione*) will be a limp affair, usually worth avoiding.

At other times of the day, **sandwiches** (*panini*) can be pretty substantial, a bread stick or roll packed with any number of fillings. Specialised sandwich bars (*paninoteche*) can be found in many larger towns, and grocer's shops (*alimentari*) are another standard source; you'll pay L1500–L3000 for most varieties. Bars may also offer *panini* and *tramezzini*, ready-made sliced white bread with mixed fillings – tasty and

slightly cheaper than the average *panino*. Toasted sandwiches (*toste*) are common too: in a *paninoteca* you can get whatever you want toasted; in ordinary bars it's more likely to be a variation on cheese or ham with tomato.

If you want **hot take-away food** there are a number of options. It's possible to find slices of **pizza** (*pizza rustica*) pretty much everywhere (buy it by the *etto* – 200g), and you can get most of the things already mentioned, plus pasta, chips, even full hot meals, in a ***tavola calda***, a sort of snack bar that's at its best in the morning when everything is fresh. Some are self-service with limited seating – found mostly in the bigger towns and inside larger train stations. Another alternative is a ***rosticceria***. Here the speciality is usually spit-roast chicken but *rosticcerie* often serve fast foods such as pizza slices, chips and hamburgers.

Other sources of quick snacks are **markets**, some of which sell take-away food from stalls, including *focacce* – oven-baked pastries topped with cheese or tomato or filled with spinach, fried offal or meat; and *arancini* or *suppli* – deep-fried balls of rice with meat (*rosso*) or butter and cheese (*bianco*) filling. **Supermarkets**, also, are an obvious stop for a picnic lunch: the major department store chains, *Upim* and *Standa*, often have food halls.

ICE CREAM

Italian **ice cream** (*gelato*) is justifiably famous: a cone (*un cono*) is an indispensable accessory to the evening *passeggiata*. Most bars have a fairly good selection, but for real choice go to a ***gelateria***, where the range is a tribute to the Italian imagination and flair for display. You'll sometimes have to go by appearance rather than attempting to decipher their exotic names, many of which don't even mean much to Italians: often the basics – chocolate, strawberry, vanilla – are best. There's no problem locating the finest *gelateria* in town – it's the one that draws the crowds, and we've noted the really special places in the text.

PIZZA

Everywhere in Italy, **pizza** comes thin and flat, not deep-pan, and the choice of toppings is fairly limited – none of the pineapple and sweetcorn variations that have taken off in Britain and

America. Most are cooked in the traditional way, in wood-fired ovens (*forno a legna*), rather than in the squeaky-clean electric ones, so that they arrive blasted and bubbling on the surface, and with a distinctive charcoal taste.

Pizzerie range from a stand-up counter selling slices (*alla taglia*) to a fully-fledged sit-down restaurant, and on the whole they don't sell much else besides pizza and drinks, though in large towns you'll come across a pizzeria that also does simple pasta dishes. Some straight restaurants often have pizza on the menu too. A basic cheese and tomato pizza (*margherita*) costs around L4000, a fancier variety anything up to L15,000, and it's quite acceptable to cut it into slices and eat it with your fingers. Check the food glossary (see box) for a rundown of varieties.

RESTAURANTS

Tuscan and Umbrian restaurant meals (lunch is *pranzo*, dinner is *cena*) are traditionally long and pretty solid affairs, starting with an *antipasto*, followed by a risotto or a pasta dish, leading on to a fish or meat course, cheese, and finished with fresh fruit and coffee. Even everyday meals are a miniaturised version of this. The minimalist ethic of nouvelle cuisine has made inroads into the more expensive restaurants, but the staple fare at the majority of places is exactly what it might have been a century ago. Vegetarianism is a concept that's also been slow to catch on – outside Florence you're unlikely to find any vegetarian places, and they are pretty scarce even there.

TYPES OF RESTAURANT

Restaurants are most commonly called either **trattorie** or **ristoranti**. Traditionally, a trattoria is a cheaper and more basic purveyor of home-style cooking (*cucina casalinga*), while a *ristorante* is more upmarket, with aproned waiters and tablecloths. These days, however, there's a fine line between the two, as its rather chic for an expensive restaurant to call itself a trattoria. It's in the rural areas that you're most likely to come across an old-style trattoria, the sort of place where there's no written menu (the waiter will simply reel off a list of what's on) and no bottled wine (it's straight from the vats of the local farm). A true *ristorante* will always have a written menu and a reasonable choice of wines, though even in smart places it's standard to choose the ordinary house wine. In popular tourist towns (again,

Florence is a sinner in this) you may well find restaurants willing to serve full meals only – no lunchtime restraint of a pasta and salad allowed.

Increasingly, too, you come across **osterie**. These used to be old-fashioned places specializing in home cooking, though recently they have had quite a vogue and the *osteria* tag more often signifies a youngish ownership and clientele, and adventurous foods. Other types of restaurant include **spaghetterie** and **birrerie**, restaurant-bars which serve basic pasta dishes, or beer and snacks, and are again often youngish hang-outs.

THE MENU AND THE BILL

The cheapest – though not the most rewarding way – to eat in bigger city restaurants is to opt for a set price *menu turistico*. This will give you a first course (pasta or soup), main course, pudding (usually a piece of fruit) and half a litre of water and a quarter litre of wine per person. Beware the increasingly common *prezzo fisso* menu, which excludes cover, service, dessert and beverages.

Working your way through an Italian menu (*la lista*, or sometimes *il menù*) is pretty straightforward. **Antipasto** (literally "before the meal") is a course generally consisting of various cold cuts of meat, seafood and various cold vegetable dishes. *Prosciutto* is a common *antipasto* dish: it's ham either cooked (*cotto*) or just cured and hung (*crudo*), served alone or with melon, figs or mozzarella cheese. Also very common are *crostini*, canapés of minced chicken liver or minced sautéed spleen (. . .*di milza*).

VEGETARIAN DISHES

Italy isn't too bad a country to travel in if you're a **vegetarian**. There are several pasta sauces and pizza varieties without meat, and if you eat fish and seafood you should have no problem at all. Salads, too, are fresh and good, and filling. Beware vegetable soups, which may be made with meat stock. The only real problem is one of comprehension: Italians don't really understand someone not eating meat, and stating the obvious doesn't always get the point across. Saying you're a vegetarian (*Sono vegetariano/a*) and asking if a dish has meat in (*c'è carne dentro?*) might still turn up a poultry or *prosciutto* dish. Better is to ask what a dish is made with before you order (*com'è fatto?*), so that you can spot the non-meaty meat. **Vegans** have a much harder time, though pizzas without cheese are a good standby, and the fruit is excellent.

A LIST OF FOODS AND DISHES

Basics and snacks

Aceto	Vinegar	*Grissini*	Bread sticks	*Patatine fritte*	Chips
Aglio	Garlic	*Maionese*	Mayonnaise	*Pepe*	Pepper
Biscotti	Biscuits	*Marmellata*	Jam	*Pizzetta*	Small cheese and
Burro	Butter	*Olio*	Oil		tomato pizza
Caramelle	Sweets	*Olive*	Olives	*Riso*	Rice
Cioccolato	Chocolate	*Pane*	Bread	*Sale*	Salt
Focaccia	Oven-baked snack	*Pane integrale*	Wholemeal bread	*Uova*	Eggs
Formaggio	Cheese	*Panino*	Bread roll/	*Yogurt*	Yoghurt
Frittata	Omelette		sandwich	*Zúcchero*	Sugar
Gelato	Ice cream	*Patatine*	Crisps	*Zuppa*	Soup

Pizzas

Calzone	Folded pizza with cheese, ham and tomato	*Margherita*	Cheese and tomato
		Marinara	Tomato, anchovy and olive oil
Capricciosa	Literally "capricious"; topped with whatever they've got in the kitchen, usually including baby artichoke, ham and egg	*Napoli/ Napoletana*	Tomato
		Quattro formaggi	"Four cheeses", usually including mozzarella, fontina and gruyère
Cardinale	Ham and olives		
Frutta di mare	Seafood; usually mussels, prawns, and clams	*Quattro stagioni*	"Four seasons"; the toppings split into four separate sections, usually including ham, green pepper, onion, egg, etc
Funghi	Mushroom; tinned, sliced button mushrooms unless it specifies fresh mushrooms, *funghi freschi*		

Antipasti and starters

Antipasto misto	Mixed cold meats and cheese	*Insalata russa*	Russian salad: diced vegetables in mayonnaise
Bruschetta	Garlic bread, often topped with tomatoes and olive oil	*Melanzane in parmigiana*	Aubergine in tomato and parmesan cheese
Caponata	Mixed aubergine, olives, tomatoes	*Peperonata*	Green and red peppers stewed in olive oil
Caprese	Tomato and mozzarella cheese salad	*Pomodori ripieni*	Stuffed tomatoes
Crostini	Mixed chicken liver canapés		
Insalata di mare	Seafood salad	*Prosciutto*	Ham
Insalata di riso	Rice salad	*Salame*	Salami

The first course (primo): soups, pasta . . .

Brodo	Clear broth	*Pastina in brodo*	Pasta pieces in clear broth
Cannelloni	Large tubes of pasta, stuffed	*Penne*	Smaller version of rigatoni
Farfalle	Literally "butterfly"-shaped pasta	*Ravioli*	Ravioli
		Rigatoni	Large, grooved tubular pasta
Fettucine	Narrow pasta ribbons	*Risotto*	Cooked rice dish, with sauce
Gnocchi	Small potato and dough dumplings	*Spaghetti*	Spaghetti
		Spaghettini	Thin spaghetti
Lasagne	Lasagne	*Stracciatella*	Broth with egg
Maccheroni	Tubular spaghetti	*Tagliatelle*	Pasta ribbons, another word for fettucine
Minestrina	Any light soup		
Minestrone	Thick vegetable soup	*Tortellini*	Small rings of pasta, stuffed with meat or cheese
Pasta al forno	Pasta baked with minced meat, eggs, tomato and cheese		
Pasta fagioli	Pasta soup with beans	*Vermicelli*	Very thin spaghetti ("little worms")

... and pasta sauce (salsa)

Arrabiata	Spicy tomato sauce, with chillies	*Parmigiano*	Parmesan cheese
Bolognese	Meat sauce	*Peperoncino*	Olive oil, garlic and fresh chillies
Burro	Butter	*Pesto*	Green basil and garlic sauce
Carbonara	Cream, ham and beaten egg	*Pomodoro*	Tomato sauce
Funghi	Mushroom	*Ragù*	Meat sauce
Matriciana	Cubed pork and tomato sauce	*Vóngole*	Clam and tomato sauce
Panna	Cream		

The second course (secondo): meat (carne) ...

Agnello	Lamb	*Fegato*	Liver	*Pancetta*	Bacon
Bistecca	Steak	*Involtini*	Meat slices, rolled	*Pollo*	Chicken
Cervello	Brain		and stuffed	*Polpette*	Meatballs
Cinghiale	Wild boar	*Lepre*	Hare	*Rognoni*	Kidneys
Coniglio	Rabbit	*Lingua*	Tongue	*Salsiccia*	Sausage
Costolette	Chops	*Maiale*	Pork	*Saltimbocca*	Veal with ham
Cotolette	Cutlets	*Manzo*	Beef	*Spezzatino*	Stew
Fagiano	Pheasant	*Mortadella*	Salami-type cured	*Tacchino*	Turkey
Faraona	Guinea fowl		meat	*Trippa*	Tripe
Fegatini	Chicken livers	*Ossobuco*	Shin of veal	*Vitello*	Veal
		Pernice	Partridge		

... fish (pesce) and shellfish (crostacei)

Acciughe	Anchovies	*Gamberetti*	Shrimps	*Sgombro*	Mackerel
Anguilla	Eel	*Gámberi*	Prawns	*Sógliola*	Sole
Aragosta	Lobster	*Granchio*	Crab	*Tonno*	Tuna
Baccalà	Dried salted cod	*Merluzzo*	Cod	*Triglie*	Red mullet
Calamari	Squid	*Ostriche*	Oysters	*Trota*	Trout
Céfalo	Mullet	*Pescespada*	Swordfish	*Vóngole*	Clams
Cozze	Mussels	*Pólipo*	Octopus		
Dentice	Dentex	*Sarde*	Sardines		

Vegetables (contorni) and salad (insalata)

Asparagi	Asparagus	*Cetriolo*	Cucumber	*Orígano*	Oregano
Basílico	Basil	*Cipolla*	Onion	*Patate*	Potatoes
Bróccoli	Broccoli	*Fagioli*	Beans	*Peperoni*	Peppers
Cápperi	Capers	*Fagiolini*	Green beans	*Piselli*	Peas
Carciofi	Artichokes	*Finocchio*	Fennel	*Pomodori*	Tomatoes
Carciofini	Artichoke hearts	*Funghi*	Mushrooms	*Radicchio*	Chicory
Carotte	Carrots	*Insalata verde/*	Green salad/	*Spinaci*	Spinach
Cavolfiori	Cauliflower	*mista*	mixed salad	*Zucchini*	Courgettes
Cávolo	Cabbage	*Melanzane*	Aubergine		

Some terms and useful words

Affumicato	Smoked	*Al dente*	Firm, not	*Milanese*	Fried in egg and
Arrosto	Roast		overcooked		breadcrumbs
Ben cotto	Well done	*Ai Ferri*	Grilled without	*Pizzaiola*	Cooked with
Bollito/lesso	Boiled		oil		tomato sauce
Brasato	Cooked in	*Fritto*	Fried	*Ripieno*	Stuffed
	wine	*Grattuggiato*	Grated	*Sangue*	Rare
Cotto	Cooked (not	*Alla griglia*	Grilled	*Allo spiedo*	On the spit
	raw)	*Al Marsala*	Cooked with	*Surgelato*	Frozen
Crudo	Raw		Marsala wine	*Úmido*	Steamed/stewed

Sweets (dolci), fruit (frutta), cheeses (formaggi) and nuts (noce)

Amaretti	Macaroons	*Gorgonzola*	Soft blue-veined cheese	*Pere*	Pears
Ananas	Pineapple			*Pesche*	Peaches
Anguria/ Coccómero	Water melon	*Limone*	Lemon	*Pignoli*	Pine nuts
		Macedonia	Fruit salad	*Pistacchio*	Pistachio nut
Arance	Oranges	*Mándorle*	Almonds	*Provolone*	Hard strong cheese
Banane	Bananas	*Mele*	Apples	*Ricotta*	Soft white sheep's cheese
Cacchi	Persimmons	*Melone*	Melon		
Ciliegie	Cherries	*Mozzarella*	Bland soft white cheese used on pizzas	*Torta*	Cake, tart
Fichi	Figs			*Uva*	Grapes
Fichi d'India	Prickly pears			*Zabaglione*	Dessert made with eggs, sugar and Marsala wine
Fontina	Northern Italian cooking cheese	*Néspole*	Medlars		
		Parmigiano	Parmesan cheese		
Frágole	Strawberries	*Pecorino*	Strong hard sheep's cheese	*Zuppa Inglese*	Trifle
Gelato	Ice cream				

Drinks

Acqua minerale	Mineral water	*Ghiaccio*	Ice	*Tónico*	Tonic water
Aranciata	Orangeade	*Granita*	Iced drink, with coffee or fruit	*Vino*	Wine
Bicchiere	Glass			*Rosso*	Red
Birra	Beer	*Latte*	Milk	*Bianco*	White
Bottiglia	Bottle	*Limonata*	Lemonade	*Rosato*	Rosé
Caffè	Coffee	*Selz*	Soda water	*Secco*	Dry
Cioccolata calda	Hot chocolate	*Spremuta*	Fresh fruit juice	*Dolce*	Sweet
Frappé	Milk shake made with ice cream	*Spumante*	Sparkling wine	*Litro*	Litre
		Succo di Frutta	Concentrated fruit juice with sugar	*Mezzo*	Half
				Quarto	Quarter
Frullato	Milk shake	*Té*	Tea	*Salute!*	Cheers!

The next course, **il primo**, consists of a soup, risotto, polenta or pasta dish. This is followed by **il secondo** – the meat or fish course, usually served alone, except for perhaps a wedge of lemon or tomato. Watch out when ordering fish or Florence's famous *bistecca alla fiorentina*, which will usually be served by weight: 250g is usually plenty for one person, or ask to have a look at the fish before it's cooked. Anything marked *S.Q.* or *hg* means you are paying by weight (hg = 100g, or around 4oz).

Vegetables – **il contorno** – or salads – **insalata** – are ordered and served separately, and often there won't be much (if any) choice: most frequent are beans (*fagioli*), potatoes (*patate*), and salads either green (*verde*) or mixed (*mista*).

For afters, you nearly always get a choice of fresh fruit (*frutta*) and a selection of **desserts** (*dolci*) – invariably focused on ice cream or a selection of home-made flans (*torta della casa*).

At the end of the meal ask for **the bill** (*il conto*). In many trattorias this amounts to no more than an illegible scrap of paper, and if you want to be sure you're not being ripped off, ask to have a receipt (*ricevuta*), something all bars and restaurants are legally bound to provide anyway. Bear in mind that almost everywhere you'll pay a cover charge on top of your food – the *pane e coperto* or just *coperto* – of around L1500 a head. As well as the *coperto*, service (*servizio*) will often be added, generally about ten percent. If service isn't included you should perhaps tip about the same amount, though trattorias outside the large cities won't necessarily expect this.

TUSCAN CUISINE

The most important ingredient of Tuscan cooking is **olive oil**, which comes into almost every dish – as a dressing for salads, as a medium for frying, and poured over bread and vegetables and into soups and stews just before serving. The olive picking begins around November, before the olives are fully ripe; the oil produced from the first pressing of these unripe whole olives is *extra virgine*, the purest and most alkaline oil,

CHECKLIST OF TUSCAN DISHES

Antipasti

Crostini di milza	Minced spleen on pieces of toasted bread	*Pinzimonio*	Raw seasonal vegetables in *extra virgine* olive oil, with salt and pepper
Donzelle or *donzelline*	Fried dough balls		
Fettunta or *Bruschetta*	Slab of toast flavoured with garlic and *extra virgine* olive oil	*Prosciutto di cinghiale*	Cured wild boar ham
		Salame toscano	Pork sausage with pepper and cubes of fat
Finocchiona	Pork sausage flavoured with fennel	*Salsicce*	Pork or wild boar sausage

Primi

Acquacotta	Onion soup served with toast and poached egg	*Pappa al pomodoro*	Tomato soup thickened with bread
Cacciucco	Fish stew with tomatoes, bread and red wine	*Pappardelle*	Wide, short noodles, often served with hare sauce (*con lepre*)
Carabaccia	Onion soup		
Garmugia	Soup made with fava beans, peas, artichokes, asparagus and bacon	*Pasta alla carrettiera*	Pasta with tomato, garlic, pepper, parsley and chilli
Gnocchi di ricotta	Dumplings filled with ricotta and spinach	*Penne strascicate*	Quill-shaped pasta in meat sauce
Minestra di farro	Wheat and bean soup	*Ribollita*	Winter vegetable soup, based on beans and thickened with bread
Minestrone alla fiorentina	Haricot bean soup with red cabbage, tomatoes, onions and herbs		
		Risotto nero	Rice cooked with cuttle-fish in its ink
Panzanella	Summer salad of tomatoes, basil, cucumber, onion and bread	*Zuppa di fagioli*	Bean soup

Secondi

Arista	Roast pork loin with garlic and rosemary	*Pollo alla diavola* or *al mattone*	Chicken flattened with a brick, grilled with herbs
Asparagi alla fiorentina	Asparagus with butter, fried egg and cheese	*Scottiglia*	Stew of veal, game, and poultry, cooked with white wine and tomatoes
Baccalà alla livornese	Salt cod with garlic, tomatoes and parsley	*Spiedini di maiale*	Skewered spiced cubes of pork loin and liver, with bread and bay leaves
Bistecca alla fiorentina	Thick grilled T-bone steak		
Cibreo	Chicken liver and egg stew	*Tonno con fagioli*	Tuna with white beans and raw onion
Cieche alla pisana	Small eels cooked with sage and tomatoes, served with Parmesan	*Triglie alla livornese*	Red mullet cooked with tomatoes, garlic and parsley
Lombatina	Veal chop		
Peposo	Peppered beef stew	*Trippa alla fiorentina*	Tripe in tomato sauce, served with Parmesan

Contorni

Fagioli all'olio	White beans served with olive oil	*Fagioli all'uccelletto*	White beans cooked with tomatoes, garlic and sage
		Frittata di carciofi	Fried artichoke flan

Dolci

Brigidini	Anise wafer biscuits	Necci	Chestnut-flour crêpes
Buccellato	Anise raisin cake	Panforte	Hard fruit, nut and spice cake
Cantucci or Cantuccini	Small almond biscuits, served with Vinsanto wine	Ricciarelli	Marzipan almond biscuits
Castagnaccio	Unleavened chestnut-flour cake containing raisins, walnuts and rosemary	Schiacciata alla fiorentina	Orange-flavoured cake covered with powdered sugar, eaten at carnival time
Cenci	Fried dough dusted with powdered sugar	Schiacciata con l'uva	Grape- and sugar-covered bread dessert
Frittelle di riso	Rice fritters	Zuccotto	Sponge cake filled with chocolate and whipped cream
Meringa	Frozen meringue with whipped cream and chocolate		

with less than one percent acidity. The other categories of good quality oil, in descending order of excellence and ascending order of acidity, are *soprafino virgine*, *fino virgine* and *virgine*. Top-quality oil is now an even more precious commodity than it used to be – a terrible frost in 1985 destroyed so many olive trees that several of Tuscany's oil producers have to use oil from other parts of the country in their blends.

The biggest influence on Tuscan cooking are the simple rustic dishes of **Florence**, the most famous of which is *bistecca alla fiorentina*, a thick T-bone steak grilled over charcoal, usually served rare. The meat for true Florentine *bistecca* comes from the Valdichiana area, south of Arezzo, from an animal no more than two and a half years old.

The Florentines are also fond of the unpretentious *arista*, roast pork loin stuffed with rosemary and garlic, and of *pollo alla diavola*, a flattened chicken marinated with olive oil and lemon juice or white wine, then dressed with herbs before grilling. Wild hare features on many menus, as *lepre in dolce e forte* – cooked in wine and tomatoes with raisins, pine nuts, candied orange peel and herbs – or as *pappardelle con lepre* – noodles topped with hare, fried bacon and tomatoes. These are basically peasant meals that have become staples of the regional cuisine, as have such tripe dishes as *trippa e zampa* – tripe with calf's feet, onions, tomatoes, white wine, garlic and nutmeg.

Each major Tuscan town has its culinary specialities, too, a vestige of the days when the region was divided into city states. **Pisa**'s treats

include black cabbage soup, new-born eels (*cieche*) fried with garlic and sage, and *torta coi bischeri*, a cake filled with rice, candied fruit, chocolate, raisins and pine nuts, and flavoured with nutmeg and liqueur. Many of the specialities of **Siena** date back to the medieval period, including *salsicce secche* (dried sausages) and *panforte di Siena*, the celebrated spicy cake of nuts and candied fruit. **Arezzo** has *acquacotta*, a soup of fried onion, tomato and bread, mixed with egg and cheese, while **Livorno** offers *cacciucco*, a mixture of fish with bread, tomatoes, garlic and white wine, and *brodatino*, a red bean and black cabbage soup.

Everywhere in the province, **soups** are central to the cuisine, the most famous being *ribollita*, a thick vegetable concoction traditionally including left-over beans (hence "reboiled"). *Pappa al pomodoro* is a popular broth with bread and tomatoes and basil cooked to a sustaining stodge. As *secondi*, you'll find a lot of **"hunters' dishes"** (*cacciatore*), most commonly *cinghiale* (wild boar). White *cannellini* **beans** are the favourite vegetables, boiled with rosemary and eaten with olive oil, or cooked with tomatoes (*all'uccelletto*). Broad beans, peas, artichokes and asparagus are other much-used vegetables, but none is as typically Tuscan as **spinach**. It's served as a side vegetable, or in combination with omelettes, poached eggs or fish, or mixed with ricotta to make gnocchi, or used as a filling for *crespoline* (pancakes).

Despite the reduction of the crop caused by recent outbreaks of tree disease, wild **chestnuts** remain another staple of Tuscan cooking, and there is a long tradition of specialities based on dried chestnuts and chestnut flour – such as the delicious *castagnaccio* (chestnut cake), made with pine nuts, raisins and rosemary.

Sheep's milk *pecorino* is the most widespread Tuscan **cheese**, but the most famous is the oval *marzolino* from the Chianti region, which is eaten either fresh or ripened, and is often grated over meat dishes. **Dessert** menus will often include *cantuccini*, hard biscuits which are dipped in a glass of Vinsanto, or *zuccotto*, a brandy-soaked sponge cake filled with cream mixed with choco-late powder, almonds and hazelnuts – like *tira-misù* elsewhere in Italy.

UMBRIAN CUISINE

Like that of Tuscany, Umbria's cooking relies heavily on rustic staples – pastas and roast meats – and tends to the simple and homely. It is, however, the only region in Italy apart from Piemonte to offer **truffles** in any abundance. Traditionally the white truffle is the most highly prized on account of its aroma, but locals swear by the Umbrian grey-white (*bianchetto*) type and the black truffle that's unique to the area around Spoleto and Norcia in the east. You're most likely to come across them as a modest sprinkling over your *tagliatelle* or meat, or on *crostini* – at a price

CHECKLIST OF UMBRIAN DISHES

Antipasti

Bruschetta	Garlic toast with olive oil	*Schiacciata*	Flat bread baked with olive oil, or flavoured with onions or cooked greens
Prosciutto di Norcia	Cured raw ham from Norcia		
Salame mezzafegato	Sausage spiced with a mixture of pine nuts, pork liver, candied orange, sugar and raisins	*Torta al testo*	Unleavened bread baked on a slab of stone

Primi

Manfrigoli	Rustic pasta made from emmer, a coarse type of wheat introduced into the region by the Romans	*Pici, stringozzi* or *ceriole*	Thread-like spaghetti, usually served with garlicky tomato sauce
Minestra di farro	Tomato, wheat and vegeta-ble soup	*Spaghetti alla norcina*	Spaghetti with an oily sauce of black truffles, garlic and anchovies
		Umbrici	Large, heavy noodles

Secondi

Anguilla alla brace	Grilled eel	*Pollo in porchetta*	Chicken cooked in the same way as suckling pig
Anguilla in úmido	Eel cooked with tomatoes, onions, garlic and white wine	*Porchetta*	Suckling pig cooked in a wood oven with fennel, garlic, mint and rosemary
Frittata di tartufi	Black truffle omelette		
Gobbi alla perugina	Deep-fried cardoons (like arti-chokes) with meat sauce	*Regina in porchetta*	Lago Trasimeno carp, cooked as above
Lepre alle olive	Hare cooked with herbs, white wine and olives	*Salsiccia all'uva*	Pork sausage cooked with grapes
Palombe or *palombacci*	Wood pigeon, usually spit-roasted	*Tegamaccio*	Freshwater-fish stew, with white wine and herbs

Dolci

Cialde	Paper-thin sweet biscuits	*Serpentone, torco-lato* or *torcolo*	Almond and dried fruit dessert in the shape of a coiled snake
Fave di morte	Almond biscuits		
Pinoccate	Pine nut biscuits		

that prohibits overindulgence. Producing truffles in controlled conditions is a culinary Holy Grail, and until there's success in this field they will remain a valuable commodity, with "no trespassers" signs common in the local woodlands. (For more on truffles, see the box on p.494)

Meat, and in particular **pork**, is the staple of the Umbrian main course, usually grilled or roasted. The region's small, free-range black pigs are famous, and have recently been joined by wild boar (*cinghiale*) – apparently escaped from Tuscany, and reproducing at a prodigious rate. Norcia is the acknowledged heart of pig country, with a superb selection of all things porcine, though other towns enjoy their own specialities. Città di Castello produces a *salame* made with spices and fennel seed; Cascia and Preci are known for their *mortadella*; Foligno has a distinctive dry *salame*; and Gualdo Tadino boasts a special sausage, the *soppressata*. Also look out for the extraordinary fruit-and-nut-flavoured *salame mezzafegato*. Endemic to the region, too, is *porchetta*, a whole roast suckling pig stuffed with herbs and spices and eaten sliced in crusty white rolls. It's an Umbrian concoction that's spread through most of central Italy, and is widely available as a snack from markets and roadside stalls.

Game may crop up on some menus, most often as pigeon, pheasant or guinea fowl. It's not unknown to be offered *tordo* (thrush), usually as a paté, so if this offends your sensibilities, watch out; other songbirds are hunted, often illegally, but they're unlikely to find their way into a restaurant. Despite the lack of a coast, some restaurants make the effort to bring in fresh **fish**, and there's a reasonably wide selection of freshwater specimens close to lakes and mountain rivers. Trout and crayfish are pulled out of the Nera, Clitunno and Scordo rivers, while Piediluco and Trasimeno yield eels, pike, tench and grey mullet.

The region's minor specialities are the tiny **lentils** of Castelluccio, the **beans** of Trasimeno, the **peas** from Bettona, and the **celery** and **cardoons** from around Trevi. Umbrian **olive oil**, though not surrounded by the hype of Tuscan oils, has a high reputation, especially that from around Trevi and Spoleto.

Umbria offers the standard Italian selection of exotically named **desserts**, most of them glorified sponges or tarts. *Perugino* chocolate is outstanding, but it's available throughout Italy.

One genuine novelty are the white **figs** of Amelia, mixed in a tooth-rotting combination of almonds and chocolate. **Cheeses** follow the standard variations, with the only genuine one-offs to be found in the mountains around Norcia and Gubbio.

DRINKING

Drinking in Tuscany and Umbria – as in Italy as a whole – is essentially as an accompaniment to food. There is little emphasis on drinking for its own sake. Locals sitting around in bars or cafés will spend hours chatting over just the one drink – whatever their age. And even in bars, most people you see imbibing one of the delicious Italian grappas or brandies will roll in just for the one shot, then be on their way. All of which, you might conclude, is a very pleasant change from Britain, which it is – the one snag being that at cafés, since Italians drink so little, prices are relatively high if you want to sit down.

WHERE TO DRINK

Bars are often very functional, brightly lit places, with a chrome counter, a *Gaggia* coffee machine and a picture of the local football team on the wall. You'll come here for **ordinary drinking** – a coffee in the morning, a quick beer, a cup of tea – but people don't generally idle away the day or evening in bars. Indeed in some, more rural places it's difficult to find a bar open much after 9pm. Where it does fit into the general Mediterranean pattern is that there are no set licensing hours and children are always allowed in; there's often a telephone and you can buy snacks and ice creams as well as drinks.

Whatever you're drinking, the **procedure** is the same. It's nearly always cheapest to drink standing at the counter (there's often nowhere to sit anyway), in which case you often pay first at the cash desk (*la cassa*), present your receipt (*scontrino*) to the barperson and give your order; sometimes you simply order your drink and pay as you leave. If you don't know how much a drink costs, there's always a list of prices (*listino prezzi*) behind the bar. It's customary to leave an extra L100 on the counter for the bar staff. Slap it down with your till receipt to guarantee prompt service. If there's waiter service, sit where you like, though bear in mind that to do this will cost perhaps twice as much, especially if you sit outside (the different prices are shown on the price list as *barra*, *tavola* and *terrazza*).

COFFEE, TEA, SOFT DRINKS

One of the most distinctive smells in an Italian street is that of fresh **coffee**, usually wafting out of a bar. The basic choice is either small and black (*espresso*, or just *caffè*), or white and frothy (*cappuccino*), but there are other varieties. If you want a longer *espresso* ask for a *caffè lungo*; a double *espresso* is *una doppia*, whilst an extra-strong *espresso* is *un ristretto*. A coffee topped with un-frothed milk is a *caffè latte*; with a drop of milk it's *caffè macchiato*; with a shot of alcohol it's *caffè corretto*. Although most places let you help yourself, some will lace your black coffee with sugar; if you don't want it, you can make sure by asking for *caffè senza zucchero*. Many places also now sell decaffeinated coffee (ask for *Hag*, even when it isn't); in summer you might want to have your coffee cold (*caffè freddo*). For a real treat, ask for *caffè granita* – cold coffee with crushed ice, usually topped with cream.

If you don't like coffee, there's always **tea**. Hot tea (*tè caldo*) comes with lemon (*con limone*) unless you ask for milk (*con latte*); or in summer you can drink it cold (*tè freddo*). **Milk** itself is drunk hot as often as cold, or you can get it with a dash of coffee (*latte macchiato*) and sometimes as milk shakes – *frappé*.

There are numerous **soft drinks** (*analcoliche*). A **spremuta** is a fresh fruit juice, squeezed at the bar, usually orange, lemon or grapefruit. You might need to add sugar to the lemon juice (. . . *di limone*) but the orange (. . . *d'arance*) is invariably sweet enough on its own, especially the crimson variety, made from blood oranges. A *succo di frutta* is a bottled fruit juice, widely drunk by Italians at breakfast. There's also crushed-ice **granite**, coming in several flavours other than coffee, and, of course, the usual range of fizzy drinks and concentrated juices: *Coke* is as prevalent as it is everywhere, while the home-grown Italian version, *Chinotto*, is less sweet – good with a slice of lemon. **Tap water** (*acqua normale*) is quite drinkable, and free in bars. **Mineral water** (*acqua minerale*) is a more common choice, either still (*senza gas, liscia, non gassata* or *naturale*) or sparkling (*con gas, gassata* or *frizzante*).

BEER AND SPIRITS

Beer (*birra*) is nearly always a lager-type brew which usually comes in one-third (*piccola*) or two-third (*grande*) litre bottles. Commonest and cheapest are the Italian brands *Peroni* and *Dreher*, both of which are very drinkable; if this is what you want, either state the brand name or ask for *birra nazionale* – otherwise you may be given the more expensive imported beer. In most bars you have a choice of this or draught beer (*alla spina*), measure for measure more expensive than the bottled variety. You may also come across darker beers (*birra nera* or *birra rossa*), which have a sweeter, maltier taste and resemble stout or bitter.

All the usual **spirits** are on sale and known mostly by their generic names. There are also Italian brands of the main varieties: the best Italian brandies are *Stock* and *Vecchia Romagna*. A generous shot of these costs about L2000, much more for imported stuff. The home-grown Italian firewater is **grappa**, originally from Bassano di Grappa in the Veneto but now made just about everywhere: the best Tuscan varieties are from Montalcino (Brunello) and Montepulciano. Grappas are made from the leftovers of the wine-making process (skins, stalks and the like) and drunk as *digestifs* after a meal; they're delicious – as well as being perhaps the cheapest way of getting plastered and savagely hung over.

You'll also find **fortified wines** like *Martini*, *Cinzano* and *Campari*; ask for a "Campari-soda" and you'll get a ready-mixed version from a little bottle. The non-alcoholic *Crodino* has recently caught on as a popular *aperitivo*. A slice of lemon is a *spicchio di limone*, ice is *ghiaccio*. You might also try *Cynar*, an artichoke-based sherry often drunk as an aperitif. There's also a daunting selection of **liqueurs**. *Amaro* is a bitter after-dinner drink, and probably the most popular way to round off a meal. The top brands, in rising order of bitterness, are *Montenegro*, *Ramazotti*, *Averna* and *Fernet-Branca*. *Amaretto* is a much sweeter concoction with a strong taste of marzipan, *Sambuca* a sticky-sweet aniseed brew, often served with a coffee bean in it and set on fire. *Strega* is another drink you'll see in every bar – the yellow stuff in elongated bottles: it's as sweet as it looks but not unpleasant.

WINE

Pursuit of wine is as good a reason as any for a visit to Tuscany. The province constitutes the heartland of Italian wine production, with sales of Chianti accounting for much of the country's wine exports, and the towns of Montalcino and Montepulciano producing two of the very finest Italian vintages. Umbria, by contrast, is low-key, except for the white Orvieto – a long-established bevvy developed by the Etruscans.

THE DENOMINAZIONE D'ORIGINE SYSTEM

The **Denominazione d'Origine Controllata** (DOC) label is the key to understanding what to look for in Italian wine, but it shouldn't be seen as any sort of guarantee. The denomination is a certification of origin, not of quality, and while it may mean a wine will be drinkable, it doesn't follow that a DOC wine will necessarily be better than a non-DOC.

Denomination **zones** are set by governmental decree. They specify where a certain named wine may be made, what grape varieties may be used, the maximum yield of grapes per hectare and how long the wine should be aged. Denominazione d'Origine Controllata (**DOC**) guarantees that the wine has been made to the specification of the rules for the zone in which it's produced; *vino da tavola* is simply wine that does not conform to the DOC laws. Denominazione d'Origine Controllata e Garantita (**DOCG**) is the only designation at the moment that actually has any qualitative meaning. Wines sold under this label not only have to conform to the ordinary DOC laws, but are also tested by government-appointed inspectors. At present there are only six such wines and three of them are Tuscan reds: Chianti, Brunello di Montalcino and Vino Nobile di Montepulciano. Two new DOCG districts will soon be operational – the Tuscan Carmignano and Torgiana Rosso Riserva from Umbria.

Though it's undoubtedly true that the DOC system has helped lift standards, the laws have come under fire from both growers and critics for their rigidity, constraints and anomalies. Chianti,

for instance, can be a quaffable lunchtime drink, a wine of pedigree to be treated with reverence, or – in the case of some of the 1984 harvest – it can be appalling. All Chianti wines, however, have a DOC. Some claim too that the restrictions of the DOCG are losing their credibility. With big reds such as Barolo the ordained ageing term can destroy all the fruitiness of the wine, while the entry of Albana di Romagna, a somewhat ordinary white, to DOCG status, with others to follow, has caused consternation.

Increasingly, producers eager to experiment have begun to disregard the regulations and make new wines that are sometimes expensive and among Italy's best wines, though they're still officially labelled "da tavola". Thus the nickname "super vini da tavola" has emerged to describe some of the excellent Tuscan table wines.

A major overhaul of the DOC system is now under way, prompted by a decline in domestic consumption and exports, and by the impending economic changes of the unified European market. To bring the hierarchy of Italian wine production closer to the French model, it is intended to increase the output of classified wines and cut back the volume from low-grade vineyards – even to the extent of eradicating the vines in certain areas. By the end of this century the percentage of Italian wines with DOC or DOCG classification should have risen from eleven percent to twenty, the number of DOCG zones should have risen to around fifty, and all DOC vintages will be subject to centralised quality control.

Until the last decade or so, most Tuscan wines – including Chianti – were criticised by wine buffs for methods geared principally to high yields, low prices, and never mind the quality. However, nudged along by the DOC laws (see below), standards have been steadily increasing in recent years. Besides the finer tuning of established names, there's a good deal of experimentation going on, with French grape varieties such as Chardonnay, Sauvignon and the Pinots being added to the blends of Tuscan wines, and producers using the French technique of *barriques,* 225-litre oak casks, for ageing reds and whites.

The snobbery associated with "serious" wine drinking in France or Britain remains for the most part, however, mercifully absent. Light reds such as those made from the *dolcetto* grape are

hauled out of the fridge in hot weather, while some full-bodied whites are drunk at near room temperature. Wine is also still very cheap. In bars you can get a glass of good local produce for L500 or so, and table wine – often decamped from the barrel – in restaurants is rarely charged at more than L3–4000 a litre. Major name bottled wine is pricier but still very good value; expect to pay from around L8000 a bottle in a restaurant, and less than half that from a shop or supermarket.

TUSCAN WINE

The wines of Tuscany are predominantly based on the local Sangiovese grape, the foundation of heavyweights such as Chianti, Brunello di Montalcino and Vino Nobile di Montepulciano. Tuscan wine is traditionally red, but new techniques have boosted the quality of many whites, especially Vernaccia di San Gimignano and Bianco di Montecarlo.

Chianti, the archetypal Italian wine, is also the most difficult to characterise, as the vintages produced by the seven Chianti districts (see p.163) vary from the lightest swillable stuff to deep-toned masterpieces aged in the cellars of ancient castles. The core of Chianti country is the Chianti Classico region between Florence and Siena, and even within this well-defined zone there are so many variables of climate and terrain that the character of the wine bottled in one estate might be quite distinct from the neighbouring product. This variety makes it as difficult to get a full grasp of the subject of Chianti wine as it is to master the intricacies of Bordeaux, but it does make a tasting tour a highly rewarding experience.

The greatest Tuscan red — **Brunello di Montalcino** — is produced just outside the Chianti region, around a hill town to the south of Siena. First created just over a hundred years back, Brunello is a powerful, complex and long-lasting wine, whose finest vintages sell at stratospheric prices. More accessible is the youthful **Rosso di Montalcino**, offering a cut-price glimpse of Brunello's majesty.

The mighty if inconsistent **Vino Nobile di Montepulciano** completes the upper tier of the Tuscan wine hierarchy, and the town again has a good regular red produced by less complex methods. **Carmignano**, from near Florence, traces its pedigree back to 1716 and is also highly regarded. Equally ancient and consistently good is **Pomino**, from the Mugello region, available as an excellent red and as a white made from Chardonnay and Pinot grapes. A rapidly improving alternative red DOC is **Morellino di Scansano**, from the coastal Maremma vineyards.

Non-DOC wines include some of the most fashionable Tuscan products at the moment. **Sassicaia**, produced near Livorno from Cabernet Sauvignon grapes, was described by Hugh Johnson as "perhaps Italy's best red wine". The Chianti-based Antinori estate, a pillar of the Tuscan wine establishment, joined the experimental wave in merging Sangiovese and Cabernet Sauvignon to make the top-rated **Tignanello**.

Cabernet-based wines have tended to steal the limelight from other innovations in recent years, with Castello dei Rampolli's **Sammarco**, Antinori's **Solaia**, and **Tavanelle** from the Villa Banfi doing especially well in blind tastings. However, Merlot and Pinot Noir grapes have begun to thrive in Tuscany, while **white-wine** producers are achieving excellent results with Chardonnay, Sauvignon Blanc, the Pinot varieties, and even Riesling and Gewurztraminer, usually considered to be best suited to cooler zones.

UMBRIAN WINE

Umbria has only a handful of DOC regions, many producing cheap, serviceable wine that rarely finds its way outside the region. Most are made from similar grapes and in similar ways to the workaday reds of Tuscany; however, as with its neighbour, innovation is beginning to produce ever more interesting high-quality vintages, and there's a trove of little-known local wines that repay searching out.

The region's most famous liquid export, **Orvieto**, is at the moment a shadow of its former self, local producers having realised that the world market was turning to dry, crisp wines. In response they've transformed the venerable vintage of antiquity — traditionally a semi-sweet *abboccato* — into a mass-produced plonk for the supermarket shelf. More ambitious producers, however, are now returning to the old wine, and with patience you'll find samples of the revamped product in and around the town. Orvieto's pre-eminence in Umbria itself has been taken over by **Grechetto**, made by countless producers across the region from the eponymous grape. It's a cheap and almost unfailingly reliable white.

Amongst the most famous of the region's new names is Giorgio **Lungarotti** at Torgiano (near Perugia), employing new grape varieties and innovative techniques to produce some of Italy's finest wines. Anything with his name on a label should be good, and in some cases — the *Rubesco Riserva* — of almost unparalleled excellence. Other key names include **Antinori**, the big Tuscan producers, who in Umbria make wine at Sala to the north of Orvieto: look out for their *Cervaro della Sala*.

Other exponents of Umbria's quest for quality are concentrated in the new **Montefalco** DOC region, a tiny area whose wines are at last becoming obtainable outside its environs; the reds are excellent, and the key producer is Adanti (for more, see p.471). Similar progress is also being made in the Upper Tiber above Perugia, where much is expected of the recent **Colli**

A WINE CHECKLIST

Tuscany

Bianco di Pitigliano Delicate dry white from southern Tuscany.

Bianco Vergine della Valdichiana Soft dry white from the area south of Arezzo.

Brunello di Montalcino Full-bodied red from south of Siena; one of Italy's finest wines.

Carmignano A dry red produced in the region to the west of Florence; this area also produces Vin Ruspo, a fresh rosé.

Chianti Produced in seven distinct central Tuscan districts, Chianti ranges from the roughest table wine to some of the most elegant reds bottled in Italy. (More details on Chianti appear in the entry on the Chianti region in Chapter Two.)

Colline Lucchesi A soft and lively DOC red from the hills east of Lucca.

Galestro Light, dry summer white – a recent development, motivated partly by the need to find some use for the surplus of low-grade white wine produced in Chianti.

Grattamacco Produced in the area to the south-east of Livorno, this non-DOC wine comes as a fruity white and as a full, dry red.

Montecarlo A full and dry white – one of Tuscany's finest – from the east of Lucca.

Morellino di Scansano A fairly dry, robust DOC red, made to the southeast of Grosseto; an up-and-coming wine.

Pomino New DOC from near Rúfina; red, white and Vinsanto.

Rosso di Montalcino A full-bodied DOC from the Montalcino area, aged less than the great Brunello di Montalcino.

Rosso di Montepulciano Excellent-value red table wine.

Sammarco Big Cabernet wine from the Chianti region.

Sassicaia Full ruby wine, best left a few years; from near Livorno.

Solaia Another Cabernet Sauvignon wine from the Antinori estate.

Spumante Sparkling wines are a relatively new departure in Tuscany, but vineyards all over the province are now using the *champenoise* or *charmat* method to produce quality vintages.

Tavarnelle California-style red from western Chianti.

Tignanello Traditional Sangiovese Chianti, again from Antinori.

Vernaccia di San Gimignano Subtle dry white DOC from the hills of San Gimignano.

Vino Nobile di Montepulciano A full, classy red DOCG from around Montepulciano, south of Siena.

Vinsanto Toscano Aromatic wine, made from semi-dried grapes and sealed in casks for at least three years. Produced all over Tuscany (and Umbria too), it ranges from dry to sweet, and is often served at dessert.

Umbria

Cabernet Sauvignon di Miralduolo Purplish dry red from Torgiano.

Cervaro della Sala A new white wine, aged in French oak.

Chardonnay di Miralduolo Flowery, dry white from Torgiano, also aged in wood.

Colli Altotiberini Tiber valley DOC; promising new arrival, best drunk young.

Colli Perugini Umbria's newest DOC – red, white and rosé.

Colli del Trasimeno Huge area producing reds and whites of ever-rising standard.

Decugnano dei Barbi Rosso Fruity red from near Lago di Corbara.

Montefalco Two types of red from the Todi area: Montefalco Rosso is a soft, dry red; the more robust Sagrantino di Montefalco itself comes in two varieties, one dry, the other bittersweet.

Orvieto Umbria's most famous DOC wine, a dry, light white, or a lightly sweet dessert wine (*abboccato*).

San Giorgio A bold, full-bodied red, made in Torgiano.

Solleone Dry, sherry-like aperitif.

Torgiano DOC region, southeast of Perugia, producing both red and white wines; look out for the fruity and dry white Torre di Giano, the wood-aged white Torre di Giano Riserva, and the opulent Rubesco Riserva, one of Italy's finest red wines.

Altotiberini DOC, and the region around Assisi is also producing ever-improving wines. Again, most of the vintages are reliable, and few of them available anywhere but Umbria. The **Colli**

Perugini and **Colli del Trasimeno** wines are the region's most humble; the latter include offerings from the Lamborghini vineyard – he of sports car fame.

COMMUNICATIONS: POST, PHONES AND THE MEDIA

Post office opening hours are usually Monday to Saturday from about 8am until 6.30pm; smaller towns won't have a service on a Saturday and everywhere the post offices close at noon on the last day of the month.

If you want **stamps**, you can buy them in *tabacchi* too, as well as in some gift shops in the tourist centres. Rates to all EU countries are L750 for a letter weighing up to 20g, L650 for a postcard; to North America the rates are L1150 and L1050. Letters can be sent **poste restante** to any Italian post office, by addressing them "Fermo Posta" followed by the name of the town. When picking something up take your passport, and make sure they check under middle names and initials – and every other letter when all else fails – as filing is diabolical.

TELEPHONES

Public **telephones**, run by SIP, the state telephone company, come in various forms, usually with clear instructions printed on them (in English too). The most common type takes both coins and phone cards. **Phone cards** (*schede telefoniche*) for L5000 and L10,000 are available from *tabacchi* or news-stands or shops displaying

the SIP *schede telefoniche* sticker. If you don't have a card, you'll need L100, L200 or L500 coins, or a token known as a *gettone* (worth L200), available from SIP offices, *tabacchi*, bars and some news-stands – they're also in common use as currency. Remember to tear the corner of the card off – they won't work until you do.

If you can't find a phone box, **bars** will often have a phone you can use (look for the yellow phone symbol), though these tend only to take *gettoni*. Alternatively, especially if you're phoning home and don't want to be bothered with piles of change, you could find a **SIP office** – we have listed addresses in the larger towns – or a bar that has a *cabina a scatti*, a soundproofed kiosk where you pay for your call afterwards. You can also make metered calls from higher-geared hotels, but this will cost you anything up to 100 percent more.

You can make **international calls** from any booth that accepts cards, and from any other booth labelled *interurbano*; the minimum charge for an international call is L2000. The cheapest way to make international calls, however, is to get hold of a **BT Chargecard** or the card issued by **AT & T Direct Service**. Both cards are free, and they work in the same way – just ring the company's international operator (BT ☎172 0044; AT & T ☎172 1011), who will connect you free of charge and add the cost of the connected call to your domestic bill.

Phone **tariffs** are highest on weekdays between 8am and 1pm, and cheapest between 10pm and 8am all week and all day Sunday.

To make an international **reversed charge** call, ring the international operators at BT or AT & T (see above), who will connect your call free of charge, even if you don't have a charge card.

NEWSPAPERS

The major **newspaper** in Tuscany is the Florence-based national paper *La Nazione*. This is technically a national paper but its sales are

---

TELEPHONE CODES

International calls

For direct **international calls**, dial the country code (given below), the area code (minus its first 0), and then the subscriber's number.

UK: ☎0044   Ireland: ☎00353   Australia: ☎0061   New Zealand:☎0064   US & Canada:☎001

Codes for major towns in Tuscany and Umbria

Arezzo ☎ 0575	Livorno ☎0586	Perugia ☎075	Siena ☎0577
Assisi ☎075	Lucca ☎0583	Pisa ☎050	Spoleto☎0743
Florence ☎055	Massa Carrara ☎0585	Pistoia ☎0573	Terni ☎0744
Grosseto ☎0564	Orvieto ☎0763	Prato ☎0574	Todi ☎075

To dial from abroad, add the prefix ☎010-39 to these codes and delete their initial **0**.

---

concentrated in the central provinces of Italy. It produces local editions, with supplements, including informative entertainments listings, for virtually every major Tuscan town. Umbria's intensely provincial and very widely read tabloid-format paper is the *Corriere dell'Umbria*.

Of the other national papers, the centre-left *La Repubblica* and authoritative right-slanted *Corriere della Sera* are the two most widely read and available; the former produces a Florence supplement called *Cronaca Firenze*, which is quite useful for background to local issues. *L'Unità*, the communist party organ, has hit hard times of late, even in the party's Tuscan strongholds, its declining appeal matched by the dip in its readership – many of whom have turned to the fresher, more radical *Il Manifesto* as an alternative.

The most avidly read papers of all, however, are without question the pink *Gazzetta dello Sport* and *Corriere dello Sport*; essential reading for the serious Italian sports fan, they devote as much attention to Marco van Basten's ankle problems as most papers would give to the resignation of the government. News magazines are also widely read in Italy, from the virtually indistinguishable *L'Espresso* and *Panorama*, through more iconoclastic magazines such as *Epoca* and *Europeo*, to the mental chocolate offerings of *Gente, Oggi* and *Novella 2000*.

English and US newspapers can be found for around L3000 a time in all the larger towns and established resorts, usually on the day of issue in bigger cities like Florence and Siena; the European editions of the *Guardian* and *Financial Times* and the Rome editions of the *International*

Herald Tribune and *USA Today* are also usually available on the day of publication.

TV AND RADIO

If you get the chance, try and watch some Italian **TV**, if only to size up the pros and cons of deregulation. The three state-run channels, *RAI 1, 2* and *3*, are controlled by the Christian Democrats, Socialists and local networks respectively (though control is breaking down in the face of Italy's current political upheavals). All three have of late also been facing a massive onslaught by independent operators, especially those owned by Silvio Berlusconi, whose *Canale 5* is one of the more successful of the new arrivals. Although the stories of stripping housewives are overplayed, the output is pretty bland across the board, with the accent on quiz shows and soaps, and a heavy smattering of American imports. The *RAI* channels carry less advertising and try to mix the dross with above-average documentaries and news coverage. Numerous channels concentrate on sport; if you want to see the weekend's Italian League football action, settle into a bar from 5pm on a Sunday.

The situation in **radio** is even more anarchic than that of TV, with the FM waves crowded to the extent that you continually pick up new stations whether you want to or not. There are some good small-scale stations if you search hard enough, but on the whole the *RAI* stations are again the more professional – though even with them daytime listening is virtually undiluted dance music. For English-language broadcasts, you can pick up the **BBC World Service** on MW 648kHz (463m).

OPENING HOURS, PUBLIC HOLIDAYS & SIGHTSEEING

Most shops and businesses in Tuscany and Umbria open from Monday to Saturday from 8 or 9am until around 1pm, and from about 4pm until 7 or 8pm, though in the biggest towns some offices work to a more standard European 9am–5pm day. Virtually everything except bars and restaurants closes on Sunday, though you might find fish shops in some coastal towns and *pasticcerie* or bakers open until Sunday lunchtime. Service stations shut on Sunday (except on motorways) and numerous businesses (restaurants included) take their holidays in August.

HOLIDAYS

You may well find your plans disrupted by **national holidays** and local **saints' days**. Local religious holidays don't generally close down shops and businesses, but they do mean that accommodation space may be tight. The country's official national holidays, on the other hand, close everything down, except some bars and restaurants. These are:

January 1
January 6 (Epiphany)
Easter Monday
April 25 (Liberation Day)
May 1 (Labour Day)
August 15 (*Ferragosto*; Assumption of the
 Blessed Virgin Mary)
November 1 (*Ognissanti*; All Saints)
December 8 (Immaculate Conception of the
 Blessed Virgin Mary)
December 25
December 26

CHURCHES, MUSEUMS AND ARCHEOLOGICAL SITES

The rules for visiting **churches** are much as they are all over the Mediterranean. Dress modestly, which usually means no shorts, and covered shoulders for women, and don't wander around during a service. Most churches open in the morning, at around 8am, for Mass, and close around noon, opening up again at 4 or 5pm until 7pm. In more obscure places, some churches will only open for early morning and evening services, while others are closed at all times except Sundays and on religious holidays. Wherever possible, the precise opening hours of major churches are given in the guide.

Another problem you'll face is that lots of churches, monasteries, convents and oratories are **closed for restoration** (*chiuso per restauro*). We've indicated in the text the more long-term closures, though you might be able to persuade a workman or priest/curator to show you around even if there's scaffolding everywhere.

Museums generally open daily from 9am until 1 or 2pm, sometimes for an additional couple of hours in the afternoon on selected days; almost all are closed on Mondays. They also often close early on Sunday, usually around noon, and for smaller museums opening hours are severely cut back during winter. The opening times of **archeological sites** are more flexible: many sites open every day of the week from 9am until one hour before sunset. Similar hours are kept by many of the **public gardens**. Museums in Florence, however, are a law unto themselves, with places shutting on almost any day of the week; check all opening times carefully before embarking on any sightseeing ventures.

Admission prices for most museums vary between L2000 and L6000, but again Florence is a law to itself – several museums charge L8000, and the Uffizi and Accademia have recently become the first to hit L10,000. Under-18s and over-60s get into public museums free on production of documentary proof; student cards are no longer accepted at many places, though possibly worth a try. Some sites, churches and monasteries are nominally free, though there'll be a custodian around to open things up and show you around, whom you are expected to tip – L1000 per person should do it.

FESTIVALS AND ANNUAL EVENTS

Both Tuscany and Umbria have a plethora of local celebrations, with saints' days being the usual excuse for some kind of binge. All cities, small towns and villages have their home-produced saint, whose mortal remains or image are normally paraded through the streets amid much noise and spectacle. There are no end of other occasions for a *festa* **– either to commemorate a local miracle or historic event, or to show off the local products or artistic talent. Many happen at Easter, in May or September, or around Ferragosto (August 15); local dates are detailed below – for more on what goes on, see the respective town entries.**

Recently there's also been a revival of **carnival** (*carnevale*), the last fling before Lent, although the anarchic fun that was enjoyed in the past has generally been replaced by elegant, self-conscious affairs, with ingenious costumes and handmade masks – at their most extravagant at the coastal resort of **Viareggio**. Carnival usually lasts for the five days before Ash Wednesday; because it's connected with Easter the dates change from year to year.

figures singing penitential hymns. The separate motivations to make some money, have a good time and pay your spiritual dues all merge in the celebrations for a town's **saint's day**, where it's not unusual to find a communist mayor and local bishop officiating side by side.

Umbria has the edge over Tuscany in religious festivities. **Assisi** – given its Franciscan associations – has a disproportionate number of events, the biggest being the *Festa di San Francesco* (Oct 3–4), a celebration of the saint's canonization which draws religious leaders and pilgrims from all over Italy. Holy Week in Assisi attracts one of the world's biggest concentrations of nuns, monks and lesser religious fanatics, and *Calendimaggio* is also huge – lasting for a week from the first Tuesday in May, it celebrates Francis's more worldly youth.

In **Cascia** another of the region's foremost saints, Santa Rita (as popular in some parts of Italy as the Virgin), attracts many thousands of devotees – mainly women – to the torchlight *Celebrazioni Ritiane* (May 21–22). Also heavily patronized is *Corpus Domini* in **Orvieto**, celebrated with a costumed procession and a panoply of associated events.

In **Tuscany**, the best traditional festivals are of a more secular nature. Top honours go to the **Palio** horse races in **Siena** – an amazing and fiercely contested spectacle, which sees jockeys careering around the central square. Other towns put on medieval-origin contests, too, though they are often a little phoney, having been revived for commercial ends over the past decade or two. Among the most enjoyable are the Gioco di Calcio Storico – a rough-and-tumble football game played between the four quarters of **Florence** in June – and the crossbow competitions between teams from **Gubbio** and **Sansepolcro**, held during May and September.

RELIGIOUS AND TRADITIONAL FESTIVALS

Many of the local **religious processions** have strong pagan roots, marking important dates on the calendar subsequently adopted and sanctified by the church. **Good Friday**, for obvious reasons, is also a popular time for processions, with images of Christ on the Cross paraded through towns accompanied by white-robed, hooded

FOOD FESTIVALS

Food- and wine-inspired festivals are more low-key affairs than the religious and traditional events, but no less enjoyable for that. They generally celebrate the edible speciality of the region to the accompaniment of dancing, music from a local brass band and noisy fireworks at the end of the evening.

CALENDAR OF TRADITIONAL AND RELIGIOUS FESTIVALS

JANUARY
Foligno *Festa di San Feliciano* – traditional fair (Jan 24).

Trevi *Festa di Sant'Emiliano* – torchlit procession (Jan 27).

Viareggio *Carnevale* (late Jan/early Feb). Also good *carnevale* processions in **San Gimignano**.

FEBRUARY/MARCH
Terni St Valentine's Day fair (Feb 14).

Norcia Crossbow competition (March 20–24).

Easter celebrations
Assisi Holy Week celebrations.

Gràssina (near Florence), **Gubbio** and **Bevagna** (near Perugia). Good Friday processions.

Florence *Scioppio del Carro* – fireworks in the Piazza del Duomo (Easter Sunday).

San Miniato National kite-flying championships (first Sun after Easter).

APRIL/MAY
Terni *Canta Maggio* – parade of illuminated floats (May 1).

Assisi *Calendimaggio* – spring festival (early May).

Gubbio *Corsa dei Ceri* – candle race (May 15).

Foligno *Giostro della Quintana* – medieval joust (May 15).

Massa Marittima *Balestro del Girifalco* – crossbow competition (first Sun after May 19).

Cascia *Celebrazioni Ritiane* – procession in honour of St Rita (May 21–22)

Gubbio Crossbow matches against team from Sansepolcro (last Sun in May).

JUNE
Orvieto and **Spello** *Corpus Domini* procession (early June).

Pisa *Luminaria* – torchlit procession – precedes *Regatta di San Ranieri* boat race (June 16 & 17). Also *Gioco del Ponte* – costumed mock battle (third Sun of month).

Florence *Festa di San Giovanni* marked by fireworks and the Gioco di Calcio Storico football game (week beginning June 24).

JULY/AUGUST
Siena The *Palio* (horse races held on July 2 & August 16 are preceded by trial races on June 29 & 30, July 1, August 14 & 15 – see entry in the guide).

Fivizzano Archery contest (second Sun of July).

Lucca *Festa di San Paolino* – torchlit parade and crossbow contest (third Sun of July).

Pistoia *Giostro dell'Orso* – joust of the bear (July 25).

Massa Marittima Second leg of the crossbow competition (second Sun in Aug).

Lucca *Luminaria di Santa Croce* – torchlit processions (Aug 14).

Florence *Festa del Grillo* – fair in the Cascine park (Aug 15).

Orvieto *Festa della Palombella* – horse race (Aug 15).

Livorno *Palio Marinaro* – boat races (Aug 17).

San Stéfano *Palio Marinaro* – parade and rowing race (mid-Aug).

Montepulciano *Bravio delle Botti* – barrel race through the town (last Sun in Aug).

SEPTEMBER
Arezzo *Giostro del Saraceno* – jousting by knights in armour (first Sun).

Cerreto Guidi (near Empoli) Renaissance processions (first Sun).

Florence *Festa delle Rificolone* – torchlit procession (Sept 7).

Prato *Festa degli Omaggi* – costume procession (Sept 8).

Foligno *Torneo della Quintana* – jousting by 600 medieval knights (second weekend).

Lucca *Festa della Santa Croce* – procession of sacred image (Sept 14).

Sansepolcro Return crossbow matches against Gubbio (second Sun).

OCTOBER
Trevi *Palio dei Terzieri* – cart race (Oct 1).

Assisi *Festa di San Francesco* – major religious festival (Oct 3–4).

NOVEMBER
Perugia *Festa dei Ognissanti* – All Saints Fair (Nov 1–5).

DECEMBER
Siena *Festa di Santa Lucia* – pottery fair (Dec 13).

Prato Display of Holy Girdle (Dec 25 & 26).

At Easter and through the summer and autumn there are literally hundreds of such events, most of them catering to locals rather than tourists; for details, ask at tourist offices or check the local newspapers – where you will find them listed as *sagre*. The more established or more interesting events are detailed in the box below.

FOOD, WINE AND ARTS FESTIVALS

FOOD AND WINE

JANUARY–MARCH

Spello Olive and *bruschetta* (garlic toast) festival (Feb 5).

.**Norcia** Truffle and sausage festival (February).

APRIL–JUNE

Montecatini Terme *Fettunta* festival – an oil and garlic speciality (April 16).

Città della Pieve *Festa della Fontana* – flooding of the town fountain with wine. A similar event takes place at nearby **Panicale**.

Montespertoli Wine festival (last Sun of May).

Orvieto Wine festival (June).

Amelia and **Bevagna** Wine and food jamborees (June).

Piediluco *Sagra del Pesce* (June).

Campello di Clitunno Trout festival (June).

JULY–SEPTEMBER

Le Ghiaie, Elba Wine festival (last week of July).

Montepulciano Food and wine festival (second Sun of Aug).

Cortona *Festa della Bistecca* – excessive consumption of local beef (Aug 15).

Greve Chianti Classico festival (second Sun of Sept).

OCTOBER

Piediluco Wine and chestnut show.

Castiglione del Lago *Cucina tipica* and wine festival.

Umbértide *Sagra della Castagna* – chestnut fair.

Todi *Festa Gastronomica*.

ARTS

APRIL–JUNE

Lucca Sacred music festival (April–June).

Florence *Maggio Musicale* – music festival (April–June).

Spoleto *Festival dei Due Mondi* (Festival of the Two Worlds). Internationally renowned, this two-month-long event is a mixture of classical concerts, films, ballet, street theatre and performance art, with its venue the open spaces of the ancient walled town (June & July).

Narni Experimental theatre season (last ten days of June).

Fiesole *Estate Fiesolana* – music, cinema, ballet and theatre (mid-June to Aug).

San Gimignano Summer festival of music and film (late June to Oct).

JULY–SEPTEMBER

Barga, near Lucca Opera and theatre festival (second half of July).

Siena *Accademia Musicale Chigiana* (July).

Perugia *Umbria Jazz* – one of Europe's foremost jazz events (July–Aug).

Siena *Settimane Musicali* (Aug).

Torre del Lago *Festival Pucciniano* (Aug).

Montepulciano *Il Bruscello* – folkloric song festival (Aug 14–16).

Arezzo International choral festival (last two weeks of Aug).

Città di Castello Chamber music festival (Aug–Sept).

Gubbio *Spettacoli Classici.* Long-established series of classical plays staged in the town's Roman amphitheatre (mid-July to mid-Aug).

Città di Castello *Festival delle Nazioni di Musica da Camera* – highly respected festival of chamber music (last week of Aug).

Perugia *Sagra Musicale Umbra* – festival of classical music, established in 1937 and now one of the region's most prestigious cultural events (last week of Sept).

Todi Increasingly well known arts festival – (ten days in Sept).

OCTOBER–APRIL

Prato Drama season at Teatro Metastasio (Oct–April).

Florence Opera and concert seasons at Teatro Comunale (Nov–Jan).

ARTS FESTIVALS

The ancient inter-town rivalries across Tuscany and Umbria – described neatly by the term *campanilismo* (ie the only things that matter are those that take place within the sound of your village's church bells) – find a highly positive expression in the willingness of local councils to put money into promoting their own **arts festivals**. For the size of the towns involved, the events are often almost ludicrously rich, celebrating the work of a native composer or artist by inviting major international names to perform or direct. Many festivals are given an added enjoyment by their sites – in summer, open-air performances take place in restored ancient amphitheatres, churches or town squares.

TROUBLE AND THE POLICE

Tuscany and Umbria are not exactly hotbeds of crime. The only real trouble you're likely to come across are gangs of *scippatori* or "snatchers", often gypsy kids, who have something of a reputation in Florence. Crowded streets or markets, railway stations and packed tourist sights are the places to beware. As well as handbags, *scippatori* whip wallets, tear off visible jewellery and, if they're really adroit, unstrap watches.

You can **minimise the risk** of this happening by being discreet: wear money in a belt or pouch; don't put anything down on café or restaurant tables; don't flash anything of value; keep a firm hand on your camera; and carry shoulder bags, as Italian women do, slung across your body. It's a good idea, too, to entrust money and credit cards to hotel managers. Never leave anything valuable in your **car** and try and park in car parks or well-lit, well-used streets. On the whole, it's sensible to avoid badly lit areas at night, and deserted inner-city areas by day.

Italy's reputation for **sexual harassment** of women is based largely on experiences in the south of the country. However, even in the "civilized north", travelling on your own, or with another woman, you can expect to be tooted and hissed at in towns from time to time and may attract occasional unwelcome attention in bars, restaurants or on the beach. This pestering is not usually made with any kind of violent intent, but it's annoying and frustrating nevertheless. There are few things you can do to ward it off. Indifference is often the most effective policy, as is looking as confident as possible, a purposeful stride and directed gaze. Sitting around in **parks** – especially Florence's unsavoury Cascine – it's best to pick a spot where there are other people around.

THE POLICE

If it comes to the worst, you'll be forced to have some dealings with the **police**. In Italy these come in many forms, their power split ostensibly to prevent any seizure of power. You're not likely to have much contact with the **Guardia di Finanza**, responsible for investigating smuggling, tax evasion and other finance-related felonies, though drivers may well come up against the **Polizia Urbana**, or town police, who are mainly concerned with directing the traffic and punishing parking offences; the **Polizia Stradale** patrol motorways.

If you're unlucky, you may have dealings with the **Carabinieri**, with their military-style uniforms and white shoulder belts, who deal with general crime, public order and drug control. These are the ones Italians are most rude about, but a lot of jokes about how stupid they are stem from the usual north-south prejudice. Eighty percent of the *Carabinieri* are from southern Italy – joining the police is one way to climb out of the poverty trap – and they are posted away from home so as to be well out of the sphere of influence of their families (the *Carabinieri* is actually part of the army). For all the digs, though, they are the most professional of the different police forces, and the ones to head for if you're in deep trouble. The **Polizia Statale**, the other general crime-fighting branch, enjoy a fierce rivalry with the *Carabinieri*, and are the ones to whom **thefts** should be reported. You'll find the address of the **Questura** or police station in the local *Tuttocittà* supplement, and we've included details in the major city listings. The office will issue you with a *denuncia*, an impressively stamped form confirming thefts and so forth which you will need for any insurance claims on your return home. The *Questura* is also where you're supposed to go to obtain a *permesso di soggiorno* **if you're staying** for any length of time, or a **visa extension** if you require one.

In any brush with the authorities, your experience will depend on the individuals you're dealing with. Apart from **topless bathing** (permitted, but don't try anything more daring) and **camping rough**, don't expect a soft touch if you're picked

---

EMERGENCIES

In an **emergency**, note the following national emergency telephone numbers.

☎112 for the police (*Carabinieri*).

☎113 for any emergency service (*Soccorso Pubblico di Emergenza*).

☎115 for the fire brigade (*Vigili del Fuoco*).

☎116 for road assistance (*Soccorso Stradale*).

---

up for any offence, especially if it's **drugs-related**: it's not unheard of to be stopped and searched if you're young and carrying a rucksack. Drugs are generally frowned upon by everyone above a certain age, and universal hysteria about *la droga*, fuelled by the serious problem of heroin addiction all over Italy, means that any distinction between the "hard" and "soft" variety has become blurred. Theoretically everything is illegal above the possession of a few grammes of cannabis or marijuana "for personal use", though there's no agreed definition of what this means. Addresses of consulates in Florence – not always that helpful – are given on p.147.

FLORA AND FAUNA

Tuscany and Umbria's countryside has been worked for centuries, but not all of it is the pastoral hill country of popular imagination. The broad sweep of the Apennines contains areas of considerable wilderness and within the coastal and hill regions there is a huge variety of sub-habitats.

A few of these areas are at last receiving protection as **national parks** (*Parco Nazionale*) or as oases supervised by the World Wide Fund for Nature (WWFN). In Tuscany there are two proposed national parks (Italy currently has just eight): the **Monti dell'Uccellina** in the Maremma, currently an excellently run nature park (*parco naturale*), and the **Migliarino-San Rossore** area between Pisa and Livorno – part-owned by the state, but prey to pollution and subject to huge commercial pressures. Two regional parks (*Parco Regionale*) are already established in the mountains north of Lucca – the excellent **Parco dell'Orecchiella**, and the

adjoining, but much more tenuous **Parco delle Alpi Apuane**.

In Umbria, where the hunting lobby is one of the most powerful in the country, there are just four parks, all still more or less paper creations. The **Monti Sibillini** in the east are a recently designated national park, and have a concerned lobby of environmentalists arguing their case. **Monte Subasio** above Assisi, **Monte Cucco** northeast of Gubbio and the **Valnerina** east of Spoleto are smaller and still fragile.

Much smaller than the state parks are the WWFN sites, which are often little more than a couple of hundred hectares in extent. However, in contrast to the state parks, protection on the ground is total, and for the dedicated naturalist they present the best opportunities for sightings if time is short. There are none as yet in Umbria, but three in Tuscany, all on the coast in or near the Maremma: **Bólgheri**, **Lago di Burano** and **Laguna di Orbetello**.

SPECIES

Amongst the larger **mammals**, the **wild boar** is best known, endemic through much of Tuscany and now spreading into Umbria. In the Maremma there is an indigenous breed, smaller than the boar of Eastern European origin common elsewhere. Both types are shy, frugal creatures and difficult to spot casually, though you may well see signs of their passage. **Porcupines** are also common and you often find quills on country walks, though again they are elusive creatures. **Roe deer** have been reintroduced into the reserves at Bólgheri and the Monti dell'Uccellina, and are readily seen. Elsewhere they've been hunted to extinction, along with the bulk of the larger mammals.

Wolves, however, are making some sort of return, drifting into the Valnerina from their heartlands in the Abruzzo mountains to the south. There are an estimated 150–200 specimens in Italy, all protected. Their largest threat comes from feral dogs – estimated to number 800,000 nationwide – both because they challenge for food and because people are increasingly dealing with the dogs by poisoning or shooting them, inevitably destroying wolves in the process.

Wild **mountain goats** are found on the island of Montecristo, a nature reserve closed to the casual visitor. Elsewhere, you may see smaller mammals – hares, rabbits, foxes and weasels – though these too have been much depleted by the hunters' guns. Wilder upland areas are seeing the return of the **wild cat**, but – like the wolf – numbers are tiny, and the chance of seeing them minimal.

You stand far more chance of observing an interesting array of **birds**, not all of which have been blasted from the sky. Coastal areas offer the richest pickings, and in particular the reserves set aside to protect them – Lago di Burano, Laguna di Orbetello and the Monti dell'Uccellina. These closely connected places collect together numerous migrant birds, many of them extremely rare. Inland, birdlife is under threat, but you can still see hoopoes, doves, woodpeckers and run-of-the-mill wrens, thrushes and starlings. **Birds of prey** are comparatively rare, though mountain areas boast a few hawks and buzzards, and perhaps a few pairs of golden eagles.

Snakes, and the viper in particular, are common, particularly around abandoned farmland – of which there's plenty. Small black **scorpions** are also quite common (see p.14 for advice on bites and stings).

The **flora** of Tuscany and Umbria is often exceptional, and spring carpets of flowers – particularly on upland meadows – can be breathtaking. The best areas in Tuscany are the Orecchiella and Alpi Apuane, at the meeting point of Alpine and Mediterranean vegetation zones. As a result they contain the vast majority of the species that grow in Italy. In Umbria, the Martani hills, Monte Subasio and the Piano Grande are smothered in orchids and fritillaries in May and June. In olive groves and on hillsides – often free of pesticides – all manner of common plants thrive: poppies, primroses, violets, grape hyacinth, cyclamen, irises, cistus and many more. Specially adapted marine species can be found in the reserves of the Maremma.

Cypresses and **parasol pines** are the icons of the Tuscan countryside, while **oak** forests blanket many of the interior hills, Chianti in particular. Elsewhere there are huge tracts of **virgin forest**, especially in the Casentino around Camáldoli, filled with oak, beech and pines, many of them huge ancient specimens. Sweet **chestnut** dominates in the Orecchiella and Alpi Apuane, rolling unbroken across mile after mile of the lower hills. On the higher hills, notably in the Sibillini, there are clumps of high beech forest, the predominant tree of the Apennines and of limestone in general. Coastal areas, especially in the Monti dell'Uccellina, have preserved the classic profiles of Mediterranean *macchia* – dwarf trees (usually oak), and a scrub of laurel, broom, lentisk, heather and fragrant plants.

DIRECTORY

BARGAINING Not really on in shops and restaurants, though you'll find you can get a "special price" for some rooms and cheap hotels if you're staying a few days, and that things like boat/bike hire and guided tours (especially out of season) are negotiable. In markets, you'll be taken for an imbecile if you don't haggle for everything except food.

BEACHES You'll have to pay a few hundred lire for access to most of the better beaches (referred to as *lido*s), a few thousand to hire a sun-bed and shade and use the showers all day. During winter most beaches look like rubbish dumps, which is what they are: it's not worth anyone's while to clean them until the season starts at Easter.

BRING ... photographic films, which are cheaper in Britain – and wait until you get home to have them developed. An **alarm clock** for early morning buses is also useful, as is **mosquito repellent** and **antiseptic cream**, not to mention **suntan lotion**. And if you're camping, don't forget a **torch**.

CAMPING GAZ Easy enough to buy for the small portable camping stoves, either from a hardware store (*ferramenta*) or camping/sports shops. You can't carry canisters on aeroplanes.

CIGARETTES The state monopoly brand – MS – are the most widely smoked cigarettes, but younger people tend to smoke imported brands these days – all of which are slightly more expensive. You buy cigarettes from *tabacchi*, recognisable by a sign displaying a white T on a blue background.

CONTRACEPTION Condoms (*profilatici*) and the Pill (*la píllola*) are available over the counter from all chemists and some supermarkets.

DEPARTMENT STORES There are two main nationwide chains, *Upim* and *Standa*, branches of which you'll see virtually everywhere. Neither is particularly upmarket, and they're excellent places to stock up on toiletries and other basic supplies; both stores sometimes have a food hall attached.

DISABLED TRAVELLERS Facilities aren't particularly geared towards disabled travellers in Tuscany or Umbria, though people are helpful enough. The Italian State Tourist Office has a list of tour operators who specialise in holidays for the disabled – see p.15 for addresses. Otherwise, in Britain the best sources of information are *Radar*, 25 Mortimer St, London W1 (☎071/637 5400) and *Mobility International*, 228 Borough High St, London SE11 (☎071/403 5688). In the US you can get information and advice from *Mobility International USA*, PO Box 3551, Eugene, OR 97403 (☎503/343 1284), or *The Society for the Advancement of Travel for the Handicapped*, 347 Fifth Ave, Suite 610, New York, NY 10016 (☎212/447 7284).

ELECTRICITY The supply is 220V, though anything requiring 240V will work. Most plugs are two round pins: a travel plug is useful.

FOOTBALL Traditionally Tuscany's premier football team is Florence's squad, Fiorentina, who won the Italian league in the not-too-distant past. At the moment they are a run-of-the-mill second-division outfit, and their standards are often matched by that of nearby Pisa. Empoli and Lucca both have strong second-division outfits; there are no decent teams in Umbria.

GAY LIFE Homosexuality is legal in Italy, and the age of consent is sixteen. Attitudes are relatively tolerant, though there's little developed gay nightlife, even in Florence. There are a few *spiagge gay* (gay beaches) dotted along the coast. The national gay organization, *ARCI-gay*, is affiliated to the youth section of the communist party. Their head office is Piazza di Porta Saragozza 2, PO Box 691, 40100 Bologna (☎051/436.700); in Florence they can be contacted through the *Arci* office at Via Ponte alle Mosse 61. *Babilonia* is the national gay magazine, published monthly. There is also a national *Lesbian Line*, based in Florence, that is open every Wednesday and Saturday 8.30–10pm (☎055/240.384), for information, advice and help.

KIDS Children are revered throughout Italy and will be made a fuss of in the street, and welcomed and catered for in bars and restaurants. Hotels normally charge around thirty percent extra to put a bed or cot in your room, for children's fares in Italy see p.18.

LAUNDRIES Coin-operated laundries are rare; far more common is a *lavanderia*, a service-wash laundry, but this will be expensive. Although you can usually get away with it, washing clothes in your hotel room has been known to cause problems, since in some parts of the country the plumbing can't cope with all the water.

PUBLIC TOILETS Almost unheard-of outside train and bus stations, and usually the only alternative is to dive into a bar or restaurant. Carry a supply of your own paper around and don't expect anywhere to be spotless.

TAX If you are thinking of splashing out on a designer outfit or some other desirable item, bear in mind that tourists are entitled to an IVA (purchase tax) **rebate** on single items valued at over L625,000. The procedure is to get a full receipt from the shop, describing the purchase in detail. This receipt must be presented to customs on your return home, and then sent back to the shop within ninety days of the date of the receipt; the shop will then refund the IVA component of the price, a saving of eighteen percent.

TIME Italy is one hour ahead of Britain except for most of October when the time is the same.

PART TWO

TUSCANY

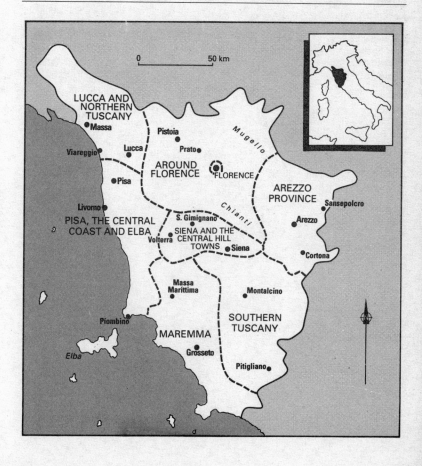

0   50 km

LUCCA AND
NORTHERN
TUSCANY

Massa

Pistoia

Viareggio

Lucca

Prato

Mugello

AROUND
FLORENCE

FLORENCE

Pisa

AREZZO
PROVINCE

Sansepolcro

Chianti

Livorno

PISA, THE CENTRAL
COAST AND ELBA

S. Gimignano

Arezzo

Volterra

SIENA AND THE
CENTRAL HILL
TOWNS

Siena

Cortona

Massa
Maríttima

Montalcino

Piombino

SOUTHERN
TUSCANY

Elba

MAREMMA

Grosseto

Pitigliano

CHAPTER ONE

FLORENCE

Since early last century **FLORENCE** (Firenze) has been celebrated as the most beautiful city in Italy: Stendhal staggered around its streets in a perpetual stupor of delight; the Brownings sighed over its idyllic charms; and E.M. Forster's *Room with a View* portrayed it as the great southern antidote to the sterility of Anglo-Saxon life. For most people Florence comes close to living up to the myth only in its first, resounding impressions. The pinnacle of Brunelleschi's stupendous dome is visible over the rooftops the moment you step out of the train station, and when you reach the Piazza del Duomo the close-up view is even more breathtaking, with the multicoloured **Duomo** rising behind the marble-clad **Baptistery**. Wander from there down towards the River Arno and the attraction still holds – beyond the **Piazza della Signoria**, site of the immense **Palazzo Vecchio**, the water is spanned by the shop-laden medieval **Ponte Vecchio**, with gorgeous **San Miniato al Monte** glistening on the hill behind it.

Yet after registering these marvellous sights, it's hard to stave off a sense of disappointment. For, away from the beaten track, much of Florence is a city of narrow streets and dour, fortress-like houses, of unfinished buildings and characterless squares. Restorers' scaffolding has become an endemic feature of the Florentine scene, and incessant traffic – right through the historic centre – provides all the usual city stresses. Just roaming the streets is a pleasure in Venice, Rome, Verona – but not in Florence.

The fact is, the best of Florence is to be seen indoors. Under the rule of the **Medici** family – the greatest patrons of Renaissance Europe – Florence's artists and thinkers were instigators of the shift from the medieval to the modern worldview, and the churches, galleries and museums of this city are the places to get to grips with their achievement. The development of the Renaissance can be plotted stage by stage in the vast picture collection of the **Uffizi**, and charted in the sculpture of the **Bargello**, the **Museo dell'Opera del Duomo** and the guild church of **Orsanmichele**. Equally revelatory are the fabulously decorated chapels of **Santa Croce** and **Santa Maria Novella**, forerunners of such astonishing creations as Masaccio's recently restored frescoes at **Santa Maria del Carmine**, Fra' Angelico's serene paintings in the monks' cells at **San Marco** and Andrea del Sarto's work at **Santissima Annunziata**.

The Renaissance emphasis on harmony and rational design is expressed with unrivalled eloquence in Brunelleschi's interiors of **San Lorenzo**, **Santo Spirito** and the **Cappella dei Pazzi**. The bizarre architecture of San Lorenzo's **Sagrestia Nuova** and the marble statuary of the **Accademia** – home of the *David* – display the full genius of **Michelangelo**, the dominant creative figure of sixteenth-century Italy. Every quarter of Florence can boast a church or collection worth an extended call, and the enormous **Palazzo Pitti** constitutes a museum district on its own – half a dozen museums are gathered here, one of them an art gallery that any city would envy.

FLORENCE

To Fiesole

River Mugnone

To Museo Stibbert

500 m

To Prato
& Pistoia

VIALE BELFIORE

VIA LUIGI ALAMANNI

VIALE FILIPPO STROZZI

Palazzo
delle Mostre

Fortezza da Basso

VIALE FILIPPO STROZZI

VIALE GIOVANNI MILTON

VIALE SPARTACO LAVAGNINI

River Mugnone

Stazione Santa
Maria Novella

VIA FAENZA

VIA VALTONDA

PIAZZA
ADUA

Cenacolo di
Foligno

S. Apollonia

PIAZZA
DELL'INDIPENDENZA

Scalzo

San Marco

Università

Museo
Botanico

VIALE GIACOMO MATTEOTTI

PIAZZA
DELLA LIBERTÀ

VIA MASACCIO

PIAZZA
G. SALVEMINI

Gardino della
Gherardesca

SS. Annunziata

English Cemetery

River Mugnone

FIRENZE NUOVA

Mass tourism was the inevitable consequence of Florence's rediscovery in the nineteenth century, and today the city's economy has become almost entirely reliant on these visitors. The latest and most ambitious attempt to break this ever-increasing dependence is the so-called **Firenze Nuova**, a Fiat-underwritten development on the northwestern outskirts that's planned as a viable industrial city, leaving Florence to develop as a cultural and small-scale commercial centre. This scheme is still very much in its early stages, and is proceeding in the face of objections that it essentially entails a surrender of the city to tourism – just as happened with the development of Venice's industrial twin, Mestre.

To enjoy a visit fully it's best to ration yourself to a couple of big sights each day (limited opening hours prevent much more anyway), and spend the rest of your hours or days exploring the **quieter spots** on the periphery, such as the **Giardino di Bóboli** behind the Palazzo Pitti – or heading out to one or two of the farther-flung places covered in the next chapter, like Fiesole, the Medici villas or the countryside of Chianti and Mugello.

Allow some time, too, to involve yourself in the life of the city. Though Florence might seem a little sedate on the surface, its university – and the presence of large numbers of language and art schools – guarantees a fair range of term-time diversions and **nightlife**. The city has some excellent **restaurants** and enjoyable **café-bars** amid the tourist joints, as well as the biggest and liveliest **markets** in Tuscany, and plenty of browsable, high-quality **shops**. And there's certainly no shortage of **special events** – from the high-art festivities of the **Maggio Musicale** to the licensed bedlam of the **Calcio Storico**, a series of costumed football matches held in the last week of July.

For a brief introduction to the history of Florence, see p.541; for the Medici family tree – essential for dispelling confusion in the first few days of church-hopping – see p.548.

Arrival, transport and information

Central Florence is a compact area, and arriving by bus or train will drop you right in the heart of it. If you're flying to Pisa – the routine approach – it's an effortless hour's journey by train from the airport into Florence.

● **By train.** Florence's station, **Santa Maria Novella** (*Firenze SMN*), is located just north of the church and square of Santa Maria Novella, a couple of blocks west of the Duomo (cathedral). The station has an information office just outside (see below), accommodation service (see p.57) and left-luggage facilities.

● **By bus.** Half a dozen bus companies run to Florence from various parts of Tuscany. The main operator is *SITA*, which has a terminal right opposite the train station at Via Santa Caterina da Siena. All the other companies are nearby: for addresses and routes see p.148.

● **By car.** Only residents are allowed to park on the streets in the centre, so you have to leave your car in one of the main **car parks**. Those nearest the centre are: underneath the train station; Fortezza da Basso (behind the train station); Mercato Centrale; Lungarno Torrigiani; Lungarno della Zecca Vecchia; Piazza della Libertà. You can also find parking spaces alongside the ring roads.

The standard tariff is L1500 per hour and all are greatly oversubscribed; the best bet with the biggest space is probably Fortezza da Basso. If you want to leave your car for a prolonged period, try Piazzale Michelangelo, the nearest substantial **free parking** area to the centre. It's about twenty minutes' walk to the Piazza della Signoria from here, if you're not burdened with luggage; if you are, it's best to take bus #12 or #13 into town.

● **By air**. Pisa's **Aeroporto Galileo Galilei** is connected by an hourly **train** service to Florence's Santa Maria Novella train station; tickets can be bought from the information desk inside the air terminal. Note that on the return journey you don't have to lug your bags all the way out to the airport, as there's a check-in desk, for most airlines, by platform 5 at Santa Maria Novella, open daily from 7am to 8pm; bags have to be checked in at least fifteen minutes before the departure of the train. Some charter companies run bus connections from Pisa airport to Florence – these usually put you down at, or close to, the main bus station.

The small airport at **Perètola**, 5km northwest of central Florence, is used by *Air UK*, which has daily flights from Stansted, and by *Meridiana* which flies daily from Gatwick. Otherwise it receives occasional flights from Munich, Paris or Nice, but is used mainly for connections with Rome, Milan and Naples. A regular bus line links Perètola with the city (L6000), or you could take a taxi for about L20,000. The journey takes about ten minutes.

Orientation and transport

Orientation is straightforward – it's just ten minutes' walk from **Santa Maria Novella** to the central **Piazza del Duomo**, along Via de' Panzani and Via de' Cerretani. You can't really miss these roads: stand with your back to the train station and they form the main thoroughfare sweeping away in front of you. The great majority of the major sights are within a few minutes of the Duomo area.

Within this historic centre, walking is generally the most efficient way of getting around, and the imposition of the **zona a traffico limitato** *(ZTL)* – which limits traffic in the centre to residents' cars, delivery vehicles and public transport – has reduced the once unbearable pollution and noise. On the other hand, the *ZTL* has increased the average velocity of the traffic, so you should be especially careful before stepping off the narrow pavements.

If you want to cross town in a hurry, or to visit some of the peripheral sights featured in Chapter Two, the orange *ATAF* **buses** are frequent and speedy; tickets are valid for 60 minutes (L1200) or 120 minutes (L1500), and can be bought from shops displaying the *ATAF* sign and from automatic machines all over Florence. From these outlets and machines you can also buy a **biglietto multiplo**, which gives you eight 60-minute tickets for L9000, and 24-hour passes for L5000. Tickets have to be stamped in a machine on board; there's a spot fine of L33,000 for any passenger without a validated ticket – checks are rare, but the inspectors will tolerate no excuses. The 24-hour passes should be validated just at the start of the first journey.

Finally there's the **Carta Arancio**, a seven-day pass valid on all buses throughout Florence province; costing L25,000, it's available to anyone not resident in Tuscany and can be obtained at the *ATAF* booth beside the train station, or at the offices of the *COPIT*, *CAP*, *SITA* and *Lazzi* companies (addresses on p.148), on presentation of a passport.

Most city **bus routes** originate at or pass by the train station and either Piazza del Duomo or Piazza San Marco; the following are the handiest.

#4:	Fortezza da Basso–Duomo–Museo Stibbert.
#7:	Train station–Duomo–Fiesole.
#10:	Train station–Duomo–San Marco–Settignano.
#11a:	Viale Calatafimi–Duomo–Porta Romana–Poggio Imperiale.
#13:	Train station–Duomo–Piazzale Michelangelo–San Miniato–Porto Romano.
#15:	Fortezza da Basso–Duomo.
#17b:	Cascine–Train station–Duomo–Via Lamarmora–Salviatino (for the Villa Camerata hostel).
#20:	Fortezza da Basso–Piazza San Marco.
#25a:	Train station–San Marco–Piazza della Libertà–Pratolino.
#28:	Train station–Via Giuliani–Castello–Sesto Fiorentino.
#31/32:	Train station–Via del Moro–Ponte alla Carraia–Santo Spirito–Palazzo Pitti.
#37:	Train station–Ponte alla Carraia–Porta Romana–Certosa di Galluzzo.

Taxi ranks are concentrated at the station and Piazza della Repubblica. The owner-drivers are generally an honest breed and all rides are metered; expect to pay L10–15,000 for a short hop within the centre. (See p.148 for phone numbers of taxi firms.)

Information

For information about Florence's sights and events the most helpful of the **tourist offices** is right outside the train station in **Piazza della Stazione** – it's the stunted tower at the end of the line of bus stops (summer Mon–Sat 8.15am–7.15pm, Sun 8.15am–1.45pm; winter Mon–Sat 8am–2pm; ☎055/212.245). There is also a tourist office at **Via Cavour 1r**, north of the Duomo, which deals with queries about the city and its province (Mon–Sat 8am–7pm; ☎055/290.832) and at **Chiasso dei Baroncelli 17–19r**, just off Piazza della Signoria (summer daily 8am–7.30pm; winter Mon–Sat 8am–2pm; ☎055/230.2124) – though the latter was damaged in the Uffizi bombing, and may take a while to get back into full operation. All of these will give you an adequate map, leaflets on a variety of subjects, and a magazine called *Concierge Information*, which gives all the latest opening hours and entrance charges. The office at Via Cavour also handles information on the whole Florence province. None of these offices will book accommodation (see opposite for the agencies that do).

Accommodation

Accommodation for the budget tourist in Florence can be a problem: **hotel** prices tend to be high and standards less than brilliant, and the city's tourist invasion has scarcely any slack spots. The "no vacancy" signs are most profuse from March to October – during these months you'd best book your room well in advance, or reconcile yourself to staying some way out of the centre – perhaps even as far afield as Prato, Pistoia, or even Arezzo or Pisa (all reasonably quick train journeys from Santa Maria Novella).

There are only a couple of **hostels** and a couple of **campsites** within the city boundaries, but the range of bottom-bracket options is extended by the relatively high number of rooms available in student houses – some of them open to visitors even during term time.

FLORENTINE ADDRESSES

Note that there is a double address system in Florence, one for businesses and one for all other properties. Business addresses are followed by the letter r, and are marked on the building with a red number on a white plate. There's no connection between the two series – thus no. 20 might be several buildings away from no. 20r.

Accommodation services

If you haven't booked ahead, the easiest course is to queue up at the **Informazioni Turistiche Alberghiere** between platforms 9 and 10 inside the train station (daily 8.30am–9pm). They make hotel reservations for incoming tourists, their charge varying with the class of accommodation chosen from a minimum L3000 for a one-star to a maximum L6000 for a four-star, or L10,000 for a five-star hotel.

Seasonal accommodation offices (April–Nov daily 10.30am–1pm & 3–7pm) are located at the Fortezza da Basso car park, at the *Agip* service station at Perètola, on the A11 road to the coast (Autostrada Firenze Mare), and at the *Chianti Est* service station, on the A1 (Autostrada del Sole) just outside the city.

Trains coming in from the airport are met by an army of **touts** for various establishments, some of them genuine hotels, others unlicensed private houses. They're only recommended if you're desperate.

Hotels

Hotels are graded in Italy on a scale running from one-star to five-star, and in Florence there's a dearth of decent places in the lower ranks – humble one-star places (often called *pensioni*, thought that category officially no longer exists in Tuscany) are regularly reborn with an extra star or two after a lick of paint and a few winter improvements. Many of the most modest establishments look more like large private flats than small hotels, and are usually installed in the upper storeys on the busiest streets.

The price codes below relate to high-season prices (see box overleaf for details). Between October and March you will pay rather less, one reason for this dip being that breakfast, which should be optional, is virtually compulsory from April to October, slapping an extra L5000–10,000 per person onto your bill. (We've noted places where it's possible to get out of breakfast without too much fuss in summer.) Some of the cheaper places have been known to charge for hot water and towels as well – but our price categories take into account all these extras. As ever in big cities, **single rooms** are at a premium – and you'll do well to pay less than two-thirds the cost of a double; the listings specify the more fruitful possibilities. The maximum cost of a room should be posted on the back of the door; if it isn't, or if you have any other complaints, contact the tourist office.

Hotels listed below are arranged in ascending order of price under headings that relate to the chief areas of the city. There are two main concentrations of lowish-cost hotels in Florence: one to the **north of the station**, centred on Via Faenza; the other to the south, centred on Via della Scala, which runs into **Piazza Santa Maria Novella**. Be warned that the whole station area, and especially the Via Faenza zone, has a sizeable night-time population of hookers and their punters. Note also that some of the places you come across in this area are unlicensed – if you're at all doubtful it's probably best to give it a wide berth. All things consid-

ACCOMMODATION PRICES

Throughout this guide, accommodation is graded on a scale from ① to ⑨. Grades ① and ② apply to **hostel** accommodation, and indicate the lowest price a **single person** could expect to pay for one night in that establishment in high season. Grades ③ to ⑨ apply to **hotels**, and indicate the cost of the **cheapest double room in high season**. The price bands to which these codes refer are as follows:

① under L20,000 per person	④ L50–70,000 per double	⑦ L120–150,000 per double
② over L20,000 per person	⑤ L70–90,000 per double	⑧ L150–200,000 per double
③ under L50,000 per double	⑥ L90–120,000 per double	⑨ over L200,000 per double

ered, if you can afford a higher expenditure on your accommodation, it's a worthwhile investment in Florence, which has plenty of colourful places to stay in the city's nicer districts.

STATION AND MARKET AREAS

Mia Cara (☎055/216.053; ③) and **Marcella** (☎055/213.232; ④), both Via Faenza 58. The first is well furnished and more characterful than most on this street; the rooms in the latter are larger. There's no breakfast in either of them to slam up the cost.

Giovanna (☎055/238.1353; ④), **Nella** (☎055/284.256; ④) and **D'Ericco** (☎055/214.059; ③), all Via Faenza 69. The first two are small, tidy and as cheap as any on Via Faenza; the third, without breakfast, is okay, but no more than that.

Erina, Via Fiume 17 (☎055/288.294). A two-star hotel located on the third floor of an old palazzo, in a street parallel to Via Faenza; open mid-July to mid-September; has just seven double rooms. ④.

Albergo Concordia, Via dell'Amorino 13 (☎055/213.233). Cheap and extremely convenient, being located at the back of San Lorenzo church; it has four private bathrooms and doesn't do breakfast. ④.

Nazionale, Via Nazionale 22 (☎055/238.2203). Halfway between the train station and the market. ④.

Ausonia e Rimini (☎055/496.547) and **Kursaal** (☎055/496.324), both Via Nazionale 24. Welcoming and recently refurbished places, run by the same management at the same prices. Both ④.

Globus, Via Sant'Antonino 24 (☎055/211.062). Well-groomed if unremarkable place, close to San Lorenzo. ④.

Albergo Azzi (☎055/213.806; ⑤), **Locanda Anna** (☎055/239.8322; ⑤), **Locanda Paola** (☎055/213.682; ⑤), **Locanda Armonia** (☎055/211.146; ⑤) and **Locanda Marini** (☎055/284.824; ④), all Via Faenza 56. With most of its rooms overlooking the garden, the *Azzi* is probably the most pleasant of the *pensioni* occupying the upper three floors of this address. The *Anna* is friendly but has a 1am curfew; *Paola* has no curfew but is the scruffiest of the bunch. None of these first three have private bathrooms. *Armonia* is well scrubbed and ordinary; and *Marini* is comfortable if bland.

Pensione Merlini, Via Faenza 56 (☎055/212.848). Cheapest of the *pensioni* at this address. ⑤.

Pensione Desirée, Via Fiume 20 (☎055/238.2382). Completely overhauled a few years back – stained-glass windows, simulated antique furniture, and a bath in every room. ⑥.

Tony's Inn, Via Faenza 77 (☎055/217.975). One for homesick Anglophones, run by a Canadian woman and her Italian photographer husband. Most rooms have a bathroom. ⑥.

SANTA MARIA NOVELLA AREA

La Mia Casa, Piazza Santa Maria Novella 23 (☎055/213.061). Free showers, free film shows on summer evenings and an excellent location make this place a regular sell-out, despite its lack of polish and boarding-school atmosphere. ③.

Giacobazzi, Piazza Santa Maria Novella 24 (☎055/294.679). Popular with Italian visitors; it has only seven rooms, with three private baths. ③.

Ottaviani, Piazza Ottaviani 1 (☎055/239.6223). The better rooms overlook Piazza Santa Maria Novella, others aren't so great. ④.

La Romagnola (☎055/211.597) and **Gigliola** (☎055/287.981), both Via della Scala 40. These two hotels, which share the same reception, would unquestionably be the pick of the bunch on Via della Scala if it weren't for the midnight curfew. With a total of 42 rooms, they often have space when the others are full. Both ④.

Elite, Via della Scala 12 (☎055/215.395). Run by one of the most pleasant managers in town – and has no curfew. All rooms have private bathrooms. ⑤.

Le Vigne, Piazza Santa Maria Novella 24 (☎055/294.449). Well-refurbished two-star – the nicest budget hotel on the square. ⑤.

CITY CENTRE

Esperanza, Via dell'Inferno 3 (☎055/213.773). Secreted away in a quiet corner just north of Santa Trinita. Curfew at 1am. ③.

Maria Luisa de' Medici, Via del Corso 1 (☎055/280.048). Slightly run-down, with painting-by-numbers portraits of the Medici in the rooms. Comfortable and quiet though. ③.

Soggiorno Bavaria, Borgo Albizi 26 (☎055/234.0313). Installed in a sixteenth-century palazzo that was built for a follower of Eleanor of Toledo. Recommended – though often booked by long-stay language students. ④.

Brunetta, Borgo Pinti 5 (☎055/247.8134). Cheap and well placed; no breakfast. ④.

Brunori, Via del Proconsolo 5 (☎055/289.648). A short walk from the Duomo, on a very busy road, this noisy and slightly run-down place has especially friendly and informative owners; single and double rooms, and breakfast. ④.

Firenze, Piazza Donati 4 (☎055/214.203). Central and unobjectionable. ④.

Orchidea, Borgo degli Albizi 11 (☎055/248.0346). Lovely twelfth-century building, with half a dozen big rooms; a bargain. ④.

Maxim, Via de' Medici 4 (☎055/217.474). Twenty-two-room hotel a few yards off Via dei Calzaiuoli; very quiet and very friendly. ④.

San Giovanni, Via Cerretani 2 (☎055/213.580). On the busy main road immediately east of Piazza del Duomo. Very popular with US visitors. ④.

Alessandra, Borgo Santi Apostoli 17 (☎055/283.438). Perhaps the best of the central *pensioni*, occupying a sixteenth-century palazzo and furnished in a mixture of antique and modern styles; used by the fashion-show crowd, so booking is essential in September. ⑤.

Aldini (☎055/214.752; ⑦), and **Costantini** (☎055/215.128; ⑤), both Via dei Calzaiuoli 13. Although both at the same address, they have quite different prices. All the doubles in both hotels come with private bathrooms; the singles come with and without.

Hotel Veneto, Via Santa Reparata 33 (☎055/294.816). Comfortable two-star, but popular with school parties. ⑦.

Porta Rossa, Via Porta Rossa 19 (☎055/287.551). Some form of hostelry has been on this site since medieval times; the present incarnation is a characterful establishment, with nineteenth-century decor, huge rooms and rambling corridors. ⑦.

Hermitage, Vicolo Marzio 1 (☎055/287.216). Very close to the Ponte Vecchio, with some of its fourteen rooms overlooking the river. The price rockets up if you want a room with all the facilities. Essential to book. ⑧.

La Residenza, Via de' Tornabuoni 8 (☎055/284.197). Right by the Strozzi palace; with similar prices to the *Hermitage*, this is the nearest thing to a bargain that you'll find on Florence's snazziest street. ⑧.

NORTH OF THE CENTRE

Rudy, Via San Gallo 51 (☎055/475.519). More than a touch quieter than the hotels on the parallel Via Cavour; 1am curfew; the doubles don't have private bathrooms. ③.

Sampaoli, Via San Gallo 14 (☎055/284.834). As restful as the *Rudy*, with no curfew, and no breakfast. ③.

Genzianella (☎055/573.909; ③), **Savonarola** (☎055/587.824; ④) and **Benvenuti** (☎055/572.141; ⑤), all Via Cavour 112. Three different *pensioni* in one building, virtually in Piazza della Libertà – two entrances (the other's on Viale Matteotti) lead to a single reception for all three. All dependable if unthrilling.

Panorama, Via Cavour 60 (☎055/238.2403). Another favourite with school parties, in the university area. ④.

Hotel Giglio, Via Cavour 85 (☎055/486.621). Close to the *Panorama*, and a touch more pleasant. ⑤.

La Colomba, Via Cavour 21 (☎055/289.139). Spick and span, run by a very friendly Australian woman. ⑤.

Casci, Via Cavour 13 (☎055/211.686). Restful hotel in a medieval building that pleasantly feels its age. Massive breakfast. ⑥.

Pensione Splendor, Via San Gallo 30 (☎055/483.427). Occupying a quiet palazzo in the university area, frescoed and antique-furnished; breakfast is included in the price. ⑦.

EAST AND NORTHEAST OF THE CENTRE

Donatello (☎055/245.870; ⑤) and **Losanna** (☎055/245.840; ④), both Via Alfieri 9. Two small hotels located between Piazza d'Azeglio and Piazzale Donatello, to the east of the university district. The former is smartly renovated, airy, and run by young management, but without private bathrooms; the latter is a clean and modest *pensione* with just eight rooms – and you can avoid breakfast if you make the point clearly when you arrive.

Pensione Jennings-Riccioli, Corso dei Tintori 7 (☎055/244.751). Forster's *Room with a View* is reputedly no. 21 – though modernisations have left little else here of the novel's atmosphere. Closed Nov–March. ⑦.

OLTRARNO

Pensione Sorelle Bandini, Piazza Santo Spirito 9 (☎055/215.308). Vast rooms, gorgeous decor (including marble fireplaces) and views from the three-sided loggia make this one of Florence's most attractive options. ⑤.

La Scaletta, Via Guicciardini 13 (☎055/283.028). In similar vein though more expensive; from the rooftop terrace you look across the Bóboli gardens in one direction and the city in the other. ⑥.

Pensione Annalena, Via Romana 34 (☎055/222.402). This *pensione* has entered the folklore of Florence on account of its longevity and its popularity with mid-twentieth-century writers and intelligentsia. It's installed in a fourteenth-century building facing one of the entrances to the Bóboli gardens, and at the reception they'll give you a leaflet on its long history. The rooms are all magnificent, and in summer the air of the hotel loggia is saturated with perfumes from the flowerbeds below; the inevitable drawback is the cost. ⑧.

Hostels and student accommodation

Florence has only two **youth hostels** and one of these is some distance from the centre, though it's one of the most pleasant hostels in Italy. To help matters a little, there are a number of **student institutions**, most of them run by religious bodies, which provide beds for non-natives at the city universities. Out of term time (June–Oct) some of these places are open to young tourists, and a few even have accommodation throughout the year. In addition to the houses listed below, there are also a number of *Case dello Studente*, which are run by the university authorities and occasionally made available to visitors; for information on these, ask at the tourist office (see p.56).

Hostels

Santa Monaca, Via Santa Monaca 6 (☎055/268.338). In Oltrarno, close to Santa Maria del Carmine. Privately owned, this is the only hostel in the centre, and is open for reservations from 8 to 9.30am. The rooms are closed from 9.30am to 4pm. Kitchen facilities, free hot showers, and no maximum length of stay. The noticeboard is useful for information on lifts. ①.

Ostello Villa Camerata, Viale Righi 2 (☎055/601.451). A half-hour journey on the #17b bus from the train station. Tucked away in a beautiful park, the Villa Camerata is one of Europe's most beautiful hostels, a sixteenth-century house with frescoed ceilings and a wide loggia. Doors open at 2pm, and if you can't be there by then, ring ahead to make sure there's a place left. If you don't have an IYHF card you can buy a special guest card that's valid in other Italian youth hostels. Breakfast and sheets are included; optional supper at L12,000 (no kitchen facilities); films in English every night; curfew at 11.30pm all year round. ②.

Student accommodation

Istituto Gould, Via dei Serragli 49 (☎055/212.576). In Oltrarno, past Ponte alla Carrara. Reception is on the second floor (the doorbell is easily missed) – open Mon–Fri 9am–1pm & 3–7pm all year. Recently renovated, the *Gould* is extremely popular, so it's wise to book in advance; rooms are especially scarce during the academic year; no breakfast. ②.

Suore Oblate dello Spirito Santo, Via Nazionale 8 (☎055/239.8202). A few steps from the station. Run by nuns, it's open from mid-June to October, to women only: minimum stay two nights. Very clean and pleasant; beds arranged in double, triple and quad rooms; breakfast included; curfew at 11pm. ②.

Suore Oblate dell'Assunzione, Via Borgo Pinti 15 (☎055/21.45.82). Not far from the Duomo, again run by nuns, but open to both men and women, this time from mid-June to the end of July and throughout September (although 4 or 5 beds are available all year round). Single and double rooms; midnight curfew; no breakfast. ②.

Pio X – Artigianelli, Via dei Serragli 106 (☎055/225.044). Probably the cheapest option in town. Don't be put off by the huge picture of Pope Pius X at the top of the steps – the management is friendly and the atmosphere relaxed. It's open all day throughout the year, but it's best to get there by 9am, as the 64 beds soon get taken. Midnight curfew; two-day minimum stay. Double, triple and quadruple rooms; free showers. ①.

Campsites

The situation for campers in Florence isn't very good: summer arrivals are almost certain to find that the only available spaces are at the *Area di Sosta*, an emergency accommodation area set aside by the city authorities every summer – it usually amounts to a patch of ground sheltered by a rudimentary roof, with a shower block attached. An alternative would be to try the site in Fiesole, to the north of the city (see p.152).

Italiani e Stranieri, Viale Michelangelo 80 (☎055/681.1977). Open from April to October, this 240-place site is always crowded, owing to its superb hillside location. Kitchen facilities and well-stocked, if expensive, shop nearby. Take #13 bus from the station.

Villa Camerata, Viale Righi 2–4 (☎055/610.300). Basic 60-place site, open all year in the hostel grounds.

Area di Sosta. The site of *Area di Sosta* is not constant: at the time of writing it was at *Villa Favard*, in Via Rocca Tedalda (☎055/690.022), reachable on the #14a bus, and open July 1– Sept 20. Check with the tourist office or train station accommodation service before setting off there. Staying there is free, and showers are available for a small charge.

THE CITY

Greater Florence now spreads several kilometres down the Arno valley and up onto the hills north and south of the city, but the major sights are contained within an area that can be crossed on foot in little over half an hour. A short walk from the train station brings you to the **Baptistery** and **Duomo**; the area south from here to **Piazza della Signoria** – site of the **Palazzo Vecchio** and the **Uffizi** gallery – is the inner core, the area into which most of the tourists are packed. A square drawn so that the Duomo and Uffizi stood in the centre of opposite sides would cover many of the best-preserved of Florence's medieval streets and the majority of its fashionable streets.

Immediately north of the Duomo is the **San Lorenzo** quarter, where market stalls surround one of the city's first-rank churches, in effect the chapel of the Medici dynasty. Within a short radius of here are the monastery of **San Marco**, with its paintings by Fra' Angelico, the **Accademia**, residence of Michelangelo's *David*, and **Piazza Santissima Annunziata**, Florence's most attractive square.

The Uffizi backs onto the Arno River, across which lies the district known as **Oltrarno**, where the **Palazzo Pitti** and Masaccio's church of **Santa Maria del Carmine** exert the strongest pull, followed by the churches of **Santo Spirito** and the colourful **San Miniato al Monte**.

Close to the eastern side of Piazza del Duomo stands the **Bargello**, the main museum of sculpture; further east, the area around the Franciscan church of **Santa Croce** forms a nucleus of activity. On the western side of the city, directly opposite the train station, the unmissable attraction is **Santa Maria Novella**, Florentine base of the rival Dominican order.

Note that you can buy a **combined ticket** for L10,000 which gives entrance to the following city museums: Palazzo Vecchio; Museo Bardini; Museo di Firenze com'era; Collezione della Ragione; Museo di Santa Maria Novella; and Museo di Santo Spirito. The ticket is valid for one month and is available from any of the above.

Piazza del Duomo

From the train station, all first-time visitors gravitate towards **Piazza del Duomo**, beckoned by the pinnacle of Brunelleschi's dome, which lords it over the cityscape with an authority unmatched by any architectural creation in any other Italian city. Yet even though the magnitude of the **Duomo** is apparent from a distance, the initial full sight of the church and the adjacent **Baptistery** still comes as a jolt, the colours of their patterned exteriors making a startling contrast with the dun-toned buildings around.

Florence doesn't make the most of these two bravura buildings: the Piazza del Duomo is not so much a square as a bit of clear space in the midst of the traffic. There are no cafés from which to admire the view, and unless you're on a shopping spree, the only place on the periphery of the piazza that you might drop in at is the summertime tourist information desk in the **Loggia del Bigallo**, opposite the south side of the Baptistery.

The loggia itself was built for the Misericordia, a charitable organisation founded in the thirteenth century and still in existence today, operating an ambulance service from offices just over Via dei Calzaiuoli. It now houses one of Florence's more problematic art museums, the small **Museo del Bigallo**, which has been closed to the public the last few years, even though it was reopened after a major refit as recently as 1976. Should it reopen once more, you'll find that it contains several religious paintings commissioned by the Misericordia and the similarly altruistic Compagnia del Bigallo, with which it merged in the fifteenth century. The fourteenth-century works – the museum's main strength – include a 1342 painting known as the *Madonna of the Misericordia*, which features the oldest known panorama of Florence. If you're really intent on getting in, you could try ringing for an appointment (☎055/215.440).

The Duomo

Some time in the seventh century the seat of the Bishop of Florence was transferred from San Lorenzo to the sixth-century church of Santa Reparata, which stood on the site of the present-day **Santa Maria del Fiore** – to give the **Duomo** its full title. Later generations modified that building until, in the thirteenth century, it was decided that a new cathedral was required, to do justice to the wealth of the city and to put the Pisans and Sienese in their place. The plan drawn up by **Arnolfo di Cambio**, who was entrusted with the project in 1294, was suitably immodest – it was to be the largest church in the Catholic world, and would "surpass anything of its kind produced by the Greeks and Romans in the times of their greatest power".

BRUNELLESCHI AND THE CONSTRUCTION OF THE DOME

Work on Arnolfo's basilica ground to a halt immediately after his death eight years later, then was resumed under a succession of architects, each of whom roughly followed his plan, which focused on a domed crossing embraced by three tribunes. By 1418 the nave was finished, the tribunes were complete, and a drum was in place to bear the weight of the **dome** that Arnolfo had envisaged as the church's crown. The conception was magnificent: the dome was to span a distance of nearly 140 feet, and rise from a base some 180 feet above the floor of the nave. It was to be the largest dome ever constructed – but nobody had yet worked out how to build the thing.

A committee of the masons' guild was set up to ponder the problem, and it was to them that **Filippo Brunelleschi** presented himself. His arrogant insistence that only he could possibly redeem the situation, and his refusal to say much more about his solution other than that he could build the dome without the use of exterior scaffolding, did little to endear him to his prospective patrons. Various alternative schemes were considered, including – according to Vasari – the ingenious notion of supporting the dome on a vast mound of earth that would be seeded with thousands of coins; when the dome was finished, the mound would be cleared away by inviting Florence's citizens to excavate the money. In the end, however, Brunelleschi was given the job on condition that he work jointly with his rival Ghiberti (see p.69) – a partnership that did not last long, though Ghiberti's contribution to the project was probably more significant than his colleague ever admitted.

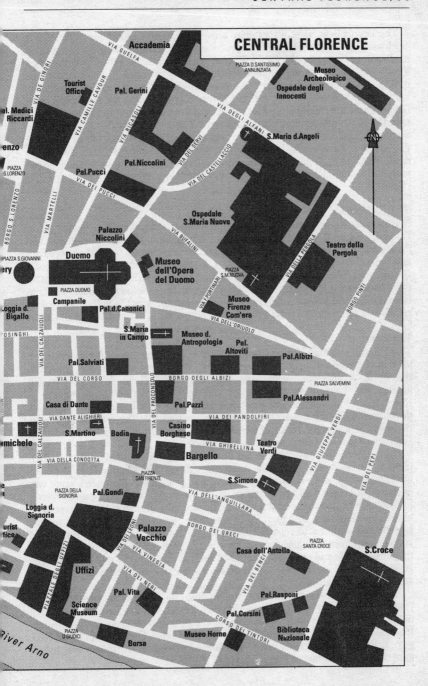

CENTRAL FLORENCE

Accademia

PIAZZA D.SANTISSIMO
ANNUNZIATA

Museo
Archeologico

VIA GUELFA

Tourist
Office

Pal. Gerini

Ospedale degli
Innocenti

VIA CAMILLE CAVOUR

VIA DEGLI ALFANI

VIA DE GINORI

al. Medici
Riccardi

VIA RICASOLI

S.Maria d.Angeli

VIA DEL SERVI

enzo

PIAZZA
S.LORENZO

Pal.Niccolini

Pal.Pucci

VIA DEL CASTELLACCIO

VIA MARTELLI

VIA DEI PUCCI

BORGO S.LORENZO

Ospedale
S.Maria Nuova

VIA BUFALINI

VIA DELLA PERGOLA

Teatro della
Pergola

Palazzo
Niccolini

PIAZZA S.GIOVANNI

Duomo

Museo
dell'Opera
del Duomo

BORGO PINTI

ery

PIAZZA DUOMO

PIAZZA
S.M.NUOVA

Campanile

Loggia d.
Bigallo

Pal.d.Canonici

VIA PORTINARI

Museo
Firenze
Com'era

OSINGHI

S.Maria
in Campo

VIA DEL CALZAIUOLI

VIA DELL'ORIUOLO

Museo d.
Antropologia

Pal.
Altoviti

Pal.Albizi

Pal.Salviati

VIA DEL CORSO

BORGO DEGLI ALBIZI

PIAZZA SALVEMINI

Pal.Alessandri

Casa di Dante

VIA DEL PROCONSOLO

VIA DANTE ALIGHIERI

Pal.Pazzi

VIA DEI PANDOLFIRI

michele

VIA DEL CALZAIUOLI

S.Martino

Badia

Casino
Borghese

VIA GHIBELLINA

Teatro
Verdi

VIA GIUSEPPE VERDI

VIA DEI PEPI

VIA DELLA CONDOTTA

Bargello

PIAZZA
SAN FIRENZE

S.Simone

PIAZZA DELLA
SIGNORIA

Pal.Gondi

VIA DELL'ANGUILLARA

Loggia d.
Signoria

BORGO DEI GRECI

PIAZZA
SANTA CROCE

urist
fice

VIA VELLEONI

Palazzo
Vecchio

VIA VINEGIA

Casa dell'Antella

S.Croce

Uffizi

PIAZZALE DEGLI UFFIZI

VIA DEI NERI

Pal. Vita

VIA DEI BENCI

Pal.Rasponi

Science
Museum

PIAZZA
D.GIUDICI

CORSO DEI TINTORI

Pal.Corsini

Biblioteca
Nazionale

River Arno

Borsa

Museo Horne

N

The key to Brunelleschi's strategy turned out to be a technique of laying the brickwork in cantilevered rings, a procedure that ensured the dome supported itself as it grew. On March 25, 1436 – Annunciation Day, and the Florentine New Year – the completion of the dome was marked by the consecration of the cathedral, a ceremony conducted by the pope himself. Yet the topmost piece, the lantern, was still not in place, and many were sceptical about the structure's capability to bear the weight. Other architects were consulted, but Brunelleschi again won the day, and this final stage commenced in 1446, a few months before the architect's death; the colossal lantern was completed in the late 1460s, when the gilded ball and cross, cast by Verrocchio, were hoisted into place. One part of the dome remains incomplete, however: the gallery around the base was abandoned with only one face finished, after Michelangelo compared it to "cages for crickets".

THE EXTERIOR

Marble quarried from three different sources was used to clad the **exterior** of the Duomo – white from Carrara, red from Maremma and green from Prato. The flanks date back to Arnolfo's era and the succeeding century or so; the overblown and pernickety main facade, however, is a nineteenth-century simulacrum of a Gothic front. The south side is the oldest part of the exterior, but the most attractive adornment is the **Porta della Mandorla**, on the other side. It takes its name from the almond-shaped frame (or *mandorla*) that contains the pollution-streaked relief of *The Assumption of the Virgin*, sculpted by Nanni di Banco around 1420.

The interior

The Duomo's interior (daily 10am–5.30pm) is the converse of the exterior – a vast, uncluttered enclosure of bare masonry. The fifth most capacious church in the world, it once held a congregation of 10,000 to hear Savonarola preach against the tyranny of the Medici and the soul-corrupting decadence of Renaissance Florence. Its ambience is more that of a great assembly hall than a devotional building, and it's not surprising to find that the most conspicuous decorations in the main body of the church are a pair of memorials to *condottieri* (mercenary commanders) on the wall of the left aisle.

Paolo Uccello's **monument to Sir John Hawkwood**, created in 1436, is often cited as the epitome of Florentine mean-spiritedness; according to local folklore – unsupported by any evidence – the mercenary captain of Florence's army was promised a proper equestrian statue as his memorial, then was posthumously fobbed off with this trompe l'oeil version. It features a strange shift of perspective, with the pedestal depicted from a different angle from what's on it; it's known that Uccello was ordered to repaint the horse and rider, presumably because he'd shown them from the same point of view as the base, which must have displayed the horse's belly and not much else. Look back at the entrance wall and you'll see another Uccello contribution to the interior – a clock adorned with four rather abstracted Evangelists.

Andrea Castagno's **monument to Niccolò da Tolentino**, created twenty years later, is clearly derived from Uccello's fresco, but has an aggressive edge that's typical of this artist (see p.85 and p.96). Just beyond the horsemen, Domenico do Michelino's *Dante Explaining the Divine Comedy*, painted in 1465, gave Brunelleschi's recently completed dome a place only marginally less prominent than the mountain of Purgatory.

Judged by mere size, the major work of art in the Duomo is the fresco of **The Last Judgement** that lurks behind the restorers' netting inside of the dome. At the time of its execution a substantial body of opinion thought Vasari and Zuccari's combined effort did nothing but deface Brunelleschi's masterpiece; quite a few people today would prefer the painting stripped away rather than cleaned up. Below the fresco are seven stained-glass roundels designed by Uccello, Ghiberti, Castagno and Donatello; they are best inspected from the gallery immediately below them, which forms part of the route to the **top of the dome** (Mon–Sat 10am–5pm; L5000). If you're queasy about heights, the narrow gallery might be troublesome, but it's the only tricky part of the ascent: most of the climb winds between the brick walls of the outer and inner shells of the dome, where you feel as secure as you would in a ground-level alleyway, while at the summit the view is so amazing it takes your mind off everything else.

When you finally come back down to earth, be sure to take a look at the entrances to the two **sacristies**, on each side of the altar. Enamelled terracotta reliefs by Luca della Robbia are placed over both, and the doors of the north sacristy were his only works in bronze. Lorenzo de' Medici took refuge in the north sacristy after his brother Giuliano had been mortally stabbed on the altar steps by the Pazzi conspirators (see p.68), the bulk of these new doors protecting him from his would-be assassins; small portraits on the handles commemorate the brothers.

The relics of Saint Zenobius, fourth-century bishop of Florence, are preserved underneath the altar of the middle **apse**, in a beautifully sculpted bronze urn designed by Ghiberti, who also executed the stained glass in all three apses. The apse is often reserved for prayer, so use your discretion.

SANTA REPARATA

In the 1960s remnants of the Duomo's predecessor, **Santa Reparata** (Mon–Sat 10am–5pm; L3000), were uncovered underneath the west end of the nave – the remains are extensive, as the nave of the Duomo was built several feet above that of the old church, which was thus not fully demolished. Subsequent excavations have revealed a complicated jigsaw of Roman, palaeochristian and Romanesque remains, plus fragments of mosaic and fourteenth-century frescoes. The explanatory diagrams tend to intensify the confusion: to make sense of it all, you'll have to keep referring to the detailed model in the farthest recess of the crypt.

Also discovered in the course of the dig was the **tomb of Brunelleschi**, the only Florentine ever honoured with burial inside the Duomo – his tombstone can be seen, without paying, through a grille to the left of the foot of the stairs.

The Campanile

The **Campanile** (daily March–Oct 8.30am–7pm; Nov–Feb 8.30am–5pm; L5000) was begun in 1334 by Giotto and continued after his death by Andrea Pisano and Francesco Talenti, who rectified the deficiencies in the artist's calculations by doubling the thickness of the walls. Erosion caused by atmospheric pollution has made it necessary to replace the tower's sculptures with copies – the originals are all in the Museo dell'Opera del Duomo (see p.70).

The first storey, the only part of the tower built exactly as Giotto designed it, is studded with two rows of remarkable bas-reliefs; the lower, illustrating the *Creation of Man* and the *Arts and Industries*, was carved by Pisano himself, the

---

THE PAZZI CONSPIRACY

The **Pazzi Conspiracy**, perhaps the most compelling of all Florence's murkier acts of treachery, had its roots in the election in 1472 of **Sixtus IV**, a pope who distributed money and favours with a largesse remarkable even by papal standards. Six of his nephews were made cardinals, one of them, the uncouth **Girolamo Riario**, coming in for particularly preferential treatment, probably because he was Sixtus's son. Sixtus's plan was that Riario should take over the town of Imola as a base for papal expansion, and accordingly he approached Lorenzo de' Medici for the necessary loan. Aware that Imola was too close to Milan and Bologna to be allowed to fall into papal hands, Lorenzo rebuffed the pope, despite the importance of the Vatican account with the Medici bank, and the family's role as agents for the papacy's alum mines in Tuscany (alum was a vital part of the dyeing industry, and therefore essential to Florence's textile trade). Enraged by the snub, and by Lorenzo's refusal to recognise **Francesco Salviati** as Archbishop of Pisa (Sixtus had ignored an agreement by which appointments within the Florentine domain could only be made by mutual agreement), Sixtus turned to the Pazzi, the Medici's leading Florentine rivals as bankers in Rome.

Three co-conspirators met in Rome in the early months of 1477: Riario, now in possession of Imola but eager for greater spoils; Salviati, incandescent at Lorenzo's veto and desperate to become Archbishop of Florence; and **Francesco de' Pazzi**, head of the Pazzi's Rome operation and determined to usurp Medici power in Florence. Any plot, however, required military muscle, and the man chosen to provide it, a plain-speaking mercenary called **Montesecco**, proved intensely wary of the whole enterprise – "beware of what you do," he counselled, "Florence is a big affair". In the end he made his co-operation conditional on papal blessing, a benediction that was readily obtained. "I do not wish the death of anyone on any account", was Sixtus's mealy-mouthed observation, "since it does not accord with our office to consent to such a thing"; yet he knew full well Lorenzo's death was essential if the plot was to succeed. "Go, and do what you wish," he added, "provided there be no killing." **Jacopo de' Pazzi**, the Pazzi's wizened godfather, was also won over by

---

upper by his pupils. Donatello and others created the figures of *Prophets* and *Sibyls* in the second-storey niches – too high to be really appreciated. The parapet at the top of the tower is a less lofty viewpoint than the dome, but a good deal more vertiginous – it feels like you're perched on top of a flagpole.

The Baptistery

Generally thought to date from the sixth or seventh century, the **Baptistery** is the oldest building in Florence, and was the city's cathedral before Santa Reparata. Though its origins lie in the depths of the Dark Ages, no building better illustrates the special relationship between Florence and the Roman world. The Florentines were always conscious of their Roman ancestry, and throughout the Middle Ages they chose to believe that the Baptistery was originally a Roman temple to Mars, a belief bolstered by the interior's inclusion of Roman granite columns. The pattern of the marble cladding – applied in the eleventh and twelfth centuries – is clearly classical in inspiration, and the Baptistery's most famous embellishments, its gilded bronze **doors**, mark the emergence of a more scholarly, self-conscious interest in the art of the ancient world.

Sixtus's disingenuous support, despite being on good terms with the Medici – indeed, one of his nephews was married to Lorenzo's sister.

After numerous false starts, it was decided to **murder Lorenzo and Giuliano** whilst they attended Mass in the cathedral. The date set was Sunday, April 26, 1478. Montesecco, however, now refused "to add sacrilege to murder", so Lorenzo's murder was delegated to two embittered priests, **Maffei** and **Bagnone**, whereas Giuliano was to be dispatched by Francesco de' Pazzi and **Bernardo Baroncelli**, a violent Pazzi side-kick deeply in debt to the family. Salviati, meanwhile, accompanied by an armed troop, was to seize control of the Palazzo della Signoria.

It all went horribly wrong. Giuliano was killed in a crazed frenzy, his skull shattered and his body rent with nineteen stab-wounds, but Lorenzo managed to escape, fleeing wounded to the duomo's new sacristy, where he and his supporters barricaded themselves behind its heavy bronze doors. Across the city, Salviati was separated from his troops, thanks to newly installed secret doors and locks in the Palazzo della Signoria, and arrested by the *Gonfaloniere*, Cesare Petrucci.

Appraised of the plot, a furious mob dispensed summary justice to several of the conspirators: Salviati's troops were massacred to a man, whilst Salviati and Francesco de' Pazzi were hanged from a window of the Palazzo della Signoria. Of the latter execution, Poliziano, the eminent humanist, noted that "as the Archbishop rolled and struggled at the end of his rope, his eyes goggling in his head, he fixed his teeth into Francesco de' Pazzi's naked body." Maffei and Bagnone, the bungling priests, were castrated and hanged. Baroncelli escaped to Constantinople but was extradited and executed. Montesecco was tortured, but given a soldier's execution in the Bargello. Jacopo's end was the most sordid. Having escaped Florence, he was recaptured, tortured, stripped naked, and hanged alongside the decomposing Salviati. He was then buried in Santa Croce, but exhumed by the mob, who blamed heavy rains on his evil spirit. His corpse was dragged through the streets, tipped in a ditch, and finally propped up outside the Pazzi palace, where his rotting head was used as door knocker. Eventually the putrefying body was thrown in the Arno, fished out, flogged and hanged again by a gang of children, and finally cast back into the river.

The doors

The **south door** was cast in 1336 by **Andrea Pisano**; twenty of its twenty-eight panels form an exquisite narrative on the life of Saint John the Baptist, patron saint of Florence and, obviously enough, dedicatee of this building. Years of financial and political turmoil, and the ravages of the Black Death, prevented any work on the other entrances to the Baptistery until 1401, when a competition was held for the commission to make a new set of doors, each entrant being asked to create a panel showing the sacrifice of Isaac.

Finding themselves equally impressed by the pieces produced by Brunelleschi and **Lorenzo Ghiberti** (both now displayed in the Bargello), the judges suggested that the pair should become partners. To this reasonable proposal Brunelleschi replied that if he couldn't do the job alone he wasn't interested in doing it at all – whereupon the contract was handed over to Ghiberti, and his rival stomped off to study architecture in Rome. Ghiberti, barely twenty years old, was to devote much of his time over the next half-century to this one project, and his fame rests almost entirely on the extraordinary result.

His **north doors** (1403–24), depicting scenes from the life of Christ, the four Evangelists and the four Doctors of the Church, show a new naturalism and classicised sense of composition, but their innovation is fairly timid in comparison with the sublime **east doors** (1425–52), which were ordered from Ghiberti as soon as the first set was finished. They have always been known as "The Gates of Paradise", supposedly because Michelangelo once remarked that they were so beautiful they deserved to be the portals of heaven. In fact, the name almost certainly comes from the fact that the area between the Baptistery and Santa Reparata was called the *Paradiso*.

As with so many exterior art works in Florence, what you now see is a reproduction: the original panels are being restored and then placed in the Museo dell'Opera as they are finished. The replicas will remain too garish until the Florentine exhaust fumes do their work, but they give a reasonable idea of the grand scheme. Unprecedented in the subtlety of their carving, the scenes are a primer of early Renaissance art, using rigorous perspective, gesture and sophisticated groupings to intensify the drama of each scene. Ghiberti has included an understandably self-satisfied self-portrait in the frame of the left-hand door: his is the fourth head from the top of the right-hand band – the bald chap with the smirk.

The pair of marble columns to the side of the east doors were presented by the city of Pisa in the twelfth century, and would have been slotted into the walls if they had not turned out to be too weak to bear any weight. Another marble column on the outside is decorated with bronze branches and leaves to commemorate the miracle brought about by the body of Saint Zenobius; as the corpse was being carried into Santa Reparata it brushed against a barren elm here, which thereupon sprang into leaf.

The interior

The baptistery **interior** (Mon–Sat 1–6pm, Sun 9am–1pm; free) is equally stunning, with its black and white marble cladding and ancient Roman columns below a blazing mosaic ceiling. Both the semi-abstract mosaic floor and the magnificent scenes in the cupola – including a fearsome platoon of demons at the feet of Christ in judgement – were created in the thirteenth century. The empty octagon in the centre of the floor marks the spot once occupied by the huge font in which every child born in the city during the previous twelve months would be baptised on New Year's Day. To the right of the altar is the **tomb of John XXIII**, the schismatic pope who died in Florence in 1419 while a guest of his financial adviser and close friend, Giovanni di Bicci de' Medici – the man who established the family at the political forefront of Florence. The papal monument, draped by an illusionistic marble canopy, is the work of Donatello and his pupil Michelozzo.

The Museo dell'Opera del Duomo

Since the early fifteenth century the maintenance of the Duomo has been supervised from the building at Piazza del Duomo 9, behind the east end of the church; nowadays this also houses the **Museo dell'Opera del Duomo** (March–Oct Mon–Sat 9am–7.30pm; Nov–Feb Mon–Sat 9am–6pm; L5000), the repository of the most precious and fragile works of art from the Duomo, Baptistery and Campanile. As an overview of the sculpture of Florence it's second only to the Bargello, and is far easier to take in on a single visit.

A family of sculptures by **Arnolfo di Cambio**, including an eerily glassy-eyed *Madonna*, are the most arresting works in the first few rooms; they were rescued from Arnolfo's unfinished facade for the Duomo, which was pulled down in the sixteenth century. Preceding rooms are dedicated to Brunelleschi, displaying his death mask and a variety of tools and machines devised by the architect. At the other end of the main room, steps lead up to a collection of models of suggested facades for the Duomo, and an assembly of reliquaries that can boast the jaw of Saint Jerome and the index finger of John the Baptist.

On the mezzanine level is **Michelangelo**'s anguished *Pietà*, moved here while restoration of the dome is in progress, but probably fated to stay. This is one of his last works, and was intended for his own tomb – Vasari records that the face of Nicodemus is a self-portrait. Dissatisfied with the quality of the marble, Michelangelo mutilated the group by hammering off the left leg and arm of Christ; his pupil Tiberio Calcagni restored the arm, then finished off the figure of the Magdalen, turning her into a whey-faced supporting player.

Although he's represented on the lower floor as well, it's upstairs that **Donatello**, the greatest of Michelangelo's precursors, really comes to the fore. Of the figures he carved for the Campanile, the most powerful is that of the prophet Habbakuk, the intensity of whose gaze is said to have prompted the sculptor to seize it and yell "Speak, speak!" Opposite poles of Donatello's temperament are represented by the bedraggled wooden figure of Mary Magdalene and his ornate *cantoria* (choir-loft) from the Duomo, with its playground of boisterous putti. Facing it is the *cantoria* created at the same time by **Luca della Robbia**; the earnest young musicians embody the text from Psalm 33 inscribed on the frame "Praise the Lord with harp. Sing unto Him with the psaltery and instrument of ten strings."

Pisano's bas-reliefs from the Campanile are on show nearby, depicting the spiritual refinement of humanity through work, the arts and, ultimately, the sacraments. Another room is evolving into a showcase for the restored panels from the Gates of Paradise, and also contains a dazzling silver-gilt altar from the Baptistery, completed in 1480 after more than a century of labour by such master craftsmen as Antonio del Pollaiuolo and Verrocchio.

Between the Duomo and the Signoria

Unless you want to construct a serpentine back-alley route, getting from Piazza del Duomo to Piazza della Signoria comes down to a choice between two streets: **Via del Proconsolo**, which leads from the eastern side of the Duomo, or **Via dei Calzaiuoli**, from the Campanile. Even the shortest stay in Florence should find time for a stroll along both, but the initial choice depends on whether it's the art you're after – in which case the former gets the nod – or the streetlife.

Via del Proconsolo: from the Duomo to the Badìa

The top of **Via del Proconsolo**, just a few yards from the Museo dell'Opera del Duomo, forms a major junction with Via dell'Oriuolo, the most direct route from the Duomo to the Sant'Ambrogio quarter (see p.116). If you've got a spare hour or so, it's worth a diversion down here for the **Museo di Firenze com'era** (Museum of Florence as it used to be) at Via dell'Oriuolo 24 (Mon–Wed, Fri & Sat 9am–2pm, Sun 8am–1pm; L3000).

Charting the growth of Florence and its environs from the fifteenth century, the museum contains a wealth of maps, prints, photos and topographical paintings, none of them masterpieces but most of them at least informative. Perhaps the most impressive item comes right at the start: a meticulous reproduction of the colossal 1470 aerial view of Florence called the *Pianta della Catena* (Chain Map), the original of which is in Berlin. The Medici villas at the end of the sixteenth century are recorded in the sequence of twelve pictures painted by Giusto Utens for the Villa dell'Artimino (see p.156), while eighteenth-century Florence is perpetuated by the elegiac engravings of Giuseppe Zocchi. There's also a poignant section recounting the destruction of the city's ancient heart to make space for the Piazza della Repubblica.

The anthropological museum

Back down Via del Proconsolo, on the nearside of the first crossroads, rises the Palazzo Nonfinito – so called because Buontalenti's project was continued but never completed after his death. Now it contains the **Museo Nazionale di Antropologia ed Etnologia** (Mon–Sat & third Sun of month 9am–1pm; closed Aug 13–17; free), Italy's first and still foremost museum of global folk costume and customs. Exhibits include Peruvian mummies, scores of skulls garnered from all over the world, a massive hoard of musical instruments, a host of objects collected on Captain Cook's last Pacific voyage and – the highlight of the collection, according to those in the know – an array of Kafiri items from Pakistan.

Dante's district

Take a right turn at Via Dante Alighieri and you'll soon come to the small piazza that fronts the **Casa di Dante** (Mon, Tues & Thurs–Sat 9.30am–12.30pm & 3.30–6.30pm, Sun 9.30am–12.30pm; free), marketed as the birthplace of the author of the *Divine Comedy*, the foundation stone of Italian literature. The museum is a homage to the poet rather than a shrine: it contains nothing directly related to his life, and in all likelihood he was born not here but somewhere in the street that bears his name. Numerous editions of the *Divina Commedia* are on show – including a poster printed with the whole text in minuscule type – along with copies of Botticelli's illustrations to the poem.

As contentious as the Casa di Dante's claim is the story that Dante got married in **Santa Margherita de' Cerchi**, the ancient little church up the street on the right. It does, however, have a nice altarpiece of the *Madonna and Four Saints* by Neri di Bicci.

Over Via Dante Alighieri from the poet's house, on Piazza San Martino, the tiny **San Martino del Vescovo** (Mon–Sat 10am–noon & 3–5pm) was once the headquarters of the charitable body called the Compagnia di Buonomini. It was they who commissioned the church's frescoes showing scenes from the life of Saint Martin and other altruistic acts; painted by the workshop of Ghirlandaio, they are as absorbing a record of daily life in Renaissance Florence as the better-known works by Ghirlandaio himself in Santa Maria Novella. The chapel also contains a couple of *Madonnas* – one Byzantine, the other possibly by Perugino.

Opposite San Martino soars the thirteenth-century **Torre della Castagna**, meeting place of the city's *priori* before they decamped to the Palazzo Vecchio. This is one of the most striking remnants of Florence's medieval townscape, when over 150 such towers rose between the river and the Duomo, many of them over two hundred feet high. Allied clans would link their towers with wooden catwalks, creating a sort of upper-class promenade above the heads of the lowlier citizens. In 1250 the government of the *Primo Popolo* ordered that the towers be reduced by two-thirds of their height; the resulting rubble was voluminous enough to extend the city walls beyond the Arno.

DANTE

Dante signed himself "Dante Alighieri, a Florentine by birth but not by character", a bitter allusion to the city he served as a politician but which later cast him into exile and was to inspire some of the most vitriolic passages in his great epic poem, *La Divina Commedia* (Divine Comedy). He was born in 1265, into a minor and impoverished noble family, then was educated at Bologna and later at Padua, where he studied philosophy and astronomy. Long before his academic career had blossomed, however, his romantic life had been forever blighted by an encounter with the eight-year-old **Beatrice Pratinari**. Boccaccio described the young girl as possessed of "habits and language more serious and modest than her age warranted." Her features, furthermore, were "so delicate and so beautifully formed, and full, besides mere beauty, of so much candid loveliness that many thought her almost an angel." Dante (himself just nine when he met Beatrice), described his own feelings after the encounter: "Love ruled my soul . . . and began to hold such sway over me . . . that it was necessary for me to do completely all his pleasure. He commanded me often that I should endeavour to see this so youthful angel, and I saw in her such noble and and praiseworthy deportment that truly of her might be said these words of the poet Homer – *She appeared to be born not of mortal man but of God."*

Sadly for Dante, Beatrice's family had decided their daughter was to marry one Simone de' Bardi – the ceremony took place when she was seventeen, and after just seven years of marriage, Beatrice was dead. Dante, for his part, was also forced into an arranged marriage, to one Gemma Donati; agreed when Dante was twelve, the wedding finally took place in 1295, when the poet was thirty.

His romantic hopes dashed, Dante settled down to a political career, joining the Apothecaries' Guild and serving on a variety of minor civic committees. In 1300 he was dispatched to San Gimignano, entrusted with the job of coaxing the town into an alliance against Pope Boniface VIII, who had designs on Tuscany, and in June of the same year he sought to settle the widening breach between the city's **Black** (anti-Imperial) and **White** (more conciliatory) factions of Florence's ruling **Guelph** party. The dispute, inevitably, had its roots in money: the Whites contained leading bankers to the Imperial powers (the Cerchi, Mozzi, Davanzati and Frescobaldi); the Blacks, by contrast, counted the Pazzi, Bardi and Donati amongst their number, all prominent papal bankers. Boniface, not surprisingly, sided with the Blacks, who eventually emerged triumphant.

Dante's White sympathies sealed his fate. In 1302, following trumped-up charges of corruption, he was sentenced with other Whites to two years exile. Whilst many of the deportees subsequently returned, Dante rejected his city of "self-made men and fast-got gain." He wandered instead between Forlì, Verona, Padua, Luni and Venice, writing much of the *Divine Comedy* as he went, finally settling in Ravenna, where he died in 1321.

The Badìa

On Via dei Magazzini, which runs south from San Martino, there's an entrance to the huge **Badìa Fiorentina** (Mon–Sat 9am–noon & 4–6pm, Sun 4.30–6pm), though you currently enter from Via Dante Alighieri due to restoration work which covers part of the building with scaffolding, and may affect opening hours. Founded late in the tenth century by Willa, widow of the Margrave of Tuscany, the Badìa was one of the focal buildings in medieval Florence – the city's sick were treated in a hospital here and the main bell marked the divisions of the working day.

The Badìa is a more authentic place of reverence for admirers of Dante than his house: this was the parish church of **Beatrice Pratinari**, for whom he conceived a lifelong love as he watched her at Mass here (see p.73). Furthermore, it was here that Boccaccio delivered his celebrated lectures on Dante's theological epic.

In the 1280s the church was overhauled, probably under the direction of Arnolfo di Cambio, architect of the Duomo and Palazzo Vecchio; later work has smothered much of the old church, but the narrow **campanile** – Romanesque at its base, Gothic higher up – has come through intact. Inside, the church itself is unremarkable save for Filippino Lippi's *Madonna and St Bernard*, and the monument to Willa's son Ugo, carved around 1480 by Mino da Fiesole, on the wall of the left transept. However, a staircase leads from the choir to the upper storey of the **Chiostro degli Aranci** (Orange Cloister – from the fruit trees that used to be grown here), brightened by a fifteenth-century fresco cycle of the life of Saint Benedict.

The Bargello

To get a full idea of the Renaissance achievement in Florence, two museum calls are essential: one to the picture galleries of the Uffizi, the other to the sculpture sections of the **Museo Nazionale del Bargello** (Tues–Sat 9am–2pm, Sun 9am–1pm; L6000), installed over the road from the Badìa in the daunting Palazzo del Bargello. In Renaissance Florence, sculpture assumed an importance unmatched in any other of the numerous states of the Italian peninsula, perhaps because this most public of artistic disciplines was especially conducive to a city with so highly developed a sense of itself as a special and cohesive community. On a less abstract level, Florence is a city surrounded by quarries, and the art of stonecutting had always been nurtured here. Whatever the reason for this pre-eminence, the Bargello's collection of sculpture from this period is the richest in Italy.

The palazzo was built in 1255, immediately after the overthrow of the aristocratic regime, and soon became the seat of the *Podestà*, the chief magistrate of the city. Numerous malefactors were tried, sentenced and executed here, the elegant courtyard being the site of the gallows and block. It became a bizarre Florentine tradition for the city authorities to commission portraits of the executed criminals, usually to be painted on the outside walls. One of Andrea Castagno's first commissions from Cosimo il Vecchio was to depict the members of the Albizzi family, hanged for subversion; according to Vasari, the painter's skill in this gruesome genre earned him the nickname Andrea degli Impiccati – Andrea of the Hanged Men. Even Botticelli took payment for this kind of work, painting the corpses of the Pazzi conspirators for the edification of his fellow citizens. (Leonardo da Vinci, meanwhile, stood in the street to make a drawing of one of the Pazzi felons, who had been hung from the windows as an example to all traitors.) The building acquired its present name in the sixteenth century, when the chief of police – the *Bargello* – was based here.

Unfortunately, the Bargello is notoriously prone to closures of whole sequences of rooms. The Donatello and Michelangelo halls will almost certainly be open, but it's common for the entire second floor to be locked – so check the notice by the ticket desk if there's something you're particularly set on seeing.

The collection

You've no time to catch your breath at the Bargello: the first room focuses on **Michelangelo**, within whose shadow every Florentine sculptor laboured from the sixteenth century onwards. The tipsy, soft-bellied figure of *Bacchus* was his first major sculpture, carved at the age of 22 – a year before his great *Pietà* in Rome. A decade later, Michelangelo's style had evolved into something less immediately seductive, as is shown by the *Pitti Tondo*, its stern grandeur prefiguring the prophets of the Sistine Chapel ceiling, which he was then about to commence. The square-jawed *Bust of Brutus*, which dates from 1540, is Michelangelo's sole work of this kind; a powerful sketch in stone, it's a coded celebration of anti-Medicean republicanism, having been made soon after the murder of the nightmarish Duke Alessandro de' Medici (see p.102). Works by Michelangelo's followers and contemporaries are ranged in the immediate vicinity; some of them would command prolonged attention in different company.

The shallower and more flamboyant art of **Cellini** and **Giambologna** is exhibited in the adjacent sections of the hall. Cellini's huge *Bust of Cosimo I*, his first work in bronze, was a sort of technical trial for the casting of the *Perseus*, his most famous work. Alongside the preparatory model for the *Perseus* are displayed the original relief panel and four statuettes from the statue's pedestal; the reproductions that took their place look rather better, seen from the intended distance. Close by, Giambologna's voluptuous *Florence Defeating Pisa* – a disingenuous pretext for a glamour display if ever there were one – takes up a lot of space, but is eclipsed by his best-known creation, the *Mercury*, a nimble figure with no bad angles. Comic relief is provided by the reliably awful Bandinelli, whose coiffeured *Adam and Eve* look like a grandee and his wife taking an *au naturel* stroll through their estate.

Part two of the sculpture collection is on the other side of the Gothic courtyard, which is plastered with the coats of arms of the *Podestà* and contains, among many other pieces, six allegorical figures by Ammannati from the fountain of the Palazzo Pitti courtyard. This second section, formerly a motley array of fourteenth-century pieces, is now getting better with the arrival of some statues which have been removed from Orsanmichele (see p.77).

THE FIRST FLOOR

At the top of the courtyard staircase, the first-floor loggia has been turned into an aviary for Giambologna's bronze birds, imported from the Medici villa at Castello. The nearer doorway to the right opens into the fourteenth-century Salone del Consiglio Generale, where the presiding genius is **Donatello**, the fountainhead of Renaissance sculpture.

Vestiges of the sinuous Gothic manner are evident in the drapery of the marble *David*, created in 1408, but there's nothing antiquated in the *St George*, carved just eight years later for the tabernacle of the armourers' guild at Orsanmichele and installed in a replica of its original niche at the far end of the room. If one sculpture could be said to embody the shift of sensibility that occurred in quattrocento Florence, this is it – whereas Saint George had previously been little more than a symbol of valour, this alert, tensed figure represents not the act of heroism but the volition behind it. The slaying of the dragon is depicted in the badly eroded small marble panel underneath, a piece as revolutionary as the figure of the saint, with its seamless interweaving of foreground and background.

Donatello's sexually ambiguous bronze *David*, the first freestanding nude figure since classical times, was cast in the early 1430s, a decade in which he later produced the strange prancing figure known as *Amor-Atys*. The *Amor-Atys* was later mistaken for a genuine antique, the highest compliment the artist could have wished for – as is attested by the story of Michelangelo's heaping soil over one of his first works, a sleeping cupid, in order to give it the appearance of an unearthed classical piece. Donatello was just as comfortable with portraiture as with Christian or pagan imagery, as his breathtakingly vivid *Bust of Niccolò da Uzzano* demonstrates; and when the occasion demanded he could produce a straightforwardly monumental piece like the nearby *Marzocco*, Florence's heraldic lion.

Donatello's master, **Ghiberti**, is represented by his relief of *The Sacrifice of Isaac*, his entry in the competition for the Baptistery doors, easily missed on the right-hand wall; the treatment of the theme submitted by Brunelleschi, effectively the runner-up, is hung alongside. Set around the walls of the room, **Luca della Robbia**'s simply sweet-natured humanism is embodied in a sequence of glazed terracotta *Madonnas*.

The rest of this floor is occupied by a collection of European and Islamic applied art, with dazzling specimens of ivory carving from Byzantium and medieval France – combs, boxes, chess pieces, devotional panels featuring scores of figures crammed into a space the size of a paperback page.

THE SECOND FLOOR

Sculpture resumes upstairs, with works from the Della Robbia family forming a prelude to the **Sala dei Bronzetti**, Italy's best assembly of small Renaissance bronzes – providing plentiful evidence of Giambologna's virtuosity at table-top scale.

Lastly, there's a room devoted mainly to **Renaissance portrait busts**, including Mino da Fiesole's busts of Giovanni de' Medici and Piero il Gottoso (the sons of Cosimo il Vecchio), Francesco Laurana's *Battista Sforza* (an interesting comparison with the della Francesca portrait in the Uffizi), and the *Woman Holding Flowers* by Verrocchio. The centre of the room is shared by Verrocchio's *David*, clearly influenced by the Donatello figure downstairs, and a powerful small bronze group of *Hercules and Antaeus* by Antonio del Pollaiuolo, who – like Leonardo – unravelled the complexities of human musculature by dissecting corpses.

Along Via dei Calzaiuoli

Connecting the western side of the Duomo to the Signoria, **Via dei Calzaiuoli** is the unchallenged catwalk of the Florentine *passeggiata*. Two distinct economies operate along here: in the daytime the street's jewellery shops and boutiques trawl in lire by the million, but after dark the mainly Senegalese **street traders** move in, laying out their groundsheets with counterfeit designer clothes, posters and tacky paintings. Every now and then the police move the hawkers on, a ritual that sometimes takes into its sweep the buskers, acrobats and dreadful mime artists who perform here on summer evenings. For some reason an exemption seems to have been granted to Via dei Calzaiuoli's nocturnal palmists and tarot-readers, presumably because the Florentine police are as superstitious as the general populace are reputed to be.

The street seems fairly congenial and self-satisfied but there's a nasty undercurrent to life on Via dei Calzaiuoli. Racist gangs have begun to take the law into their own hands, attacking the foreign traders with knives, chains and other lumps of dangerous metalware – and it appears that the thugs have allies in the Florentine business community. Naturally, Florence's politicians and media deplore the violence, characterising it as an aberration in a country that prides itself on its racial tolerance. Yet this tolerance has only been put to the test in the last few years with the increase in immigration from north and west Africa, and the tacit attitude of many Florentines can be surmised from the fact that the traders are generally known as *marocchini* (Moroccans), a tag that displays a blithe contempt for their identity.

Piazza della Repubblica

Halfway down the street, Via dei Speziali connects with the great void of the **Piazza della Repubblica**. Impressive solely for its size, this square was created in the last century in an attempt to give Florence the sort of grand public space that is a prerequisite for any capital city. On the west side a vast arch bears the triumphant inscription: "The ancient city centre restored to new life from the squalor of centuries". Most people would have preferred a few more traces of the squalor: this was once the site of the Roman forum, before becoming the city's Jewish quarter and central marketplace. In 1431 Donatello was commissioned to make a statue of *Abundance* to top a column amid the stalls, and a bell was mounted underneath the figure to ring the start and close of trading. The column was taken down during the piazza's creation, long after the statue had rotted away; replaced in 1956, it stands as the sole reminder of the square's more active past.

Maintaining the flat tone, the piazza's four large and once-fashionable cafés – *Donnini*, *Giubbe Rosse*, *Gilli* and *Paszkowski* – similarly lack the charisma to which they aspire. The *Paszkowski* in recent years brought attention to bear on racism in the upper economic echelons of Florentine society, through its pioneering employment of a black waiter; itself perhaps an instance of mere radical chic, the move prompted abusive letters and boycotts.

Orsanmichele

Standing foursquare like a truncated military tower at the southern end of Via dei Calzaiuoli, **Orsanmichele** (daily 8am–noon & 3–6pm) is the oddest-looking church in Florence. Not only is the church itself a major monument but its exterior was once the most impressive outdoor sculpture gallery in the city. However, several of the pieces are currently away for restoration, after which they will be displayed in the Bargello, while their places at Orsanmichele are taken by replicas. We've described the church as it was at the time of going to press.

From the ninth century until the thirteenth the church of San Michele ad hortum stood here – hence the compacted form of Orsanmichele. Towards the end of that century a grain market was raised on the site, which was in turn replaced, after a fire in 1304, with a vast loggia that served as an oratory and a trade hall for the *Arti Maggiori*, the Great Guilds which governed the city. In 1380 the loggia was walled in and dedicated exclusively to religious functions, while two upper storeys were added for use as emergency grain stores. Not long after, each guild was charged with decorating one of the exterior tabernacles of the building, a scheme which spanned the emergent years of the Renaissance.

THE EXTERIOR

Beginning on the far left of the Via dei Calzaiuoli side, and moving round the building to the right, the first tabernacle should soon be occupied by a replica of Ghiberti's *John the Baptist*, the earliest life-size bronze statue of the Renaissance period. It was made for the *Calimala*, the guild of the wholesale cloth importers, who were the wealthiest of the guilds but nonetheless very cautious patrons; doubtful whether Ghiberti could cast the figure in one piece as planned, they made him liable for the cost of the metal should he fail. In the event it did come out intact, except for one toe, which had to be welded on. The other niches on this side are soon to be occupied by replicas of *The Incredulity of St Thomas* by Verrocchio and Giambologna's *St Luke*.

Round the corner, Donatello's *St Peter* is followed by two works from Nanni di Banco, *St Philip* and the so-called *Quattro Coronati* – four Christian sculptors executed by Diocletian for refusing to make a pagan image. The story goes that Nanni slightly miscalculated the size of the available space, and found that he could fit only three of the figures into the niche; to solve the crisis he is said to have consulted his friend Donatello, who simply had his assistants file and chip away at the four saints until they were slim enough to occupy their slot. A copy of Donatello's own *St George* comes next – the original is in the Bargello.

On the west side stand *St Matthew* and *St Stephen* by Ghiberti and *St Eligius* by Nanni di Banco; the *St Matthew*, posed and clad like a Roman orator, makes a telling comparison with the same artist's *St John*, cast just ten years before but still semi-Gothic in its sharp-edged drapery and arching lines.

Earlier than either is Donatello's *St Mark*, made in 1411 when the artist was twenty-five; this is often considered the first freestanding statue of the Renaissance, a title based on the naturalism of his stance and the brooding intensity of his gaze. A replica of Pietro Lamberti's *St James* precedes an uncomplicatedly benign *Madonna and Child*, probably by Giovanni Tedesco. It was damaged in 1493 when one Signor Marrona went berserk and set about axing lumps out of every statue of the Madonna he could find. Retribution in the form of a lynch mob of Savonarola's monks caught up with him just after he'd gouged out one of the eyes of the infant Christ. The weakest of Orsanmichele's sculptures brings up the rear, Baccio da Montelupo's *John the Evangelist*.

THE INTERIOR

Inside Orsanmichele, the centrepiece is the pavilion-sized glass and marble **tabernacle** by Orcagna, the only significant sculptural work by the artist. It frames a *Madonna* painted in 1347 by Bernardo Daddi as a replacement for a miraculous image of the Virgin that was destroyed by the 1304 fire, and whose powers this picture is said to have inherited. The brotherhood that administered Orsanmichele paid for the tabernacle from thanksgiving donations in the aftermath of the Black Death; so many people attributed their survival to the Madonna's intervention that the money received was greater than the annual income of the city coffers. Other paintings can be seen on the pillars – devotional images commissioned by the guilds, they are the low-cost ancestors of the Orsanmichele statues.

The vaulted halls of the **upstairs granary** – one of the city's most imposing medieval interiors – are entered via the footbridge from the Palazzo dell'Arte della Lana; they are usually open only when being used as an exhibition space.

Piazza della Signoria

Even though it sets the stage for the Palazzo Vecchio, Florence's main civic square – the **Piazza della Signoria** – doesn't quite live up to its role. Too many of the buildings round its edge are bland nineteenth-century efforts, now occupied by banks, and the surface of the square itself resembles nothing so much as the deck of an aircraft carrier.

It should look better than it does. Back in the 1970s it was decided to restore the piazza's ancient paving stones. The government minister in charge of archaeological work decided that, since the stones were coming up anyway, it might be an idea to turn it into a full-blown dig to uncover the traces of Roman Florence. Unappreciative of the disruption, the city authorities tussled with their political bosses, and the excavation proceeded on a stop-start basis, turning the piazza into a part-time building site. Then a double scandal broke. When the company in charge of cleaning the old slabs returned the first batch, it was found that they had simply sandblasted great chunks off them, rather than rinsing them carefully in the prescribed manner; it turned out that they were not actually conservation experts – and the chief engineer of the city was promptly accused of taking a bribe to award the contract. Then some of the slabs turned up in the yard of a stone merchant on the city outskirts and on the front drives of a number of Tuscan villas. The contractor was dragged through the courts, and the piazza relaid with what looks like a job lot from a DIY warehouse. There's talk of hammering the stones with ice-picks to make them look as ancient as the stones they replaced.

The piazza is liveliest on May Day and other occasions in the political calendar, when speakers address the crowds from the terrace in front of the Palazzo Vecchio. (The terrace is called the *arringhiera*, from the same root as the English word "harangue".) Tempers can get frayed, but the temperature is cooler than it often used to be – in 1343, for example, one inflammatory meeting ended with a man being eaten by a mob. Most famously, it was in the piazza that Savonarola held his "Bonfire of Vanities" – on the very spot where, on May 23, 1498, he was to be executed for heresy. A plaque near the fountain marks the place.

The statues

Florence's political volatility is encapsulated by the Piazza della Signoria's peculiar array of statuary. The line-up, arranged in the sixteenth century to accentuate the axis of the Uffizi, starts with Giambologna's equestrian statue of Cosimo I, the only such equestrian bronze figure produced in the late Renaissance, and continues with Ammannati's fatuous *Neptune Fountain*, a tribute to Cosimo's prowess as a naval commander. Neptune himself is a lumpen lout, who provoked Michelangelo to coin the rhyming put-down – "Ammannato, Ammannato, che bel marmo hai rovinato" (. . . what a fine piece of marble you've ruined); Ammannati doesn't seem to have been too embarrassed, though in a late phase of piety he did come to regret the lasciviousness of the figures round the base, created with the assistance of Giambologna and other junior sculptors.

After a copy of Donatello's *Marzocco* (original in the Bargello) comes a copy of his *Judith and Holofernes* (original in the Palazzo Vecchio), which freezes the action at the moment Judith's arm begins its scything stroke – a dramatic conception that no other sculptor of the period would have attempted. Commissioned by

Cosimo il Vecchio, this statue originally served as a fountain in the Palazzo Medici, but was removed to the Piazza della Signoria after the expulsion of the family in 1494, and displayed as an emblem of vanquished tyranny; a new inscription on the base reinforced the message for those too obtuse to get it.

Michelangelo's *David* (original in the Accademia), at first intended for the Duomo, was also installed here as a declaration of civic solidarity by the short-lived Florentine Republic. It was not a trouble-free project: during its four-day journey from Michelangelo's studio to the Palazzo Vecchio the statue was stoned by gangs of Medici supporters, and then the Republic's leaders found themselves somewhat abashed by David's nudity – so they kept him under wraps for a couple of months while a skirt of copper leaves was made for him.

Keeping David company is Bandinelli's *Hercules and Cacus*, a personal emblem of Cosimo I, but dismissed by Benvenuto Cellini as "a sackful of melons". The marble might have ended up as something more inspiring. In the late 1520s, when the Florentines were once again busy tearing the Medici emblem from every building on which it had been stuck, Michelangelo offered to carve a monumental figure of Samson to celebrate the Republic's latest victory over tyranny; other demands on the artist's time put paid to this project, and the stone passed to Bandinelli, who duly vented his mediocrity on it.

The Loggia

The square's grace note, the **Loggia della Signoria**, was built in the late fourteenth century as a dais for city officials during ceremonies; its alternative name, the Loggia dei Lanzi, comes from Cosimo I's bodyguard of Swiss lancers, who used the loggia as their rest room. Though the *Judith and Holofernes* was placed here as early as 1506, it was only in the late eighteenth century that the loggia became exclusively a showcase for melodramatic sculpture.

In the corner nearest the Palazzo Vecchio stands a figure that has become one of the iconic images of the Renaissance, Benvenuto Cellini's *Perseus*. Made for Cosimo I, it symbolises the triumph of firm Grand Ducal government over the monstrous indiscipline of all other forms of government. The traumatic process of its creation is vividly described in Cellini's riproaring and self-serving autobiography – the project seemed doomed when the molten bronze began to solidify too early, but the ever-resourceful hero saved the day by flinging all his pewter plates into the mixture. Equally attention-seeking is Giambologna's last work, *The Rape of the Sabine*, epitome of the Mannerist obsession with spiralling forms.

For a considerable period the loggia has been encased in scaffolding, and it seems likely to remain that way for some time to come. Here, as elsewhere in Florence, scaffolding doesn't necessarily imply that work is in progress – it's more than likely that the cover is there to stop a lump of stone falling on a passing pedestrian and triggering a law suit against the council.

The Ragione museum

Occupying a suite of rooms over the Cassa di Risparmio bank is the **Collezione della Ragione** (Mon & Wed–Sat 9am–1pm, Sun 8am–noon; L4000), the nearest thing in Florence to a general collection of modern Italian art. A civil engineer by profession, Alberto della Ragione was an extremely active patron, subsidising young artists and hustling other collectors to buy their work. Now administered by the *comune*, his gallery includes paintings by many of the people you'd expect to find (de Chirico, Carrà, Morandi), a miscellany of Tuscan landscapes, and sculpture by Manzù and Marini. Not much of a treat by the standards of Paris or London, but it might be a welcome aesthetic break from the world of the Medici.

THE FLORENTINE REPUBLIC

Dante compared Florence's constant political struggles to a sick man forever shifting his position in bed, and indeed its medieval history often appears a catelogue of incessant civic unrest. Yet between 1293 and 1534 – bar the odd ruction – the city maintained a republican constitution that was embodied in well-defined institutions. The nucleus of this structure was formed by the city's **merchants** and **guilds**, who covertly controlled Florence as early as the twelfth century and formalised their influence during the so-called **Primo Popolo** (1248–59), a quasi-democratic regime whose ten-year rule, claimed Dante, was the only period of civic peace in Florence's history. During the **Secondo Popolo** (1284), the leading guilds, the *Arti Maggiori*, introduced the **Ordinamenti della Giustizia** (1293), a written constitution that entrenched mercantile power still further and was to be the basis of Florence's government for the next two hundred and fifty years.

The **rulers** of this much-vaunted republic were drawn exclusively from the ranks of guild members over the age of thirty, and were chosen in a public ceremony held every two months – the short tenure being designed to prevent individuals or cliques assuming too much power. At this ceremony, the names of selected guild members were placed in eight leather bags (*borse*) kept in the sacristy of Santa Croce, and the ones picked from the bags duly became the **Priori** (or *Signori*), forming a government called the **Signoria**, usually comprising nine men, most of them from the *Arti Maggiori*. Once elected, the *Priori* moved into the Palazzo della Signoria, where they were expected to stay, virtually *incomunicado*, for their period of office – though they were waited on hand and foot, and enjoyed the services of a professional joke-teller, the *Buffone*.

Headed by the **Gonfaloniere** (literally the "standard bearer") the *Signoria* consulted two elected councils or **Collegi** – the **Dodici Buonomini** (Twelve Citizens) and **Sedici Gonfalonieri** (Sixteen Standard Bearers) – as well as committees introduced to deal with specific crises (The Ten of War, the Eight of Security, the Six of Commerce . . .). Permanent officials included the Chancellor (Machiavelli once held this post) and the **Podestà**, a chief magistrate brought in from a neighbouring city as an independent arbitrator, and housed in the Bargello. In times of extreme crisis, such as the Pazzi Conspiracy (see p.68), all male citizens over the age of fourteen were summoned to a **Parlemento** in Piazza della Signoria by the tolling of the Palazzo Vecchio's famous bell – known as the *Vacca* (cow), after its deep bovine tone. When a two-thirds quorum was reached, the people were asked to approve a **Balìa**, a committee delegated to deal with the siutation as it saw fit.

All this looked good on paper but in practice the set-up was far from democratic. The lowliest workers, the **Popolo Minuto**, were totally excluded, as were the **Grandi**, or nobles. And despite the *Signoria*'s apparently random selection process, political cliques had few problems ensuring that only the names of likely supporters found their way into the *borse*. If a rogue candidate slipped through the net, or things went awry, then a *Parlemento* was summoned, a *Balìa* formed, and the offending person replaced by a more pliable candidate. It was by such means that the great mercantile dynasties of Florence – the Peruzzi, the Albizzi, the Strozzi, and of course the Medici – retained their power even when not technically in office.

The Palazzo Vecchio

Florence's fortress-like town hall, the **Palazzo Vecchio** (Mon–Fri 9am–7pm, Sun 8am–1pm; L8000), was begun in the last year of the thirteenth century as the home of the *Signoria*, the highest tier of the city's republican government. Local folklore has it that the eccentric plan was not devised by the original architect (thought to be Arnolfo di Cambio), but is rather a product of factional division – the Guelph government refusing to encroach on land previously owned by the Ghibellines (see p.542).

Changes in the Florentine constitution entailed alterations to the layout of the palace, the most radical overhaul coming in 1540, when Cosimo I moved his retinue here from the Palazzo Medici and grafted a huge extension onto the back. The Medici were in residence for only nine years – they moved to the Palazzo Pitti, largely at the insistence of Cosimo's wife, Eleanor of Toledo – but the enlargement and refurbishment instigated by Cosimo continued throughout the period of his rule. Much of the decoration of the state rooms comprises a relentless eulogy of Cosimo and his relations; the propaganda is made tolerable, though, by some of the palace's examples of Mannerist art – among the finest pieces produced by that ultra-sophisticated and self-regarding movement.

The interior

Giorgio Vasari, court architect from 1555 until his death in 1574, was responsible for much of the sycophantic decor in the state apartments. His limited talents were given full rein in the huge **Salone dei Cinquecento**, built at the end of the fifteenth century as the assembly hall for the Great Council of the penultimate republic. Instead of these drearily bombastic murals – painted either by Vasari or under his direction – the chamber might have had one of Italy's most remarkable decorative schemes. Leonardo da Vinci and Michelangelo were employed to paint frescoes on opposite sides of the room; Leonardo's work – *The Battle of Anghiari* – was abandoned after his experimental technique went wrong, and Michelangelo's project – *The Battle of Cascina* – existed only as a fragment when he was summoned to Rome by Pope Julius II in 1506. Michelangelo's *Victory*, by the far wall on the left, was carved for Julius' tomb, and was at some point converted by the sculptor from a female to a male figure; donated to the Medici by the artist's nephew, it was installed here by Vasari to mark Cosimo's defeat of the Sienese.

A door to the right of the entrance to the hall, at the far end, opens onto the most bizarre room in the building – the **Studiolo di Francesco I**. Created by Vasari in the 1570s and decorated by several Mannerist artists, this windowless cell was created as a retreat for the introverted son of Cosimo and Eleanor. Each of the miniature bronzes and nearly all the paintings reflect Francesco's interest in the sciences and alchemy: the entrance wall illustrates the theme of "Earth" and the others, reading clockwise, signify "Water", "Air" and "Fire". The outstanding paintings are the two which don't fit the scheme, Bronzino's portraits of the occupant's parents, facing each other across the room.

Bronzino's major contribution to the palace can be seen on the floor above, reached after the **Quartiere di Leone X**, where each room is slavishly devoted to a different member of the Medici clan. Upstairs, Eleanor of Toledo's tiny **chapel** was decorated by Bronzino in the 1540s; it seems that the artist used a novel and time-consuming technique to give these wall paintings the same glassy surface as his canvases, executing a first draft in fresco and then glazing it with a layer of tempera.

Those who find all this Mannerist stuff unhealthily airless can take refuge in the summery **Sala dei Gigli**, which was fitted out in the decade after 1475. Named after the lilies which adorn the room (the city's symbol), it has a splendid ceiling by the brothers Giuliano and Benedetto da Maiano, and frescoes by Domenico Ghirlandaio. Two small rooms are attached to the Sala dei Gigli: the Cancelleria, once Macchiavelli's office and now containing a portrait of the often-maligned political thinker, and a chamber decorated with 57 maps painted in 1563 by the court astronomer Fra' Ignazio Danti, depicting the entire known world.

The adjoining **Sala d'Udienza**, originally the audience chamber of the republic, has an equally fine ceiling by Giuliano and assistants, and a magnificent doorway by the brothers in partnership; the Mannerists reassert themselves here, however, with a vast fresco sequence by Cecchino Salviati: this is generally held to be his most accomplished work. In here is also Donatello's *Judith and Holofernes*.

Very occasionally it's possible to climb from this floor to the top of the Palazzo Vecchio's **tower**, passing the cell known as the Alberghinetto (little hotel), where such troublemakers as Cosimo il Vecchio and Savonarola were once imprisoned.

The Uffizi

Florence's prime tourist attraction is housed in what was once a government office block, built by Vasari for Cosimo I in 1560 on a site then occupied by a church and some houses between the Palazzo Vecchio and the river. After Vasari's death, work on the elongated U-shaped building was continued by Buontalenti, who was asked by Francesco I to glaze the upper storey so that it could house his art collection. Each of the succeeding Medici added to the family's trove of art treasures, and the accumulated collection was preserved for public inspection by the last member of the family, Anna Maria Lodovica, whose will specified that it should be left to the people of Florence and never be allowed to leave the city. Last century a large proportion of the statuary was transferred to the Bargello, while most of the antiquities went to the Museo Archeologico, leaving the **Galleria degli Uffizi** (Tues–Sat 9am–7pm, Sun 9am–1pm; L10,000) as essentially a gallery of paintings supplemented with some classical sculptures.

Florence can prompt an over-eagerness to reach for the superlatives; in the case of the Uffizi, superlatives are simply the bare truth – this is the finest picture gallery in Italy. So many masterpieces are collected here that it's not even possible to skate over the surface in a single visit; it makes sense to limit your initial tour to the first fifteen rooms, where the Florentine Renaissance works are concentrated, and to explore the rest another time. And as this is the busiest single building in the country, with over one and a half million visitors each year, you should anticipate queues at most times of the day except in the depths of winter; in summer the best way to beat the crowds is to visit for the last couple of hours. Finally, be prepared to find some of the rooms closed for one reason or another – at the height of the summer it's not unusual to find that nearly half the gallery is locked up.

THE UFFIZI BOMBING

At 1am on May 27, 1992, a colossal explosion occurred on the west side of the Uffizi, killing five people, demolishing the headquarters of Europe's oldest agricultural academy, blasting holes through the walls of the Uffizi itself, and damaging numerous paintings inside, some of them irreparably. Initially it was supposed that a gas leak might have been responsible, but within hours the country's head prosecutor, after discussions with forensic experts and the anti-terrorist squad, issued a statement – "Gas does not come into it. We have found a crater one-and-a-half metres wide. The evidence is unequivocal." Fragments of the car that had carried the estimated 100kg of TNT had been found some thirty metres from the rubble.

Instantly it was put about that the Mafia lay behind the atrocity, though it was not explained what the Mafia had to gain from the killing of the academy's curator and her family, or from the mutilation of a few Renaissance paintings. While many were willing to believe that the Mafia may have planted the bomb, most Florentines were convinced that the orders had originated within the country's political and military establishment. Frightened by the political realignments taking place all over Italy, with the rise of northern separatists, the reformed communist party and various newly formed groupings, the reactionary old guard were evidently employing the tactics of destabilisation – a repeat of the 1970s' "Strategy of Tension", when organised criminals and right-wing politicians colluded in a sequence of terrorist attacks to ensure the public's loyalty to the supposedly threatened state. Just days before the Uffizi bombing, the Italian secret service had been implicated in the murders of Giovanni Falcone and Paolo Borsellino, the country's most powerful anti-Mafia investigators, and it seemed plain that the same unholy alliances had been at work in Florence. The aftermath of the explosion has done nothing to dispel these suspicions: the car that carried the bomb was recorded by video-cameras at several places in the city, yet no-one has been charged with the outrage to this day.

Much of the superficial damage has now been repaired, but deep structural repairs will take years, so you can expect large areas of the Uffizi to be smothered in scaffolding for a long time to come.

From Cimabue to Uccello

The main picture galleries are ranged on the third floor, but on the ground floor, in rooms that once formed part of the eleventh-century church of San Pier Scheraggio, are shown **Andrea del Castagno**'s frescoes of celebrated Florentines; the imaginary portraits include Dante and Boccaccio, both of whom spoke in debates at the church. Close to a Botticelli *Annunciation*, a lift goes up to the galleries; if you take the staircase instead, you'll pass the entrance to the prints and drawings collection, the bulk of which is reserved for scholarly scrutiny, though samples are often on public show.

Room 1, housing an assembly of antique sculptures, many of which were used as a sort of source book by Renaissance artists, is often shut. The beginnings of the stylistic evolution of that period can be traced in the following room, where three altarpieces of the *Maestà* (Madonna enthroned) by **Cimabue**, **Duccio** and **Giotto**, dwarfing everything around them, show the softening of the hieratic Byzantine style into a more tactile form of representation. Painters from fourteenth-century Siena fill **room 3**, with several pieces by Ambrogio and Pietro Lorenzetti and **Simone Martini**'s glorious *Annunciation*, the Virgin cowering from the angel amid a field of pure gold.

Other trecento artists follow in **rooms 5 and 6**, among them Florence's first-rank Gothic painters, Orcagna and **Lorenzo Monaco**, whose majestic *Coronation of the Virgin* and *Adoration of the Magi* catch the eye first. The version of the latter subject by **Gentile da Fabriano** is the summit of the precious style known as International Gothic, spangled with gold that in places is so thick that the crowns of the kings, for instance, are like low-relief jewellery. It's crammed with so much detail that there's no real distinction between what's crucial and what's peripheral, with as much attention lavished on incidentals such as a snarling cheetah as on the supposed protagonists. Also in this room is Starnina's *Thebiad*, a baffling but beguiling little narrative that can perhaps best be described as a monastic fairy tale.

Madonna with SS. Francis, John the Baptist, Zenobius and Lucy is one of only twelve extant paintings by **Domenico Veneziano** (**room 7**), who spent much of his life in Venice but died destitute in Florence. Veneziano's greatest pupil, **Piero della Francesca**, is represented with *Federico da Montefeltro and Battista Sforza*, backed by images of the Duke surrounded by the cardinal virtues and his wife by the theological virtues. Elevating the couple to the status of mythic lovers, these panels were painted two years after Battista's death – in the background of her portrait is the town of Gubbio, where she died giving birth to her ninth child and first son, Guidobaldo.

Paolo Uccello's *The Battle of San Romano* once hung in Lorenzo il Magnifico's bed chamber, in company with the depictions of the battle now in the Louvre and London's National Gallery. Warfare is the ostensible subject, but this is really a compendium of perspectival effects: a toppling knight, a horse and rider keeled onto their sides, the foreshortened legs of a kicking horse, a thicket of lances: every object exists in a self-contained space, creating a fight scene with no sense of violence.

Filippo Lippi to Botticelli

Most space in **room 8** is given to **Filippo Lippi**, whose *Madonna and Child with Two Angels* supplies one of the gallery's most popular faces, and one of its least otherworldly devotional images – the model was Lucrezia Buti, a convent novice who became the object of one of his more enduring sexual obsessions (see p.171). There's a fine *Madonna* here by Lippi's pupil **Botticelli**, who also steals some of the thunder in the next room, where the artists centre stage are **Piero and Antonio del Pollaiuolo**; their sinewy *SS. Vincent, James and Eustace*, one of their best works, is chiefly the work of Antonio. This room also contains the *Portrait of Young Man in a Red Hat*, sometimes referred to as a self-portrait by Lippi and Lucrezia Buti's son, Filippino, but now widely believed to be an eighteenth-century fraud.

It's in the merged **rooms 10–14** that the greatest of **Botticelli**'s productions are gathered. A century ago most people walked past his pictures without breaking stride; nowadays – despite their elusiveness – the *Primavera* and *The Birth of Venus* stop all visitors in their tracks. The identities of the characters in the *Primavera* are not contentious: on the right Zephyrus, god of the west wind, chases the nymph Cloris, who is then transfigured into the goddess of spring; Venus stands in the centre, to the side of the three Graces, who are targeted by Cupid; on the left Mercury wards off a cloud. What this all means, however, has occupied scholars for decades. Some see it as an allegory of the four seasons, but the consensus now seems to be that it shows the triumph of Venus, with the Graces as the physical embodiment of her beauty and Flora the symbol of her fruitfulness – an interpretation supported by the fact that the picture was placed outside the wedding suite of Lorenzo di Pierfrancesco de' Medici.

Botticelli's most winsome painting, the *Birth of Venus* probably takes as its source the grisly myth that the goddess emerged from the sea after it had been impregnated by the castration of Uranus – an allegory for the creation of beauty through the mingling of the spirit (Uranus) and the physical world. A third allegory hangs close by – *Pallas and the Centaur*, perhaps symbolising the ambivalent triumph of reason over instinct.

His devotional paintings are generally less perplexing. The *Adoration of the Magi* is traditionally thought to contain a gallery of Medici portraits: Cosimo il Vecchio as the first king, his sons Giovanni and Piero as the other two kings, Lorenzo il Magnifico on the far left, and his brother Giuliano as the black-haired young man in profile on the right. Only the identification of Cosimo is reasonably certain, along with that of Botticelli himself, on the right in the yellow robe. Profoundly influenced by Savonarola's teaching, Botticelli in later life confined himself to devotional pictures and moral fables, and his style became increasingly severe. The transformation is clear when comparing the easy grace of the *Madonna of the Magnificat* and the *Madonna of the Pomegranate* with the more rigidly composed *Enthroned Madonna with Saints* or the *Calumny*, a painting so angular and agitated it seems like a recantation of his former self.

Not quite every masterpiece in this room is by Botticelli. Set away from the walls is the *Adoration of the Shepherds* by his Flemish contemporary **Hugo van der Goes**. Brought to Florence in 1483 by Tomasso Portinari, the Medici agent in Bruges, it provided the city's artists with their first large-scale demonstration of the realism of Northern European oil painting, and had a great influence on the way the medium was exploited here.

Leonardo to Mantegna

Works in **room 15** trace the formative years of **Leonardo da Vinci**, whose distinctive touch appears first in the *Baptism* by his master Verrocchio – the wistful angel in profile is by the eighteen-year-old apprentice, as is the misty landscape in the background. A similar terrain of soft-focus mountains and water occupies the far distance in Leonardo's slightly later *Annunciation*, in which a diffused light falls on a scene where everything is observed with a scientist's precision – the petals of the flowers on which the angel alights, the fall of the Virgin's drapery, the carving on the lectern at which she reads. In restless contrast to the aristocratic poise of the *Annunciation*, the sketch of *The Adoration of the Magi* – abandoned when Leonardo left Florence for Milan in early 1482 – presents the infant Christ as the eye of a vortex of figures, all drawn into his presence by a force as irresistible as a whirlpool.

Usually this room also contains a brace of pictures by **Piero di Cosimo**, the wild man of the Florentine Renaissance. Shunning civilised company, Piero did everything he could to bring his life close to a state of uncompromised Nature, living in a house that was never cleaned, in the midst of a garden he refused to tend, and eating nothing but hard-boiled eggs. Where his contemporaries might seek inspiration in commentaries on Plato, he would spend hours staring at the sky, at peeling walls, at the pavement – at anything where abstract patterns might conjure fabulous scenes in his imagination.

Room 18, the octagonal *Tribuna*, now houses the most important of the Medici sculptures, chief among which is the **Medici Venus**, a first-century BC copy of the Praxitelean *Aphrodite of Cnidos*. She was kept in the Villa Medici in Rome until Cosimo III began to fret that she was having a detrimental effect on the morals of the city's art students, and ordered her removal to Florence. Around the walls are hung some fascinating portraits by **Bronzino** – Cosimo de' Medici, Eleanor of Toledo, Bartolomeo Panciatichi and his wife Lucrezia Panciatichi, all painted as figures of porcelain, placed in a bloodless, sunless world. More vital is Andrea del Sarto's flirtatious *Portrait of a Young Woman*, and there's a deceptive naturalism to Vasari's portrait of Lorenzo il Magnifico and Pontormo's of Cosimo il Vecchio, both painted long after the death of their subjects.

Signorelli and **Perugino** – with some photo-sharp portraits – are the principal artists in **room 19**, and after them comes a room largely devoted to **Cranach** and **Dürer**. Each has an *Adam and Eve* here, Dürer taking the opportunity to show off his proficiency as a painter of wildlife. Dürer's power as a portraitist is displayed in the *Portrait of the Artist's Father*, his earliest authenticated painting, and Cranach has a couple of acute pictures of Luther on display, one of them a double with his wife.

Highlights in the following sequence of rooms (**20–24**) are an impenetrable *Sacred Allegory* by **Giovanni Bellini**, **Holbein**'s *Portrait of Sir Richard Southwell* and a crystalline triptych by **Mantegna** – not in fact a real triptych, but rather a trio of small paintings shackled together after the event. To the side are a couple of other pictures by Mantegna – a swarthy portrait of Carlo de' Medici and the tiny *Madonna of the Stonecutters*, set against a mountain that looks like a gigantic fir-cone.

Michelangelo to Titian

Beyond the stockpile of classical pieces in the short corridor overlooking the Arno, the main attraction in **room 25** is **Michelangelo**'s *Doni Tondo*, the only easel painting he came close to completing. (Regarding sculpture as the noblest of the visual arts, Michelangelo dismissed all non-fresco painting as a demeaning chore.) Nobody has yet explained the precise significance of every aspect of this picture, but plausible explanations for parts of it have been put forward. The five naked figures behind the Holy Family seem to be standing in a half-moon-shaped cistern or font, which would relate to the infant Baptist to the right, who – in the words of Saint Paul – prefigures the coming of Christ just as the new moon is "a shadow of things to come". In the same epistle, Paul goes on to commend the virtues of mercy, benignity, humility, modesty and patience, which are perhaps what the five youths represent. The tondo's contorted gestures, hermetic meaning and virulent colours were greatly influential on the Mannerist painters of the sixteenth century, as can be gauged from the nearby *Moses Defending the Daughters of Jethro* by **Rosso Fiorentino**, one of the seminal figures of the movement.

Another piece by Rosso is on show in **room 27**, along with several works by Bronzino and his adoptive father, **Pontormo** – one of the very few painters not seen at his best in the Uffizi. Separating the two Mannerist groups is a room containing **Andrea del Sarto**'s sultry *Madonna of the Harpies* and a number of compositions by **Raphael**, including the lovely *Madonna of the Goldfinch* and the late *Pope Leo X with Cardinals Giulio de' Medici and Luigi de' Rossi* – as shifty a group of ecclesiastics as was ever gathered in one frame.

Room 28 is entirely given over to another of the titanic figures of sixteenth-century art, **Titian**, with nine paintings on show. His *Flora* and *A Knight of Malta* are stunning, but most eyes tend to swivel towards the *Venus of Urbino*, the most fleshly and provocative of all Renaissance nudes – or, in the opinion of Mark Twain, "the foulest, the vilest, the obscenest picture the world possesses".

Parmigianino to Chardin
A brief diversion through the painters of the sixteenth-century Emilian school follows, centred on **Parmigianino**, whose *Madonna of the Long Neck* is one of the pivotal Mannerist creations. Parmigianino was a febrile and introverted character who abandoned painting for alchemy towards the end of his short life, and many of his works are marked by a sort of morbid refinement – none more so than this one. The Madonna's tunic clings to every contour, an angel advances a perfectly turned leg, the infant Christ drapes himself languorously on his mother's lap, while in the background an emaciated figure unrolls a scroll of parchment by a colonnade so severely foreshortened that it looks like a single column.

Rooms 31 to 35 feature artists from Venice and the Veneto, with outstanding paintings from **Moroni** (*Portrait of Count Pietro Secco Suardi*), **Paolo Veronese** (*Annunciation* and *Holy Family with St Barbara*), and **Tintoretto** (*Leda*). This is the part of the Uffizi that took the brunt of the terrorist bomb, an explosion which reduced Sebastiano del Piombo's *Death of Adonis* to postage-stamp tatters, though the restorers are confident of retrieving the masterpiece.

In **room 41**, dominated by **Rubens** and **Van Dyck**, the former's *Portrait of Isabella Brandt* makes its point more quietly than most of the stuff around it. Rubens lets rip in *Henry IV at the Battle of Ivry* and *The Triumphal Entry of Henry IV into Paris* – Henry's marriage to Marie de' Medici is the connection with Florence. Rubens' equally histrionic contemporary, **Caravaggio**, has a cluster of pieces in **room 43**, including a screaming severed head of *Medusa*, a smug little bore of a *Bacchus*, and a *Sacrifice of Isaac* – religious art as tabloid journalism.

The next room (**44**) is in effect a showcase for the portraiture of **Rembrandt**. His sorrow-laden *Self-Portrait as an Old Man*, painted five years or so before his death, makes a poignant contrast with the self-confident self-portrait of thirty years earlier. Although there are some good pieces from Tiepolo, portraits again command the attention in the following room of eighteenth-century works, especially the two of Maria Theresa painted by **Goya**, and **Chardin**'s demure children at play. On the way out, in the hall at the top of the exit stairs, squats one of the city's talismans, the *Wild Boar*, a Roman copy of a third-century BC Hellenistic sculpture; it was the model for the *Porcellino* fountain in the Mercato Nuovo.

The Corridoio Vasariano
A door on the west corridor, between rooms 25 and 34, opens onto the **Corridoio Vasariano**, a passageway built by Vasari to link the Palazzo Vecchio to the Palazzo Pitti through the Uffizi. Winding its way down to the river, over the Ponte Vecchio, through the church of Santa Felìcita and into the Giardino di Bóboli, it gives a fascinating series of clandestine views of the city. As if that weren't pleasure enough, the corridor is completely lined with paintings, the larger portion of which comprises a **gallery of self-portraits**. Once past the portrait of Vasari, the series proceeds chronologically, its roll-call littered with illustrious names: Raphael, Andrea del Sarto, Bronzino, Bernini, Rubens, Rembrandt, Velasquez, David, Delacroix, Ingres.

Visits to the corridor have to be arranged the previous day at the gallery's offices, on the third floor near the entrance (or ring ☎055/238.85); tours are conducted in the morning, usually from Tuesday to Saturday, the precise time varying with the availability of staff.

The science museum

Down the east flank of the Uffizi runs Via dei Leoni, named after the lions housed in this street by the *comune* – the ferocious mascots used to be kept in the Piazza della Signoria, but Cosimo I had problems with the smell from their cages, so new ones were built here. At the river end, the street opens into Piazza dei Giudici, so called from the civil tribunal that used to meet in the building now housing the **Museo di Storia della Scienza** (Mon–Sat 9.30am–1pm; L10,000).

Long after Florence had declined from its artistic apogee, the intellectual reputation of the city was maintained by its scientists, many of them directly encouraged by members of the ruling Medici-Lorraine dynasty. Grand Duke Ferdinando II and his brother Leopoldo, both of whom studied with Galileo, founded a scientific academy at the Pitti in 1657 – called the Accademia del Cimento (Academy of Experiment), its motto was "Try and try again". The instruments made and acquired by this academy are the core of the science musuem's collection.

The museum has recently received a major overhaul: the exhibits now take up the first two floors, with a large research library on the ground floor. Lists of the exhibits in English are handed out to visitors, providing a full background to some of the more extraordinary items.

The eleven rooms on the **first floor** feature some marvellous timepieces and measuring instruments (such as beautiful Arab astrolabes), as well as a massive armillary sphere made for Ferdinando I to provide visual demonstration of the veracity of the earth-centred Ptolemaic system, and the fallacy of Copernicus' heliocentric universe. Galileo's original instruments are on show here, such as the lens with which he discovered the four moons of Jupiter, which he tactfully named the Medicean planets. On this floor you'll also find the museum's religious relic – a bone from one of Galileo's fingers.

On the **second floor** there is all kinds of scientific and mechanical equipment – such as a perpetual motion machine from the quasi-magical realms of scientific endeavour. There are a couple of remarkable outsized pieces: the huge lens made for Cosimo III, with which Faraday and Davy managed to ignite a diamond by focusing the rays of the sun, and the enormous lodestone given by Galileo to Ferdinando II. Other rooms are filled with clocks, or pharmaceutical and chemical apparatus. Finally there is a medical section full of alarming surgical instruments and wax anatomical models for teaching obstetrics. The covered roof-terrace on the third floor sometimes houses temporary exhibitions.

West from the Signoria

Despite the urban improvement schemes of the last century and the bombings of the last war, several streets in central Florence retain their medieval character, especially in the district to the west of Piazza della Signoria. Forming a border post to this quarter is the **Mercato Nuovo** (summer daily 9am–7pm; winter

Tues–Sat 9am–5pm), where there's been a market since the eleventh century, though the present loggia dates from the sixteenth. Having forked out their lire at the souvenir stalls, most people join the small group that's invariably gathered round the bronze boar known as *Il Porcellino* – you're supposed to earn yourself some good luck by getting a coin to fall from the animal's mouth through the grille below his head. It's a superstition with a social function, as the coins are collected by an organisation that runs homes for abandoned children.

From here, an amble through streets such as Via Porta Rossa, Via delle Terme and Borgo Santi Apostoli will give you some idea of the feel of Florence in the Middle Ages, when every important house was an urban fortress.

Palazzo Davanzati

Perhaps the most imposing exterior in this district is just to the south of the market – the thirteenth-century **Palazzo di Parte Guelfa**, financed from the confiscated property of the Ghibelline faction and later expanded by Brunelleschi. However, for a more complete recreation of medieval Florence you should visit the fourteenth-century **Palazzo Davanzati** in Via Porta Rossa. In the last century the palazzo was divided into flats, but at the beginning of this century it was restored to something very close to the modified appearance of the 1500s, when a loggia replaced the battlements on the roof, and the Davanzati stuck their coat of arms on the front. Apart from those haute-bourgeois emendations, the place now looks much as it did when first inhabited.

Nowadays the palazzo is maintained as the **Museo della Casa Fiorentina Antica** (Tues–Sat 9am–2pm, Sun 9am–1pm; L4000), and virtually every room is furnished and decorated in predominantly medieval style, using genuine artefacts gathered from a variety of sources. As soon as you enter it's clear that the owners of this house were well prepared for the adversities of urban living: note the siege-resistant doors, the private water supply and the huge storerooms for the hoarding of life-supporting provisions. Upstairs, the Sala Grande reinforces the dual nature of the house – furnished in the best style of the day, it also has hatches in the floor for bombarding the enemy.

Merchants' houses in the fourteenth century would typically have had elaborately painted walls in the main rooms, and the Palazzo Davanzati preserves some fine examples of such decor – especially in the dining room, where the imitation wall hangings of the lower walls are patterned with a parrot motif, while the upper walls depict a garden terrace. Before the development of systems of credit, wealth had to be sunk into tangible assets such as the tapestries, ceramics, sculpture and lacework that alleviate the austerity of many of these rooms; any surplus cash would have been locked away in a strongbox like the extraordinary example in the Sala Piccola, whose locking mechanism looks like the innards of a primitive clock. There's also a fine collection of *cassoni*, the painted chests in which the wife's dowry would be stored.

Plushest of the rooms is the first-floor **bedroom**, with a Sicilian linen bed cover woven with scenes from the story of Tristan. But the spot where the occupants would have been likeliest to linger is the **kitchen**. Located on the top floor to minimise the damage that might be caused by the outbreak of a fire, it would have been the warmest room in the house. A load of ancient utensils are on show here, and set into one wall you'll find the most civilised of amenities, a service shaft connecting the kitchen to all floors of the building.

Santi Apostoli

Between Via Porta Rossa and the Arno, on Piazzetta del Limbo (the former burial ground of unbaptised children), stands the ancient church of **Santi Apostoli**. Legend has it that this was founded by Charlemagne, but it's not quite that ancient – the eleventh century seems the likeliest date of origin. Santi Apostoli possesses some peculiar relics, in the form of stone fragments allegedly brought from the Holy Sepulchre in Jerusalem by a crusading Florentine; on Holy Saturday sparks struck from these stones are used to light the flame that ignites the dove that in turn sets off the fireworks in front of the Duomo (see p.141). Orderly and graceful, the interior of grey *pietra serena* against white walls looks like an anticipation of the architecture of Brunelleschi. You would be lucky to see it, though, for the church is hardly ever open.

The Santa Trìnita area

Westward of the Palazzo Davanzati, Via Porta Rossa runs into **Piazza Santa Trìnita** – not really a square, just a widening of the city's most expensive street, Via de' Tornabuoni. Sweeping past the Column of Justice – which Pope Pius IV uprooted from the Baths of Caracalla and sent to Cosimo I – the traffic crosses the Arno on the sleek **Ponte Santa Trìnita**, which was built on Cosimo's orders after its predecessor was demolished in a flood. The roads on both sides of the river were raised and widened to accentuate the dramatic potential of the new link between the city centre and Oltrarno, but what makes this the classiest bridge in Italy is the sensuous curve of its arches, a curve so shallow that engineers have been baffled as to how the bridge bears up under the strain. Ostensibly the design was conjured up by Ammannati, one of the Medici's favourite artists, but the curves so closely resemble the arc of Michelangelo's Medici tombs that it's probable the credit should go elsewhere.

In 1944 the Nazis blew the bridge to smithereens and a seven-year argument then ensued before it was agreed to rebuild it using as much of the original material as could be dredged from the Arno. To ensure maximum authenticity in the reconstruction, all the new stone that was needed was quarried from the Bóboli gardens, where the stone for Ammannati's bridge had been cut, and hand tools were used to trim it, as electric blades would have given the blocks too harsh a finish. Twelve years after the war, the reconstructed bridge was opened, lacking only the head from the statue of *Spring*, which had not been found despite the incentive of a hefty reward. At last, in 1961, the missing head was fished from the riverbed; having lain in state for a few days on a scarlet cushion in the Palazzo Vecchio, it was returned to its home.

SANTA TRÌNITA CHURCH

The antiquity of the church of **Santa Trìnita** (daily 9–10am & 4–7pm) is manifest in the Latinate pronunciation of its name – modern Italian stresses the last, not the first syllable. Founded in the eleventh century, it was rebuilt between 1250 and the end of the following century, though the inside face of the entrance wall remains from the Romanesque building. The plainness of the architecture is softened by a number of works of art, the best of which all date from the fifteenth century.

Lorenzo Monaco frescoed the fourth chapel in the right aisle and painted its *Annunciation* altarpiece. The decoration of the Cappella Sassetti, second to the right of the altar, was undertaken by **Ghirlandaio**, who provided an altarpiece of *The Adoration of the Shepherds* and a fresco cycle depicting *Scenes from the Life of St Francis*. Set in the Piazza della Signoria, the scene showing Francis receiving the rule of the order (in the lunette above the altar) includes portraits of Lorenzo il Magnifico and Francesco Sassetti, the patron of the chapel, in the right foreground; on the steps below them are Lorenzo's children and their tutor Poliziano, scholar, philosopher and author of a book on the Pazzi conspiracy – in Latin.

Displayed in the neighbouring chapel is the miraculous Crucifix, formerly in San Miniato church, that bowed to **Giovanni Gualberto** in approval of the mercy he showed to the murderer of his brother. Giovanni went on to found the reforming Vallombrosan order and – notwithstanding the mayhem created on Florence's streets by his militant supporters – was eventually canonised. Frescoes in the fourth chapel of the left aisle show scenes from his life.

A powerful composition by **Luca della Robbia** – the tomb of Benozzo Federighi, Bishop of Fiesole – occupies a wall of the chapel second to the left of the altar; moulded and carved for the church of San Pancrazio, it was transported here in 1896.

THE GALLERIA CORSINI

A little way west, on Lungarno Corsini, stands the pompous Palazzo Corsini, once owned by gentry so landed that they could ride from Florence to Rome without straying off their own territory. Much of their wealth was sunk into the contents of the still private **Galleria Corsini** (Mon, Wed & Fri afternoons; appointments only, ☎055/218.994), which retains custody of pieces by Giovanni Bellini, Pontormo and Filippino Lippi, to name just three.

Via de' Tornabuoni and the Palazzo Strozzi

The shops of **Via de' Tornabuoni** are effectively out of bounds to those who don't travel first class. Versace, Ferragamo, Gucci and Armani have their outlets here (see p.143), sharing the territory with jewellery and leather showrooms, perfumiers and upmarket cafés.

Conspicuous wealth is nothing new on Via de' Tornabuoni. Looming above everything is the vast **Palazzo Strozzi**, the last, the largest and the least subtle of all Florentine Renaissance palaces, with windows as big as gateways and embossed with lumps of stone the size of boulders. It was begun by the banker Filippo Strozzi, a figure so powerful that he was once described as "the first man of Italy", and whose family provided the ringleaders of the anti-Medici faction in Florence. He bought and demolished a dozen town houses to make space for Giuliano da Sangallo's strongbox in stone, and the construction of it lasted from 1489 to 1536. The **Museo di Palazzo Strozzi** is only open when holding temporary – and sometimes contemporary – art exhibitions; ask at the tourist office for information.

The Palazzo Rucellai

Some of Florence's other plutocrats made an impression with rather more élan. In the 1440s Giovanni Rucellai, one of the richest businessmen in the city and an esteemed scholar too, decided to commission a new house from Leon Battista Alberti, whose accomplishments as architect, mathematician, linguist and theorist of the arts prompted a contemporary to exclaim "Where shall I put Battista

Alberti: in what category of learned men shall I place him?" The resultant **Palazzo Rucellai**, two minutes' walk from the Strozzi house at Via della Vigna Nuova 18, was the first palace in Florence to follow the rules of classical architecture; its tiers of pilasters, incised into smooth blocks of stone, evoking the exterior wall of the Colosseum. Alberti later produced another, equally elegant design for the same patron – the front of the church of Santa Maria Novella (see p.94). In contrast to the feud between the Medici and the Strozzi, the Rucellai were on the closest terms with the city's royal family. The frieze on the Palazzo Rucellai features the heraldic devices of the two families, the Medici emblem alongside the Rucellai sail; moreover, the Loggia dei Rucellai, across the street, was in all likelihood built for the wedding of Giovanni's son to the granddaughter of Cosimo il Vecchio.

A portion of the palazzo is occupied by the **Museo di Storia della Fotografia Fratelli Alinari**, displaying a changing selection of the archive amassed by the Alinari brothers, founders of the very first photography club (daily except Wed 10am–7.30pm; L5000). From time to time it gives over its gallery space to prestigious travelling shows.

The Marini museum and Rucellai chapel

Round the corner from the Palazzo Rucellai stands the ex-church of San Pancrazio, deconsecrated by Napoleon, then successively the offices of the state lottery, the magistrates' court, a tobacco factory and an arsenal. It has now been converted into the swish **Museo Marino Marini** (June–Aug daily except Tues 10am–1pm & 4–7pm; Sept–May same days 10am–1pm & 3–6pm; L5000), where the attire and demeanour of the attendants might make you think you'd strayed into a well-appointed fashion house. Holding around 200 works left to the city a few years ago in Marini's will, the museum itself is perhaps the most intriguing artefact and it's debatable whether Marini's pieces can stand up to the reverential atmosphere imposed by the display techniques. Variations on the sculptor's trademark horse-and-rider theme – familiar from tasteful civic environments all over Europe – make up much of the show.

Once part of the church but now corralled off from the museum, the **Cappella di San Sepolcro** is the most exquisite of Alberti's buildings (open Oct–June Saturdays only at 5.30pm for Mass, or by appointment ☎055/287.707). Designed as the funerary monument to Giovanni Rucellai, it takes the form of a diminutive reconstruction of Jerusalem's Church of the Holy Sepulchre.

The Santa Maria Novella district

Scurrying from the platforms in search of a room, or fretting in the queues for a rail ticket, most people barely give a glance to **Santa Maria Novella train station**, but this is a building that deserves as much attention as many of the city's conventional monuments. Its principal architect, **Giovanni Michelucci** – who died in January 1991 just two days short of his hundredth birthday – was one of the leading figures of the modernist movement, which in Mussolini's Italy was marginalised by the officially approved pomposities of the neoclassical tendency. Accordingly there was some astonishment when, in 1933, Michelucci and his colleagues won the open competition to design the main rail terminal for one of the country's showpiece cities. Although the obstructiveness of some of the staff goes a long way to disguise the fact, the station is a piece of impeccably rational planning, so perfectly designed for its function that no major alterations have been necessary in the half century since its completion.

Cross the road from the front of the train station, and you're on the edge of a zone free from the hazards of speeding traffic and petrol fumes. On the other side of the church of Santa Maria Novella – whose back directly faces the station – lies **Piazza Santa Maria Novella**, a square with a lethargic backwater feel, much favoured as a spot for picnic lunches and after-dark loitering.

Santa Maria Novella

From the gay green and white patterns of its marble facade, you'd never guess that the church of **Santa Maria Novella** (daily 7–11.30am & 3.30–6pm) was the Florentine base of the Dominican order, the fearsome vigilantes of thirteenth-century Catholicism. A church was founded here at the end of the eleventh century and shortly afterwards was handed over to the Dominicans, who set about altering the place to their taste. By 1360 the interior was completed but only the Romanesque lower part of the facade was finished, a state of affairs that lasted until 1456, when Giovanni Rucellai paid for Alberti to design a classicised upper storey that would blend with the older section while improving the facade's proportions. Running round the cemetery to the right of the church is a feature unique in Florence – an arcade of *avelli*, the collective burial vaults of upper-class families.

The interior

The architects of the Gothic interior were also capable of great ingenuity – the distance between the columns diminishes with proximity to the altar, a perspective illusion to make the nave seem longer. In the 1560s Vasari and his minions ran amok here, ripping out the rood screen and the choir, and bleaching over the frescoes; restorers in the last century managed to reverse much of his handiwork.

Masaccio's extraordinary fresco of *The Trinity*, one of the earliest works in which perspective and classical proportion were rigorously employed, is painted onto the wall halfway down the left aisle. Surmounting a stark image of the state to which all flesh is reduced, the main scene is a dramatised diagram of the mechanics of Christian redemption, with the lines of the painting leading from the picture's donors, through the Virgin and the Baptist, to the crucified Christ and the stern figure of God the Father at the pinnacle.

Nothing else in the main part of the church has quite the same innovative impact, but the wealth of decoration is astounding. In the right transept lies the **tomb of the Patriarch of Constantinople**, who died in the city after unsuccessful negotiations to unite the Roman and Byzantine Churches at the 1439 Council of Florence. The cultural repercussions of the failed mission were enormous, however, with the influx of Greek scholars from Constantinople playing a major part in the introduction of classical texts to the Florentine intelligentsia. Raised above the pavement of the transept, the Cappella Rucellai contains a *Madonna and Child* signed by Nino Pisano, and Ghiberti's bronze tomb of the Dominican general Francesco Lionardo Dati.

In 1486 the chapel immediately to the right of the chancel was bought by Filippo Strozzi, who then commissioned a fresco cycle on the *Life of St Philip*

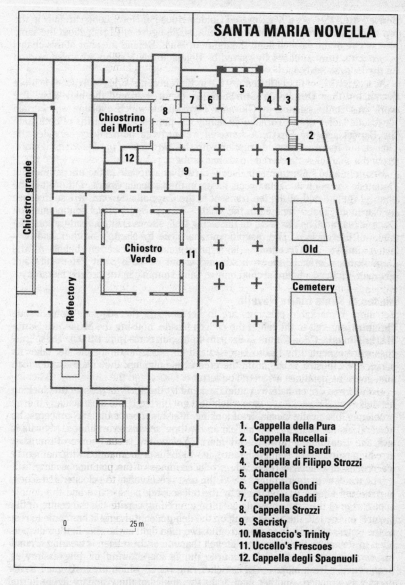

SANTA MARIA NOVELLA

1. Cappella della Pura
2. Cappella Rucellai
3. Cappella dei Bardi
4. Cappella di Filippo Strozzi
5. Chancel
6. Cappella Gondi
7. Cappella Gaddi
8. Cappella Strozzi
9. Sacristy
10. Masaccio's Trinity
11. Uccello's Frescoes
12. Cappella degli Spagnuoli

Chiostrino dei Morti

Chiostro grande

Chiostro Verde

Refectory

Old Cemetery

0   25 m

from **Filippino Lippi**. Before starting the project Filippino spent some time in Rome, and the work he carried out on his return displays an archaeologist's obsession with ancient Roman culture. In the bizarre *Exorcism of a Demon from the Temple of Mars*, for example, the figures swooning from the nauseous fumes emitted by the demon are almost overwhelmed by an architectural fantasy derived from the recently excavated Golden House of Nero. Look carefully in the top right-hand corner and you'll see a minuscule figure of Christ, about the same size as one of the vases behind the figure of Mars. Behind the altar of this chapel is **Strozzi's tomb**, beautifully carved by Benedetto da Maiano, who also worked on the Palazzo Strozzi.

As a chronicle of fifteenth-century life in Florence, no series of frescoes is more fascinating than **Domenico Ghirlandaio**'s pictures around the high altar. The work was commissioned by Giovanni Tornabuoni, which explains why certain illustrious ladies of the Tornabuoni family are present at the births of both John the Baptist and the Virgin. A sense of well-ordered domesticity pervades the chapel, but there's a nasty disruption with the *Massacre of the Innocents*, its foreground a shambles of severed heads and limbs.

Brunelleschi's *Crucifix*, supposedly carved as a riposte to the uncouthness of Donatello's version in Santa Croce, hangs in the Cappella Gondi, to the left of the chancel. At the end of the left transept is the **Cappella Strozzi**, whose frescoes by Nardo di Cione – painted in the 1350s – incorporate a visual commentary on Dante's *Inferno*. The *Paradise*, on the facing wall, shows Dante already among the ranks of the blessed. The magnificent altarpiece by Nardo's brother Andrea – better known as **Orcagna** – is a propaganda exercise on behalf of the Dominicans: Christ is shown bestowing favour on both Saint Peter and Saint Thomas Aquinas, a figure second only to Saint Dominic in the order's hierarchy.

Museo di Santa Maria Novella

Yet more remarkable paintings are to be found in the spacious Romanesque **cloisters**, entered to the left of the church facade, housing the **Museo di Santa Maria Novella** (Mon–Thurs & Sat 9am–2pm, Sun 8am–1pm; L4000). These frescoes were executed by **Paolo Uccello** and his workshop – the cloister takes its name, the Chiostro Verde, from the green base pigment they used – and which now gives the paintings a spectral undertone.

Uccello was driven halfway round the bend by the study of perspective, locking himself away for weeks at a time when he'd got his teeth into a particularly thorny problem. Chronically incapable of looking after his more mundane concerns, he finished his life destitute – "I am old and without means of livelihood. My wife is sick and I am unable to work any more". Yet he left behind some of the most arresting paintings of the Renaissance, in which his preoccupation with mathematical precision sometimes, ironically, produced images of fascinating obscurity.

The windswept image of *The Flood*, the best preserved of the cloister's frescoes, is rendered almost unintelligible by the telescoping perspective and the double appearance of the ark, whose flanks form a receding corridor in the centre of the picture: on the left, the ark is rising on the deluge, on the right it has come to rest as the waters subside. In the foreground, two men fight each other in their desperation to stay alive; the chequered lifebelt that one of these men is wearing around his neck is one of Uccello's favourite motifs for showing off his mastery of perspective – it's a *mazzocchio*, a wicker ring round which the turbanned headdress was wrapped. Another man grabs the ankles of the visionary figure in the foreground – presumably Noah, though he doesn't look much like the Noah peering out of the ark on the right, nor the bearded patriarch in the other frescoes here. In the right foreground there's a preview of the universal devastation, with tiny corpses laid out on the deck, and a crow gobbling an eyeball from one of the drowned.

THE PATERENES AND SAINT PETER MARTYR

In the twelfth century Florence became the crucible of one of the reforming religious movements that periodically cropped up in medieval Italy. The **Paterenes**, who were so numerous that they had their own clerical hierarchy in parallel with that of the mainstream Church, were convinced that everything worldly was touched by the devil. Accordingly they despised the papacy for its claims to temporal power and spurned the adoration of all relics and images. Furthermore, they rejected all forms of prayer and all contracts – including marriage vows – and were staunch pacifists.

Inevitably their campaign against the financial and moral corruption of the Catholic Church brought them into conflict with Rome, and eventually the displeasure of the Vatican found its means of expression in the equally zealous but decidedly non-pacific figure of the Dominican known as **Saint Peter Martyr**. Operating from the monastery of Santa Maria Novella, this papal inquisitor headed a couple of anti-Paterene fraternities, the Crocesegnati and the Compagnia della Fede, which were in effect his private army. In 1244 he led them into battle across the Piazza Santa Maria Novella, where they proceeded to massacre hundreds of the theological enemy. The epicentre of the carnage is marked by the Croce del Trebbio in Via delle Belle Donne, off the eastern side of the piazza.

After this, the Dominicans turned to less militant work, founding the charitable organisation called the Misericordia, which is still in existence today (see p.000). In 1252 Peter was knifed to death by a pair of assassins in the pay of a couple of Venetians whose property he'd confiscated, which is why he's usually depicted with a blade embedded in his skull. Allegedly the dying man managed to write out the creed with his own blood before expiring. Within the year he had been made a saint.

Once the chapterhouse of the immensely rich convent of Santa Maria, the **Cappella degli Spagnuoli** (Spanish Chapel) received its new name after Eleanor of Toledo reserved it for the use of her Spanish entourage. Presumably she derived constant inspiration from its fresco cycle by **Andrea di Firenze**, an extended depiction of the triumph of the Catholic Church that was described by Ruskin as "the most noble piece of pictorial philosophy in Italy". The sponsors of the project, the Dominicans, appear in emblematic guise on the right wall – the "Domini canes" or hounds of the Lord, unleashed by Saint Peter Martyr (see box above). The prominent representation of the Duomo was purely speculative – the cycle dates from the 1360s, long before Brunelleschi won the contract for the dome.

The contemporaneous decoration of the **Chiostrino dei Morti**, the oldest part of the complex, has not aged so robustly; the Chiostro Grande is off bounds, being the property of the army.

Ognissanti

In medieval times one of the main areas of cloth production – the mainstay of the Florentine economy – was in the western part of the city. **Ognissanti**, the main church of the quarter between Santa Maria Novella and the river, was founded in the thirteenth century by a Benedictine order whose speciality was the weaving of woollen cloth. Three hundred years later the Franciscans took it over, and the new tenure was marked by a Baroque overhaul which spared only the medieval campanile.

The facade of the church is of historical interest as one of the earliest eruptions of the Baroque style in Florence, but the building is made appealing by earlier features – the frescoes by **Domenico Ghirlandaio** and **Sandro Botticelli**. The young face squeezed between the Madonna and the dark-cloaked man in Ghirlandaio's *Madonna della Misericordia*, over the second altar on the right, is said to be that of Amerigo Vespucci – later to set sail on voyages that would give his name to America. Just beyond this, on opposite sides of the nave, are mounted Botticelli's *St Augustine* and Ghirlandaio's more earthbound *St Jerome*, both painted in 1480. In the same year Ghirlandaio painted the *Last Supper* that covers one wall of the **refectory**, reached through the cloister (Mon, Tues & Sat 9am–noon; free). It's a characteristically placid scene, the most animated characters being the birds in flight over the fruit-laden lemon trees above the heads of the disciples.

The San Lorenzo district

Walk a couple of blocks east from the train station and you'll see both the tawdriest and the liveliest aspects of central Florence. Beyond the hustle of Via Nazionale and Via Faenza, with their rabbit-hutch hotels and nocturnal hustle, lies the city's main market area, with scores of stalls encircling a vast food hall that rarely sees a foreign face. The racks of T-shirts, leather jackets and belts almost engulf the church of San Lorenzo – like Santa Maria Novella, a building of major importance that's often overlooked in the rush to the Duomo and the Uffizi.

San Lorenzo

Founded back in the fourth century, **San Lorenzo** (daily 7am–noon & 3.30–6.30pm) has a good claim to be the oldest church in Florence, and for the best part of three hundred years it was the city's cathedral. As this was the Medici's parish church, it inevitably benefited from the family's patronage: in 1420 Giovanni di Bicci de' Medici commissioned Brunelleschi to rebuild San Lorenzo, beginning with the old sacristy, a move which started a long association between the family and the building. Although Michelangelo laboured over a scheme for San Lorenzo's facade, the bare brick of the exterior has never been clad. It's a stark, inappropriate prelude to the powerful simplicity of Brunelleschi's interior, one of the earliest Renaissance church designs.

The church

Close to the entrance of the church, in the second chapel on the right, is **Rosso Fiorentino**'s *Marriage of the Virgin*, a painting with a uniquely golden-haired and youthful Joseph. Though you might not think so from the acreage of self-congratulatory works in the Palazzo Vecchio, few artists found sixteenth-century Florence a congenial place in which to work, and many followed Rosso's example in leaving the city. No sooner had the Medici returned to the city after the siege of 1530 than he had packed his bags for France, in order – to quote Vasari – "to raise himself . . . out of wretchedness and poverty, which is the common lot of those who work in Tuscany". He eventually found gainful employment with Francis I at Fontainebleau, where he and Primaticcio became the most influential artists in France.

At the end of the right aisle there's a fine tabernacle by Desiderio da Settignano, but far more striking are the two **bronze pulpits** by **Donatello**, in the centre of the church. Chiefly of scenes preceding and following the Crucifixion, these are the artist's last works, and were completed by his pupils as increasing paralysis limited their master's ability to model in wax. Jagged and discomforting, charged with more energy than the space can contain, these panels are more like brutal sketches in bronze than conventional reliefs. The overpopulated *Deposition*, for example, has demented mourners screaming underneath crosses which disappear into the void beyond the frame, while in the background a group of horsemen gather on a hill whose contours are left unmarked.

Close by, underneath the dome, an inscription and the Medici arms mark the grave of Donatello's main patron, **Cosimo il Vecchio**, bearing the plain dedication "Pater Patriae" – Father of the Fatherland. Donatello is buried in the chapel on the west side of the left transept, currently covered for restoration, where there's also a Filippo Lippi *Annunciation*.

Much of the decorative work in the neighbouring **Sagrestia Vecchia** or Old Sacristy (Mon, Wed, Fri & Sat 10–

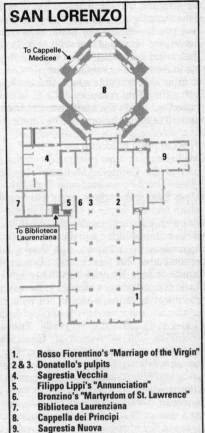

1. Rosso Fiorentino's "Marriage of the Virgin"
2 & 3. Donatello's pulpits
4. Sagrestia Vecchia
5. Filippo Lippi's "Annunciation"
6. Bronzino's "Martyrdom of St. Lawrence"
7. Biblioteca Laurenziana
8. Cappella dei Principi
9. Sagrestia Nuova

11.45am, Tues & Thurs 4–5.45pm) is by Donatello too: the two bronze doors with their combative pairs of martyrs and disciples, the large reliefs of *SS. Cosmas and Damian* and *SS. Lawrence and Stephen* (high on the wall facing the entrance), and the eight terracotta tondoes of the *Evangelists* and *Scenes from the Life of St John the Evangelist*. The table of milky marble in the centre of the room is the tomb of Cosimo il Vecchio's parents, Giovanni di Bicci de' Medici and Piccarda Bueri; Cosimo's sons, Piero and Giovanni, are buried in the Verrocchio-designed sarcophagus to the left of the entrance.

Biblioteca Medicea-Laurenziana

At the top of the left aisle, beside an enormous Bronzino fresco of *The Martyrdom of St Lawrence*, a door leads out to the cloister, and to a staircase going up to the **Biblioteca Medicea-Laurenziana** (Mon–Sat 9am–1pm; free). Wishing to create a suitably grandiose home for the precious manuscripts assembled by Cosimo il

Vecchio and Lorenzo il Magnifico, Pope Clement VII (Lorenzo's nephew) asked Michelangelo to design a new Medici library in 1524. The vestibule of the building he came up with is a showpiece of Mannerist architecture, delighting in paradoxical display – brackets that support nothing, columns that sink into the walls rather than stand out from them, a flight of steps so large that it almost fills the room, spilling down like a solidified lava flow.

From this eccentric space, the visitor passes into the tranquil, architecturally correct **reading room**; exhibitions in the connecting rooms draw on the Medici collection, which includes manuscripts as diverse as a fifth-century copy of Virgil and a treatise on architecture by Leonardo.

The Cappelle Medicee

Michelangelo's most celebrated contribution to the San Lorenzo buildings forms part of the **Cappelle Medicee** (Tues–Sat 9am–2pm, Sun 9am–1pm; L9000), entered from Piazza Madonna degli Aldobrandini, at the back of the church. After filing through the subfusc crypt where many of the Medici are actually buried, you climb into the larger of the chapels, the **Cappella dei Principi** (Chapel of the Princes), a gloomy, marble-plated hall built as a mausoleum for Cosimo I and his descendants. Morbid and dowdy, with tombs like armoured personnel carriers, it epitomises the mentality that thinks magnificence is directly proportional to expenditure. This was the most expensive building project ever financed by the family, and the Medici were still paying for it when the last of the line, Anna Maria Ludovica, joined her forebears in the basement. It could have looked even worse – the massive statues in the niches were intended to be made from semiprecious stones, like those used in the heraldic devices set into the walls.

Begun in 1520, the **Sagrestia Nuova** was designed by Michelangelo as a tribute to, and subversion of, Brunelleschi's Sagrestia Vecchia. Architectural connoisseurs go into raptures over the complex cornices of the alcoves, the complex relationship between those alcoves and the plane of the walls, and other such sophistications, but the lay person will be drawn to the fabulous **Medici tombs**, carved by Michelangelo between 1524 and 1533. To the left is the tomb of **Lorenzo, Duke of Urbino**, the grandson of Lorenzo il Magnifico; he is depicted as a man of thought, and his sarcophagus bears figures of *Dawn* and *Dusk*, the times of day whose ambiguities appeal to the contemplative mind. Opposite is the tomb of Lorenzo il Magnifico's youngest son, **Giuliano, Duke of Nemours**; as a man of action, his character is symbolised by the clear antithesis of *Day* and *Night*.

As a contemporary writer recorded, these are not true portraits: "He did not take from the Duke Lorenzo nor from the Lord Giuliano the model just as nature had drawn and composed them, but he gave them a greatness, a proportion, a dignity . . . which seemed to him would have brought them more praise, saying that a thousand years hence no one would be able to know that they were otherwise." They were very much otherwise, flattered by their ducal titles and genealogies as much as by these noble memorials: action man Giuliano was an easy-going but feckless individual, while Lorenzo combined ineffectualness with insufferable arrogance. Both died young and unlamented – Giuliano being killed by tuberculosis, Lorenzo by a combination of the same disease and syphilis.

Their effigies were intended to face the equally grand tombs of Lorenzo il Magnifico and his brother Giuliano; the only part of the project realised by Michelangelo is the preoccupied *Madonna and Child*, the last image of the Madonna he ever sculpted. In 1534, four years after the Medici had returned to

THE MEDICI BALLS

You come across the Medici emblem – a cluster of red balls (*palle*) on a gold background – all over Florence, yet its origins are shrouded in mystery. Legend claims the family descended from a Carolingian knight named Averardo, who fought and killed a giant in the Mugello, north of Florence. During the encounter his shield received six massive blows from the giant's mace, so Charlemagne, as a reward for his bravery, allowed Averardo to represent the dents as red balls on his coat-of-arms. Others say the balls had less exalted origins, that they were medicinal pills or cupping glasses, recalling the family's origins as apothecaries or doctors (*medici*). Others claim they are *bezants*, Byzantine coins, inspired by the arms of the *Arte del Cambio*, the money-changers' guild to which the Medici belonged. In a similar vein, some say the balls are coins, the traditional symbols of pawnbrokers.

Whatever the origin, the number of *palle* was never constant. In the thirteenth century, for example, there were twelve. By Cosimo de' Medici's time the number had dropped to seven, though San Lorenzo's Old Sacristy, a Cosimo commission, strangely has eight, while Verrocchio's roundel in the same church's chancel has six and Grand Duke Cosimo I's tomb, in the Cappella dei Principi, has five.

Florence in the unfathomably wretched form of Alessandro, Michelangelo decamped to Rome, where he stayed for the rest of his life. There are more Michelangelo drawings behind the altar which can be seen on supervised (free) trips every 30 minutes.

The Palazzo Medici-Riccardi

On the edge of the square in front of San Lorenzo stands the **Palazzo Medici-Riccardi** (Mon, Tues & Thurs–Sat 9am–1pm & 3–5pm, Sun 9am–noon; L6000), built for Cosimo il Vecchio by Michelozzo in the 1440s, and the family home until Cosimo I installed the clan in the Palazzo Vecchio. With its heavily rusticated exterior, this monolithic palazzo was the prototype for such houses as the Palazzo Pitti and Palazzo Strozzi, but in the seventeenth century it was greatly altered by its new owners, the Riccardi.

Of Michelozzo's original palazzo only the **chapel** remains intact, its interior covered by lively frescoes by **Benozzo Gozzoli**, of which the centrepiece is the *Journey of the Magi*, painted around 1460 and recently restored to blazing colour. It shows the pageant of the Compagnia dei Magi, the most patrician of the city's religious confraternities; their procession took place on Epiphany, with members of the Medici usually participating. It's known that several of the Medici household are featured in the procession, but putting names to these prettified faces is a problem. The man leading the cavalcade on a white horse is almost certainly Piero il Gottoso, sponsor of the fresco. Lorenzo il Magnifico, eleven years old at the time the fresco was painted, is probably the young king in the foreground, riding the grey horse detached from the rest of the procession, while his brother, Giuliano, is probably the one preceded by the black bowman. The artist himself – almost impossible to find – is in the crowd on the far left, his red beret signed with the words "Opus Benotii" in gold. Finally, the bearded characters in among the gallery of faces might be portraits of the retinue of the Byzantine emperor John Paleologus III, who had attended the Council of Florence twenty years before the fresco was painted.

Stairs ascend to the first floor, where a display case in the lobby of the main gallery contains a *Madonna and Child* by **Filippo Lippi**, one of Cosimo de' Medici's more troublesome protegés. Even as a novice in the convent of Santa Maria del Carmine, Filippo managed to earn himself a reputation as a drunken womaniser: in the words of Vasari, he was "so lustful that he would give anything to enjoy a woman he wanted . . . and if he couldn't buy what he wanted, then he would cool his passion by painting her portrait". Cosimo set up a workshop for him in the Medici palace, from which he often absented himself to go chasing women. On one occasion Cosimo actually locked the artist in the studio, but Filippo escaped down a rope of bed sheets; having cajoled him into returning, Cosimo declared that he would in future manage the painter with "affection and kindness", a policy that seems to have worked more successfully.

The ceiling of the main room is covered by Luca Giordano's fresco of *The Apotheosis of the Medici*, from which one can only deduce that Giordano had no sense of shame. Accompanying his father on the flight into the ether is the last male Medici, Gian Gastone (d. 1737), in reality a man so inert that he could rarely summon the energy to get out of bed in the morning.

The Mercato Centrale and around

The **Mercato Centrale**, the largest covered food hall in Europe, was built in stone, iron and glass by Giuseppe Mengoni, architect of Milan's Galleria, and opened in 1874; a century later it was given a major overhaul, reopening in 1980 with a new first floor. Butchers, *alimentari*, tripe sellers, greengrocers, pasta stalls, bars – they're all gathered under the one roof, and all charging prices lower than you'll readily find elsewhere in the city. The market is open Monday to Saturday from 7am to 2pm, and on Saturdays additionally from 4 to 8pm. Get there close to the end of the working day and you'll get some good reductions. And for a taste of simple Florentine food at its best, call in at *Ottavino*, a small bar that's the established meeting place of the market workers – it's on the Via dell'Ariento side and is open until 1.30pm.

Each day from 8am to 7pm the streets around the Mercato Centrale are thronged with stalls selling bags, belts, shoes, trousers – everything, in fact, that your wardrobe might need. This is the busiest of Florence's daily **street markets**, and a half-hour's immersion in the haggling mass of customers provides as good a break as any from pursuit of the city's art.

North of the market – the Cenacolo di Foligno and the Fortezza da Basso
One of Florence's more obscure *cenacoli* (Last Suppers), the **Cenacolo di Foligno**, is to be found a short distance west of the market at Via Faenza 42, in the ex-convent of the Franciscans of Foligno (visit has to be booked: ☎055/238.85 for individuals; ☎055/284.272 for groups). It was once thought to be by Raphael but is now reckoned to have been painted in the 1490s by Perugino. Certainly it shows many of Perugino's stylistic idiosyncrasies – the figures arranged in screen-like ranks, their gestures compiled from the same repertoire of standard poses that can be seen in his other works.

Beyond Via Faenza, the **Fortezza da Basso** was built to intimidate the people of Florence by the vile **Alessandro de' Medici**, who ordained himself Duke of Florence after a ten-month siege by the army of Charles V and Pope Clement VII (possibly Alessandro's father) had forcibly restored the Medici. The most talented Florentine architect of the day – Michelangelo – had played a major role in the defence of the city during the siege; the job of designing the fortress fell to the more pliant Antonio da Sangallo.

Within a few years the cruelties of Alessandro had become intolerable; a petition to Charles V spoke of the Fortezza da Basso as "a prison and a slaughter house for the unhappy citizens". Charles's response to the catalogue of Alessandro's atrocities was to marry his daughter to the tyrant. In the end, another Medici came to the rescue: in 1537 the distantly related **Lorenzaccio de' Medici** stabbed the Duke to death as he waited for an amorous assignation in Lorenzaccio's house. The reasons for the murder have never been clear but it seems that Lorenzaccio's mental health was little better than Alessandro's – in his earlier years he and Alessandro had regularly launched lecherous sorties on the city's convents, and he had been expelled from Rome after lopping the heads off the statues on the Arch of Constantine. The assassination, however, had favourable consequences for the city: as Alessandro died heirless, the council proposed that the leadership of the Florentine republic should be offered to **Cosimo de' Medici**, the great-grandson of Lorenzo il Magnifico. Subsequent Medici dukes had no need of a citizen-proof fort, and the Fortezza da Basso fell into dereliction after use as a gaol and barracks.

Since 1978 there's been a vast modern shed in the centre of the complex, used for trade fairs and shows such as the *Pitti Moda* fashion jamborees in January and July. The public gardens by the walls are fairly pleasant, but unless you want an open-air spot to relax before catching a train, you'd be better off on the other side of the Arno, in the Bóboli gardens.

The San Marco district

Much of central Florence's traffic is funnelled along **Via Cavour**, the thoroughfare connecting the Duomo area to Piazza della Libertà, a junction of the city's *viale* ring roads. Except as a place to catch buses out to Fiesole and other points north, the street has little to recommend it, but halfway along it lies **Piazza San Marco**, the core of the **university district**. On the square itself stands one of the city's top attractions, the **San Marco** monastery, with its Fra' Angelico paintings; and a couple of minutes away there's the museum that comes second only to the Uffizi in the popularity stakes, the **Accademia**, home of Florence's main assembly of Michelangelo sculptures.

San Marco

A whole side of Piazza San Marco is taken up by the Dominican convent and church of **San Marco**, recipient of Cosimo il Vecchio's most lavish patronage. In the 1430s he financed Michelozzo's enlargement of the conventual buildings, and went on to establish a vast library here. Abashed by the wealth he was transferring to them, the friars of San Marco suggested to Cosimo that he need not continue to support them on such a scale, to which he replied "Never shall I be able to give God enough to set him down as my debtor". Ironically, the convent became the centre of resistance to the Medici later in the century – Girolamo Savonarola, leader of the government of Florence after the expulsion of the Medici in 1494, was the prior of San Marco (see p.104).

As Michelozzo was altering and expanding the convent, its walls were being decorated by one its friars, **Fra' Angelico**, a painter in whom a medieval simplicity of faith was uniquely allied to a Renaissance sophistication of manner. He was born in Vicchio di Mugello (see p.165) some time between the late 1380s and 1400, and entered the Dominican monastery of nearby Fiesole, where he was known simply as Fra' Giovanni da Fiesole. He was then already known as an accomplished artist, but his reputation really flourished when he came to San Marco, where he was encouraged by Antonino Pierozzi – the future Saint Antonine. By the time Fra' Giovanni succeeded Pierozzi as prior of San Marco, the pictures he had created for the monastery and numerous other churches in Florence had earned him the title "the angelic painter", hence the name by which he's been known ever since.

The Museo di San Marco

Now deconsecrated, the convent today houses the **Museo di San Marco** (Tues–Sat 9am–2pm, Sun 9am–1pm; L6000), in essence a museum dedicated to the art of

SAVONAROLA

Girolamo Savonarola was born in 1452, the son of the physician to the Ferrara court. He grew up to be an abstemious and melancholic youth, sleeping on a bare straw mattress and spending much of his time reading the Bible and writing dirges. At the age of 23 he absconded to a Dominican monastery in Bologna, informing his father by letter that he was "unable to endure the evil conduct of the heedless people of Italy".

Within a few years, the Dominicans had dispatched him to preach all over northern Italy, an enterprise which got off to an unpromising start. Not the most attractive of men – he was frail, with a beak of a nose and a blubbery mouth – Savonarola was further hampered by an uningratiating voice and a particularly inelegant way of gesturing. Nonetheless, the intensity of his manner and his message attracted a committed following when he settled permanently in the monastery of San Marco in 1489.

By 1491, Savonarola's sermons had become so popular that he was asked to deliver his Lent address in the Duomo. Proclaiming that God was speaking through him, he berated the city for its decadence, for its paintings that made the Virgin "look like a whore", and for the tyranny of its Medici-led government. Following the death of Lorenzo il Magnifico, the rhetoric became even more apocalyptic. "Wait no longer, for there may be no more time for repentance" he told the Duomo congregation, summoning images of plagues, invasions and destruction.

When Charles VIII of France marched into Italy in September 1494 to press his claim to the throne of Naples, Savonarola presented him as the instrument of God's vengeance. Violating Piero de' Medici's declaration of Tuscan neutrality, the French army massacred the garrison at Fivizzano, and Florence prepared for the onslaught, as Savonarola declaimed "the Sword has descended; the scourge has fallen". With support for resistance ebbing, Piero capitulated to Charles; within days the Medici had fled and their palace had been plundered. Hailed by Savonarola as "the Minister of God, the Minister of Justice", Charles and his vast army passed peacefully through Florence on their way to Rome.

The political vacuum in Florence was filled by the declaration of a republican constitution but Savonarola was now in effect the ruler of the city. Continual decrees were issued from San Marco – profane carnivals were to be outlawed, fasting was to

Fra' Angelico. Around twenty paintings by him are gathered in the **Ospizio dei Pellegrini** (Pilgrims' Hospice) to the right of the entrance, many of them brought here from other churches in Florence. Here a *Last Judgement* and *Deposition* are outstanding, with their typically brilliant colouring and spatial clarity, and their air of imperturbable piety. The so-called *San Marco Altarpiece*, though badly damaged by the passage of time and a disastrous restoration, demonstrates Fra' Angelico's familiarity with the latest developments in artistic theory – its figures are arranged in lines that taper towards a central vanishing point, in accordance with the principles laid out in Alberti's *Della Pittura* (On Painting), which had appeared in Italian only two years before this picture was executed.

Across the cloister, in the **Sala Capitolare**, is a powerful fresco of the *Crucifixion*, painted by Angelico and assistants in 1441. At the rear of this room, the **refectory** – with a lustrous *Last Supper* by **Ghirlandaio** – forms an anteroom to the **foresteria** (guest rooms), which is cluttered with architectural bits and pieces salvaged during the urban improvement schemes of the latter half of the last century.

be observed more frequently, children were to act as the agents of the righteous, informing the authorities whenever their parents transgressed the Eternal Law. Irreligious books and paintings, expensive clothes, cosmetics, mirrors, board games, trivialities and luxuries of all types were destroyed, a ritual purging that reached a crescendo with a colossal "Bonfire of the Vanities" on the Piazza della Signoria.

Meanwhile, Charles VIII was installed in Naples and a formidable alliance was being assembled to overthrow him – the papacy, Milan, Venice, Ferdinand of Aragon and the Emperor Maximilian. In July 1495 the army of this Holy League confronted the French and was badly defeated. Charles's army continued northwards back to France, and Savonarola was summoned to the Vatican to explain why he had been unable to join the campaign against the intruder. He declined to attend, claiming that it was not God's will that he should make the journey, and thus set off a chain of exchanges that ended with his excommunication in June 1497. Defying Pope Alexander's order, Savonarola celebrated Mass in the Duomo on Christmas Day, which prompted a final threat from Rome: send Savonarola to the Vatican or imprison him in Florence, otherwise the whole city would join him in excommunication.

Despite Savonarola's insistence that the Borgia pope was already consigned to hell, the people of Florence began to desert him. The region's crops had failed, plague had broken out again, and the city was at war with Pisa, which Charles had handed over to its citizens rather than return to Florence's control, as he had promised. The Franciscans of Florence, sceptical of the Dominican monk's claim to divine approval, now issued a terrible challenge. One of their community and one of Savonarola's would walk through an avenue of fire in the Piazza della Signoria: if the Dominican died, then Savonarola would be banished; if the Franciscan died, then Savonarola's main critic, Fra' Francesco da Puglia, would be expelled.

A thunderstorm prevented the trial from taking place, but the mood in the city had anyway turned irrevocably. The following day, Palm Sunday 1498, a siege of the monastery of San Marco ended with Savonarola's arrest. Accused of heresy, he was tortured to the point of death, then burned at the stake in front of the Palazzo Vecchio, with two of his supporters. When the flames had finally been extinguished, the ashes were thrown into the river, to prevent anyone from gathering them as relics.

For the drama of its setting and the lucidity of its composition, nothing in San Marco matches Angelico's **Annunciation** at the summit of the staircase by the entrance to the *foresteria*. The pallid, submissive Virgin is one of the most touching images in Renaissance art, and the courteous angel, with his scintillating unfurled wings, is as convincing a heavenly messenger as any ever painted.

An inscription on this fresco reminds the passing monks to say a Hail Mary as they venerate the image. A less admonitory function is performed by the pictures which Angelico and his assistants painted in each of the 44 **cells** on the upper floor, into which the brothers would withdraw for solitary contemplation and sleep. The outer cells of the corridor on the left almost all have works by Angelico himself – don't miss the *Noli me tangere* (cell 1), the *Annunciation* (cell 3), the *Transfiguration* (cell 6) and the *Coronation of the Virgin* (cell 9). The marvellous *Madonna Enthroned*, on the wall facing these cells, is probably by Angelico too. Several of the scenes include one or both of a pair of monastic onlookers, serving as intermediaries between the occupant of the cell and the personages in the pictures: the one with the star above his head is Saint Dominic; the one with the split skull is Saint Peter Martyr. At the end of the corridor adjoining the far end of this one there's a knot of rooms once occupied by **Savonarola**; they are usually closed, but if you're lucky you'll be able to see the portrait of him as Saint Peter Martyr, painted by his acolyte Fra' Bartolomeo.

Michelozzo's **library**, a design that exudes an atmosphere of calm study, is off the corridor to the right of the *Annunciation*. Cosimo il Vecchio's agents roamed as far as the Near East garnering precious manuscripts and books for him; in turn, Cosimo handed all the religious items over to the monastery, stipulating that they should be accessible to all – thus making it Europe's first public library. Beyond the library is the pair of rooms used by the monastery's benefactor when he came here on retreat.

San Marco church
Greatly altered since Michelozzo's intervention, **San Marco church** is worth a visit for two works on the second and third altars on the right: a *Madonna and Saints* painted in 1509 by Fra' Bartolomeo, and an eighth-century mosaic of *The Madonna in Prayer*, brought here from Constantinople.

Sant'Apollonia, the Scalzo and the Giardino dei Semplici

Within a couple of minutes' stroll of San Marco are two major but little-visited art attractions, one of the city's obscurer parks, and a cluster of specialist museums. Perhaps none would feature in a rushed itinerary, but the first pair in particular are worth the diversion on any high culture point-to-point.

The Cenacolo di Sant'Apollonia
Running off the west side of Piazza San Marco, Via Arazzieri soon becomes Via XXVII Aprile, where the former Benedictine convent of **Sant'Apollonia** stands at no. 1. Most of the complex has now been turned into flats, but the former refectory houses one of **Castagno**'s masterpieces, the *Last Supper* (Tues–Sat 9am–2pm, Sun 9am–1pm; free).

Painted around 1450, after the artist's return from Venice, the *cenacolo* was whitewashed out by the nuns, before being uncovered in the middle of the last century. It is perhaps the most disturbing version of the event painted in the Renaissance. Blood red is the dominant tone, and the most commanding figure is the diabolic black-bearded Judas, who sits on the near side of the table. The seething patterns in the marble panels behind the Apostles seem to mimic the turmoil in the mind of each, as he hears Christ's announcement of the betrayal.

Above the illusionistic recess in which the supper takes place are the *sinopie* of a *Crucifixion*, *Deposition* and *Resurrection* by Castagno, revealed when the frescoes were taken off the wall for restoration.

The Chiostro dello Scalzo

To the north of San Marco, at Via Cavour 69, is **Lo Scalzo**, the home of the Brotherhood of Saint John, whose vows of poverty entailed walking around barefoot – *scalzo*. The order was suppressed in 1785 and their monastery sold off, except for the **cloister** (Mon–Thurs 9am–1pm; free; ring the bell).

This was the training ground for **Andrea del Sarto**, an artist venerated in the nineteenth century as a painter with no imperfections, but now regarded with slightly less enthusiasm on account of this very smoothness. His monochrome paintings of the *Cardinal Virtues* and *Scenes from the Life of the Baptist* occupied him off and on for a decade from 1511, beginning with the *Baptism*, finishing with the *Birth of St John*. A couple of the sixteen scenes – *John in the Wilderness* and *John meeting Christ* – were executed by his pupil Franciabigio in 1518, when del Sarto was away in Paris.

The Giardino dei Semplici and the university museums

The **Giardino dei Semplici** (Mon, Wed & Fri 9am–noon, plus mid-April to mid-May Sun 9am–1pm; closed Aug 11–18; free), northeast of San Marco, was set up in 1545 for Cosimo I as a medicinal garden, following the examples of Padua and Pisa. Entered from Via La Pira, it now covers five acres, most of the area being taken up by the original flowerbeds and avenues. It's a shady place to catch your breath.

The garden entrance at Via P.A. Micheli 3 also gives access to a number of museums administered by the university. The **Museo Botanico** (Mon–Fri 9am–noon; free), set up for Leopoldo II of Lorraine, contains over four million botanical specimens, supplemented by plaster mushrooms and wax models of plants; most people will get more fun from the living specimens outside. Masses of rocks are on show in the **Museo di Mineralogia e Litologia** (Mon–Sat 9.30am–12.30pm, plus first Sun in month except July & Aug same hours; closed Aug 13–17; free), including a 150-kilo topaz from Brazil and a load of worked stones from the Medici collection – snuff boxes, little vases, a quartz boat. The **Museo di Geologia e Paleontologia** (Mon 2–6pm, Tues–Thurs & Sat 9am–1pm, plus first Sun in month 9.30am–12.30pm except July–Sept; free) is one of Italy's biggest fossil shows, featuring such delights as prehistoric elephant skeletons from the upper Valdarno and a skeleton from Grosseto once touted as the missing link between monkeys and homo sapiens.

Sooner or later all these natural history museums are to be moved into a new home on Via Circondaria, making what will be the largest museum of its kind in Italy.

The Galleria dell'Accademia

Florence's first academy of drawing – indeed, Europe's first – was founded in the mid-sixteenth century by Bronzino, Ammannati and Vasari. Initially based in Santissima Annunziata, this Accademia del Disegno moved in 1764 to Via Ricasoli 66, and soon afterwards was transformed into a general arts academy, the Accademia di Belle Arti. Twenty years later the Grand Duke Pietro Leopoldo founded the nearby **Galleria dell'Accademia** (Tues–Sat 9am–2pm, Sun 9am–1pm; L10,000), filling its rooms with paintings for the edification of the students. Later augmented with pieces from suppressed religious foundations and other sources, the Accademia has an extensive collection of paintings, especially of Florentine work of the fourteenth and fifteenth centuries.

Yet the pictures are not what draw the crowds in numbers equalled only by the Uffizi. The real attraction is **Michelangelo**, half a dozen of whose major sculptures are here, among them the **David** – symbol of the city's republican pride and of the illimitable ambition of the Renaissance artist. Finished in 1504, when Michelangelo was just 29, and carved from a block of marble whose shallowness posed severe difficulties, it's an incomparable show of technical bravura. But the *David* is a piece of monumental public sculpture, not a gallery exhibit. After being considered as an adornment for the exterior of the Duomo, it was instead installed outside the Palazzo Vecchio, where it remained until 1873, when it was removed to the Accademia's specially built tribune. Closely surveyed in this chapel-like space, the *David* appears a monstrous adolescent, with massive head and hands and gangling arms – the ugliest masterpiece of western sculpture.

Michelangelo once described the process of carving as being the liberation of the form from within the stone, a notion that seems to be embodied by the remarkable unfinished **Slaves** nearby. His procedure, clearly demonstrated here, was to cut the figure as if it were a deep relief, and then to free the three-dimensional figure; often his assistants would perform the initial operation to his instructions, so it's possible that Michelangelo's own chisel never actually touched these stones. Carved in the 1520s, they were intended for the tomb of Julius II, a project that underwent innumerable permutations before its eventual abandonment; in 1564 the artist's nephew gave them to the Medici, who installed them in the grotto of the Bóboli gardens. Close by is another unfinished work, *St Matthew*, which was started immediately after completion of the *David* as a commission from the Opera del Duomo; they actually requested a full series of the Apostles from Michelangelo, but this is the only one he ever began.

The Accademia's **picture galleries** are big but unexciting, with copious examples of the work of "Unknown Florentine" and "Follower of . . .". The pieces likeliest to make an impact are Pontormo's *Venus and Cupid*, Botticelli's attributed *Madonna of the Sea* and the painted fifteenth-century *Adimari Chest*, showing a Florentine wedding ceremony in the Piazza del Duomo.

Piazza Santissima Annunziata

Nineteenth-century urban renewal schemes left many of Florence's squares rather grim places, which makes **Piazza Santissima Annunziata**, with its distinctive arcades, all the more attractive a public space. It has a special importance for the city, too. Until the end of the eighteenth century the Florentine year used to begin on March 25, the Festival of the Annunciation – hence the Florentine predilection for paintings of the Annunciation, and the fashionableness of the Annunziata church, which has long been the place for society weddings. The festival is still marked by a huge fair in the piazza and the streets leading off it; later in the year, on the first weekend in September, the square is used for Tuscany's largest crafts fair.

The **equestrian statue of Grand Duke Ferdinand I** in the centre of the square was Giambologna's final work, and was cast by his pupil Pietro Tacca from cannons captured at the Battle of Lepanto. Tacca was also the creator of the bizarre **fountains**, on each of which a pair of aquatic monkeys dribble water at two whiskered sea-slugs.

The Spedale degli Innocenti

The tone of the piazza is set by Brunelleschi's **Spedale degli Innocenti**, which was opened in 1445 as the first foundlings' hospital in Europe, and is still an orphanage. Luca della Robbia's ceramic tondoes of well-swaddled babies advertise the building's function, but their insouciance belies the misery associated with it. Slavery was part of the Florentine economy even as late as the fifteenth century, and many of the infants given over to the care of the Innocenti were born to domestic slaves. A far from untypical entry in the Innocenti archives records the abandonment of twins "from the house of Agostino Capponi, born of Polonia his slave ... They arrived half dead: if they had been two dogs they would have been better cared for."

The attached convent, centred on two beautiful cloisters, now contains the **Museo dello Spedale degli Innocenti** (Mon, Tues & Thurs–Sat 8.30am–2pm, Sun 8.30am–1pm; L3000), a miscellany of Florentine Renaissance art that includes one of Luca della Robbia's most charming Madonnas and an *Adoration of the Magi* by Domenico Ghirlandaio which has a massacre of the innocents going on in the background. No collection of pictures from this period could be entirely unengrossing, but Florence has several museums you should check out before this one.

Santissima Annunziata

Santissima Annunziata (daily 7.30am–12.30pm & 4–7pm) is the mother church of the Servite order, which was founded by seven Florentine aristocrats in 1234. The church's dedication to the Virgin Annunciate took place in the fourteenth century, in recognition of its miraculous image of the Virgin, which was said to have been completed by an angel when the monastic artist left it unfinished. So many pilgrims came to adore the painting that the church was rebuilt to accommodate them in the second half of the fifteenth century: the architect was Michelozzo (brother of the prior), the paymasters the Medici.

A customary act of devotion was to leave behind a life-size wax effigy of oneself in the **Chiostro dei Voti**, the atrium that Michelozzo built onto the church. None of these ex-votoes remains in the now glazed atrium, but it does retain – albeit in battered shape – a fine set of frescoes. Mostly painted in the 1510s, these include a *Visitation* by Pontormo, Rosso Fiorentino's *Assumption*, a bucolic *Nativity* by Baldovinetti, and a *Birth of the Virgin* by Andrea del Sarto that achieves a perfect balance of spontaneity and geometrical order.

Much of the gilt and stucco fancy dress of the main **church interior** was perpetrated in the seventeenth and eighteenth centuries, but the ornate **tabernacle** of the miraculous image (to the left of the entrance) was produced by Michelozzo. His patron, Piero di Cosimo de' Medici, made sure that nobody remained unaware of the money he sank into the shrine – an inscription reads

"Costò fior. 4 mila el marmo solo" (The marble alone cost 4000 florins). The painting encased in the marble has been repainted into illegibility, and is usually kept covered anyway.

Far more interesting are the raw-nerved frescoes by **Andrea del Castagno** in the first two chapels on the left, *The Vision of St Jerome* and *The Trinity*. Now restored, they were obliterated after Vasari publicised the rumour that Castagno had poisoned his erstwhile friend, Domenico Veneziano, motivated by envy of the other's skill with oil paint. Castagno was saddled with this guilt until the last century, when an archivist discovered that the alleged murderer in fact predeceased his victim by four years.

Separated from the nave by a triumphal arch is the unusual **tribune**, begun by Michelozzo but completed to designs by Alberti; you get into it along a corridor from the left transept. The chapel at the furthest point was altered by Giambologna into a monument to himself, complete with bronze reliefs and a Crucifix by the sculptor.

The adjoining **Chiostro dei Morti** is worth visiting for Andrea del Sarto's intimate *Madonna del Sacco*, painted over the door leading into the church; the cloister is entered through a gate to the left of the church portico or from the left transept, but both are often locked, so a word with the sacristan might be in order.

The Museo Archeologico – and the Pazzi church

On the other side of Via della Colonna from the side wall of Santissima Annunziata is the **Museo Archeologico** (Tues–Sat 9am–2pm, Sun 9am–1pm; L6000), the most important collection of its kind in northern Italy. It suffered terrible damage in the flood of 1966 and the task of restoring the exhibits is still not finished, so the arrangement of the rooms is subject to sudden changes.

The museum's special strength is its showing of **Etruscan** finds, many of them part of the Medici bequest. On the ground floor there's a comprehensive display of Etruscan funerary figures, but even more arresting than these is the *François Vase*, an Attic krater from the sixth century BC, discovered in an Etruscan tomb at Chiusi. Pride of place in the first-floor **Egyptian collection** goes to a Hittite chariot made of bone and wood and dating from the fourteenth century BC.

The rest of this floor and much of the floor above are given over to the **Etruscan, Greek and Roman collections**, arranged with variable clarity. Of the Roman pieces the outstanding item is the *Idolino*, probably a copy of a fifth-century BC Greek original. Nearby is a massive Hellenistic horse's head, which once adorned the garden of the Palazzo Medici, where it was studied by Donatello and Verrocchio. In the long gallery you'll find the best of the Etruscan pieces: the *Arringatore* (Orator), the only known Etruscan large bronze from the Hellenistic period; and the *Chimera*, a triple-headed monster of the fifth century BC. A symbol of the three-seasoned pre-Christian Mediterranean year, the *Chimera* was much admired by Cosimo I's retinue of Mannerist artists and all subsequent connoisseurs of the offbeat.

Santa Maria Maddalena dei Pazzi and around

Further along Via della Colonna, a right turn into Borgo Pinti brings you to the church of **Santa Maria Maddalena dei Pazzi**, named after a Florentine nun who was prone to demonstrating her saintliness by pouring boiling wax over her arms. Her piety was of the uncompromising sort much honoured during the Counter-

Reformation: when Maria de' Medici went off to marry Henry IV of France, Maria Maddalena transmitted the news that the Virgin expected her to readmit the Jesuits to France and exterminate the Huguenots, which she duly did.

Founded in the thirteenth century but kitted out in Baroque style, the church is not itself much of an attraction, but its chapterhouse – reached by a strange subterranean passageway – is decorated with a radiant **Perugino** fresco of the *Crucifixion* (Tues–Sun 9am–noon & 5–7pm; L1000). The scene is painted as a continuous panorama on a wall divided into three arches, giving the effect of looking out through a loggia onto a springtime landscape. As always with Perugino, there is nothing troubling here, the Crucifixion being depicted not as an agonising death but rather as the necessary prelude to the Resurrection.

The enormous building behind the church is the **Synagogue**; the ghetto established in this district by Cosimo I was not demolished until the mid-nineteenth century, which is when the present Moorish-style synagogue was built. It contains a small museum charting the history of Florence's Jewish population (daily 9.30am–5pm, closes 2pm Fri).

To the north of the Pazzi church, at the end of Borgo Pinti, you come to the **English Cemetery** at Piazza Donatello (daily 9am–noon & 3–6pm). Now a funerary traffic island, this patch of garden is the resting place of Elizabeth Barrett Browning and a number of contemporaneous artistic Brits, among them Walter Savage Landor and Arthur Hugh Clough.

East of the Signoria: the Santa Croce district

The 1966 flood completely changed the character of the area around **Santa Croce**. Prior to then it had been one of the more densely populated districts, packed with tenements and small workshops. When the Arno burst its banks, this low-lying zone was virtually wrecked, and many of its residents moved out permanently in the following years.

Traditionally the **Piazza Santa Croce** has been one of the city's main arenas for ceremonials and festivities. Thus when Lorenzo il Magnifico was married to the Roman heiress Clarice Orsini, the event was celebrated on this square, with a tournament that was more a fashion event than a contest of skill – Lorenzo's knightly outfit, for instance, was adorned with pearls, diamonds and rubies. During the years of Savonarola's ascendancy, the piazza became the principal site for the execution of heretics. It's still used as the pitch for the *Gioco di Calcio Storico*, a football tournament between the city's four *quartieri*; the game is held three times in Saint John's week (the last week of June), and is characterised by incomprehensible rules and a level of violence which the sixteenth-century costumes do little to inhibit (see p.141).

The Church of Santa Croce

Though traditionally said to have been founded by Saint Francis himself, the Franciscan church of Florence, **Santa Croce** (Mon–Sat 8am–6.30pm, Sun 8am–12.30pm & 3–6.30pm), was probably begun seventy or so years later, in 1294, possibly by the architect of the Duomo, Arnolfo di Cambio. In the following century the first of the church's remarkable **fresco cycles** – by Giotto, the Gaddi family and others – were completed. Construction of the building, though, was

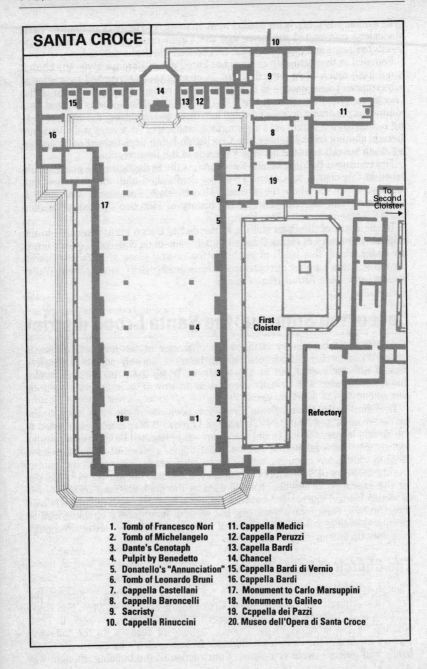

SANTA CROCE

1. Tomb of Francesco Nori
2. Tomb of Michelangelo
3. Dante's Cenotaph
4. Pulpit by Benedetto
5. Donatello's "Annunciation"
6. Tomb of Leonardo Bruni
7. Cappella Castellani
8. Cappella Baroncelli
9. Sacristy
10. Cappella Rinuccini
11. Cappella Medici
12. Cappella Peruzzi
13. Capella Bardi
14. Chancel
15. Cappella Bardi di Vernio
16. Cappella Bardi
17. Monument to Carlo Marsuppini
18. Monument to Galileo
19. Cappella dei Pazzi
20. Museo dell'Opera di Santa Croce

held up by a split in the Franciscan ranks and not resumed until the early fifteenth century, the period when Santa Croce acquired its status as the mausoleum of Florence's eminent citizens.

Today, over 270 tombstones pave the floor of the church, while grander monuments commemorate the likes of Ghiberti, Michelangelo, Machiavelli, Galileo and Dante – though the last of the group is actually buried in Ravenna, where he died in exile. The glum statue of the poet outside the church is a nineteenth-century job, as is the facade, which is based on the Orcagna tabernacle in Orsanmichele.

Santa Croce played a significant role in the evolution of Renaissance thought. It was here that the full sessions of the Council of Florence took place in 1439, in an attempt to reconcile the differences between the Roman and Eastern churches. Attended by the pope, the Byzantine emperor and the Patriarch of Constantinople, the council culminated in a compromise that lasted only until the Byzantine delegation returned home. Its more lasting effect was that it brought scores of classical scholars to the city, some of whom stayed on, to provide the impetus behind such bodies as Cosimo de' Medici's academy of Platonic studies, perhaps the single most influential intellectual gathering of the Florentine Renaissance.

The interior

In the nave, almost every object of interest is a funerary monument. Against the first pillar on the right is the tomb of one of the victims of the Pazzi conspiracy, **Francesco Nori**, surmounted by a lovely relief by Antonio Rossellino. Nearby is Vasari's monument to **Michelangelo**, whose body was brought back from Rome to Florence in July 1574, a return marked with a spectacular memorial service in San Lorenzo. On the opposite side of the church is the tomb of **Galileo**, built in 1737, which was when it was finally agreed to give the great scientist a Christian burial. Back in the right aisle, the Neoclassical cenotaph to **Dante** is immediately after the second altar, while against the third pillar there's a marvellous **pulpit** by Benedetto da Maiano, decorated with scenes from the life of Saint Francis. The side door at the end of the aisle is flanked by **Donatello**'s gilded stone relief of *The Annunciation* and Bernardo Rossellino's much-imitated tomb of the humanist **Leonardo Bruni**, author of the first history of the city – a copy of which his effigy is holding.

The chapels at the east end of Santa Croce are a compendium of Florentine fourteenth-century painting, showing Giotto's art at its most eloquent and the extent of his influence. The **Cappella Castellani**, on the west side of the right transept, was completely frescoed in the 1380s by **Agnolo Gaddi** and his pupils, while the adjoining **Cappella Baroncelli** was decorated by Agnolo's father, **Taddeo**, a long-time assistant to Giotto himself. Taddeo's cycle features one of the first night scenes in Western painting, *The Annunciation to the Shepherds*.

A doorway halfway down the corridor, alongside the Castellani chapel, opens into the **sacristy**, where the centrepiece is a marvellous *Crucifixion* by Taddeo; the tiny **Cappella Rinuccini**, separated from the sacristy by a grille, is covered with frescoes by the more solemn **Giovanni da Milano**. The corridor ends at the **Cappella Medici**, open only for those taking mass, notable for its large terra-cotta altarpiece by Andrea della Robbia and a nineteenth-century forged Donatello; like the corridor, the chapel was designed by Michelozzo, the Medici's pet architect.

Both the **Cappella Peruzzi** and the **Cappella Bardi** – the two chapels on the right of the chancel – are entirely covered with frescoes by **Giotto**, with some assistance in the latter. Their deterioration was partly caused by Giotto's having painted some of the pictures onto dry plaster, rather than the wet plaster employed in true fresco technique. But the vandalism of later generations was far more destructive. In the eighteenth century they were covered in whitewash, then they were heavily retouched in the nineteenth; restoration in the 1950s returned them to as close to their pristine state as was possible. Scenes from the lives of Saint John the Evangelist and Saint John the Baptist cover the Peruzzi chapel, while a better-preserved cycle of the life of Saint Francis fills the Bardi. Despite the areas of paint destroyed when a tomb was attached to the wall, the *Funeral of St Francis* is still a composition of extraordinary impact, the grief-stricken mourners suggesting an affinity with the lamentation over the body of Christ – one of them even touches the wound in Francis's side, echoing the gesture of Doubting Thomas. The *Ordeal by Fire*, showing Francis about to demonstrate his faith to the Sultan by walking through fire, shows Giotto's mastery of understated drama, with the Sultan's entourage skulking off to the left in anticipation of the monk's triumph. Above the chapel is the most powerful scene of all, *St Francis Receiving the Stigmata*, in which the power of Christ's apparition seems to force the chosen one to his knees.

Agnolo Gaddi was responsible for the design of the stained glass in the lancet windows round the high altar, and for all the chancel frescoes, depicting the legend of the True Cross (see p.384 for the story). The **Cappella Bardi di Vernio**, the fifth after the chancel, was painted in the 1330s by **Maso di Banco**, perhaps the most inventive of Giotto's followers; as tradition dictated, his *Scenes from the Life of St Sylvester* depict the saint baptising the Emperor Constantine, notwithstanding the fact that Sylvester died some time before the emperor's actual baptism. At the end of the left chancel, the second Cappella Bardi houses a wooden crucifix by **Donatello** – supposedly criticised by Brunelleschi as resembling a "peasant on the Cross".

THE CAPPELLA DEI PAZZI, CLOISTERS AND MUSEUM

Brunelleschi's **Cappella dei Pazzi** (March–Sept daily except Wed 10am–12.30pm & 2.30–6.30pm; Oct–Feb same days 10am–12.30pm & 3–5pm; L3000), which stands at the end of Santa Croce's first cloister, typifies the spirit of early Renaissance architecture. Planned in the 1430s and completed in the 1470s, several years after the architect's death, the chapel is geometrically perfect without seeming pedantic, and is exemplary in the way its decorative detail harmonises with the design. The polychrome lining of the shallow cupola of the portico is by Luca della Robbia, as is the tondo of *St Andrew* over the door; inside, Luca also produced the blue and white tondoes of the *Apostles*. The vividly coloured tondoes of the *Evangelists* were produced in the Della Robbia workshop, possibly to designs by Donatello.

Off this cloister, the **Museo dell'Opera di Santa Croce** (same hours & ticket) houses a miscellany of works of art, the best of which are gathered in the refectory. Cimabue's *Crucifixion* was very badly damaged in 1966, and has become the emblem of the havoc caused by the flood; the high-water tide mark is still clearly visible on the walls. The other highlights are the detached fresco of the *Last Supper*, valued as the finest work by Taddeo Gaddi, and Donatello's enormous gilded *St Louis of Toulouse*, made for Orsanmichele.

FLORENCE'S FLOODS

The calamity of the November 1966 flood had plenty of precedents. Great areas of the city were destroyed by a flood in **1178**, a disaster exacerbated by plague and famine. In **1269** the Carraia and Trinita bridges were carried away on a torrent so heavy that "a great part of the city of Florence became a lake". The flood of **1333** was preceded by a four-day storm, with thunder and rain so violent that all the city's bells were tolled to drive away the evil spirits thought to be behind the tempest: bridges were demolished and the original Marzocco – a figure of Mars rather than the leonine figure that inherited its name – was carried away on the raging Arno. Cosimo I instituted an urban beautification scheme after a deluge put nearly twenty feet of muddy water over the city in **1557**; on that occasion the Trinita bridge was hit so suddenly that everyone on it was drowned, except for two children who were left stranded on a pillar in midstream, where for two days they were fed by means of a rope slung over from the bank.

It rained continuously for forty days prior to **November 4, 1966**, with nearly half a metre of rain falling in the preceding two days. When the water pressure in an upstream reservoir threatened to break the dam, it was decided to open the sluices. The only people to be warned about the rapidly rising level of the river were the jewellers of the Ponte Vecchio, whose private nightwatchman phoned them in the small hours of the morning with news that the bridge was starting to shake. Police watching the shopkeepers clearing their displays were asked why they weren't spreading the alarm – they replied "We have received no orders".

When the banks of the Arno finally broke down, a flash flood dumped around 500,000 tons of water and mud on the streets, moving with such speed that people were drowned in the underpass of Santa Maria Novella train station. In all, 35 Florentines were killed, over 15,000 cars wrecked, and thousands of works of art damaged, many of them ruined by heating oil flushed out of basements.

Within hours an impromptu army of rescue workers had been formed – many of them students – to haul pictures out of slime-filled churches and gather fragments of paint in plastic bags. Donations came in from all over the world, but the task was so immense that the restoration of many pieces is still unaccomplished. Some rooms in the archaeological museum, for example, have remained closed since the flood, and many possessions of the National Library are still in the laboratories. In total around two-thirds of the 3000 paintings damaged in the flood are now on view again, and two massive laboratories – one for paintings and one for stonework – are operating full time in Florence, developing restoration techniques often taken up by galleries all over the world.

The spacious **second cloister**, another late project by Brunelleschi, is the most peaceful spot in the centre of Florence – or will be once again, when the restoration work is finished.

The Casa Buonarotti and the Sant'Ambrogio area

The enticing name of the **Casa Buonarotti** (Mon & Wed–Sun 9.30am–1.30pm; L8000), north of Santa Croce at Via Ghibellina 70, is slightly misleading – though Michelangelo Buonarotti owned the property, he never actually lived here. The sculptor's nephew, his sole descendant, was given the house, and his son in turn converted part of the property into a gallery dedicated to his great-uncle. Among the jumble of works collected here – many of them created in homage to him – are a few pieces by the great man himself.

Reproductions of some of Michelangelo's drawings are displayed on the ground floor, the authentic stuff being housed upstairs. The two main treasures are to be found in the room on the left at the top of the stairs: *The Madonna of the Steps* is Michelangelo's earliest known work, carved when he was no older than sixteen, and the similarly unfinished *Battle of the Centaurs* was carved only a few weeks afterwards, when the boy was living in the Medici household. In the adjacent room you'll find his wooden model for the facade of San Lorenzo, while the room in front of the stairs houses the largest of all the sculptural models on display, the torso of a *River God* intended for the Medici chapel in San Lorenzo. To the right is a room containing a slim wooden *Crucifix* discovered in Santo Spirito in 1963, and now generally thought to be a work whose existence had long been documented, but was feared lost.

The markets

Two of Florence's markets lie within a few minutes of the Casa Buonarotti. To the north, the Piazza dei Ciompi is the venue for the **Mercato delle Pulci** or flea market (Tues–Sat 8am–1pm & 3.30–7pm, plus first Sun of month 9am–7pm). Much of the junk maintains the city's reputation for inflated prices, though you can find a few interesting items at modest cost – old postcards, posters and so on. Vasari's **Loggia del Pesce** gives the square a touch of style; built for the fishmongers of what's now Piazza della Repubblica, it was moved here when that square was laid out.

A short distance to the east, out of the orbit of ninety percent of tourists, is the **Mercato di Sant'Ambrogio** (Mon–Fri 7am–2pm), a smaller, tattier and even more enjoyable version of the San Lorenzo food hall. The *tavola calda* here is one of Florence's lunchtime bargains (see p.137), and – as at San Lorenzo – the stalls bring their prices down in the last hour of trading.

Unassuming on the outside, **Sant'Ambrogio** church is worth a visit for its Orcagna fresco of *The Madonna and Saints* (second altar on the right), and for the chapel to the left of the chancel, containing a tabernacle carved in 1481 by Mino da Fiesole and a fresco by Cosimo Rosselli that's another one of Florence's pieces of Renaissance social reportage. Commemorated by a simple slab, Verrocchio is buried in the fourth chapel of the left aisle.

The Museo Horne

On the south side of Santa Croce, down by the river at Via dei Benci 6, is one of Florence's more recondite museums, the **Museo Horne** (Mon–Sat 9am–1pm; L6000). Left to the nation by the nineteenth-century English art historian Herbert Horne, who was instrumental in rescuing Botticelli from neglect, this houseful of paintings, sculptures, pottery, furniture and other domestic objects contains no real masterpieces, but is diverting enough if you've already done the major collections. The building itself is worth a glance even if you're not going into the museum; commissioned by the Corsi family around 1490, it's a typical merchant's house of the period, with huge cellars in which wool would have been dyed, and an open gallery above the courtyard for drying the finished cloth.

The pride of Horne's collection was its drawings, which are now salted away in the Uffizi. Of what's left, the pick is Giotto's *St Stephen* (a fragment from a polyptych), a *Deposition* by Gozzoli, his last work, and Beccafumi's *Holy Family*, shown in its original frame. One of the main exhibits is a piece of little artistic merit but great historical interest – a copy of part of Leonardo's *Battle of Anghiari*, once frescoed on a wall of the Palazzo Vecchio.

Oltrarno

Visitors to Florence might perceive the Arno as just an interruption in the urban fabric, but Florentines still tend to talk as though a ravine runs through their city. North of the river is known as *Arno di quà* (over here), while the other side, hemmed in by a ridge of hills that rise a short distance from the river, is *Arno di là* (over there). More formally, it's known as the **Oltrarno**, a terminology which has its roots in medieval times, when the district to the south was not as accessible as the numerous bridges now make it.

Traditionally an artisans' quarter, Oltrarno has nonetheless always contained more prosperous enclaves – many of Florence's ruling families chose to settle in this area, and nowadays some of the city's plushest shops line the streets parallel to the river's southern bank. Window-shopping is not the principal pleasure of a roam through Oltrarno, however, as this is also the district of the **Palazzo Pitti**, the Masaccio frescoes in **Santa Maria del Carmine**, Brunelleschi's marvellous church of **Santo Spirito** and – looking down from a hill to the southeast – the Romanesque **San Miniato al Monte**.

From the Ponte Vecchio to Santa Felìcita

The direct route from the city centre to the heart of Oltrarno crosses the river on the **Ponte Vecchio**, the only bridge not mined by the retreating Nazis in 1944. Built in 1345 to replace an ancient wooden bridge, the Ponte Vecchio has always been loaded with shops like those now propped over the water, but the plethora of jewellers dates from 1593, when Ferdinando I evicted the butchers' stalls then in occupation. Florence had long revered the art of the goldsmith, and several of its major artists were skilled in the craft: Ghiberti, Donatello and Cellini, for example. The third of the trio is celebrated by a bust in the centre of the bridge, the night-time meeting point for Florence's unreconstructed hippies and local lads on the make.

Santa Felìcita

The reason for Ferdinando's objection to the Ponte Vecchio's butchers was that the noisome slabs of meat lay directly beneath the corridor that Vasari had constructed between the Palazzo Vecchio and the Medici's Palazzo Pitti. It was to accommodate this corridor that Vasari stuck a portico onto the nearby **Santa Felìcita**, probably the oldest church in Florence after San Lorenzo. It's now thought that the Syrian Greek tradesmen who came to this district in the second century were the settlement's first practising Christians.

Remodelled in the sixteenth century – when it became the Medici chapel – and again in the eighteenth, the interior demands a visit for the paintings by **Pontormo** in the **Cappella Capponi**, surrounded by irritating railings immediately to the right of the door. Under the cupola are four tondoes of the *Evangelists* (Bronzino supplied the *St Mark*), while on opposite sides of the window are the

Virgin and the angel of Pontormo's *Annunciation*, the arrangement alluding to incarnation as the means by which the Light came into the world. The low level of light admitted by this window was a determining factor in the startling colour scheme of the weirdly erotic *Deposition*, one of the masterworks of Florentine Mannerism. There's no sign of the cross, the thieves, the Roman soldiers or any of the usual scene-setting devices, as the body of Christ is carried like a mournful trophy by androgynous figures clad in billows of acidic sky-blue, green and pink drapery.

Pontormo himself was every bit as strange as this picture suggests. A relentless hypochondriac – his diary is a tally of bowel disorders and other assorted ailments – he seems to have found the company of others almost intolerable, spending much of his time in a top-floor room that could be reached only by a ladder, which he drew up behind him. So eccentric was his behaviour that he was virtually mythologised by his contemporaries, whose stories are often united only by the conviction that Pontormo was a very odd case. Thus one writer attributed him with an all-consuming terror of death, while another insisted that he kept corpses in a tub as models for a *Deluge* that he was painting – an antisocial research project that allegedly brought protests from the neighbours.

Palazzo Pitti

Beyond Santa Felicita, the street opens out at Piazza Pitti, forecourt of the largest palazzo in Florence – the **Palazzo Pitti**. The man for whom this house was built, Luca Pitti, was a prominent rival of Cosimo il Vecchio, and the motive for the commission was in large part a desire to trump the Medici. The building was started around 1457, possibly using a design by Brunelleschi which the architect had intended for the Palazzo Medici but which had been rejected by Cosimo for being too grand. In time the fortunes of the Pitti declined and in 1459 they were forced to sell out to the enemy. The Pitti subsequently became the Medici's base in Florence and the building was continually expanded up to the early seventeenth century, when it finally achieved its present gargantuan bulk.

Today the Palazzo Pitti and the pavilions of the **Giardino di Bóboli** contain eight museums, of which the foremost is the **Galleria Palatina**, an art collection second in importance only to the Uffizi. As with the Uffizi, you should anticipate closure of some parts of the Pitti, a building with notorious operational problems – for example, the restoration of the facade, which has been in progress for several years now, is budgeted to cost around one hundred billion lire, or about one-third of the entire annual governmental fund for the upkeep of Italy's artistic heritage.

THE PITTI MUSEUMS

All the museums in the Pitti complex are open Tues–Sat 9am–2pm & Sun 9am–1pm, with last admission 45min before closing. The ticket for the Galleria Palatina, costing L8000, covers admission to the Appartamenti Monumentali, while the ticket for the Museo degli Argenti, costing L6000, covers admission to the Galleria del Costume and the Museo delle Porcellane – though you have to book to see the porcelain. The ticket for the Galleria d'Arte Moderna, costing L8000, admits solely to that collection.

The Galleria Palatina

Many of the paintings gathered by the Medici in the seventeenth century are now arranged in the **Galleria Palatina**, a suite of 26 rooms in one first-floor wing of the palace. Stacked three deep in places, as they would have been in the days of their acquisition, the pictures are not arranged in the sort of didactic order observed by most galleries, but rather are hung to make each room pleasurably varied. You'll need the best part of the morning to see it properly.

The art of the sixteenth century is the Palatina's real strength – in particular, the art of **Raphael** and **Titian**, with eleven pictures by the former, fourteen by the latter. When Raphael settled in Florence in 1505, he was besieged with commissions from patrons delighted to find an artist for whom the creative process involved so little agonising. In the next three years he painted scores of pictures for such people as Angelo Doni, the man who commissioned Michelangelo's *Doni Tondo* (in the Uffizi); Raphael's portraits of Doni and his wife, hung side by side, display the same unhesitating facility and perfect poise as the *Madonna of the Chair*, in which the figures are curved into the rounded shape of the picture with no sense of artificiality.

The contingent of works by Titian includes a number of his most trenchant portraits. The lecherous and scurrilous Pietro Aretino – journalist, critic, poet and one of Titian's closest friends – was so thrilled by his portrait that he gave it to Cosimo I; Titian painted him on several other occasions, sometimes using him as the model for Pontius Pilate. Also here are likenesses of Philip II of Spain and the young Cardinal Ippolito de' Medici – who fought in the defence of Vienna against the Ottomans only to be poisoned at the age of 24 – and the so-called *Portrait of an Englishman*, who scrutinises the viewer with unflinching sea-grey eyes.

Andrea del Sarto is represented in strength as well, his seventeen works including a beautifully grave *Annunciation*. Other individual works to look out for are Rosso Fiorentino's *Madonna Enthroned with Saints*, Fra' Bartolomeo's *Deposition*, a tondo of the *Madonna and Child* by Filippo Lippi, his son Filippino's *Death of Lucrezia*, a *Sleeping Cupid* by Caravaggio, and Cristofano Allori's sexy *Judith*. The outstanding piece of sculpture is Canova's *Venus Italica*, commissioned by Napoleon as a replacement for the Venus de' Medici, which he had whisked off to Paris.

Much of the rest of the first floor comprises the **Appartamenti Monumentali**, the Pitti's state rooms. They were renovated by the Dukes of Lorraine in the eighteenth century, and then by Vittore Emanuele when Florence became the country's capital, so the rooms display three distinct decorative phases. At the moment, though, a restoration of the chambers keeps this wing shut.

The Pitti's other museums

On the floor above the Palatina is the **Galleria d'Arte Moderna**, a chronological survey of primarily Tuscan art from the mid-eighteenth century to 1945. Most rewarding are the products of the *Macchiaioli*, the Italian division of the Impressionist movement; most startling, however, are the sculptures, featuring sublime kitsch such as Antonio Ciseri's *Pregnant Nun*.

The Pitti's **Museo degli Argenti**, entered from the main palace courtyard, is a museum not just of silverware – as its name implies – but of luxury artefacts in general. The lavishly frescoed reception rooms themselves fall into this category: the first hall, the Sala di Giovanni di San Giovanni, shows Lorenzo de' Medici giving refuge to the muses; the other three ceremonial rooms have trompe l'oeil paintings by seventeenth-century Bolognese artists. As for the exhibits, the least ambivalent response is likely to be aroused by Lorenzo il Magnifico's trove of antique vases, all of them marked with their owner's name. The later the date of the pieces, though, the greater the discordance between the skill of the craftsman and the taste by which it was governed; by the time you reach the end of the jewellery show on the first floor, you'll have lost all capacity to be surprised or revolted by seashell figurines, cups made from ostrich eggs, portraits in stone inlay, and the like.

Visitors without a specialist interest are unlikely to be riveted by the two remaining museums currently open. In the Palazzina della Meridiana, the eighteenth-century southern wing of the Pitti, the **Galleria del Costume** provides the opportunity to admire the dress that Eleanor of Toledo was buried in, though you can admire it easily enough in Bronzino's portrait of her in the Palazzo Vecchio. Also housed in the Meridiana is the **Collezione Contini Bonacossi** (free tours usually Thurs & Sat 9.45am – appointments have to be made a week before at the Uffizi ☎055/238.85), on long-term loan to the Pitti. Its prize pieces are its Spanish paintings, in particular Velasquez's *Water Carrier of Seville*.

The **Museo delle Porcellane**, on the other side of the Bóboli, is well displayed but dull, and can only be visited by prior arrangement at the Pitti ticket office. The **Museo delle Carrozze** (Carriage Museum) has been closed for years and, despite what the Pitti handouts tell you, will almost certainly remain so for years, to the chagrin of very few.

The Giardino di Bóboli and the Belvedere

The creation of the Pitti's enormous formal garden, the **Giardino di Bóboli** (Tues–Sun March, April, Sept & Oct 9am–5.30pm; May–Aug 9am–6.30pm; Nov–Feb 9am–4.30pm; L5000), began when the Medici took over the house, and continued into the early seventeenth century, by which stage this steep hillside had been turned into a maze of statue-strewn avenues and well-trimmed vegetation. Opened to the public in 1766, it is the only really extensive area of accessible greenery in the centre of the city, and can be one of the pleasantest spots for a midday picnic or siesta. There's a café in the gardens, but it's best to bring your own supplies.

THE BIRTH OF OPERA

The Medici pageants in the gardens of the Pitti were the last word in extravagance, and the palace has a claim to be the birthplace of the most extravagant modern performing art, **opera**. The roots of the genre are convoluted, but its ancestry certainly owes much to the singing and dancing tableaux called *intermedii*, with which the high-society Florentine weddings were padded out. Influenced by these shows, the academy known as the Camerata Fiorentina began, at the end of the sixteenth century, to blend the principles of Greek drama with a semi-musical style of declamation. The first composition recognisable as an opera is *Dafne*, written by two members of the Camerata, Jacopo Peri and Ottavio Rinucci, and performed in 1597; the earliest opera whose music has survived in its entirety is the same duo's *Euridice*, premiered in the Pitti palace on the occasion of the proxy marriage of Maria de' Medici to Henry IV.

Aligned with the central block of the palazzo, the garden's **amphitheatre** was designed in the early seventeenth century as an arena for Medici entertainments, the site having previously been laid out by Ammannati as a garden in the shape of a Roman circus. For the wedding of Cosimo III and Princess Marguerite-Louise, cousin of Louis XIV, 20,000 guests were packed onto the stone benches to watch a production that began with the appearance of a gigantic effigy of Atlas with the globe on his back; the show got under way when the planet split apart, releasing a cascade of earth that transformed the giant into the Atlas mountain. Such frivolities did little to reconcile Marguerite-Louise to either Florence or her husband, and after several acrimonious years this miserable dynastic marriage came to an effective end with her return to Paris, where she professed to care about little "as long as I never have to set eyes on the Grand Duke again".

Of all the garden's Mannerist embellishments, the most celebrated is the **Grotta del Buontalenti**, to the left of the entrance, beyond the hideous and much-reproduced statue of Cosimo I's favourite dwarf astride a giant tortoise. Embedded in the grotto's faked stalactites and encrustations are replicas of Michelangelo's *Slaves* – the originals were lodged here until 1908. Lurking in the deepest recesses of the cave, and normally viewable only from afar, is Giambologna's *Venus*, leered at by attendant imps. Another spectacular set piece is the fountain island called the **Isolotto**, which is the focal point of the far end of the gardens; from within the Bóboli the most dramatic approach is along the central cypress avenue known as the **Viottolone**, many of whose statues are Roman originals – or you come upon it quickly if you enter the Bóboli by the Porta Romana entrance, a little-used gate at the southwestern tip of the gardens.

THE BELVEDERE – AND ON TO SAN LEONARDO

The **Forte di Belvedere** (daily 9am–8pm; free), at the crest of the hill up which the gardens spread, is a star-shaped fortress built on the orders of Ferdinando I in 1590, ostensibly for the city's protection but really to intimidate the Grand Duke's subjects. The urban panorama from here is incredible, and added attractions are the exhibitions held in and around the shed-like palace in the centre of the fortress, and the summer evening film screenings. The Bóboli gate is very rarely open, so if you want to be certain of the view, approach the fort from the Costa San Giorgio, a lane which begins at the back of Santa Felicita, winding past the villa (at no. 19) that was Galileo's home from 1610 to 1631.

East from the Belvedere stretches the best-preserved stretch of Florence's fortified walls, paralleled by Via di Belvedere. South of the Belvedere, Via San Leonardo leads past olive groves to the rarely open church of **San Leonardo in Arcetri**, now the home of a beautiful thirteenth-century pulpit brought here from the church now incorporated into the Uffizi.

Casa Guidi and La Specola

Within a stone's throw of the Pitti, on the opposite side of the road, on the junction of Via Maggio and Via Romana, you'll find the home of Robert Browning and Elizabeth Barrett Browning, the **Casa Guidi** (summer Mon–Fri 9am–noon & 3–6pm; winter 3–6pm only; free, but donations welcome). It's something of a shrine to Elizabeth, who wrote much of her most popular verse here (including, naturally enough, *Casa Guidi Windows*) and died here, but it's an unatmospheric spot – virtually all the Casa Guidi's furniture went under the hammer at Sotheby's in 1913, and there's just one oil painting left to conjure the missing spirit.

There's more to enjoy on the third floor of the university buildings at Via Romana 17, in what can reasonably claim to be the strangest museum in the city. The first part of the twin-sectioned **Museo di Zoologia** (Mon, Thurs & Fri 9am–noon; closed Aug; free), popularly known as "La Specola" from the telescope on the roof, is conventional enough – a mortician's ark of animals stuffed, pickled, dessicated and dissected. It includes a hippo given to Grand Duke Pietro Leopardo, which used to reside in the Bóboli gardens, and finishes with a display of wax models of animals and human joints.

This is a hint at what lies behind the door of the section called the **Cere Anatomiche** (Tues & Sat 9am–noon; closed Aug; free). Wax arms, legs, body sections and organs cover the walls, arrayed around satin beds on which recline wax cadavers in progessive stages of deconstruction, each muscle fibre and nerve cluster moulded and dyed with absolute precision. Most of the 600 models were made between 1775 and 1814 by the artist Clemente Susini and the physiologist Felice Fontana, and were intended as teaching aids in an age when medical ethics and refrigeration techniques were not what they are today. In a room on their own, however, are some models created by one Gaetano Zumbo, a cleric from Sicily, to satisfy the hypochondriacal obsessions of Cosimo III, a Jesuit-indoctrinated bigot who regarded all genuine scientific enquiry with suspicion. Enclosed in tasteful display cabinets, they comprise four tableaux of Florence during the plague – rats teasing the intestines from green-fleshed corpses, the pink bodies of the freshly dead heaped on the suppurating semi-decomposed. It's the grisliest show in town, and a firm favourite with school parties.

Santo Spirito

Some indication of the importance of the parish of **Santo Spirito** is given by the fact that when Florence was divided into four adminstrative *quartieri* in the fourteenth century, the entire area south of the Arno was given its name. The slightly run-down square in front of Santo Spirito church, with its market stalls and cafés, encapsulates the self-sufficient character of Oltrarno, an area not hopelessly compromised by the encroachments of tourism.

Santo Spirito church

Designed by Brunelleschi as a replacement for a thirteenth-century church, **Santo Spirito church** (daily 8.30am–noon & 4–6pm) was one of his last projects, and was described by Bernini as "the most beautiful church in the world". The paper-smooth facade is just a plastering job to disguise the unfinished front, but inside it's so perfectly proportioned that nothing could seem more artless. Yet the plan is extremely sophisticated – a Latin cross with a continuous chain of 38 chapels round the outside and a line of 35 columns running without a break round the nave, transepts and chancel. Only the Baroque baldachin, about as nicely inte-grated as garden gnome in a Greek temple, disrupts the harmonics.

The best paintings are in the transepts: in the right there's Filippino Lippi's *Nerli Altarpiece*, and in the left a *St Monica and Augustinian Nuns* by Verrocchio that's virtually a study in monochrome, with black-clad nuns flocking round their black-clad paragon. Also worth a peep is the sacristy, which is entered through a vestibule that opens onto the left aisle; both rooms were designed at the end of the fifteenth century by Giuliano da Sangallo.

A fire in 1471 destroyed all the monastery with the exception of its refectory, now the home of the **Museo Santo Spirito** (Tues–Sat 9am–2pm, Sun 8am–1pm; L3000), a one-room collection comprising an assortment of carvings, many of them Romanesque, and a huge fresco of *The Crucifixion* by Orcagna and his workshop.

Santa Maria del Carmine

Nowhere is the Florentine contrast of exterior and interior as stunning as in the plain brick box of **Santa Maria del Carmine**, a couple of blocks west of Santo Spirito. Outside it's a bleak mess; inside – in the frescoes of the **Cappella Brancacci** – it provides one of Italy's great artistic thrills. The decoration of the chapel was begun in 1424 by **Masolino** and a certain Tommaso di Ser Giovanni di Mone Cassai – known ever since as **Masaccio**, a nickname meaning "Mad Tom". The former was aged 41 and the latter just 22, but within a short while the teacher was taking lessons from the supposed pupil, whose grasp of the texture of the real world, of the principles of perspective, and of the dramatic potential of the Biblical texts they were illustrating, far exceeded that of his precursors.

Three years later Masaccio was dead, but in the words of Vasari – "All the most celebrated sculptors and painters since Masaccio's day have become excellent and illustrious by studying their art in this chapel." Michelangelo used to come here to make drawings of Masaccio's scenes, and had his nose broken on the chapel steps by a young sculptor whom he enraged with his condescension.

Public taste had performed a complete about-face by the mid-eighteenth century, when it was seriously proposed that the Brancacci frescoes be removed. That suggestion was overruled but approval was given for building alterations that destroyed frescoes in the lunettes above the main scenes. The surviving scenes were blurred by smoke from a fire that destroyed much of the church and adjoining convent in 1771, and subsequent varnishings smothered them in layers of grime that continued to darken over the decades. Then in 1932 an art historian removed part of the altar that had been installed in the eighteenth century, and discovered areas of almost pristine paint; half a century later, work finally got under way to restore the chapel to the condition of the uncovered patch.

This **restoration** provided the Italian art world with one of its characteristic controversies. The scaffolding went up in 1981, but for the next three years scarcely a brush was raised. At last Olivetti waved a cheque, and the work was pretty well finished by 1988. A couple of years' delay then occurred, ostensibly because the authorities couldn't decide whether to replace that Baroque altar, though cynics maintained that somebody somewhere was making a lot of money by protracting the work – perhaps people with influence were profiting from the rental charges for scaffolding and other incidental costs. Finally the mayor of Florence forced the central government into opening the chapel to catch the anticipated influx of Masaccio fans for the 1990 World Cup.

The frescoes

The Cappella Brancacci (Mon & Wed–Sat 10am–5pm, Sun 1–5pm; L5000) is now barricaded off from the rest of the Carmine, and has to be entered through the cloister. Your L5000 allows you into the chapel, in a maximum group of thirty, for an inadequate fifteen minutes.

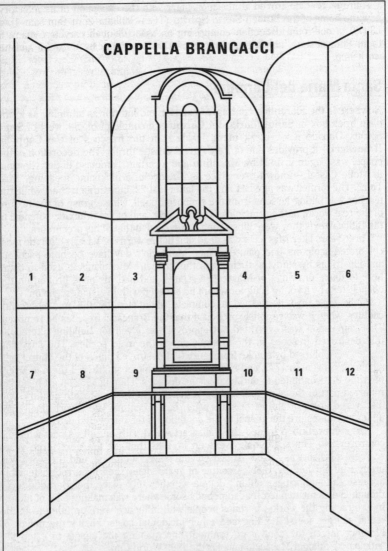

CAPPELLA BRANCACCI

1. The Expulsion 2. The Tribute Money 3. St Peter Preaching
4. The Baptism of the Neophytes 5. The Healing of the Cripple
and the Raising of Tabitha 6. The Temptation 7. St Paul Visits
St Peter in Prison 8. The Raising of the Son of Theophilus and
St Peter Enthroned 9. St Peter Healing the Sick with his Shadow
10. The Distribution of Alms and the Death of Ananias
11. The Disputation 12. St Peter Freed from Prison

The frescoes are now as startling a spectacle as the restored Sistine Chapel, the brightness and delicacy of their colours and the solidity of the figures exemplifying what Bernard Berenson singled out as the tactile quality of Florentine art. The small scene on the left of the entrance arch is the quintessence of Masaccio's art. Plenty of artists had depicted *The Expulsion of Adam and Eve* before, but none had captured the desolation of the sinners so graphically: Adam presses his hands to his face in bottomless despair, Eve raises her head and screams. The monumentalism of these stark naked figures – whose modesty was preserved by strategically placed sprigs of foliage prior to the restoration – reveals the influence of Donatello, who may have been involved in the planning of the chapel. In contrast to the emotional charge and sculptural presence of Masaccio's couple, Masolino's almost dainty *Adam and Eve*, on the opposite arch, pose as if to have their portraits painted.

Saint Peter is chief protagonist of all the remaining scenes. It's possible that the cycle was intended as propaganda on behalf of the embattled papacy, which was at the time being undermined by the **Great Schism**, with one pope holding court in Rome and another in Avignon; by celebrating the primacy of Saint Peter, the rock upon whom the Church is built, the frescoes by implication extol the apostolic succession from which the pope derives his authority. Two scenes by Masaccio are especially compelling: the *Tribute Money* (on the upper left wall), a complex narrative showing Peter, under Christ's instruction, fetching money from the mouth of a fish to pay the sum demanded by the city authorities; and the scene to the left of the altar, in which the shadow of the stern and self-possessed saint cures the infirm as it passes over them, a miracle invested with the aura of a solemn ceremonial.

The cycle was suspended when Masaccio left for Rome, where he died, and not resumed for some sixty years, when it was completed by **Filippino Lippi**. He finished the *Raising of the Emperor's Nephew* (lower left-hand wall) and painted the lower part of the wall showing the crucifixion of the saint; his most distinctive contribution, though, is *The Release of St Peter* on the right-hand side of the entrance arch, where there's a touching intimacy in the relationship between saint and counselling angel. Lippi also made a rather odd intervention on the opposite wall. To the right of the enthroned Saint Peter stands a trio of men, now identified as Masaccio, Alberti and Brunelleschi, who made a trip to Rome together. Masaccio originally painted himself touching Peter's robe, a reference to the enthroned statue of Peter in Rome, which pilgrims touch for good luck. Lippi considered the contact of the artist and saint to be improper and painted out the arm; at the moment, his fastidious addition has been allowed to remain, but you can clearly see where the arm used to be.

East of the Ponte Vecchio

On the tourist map of Florence, the Oltrarno area immediately to the **east of the Ponte Vecchio** is something of a dead zone: as with the opposite bank of the river, blocks of historic buildings were destroyed by mines left behind by the Nazis in 1944. Some characterful parts remain, however, such as the medieval **Via de' Bardi** and its continuation, **Via San Niccolò**. Following these narrow, palazzo-lined streets will take you past the obsessively eclectic **Museo Bardini** and the medieval church of **San Niccolò**, both perhaps best visited on the way up the hill to San Miniato (see overleaf).

The Museo Bardini

Like the Horne museum close by across the Arno, the **Museo Bardini** at Piazza de' Mozzi 1 (Mon, Tues & Thurs–Sat 9am–2pm, Sun 8am–1pm; L5000) was founded on the bequest of a private collector. Whereas Horne was just a moderately well-off connoisseur, his contemporary Sergio Bardini was the biggest art dealer in Italy, and was determined that no visitor to his native city should remain unaware of his success. Accordingly he ripped down the church that used to stand here and built a vast house for himself, studding it with fragments of old buildings to advertise his affinity with Florence's past. Doorways, ceiling panels and other orphaned pieces are strewn all over the place: the first-floor windows, for instance, are actually altars from a church in Pistoia. The more portable items on display are equally wide-ranging: musical instruments, carvings, ceramics, armour, carpets, pictures – if it was vaguely arty and had a price tag, Bardini collected it.

On the lower floors Tino da Camaino's *Charity* stands out from the clutter, and there's a room of funerary monuments done out like a crypt, with an altarpiece thought to be by Andrea della Robbia. Upstairs, three pieces grab the attention: a stucco, mosaic and glass relief of the *Madonna* that's probably by Donatello; a beautiful *Virgin Annunciate*, an anonymous piece from fifteenth-century Siena; and a *St Michael* painted by Antonio del Pollaiuolo.

To San Niccolò and the city gates

Beyond the Bardini museum, Via San Niccolò swings towards the church of **San Niccolò sopr'Arno**, this quarter's only interesting church. Restoration work after the 1966 flood uncovered several frescoes underneath the altars, but none is as appealing as the fifteenth-century fresco in the sacristy: known as *The Madonna of the Girdle*, it was painted probably by Baldovinetti.

In medieval times the church was close to the edge of the city, and two of Florence's fourteenth-century gates still stand in the vicinity: the dinky **Porta San Miniato**, set in a portion of the walls, and the huge **Porta San Niccolò**, overlooking the Arno. From either of these you can begin the climb **up to San Miniato** (see below): the path from Porta San Niccolò weaves up through **Piazzale Michelangelo**, with its replica *David* and bumper-to-bumper tour coaches; the more direct path from Porta San Miniato offers a choice between the steep Via del Monte alle Croce or the stepped Via di San Salvatore al Monte, both of which emerge a short distance uphill from Piazzale Michelangelo.

San Miniato al Monte

The brilliant multicoloured facade of **San Miniato al Monte** (daily 8am–noon & 2–7pm) lures troops of visitors up the hill from Oltrarno, and the church more than fulfils the promise of its distant appearance. If you don't feel up to the walk, you can take bus #13 up from the station or Duomo.

Arguably the finest Romanesque structure in Tuscany, San Miniato is also the oldest surviving church building in Florence after the Baptistery. It recently began to show signs of its age, though, and the authorities become so concerned about the dangers of subsidence that a project was initiated to shore up the downhill side of the church and the adjoining cemetery. Then, in a depressing re-run of the Piazza della Signoria fiasco, it was discovered that a degree of financial impropriety may have been involved in awarding the contract; work has now been suspended for an indefinite period.

The church's dedicatee, Saint Minias, belonged to a Christian community which settled in Florence in the third century. Legend has it that after martyrdom by decapitation the saintly corpse was seen to carry his severed head over the river and up the hill to this spot, where a shrine was subsequently erected to him. Construction of the present building began in 1013, with the foundation of a Benedictine monastery. The gorgeous marble **facade** – alluding to the Baptistery in its geometrical patterning – was added towards the end of that century and paid for by the Arte di Calimala (cloth merchants' guild), whose trade mark, a gilded eagle, perches on the roof. The mosaic of *Christ between the Virgin and St Minias* dates from the thirteenth century.

The interior
With its choir raised on a platform above the large crypt, the interior of San Miniato is like no other in the city, and its general appearance has changed little since the mid-eleventh century. The main additions and decorations in no way spoil its serenity, though the nineteenth-century recoating of the marble columns is a little lurid. The intricately patterned panels of the **pavement** are dated 1207 on the panel of the zodiac, and the lovely **tabernacle** between the choir stairs was designed in 1448 by Michelozzo, to house the miraculous Crucifix that nodded to Giovanni Gualberto (see p.92 and p.380).

Dating from a few years later is the **Cappella del Cardinale del Portogallo**, which was built into the left wall as a memorial to Cardinal James of Lusitania, who died in Florence in 1459, aged twenty-five. His chapel is a marvellous example of artistic collaboration: the basic design was by Antonio Manetti, a pupil of Brunelleschi; the tomb itself was carved by Antonio Rossellino; the *Annunciation* was painted by Baldovinetti; Antonio and Piero del Pollaiuolo produced the altarpiece (the original is now in the Uffizi); and the terracotta decoration of the ceiling was provided by Luca della Robbia.

Beyond the slender columns of the **crypt** is the church's first altar, containing the relics of Minias. The magnificently carved balustrade and pulpit in the **choir** were both created at the same time as the zodiac pavement; artists from Ravenna executed the mosaic in the apse at the end of that century. Finally, the **sacristy** is completely covered with *Scenes from the Life of St Benedict*, a beguiling fresco cycle painted by Spinello Aretino in 1387.

The city outskirts

The peripheral attractions covered in this section – the **Cascine park, Museo Stibbert**, Andrea del Sarto's *cenacolo* at **San Salvi**, and **Fiorentina's football ground** – are all a stiff walk from the centre of town, though all can be reached by *ATAF* bus. Sights lying within the city boundaries but definitely requiring transport – such as the Medici villas – are dealt with in the following chapter.

West: the Cascine

Florence's public park, the **Cascine**, begins close to the Ponte della Vittoria, a half-hour walk west of the Ponte Vecchio (or bus #17c from the Duomo, station or youth hostel). It dwindles away three kilometres downstream, at the confluence of the Arno and the Mugnone, where there's a statue of the Maharajah of

Kohlapur – he died in Florence in 1870 and the prescribed funeral rites demanded that his body be cremated at a spot where two rivers met.

Once the Medici's dairy farm (*cascina*), then a hunting reserve, this narrow strip of green mutated into a high-society venue in the eighteenth century: if there was nothing happening at the opera, all of Florence's *belle monde* turned out to promenade under the trees of the Cascine. A fountain in the park bears a dedication to Shelley, who was inspired to write his *Ode to the West Wind* while strolling here on a blustery day in 1819.

By day, Florentines take their kids out to Cascine to play on the grass or visit the small zoo, and thousands of people come out here on Tuesday mornings for the colossal **market** (see p.143). But the Cascine is not a great park by any stretch of the imagination – and it has a pretty seedy reputation. The situation isn't as bad as it has been, but junkies still shoot up here in the middle of the day, and the Cascine is emphatically not a place for a nocturnal stroll, as it has long been a playground for the city's hookers and pimps (see box opposite).

North: Museo Stibbert

About a kilometre and a half north of San Marco, at Via Stibbert 26 (bus #4 from the station), is the loopiest of Florence's museums, the **Museo Stibbert** (Mon–Wed, Fri & Sat 9am–1pm, Sun 9am–12.30pm; L5000, free on Sun). This rambling, murky mansion was the home of the half-Scottish half-Italian Frederick Stibbert, who in his twenties made a name for himself in Garibaldi's army. Later he inherited a fourteenth-century house from his mother, then bought the neighbouring mansion and joined the two together, thus creating a place big enough to accommodate the fruits of his compulsive collecting. The sixty-four rooms contain over fifty thousand items, ranging from snuff boxes to paintings by Carlo Crivelli and a possible Botticelli.

Militaria was Frederick's chief enthusiasm, and the Stibbert **armour** collection is reckoned one of the world's best. It includes Roman, Etruscan and Japanese examples, as well as a fifteenth-century *condottiere's* outfit and the armour worn by Giovanni delle Bande, retrieved from his grave in San Lorenzo in 1857. The big production number comes in the great hall, between the two houses, where a platoon of mannequins is clad in full sixteenth-century gear. Also on show is the regalia in which Napoleon was crowned King of Italy.

East: San Salvi and Campo Marte

Twenty minutes' walk beyond Piazza Beccaria (or bus #10 from the station, or #2 from Piazza San Marco) is the ex-convent of **San Salvi**, which was reopened in 1982 after the restoration of its most precious possession, the *Last Supper* by Andrea del Sarto (Tues–Sat 9am–2pm, Sun 9am–1pm; L2000). As a prelude to this picture, there's a gallery of big but otherwise unremarkable Renaissance altarpieces, a gathering of pictures by various del Sarto acolytes, and the beautiful reliefs from the tomb of Giovanni Gualberto, founder of the Vallombrosan order to whom this monastery belonged.

The tomb was smashed up by Charles V's troops in 1530 but they refused to damage the *Last Supper*, which is still in the refectory for which it was painted, accompanied by three del Sarto frescoes brought here from other churches in Florence. Painted around 1520 and evidently much influenced by Leonardo's

CRIME IN FLORENCE

There's a catchphrase much used by the Florentine press: "Firenze snaturata", meaning "Florence corrupted". It's a cry directed at both the city's violation by the tourists and its rising crime problem – two aspects of the same problem, in many eyes.

Heroin is the source of most anguish: in recent years around seventy percent of all cases heard in the city courts have been drug-related offences, and the percentage shows no sign of decreasing. Piazza Santo Spirito and Piazza Santa Croce recently became notorious for the detritus of syringes and phials found by the road-sweepers in the morning; these squares were cleaned up, but the operation amounted to little more than window-dressing. Stroll along Via de' Neri, at the back of the Palazzo Vecchio, during the midday siesta, and you'll see gear being set up in doorways and groups waiting for the man. Dealers from the *cosa nostra* strongholds of southern Italy take much of the popular blame, but the poorer half of the country provides as many victims as villains, as young southerners come up to Florence to pick up drugs from foreign dealers.

The other high-profile – and closely associated – problem is **prostitution**, with under-age, transvestite and transsexual prostitutes especially conspicuous round the station area and in the Cascine. Many of the transsexuals come here from Brazil and Argentina – for some reason, more sex-change operations are performed in Florence than in any other Italian city. Their trade covers the entire spectrum of Florentine society – many are caught up in the Florentine underworld, but some of the Florentine smart set also think it's chic to have a South American transsexual hostess for a cocktail party.

Kidnapping, on the other hand, remains a relatively hidden problem. Since 1975 there have been around thirty publicised kidnappings in Florence, but the true statistic is certainly higher. The perpetrators – often Sardinian shepherds based around Prato, up in the Mugello hills, or even in bourgeois Chianti – do not mess about, and many hostages have been returned alive but mutilated after their relatives showed reluctance to come up with the ransom. Terrified of retribution if the kidnappers find out that the authorities are party to the negotiations, the families of victims often do not inform the police.

But by far the most sensational crimes of recent years were the killings committed by the so-called **Mostro di Firenze** (Monster of Florence), one of Italy's few cases of serial murder. Between the mid-1970s and mid-1980s he hacked fourteen people to death, mostly young couples camping out on the hills above the city. Even after the killings had apparently stopped, nobody would risk camping wild in the Florence region, and houses in Chianti were still being shuttered as though to withstand a siege. Towards the end of 1993 a farmer from Mercatale was charged with the murders.

work, this is the epitome of del Sarto's soft, suave technique – emotionally undernourished for some tastes, but faultlessly carried out.

The Stadio Comunale

As befits the football team of this monument-stuffed city, **A.C. Fiorentina** play in a stadium that's listed as a building of cultural significance, the **Stadio Comunale** at Campo Marte. It was designed by Pier Luigi Nervi in 1930, as a consequence of two decisions: to create a new football club for Florence and to hold the 1934 World Cup in Italy.

The stadium was the first major sports venue to exploit the shape-making potential of reinforced concrete and its spiral ramps, cantilevered roof and slim central tower still make most other arenas look dreary. From the spectator's point of view, however, it's far from perfect: for instance, the peculiar D-shape of the stands – necessitated by the straight 200-metre sprint track – means that visibility from some parts of the ground is awful. But the architectural importance of Nervi's work meant that when Florence was chosen as one of the hosts for the 1990 World Cup there could be no question of simply building a replacement (as was done brilliantly at Bari), nor of radically altering the existing one (as happened at most grounds). Much of the seventy billion lire spent on the refurbishment of the Stadio Comunale was thus spent ensuring that the improvements did not ruin the clean modernistic lines, and most of the extra space in the all-seater stadium was created by lowering the pitch a couple of metres below its previous level, in order to insert another layer of seats where the track had been. Visitors familiar with the old ground might notice another couple of additions right behind the goals: they are water hydrants, the latest thing in Italian crowd control.

Their violet shirts might be quite natty – hence their nickname, the *Viola* – but Fiorentina are no longer one of Italy's glamour sides, even though they produced the most lavishly talented Italian currently playing – the mercurial **Roberto Baggio**, transferred to Juventus for what was then a world record transfer fee of £7,700,000, amid scenes of fervent protest in Florence. Fiorentina last won the league title in 1969, and in 1993 – the year golden boy Baggio was voted European Footballer of the Year – they suffered the ultimate ignominy. Halfway through the season they sacked the team coach, went on to win just three games out of nineteen, and were relegated for the first time in fifty-five years, despite the services of such world-class players as Brian Laudrup and Stefan Effenberg. They will probably be back in the top division soon, but for the time being most of the thrills at Campo Marte are likely to come from the visiting team rather than the *Viola* themselves.

Match tickets cost from L30,000 to L200,000 and can only be bought at the ground itself (information on ticket availability and fixtures ☎055/292.363); to get there, take bus #17 from the station.

CONSUMER'S FLORENCE

Florence might not have the metropolitan dash of Milan or Rome, but it has most of the big-city attractions you'd expect to find – plenty of **cultural events**, scores of **cafés** and **restaurants**, and a lot of very chic **shops** to give focus to the evening *passeggiata*. The main problem is one of identity, in a city whose inhabitants are heavily outnumbered by outsiders from March to October. Restaurant standards are often patchy and prices pitched at whatever level the tourists can bear, while many of the locals swear there's scarcely a single genuine Tuscan place left in the city – an exaggeration, of course, but not altogether groundless. Yet the situation is nowhere near as bad as some reports would have it, and it doesn't require much effort to have a good time in Florence, whatever your budget. As for **nightlife**, the university and the influx of language students keep things lively, and **seasonal events** such as the *Maggio Musicale* maintain Florence's standing as the pivot of cultural life in Tuscany.

Cafés, bars and pasticcerie

Pavement cafés are not really part of the Florentine scene. Smaller, less ostentatious venues are more the city's style – one-room **cafés**, **bars** and **pasticcerie**, and places that combine the functions of all three.

Predictably enough, the main concentrations are found on the big tourist streets – Via de' Tornabuoni, Via de' Panzani, Via de' Cerretani, Via Por Santa Maria, Via Guicciardini and Via dei Calzaiuoli. Many are expensive and characterless, but others, as listed below, are expensive and very good, especially when it comes to cakes and other sweet delicacies. To find places where prices are lower and non-Florentine faces fewer, only a little effort is needed: a short walk north from the Duomo gets you into the university area around Piazza San Marco, and it's just as easy to get over into Oltrarno, the most authentic quarter of the historic centre.

Most of the places listed in the first two sections below are at their busiest first thing in the morning, as the natives stop off on the way to work at a **caffè-pasticceria** for a quick coffee and a pastry such as a *budino di riso* (small rice cake) or a simple brioche or *cornetto* (croissant). Every other street in the centre has a café or bar of some sort; what follows is a guide to the best and the most popular. **Late-night** bars and cafés are covered under their own heading, while places that have music are listed in the "Nightlife" section (see p.138).

North of the river

Apollo, Piazza del Mercato Centrale. Very cool minimalist bar – metal tables, marble floor, leather benches – serving decent food. Doesn't charge extra if you sit down. Ray-Bans de rigueur.

Caffellatte, Via degli Alfani 39r. Housed in a former dairy shop, this is good for breakfast and brunch; features a wide range of teas.

Donnini, Piazza della Repubblica 15r. Smallest of the square's cafés; the hot sandwiches are the chief draw. Closed Mon.

Giacosa, Via de' Tornabuoni 83r. Public living room of Florence's gilded youth, this was the birthplace of the *Negroni* cocktail – equal parts Campari, sweet Martini and gin. Closed Mon.

Gilli, Piazza della Repubblica 39r. Across the way from the *Giubbe Rosse*, this place was founded in the 1730s and is the grandest of all Florence's cafés. Renowned mainly for its delirious cocktails. Closed Tues.

Giubbe Rosse, Piazza della Repubblica 13–14r. A former hang-out of the Florentine intellectual elite, this swanky café-restaurant is now patronised most conspicuously by the American high-income set. Open until 1.30am; closed Thurs.

Gran Caffè San Marco, Piazza San Marco. Busy café-bar-pasticceria; a standard stopoff for the university students on their way home.

Manaresi, Via de' Lamberti 16r. In the opinion of some, the coffee roasted, milled and poured at this place, at the back of Orsanmichele, is the best in the city; serves snacks too.

Paszkowski, Piazza della Repubblica 6r. Third of the Repubblica high-life quartet; big, plush and more than slightly sterile. Closed Mon.

Penna, Borgo degli Albizi 39r. One of the contenders for the title of best pasticceria in Florence.

Procacci, Via de' Tornabuoni 64r. Famous café-shop that doesn't serve coffee, just cold drinks. Its fame comes from the extraordinary truffle rolls (*tartufati*), which are delicious if not exactly filling. Closed Mon.

Rivoire, Piazza Signoria 5r. A classy and very expensive café, with outdoor tables in summer. Popular with tourists and Florentines alike, it specialises in chocolate and pastries: go for their *cantuccini con vin santo* – hard almond biscuits soaked in sweet white wine. Closed Mon.

Robin Hood's Bar, Via dell'Oriuolo 59r. English-style pub, serving a range of beers and all-day English breakfast; 30 percent reductions 6–9pm.

Ruggini, Via de' Neri 76r. Close to the Uffizi; smart without being intimidating.

Caffè Strozzi, Piazza Strozzi 16r. Stylish in a posey sort of way, but the outdoor tables are good for viewing the streetlife. Closed Mon.

Oltrarno

Cabiria, Piazza Santo Spirito. Regular café-bar, which has a room covered with an intriguing range of artists' proposals for the decoration of the still blank facade of Santo Spirito church.

Caffè, Piazza Pitti 11–12r. Right opposite the Pitti Palace, this is as elegant a café as any in Tuscany, with huge antique tables and benches. You pay a fair whack for this decor – even more for the summer outside tables – but it's as restful and diverting a place to read and recover as you'll find. Closed Wed.

Cennini, Borgo San Jacopo 51r. Tiny, immaculate café, with perfect coffee and pastries. Closed Mon.

Pasticceria Maioli, Via Guicciardini 43r. A less expensive place to stop for a home-made pastry after the rigours of the Pitti. Closed Tues.

Maria, Piazza Nazario Sauro 19r. Excellent spot for a stand-up breakfast of home-made brioche and coffee. Closed Mon.

Caffè Santa Trìnita, Via Maggio 2r. Just over Santa Trìnita bridge, this spacious, marble-tabled café varies its clientele through the day – quiet in the earlier part of the day, more teen-oriented later on.

Late-night bars and cafés

Dolce Vita, Piazza del Carmine. Trendy bar that's often a venue for small-scale art exhibitions; open Mon–Sat 10pm–1am.

Rifrullo, Via San Niccolò 55r. Calls itself a pub – indicative of its affluent young clientele – and has a garden that's open in summer. It shares the building with a small family-run *latteria* which makes ice cream on the premises. Closed Wed.

Sant'Ambrogio Caffè, Piazza Sant'Ambrogio 7. Designer bar, similar in feel to the *Dolce Vita*, but less intimidating for novices. Closes 1am.

Tiratoio, Piazza de' Nerli. Near to the *Dolce Vita*, a large easy-going place, with a couple of video jukeboxes and a wide range of food. Closes around midnight.

Video Diva, Via San Zanobi 114r. Always packed with students from the nearby university; serves good cocktails; daily 9.30pm–1.30am.

Gelaterie

Devotees of Italian ice cream will find plenty of occasions to sample some wacky concoctions without straying far off the main drags – though, as with the bars and cafés, the most rewarding spots are less central.

Badiani, Viale dei Mille 20r. Known for its eggy *Buontalenti* ice cream, the recipe of which is known only to the proprietors; closed Tues.

Banchi, Via dei Banchi 14r. Close to Santa Maria Novella, this is known not so much for its ice creams as for its wonderful *granite* – fragmented ice soaked in coffee or fruit juice. Closed Sun.

Bondi, Via Nazionale 61r. Some of the daftest concoctions in town – rhubarb, for instance, or vanilla-orange-anise. Closed Mon.

Festival del Gelato, Via del Corso 75r. Over 100 varieties, with some very exotic combinations; good *semifreddi*. Closed Mon.

Frilli, Via San Niccolò 57. Excellent ice creams made from seasonal fruit. Closed Wed.

Il Giardino delle Delizie, Piazza della Felicità 3r. Does a gorgeous chocolate ice cream. Closed Mon.

Perchè No!, Via de' Tavolini 19r. Very central *gelateria*; go for the rum-laced *tiramisù* ice cream. Closed Tues.

Pomposi, Via dei Calzaiuoli 9r. Small selection, but great fruit flavours – including a delicious kiwi fruit. Closed Sun.

Vivoli, Via Isola delle Stinche 7r. Operating from deceptively unprepossessing premises in a side street close to Santa Croce, this is the best ice cream maker in Florence – and some say in Italy. At least one daily visit is a must. Closed Mon and Aug.

Snacks

Bars and cafés are far from being the only places where you can get a quick bite to eat in Florence. One of the focal points of a Florentine parish is the **vinaio**, an institution that's part wine cellar, part snack bar and part social centre, where the typical customer calls in for a quick chat, a glass of wine and a few *crostini* (bread with savoury topping). Another option for a rapid filler is the **friggitoria**, an approximate equivalent of the fish and chip shop, serving fried food such as *polenta* (maize-cake) and croquettes; these are often so basic they don't even have a name.

A good alternative to the trattoria is the **rosticceria**, a sort of delicatessen serving first courses and roast meat dishes; usually these are takeaway places, but there are seats at the ones we've listed. **Pizza** by the slice (*a taglio*), a routine tourist stand-by, often amounts to just a slab of dough with a smear of tomato paste, but you can get something a touch more tasty at the addresses below. Most of the places given in this section are open from around 8am to 8pm from Monday to Saturday.

Note also that *alimentari* and wine shops (listed below) often sell sandwiches and local delicacies, especially pastries.

Vinaii

La Mescita, Via degli Alfani 70r. Low-key student bar in the university area; serves stuffed tomatoes and a range of other vegetables in addition to the traditional *crostini*.

Piccolo Vinaio, Via Castellani 25. At the back of the Palazzo Vecchio; the only space for tables is on the pavement outside, so if the weather's lousy the bar doesn't open. Try their *panzanella*, a salad made with stale bread, onions and parsley.

Il Vecchio Vinaio, Via de' Neri 65r. Rough and ready joint, close to the Uffizi.

Vineria, Via dei Cimatori 38r. A perfect example of the Florentine *vinaio*, just off Via dei Calzaiuoli.

Friggitorie, rosticcerie and takeaway pizza

Aliseo, Via dei Serragli 75r. Decent *rosticceria*, close to the Carmine; closed Mon.

Il Fornaio Renzo, Via Guicciardini 3. Best place for a pizza slice in the Pitti area.

Luisa, Via Sant'Antonino 50. Sells slices of pizza as well as the traditional *friggitoria* fare.

Alla Marchigiana, Via del Corso 60r. Good source of takeaway pizza in the centre of town; closed Tues.

Da Moreno, Via Val di Lamona. Busy *rosticceria* at the back of the *Porcellino* market.

Rosticceria la Spada, Via della Spada 62. Recommended place near S. Maria Novella.

Via de' Neri 40r. Calls itself a *friggitoria*, but in fact serves virtually nothing but pizza.

Via de' Neri 74. Midway between a *rosticceria* and a trattoria.

Volta di San Piero 5. Highly recommended place in a tiny alley off Borgo degli Albizi (between the Duomo and Sant'Ambrogio). Serves hamburgers, sausages and salads and you can wash your snack down with a glass of wine from *All'Antico Noè*, in front of the *friggitoria*, or with a coffee from the bar on the corner with Via dell'Oriuolo.

Tripe, lamprey and fast food

Fans of Florentine **tripe or lamprey sandwiches** extol the virtues of the stalls that set up at the Mercato Centrale, in Piazza dei Cimatori and behind the *Porcellino* market on weekdays.

There's a variety of places for hamburger addicts, but for more Italianate **fast food**, try *Italy & Italy* in Piazza della Stazione 25r, in front of the train station, where spaghetti and pizza are churned out at the speed of Big Macs.

Food markets, shops and wine

An obvious and enjoyable way to cut down costs is to put together a picnic and retire to the Bóboli gardens or squares such as Piazza Santissima Annunziata, Piazza Santa Croce or Piazza Santa Maria Novella.

For **provisions**, the easiest option is to call in at the **Mercato Centrale** by San Lorenzo church (Mon–Sat 7am–2pm, plus Sat 4–8pm), where everything you could possibly need can be bought under one roof – bread, ham, cheese, fruit, wine. Almost as comprehensive, and even cheaper, is the **Mercato Sant' Ambrogio** over by Santa Croce (Mon–Fri 7am–2pm). For fresh fruit and vegetables, you could drop by at **Piazza Santo Spirito**, where there are usually a few stalls run by local farmers (Mon–Sat 7am–1pm).

If you're right in the thick of the main sights with closing time approaching, **Via dei Tavolini**, off Via dei Calzaiuoli, is a good central street in which to assemble a picnic: *Grana Market* at 11r has a fabulous cheese selection, *Chellini* at 1r is a good *alimentari*, and *Semelino* at 18r bakes wonderful bread.

Every district has its **alimentari**, which in addition to selling the choicest Tuscan produce might also provide sandwiches. The simply named *Alimentari*, close to Santa Trinita at Via Parione 19, prepares perhaps the most delicious sandwiches in town (eg smoked salmon and stracchino cheese), and has a few seats, so you can linger over a glass of wine. *Vera*, at the southern end of Ponte Santa Trinita at Piazza Frescobaldi 3r, takes the prize for the ultimate Florentine deli; other excellent central *alimentari* include *Tassini* at Borgo Santi Apostoli 24r and *Alessi Paride* at Via delle Oche 27–29r.

If the stalls and the *alimentari* are shut, there's the last resort of the *Standa* **supermarkets** at Viale dei Mille 140, Via Pietrapiana 42–44 and Via de' Panzi 31 (Mon 2–8pm, Tues–Sun 9am–8pm).

Wine outlets

Alessi Paride, Via delle Oche 27–29r. Renowned for its vast stocks of Tuscan wines – one room is stacked with nothing but Chianti. Closed Sun, plus Sat in summer.

Bottigliera, Via de' Banchi 55–57. Wide choice of mainly Tuscan and northern Italian wines. Closed Mon morning & Sat afternoon in summer, and Aug.

Cantina Guidi, Viale dei Mille 69. Wine is stacked so high here that you have to go up into a kind of loft to reach the upper shelves.

Cantinone del Gallo Nero, Via Santo Spirito 6r. Top-of-the-range local wines.

Fiaschetteria Zanobini, Via Sant'Antonino 47. Not far from the Mercato Centrale. Tuscan wines predominate, and there's a small bar where you can taste before buying. Closed Sun.

Murgia Florio, Piazza Santa Maria Novella 15. Easily missed, this cramped but well-stocked wine store is tucked under the arcade opposite Santa Maria Novella church. Closed Mon morning plus Sat afternoon in summer.

R. F., Via Ghibellina 142. Probably the best place for Italian spirits.

Restaurants

In gastronomic circles, Florentine cuisine is accorded as much reverence as Florentine art, a reverence encapsulated in the myth that French eating habits acquired their sophistication in the wake of Catherine de' Medici's marriage to the future Henry II of France. In fact, Florentine food has always been characterised by modest raw materials and simple technique – beefsteak (*bistecca*), tripe (*trippa*) and liver (*fegato*) are typical ingredients, while grilling (*alla Fiorentina*) is a favoured method of preparation. In addition, white beans (*fagioli*) will feature on most menus, either on their own, garnished with liberal quantities of local olive oil, or as the basis of such dishes as *ribollita* soup.

Unfussy it might be, but quality cooking doesn't come cheap in Florence – most of the restaurants that meet with local approval cost L40,000-plus per person, wine included. Yet there are some decent low-budget places serving food that at least gives some idea of the region's characteristic dishes, and even the simplest trattoria should offer *bistecca alla Fiorentina* – though you should bear in mind that this dish is priced per hundred grammes, so your bill will be considerably higher than the figure written on the menu. Another thing to be aware of is that many restaurants will only serve full meals – so check the menu outside if you're thinking of just popping in for a quick lunchtime plate of pasta.

As a very rough guideline, the cheapest places tend to be near the station, the best places on or near the main central streets, and the best mid-range restaurants tucked away in alleys on the north of the river or over in Oltrarno.

Station, market and Santa Maria Novella areas

Antellesi, Via Faenza 9r. Constantly changing menu of Florentine specialities, served in a fifteenth-century building just a few steps from the entrance to the Medici chapels. Run by an expat Arizonan and her Florentine chef husband, this is one of the best and friendliest restaurants in the area. Around L30,000. Closed Sun.

Antichi Cancelli, Via Faenza 73r. Not a gourmet experience, but more than tolerable at the price. Closed Mon.

Il Biribisso, Via dell'Albero 38r. Just off Via della Scala, to the south of the station; offers one of the best low-price set menus in Florence.

Il Contadino, Via Palazzuolo 69r. Very basic meals at around L15,000; often a lot of backpackers in the queue. Closed Sat & Aug.

Da Giorgio, Via Palazzuolo 100r. Another bargain basement joint. Closed Sun.

Gozzi, Piazza San Lorenzo 8r. Over the road from the market, this is a fairly inexpensive, homely trattoria.

Da Mario, Via Rosina 2r. Popular with students and market workers, so be prepared to queue and share a table; atmosphere is friendly and the prices low. Closed Sun & Aug.

Mensa Universitaria, Via San Gallo 25a. Not far from the San Lorenzo market, this is the cheapest deal in town – L8000 for two-course meal plus fruit and drink. Open to all student card holders Mon–Sat noon–2.15pm and 6.45–8.45pm; closed mid-July to mid-Sept. There are smaller *mensas* at Via dei Servi 25a (same hours) and at Piazza Santissima Annunziata 2 (lunchtime only).

Palle d'Oro. Via Sant'Antonio 43r. Plainest possible type of trattoria; besides full meals, they do sandwiches to take away.

Pepe Verde, Piazza del Mercato 17–18r. Bar/café/low-cost eatery, with mainly young clientele. Closed Wed & two weeks in Aug.

Za-za, Piazza del Mercato 26r. Set up in 1977, *Za-Za* has made itself a good reputation; a few tables on ground level and a bigger canteen below; *fettunta con fagioli* (olive oil and white beans on bread) is a speciality, but it requires a strong stomach. Closed Sun & Aug 1–21.

OVER L40,000

La Lampara, Via Nazionale 36r (☎055/215.164). Don't be put off by the multilingual menus – the food is very good (around L45,000 per head) and the waiters chattily attentive. Packed with locals at lunchtime and evening – so try to book a table.

City Centre

Acqua al Due, Via dell'Acqua 2r. Always packed, chiefly on account of its *assaggio di primi* – a succession of pasta dishes shared by everyone at the table (L10,000 per person). Closed Mon.

Antico Fattore, Via Lambertesca 1–3r. Simple Tuscan dishes dominate the menu, and the soups are particularly good; close to the Piazza della Signoria, but not as expensive as the locale might suggest. Grim service though. Closed Sun plus Sat in summer, Mon in winter, and Aug.

Belle Donne, Via delle Belle Donne 16r. Bustling, basic trattoria with blackboard menu; especially busy at lunchtime. Closed Sat & Sun.

La Bussola, Via Porta Rossa 58r. Fashionable joint whose main attraction is that it stays open until past 2am every night except Monday.

Il Cuscussù, Via Farini 2a (☎055/241.890). Florence's kosher restaurant is on the first floor of the building next door to the synagogue, some distance east of the centre near Piazza D'Azeglio. Specialities of Jewish cuisine from Livorno, Rome and Ferrara include *cuscus*, goulash and *spaghetti al paté di olive*. Usually advisable to book. A full meal should cost under L40,000. Closed Sun.

Da Ganino, Piazza dei Cimatori 4r (☎055/214.125). Produces wonderful home-made pastas and desserts; *osteria* atmosphere, *ristorante* prices. In summer, when tables are moved out onto the tiny square, it's essential to book.

I Ghibellini, Via San Pier Maggiore 8r. Inexpensive but always crowded ristorante-pizzeria, with some pleasant outside tables if you strike lucky.

Latini, Via Palchetti 6r. Good local fare in semi-rustic atmosphere; always busy – turn up after 8pm and you'll have to queue. Closed Mon.

Alle Mossacce, Via del Proconsolo 55r. Once the fashionable haunt of Florence's young artists, who occasionally paid for their meals with a painting or two; the bohemian element has since fled, and the food is nothing exceptional, but it's inexpensive by Florentine standards. Closed Sun, and Aug 1–19.

Pizza Nuti, Borgo San Lorenzo 39r. Massive place that claims to be the oldest trattoria in town; the menu isn't limited to pizzas and prices are reasonable – though the service often isn't.

Silvio, Via del Parione 74r. Mid-market and straightforward in its menu, this is one of the best places in town for fish. Closed Sun.

Sostanza, Via della Porcellana 25r. Solid Tuscan fare (*trippa alla Fiorentina*, *bistecca alla Fiorentina*) at solid Tuscan prices – L30,000 and upwards. Closed Sat, Sun & Aug.

OVER L40,000

Cantinetta Antinori, Piazza Antinori 3r. Extremely classy bar-restaurant, many of whose dishes use wine, cheese and oil from the Antinori estates. Costs upward of L50,000; booking always a good idea (☎055/292.234). Closed Sat, Sun & Aug.

Coco Lezzone, Via del Parioncino 26r. Self-consciously plain, white-tiled, noisy trattoria near Santa Trinita; go for the *porcini* (wild mushroom) pasta. A really full meal should come in at around L50,000. Closed Sat & Sun in summer, Tues evening & all Sun in winter, and Aug.

Garga, Via del Moro 48r. Small place that serves up some inventive variations on Tuscan standards – such as *pasta Lorenzo il Magnifico*, with a parmesan and mint sauce. Minimum L50,000 per person. Open until midnight Tues–Sun.

Santa Croce area

Benvenuto, Via Mosca 16r, off Via de' Neri. Don't be misled by the entrance, which looks more like the doorway to a delicatessen than a trattoria; the *gnocchi* and *arista* are delicious. Closed Sun & Wed.

Cantina Sabrosa, Via Ghibellina 70r. Recently opened Mexican restaurant.

Danny Rock, Via Pandolfini 13. Looks a bit like a fast-food place with its green metal chairs but employs a French cook who creates marvellous crêpes, among other things; large suspended screens show concerts and sporting events; open from 7.30pm to 1am (2am Sat).

La Maremmana, Via de' Macci 77r. Very good set menus for L18,000, L25,000 and L30,000. Closed Sun & Aug.

Bar Santa Croce, Borgo Santa Croce 31r. Offers a good lunchtime L18,000 *menu fixe* and has a highly esteemed kitchen. Closed Sun.

OVER L40,000

Il Cibrèo, Via de' Macci 118r. Influenced by nouvelle cuisine in its menu and its prices, but not too precious; desserts are wonderful. Allow around L65,000 in the posh part of the restaurant – but round the corner in Via del Verrocchio there's the entrance to a backroom section where the menu is basically the same but the prices are lower. Closed Sun & Mon, plus Aug.

Enoteca Pinchiorri, Via Ghibellina 87 (☎055/242.777). The unsurpassed wine cellar and imaginative nouvelle-Tuscan cuisine of the *Pinchiorri* have earned it the title Best Restaurant in Italy in most Italian gastronomic guides – though the odd writer rubbishes the pomp and ceremony. It's essential to book if you want the privilege of dropping at least L100,000 to make up your own mind. Closed Sun, Mon lunchtime, Aug & Christmas.

Da Noi, Via Fiesolana 46r (☎055/242.917). Run by ex-employees of the *Pinchiorri*; similar fare at about two-thirds of the cost, sometimes less. Again, essential to book. Closed Sun, Mon & Aug.

La Vie en Rose, Borgo Allegri 68r. Excellent game dishes in this cosy little restaurant, where a full meal with wine will set you back in the region of L50,000. Closed Tues & Sun.

East of Santa Croce

Tavola Calda, Sant'Ambrogio market. A superb daytime place for mouthwatering Tuscan dishes such as *topini di patate*, a first course of potatoes topped with a variety of sauces. A full three-course lunch costs just L18,000.

Oltrarno

Angiolino, Via Santo Spirito 36r. Erratic service and cooking – can be good, can be dreadful. Closed Sun & Mon.

Cantinone del Gallo Nero, Via Santo Spirito 6r. Downstairs from an easily missed door, this place serves appetisers, first courses and special *crostini*; its main claim to fame, though, is as a stockist of the best Tuscan wines – wine at the table is sold by the bottle, starting at L1000. Closed Sun & Aug.

Trattoria del Carmine, Piazza del Carmine 18r. Reasonable food, reasonable prices, charmless service. Closed Sun in winter, Sat & Sun in summer, plus Aug.

Trattoria Casalinga, Via Michelozzi 9r. About the best low-cost authentic Tuscan dishes in town; understandably popular despite the drop-dead demeanour cultivated by the workforce. The *lesso con le cipolle* (chopped beef with onions) is marvellous. Closed Sun.

Cinghiale Bianco, Borgo San Jacopo 43r. As the name tells you, wild boar is the pride of this restaurant. Closed Wed.

Dante, Piazza Nazario Sauro 10r. Popular pizzeria that also serves around a dozen types of spaghetti. Closed Wed.

Trattoria Oreste, Piazza Santo Spirito. A place to go to in fine weather, when it sets up its tables on the square; the *menu fixe* is good, as is the *salsiccia e fagioli* – sausage and beans Tuscan-style.

Perbacco, Borgo Tegolaio 21r. Offers both a full and·a L15,000 half-portion *menu fixe* at lunchtime, an option that invariably packs the place out; in the evenings it's possible to get an excellent *à la carte* meal for under L25,000.

Dei Quattro Leoni, Via Vellutini 1r. A genuine, extremely plain trattoria with irresistible prices – around L20,000. As a starter try the *finocchiona*, a type of Tuscan salami. Closed Sun & Aug.

Trattoria i Raddi, Via Ardiglione 47r. One of the area's newer places, recommended for its *peposa*, veal casseroled with pepper but no salt.

Ruggero, Via Senese 89r. Magnificent *pappa al pomodoro* and *braciola della casa* more than make up for the frosty staff and the rather distant location, beyond the tip of the Bóboli gardens. Closed Tues & Aug.

San Tomaso, Via Romana 80r. Good macrobiotic restaurant.

Trattoria le Sorelle, Via San Niccolò 30r. Unpretentious local restaurant; specialises in salami and *penne*. Beware high charges for drinks, though. Closed Thurs.

I Tarocchi, Via de' Renai 12r. Busy restaurant-pizzeria. Closed Mon.

Alla Vecchia Bettola, Viale Lodovico Ariosto 32r. Long trestle tables give this place something of the atmosphere of a drinking den, which is what it once was; the menu is a good repertoire of Tuscan meat dishes. Closed Sun & Mon.

OVER L40,000

Le Quattro Stagioni, Via Maggio 61r. A fair number of the district's antique dealers seem to gravitate here of an evening, which gives you some idea of the tone. The risotto and gnocchi are extremely good. Closed Sun, Aug & Dec 23–March 1.

Nightlife and cultural events

Florence has a reputation for catering primarily to the middle-aged and affluent, but like every university town it has its pockets of activity, and by hanging around the San Marco area you should pick up news of any impromptu term-time events. Full details of the city's dependable venues are given below; for up-to-the-minute **information** about what's on, call in at *Box Office* at Via della Pergola 10ar, or the Via Cavour tourist office. Tickets for most events are available at the offices and agencies listed in the box below.

Florence's cultural impresarios make a good job of ensuring that the city doesn't ossify. Art exhibitions are held all through the year in various galleries and palazzi, and seasons of opera, theatre and ballet performances punctuate the year, as do one-off concerts of classical music, folk and jazz. In addition to *Box Office*, you can usually find information in English about concerts and shows at the city council kiosk inside the Palazzo Vecchio, or at the agencies listed in the box below; otherwise, keep your eyes peeled for advertising posters, or take a look at monthly magazines such as *Metró, Time Off* or *Firenze Spettacolo*.

The streets of central Florence are generally safe at night, but women should be wary of strolling through the red-light districts alone – the station area and Piazza Ognissanti have a particularly dodgy reputation, and kerb-crawling is prev-

TICKET OFFICES AND AGENCIES

Box Office, Via della Pergola 10ar (☎055/242.361).

Agenzia Universalturismo, Via Speziali 7r (☎055/217.241).

Agenzia Arno, Piazza degli Ottaviani 7r (☎055/219.512).

Agenzia Newtours, Via G. Monaco 20a (☎055/321.155)

Agenzia Globus, Piazza Santa Trinita 2r (☎055/214.992).

alent on the *viali*, the wide avenues circling the centre (not that anyone would want to wander along them at night). Unaccompanied tourists of either gender should stay well clear of the Cascine park at night.

Live music venues

Auditorium Flog, Via Mercati 24. Hottest rock and jazz venue.

Betty Boop, Via Alfani 26r. Jazz and rock, plus cabaret acts on Thurs & Sun; especially recommended; membership at the door; closed Mon.

Chiodo Fisso, Via Dante Alighieri 16r. A good spot for folk guitar music and occasionally for jazz – the wine's good as well; open every night.

Dottor No, Via dei Benci 19r. Underground music venue open all night.

Drunk Ladder, Piazza IV Novembre, Sesto Fiorentino (bus #28). Video-pub (with English beer) which hosts jazz groups from time to time; open from 8pm every night except Wednesday.

Eskimo, Via dei Canaccii 12r. Live music and alternative theatre; open 9.30pm–2.30am.

Genius, Via San Gallo 22r. Jazz sessions organised by the local Red Bean Jazz group, every night except Sat from 10pm; serves good food and drink, but the decor is off-puttingly cold.

Jazz Club, Via Nuova dei Caccuni 3. One of Florence's two main jazz venues. Buses #6, 12, 14 or 23.

Mexcal, Via Ghibellina 69r. Latin American sounds; open 9pm–3am.

Palasport, Viale Paoli. Huge venue for international megastars.

Pegaso, Via Palazzuolo 82r. Jazz sets from 10pm to 2.30am; inexpensive membership.

Rex Cafe, Via Fiesolano 25r. Trendy music bar open 7pm–late.

Salt Peanuts, Piazza Santa Maria Novella 26r. The other main jazz joint.

Stonehenge, Via dell'Amorino 16r. Rock venue, operating under the slogan "Do it, then come here"; open from 10pm to 4am every night except Mon.

Teatro Tenda, Lungarno Aldo Moro. Forty-something rockers' venue.

Clubs and discos

Andromeda, Via dei Cimatori 13. Changes its look every year; closed Mon.

Caffè Voltaire, Via della Scala 9r. Took its name from the Dadaist meeting place in Zurich and is the base of an association well known for its left-wing political commitments and work in the field of international relations; a tourist agency operates from one of the rooms during the day, and temporary exhibitions and video shows are regular events; an annual membership is compulsory but inexpensive – which is more than can be said for its restaurant.

KGB, Borgo Albizi 9. Vaguely underground/avant-garde, and entirely yuppie-free; the interior design is constantly changing; open from 10pm into the small hours every night, except for a few weeks in July/Aug.

Manila, Piazza Matteucci, Campo di Bisenzio. A strongly Afro-Cuban disco that doubles as a showcase for young fashion designers and better-known names in the field; open Fri–Sun.

Meccanò, Piazza Vittorio Veneto. Florence's best and most popular disco, by the entrance to the Cascine. Closed Mon & Wed.

Rockafe, Borgo Albizi 66r. Solid mainstream disco; open Thurs–Sun.

Space Electronic, Via Palazzuolo 37. The first disco to introduce videos in Florence and has remained at the top of the tree; now fitted out with a glass dance floor and lasers, it's a favourite with young foreigners; open every night.

Tenax, Via Pratese 46a, Perètola. The biggest disco in Florence, and one of its leading venues for new and established bands – the cocktails are great too; open Wed–Sun.

Xenon, Via Pisani 683, Scandicci. Plays straight disco on weekends and stronger stuff on Friday nights; mainly for the teenies.

Yab Yum, Via de' Sassetti 5r. Right in the centre, so its vast dance floor is heaving in summer; closed Mon.

GAY CLUBS

Crisco Club, Via S. Egidio 42a. Men only pub/bar.

Flamingo, Via Pandolfini 26. Mixed gay and lesbian club.

Tabasco, Piazza Santa Cecilia 3r. Men only, and rather seedier than the Flamingo.

Classical music – festivals and concerts

The highlight of Florence's cultural calendar is undoubtedly the **Maggio Musicale Fiorentino,** one of Europe's leading festivals of opera and classical music; confusingly, it isn't limited to May (*Maggio*), but lasts from late April to early July. The *Maggio* has its own orchestra, chorus and ballet company, whose performances alternate with guest appearances from foreign ensembles such as the BBC Symphony Orchestra. Events are staged at the *Teatro Comunale* (or its Teatro Piccolo), the *Teatro della Pergola,* the *Palazzo dei Congressi* (by the train station), the *Teatro Verdi* and occasionally in the Bóboli gardens – and tickets don't come cheap. Information and tickets can be obtained from the festival HQ in the *Teatro Comunale,* at Corso Italia 16 (Tues–Sun 9am–1pm & 2.30–4.30pm; ☎055/277.9236). See p.142 for addresses of the theatres themselves.

Slightly less exclusive is the **Estate Fiesolana,** a festival concentrating more on chamber and symphonic music, held in Fiesole every summer – usually from June to late August. Films and theatre groups are also featured, and most events are held in the open-air *Teatro Romano.*

Outside these festival seasons, numerous other **concerts and events** are held at venues all over Florence, often in major churches. The *Teatro Comunale*'s season of recitals and concertos begins in September, lasting until mid-December; the opera season then begins, finishing in mid-January; and from then until April the *Comunale* holds a series of symphony concerts. There's also opera (and ballet) at the *Teatro Verdi* from January to April. Other concerts are arranged by the *Orchestra Regionale Toscana* (whose hall is Santo Stefano church, by the Ponte Vecchio), the *Amici della Musica* (usually at the *Teatro della Pergola*), the *Teatro di Rifredi* and the *Musicus Concentus,* a classical music company which organises concerts from October to June at various venues in the city (sometimes diversifying into jazz).

Theatre

If your Italian is up to a performance of the plays of Machiavelli or Pirandello in the original, Florence's theatres offer year-round entertainment, some of it riskier than the repertoire of the concert halls. In addition to the places listed below, vari-

FLORENCE'S FESTIVALS

Florence's various cultural festivals are covered in the previous sections; what follows is a rundown on its more folkloric events.

Scioppio del Carro

The first major folk festival of the year is Easter Sunday's **Scioppio del Carro** (Explosion of the Cart), when a cartload of fireworks is hauled by six white oxen from the Porta a Prato to the Duomo; there, during the Gloria of the midday mass, the whole lot is set off by a "dove" that whizzes down a wire from the high altar. The origins of this incendiary descent of the Holy Spirit lie with one Pazzino de' Pazzi, leader of the Florentine contingent on the First Crusade. On getting back to Florence he was entrusted with the care of the flame of Holy Saturday, an honorary office which he turned into something more festive by rigging up a ceremonial wagon to transport the flame round the city. His descendants continued to manage the festival until the Pazzi conspiracy of 1478, which of course lost them the office. Since then, the city authorities have taken care of business.

Festa del Grillo

On the first Sunday after Ascension Day (forty days after Easter), the **Festa del Grillo** (Festival of the Cricket) is held in the Cascine park. In amongst the stalls and the picnickers you'll find people selling tiny wooden cages containing crickets, which are then released onto the grass – a ritual that may hark back to the days when farmers had to scour their land for locusts, or to the tradition of men placing a cricket on the door of their lovers to serenade them.

Saint John's Day and the Calcio Storico

The saint's day of **John the Baptist**, Florence's patron, is June 24 – the occasion for a massive fireworks display up on Piazzale Michelangelo, and for the first game of the **Calcio Storico**. Played in sixteenth-century costume to perpetuate the memory of a game played during the siege of 1530, this uniquely Florentine mayhem is a three-match series played in this last week of June, with fixtures usually held in Piazza Santa Croce (scene of that first match) and Piazza della Signoria. Each of the four historic quarters fields a team, Santa Croce playing in green, San Giovanni in red, Santa Maria Novella in blue and Santo Spirito in grossly impractical white. Prize for the winning side is a calf, which gets roasted in a street party after the tournament and shared among the four teams and the inhabitants of the winning quarter.

Festa delle Rificolone

The **Festa delle Rificolone** (Festival of the Lanterns) takes place on the Virgin's birthday, September 7, with a procession of children to Piazza Santissima Annunziata. Each child carries a coloured paper lantern with a candle inside it – a throwback to the days when people from the surrounding countryside would troop by lantern-light into the city for the Feast of the Virgin. The procession is followed by a parade of floats and street parties.

Festa dell'Unità

October's **Festa dell'Unità** is part of a nationwide celebration run by the Italian communists. Florence's is the biggest event after Bologna's, with loads of political stalls and restaurant-marquees. *Box Office* will have details of venues, while news about the *Feste* and other political events in Florence can be found in *Anteprima*, a local supplement published with Friday's edition of the communist daily *L'Unità*.

ous halls and disused churches are enlisted for one-off performances – keep an eye out for posters, or drop into *Box Office*.

Teatro Comunale, Corso Italia 16 (☎055/277.9236). Mainstream, uncontentious theatre.

Teatro Niccolini, Via Ricasoli 3 (☎055/239.6653). One of the oldest in town, but its repertoire has a decidedly modern look, featuring from October to May a mixture of innovative Italian works and milestones of contemporary drama.

Teatro Nuovo Variety, Via del Madonnone 47 (☎055/676.942). Although not quite in the *Pergola*'s league, the *Variety* often has good Italian touring companies – and occasional foreign groups too.

Teatro della Pergola, Via della Pergola 12 (☎055/247.9651). Florence's main classical theatre, hosting the best-known Italian companies from October to May.

Teatro dell'Oriuolo, Via dell'Oriuolo 31 (☎055/234.0507). Specialises in productions of particular local interest; entrance is sometimes free, and when it isn't you can get a student discount.

Teatro Regionale Toscano, Via dei Pucci 4 (☎055/219.854). Shows by Tuscany's highly esteemed regional theatre company are held in various theatres in town.

Teatro di Rifredi, Via Vittorio Emanuele 303 (☎055/422.0361). Currently run by *Pupi and Fresedde*, a youngish group founded in the mid-1970s with a progressive popular culture bias.

Teatro Verdi, Via Ghibellina 101 (☎055/239.6242). Much like the fare at the *Comunale*, but with occasional musical shows.

Cinema

Florence has a large number of **cinemas**, but very few show subtitled films, and nearly all English-language films are dubbed. Cineastes for whom language is no barrier will get most out of the programmes at the *Alfieri Atelier*, Via Ulivo 6. Other places with often interesting programmes are *Spazio Uno* at Via del Sole 10 (occasional films in English), *Universale* at Via Pisana 43, and *Cine Città* at Via Pisana 576. *Astro*, on Via Isola delle Stinche, near Santa Croce, shows exclusively English-language films in a ramshackle village-hall kind of way; *Cinema Goldoni* at Via dei Serragli shows English films on Mondays from 3.30pm until 10.45pm.

From June to September there's a season of **open-air** cinema at the Forte Belvedere, above the Bóboli gardens; the ambience is beautiful and the films are usually good. High quality **videos**, usually documentaries about non-European cultures, are shown frequently at *Caffè Voltaire* (see p.139).

The *Festival dei Popoli*, an academic institution concerned with documentary film and its connection with socio-anthropological research, organises an annual event, usually in November. Its reputation rests on such projects as "The Depiction of Terrorism in Television Programming", but it does conduct less earnest surveys as well – on François Truffaut, for example, or jazz in the cinema. The festival's offices are at Via Fiume 14, near the train station.

Shopping

Florence's best-known area of manufacturing expertise is **leather goods**, and top-quality shoes, bags and gloves are sold in every part of the city, with a concentration of outlets round **Via de' Tornabuoni**. Here, and in the tributaries of Via degli Strozzi and Via della Vigna Nuova, virtually all of Italy's top **fashion designers** have their shops. If their prices are too steep, passable imitations (and outright fakes) can be unearthed at the various **street markets**. Marbled **paper** is another

Florentine speciality, and, as you'd expect in this arty city, Florence is also one of the best places in the country to pick up books on Italian art, architecture and general culture. Most shops are closed at lunchtime, on Sunday, and on Monday morning – though food shops tend to close on Wednesday morning instead.

Street markets

Biggest of all Florence's **markets** is the Tuesday morning one at the **Cascine** park (bus #17c), where hundreds of stallholders set up an al fresco budget-class department store. Go along for a look and you're certain to come back having bought something. Clothes and shoes are the best bargains, though for the cheapest clothes in Florence you should check out the weekday morning stalls at **Piazza delle Cure**, just beyond Piazza della Libertà (bus #1 or #7).

The market around **San Lorenzo** church is another open-air warehouse of cheap clothing, with fakes of well-known brands accounting for a large percentage of turnover. Some of these fakes are so good that the big-name companies have formed gangs of counterfeit-busters to root them out – and to their embarrassment, they've not always been able easily to distinguish the fake from the real thing. San Lorenzo is as well organised as a shopping mall: huge waterproof awnings ensure that the weather can't stop the trading, and some of the stallholders even accept credit cards.

The **Mercato Nuovo** (or *Porcellino* market), just to the west of Piazza della Signoria, is the main emporium for straw hats, plastic *Davids* and the like. Finally, a flea market, stacked with antiques and bric-a-brac, is pitched every day in **Piazza dei Ciompi**, near the Sant'Ambrogio food market; more professional antique dealers swell the ranks on the last Sunday of each month, from 9am to 7pm.

Clothes

Alex, Via della Vigna Nuova 5r & 19r. Small but select range of international fashion for women – Alaïa, Byblos, Mugler, Genny – displayed with minimalist panache. The branch at no. 5 concentrates each season on one or two classic lines, such as Equipment silk shirts in every conceivable hue.

Armani, Via de' Tornabuoni 35–37r. Gorgeous clothes from the most astute designer in Italy, at prices that make you think you must have misread the tag.

Emilio Cavallini, Via della Vigna Nuova 52r. Youth-oriented, with splashy colours and occasionally wacky designs, something like a toned-down Katharine Hamnett. Good reductions in the winter sales, which sometimes drag on into March.

Coin, Via dei Calzaiuoli 56r. Clothes-dominated chain store, occupying a similar niche to M&S, with a touch more dash and bit more dosh.

Enrico Coveri, Via della Vigna Nuova 27–29r & Via de' Tornabuoni 81r. Born in nearby Prato, Coveri specialised in bold multicoloured outfits that contrast sharply with the prevailing sobriety of Florentine design – the designs produced by his firm since his death continue along the founder's path.

Emporio Armani, Piazza Strozzi 14–16r. The lowest-priced wing of the Armani empire, this is really only a place to go if you're desperate to get Italy's number one label on your back – you're paying a fair premium for the name, and the quality isn't all it could be at the price.

Ferragamo, Via de' Tornabuoni 16r. Salvatore Ferragamo emigrated to the US at the age of 14 and before long had become the most famous shoemaker in the world, producing everything from pearl-studded numbers for Gloria Swanson to gladiators' sandals for Cecil B. de Mille's blockbusters. Managed by Salvatore's widow and children, Ferragamo now produces complete ready-to-wear outfits, but the company's reputation still rests on its beautiful, comfortable and expensive shoes.

Gucci, Via de' Tornabuoni 73r. The Gucci empire was founded at no. 73, which remains the flagship showroom; everything is impeccably made, but even if it weren't, the demand for the linked Gs would probably keep going under its own momentum.

Luisa Via Roma, Via Roma 19–21r. The pinnacle of Florentine chic, featuring the leading edge of world fashion – for instance, this is the city's only outlet for the hyper-fashionable Comme des Garçons, Yohji Yamamoto and Issey Miyake. Gold Cards essential. The branch at Via del Corso 54–56r – *Luisa il Corso* – sells only the Luisa Via Roma lines for women.

Max Mara, Via Pecori 23r. Economically the most accessible of Italian high-fashion houses, *Max Mara* turns out clothes to suit every wardrobe.

Pucci, Via dei Pucci 6. The Pucci family was known primarily as one of the city's mercantile dynasties until Marchese Emilio Pucci stunned the catwalk shows in the 1950s with his vividly dyed, swirling-patterned silks. Garish Pucci prints were the hottest items in town during the Sixties, then the company hit a lull. In 1990, however, Pucci suddenly became the London clubland uniform, and their £400 shirts were selling so fast that supply couldn't keep up. The wave may have broken now, but a pair of Pucci leggings (under £100) still carries some clout in fashion victim circles.

Sem, Via Cimatori 25r. Provides the city's young and youngish women with affordable derivatives of the latest Italian *haute couture*.

Versace, Via de' Tornabuoni 13–15r. The most blatantly sexy clothes in Italy – Versace makes you feel like a million dollars, if you have the loot to start with.

SPORTSWEAR

Camping Sport, Via dei Servi 70–72r & Via Castellaccio 70–72r. Big outlet for Fila, Tacchini and Kappa, and normally has a few cut-price sportswear items.

Casa dello Sport, Via Tosinghi 8–10r. If this place doesn't have the sports accessory you're looking for, it isn't on sale in Italy.

Shoes, gloves and leather

Arturo, Viale Segni 6. *Arturo* sells Coveri, Basile and Moschino leather goods, aimed at younger customers.

Beltrami, Via de' Tornabuoni 48r. Department store selling high-fashion, high-price shoes, bags, leather, and other clothes, for men and women.

La Calzoleria, Via dei Conti 39r. Close to San Lorenzo; low-price smart shoes.

Capanna O, Via dell'Albero 19r. Does special discounts for students.

Cellerini, Via del Sole 37r. Everything sold here is made on the premises, under the supervision of the firm's founders, thought by many to be the city's premier exponents of the craft; bags don't come more elegant, durable – and costly.

Desmo, Via Solferino 10r. One of Italy's main fashion leather shops.

Eusebio, Via del Corso 5r. Main source of bargain shoes for men and women.

Francesco da Firenze, Via Santo Spirito 62r. Handmade shoes for men and women – some striking designs and good prices.

Gestri, Via Oriuolo 45r. Incredibly cheap footwear – especially sandals and canvas shoes.

John F, Lungarno Corsini 14r. Popular outlet for stylish – and expensive – clothes and bags; worth checking out during the sales for their large discounts.

La Pelle, Via Guicciardini 11r. Modern leather clothes for the young and hip.

Madova, Via Guicciardini 1r. Glove emporium – every colour, every size, every shape.

Pollini, Via Calimala 12r. Typically Florentine, Pollini shoes are very smart, rather formal and very expensive.

Franco Rizzo, Via Fornace 22r. A preferred outlet for young Florentine women with money to spend on their feet.

Valentina, Via Nazionale 98r. Inexpensive and fairly trendy shoes, built to last the year and not much longer.

Jewellery

The whole **Ponte Vecchio** is crammed with jewellers' shops, all of them catering strictly to the financial stratosphere. Those of more limited means could either take a chance on the counterfeits and low-cost originals peddled by the street vendors on and around the bridge, or check out the places below.

Bijoux Cascio, Via de' Tornabuoni 32r & Via Por Santa Maria 1r. *Cascio* has made a name for itself over the last thirty years as a maker of imitation jewellery. It takes a trained eye to distinguish much of the stuff from the window displays on the Ponte Vecchio.

COI (*Commercio Oreficeria Italiana*), Via Por Santa Maria 8r. Massive selection of gold trinkets in an upstairs showroom that knocks up what must be the highest turnover of any jewellers' in Florence.

Gatto Bianco, Borgo SS. Apostoli 12r. Strange combinations of precious and everyday materials are the signature of this outlet, one of the more adventurous jewellery workshops in the city.

Angela Caputi, Borgo San Jacopo 82r. Though she's now branching out into clothing, Caputi made her name with magnificent chunks of plexiglass and plastic costume jewellery, at very affordable prices. Not for shrinking violets.

Ceramics

Hand-painted pottery is produced by several Florentine firms, and their work is often indistinguishable. Two of the more distinctive ones are the family-run *Borgopinti*, at Borgo Pinti 40r, and *Luca della Robbia*, at Via del Proconsolo 19r – founded in 1904, but a modern-looking outfit. *Sbigoli*, Via San Egidio 4r, is the best place for unglazed pottery.

Paper

& C, Via della Vigna Nuova 82r. Florence's flashiest stationery: the handmade envelope as sculptural object.

Bottega Artigiana del Libro, Lungarno Corsini 38–40r. Sells traditional Florentine marbled paper, glued to folders, pencils, address books etc.

Giannini, Piazza Pitti 37r. Established in 1856, this firm was recently honoured with an exhibition dedicated to its work. Once the only place in Florence to make its own marbled papers, now its exclusivity is more of an economic one.

Il Papiro, Piazza Duomo 24r. Same sort of place as the *Bottega Artigiana*.

Pineider, Piazza della Signoria 13r & Via de' Tornabuoni 76r. Florence's gentry would rather die than use anything except *Pineider*'s colour co-ordinated calling cards, handmade papers and envelopes.

Lo Scrittoio, Via Guelfa 112r. Another place for fancy papers and bindings.

Il Torchio, Via dei Bardi 17. Marbled paper workshop, made appealing by its slightly lower prices.

Books, posters and cards

L'Affiche Illustrée, Via dei Servi 69r & Via Guelfa 14r. Posters and postcards by contemporary artists.

After Dark, Via del Moro 86r. English bookshop with a seedy side that stocks soft porn mags.

Alinari, Via della Vigna Nuova 46r. Owners of the best archive of old photographs in Italy, *Alinari* will print any image you choose from their huge catalogues. They also publish books, calendars, posters and cards.

BM, Borgo Ognissanti 4r. Includes a wide selection of guidebooks and general English and American titles.

Centro Di, Piazza de' Mozzi 1r. Retailer, publisher and distributor of art and architecture books, with the emphasis on exhibition catalogues; the slightly shambolic air is deceptive – name any artist and they'll locate a relevant book in seconds.

Feltrinelli, Via Cavour 12r. International stock, including large English-language sections; the best-organised of the large central shops.

Franco Maria Ricci, Via Belle Donne 41r. Very posh outlet of Italy's poshest publisher; the problem is finding a coffee table good enough for the books.

Le Monnier, Via San Gallo 53r. Run by one of Florence's oldest publishing houses, this is a very good international bookshop.

Libreria delle Donne, Via Fiesolana 2b (open afternoons only). Women's bookshop; also the best place for contacting women's groups in Florence.

Libreria della Signoria, Via dei Magazzini 3r. Specialises in the graphic arts, with a good stock of posters.

Marzocchino, Via Cavour 14r. Has masses of Italian kids' books and paper models.

Paperback Exchange, Via Fiesolana 31r. Always has a good stock of English and American books, with the emphasis on Italian-related titles and second-hand stuff; operates an exchange scheme for second-hand books and has informative and very friendly staff.

Salimbeni, Via Matteo Palmiri 14–16r. Yet another place where lavishly produced art books predominate. *Salimbeni* is also a publishing house, specialising in books on Italian culture.

Seeber, Via de' Tornabuoni 68r. Probably the best-stocked general bookshop in the city.

Tempi Futuri, Via de' Pilastri 20–22r. Mainly comics and graphic books.

Il Viaggio, Via Ghibellina 117r. Specialises in travel books, guides and maps.

Records

Alberti, Via de' Pucci 16r & Borgo S. Lorenzo 45–49r. Founded in 1873, this is the city's leading mainstream supplier.

Contempo Records, Corso dei Tintori 8/16. Florence's hippest record store; this is the place to go if you're looking for the latest from Tuscan bands like Litfiba and Diaframma.

IRA, Via Pietrapiana 64r. Like *Contempo*, its main rival, this shop is also an independent record and tape producer.

Mastelloni, Piazza del Mercato Centrale 21r. Small and very noisy; the focal point for Florence's Anglophile rock fans.

Sala, Via Zannetti 6–8r. Sells fairly recent Italian records at reduced prices.

Setteclavio, Piazza Duomo 16. Classical music specialist, with virtually every disc currently in the Italian catalogue and thousands of imports.

Designer artefacts

Emporium, Via Guicciardini 122r. Temple dedicated to the cult of modern design; most of the objects displayed are from Italy.

Flos, Borgo San Jacopo 62r. Milanese lamp designer – polychromatic plastics, black steel and spartan lines.

Proforma, Borgo SS. Apostoli 47r. Very slick design emporium, displaying the trendiest Italian household accessories – Alessi stainless steel, Baldelli ceramics and so on.

Soluzioni, Via Maggio 82r. Specialises in household objects, some ingenious, some peculiar and some kitsch.

Vice Versa, Via Ricasoli 53. Postmodern design principles applied to objects that sometimes don't warrant the attention: architect-designed teapots and so on.

Perfumes and toiletries

Farmacia Santa Maria Novella, Via della Scala 16. Occupying the virtually unaltered pharmacy of the Santa Maria Novella monastery, this shop is as famous for its antique furniture and decor as for its face-creams and soaps, whose white packages are distributed worldwide.

Listings

Airlines *Air France*, Borgo SS. Apostoli 9 (☎055/284.304); *Alitalia*, Lungarno Acciaioli 10–12 (☎055/27.881); *British Airways*, Via della Vigna Nuova 36r (☎055/218.655 or 218.659); *Lufthansa*, Piazza Antinori 2 (☎055/238.1444); *TWA*, Piazza Santa Trìnita 2 (☎055/284.691).

Airport enquiries *Aeroporto Galileo Galilei*, Pisa (☎050/28.088); information also from the check-in desk at Santa Maria Novella train station, platform 5 (daily 7am–8pm; ☎055/216.073). Information for flights from Perètola airport: ☎055/317.123.

Banks and exchange Banks are concentrated in the Piazza della Repubblica area, especially around Via degli Strozzi. For exchange out of normal banking hours, try *American Express*, Via Dante Alighieri and Via Guicciardini (Mon–Fri 9am–5.30pm, Sat 9am–12.30pm), or the *Esercizio Promozione Turismo*, just north of Piazza Signoria at Via Condotta 42 (Mon–Sat 10am–7pm, Sun 10am–6pm). The *Banca delle Comunicazione* in the station is open 8.20am–7.20pm, though be prepared for a commission in the region of L5000. The best of the central exchange booths is *Carlo Alunno*, right by the Uffizi at Via della Ninna 9r. Several banks on the main shopping streets now have hole-in-the-wall machines that exchange banknotes in dollars and all major European currencies into lire.

Bicycle rental *Alinari*, Via Guelfa 85r (☎055/280.500), Via dei Bardi 35r (☎055/234.6436), Piazza Cavalleggeri (☎055/682.725); *Ciao & Basta*, Lungarno Pecori Girardi 1 (☎055/234.2726); *Motorent*, Via S. Zanobi 9r (☎055/490.113); *Promoturist*, Via Baccio Bandinelli 43 (☎055/701.863).

Bus enquiries For local services: *ATAF*, Piazza della Stazione (☎055/580.528). For routes outside the city, see "Travel Details" below.

Car rental *Avis*, Borgo Ognissanti 128r (☎055/213.629); *Europcar*, Borgo Ognissanti 53r (☎055/293.444); *Excelsior*, Via Agnelli 33 (☎055/644.437); *Hertz*, Via Maso Finiguerra 33r (☎055/282.260); *Italy by Car*, Borgo Ognissanti 134r (☎055/293.021); *Maggiore*, Via Maso Finiguerra 31r (☎055/210.238); *Program*, Borgo Ognissanti 135r (☎055/282.916).

Consulates *UK*, Lungarno Corsini 2 (☎055/284.133); *US*, Lungarno Vespucci 38 (☎055/239.8276); *Belgium*, Via dei Servi 28 (☎055/282.094); *Denmark*, Via dei Servi 13 (☎055/212.732); *Netherlands*, Via Cavour 81 (☎055/475.249); *Norway*, Via G. Capponi 26, c/o Ufficio Fiduciaria Toscana (☎055/247.9321); *Sweden*, Via della Scala 4 (☎055/239.6865). Travellers from Ireland, Australia, New Zealand and Canada should contact their Rome embassies.

Dental surgery Dr Donatella Diamante, Via Puccinotti 71 (☎055/486.969) is an excellent English-speaking dentist.

Doctors For medical complaints that require more than simple first aid (see below) but don't warrant a hospital visit, the *Tourist Medical Service*, Via Lorenzo il Magnifico 59 (☎055/475.411), has English-speaking doctors on 24-hr call.

First aid *Misericordia*, Piazza del Duomo 20 (☎055/287.788).

Hospital Santa Maria Nuova, Piazza Santa Maria Nuova 1 (☎055/27.581). Should you require the services of an interpreter, the *Associazione Volontari Ospedalieri* can be called out by ringing ☎055/403.126; it's a volunteer organisation, and its services are free.

Laundry *Lavamatic*, Via degli Alfani 44r, is the cheapest and most central; *Guelfa*, Via Guelfa 106r, is the next best.

Left luggage Train station left-luggage desk open 24hr; L1500 per item.

Lost property Via Circondaria 19 (Mon–Wed & Fri–Sat 9am–noon; ☎055/367.943).

Pharmacies All-night pharmacies are as follows: *Comunale della Stazione*, at the train station; *Molteni*, Via dei Calzaiuoli 7r; *Taverna*, Piazza San Giovanni 20. In addition there's a rota system by which the city pharmacies take it in turn to stay open at night: each pharmacy displays the roster in its window, or you can ring ☎192 for information.

Police Carabinieri ☎055/112; Polizia Urbana ☎055/36.911. The *Questura*, for passport problems, reporting thefts and so on, is at Via Zara 2 (☎055/49.771).

Post office Central post office at Via Pellicceria 8 (Mon–Fri 8.15am–6pm, Sat 8.15am–12.30pm; international telegrams 8am–11.30pm); poste restante at counters 23 & 24.

Florence's main post office is at Via Pietrapiana 53–55 (same hours) – this is the one that poste restante mail will be sent to, unless specified otherwise.

Scooter and motorbike rental *Alinari*, Via Guelfa 85r (☎055/280.500), Via dei Bardi 35r (☎055/234.6436), Piazza Cavalleggeri (☎055/682.725); *Eurodrive*, Via della Scala 48r (☎055/239.8639); *Excelsior*, Via Agnelli 33 (☎055/644.437); *Motorent*, Via San Zanobi 9r (☎055/490.113); *Program*, Borgo Ognissanti 135r (☎055/282.916); *Sabra*, Via Artisti 8 (☎055/576.256); *Vespa Rent*, Via Pisana 103r (☎055/715.691).

Swimming pools *Costoli*, Viale Paoli, at Campo Marte; *Amici del Nuoto*, Via del Romito 38; *Tropos*, Via Orcagna 20; *Le Pavoniere*, Viale degli Olmi, at the Cascine (open-air); *Bellariva*, Lungarno Colombo 6 (open-air).

Taxis Main ranks by the train station and in Piazza della Repubblica; radio cabs ☎055/4798 or ☎055/4390.

Telephones Booths at SIP office in train station (8am–9.45pm, closed Sun); Via Pellicceria post office (8am–10.30pm); SIP office, Via Cavour 21r (24hr); Palazzo delle Poste, Via Pietrapiana (8am–7.45pm, closed Sat & Sun).

Train enquiries ☎055/288.785.

travel details

Trains

From Florence to Arezzo (hourly; 1hr); Bari (12 daily; 8hr 15min–9hr), 7 continuing to Lecce (10hr 25min–12hr); Bologna/Ancona/Rimini (hourly; 1hr 30min/2hr 30min–4hr/3hr 30min–6hr); Bologna direct (every 30min; 1hr 5min–1hr 40min); Genoa (hourly; 3hr 10min–4hr 30min); Empoli (every 20min; 25min; hourly connections for Siena – 50min–1hr 20min); Naples (2 daily; 4hr); Livorno (12 daily; 1hr 30min); Milan (18 daily; 2hr 50min–4hr 50min); Perugia/Assisi/Foligno (11 daily; 2hr 10min/2hr 35min/2hr 55min), plus 1 daily to Perugia only; Pistoia/Lucca/Viareggio (hourly; 30–45min/1hr 5min–1hr 50min/1hr 30min–2hr 25min); Pisa central (every 30min; 55min); Pisa airport (hourly; 1hr); Prato (every 30min; 20min); Reggio Calabria (from Campo Marte, 4 direct trains daily; 11hr/from Santa Maria Novella, changing at Rome, 7 daily; 11hr); Rome (hourly; 2hr 15min–3hr 30min); Trieste, usually changing at Venice-Mestre (9 daily; 5hr–6hr 15min); Udine via Venice-Mestre (10 daily; 5hr 20min–6hr/2hr 45min–3hr 20min); Venice central (hourly; 3hr 25min–4hr 10min); Verona/Bolzano (14 daily; 2hr 40min–3hr 40min/4hr 10min–5hr 50min).

Buses

In addition to the state-owned *SITA*, numerous independent bus companies operate from Florence. After the details of *SITA* routes comes a list of the most useful private routes, with the address and information number of each company. Buses depart from the addresses given.

SITA, Via Santa Caterina da Siena 15 (☎055/211.487): to Barberino di Mugello (17 daily; 40min); Bibbiena (8 daily; 2hr 15min); Castellina in Chianti (1 daily; 1hr 35min); Certaldo (4 daily; 2hr 20min); Gaiole (2 daily Mon–Fri; 2hr); Greve (around 25 daily; 1hr 5min); Poggibonsi (10 daily; 1hr 20min); Pontassieve (12 daily; 50min); Poppi (9 daily; 2hr 5min); Radda in Chianti (1 daily Mon–Sat; 1hr 40min); San Casciano (14 daily; 40min); Siena (12 express daily, plus 9 stopping services; 1hr 15min express); Volterra (6 daily; 2hr 25min).

CLAP, Piazza della Stazione 15 (☎055/283.734): to Lucca and Lucca province.

CAP, Via Nazionale 13 (☎055/214.637): to Borgo San Lorenzo, Impruneta, Montepiano and Prato.

CAT, Via Fiume 2 (☎055/283.400): to Anghiari, Arezzo, Caprese, Città di Castello, Figline Valdarno, Incisa Valdarno, and Sansepolcro.

COPIT, Piazza Santa Maria Novella (☎055/215.451): to Abetone, Pistoia, Poggio a Caiano and Vinci.

LAZZI, Piazza della Stazione 4 (☎055/298.840): to Abetone, Calenzano, Cerreto Guidi, Empoli, Forte dei Marmi, Incisa Valdarno, Livorno, Lucca, Marina di Carrara, Marina di Massa, Montecatini Terme, Montevarchi, Pescia, Pisa, Pistoia, Pontassieve, Pontedera, Prato, Signa, Tirrenia, Torre del Lago and Viareggio.

RAMA (same address & phone as *Lazzi*): to Grosseto.

CHAPTER TWO

AROUND FLORENCE

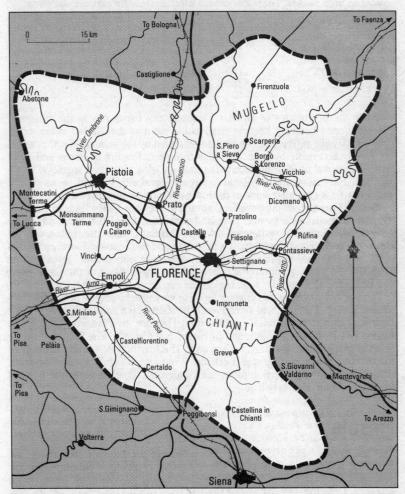

Having paid their respects to the sights of Florence, most people doing a Tuscan tour set off for another of the big-league towns, such as Siena or Pisa, leapfrogging the city's immediate surroundings. Yet there's a lot to be gained by lingering a few days in this area, either using Florence as a base, or staying at a couple of the smaller places within the city's orbit.

ACCOMMODATION PRICES

Throughout this guide, accommodation is graded on a scale from ① to ⑨. Grades ① and ② apply to **hostel** accommodation, and indicate the lowest price a **single person** could expect to pay for one night in that establishment in high season. Grades ③ to ⑨ apply to **hotels**, and indicate the cost of the **cheapest double room in high season.** The price bands to which these codes refer are as follows:

- ① under L20,000 per person
- ② over L20,000 per person
- ③ under L50,000 per double
- ④ L50–70,000 per double
- ⑤ L70–90,000 per double
- ⑥ L90–120,000 per double
- ⑦ L120–150,000 per double
- ⑧ L150–200,000 per double
- ⑨ over L200,000 per double

Inside the boundaries of Greater Florence, city buses run to the village of **Fiesole**, once Florence's keenest rival, and to many of the **Medici villas**, originally countryside retreats but now all but engulfed by the suburbs. Further afield but readily accessible by train, the busy commercial centre of **Prato** and quiet provincial capital of **Pistoia** each make fine day trips, with their medieval buildings and Florentine-inspired Renaissance art – and either could be used as a springboard for exploring some of the more obscure corners of Tuscany.

West of Florence, an industrialised stretch of the Arno valley leads to **Empoli**, the point of access for a number of upland attractions: **Vinci** (Leonardo da Vinci's village), the imperial settlement of **San Miniato**, and the hill towns of **Castelfiorentino** and **Certaldo**. To the north and the south of Florence lie two rural regions that require independent transport for proper investigation: **Mugello**, the lush agricultural area around the upper valley of the Sieve river; and **Chianti**, Italy's premier wine region and expatriate settlement.

The places covered in this chapter lie on or very near to several of the principal routes through Tuscany, and so can easily be visited on a journey between major centres. Three of these routes radiate from Florence: **to Pisa** (via Empoli); **to Lucca** (via Prato and Pistoia); and **to Siena** (via Chianti). The first two can be done by bus or train, the third by bus only. The fourth route – **from Empoli to Siena** via Castelfiorentino and Certaldo – is again possible by bus or train, though if you intend stopping off at San Gimignano, which is really the point of this trip, only the former will do.

Fiesole

The hill town of **FIESOLE**, which spreads over a cluster of hills above the Mugnone and Arno valleys some 8km northeast of Florence, is conventionally described as a pleasant retreat from the crowds and heat of summertime Florence. Unfortunately, its tranquillity has been so well advertised that it's now hardly less busy than Florence itself in high season, and you'd need paranormal sensitivity to detect any climatic difference on an airless August afternoon.

That said, Fiesole offers a grandstand view of the city, has something of the feel of a country village, and bears many traces of its history – which is actually lengthier than that of Florence. First settled in the Bronze Age, then by the

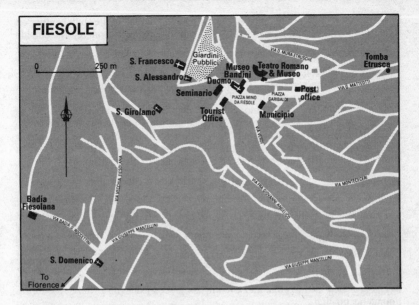

Etruscans, then absorbed by the Romans, it rivalled its neighbour until the early twelfth century, when the Florentines overran the town. From that time it became a satellite, especially favoured as a semi-rural second home for wealthier citizens such as the inevitable Medici.

Fiesole is one of the easiest short trips from the city: the #7 *ATAF* **bus** runs every quarter of an hour from Santa Maria Novella train station to Fiesole's central Piazza Mino da Fiesole. The journey takes around twenty minutes, and costs the standard city fare of L1100.

The Town

When the Florentines wrecked Fiesole in 1125, the only major building they spared was the **Duomo**, on the edge of Piazza Mino. Subsequent, nineteenth-century, restorers, however, managed to ruin the exterior, which is now notable only for its lofty campanile. The most interesting part of the bare interior is the raised choir: the altarpiece is a polyptych painted in the 1440s by Bicci di Lorenzo, and the Cappella Salutati, to the right, contains two fine pieces carved around the same time by Mino da Fiesole – an altar frontal of *The Madonna and Saints* and the tomb of Bishop Salutati. Fiesole's patron saint, Saint Romulus, is buried underneath the choir in the ancient crypt.

Behind the duomo at Via Dupré 1, the **Museo Bandini** (summer 9.30am–1pm & 3–7pm; winter 10am–1pm & 3–6pm; closed Tues; L3000, or L6000 combined ticket including admission to Museo Archeologico and Antiquarium Costantini) possesses a collection of glazed terracotta in the style of the Della Robbias, the odd case of Byzantine ivory work and a few thirteenth- and fourteenth-century Tuscan pictures – worthy but uninspiring.

Fiesole's other major churches, Sant'Alessandro and San Francesco, are reached by the steep Via San Francesco, which runs past a terrace offering a knockout view of Florence. **Sant'Alessandro** was founded in the sixth century on the site of Etruscan and Roman temples; recent repairs have rendered the outside a whitewashed nonentity, but the beautiful *marmorino cipollino* (onion marble) columns of the basilical interior make it the most atmospheric building in Fiesole.

Again, restoration has not improved the Gothic **San Francesco**, which occupies the site of the acropolis – the interior is a twentieth-century renovation, but the tiny cloisters are genuine. The church itself contains an *Immaculate Conception* by Piero di Cosimo (second altar on right), and attached to the church is a small museum featuring material gathered mainly by missions to the Far East, much of it from China (daily summer 10am–noon & 3–6pm; winter 10am–noon & 3–5pm; free). From the front of San Francesco a gate opens into a wooded public park, the most pleasant descent back to Piazza Mino.

The Roman Theatre and Etruscan Tombs

Back down in the main part of Fiesole, beyond the Duomo in Via Marini, is the entrance to the **Teatro Romano** and **Museo Archeologico** (April–Sept daily 9am–7pm; Oct–March daily except Tues 9am–6pm; L5000, or L6000 including admission to Antiquarium Costantini and Museo Bandini). Built in the first century BC, the 3000-seater theatre was excavated towards the end of the last century and is in so good a state of repair that it's used for performances during the *Estate Fiesolana* festival. Most of the exhibits in the site's small **museum** were excavated in this area, and encompass pieces from the Bronze Age to the Roman occupation.

Close by, at Via Portigiana 9, the **Antiquarium Costantini** (same hours as Teatro Romano) is basically a run-of-the-mill collection of old ceramics. And from here, if you want to wring every last drop of historical significance from Fiesole, you could follow the signposts up the hill to the east of the Teatro, where there are the ruins of a couple of **Etruscan tombs** from the third century BC.

To San Domenico

The most enjoyable excursion from Fiesole is to wander down the narrow **Via Vecchia Fiesolana**, which passes the **Villa Medici** – built for Cosimo il Vecchio by Michelozzo – on its way to the hamlet of **SAN DOMENICO**, 1.5km southwest of Piazza Mino.

Fra' Angelico was once prior of the Dominican **monastery** at this village and the church retains a *Madonna and Angels* by him, in the first chapel on the left; the chapterhouse also has a Fra' Angelico fresco of *The Crucifixion* (ring at no. 4).

Five minutes' walk northwest from San Domenico stands the **Badia Fiesolana**, Fiesole's cathedral from the ninth century to the eleventh. Cosimo il Vecchio had the church altered in the 1460s, a project which left the magnificent Romanesque facade intact while transforming the interior into a superb Renaissance building (open Mon–Fri 8.30am–6.30pm).

Fiesole practicalities

The Fiesole **tourist office** is at Piazza Mino da Fiesole 37 (Oct–March & Aug Mon–Sat 8am–2pm; April–July & Sept same days 8.30am–1.30pm & 3–6pm). Fiesole itself is small enough to be explored in a morning, but the country lanes of its surroundings invite a more leisurely tour, and might even tempt you to stay.

Accommodation on a tight budget is a problem. *Villa Sorriso*, Via Gramsci 21 (☎055/59.027; [5]), is the cheapest close to the centre; about a kilometre further out, *Villa Baccano*, Via Bosconi 4 (☎055/59.341; ⑨), is in the same price range. Fiesole's **campsite**, *Camping Panoramico* (☎055/59.90.69), is 3km out of town in Via Peramonda; the *Linea A* bus goes to the foot of the hill on which it's situated.

There are a couple of good **pizzerias** on Piazza Mino da Fiesole, and if you have a car you could try the excellent *Cave di Maiano* (closed Sun evening, Thurs & Aug), 3km southeast of Fiesole in the village of Maiano.

The Medici villas

The finest country houses of the Florentine hinterland are, predictably enough, those built for the **Medici**. The earliest of these villas were primarily intended as fortified refuges to which the family could withdraw when the political temperature in the city became a little too hot, but as the Medici became more secure the houses acquired the role of advertisements for the humanistic culture of their owners. In the sixteenth and seventeenth centuries, with the Medici established as the unchallenged rulers of the city, the villas became more ostentatious, signifying the might of the dynasty through their sheer luxuriousness. They had an investment function too – as Florence's importance as a manufacturing city began to dwindle, the Medici decided to divert some of their resources into agriculture.

Not every Medici villa is covered in this section – just the ones that are easily accessible on a day trip from Florence and whose interior or grounds are open to the public. Thus the villas of Trebbio and Cafaggiolo, both of which can be viewed only from outside, are described later in this chapter, on p.167, while the Villa Medici at Cerreto Guidi, far closer to Empoli than to Florence, is dealt with on p.182.

Apart from the selection of Medici villas, this section also includes a few sights best visited on an excursion to one of the houses – the church at **Carmignano**, for example, with its remarkable Pontormo altarpiece.

Villa Medicea della Petraia

The **Villa della Petraia** (bus #28 from train station to Castello) was adapted from a medieval castle in the 1570s and 1580s by Buontalenti, working to a commission from the future Grand Duke Ferdinando I. Only the watchtower of the fortress was retained, to serve as a high-rise belvedere above the simple two-storey house.

The **interior** (Tues–Sun March & Oct 9am–4.30pm; April, May & Sept 9am–5.30pm; June–Aug 9am–6.30pm; Nov–Feb 9am–3.30pm; L4000) was altered in turn by Vittorio Emanuele II, who glassed over the interior courtyard to convert it into a ballroom. Its walls are covered by a seventeenth-century fresco cycle glorifying the Medici and the Knights of St Stephen, a pseudo-chivalric order founded by Cosimo I to rid the Tuscan coast of pirates. The suffocating style of the House of Savoy tends to prevail in the villa's apartments, though there's the occasional sixteenth-century tapestry or painting, and Giambologna's bronze statue of *Venus* has now been transplanted indoors from the fountain on the upper terrace of the garden, having been moved from the Castello house (see below).

Laid out in geometrical order, in half-hearted imitation of the Castello estate, the garden isn't much to get excited about, but the park behind the villa to the east is glorious, with its ancient cypress trees (grounds close 1hr later than the villa).

Villa Medicea di Castello

From La Petraia follow Via della Petraia past Villa Bel Riposo (where Carlo Lorenzini wrote *Pinocchio*) to the Baroque Villa Corsini, from where Via di Castello leads to the **Villa di Castello**. This house was bought in 1477 by Lorenzo and Giovanni de' Medici, second cousins of Lorenzo il Magnifico and the principal patrons of Botticelli – the *Birth of Venus* and the *Primavera* both used to hang here. Wrecked after the expulsion of the Medici, it was rebuilt for Cosimo I, and is now the headquarters of the Accademia della Crusca, the society that maintains the purity of the Italian language.

The society doesn't allow visitors into the house, but that's no great hardship, as its Pontormo and Bronzino frescoes perished a long time back, and the villa's fame rests entirely on its **gardens** (Tues–Sun 9am–sunset; L4000), which were laid out by Tribolo for Cosimo and continued by Buontalenti, who also redesigned the house. Had the full scheme ever been carried out, over fifty sculptural tableaux would have represented the seasons, the virtues, the landscapes of Tuscany and, inevitably, the triumphs of the Medici. Even in a state of semi-completion, Castello's gardens were astonishing – delighted by their labyrinths, sculptures, fountains and myriad water tricks, Montaigne judged them to be the best in Europe. Of the surviving eccentricities, the outstanding set pieces are Ammannati's colossal shivering figure of *January*, the triple-bowled fountain topped by the same sculptor's *Hercules and Antaeus*, and the *Grotto degli Animali*, a man-made cave against the walls of which are stacked a menagerie of plaster birds and animals. (The bronze originals of some of these are now on show in the Bargello in Florence.)

Villa Medicea di Careggi

Originally a fortified farmhouse, the **Villa di Careggi**, 5km northwest of central Florence, came into the possession of the Medici in 1417 and was altered by Michelozzo for Cosimo il Vecchio in the 1430s. It was always the old man's favourite home: he brought his private library out here and hung the walls with paintings by his protégés. Cosimo died here, too, as did his son Piero and grandson Lorenzo il Magnifico, with whom the house is particularly associated, as it was here that his academy of Platonic scholars used to meet.

Low-slung and blank-faced, Careggi is not a gracious building, its one amusing touch being a fresco in one of the garden loggias: showing a man being thrown down a well, it depicts the fate of the doctor whose incompetence was unjustly alleged to have brought about the death of Lorenzo.

The villa is now a nurse's home, and written permission to visit the interior has to be obtained from *Unità Operativa Affari Generali*, U.S.L. 10/D, Viale Pieraccini 17, Firenze (☎055/427.7501). The extensive surrounding gardens and woodland can be explored freely, however. The #14C bus runs from Santa Maria Novella train station to the villa, or you can walk from La Petraia (see p.153).

Poggio a Caiano – and Carmignano

For the most complete image of what life was like in the Medici villas in the family's heyday, you should make the trip to the **Villa Medici di Poggio a Caiano** (Tues–Sun 9am–1.30pm; L3000), 18km northwest of Florence, on the crest of the main road through the village of Poggio a Caiano. A *LAZZI* bus service leaves from Piazza Santa Maria Novella every half-hour, and takes around half an hour to get there; an alternative approach is the #1 local service from Prato.

Lorenzo il Magnifico bought a farmhouse on this site in 1480 and commissioned Giuliano da Sangallo to rebuild it as a classical rural palace – the only architectural project instigated by Lorenzo that has survived, and the first Italian house to be built specifically as a place of country leisure. Raised on a kind of arcaded podium, it is the most elegant of the Medici villas and its impact is enhanced by later additions – the entrance loggia, for instance, was commissioned by Lorenzo's son Giovanni, the future Pope Leo X, and the curving double stairway was added in the eighteenth century. The house was often used to accommodate guests of state before a ceremonial entrance into Florence – Charles V stayed here, and it was at Poggio a Caiano that Eleanor of Toledo was introduced to her future husband, Cosimo I.

You enter the **villa** through the basement, where the plush games room and private theatre hint at the splendour to come. Upstairs, the focal point is the double-height *salone* which Sangallo made out of the courtyard between the two main blocks, and which Vasari pronounced the most beautiful room in the world. Its sixteenth-century frescoes include del Sarto's *Caesar Receiving Egyptian Tribute* (note the giraffe in the background, a gift to Lorenzo from the Sultan of Egypt), Franciabigio's *Triumph of Cicero* (a reference to Cosimo il Vecchio's return from exile) and, best of the lot, Pontormo's gorgeous *Vertumnus and Pomona*, the perfect evocation of a sun-stunned Tuscan afternoon.

Also on this floor is a reconstruction of the salon of the Villa Topaia, built by Cosimo III at Castello but now destroyed. The villa was set among orchards, and the literal-minded Cosimo duly ordered scores of horticultural paintings to fill the house; the Dutch still lifes are like ideal fruit stalls, each variety of grape, peach and apple assiduously numbered and labelled. Other such pictures from La Topaia are scattered throughout the main floor.

Many of the rooms were redecorated in the last century, but one part that escaped was the apartment of Bianca Cappello, wife of Francesco I and inspiration of many a romantic yarn. Born into an upper-class Venetian family, she fled her native city with a young man whom she promptly dumped to become Francesco's mistress. Banned from the city by Francesco's first wife, she remained an outcast even after she had become his second, being blacklisted by many of Florence's elite. In October 1587 both she and her husband died here on the same day – perhaps poisoned, perhaps victims of a particularly virulent virus.

In Lorenzo's time the grounds of Poggio a Caiano were far more extensive than they are today, and included a farm and a hunting estate; the Lorraine princess converted the **gardens** (daily 9am–2pm) into an English-style landscape, now containing some magnificent old trees.

CARMIGNANO

Five kilometres to the west of Poggio a Caiano, the church of San Michele in the village of **CARMIGNANO** contains one of Pontormo's greatest paintings, the *Visitation*. Created in 1530, it's as unusual an interpretation of a common theme as his *Deposition* in Florence – clad in bright pink, green and orange, the women seem to be clutching each other in an almost static dance.

There is a fairly regular *CAP* bus service to Carmignano from Poggio, the journey taking between ten and twenty minutes. If you feel like staying there's a two-star **hotel**, *Montalbino*, Via Borri 14 (☎055/879.9008; ③).

Villa dell'Artimino

Some of the buses from Poggio a Caiano to Carmignano stop on the way at Comeana, 3km south, where a couple of large **Etruscan tombs** dating from the seventh century BC have been excavated (Tues–Sun 9am–noon). A few of these bus services then loop through the walled village of Artimino, site of the Villa dell'Artimino, another 3km on.

Villa dell'Artimino is sometimes known as *La Ferdinanda* after Grand Duke Ferdinando I, for whom Buontalenti designed the house as a hunting lodge, with no intervening garden to smooth the transition from civilisation to nature. Unlike most of the other Medici villas it's still out in the country, with brilliant views towards Florence in one direction and west along the Arno in the other.

A white rectangular block with details picked out in grey *pietra serena*, the house has the appearance of a rather dandified fortress, and its most distinctive external feature has earned it the nickname "the villa of the hundred chimneys". Most of the **interior** is now shut to the public, and the paintings of the various Medici villas that once hung here are now on show in Florence's *Firenze com'era* museum. In the basement there's a dreary museum of Etruscan finds from the Comeana tombs (Mon, Tues, Thurs–Sun 9am–12.30pm, plus Sat 3.30–6.30pm; L5000).

While you're here, take a look at the village church of **San Leonardo**, which was put together in the twelfth century from stones garnered from an Etruscan necropolis. And if you can hang around until the evening, you should sample the menu at the village **restaurant**, *Da Delfina* (closed Mon, Tues, Aug and first two weeks of Jan), where a wonderful Tuscan meal costs around L50,000.

Pratolino and Monte Senario

Nothing remains of Francesco I's favourite villa at **Pratolino**, 12km north of the city, except for its huge park – and even this is but a shadow of its earlier self (May–Sept Fri–Sun 10am–8pm; L4000, free on Fri).

The mechanical toys, trick fountains and other practical jokes that Buontalenti installed in the grounds of Pratolino were the most ingenious ever seen, and required so much maintenance that there was a house in the grounds for the court plumbers. The only survivals from the original garden are a couple of fountains, a little temple by Buontalenti, and Giambologna's immense *Appennino*, a shaggy man-mountain who gushes water. Nonetheless, the park – known as the **Parco Demidoff**, after the nineteenth-century owners of the estate – is still one of the pleasantest green spaces within a bus ride of Florence, and is easily reached by the #25 service.

MONTE SENARIO

If you're travelling under your own steam, you could take an eight-kilometre diversion northeast off the main road into the Mugello to **Monte Senario**, a monastery established by the seven founder members of the Servite order in 1233. The complex is impressive, with its gilded Rococo basilica and hermitages scattered up the hill, but the architecture is less exciting than the views of Mugello from the terrace.

Poggio Imperiale

South of central Florence, Viale del Poggio Imperiale rises from the Porta Romana to the **Villa di Poggio Imperiale**, built by the Salviati family but confiscated by Cosimo I. The Medici did little to improve the place when they enlarged it, and neither did the post-Medici rulers of the city, who glued a Neoclassical facade onto the house. The goverment department that now occupies most of the villa allows pre-arranged visits on Wednesday from 10am to noon, except in August (☎055/220.151; free) – but it's only a trip for the committed Medicean.

Chianti

Ask a sample of northern Europeans to define their idea of paradise and the odds are that several will come up with something that sounds much like **Chianti**, the territory of vineyards and hill towns that stretches between Florence and Siena. Every aspect of life in Chianti is in perfect balance: the landscape is the sort of terrain devised by painters to evoke the Golden Age; one of the most fascinating cities in the world is nearby; the climate for most of the year is balmy, and even in the pit of winter rarely too grim; and on top of all this, there's the wine, the one Italian vintage everyone knows.

The British and others from similarly ill-favoured zones were long ago alerted to Chianti's charms and the rate of immigration has been so rapid since the 1960s that the region is now popularly known as "Chiantishire". Gentrification has pushed property prices beyond the reach of the local population and altered the tone of certain parts irreparably. Tourist handouts might talk of the charm of Chianti's medieval hamlets, but many of them are places where history has become just another commodity and where the abiding impressions are of newly varnished shutters and locks the size of letter boxes.

Away from the Volvo-infested villages, though, there is much to enjoy in Chianti – quiet backroads, hundreds of acres of woodland, and of course the vineyards. Buses from Florence and Siena connect with the main Chianti towns, but the only way to really get to know the region is **by car**. Your own transport allows you to roam into the quieter recesses of the hills, and to stop off at one of the 800-odd **wine producers** to sample the local produce. (Every village mentioned in the text will have wine tastings on offer within a few hundred yards of the main street.) There is basically a choice of two main roads to follow through Chianti: the old **Florence to Siena** road (N2) along the western edge of the region, or the so-called *Chiantigiana* (N222), through the Chianti heartland to the east.

If you pick up a detailed survey map of the region, you can also pick out some of the innumerable miniature **lakes** – offering the quietest swimming you'll find anywhere in Tuscany in the summer. **Hotel** accommodation in Chianti is generally expensive; the only low-budget options are two youth hostels and a few **campsites**. The area's **restaurants** are mostly on the pricey side, too – we've singled out the more attractive propositions.

Western Chianti

A stretch of *autostrada* now connects Florence to Siena along the western edge of Chianti, but to get some sense of the character of the land it's better to take the older N2, which takes in a few of the major Chianti towns en route. Apart from being a far more diverting drive, it's actually not that much slower than the motorway: even with a few stops on the way, you could reach San Gimignano or Siena comfortably in a half-day drive from Florence.

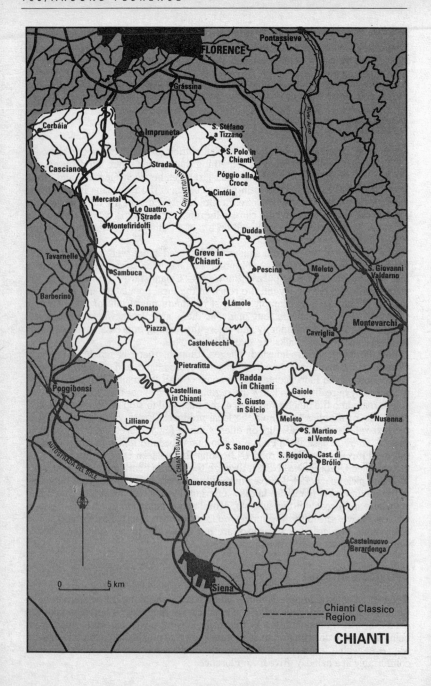

FLORENCE

Pontassieve

Grássina

Cerbáia

Impruneta

S. Stéfano a Tizzano

S. Polo in Chianti

S. Casciano

Strada

Póggio alla Croce

Mercatal

Cintóia

Le Quattro Strade

Montefiridolfi

Dudda

Tavarnelle

Greve in Chianti.

Pescina

Meleto

S. Giovanni Valdarno

Barberino

Sambuca

S. Donato

Lámole

Piazza

Montevarchi

Castelvécchi

Cavriglia

Pietrafitta

Poggibonsi

Radda in Chianti

Castellina in Chianti

Gaiole

S. Giusto in Sálcio

Lilliano

Meleto

Nusenna

S. Martino al Vento

S. Sano

S. Régolo

Cast. di Brólio

AUTOSTRADA DEL SOLE

Quercegrossa

Castelnuovo Berardenga

0   5 km

Siena

LA CHIANTIGIANA

------- Chianti Classico Region

CHIANTI

The Certosa di Galluzzo

On the city side of the Autostrada del Sole, beyond Poggio Imperiale, the N2 sweeps by the Carthusian monastery of the **Certosa di Galluzzo** (Tues–Sun 9am–noon & 3–7pm; closes 5pm in winter; free), founded in the fourteenth century by the Florentine banker Niccolò Acciaioli. Buses #36 and #37 run here from Santa Maria Novella train station, so it can easily be visited as an excursion from Florence.

The Certosa is now occupied by Cistercian monks, one of whose number shows visitors round the enormous complex. Its main architectural attraction is the **Chiostro Grande**, with its tondoes of prophets and saints by Andrea and Giovanni della Robbia and their workshop. One of the eighteen monks' cells adjoining this cloister is open – a very homely arrangement, each with three rooms and its own patch of garden.

Beyond, the tour reaches the **Palazzo degli Studi**, now a picture gallery though built as a study centre by the well-educated Acciaioli, who counted Boccaccio and Petrarch among his friends. The Certosa was once so rich that it owned over 500 works of art, most of which were carried off by Napoleon; the best of what remains are the five scenes of the Passion painted for the Chiostro Grande by Pontormo in 1522, while he and his pupil Bronzino were taking refuge from a plague outbreak in the city.

In the **church** itself, down in the crypt of the lay brothers' choir are the tombs of the monastery's founder and his descendants, including a beautiful slab once thought to have been by Donatello, now attributed to Francesco da Sangallo.

Sant'Andrea and San Casciano Val di Pesa

South of the Certosa, the N2 passes to the east of **SANT'ANDREA IN PERCUSSINA**, where **Machiavelli** allieviated the boredom of exile by writing *The Prince*, the manual of statecraft that he hoped, in vain, would seal his rehabilitation. A house has been identified as his residence but it is not open to visits.

SAN CASCIANO VAL DI PESA, 17km from Florence, is the first real town on the road itself. In fact, with a population of around 15,000, it is the only place in Chianti that is really more than an extended village. It is also home to one of the slickest commercial operations in Tuscany, the six-hundred-year-old **Antinori wine house**, and to one of Chianti's most interesting churches, **Santa Maria del Prato**, which stands by the one surviving gateway in the town walls. Santa Maria was built in the fourteenth century and contains some beautiful works of art from the same period: a crucifix by an anonymous follower of Giotto, an altarpiece of the Madonna and Child, and a pulpit by a pupil of Andrea Pisano.

For **accommodation**, San Casciano town offers the well-appointed *Antica Posta*, Piazza Zannoni 1 (☎055/820.116; ⑥); the attached **restaurant** (closed Mon) is marvellous, offering a superb set meal with wine from L60,000 – booking is essential. Alternatively, for L20,000 less you can get a fine meal at *Da Nello*, Via IV Novembre 64, where the Friday fish menu is especially good (closed Wed evening & Thurs).

Mercatale and around

The road east from San Casciano passes the Chianti-producing **Villa Le Corti**, one of many Florentine gentry residences in this part of the region, before reaching the once-major market town of **MERCATALE**, 5km from San Casciano. Mercatale has a tiny **hotel**, the *Soggiorno Paradise*, right in the centre at Piazza

Vittorio Veneto 28 (☎055/821.327; ④). There's also a couple of good **restaurants**: *La Biscondola* on Via Grevigiana (the road from San Casciano), at around L40,000 per head (closed all Mon & Tues lunchtime); and *Trattoria Da Poldo*, in an old farmhouse a bit further along the same road, at about the same price, with fried rabbit and chicken their speciality.

A couple of kilometres further east, on the road towards Greve (see facing page), stands the eleventh-century **Castello di Gabbiano**, built by the Bardi, the wealthiest Florentine banking dynasty before the coming of the Medici. As with Le Corti, it produces wine – and olive oil, another great Chianti speciality.

Bargino and southwards

Back on the N2 south of San Casciano, you pass the castle of **Bibbione** – home of the Buondelmonte family, who triggered the Guelph versus Ghibelline battles – before coming into **BARGINO**, which has low-cost rooms at the one-star *Bargino*, Via Cassia 122 (☎055/824.9055; ③). From here it's a short diversion east to the fortified village of **MONTEFIRIDOLFI**, whose castle once belonged to the sons of Ridolfo Buondelmonte (*figli di Ridolfo*).

Beyond Bargino, the N2 rolls into **TAVARNELLE VAL DI PESA**, which expanded as an agricultural centre in the nineteenth century. There's a reasonable **restaurant** here, *La Fattoria* at Via del Cerro 11, and one of two **youth hostels** in Chianti, at Via Roma 137 (March–Oct; ☎055/807.7009; ①).

A couple of kilometres further lies the more ancient **BARBERINO VAL D'ELSA**, site of one of the rare **campsites** in Chianti (☎055/807.5454). The beautiful Romanesque **Pieve di Sant'Appiano**, parts of which date back to the tenth century, is a few kilometres southwest of the village (well signposted); due south, on the main road, is Poggibonsi, nexus for buses to San Gimignano and Siena (see p.322).

The Chianti heartland

There's no better way to experience the village life of Chianti than to drive along the **Chiantigiana** (N222), which cuts right across the hills from Florence to Siena, connecting with a tangle of minor roads that supply the most unspoiled parts of the region. If you put your foot down, the twists and turns of the *Chiantigiana* can be negotiated in only a little longer than the major road to the west, but really this is a route to dawdle along, taking side turnings on a whim and dropping by at any vineyard that takes your fancy.

Santa Caterina d'Antella and Impruneta

Leaving Florence on the N22 (the access road for the *Chiantigiana*), a short detour just before the *autostrada* will bring you to the village of **PONTE A EMA** and, a kilometre beyond, to the church of **Santa Caterina d'Antella**. This has a fine cycle of scenes from the life of Saint Catherine of Siena, painted by Spinello Aretino in 1387. Executed immediately prior to his work at San Miniato al Monte, they make an interesting comparison with Agnolo Gaddi's less monumental fresco cycle in Florence's church of Santa Croce, painted at the same time. (For an account of the life of the saint, see p.313.)

Another rewarding detour, this time just south of the *autostrada*, presents itself at Grássina. Take a right turn here and, after 9km of winding minor road, you arrive at **IMPRUNETA**. The **Collegiata** here, now restored after heavy bomb damage in 1944, was founded in the eleventh century to house a miraculous icon of the Madonna and Child dug up in a nearby field and said to have been painted – as these things so often are – by Saint Luke. It's housed in one of a pair of matching chapels by Michelozzo, the other one of which contains a fragment of the True Cross; both have lovely enamelled terracotta decoration by Luca della Robbia. Impruneta has long been a centre of the terracotta industry, and holds a big fair in October on the main square. In nearby Bottai there's a **campsite** at Via San Cristoforo 2 (☎055/237.4704; April–Oct) and a two-star **hotel**: *Scopeti* at Via Cassia 183 (☎055/202.2008; ④).

Grássina to Strada

Go east rather than west at Grássina and you'll come to **SANTO STEFANO A TIZZANO**, with its Romanesque church and contemporaneous **Castello di Tizzano**, a producer of good wines but best known for its *extra vergine* olive oil. A couple of kilometres further is **SAN POLO IN CHIANTI**, where a massive iris festival in May celebrates the village's crop of Florence's floral emblem. One of Chianti's best wine shops is here, the *Antico Toscana* – though the pleasure of the visit is very much dependent on who's on duty that day.

From San Polo a minor road reconnects with the *Chiantigiana* at **STRADA IN CHIANTI**. The road southeast from Strada to Dudda is overlooked by the mighty **Castello di Mugnana**, once echoed by a second castle across the hillside, protecting this stretch of the road down into the Arno valley. This renovated fort is now the headquarters of a massive wine estate which organises excellent tastings – but they have to be arranged five days in advance (☎055/857.2021).

Greve and around

For more casual oenophiles, perhaps the best target is **GREVE**, 10km down the *Chiantigiana* from Strada. The venue for Chianti's biggest **wine fair** (held in September), this is a town with a **wine shop** on every street: the best outlet is the *Enoteca di Gallo Nero*, Piazzetta Santa Croce 8. The hub of the town, and site of the Saturday market, is the funnel-shaped **Piazza Matteotti**, whose irregular arcades are explained by the fact that different merchants paid for their own stretches of colonnade. The statue in the centre is of Giovanni da Verrazzano, the man who discovered New York harbour; he was born in the nearby village of Verrazzano.

As the chief town of the *Gallo Nero* region, Greve is equipped with a vineyard-oriented **tourist office**, in Via Luca Cini (Mon–Sat 10am–12.30pm & 4.30–7pm). A couple of three-star **hotels** on Piazza Matteotti offer comfortable accommodation: the clean-cut *Del Chianti* at no. 86 (☎055/853.763; ⑥) and *Da Verrazzano* at no. 28 (☎055/853.189; ⑤). The latter also has a very good **restaurant**, at around L40,000 for a full meal (closed Mon & Jan 15–Feb 15). There are several recommended pizzeria-restaurants too: *Gallo Nero*, Via Cesare Battista 9; *La Cantina*, Piazza Trento; and *Casa del Popolo*, Via Luca Cini. For travellers on a tight rein, there's a well-signposted **campsite**, the *Girasole*, just outside the village, and a new **youth hostel** in Lucolena, 10km east of Greve – the *San Michele*, Via Casole 42 (☎055/851.034; mid-March to Oct; ①).

Five minutes' drive from Greve, up a steep zigzagging road, lies the much-restored hamlet of **MONTEFIORALLE**, where a single elliptical street – Via di Montefioralle – encompasses a few tower houses and a pair of Romanesque churches. This street has one of the nearest approximations to a simple **trattoria** in Chianti, the *Taverna del Guerrino*; a menu of locally produced sausages, beans and vegetables provides a good Tuscan meal for around L30,000.

Continuing west from Montefioralle, the road passes the vestiges of the castle of **Montefili**, whose owners were generous benefactors of the **Badìa a Passignano**, which is a few kilometres on towards the N2. Once one of the wealthiest religious houses in Tuscany, the Badìa a Passignano has now become a private residence, but the abbey church of **San Michele** is unaltered; it contains pictures by Ghirlandaio and Alessandro Allori, and a bust of Giovanni Gualberto, founder of the Vallombrosan order, whose arrival here in 1050 led the monastery to dedicate itself to the care of the sick.

South to Castellina

Six kilometres south of Greve along the *Chiantigiana*, the hilltop town of **PANZANO** overlooks a circle of hills known as the *Conca d'Oro* (Golden Valley) because of their sun-trap properties; the resultant wines can be sampled at the *Enoteca del Chianti Classico*, Via Giovanni da Verrazzano 8. Signposted down a branch road, the Romanesque **Pieve di San Leolino**, 3km south of the village, is one of the oldest churches in Chianti, tracing its origins to the first Christian settlers; it's much favoured for local weddings.

The summit of the next main hill, 15km on, is occupied by well-heeled **CASTELLINA IN CHIANTI**, which formerly stood on the front line of the continual wars between Florence and Siena. The walls, fortress and the covered walkway known as the **Via delle Volte** – a kind of gallery looking east from underneath the town – all bear testimony to an embattled past; marks of a more distant era can be seen ten minutes' walk out of the village, in the form of the **Ipogeo Etrusco di Montecalvario**, a sixth-century BC Etruscan tomb. The power-station bulk of the **wine co-operative** on the main road declares Castellina's modern preoccupations; the local wine and oil are on sale in the compendious *Bottega del Vino Gallo Nero*, at Via della Rocca 10.

Radda and around

The best of Chianti lies east of Castellina and the *Chiantigiana*, in the less domesticated terrain of the **Monti del Chianti** – the stronghold of the medieval Lega di Chianti, whose power bases were Castellina itself and the two principal towns of this craggy region. The nearer of these, **RADDA IN CHIANTI**, was the league's capital, and the imprint of that period is stronger here than anywhere else in Chianti. The street plan of this minuscule historic centre is focused on Piazza Ferrucci, where the frescoed and shield-studded Palazzo Comunale faces a church raised on a high platform. Neither is an outstanding individual building – it's the ancient core as a unit that gives the place its appeal.

Close to the piazza, at Via Roma 41, the *Girarrosto* **restaurant** has an annexe with double **rooms** (☎0577/738.010; closed Wed; ③). The newsagent at Via Roma 46 has rooms and houses to rent (☎0577/738.556; ④), while the *Villa Miranda*, a short distance east of the village in Villa a Radda (☎0577/738.021; ④) has scruffy rooms and a rather grubby if occasionally inspired restaurant. Meals at around L60,000 per head, are served at the *Vignale*, Via XX Settembre 23 (closed Thurs & Jan 10–March 10), and there's a pizza place down the ramp opposite here. Far better are a couple of trattorie in old, isolated farmhouses with spectacular scenery, serving good, local food at around L30–35,000 per head: *Le Vigne*, just off the road between Villa a Radda and Radda in Chianti; and *Dominic Montevarchi*, on the road between Villa and Badìa a Coltibuono (see p.164).

CHIANTI WINES

Chianti became the world's first officially defined wine-producing area in 1716, the year Cosimo III drew the boundaries within which vineyards could use the region's name on their product. Modern Chianti wine, however, came into being last century, with the oenological experiments of Bettino Ricasoli, second prime minister of unified Italy, who refined the blend of grapes at his residence in Brolio. Since then the **Sangiovese** variety has been the basis of Chianti wines, as of many of the country's other big-league reds, such as Brunello di Montalcino and Vino Nobile di Montepulciano.

White grapes used to be an important component of the mix, but all over the Chianti area there's now a trend to replace these with dark grapes like Cabernet, Merlot and Pino Nero – a development that nonetheless has not altered the tremendous variety of wines bearing the Chianti name. The re-evaluation of Chianti as a **DOCG** wine in the 1980s led to a severe dip in production, the 1979 output of 180 million litres rapidly falling by a half, but it's Italy's highest-volume DOCG producer.

The better Chianti wines mature at around 4–7 years and the best recent vintages to look out for are 1982, 1983, 1985 and 1986. The seven classified **regions** – which extend well beyond the geographical area known as Chianti – are as follows.

● **Chianti Classico.** The central Chianti district, delineated on the map on p.158. In 1924 Chianti Classico was institutionalised, taking as its trademark the black cock (*Gallo Nero*) that was once the heraldic symbol of the baronial alliance called the Lega di Chianti. Most producers within this zone belong to the Gallo Nero consortium, a further guarantee of the reliability of the wines produced here.

● **Chianti Colli Aretini.** From the hills on the east side of the Arno valley, to the north of Arezzo. Generally softer than Classico.

● **Chianti Colli Fiorentini.** From the area immediately south and east of Florence, and along the Arno and Pesa valleys. Much of the house wine served in Florence's restaurants comes from here, as do most of the traditional straw-jacketed flasks.

● **Chianti Colli Senesi.** The largest Chianti zone, comprising three distinct districts: around Montalcino, around Montepulciano, and south of the Classico region, east of San Gimignano. Quality often very good, but variable.

● **Chianti Colline Pisane.** The lightest Chianti comes from this region, southeast of Pisa around Casciana Terme.

● **Chianti Montalbano.** From the hills west of Florence and south of Pistoia. Known for its fruitier wines.

● **Chianti Rúfina.** From the lower Sieve valley, in eastern Mugello. Produces some of the beefier Chiantis.

Seven kilometres north of Radda is the unspoilt village of **VOLPAIA**, which from the tenth to the sixteenth century was an important military lookout over the valley of the Pesa. The medieval donjon still stands, but the most interesting structure in Volpaia is the deconsecrated Commenda di Sant'Eufrosino, the unlikely venue for an annual **festival of avant-garde art**, sponsored by the **Castello di Volpaia** wine estate.

The same distance south of Radda is **AMA**, once a fortification on the southern edge of Florentine territory. Round the village are ranged the vineyards of one of

Chianti's first-rank wine estates, **Castello di Ama**, which offers tastings throughout the year except in August.

Gaiole and Brolio

Leaving Radda, the first turning left after the *Villa Miranda* passes the foot of the hill on which stands the **Badìa a Coltibuono**, 6km from Radda. This Vallombrosan abbey (see p.380) was founded on the site of an eighth-century hermitage, and its church of San Lorenzo, built in 1050, is one of Tuscany's finest Romanesque buildings; unfortunately, it's rarely open except for daily Mass (4pm in spring, 4.30pm in summer, 3.30pm in autumn, 3pm in winter). The monastic complex is now owned by a wine estate, whose vintages are served at *Badìa a Coltibuono*, the **restaurant** adjoining the abbey – a wonderful meal here will cost anything from L35,000 to L80,000 per head, depending on which wine you select. *Club Alpino* **walks** are laid out through the oak and pine woods on the surrounding slopes.

Modern times have caught up with the third of the Lega di Chianti triad, **GAIOLE**, 5km south of Coltibuono. Now a brisk market town, it has a **wine co-operative** at Via Mulinaccio 10, which offers splendid tasting opportunities, as does the *Enoteca Montagnani*, at Via Bandinelli 9, which has a superlative range of Chianti Classico. The most impressive sights in the immediate area are the ruins of the **Castello di Vertine**, occupying the heights 3km west of the village, and the fortified village of **Barbischio**, up a winding little road to the east. Devotees of military ruins could follow the signposted *Strada dei Castelli* from Gaiole, an itinerary of half a dozen fortresses between Spaltena (1km) and Vistarenni (6km). There are a couple of pricey hotels in the Gaiole vicinity, but it's not the pick of the Chianti towns, so it's better to drive on; the same goes for places to eat.

A couple of kilometres south of Gaiole, the twin circular towers of the **Castello di Meleto** peer from behind a screen of cypresses over the road leading to **Castagnoli**, where the houses form a fringe to a thickset fortress. If you are interested in visiting a classic Chianti *cantina*, perhaps the best place to make for is **Castello di Brolio**, just outside the nearby village of **BROLIO**: from Castagnoli you should take the minor road through San Martino al Vento; or, coming from Gaiole, you could take the turning off the N408 after Meleto.

The building itself passed to the Ricasoli family as far back as the twelfth century, and was the subject of frequent tussles between the Florentines and the Sienese. Demolished by the Sienese army, it was rebuilt in the sixteenth century, then in the last century it was converted into a colossal mock-medieval country residence by the vinicultural pioneer **Baron Bettino Ricasoli**. The baron's apartments can be visited on a tour of the house (daily 9am–noon & 3–6pm) – but a far more rewarding experience is to sample the fruits of his labours in the estate's salerooms. Castello di Brolio wine is the routine accompaniment in the *castello*'s unpretentious *Da Gino* **restaurant**, one of the least expensive places to eat in Chianti (closed Tues). However, for quality it's surpassed by *Carlino* at San Règolo (just next to Castello di Brolio), a trattoria where you can eat exquisitely for L30,000.

Back on the N408, 9km south of Gaiole there's the option of a diversion to the pleasant, regular *Trattoria San Sano* in **SAN SANO**, just to the west of the road to Ama (see above) – it's a combined restaurant, bar and general store, with tables outside.

Mugello

For every ten tourists who give over a day to the vineyards of Chianti, perhaps one gives a few hours to the **Mugello**, the lushly fertile region on the Tuscan side of the Apennine ridge separating the province from Emilia-Romagna. Like Chianti this is a benign, humanised sort of landscape, with nothing that will take your breath away – but it's easier to leave the crowds here, even though it's a favourite weekend hang-out of the Florentine bourgeoisie. Its celebrated olive groves and vineyards are concentrated in the central Mugello basin, formed by the Sieve and its tributary valleys; elsewhere the vegetation is principally oak, pine and chestnut forest, interspersed with small resorts whose customers tend to be short-stay vacationers from the city. Accommodation is quite expensive – unless you're camping, this is a region to nip into from Florence for the day.

As with Chianti, you'll need a car to see anything much. **Three main roads** run from Florence: the **Via Bologna** (N65), which passes Pratolino on its way to the Passo della Futa, the **N302** direct to Borgo San Lorenzo, and the **N67/551**, which winds up to Borgo San Lorenzo along the Sieve. By public transport, there's choice between the **Sieve valley train line** to Borgo San Lorenzo, or *SITA* and *CAP* buses along the same route; buses run from Borgo San Lorenzo to the western and northern parts of Mugello. The layout of this section follows the Sieve upstream.

Eastern Mugello

The Sieve flows into the Arno at the unprepossessing town of **PONTASSIEVE**, which makes its money from the **Rúfina wine** district immediately to the north. From here the N70 clambers over the Passo della Consuma, then drops south into the Casentino district towards Poppi (see p.393). The N67 trails the valley through the moderately industrialised area up to Rúfina, then on through Dicomano, where it veers off towards Faenza (in Emilia-Romagna), passing through the **Alpe di San Benedetto**. The main settlement in this zone of Mugello is San Godenzo, which boasts an eleventh-century abbey and not a lot else.

Hugging the course of the Sieve beyond Dicomano, the N551 runs on through **VICCHIO**, the birthplace of Fra' Angelico. Unsurprisingly the village makes the most of the Angelico connection, but the **Museo Comunale Beato Angelico** (by appointment only ☎055/849.7026) in fact possesses nothing directly connected with the man; unless Etruscan bits and pieces sound enticing, it's not worth making the call. Vicchio has a **campsite**, the *Vecchio Ponte*, at Via Costoli 10 (☎055/844.8306).

Next stop along the main road is another exalted birthplace, **VESPIGNANO**, where **Giotto** was born in around 1266. His career started, so the story goes, when Cimabue happened to pass by the spot where the boy was tending his father's flock; Giotto was drawing a picture of one of the sheep on a stone, and Cimabue was so astonished by the shepherd's proficiency that he immediately took him on as an apprentice. The bridge where the crucial encounter is said to have occurred is a few hundred yards out of Vespignano, and is well signposted. The farmhouse in which Giotto was actually born – the **Casa di Giotto** (summer Thurs, Sat & Sun 3–7pm; winter Sun only; L1000) – is a kilometre off to the north, also well signposted; as with the homes of Leonardo and Michelangelo, the point of going there has nothing to do with what's in the museum.

Borgo San Lorenzo

With a population of 15,000 or so, **BORGO SAN LORENZO** is the giant of
Mugello towns, with industrial plots and tracts of new housing spreading further
with each year. Substantially rebuilt after a massive earthquake in 1919, it has just
one major building, the church of **San Lorenzo**, an eleventh-century foundation
that was renovated in the sixteenth but still retains its irregularly hexagonal
Romanesque tower. This isn't the most photographed sight in town, though –
that honour goes to the ghastly statue of *Fido* in Piazza Dante, a rare example of
overt Italian sentimentality towards animals. Borgo San Lorenzo has lots of hotels
for visiting traders, the only people who would really want to hang about here.

If you're travelling by public transport from Florence and want to carry on westward into Mugello, you'll have to change here for the local **bus** route through San
Piero a Sieve and Scarperia to Barberino di Mugello. The **rail** line heads north
from Borgo San Lorenzo to Faenza, while the road north divides after about 20km,
one branch going to the bland resort of Palazzuolo sul Sénio, the other to the similar Marradi. If you're driving that way, or waiting for a train in Borgo San Lorenzo,
you could call at **San Giovanni Maggiore**, 3km north of the town at the end of an
avenue of cypress trees. Like San Lorenzo, it too has a fine Romanesque campanile, and inside there's a twelfth-century marble pulpit inlaid with symbolic figures.

San Piero a Sieve

The N551 continues up the Sieve from Borgo San Lorenzo to **SAN PIERO A
SIEVE**, crossing the N65 coming up from Florence. The Mugello landscape is at
its best here, with ploughed fields foregrounding the slopes of tree-crested conical
hills. San Piero's Romanesque church, semi-ruined by an eighteenth-century
facade, houses a beautiful coloured terracotta font, possibly by Luca della Robbia;
its other main monument is the Medici fortress overlooking the town, built by
Buontalenti in 1571.

San Piero has a fine **hotel** in Via Provinciale, the *Ebe* (☎055/848.019; ⑦); the
hotel **restaurant** is more than acceptable, its menu tending to favour dishes from
Emilia-Romagna rather than Tuscany. The *Ebe* has less expensive rooms at its
dipendenza, Via di Cafaggio 11 (☎055/848.019; ③). There's also a **campsite** a
short distance outside the town at La Fortezza – the *Mugello Verde* (☎055/
848.511; open all year).

Bosco ai Frati

The secluded monastery of **Bosco ai Frati**, reached by taking a left turn off the
N503 immediately north of San Piero (it's a rough 4-km track), traces its roots
back to a community of Greek monks who arrived here in the seventh century. In
the early eleventh century the settlement was abandoned, but at the start of the
thirteenth Saint Francis established his order here. One of the earliest Franciscan
saints, **Bonaventure**, was the prior at Bosco ai Frati; a man of exemplary
modesty, he refused to put on the cardinal's attire brought to him by a papal delegation until he'd finished washing up his brothers' pots and pans – the tree where
the outfit was hung is still there.

Cosimo il Vecchio sank a lot of money into this monastery, hiring Michelozzo
to redesign the complex in the plainest early Renaissance style; in the sacristy of
Michelozzo's porticoed church (open daily 8.30am–7pm) there's the most
remarkable work of art in the Mugello, a stripped and pain-racked **crucifix** probably carved by Donatello.

Scarperia and beyond

Beyond the turning for Bosco ai Frati, the N503 continues to **SCARPERIA**, once the biggest producer of cutlery in Tuscany and now a low-output high-quality centre of the industry. Sitting on a platform of rock above a valley 5km from San Piero, it's essentially a one-street town, laid out by the Florentines after they turned it into their chief military base in Mugello in 1306. The **Palazzo Pretorio**, built in the same year along the lines of Florence's Palazzo Vecchio, has a rash of coats of arms on the outside, and extensive frescoes on the inside, some of them by followers of Giotto. None of its churches is remarkable, though one of them bears an unusual dedication to Our Lady of the Earthquakes.

If you're perplexed by the crowds around the town, they are on their way to the **motor racing track** on the eastern outskirts; built in the 1970s, this is a venue for Formula Two car races and motorcycle events, but may become Italy's grand prix circuit. At present the town has a neat little **hotel**, *Cantogallo*, at Via Kennedy 17 (☎055/843.0442; ⑤).

A small road climbs northwest from Scarperia to the tiny village of **SANT'AGATA**, where the Romanesque parish church contains some beautiful inlaid panels from a dismantled twelfth-century pulpit, and a tabernacle by Giovanni della Robbia. The N503 becomes a switchback after this turnoff, swooping through the region known as Mugello's "Little Switzerland" to the hill resort of **FIRENZUOLA**, 22km from Scarperia. Rebuilt after a fierce battle in 1944, Firenzuola has few blandishments – only those pressing on into Emilia-Romagna need bother with it.

Trebbio and Cafaggiolo

The Medici were originally from Mugello, and the environs of San Piero contain two rough-hewn villas which encapsulate something of the flavour of the period when the family secured its political ascendancy.

Near Novoli an unsurfaced road runs west from the Via Bologna to the Medici villa of **Trebbio**, whose fortified tower peeps over a cordon of cypresses from the top of its hill. This fourteenth-century castle was converted into a country abode by Michelozzo in 1461 and became a particular favourite with Giovanni delle Bande Nere and his branch of the clan: it was from here that Giovanni's son, Cosimo, rode down to Florence to assume power after the assassination of Alessandro de' Medici. The small garden is often open to the public, but the house can at present only be visited on the first Tuesday of each month – don't set out to visit the villa without first checking its times with one of the Florence tourist offices.

A short distance north, right on the Via Bologna, lies the villa of **Cafaggiolo**, which like Trebbio was a fortress converted for less bellicose use by Michelozzo. When Cosimo il Vecchio set about consolidating the family fortune through land investment in their ancestral domain, one of his first ventures was to buy this estate, which comprised the castle and tracts of land for hunting and agriculture. It was at Cafaggiolo that Cosimo's immediate descendants Lorenzo il Magnifico and his brother grew up, and Lorenzo's own children – Piero, Giovanni (Pope Leo X) and Giuliano – were taught here by such luminaries as Ficino, Poliziano and Pico della Mirandola. In those days the house would have had an even less suave appearance than it does now – alterations in the last century did away with the surrounding walls, the moat, the drawbridge and one of its towers. Now neglected and ailing, the villa can only be inspected from the road.

Barberino di Mugello – and over the Apennines

North of Cafaggiolo the gradient of the road gets pretty savage as it begins the climb to Passo della Futa; if you don't have enough under the bonnet to do the climb comfortably, there's a less strenuous loop that goes through the main market town of western Mugello, **BARBERINO DI MUGELLO**. In the early fourteenth century this became a Florentine border post, and in later years Michelozzo picked up some work here, too, giving the main square its loggia – the **Loggie Medicee**, naturally; the neighbouring much-decorated Palazzo Pretorio and the Castello dei Cattani are the only other buildings to catch the eye.

Barberino has one of the few reasonable Mugello **hotels**, *Il Cavallo* at Via della Repubblica 7 (☎055/841.363; ④), and there's a good **restaurant** attached, specialising in seafood, at L40–45,000 a head. Another decent restaurant is to be found close to the exit from the *autostrada* to the west of the village – *Le Capannine*, Viale Don Minzoni 88, Cavallino Mugello (closed Mon). Outside Barberino, at Via Santa Lucia 26 in Monte di Fo, is the *Sergente* **campsite** (☎055/ 842.3018; open March–Oct).

When the Barberino loop rejoins Via Bologna it's an unrelenting haul up to **Passo della Futa**, from whose 900-metre vantage all of Mugello's valleys and ridges are visible. This isn't the highest point on Mugello's road network – Passo della Raticosa, 13km on, is a few metres higher – but it is easily the best view-point; there's no reason to go further unless you're off to Bologna.

Prato

Taking its name from the meadow (*prato*) where the ancient settlement's great market used to be held, **PRATO** has long been a commercial success, and is now the third largest city in Tuscany, after Florence and Livorno. It's been Italy's chief textile city since the early Middle Ages, and even though recession has cut exports by a quarter over the last five years, it still produces three-quarters of all the woollen cloth sold from Italy. It might not feature on a list of the most attractive places in the province, but its long-time wealth has left a fair legacy of buildings and art, including Filippo Lippi's most engaging cycle of frescoes.

A close Florentine connection goes back to 1350, when the self-governing *comune* of Prato was besieged by its neighbour, which by then was becoming alarmed at the economic threat of Prato's cloth mills. The year after, Florence bought the titles to the town from its Neapolitan rulers, thus legally sealing their union. Thenceforward, political events in the capital were mirrored here, a relationship that was to cost Prato dear after Savonarola's example led the Pratese to join him in rejecting the Medici. Under the direction of Leo X, the imperial army sacked Prato in 1512 as a warning to the rebellious Florentines; two days of slaughter and pillage ensued, and the historian Guicciardini remarked – "Nothing would have escaped the avarice, lust and cruelty of the invaders had not the Cardinal de' Medici placed guards at the main church and saved the honour of the women who had taken refuge there. More than two thousand men died, not fighting . . . but fleeing or crying for mercy". A more pacific relationship was soon established and Florence limited its bullying to the imposition of quotas on Prato's factories. Today the balance has shifted: Prato is fairly self-sufficient, while Florence struggles to find some alternative to a service-based economy.

The City

The historic centre remains enclosed within its hexagon of grey stone walls, making orientation very straightforward. Buses from Florence run direct to the Piazza del Duomo; if you're coming from the main train station it's basically a question of following your nose – cross the Ponte della Vittoria over the Bisenzio river, and Viale Vittorio Veneto leads you through the walls at Piazza San Marco.

The Castello area

Directly ahead of the train station, past a Henry Moore sculpture, is the white-walled and sharp-angled **Castello dell'Imperatore** (Mon & Wed–Sat 9.30am–12.30pm & 3–6.30pm, Sun 9.30am–12.30pm; free), built in the 1230s for Emperor Frederick II as a base for his representative in the city and as a way-station for imperial progresses between Germany and his domains in southern Italy and Sicily. The castle is heavily restored, and empty except for the rooms used for temporary exhibitions, but you can wander around the ramparts for views over the old city and the industrial suburbs.

Round the back is Prato's major Renaissance monument, Giuliano da Sangallo's church of **Santa Maria delle Carceri** (closed noon–4.30pm), built to honour a miraculous talking image of the Virgin that was painted on the walls of the gaol here – hence the name "Mary of the Prisons". With its perfect proportions and uncluttered lines, the church feels less like a place for worship than a demonstration of the correctness of the Brunelleschian style. The exterior makes a decorative gesture towards the Romanesque with its half-completed bands of green and white marble, while the interior is lightened by Andrea della Robbia's tondoes of the Evangelists and ceramic frieze.

Twin-coloured marble cladding also features on the facade of the thirteenth-century **San Francesco**, which presents one massive flank to the other side of the square. Inside, there are a couple of fine monuments: on the left wall of the single aisle you'll find Bernardo Rossellino's worn-down tomb of Gemignano Inghirami, and set into the floor near the high altar is the slab of **Francesco di Marco Datini**, the city's most celebrated personality. The subject of Iris Origo's classic study, *The Merchant of Prato*, Datini became one of Europe's richest men through his dealings in the cloth trade, and played a crucial role in the rationalisation of accounting methods – on his death, his offices were found to contain tens of thousands of scrupulously kept ledgers, all inscribed "To God and profit". Off the cloister, the Cappella Migliatori has lovely frescoes of *The Lives of St Anthony Abbot and St Matthew* and *The Crucifixion*, painted in the 1390s by Niccolò di Pietro Gerini.

Datini's house, **Palazzo Datini**, is a couple of minutes from the church, across Piazza San Francesco and up Via Rinascelda. Built in the 1390s, this is now home to the *Ceppo*, a charity he established a few years later. The inscrutable frescoes on the facade show scenes from the life of Datini; the interior is completely frescoed as well, but access is rarely possible.

The Piazza del Comune

A short distance north of here, Datini is commemorated with a statue and bronze reliefs at the centre of the trim little **Piazza del Comune**, and inevitably he crops up again in the **Museo Civico**, which occupies much of the medieval Palazzo Pretorio (Mon & Wed–Sat 9.30am–12.30pm & 3–6.30pm, Sun 9.30am–12.30pm; L5000, including entry to the other two town museums). Here Filippo Lippi's

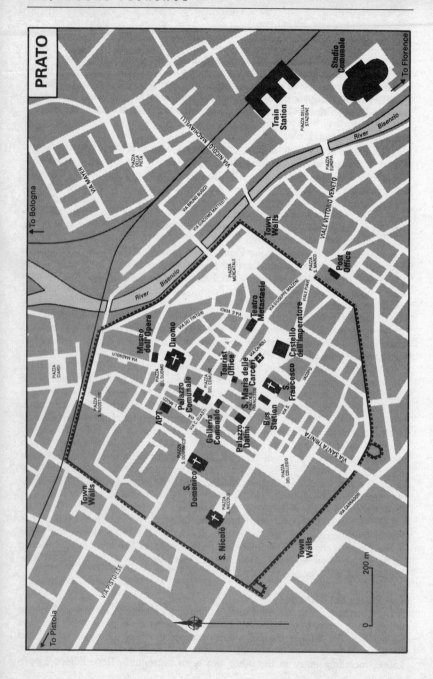

Madonna del Ceppo includes portraits of the five men who financed the picture; Datini coughed up more than the other four, so he's the one depicted large-scale. The gallery's ramshackle collection of Florentine art also includes work by Lippi's son Filippino, and a selection of fourteenth-century altarpieces including a predella by Bernardo Daddi narrating the story of Prato's holy relic, the Girdle of the Madonna (see below). The collections fizzle out with a stream of forgettable seventeenth- and eighteenth-century pieces, alleviated by Giovanni Caracciolo's *Noli me tangere*, featuring a Christ who looks like a refugee from Woodstock.

Facing the Palazzo Pretorio is the **Palazzo Comunale**, which retains its frescoed council chamber, but little else that bears testimony to its long history.

The Duomo and its museum

The wide and lively Piazza del Duomo, a couple of blocks further in, forms an effective space for the Pisan-Romanesque facade of the **Duomo** (7am–noon & 3.30–6.30pm), distinguished by another Andrea della Robbia terracotta over the portal and by Donatello and Michelozzo's beautiful **Pulpit of the Sacred Girdle**, its canopy lodged like a halo on the corner of the church. This unique addition was constructed for the ceremonial display of the girdle of the Madonna, a garment handed to the ever-incredulous Thomas the Apostle at her Assumption. The girdle was supposedly bequeathed by Thomas to a priest, one of whose descendants married a crusader from Prato, who in turn brought it back to his home town in the twelfth century. Replicas have replaced the Donatello reliefs of gambolling children, the originals now being shown in the cathedral museum. The pulpit is put to its intended use five times a year: on Easter Day, May 1, August 15, September 8 and Christmas Day.

The story is detailed in the chapel immediately left of the entrance in Agnolo Gaddi's fresco cycle of *The Legend of the Holy Girdle* (1392–95) – though unfortunately it's all but invisible behind the grating, as is the *Madonna and Child* carved by Giovanni Pisano. Close by, in the left aisle, there's another fine piece of stonework, a chalice-shaped pulpit by Antonio Rossellino and Mino da Fiesole.

Filippo Lippi's famous frescoes, around the high altar, were completed over a period of fourteen years (1452–66) and depict the lives of John the Baptist and Saint Stephen. (A long-term restoration has hidden much of this cycle for the last three years; if the work has been completed, you'll need coins for the light boxes.)These are marvellously sensuous paintings in which even the Baptist's wilderness looks enticing, a whisked-up landscape like a confectioner's fantasy. Especially decadent is the *Feast of Herod*, where the decapitation seems like a regrettable incident that won't ruin the party. There's a scandalous story to the creation of these pictures. During the period of their creation, Lippi – himself a monk, at least in name – became so besotted with a young nun named Lucrezia Buti that he abducted her as she was preparing to attend the ceremony of the girdle. Later to become the mother of Filippino Lippi, Lucrezia is said to have been the model for the dancing Salome. Her lover has depicted himself among those mourning Saint Stephen – he's third from the right.

The chapel to the right of the high altar has scenes from *Lives of the Virgin and Saint Stephen*, still cussedly labelled as being by Paolo Uccello, even though a study of the *sinopie* has established that they can't possibly be.

Housed alongside the Duomo, around the cloister of the bishop's palace, the **Museo dell'Opera del Duomo** (Mon & Wed–Sat 9am–12.30pm & 3–6.30pm, Sun 9.30am–12.30pm) contains the Donatello panels from the great pulpit; they are badly cracked and stained by exhaust fumes but their sculpted putti make a sprightly contrast with the lumbering little lads on Maso di Bartolomeo's tiny silver *Reliquary for the Sacred Girdle*, the museum's other main treasure. Also on show is Filippino Lippi's plucky *Saint Lucy*, unperturbed by the gigantic sword lodged in her neck, and the painting that Filippo Lippi produced to demonstrate his suitability for the fresco commission, *The Death of Jerome*. A doorway on the far side of the cloister opens into the Duomo's frescoed **crypt**; beside the altar is the head of one of the city's main wells, which – as the inscription records – was choked with corpses by the barbarian invaders of 1512.

West and east of the Duomo

A five-minute walk west of the Duomo, in the ex-monastery adjoining the mainly fourteenth-century church of San Domenico, the **Museo Pittura Murale** (9am–noon; closed Tues) contains a hotch-potch of minor frescoes, culled mostly from churches in and around Prato. After that, there's nothing more to see in Prato, unless you happen to be in town on market day (Monday), in which case you could stroll down to the **Piazza Mercatale**, which makes a large hole in the city close to the river east of the Duomo. War damage reduced the square's visual impact to virtually zero, and for the rest of the week it's a vast car park.

Practicalities

Prato has two **tourist offices**: behind the Carceri church at Via Cairoli 48 (Mon–Sat 8.30am–1.30pm & 4–7pm; ☎0574/24.112) and at Via Muzzi 51, by the Duomo (same hours; ☎0574/35.141). Prato, under half an hour from Florence by bus or train, can be an alternative for **accommodation** when there's nothing available there. It has a one-star hotel, the *Roma*, outside the southern gate at Via Carradori 1 (☎0574/31.777; ④), and two two-stars, the *Stella d'Italia* at Piazza Duomo 8 (☎0574/27.910; ④) and *Il Giglio* at Piazza San Marco 14 (☎0574/37.049; ④).

Prato has plenty of **restaurants**. The *Trattoria Lapo* is a basic local place at Piazza Mercatale 140 (closed Sun); there are two neon-lit birreria-pizzeria places on the square as well. Moving upmarket, *Ristorante Osualdo Baroncelli*, Via Fra Bartolomeo 13 (off Piazza S. Marco), comes up with imaginative variations of traditional Tuscan meat and fish dishes for around L50,000 per head without wine. And for a little more you can eat at one of Tuscany's best seafood restaurants, *Il Piraña*, Via Valentini 110, ten minutes' drive out of the centre (☎0574/25.746; closed Mon & Sat lunchtimes, all Sun & Aug). Also worth trying are *Lo Scoglio*, Via G. Verdi 42, which specialises in fish dishes, and *Baghino*, Via dell'Accademia 9, for local food in a traditional atmosphere (closed Sun evening & Mon lunch): both about L30,000 a head.

A Prato speciality is the *Biscotto di Prato*, a very hard yellow biscuit, tradition-ally eaten over the Christmas period, and made a touch less resistant by dipping in wine or coffee. The best outlet for these and other Prato pastries is *Antonio Mattei*, Via Ricasoli 22.

If you're staying, you could check out the adventurous *Terminale* **cinema**, at Via Frascati 36, or the **Teatro Metastasio** at Via Cairoli 59, a world-famous venue for concerts and theatre productions (☎0574/6084; Sept to mid-June). Excellent modern art exhibitions and cultural events are organised year-round by the smart new **Centro per l'Arte Contemporanea L. Pecci**, a kilometre or so southeast of the centre in Viale della Repubblica (☎0574/570.620). Finally, summer concerts are also held in the castle courtyard.

Pistoia

The provincial capital of **PISTOIA** is one of the least visited cities in Tuscany, an unjustified neglect for this quiet, well-preserved medieval settlement at the base of the Apennines. Just thirty-five minutes by train from Florence (about the same by bus), it is an easy and enjoyable day trip – and also forms the most attractive approach to Lucca and Pisa, with both of which it has strong architectural links.

The Roman forerunner of Pistoia – Pistoria – was where Catiline and his fellow conspirators against the republic were finally run to ground, and the town later earned itself a reputation as a lair of malcontents. It was a Ghibelline city until its conquest by Guelph Florence in 1254, whereupon it allegedly brought about the division of the **Guelphs** into the **Black** and **White factions**. According to the folkloric version, one Pistoiese child injured another while playing with a sword; the miscreant's father sent him to apologise, whereupon the father of the injured party chopped the offender's hand off, telling him "iron, not words, is the remedy for sword wounds". The city promptly polarised into the Neri and the Bianchi camps (taking the names from ancestors of the two parties), and by some osmotic process the battle names were taken up in Florence. In view of this sort of mayhem, Dante found it entirely appropriate that Pistoia should have been the home of Vanni Fucci, a thuggish factional leader whose exploits included stealing the silver from the cathedral; he's encountered in the *Inferno*, enmeshed in a knot of snakes and cursing God.

Except for a brief spell at the start of the fourteenth century, when Castruccio Castracani held the city for Lucca, Pistoia remained a Florentine fief, yet for centuries the mythology of murderous Pistoia endured, and Michelangelo spoke for many when he referred to the Pistoiese as the "enemies of heaven". It's fitting that, according to one school of thought, the word "pistol" should be derived from this violent town; meaning "from Pistoia", a *pistole* was originally a dagger, but the name was tranferred to the first firearms made here in the sixteenth century. These days, Pistoia maintains its industrial tradition with a large rail plant, but is better known for the acres of garden nurseries on the slopes around. In terms of art attractions, its appeal lies in a sequence of Romanesque churches and medieval sculptures, and one of the masterpieces of the Della Robbia workshop.

The City

Arriving by train or by bus from Florence you are just a couple of minutes' walk south of the historic centre – Viale XX Settembre points the way through the city walls, which were raised in the fourteenth century and reinforced by the Medici. The interesting part of the city begins one block north of Piazza Treviso, at the junction with the centre's widest avenue, Corso Gramsci.

Around Piazza Garibaldi

A right turn at this junction takes you to Piazza Garibaldi and the thirteenth-century church of **San Domenico**, which was rebuilt in the 1970s after terrible damage during the war. Scraps of medieval frescoes remain inside, where the most arresting feature is the Rossellino brothers' tomb of the teacher Filippo Lazzari, on the right near the door. In the cloister (entered from the aisle) there are remnants of a fresco of *The Journey of the Magi* by Benozzo Gozzoli, who died of the plague in Pistoia and is buried here.

Opposite San Domenico, the **Cappella del Tau** (or Sant'Antonio Abate) preserves a chaos of fourteenth- and fifteenth-century frescoed scenes from the lives of Adam and Eve, Christ and various saints. A couple of doors away, in the Palazzo del Tau, there's the new **Museo Marino Marini** (Tues–Sat 9am–1pm & 3–7pm, Sun 9am–12.30pm; free), showing a selection of work by Pistoia's most famous modern son. Marini found an early influence in the realism of Etruscan sarcophagi, expressed in the sculptures of horses and riders that he churned out throughout his life; in the 1940s he diversified into portraiture – subjects here include Thomas Mann, Henry Miller and Marc Chagall.

On the other side of the Cappella del Tau, a couple of minutes' walk east, rises the late thirteenth-century facade of **San Paolo**; the front of greenish stone with dark green and white inlays is topped by a statue of Saint James, possibly by Orcagna. The exterior is the best bit.

San Giovanni Fuorcivitas

All streets north from Piazza Garibaldi link with Via Cavour, now the main street of the city's inner core but once the settlement's outer limit – as the name of the majestic **San Giovanni Fuorcivitas** ("outside the walls") proclaims. The church was founded in the eighth century, but rebuilt between the twelfth and fourteenth centuries, when it received the dazzling green and white flank that serves as its **facade**. Rather than being the focal point of the wall, the doorway is just a brief interruption in the infinitely repeatable pattern of the triple arcade – a pattern echoed in the oratory across the alleyway. The **interior**, though only feebly lit by the slit windows, is just as remarkable, as this is one of three Pistoia churches distinguished by pulpits showing state-of-the-art Tuscan sculpture in the thirteenth century. The **pulpit** here was carved in 1270 by a pupil of Nicola Pisano, whose son, Giovanni, executed the four figures of cardinals on the holy water stoup. Just about visible in the murk is a glazed terracotta *Visitation* on the left wall, probably by Luca della Robbia.

From here, a left up Via Roma is the quickest way into the central square, but if you want to prolong the pleasure for a while and make sure you don't miss any of Pistoia's architectural sights, you could follow the westward arc of Via Cavour and Via Buozzi until you come to **Madonna dell'Umiltà**. This handsome colossus was designed by a pupil of Bramante and finished off by Vasari with a dome so heavy that the walls had to be reinforced to stop the church collapsing.

The direct path from Via Cavour to Piazza del Duomo crosses the **market square**, Piazza della Sala; a marginally more long-winded alternative is to walk through the minuscule **Piazza San Leone**, a few blocks east. This was the centre of the ancient Lombard settlement, and its stocky tower was later the bolt hole of Vanni Fucci.

Piazza del Duomo

The medieval complex of the **Piazza del Duomo** is a superb and slightly eccentric ensemble, reversing the normal priorities of the Italian central square: the ornate baptistery lurks in a recess off one corner and the duomo faces it, turning its unadorned side to the open space and leaving the huge campanile and monolithic civic buildings to take the limelight. There's something odd about the expanse of the piazza too, as if it were conceived for a town considerably larger than present-day Pistoia. Once a year, though, the square is packed to capacity – for the **Giostro dell'Orso**, Pistoia's answer to the medieval shenanigans of Siena's Palio (see p.176).

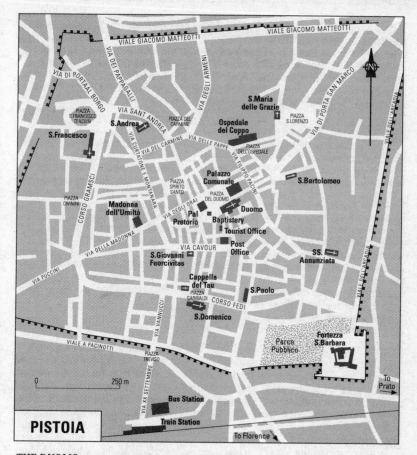

PISTOIA

THE DUOMO

If you have come from Pisa or Lucca, the style of Pistoia's **Duomo** will be immediately familiar, with its tiered arcades and distinctive Pisan-Romanesque decoration of striped black and white marble. Set into this soberly refined front is a
tunnel-vault portico of bright terracotta tiles by Andrea della Robbia, creator also
of the *Madonna and Child* above the door.

The interior (Mon–Sat 7am–noon & 4–7pm, Sun 7am–1pm) has an outstanding
array of sculptural pieces, one of which is part of the entrance wall – a marvellous
font designed by Benedetto da Maiano, showing incidents from the life of the
Baptist. Close by, on the wall of the right aisle, is the monument to Dante's
friend, the diplomat, teacher and poet **Cino da Pistoia**; it is said that Boccaccio
is one of the pupils to whom he's shown lecturing in the bottom panel.

Just beyond this monument is the Cappella di San Jacopo (L1500), endowed
with one of the richest pieces of silverwork to be seen in Italy, the **Altarpiece of
St James**. Weighing almost a ton and populated with 628 figures, it was begun in
1287 and completed in the fifteenth century, when Brunelleschi cast the two half-

THE GIOSTRO DELL'ORSO

The earliest forerunner of the **Giostro dell'Orso** was a peculiar ritual mentioned in a chronicle of 1300. On March 10 of that year, the feast day of San Francesca Romana, a dozen knights fought a ceremonial battle against a bear dressed in the town's coat of arms. The precise form of this joust changed many times over the following centuries but some version of it was fought every year until 1666, when it seems suddenly to have been abandoned. In 1947 it was revived in more humane form and now takes place on July 25, feast of the city's patron, Saint James. It forms the centrepiece of the festival season known as the *Luglio Pistoiese* – the Pistoia July.

The fun begins with a procession of around 300 standard-bearers, trumpeters, knights, halberdiers and assorted costumed extras from the Porta Lucchese to the Piazza del Duomo. These characters represent the villages around Pistoia, the city's crafts and trades, and the four districts of the historic centre. Each of these four districts is represented in the joust by three knights, their regalia bearing the heraldic emblems of the Lion, the Stag, the Griffon and the Dragon. Having led the procession into the arena laid out on the piazza, the knights are separated into pairs, who then ride against each other around the track, scoring points by hitting the two highly stylised "bears" set on bales on opposite sides of the circuit. Points are awarded according to which parts of the target are hit with the lance, and at the end of the day two prizes are awarded – to the highest-scoring district and the highest-scoring knight.

The *giostro* is always a sell-out; to be sure of tickets, contact the regional tourist office at least a couple of months in advance. The address is Ente Provinciale per il Turismo, Corso Gramsci 110, Pistoia (☎0573/34.326).

figures of prophets on the left-hand side. The length of time taken on the work is clear if you compare the scenes on the front with the bolder figures in the scenes from the life of Saint James on the left-hand flank, where an extra suppleness and vitality is evident. The artist responsible for these latter panels was a certain Leonardo di Ser Giovanni, who immediately after completing them was given the commission to begin the only other piece of silverwork that can stand comparison with this one – the altarpiece now in Florence's Museo dell'Opera del Duomo.

In the chapel to the left of the high altar is Antonio Rossellino's bust of bishop Donato de' Medici, and the so-called *Madonna di Piazza*, begun by Verrocchio and finished by Lorenzo di Credi (often kept under wraps); Verrocchio, with his workshop, was also responsible for the flurried tomb of Cardinal Forteguerri, in the left aisle by the door.

The duomo's adjacent **Campanile** was originally a Lombard watchtower, then was spruced up with Romanesque arcades in the twelfth century and a Gothic turret in the sixteenth; the swallowtail crenellations near the summit of this bizarre hybrid give away the town's old Ghibelline loyalties.

AROUND THE PIAZZA

Adjoining the duomo is the partly clad Palazzo dei Vescovi, now home of the small **Museo della Cattedrale** (tours Tues, Thurs & Fri 10am, 11.30am & 3.30pm; L2000), where the chief exhibit is Ghiberti's reliquary of Saint James. The basement has an even more modest archaeological collection, with relics from the Roman settlement.

Opposite is the tall, dapper Gothic **Baptistery**, designed by Giovanni Pisano, completed in the mid-fourteenth century by Cellino di Nese, creator of the duomo's monument to Cino da Pistoia. There's nothing under the conical brick ceiling but an old font; the vacancy is sometimes filled by commercial art shows.

Though its interior is closed to the public, you can take a look at the courtyard of the **Palazzo del Podestà**, the law court building to the side of the baptistery. From the stone benches half-sheltered by the portiço the Pistoian judges used to pronounce sentences notorious for their severity; a speciality was to sentence the guilty to be elevated to the ranks of the nobility – thus depriving them of any civic rights under the town's republican constitution.

On the far side of the square, the flaking pale limestone facade of the **Palazzo Comunale** bears a black marble head that's probably a portrait of the Moorish king of Majorca whom the Pistoiese defeated in the twelfth century; local folk-lore, tending to the conspiratorial, prefers to interpret it as the head of a man who betrayed the city to the Lucchesi. The building contains the **Museo Civico** (Tues–Sat 9am–1pm & 3–7pm, Sun 9am–12.30pm; L4000), where the customary Tuscan welter of medieval and Renaissance pieces is counterweighted by an impressive showing of Baroque hyperactivity – including a couple of hideous battle scenes by the evidently disturbed Ciccio Napoletano.

There's a **Nuovo Museo Diocesano** (Tues, Thurs & Fri 10am–1pm & 4–7pm, Wed & Sat 10am–1pm; L4000) opened in the Ripa del Sale, next to the Palazzo Comunale, with the furniture and paraphernalia of Pope Clemento IX.

From the Piazza to San Francesco

At the back of the Palazzo Comunale, Via Pacini is the obvious route to take to explore the northern part of the town. Across this road, on Piazza San Bartolomeo, is **San Bartolomeo in Pantano** – "Saint Bartholomew in the Swamp", from the marshy ground on which it was raised in the eighth century. The semi-complete facade is as appealing as any of the city's more polished fronts, the marble plating giving way to powdery red brick. Inside there's the earliest of Pistoia's trio of pulpits. Executed in 1250 by Guido da Como, and reconstructed from its dismantled parts, it's far less sophisticated than the other two, a rectangular box whose principal scenes are filled with figures arrayed in level ranks like an audience in a stadium.

The most publicised episode of the Pistoia townscape is not a church but a hospital in a square at the end of Via Pacini – the **Ospedale del Ceppo**, which takes its name from the hollowed-out tree stump (*ceppo*) in which alms were traditionally gathered. Established in the thirteenth century, it was embellished in the fifteenth with a portico like the one Brunelleschi designed for the Innocenti in Florence. Emblazoned along its length is the feature that makes it famous – Giovanni della Robbia's painted terracotta **frieze** of the *Theological Virtues* and the *Seven Works of Mercy*. Completed in the early sixteenth century, it is a startlingly colourful panoply of Renaissance types and costume: pilgrims, prisoners, the sick, the dead, all committed with a precise attention to domestic realism.

A couple of minutes over to the west, the twelfth-century **Sant'Andrea** has a typically Pisan facade with a pair of Romanesque lions and a panel of *The Journey of the Magi* stuck onto it. The corridor-slim aisle contains the third and greatest of the pulpits, by **Giovanni Pisano**; carved in 1297, it is based on his father's design for the Pisa baptistery pulpit and only marginally less elaborate than his own slightly later work in Pisa cathedral. It shows scenes from the life of Christ and the Last Judgement, the figures carved so thickly and in such deep relief that they seem to be surging out of a limitless depth. Giovanni was the first to appreciate the glory of his achievement: Nicola Pisano had boasted of being the greatest living sculptor, and Giovanni's inscription brags that he had now surpassed his father. The church also has a second piece by Giovanni – the crucifix mounted on the wall of the right aisle.

The plainest of the city's churches, the Franciscans' **San Francesco al Prato**, is a little further to the west, on the edge of one of the main bus terminals. Tattered fourteenth-century frescoes are preserved in the single nave and some healthier specimens adorn the chapels at the east end, where there's a fine *Triumph of Augustine* in the chapel to the left of the high altar. To the side of the church there's an unusual memorial to Aldo Moro, the Italian prime minister killed by the Red Brigade on May 7, 1978; the bronze plaques are imprinted with the newspaper headlines from the day his body was found.

Out of town – the zoo and the Celle arts centre

Four kilometres southwest of the city at Via Pieve a Celle 160, the **Giardino Zoologico** (daily 9am–7pm in summer; 9am–5pm in winter; L10,000) is a good stand-by for anyone with kids who aren't responding to the charms of Romanesque architecture and Della Robbia ceramics. Opened in 1970, it's one of Italy's more spacious zoos – though it has to be said that the captives don't include any rarities.

Adult palates jaded by too much venerable Tuscan art can give their systems a jolt at the **Fattoria di Celle**, a short drive east of town at Santomato. Occupying the rooms and park of the Villa Celle, this arts centre was established in 1982 to give Italy an international forum for contemporary work comparable to such centres as the Kroller-Müller in Holland. Everything here could be described as environmental art – the large-scale outdoor pieces are conceived as interactions with the natural world, while the smaller installations inside take their cue from the enclosing space of the rooms.

Artists from all over Europe and the United States have contributed to the sculpture park, devising a variety of responses to its woodlands and grassy slopes, and to the wider cultural environment of Tuscany. Alice Aycock's steel constructions recall such Renaissance mechanisms as the astrolabe, but are built on a scale to echo the curves and angles of the landscape. A labyrinth of polished green and white marble by Robert Morris recalls the Romanesque churches of the region, and is so perfectly placed on the gradient of the hill that it seems to be a single mass of stone until you come to the entrance. An artificial stream and grotto laid out in the last century has been used by Anne and Patrick Poirier to evoke the epic struggle between Zeus and the Giants, with steel lightning flashes and fragments of huge marble heads littering the water course. In hi-tech contrast, Dennis Oppenheim's massive contraption of steel towers, immovable pulleys and functionless wires looks like a visual pun on the ski-lifts of the winter resorts north of Pistoia. Most of the installations date from the inaugural year, but new pieces are being commissioned all the time, maintaining the Fattoria di Celle's status as one of the most vital art centres in the country. The centre is open from Monday to Saturday, and visitors are asked to ring for an appointment a day in advance (☎0573/479.907 or 479.562). The entrance gate is not signposted, but rather signalled by a huge spherical metal construction.

Practicalities

Pistoia's central **tourist office** is at Piazza del Duomo 4 (Mon–Sat 9am–1pm & 3.15–6.30pm; plus July & Aug Sun 9am–1pm; ☎0573/21.622). The main **post office** is off the south side of Piazza del Duomo at Via Roma 5; the SIP **telephone** booths are on Corso Gramsci.

The city's low tourist profile means a dearth of **accommodation** – so if you plan to stay, phone ahead. There's just one one-star hotel, the clean and friendly *Albergo Autisti*, close to Piazza Treviso at Viale Pacinotti 93 (☎0573/21.771; ③), but with semi-permanent guests during the week it is unlikely to have many free rooms, and within the city walls there's only one two-star, the *Albergo Firenze*, a short walk west of Piazza del Duomo at Via Curtatone e Montanara 42 (☎0573/23.141; ⑤). Central alternatives are the three-star *Leon Bianco*, Via Panciatichi 2 (☎0573/26.675; ⑥), or the *Patria*, Via Crispi 6 (☎0573/25.187; ⑤) – both are within a minute of San Giovanni Fuorcivitas.

The **restaurant** scene in central Pistoia isn't a lot better, with no real rivals to the straightforward Tuscan menu of *Da Mone*, Via Verdi 3, where a fixed menu of L25,000 changes daily (closed Sun), or *Leon Rosso*, at Via Panciatichi 4 (closed Sun), where a full meal costs around L40,000. For wood-oven pizzas and excellent *frutti di mare*, check out *Pollo d'Oro*, Via A. Frosini 132 (closed Mon). The most interesting food for vegetarians and carnivores is at *S. Jacopo*, Via Crispi 15, with a likely charge of L30,000 for a full meal.

The liveliest time to be in Pistoia is late July, for the *Luglio Pistoiese* – a month-long programme of concerts and events, culminating in the *Giostro dell'Orso*. Other times of year, the city stirs a little for Wednesday and Saturday **markets** in the Piazza della Sala.

Leaving Pistoia, *Lazzi* **buses** for Florence and Prato run from by the train station; *COPIT* buses for Vinci and Empoli from Piazza San Francesco. The route to Vinci goes over beautiful Monte Albano and allows a loop to Florence or Pisa if you set out early in the day.

Montecatini and Monsummano

Known as the **Valdinievole** (Valley of Mists), the area to the west of Pistoia is a region of subterranean streams and springs that now harbours one of Italy's main concentrations of **spa towns**. As with the German spas, such resorts as a rule don't have the same aura of social exclusivity in Italy as they do in Britain. But Tuscany has more than its share of the leisured classes, and the two big centres of the Valdinievole, **Montecatini Terme** and **Monsummano Terme**, are definitely not places for hoi polloi. Dauntless individuals can join the smart set for an afternoon of sweltering and sipping, but most people will probably prefer to spend more time in the old hill towns above the modern spas.

The Florence to Viareggio **trains** stop at Montecatini; Monsummano is really only worth a call if you're driving through.

Montecatini Terme

No spa in Italy has a glossier reputation than **MONTECATINI TERME**, as can be gauged from the fact that the likes of Gucci and Gianfranco Ferre find it profitable to have a branch here. Sedated rather than sedate, most of the town is a leafy grid of indistinguishable apartment blocks and villas where it's eternally siesta.

The centre of the town is delineated by the **Parco delle Terme** (a ten-minute walk from the train station), where each of the nine sulphur springs is encased in its own separate building. Fronting the piazza at the edge of the park is the pompous **Terme Leopoldine**, a shrine to the healing properties of mud baths. North of this is the oldest of the springs, the **Tettuccio**, discovered in the fourteenth century but not exploited to the full until Grand Duke Leopoldo I gave it the works in the eighteenth. Inside, Art Nouveau paintings and ceramics create a suitably sybaritic environment in which to compose your letters in the spa café or imbibe the acrid water. Across the way, the Palladian home of the **Regina** spring suggests more astringent regimes, while at the back of the park, the mock-medieval **Torretta** embodies the straightforwardly escapist eiement of all spa resorts.

All these spas are open from May to October; there's one establishment, the hybrid Neo-Renaissance-modernist **Excelsior**, that's open all year. An office at Viale Verdi 41, near the entrance to the park, sells entry tickets for all of them: expect to pay, for a half-day pass, somewhere in the region of L7–17,000 just for drinking the waters, L26–58,000 for a bath or mud, depending on the season and time of day.

The non-thermal delights of Montecatini can all be sampled by following Viale Diaz, which curves round the north side of the park. Here, across the road from the Regina spa, you'll find the **Accademia d'Arte** (summer Tues–Sun 4–7.30pm; winter Mon–Sat 3–6pm; L2000), a mishmash of gifts from illustrious guests such as Verdi, who composed *Otello* while staying in Montecatini, refining the score on the piano that's kept here. Ten minutes' walk beyond is the relatively unkempt verdure of **Le Panteraie**, a wooded park with a swimming pool and deer reserve.

Halfway between the gallery and the woods is the most enjoyable thing in Montecatini: the **funicular** to **Montecatini Alto**, a few hundred metres above the spa (April–Oct Tues–Sun every 30min); if you drive, it's a five-kilometre haul. The original Montecatini settlement here offers excellent views, especially of Monsummano, and in summer the tiny Piazza Giusti becomes a pleasant outdoor extension of its cafés and pizzerias. If you want to get out of the sun for a while, there's the stalactite-heavy **Grotta Maona** (April–Nov Tues–Sun 9am–noon & 2.30–6.30pm; L7000), a couple of kilometres below Montecatini Alto. Outside you'll find ballroom dancing going on in the afternoons and evenings.

MONTECATINI PRACTICALITIES

The Montecatini **tourist office**, at Viale Verdi 66 (Mon–Sat 9am–12.30pm & 4–7pm, Sun & hols 9am–noon) has full details of Montecatini's plentiful **accommodation** – it has around three hundred places to stay, predominantly top-bracket, but with about fifty one-star hotels. In the main town, the best deal is at the *Corallo*, Viale Cavallotti 116 (☎0572/78.288; full board ⑥) – and there's a pool. Even more reasonable is the one-star *Daniela*, Viale Cavallotti 127 (☎0572/78.858; full board ④) with a garden. There are two hotels in Montecatini Alto, both one-star: *Miravalle*, Via Leon Livi 4 (☎0572/74.561; ⑤) and *Trattoria Albergo L'Etrusco*, Via Talenti 2 (☎0572/79.645; full board ⑤). With so many choices, the best bet is to go straight to the tourist office for details of vacancies.

Most of Montecatini's **restaurants** are attached to the posh hotels; of the independent places, the best are *Enoteca da Giovanni* at Via Garibaldi 25 (closed Mon

& Aug), and *Pier Angelo* at Viale IV Novembre 99 (closed Sun), both of which will set you back around L70,000 per person.

The tourist office organizes various afternoon trips to the more inaccessible places in the surrounding area (June–Oct Mon, Wed & Fri leaving 2.30pm returning 7.15pm), costing L12,000 including a drink. One of the more remarkable trips takes you to **Villa Di Bellavista** (open first Sunday of every month throughout the year; free), 3km from Montecatini, which was designed by Antonio Maria Ferri for Francesco Feroni and finished in 1689. Feroni made his fortune selling spices and slaves in Amsterdam, but soon squandered it, giving rise to the popular Italian proverb "Fare come il Feroni" (to be like Feroni), meaning to waste money. The villa was said to be the most beautiful after Villa Caserta, with frescoes by both Pier Dandini (in the spectacular ballroom) and Niccolo Nannetti, and stucco work by Battista Ciceri. But Feroni didn't enjoy the villa for very long: after blowing his fortune he had to give it up.

Monsummano Terme

Montecatini's sister-spa, **MONSUMMANO TERME**, a few kilometres southeast, has a peculiar speciality act: the steam cave. The family of the satirist Giuseppe Giusti – a native of Monsummano – set the town in motion when they discovered a flooded cave filled with mineral-saturated steam. Divided into chambers known as *Inferno*, *Purgatorio* and *Paradiso*, the **Grotta Giusti** (April–Oct) is still the big draw, half luxury hotel, half medical centre. The Giusti cave is on the eastern outskirts; competition is provided by the artificial **Grotta Parlanti** (May–Oct) to the north, whose vapours are allegedly even more efficacious.

The old town of **Monsummano Alto**, three kilometres from the centre up a relentlessly steep and narrow road, now amounts to little more than a twelfth-century church, a few very ruined castle ruins and an extremely aggressive dog; the panorama is spectacular though, with the massed glasshouses of Pescia catching the sun like a lake (see p.204).

Empoli and around

The N67, tracking the Arno west of Florence, is as dispiriting as the road that follows the river to the east. Busy and slow, it's strung with drab towns, industrial developments, megastores and warehouses, and – apart from a handful of attractions in **Empoli** – is only worth bothering with for the diversions to be found off it.

Empoli

The manufacturing town of **EMPOLI**, purveyor of glass and raincoats to the nation, is a major junction of road and rail routes between Florence, Pisa, the coast and Siena, and thus might well be a place you'll find yourself passing through. Most people limit their exploration to a change of platforms at the train station, or a confused tour of the one-way road system.

If you want to spare time for a quick look around, though, head for the central **Piazza Farinata degli Uberti**, named after the commander of the Ghibelline army of Siena which defeated the Florentine Guelphs at Montaperti in 1260; he's revered not for his military prowess, however, but for his advocacy at the "parliament of Empoli", when he dissuaded his followers from wrecking Florence. The green and white **Collegiata**, on the square, was founded as far back as the fifth century; its lower portion is the most westerly example of Florentine Romanesque architecture, the top a postwar reconstruction of a nineteenth-century imitation.

Adjacent is the **Museo Collegiata**, entrance in Piazzetta S. Giovanni (Tues & Wed 9am–noon, Thurs–Sun 9am–noon & 4–7pm; L4000, including entrance to Museum of Paleontology), which has a pretty good collection of sculpture and painting: Lorenzo Monaco's *Madonna and Saints*, a couple of panels by local-born Pontormo, a possible Filippo Lippi, a Masolino *Pietà*, sculptures by Bernardo Rossellino and Mino da Fiesole, and Lorenzo di Bicci's *St Nicholas of Tolentino Saving Empoli from the Plague* – with a view of the town in the 1440s. The museum also possesses an item relating to one of Tuscany's stranger Easter rituals, a winged mechanical donkey that used to perform a version of Florence's incendiary dove ceremony – the donkey being propelled from the Collegiata tower down to Piazza degli Uberti, where it would ignite a pile of fireworks. Nowadays a papier-mâché beast performs the role.

Finally, it's worth recording that Empoli was the birthplace of composer-pianist **Ferruccio Busoni** (1866–1924), a musician of such virtuosity that whenever a new keyboard star emerges it's inevitable that some hack will re-mint the phrase "the greatest pianist since Busoni". The town commemorates him with a **festival of piano music** each October and November – details are available from the **tourist office**, at no. 8 on the piazza (daily 7.30am–1.30pm), next door to the **Museum of Paleontology** (same hours as Museo Collegiata, see above).

Cerreto Guidi

From the time of Cosimo I to the end of the dynasty, the Medici administered their estates in this northern part of Tuscany from the villa at **CERRETO GUIDI** (Tues–Sat 9am–2pm & Sun 9am–1pm; L3000), 8km northwest of Empoli (*COPIT* bus service). Having converted this former castle into something more domesticated, and having got Buontalenti to build the huge approach ramps that remain the villa's most distinctive feature, the clan set about making it the focus of rural life in the Empoli district: they instituted a weekly fair here, with compulsory attendance for the local peasants.

The **villa** is in fact a plain box of a house and the church that Cosimo built next door is no more exciting – though there's a good view from the top of the ramps, with Frederick's tower at San Miniato (see below) standing out in the middle distance. The main point of visiting the **interior** is to see the gallery of Medici portraits, and even these are fairly dull – if they weren't, they wouldn't be stuck out here. One section is entitled "Unhappy marriages among the descendants of Cosimo I", and includes a likeness of Cosimo's daughter Isabella, murdered here by her husband in 1576, for her infidelity. The Medici hitmen caught up with her alleged lover in Paris the following year.

Vinci

Sitting on the southern slopes of Monte Albano, 11km north of Empoli, **VINCI** is set amid a rolling swathe of vineyards and olive groves. The landscape is not what draws people along the road between Empoli and Pistoia, however – it's the village's association with **Leonardo da Vinci**, who in April 1452 was born in the nearby hamlet of Archiano, and baptised in Vinci's church of Santa Croce.

Vinci itself is a torpid place but preserves a thirteenth-century castle, in which the **Museo Leonardiano** (daily 9.30am–6pm; L5000) has been set up. Opened on the five-hundredth anniversary of Leonardo's birth, the museum is dedicated to Leonardo the inventor and engineer, honoured with a large and fairly imaginative display of models – tanks, water cannon, flying machines, gearboxes, looms, gear mechanisms, all manner of pulleys. The models are all reconstructed from Leonardo's notebook drawings, which are reproduced alongside the relevant contraptions. The museum doesn't do Leonardo any favours, though, in giving as much space to his half-baked jottings as to his sounder propositions – thus half a room is wasted on a mock-up of his skis for walking on water. Avoid the museum on a Sunday, when half the population of northern Tuscany seems to come out here.

Leonardo's actual **birthplace** (Mon, Tues & Thurs–Sun 9.30am–noon & 2.30–6pm; free) is a couple of kilometres further north into the hills, a pleasant walk past fields of poppies. The house was owned by his father, a Florentine clerk called Ser Pietro; of his mother little is known except that she was a serving maid and that her name was Caterina. It's now filled with placard-size captions and a couple of reproduction drawings – otherwise there's nothing to see.

From Vinci you could make a circuit **north to Pistoia**, along a fine scenic road. Buses from Empoli pass through the village three times daily.

San Miniato

The strategic hilltop site of **SAN MINIATO**, more or less equidistant from Pisa and Florence, has been exploited since the era of Augustus, when the Roman settlement of Quarto was founded here. A Lombard town succeeded it, and at the end of the tenth century Otto I made this an outpost of the Holy Roman Empire. A later emperor, Frederick II, gave the town its landmark fortress, and the imperial connection led to the nickname "San Miniato dei Tedeschi" – San Miniato of the Germans. Today San Miniato is a brusque little agricultural town, good for a couple of hours' break of journey, but unlikely to tempt anyone to give it longer.

The train station and main, predominantly modern, part of town – **San Miniato Basso** – is sited down in the valley. From here it's a steep four-kilometre climb to **San Miniato Alto**, the old quarter. If you get a **bus** from the train station, it will deposit you just below the walls in **Piazzale Dante Alighieri**, which is also the place to park. From here, once through the town gate, a right turn leads to **Piazza del Popolo**, where a plan of the town is displayed outside the helpful **tourist office** (9am–1pm & 3.30–7.30pm). At the top end of the square is the much-rebuilt **San Domenico**, which contains the fine tomb of a Florentine doctor named Giovanni Chellini. Carved by one Pagno di Lapo Portigiani, it's modelled on the tomb of Leonardo Bruni in Florence's Santa Croce.

From here Via Conti rises to the **Piazza della Repubblica**, which is jazzed up by seventeenth-century *sgraffiti* on the long facade of the seminary, part of whose ground floor is a row of restored fourteenth-century shops, a rare survival. Opposite the seminary a flight of steps rises to the **Prato del Duomo**, where a tower of the imperial fortress now houses the expensive *Miravalle* hotel (☎0571/418.075; ⑦) and its more affordable restaurant. The neighbouring **Palazzo dei Vicari dell'Imperatore** is a relic of the time when San Miniato was the seat of the vicars of the Holy Roman Empire – Countess Matilda of Tuscia, daughter of one of these vicars, was born here (see p.542).

The red brick **Duomo** itself, dedicated to Saint Genesius, the patron saint of actors, is hacked-about Romanesque, with an interior of Baroque gilding and marbling. Next door, the tiny **museum** (July–Oct Tues–Sun 9am–noon & 3–6pm; Nov–Dec same days 9am–noon & 2.30–5.30pm; Jan–June Sat & Sun 9am–noon & 2.30–5.30pm; L1000) has a *Crucifixion* by Filippo Lippi and a terracotta bust of Christ by Verrocchio. At the back of the duomo, the ponderous **Santuario del Crocifisso** was built to house a crucifix that was thought to have played a part in saving the town from the plague of 1637; the crucifix is still there, but the sanctuary is rarely open. From the Prato del Duomo it's a short walk up to the tower of the **Rocca**, which was rebuilt by Frederick II and restored brick by brick after damage in the last war; the view is the main point of the climb. Dante's *Inferno* perpetuates the memory of Pier della Vigna, Frederick's treasurer, who was imprisoned and blinded here, a fate that drove him to suicide by jumping from the tower – as the inscription at its foot records. On the first Sunday after Easter this zone is packed with competitors in the national **kite-flying championships**, the liveliest event in the San Miniato calendar.

Below the tower, on the opposite side from the duomo, stands the church of **San Francesco**, occupying the site where the Lombards dedicated the chapel to San Miniato that gave the town its name. The church was altered by the Franciscans, who were given the property after Francis himself had visited the town, and traces of their Romanesque building can still just about be discerned through the later Gothic. If you want to eat in San Miniato there's a **restaurant** in Piazza Buonaparte, *Da Canapone*, serving local food at reasonable prices.

South of Empoli: Castelfiorentino and Certaldo

The **N429** road and Empoli–Siena **rail line**, which head south between Empoli and San Miniato, provide an easy and direct approach to San Gimignano and Siena. Along the way are two interesting, if modest, hill town attractions: **Castelfiorentino**, home to a couple of delightful Gozzoli fresco cycles, and **Certaldo**, where Boccaccio spent his last years.

Castelfiorentino

A fief of the bishops of Florence from the twelfth century onwards, **CASTELFIORENTINO** remained in the city's orbit through most of its uneventful history. Today it's a fairly large urban centre, with light industry and block housing spreading out in the modern, lower quarter of town, across the river Elsa. It's not an obvious or particularly pretty stop and, for once in Tuscany, you may well find yourself the only visitor in the place.

From the **train station**, the expansive **Piazza Gramsci** can be seen straight ahead. It is flanked by cafés, bars and the only central **hotel**, the two-star *Hotel-Ristorante Lami* at no. 82–83 (☎0571/64.076; ④); the town's other hotel, the three-star *La Pieve*, at Via V. Orazio Bacci 2 (☎0571/64.045; ④), is out on the road for Montespértoli. Best of a dozen or so **restaurants**, most grouped in the area around the square, is *La Magona* at Via Ridolfi 10 (closed Mon), on the street to your right out of the station.

The Gozzoli frescoes and the town

To look around the **Castello** – the old, upper town – head up the stairs at the corner of Piazza Gramsci, by the Teatro del Popolo, and you'll reach a patch of garden square, to either side of which runs Via dei Tilli. Turn left and you come to the **Biblioteca Comunale** (Mon–Fri 2.30–7.30pm; closed mid-Aug; free), where the Gozzoli frescoes are displayed.

The **frescoes** occupy the top floor of the Biblioteca, having been detached from a pair of local sanctuary chapels. To the left of the gallery entrance is a complete reconstruction of the *Madonna della Tosse* chapel, including a frescoed "altar-piece" and side wall scenes of the death and assumption of the Virgin, their land-scapes studded with cypress trees and rolling Tuscan hills. More fragmentary but more interesting are the flood-damaged frescoes and *sinopie* from the *Sanctuary of the Visitation*. These again depict episodes from the life of the Virgin, and of her parents, Joachim (Gioacchino) and Anne, the best of them full of genre detail of everyday fifteenth-century life. Both sets of frescoes were completed in the 1480s, late in Gozzoli's career, possibly during periods when the plague had hit Florence.

Had you turned right along Via dei Tilli, you would have come to the **Piazza del Popolo**, the castello's main square, flanked by the Collegiata of San Lorenzo – built on Lombard foundations – and a nineteenth-century Municipio. The stepped street above the piazza leads to the summit of the town, marked by the Romanesque **Pieve di San Ippolito**. It was here in 1197 that the rectors of the Tuscan League, formed to defend the cities against "any emperor, king, or prince", were sworn in – Castelfiorentino's only real episode in the limelight.

Down in the **lower town**, east of Piazza Gramsci (left as you face the station and river), a small park gives onto the Baroque church of **Santa Verdiana**, where a gallery is being built to house paintings from churches in the town and region, including works by Duccio, Taddeo Gaddi and Gozzoli. Many of these panels came from nearby **San Francesco** (usually locked), which has two frag-mentary fresco cycles of the *Life of St Francis* – the finest, by Cenno di Cenni, in the nave. As so often in these parts, the church claims foundation by the saint himself. Saint Verdiana – the local patron saint – was his contemporary and ordained by him into the order; she's generally depicted with a couple of serpents whose lives she saved, in a pause between other miracles.

San Vivaldo

If you're driving and feel like a rambling, fourteen-kilometre cross-country route down to San Gimignano, follow the road southwest of Castelfiorentino through either Montaione, a quiet little hill town with a not very essential palaeontology museum, or through the minor spa of Gambassi Terme – with the lovely Romanesque **Pieve a Chianni** on its outskirts – to the village of **SAN VIVALDO**.

Here, amid the woods, a fourteenth-century Franciscan hermit founded the monastery of **Sacro Monte**, which between 1500 and 1515 was endowed with thirty-four chapels, representing the Stations of the Cross and other scenes from the life of Christ. The surviving fifteen chapels are not quite the "Jerusalem in Tuscany" the local tourist literature promotes – clustered together by the entrance gate to the monastery, they look more like a miniature cemetery and hardly a credible alternative to a pilgrimage to the Holy Land. However, each of the chapels is endowed with a large-scale painted terracotta tableau, completed with impressive animation by artists from the Della Robbia school.

Certaldo

Even without the Boccaccio connection **CERTALDO** would justify a visit. A very striking hill town – all red brick towers, battlements and mansions – it is visible for miles along the Elsa valley, and itself has views out to San Gimignano. For a spell in the twelfth century, its rulers, the Alberti, controlled a domain stretching north to the Arno, but subsequent domination by Florence and incursions by Siena led to a largely provincial role. These days its lower town, built along the N429, is a prosperous place, making its money from wine and agriculture, glass, brick and pasta factories.

   Arriving by bus or train, you will find yourself close to the central **Piazza Boccaccio** in the **lower town**. From here, two stone-flagged paths – Costa Alberti and Costa Vecchia – and a road, the Via del Castello, make the steep ascent to the upper town or **Castello**.

Castello

Certaldo's upper town is little more than a single street, predictably dubbed the **Via Boccaccio**. At its western end, by the Piazza SS. Annunziata, stands a group of privately owned palazzi. Moving up from here, towards the archetypally Tuscan town hall, or Palazzo Vicariale, you pass the Casa del Boccaccio (on the left) and, fronting a tiny piazza, the church and convent of SS. Jacopo e Filippo.

   The **Casa di Boccaccio** (daily 10am–12.30pm & 3–6.30pm; free) is as likely a candidate as any of the town mansions for the home of the poet, though scholars continue to dispute quite which towers were specified in his will. If Boccaccio's home it is, it was here that he spent the last twelve years of his life and here that he died, despite a considerable reputation, in very modest circumstances. Giovanni Boccaccio was actually born, according to the account he gave his friend Petrarch, in Paris, probably in 1313. The son of a banker from Certaldo, he returned fairly early in his childhood to Tuscany. As a youth he rejected the banking career planned by his family, instead going to study in Naples, where he fell in love with Fiammetta, an illegitimate princess and the inspiration for numerous sonnets. He returned to Florence reluctantly, after the collapse of his father's business, and there – and in Milan and Avignon, where he worked as a diplomat – wrote his major works, including the **Decameron**. Aged around fifty, after meeting a monk who impressed him with a vision of his death, he repented the worldly excesses of his life and retired to Certaldo. The rest of the years here were spent producing learned volumes on geography, the vanity of human affairs, and mythology, and preparing lectures on Dante, which he delivered in Florence. He died on December 21, 1375.

   As you'd expect given its uncertainty even of attribution, the house contains no direct links with the man, but does give a reasonable impression of the kind of house Boccaccio would have lived in. The actual exhibits comprise a colourful group of illustrations from the *Decameron* and a murky display case of drawings from various editions – by Rubens, Hogarth and D.H. Lawrence, among others.

   Perhaps more interesting is the church of **SS. Jacopo e Filippo**, alongside, which Boccaccio attended and where he was buried. Between the first and second altars on the right is his **monument** – a sixteenth-century bust and the lines he wrote as an epitaph – on the site of what was, until 1783, his grave. In that year the floor of the church was relaid and the good burghers of Certaldo – having come to the same conclusion as the author that the *Decameron* was an ungodly work – ripped up the original tomb and scattered the ashes. Byron, who came to pay his respects a few years later, was scandalised:

> *... even his tomb*
> *Uptorn must bear the hyena bigot's wrong;*
> *No more amidst the meaner dead find room.*

His verses had an effect, prompting the Marquise Lenzoni – a straggler from the Medici family – to buy up and restore the Boccaccio house and arrange the monument. But there's still a sense of incredulous shame in the local pamphlets. Of some note, also, in the church are a pair of Della Robbia tabernacles, an altar-piece by the same family (*Our Lady of the Snow*), and a fourteenth-century Sienese fresco of the Madonna and Child.

Boccaccio aside, the **Palazzo Vicariale** (summer Tues–Sun 9.30am–12.30pm & 4.30–7.30pm; winter same days 10am–noon & 3–6pm; L2000) is by far the most interesting building in Certaldo. Arms on its exterior – including further examples of the Della Robbia mastery of painted terracotta – attest to its use as the governor's residence, after the decline of its original owners, the Alberti. Inside, the arcaded entrance hall displays further coats of arms and a mostly fragmentary array of frescoes, many either painted or repainted at the end of the fifteenth century by Pier Francesco Fiorentino. The *Doubting Thomas*, over a small door by the stairway, is attributed to Gozzoli. Other fine patches of fresco are to be seen in the "Court of Justice", to the left, including a very faint *Allegory of Truth* on the wall with the door. To the right of the hall was the old civil prison, apparently frescoed by its inmates, and beyond, a series of grimmer dungeons for serious offenders. Virtually windowless, these retain graffiti etched by prisoners, including a diagram of the sun, each beam numbering a day spent confined.

Upstairs, you move into the more spacious environs of the governor's and servants' chambers, again with the odd faded fresco. These rooms are used on and off for special exhibitions, with an international showing inspired by Boccaccian themes filling the lulls.

Through the garden to the right of the palazzo, and entered on the same ticket, is the chapel of San Tommaso e Prospero, which was used as a storeroom from the eighteenth century, before restoration after the last war. The work was just in time to save Gozzoli's *Tabernacle of the Condemned* – a group of frescoes of Christ and the two thieves crucified with him, which are now displayed detached from the wall; traces of *sinopie* show their original position.

Practicalities

There's just one **hotel** up in Certaldo Alto, the three-star *Il Castello* at Via della Rena 6 (☎0571/668.250; ⑥), at the western end of Via Boccaccio. This has a **restaurant**, too, which has its only competition from the *Osteria del Vicario*, in Via Rivellino, just beyond the Palazzo Vicariale. For more choice, head down to the area around Piazza Boccaccio in the lower town, where there are two reasonably priced hotels: *Albergo Gelli*, Via Romana 30 (☎0571/668.135; ④) and *La Speranza*, Borgo Garibaldi Giuseppe 80 (☎0571/668.014; ④), close to the piazza.

As for other pursuits, Certaldo runs a **cultural festival** in September, on the first Sunday of which is the **Feast of San Giulia della Rena**, signal for a reunion of all the town's emigrants. In July there are courses and occasional concerts of **medieval music**, at the *Ars Nova* centre in the Palazzo Vicariale. And, lastly, a little incongruous in this company, the *comune* once sponsored a fortnight's **festi-**

val of rock bands in 1991 at the *Discoteca Y* in Certaldo Basso: an initiative that is unlikely to be repeated.

Moving south from Certaldo, there are **trains and buses** to Siena. Heading for **San Gimignano** by public transport you need to change at Poggibonsi; by car, the most direct and attractive route is the minor road due south.

travel details

Trains

From Florence to Prato (every 30min; 20min); Prato, Pistoia, Montecatini, Lucca, Viareggio (hourly; 20min, 35min, 50min, 1hr 20min, 1hr 50min); Empoli (every 30min; 25min); Borgo San Lorenzo (hourly; 1hr).

From Pistoia to Florence (hourly; 30–45min); Montecatini, Lucca, Viareggio (hourly; 15min, 45min, 1hr 15min); Bologna (hourly; 1hr).

From Prato to Florence (every 30min; 20min); Pistoia, Montecatini, Lucca, Viareggio (hourly; 15min, 30min, 1hr, 1hr 30min); Bologna (10 daily; 1hr).

From Empoli to Florence (every 30min; 25min); Pisa (every 30min; 25min) Castelfiorentino, Certaldo, Poggibonsi, Siena (hourly; 20min, 30min, 40min, 1hr).

Buses

From Florence

ATAF to La Petraia, Careggi, Pratolino and Fiesole.

SITA to Impruneta, Castellina in Chianti, Greve, Radda in Chianti, Gaiole, Barberino di Mugello, Certaldo, Pontassieve, Borgo San Lorenzo and San Casciano.

Lazzi to Cerreto Guidi, Empoli, Incisa Valdarno, Montecatini Terme, Prato, Pistoia and Pontassieve.

CAP to Borgo San Lorenzo, Impruneta and Prato.

COPIT to Pistoia, Poggio a Caiano and Vinci.

From Prato

Lazzi to Montecatini, Pistoia, Florence, Lucca, Pisa and Viareggio.

CAP to Florence, Siena, Barberino and Mugello.

From Pistoia

Lazzi to Montecatini, Prato, Florence, Lucca, Pisa and Viareggio.

COPIT to Montecatini, Poggio a Caiano, Empoli and Vinci.

From Empoli to Cerreto Guidi and Vinci (from outside railway station), Castelfiorentino and Certaldo (from Piazza della Vittoria).

From Castelfiorentino to Empoli, Florence, Certaldo and Volterra.

From Montecatini Terme to Monsummano, Pescia, Collodi, Pistoia, Prato, Florence, Pisa and Livorno.

From Borgo San Lorenzo to San Piero a Sieve, Scarperia, Barberino di Mugello and other villages in the Mugello.

CHAPTER THREE

LUCCA AND NORTHERN TUSCANY

The north of Tuscany is one of the province's least known regions. Very few non-Italians holiday on its resort-lined coast, the so-called Riviera della Versilia, and fewer still penetrate inland to the mountains of the Alpi Apuane or the remote hills and valleys of the Garfagnana and Lunigiana. The one city on the Tuscan sightseeing trail is Lucca – and even there tourism is very much a secondary consideration.

Lucca's proximity to Pisa airport – half an hour by road or rail – makes it an excellent first or last Tuscan stop. Contained within vast, park-lined Medicean walls, it's an urbane, affluent place, with as rewarding an ensemble of Romanesque churches as any you'll find in Italy.

For a quick break by the sea, the sands of the **Riviera della Versilia** are functional enough, and easily reached from Lucca. Though there is often little to distinguish the resorts, where the sands are usually staked out by private operators, the towns of **Viareggio** and **Forte dei Marmi** have their moments – Viareggio's at carnival time, when it mounts Italy's most amazing procession of floats. And from this coast it is a simple matter to explore the jagged peaks of the **Alpi Apuane**, which run parallel to the sea for some forty kilometres. The mountains are best known for the **marble quarries** around **Carrara**, but head beyond these and you will find yourself amid steep forested valleys, threaded by a network of clearly marked **footpaths**. Many of these can be trekked in a day from their village trailheads, though there are refuges and longer trails if you fancy something more strenuous.

Equally easy to visit from Lucca, is the **Garfagnana**, a lovely rural enclave that focuses on the **Serchio valley** and is flanked by the eastern slopes of the Apuane on one side and by the more rounded mountains of the **Orecchiella** on the other. Plenty of trails strike off into these upland regions, each of which is protected by a regional nature reserve. **Castelnuovo di Garfagnana** is the only town of any size, a good base for excursions to the hills or a visit to nearby **Barga**, the one outstanding medieval centre. North of the Serchio is one of the most marginalised areas of Tuscany, the **Lunigiana**, a wild and unspoilt region of rocky, forested landscape peppered with castles and tiny hamlets.

By virtue of their microclimates and a position that puts them at a meeting point of Alpine and Mediterranean vegetation zones, the Apuane and Orecchiella constitute one of the finest **floral** zones in the country: two-thirds of Italy's known species grow here, and in late spring the upland meadows are an incredible carpet of flowers. As well as flowers and a wide variety of funghi, their nature reserves abound in often spectacular **wildlife** – such as wolves, red deer and golden eagles. At the last count 165 bird species have been reported, some 85 of them breeding here, including kestrels, buzzards and sparrowhawks.

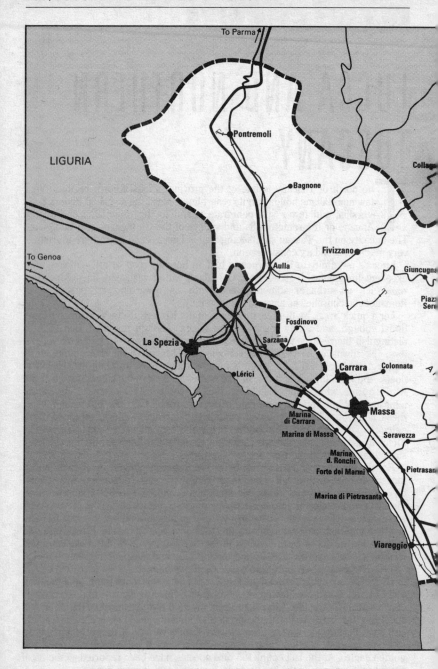

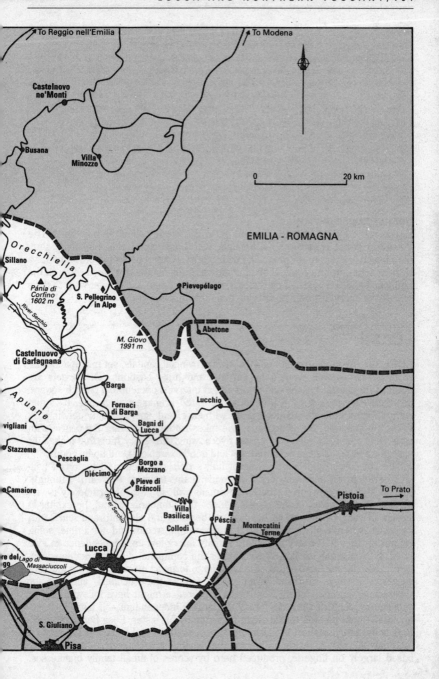

ACCOMMODATION PRICES

Throughout this guide, accommodation is graded on a scale from [1] to [9]. Grades [1] and [2] apply to **hostel** accommodation, and indicate the lowest price a **single person** could expect to pay for one night in that establishment in high season. Grades [3] to [9] apply to **hotels**, and indicate the cost of the **cheapest double room in high season**. The price bands to which these codes refer are as follows:

[1] under L20,000 per person	[4] L50–70,000 per double	[7] L120–150,000 per double
[2] over L20,000 per person	[5] L70–90,000 per double	[8] L150–200,000 per double
[3] under L50,000 per double	[6] L90–120,000 per double	[9] over L200,000 per double

Getting around the region

Lucca is the hub of a broad transport network covering all of the northwest. **The Versilian coast** is extremely accessible, with buses and trains constantly shuttling beach-seekers in summer. The **train routes** offer a perfect opportunity for a circular tour – up the coast, then changing at Aulla for the trip down through the Lunigiana and Garfagnana, on the east side of the Apuane. If all you want to do is scan the scenery, it would be feasible to do this in a day from Lucca.

Lucca

LUCCA is the most graceful of Tuscany's provincial capitals, set inside a swathe of Renaissance walls fronted by gardens and huge bastions. The streets are dotted with palazzi and the odd tower and at intervals open onto a church square, invariably overlooked by a brilliantly decorated Romanesque facade. It's quiet without being dull, absorbs its tourists with ease, and – perhaps uniquely in Italy – has a population that chooses to ride bikes rather than cram the centre with cars. Henry James's eulogy – "a place overflowing with everything that makes for ease, for plenty, for beauty, for interest and good example" – still holds good.

The city lies at the heart of one of Italy's richest agricultural regions ("half-smothered in oil and wine and corn and all the fruits of the earth", thought James) and has prospered since the Romans, whose gridiron orthodoxy is still obvious in the layout of the streets. Under the Lombards it was the capital of Tuscia (Tuscany), though its heyday was between the eleventh and fourteenth centuries, when banking and the silk trade brought wealth and, for a time, political power. In a brief flurry of military activity Lucca lost its independence to Pisa in 1314, soon regaining it, however, under the command of a remarkable adventurer, **Castruccio Castracani**, who went on to forge an empire covering much of western Tuscany. Pisa and Pistoia both fell to the Lucchesi, and but for Castracani's untimely death from malaria, Florence might have followed too. In subsequent centuries the city remained largely independent – if fairly inconsequential – until passing to Napoleon (and rule by his sister, Elisa Baciocchi), the Bourbons, and, just short of Italian unification, to the Grand Duchy of Tuscany.

Today the city is reckoned among the wealthiest in Tuscany – a prosperity based largely on lingerie, produced here by scores of small family businesses,

and on the region's high quality olive oil and other produce. The Lucchesi themselves have a reputation for tight family links – money never leaves the area – and
conservatism; where neighbouring towns are communist, Lucca owes its political
allegiance to the Christian Democrats. There is, too, a tradition of decorum, a
tradition traceable to eighteenth- and nineteenth-century court life; up until the
turn of the present century, smart Italian families sent their daughters to the city
to pick up the better manners presumed to prevail here.

Orientation, arrival and information

Confined within its walls, Lucca is a pretty easy place to get your bearings. The
centre of town is ostensibly **Piazza Napoleone**, a huge expanse carved out by
the Bourbons to house their administration. From here, **Via Fillungo** – the "long
thread" – heads north through the heart of the medieval city to the Piazza
Anfiteatro, built on the Roman arena. To the west of Via Fillungo is Lucca's social
heart, **Piazza San Michele**, while to the east, fronting a rather anonymous
square, is the **Duomo**. Further east still, the **Fosso** ("ditch") cuts off the quarter
around **San Francesco**.

Arriving by **bus**, you'll find yourself just inside the western stretch of walls, in
Piazza Giuseppe Verdi. The **train station** is a short way outside the walls to the
south, an easy walk or short bus ride to the centre.

The lone building on the north side of Piazza Verdi is the **tourist office** (daily
9am–7pm; ☎0583/419.689), a swish affair with plenty of information. The office
also rents **bikes** (April–Oct; L12,000 per day), good for a circuit of the walls or
getting to the outlying villas (see p.201).

The City

Lucca is once reputed to have had seventy churches to service its spiritual needs,
and even today you can hardly walk for five minutes without coming on a small
piazza and marble-fronted facade. Most were built obliquely to the grid of streets,
so you rarely confront a church head on, but rather as a sudden apparition as you
enter a square. The Romanesque trio of the **Duomo**, **San Michele** and **San
Frediano** are the city's chief monuments.

The Duomo di San Martino

It needs a double-take before you realise why the **Duomo di San Martino**
(closed 3.30–6.30pm) looks odd. The city's cathedral is fronted by a severely assy-
metric **facade** – its right-hand arch and loggias squeezed by the bell tower,
which was already in place from an earlier building. Nonetheless, the building
sets a tone for Lucca's Romanesque churches and little detracts from the overall
grandeur, created by the repetition of tiny columns and loggias and by the stunning **atrium**, whose bas-reliefs are some of the finest sculptures in the city.

It's well worth looking closely at these **carvings**, some dated as early as the
fifth century, and executed by a variety of mainly Lombard artists, most of whom
are unknown. Part of the sculpture, however, is by **Nicola Pisano**, and may well
be his first work after arriving in Tuscany from Apulia. His are the offerings
around the left-hand door – the *Deposition* (in the lunette), *Annunciation*, *Nativity*
and the *Adoration of the Magi*. Other panels display a compendium of subjects: a
symbolic labyrinth, a Tree of Life (with Adam and Eve at the bottom and Christ at
the top), dragons, bears, a bestiary of grotesques, and the months of the year

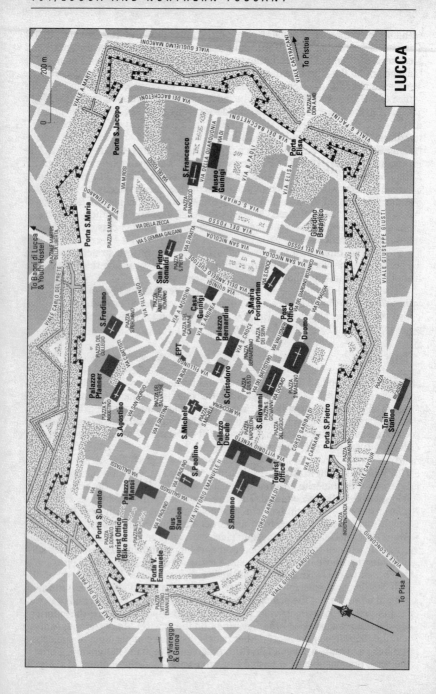

with their associated activities – December has a particularly graphic pig-sticking. The panels of the *Life of St Martin* (1210), between the doors, are the masterpiece of the facade's architect, **Guidetto da Como**. Walk along the flanks of the building for the ornate apse and transepts, as well as the extraordinary patterns of arches and marbles in the bricked-up side walls.

The **interior** is best known for the contribution of **Matteo Civitali** (1435–1501), who only gave up his daytime job as a barber to become a sculptor in his mid-thirties. He's represented here by a couple of fonts, the pulpits and several tombs, but his most famous work is the **Tempietto**, the gilt and marble octagon halfway down the church. Some fanatically intense acts of devotion are performed in front of it, directed at the **Volto Santo** (Holy Face), Lucca's most famous relic. A cedarwood crucifix with bulging eyes, it's said to be a true effigy of Christ carved by Nicodemus, an eyewitness to the crucifixion, but is probably a thirteenth-century copy of an eleventh-century copy of an eighth-century original.

Legend has it that the *Volto Santo* came to Lucca of its own volition in 782, first journeying by boat from the Holy Land, and then brought by oxen guided by divine will – a story similar to the ecclesiastical sham of Saint James's bones at Santiago di Compostela in Spain. As at Santiago, the icon brought considerable power to the local church: it may be no coincidence that it appeared during the bishopric of Anselmo di Baggio, later elevated to the papacy. The effigy attracted pilgrims from all over Europe and inspired devotion in all who heard of it: King William Rufus in England used to swear by it (*per sanctum vultum de Lucca*), London merchants kept a copy of it, and in France a certain Saint Vaudeluc was conjured into existence from a corruption of the French for the icon's name – Saint Vault de Lucques.

Elsewhere in the church the works of art are of less disputed origin. The finest of them is the **tomb of Ilaria del Carretto** (1410), a little beyond the Tempietto in the left transept. Considered the masterpiece of Jacopo della Quercia, it consists of a raised dais and the sculpted body of Ilaria, second wife of Paolo Guinigi, one of Lucca's medieval big shots. In a touching, almost sentimental gesture, the artist has carved the family dog – a spitting image of the HMV mutt – at her feet. Recent restoration of the work led to accusations that the restorer's cleaning techniques were extremely overenthusiastic, and had robbed the stone of its variegated textures. The craftsman concerned promptly sued his chief critic, Professor James Beck, the world's leading authority on Jacopo della Quercia, for defamation of character.

Immediately before the sculpture is a *Madonna and Child*, painted in 1509 by Bartolomeo della Porta, the first of several paintings – all recently restored – by surprisingly big names. The first chapel on the left has a *Presentation of the Virgin* by **Bronzino** (1598), and the third altar on the right a garish *Last Supper* by **Tintoretto**. In the sacristy off to the right, there's a superb *Madonna Enthroned with Saints* by **Domenico Ghirlandaio**, facing a *Trinity* attributed to Filippino Lippi.

Occupying a converted twelfth-century building across Via Archivescovale from the cathedral, the **Opera del Duomo** (June–Sept Tues–Sun 10am–6pm; Oct–May closed 1–3pm; L5000 or L7000 with San Giovanni) is a glossy new showcase for a generally unexceptional array of artefacts, though it does contain some unnerving Romanesque stone heads – human and equine – and some lavish metalwork, including the festive regalia for the *Volto Santo*.

On the north side of the square stands the large basilica of **San Giovanni** (same hours as Opera del Duomo; L3000 or L7000 joint ticket), Lucca's original cathedral. Rebuilt in the twelfth century, and again in the seventeenth, it preserves a lion-flanked carved Romanesque portal. Inside, recent excavations have uncovered a tangle of architectural remains, from Roman villa mosaics to traces of a Carolingian church.

San Michele – and the western quarter

Head west from San Giovanni and the duomo and across Via Fillungo, or more directly north from Piazza Napoleone, and you emerge on the site of the Roman forum, now the square surrounding **San Michele in Foro**, a church with one of Tuscany's most exquisite **facades**. The church is unfinished, the money running out before the body of the church could be raised to the level of the facade. The effect is wonderful, the upper loggias and the windows fronting air, like the figure of the archangel at their summit. Its Pisan-inspired intricacy is a triumph of poetic eccentricity, mirrored in many of Lucca's churches. Each of its myriad columns is different – some twisted, others sculpted or candy-striped. The impressive **campanile** is the city's tallest.

It would be hard to follow this act and the **interior** barely tries. Italians flock for spiritual regeneration to the second altar on the left, the so-called *Rifugio dei Peccatori* – "The Refuge of Sinners". On the neighbouring altar there's a modest terracotta *Madonna and Child* by Luca della Robbia; the best work of art is a beautifully framed painting of *SS. Jerome, Sebastian, Roch and Helena* by **Filippino Lippi**, at the end of the right-hand nave. Look out also for the **organ**, marvellously painted with intricate fleurs-de-lys.

Giacomo Puccini was born almost opposite San Michele at Via di Poggio 30; his father and grandfather had both been organists in the church. Their home, the **Casa di Puccini** (Tues–Sun April–Sept 10am–6pm; Oct–March 10am–4pm; L3000) is now a school of music, and maintains a small museum containing the Steinway on which he wrote *Turandot*, scores, photographs, even his overcoat. Students take it in turns to show visitors around and put on records of the master's compositions.

Just a couple of blocks to the west of San Michele is **San Paolino**, where Puccini cut his teeth as organist. A dull Baroque church, it was founded in honour of Lucca's first bishop and patron saint, whose remains are kept behind the high altar. Some third-rate eighteenth-century frescoes are his only memorial. South of San Paolino, tucked behind the Palazzo Ducale, is **San Romano**, a big, blunt Romanesque hall adapted and enlarged in a bizarre hotch-potch of styles; it would be one of the city's more interesting churches if the restoration started in 1987 had actually shown any progress. At the moment the whole place is sadly dilapidated.

North of San Paolino, in Via Galli Tassi, the seventeenth-century Palazzo Mansi houses a **Pinacoteca Nazionale** (Tues–Sat 9am–7pm, Sun 2–7pm; L6000). This is an indifferent collection of pictures – its only real highlight Pontormo's portrait of Alessandro de' Medici (see p.103 for the dirt on this sensitive youth) – but the palace itself is a sight: all over-the-top Rococo, which reaches its zenith in a spectacularly gilded bridal suite.

North to San Frediano

Back to the east of San Michele, **Via Fillungo** cuts through Lucca's luxury shopping district, a tight huddle of streets and alleys where medieval fragments and bricked-up loggias compete with Liberty-style shop fronts and lunchtime and early-evening throngs. Amid the crowds it's easy to miss the gorgeous facade of **San Cristoforo**, the deconsecrated church at the southern end; inside, the left-hand wall is completely covered in writing – the names of Lucca's dead in the two world wars. Further on is the **Torre delle Ore**, the city's clock tower since 1471; then at no. 58 there's the famous *Caffè di Simo*, a bar worth the price of a drink just for the turn-of-the-century ambience. Beyond, the street branches into a warren of lanes that lead to Piazza San Frediano.

San Frediano is again Pisan-Romanesque, though in place of the characteristic multiple loggias of the other great facades is a magnificent thirteenth-century mosaic of *Christ in Majesty* with the apostles gathered below. The **interior** lives up to the facade's promise – a delicately lit, hall-like basilica, with subtly varied columns and capitals and some fine treasures. Immediately facing the door is one of the best, the **Fonte Lustrale**, a huge twelfth-century piece executed by three different craftsmen. The first, an unknown Lombard, carved the stories of Moses on the outer slabs of the basin – including a superb *Crossing of the Red Sea*, with the Egyptian soldiers depicted as medieval knights. The second, one Maestro Roberto, added the Good Shepherd and six prophets on the other two basin slabs, their enframing arches showing a clear Byzantine influence. To the third sculptor, an unknown Tuscan, is owed the decoration of the Apostles and the Months on the cup above the basin and the beautiful fantasy masks from which the water is disgorged. Set behind the font is an *Annunciation* by Andrea della Robbia, festooned with trailing garlands of ceramic fruit.

Another Della Robbia composition, a figure of San Bartolomeo, is to be found on the pillar of the neighbouring chapel, which houses the incorrupt body of **Santa Zita**. A thirteenth-century Lucchese maidservant, Zita achieved sainthood from a fortunate white lie: she used to give out bread from her household to the poor and when challenged one day by her boss as to the contents of her apron, replied "only roses and flowers" – into which the bread was duly transformed. She is commemorated on April 26 by a flower market outside the church and by the Lucchesi freeing her of her finery and bringing her out to touch.

More fine carving is displayed by the Jacopo della Quercia altarpiece and pavement tombs in the **Cappella Trenta** (fourth on the right). The best frescoes in the city, meanwhile, are to be found in the second chapel of the left aisle: **Amico Aspertini**'s sixteenth-century scenes of the *Arrival of the Volto Santo* (see p.195), the *Life of St Augustine* and *The Miracle of St Frediano*. Frediano, an Irish monk, is said to have brought Christianity to Lucca in the sixth century and is depicted here saving the city from flood. A course of restoration is in progress on the frescoes, whose style is much influenced by the realism of Flemish and German painters; they could be out of circulation for some time. The large fresco of the Madonna on the right of the entrance door is also by Aspertini.

Close by San Frediano, at Via degli Asili 33, is the **Palazzo Pfanner**, whose outstanding rear loggia and statued gardens can be seen to good effect from the city walls, which also yield a good overview of another fine church, **Sant'Agostino**, currently in the throes of what looks like long-term restoration.

Piazza Anfiteatro and around

East of San Frediano you reach the remarkable **Piazza Anfiteatro**, aerial shots of which are featured in all Lucca's tourist literature. A ramshackle circuit of medieval buildings, as yet unprettified, it incorporates elements of the Roman amphitheatre that once stood here. Much of the original stone was carted off in the twelfth century to build the city's churches, but arches and columns can still be seen embedded in some of the houses, particularly on the north side of the outer walls. Medieval slums used to occupy the centre of the arena, but these were cleared in 1830 on the orders of the Bourbon ruler, Marie Louise.

This quiet neighbourhood is at its most dilapidated just north of Piazza Anfiteatro in Piazza del Carmine, a square distinguished by a huge brick campanile. The unappealing frontage of the market building gives way to a lovely arcaded interior, but unfortunately the market itself has been moved to Via Dei Bacchettoni, along the eastern city wall.

A couple of blocks east is **San Pietro Somaldi**, with the usual delicate facade, this time stone on the lower levels, topped with two tiers of Pisan marbling and tiny columns. Above the lovely **portal** is a good carved frieze and the customary pair of lions. The interior is whitewashed and blank, save for a sumptuous detached fresco of the Assumption on the right wall, and an uncredited fifteenth-century work above the first left-hand altar.

The **Casa Guinigi**, south of San Pietro, is the strangest sight in Lucca's cityscape. The fifteenth-century home of Lucca's leading family, its battlemented tower, Torre Guinigi, is surmounted by a holm oak whose roots have grown into the room below. Much of the stolid, red-brick tower is still undergoing repairs, but from Via San Andrea you can climb up for a close look at the tree and for one of the best views over the city (daily March–Sept 9am–7.30pm; Oct 10am–6pm; Nov–Feb 10am–2.30pm; L4500). The adjacent fortress, which has some wonderful austere medieval details, fronts a startling number of streets.

Continue south along Via Guinigi and you come to the twelfth-century **Santa Maria Forisportam** ("outside the gate"), signalling the limit of the Roman and medieval city. Ruskin claimed that it was this church that sparked his interest in medieval architecture. The facade in fact sports just two unfinished tiers and none of its relatives' decorative columns, but it's appealing for all that, with a few carvings above the doors and the usual jutting animals high on the front. The interior has the angular simplicity of the other churches, though no particular works of art.

Across the Fosso: San Francesco and the Museo Nazionale

The city's canal and parallel road, the **Via del Fosso**, mark the entry to Lucca's more lacklustre eastern margins. The most attractive part of this quarter is the **Giardino Botanico** (May–Sept Tues–Sun 9am–noon & 3.30–6.30pm; Oct–April Tues–Sun 8am–1pm; L3000) at the southern end of Via del Fosso, an extensive patch of green neatly complementing the ramparts.

Otherwise, the only significant sights are in the north of this quarter, around the church of **San Francesco**, fronted by a relatively simple facade and adjoining a crumbling brick convent. The inside of the church is a vast empty barn, relieved only by a delicate rose window.

Across the street is the much-restored **Villa Guinigi**, built to supplement the family's medieval town house. This is now home to the city's major museum, the **Museo Nazionale Guinigi** (Tues–Sun 9am–2pm; L4000), an extremely varied collection of painting, sculpture, furniture and applied arts. The lower floor is mainly sculpture and archaeological finds, with numerous Romanesque pieces and works by della Quercia and Matteo Civitali. Upstairs, the gallery moves onto paintings, with lots of big sixteenth-century canvases, and more impressive works by early Lucchese and Sienese masters, as well as fine Renaissance offerings from such as Fra' Bartolomeo.

Around the walls

Climbing up at one of the bastions, you can follow the four-kilometre circuit of the city **walls**, either on bike or on foot. It's worth taking time to savour them, the mid-afternoon shut-down being perhaps the best time to walk their broad promenade, which is lined successively with plane, lime, ilex and chestnut.

Construction of the walls started around 1500, prompted by the need to replace medieval ramparts made inadequate by advances in weapon technology. By 1650 the work was completed, with eleven bastions to fortify walls that were thirty metres wide at the base, twelve metres high and surrounded by moats thirty-five metres across. Perhaps the best feature, from the present-day perspective, was the destruction of all trees and buildings within a couple of hundred metres of the walls, creating a green belt of lawns that has shielded the old town from the ugliness that's sprouted on the outside.

Ironically, having produced a perfect set of walls, Lucca was never called on to defend them. The only siege was against the floodwaters of the River Serchio in 1812, when the gates were sealed against the deluge that had flooded the countryside. Napoleon's sister and city governor, Elisa Baciocchi, one of the last people allowed in, had to be winched over the ramparts by crane. Marie Louise of Bourbon, her successor, had the walls transformed to their present garden aspect, arranging them, as the local tourist handout puts it, "with unparalleled good taste and moderation".

Practicalities

Though Lucca isn't a major stop on the tourist trail, its limited **accommodation** always seems in demand – and it's wise to book ahead at any time of year. There is no such problem finding **restaurants**, though the city goes to bed early, leaving just a couple of **bars** open around San Michele.

Accommodation

Lucca's dozen one- and two-star **hotels** are scattered about the city, with a couple (usually the last to fill) located outside the walls. If you turn up without a booking and can't find a room, be prepared to press on to Viareggio. The listings below cover all of the one- to three-star places, in ascending order of price. There is also a **youth hostel** and **campsite**, listed at the end.

Cinzia, Via della Dogana 9 (☎0583/491.323). Near the duomo; shabby and not exactly welcoming, but quiet. ③.

Il Giardinetto, Via Nazionale 173 (☎0583/406.272). Well outside the walls to the northeast. ③.

Melecchi, Via Romana 37 (☎0583/950.234). A couple of blocks outside the walls: follow Via Elisa from Porta Elisa onto Viale Cardona and take the first left, Via del Tiglio – Via Romana is the first right off this street. ③.

Stipino, Via Romana 109 (☎0583/495.077). Adequate hotel: see above for directions. ④.

Diana, Via del Molinetto 11 (☎0583/492.202). Located a block west of the duomo, this would be a fine choice if it weren't for the frequency of complaints about surly staff. ⑤.

Moderno, Via V. Civitali 38 (☎0583/55.840). Outside the walls, southwest of the train station. ⑤.

Bernardino, Via di Tiglio 109 (☎0583/953.356). On the corner of Via Romana (see the *Melecchi*, above). ⑤.

Ilaria, Via del Fosso 20 (☎0583/47.558). Nice location by the canal; erratic staff. ⑨.

Universo, Piazza del Giglio 1 (☎0583/493.678). Positioned bang on the central Piazza Napoleone. ⑥.

Rex, Piazza Ricasoli 19 (☎0583/955.443). A modern, characterless hotel, a couple of blocks west of the train station. ⑥.

Celide, Viale Giusti 27 (☎0583/954.106). Posh, friendly hotel on the main street east of the station. ⑦.

La Luna, Corte Compagni 12 (☎0583/493.634). Nice location to the west of Piazza Anfiteatro. ⑧.

HOSTEL AND CAMPSITE

Ostello Il Serchio, Via del Brennero 673 (☎0583/341.811). Located 3km out of town: to get there take buses #1/1a, #6 or #7, or leave the city at Porta Santa Maria, turn right at the roundabout onto Viale Batoni, then first left up Viale Civitali and first right onto Via del Brennero – the hostel is on the left, next to a service station. Reception 4.30–11pm, midnight curfew. Food available, but not good. It's rarely full, and you can camp at the back for the same price. Open March 1–Oct 15. ①.

Eating

As a wealthy, gastronomic centre, Lucca has some high quality restaurants. Local specialities often feature the characteristic *Garfagnana farro* (chestnut flour) and roast mountain goat (*capretto*). If you're buying your own food, the **central market** is in Via dei Bacchettoni, along the eastern wall, on Wednesday and Saturday mornings. There's also an **open-air market** in Piazza Anfiteatro on Wednesday and Saturday (8am–1pm). For excellent pizza by weight try *Pizzeria Castagnacci*, Piazza San Michele 25 (closed Sun).

RESTAURANTS

La Buca di San Antonio, Via della Cervia 1 (☎0583/55.881). Lucca's finest – has been accorded a Michelin star. From L45,000; booking essential. Closed Sun & Mon.

Canuleia, Via Canuleia 14. Excellent cooking, with odd desserts like *salami di cioccolata*. Around L35,000. Closed Sat & Sun.

Da Giulio, Via del Tommaso 29. The city's best known local trattoria, very close to the Palazzo Mansi. It's always packed, so get there before 8pm if you don't want to queue. Around L30,000. Closed Sun & Mon.

Da Guido, Via Cesare Battisti 28. Cheapest in town at around L16,000. Closed Sun & Mon.

Da Leo, Via Tegrimi 1, near Piazza del Salvatore. Another good-value trattoria. Closed Sun.

Pizza Italia, Corte Compagni 2, off Via Fillungo. Very reasonable pizzas, popular with tourists and locals alike.

Pizzeria Queen, Via Cenami 13. Good pizzas and a range of beers.

Festivals

Lucca's festival entertainment centres around classical music and ballet. During the summer **Festival di Marlia** there are concerts and events at the Villa Reale, 8km towards the Garfagnana mountains (see opposite), while in September the focus shifts back to the city with the **Settembre Lucchese**. Both festivals usually feature at least one Puccini opera, staged during the *Settembre* at the intimate, four-tiered **Teatro Comunale** in Piazza del Giglio.

A vast **antiques market** takes place over the weekend of the third Sunday in every month, in and around Piazza San Martino.

Buses and trains

Two **bus** companies operate out of Piazza Verdi – *LAZZI* and *CLAP* – with some overlap of services. Most of the *CLAP* routes, departing from the south side of the piazza, are to local villages or to towns and villages in the inland area north of the city (Barga, Castelnuovo di Garfagnana), but they also run to Viareggio, Forte dei Marmi, Massa and other places (information ☎0583/587.897). Occupying the east side of the square, *LAZZI* concentrate more on long-distance routes; destinations include Rome, Florence, Siena, La Spezia, Pistoia, Prato, Pisa (and Pisa airport), Empoli, Massa, Lerici, Livorno and Viareggio (information ☎0583/584.876). **City buses** leave from Piazza Napoleone and Piazza Verdi.

Trains are considerably less frequent than buses for connections to Pisa, Pistoia, Prato, Florence and Viareggio.

East of Lucca: the villas, Collodi and Pescia

As with Florence's hinterland, Lucca's surroundings are dotted with outstanding **villas**, built by wealthy merchants as retreats from the rigours of city life, or simply as an indulgence on the part of aristocratic landowners. Some of these started life as simple country houses, others had grandiose ambitions from the word go; most have been repeatedly altered since their inception. Many involved the leading architects of their day, either in the construction of the villas themselves, or in the design of the magnificent **gardens** that accompanied them.

Three of the villas – **Villa Reale**, **Villa Mansi**, **Villa Torrigiani** – lie within a ten-kilometre radius of the city to the northeast, so if you rent a bike from Lucca's tourist office they can all be reached in a hour or so. Slightly further afield is the **Villa Garzoni** at **Collodi**, which competes for attention with the **Parco di Pinocchio** – an attraction advertised on roadside hoardings all over Tuscany.

The Villa Reale at Marlia

By general consent, the **Villa Reale** at Marlia is the most beautiful of the villas close to Lucca. **Access** is via the SS445 from Lucca to Barga, turning off to Marlia after eight kilometres; a less direct but better signposted route takes the SS435 for Montecatini Terme, with a left turn after seven kilometres, also signed for the Villa Reale.

The Villa Reale's life as a country house started with the destruction of a fortress on this site in the fourteenth century, its first gardens being laid out a century later. The present Neoclassical look dates from 1806, when Napoleon's sister, Elisa Baciocchi, compelled the Orsetti family to sell up. Having ousted the owners she and her personal architect, Morel, set about a radical remoulding of the villa and garden, completely refurbishing the interior and planning an English park complete with huge monumental lake. Some of the garden's most important earlier fixtures were respected, though Napoleon's downfall and Elisa's subsequent eviction undoubtedly saved some earlier components due for destruction. Sadly, the vigour of court life at the Villa Reale also vanished with Elisa. The violinist Paganini, for example, had been employed as resident composer – he later claimed his playing had caused his patroness to swoon with ecstasy.

The most striking aspect of the **garden** (guided tours July–Sept Tues–Thurs & Sun 10am, 11am, 4pm, 5pm & 6pm; Oct–Nov & March–June Tues–Sun 10am, 11am, 3pm, 4pm, 5pm & 6pm; L5000 Nov–June, L6000 July–Oct) is the sweeping lawn that runs from the house down to the lake, a feature of the original layout that was enlarged under the Baciocchi regime. To its left, set deep in the woods, is the **Grotto of Pan**, an elaborate two-storey hideaway with mosaic floor, much trailing greenery and a ceiling of stone plants and flowers. The hidden fountains which once sprayed the unwary are regrettably no longer working.

To one side of the lawn, an avenue of ilex trees leads to the heart of the original garden, centred on a trio of so-called **garden rooms**, which become progressively more confined. The first has a collection of lemon trees and a pool on which swans drift; the second features a high-spouting fountain; the third is a tiny and intimate "green theatre", its orchestra pit and seats all made of box and yew hedges, and edged with a variety of exotic flora. This and other parts of the garden are used as a setting for concerts in Lucca's summer music festival.

The Villa Mansi

Arguably the least interesting of the villa quartet is the **Villa Mansi** at Segromigno, 5km east of Marlia. Originally a plain sixteenth-century country house, the villa was enlarged in 1635 by Muzio Oddi and expanded many times in subsequent centuries. The harmonious late-Renaissance facade remains, much adorned with statuary, and flanked by two pavilions joining the three-arched portico.

The **garden** (summer Tues–Sun 9am–1pm & 3.30–8pm; winter same days 10am–12.30pm & 2.30–5pm; L7000 garden & villa, L5000 garden only) has suffered more brutal treatment. The few early sections that remain intact are the best: the French-inspired eastern part, with its star-shaped avenues and irregular arrangement of fountains and basins; and the western part, laid out between 1725 and 1732 by the Sicilian architect Filippo Juvarra – the man who refashioned Turin. At the beginning of the nineteenth century much of Juvarra's geometric work was replaced by haphazard borrowings from English garden design. Innovations by the present owners have continued the garden's dubious development.

The Villa Torrigiani

Situated just two kilometres from the Villa Mansi, the **Villa Torrigiani** at Camigliano (March to mid-Nov daily 9.30–11.30am & 2.30–5pm; Mid-Nov to Feb Sun & holidays 9.30–11.30am & 3–7.30pm; L7000) was built for the Buonvisi family in the sixteenth century, and transformed almost entirely by Alfonso Torrigiani in the eighteenth century to conform with the prevailing taste for villas and gardens in the English manner. Though little from the original survives, the present ensemble is a fine example of less formal garden design.

From Lucca, the **approach** to Camigliano village is to take the SS435 for Montecatini Terme, and fork left at Borgonuovo (11km) on the signed road to the village. In Camigliano on Corte Pianeta, is *I Diavoletti*, a **restaurant** with excellent cooking (closed Wed); expect to pay L20–30,000. The villa is clearly marked from the village centre.

A magnificent avenue of cypresses leads to the villa's stately Baroque facade, adorned with a similar surfeit of statuary to the Villa Mansi's – Oddi was probably the architect here, too. The **interior** has been slightly diminished by a spate of recent thefts, but there's still a wealth of furniture and incidental interest. The extravagantly decorated central hall and the elliptical staircase are outstanding, both products of the eighteenth-century modifications.

The **gardens**, and larger park alongside, are complex and beautiful affairs, noted above all for their *giochi d'acqua* (water games). Intended to drench unsuspecting visitors with hidden sprays and fountains activated by the owner, or by the pressure of footsteps on levered flagstones, these tricks were especially popular with Mannerist gardeners, but in fact were first used in Roman times.

The games here, initiated by the fun-loving Marquis Niccolò Santini – Lucca's ambassador to the court of Louis XIV – are among the finest examples still functioning. They're all contained in the so-called **Garden of Flora**, a sunken garden to the east of the villa, and all that has survived the garden's eighteenth-century Anglicisation. The Marquis would first herd his guests into the garden from an upper terrace, whereupon they would find their path blocked by a wall of spray. Attempting to retreat down the beautiful pebble-mosaic path they had just come down, they would discover that this too was now awash with water. Seeking sanctuary on the roof of the Temple of Flora, a small cupola-topped grotto, they would blunder into the biggest soaking of all – water gushed from the domed roof, from the four statues set in the walls (representing the four winds), and, as if this weren't enough, shot up from the floor as well. The frosts of 1985 damaged some of the underground piping, but the gardeners occasionally provide impromptu demonstrations of the Temple's aquatic abilities.

Collodi and around

When Carlo Lorenzini published the children's book that was to make him famous, he exchanged his surname for the name of his birthplace, **COLLODI**, a little town 15km east of Lucca. Thus, whereas other Tuscan towns adopt the Baptist or the Mother of Christ as their patron, Collodi has dedicated itself to a puppet with an erectile nose – **Pinocchio**. To English-speakers reared on the glutinous Disney version, it's difficult to appreciate the adult reverence afforded to Pinocchio in his homeland, but the tale's moral simplicity and exemplary Tuscan prose ensures it a massive following. The saintly Pope John Paul I used to address missives to the novel's hero, and a recent Italian newspaper poll to ascertain the Greatest Novel of All Time seriously included *Pinocchio* in its shortlist.

Parco di Pinocchio

Created in the 1950s, the **Parco di Pinocchio** (daily 8.30am–sunset; L7000, under-10s L5000) honours the book with statues of its characters, a sequence of mosaics depicting moments from Pinocchio's life, and various tableaux scattered around the paths that wind through the park.

The monsters and mazes are fun without any background knowledge, but you'll need to have read the book in order to get the most from the park – and to field questions from curious children. Pinocchio's importance to the nation can be gauged from the fact that Michelucci – architect of Florence's train station and several prestigious churches – was commissioned to design the **museum** near the entrance, which usually contains a display of drawings for a special edition. Be warned that you'll be lucky to get out of the park having forked out only for the tickets – there's a very inviting toy shop ready to hook the kids as you leave.

The Villa Garzoni

Overshadowing the Pinocchio park, the vast **Villa Garzoni** evolved from a castle that stood here in the days before Lucca surrendered this region to Florence. The house took on its present form in the second half of the seventeenth century, but it was towards the end of the following century that it acquired the magnificent formal **garden** (summer 8am–8pm; winter 8am–5pm; L8500 garden, L6500 villa) that makes this one of Italy's finest villas.

Access is usually through a gate on the main road, but the garden was designed to be entered through the wood adjoining the villa, so that the visitor would emerge from the wilderness into this precisely orchestrated landscape. Maximising the theatrical possibilities of the steep slope, the Garzoni deploys the full resources of the Baroque garden: circular fountains, topiary animals, patterns of flowers and coloured stones, a water staircase, a zigzagging cascade of steps and terraces, and terracotta figures cropping up in every corner. The villa itself contains some impressive frescoed rooms – but not impressive enough to justify the extra L6500 entry fee.

Villa Basilica

One of the most dramatically sited Romanesque churches in Tuscany is a short distance north from Collodi at **VILLA BASILICA**, a tiny village clinging to a ridge below Monte Pietra Pertusa. To get to it just follow the main road out of Collodi for 3km, then keep an eye out for an acute turn to the left. It's a sternly unadorned building, made attractive by the backdrop of woods and terraces on the other side of the valley; to get the best view of all, you could clamber up to the ruins of the fortress above the village.

Pescia – and Castelvecchio

In summer, every second person on the streets of **PESCIA** is a florist: this medium-sized town, 8km west of Montecatini Terme (see p.179), is Italy's top producer of cut flowers, boxing around three million lilies, carnations, gladioli and other blooms per day at the height of the season. Each September of even-numbered years it hosts the technicolour **Biennale del Fiore**, held in the gargantuan market hall on the outskirts.

Split by the Pescia river, the town has two distinct zones: the left bank forms the ecclesiastical quarter, the right is the secular and commercial district. The **Duomo**, rebuilt Baroque but with a fourteenth-century campanile, takes second slot to **San Francesco** in Via Battisti – reached by walking towards the river from the cathedral and turning right before the bridge. Here Bonaventura Berlinghieri's panel of *Six Scenes from the Life of St Francis* (third altar on the right), painted nine years after the saint's death, provides what's publicised as the most accurate surviving portrait of him, but is in fact a routinely stylised image of the saint. On the other side of the nave, the Cappella Cardini was added to the Gothic church by the architect known simply as Buggiano, employing the style of his adoptive father, Brunelleschi. The nearby oratory of **Sant'Antonio Abbate**, just before San Francesco, has a *Deposition* that's an outstanding specimen of thirteenth-century woodcarving.

Over on the right bank, at one end of the elongated **Piazza Mazzini**, the church of **Madonna di Piè di Piazza** is another worthy creation by Buggiano. At the other end of the square stands the bemedalled **Palazzo dei Vicari**, Romanesque home of the local council. For admission to the **Museo Civico**, in the Palazzo Galeotti on Piazza Santo Stefano (follow the signs from the Palazzo dei Vicari), you normally have to ask at the library on the ground floor; inside there's an endearingly shambolic assembly of Tuscan paintings, illuminated manuscripts and prints, as well as a section dedicated to the Sicilian-born opera composer Giovanni Pacini; one of the most successful musicians of his time, he is now held in such low regard that his manuscripts are just strewn round the room like out-of-date theatre programmes.

There's no reason to hang around in Pescia unless it's to sample the town's edible specialities – asparagus and a questionable stew known as *cioncia*, made from ox's muzzle. For around L40,000 you can get an excellent **meal** at *Cecco*, Via Forti 84 (closed Mon) – try the *pollastrino*, chicken cooked in a terracotta vessel with lemon and garlic. A slightly more routine experience is to be had at the cheaper *La Buca*, at Piazza Mazzini 4 (closed Tues).

Castelvecchio

Thirteen kilometres upstream from Pescia – past the paper mills that keep Pescia's second industry going – stands the strange **Pieve San Ansano** in the village of **CASTELVECCHIO**. Founded in the eleventh century, it bears a frieze of ghoulish faces on the facade and apse, suggesting a strong pagan undertow to the Christian piety of this area. Inside are some wonderfully carved capitals and a gloomy crypt that intensifies the threatening aura of the grimacing heads.

The Versilia coast and the Alpi Apuane

The northern coast of Tuscany – **the Riviera della Versilia** – is dominated by the mountains of the **Alpi Apuane**, a forty-kilometre spread of genuinely alpine spectacle. Now a protected *Parco Naturale* (and earmarked for promotion to *Parco Nazionale* status), they are crisscrossed by well-marked **footpaths**, and offer huge rewards for the walker and naturalist. **Carrara** and **Massa** are the littoral's main towns, known above all else as the marble capitals of Italy – huge blocks of stone, fine white dust and mine-scarred rockfaces are the memories likeliest to endure from a visit.

The beach resorts that run unbroken between **Viareggio** and **Forte dei Marmi** offer Italian beach culture in all its glory. Much of the sand is leased to the virtually indistinguishable *stabilimenti*, who in turn charge admission to their strips and rent out chairs and umbrellas; if you blanch at paying, there are public beaches (*spiaggia pubblica*) at regular intervals. For a swim and some sun in cheerfully crowded conditions, this coast is not as black as it's usually painted: the water may be cleaner elsewhere but it's not filthy, and the sand is immaculately groomed. And **bus** and **train** links to all points are excellent, especially in the summer, when you can move up and down the coast with more ease than anywhere else in Tuscany.

Viareggio and Torre del Lago

The best town on the coast, **VIAREGGIO** is also Tuscany's biggest seaside resort, the so-called Biarritz of the Riviera della Versilia. More pleasant and less pretentious than its supposed model, it nonetheless shares its air of elegance, thanks mainly to the long avenue of palms that runs the length of its seafront promenade. A modest collection of Liberty-style frontages – designed by the father of the Italian Art Nouveau, Galileo Chini – add to the sense of refinement, though for the most part the buildings are the old-style hotels you'd find in British seaside towns.

In its early days as a resort, at the turn of the century, the town's reputation for exclusivity was well deserved; these days all that survives are the high prices. The excellent **beaches are** all private, charging L25,000 and upwards for admission – except for the free stretch between Viareggio and Torre del Lago – and in summer the few hotels that aren't full usually hold out for *pensiona completa*. You may well prefer to join the majority and cram into the train for a day trip. This is certainly what Florentines do: in summer, special early morning trains from the city are packed with day-glo *ragazzi* and about a dozen ghetto blasters per carriage.

The town

Arriving at the **train station**, ten minutes' walk back from the seafront, you can pick up details from the summer-only **tourist office**, or from the main office (daily 9am–1pm plus summer 4–7pm) one block back from the beachside boardwalk at Viale Carducci 10. **Buses** stop near the centre at Piazza d'Azeglio and Piazza Mazzini.

Lacking any real centre, Viareggio's main focus is its promenade, the **Passeggiata Margherita**, a broad thoroughfare that runs along the seafront for three kilometres. Most of the Art Nouveau fronts are crowded together around the town's best-known spot, the chocolate-coloured *Gran Caffè Margherita*, at the very end of the Passeggiata alongside the marina. Across the marina and distinct from the town, the **Viale dei Tigli**, is a beautiful six-kilometre avenue of lime trees that stretches to the south. Along its length there's access to various beaches, and to the bulk of the town's campsites.

The town has over one hundred one-star **hotels**, with the biggest concentrations near the tourist office on Viale Carducci, and along Via Vespucci and Via Leonardo da Vinci. More upmarket options are equally numerous, so if you fail to strike lucky at one place, the next hotel is rarely more than a few seconds' walk away. There's almost nothing to choose between hotels, but among the cheaper options you might try first are the *Piera*, Via Fratti 684 (☎0584/50.737; [4]) with garden and all rooms with private bathrooms; *Villa Amadei*, Via F. Gioia 23 (☎0584/45.517; [4]) and *Ely*, Via Carrara 16 (☎0584/50.758; [4]) which are both by the sea; the more pricey two-star *Lupari*, Via Galvani 6 (☎0584/962.266; [5]).

If you're **camping**, head out along Viale dei Tigli. There are several sites off this avenue: the first is the *Paradiso* (☎0584/392.005), on the left after about a kilometre, and there are half a dozen more beyond it. There are several obvious spots to **hire a bike** in the centre if you want to ride down here.

As for **restaurants**, you're spoilt for choice, though prices here are considerably over the odds – even at basic pizzerias. If you can afford the prices, the best include the *Michelin*-starred *Patriarca*, Viale Carducci 79 (☎0584/53.126; closed Wed except in summer); the *Margherita*, Piazzale Margherita (☎0584/962.553; closed Wed); and the *Montecatini*, Viale Manin 8 (☎0584/962.129; closed Mon).

On a tight budget, you're more likely to depend on pizzas or takeaway food from the **market**, held on Piazza Cavour.

CARNEVALE

The one time Viareggio hits national headlines is during the two-week **Carnevale** (late Jan/early Feb), one of the liveliest in Italy. Each Sunday there's an amazing parade of colossal floats, or *carri*, carrying lavishly designed papier-mâché models of politicians and celebrities. The top *carri* designers are feted as artists, and their highly imaginative creations are displayed for the rest of the year in the **Hanger-Carnevale** at the top of Via Marco Polo. Ask at the tourist office for opening times.

Torre del Lago and the Lago di Massaciuccoli

The journey south from Viareggio along the Viale dei Tigli is worth it just for the lime trees; whether you press onto **TORRE DEL LAGO** depends on how much you value Puccini, who spent the later part of his life in a villa on the edge of the **Lago di Massaciuccoli** (bus from Piazza d'Azeglio).

No more than two metres deep, yet covering an area the size of Pisa, the **lake** itself is one of the few Tuscan lagoons not lost to land reclamation. Once it supported virtually all the aquatic birds it was possible to see in Italy, but many species have been wiped out by pollution and hunters – Puccini himself came here so he could practise "my second favourite instrument, my rifle". Now the lake forms part of the proposed Migliarino-San Rossore national park (currently only a *Parco Naturale*), and is also a protected bird reserve; as a result there are some 80 breeding and another 65 occasional species on the lake. You can take **boat trips** (ask in *Albergo Antonio* or ☎0337/712.530) on it for about L5000 to get across the lake, or L6000 for a bird-spotting trip.

In the hamlet itself, it's easy to miss the **Villa Puccini**, set back from the shore and surrounded by bars, trees and high iron railings. Visits are in guided groups of no more than twenty-five people for a maximum of thirty minutes (Tues–Sun half-hourly April–July 10–12.30am & 3.30–5.30pm; July–Aug 10am–12.30pm & 4–7pm; Oct–March 10am–12.30pm & 2.30–5pm; L4000); the rooms feature original furnishings, mementoes, and the piano on which Puccini bashed out many of his operas.

In July and August the **Festival Pucciniano** presents the master's works in Torre del Lago's outdoor theatre and other changeable venues (information from the festival office, Piazzale Belvedere Puccini; ☎0584/350.567). It's an extremely popular show, as are the international regattas held on the lake through the summer, both events turning the place into a chaotic mess.

Torre del Lago has a huge **campsite** – to the left of the road as you arrive from Viareggio – and no fewer than ten **hotels**, all one-star, mostly along the main Viale Marconi, except for: *Butterfly*, Via Belvedere Puccini 24 (☎0584/341.024; ④), right by the lake; the *Albergo Antonio*, Via G. Puccini 260 (☎0584/341.053; ④), near the Villa Puccini; *Pina*, Viale John Kennedy 27 (☎0584/341.025; ④), on the way to the sea. Along the *lungomare* there are plenty of good restaurants and pizzerias; also a **disco** *Frau Marleen*, at the end near Viale John Kennedy, open till the early hours, which draws people of all persuasions from as far afield as Florence.

Pietrasanta to Forte dei Marmi

North of Viareggio, the resorts of Lido di Camaiore and Marina di Pietrasanta are merely continuations of the Versilia's ribbon development, distinguishable only by a gradual shift downmarket as you move towards Forte dei Marmi.

The town of **PIETRASANTA**, two kilometres back from the beach, passes for an interesting place in these parts, but is no more than a busy marble centre with one or two old buildings. However, there are useful buses into the mountains from Piazza Matteotti in the town centre, with several services daily to Seravezza, where you can change for connections to Levigliani and Stazzema, and one to Castelnuovo di Garfagnana. The bus stop is by the **hotel** *Palagi*, Piazza Carducci 23 (☎0584/70.249; ④), which has full details of departures. The **tourist office** is in Tonfano, at Via Donizetti 14.

Another inland town, **CAMAIORE**, has a couple of Romanesque churches and the eighth-century **Badìa dei Santi Benedetti**, but it's an ugly semi-industrial spot, worth passing through only if you're taking the minor road back to Lucca.

Forte dei Marmi

As these places go, **FORTE DEI MARMI** is a pleasant resort, with lush, tree-lined streets and a good beach – but there's nothing here to justify its reputation as the trendiest spot on the coast, nor the high prices in its top hotels and restaurants. Once a major port for marble from the Apuane, it's now one of the second-home capitals of Tuscany, and a retreat for writers and artists who hole up in its more isolated, tree-surrounded villas.

The town, however, is again a good point of access to the mountains, with **buses** to Seravezza, Levigliani, Stazzema and Farnocchia (see below). *CLAP* services run to the interior and to Lucca, Viareggio and Pietrasanta from the **train station** (at Querceta, 3km inland) and from Via Matteotti in the town itself. *LAZZI* services run from nearby Via Pascoli to La Spezia, Pisa, Lucca and Florence. The **tourist office** at Via Achille Franceschi 8b can provide full lists of the hundred-odd hotels if you get the urge to stay. **Restaurants** largely cater to the well-heeled, though there are the usual seafront pizzerias. For L60,000-plus you can have one of the region's finest culinary experiences at *Lorenzo*, Via Carducci 61 (☎0585/84.030; closed Mon).

For a few hundred metres to the north of Forte di Marmi there's actually a stretch of **dunes** with no development at all; it looks a tempting camping option, but local police will shift you within minutes if you try to pitch a tent. Beyond the dunes, nondescript Cinquale and Ronchi resume the corridor of beachfront commercialism.

The Western Apuane

If you want to do more than admire the jagged knife-edge ridge of the **Alpi Apuane** from afar, there are numerous **marked trails** starting from roadheads deep in the mountains, and the biggest concentration of these tracks is in the peaks east of Forte dei Marmi and Pietrasanta, centred on Pania della Croce (1859m) and Monte Forato (1223m).

Thanks to their position and height, the Apuane are a perfect combination of different ecological habitats, from tundra through Alpine meadow to Mediterranean grassland. An extraordinary variety of **wild flowers** makes this one of the country's richest botanic enclaves, but the most noticeable vegetation are the immense forests of **chestnut and beech** which cover virtually all the lower slopes. These shelter some of the mountains' 300 species of **birds**, all now protected by a *Parco Regionale* encompassing virtually the entire range. Protection came too late to preserve many larger mammals from hunters, though you may see marmots – rare in the Apennines – on the higher, sunnier slopes.

The Apuane are also the Italian **speleology** capital, riddled with some of the greatest challenges in European caving. An estimated 400 kilometres of galleries run through the mountains, the deepest – the *Antro del Corchia* – touching minus 1120 metres. For information contact the **tourist office** in Seravezza, at 11 Via Corrado del Greco (☎0584/757.325).

Walking in the Apuane

Detailed *Multigraphic-Wanderkarte* 1:25,000 **maps** of the Apuane (widely available in the area) mark all the main trails with the international convention of red and white stripes and black number, though some short diversions to the summits are marked in blue without numbers. On maps and on the ground you'll also find paths marked "A", a reference to **Apuane Trekking**, an eight-day path along the ridge, following a route roughly north to south.

The main approach to the northern group of peaks, round **Pania della Croce**, is from **LEVIGLIANI**, reached by bus from Forte dei Marmi and Pietrasanta, from where a mining road runs towards Monte Corchia (1677m) – about half of which has been removed by quarrying. You can sometimes get lifts up this far from mining lorries, although going up it on the mine's working days is officially prohibited. Then from the top of the mining road you can pick up trail #9 to the **Rifugio del Freo** (2hr 30min walk from Levigliani; open daily April–Oct, Sat & Sun Nov–March; ☎0584/778.007). From the refuge you can climb Pania della Croce (trail #126; 2hr 30min from the refuge), one of the best walks locally, or choose from seven other paths. If you'd prefer **hotel** comfort to the rigours of the refuge, Levigliani has a couple of options: the *Vallechiara* (☎0584/778.054; ④) and the *Raffaello* (☎0584/778.063; ④).

For the southern peaks, round **Monte Forato**, the best access point is **STAZZEMA**, a lovely village in its own right, with **hotel** accommodation at the *Procinto*, Via IV Novembre (☎0584/78.004; ④). The bus from Forte dei Marmi and Pietrasanta goes to Farnocchia – itself the starting point for some easy paths through the trees – and then to Stazzema. The classic walk from Stazzema (trail #5) is a gentle climb through chestnut woods to the **Procinto**, a huge table-top crag mentioned by Dante. Below the crag is the **Rifugio Forte dei Marmi** (June–Sept daily; Oct–May Sat & Sun; ☎0584/777.051), a perfect base for walks along the main ridge – to the *Rifugio del Freo*, for example, in a couple of hours. The Procinto walk is a comfortable day's outing, with time to walk up to Monte Nona (1279m), drop back to the refuge, and then return to Stazzema by trails #121/126.

Massa

It might have a castle and cathedral, but the character of busy, modern **MASSA** is encapsulated more by its bland broad streets and fascist civic architecture. The town's most distinctive sight is on the main street, a **fountain** consisting of a big marble ball and fat babies – easily seen from a passing bus or car. If you do stop off, the **Castello Malaspina** (Tues–Sun 8.30am–12.30pm & 3–6pm; L3000) is worth an hour if you've time to spare, with its loggia and spread of Renaissance rooms clustered around the eleventh-century kernel. The castle was the base of the Malaspina family, lords of Massa from the sixteenth to the eighteenth centuries. Otherwise there's only the two-tiered **duomo** – in local marble, of course – and the **Piazza degli Aranci**, hub of what remains of the old town.

Practicalities

Buses come and go from Massa's **train station**: if you want to take a trip down the Versilia's beach strip, take the bus to Marina di Massa, and then transfer to one of the frequent services that run up and down the coast – they stop every few hundred metres.

Most of the hotels are in Marina di Massa. A good one is the *Miramonte* at Via Monte Grappa 7 (☎0585/241.067; ⑥). There's also a **youth hostel**, the *Ostello Apuano* (☎0585/789.034; open March–Sept; curfew 11.30pm; ①), on the seafront between Marina di Carrara and Marina di Massa, at Via delle Pinete 89, Partaccia; you can take a direct bus from Carrara train station, or from Marina di Massa for a northbound coast bus. There's a free beach nearby, but the sand's poor; you're better off heading south to stretch out. The best known **restaurant** is the *Riccà*, Via Lungo Mare (☎0585/241.070; closed Mon), which is good but expensive. Alternatively, cheap snack and pizza outlets abound.

Into the mountains

Behind Massa, a road climbs up into the Alpi Apuane **to Castelnuovo di Garfagnana** (see p.217), a scrappy ride, with new villas and ramshackle pizzerias taking the edge off the views. Two kilometres above the village of Antona there's a council-owned refuge, the **Rifugio-Albergo di Massa** (open all year; ☎0585/ 319.923; ①). It's not in the best part of the Apuane, but if you go through the road tunnel just beyond it, Club Alpino Italiano trails #41/188 lead up to Monte Altissimo (1589m) and a couple of low ridge walks. Just before the refuge, at Pian della Fioba, there's a small **botanical garden** with some of the Alps' many hundreds of different wild flowers.

Carrara

You can't get away from marble in **CARRARA**, a town whose very name is said to derive from *kar*, the Indo-European word for stone. However, the town itself is a surprisingly attractive place, once you get away from the sprawling factories around the station. Set in the hills above this mess, central Carrara has a rural hill-town feel, with peeling pastel stucco on its houses, elegant side streets lined with rows of green shutters, and a couple of piazzas and a **duomo** that would do credit to any Tuscan town. By contrast, the town's "resort", **Marina di Carrara**, is grim – more a container port than a beach. If you want the sea, it's best to drive inland to Massa, and then drop down to the coast.

Carrara feels like a self-sufficient town, and its people have always had a reputation as a breed apart – something they preserved even under the long-term domi-

nation of the Malaspina nobles, the local medieval big shots. Before their rule, the town had developed as a trading centre poised between Tuscany, the mountains and the Ligurian coast. Roman exploitation of the marble made trade with the nearby colony of Luni particularly brisk, and something of its scale can be seen in the ruins of the colony currently being excavated over the Ligurian border.

The Town

The old town, connected to the train station by a regular bus service, centres on **Piazza Alberica**, a gracious square whose beauty owes much to the hills which come down on two sides, and to the elegant colours and tone more often associated with Liguria than Tuscany. Stray blocks of marble sit at its centre, a legacy of the annual *Scolpire all'Aperto*, a festival in which sculptors from around the world are invited to the town, given a block of marble, and left to work in the middle of the square. If you're here between late July and early October, watching them chipping away makes a pleasant way to idle away an hour.

A short walk brings you to the eleventh-century **Duomo**, rather squashed into its piazza, but graced with a huge tower and a lovely facade built to the inevitable Pisan Romanesque pattern. Only the intricate rose window, a superb fourteenth-century addition, departs from the norm. The interior has a more severe simplicity but contains some beautiful works – a fifteenth-century **pulpit** and five appealing statues by the fourteenth-century sculptor Bergamini. The piazza's fountain, known locally as Il Gigante (The Giant), is an incomplete work by the lacklustre Florentine Bandinelli. Also in the square is the house where Michelangelo put up while checking out his marble supplies, while nearby are Petrarch's digs at Casa Repetti in Via Santa Maria. The castle on Piazza Gramsci was once a Malaspina fortress and is now the **Accademia delle Belle Arti**. It looks much as a castle should and has a few Roman fragments and plaster casts around its courtyard.

Closed for restoration at the time of writing, but worth a look when it re-opens, is the **Museo Civico di Marmo** in Via XX Settembre, 2km out of town on the road down towards Marina di Carrara (May–Sept Mon–Fri 8.30am–12.30pm & 3–6pm; L4000). Run as a promotional exercise by the local Chamber of Commerce, it's an impressive display that looks at the history and production of the stone – lots of photographs, examples of different types of marble, and a room devoted to rather dubious examples of marble art. A bus runs there from Piazza Matteotti.

The Quarries

Any short trip into the interior brings you across the huge scars of the marble **quarries**, some of the most startling sights in Tuscany. A particularly accessible site is at **Colonnata** (taking its name from a column of Roman slaves brought in to work the mines), just 8km from Carrara and served by **buses** (8am, 10am, noon, 2pm & 3pm) from Via Don Minzoni, five minutes from the main terminus in Piazza Matteotti. Don't go all the way to Colonnata village, but get off at the *Visita Cave* signs by the mine; if you're driving, follow the *Cava di Marmo* signs from the town up the twisting road. You'll see a huge, blindingly white marble basin, its floor and sides perfectly squared by the enormous wire saws used to cut the blocks that litter the surroundings. There are even bigger quarries further south, notably at Monte Corchia.

Walking
Colonnata village also marks an entrance point for **walks** in the Alpi Apuane, the CAI trail #38 behind the village leading to a dense web of paths around **Monte Rasore** (1422m) and **Monte Grondice** (1805m); the 1:25,000 *Multigraphic-Wanderkarte* **map** #101/102 is useful for making sense of this. As an alternative, take the SS446 north from Carrara to Campo Cecina (18km), where the all-year **Rifugio Carrara** (1320m; ☎0585/841.972; ①) offers accommodation and a rather more limited and gentle selection of paths.

Carrara practicalities
Carrara's **tourist office** is at the Marina, Piazza Menconi 6b. The SIP **telephone** office is on the corner of Via Roma and Via Aronte (Mon–Sat 9am–12.30pm & 3–7.30pm); the **post office** is in Via Mazzini, on the corner with Via Aronte.

   Accommodation is tight in the old town, most of the hotels clustering around Marina di Carrara – your best bet there, though, is to move down the coast to the **youth hostel** which serves the Marina di Massa (see p.210). In Carrara itself there's budget **hotel** accommodation at *Albergo da Roberto*, just north of Piazza

CARRARA MARBLE

Ever-present on the Versilia coast, whether as blocks waiting shipment or as huge snow-like scars on the mountains, **marble** has been the lifeblood of the region for over two thousand years. Over 200 working concerns extract 700,000 tonnes of stone annually, making this still the world's single largest producer of marble, despite the effects of recent recessions. Huge wire saws slice into the mountains at a rate of about 8cm an hour, their twenty-four-hour hum the bane of local residents. Environmentalists oppose the speed of extraction, and the industry is threatened by government plans to give national park status to the Apuane, but the quarry owners will fight all the way to preserve the 2000 jobs that remain in an industry which employed as many as 14,000 men at the start of this century. With an estimated 1000 jobs ultimately depending on each job in the quarries, the Carrara employers have no lack of supporters elsewhere in Italy.

   Marble is a metamorphic form of limestone, changed and hardened by colossal heat and pressure. Though it takes many forms, **Carrara stone** is usually white-grey and is prized for its flawless lustre. The many other types you'll see are mostly blocks which have been imported – from as far away as the Soviet Union – to be worked by the highly reputed local factories.

   The Romans were the first to extract this stone commercially, driving pegs of fig-wood into natural faults and then soaking them until the swollen wood split the stone. In time they used scored lines and iron chisels to produce uniform blocks about two metres square – still the basic measure.

   Practices remained little changed until the Renaissance, when **Michelangelo** began to visit the area. His wet nurse was from this part of Tuscany, and he claimed he became a sculptor by ingesting the marble dust in her milk; he also claimed to have "introduced the art of quarrying" to Carrara, a process he considered as important as sculpting itself. The *David* is sculpted from Carrara marble and local folklore is full of his pilgrimages to distant corners of the mountains in search of perfect stone. Benvenuto Cellini's *Autobiography* is illuminating on the anxiety of the artist's search for a good slab of marble – not to mention the huge financial value of the perfect stone. Such on-site concern has continued to the present day, artists of the calibre of Henry Moore having spent time picking over the quarries.

Alberica on Via Apuana 3 (☎0585/70.634; ④). For a more salubrious room, head for the *Michelangelo*, Corso Fratelli Rosselli 3 (☎0585/777.161; ⑥).

Restaurants are numerous, few of them tourist-oriented. For around L30–60,000 you can eat at the excellent *Soldaini*, Via Mazzini 11 (closed Mon & Sun evening); best mid-price option is the *Roma di Prioreschi*, Piazza Cesare Battisti 1 (closed Sat). An excellent little spot for snacks is the **bar** at Via Santa Maria 12, just off Piazza Accademia.

The **train station** is close to the sea, with a regular bus service to the old town (Piazza Matteotti – which is also the terminal for local buses to Massa, Marina di Massa and the youth hostel). Frequent trains run to La Spezia, Viareggio, all points on the coast and Pisa. *LAZZI* bus connections for La Spezia and Florence leave from Piazza Menconi, in the Marina. Finally, for detailed **walking** and **climbing** information contact the CAI office at Via L. Giorgi 1 (☎0585/76.782).

The Garfagnana

The Garfagnana is the general name for the area encompassing the Serchio valley north of Lucca, one of Tuscany's least explored yet most spectacular corners. The paucity of visitors is accounted for by the lack of any great sights – medieval **Barga** and the spa town of Bagni di Lucca are the only historic towns – but for anyone with an interest in **hiking**, there are rewards in plenty.

Much of the Garfagnana is protected as a regional **nature reserve**, whose excellent on-the-ground organisation has mapped and signposted a good range of walks. The best of these are on the east of the Serchio valley, up in the mountainous **Orecchiella** range. The Serchio's western flanks are the equally spectacular mountains of the **Alpi Apuane**, but as the main ridge here is better reached from the coastal side, it is covered in an earlier section (see p.209).

Transport

If you don't have a car, the best way to see the Garfagnana is on the **train** line which runs the entire length of the Serchio, past Barga and the region's major centre, **Castelnuovo di Garfagnana**, and then cuts through the head of the valley to **Aulla**, centre of the Lunigiana (see p.221). From there you can drop down by train to La Spezia, and complete a loop back to Lucca via Massa and Viareggio. For Bagni di Lucca, it's easiest to travel by bus from Lucca, as the Bagni di Lucca train station is about 4km out of town.

The Lower Serchio valley

Although the road north up the Serchio soon leaves Lucca behind, there's something laborious about the first part of the journey along the **Serchio valley**, with dusty hills and snatches of light industry dotting the way to Barga, 50km north. Buses from Lucca call at all the peripheral villages but you're unlikely to want to stop at any of them if you don't have your own transport.

A first possible detour for the mobile is the **Pieve di Brancoli**, a twelfth-century abbey, reached by a twisting, hillside road on the east bank of the valley, 10km out of Lucca. More easily visited, with its own rail stop, is **DIECIMO**, over on the west bank. Its Latin name is explained by a past as a Roman outpost, positioned ten Roman miles (17km) from Lucca. No more than a hamlet, it is dominated by a large, white **Romanesque campanile** – clearly visible from the river.

Four kilometres on, road and rail line bypass **BORGO A MOZZANO**, which basically comprises a single cobbled street of medieval houses and the famous **Ponte della Maddelena** (or Ponte del Diavolo). Narrow, steep and elegant, this strange five-arched bridge was constructed in the eleventh century. According to legend it was built by the devil in exchange for the soul of the first person to cross it; here, as in every European village where a version of this tale survives, the villagers outfoxed the devil by sending across an unsuspecting animal – in this case a dog. If you need to stay, Borgo has a couple of **hotels**: the one-star *Gallo d'Oro*, Via del Brennero 3 (☎0583/88.380; ④), and two-star *Il Pescatore*, Via Maggio 2 (☎0583/88.071; ⑤).

Bagni di Lucca and the Lima valley

Though it had been a spa for centuries, **BAGNI DI LUCCA**, 25km from Lucca, hit the social big time only in the early nineteenth century, when the patronage of Elisa Baciocchi brought in Europe's fashionable elite. The town boasted one of Europe's first official casinos – roulette was invented here – and was graced by the presence of such romantic luminaries as Byron, Shelley, Browning and Heine.

Today, Bagni di Lucca retains its elegance and pretty surroundings and the atmosphere is fairly subdued. If you want to spend a day or two soaking in the salty or sulphurous waters, there are a dozen **hotels** spread out along the valley – most of them reasonably priced, despite claims to famous names as past guests. Try the old-world *Svizzero*, Via C. Casalini 30 (☎0583/87.114; ④), or the *Roma*, Via Umberto I 110 (☎0583/87.278; ③); or the *Bridge*, in the old centre at Piazza Ponte a Serraglio (☎0583/87.147; ④).

The best place for **eating** is *Circolo Dei Forestieri*, Piazza Varraud 10 (☎0583/86.038), where you will be served food which is both exquisite and inexpensive (about L20,000), in a beautiful building with a columned terrace; best to book in advance. Or visit the busy pizzeria *Da Vinicio*, a block downstream from Bagni's bridge (closed Mon).

The pace of the town may quicken in the summer, since Bagni di Lucca has recently become host to an **opera festival** (late July to early August), in which musicians who have recently finished their training appear here in productions under the direction of established professionals. As well as reviving works that have fallen out of the standard repertory, the festival also commissions new pieces – as with the 1990 performance of *Die Traumenden Knaben*, by the young Italian composer Ruggero Laganà. You can get information about the festival from the **tourist office** at Via Umberto I 139, or by ringing the box office (☎0583/723.702).

The Lima valley

East of Bagni, the **Lima valley**, a tributary of the Serchio, rises towards the border with Emilia-Romagna. Two **buses** daily (morning and afternoon) make the run over the hills to San Marcello Pistoiese, the afternoon service continuing to the skiing and walking centre of Abetone.

In the valley itself, there are several possible rough road diversions to villages with **ancient churches** and spectacular mountain surroundings. Pieve Di Controne, just 3km northeast of Bagni, has a strange old church in red stone, fronted by a facade covered with odd diagonal motifs. San Cassiano, 10km from Bagni, has a twelfth-century church of the same name, with a wonderful carved facade, three tiers of very shallow arches, and a much older and dirtier tower that cuts off half the marble-faced front. Just south of the valley, Lucchio (22km from Bagni), cascading down the mountainside, is crowned by a castle ruin.

Past Lucchio, you enter the province of Pistoia, as **SAN MARCELLO PISTOIESE** proclaims. The business centre of the Pistoian mountains, San Marcello observes one of the quirkier Tuscan rituals: the releasing of a hot-air balloon on September 8 as a valediction to summer. Buses follow the main road north of here – a continuation of the N66 from Pistoia – to **ABETONE** (18km from San Marcello) which is the nearest winter sports resort to Florence. Its six chair lifts can cope with an hourly capacity of 14,000 people and at the height of the skiing season the system is tested to the fullest; even in summer there's often not too much space in the town's thirty-odd hotels, as thousands come up from the sweltering lowlands to revive themselves in the mountain air. As a package-tour destination it's not too bad, but Abetone isn't a place to go out of your way to see.

With your own transport, you could make a more exciting **approach to Abetone from Bagni di Lucca** by taking the high mountain road to Montefegatesi, and then over the main ridge of the Orecchiella (impassable in bad weather), passing the dramatic gorge called the **Orrido di Botri** before crossing the mountains at the pass of **Foce a Giovo** (1674m).

Barga

The ancient hill town of **BARGA** – poised 3.5km to the east of its train station on the Serchio – marks the start of the valley's best scenery. The village itself is quiet and pretty, with a long tradition of independence. It grew up originally around a Lombard castle, and was besieged by Lucca and Pisa before falling to Florence, under whose influence it remained until 1859. Where it differed from other Lucchesi strongholds was in its rule by elected council, a system it retained even under the Florentines.

Definitely worth a visit if you're up this way, Barga's surroundings also repay attention, dominated by hills and an incredibly lush vegetation. If you have transport of your own and fancy some mountain driving, a couple of tempting minor roads lead into the wild country of the Orecchiella, offering stunning views over steep wooded slopes and across to the jagged profiles of the Apuan mountains.

The Duomo

Barga's **Duomo**, founded in the tenth century and expanded over the next four hundred years, stands at the village's highest point, fronted by a terrace that provides a huge panorama of rooftops, mountains and villa-spotted hills. Built in a honey-blonde stone known as *albarese di Barga*, the **facade** is decorated in a shallow pattern of reliefs and tiny arches, a delicate contrast to the **campanile**, which seems to have erupted from the tiled roof. Left of the door is a wonderful little relief of an obviously convivial feast, sculpted in 1200; on the architrave is an equally rustic harvest scene and twin lions.

Inside, the naves are beautifully divided by low walls of inlaid marble and overlooked by a superlative and idiosyncratic **pulpit**. Created by the thirteenth-century sculptor Bigarelli da Como, it consists of a huge rectangular stand – lavishly carved with scenes from the Scriptures – supported by four red marble pillars, the front pair of which are propped up by another pair of lions. One, with an inane smirk, surmounts a dragon (a symbol of evil), while the other stands on a man (a symbol of heresy) who is simultaneously stroking and stabbing the animal. The rear left pillar is supported by a grotesque dwarf, snub-nosed symbol of the pagan world. The church's other unmissable artefact is a tenth-century **statue of Saint Christopher**, looking rather like a huge wooden puppet. Continuing the building's eccentric streak, the saint carries a child on one shoulder and a club the size of a small tree on the other. There are many less unconventional touches around the church: a cluster of **Della Robbia terracottas** in the right chapel, **frescoes** on several pillars, a carved choir screen and two Giottoesque **crucifixes** – the overpoweringly framed example above the altar is particularly good.

Just below the duomo to the left, the *centro storico* signs point the way to the Baroque chapel of **Santissimo Crocifisso dei Bianchi**, an oddly attractive extravagance, with a blue-gilt altar and four diversely excessive side chapels.

Practicalities

It's a long haul up from Barga's **train** station to the town and coming from Lucca it's easier to use the regular *CLAP* **bus**, which takes an hour and a quarter. Moving on, there are four buses daily to Castelnuovo di Garfagnana and two to Bagni di Lucca; all buses depart from the Porta Reale, alongside the big car park where the road stops outside the walls.

Barga's small **tourist office** is at Piazza Angelio 2 (daily 10am–noon), a straight walk down from Santissimo Crocifisso. Several **hotels** and **restaurants** are on the road north down to the Serchio at **ALBIANO**, a rather scrappy neighbourhood in comparison with the town itself, but with good views. Aim to stay in the *Villa Libano*, Via del Sasso 6 (☎0583/723.059; [5]), next to the town park and linked to a nice restaurant with a garden terrace, or at the *Alpino*, Via Mordini 16 (☎0583/723.336; [5]). Just to the south of Barga, in Fornaci di Barga, is *Gorizio*, Viale Battisti (☎0583/75074; [4]), with a garden and restaurant.

The Grotta del Vento

From Gallicano, across the river from Barga train station, you can drive west for 9km, following the bottom of the Túrrite valley, to what is rated as Tuscany's best cave, the **Grotta del Vento** in Fornovo Lasso. From April to September the cave guides put on three different daily tours through the caverns and lakes of this bizarre subterranean landscape, lasting one hour (on the hour 10am–noon & 3–6pm; L8500), two hours (11am, 3pm, 4pm & 5pm; L16,000), or three hours (10am & 2pm; L22,000). For the rest of the year the cave is open only on Sundays and public holidays. Whenever you go, get there in the morning to miss the crowds.

Castelnuovo di Garfagnana

Despite its mountain-ringed location, Garfagnana's main town, **CASTELNUOVO DI GARFAGNANA**, is a disappointment – a rather featureless sprawl, with a daytime market bustle to its centre but virtually no life after 5pm. The only thing to see is the fourteenth-century **Rocca**, built by the Este dukes of Ferrara and best known for its former commander, the poet Ariosto, author of *Orlando Furioso*. By all accounts he didn't much enjoy his tour of duty in the 1520s, and mournful evocations of the area's landscape were to colour much of his later poetry. The rest of the town was badly damaged by bombing in the last war.

However, if you intend to explore the Orecchiella, Castelnuovo is the obvious base. Some of the mountain roads that radiate east and west offer astounding views for car drivers, and the villages around are highly attractive. For serious hiking, it's also well worth a stop in order to pick up maps and information.

Hiking information

The **tourist office**, alongside the Rocca at Loggiato Porta 10 (Mon–Sat 9am–noon & 3–7pm, Sun 10am–12.30pm) is geared up to promote the area's attractions – from **Piazza Umberto I**, the town's main square, walk through the arch, and the office is under the arcade up on the right. A better source of hiking information is the **Comunità Montana** office in the *Centro Accoglienza* at Via Vittorio Emanuele 9 (open all year; ☎0583/658.990), reached by walking straight past the arcade to Piazza delle Erbe and taking the first left. The office is crammed with maps and pamphlets, and the friendly staff can book you into mountain refuges and advise on accommodation and long-distance paths. Note that the only two campsites in Garfagnana are at Piella (see below) and the *Monte Argegna* (☎0583/611.182; June 15–Sept 15), near Giuncugnano, in the north of the valley above Piazza al Serchio.

For specialised **climbing** information contact the *Club Alpino* office in Cortile Carrara. And lastly, you can rent **mountain bikes** at *Tutto Sport*, Via Rosa 11a (☎0583/628.58).

Accommodation and buses

There are several **hotels** in Castelnuovo, the most central being the *Pensione Aquila d'Oro*, Vicolo al Serchio 6 (☎0583/622.59; ③), jammed in an alley above a very squalid-looking bar, but extremely cheap. Most people stay in the *Da Carlino*, Via Garibaldi 413 (☎0583/644.270; ④), up the steep street out of Piazza Umberto I, a modernish place with rather expensive **restaurant** (from L35,000). For good, typical home-made food, at a better price (L20–25,000), try the trattorie out of town: *Il Triti*, Via Roma 29c (closed Wed), across the bridge on the road for Medena; *La Lanterna*, about 1km further on from *Il Triti* in Le Monarche; and *Da Beppe* in La Costa, further on still down the same road. In town itself, *Il Baretto*, Via Farini 5, is a cheap spaghetteria. Directly opposite the tourist office is the *Bar Costanza*, a nice spot in a dull town, with good snacks and lots of seating space at the rear.

There's a **campsite**, the only one for miles, in a wooded setting close to the train station at Piella, the *Parco di Piella* (open all year; ☎0583/63.016). To get there walk down from Piazza delle Erbe to the river, cross the bridge, take Via XX Settembre left into Via G. Marconi, and then walk up the narrow alley straight ahead, Via dei Cappuccini. From the **train station**, which is ten minutes from the centre, turn right and first left up Viale della Rimembranza.

Bus services run from Piazza Umberto to a variety of destinations. There are eleven daily connections to Lucca; nine to Barga; two to Florence; two to Massa; three to Corfino (for the Orecchiella park centre – see opposite); eight to Castiglione; two to Passo delle Radici (for San Pellegrino); and six to Piazza al Serchio.

The Orecchiella

Though higher than the spectacular Apuane on the other side of the valley, the **Orecchiella mountains** are a generally tamer terrain, rounded and thickly wooded, with steep lateral valleys and gentle grassy slopes above the tree line. The headquarters of the park which protects these uplands is located at a new **park centre** near the village of **Corfino**. The one monument of note is the monastery at **San Pellegrino**, now home to a museum of Garfagnana traditions.

San Pellegrino in Alpe

The sixteen-kilometre drive up the minor road northeast from Castelnuovo to **SAN PELLEGRINO IN ALPE** (1524m) offers stunning views over the steep valleys and ridges of the Orecchiella. If you don't have a car, there's the option of the two daily summer **buses** from Castelnuovo, which take the parallel and almost equally impressive major road via Castiglione.

San Pellegrino's magnificently sited **monastery** is partly given over to an excellent **Museo della Campagna**, Via del Voltone 14 (Tues–Sun June–Sept 9.30am–1pm & 2.30–7pm; Oct–May 9am–noon & 2–5pm; closed Mon except in July & Aug; L3000). Similar museums chronicling the art and culture of rural life can be pretty dire but this is a huge and fascinating display of the Garfagnana's peasant traditions. The exhibits cover four floors, and range over every imaginable aspect of country life: whole rooms are devoted to single themes – one contains dozens of different spinning wheels, for example. Elsewhere are tiny objects of mind-boggling ingenuity for things like bilberry-picking, many crafted from wood or crudely cast iron, all displayed with great clarity. Great care and thought has gone into the place, and it's no surprise to find that it's also a respected centre of anthropological research.

The adjacent hamlet has a bar, a couple of run-down **pensioni**, and reasonably priced shops where you can buy local honey, oil, mushrooms, grappa and sweet chestnut flour, once the area's staple diet.

Other **accommodation** is to be found on the pass at the top of the road – the **Foce delle Radici** – where there's a high, bleak and isolated hotel, the two-star *Lunardi* (☎0583/649.071; ④). Down the parallel road towards Castiglione and Castelnuovo there are a couple more hotels, both in great locations about 5–7km from the pass (ask the bus driver to drop you off): the *Casone* (☎0583/649.096; ⑤), perched at over 1300 metres and the *Filippe* (☎0583/649.081; ③), at 1200m.

Be warned, if you are using the green TCI map, that the apparent short cut between Castiglione and the Castelnuovo–Corfino road does not in fact exist.

Corfino and the park centre

Reached from Castelnuovo by a beautiful road past meadows, thatched barns and views over the Apuane and Orecchiella, **CORFINO** is a small hill village which provides walkers with a choice of half a dozen **hotels**: *La Pania*, Via della Madonna (☎0583/660.087; ③), and the *Panoramico*, Via Fondo la Terra 9 (☎0583/660.161; ④).

Whatever standard of walk you want, or if you just fancy a drive in the area, it's worth visiting the excellent **park centre** (open daily July & Aug; June & Sept weekends only; Oct–May booked groups only; ☎0583/619.098 or 65.169), a Swiss chalet-type development in wild countryside, five kilometres to the north. It has a small bar, telephones, information and exhibition centre, a lake with nicely sited picnic spots, and an excellent **botanical garden**. There's nowhere to stay at the centre itself but in the park is the all-year *Rifugio Orecchiella* (☎0583/619.010; ②), and about two kilometres beyond is the – also all-year – *Rifugio Miramonti* (☎0583/619.012; ②), whose owner knows every walk that can be plotted across these hills.

Walks from the centre

If you're going in for serious **walking**, you should pick up one of the widely available *Multigraphic-Wanderkarte* 1:25,000 maps (sheets #15 or #18), which show all the marked trails in the area. However, there are three **marked circular walks** laid out by the centre which you can tackle without too much planning.

Walk 1 (5hr) takes in the summit of the craggy limestone Cima Pania (1602m) and the nature reserve of the Pania di Corfino, the most important of the three special reserves in the park and a noted area for nesting birds of prey, including peregrine falcons. **Walk 2** (4hr) passes through oak and beech forest and a stretch of grassy meadow. **Walk 3** needs two days, with a choice of three overnight stops: *Rifugio C. Battisti, Rifugio La Bargetana* or *Rifugio di Monte Prado*.

In addition to these walks, there are also seven **Club Alpino paths** (2–3hr), and three paths pioneered by **Airone**, the leading Italian natural history magazine. The centre's board-plan or staff will make sense of the paths if you need help.

Long-distance paths

If you want a real challenge, there's also a long-distance marked path known as **Garfagnana Trekking**, which starts and finishes at **Castelnuovo** and is designed to take about ten days. The Castelnuovo *Centro Accoglienza* has full details, and it's marked as a separate route on the *Wanderkarte* maps. As well as taking in the best of the Orecchiella, five of the stages of this walk go through the Alpi Apuane.

An even more ambitious long-distance route, the linear **Grande Escursione Apenninica**, runs through the Orecchiella on its 24-stage trail from Sansepolcro across the roof of Tuscany to the Passo dei due Santi above La Spezia.

The Eastern Apuane

North of Castelnuovo di Garfagnana the Serchio valley floor is itself not very memorable but if you have transport – or can fit in with very sparse bus services – there are several possible diversions into the **Apuane mountains** to the west.

Over the ridge to Massa

The most obvious of these Apuane forays is the road which climbs **over the main ridge to Massa** – a route covered by one lunchtime bus a day from Castelnuovo. The road is not quite the scenic backwater it appears on the map, but the early stretch, up the **Túrrite valley**, is verdant and tree-lined, with good views of the vast crags of the Pania della Croce (1859m). Much of the road is newly widened, following the opening of the hydroelectric station at Tórrite, but it degenerates suddenly after the tunnel into Massa province.

The one hamlet of consequence is **ISOLA SANTA**, with a rustic **restaurant**, *Da Giacco*, especially good during the mushroom season (Sept–Oct), overlooking the river and a small lake. A section of the long-distance *Garfagnana Trekking* (GT) passes a hundred metres west of the hamlet, and you can follow it north towards Lago di Vagli (about 4hr walking; see opposite) or south for a couple of hours to the above average bar and accommodation of *Rifugio Freo* (April–Oct; ☎0584/778.007; accessible only on foot). The best circular walk from Isola Santa is north on the GT/CAI-marked trail #145 to Monte Sumbra (1764m), and back the same way, a stiff climb but only about 8km in total.

Back on the main road, 6km beyond Isola, and shortly before the tunnel, a road leads off north to Arni (2km).

Lago di Vagli and some walks

North of Castelnuovo, the best diversion comes at Poggio (8km), where there's a choice of two roads. One runs to the high village of **CAREGGINE** (882m), notable for little except its views over the valley and the mountains to the rear. It has three one-star **hotels** – the cheapest the *Belvedere*, Via Taccino 3 (☎0583/661.005; ③). The other leads to **Lago di Vagli**, an artificial creation that submerged the village of Fabbriche (whose church tower is still visible above the water), but left three others intact – Roggio, Vagli Sotto and Vagli Sopra.

ROGGIO is immersed in chestnut trees, and boasts the biggest single specimen in Italy, ten metres round and twenty-six high. It has a small one-star **hotel**, *La Guardia*, Piazza La Guardia (☎0583/649.121; ④).

Equally enticing, **VAGLI DI SOTTO** sits on an arm of the lake, hires out boats for messing around on the water, and has a popular two-star **hotel**, *Le Alpi*, Via Vandelli 8 (☎0583/664.057; ⑤). It also provides the starting point for a couple of excellent **walks** onto the highest ridges of the Apuane – for which the *Multigraphic-Wanderkarte* map (#101/102) is invaluable. Vagli di Sopra, above the lake, has a few **rooms** for rent. All of these villages have a trattoria which, though small, does excellent cooking.

The **first path** from Vagli di Sotto follows the road southwest up the Tambura valley, before linking with the CAI-marked trail #35; you can then follow this west to **Monte Focoletta** (1620m), or, more interestingly, east to CAI #144, which takes you to the top of **Monte Sumbra** (1764m) and then in a wide circle via the Tassetora valley back to Vagli di Sotto – a fantastic and varied day's walk (16km).

The **second path**, CAI #177, climbs to the Passo della Foccolacia (1650m), a meeting point of several other trails. The pass offers excellent views to the Apuane's highest point, **Monte Pisanino** (1947m), just to the north, and access to a superb ridge (trail #179/186) that takes you to the top of **Monte Grondilice** (1805m). From the summit you can carry on to Carrara, or north (on the GT) to the *Rifugio Donegani* (May–Nov; ☎0583/610.085), the starting point for many trails. The refuge is also accessible by road from the Serchio valley to the north via Piazza al Serchio and Gramolazzo.

The Lunigiana

Few people make it to Tuscany's northernmost tip, the **Lunigiana**. A land of rocky, forested landscape, with just two sizeable towns – **Aulla** and **Pontrémoli** – this is one of the most insular regions in Tuscany. Its isolation was ensured over centuries by its mountainous approaches – only broken this century by the carving out of a rail tunnel and twisting mountain road at Piazza al Serchio.

The Lunigiana's name derives from the **Luni**, an ancient tribe who proved a tough lot for the Romans to crack and were equally impervious for some centuries to Christianity. In later centuries the tradition continued as numerous would-be rulers built castles to exact tolls from anyone passing through the valley – hence the tourist-board name for the Lunigiana, "Land of the Hundred Castles". Further proof of individualism came after Unification, when the region gained a reputation for its anarchists, and in the last war, when it was liberated early by local Partisans.

Many of the touted **castles** are now in private hands and numerous others were left in ruins by the last war, but the region still repays a visit for the scenery and self-contained feel. If you want to do more than scoot through on the train, there's an extensive **bus network**, with Aulla the hub of a system that connects within the region itself and with Massa and Carrara further afield. **Train** connections are frequent to Parma, La Spezia, Massa, Lucca and Pisa.

Equi Terme, Fosdinovo and Fivizzano

The train from the Garfagnana emerges from its long tunnel at **EQUI TERME**, which advertises itself for visits to the **Buca del Cane**, "Dog's Hole" cave (daily from 2.30pm "until there are no more people"; L8000), inhabited in prehistoric times. It's not perhaps enough to merit a special diversion, though the tiny village has a superb scenic backdrop of crags and knife-edge peaks. If you need it, there's a single **hotel**, the *Posta* at Via Provinciale (☎0585/97.937; ④), with a fine **restaurant**.

Heading towards the coast from here by road, the most interesting route is via **FOSDINOVO**, a beautifully situated village that sits along a spur overlooking steep, wooded valleys. Host to Dante in 1306, the **Castello della Malaspina** here is certainly the best of the region's fortresses, and houses a museum of arms, armour and bric-a-brac from local tombs (Tues–Sun 10am–noon & 4–7pm; L5000).

FIVIZZANO – to the north, on the N63 road into Emilia – is a more substantial place, with its medieval **Piazza Medicea**, dominated by a Medici fountain and a retinue of Florentine palazzi. The village also has a fine thirteenth-century church, **SS. Jacopo e Antonio**, with a handful of Renaissance paintings. If you want a **room** or **meal**, the obvious choice is the central *Hotel-Ristorante Giardinetto* in Via Roma 151 (☎0585/92.060; ④); the restaurant is closed Monday. You might pass this way heading for the **Passo di Cerreto** (1261m), a walking and skiing centre on the Emilia-Romagna border. En route, 6km out of Fivizzano, look for the hamlet of Vendaso on the right, home to the Romanesque church of **San Paolo**.

Aulla and around

AULLA, squeezed onto a green strip at the confluence of two rivers, was almost totally destroyed in the last war and has virtually nothing of note except for the **Fortezza della Brunella**, a sixteenth-century Genoese castle that testifies to the town's early strategic importance (daily summer 9am–noon & 4–6pm; winter 9am–noon & 3–5pm; L1000). With time on your hands, you might look into the parish church, built within the ruins of the eighth-century **San Caprasio**, an abbey that long dominated the hinterland.

Your best bet if you have the inclination for really getting to grips with Lunigiana is to head to some of the surrounding villages, most of which were fortified by the Malaspina nobles. Try Licciana Nardi, named for an early freedom fighter shot in 1844 while leading an uprising in southern Italy (his remains are in the big sarcophagus in the village's Piazza del Municipio), Caprigliola (6km south on the border with Liguria), Bibola or Ponzanello.

A more well-defined target is **VILLAFRANCA IN LUNIGIANA**, halfway from Aulla to Pontrémoli, again with the ruins of a Malaspina castle, but of more interest for its **Museo Ethnografico** (Tues–Sat 9am–1pm & 3–6pm; L3000). Occupying an old mill in Via Borgo, this documents the area's rural traditions, with a special nod to the omnipresent sweet chestnut. From **BAGNONE**, 5km east, there are opportunities for walks into the remote chestnut-covered ridges of Monte Sillara (1867m) and Monte Marmagna (1851m).

If you're in the Aulla area overnight, the best place for **food** and **accommodation** is the one-star *Alpi Apuane* (☎0187/418.045; ③), 3km east of the town at Pallerone. The food, in particular, is splendid.

Pontrémoli

PONTRÉMOLI is the Lunigiana's biggest centre, and the northernmost town in Tuscany. Part is still evocatively medieval, especially the area rambling north of the **Torre del Campanone**. The tower, now the duomo's campanile, originally formed part of a fortress built by Lucca's Castruccio Castracani in 1322 to keep the town's warring factions apart: hence its nickname, the *Cacciaguerra* – "chaser-away-of-war". The **Duomo** itself is an extraordinary Baroque affair.

The most captivating things in the town, however, are the twenty or so prehistoric **stele** housed in the **Museo del Comune** – whose home is the **Castello del Piagnaro**, a bleak fourteenth-century castle (Tues–Sun June–Sept 9am–noon & 4–7pm; Oct–May 9am–noon & 2–5pm; L1000). These highly stylised statues fall into three groups. The oldest date from 3000–2000 BC, and are crude rectangular blocks with just a "U" for a face, and only the suggestion of arms and trunk. The second group (2000–800 BC) have more angular heads and more detail; the last pieces (700–200 BC) are more sophisticated still, and usually have a weapon in each hand. Most stele were funerary headstones, but here it's thought they represented a pagan communion between heaven (the head), earth (the arms and their weapons) and the underworld (the buried bottom third). Those with heads missing perhaps suffered at the hands of Christians intent on doing away with idolatry.

Fifteen minutes' walk south of the town, the small church of **SS. Annunziata** was built to celebrate an appearance of the Virgin in 1471; it contains a trio of treasures, the most important an octagonal marble **tempietto** by Jacopo Sansovino, the others a fifteenth-century *Annunciation* and a Florentine altarpiece by an unknown artist.

Pontrémoli has the only **tourist office** in the Lunigiana, in the central Piazza Municipio. Enquire here about the plentiful **accommodation** possibilities, or call at the three-star *Napoleon*, Piazza Italia 2 (☎0187/830.544; ⑤) which has its own **restaurant**. The local culinary speciality is a type of pasta, *testroli*, available in most of the many restaurants: try the *Da Ferdinando*, Via San Gemignano 52, or the long-established *Da Bussè*, Via del Duomo 9 (closed Fri).

travel details

Trains

From Lucca to Pisa (hourly; 30min); Florence, via Pescia, Montecatini, Pistoia and Prato (hourly; 1hr 5min–1hr 50min); Viareggio (hourly; 35min); Aulla, via Barga and Castelnuovo di Garfagnana (10 daily; 2hr).

From Massa to Viareggio/Pisa/Livorno/Rome (hourly; 20min/35min/55min/4hr 30min).

From Aulla to Lucca via Castelnuovo di Garfagnana and Barga (10 daily; 2hr).

Buses
From Lucca

LAZZI services to Abetone (1 daily; 2hr 20min); Bagni di Lucca (10 daily; 50min); Camaiore (6 daily; 1hr); Empoli (1 daily; 1hr 45min); Florence (27 daily; 1hr 15min); Forte dei Marmi (16 daily; 1hr 15min); La Spezia (6 daily; 2hr 50min); Lerici (1 daily; 2hr 20min); Livorno (3 daily; 1hr 20min); Marina di Carrara (10 daily; 1hr 40min); Marina di Massa (10 daily; 1hr 30min); Pisa (26 daily; 40min); Pisa Airport (3 daily; 1hr 30min); Prato (5 daily; 2hr 15min); Viareggio (18 daily; 40min).

CLAP services to Barga (10 daily; 1hr 15min); Castelnuovo di Garfagnana (9 daily; 1hr 20min); Forte dei Marmi (14 daily; 1hr 15min); Marina di Massa (13 daily; 1hr 40min); Massa (8 daily; 1hr 35min); Pescia (20 daily; 40min); Pietrasanta (15 daily; 1hr); Viareggio (16 daily; 50min).

From Barga to Bagni di Lucca (2 daily; 40min); Castelnuovo di Garfagnana (4 daily; 30min); Lucca (8 daily; 1hr 15min).

CHAPTER FOUR

PISA, THE CENTRAL COAST AND ELBA

Flying to Tuscany you'll most likely arrive at **Pisa**, a city which – thanks to its tower – is known, at least in name, to almost every visitor to the province. Like Lucca, a little way to the north, Pisa bears the architectural stamp of the Middle Ages, the Torre Pendente being just one element of Italy's most refined medieval ensemble, the Campo dei Miracoli, or Field of Miracles. Since before the time of Galileo it has had one of Italy's major universities, and its student life is a major aspect of Pisa's strong sense of identity. It's an underrated place, seen by most outsiders on a whistle-stop trip – which means that finding accommodation here is often less troublesome than in Tuscany's more overtly enticing towns. Furthermore, its excellent road and rail connections to Florence and to the north and south makes it a good base for wider exploration.

The chief city of the central Tuscan coast is the no-nonsense port of **Livorno**, which is worth a call more for its food than for its sights. To the south, the so-called **Etruscan Riviera** is one of the least attractive areas of Tuscany, with its dingy resorts and drab hinterland of low hills and reclaimed swampland – known often as the Pisan Maremma. Most of it is best seen from the coastal train, as the parallel road is a slow drive and has a reputation as one of the country's most dangerous pieces of tarmac, owing to the huge numbers of Italian holidaymakers who pour into the seaside villages in summer. However, the coast is not unremittingly bad. There are pockets of unspoilt sand around **Baratti**, and some beautiful areas of pine woodland (*pineta*) have been preserved at the important **nature reserve** at **Bólgheri**.

ACCOMMODATION PRICES

Throughout this guide, accommodation is graded on a scale from ① to ⑨. Grades ① and ② apply to **hostel** accommodation, and indicate the lowest price a **single person** could expect to pay for one night in that establishment in high season. Grades ③ to ⑨ apply to **hotels**, and indicate the cost of the **cheapest double room in high season**. The price bands to which these codes refer are as follows:

① under L20,000 per person
② over L20,000 per person
③ under L50,000 per double
④ L50–70,000 per double
⑤ L70–90,000 per double
⑥ L90–120,000 per double
⑦ L120–150,000 per double
⑧ L150–200,000 per double
⑨ over L200,000 per double

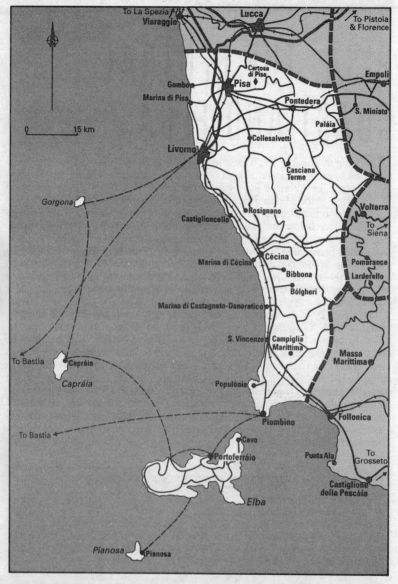

Close to Baratti, at the southern tip of the flatlands, **Piombino** provides the main point of embarkation for the biggest island of the Tuscan archipelago – **Elba**. Though peak-season crowds fill every hotel room on the island, Elba can be a seductive place in spring or early autumn, when it almost rivals the charm of outlying **Capraia**, a spot still remarkably untouched by tourism. Capraia was once a prison island, a function still performed by two other islands – Gorgona and Pianosa. There are plans to close the gaol on Pianosa and convert the island into a nature reserve like the tiny Montecristo, which is now accessible only to research scientists.

Pisa

Since the beginning of the age of the tourist brochure, **PISA** has been known for just one thing – the **Leaning Tower**, the favourite shorthand image for the idea of Italy. It is indeed a freakishly beautiful building, a sight whose impact no amount of prior knowledge can blunt. Yet it's just a single component of the city's amazing religious core – the **Campo dei Miracoli** – where the Duomo, Baptistery and Camposanto complete an unrivalled quartet of medieval masterpieces. These, and a dozen or so churches and palazzi scattered about the town, belong to Pisa's "Golden Age", from the eleventh to the thirteenth century, when the city, then still a port, was one of the maritime powers of the Mediterranean. The Pisan Romanesque architecture of this period, distinguished by its white and black marble facades, is complemented by some of the finest medieval sculpture in Italy, much of it from the workshops of Nicola and Giovanni Pisano.

The city's political zenith came in the second half of the eleventh century with a series of victories over the Saracens, whom the Pisans drove out from Corsica, Sardinia and the Balearic islands, and harassed even in Sicily. Decline set in early, however, with defeat at sea by the Genoese in 1284 followed by the silting

---

PISA AIRPORT

Pisa city centre is just a five-minute **train** ride from **Galileo Galilei airport**, most visitors' point of entry to Tuscany. Trains leave the airport station every hour for Florence, calling at **Pisa Centrale** on the way; there's almost no chance of your arriving too late for a connection, as the last train leaves just before midnight. If your destination is Siena, you'll have to change at Empoli, thirty-five minutes' ride away. Bus departures are more frequent than the trains, but they are no quicker and no cheaper.

The airport concourse has the usual **exchange** facilities, where the rates are a shade less favourable than you'll get in the city. There's also an impressive turnout of **car-hire** firms, though on-the-spot deals are more expensive than those arranged in advance. If you've pre-booked a car and your flight is delayed, the rental desk will remain open until your arrival, so don't panic. All the firms will demand a deposit to cover the full fuel tank – expect to leave around L80,000. The deposit is returned if you bring the car back with a full tank; always refuel before getting to the airport, as petrol is even pricier here than elsewhere, and the airport petrol station takes a long lunch break.

The drive from the airport to Florence is straightforward, but **the road into Pisa** is so confusing that you'll end up driving four times the necessary distance if you don't get detailed directions from the car-hire desk.

One last point – Pisa's **duty-free shop** is one of the worst in Europe. If you're contemplating taking back a bottle of grappa or crate of Brunello, don't bank on finding it here.

up of the harbour. From 1406 the city was governed by Florence, whose Medici rulers re-established the University of Pisa, one of the intellectual forcing houses of the Renaissance; **Galileo**, Pisa's most famous native, was one of the teachers there. Subsequent centuries saw the city fade into provinciality – its state when the Shelleys and Byron took palazzi here, forging what Shelley termed their "paradise of exiles". The modern city has been revitalised by its airport and industrial suburbs and, of course, money from tourism.

Arrival and accommodation

Coming in by **train** you arrive at the Piazza della Stazione on the south bank of the Arno; by **bus** at the nearby Piazza Vittorio Emanuele II or adjacent Piazza San Antonio. From here, the **Campo dei Miracoli** is about twenty minutes' walk, across the Ponte di Mezzo, or a five-minute bus ride (#1) from outside the train station; local bus tickets are sold at a kiosk to the right of the station as you leave. If you arrive by **car**, follow the signs to the official car park outside the Porta Nuova, just west of the Campo dei Miracoli.

To pick up a **map** – and full hotel lists for the city and province – look in at one of the **tourist offices**: to the left (as you leave) of the train station (Mon–Sat 9.30am–1pm & 3.30–7pm), or tucked into the northeast corner of the Campo dei Miracoli, close to the Leaning Tower (Mon–Fri 9am–noon & 3–6pm, Sat 9.30am–1pm & 3.30–7pm).

There are **currency exchange** bureaux at the station, the airport, and in the middle of the row of stalls at the Campo dei Miracoli. The station also has a **telephone office** (daily 7.30am–10.45pm) and a **left luggage office**, while the main post office is a hundred metres away in Piazza Vittorio Emanuele II.

Accommodation

People tend to cover Pisa as a day trip, or stay just a night, so **accommodation** is usually not too hard to find. In summer, however, it's still best to phone ahead or arrive early in the day. Pisa's prospects for budget accomodation are improving with a newly-opened youth hostel with a campsite, another fairly central campsite, and a women-only hostel; if these are full, high-season campers or hostellers may have to head for the coastal sites.

The most attractive of Pisa's budget **hotels** are grouped around the Campo dei Miracoli, and these are obviously the ones that are quickest to fill. Similar-cost places in the centre of the city, around Piazza Dante and Piazza dei Cavalieri, are often filled with students in term time, but in midsummer are likelier to have rooms than the ones near the Campo; hotels near the station tend to be tattier and cheaper. The hotels below are listed in ascending order of price.

HOTELS

Rinascente, Via del Castelletto 28 (☎050/502.436). Occupies an old palazzo near Piazza dei Cavalieri; very popular. ③.

Serena, Via D. Cavalca 45 (☎050/580.809). Off the east side of Piazza Dante; a favourite with students. ③.

Di Stefano, Via Sant'Apollonia 35 (☎050/553.559). Tidy if characterless hotel in quiet street just off the east side of Piazza dei Cavalieri. ③.

Gronchi, Piazza Arcivescovado 1 (☎050/561.823). Just east of the Campo; elegant in a run-down sort of way, and a definite first choice, despite the midnight curfew. ③.

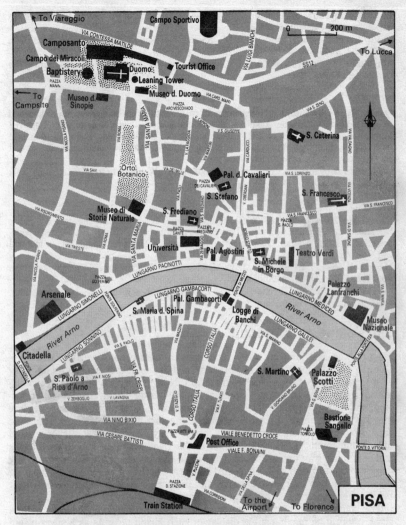

Galileo, Via Santa Maria 12 (☎050/40.621). Nine big, nicely decorated rooms; not the quietest hotel in town, but central and good value. ③.

Giardino, Via Cammeo (☎050/562.101). Tucked behind a self-service restaurant just west of the Baptistery. ③.

Helvetia, Via Don G. Boschi 31 (☎050/553.084). Spotless and friendly place off Piazza Arcivescovado; midnight curfew. ③.

Milano, Via Mascagni 14 (☎050/23.162). In side street leading into Piazza della Stazione; one of the better hotels in the station area. ③.

Clio, Via San Lorenzino 3 (☎050/28.446). Clean and welcoming place at the river end of Corso Italiana. ③.

Leon Bianco, Piazza del Pozzetto 6 (☎050/28.446). Smartish two-star hotel, well-situated in the centre, near Ponte di Mezzo. ④.

Bologna, Via Mazzini 57 (☎050/502.120). Another two-star, on the station side of the river, parallel to Corso Italia. ④.

Amalfitana, Via Roma 44 (☎050/29.000). Pleasant two-star, a couple of minutes south of the Campo dei Miracoli. ⑤.

HOSTELS

Ostello della Gioventù, Via Pietrasantina 15 (☎050/890.622). New hostel, with an attached campsite due to open soon. Take bus #3 from the station – signs close to the Campo dei Miracoli suggest that it's just a brief walk away, but it's a 40-minute slog. Make sure you have mosquito repellent in summer, as the hostel is right by a swamp. Nearby supermarket, and very friendly staff. Reception opens 6pm. ①.

Casa della Giovane, Via Corridoni 31 (☎050/43.061). Women's hostel, five minutes' walk from the station. ②.

CAMPSITES

Campeggio Torre Pendente (☎050/560.665). Large, well-maintained site, with a laundry, bar, restaurant and shop; 1km west of the Campo dei Miracoli at Viale delle Cascine 86 (signposted from Piazza Manin). Open mid-March to Sept. L8000 per person, L6000 per tent and L6000 per car.

Marina di Pisa, Via Litoranea, Marina di Pisa (☎050/36.553). Largish beach site, 10km from central Pisa. Open mid-April to Oct.

Mare e Sole, Viale del Tirreno (☎050/32.757). Another beach campsite, 15km from Pisa, near Tirrenia; bus #7. Open April–Sept.

The Campo dei Miracoli

Since it was first laid out, Pisa's ecclesiastical centre has been known as the **Campo dei Miracoli** (Field of Miracles), and the sight of it is as stunning today as it must have been to medieval travellers. Nowhere in Italy are the key buildings of a city – the cathedral, baptistery and bell tower – arrayed with such precision, and nowhere is there so beautiful a contrast of stonework and surrounding meadow. Underneath the pavements and the turf lies a platform of saturated sandy soil, whose instability accounts for the crazy tilt of the Leaning Tower, and of its companions. Take a close look at the Baptistery and you'll see that it's inclined some way out of the vertical, while the facade of the Duomo is a few degrees out of true as well. The weird angles aren't the only oddity – the tapering domes of the Baptistery and Duomo, with the precarious top storey of the Tower behind them, comprise the strangest skyline in Tuscany.

The souvenir stalls around the edge of the Campo are in themselves quite a sight, offering an inexhaustible display of such kitsch delights as a silver-plated plastic replica of the Leaning Tower with a comely mermaid wrapped round its base – presumably an arcane reference to Pisa's maritime history.

TICKETS FOR THE CAMPO DEI MIRACOLI SIGHTS

For L12,000 you can buy a **combined ticket** which gives entry into the Baptistery, the Camposanto, the Museo dell'Opera del Duomo and Museo delle Sinopie – a saving of L8000. The ticket is available at all of these sights.

The Leaning Tower

Perhaps the strangest fact about the **Leaning Tower** – the Torre Pendente – is that it has always tilted. Begun in 1173, it started to subside when it had reached just three of its eight storeys, but it leaned in the opposite direction to the present one. Odd-shaped stones were inserted to correct this deficiency, whereupon the tower went over the other way. Over the next 180 years a succession of architects continued to extend the thing upwards, each one endeavouring to compensate for the angle, the end result being that the main part of the tower is slightly banana-shaped. Around 1350, Tomasso di Andrea da Pontedera completed the magnificent stack of marble and granite arcades by crowning it with a bell-chamber, set closer to the perpendicular than the storeys below it, so that it looks like a hat set at a rakish angle. Galileo exploited the overhang in one of his celebrated experiments, dropping metal balls of different mass to demonstrate his theory of the constancy of gravity.

Eight centuries on, the tower leans more than five metres from the upright and is nearing its limits. In 1989 the Ministry of Public Works in Rome suggested its closure to visitors; facing the loss of a revenue totalling over £2 million a year, the Pisans disagreed. However, the collapse of a church tower in Pavia, killing four people, concentrated minds on the risks of keeping the tower open and in January 1990 it was finally shut. Since then the situation has worsened: having moved annually by about one millimetre over the last couple of decades, the tower shifted that amount in the first ten weeks of 1991 alone.

Soon after the closure, ten steel bands were wrapped round the lowest section of the tower, to prevent the base from buckling under the weight of the 14,000 tonnes of marble above. Various schemes aimed at arresting the effects of gravity were then discussed. A Japanese consortium – rather missing the scenographic importance of the tower – submitted a plan for encasing it in a structure that would double as a viewing platform and a prop, while from the US came the idea of installing a vast underground refrigerator that would grip the foundations in a block of permafrost. In the end it was decided to hang enormous lead weights off the tower's foundations to counterbalance the force of the leaning stonework, but even this straightforward plan has run into problems, with the discovery of ancient subterranean ruins during the early stages of the work. A classic Tuscan conundrum has thus arisen – should one damage an historically valuable site in order to preserve a younger one? However things turn out, the tower is unlikely to reopen before the end of the century.

The Duomo

The **Duomo** (daily summer 7.45am–1pm & 3–7pm; winter closes 5pm) was begun a century before the campanile, in 1064. With its four levels of variegated colonnades and its subtle interplay of dark grey marble and white stone, it's the archetype of the Pisan Romanesque style, a model often imitated but never surpassed. Squares and discs of coloured marble are set into the magnificent facade, but the soberly graceful overall effect of the primary grey and white is such that you notice these strong tones only when you look closely.

The original bronze doorway, the **Portale di San Ranieri**, stands opposite the Leaning Tower. Its scenes from the Life of Christ, cast around 1180 by Bonnano Pisano, first architect of the Leaning Tower, are powerfully diagrammatic; the Massacre of the Innocents, for example, is represented by the smallest possible cast – Herod, one mother and one soldier. The Portale's place on the main facade has been taken by massive doors from the workshop of Giambologna, a panoply of Renaissance detail.

Inside the Duomo, the impact of the crisp black and white marble of the long arcades – recalling the Moorish architecture of Córdoba – is slightly diminished by the incongruous gilded ceiling, the fresco in the squashed circle of the dome, and the massive air vents bunged through the upper arches. Much of the interior was redecorated, and some of the chapels remodelled, after a fire in 1595, so most of the paintings and sculpture are Renaissance or later.

A notable survivor from the medieval building is the apse mosaic of *Christ in Majesty*, completed by Cimabue in 1302, but the acknowledged highlight is the **pulpit** sculpted by **Giovanni Pisano**. This was packed away after the fire, sixteenth-century Pisans evidently no longer concurring with the Latin inscription around the base, which records that Giovanni had "the art of pure sculpture . . . and would not know how to carve ugly or base things, even if he wished to". Only in 1926 was it rediscovered and put back together in the nave.

The last of the great series of pulpits created in Tuscany by Giovanni and his father Nicola (the others are in Siena and Pistoia), it is a work of amazing virtuosity, the whole surface animated with figures almost wholly freed from the block. Its narrative density rewards close attention – the story of the Passion from Judas's betrayal to the scourging of Christ, for instance, is condensed into a single panel. Unfortunately the most tumultuous panel of all – the *Last Judgement* – can't be seen properly because a column gets in the way. You'll need plenty of L200 coins for illumination.

In the right transept is the other principal relic from before the blaze, the tomb of the Holy Roman Emperor **Henry VII**, who died near Siena, allegedly from eating a poisoned wafer at Mass. Having laid Siena to waste, the Ghibelline (ie pro-Imperial) Pisans bore the body of their hero back to the Camposanto, where Tino da Camaino carved the effigy in 1315. In photographs the sculpture looks wonderful, but it's now mounted so high on the wall that you can see little more than its delicate profile.

Lastly, the cathedral has a piece of scientific legend. It is said that the forerunner of the huge bronze incense lamp, swung to fumigate the central aisle, provided the inspiration for Galileo's theory of the movement of the pendulum.

The Baptistery

The third building of the Miracoli ensemble, the circular **Baptistery** (daily summer 8am–8pm; winter 9am–5pm; L5000), is a slightly bizarre mix, with three storeys of Romanesque arcades peaking in a crest of Gothic pinnacles and a dome shaped like the stalk end of a lemon. It was begun in the mid-twelfth century by a certain Deotisalvi ("God save you"), who left his name on the column to the left of the door. Lack of money – caused mainly by Genoa's incursions into the Pisan trade network – prevented its continuation in the style in which it had been started. In the latter half of the thirteenth century the Gothic top storeys and attendant flourishes were applied by Nicola and Giovanni Pisano, who rounded off the job with a glorious gallery of statues – the originals of which are now displayed in the Museo dell'Opera del Duomo (see p.234).

This is the largest baptistery in Italy, and the plainness of the vast interior is immediately striking, with its unadorned arcades and bare dome. The acoustics are astonishing too – as demonstrated at intervals by the custodian. At the centre, continuing the exotic strain of Pisan Romanesque, is a mosaic-inlaid **font** by Guido da Como (1246), raised on stone steps for ease of immersion.

Overlooking it is Nicola Pisano's **pulpit**, sculpted in 1260, half a century before his son's work in the cathedral. This was the sculptor's first major commission and manifests a classical spirit in part attributable to the influence of the court of Emperor Henry II, whose Italian power base was in Nicola's native Apulia. Thus the seated Virgin in the *Adoration of the Magi* is almost a literal copy of a figure of Phaedra on a Roman sarcophagus now housed in the Museo dell'Opera del Duomo, while the nude figure of Daniel (underneath the *Adoration*) is evidently Hercules under an alias. The complexity of the cultural make-up of fourteenth-century Pisa is shown by the Gothic sharp-angled drapery and by the architectural elements of the pulpit – the decoration of the arches and the foliage of the capitals recalling the stonework of French Gothic cathedrals.

The Camposanto
The screen of sepulchral white marble running along the north edge of the Campo dei Miracoli is the perimeter wall of what has been called the most beautiful cemetery in the world – the **Camposanto** (daily winter 9am–5pm; summer 8am–8pm; L5000). According to Pisan legend, at the end of the twelfth century the city's archbishop brought back from the Crusades a cargo of soil from Golgotha, in order that eminent Pisans might be buried in holy earth. The building enclosing this sanctified site was completed almost a century later.

The Camposanto basically takes the form of an enormous Gothic cloister, each of whose long sides is as big as a cathedral nave. A few **tombs** are set into the rectangle of lawn at its centre, but most are housed under the shelter of the arcades. Some of the memorials, such as the Egyptian examples, are installed here as museum pieces, but most are for people who were actually buried in the Camposanto. Together they constitute a virtual encyclopaedia of the ways in which death has been accommodated, from the terse classical style – recording the occupant's name, status and nothing else – to the opposite extreme, where the focus of interest is not on the deceased but on those left behind – as in the romantic tomb surmounted by a woman identified as "The Inconsolable".

However, when Ruskin described the Camposanto as one of the three most precious buildings in Italy, along with the Sistine Chapel and the Scuola di San Rocco in Venice, it was not its tombs but rather its **frescoes** that he was praising. Paintings once covered over 2000 square metres of cloister wall, but now the brickwork is mostly bare. Incendiary bombs dropped by Allied planes on July 27, 1944 set the roofing on fire and drenched the frescoes in a river of molten lead; the masterpieces of **Benozzo Gozzoli** were all but destroyed – just a few patches of his Old Testament scenes remain, to the left of the entrance. Close by there's another picture that came through the bombing: a fascinating fourteenth-century **Theological Cosmograph**, showing the concentric spheres of the universe and the tripartite division of the earth into Europe, Asia and Africa.

The most important surviving frescoes are the remarkable fourteenth-century cycle by the painter known as the *Maestro del Trionfo della Morte*, the **Master of the Triumph of Death**. These have been detached from the wall and put on show in a room opposite the entrance, beyond a photographic display of the Camposanto before the bombing. Painted within a few months of the Black Death of 1348 – a pestilence which hit Tuscany so badly that it was known throughout Europe as the Florentine Plague – the *Triumph* shows a trio of aristocratic huntsmen stopped in their tracks by a trio of coffins, the contents of which are so putrescent that one of the riders has to pinch his nose. Over to the right, squadrons of angels and demons bear away the souls of the dead, whose final resting place is determined in the terrifying *Last Judgement* at the far end of the room. There's no more ruthless catalogue of horrors in western art than this.

The Museo dell'Opera del Duomo

A vast array of statuary from the Duomo and Baptistery, plus ecclesiastical finery, paintings and other miscellaneous pieces are displayed in the recently revamped **Museo dell'Opera del Duomo** (daily summer 8am–8pm; winter 9am–5pm; L5000), at the southeast corner of the Campo.

The collection kicks off with pieces dating from the period of the Duomo's construction, showing how Islamic influences, filtered through the intermediary of Byzantium, came to be expressed in the city's art – notably in the marble inlays from the Duomo facade. The large bronze griffon is a more direct borrowing from Islam, having been thieved from the Middle East by a Pisan war party in the eleventh century. The other main cultural input shown here is from Burgundy, source of the strange painted wooden Crucifix, a gigantic figure with a tiny head and mantis-thin arms.

Sculptures by the various Pisanos are the high points of the museum, but the first pieces you encounter – Nicola and Giovanni's figures from the Baptistery – are too eroded and pitted to give much of an idea of their power. Room 5, however, which is given over to works by **Giovanni Pisano**, contains the most affecting statue in Pisa, the *Madonna del Colloquio*, so called because of the intensity of the gazes exchanged by the Madonna and Child. Giovanni's great contemporary, **Tino da Camaino**, monopolises the next room, where fragments from the tomb of Emperor Henry VII are assembled; the magnificent figures of the emperor and his counsellors may have come from the tomb as well.

Nino Pisano – no relation to Nicola and Giovanni – is the subject of room 7, where his creamy marble monuments to archbishops Giovanni Scherlatti and Francesco Moricotti show the increasing suavity of Pisan sculpture in the late fourteenth century. Giovanni Pisano returns in the **treasury**, his ivory *Madonna and Child* showing a remarkable ingenuity in the way it exploits the natural curve of the tusk from which it's carved. The other priceless object here is the *Pisan Cross*, which was carried by the Pisan contingent on the First Crusade.

Upstairs, big and witless altarpiece paintings take up a lot of room, as do cases of ecclesiastical clothing and lavish examples of intarsia, the art of inlaid wood, much practised here in the fifteenth and sixteenth centuries. Strangest objects on view are the two ancient parchment rolls known as **Exultets**, from the opening word of the chant on the eve of Holy Saturday. It was during this service that the cantor would unfurl these scrolls from the pulpit, so that the congregation could follow his words through the pictures painted on them.

A fine collection of engravings by **Carlo Lasinio** comes near the end of the museum; it was mainly thanks to his efforts that the Camposanto was rescued from ruin at the beginning of the last century, and his fastidious record of the cloister frescoes is one of the most poignant things in the city. Finally, the museum has a large collection of **Roman and Etruscan** pieces, many of which were slotted into odd corners of Pisa's churches to brighten them up a bit. The most famous image is a thin-lipped bust of Julius Caesar, featured on a dozen editions of his writings.

The Museo delle Sinopie

On the south side of the Campo, the only gap in the souvenir stalls is the entrance to the **Museo delle Sinopie** (daily 9am–1pm & 3pm to sunset; L5000). After the catastrophic damage wreaked on the Camposanto by the bombers, the building's restorers removed its *sinopie*, the monochrome sketches for the frescoes. These great plates of plaster are now hung from the walls of this hi-tech museum, where gantries and galleries give you the chance to inspect the painters' preliminary ideas at close range, but it's a rather scholastic enterprise.

The rest of the city

Away from the Campo dei Miracoli, Pisa takes on a very different character, as few tourists penetrate far into its squares and arcaded streets, with their Romanesque churches and – especially along the banks of the Arno – ranks of fine palazzi. With the large student population it can be quite a lively place, particularly during the summer festivals and the monthly market, when the main streets on each side of the river become one continuous bazaar.

Piazza dei Cavalieri and the eastern districts

The **Piazza dei Cavalieri** is an obvious first stop from the Campo, a large square that opens unexpectedly from the narrow backstreets. Perhaps the site of the Roman forum, it was the central civic square of medieval Pisa, before being remodelled by Vasari as the headquarters of the Knights of Saint Stephen. This order was established by Cosimo I, ostensibly for crusading, though in reality they amounted to nothing more than a gang of licensed pirates, given state sanction to plunder Turkish shipping. Their palace, the curving **Palazzo dei Cavalieri** (now a school), covered in *sgraffiti* and topped with busts of the Medici, faces a statue of Cosimo and adjoins the order's church of **Santo Stefano**, designed by Vasari and housing banners captured from the Turks.

On the other side of the square is the Renaissance-adapted **Palazzo dell'Orologio**, with its archway and clock tower. This was a medieval palace, in whose tower the military leader Ugolino della Gherardesca was starved to death in 1208, with his sons and grandsons, as punishment for his alleged duplicity with the Genoese enemy – an episode described in Dante's *Inferno* and Shelley's *Tower of Famine*.

Northeast from here, across the wide Piazza dei Martiri della Libertà, stands the Dominican church of **Santa Caterina**, whose Romanesque lower facade dates from the year of its foundation, 1251. Inside, there's an *Annunciation* and a tomb by Nicola Pisano, and a fourteenth-century painting of the *Triumph of Thomas Aquinas*, the ideological figurehead of the Dominicans. Nearby, in front of the **Porta Lucca** – the main northern gate of medieval Pisa – you can see the unimpressive remnants of the city's Roman baths, while tucked into the northeast corner of the city walls is the church of **San Zeno**, parts of which go back to the fifth century.

From Via San Zeno, Via Valdagno runs south to the plain Gothic **San Francesco**, whose well-preserved frescoes include work by Taddeo Gaddi and Niccolò di Pietro Gerini. Count Ugolino and his offspring are buried in the second chapel on the right. If you continue down Via di Simone from the back of the church, you'll come out at the Museo Nazionale.

Borgo Stretto to the Museo Nazionale

Heading from Piazza dei Cavalieri towards the Arno, Via Dini swings into the arcaded **Borgo Stretto**, Pisa's smart street, its windows glistening with Laura Biagiotti jewellery, Romeo Gigli shades and other desirables that seem slightly out of tune with the city's unshowy style. More typically Pisan is the **market** just off Via Dini (weekday mornings and all day Saturday), its fruit, vegetable, fish, meat and clothing stalls spilling onto the lanes around Piazza Vettovaglie.

Past the Romanesque-Gothic facade of **San Michele** – built on the site of the Roman temple to Mars – the Borgo meets the river at the traffic-knotted Piazza Garibaldi and **Ponte di Mezzo**, the city's central bridge. A left turn along Lungarno Mediceo takes you past the **Palazzo Toscanelli** (now the city archives), which was rented by Byron in 1821–22, after his expulsion from Ravenna for seditious activities. The poet's lunatic reputation, already well established thanks to his menagerie of horses, cats and dogs, was given a further boost when he got into a scrap with a bunch of Pisan soldiers, a contretemps that brought his brothers in exile – Shelley, Leigh Hunt, Walter Savage Landor – out onto the streets. This display of hot-blooded solidarity prompted the writer Guerrazzi to muse that he at last understood "why the English are a great people, and the Italians a clump of rags in the shop of a secondhand dealer".

A couple of doors further along the *lungarno* is the **Museo Nazionale di San Matteo** (Tues–Sat 9am–7pm, Sun 9am–1pm; L6000), where most of the major works of art from Pisa's churches are now gathered. Supposedly for reasons of security, the Pisan authorities have decided that visitors to this and certain other museums under their jurisdiction must present some form of ID before going into the gallery; for foreigners this basically means that if you don't have your passport with you, you don't get in. Quite why they should make so much fuss about one of Tuscany's minor galleries, while letting anyone get within felt-pen range of the Camposanto frescoes, is a mystery.

Fourteenth-century religious paintings make up the meat of the collection, with a Simone Martini polyptych and work by Antonio Veneziano outstanding in the early sections. Later on, there's a stash of Middle Eastern ceramics pilfered by Pisan adventurers, a panel of *St Paul* by Masaccio, Gozzoli's strangely festive *Crucifixion* and Donatello's reliquary bust of the introspective *St Rossore*. Also housed in the museum are the antique armour and wooden shields used in the annual *Gioco del Ponte* pageant (see p.239).

West of Ponte di Mezzo

The faculty buildings of Pisa's **university** – still one of the most important in the country – are scattered all over the city, but the main concentration is to the west of the Ponte di Mezzo, around **Piazza Dante**. The general tone of the streets – especially the *osterie* and bars – is the attraction of this quarter, though it does have a couple of sights worth singling out.

Immediately to the north of the piazza, the bare stone nave of the eleventh-century **San Frediano** preserves some capitals from that period. To the west, at the end of Via Santa Maria, rises Pisa's second **leaning tower**, the thirteenth-century campanile of **San Nicola**. Cylindrical at its base, mutating into an octagon then a hexagon, it contains a majestic spiral staircase that was Bramante's inspiration for his grand Belvedere staircase in the Vatican. Inside the church, the *Crucifix* in the first chapel on the left is attributed to Giovanni

Pisano, while Nino Pisano is credited with the wooden *Madonna and Child* in the fourth chapel on this side. In the chapels on the other side of the nave, there's a *Madonna* by Francesco Traini and a painting showing Pisa around 1400, being protected from the plague by St Nicholas of Tolentino.

Across the river

The more down-at-heel districts south of the Arno are popularly known as the **Mezzogiorno**, the name disparagingly used by northern Italians when referring to the semi-developed south of the country. On the second Sunday and the preceding Saturday of each month the opposite banks are linked by a big **street market**, with hippy earrings, candles and other craft stuff filling the lower reaches of Borgo Stretto, and furniture and general bric-a-brac around the south-bank **Logge di Banchi**. Formerly the city's silk and wool market, this vast and usually deserted loggia stands at the top of the main shopping street of the *mezzogiorno*, Corso Italia, which starts off classy and gets progressively shabbier as it nears the train station.

East along the **Lungarno Galilei**, the only real sight is the octagonal San Sepolcro, built for the Knights Templar by Diotisalvi, first architect of the Baptistery. A short way past here is the ruined **Palazzo Scotti**, Shelley's home during the period when Byron was in residence on the other side of the river.

Along the *lungarni* to the **west** of the Ponte di Mezzo, the rather monotonous line of palazzi – mirroring those on the facing bank – is suddenly enlivened by the spry turreted oratory of **Santa Maria della Spina**. Rebuilt in 1323 by a merchant who had acquired one of the thorns (*spine*) of Christ's crown, it's the finest flourish of Pisan Gothic. Originally built closer to the river, it was moved here for fear of floods in 1871. The interior is a disappointment that visitors are usually spared by extremely erratic opening hours.

Further west again, **San Paolo a Ripa d'Arno** probably occupies the site of Pisa's very first cathedral. The arcaded facade was built in imitation of the present cathedral in the twelfth century; the interior, badly damaged in the last war, has a handsome Roman sarcophagus and a finely carved capital (second on left), but nothing else to detain you. Behind the church is the octagonal **Cappella di Sant'Agata**, also built in the twelfth century.

Out of town – San Michele

A couple of kilometres east of the centre, secreted in a residential area, stands Pisa's third leaning tower, the campanile of **San Michele dei Scalzi** – you get to it by walking along the riverbank upstream from Ponte di Mezzo. Everything in this building is severely askew: the columns in the nave lurch this way and that, the windows in the apse are all over the place, and the walls set up a drunken counterpoint to the tilt of the tower.

Eating, drinking and entertainment

Pisa's proximity to the coast means that seafood is the staple of its **restaurant** menus. As for the atmosphere in the city's eating places, the university is as strong an influence as the tourist trade, supporting a range of genuine places that cater for a regular clientele of impecunious students at one end of the range, and for their less inhibited teachers at the other. There's the usual scattering of city centre bars, but at night Pisa can be an eerily quiet place, as the majority of its students are Pisan natives who still live at home. In term time, though, there's usually a fair number of one-off events going on – the walls around Piazza Dante are the place to look for posters.

Restaurants

The restaurants in the environs of the Leaning Tower are generally not good value, though any of the numerous pizzerias down Via Santa Maria will do for a quick refuel if that's all you need. Head a few blocks south, to the areas **around Piazza dei Cavalieri and Piazza Dante**, and you'll find predominantly local places, many with prices reflecting student custom. The restaurants below are listed in ascending order of cost.

As with all touristic Italian cities, many of the residents head out of town for their weekend treat – and our listings finish with one recommendation some way outside the city limits.

Mensa Universitaria, Via Martiri. Housed in the modern university building off Piazza dei Cavalieri, the student refectory does meals from L5000. Open mid-Sept to mid-July Mon–Fri noon–2.30pm & 7–9pm; Sat & Sun noon–2.30pm.

Pizzeria da Cassio, Piazza Cavallotti 14. Just off Via Santa Maria, this excellent *tavola calda* is the place to come for a midday pit-stop. Closed Sat & Sun.

San Francesco, Vicolo dei Tinti 26. Friendly, inexpensive spaghetteria.

Trattoria Stelio, Piazza Dante 11. Very busy student place, good for meals around L18,000 and impressive pizzas for a lot less. Closed Sat night and Sun.

Il Vecchio Dado, Lungarno Pacinotti 22. Next to the *Royal Victoria Hotel*, on the waterfront; classy pizzas and lively atmosphere.

La Mescita, Via Cavalca 2. Patronised by students and professors in equal numbers, this small restaurant is virtually an academic institution. Vegetarian fixed menu L30,000; other fixed menus L35,000. Closed Sat lunchtime, Sun & Aug.

Il Paiolo, Via C. Montanara 9. Lively place with outside seats, half a block north of the river. Open until 2am. Closed Aug.

La Cereria, Via Pietro Gori 33. Popular unpretentious restaurant tucked away to the north of Via Benedetto Croce, not far from the train station. Excellent seafood and pasta dishes, and a pleasant courtyard. Closed Tues.

Il Viale, Viale Bonaini 78. Excellent seafood restaurant, five minutes' walk from the train station.

Da Bruno, Via Bianchi 12. To the east of the Campo dei Miracoli, this place specialises in simple Pisan dishes such as the local *baccalà*. From L45,000 per person. Closed Mon, Tues & two weeks in Aug.

Il Cucciolo, Vicolo Rosselini 9. Always reliable, offering unfussy, delicious meals from around L30,000 without wine. Closed Sun & Aug.

Taverna Kostas, Via del Borghetto 39. Long-standing local favourite, its menu mixing Greek and predominantly marine Pisan dishes. Closed Mon & Aug.

Lo Schiaccianoci, Via Vespucci 104 (☎050/21.024). Wonderful fish restaurant, but a tiny place – so it's almost essential to book ahead. Around L70,000 per person. Closed Sun, Mon & Aug.

OUT OF TOWN

La Gattaiola, Via San Lorenzo 2–4, Fauglia (☎050/650.852). High-class trattoria, installed in an old cellar in the village of Fauglia, 20km from central Pisa off the main road to Rome – so only feasible if you have a car. Excellent meals for around L45,000. A lot of Pisans make the trip at weekends, when it's best to ring ahead. Closed Mon & Jan.

Festivals and events

The city's big traditional event is the **Gioco del Ponte**, held on the last Sunday of June, when twelve teams from the north and south banks of the city stage a series of "push-of-war" battles, shoving a seven-ton carriage over the Ponte di Mezzo. The event has taken place since Medici times and continues in Renaissance costume. Other celebrations – concerts, regattas, art events – are held around the same time, and the city has a festive feel for most of the month, with banners and pavement drawings brightening the streets. Most spectacular of the ancillary shows is the **Luminaria di San Ranieri**, when blazing torches light up both river banks. Among **regular events**, look out for concerts at the *Teatro Comunale Verdi* in Via Palestro, and for more offbeat and contemporary shows (even the odd rock concert) held in a former church at the end of Via San Zeno. The city also has an adventurous **arts cinema**, *Cinema Nuovo*, in Piazza della Stazione.

On from Pisa

Moving on from Pisa, the easiest destinations are **Lucca**, half an hour by train or bus, or **Florence**, an hour up the Arno by train. Along the Arno, the most interesting diversions come east of San Miniato and are covered on pages 181–84; on the Pisan side, the only compelling detour is to the **Certosa di Pisa**, a marvellous Baroque Charterhouse, which you could take in on a brief loop from the main road. Beyond, there is little to be said for **Cáscina**, whose medieval core is firmly entrenched in industrial sprawl, and nothing for **Pontedera**, home of the Piaggio factory, producer of the inescapable Vespa scooter.

Heading for **Siena**, the simplest approach by public transport is to take the Florence train, changing for the journey south at Empoli. Driving, you have more choice. You could roam through the Pisan hills to **Volterra**, via Casciano Terme, or – faster but less scenic – via Cáscina, or follow a stretch of the coast, turning inland to Volterra at Cécina.

For just a quick taste of the coast, **Marina di Pisa** and **Tirrenia** are the city's local resorts. Neither is very inspiring but the area just inland has the intermittently open San Rossore park and the ancient church of **San Piero a Grado**.

The Certosa di Pisa

Of the thirty Carthusian monasteries left intact in Italy none makes a more diverting excursion than the fourteenth-century **Certosa di Pisa**, set at the foot of the forested Monte Pisano, close by the village of Calci, 10km east of Pisa. A regular *APT* bus service runs to the village (from 100m west of Piazza Vittorio Emanuele II); if you're in a car, just get to the amazing Medici aqueduct – immediately visible on the eastern outskirts of the city – and follow it all the way. The guided tour of the monastery (May–Sept Tues–Sat 9am–6pm, Sun 9am–noon; Oct–April Tues–Sat 9am–4pm, Sun 9am–noon; L4000) gives a remarkable sense of how the building related to the lives of this order. As with the Museo Nazionale in Pisa, you may need your passport to get in.

The size of the Certosa is startling. From the frescoed central **church**, where a freestanding marble angel does service as a lectern, the tour passes through eleven other **chapels** in which Sunday Mass was conducted simultaneously.

Looking as fresh as the day they were decorated (they have not been restored), these are strangely sybaritic interiors – all powder blue, baby pink, pale violet and pallid green, with stucco details and trompe l'oeil pillars and balustrades to perk things up. Floors are covered with tiles that are only paint-deep, and there's a rectangular chapel tricked out to look like an oval room with a dome.

This ballroom decor contrasts with the more conventional monasticism of the **cloister** and its cells. Each of the monks had a suite of three sparse rooms – a bedroom, a study and a workroom, as the order placed great emphasis on the importance of manual occupation. Attached to every suite is a self-contained garden, walled so that the monks could maintain their soul-perfecting isolation. Except on a Sunday – the one day when conversation was permitted and all the monks ate together – their meals were served through hatches, positioned to minimise the possibility of coming face to face.

From the cloister the tour progresses to the **refectory**, where frescoes of semi-nal moments in the history of the monastery are interspersed with images of the months and their associated crops – a reminder of the order's agricultural self-sufficiency. Nearby are the luxuriously appointed **guest rooms**, where high-born VIPs – various Medici among them – would stay for a bout of not too rigorous scourging of the spirit. Their private cloister features yet more trompe l'oeil, its windows "opening" onto the dining room and monks' cloister.

The visit is made especially absorbing by little details that the guide points out – like the panel with sliding wooden paddles to designate the day's duties (eg head-shaving), or, at the end of the tour, the measuring machines in the **pharmacy**. Above the gate as you leave, an inscription reads "Egredere sed non omnis" (Leave, but not entirely) – once addressed to any monk who had to go out on some mission in the wider world.

Parts of the Certosa complex are owned by the university of Pisa, who have installed their **natural history** collections here –"of great interest for the material on reptiles' respiratory apparatus", according to the official guide. To ascertain the truth of this, you'll have to make an appointment (☎050/937.092).

Over Monte Serra

If you're in a car, you could make a loop down to the Arno from the Certosa by following the scenic mountain pass over **Monte Serra** – where the *Rosa dei Venti* bar-restaurant provides an opportunity for a quick bite. Beyond the summit, the road meanders down to the village of **BUTI**, its Gothic-windowed castle looking down on the main square and over the Arno valley.

The descent has flattened out by the time you get to **VICOPISANO**, a couple of kilometres north of Cáscina (see below). Built on a plump little hummock of a hill, the core of the village retains four towers of its fortifications, one of which was built by Brunelleschi after the Florentines had conquered Pisa. In the lower part of the village there's a handsome Romanesque church, fronted by a green piazza and backed by hills that have been blackened by forest fires.

Along the Arno and over the Pisan hills

The Arno valley commences with a glum stretch of unrelievedly industrialised development. **CÁSCINA**, a town you wouldn't know you'd entered if there weren't the road signs to tell you so, might have been well known if Michelangelo's ill-fated fresco for Florence's Palazzo Vecchio had survived – this was the scene of the battle he depicted. As for its own monuments, a clutch of **churches** within the medieval walls might justify a car stop: the frescoed San Giovanni Evangelista, built by the Knights of Saint John, and the Romanesque San Casciano and San Benedetto a Settimo, the latter with a fourteenth-century alabaster altarpiece carved in Ireland. Otherwise the dominant sights are the workshops which turn out the low-grade furniture that's the town's economic mainstay.

Into the hills

From Cáscina or Pontedera, the road south goes through Ponsacco and then past the **Medici villa** at **CAMUGLIANO**. Built by Alessandro de' Medici and continued by his successor, Cosimo I, it's one of the less scintillating of the family homes and anyway closed to the public.

Over to the west, **CASCIANO TERMO** is a pleasant, workaday spa town, and the little town of Rivalto, 6km south, an attractively medieval settlement. The road southwest from Casciano, emerging on the N68 near Cécina, takes in the best of the Pisan hills, though with little to suggest any great rewards in more prolonged exploration.

To the east of the main N439 road to Volterra, there's a fine thirteenth-century church at **PALAIA**, though only devout admirers of the Romanesque will want to drive the 10km from Capánnoli to see it. Past Capánnoli you're into a rather more humdrum swathe of hills until Volterra and its eroded cliffs rear up ahead (see p.331).

West of Pisa: San Piero, San Rossore and the coast

Six kilometres west of Pisa, on the road to the coast, the monastic complex of **San Piero a Grado** was allegedly founded by Saint Peter himself, on his way to Rome and martyrdom. The site is now in ruins except for the glorious eleventh-century **basilica**, a double-apsed church built from lustrous local yellow sandstone. Saint Peter's story is detailed in a sequence of pale fourteenth-century frescoes inside the basilica (daily 9am–noon & 3–6pm), where the whiff of the sea conjures a uniquely evocative atmosphere. At one end of the basilica a section of a fourth-century oratory has been excavated, the most ancient Christian site in this part of Tuscany.

Marina di Pisa and Tirrenia

MARINA DI PISA is an unobjectionable little town cursed with water made grubby by industrial waste. The view out to sea is impaired by a long breakwater parallel to the shore, and is frequently worsened by passing tankers. These factors, combined with the usual private beach strips, don't exactly entice.

TIRRENIA, 5km south, is a better bet – with finer sand, separated from the road by pines and parkland. It has a good spread of hotels and a couple of campsites. **Buses**, taking thirty minutes, run from Pisa to both resorts every fifteen minutes in summer, every thirty minutes in winter; they are best avoided on a Sunday, when hundreds of locals nip down to the ocean.

Parco Naturale di San Rossore

The **Parco Naturale di San Rossore** spreads over much of the coastal hinterland between Lucca and Livorno. Its pine woods are among the densest in Tuscany, supporting populations of deer, goats and wild boar, and until World

War II were also home to a herd of dromedaries, descendants of the animals placed here by Grand Duke Ferdinando II in the 1620s, then bred for their load-carrying capacities. There are plans to grant the Rossore area national park status, but at the moment general access is restricted to national holidays only – though permission might be given to anyone with specialist interest (park information ☎050/539.111).

At the park's centre is the village of **GOMBO**, scene of the most celebrated cremation of the nineteenth century. In 1822 Percy Bysshe Shelley, drowned while sailing from Livorno, was here reduced to ashes in front of his friends Edward Trelawny and Lord Byron. Trelawny recorded the suitably extraordinary culmination – "the brains literally seethed, bubbled and boiled as in a cauldron . . . what surprised us all was that the heart remained entire. In snatching this relic from the fiery furnace, my hand was severely burnt; and had anyone seen me do the act I should have been put into quarantine."

Livorno and around

As Tuscany's second largest city – after Florence – and Italy's second biggest port – after Genoa – **LIVORNO** should really have more going for it than it does. Unfortunately Henry James's observation still holds true: "It has neither a church worth one's attention, nor a municipal palace, nor a museum, and it may claim the distinction, unique in Italy, of being the city of no pictures." Livorno's principal appeal – apart from its **ferry connections** – is the excellent seafood.

Livorno's poor showing has a lot to do with the last war, when its port facilities invited blanket bombing. In fact, its origins go back to Roman times, though the port was only developed under Cosimo I as an alternative to Pisa, whose harbour was silting up. Later Medici dukes declared it a **free port** and instituted a liberal constitution, an extraordinarily enlightened move which prompted an influx of Jews, Greeks, Spanish Muslims, English Catholics and a cosmopolitan throng of other refugees – making it the Tangier of its day. As one of few Italian harbours safe from the Spanish, it flourished on the back of trade with England and Holland, and attracted a community of British expatriates (such as Shelley), whose anglicisation of the city's name – **Leghorn** – is still used by the tourist brochures.

Greater freedom of European trade brought some decline, though the city retained a reputation for enterprise that was especially manifest after World War II, when it was amongst the first to realise the importance of container traffic – the basis of its current prosperity.

The City

The Livorno **train station** is 2km east of the centre; local bus services (#1, #2 or #8) run from here to **Piazza Grande**, the heart of what's left of the old town. Out of town buses, except those from Florence, terminate in Piazza Grande; *LAZZI* buses to and from Florence use Via Saffi on the Fosse Reale, off Piazza Cavour, a five-minute walk from the old town down Via Grande.

The **Porto Mediceo** is the town's most picturesque corner, still conforming to the pentagonal canal-enclosed plan devised for the Medici by Buontalenti in 1557. The **Duomo** in Piazza Grande – now a postwar reconstruction – is its focal point, of interest mainly for its doorway by Inigo Jones, whose subsequent plan for London's Covent Garden was a direct copy of the square. More absorbing is the bustle of the port itself, with fishing boats spilling back into the canals of the so-called "Little Venice", a liner often blocking the view out to sea, and Sangallo's **Fortezza Vecchia** flanking the harbour on the right.

Further down the quay, at the centre of Piazza Micheli, is Livorno's only artwork of note, the famous *Quattro Mori* (1623) by the Carraran sculptor Pietro Tacca. Though Ferdinando I is the centrepiece, the key figures are the four "Moors", alternatively considered to be slaves, or memorials to the success of Tuscan raids against North African shipping.

The bulky **Fortezza Nuova** (daily 10am–7pm; free), a moated, semi-derelict recreation area, is where Livorno's citizens turn out for their Sunday walk. Of more general interest on this northern side of the inner pentagon is the **Mercato Americano** (Tues–Sat 9am–7pm, Mon 2–7pm), across Piazza Repubblica in Piazza XX Settembre. So called because of the amount of GI surplus on sale here after the war, it still deals in military gear (there's a big US naval base in the city) and the usual flea-market paraphernalia. The streets around Piazza XX Settembre – **Via Oberdan** in particular – are good territory for cafés, pizzerias and trattorias.

MODIGLIANI

There's a nice irony to the fact that the most famous son of this sensible mercantile city was the archetypal bohemian – hard-drinking, womanising **Amedeo Modigliani**. By the time Modigliani reached his mid-twenties he was renowned as the most dissolute figure in Montparnasse, but his family background in Livorno could not have been more respectable. His mother, Eugenia Garsin, was from a prosperous and highly intellectual family, brought up speaking French, Italian, English and Hebrew. His father's ancestors, also Sephardic Jews, were equally grand – Amedeo's great-grandfather, for example, had been an adviser to Napoleon.

Amedeo was born in Via Roma in 1884, the year that his father's wood and coal company was declared bankrupt. The Modiglianis were obliged to move from their villa to a more humble property in Via delle Ville, and it was there that Amedeo was living when he began his studies at the Livorno art school. By 1900, aged 16, he had become bored with the academicism of his training, and he soon embarked on a travelling apprenticeship that was to take him to Naples, Florence and Venice. In 1906 he arrived in Paris, where he was to spend most of the rest of his life. He returned to Livorno briefly in 1909 for a vacation by the sea, and came back again four years later, antagonising most people he met with his arrogance and wild behaviour. A friend tried to persuade him to take a studio near the Carrara marble quarries, but he missed the big city too much, and was on his way after a few months. He lived for just one more decade. "I am going to drink myself dead", he declared, and in effect he did, dying of meningitis at the age of 35 – and leaving the latest of his innumerable mistresses nine months pregnant. She committed suicide on the afternoon of his death.

Before leaving Livorno for the last time, he had asked some students at his former art school if they knew of somewhere he could store a group of sculptures he had carved. "Throw them in the canal", they are alleged to have replied. In 1984 the city authorities decided to follow up the lead by dredging the canal round the old town, and duly discovered three stone heads. They turned out to be fakes – the three schoolboys responsible for the hoax appeared on TV to demonstrate how they used Black & Decker power tools to create the sculptures that nearly sold for millions.

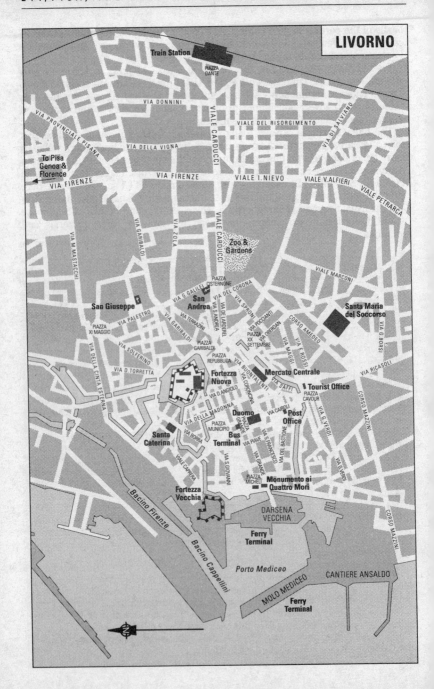

LIVORNO

Train Station

PIAZZA
DANTE

VIA DONNINI

VIALE DEL RISORGIMENTO

VIA DI SALVIANO

VIA PROVINCIALE PISANA

VIA DELLA VIGNA

VIALE CARDUCCI

To Pisa
Genoa &
Florence

VIA FIRENZE

VIA FIRENZE

VIALE I. NIEVO

VIALE V. ALFIERI

VIALE PETRARCA

VIA M MASTACCHI

VIA GARIBALDI

VIA ZOLA

VIALE CARDUCCI

Zoo &
Gardens

VIALE MARCONI

VIA B BORSI

PIAZZA
CISTERNONE

San Giuseppe

VIA G.GALILEI

San
Andrea

VIA DEL CORONA

VIA DEL SPRONI

VIA PUCCIANTI

Santa Maria
del Soccorso

VIA PALESTRO

VIA S.ANDREA

VIA S.SANDRIA

VIA DE'LARDEREL

CORSO AMEDEO

VIA ORERDAN

PIAZZA
XI MAGGIO

VIA TERRAZINI

VIA GARIBALDI

PIAZZA
XX
SETTEMBRE

VIA MAGGI

VIA E.ROSSI

VIA SOLFERINO

PIAZZA
GARIBALDI

VIA D TORRETTA

PIAZZA
REPUBBLICA

VIA BIGNAMI TALENTI

Mercato Centrale

VIA RICASOLI

VIA DELLA CINTA ESTERNA

Fortezza
Nuova

VIA S.FAFFI

VIA CORONINA

Tourist Office

PIAZZA
CAVOUR

CORSO MAZZINI

VIA D.ANGIOLO

Duomo

PIAZZA
GRANDE

VIA CARDU

Post
Office

VIA E.VEDI

VIA DELLA MADONNA

PIAZZA
MUNICIPIO

Bus
Terminal

VIA PIAVE

VIA DEL BASTIONE

VIA FRANCESCO

Santa
Caterina

VIA BORRA

VIA S.GIOVANNI

VIA GRANDE

VIA G.VEDI

VIALE CAPITRA

Fortezza
Vecchia

PIAZZA
MICHEL

Monumento ai
Quattro Mori

CORSO MAZZINI

Bacino Firenze

DARSENA
VECCHIA

Ferry
Terminal

Bacino Cappellini

Porto Mediceo

CANTIERE ANSALDO

MOLO MEDICEO

Ferry
Terminal

N

Around Livorno

For good views over Livorno and the hillside villas which were home to expatriates like Byron, Shelley and Napoleon III, you could take a bus out to hilltop
MONTENERO, 5km to the southeast – or take the bus to the outskirts then hop
onto the funicular. The sanctuary here has been a place of pilgrimage since an
apparition of the Virgin in the fourteenth century; the present church is less interesting than the panorama.

If all you want is a quick dip before leaving town, **ARDENZA** is Livorno's nearest beach, a one-time village but now a suburb, just ten minutes on bus #1 from
Piazza della Repubblica. It's all very urban and tacky, with crowded swimming off
a paved promenade, or – for a small fee – from a couple of concrete *bagni*. A
better alternative is to head north to **Tirrenia** (25min by bus from Piazza Grande;
see p.241).

Practicalities

Livorno's **tourist office** is on the second floor at Piazza Cavour 6 (Mon, Wed, Fri
& Sat 8.30am–1.30pm, Tues & Thurs 8.30am–1.30pm & 3.30–6.30pm); in summer
there's a small booth on the Mole Mediceo, the dock for ferries. As a port, the city
has a rash of basic **hotels**, some of which – around the harbour and station – are
grim dives to be avoided by all but the desperate. It's best to head for the centre of
the old town, especially around Corso Mazzini or the Fortezza Nuova where you
should have no problems finding a reasonable room. Possibilities in this price
range include: the two-star *Corsica*, Corso Mazzini 148 (☎0586/882.103; ④); the
Cremona, Corso Mazzini 24 (☎0586/899.681; ③); the *Ariston*, Piazza della
Repubblica 11 (☎0586/880.149; ③); the *Europa*, Via dell'Angiolo 23 (☎0586/
888.581; ④); and the *Milano*, Via degli Asili 48 (☎0586/894.348; ③) which has a
garden.

In 1994 a new **youth hostel** will open at Monterotondo, about 7km away, east
of Ardenza – you can get details on the current situation from the tourist office.
The nearest **campsite** is *Camping Miramare* (☎0586/580.402), on the Via Aurelia

---

LIVORNO FERRIES

There are regular car and passenger ferry services from Livorno to Capraia,
Sardinia and Corsica, with less frequent departures for Sicily. Ferries to Capraia
leave from Porto Mediceo; ferries to Sardinia and Corsica leave from Calato
Carrara, near the Stazione Marittima. Boats are often fully booked – for cars at least
– through July and August.

Corsica Ferries, Stazione Marittima
(☎0586/881.380). To Corsica (Bastia).

NAV.AR.MA, c/o *Agenzia Marittima
Ghianda*, Via Veneto 24
(☎0586/893.327). To Sardinia (Olbia);
three times a week, daily in high
season.

Sardinia Ferries, Stazione Marittima
(☎0586/881.380). To Corsica (Bastia);
daily from the end of March to early
November.

TO.RE.MAR, Via Calafati 6 (☎0586/
896.372). To Capraia; one daily most of
the year, twice daily on Thurs & Sat
June–Sept.

Note: US citizens travelling to Corsica will need to obtain a **visa** from the French
consulate at Piazza Attius 37 (☎0586/899.295).

past Antignano, a short distance to the south; there's another, the *Collina 1*, Via di Quercianella 269 (☎0586/579.573) on the road to Castellaccio.

For **meals** the great temptation is the seafood. The local speciality is *cacciucco*, a spicy fish stew, traditionally made from scraps the boats couldn't sell. There are dozens of good **trattorias**, the more esteemed being the *Antico Moro* at Via di Franco 59, *Aragosta* at Piazza Arsenale 6, *Il Sottomarino* off Piazza Repubblica in Via dei Terrazini 22, and the big, busy *La Barcarola*, Viale Carducci 63. These are relatively upmarket at around L50–60,000 per person, but you'll have no problem digging out a regular neighbourhood choice such as *L'Attias* at Via Ricasoli 127 or *Trattoria Galileo* in Via delle Campare. For pizza, try *Pizzeria Umbra*, Via E. Mayer 1, or the *Rustic Inn*, Via Bosi 16.

The Etruscan Riviera

There's little to distinguish the resorts that cling to the road south from Livorno along the absurdly titled **Etruscan Riviera**. Most are remorselessly developed and edged with stony or scrubby beaches, and have an appeal only if you want to share the Italian cheek-by-jowl seaside experience. All points on the coast as far south as Follonica can be reached by **bus** or **train** from Livorno; the faster Rome–Pisa expresses often stop only at Cécina, which has inland connections for Volterra.

Quercianella to Vada

Thirteen kilometres south of Livorno, **QUERCIANELLA** is a relatively small resort which has clung onto a hinterland of scrub-covered hills and rocky headlands. The beach is pebbly, but nevertheless popular and well developed. If you want to **stay**, the one-star *Pensione Villa Verde*, Via G. Pascoli 32 (☎0586/491.027; ④), overlooking the sea, is a reasonable bet.

Next stop is **CASTIGLIONCELLO**, the biggest of the resorts, sprawled over several small bays, some with sand, most with pebbles, and all crammed with boats and beach huts. Probably the best beach is the fee-charging Quercetano; the bay at Caletta is one to avoid, as is Rosignano (1km south), graced as it is with a vast chemical works with outlets into the sea. Castiglioncello has a summer **tourist office** at Via Aurelia 967; in addition to accommodation lists, they hand out details of a small July **dance festival** and September **literary festival**.

Smaller **VADA**, 5km south of Rosignano, has a featureless modern centre but is preferable to Castiglioncello, with a good beach and a long flat stretch of sand and pines to the south. These shade a couple of large **campsites**, the better being the *Tripesce*, Via Cavallaggeri 88 (April 1–Oct 20; ☎0586/789.159).

Cécina

The town of **CÉCINA**, 3km inland, marks the start of the Maremma's coastal plains. It has a small **museum**, in Via Guerrazzi (Tues–Sat 4.30–7.30pm, Sun 9.30am–1.30pm; L3000), with a few Etruscan and Roman remains, and a **tourist office** at Largo Cairoli 17, in Marina di Cécina, a source of information on the town's back-to-back **festivals** – antiques in July, arts and music in September and a miscellaneous "October Fair". Essentially, though, it is a place to pick up **bus** and **train** connections for Saline di Volterra (see p.333). If these leave you stranded in town, there are cheap **rooms** at the one-star *Iolanda*, Piazza Gramsci 12 (☎0586/680.724; ③), opposite the station.

At **MARINA DI CÉCINA**, a quite pleasant coastal strip, there are fair sections of beach, most freely accessible save for a patch cordoned off by the local military academy. A range of **hotels** are to be found on Viale della Vittoria, among them the two-star *Miramare* (☎0586/620.295; ④) and *Azzurra* (☎0586/620.595; ④). To the north there's also a huge conglomeration of **campsites**. For cheapish food, there's *La Triglia*, a good *rosticceria* in Viale Galliano 5 (May–Sept).

The Bólgheri reserve and Bibbona

South of Cécina the main road pulls back from the coast, leaving a few tracts relatively unspoilt. If you take any of the minor turnings to the sea you'll find pine forest and beaches only slightly touched by development, but the best stretch is the exquisite **Rifugio Faunistico di Bólgheri** (Oct 15–April 15 Fri & first and third Sat of the month 9am–noon & 2–4.30pm; L3000), a nature reserve run by the Worldwide Fund for Nature. The entrance is off the main SS1, just south of the glorious avenue of trees that runs to Bólgheri village; take the lane that runs over the railway towards the sea.

Founded in 1962, this was the first private nature reserve in Italy, and is now recognised as a wildlife centre of international importance. The reserve is a microcosm of the various habitats associated with the ancient Maremma: seashore, dunes (full of rare plants), marsh and lakeland, pine groves, tracts of juniper and mixed scrub forest, *macchia*, grassland and some of the most ancient stands of cypress in Italy. Such is the tranquillity of the area that even in daylight you can expect to see **boar**, **roe-buck**, **martens**, black and white **porcupines**, even **otters** – an extremely rare species in Italy. Thousands of **birds** also settle here: it's the southern limit of the lapwing and a spot for rarities like blue throats, Blyth reed warblers (their first sighting in Italy), grey herons, cranes, black storks and hunters like the osprey and lesser-spotted eagle.

The nearby resort of **MARINA DI BIBBONA** has an immensely broad stretch of sand running for miles south from the village along a pinewood backdrop: all it takes for privacy is the patience to walk beyond the beach umbrellas. For a cheap **beach hotel**, bear left on the approach road to Forte di Bibbona and try the two-star *Hotel Nina*, Via del Forte 5 (☎0565/600.039; ④) or the next door *Paradiso Verde* (☎0565/600.022; ④) with a garden.

SAN VINCENZO is the fast-growing resort of the moment, though again there's a good beach with plenty of quieter spots out on the fringes. Summer **accommodation**, however, is at a premium, and if you arrive on a whim and want to stay, you'll probably have to camp at the only **campsite**, the *Park Albatross*. Otherwise try the **tourist office** at Via B. Alliata.

Inland – Castagneto Carducci to Campiglia

If you're driving along the sluggish Via Aurelia from Pisa, you could take time out from the plain-induced monotony by turning off at Donaratico – 8km before San Vincenzo – for a 35-kilometre loop into the hills and a handful of scarcely visited **medieval villages**.

CASTAGNETO CARDUCCI, 6km on from Donaratico, is renowned for two things: it was the birthplace of the poet Carducci, winner of the Nobel Prize in 1906; and it produces what is widely believed to be the best **olive oil** in all Italy.

The village is riddled with little alleyways and has a parish church filled with faded frescoes and painted terracotta saints.

Beyond, the road is a rollercoaster of sea views and woods, with a single **hotel**, the two-star *La Selva*, Via delle Fornaci 32 (☎0565/794.239; ④), just before the road touches the little village of **SASSETTA**, a car-free maze of minute streets. During the October *festa* (last three Sundays of the month), the alleys are laid with tables for the traditional meal of thrushes and chestnuts. The road then twists down to **SUVERETO**, whose thin shield of modern outskirts hides another old centre, with its thirteenth-century **Palazzo Comunale** and the church of **San Giusto**, built in Pisan Romanesque mode. The village's December festival addresses itself to the local wild boar.

A slight detour on the return to the coast takes in **CAMPIGLIA MARÍTTIMA**, another little gem, partly spoilt by new houses and holiday homes, but with a perfect central piazza, composed of civic palazzi and a fine Romanesque church. For something to **eat**, the trattoria opposite the train station is very popular, with good local food at L10–12,000; there's also a reasonable two-star hotel, *Il Piave*, Piazza Nicciolini 18 (☎0565/33.050; ④), near the Campiglia station.

Populonia and the Golfo di Baratti

Perched on a high rocky headland 5km off the main coast road, **POPULONIA** was once a centre of Etruscan and Roman iron production, using ore from Elba. Now it's a tiny place looking down on the broad, half-moon bay of the **Golfo di Baratti**, with some of the nicest beaches for miles around. There's an impressive-looking fortress at the edge of the village, disappointing inside except for the fine views across the hills of southern Tuscany and as far as Livorno on a clear day. The enterprising inhabitants in Via S. Giovanni di Sotto (off the main street) have opened a small private **museum** of Etruscan odds and sods (daily 9am–9pm; if closed ask for owner in nearby bar; L2500). The same street has a **restaurant**, the *Populonia*, with very good meals but expect to pay about L40,000.

On the bay below, once Populonia's port, there's a cluster of houses glorified with the name of **BARATTI**, a colourful base for fishing boats. Behind the church of San Cerbone a dead-end lane leads to an **Etruscan necropolis** (9am–sunset; free) – several official wardens are on hand to take you round the site; if you need an English-speaking guide contact the tourist office in Piombino (see below). There's scope for some freelance **camping** locally or try the campsite *Sant'Albinia*, Via della Principessa (☎0565/29.389; open May to mid-Sept); if you want a **hotel** try the seafront *Alba* (☎0565/29.591; ④) with a garden.

Piombino

PIOMBINO, the nearest port to Elba, is not a place to linger, being dominated by a massive steelworks to the south that was rebuilt after wartime bombing and is likely soon to be closed. The only point in passing through is to take the **ferry to Elba**. If you come down the coast by train, get out at Campiglia Maríttima, from where there's a connecting train to Piombino port (don't get out at Piombino town).

In the event that you have to spend a night here, try the two-star *Roma* in Via San Francesco 43 (☎0565/220.165; ⑤), a relatively peaceful side street, or the hotel in Campiglia (see above). There are also three vast **campsites** on the road to Follónica; for emergencies only. The **tourist office** is at Via B. Callini 102 (☎0565/49.121).

Elba

Nearly thirty kilometres long and twenty across, **ELBA** is the third largest Italian island after Sicily and Sardinia, yet until about twenty years ago it was known only for its mineral resources and as Napoleon's place of exile. Now, however, it's suffering the fate of many a Mediterranean idyll, devoured by tourism in the summer and all but deserted in the long closed season. If you come here in August, when an estimated one million visitors flood onto Elba, you'll have trouble finding a room or even campsite space. To get the most out of the island, visit in spring or late summer.

Elba's enduring appeal comes from its exceptionally clear water, fine white beaches and a mountainous interior ideally suited to easy summer strolls. Development is spread over a series of fairly restrained resorts and the towns and villages retain their distinct characters. **Portoferraio** is very much the capital, and centre of the road and transport network that makes the island an easy place to explore; **Marina di Campo**, over on the south coast, has the best beach. The least-visited and loveliest part of the island centres on **Monte Capanne** (1018m) and the western coast from **Marciana** to **Fetovaia**. The flatter **southern coast** from Marina di Campo to Capoliveri has the island's main concentration of **campsites**, though there are sites in or near most centres. **Poggio** and the central **interior villages** are sheltered by lush woods and give access to hikes in the hills. In the island's eastern segment – the old mining district – **Porto Azzurro**, and the more pleasant **Capoliveri**, give access to a string of smaller but much visited villages.

The island has been inhabited since about 3000 BC thanks to its **mineral** wealth. The Greeks named it Aethalia (Sparks) after its many forges, and it was Elban iron in the Roman swords that conquered an empire. The last iron ore mine closed as recently as 1984, but it's still a geologist's dream, with an estimated thousand different minerals running the A to Z from andalusite to zircon.

Getting around the island

Buses run to just about everywhere on the island, whether or not they're main tourist centres. The key services **from Portoferraio**, the main terminal, are to **Procchio** (14 daily), **Marina di Campo** (10 daily) and **Porto Azzurro** (12 daily), all less frequent in low season; other services are more sporadic, and there are none going anywhere after 8pm. For general information on Elba buses

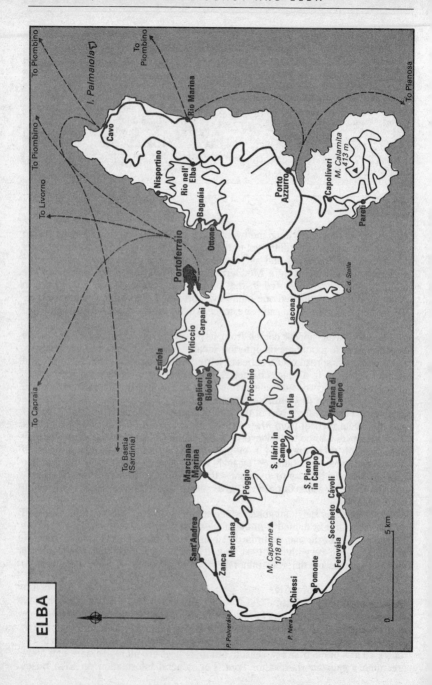

ELBA

To Piombino
I. Palmaiola
To Piombino
To Piombino
To Livorno
To Capraia
To Bastia (Sardinia)
To Pianosa

Cavo
Rio Marina
Nisportino
Rio nell' Elba
Bagnáia
Ottone
Porto Azzurro
Capoliveri
M. Calamita 413 m
Parete
C. d. Stella
Portoferráio
Viticcio
Carpani
Lacona
Enfola
Scagliéri
Biódola
Prócchio
La Pila
Marina di Campo
S. Ilário in Campo
Marciana Marina
Póggio
S. Piero in Campo
Seccheto
Cávoli
Sant'Andrea
Marciana
Zanca
M. Capanne 1018 m
Fetovaia
Pomonte
Chiessi
P. Polveráio
P. Nera

0   5 km

services, contact *ATL* at Viale Elba 20, Portoferraio (☎0565/914.392); they also do an eight-hour tour of the island in July and August. **Boats** are much used to reach out-of-the-way beaches, and they're well advertised at all the ports.

Bike or **moped rental** is a good way of exploring the island. Both are available from *Rent Ghiaie*, Via Cairoli 26 or at the bus station (☎0565/914.666); mopeds cost around L35–60,000 per 24 hours, bikes L20,000.

There are also several **car hire** agencies in Portoferraio: in the port area try *Maggiore*, Calata Italia (☎0565/930.222), or *Segnini*, in the same street (☎0565/916.374); in town, try *Arrighi*, Via Mercato Vecchio (☎0565/914.062), or *Mario Ridi*, Via del Carmine 40 (☎0565/914.731). Reckon on at least L80,000 a day – although some places offer small cars for L60,000 – and be ready for considerable summer congestion, especially anywhere near a decent beach.

Portoferraio and around

PORTOFERRAIO is most people's first port of call, and unless you're interested solely in beachlife it's a place you'll come back to: it's probably the island's liveliest town – closely followed now by Capoliveri – and has the widest range of accommodation. Beyond the busy port area, it also retains an **old town** which might be low on sights but has more than a little charm, and a few kilometres inland there's one of the crucial sights on the Napoleonic trail, the villa at **San Martino**.

Information and accommodation

The bus terminal and **tourist office** (Mon–Sat summer 8am–8pm; winter 8am–2pm) are both at Viale Elba 20. The tourist office provides a map, bus timetable and a list of the island's hotels, apartments and campsites, and will often phone around to try and find space. So, too, will the **Associazione Albergatori** at Calata Italia 21 (summer daily 9am–12.30pm & 3.30–7pm).

If these fail to turn up something – as is all too likely in August – tour the bars and ask about **private rooms**; in season prices are on a par with hotels. If you can get a group together, an **apartment** may work out cheaper. Bookable through the tourist office, most have two double rooms with cooking facilities, and can be rented by the day, or for less by the week (week only in July and August).

Portoferraio's better **hotel** options are: the two-star *Nobel*, Via Manganaro 72 (☎0565/915.217; ④), which is probably the cheapest place to stay; the *Villa Ombrosa*, Via de Gasperi 3 (☎0565/914.363; ⑤), near the beach at Le Ghiaie; *L'Ape Elbana*, Salita Cosimo de' Medici 2 (☎0565/914.245; ⑤), just off Piazza della Repubblica in the oldest part of town; and *Il Touring*, Via Roma 13 (☎0565/915.851; ⑥). If you are really stuck for a bed, the *Massimo*, Calata Italia 23 (☎0565/92.766; ⑧), with 68 rooms, should have some chance of space. The plushest place is the *Crystal*, Via Cairoli (☎0565/917.971; ⑨), virtually on Le Ghiaie beach.

The nearest **campsites** are *La Sorgente* (☎0565/917.139), the nearby *Acquaviva* (☎0565/915.592) and *La Enfola* (☎0565/939.001); all between 5km and 6km along the road west to Viticcio and quite accessible by bus.

If you fail to find accommodation you can get by for a few days sleeping on beaches, though this is officially prohibited. Leave your bags at the **left luggage** at the tourist office (L1500 a day), rent a moped if you can afford it, and set out in search of a secluded spot.

The Town

Portoferraio consists of a modern sector – where the ferries arrive – and the old Medicean port with its fortifications and fishing harbour. To get to the latter, turn right off the ferry along Calata Italia, past all the car parks, to the harbourside Calata Mazzini, the town's *passeggiata* parade. Midway round Calata Mazzini is the entrance to the old town, the **Porta a Mare**, from where an ampitheatre of streets rises towards the walls on the high cliffs.

The town's most obvious features are the **fortifications**, built – like Livorno's – by the Medici; you can pass an hour or so wandering around them, even though many of the main bastions are now in private hands. Most visitors walk up Via Garibaldi and make straight for Napoleon's home in exile, the **Villa dei Mulini** (Tues–Sat 9am–1.30pm, Sun & hols 9am–1pm; L6000, including same-day entry to San Martino). Built specifically for the ex-Emperor on a site chosen for its fine views of the bay, the villa features a stunning Baroque bedroom, a library sent over from Fontainebleau, and various pieces of memorabilia – including the Napoleonic Elban flag (see box below).

A small, rock-enclosed **beach** called Le Viste is signposted from the Palazzina, but otherwise there's little else to see, unless you're determined to check out every Napoleon-related scrap. In that case you could drop into the small Napoleonic museum in Via Garibaldi's **Chiesa della Misericordia** and the similar place lower down in **Santissimo Sacramento** – both contain death masks of the emperor and not a lot more. There's a **Museo Archeologico** in the fort (July

---

NAPOLEON AND ELBA

Elba is indissolubly linked with Napoleon, even though he was exiled here for little more than nine months – from May 4, 1814 to February 26, 1815. According to island tradition, after renouncing the thrones of France and Italy by the Treaty of Fontainebleau, Napoleon chose Elba as his place of exile for the "gentleness of its climates and its inhabitants". In fact, he had no choice – the allies packed him off here, sweetening the pill by ordaining that Elba would be "a separate principality for his lifetime, held by him in complete sovereignty". The dethroned emperor spent the journey south doodling a new flag for his pocket-sized domain: a red diagonal on a white background – echoing the Medici banner – plus the bees of his own imperial emblem.

After a confusing episode in which his ship was shelled from Portoferraio, Napoleon came ashore to a rousing welcome, and soon set about reorganising the island's economy and infrastructure. Some of this work might have been motivated by altruism or an inability to forgo politics, but much of what he achieved was for his own ends. The iron ore mines were revamped to supplement his income, his promised salary from Louis XVII having never materialised; the public works were to occupy and pay for the 500-strong Napoleonic Guard that had stuck by him. Portoferraio was given drains because the stench offended the imperial nostrils.

Some of the longer-term planning, however, undoubtedly paid dividends to the islanders – education and the legal system were overhauled, roads were built, agriculture was modernised, land was cleared, defences were repaired. These multifarious schemes suggested that Napoleon had resigned himself to his life sentence, but intrigue, rumour and unrest in France persuaded him to have another go. The day after Sir Neil Campbell, his British keeper, left for Livorno, he returned to France and the "Hundred Days" that were to culminate in Waterloo.

& Aug Mon–Sat 9am–noon & 4–7pm; Sept–June same days 4–7pm; L4000) displaying mainly Roman remains found in the sea around Elba and pieces from pre-Romanic sites on the island.

San Martino

Napoleon's sister Elisa bought the **Villa Napoleonica di San Martino** (Tues–Sat 9am–1.30pm, Sun & hols 9am–1pm; L6000 including same-day entry to Villa dei Mulini) as a summer residence just before the emperor – who had built it as a summer retreat – left the island for good. It's located 6km from Portoferraio on the #1 bus route, which passes the **Museo delle Ceramiche**, where artist Italo Bolano has landscaped huge walls of ceramic tiles into the countryside.

Engulfed by a vast car park and trolleys flogging Napoleonic souvenirs, the villa is a rather chilly affair, but its drab Neoclassical facade is at least sprinkled with exuberant N motifs. The monograms were the idea of Prince Demidoff, husband of Napoleon's niece – and it was he who bought up the villa to create a Napoleonic museum. By all accounts, the great man himself hardly spent any time here, and the permanent exhibits are no great shakes, though special annual exhibitions are held on a Napoleonic theme. Highlight of the house is the **Sala Egizia**, with friezes outlining Napoleon's Egyptian campaign, one of his more successful. At the back of the palazzo is Napoleon's own modest summer retreat – in some respects he had simple tastes – with its famous graffito "Ubicunque felix Napoleon" (Napoleon is happy anywhere).

Food and other practicalities

Portoferraio's **restaurants** are expensive and few have food to merit the prices. The well-patronised *Pizzeria Il Castagnacciaio* in Via del Mercato Vecchio (parallel to Piazza della Repubblica) sells the cheapest – and smallest – pizzas; a better bet is the *Albatros*, Via Roma 10 (on the steps above Piazza della Repubblica). *L'Ape Elbana* hotel restaurant has a choice of six tourist menus from L15,000, and *Trattoria Granchio*, Via Dietro la Pieve 13, has reasonable prices and good food. Best-known of the more upmarket choices are *La Ferrigna*, Piazza della Repubblica (☎0565/914.129; closed Tues), and the *Trattoria La Barca* in Via Guerazzi (closed Wed except in summer), both at around L60,000 per head. Another reliable spot, close to the port, is *Zi'Rosa*, on Piazza del Popolo.

For **bars**, pick from any of the places around Piazza della Repubblica in the heart of the old town, or Piazza Cavour, particularly *Bar Roma* which is the most popular bar with locals, with music in the summer and upmarket prices; or for a bit more elbow room, try the *Enoteca Torchio*, close to the square in Via dell'Amore.

PORTOFERRAIO FERRIES

If you're coming to Elba in the summer, it's worth booking your ticket back to the mainland well in advance, especially if you're taking a car. The offices below are for advance reservations; if you're buying a ticket on the day you leave, go to the kiosks on the quay.

TO.RE.MAR, Calata Italia 22 (☎0565/ 918.080).

NAV.AR.MA, Viale Elba 4 (☎0565/ 914.133).

The town **post office** is in Piazza Hutre, off Piazza della Repubblica. If you plan on **hiking**, the *Comunità Montana*, Viale Carducci 152, should provide a contour map of the Monte Capanne area, and helpful advice.

Eastern Elba

Eastern Elba is a distinct geographical area, basically comprising two tongues of land, each dominated by mountain ridges. Away from the main seaside centres of **Rio Marina** and **Porto Azzurro** the beaches are comparatively quiet, but much of the southern isthmus – **Monte Calamita** – was the heart of the mining industry, and is still owned by the quarrying companies. Close by, on the southern coast, **Lacona** boasts one of the island's main concentrations of **campsites**; **Barbarossa** is another popular camping spot, with some particularly fine beaches.

Portoferraio to Rio nell'Elba

South of Portoferraio the main road divides, one spur heading west, the other east towards Porto Azzurro. Following the latter, the first stop is the spa of **SAN GIOVANNI**, where Germans and Italians pay through the nose for the privilege of wallowing in its sulphurous marine mud. A few kilometres on at **LE GROTTE** are the ruins of a **Roman villa**, little more than a few stones and mosaic fragments among the gorse, but worth a stop for a great view over the sea, into which most of the building has tumbled.

Soon after comes a left turn for Rio nell'Elba and **MAGGAZZINI**, a little place with a sand and shingle beach and a couple of hotels: the three-star *Mare* (☎0565/933.069; ⑤) and two-star *Tirrenia* (☎0565/933.002; ⑤). Moving on to **OTTONE**, there's the one-star *Villa Gaia* (☎0565/933.160; ④), and the *Rosselba le Palme* **campsite** (May–Sept; ☎0565/933.101), rated by many the island's best.

West-facing **BAGNAIA**, just beyond Ottone (off the direct road to Rio nell'Elba), is famous for its sunsets. There are two **hotels** here, the *Punta Pina* (☎0565/961.077; ⑥) and *La Feluca* (☎0565/961.084; ⑥), and a bar, the *Villino Marte*. If you have the patience to drive the twisting road beyond, the twin tiny hamlets of Nisporto and Nisportino mark the beginning of the most unspoilt beaches and coastline on Elba's north shore. You can walk into the hills behind, or take boats out to the beaches beyond the end of the road. The only **accommodation** in the immediate vicinity is the *Camping-Villagio Sole e Mare* at Nisporto (all year; ☎0565/934.907) or the neighbouring campsite *Ut Cala di Nisportino* (mid-June to mid-Sept; ☎0565/934.908). There's a **hotel** 2km from the sea at La Ginestra – the three-star *La Ginestra* (☎0564/943.181; ⑥).

A narrow, scenic road climbs from Nisportino to Rio nell'Elba through La Ginestra; if you've taken the more direct route from Maggazzino you'll pass the old castle at **VOLTERRAIO**, once the strongest in Elba and now a silent and evocative ruin, with a great view over its desolate surroundings. It's a stiff climb from the road.

RIO NELL'ELBA itself is a graceless place, though old enough in parts and almost unique in appearing to have resisted Elba's tourist boom. From its high vantage it surveys a wild countryside devastated by repeated forest fires. There's nowhere to stay, and just one place to **eat**, *Da Cipolla* in the main square (closed Tues, except in summer).

Cavo and Rio Marina

CAVO, on the northern extremity of Elba, is a shabby, isolated and polluted place, its beach a very un-Elban grey; car ferries from Piombino to Portoferraio stop off here, but there's little to invite a stay.

The main town on Elba's east coast is **RIO MARINA**, a ferry terminal for connections to Piombino, Portoferraio and Porto Azzurro. Tourism and a busy harbour have replaced iron ore as the source of revenue, but this again isn't one of the better Elban towns. Its only sight is the **Museo dei Minerali Elbani** next to the Palazzo Comunale, a display of some two hundred Elban minerals (Tues–Sat 9am–noon & 3–6pm, Sun 9am–noon; L2000). There's just one **hotel**, the *Rio* at Via Palestro 31 (☎0565/962.722), next to the scrubby public gardens overlooking the port. Close by is one of the island's best **restaurants**, *La Canocchia* (closed Mon in winter), where a fine meal comes to around L70,000. Cheaper eating options abound in the lower port, where there's also a very good fish restaurant, the *Osteria della Strega*, in Piazza V. Emanuele.

For a **beach**, head south to the hamlet of **ORTANO**, dominated by a big tourist complex, but with public sand too; there's an on-beach **campsite**, the *Canapai* (☎0564/939.165) and a **hotel**, *Easytime*, Via Pan Porticciolo (☎0564/962.531; ⑥). You get to it by a turning 1500 metres back along the road to Rio nell'Elba.

Porto Azzurro

The resort of **PORTO AZZURRO** was heavily fortified by Philip III of Spain in 1603 as protection against continual raids by the French and the Austrians. Today his fortress is the island's prison; a walk round the outer ramparts brings you to a shop selling pottery and other prison crafts. The town's small old quarter, closed to cars, centres on **Via d'Alarcon**, a bustle of bars, shops and restaurants, with traditional open-front shops and balconied houses in the cobbled area near Piazza Matteotti. The best place to swim is from the rocks east of the harbour.

Porto Azzurro's **accommodation** is limited and lacklustre: best bets are the *Belmare*, Banchina IV Novembre 25 (☎0564/95.012; ⑥), the *Arrighi*, Via V. Veneto 18 (☎0565/95.315; ④), and the *Villa Italia*, Viale Italia (☎0564/951.119; ④). The best of the **campsites** are at the small nearby resort of Barbarossa – the *Da Mario* (☎0565/958.032) and *Arrighi* (☎0565/95.568) sites both give straight onto the beach; there's a one-star hotel here too, the *Barbarossa* (☎0565/95.087; ④).

For **food** there are plenty of identikit joints, the best-known being the *Delfino Verde* in Lungomare Vitaliani (☎0565/95.197); *Da Paride*, the third restaurant along the beach, is good for fish. Of the town centre **bars**, try *Il Sottoscala* at Via Ricosoli 11. Other local nightspots are the two discos – *Aris*, on Via Kennedy, and *Ovè*, on Via Romita – and the *Rock Bar*, a restaurant which fails to live up to its name, usually playing waltzes.

Out of town, **boat trips** run along the coast to the south twice daily in summer, costing L30,000 for a stretch of coast, or L60,000 to go around the island; contact the harbourside *Agenzia Pianotta* for details and tickets.

Off the Rio Marina road to the north, at **TERRANERE**, there's a bizarre sulphurous pond, its half-stagnant waters a violent yellow contrast to the sea; the beach here is scattered with mine debris. Nearby, up an unsignposted left turn off the same road, is the **Santuario della Madonna di Monserrato**, about one kilometre beyond the so-called Piccolo Miniera, a tourist-trap mine reconstruction. The short walk at the end of the road brings you to the church whose chief claim to fame is its replica of the Black Madonna of Montserrat; chapel and Madonna were both commissioned in 1606 by the island's Spanish governor, who was reminded by this site of the holy mountain outside his native Barcelona.

Naregno

East of the road between Porto Azzuro and Capoliveri, **NAREGNO** is a small resort with a good beach, though not as good as the less accessible sand to the south at Côte Piane, Liscolino and Buzzancone. None can match the village's **accommodation** possibilities, however, which include the seafront *Villa Rodriguez* (☎0565/968.423; ⑤), *Frank's Hotel* (☎0565/968.144; ⑥), and *La Voce del Mare* (☎0565/968.455; ⑤).

Capoliveri

CAPOLIVERI, 3.5km south of Porto Azzurro, is the best of the towns on Elba's eastern fringe, a prosperous centre whose close-knit streets have made few concessions to tourism. Occupying a naturally fortified spot, it's amongst the oldest settlements on the island – in Roman times it was known as Caput Liberi and was a place of sanctuary for anyone who could escape to it. Its hinterland remains undeveloped, as the mining companies have not sold their disused plots to the hoteliers – though much of the area is thus out of bounds.

There's nothing specific to see, but **old streets** such as Via Roma, Via Cavour and Vicolo Lungo are pleasant places to roam, and there are numerous half-hidden bars in the alleyways, as well as a sprawl of outside tables in the central piazza. The town is at its busiest on Thursdays, when locals and tourists flood in for the weekly **street market**; it is also very lively in the evenings, with a reputation for being the place to go for a night out.

Capoliveri makes an ideal base for visits to the fine **beaches** at Naregno, Morcone and Innamorata (see below). However, the town has become very upmarket and it is practically impossible to stay there cheaply: it only has **apartments**, rented out by numerous private agencies, which are all very expensive with few high-season vacancies; try the **information office**, Via Melina 9. Amongst the **restaurants**, *Il Chiasso*, Via Sauro (☎0565/968.709; closed Tues), is outstanding at around L70–80,000 a head. Its more reasonable rivals include *Summertime*, Via Roma 56, with friendly service and excellent food, and the rustic and informal *L'Arco Vecchio*, off the main piazza. To sample local **wines** make for the *Enoteca Elba* in Piazza Matteotti; for beer try *Le Piccole Ore*, Via P. Gori; and for delicious home-made ice cream drop in at *Patelli Gelateria* in Via Roma. As for **nightlife** Capoliveri brims with life well into the small hours: *Deco* disco, 2km away at La Trappola, is the chosen dancing spot, with *Sugareer*, a friendly late night jazz bar, just below it.

South of Capoliveri

The much-touted local church at **Madonna delle Grazie** – another place of pilgrimage – has a school-of-Raphael altarpiece but is otherwise more or less a waste of time, as is the overbuilt area around.

It's better to continue to the trio of resorts at **MORCONE**, **PARETI** and **INNAMORATA**. The last is the quietest and has a fine sand and shingle beach; the other hamlets have large beaches, the one at Morcone being more regimented than its neighbour. Parking is difficult, as is **accommodation**. Morcone has no hotels, though there are some **rooms** to rent and *Residency la Scogliera* will put people up on a nightly basis in mini-apartments (☎0565/935.205; ⑤). Pareti offers the *Pensione Villa Miramare* (☎0565/968.673; ⑤) and *Dino* (☎0565/939.103; ⑤). There's nowhere to stay in Innamorata except a tourist village, but it's worth visiting for the **restaurant** *I Gemini di Pietro*, with a friendly owner, well-cooked fish and a terrace overlooking the sea – perfect for sunsets.

Roads continue south into the hills of **Monte Calámita**, and to the stretch of unspoilt coast known as the **Costa dei Gabbiani**, both areas with mine-restricted access and with some of the beaches reserved for the newly emerging tourist villages. The area's name (Calamity) is a pun referring to the magnetic properties of the rocks, which allegedly draw boats towards the rocks – *calamita*, without the accent, means "magnet".

Lacona

LACONA, well round the coast to the west of Porto Azzurro, is one of the island's main camping centres, and its flat foreshore is crowded with **bars and discos** designed to cater to the beach crowd once the sun's gone down. The **campsites** to head for are *Il Lacona* (☎0565/964.161) or the nearby *Lacona Pineta* (☎0565/964.322), both set in the pine woods on the eastern arm of the Golfo di Lacona. *Stella Mare* (☎0565/964.007) is on the beach a bit further out along the headland, also amidst plenty of greenery. The best-value **hotel** is the *Pensione Giardino* (☎0565/964.059; ⑤).

Western Elba

Western Elba's road system allows for a circular tour of the area, but many people make immediately for specific targets – usually **Marina di Campo**, with its huge beach and the island's major concentration of hotels after Portoferraio. Upmarket alternatives are offered by the north-coast resorts of **Procchio** and **Marciana Marina**, while backpackers favour the relatively less commercialised **Énfola** area. Fewer visitors go inland to **Marciana**, one of Elba's nicest villages, or to the long sweep of the **western coast**, whose hamlets and beaches are amongst the island's most tranquil. Though the western zone tends to be rockier than the east, it's better for **walking**, the obvious highlights being **Monte Capanne** and its surrounding ridges.

Énfola

If you want a spread of beach and a choice of **campsites** near Portoferraio, follow the scenic road below Monte Poppe to the headland at **Capo d'Énfola**. You pass through the busy but pretty hamlets of Sorgente and Punta Acquaviva (both with a campsite), and a rare bargain for accommodation in Acquaviva, the one-star *Stella Del Mare* (☎0565/916.352; ③), before reaching **ÉNFOLA**, where the land narrows to a 75-metre-wide isthmus with beaches on both sides. The road ends at a small car park next to the *Bar Emanuel*, where you can get down to either strip of sand. Two hundred metres back from the bar, a road strikes off left to **VITICCIO**, another small spot with a dead-end road, parking area, and sand and shingle beach.

There are numerous **hotels** in the area, pick of the bunch being the three-star *Paradiso* at Viticcio (☎0565/939.034; ⑥) or two-star *Scoglio Bianco* (☎0565/939.036; ⑤). Énfola has a shady **campsite**, *Énfola Camping* (April to mid-Oct; ☎0565/915.390). On the bus route between Énfola and Viticcio is the recommended, but not yet too popular, Sanzone **beach**; ask the driver for the stop.

Biodola and Scaglieri

From Viticcio a footpath runs a couple of kilometres round the coast to Scaglieri and Biodola, otherwise reached by a side road from the main highway out of Portoferraio. **BIODOLA** consists simply of a road, two big hotels and a superb **beach**, which inevitably gets a summer blitz of visitors. Parking is difficult, but there are no buses. Biodola's two **hotels** are very expensive, though there's a cheaper and beautifully situated place two minutes from the beach, the *Casa Rosa* (☎0565/969.919; full pension ⑥).

SCAGLIERI is a similar sort of place but a touch livelier and more picturesque, fronted by a shop, two bars (the *Piccola Bar* rents bikes and mopeds) and a couple of places to **eat**: *I due Pini* is the better of the two pizzerias. You can **stay** at the *Albergo-Ristorante Danila* (☎0565/969.915; full pension ⑥) or there's a new **campsite**, the *Scaglieri* (☎0565/969.940), on the hillside.

Procchio

PROCCHIO suffers from being at the junction of main roads south and west, the greenery of its surroundings offset by an incessant stream of summer traffic. With its buzzing bars and shops it's not a place to get away from it all, but the sea is good and the white beach excellent – access to much of the sand is free and it's large enough not to seem overcrowded. However, this is a relatively expensive town. The cheaper **hotels** are the *Hotel di Procchio* (☎0565/907.477; ④); *Delfino* (☎0565/907.455; ④); *Da Renzo* (☎0565/907.505; ⑤); and *Fontalleccio* (☎0565/907.431; ⑤). More expensive, but not unreasonable, are the *Edera* (☎0565/907.525; ⑥) and *Monna Lisa* (☎0565/907.519; ⑥). Campsites don't exist. **Restaurants** along the roadside strip are much of a muchness; the *Orso Bianco* does good ice cream.

Marciana Marina and Poggio

Further round the north coast, **MARCIANA MARINA** has the minor distinction of being the smallest *comune* in Tuscany, a status it's proud of, allowing few hotels and aiming to preserve an air of residential order away from the seafront. The traffic-filled promenade of bars, restaurants and trinket shops does nothing to lure you into staying. Even the beach, overlooked by a Pisan watchtower, is shingly and forgettable. There are no campsites and accommodation is largely restricted to private houses and apartments.

Situated 5km inland from Marciana Marina, **POGGIO** is renowned for its **spring water**, from the *Fonte di Napoleone*. It also has a tight medieval centre whose decorated doorways and patchwork of cheerful gardens make this an attractive place to **stay**. Best overnight option is the *Albergo-Ristorante Monte Capanne*, Via Pini 1 (☎0565/99.083; ④), in a lovely, peaceful setting. **Food** here is good and the village claims one of the island's leading restaurants, the *Publius*, Via XX Settembre 13 (☎0565/99.208) – great views, classic Tuscan cooking and steep prices.

Poggio is a good base for a **walk** to the summit of **Monte Capanne** (1018m), Elba's highest point. Before setting off, pick up the local *Comunità Montana* **map** or a less detailed equivalent on sale in Poggio and Marciana. The marked trail (#2 on maps) climbs the spur to the south of the village, the quickest of the many paths that radiate from villages around the west coast. Allow about two hours at a leisurely pace, and be prepared for the bar and crowded terrace at the summit.

Marciana

The high and isolated village of **MARCIANA**, the oldest settlement on Elba, is perfectly placed between great beaches (Promonte and Sant'Andrea), mountainous interior (Monte Capanne), and a modern centre for supplies (Procchio). Its **old quarter** is a delight, too, its narrow alleys, arches, belvederes and stone stairs festooned with flowers and climbing plants. There's virtually no traffic or commercial development, and with the skeletal outline of its old fortifications it feels very distinct from the rest of the island's towns.

Marciana's history is encapsulated in the Roman and prehistoric remains in the small **Museo Archeologico** in Via del Pretorio (daily June–Sept 9am–noon & 4–7pm; early Oct & mid-April to June 9am–noon; L3000), in the **Fortezza Pisano** above the village (closed to the public), and in the palaces of the Appiani, Elba's leading fifteenth-century family, who made Marciana their home base.

Outside the village there's a trio of interesting **churches**, the oldest of which is the twelfth-century Pisan-influenced **San Lorenzo**; now largely in ruins, it's on a track off the road to Poggio. More intriguing is the **Santuario della Madonna del Monte**, about half an hour's walk along the road curving uphill west of the village. Though it dates from the eleventh century – and was probably a pagan temple well before that – its appearance is largely sixteenth-century, the Renaissance church serving to house a stone painted by a heavenly hand with the image of the Virgin. The island's most important shrine, it's also featured on the Napoleonic trail, as the ex-emperor came here to seek spiritual solace from the monks; by all accounts he received solace of a different kind when he was joined by his Polish mistress, Maria Walewska.

The third church, the **Santuario di San Cerbone**, is passed on the **walk** to Monte Capanne (trail #1; 3hr). The track starts from the southern tip of the village, the church appearing after an hour at the junction with trail #6. San Cerbone was buried here during a miraculous cloudburst that hid the ceremony from the Lombards who had the saint's valuable remains in their sights.

If you don't want to walk up Monte Capanne, there's a popular **cable car** to the top (daily 10am–12.15pm & 2.45–6pm; L14,000 return, L9000 single); most people choose to walk down either to Marciana or Poggio, though if you're trekking with your gear you could drop down to the south coast: Pomonte is on trail #5/30, Fetovaia on #5/31/35, and San Piero on #7/5.

Marciana's only drawback is its shortage of **accommodation**, restricted to rented rooms and apartments available through the *Birreria La Porta*, Piazza Umberto I (☎0565/904.253) at the entrance to the village, which also serves good sandwiches and salads; the other decent place to eat is the reasonably priced *Ristorante Bellavista* which is in the same piazza.

Sant'Andrea and around

The dispersed village of **SANT'ANDREA**, 6km west of Marciana, just off the coast road, is currently one of Elba's trendiest retreats, with villas and hotels creeping further into the wooded hinterland each year. It's popular with divers, drawn here by what is reputedly some of the clearest sea water around Elba. **Accommodation** is at a premium, but it's not necessarily expensive, and most is discreetly set amid almost tropical vegetation. On the beach itself there's the small *Bambu* (☎0565/908.012; [5]); top hotel of the moment is *La Cernia* (☎0565/908.194; [6]), midway between the coast and the main road. Or try *L'Oleandro*

(☎0565/908.088; [4]); *Piccola Pineta* (☎0565/908.022; [5]); or *Bella Vista* (☎0565/908.015; [5]).There are also plenty of apartments to rent.

Immediately south are the linked hamlets of **PATRESI**, **MORTAIO** and **LA GUARDIA**, rated as having the island's finest seas and still fairly unspoilt into the bargain. Cliffs drop to the sea, as they do all round this section of coast, with plenty of rock pillars and stacks for underwater enthusiasts. Most local **accommodation** is in apartments, though there are two **hotels**, the eleven-room *Villa Rita* (☎0565/908.095; [5]) and the two-star *Belmare* (☎0565/908.067; [5]), at Patresi. For pizza and full **meals**, eat at *Il Faro*, on the road near Patresi, with a veranda and sea view.

Chiessi to Cavoli

CHIESSI and **POMONTE**, further round the coast road, each has a small stony beach, beautifully clear water, a rocky hinterland and little commercialism. By **FETOVAIA** you're back to beach development, but the sand is superb – and a big car park prevents some of the chaos of other Elban resorts. There's lots of apartment accommodation and several top-whack hotels. Try the central *Lo Scirocco* (☎0565/988.030; [6]); the *Pensione Montemerlo* (☎0565/988.051; [6]), out of town on the hill; *Anna* (☎0565/988.032; [5]); or *Da Alma* (☎0565/988.040; [5]).

Further on, **SECCHETO** is good for a swim from the rocks at the western end of town, or for tanning on the largely nudist stretch beyond – *le piscine* – where the water forms deep pools in the hollows of a Roman granite mine. Two **hotels** with average-priced rooms are *La Stella* (☎0565/987.013; [6]), at the end of the road to the sea, and the nearby *Da Fine* (☎0565/987.017; [5]). Better than either, if you don't mind being away from the coast, is the *Locanda dell'Amicizia* (☎0565/987.051; [4]), set in a peaceful spot at **Vallebuia**, in the little valley north of Seccheto. The **bar** on the main road, which can sometimes direct you to available apartments, is popular, fairly cheap and does excellent pizzas. As on much of this section of coast there is no campsite, and no shelter if you want to pitch a tent on the quiet.

Nearby **CAVOLI** is more upmarket, though the beach is good if you don't mind the crowds. There are two similar beach-side *pensioni*, the *Lorenza* (☎0565/987.054; [5]) and the *Conchiglia* (☎0565/987.010; [5]).

Marina di Campo

Set in one of the island's few areas of plain, **MARINA DI CAMPO** was the first and is now the largest resort on Elba. The huge white **beach** is what makes the place popular: the water's clean, and there's space on land if you walk to the east end or out to the rockier west. There's also all the tourist frippery and **nightlife** you'd expect in any major seaside centre, with key discos and clubs changing by the month.

Pick of the numerous **hotels** are: *Lido*, Via Mascagni 29 (☎0565/976.040; [3]); *Pensione Elba*, Via Mascagni 43 (☎0565/967.224; [5], plus two- or four-bed apartments); *Santa Caterina*, Viale Elba (☎0565/967.452; [6]); *Barracuda*, Viale Elba (☎0565/976.893; [6]); and *Thomas*, Viale degli Etruschi 32 (☎0565/977.732; [6]). If you arrive early in the day you might find space at one of the four **campsites**. Best deals for a **meal** are *Rosticceria Mazzarri*, at Via Roma 19, *Il Golfo* situated at the eastern end of the beach, *Kontiki* in the port (for fish), and *La Triglia* at Via Roma 58, the town's best-known restaurant (L30–50,000 per person).

You can **hire bicycles** and **boats** from *Residency Montauti*, Via Pisa 3 (☎0565/ 976.194). For a break from the crowds you might take a bus trip out to two smaller **hill villages** close by: the very pretty Sant'Ilario in Campo and San Piero in Campo, whose parish church has a hotchpotch of frescoes.

Capraia

CAPRAIA, 30km northwest of Elba, is a Mediterranean island in the old sense: unspoilt, with just a couple of hotels and one road that links the small port to the old town on the hill. Its former use as a penal colony ensured that the terrain remained largely untouched, and now – despite considerable pressure from potential hoteliers – the local council have held back on commercial development, instead promoting the formation of a *Parco Naturale* to protect the island's natural heritage. This makes it difficult to visit, and the two hotels and single campsite come close to saturation point in summer; again, it's best to come slightly out of season.

Getting to Capraia is no problem, with a daily **ferry** from Livorno throughout the year – twice daily on Thursdays and Saturdays in summer.

Capraia Isola

From the tiny harbour to the town of **CAPRAIA ISOLA** – the only inhabited part of the island except the port – is a gentle walk of about a kilometre; there's a bus if you're feeling lazy. The island's long periods of desolation – mainly due to pirate raids – have done little for its monuments. Capraia Isola's Baroque church and convent of **Sant'Antonio** is largely ruined and the big castle, the privately owned **Fortezza di San Giorgio**, has seen considerably better days. Tourist sights, however, are not the reason for a visit to Capraia.

The **tourist office**, at Via Assunzione (☎0586/905.071), has a map of the island and a variety of information on wildlife, walking, accommodation and boat trips; this is also the office of the **park Cooperativa**, who will supply details of the courses and guided visits they run in spring and autumn.

The main **hotel**, the four-star *Il Saracino* (☎0586/905.018; ⑨), is in the upper part of town; prices are high, and you'll have to pay at least half-pension in peak periods. There are, however, numerous private **rooms** and **apartments** for rent; the tourist office will ring around for you, or you can just wander round town and look for the signs – virtually everyone can point towards a room.

There's a single **campsite**, *Le Sughere* (May 1–Sept 15; ☎0586/905.066), behind the town's small church of the Assumption. **Free camping** is feasible, but the terrain is rocky, and there's little cover or fresh water.

The best **restaurant** is *La Garitta*, up in the top of the town near the castle; run as a bar during the day, it's an informal place, dedicated to simple seafood. Still in the upper town, the *Cala Rossa* is a homely trattoria. There are a couple of other basic places down on the harbour: *Da Beppone*, Via Assunzione, is the best of these.

The interior and the beaches

From Capraia Isola you can easily strike off into the interior, which is dominated by a spine of steep hills, largely rocky and covered in scrub. Tracks crisscross the whole island, but there are four distinct and fairly obvious **walks**: to the **Torre**

dello Zenobito, a Genoese watchtower on the island's southernmost tip; to **Il Piano** and the Pisan church of **Santo Stefano**, using the rough road south of the town; to the lighthouse on the west coast, further down the same track; and to the **Laghetto**, a tiny lake in the hills and the focus of the *Parco Naturale*.

Isolation has favoured the development of various indigenous animal and vegetable species, several of them similar to species otherwise confined to Corsica and Sardinia. These include sub-species of buzzard, sparrow, large finch and La Marmora's warbler amongst the birds, and campion, toad flax and blue button amongst the plants. Birds are the main natural interest, with numerous itinerant visitors, and forty resident species including peregrines, shearwaters and up to a hundred pairs of the rare Corsican gull.

There is only one proper **beach**, at the **Cala della Mortola**, a bay a couple of kilometres north of the town. However, there are plenty of rocky coves and the water's clean and clear everywhere – even in the port area. It's easy to rent pedaloes, canoes and small launches, the motor boats costing from about L10,000 an hour to L70,000 for the day. Try the park *Cooperativa*, or the *House and Boat* agency in the port.

Both outfits also run a trip **round the entire island** (twice daily in season; about L15,000 per person for groups of 12 and up). *House and Boat* also operate the **taxi boat**, which will take you to the bay of your choice, and pick you up at a specified time (from about L10,000 per person). For **subaqua** enthusiasts there are a couple of clubs based in the port – contact the *Capraia Diving Club* on the harbour (☎0586/905.137) for help and equipment hire.

travel details

Trains

From Pisa to Florence (hourly; 1hr), via Empoli (35min; change for Volterra and Siena); Lucca (hourly; 30min); Viareggio (every 30min; 20min); Livorno (every 30min; 15min).

From Livorno to Rome (every 30min; 3–4hr); La Spezia (5 daily; 1hr 20min); Pisa (every 20min; 15–30min); Florence (12 daily; 1hr 30min).

Buses

From Pisa to Viareggio, Florence, Livorno and La Spezia.

From Livorno to Piombino and Pisa

Ferries

From Livorno to Capraia, Portoferraio (Elba), Bastia (Corsica) and Olbia (Sardinia).

From Piombino to Portoferraio (Elba).

CHAPTER FIVE

THE MAREMMA

The **Maremma** – the coastal plain that runs south from the Piombino headland – was the northern heartland of the **Etruscans**, whose drainage and irrigation canals turned it into an area of huge agricultural potential. Their good work, however, was largely lost under the Romans, who abandoned much of the land and left it to revert to marsh – a decline that continued through the Middle Ages, when war and further dereliction turned the region into an area of malarial swamp. For years, virtually the only inhabitants were migrant charcoal burners and shepherds – who in summer abandoned the infested lowlands for the hill villages of Amiata – and the famous *butteri*, the cowboys who tend the region's oxen and horses.

Modern attempts to revive the Maremma were started in 1828 by Grand Duke Leopoldo of Tuscany, who instigated new drainage schemes and introduced a crude health service, with free quinine for malaria sufferers. At the turn of this century, though, Grosseto's regional council still had to move its offices annually to the healthier surroundings of Scansano, and real progress was only made under Mussolini and after the last war. The malarial mosquito was definitively banished as recently as 1950, and something of the Maremma's grim reputation lives on in its common Italian nickname, *La Miseria*.

Drainage has returned a measure of prosperity to the Maremma, but at the cost of destroying its ancient landscapes and prompting the expansion of **Grosseto**, one of Tuscany's more miserable towns. A few efforts have been made to preserve the old world, mainly in the **Monti dell'Uccellina** but also in the **nature reserves** at **Burano** and **Orbetello**, two of the finest **birdwatching** spots in the country. You'll also stand a chance of seeing wild boar – a hoary-skinned sub-species (*Sus scropha Majori*) has developed in the isolation of its swamp-encircled habitats.

THE BUTTERI

The *butteri*, the Maremma's very own cowboys, have for centuries taken care of the region's half-feral horses and its celebrated white cattle, a special breed imported from Asia for their resilience to the rigours of the Maremman climate and terrain. For most of the year they ride with the herds on the Maremma's grasslands, the key event of the year being the so-called *merca* in April, when the one-year-old calves and foals are rounded up, counted and branded. You stand most chance of seeing them on the Ombrone estuary, particularly on the road to Marina di Alberese.

From time to time the *butteri* make an appearance in local festivals and special events. Such performances are nothing new: in 1911 Buffalo Bill brought a travelling troupe of cowboys to Rome, where they were trounced by the *butteri* in a series of rodeo events in the Piazza del Popolo. Today the best-known of their tourist shows is the August rodeo in Alberese, and they also prove their skills in perhaps the most demanding equestrian arena in the world – as the riders in the Siena Palio.

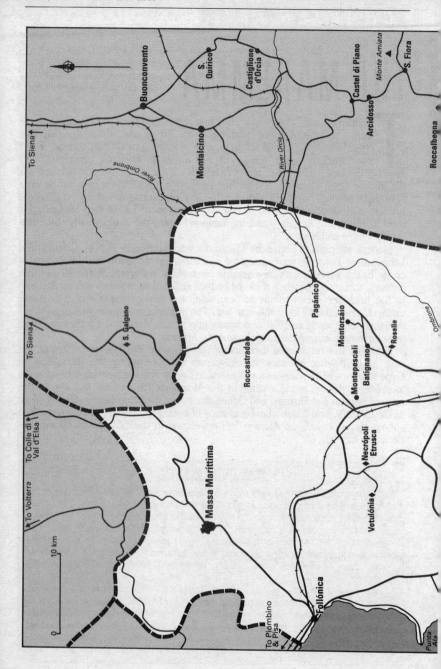

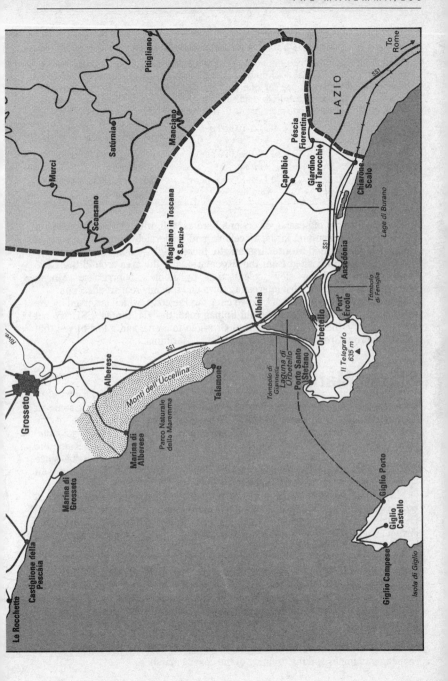

ACCOMMODATION PRICES

Throughout this guide, accommodation is graded on a scale from ① to ⑨. Grades ① and ② apply to **hostel** accommodation, and indicate the lowest price a **single person** could expect to pay for one night in that establishment in high season. Grades ③ to ⑨ apply to **hotels**, and indicate the cost of the **cheapest double room in high season**. The price bands to which these codes refer are as follows:

① under L20,000 per person	④ L50–70,000 per double	⑦ L120–150,000 per double
② over L20,000 per person	⑤ L70–90,000 per double	⑧ L150–200,000 per double
③ under L50,000 per double	⑥ L90–120,000 per double	⑨ over L200,000 per double

There are plenty of seaside diversions here as well, with glorious **beaches** at **Marina di Alberese** and in the Uccellina, and moderately upmarket resorts at **Punta Ala** and around **Monte Argentario**. Increasingly well-known are the idyllic island of **Giglio**, visited from the Argentario, and the area around the Lazio border, both suffering slow colonisation by Rome's bourgeoisie. **Massa Maríttima** is the area's most interesting town and the only real art attraction.

Almost everything you'll want to see clings to the coast, which is served by the main Rome–Pisa **railway** and the old Roman road, the Via Aurelia (SS1). To cut across country, there's a rail link from Grosseto to Siena, and a few **buses** that run inland from Grosseto, Orbetello and Massa Maríttima.

Massa Maríttima

Once the second city of the Sienese Republic and still graced with some of Siena's civic style, **MASSA MARÍTTIMA** is the finest historic town of the Maremma. Named simply "Massa" by the Romans – their word for a large country estate – it gained its maritime suffix in the Middle Ages, when it became the pre-eminent town of this coastal region. The sea has receded somewhat since that time, and is now twenty kilometres distant across a silt-filled plain, and scarcely visible from the town's hilltop.

Massa, like Volterra to the north, has long been a **mining** town, its silver, copper and other metal deposits accruing wealth from as early as Neolithic times. Designation as a bishopric in the ninth century – in place of declining Populonia – gave it an additional impetus, leading to the formation of an independent republic in 1225, the same year that it produced Europe's first charter for the protection of miners, the *Codice Mineraio*.

Sadly for Massa, its mineral riches attracted the rival attentions of Pisa and Siena, the latter finally absorbing the town in 1335. Its hundred years of glory, however, funded the building of its monuments – notably the exquisite duomo – and saw the doubling of the population, a trend reversed after absorption into the Grand Duchy of Tuscany in 1555. Subsequent plague, malaria and a downturn in mining had created a virtual ghost town by 1737, when Massa had just 537 inhabitants. Like other Maremma towns, its recovery only began in the 1830s with the reopening of mines and the draining of the coastal marshes.

The Town

A small industrial estate mars the approach to Massa and blocks of new buildings don't improve the prospect. However, all is soon overshadowed by the medieval splendours of Piazza Garibaldi in the lower, mainly Romanesque **Città Vecchia**. The upper town, **Città Nuova**, is more Gothic in appearance and was built largely as a residential centre. An immensely steep and picturesque lane, **Via Moncini**, connects the two. For most of the Middle Ages the lower town was inhabited by a Pisan clan, the Todini, the upper by their Sienese rivals, the Pannochieschi.

Most of the upper town's interest centres on **Piazza Garibaldi**, a small, eccentric and exquisite example of Tuscan town planning, whose medieval ensemble is climaxed by the thirteenth-century duomo, set on broad steps at a dramatically oblique angle to the square.

The Duomo

The **Duomo** is essentially Pisan Romanesque, with a few later additions blending harmoniously with the blind arches and tiny columns – most notably the extraordinary Gothic **campanile**, added in about 1400. The cathedral's dedication is to Saint Cerbone, the Bishop of Populonia in the sixth century. He's

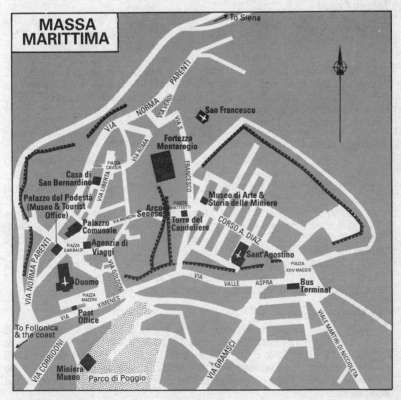

most famous for persuading a flock of geese to follow him when he was summoned to Rome on heresy charges, but is usually shown with a bear licking his feet – a reference to the beast he tamed when Totila the Hun threw him into a pit of wild animals. Bas-reliefs in the architrave of the main door show scenes from the saint's life.

Inside, the bare stone walls set off some superb carvings and works of arts. The most admired of the carvings are the thirteenth-century work by Giraldo da Como, on the huge **baptistery** and also the quadrangular **font**. Almost as arresting are the fifteenth-century tabernacle, under the marble canopy of the baptistery, and some eleventh-century Romanesque carvings close to the entrance – featuring powerful and primitive grinning faces that make a dramatic contrast with the severe, polished Roman sarcophagus to their right. Over the altar is a large Giovanni Pisano altarpiece, and behind it the *Arco di San Cerbone*, an arch of bas-reliefs on the life of the saint, carved by Gori di Gregorio in 1324. Take a look, too, at the *Madonna delle Grazie* at the end of the left transept, a damaged but gorgeous Sienese work attributed to Duccio or Simone Martini. Finally, the fine little crypt has a single fresco featuring both Cerbone and St Bernardino.

Museo Civico

The smaller of the two palaces on the piazza, the Palazzo del Podestà, contains the **Museo Civico** (Tues–Sun April–Oct 10am–12.30pm & 3.30–7pm; Nov–March 10am–12.30pm & 3–5pm; closed Mon except July & Aug; L4000), where the chief exhibit is one of the finest altarpieces in Tuscany, a *Maestà* painted in 1330 by **Ambrogio Lorenzetti**. Vivid pink, green and tangerine illuminate the figures of Faith, Hope and Charity below the Madonna, while Cerbone and his geese lurk in the right-hand corner. This apart, the museum comprises a handful of very minor paintings and a few archaeological finds; most of the best pieces have been removed to Florence.

Città Nuova

The town council has organised what it calls a "tourist itinerary", a signposted route that takes you to some very dull spots. The best thing to do is to wander up to the **Città Nuova** by Via Moncini, whose tributary alleyways reveal small gardens and good views.

At the end of the street is **Piazza Matteotti**, flanked by a segment of the town wall, a tower and an impressive but militarily useless arch, the **Arco dei Sienesi**. There's also a small park, ideal for a picnic or siesta. Across the piazza stands the **Museo di Arte e Storia delle Miniere**, which houses a puny collection of fossils and archive photographs of local history (Tues–Sun 10am–12.30pm & 3.30–6pm; L5000). Otherwise the only thing to see up here is the church of **Sant'Agostino**, graced with simple cloisters and little else.

The Mining Museum

Inevitably, given its mining heritage, Massa boasts a **Miniera Museo** (guided tours Tues–Sun April–Sept 10am–12.30pm & 3.30–7pm; Oct–March 11am–1pm & 4–5pm; L2000). It is situated five minutes from Piazza Garibaldi off Via Corridoni – suitably enough in an underground air-raid shelter. The mock-up mine has 700 metres of galleries, and a chronological display of the area's mining methods and equipment.

East of the town – Roccatederighi

Situated fifteen kilometres east of Massa, **ROCCATEDERIGHI** is difficult to fit into any logical itinerary, but with transport is well worth the twenty-minute diversion. Perched on a needle of rock, the village has been literally carved from stone, and offers one of the finest **views** of the Maremma. Gird yourself for the haul up one of the impossibly steep alleys to the rock pillars that command the area.

Practicalities

Most **buses** stop on Via Corridoni close to Piazza Garibaldi – get off when you see the campanile of the duomo. There are three or four services daily between Massa and Volterra (changing at Monterotondo) plus one to Grosseto and two to Florence and Siena. The nearest train **station** is Massa-Follónica, 19km away on the main Pisa–Rome rail line; a bus shuttle meets the incoming trains. The **tourist office** is close by the bus office in Piazza Garibaldi.

Despite Massa's popularity – especially with Germans – there are surprisingly few places to stay. A brand new **hotel**, the three-star *Il Sole*, is now open in Corso della Libertà 43 (☎0566/901.971; ⑤) and the only other central accommodation is the one-star *Cris*, Via degli Albizzeschi (☎0566/903.830; ③). If that's full, there are two modern hotels on the approaches to Massa: the two-star *Duca del Mare*, Via Dante Aligheri 1–2 (☎0566/902.284; ④), and the two-star *Girifalco*, Via Massetana Nord 25 (☎0566/902.177; ④). The nearest **campsites** are on the coast at Follónica (see below); there are plenty of wooded spots on the road north if you fancy pitching a tent on your own; however, be warned, unofficial campers are not welcomed and may be moved on.

Piazza Garibaldi has some pleasant **bars**, especially the one under the arches in the corner by Via Moncini, though its restaurants are geared straight to tourist trade. Better options include the **restaurant** at the *Hotel Cris*; the cheap and excellent value *Vecchio Borgo*, just behind Piazza Garibaldi at Via Parenti 12 (☎0566/903.950); or the nearby *Roma* at Via Parenti 19, something of a tourist trap but with good food and a strange local wine from Monte Regio. For **pizza**, served at outside tables, try the *Pizzeria La Torre*, Piazza Matteotti 5; or, for a snack, the no-nonsense *pizza alla taglia* at Via Moncini 44.

Follónica to Marina di Grosseto

The popular downmarket resort of **Follónica** marks something of a watershed on the Maremma coast. To the north the real flatlands drag up towards Cécina, but to the south lies a tract of relatively unspoilt hilly countryside, a landscape similar to that of the Tuscan heartland. Pick of the mixed bag of small resorts along this stretch is **Castiglione della Pescaia**, beyond which lies a magnificent swathe of classic Maremma pine forest.

Follónica and its gulf

FOLLÓNICA, rail access point for Massa Maríttima, is a large and scruffy town, its long untidy beach spoilt by high-rise buildings and, at the far southern end, by factory outlet pipes. It's very much a family resort – packed out in summer and with a big, colourful Friday **market**, the only real "sight".

The **train station** is at the top of Via Matteotti, which leads straight down to the sea. If you're passing through and want an hour's sun and sea, the best part of the **beach** lies along the stands of pines to the south, before the pipes: follow the main road for about a kilometre from the centre, then strike off through the trees at the garage on the left – there will be cars parked on the roadside.

The **tourist office** is one street back from the beach, a couple of hundred metres west of the central Piazza XXV Aprile, on the intersection of Viale Italia and Via Matteotti; they produce a detailed map, and offer plenty of help with accommodation.

Of the numerous **hotels**, most on or near the seafront, good choices are the two-star *Miramare*, Lungomare Italia 186 (☎0566/41.521; ④), and *Orchidea*, Viale Italia (☎0566/40.334; ④). There are also two **campsites** ranged along the seafront: *Campsite Thaiti*, Viale Italia 320, Pratoranieri (☎0566/60.255), is not as nicely situated as the *Pineta del Golfo*, at Via delle Collachie 2, Pineta di Levante (June–Sept; ☎0566/53.369), which is at the southern edge of town off the main SS322.

For **food** there are plenty of modest restaurants. If you want to splash out on the Follónica gastronomic exprience, try the *Leonardo Capelli*, Piazza XXV Aprile 33 (☎0566/44.637; closed Sun & Mon).

Scarlino and Tirli

Nine kilometres east of Follónica, **SCARLINO** is invitingly situated on a steep, wooded hillside – beyond a huge red-striped chimney that does its best to wreck the view. The village itself is medieval in an attractive if unexceptional sort of way, while the hills behind are dotted with fragments of castles and monasteries.

Further south, and accessible by minor roads through the hills, is **TIRLI**, where – as in other local villages – they venerate the hermit Saint Guglielmo. He is renowned for slaying a dragon, a "rib" of which is contained in the village church. There are walks into the woods behind the village, one to the ruins of **Malavalle monastery** – scene of the slaying – and to the miraculous **spring of Santa Anna**, a point of pilgrimage on July 24. Guglielmo's feast day is the first Sunday in May, an excuse for a *festa* which involves the saint's old drum and some so-called "miracle herbs".

Punta Ala and Le Rocchette

Unless you're feeling particularly flush, there's not a lot of point in making the detour to **PUNTA ALA**, a ritzy, purpose-built resort on the southern spur of the gulf of Follónica (buses from Follónica and Castiglione della Pescaia). Though beautifully situated below a castle-topped headland, Punta Ala is dominated by its millionaires' marina. All but a couple of the **hotels** are four-star jobs, as are the **campsites**, most of which are at Capo Civinini, north of the resort where the lane from the main road meets the coast. The cheapest place to stay in Punta Ala is the three-star *Punta Ala*, Via del Pozzino 5 (☎0564/922.636; ⑦): prices drop considerably out of season. The most acclaimed restaurant is at the very pricey *Hotel Gallia* (☎0564/922.022).

The minor road marked on the TCI road map between Punta Ala and **LE ROCCHETTE** to the south is little more than a footpath: car access is from the main SS322. There's a handful of bars close to a good beach, whose tiny approach lane is chaotic in high summer. With transport, it could be a convenient point to camp, though the **campsites** have little free space in August. Try the 150-pitch *Rocchette* (April–Oct; ☎0564/941.123), the similar-sized *Baia delle Rocchette* (April–Oct; ☎0564/941.092), or the 350-pitch *Santapomata* (March 15–Oct 15; ☎0564/941.037).

Castiglione della Pescaia

Set among low, wooded hills that are a welcome break from the plain around Grosseto, **CASTIGLIONE DELLA PESCAIA** still affects the air of a fishing village. It does admittedly have a marina and tourist centre, but it lacks Punta Ala's exclusivity, and of all the Maremma resorts, this is the one that's likeliest to give you a good time. The bars are enjoyable, the beach is okay, and there's a fair amount of action on a summer's evening. On top of this, the walled **old town** on the hill – believed to have been an Etruscan port – is a characterful spot to wander, with spectacular views from the castle, and is kept free of cars for the best part of the day.

The best-sited **hotels** are on the main road north, an area still blessed with stands of umbrella pines. The modern three-star *Miramare* overlooks the sea at Via Vittorio Veneto 27 (☎0564/933.524; [5]), while the two-star *Iris*, Via Movi 5 (☎0564/933.639; [4]), is near the water at the foot of the old town. In the old town itself, look up the two-star *Gli Archi*, Via della Libertà 28 (☎0564/933.083; [4]). The best of the seven local **campsites** are on the road towards Grosseto – the pick of them is the *Etruria* (April 15–Sept 30; ☎0564/933.483), about 1km south.

There are a lot of cheap **restaurants** and **pizzerias**, but for a splurge go to the *Miramare*, which is renowned for its innovative fish restaurant; expect to pay up to L75,000 a head with wine. Also excellent and pricey is *Il Corallo*, Via Nazario Sauro 1 (☎0564/933.668; closed Tues except in summer & Nov–Jan).

For general information, there is a **tourist office** at Piazza Garibaldi 78. The fish **market** at the harbour, in the morning and late afternoon, is worth checking out if you're self-catering.

South to Marina di Grosseto

The road south from Castiglione runs through a stunning woodland of **umbrella pines** (*pineta*), a small part of which is administered as a nature reserve by the World Wide Fund for Nature (entry is very limited; for details contact Giuseppe Anselmi, ☎0564/26.588). Most of the *pineta* – about twelve kilometres in extent – is accessible by foot, however, and the thing to do is to leave a car on the roadside and walk down to the sea on one of the many tracks through the trees. The beaches are superb and unspoilt. A **bus** service between Grosseto and Castiglione stops en route if you're without transport.

Marina di Grosseto

At first glance **MARINA DI GROSSETO** looks a dreadful place, with its gridiron streets and scattering of big, brand-new houses. As Maremma resorts go, however, it's surprisingly upbeat, and the clean and broad **beach** is backed by restrained bars and restaurants. Trees shade the open-plan residential district, giving a touch of style.

You could bus out here from Grosseto for the day, though with a car or bike you'd be better off on the superior beaches at Marina di Alberese (see p.275). There is at least no shortage of **accommodation** in Marina's purpose-built modern hotels, ranging from the *Tre Stelle*, Via dei Platani 15 (☎0564/34.538; ③), to the three-star *Lola Piccolo*, Via XXIV Maggio (☎0564/34.402; ⑥). For assistance in finding a room there's a small summer **tourist office** at Via Piave 10.

Campsites are plentiful in and around Marina, the more enticing strung out on the main road north through the *pineta*. Most convenient of these is the *Rosmarino* site in Via delle Colonie (April–Sept; ☎0564/36.319), 1km north; it also has hotel accommodation (⑥). A couple of kilometres south at Principina a Mare there's a huge campsite, the *Principina* (☎0564/35.421).

Grosseto

Travelling by train, the chances are that you'll pass the provincial capital, **GROSSETO**, with no more than a glance – by and large all it deserves – but by bus or car you'll be forced into the heart of its unappealing new centre. Ringed by a factory-pocked plain, and composed mainly of characterless condominiums, it's a commercial and administrative city, raised from the ruins of heavy bombing. Urban dreariness may explain its high incidence of drug addiction (apparently the highest in Italy) and maybe even its odd penchant for American football – there's a local team, the Grosseto 61'ers.

Most **trains** on the main Rome–Genoa line stop at Grosseto, where you can change for Siena, or for *locale* connections to Orbetello, Cécina (for Volterra) and Follónica (for Massa Maríttima). Timetabling often leaves about an hour or so between trains – which is about all you need for the **old centre**, contained within a largely intact hexagon of walls commissioned by Cosimo I after the Florentines finally wrested control of the city from the Sienese.

The Town

To reach the old centre, walk down Via Carducci from the station, a road interrupted by an over-the-top post office and bleak piazza, both monuments to fascist architectural endeavour. The best of what survives in Grosseto is on **Piazza Dante**, where a quirky statue shows Leopoldo II protecting Mother Maremma and crushing the serpent malaria under his foot. The **Duomo** was started in 1294 but virtually nothing is left to suggest antiquity: the white and pink marble facade is a product of the nineteenth century, while the interior has suffered repeated butchery. Above the sacristy, the **Museo Diocesano di Arte Sacra** (closed Tues) gathers together a few ecclesiastic bits.

The best pieces from the duomo have been transferred to the **Museo Archeologico** at nearby Via Mazzini 34 (9am–1pm & 4–7.30pm, Sun 9am–1pm; closed Wed; L3000), which, at the time of writing, is closed for restoration. The second-floor **Pinacoteca** has a handful of good Sienese paintings, notably Sassetta's *Madonna of the Cherries* and a *Madonna and Child* attributed to Simone Martini. Most of the archaeological finds are from the Etruscan settlements at Vetulonia and Roselle (see opposite), neatly arranged and well-labelled, but unlikely to set the pulse racing.

The town's only other significant work is an early *Crucifix* by Duccio in **San Francesco**, just north of the museum, also home to a few patches of fresco. Look out for the cloisters alongside the church, distinguished by a well known as the *Pozzo della Bufala* (Well of the Buffalo).

From San Francesco you can walk round the **walls**, a trip of about forty minutes, and one of the more rewarding things the place has to offer. Public gardens, some well kept, others virtual jungle, fill the spaces in the corner turrets – bar one, which retains some Florentine fortifications.

Practicalities

The city has two **tourist offices**: a provincial one at Via Monterosa 206 (Mon–Sat 8am–2pm) and a smaller town one through the gateway on the main Corso Carducci (June–Sept 9am–1pm & 4–8pm).

You'd have to be desperate to stay overnight, but in emergencies there are plenty of bottom-line **hotels**. Central options include the one-star *Appennino*, Viale Mameli 1 (☎0564/23.009; ③); the *Mulinacci*, Via Mazzini 78 (☎0564/28.419; ③); and the *Duomo*, Via D'Azeglio 3 (☎0564/29.093; ③). The nearest **campsites** are at Marina di Grosseto (bus from the station).

If you have money to burn, the town claims the Maremma's best **restaurant**, the *Enoteca Ombrone*, Viale Matteotti 69 (☎0564/22.585; closed Sun, Jan, and two weeks in July); prices start at L70,000 for local specialities. The *Buca di San Lorenzo*, Via Manetti 1, has an equally exalted reputation and prices (☎0564/25.142; closed Mon). On a more earthy scale, there are many basic **pizzerias**, including the homely *Maremma* in Via F. Calboli, the *Dal Ghepa* in Via Vinzaglio, and the *Italiana* in Via Aurelia Saffi.

The **market** is on Thursday and draws in people from all over the province. The liveliest day in Grosseto's year is August 10, when the local **festa** features a group of *butteri* leading an ox-drawn cart that bears a statue of Saint Laurence.

Rusellae and Vetulonia

Etruscan enthusiasts might want to visit **Rusellae** and **Vetulonia**, two ancient sites north of Grosseto. To reach either, you really need your own transport.

Rusellae

For **RUSELLAE**, the nearer of the sites, take the SS223 Siena road for ten kilometres and watch for the signpost to the ruins on the plateau above – don't take the turn for modern Roselle about a kilometre earlier. The track leads to a small car park, with the site about five minutes away on foot. One of the twelve towns of the Etruscan federation, Rusellae rose above the lake and marshy ground now occupied by Grosseto, and survived the arrival of the Romans. By the fifth century, however, it had been all but abandoned as Grosseto rose in its wake. Most of the finds are in Grosseto's museum, and all that's visible are the foundations of some buildings, scattered necropolises, and the outlines of a Roman amphitheatre. The tombs at Rusellae are perhaps more interesting than those at Vetulonia, but unfortunately they are closed – which is probably why they are also better preserved.

Vetulonia

Twenty kilometres north of Grosseto off the Follónica road (the SS1), **VETULONIA** is a more rewarding destination. This ancient city was another member of the Etruscan federation and survived through to the Middle Ages, though Massa Maríttima had long taken over its pivotal function. It was probably destroyed during a revolt against the Pisans in the fourteenth century: blocks from its buildings are now incorporated into the village above the ruins, which stand at the road junction for Buriano to the south.

Little of genuine Etruscan vintage remains apart from a couple of big **tombs** – the Tomba della Pietrera and the Tomba del Diavolino – though scholars claim to have unearthed an Etruscan brothel, along with lewd graffiti apparently left by the women who staffed it. Much of the area is still being excavated.

Perhaps the best reason for a visit to the area, though, is the fine **restaurant** in the main square of modern Vetulonia, the *Taverna Etrusca* (closed Thurs). It looks like an ordinary bar, with the dining room at the back through a beaded curtain, but the regional specialities – including wild boar – and the views are superb. The pizzeria, in front of the now closed museum, does the best pizzas in the area and delicious desserts; there's a garden and stables at the back.

Monti dell'Uccellina

Currently designated a *Parco Naturale*, the hills and coastline of the **MONTI DELL'UCCELLINA** are set to become a fully-fledged *Parco Nazionale*, recognition for an area that is claimed to be the last virgin coastal landscape on the Italian peninsula.

The heart of the park is a hump of hills that rises suddenly from the plain, about a dozen kilometres south of Grosseto. A breathtaking piece of countryside that combines cliffs, coastal marsh, *macchia*, forest-covered hills, pristine beaches and some of the most beautiful stands of umbrella pines in the country, it is a microcosm of all that's best in the Maremma – devoid of the bars, marinas, hotels, roads and half-finished houses that have destroyed much of the Italian littoral. Kept remote for centuries by malaria and impassable swamp, it's now preserved by the determination of its owners to keep the region sacrosanct. All has been to the benefit of the visitor, producing an area that rewards the casual walker, birdwatcher, botanist, or anyone simply in search of unspoilt sand.

The park

There is no public road access into the park – all drivers should park near the reserve headquarters in the main square at **ALBERESE**. Without a car it is difficult to get here from Grosseto. Irregular buses run from the station every day except Sunday; otherwise it's a choice between taking a taxi from the station (L30,000) or one of the two daily **trains** to the Stazione di Alberese, a four-kilometre walk from the village. Alberese's **park headquarters**, in Via del Fante (☎0564/407.098), offers details about a huge range of guided and unguided tours – we've detailed the pick of the marked trails opposite.

Admission to the park (see box opposite) secures a basic **map** and a place on an hourly **bus** which runs 10km into the hills, drops you at Pratini (virtually just a field) and leaves you to your own devices. It's about a twenty-minute stroll from there to the beach. Really energetic types can walk all the way from Alberese; if you want to see the wildlife at dusk (the best time) you'll have to walk back anyway, as the last bus from Pratini departs at 5.30pm in summer. It'll usually take you back to Grosseto.

Walking in the Uccellina

Once off the bus at Pratini you've the choice of **walking** either to the beach (follow the *Strada degli Olivi*), or along one of the seven **marked trails** which crisscross each other within the park. Most people rush headlong for the **beach**, an idyllic curving bay backed by cliffs and wooded hills. The obvious stretch is to the left, though you can trudge the beach for miles to the right, round the huge *pineta* towards the mouth of the Ombrone, Tuscany's second longest river.

The best of the marked trails is **Trail 1** (*San Rabano*; 6km; 3hr 30min), which starts from the drop-off point. The track climbs quickly to Uccellina's main ridge (417m), with views to the coast and to Monte Amiata in the interior, reaching the abbey of **San Rabano** after about ninety minutes. Built in the eleventh century and abandoned five hundred years later, the church is now an evocative ivy-covered ruin, with stone carvings littering the grass. The path then drops right, returning below the ridge to the *Strada degli Olivi* through evergreen woods.

Trail 2 (*Le Torri*; 5km; 1hr 30min) starts nearer the beach and connects some of the medieval **watchtowers** built by the Spanish, who, with the Sienese, were virtually the only people to bother with the area, using it as a source of cork and charcoal. Taking in several coastal habitats, it's best for its extraordinary view over the woods of **umbrella pines** (*Pinus pinea*) on the sand bar and dunes below. These are the park's crowning glory and one of the most memorable natural sights in Tuscany – a vast, unique canopy of emerald green that stretches almost as far as the eye can see. It's well worth dropping down from the tower to enjoy the woods, where you could roam for hours, limited only by the areas of marsh at their fringes. Many of these pines were planted: the domestic variety for their crop of pine nuts (still harvested) and the maritime variety (undergoing rampant expansion) to consolidate the dunes on the estuary.

The level **Trail 3** (*Le Grotte*; 8km; 3hr) takes in a long stretch of the woods and of the canals that divide the park, but is one of the less rewarding walks. It starts near no. 2 and its ultimate destination is a group of caves, one of which (*La Grotta della Fabbrica*) has yielded some of the oldest human remains found in Italy. The trail is remote, however, and offers good chances of wildlife sightings.

Trail 4 (*Cala di Forno*; 12km; 4hr) is the longest, most varied, and least walked of the trails, taking in hill, coast and cliff scenery, and reaching the large headland (the Cala di Forno) that dominates the bay to the south. The return takes you along the dunes and a superb stretch of beach at Portovecchio.

There are several other shorter trails if you are looking for no more than a quick stroll.

Marina di Alberese

Although part of the park, stringent entry restrictions do not apply to the **MARINA DI ALBERESE**, whose **beach** – whilst not as superb as that in the park proper – rates as one of the best in Tuscany. It's open all year, but there's a

FLORA AND FAUNA IN THE UCCELLINA

Even if you're not looking out for it, you'd have to be extremely unlucky not to see any interesting wildlife in the protected environment of the Uccellina. An extraordinary range of species thrive here, in what is effectively a textbook compendium of Mediterranean coastal **habitats** – wooded hills, olive groves, pastures, marshland, *pineta*, primary and secondary *macchia*, dunes, retro-dunal areas, estuary and mudflats.

The Monti dell'Uccellina take their name (the mountains of the little bird) from the number of **birds** that use the hills as a stepping stone between Europe and North Africa. The **Ombrone estuary** is the key target for serious birdwatchers during the spring and autumn migratory cycles, when a varied assortment of waders, ducks, herons and egrets can be seen. Rarities like ospreys, bee-eaters, flamingoes, and even falcons and short-toed eagles can be spotted in the rockier hinterland, and you're almost guaranteed the sight of herons wheeling away from the canals, perhaps with hoopoes, shrikes, kingfishers and the rare, brightly coloured Knight of Italy.

Other wildlife species are most likely to be encountered towards dusk with roe-deer prevalent in the hills, and the famous **wild boar** an often audible (if not visible) inhabitant of the scrub and pine forest. An indigenous Maremman breed, it's a smaller specimen than other Italian boar, most of which are descended from bulky Eastern European stock. The crested **porcupine**, introduced by the Romans, is also reasonably common (Italy is the only place it's found outside Africa), as are badgers and foxes; it is hoped that the increasingly rare otter will flourish here too. In the cultivated land to the north and on the flat fringes of the estuary you'll see the semi-wild **horses** for which the Maremma is famous.

Tracking down **flora** is more a job for the specialist, though the pines and cork oaks are unmissable, as are the huge banks of rosemary bushes, purple with flowers in the late summer. The dwarf pine, Italy's only indigenous palm, has its northernmost natural limit in the park, and numerous floral rarities scatter the park's dunes, *macchia* and marshes.

The World Wide Fund for Nature's main branch in Florence runs summer **work camps** in the park; for details contact WWFN, Via Canto dei Nelli 8 (☎055/230.2675). Grosseto's local birdwatching group also runs summer work camps, and provides information on the park's birds (☎0564/454.527).

barrier at Spergolaia, brought down when pressure of numbers becomes too great. Campers, caravans and trailers in theory are excluded, but in practice no one seems to take much notice. There's nowhere to stay here and camping is prohibited, though people doubtless get away with it.

The arrow-straight access road is a pleasure in itself, shaded by a continuous avenue of pines, and flanked by hills, corrals of horses and fields of white oxen. Towards the sea it enters a dense *pineta*, and ends with a car park (L1500) laid out under the trees. Except for a mobile bar and pleasant picnic area, there's no other development. The pines come right down to the beach, and in places into the sea itself, their bleached, smooth trunks giving the place the feel of a tropical island. The Italians, gregarious as ever, stick to the area at the end of the road, and you don't have to walk far to find solitude. The sand is clean, the sea a dream – shallow and perfect for swimming – and the experience rounded off with beautiful views to the Argentario, Giglio and the tree-covered backdrop of the Uccellina.

Talamone

At the southern tip of the Uccellina, and just outside the park's confines, **TALAMONE** is a fishing village and discreet summer resort. Save for a yacht-filled marina, most of its old charm is still, so far, intact. The Sienese – who never had a proper outlet to the sea – once planned to make its hole-in-the-wall harbour into a port to rival Pisa, but extended lines of communication and clogging weed doomed the project to failure. In the *Inferno* Dante used it as a metaphor for pointless enterprise. The town's greatest moment came in 1860, when Garibaldi and the Thousand stopped here for three days on their way to Sicily.

The main sight in the town is the sixteenth-century Spanish **castle**, home to the **Museo della Maremma** (9.30am–12.30pm & 4.30–8pm, Sun 9.30am–12.30pm; closed Wed; free), which documents the social and natural history of the whole Maremma. Most of the ground floor of this immense museum is given over to finds from the Etruscan town at Roselle (see p.273); other rooms are dedicated to individual towns or regions of the Maremma, or to artists associated with the region. Close at hand, the church of **San Francesco** contains a crucifix by Duccio, painted in 1289.

Three trails lead off into the hills from Talamone, making it a good base for exploring the southern edge of the park. There are two three-star **hotels** here: the central *Telamonio*, Piazza Garibaldi (☎0564/887.008; ⑧) with breakfast included – and so it should be at the price – and the *Capo d'Uomo*, Via Cala di Forno 7 (☎0564/887.077; closed Oct–March; ⑦), with sea views. There's also a **campsite**, the *Village Camping Talamone* (☎0564/887.026; April 15–Sept 30). Among the **restaurants**, try the central *La Buca*, Piazza Garibaldi (☎0564/887.067; closed Mon), which is small, rustic and pricey, or the *Da Flavia*, on Via Garibaldi, known for its fish and seafood.

Scansano and Magliano

The settlements of **Magliano** and **Scansano** offer one of the Maremma's few rewarding inland diversions. If you're spending any time in the region, Scansano is worth considering as an alternative base to Grosseto, and even if you're just passing through, the enclosing walls of Magliano are a sight not to be missed. The landscape here is more inviting than most of the coast, with vineyards and woods of sweet chestnut reminiscent of Chianti – and excellent vistas of the Uccellina.

Both villages are somewhat off the beaten track: just four buses a day run to them from Grosseto, plus a couple from Orbetello on school days. A car is thus a distinct advantage, allowing you to combine the two in a cross-country route from the coast or Grosseto to Monte Amiata, via Roccalbegna.

Scansano

Twenty-five kilometres southeast of Grosseto (on the SS323), **SCANSANO** is a cramped little hill village with fine clear views to the ridges of the Uccellina. It is sited 500 metres above sea level, on a spur that pushes into an impressive wooded gorge; the end of the spur is picturesquely capped by the bulk of the parish church. The main road climbs into the **Piazza Garibaldi**, occupied by a stern statue of the eponymous hero, several tiny **trattorias** and the one-star **hotel**, *La Posta* (☎0564/507.189; ③).

There's quieter but more upmarket accommodation in the **old town**, entered through the arch off Piazza Garibaldi, and little more than a single street that runs the length of the spur. The mid-price option here is the two-star *Magini* (☎0564/507.181; ④). Alternatively, three kilometres out of town at Castagneta, on the SS322 to Manciano, there's the *Antico Casale* (☎0564/507.219; ⑧) which also has a **restaurant** with a good reputation.

The Scansano area produces a fine DOC wine, **Morellino di Scansano**, which, like the better-known Brunello di Montalcino, is made entirely from Sangiovese grapes. It's marked by experts as one of the Tuscan wines to watch, and should be on offer in all the local restaurants.

Magliano in Toscana

South of Scansano the road passes through the hamlet of Pereta, where one huge tower crowns a fortified *borgo* and a couple of streets, before reaching **MAGLIANO IN TOSCANA**, descendant of the Etruscan town of Heba. The place today is essentially a village, and its most remarkable feature an almost completely intact circle of **walls**, those on the village's south side dating from the thirteenth century, the rest a fifteenth-century legacy of the Sienese. The bastions are so impressive from a distance that they draw you into the town, through the ugly new estate that suddenly appears round a bend in the road. Close up, the village itself is a strange, crumbling mixture of old and new, with concrete houses squeezed in with little thought for the medieval fabric.

The main **church**, in Corso Garibaldi, is a Baroque mess, but retains some well-preserved frescoes from the original building. Close by is the tiny Piazza del Popolo and the abandoned **Palazzo dei Priori**, built by the Sienese. The ghost-town atmosphere doesn't invite further exploration, but you should carry on to the end of the main street, where an arch in the walls frames a view over the classic Tuscan countryside.

The town's other talking point is the extraordinarily gnarled **Ulivo della Strega** (the Witch's Olive); over a thousand years old, the tree is said have been the scene of pagan rituals in days past and is now allegedly haunted. To see it, leave the town by the road to the south and stop at the Romanesque church of **Sant'Annunziata**, beyond the estate on the left. Knock on the first house on the left (no.47) and the woman will show you the tree – with some reluctance, as she says it's been hacked for souvenirs and lost half its branches since appearing in an English guide several years ago.

Less prone to desecration are the ruins of **San Bruzio**, 2km south of the village on the road to Marsiliana. A single, bleached white stump of a tower is all that remains of this twelfth-century abbey, but it's an evocative place, set in a large olive grove. Local tradition suggests it was built on the site of a pagan temple and, more salaciously, that it was connected by a tunnel to the now-vanished nunnery of Sant'Anna.

There's a single one-star **hotel** in Magliano, *I Butteri* (☎0564/589.824; ③), and a good little **restaurant-pizzeria**, the *Sandra*, Corso Garibaldi 20. For rather more upmarket cuisine try the *Aurora*, Chiasso Lavagnini 12–14 (closed Wed & Sept).

Orbetello and its lagoon

ORBETELLO is principally distinguished by its strange location on a narrow isthmus in the middle of the **Laguna di Orbetello**. Little in the place excites real attention but it has become something of a resort, thanks to its function as the gateway to the dramatic rocky outcrop of **Monte Argentario**. On summer weekends it becomes a bottleneck of cars as tourists pile in to Porto Ercole and Porto San Stefano, the Argentario's supposedly chic resorts. As well as seafront attractions, the Orbetello area offers much to naturalists, its lagoon boasting a **nature reserve** renowned as the Italian birdwatchers' El Dorado.

The **train station** is four kilometres away at Orbetello Scalo, on the mainland edge of the lagoon, a prominent stop for trains on the Rome–Pisa line. There are connections for Siena and slow trains to smaller stations to the north and south. Connecting buses run from the station to the **bus terminal** just off Piazza della Repubblica; from here there are regular services to Grosseto, Porto Ercole and Porto San Stefano, as well as daily buses to Capálbio and Pitigliano.

The Town

Orbetello is an unassuming and pleasant place, graced with palm trees, the pastel-coloured remnants of Spanish walls, and a single main street – Viale Italia – thronged each evening with a particularly vigorous *passeggiata*. It was probably Etruria's leading port, though little evidence of its ancient past remains except for a few blocks of Etruscan wall underwater near the causeway. The Byzantines took advantage of its easily defended position, holding out longer here than anywhere else on the Tyrrhenian coast. Thereafter the papacy gained a control that was not relinquished until 1559, when the Spanish became rulers of a military *Presidio* with Orbetello as its capital. The town's last claim to fame was as the headquarters of Mussolini's seaplane squadrons; the surviving **aircraft hangar** is one of Tuscany's more bizarre architectural attractions.

The **Spanish fortifications** are the town's conspicuous feature, a fine example of military architecture; the elegant arsenal, the **Polveriera de Guzman**, houses a small archaeological museum. Nearby, the **Duomo** in Piazza della Repubblica diverts with a lovely Gothic facade, before disappointing with a grim Baroque interior. Orbetello's lively **street market** is held on Saturdays.

The nature reserve

Orbetello's **lagoon** was formed when Monte Argentario became joined to the mainland by two narrow sand spits (or *tomboli*): one to the north – Tombolo di Giannella – and one to the south – Tombolo di Feniglia. In the lagoon's northernmost corner, near the hamlet of Albinia, the World Wide Fund for Nature has established an eight-square-kilometre **nature reserve** (guided tours Sept–April Sun & Thurs at 10am & 2pm; L8000, WWFN members L4000; ☎0564/82.097). The entrance to the reserve is off the main road two kilometres east of Albinia, marked by a small panda sign; the warden can be contacted at the building at the end of the track.

The reserve, and the lagoon in general, offers exceptional **birdwatching**, with confirmed sightings of 200 of Italy's estimated 450 species. Rarities are numerous and many of them are known to breed in the area. Most notable are the stone curlew, osprey, black-winged stilt, bee-eater, Montagu's harrier, and – most importantly – the Knight of Italy, known to breed elsewhere only in Sardinia and the Po delta. Little egrets, terns, storks and herons arrive in large numbers, glossy ibis and cranes are regular visitors, and it's not unknown for flamingoes to stay for the summer.

One reason for the variety is the relative lack of avian refuge on Italy's west coast. Another is the lagoon's modest one-metre depth, source of an accessible mulch of fish and assorted food – and there's also a wide variety of marsh, *macchia*, dune and reed habitats for nest building. Evening is the best time to be around the lagoon: not only is the wildlife most visible then, but the **sunsets** over the water and the mountains of the Argentario are fabulous too.

The *tomboli*

It's possible to see wildlife from almost any point on the lagoon, and if time is tight, exploring the southern *tombolo* is a good substitute for a tour of the reserve – the campsites and driveable road detract from the appeal of the northern Tombolo di Giannella. The **Tombolo di Feniglia** has one of Italy's most beautiful *pinete*, a long sandy dune covered in parasol pines, and is protected by a small nature reserve where roe deer are usually to be seen. The road along it is off-limits for cars, though you can walk its whole course, dropping down to the lagoon side for great views, or to the other for a fine beach. You could continue this walk to the **Lago di Burano** (see p.285), if you carry on through Ansedonia, and then along the beach south for about an hour.

Practicalities

The Orbetello **tourist office** in Piazza della Repubblica is a useful source of information on **accommodation** in Orbetello itself, on the *tomboli* and in the mainland hamlets of Albinia and Ansedonia – both of them served by local buses.

Orbetello is the nicest option, and has two **hotels** with similarly priced rooms: *La Perla*, Via Volontari del Sangue 10 (✆0564/863.546; ④); and the *Piccolo Parigi*, Corso Italia 159 (✆0564/867.233; ④), the best choice. The town's best budget **restaurant** is the *Pizzeria Gennaro* in Viale Italia. For something ritzier – though they do pizzas too – try *La Goletta* in Via del Pino, towards the Tombolo di Giannella (✆0564/820.034). The nearest modest-priced **hotel** to the WWFN reserve is Albinia's one-star *Fagiano* on the main road (✆0564/870.143; ③).

Most of the area's fourteen **campsites** are on and around the lagoon and along the main SS1 Via Aurelia. The most attractive is the all-year *Feniglia* (✆0564/831.090), the only site on the Tombolo di Feniglia. Two more are to be found out on the Tombolo di Giannella: the three-star *Il Vegliero* (April 15–Sept 15; ✆0564/820.201) is a vast affair; the *Comunale Giannella* (March–Dec; ✆0564/820.049) is perhaps the better, if tattier choice. Albinia also has a couple of sites and four more within six kilometres on the SS1 to the west; *Campo Regio* (✆0564/870.163), 4km west, is the only one of these open all year.

Monte Argentario

The high, rocky terrain of **Monte Argentario** is as close to wilderness as southern Tuscany comes: the interior is mountainous, reaching 635m at its highest point – **Il Telegrafo** – and the coast dramatically cut into headlands, bays and shingle beaches. Away from the villas of rich Romans, much is still uninhabited scrub and woodland, badly prone to forest fires but still superb **walking** country.

In their day, the main centres of **Porto Santo Stefano** and **Porto Ercole** had a reputation for upmarket exclusivity, but these days they're too well known to pander solely to the upper market. Prices can be manageable, as are the crowds, though you'll probably need to book ahead for peak periods.

With your own transport you might follow the touted **scenic drive** (*gita panoramica*) around the entire island, a tortuous trip of about 24km, not all of it on paved roads; you will need a four-wheel drive for the stretch near Porto Ercole which is otherwise impassable. There is a **car hire** outlet in Porto Santo Stefano – *Fanciulli*, Via Campone 96 (☎0564/817.291).

Porto Santo Stefano

PORTO SANTO STEFANO is the more developed of the Argentario resorts, and also the more fashionable – which in Italy is a lot worse than being plain popular. Something of the charm which first brought people here, however, still shines through, despite the hotels, villas and yachts that have all but obliterated the original village. A few fishing boats still cluster in the town's smaller harbour, having relinquished the main port to the marina and its mega-yachts.

If you're on a budget, you'll probably stay only as long as it takes to get a **ferry** to the island of Giglio (see p.282). Information and sailing times are available from the quayside *TO.RE.MAR* office (☎0564/814.615), or the neighbouring *Maregiglio* (☎0564/812.920), or the **tourist office** at Corso Umberto 55a (daily summer 8am–2pm & 4–6.30pm; winter 8am–2pm). Boats make the one-hour trip three times daily year-round, with five extra sailings in the summer (one-way tickets L6000–8000 for foot passengers, L31,500–63,000 for cars). **Buses** run to the port from the train station at Orbetello Scalo, so you could avoid almost any contact with the place at all.

Affordable **accommodation** does exist, though mainly in private rooms – for which the tourist office supplies lists. You'll need to book well ahead in season to secure a place at either of the town's one-star **hotels**: the central *Da Alfiero*, Via Cuniberti 14 (☎0564/814.067; ⑤), and less central *Week End*, Via Martiri d'Ungheria 3 (☎0564/812.580; ⑤). If money is no object try Porto Santo Stefano's finest, the three-star *Belvedere* (☎0564/812.634; ⑦), near the beaches at Poggio Calvella, a short way west. The nearest campsites are those listed in the Orbetello entry, opposite.

Restaurants are generally swanky and overpriced, making back street pizzerias and bar snacks the best options. The *Mini Mouse Pub* is one of many waterfront **bars** – good sandwiches and a big selection of beers; or try *Pub Baracuda*, overlooking the port. If you're going for a blow out, *Da Siro*, Corso Umberto I 102 (☎0564/812.538; closed Mon & Nov), has quite a reputation. *La Bussola*, Piazzale del Valle, is good for fish, or try *La Formica*, one of the more popular and reasonable fish restaurants, out at Pozzerella, 1500 metres east of the village.

Porto Ercole

PORTO ERCOLE is a more intimate place than Santo Stefano, with an attractive old quarter and a more genuine fishing-village atmosphere. Though founded by the Romans, its chief historical monuments are two **Spanish fortresses**, facing each other on opposing sides of the harbour, and a third one above the new town. At the entrance to the old town, a plaque on the stone gate commemorates the painter **Caravaggio** , who in 1610 keeled over with sunstroke on a beach nearby; taken to a local tavern, he soon died of a fever, and was buried in the parish church of Sant'Erasmo.

A couple of good **walks** suggest themselves from the village. The most obvious is along the Tombolo di Feniglia (see p.280). The other is to the top of **Il Telegrafo**, accessible either partly by road and track from the ridge that runs up from the lighthouse to the south, or on a rough road that leaves the port to the north and then runs west under the main ridge. The way is fairly open and clear and there are superb views to make the haul worthwhile.

Reasonably priced **hotels** in Porto Ercole are limited to the one-star *Conchiglia* in Via della Marina (☎0564/833.134; [4]), and the *Albergo-Gelateria Stella Marina* in Lungomare A. Doria (☎0564/833.055; [6]). For information about **rooms**, ask in *Bar Centrale* on the main road opposite the bus stop. The nearest **campsite** is on the Tombolo di Feniglia (see p.280). For a **meal**, try the excellent *La Lampara*, Lungomare A. Doria 67 (☎0564/833.024), which serves Neapolitan specialities, pizza included; many of the Argentario's inhabitants have Neapolitan and southern forebears.

The island of Giglio

The largest of the Tuscan islands after Elba, **GIGLIO** is visited by an ever-increasing number of foreign tourists and is so popular with Romans that in high season there's standing room only on the boats. Yet it's well worth making the effort to stay on this fabulous island. The rush is fairly short-lived, most visitors are day-trippers, and few of them explore the tracks across the unspoilt interior, a mix of barren rock and reforested upland. The island is rich in such **fauna** as peregrine falcons, mouflon, kestrels and buzzards, and in **wild flowers** too – this is the only place outside North Africa to shelter wild mustard, and the sole spot in Tuscany to support the yellow flowers of artemisia.

The island derives its name not from *giglio* (lily), but from the Roman colony **Aegilium**, in its day a resort for the rich and famous, a function it continued to fulfil through most of the Middle Ages. Granite quarries kept the economy buoyant and Giglio stone was used to construct many medieval churches. Later, pirate incursions took the edge off its appeal, despite the miraculous defensive power of Saint Mamiliano's right arm, a relic hacked from a sixth-century Sicilian bishop exiled on the island of Montecristo. The limb proved effective when waved at Tunisian pirates in 1799, but less so on other occasions, notably in 1534, when Barbarossa carried off most of the island's population.

Transport

There are up to eight **ferry** connections daily in summer from Porto Santo Stefano to **Giglio Porto** (see opposite); the rest of the year daily sailings drop to three. (Porto Santo Stefano is also the embarkation point for the tiny island of **Giannutri**, dealt with at the end of this section.)

From Giglio Porto there's an excellent **bus** service to Giglio's two main villages, **Giglio Castello** and **Campese**. It's best not to come by car – it's expensive at any time of the year, and in summer you need a permit to bring a car onto the island.

Around the island

Small, rock-girdled **GIGLIO PORTO** is the place you're likeliest to stay on Giglio, as it hosts eight of the island's twelve hotels. It has no sights to be visited, but the whole scene is wonderful, the pale-coloured houses offset by a backdrop of terraced vineyards. As much of the land around rises sheer from the sea, the **beaches** are modest: you'll find one to the north of the port at Punta Aranella, and a couple to the south at Cala delle Canelle and Cala delle Caldane; all three are more or less developed. The port's big day is August 10, when locals vie with each other to retrieve a flag tied to the end of a greasy pole over the harbour (the *Cuccagna a Mare*). Further frolics ensue later in the day during the *Palio Marinaro*, a competition at sea between the port's three districts.

There's a **tourist office** opposite the ferry ramp at Via Umberto I 48, which can provide details of accommodation possibilities – including a fair number of houses around the port which have **rooms to let** (most also place advertisements in their windows). The **hotels** generally offer only full board in high season, and most are open only from June to September. If you can spare the amount for full board, the one to go for is the three-star *Pardini's Hermitage Hotel* in the Cala degli Alberi cove, only accessible by boat or on foot (☎0564/809.034; [7]); it has just ten rooms, so book ahead – for boat access enquire at the *Giglio Sub* shop in the port. A more modest choice is *La Pergola,* in the port's Via Thaon de Revel (☎0564/809.051; [6]). Cheapest of all is the two-star *Da Ruggero*, in Via del Saraceno 86 (☎0564/809.121; [5]).

Giglio Castello

GIGLIO CASTELLO, hidden away in the hills just under six hairpin kilometres from the port, was for a long time the island's only settlement and the sole spot safe from pirate attack. Surprisingly well-preserved, its maze of arches and medieval alleyways is still surrounded by thick defensive walls. Buses from the port stop near a vine-covered patio **bar** in the large main square, also the entrance to the granite fortress and medieval quarter.

Started by the Pisans, the **castle** was completed by the Grand Duchy of Tuscany; rough paths around the walls enable you to clamber over the rocks for superb views over the island and ruins far below. For a look at San Mamiliano's miraculous arm, check out the Baroque **church**; to explore Giglio's interior, take the road that runs south from the village towards the island's main ridge.

Accommodation is limited to private rooms; the first bungalow up a path from the bar in the square is one possibility (☎0564/806.074; [5]). *Da Maria* in Via Casamatta is the island's best **restaurant** (☎0564/806.062), though the seafood doesn't come cheap. In summer an open-air **disco** opens up near the square.

Giglio Campese

Sited at the western end of the island road, **GIGLIO CAMPESE** is a growing resort. It has Giglio's best **beach** – a fine stretch of sand, overlooked by a Medici tower, and curving for two kilometres from a huge phallic rock which the tourist brochures are too modest to photograph. Around the base of the tower is a modern, turreted apartment complex with a couple of restaurants, tennis courts and all manner of water-sport facilities – including diving gear for hire and lessons in how to use it.

The resort has four **hotels**, cheapest of which is *Giardino delle Palme*, Via della Torre (☎0564/804.037; ⑤). *La Lampara*, Via Provinciale 66 (☎0564/804.022; ⑥), costs slightly more but it includes breakfast in the price, unlike *Da Giovanni*, Via di Mezzo Franco 10 (June–Sept; ☎0564/804.010; ⑥). Top of the range is the three-star *Campese*, Via della Torre 18 (☎0564/804.003; ⑦). There's also a **campsite**, the *Baia del Sole* (May–Sept; ☎0564/804.036).

Giannutri

The southernmost Tuscan island, **GIANNUTRI**, is privately owned, and overnight stays are impossible unless you're a friend of the inhabitants. The few people who come over for the day do so to visit the ruins of a **Roman villa** at Cala Maestra. The island policeman asks travellers to remove backpacks before stepping ashore.

Given this sort of attitude, and the island's physical make-up – flat, dull and walkable end-to-end in two hours – it's a place for island obsessives only. If you're curious, the tiny **boat** *M/S Gabbiano II* leaves Porto Santo Stefano daily from May 1 to September 15 at 10.30am, returning at 4.30pm; out of season it runs only Saturday and Sunday.

South from Orbetello

South of Orbetello most of the terrain is a drab foretaste of the expanses of Lazio, but there are several worthwhile diversions if you're headed this way. At **Ansedonia** you can inspect one of Tuscany's few ancient Roman sites before moving on to the important **nature reserve** at **Lago di Burano**. Inland **Capálbio** rates as one of the area's loveliest villages, while near **Chiarone** – which has fine beaches – there's the **Giardino dei Tarocchi**, a series of monumental sculptures that's quickly becoming both a tourist attraction and artistic talking point.

Ansedonia and Lago di Burano

ANSEDONIA crouches under a rocky crag at the end of the Tombolo di Feniglia. Scattered with holiday villas, it has a long beach and – on the hilltop above the village – the remains of **Cosa**, founded by the Romans in 273 BC as a frontier post against the Etruscans. It was one of their most important commercial centres in the area until its population – according to the historian Rutilius – was driven out by an army of mice. Most of the old *municipium* was devastated by the Visigoths in the fourth century, and what survived was ruined when medieval Ansedonia was sacked by the Sienese in 1330. Current excavations have exposed enough of the Roman colony to suggest some idea of its former layout.

To reach **the site**, leave Ansedonia on the road east, passing a couple of medieval towers (converted into houses) and the so-called **Tagliata Etrusca**, a none-too-exciting series of cuts into the rock believed to have been part of a system to drain the marshland. After about a kilometre, where the road bends sharp right, there's a signed track to Cosa off to the left. You'll find a ring of **walls** eight metres high in places, the remains of a defensive circuit of eighteen towers, the outline of the grid-iron **street plan**, a **forum** (with basilica and senate discernible nearby), two **temples**, and some recently uncovered **mosaics** and **wall paint-**

ings. It's worth climbing to the top of the hill, not only for the remains of the **acropolis**, but also for fine views across to Giannutri and Monte Argentario.

If you need a local place to stay, there's a **hotel** near the Tagliata, the one-star *Le Rocce* (☎0564/881.275; ③). The best of Ansedonia's **restaurants** is the quiet *Il Pescatore*, Via della Tagliata (closed Tues).

Lago di Burano

You can walk to the **Lago di Burano** along the beach from Ansedonia, or catch a slow train from Orbetello to Capálbio Scalo, less than 100 metres from the water. Technically a lagoon rather than a lake, Burano is a placid stretch of water, shielded from the sea by vegetation-covered dunes. Completing the scenic picture – which is captivating at dusk with the sun behind the Argentario – is a superb and mysterious-looking tower, the **Torre di Burinaccio**.

Though you can just walk onto the enclosing beach, access to the lagoon itself is restricted, as the WWFN runs Burano as a **nature reserve**. Recognised as a wetland habitat of international significance, this and the Orbetello lagoon are together rated as the most important area for **birds** on Italy's western coast. The lagoon shares many of the species found in Orbetello, and for similar reasons – Burano is also only a metre deep. Notable species include the bluethroat, great spotted cuckoo, great white heron and velvet scoter.

The entrance to the reserve is on the perimeter road 500m east of the station. Warden Guido Manfredi conducts visits (May–Aug Thurs & Sun 10am & 2pm; Sept–April same days 10am & 2.30pm; L8000, L4000 WWFN members; ☎0564/820.297), picking out observation points and explaining the **nature trail** that takes in the dune, woodland and scrub habitats around the lake. With prior arrangement it's possible to stay overnight in the twelve-bed forestry hut on site. **Camping** nearby is prohibited, but the **beach** here stretches for miles and is perfect for pitching a tent in private. There are also two **hotels** near the Capálbio Scalo train station: the one-star *Del Lago* (☎0564/898.820; ③), and the two-star *La Palma* (☎0564/890.341; ④).

Chiarone, the Tarot Garden and Capálbio

CHIARONE is nothing more than a station and a couple of bars, though its **beaches** – fifteen minutes' walk away – are some of the best and quietest on this part of the coast. The virgin stretch was singled out in a recent report as enjoying the first unpolluted water north of Rome. Fifteen kilometres of unbroken sand stretch away towards the Argentario, with plenty of opportunities for **camping** in the dunes. Things get grubby on-shore as the summer wears on, but the gentle, shelving seabed makes for good swimming, and all it takes for solitude on the sand is a few minutes' walk.

A handful of **trains** to and from Grosseto stop at Chiarone station and there's a beach **bar** and **campsite** – the *Chiarone* (May–Sept; ☎0564/890.101) – at the end of the road to the dunes.

Il Giardino dei Tarocchi

With a car it's possible from Chiarone to visit one of Italy's oddest and increasingly well-known works of modern art: **Il Giardino dei Tarocchi** (The Tarot Garden), a huge set of monumental sculptures by Niki di Saint Phalle, most famous for the Fontaine Stravinsky, created with her then-husband Jean Tinguely outside the Pompidou Centre in Paris. The brightly coloured pieces are clearly visible from the Via Aurelia: to reach them it's a five-kilometre drive on the road from Chiarone to Pescia Fiorentina.

Using land donated by friends, the work has been ten years in the making, and is still some way from completion, hence its limited opening hours (June–Sept Sat & Sun 2–4pm; free). Nonetheless it's already a staggering sight – a whimsical mix of Gaudí, arcane symbolism and sheer fun that tends to be loved by children and arouse bewildered admiration in adults. The bigger pieces will each represent one of the Tarot's twenty-two major arcana. Amongst those already finished are **The Tower** – three storeys of glittering broken mirrors – and **The Goddess**, a sphinx-like creation with the head of Queen Victoria, in which the artist lives. Plants and fountains form an integral part of the scheme.

Capálbio

Stranded in empty country, the hill village of **CAPÁLBIO** is virtually unknown to outsiders, though not to Rome's cultural and political elite, many of whom – the head of the communist party included – have homes in the locality. Most have been attracted by the almost perfect medieval interior, which at night is a deathly quiet maze of streets straight out of the Middle Ages. Views are superb – the place is visible for miles around – and though there's little to see apart from a few frescoes and the Aldobrandeschi fortifications, it definitely warrants a look if you're touring by car. There are also two **buses** daily from Orbetello.

Near the entrance to the old town, the obvious wooden building perched above the valley contains a superb **restaurant**, *Trattoria la Torre da Calla* – this is the heart of wild boar country. There are two **hotels**: the two-star *La Mimosa*, Via Torino (☎0564/890.220; [4]), and the three-star *Bargello* in Via della Circonvallazione (☎0564/896.020; [5]), which is popular, so book ahead.

travel details

Trains

From Grosseto to Orbetello (10 daily; 30min), going on to Tarquinia (50min), Civitavecchia (1hr 5min) and Rome (1hr 30min); Piombino, changing at Campiglia Maríttima (10 daily; 20min); Follónica (13 daily; 35min); San Vincenzo (10 daily; 45min); Cécina (10 daily; 1hr); Livorno (21 daily; 1hr 15min), going on to Pisa (1hr 40min; connections for Lucca, Pistoia, Prato and Florence); Siena (6 daily; 1hr 20min); Florence (7 daily via Siena and Buonconvento; 3–4hr depending on train).

From Orbetello to Tarquinia (10 daily; 35min), going on to Civitavecchia (35min) and Rome (1hr); Grosseto (14 daily; 30min); Piombino, changing at Campiglia Maríttima (10 daily; 50min); Follónica (18 daily; 30min); San Vincenzo (4 daily; 50min); Cécina (15 daily; 1hr 10min); Livorno (21 daily; 1hr 45min), going on to Pisa (18 daily; 2hr); Siena (3 daily; 1hr 50min); Florence (3 daily direct; 2hr 50min).

Buses

From Massa Maríttima to Follónica (every 45min; 10min); Piombino (2 daily; 25min); Siena (2 daily; 1hr 40min); San Galgano (2 daily; 1hr).

From Grosseto Frequent buses to all main towns in Grosseto province, especially Castiglione della Pescaia (via Marina di Grosseto), Orbetello, Alberese (for the Monti dell'Uccellina), Magliano in Toscana and Scansano. Also frequent services to Arcidosso, Pitigliano and villages en route. Less frequent connections to Siena and Rome.

From Orbetello to Porto Santo Stefano, Porto Ercole, Grosseto, Capálbio and Pitigliano and villages en route.

Ferries

From Porto Santo Stefano to Giglio Porto (8 daily in summer, 2 for rest of year); Giannutri (1 daily in summer, 2 weekly for rest of year).

CHAPTER SIX

SIENA AND THE CENTRAL HILL TOWNS

Siena is the perfect counterpoint to Florence. Self-contained and still partly rural behind its medieval walls, its attraction lies in its cityscape: a majestic Gothic whole that could be enjoyed without venturing into a single museum. In its great scallop-shaped piazza, **Il Campo**, it has the loveliest of all Italian public squares; in its zebra-striped **Duomo**, a religious focus to match; and the city's whole construction, on three ridges, presents a succession of amazing vistas. It is a place of immediate charm: airy, easy-going and pedestrianised, where Florence is cramped, busy and traffic-ridden, and it is startlingly untouristed away from the few centres of day-trip sightseeing. Perhaps most important of all, though, the city is host to the undisputed giant of Italian festivals, the **Palio**, a bareback horse race around the Campo, whose sheer excitement and unique importance to the life of the community is reason enough to plan your holiday around one of the two race dates – July 2 and August 16.

The contrasts with Florence are extended in Siena's **monumental** and **artistic highlights**. The city's Duomo and Palazzo Pubblico are two of the purest buildings of Italian Gothic, and the finest of their paintings are in the same tradition. **Sienese painting** remained stamped with Byzantine, Romanesque and Gothic influences long after classical humanism had transformed Florence. It is a style characterised by brilliance of colour and decorative detail and an almost exclusive devotion to religious subjects – principally the city's patroness, the Virgin. Its traditions were shaped by a group of artists working in the last half of the thirteenth century and the first half of the fourteenth: **Duccio di Boninsegna**,

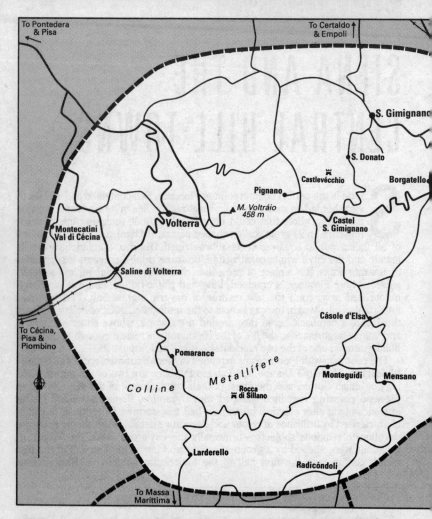

Simone Martini, and the brothers **Ambrogio and Pietro Lorenzetti**. In its **sculpture**, Siena drew mainly on foreign artists: the Florentines Donatello and Ghiberti worked on the font in the Baptistery, while Michelangelo and Nicola and Giovanni Pisano left their mark on the Duomo.

As a provincial capital, Siena has good transport links with some of the finest sights and countryside of Tuscany. The city makes a good base for much of the territory covered in the following, southern Tuscany chapter, while to the north is the wine heartland of Chianti (see p.157). Covered in this chapter are the hill towns to the west, of which **San Gimignano**, with its amazing skyline of towers, is the major target: a stunningly preserved reminder of how most Tuscan towns must have looked in the thirteenth century. It's an easy day trip from Siena but

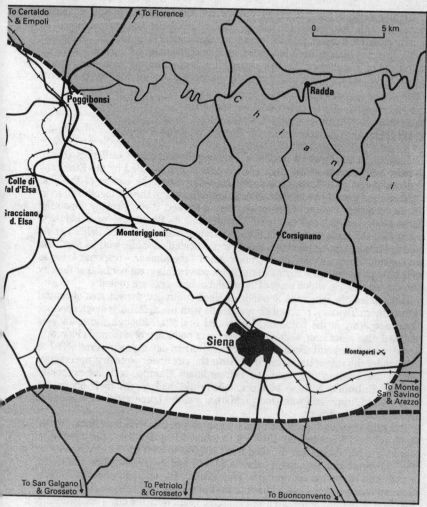

really demands a stay to get the most from its fresco cycles, setting and atmosphere. So too does the ancient Etruscan town of **Volterra**, isolated on a windswept ridge midway between Siena and the coast – a useful staging post en route between Siena and Pisa. For a rewarding few hours out of Siena, the best short trips are to **Monteriggioni**, a tiny walled hamlet, and the little-known **Colle di Val d'Elsa**; both are also promising gastronomic stops.

Getting around
Siena is just an hour from Florence by express *SITA* **bus**, a little longer by **rail**, either on a direct train or with a change at Empoli, and then a bus into the town centre – details on Siena's points of arrival are given below.

Getting around the hill towns, **buses** are the principal means of public transport, with **Poggibonsi** the hub for connections to San Gimignano, though in summer there's a direct *TRA-IN* tourist bus that connects Siena, San Gimignano and Volterra. **Volterra** itself has buses to **Massa Marítimma** – a route covered at the end of this chapter. There's also rail line connecting the Rome–Pisa line to Saline di Volterra, from where there are connecting bus services on to Volterra itself.

Siena

Though myth attributes its origins to Senius and Acius, sons of Remus (hence the she-wolf emblem of the city), **SIENA** was in fact founded by the Etruscans and refounded as a Roman colony by Augustus. Over the course of the next millennium it grew to be an independent republic, and in the thirteenth and fourteenth centuries was one of the major cities of Europe. It was virtually the size of Paris, controlled most of southern Tuscany and its flourishing wool industry, dominated the trade routes from France to Rome, and maintained Italy's richest banks. The city also developed a highly sophisticated civic life, with its own written constitution and a quasi-democratic council – the *comune* – responsible for as wide a range of duties as any modern city. It was in this great period that the city was shaped – and in which most of its art and monuments are rooted.

This golden era, when the Republic of Siena controlled a great area of central and southern Tuscany, reached an apotheosis with the defeat of a much superior Florentine army at the battle of **Montaperti** in 1260. Although the result was reversed nine years later, shifting the fulcrum of political power towards Florence, Siena's merchants embarked on an unrivalled urban development. From 1287 to 1355, under the rule of the **Council of Nine**, the city underwrote first the completion of the **Duomo** and then the extraordinary **Campo**, with its exuberant **Palazzo Pubblico**. Sienese bankers, meanwhile, had spread their operations throughout Europe, and with Duccio, Martini and the Lorenzettis, the city was at the forefront of Italian art.

The prosperity and innovation came to an abrupt halt with the **Black Death**, which reached Siena in May 1348. By October, when the disease exhausted its course, the population had dropped from 100,000 to 30,000. The city was never fully to recover (the population today is 60,000) and its politics, always factional, moved into a period of intrigue and chaos. Its art, too, became highly conservative, as patrons looked back to the old hierarchical religious images. The chief figures in these war-ridden and anarchic years were the city's two nationally renown^d saints, **Caterina** (1347–80) and **Bernardino** (1380–1444), who both exercised an enormous grip on the age, amid two further outbreaks of the plague.

As the sixteenth century opened, a period of autocratic rule under the tyrannical Pandolfo Petrucci brought a further victory over Florence, but ended with the city embroiled in ever-expanding intrigue involving the Borgias, Florentines, papacy, French, and the empire of **Charles V**. The latter proved too big a figure for the Sienese, imposing a fortress and garrison, and then, after the city had turned to the French to expel the imperial troops, laying siege to it and the Sienese countryside. The effects of the siege (1554–55) proved more terrible even than the Black Death, with the population slumping from 40,000 to as little as 8000. The republic was over, although a small band of loyalists took refuge at Montalcino and prolonged it there for a while, at least in name.

Two years after the siege, Philip II, Charles's successor, gave up Siena to **Cosimo I** in payment for war services, and the city subsequently became part of Cosimo's Grand Duchy of Tuscany. This was the real death knell. For sixty years the Sienese were forbidden even to operate banks, while control of what was by now an increasingly minor provincial town reverted, under Medici patronage, to the nobles.

The city today

Siena's swift decline from republican capital to little more than a market centre explains the city's astonishing state of medieval preservation. Little was built and still less demolished, while allotments and vineyards occupied the spaces between the ancient quarters, as they do today.

Since the last war, however, Siena has again become prosperous, partly due to **tourism**, partly to the resurgence of the **Monte dei Paschi di Siena**. This bank, founded in Siena in 1472, is one of the major players in Italian finance and in its home base is by far the largest employer. It today sponsors much of the cultural life of the city, which climaxes in a series of classical music performances at the highly respected **Accademia Musicale Chigiana**.

THE CONTRADE

Within the fabric of the medieval city, Siena preserves its ancient division into wards, or *contrade*. These are integral to the competition of the Palio (see p.298) and sustain a unique neighbourhood identity, clearly visible as you wander around the streets. Each of the seventeen *contrade* has its own **church**, **social centre** and **museum**. Each, too, has its individual **flag** and a heraldic **animal motif**, after which most of them take their names. The animals – giraffe, snail, goose, porcupine, etc – can be seen all around the city on wall plaques and are represented in a series of modern fountains near the *contrada* churches or headquarters.

There were once social distinctions between the *contrade* and although these today are blurred to the point of extinction, **allegiance to one's contrada** – conferred by birth – remains a strong element of social life. After a conventional church baptism, anyone born in a ward division is baptised for a second time in their *contrada* fountain. Subsequently, the *contrada* plays a central role in activities: for kids, in the flag-twirling and drumming for the Palio and local *contrada* festivals, for adults in the social clubs – a mix of bar and dining club – and in the attendance of a herald at marriages and funerals. *Contrade* also dispense social assistance to needy members and the respect accorded to the institution is said to have a significant effect on the city's social cohesion. Certainly, for a city of its size, Siena has remarkably low levels of crime and drug usage. Indeed, the only violence tolerated is during the Palio, when *contrada* members may well get into fights with their ancient rivals.

For an insight into the workings of the *contrade*, it is worth paying a visit to one of their **museums**, each of which gives pride of place to its displays of Palio trophies. All of the museums are open to visitors during the build-up to the Palio and at other times by appointment; if you're interested, ask the tourist office to phone. Each *contrada* also has its own **annual celebration**, accompanied by parades and feasts. And at almost any time of year, you will see groups practising flag-waving and drum-rolling in the streets.

The Monte dei Paschi co-exists, apparently easily enough, with Italy's strongest **communist council**. Though this quiet, rather bourgeois provincial capital may not look like a red city, some 35,000 of the 250,000 population of Siena province are card-carrying party members – a loyalty won by the communists' role in the resistance during the last war, and sustained by imaginative community projects. In Siena itself, the council perceives its major problem as too great a reliance on tourism. Building on the existing strengths of the university, it has plans for rejuvenation through a biotechnology park and other hi-tech projects. Meanwhile, the town's most famous and successful export is Gianna Nannini – Italian hard rock supremo and daughter of the city's pasticceria chain owner.

Arrival, information and accommodation

The centre of Siena is its great square, **Il Campo**, built at the convergence of the city's principal roads, the **Banchi di Sopra**, **Banchi di Sotto** and **Via di Città**. Each of these roads leads out across a ridge, straddled by one of the city's three medieval *terzi*, or quarters: the **Terzo di Città** to the southwest, the **Terzo di San Martino** to the southeast, and the **Terzo di Camollia** to the north.

This central core – almost entirely medieval in plan and appearance – has been effectively pedestrianised since the 1960s. Everywhere of use or interest in the city is within easy walking distance, with the exception of Saint Bernardino's monastic retreat, L'Osservanza, and the youth hostel and campsite.

Points of arrival

Arriving by **bus**, you are dropped in Piazza Matteotti (local buses) or along Via Curtatone, by the church of San Domenico, from where you can see the city – dominated by the cathedral and town hall bell towers – spread out below.

The **train station** is less convenient, sited 2km to the northeast in the valley below the city. Connecting buses (#15 is the most direct) shuttle between here and Piazza Matteotti, at the top end of Via Curtatone. Alternatively, local **city taxis** are to be found at ranks by the train station (☎0577/44.504) and on Piazza Matteotti (☎0577/289.350), or can be called elsewhere by phone (☎0577/49.222). Note, however, that in Siena it's impossible to book taxis in advance and you should allow plenty of time for cabs to reach you through the city's labyrinthine one-way system.

If you are **driving into Siena**, follow signs to the *centro* and try to find a parking space at one of the following: around **Piazza Gramsci** or the large triangle of **La Lizza**, just north of Piazza Matteotti; opposite San Domenico in the car park **alongside the stadium**; or **off the Viale Minzoni**, which loops around the northeast wall of the city. The last is free parking, at the others an attendant issues tickets by the day or half-day. Note that you cannot park around La Lizza on **Wednesday mornings** (8am–2pm), when the market takes place; offending cars are towed away.

Information

Siena's main **tourist office** is at Via di Città 43 (Mon–Fri 9am–12.30pm & 3.30–7pm; ☎0577/42.209), although this is largely an administrative office, and will refer you to the new but tiny **office** on the Campo, inside the travel agent *SETI* at no. 56 (☎0577/280.551). The latter can provide, in addition to the usual maps, a list of addresses offering accommodation in private houses (see below).

The offices provide a wide range of leaflets on the major sites, hotel lists for the town and province, and a handy booklet listing the festival and cultural events of the year. The most useful freebie, though, is the tourist office's superb, contoured **city map**; better than any of those on commercial sale, it is complete with a street key, a map of the environs, and details of hotel locations inside and outside the city.

Accommodation

Except during the Palio, finding a room is much less of a struggle than in Florence. As ever, though, it pays to phone ahead. If you haven't done so, and all the options listed below are booked solid, make your way to the **Cooperativa "Hotels Promotion"** booth (mid-March to Oct Mon–Sat 9am–8pm; rest of year Mon–Sat 9am–1pm & 3–7pm; ☎0577/288.084 or 288.480), opposite the church of San Domenico on Via Curtatone. The staff here are generally very helpful and will book you a room in any of the city's hotels.

For budget accommodation, call in at the **tourist office** at Piazza del Campo 56 (see above), which provides daily lists of **rooms** available in private houses, usually totalling around two hundred places. These are offered mainly to students, either at the university or on the numerous language and art courses held in the city, but some are willing to offer shorter lets. They're certainly worth a try if you're staying for a week or more; rates are around L25,000 per person a night (less for long-term lets), usually for a shared room.

Another option for **longer stays** is to arrange a let through one of the local **agriturismo agencies**; most rent out villas and farmhouses, as well as rooms or flats on farms, in the countryside around. Siena-based companies include: *Casa Club*, Piazza Indipendenza 2 (☎0577/44.041); *Casa Toscana*, Via dei Termini 85 (☎0577/270.279); *Sudcar*, Via Castelvecchio 3 (☎0577/40.522); and *Turismo Verde*, Via dei Termini 6 (☎0577/47.157). The tourist office has full lists of the dozen or so other agencies in the Siena region.

All hotels listed below are in the city proper: they include all the one- and two-star places and the best and most central of the three-stars, and are arranged in ascending order of price. The price codes are for a double room in the April to October season: expect to pay from ten to twenty percent less outside these times (the lower end of this range is more common), but at least fifty percent more during the Palio.

HOTELS

Bernini, Via della Sapienza 15 (☎0577/289.047). Inexpensive but rather pokey rooms on a street running downhill and east from San Domenico. ④.

Garibaldi, Via Giovanni Dupré 18 (☎0577/284.204). A good, no-nonsense *locanda*, sited above one of the city's better low-cost restaurants, just south of the Campo (off to the right-hand side of the Palazzo Pubblico). Midnight curfew. ④.

Lea, Viale XXIV Maggio 10 (☎0577/283.207). Modern hotel, a bit of a climb from the centre on the road looping around the Forte di Santa Barbara. ④.

La Perla, Via delle Terme 25 (☎0577/47.144). Regular *pensione*, in a very central location, two blocks north of the Campo on a street parallel to Banchi di Sopra. Curfew 1am. ④.

Piccolo Hotel Il Palio, Piazza del Sale 19 (☎0577/281.131). Good location in the earthier quarter of Terzo di Camollia, but the rooms are dark and cramped, and the staff less than welcoming on occasion. Something of a last resort. ④.

Santa Caterina, Via E.S. Piccolomini 7 (☎0577/221.105). Ten minutes' walk from the Campo, on the street that leads out of town from Porta Romana. ④.

Cannon d'Oro, Via Montanini 28 (☎0577/44.321). A stylish small two-star hotel tucked down an alleyway just beyond the point where Banchi di Sopra becomes Via Montanini. Friendly and immaculately maintained, this is the best choice among the central low-cost hotels. ⑤.

Centrale, Via Cecco Angiolieri 26 (☎0577/280.379). As the name suggests – a block north of the Campo; large rooms. ⑤.

Il Giardino, Via B. Peruzzi 43 (☎0577/220.090). Not the handiest of locations, outside the walls in the northeast of the city. A reasonable standby, though. ⑤.

Piccolo Hotel Etruria, Via Donzelle 1–3 (☎0577/288.088). Almost next door to the *Tre Donzelle* (see below), just off Banchi di Sotto. A neat little hotel, and very popular – two months' advance booking recommended in high season. ⑤.

La Toscana, Via Cecco Angiolieri 12 (☎0577/46.097). Atmospheric, central location on an alley behind Piazza Tolomei (on Banchi di Sopra). ⑤.

Tre Donzelle, Via Donzelle 5 (☎0577/280.358). Budget option right in the heart of town, just off Banchi di Sotto, north of the Campo. Good, clean rooms, but has a curfew at 12.30am and is often booked solid. ⑤.

Alex, Via G. Gigli 5 (☎0577/220.338). The most expensive two-star in town, way out east near Porta Pispini. ⑥.

Chiusarelli, Via Curtatone 9 (☎0577/280.562). A nice old villa, with a garden at the back, but it's on a busy street near the bus station, so this is probably not a first choice for light sleepers. ⑥.

Duomo, Via Stalloreggi 34 (☎0577/289.088). Probably the best of the city's three-star hotels, located south of the Duomo on the westward continuation of Via di Città. ⑥.

Palazzo Ravizza, Pian dei Mantellini 34 (☎0577/280.462). Quiet hotel in a pleasant backwater of town, near San Niccolò al Carmine. ⑥.

HOSTELS

Ostello della Gioventù "Guidoriccio", Via Fiorentina 89 (☎0577/52.212). The city youth hostel is located 2km northwest of the centre. Take bus #3, #10 or #15 from Piazza Gramsci and ask for "Ostello"; or, if you're coming from Florence, ask to be let off at "Lo Stellino", just after the Siena city sign. Dormitory beds and also several double rooms, with breakfast included; restaurant (meals L12,000) and bar. IYHF card required. Curfew 11pm. ①.

Casa del Pellegrino (Santuario di Santa Caterina), Via Camporegio 31 (☎0577/44.177). This old pilgrim hostel behind San Domenico offers single, double and triple rooms. The only couples they'll accept are married ones. Try to get a room in the annexe on Vicolo del Tiratoio, where there's no curfew, as they just give you the door key. ②.

Conservatori Femminili Riuniti, Via del Refugio 4 (☎0577/280.376). Women-only hostel. Off Via Roma in the Terzo di San Martino. It's advisable to phone in advance to check that it's operating. ①.

CAMPSITE

Campeggio Siena Colleverde, Strada di Scacciapensieri 37 (☎0577/280.044). Secure, well-maintained campsite, 2km out to the north; take bus #8 from Piazza Gramsci (last one runs at 10pm). Shop, bar and swimming pool. Open late March to mid-Nov.

The Campo

The Campo is in every sense the centre of Siena: the main streets lead into it, the Palio takes place around its perimeter, and in the evenings it is the natural place to gravitate towards, for visitors and residents alike. Four hundred years ago, Montaigne described it as the most beautiful square in the world – an assessment that still seems pretty just.

With its amphitheatre curve, the Campo appears an almost organic piece of city planning. In fact, when the Council of Nine began buying up land in 1293, they were adopting the only possible site – the old marketplace, which stood at the convergence of the city quarters but was a part of none. To build on it, it was necessary to construct an enormous buttress beneath the lower half of the square, where the Palazzo Pubblico was to be raised. The piazza itself was completed in 1349, when the council laid its nine segments of paving to commemorate their highly civic rule, and to pay homage to the Virgin – the folds of whose cloak it was intended to symbolise.

The stage-like Campo was from the start a focus of city life. As well as its continuing role as the city's marketplace – for livestock as well as produce – it was the scene of executions, bull fights, communal boxing matches, and, of course, the Palio. Saint Bernardino preached here, too, holding before him the monogram of Christ's name in Greek – IHS – which he urged the nobles to adopt in place of their own vainglorious coats of arms. A few did so (the monogram is to be seen on various palazzi), and it was adopted by the council on the facade of the Palazzo Pubblico, alongside the city's she-wolf symbol, itself a reference to Siena's legendary foundation by the sons of Remus.

Making no bones about its expression of civic pride, the **Palazzo Pubblico**, with its 320-foot bell tower, the **Torre del Mangia**, occupies virtually the entire south side of the Campo. Built largely in the first decade of the fourteenth century, the palace's lower level of arcading is a characteristic of Sienese Gothic, as are the columns separating the windows. The council were so pleased with this aspect of the design that they ordered its emulation on all other buildings on the square – and it was indeed gracefully adapted on the twelfth-century **Palazzo Sansedoni** across on the north side.

The other main exterior feature of the Palazzo Pubblico is the **Cappella di Piazza**, a stone loggia set at the base of the tower, which the council vowed to build at the end of the Black Death in 1348. Funds were slow to emerge, however, and by 1376, when the chief mason at the cathedral turned his hand to its design, new Florentine ideas were already making their influence felt. The final stage of construction, a century later, when the chapel was heightened and a canopy added, was wholly Renaissance in concept.

At the highest point of the Campo, the Renaissance again makes an appearance in the **Fonte Gaia** (Gay Fountain), designed and carved by Jacopo della Quercia in the early fifteenth century. Its panels are poor, nineteenth-century reproductions – the badly eroded originals can be seen on the rear loggia of the Palazzo Pubblico – but they give an idea of what was considered one of the city's masterpieces. Its conception – the Virgin at the centre, flanked by the Virtues – was a conscious emulation of the Lorenzetti frescoes on *Good and Bad Government* in the Palazzo Pubblico (see below). It took its name from festivities celebrating its inauguration: the climax of a long process that began in the 1340s, when masons managed to channel water into the square, and was completed some seventy years later, following the restoration of the republic.

The Museo Civico and Torre del Mangia

In the days of the *comune*, the lower floors of the Palazzo Pubblico housed the city accounts, and the upper storeys, as today, the council. Nowadays, the principal rooms have been converted into the Museo Civico, entered through the courtyard to the right of the Cappella di Piazza.

THE SIENA PALIO

"The Palio helps Siena to survive in its own mind. It is a metaphor for the continuity of the life of the people."

Roberto Barzanti, Siena MEP and former mayor.

The **Siena Palio** is the most exciting and spectacular festival event in Italy, a twice-yearly bareback horse race around the Campo, supported by days of preparation, pageantry and intrigue. It has been held since at least the thirteenth century, in honour – like almost everything in Siena – of the Virgin, and it remains a living tradition, felt and performed with an intensity that comes as a shock in these days of cosily preserved folklore. For days around the festivals there's a palpable air of rivalry, quite often breaking into violence amid the bragging celebration of victory by one or other of the *contrade*.

Except at times of war, the Palio has virtually always taken place. In 1798, for example, when the city was in chaos after an earthquake, the July Palio was cancelled but the August race took place. The following year, however, the Palio was again cancelled, due to political unrest: Sienese counter-revolutionaries took the opportunity to rise against the French-held fortress, and sacked the ghetto area of the city. In 1919, when half of Italy was in the throes of strikes and rioting, Siena's factions of the left and right agreed to defer such politics until after the Palio.

The Race

Originally the Palio followed a circuit through the town, but since the sixteenth century it has consisted of three laps of the **Campo**, around a track covered with sand and padded with mattresses in an attempt to minimise injury to horses and riders. Despite all probabilities no jockey has ever been killed.

The Palio is unlike any other horse race, with fortune playing the pre-eminent part. As there is only room for ten riders, each year the *contrade* have to draw lots to take part. The participants also draw lots both for the horses and the jockeys, and for starting positions in the race itself. The result of all this is that in any one year perhaps three or four *contrade* have a serious chance of victory; for those disadvantaged by poor horses or riders, and the seven *contrade* who aren't even taking part, the race becomes a vehicle for schemes, plots and general mayhem. Each *contrada* has its traditional rival, and ensuring that the other loses is as important as winning for oneself. The only rule of the race is that the jockeys cannot interfere with each others' reins; everything else is accepted and practised. The jockeys are professional outsiders, traditionally the *butteri*, or cowboys, of the Maremma area, who spend most of the race period living in fear of the threats of rival *contrade* and the suspicions of their own. They may be bribed to throw the race, or to whip a rival or his horse; *contrade* have been known to drug horses, and even to mount an ambush on a jockey making his way to the race. And it's the horse that wins – it doesn't matter if the jockey has been thrown en route to victory.

The Calendar

There are two annual Palios, held on **July 2** (Feast of the Visitation) and **August 16** (day after Feast of the Assumption), each of which is preceded by a fascinating sequence of events.

June 29/August 13. The year's horses are presented in the morning at the town hall and drawn by lot. At 7.15pm the first trial race is held in the Campo.

June 30/August 14. Further trial races at 9am and 7.45pm. The evening race is usually followed by a concert in the Campo.

July 1/August 15. Two more trial races at 9am and 7.45pm, followed by a street banquet and pretty much all-night revelry in each of the *contrade*. Restaurants also move their tables outside for these Palio nights.

July 2/August 16. The **day of the Palio** begins with a final **trial race** at 9am, then in the early afternoon each of the ten chosen *contrade* takes its horse to be blessed in its church – "Go little horse and return a winner" are the priest's words. It's worth trying to see one of these **horse blessings**, which are often preceded by an extraordinary struggle to get the animal up or down the entrance steps; if the horse defecates in church, it's taken as a good omen.

At around 5pm the town hall bell begins to ring and the **corteo storico**, a pageant of horses, riders and medieval-costumed officials, processes through the city to the Campo. The *corteo* includes *comparse* – symbolic groups of equerries, ensigns, pages and drummers – from each of the *contrade*, who perform various *sbandierata* (flag-twirling) and athletic feats in the square. They are preceded by officials of the *comune* of Siena and representatives from all the ancient towns and villages of the Sienese Republic, led by the standard-bearer of Montalcino, which offered refuge to the last republicans.

The **race itself** begins at 7.45pm in July, 7pm in August, and lasts for little more than ninety seconds of demented excitement. There's no PA system to tell you what's going on. At the start (in the northwest corner of the Campo) all the horses except one are penned between two ropes; the free one charges the group from behind, when his rivals least expect it, and the race is on. It's a hectic, violent and bizarre spectacle, and even after the circuit the jockeys don't stop at the finishing line but keep going at top speed out of the Campo, followed by a frenzied mass of supporters. Losers can be in danger of assault, especially if there are rumours of bribery and thrown races flying around.

The **palio** – a silk banner – is subsequently presented to the winning *contrada*, who then make their way to the church of **Provenzano** (in July) or the **Duomo** (in August) to give thanks. The younger *contrada* members spend the rest of the night and much of the subsequent week swaggering around the town celebrating their victory, even handing out celebratory sonnets. In the evening all members of the *contrada* hold a jubilant street banquet.

Palio Practicalities

It's not hard to get a view of any of the practice races or ceremonies, but for the Palio proper you need a little planning. Most ordinary spectators crowd for free into the centre of the Campo. For the **best view** you need to have found a position on the inner rail by 2pm (ideally at the start and finishing line), and to keep it for the next six hours. If you haven't done so, there's no great hurry, as you'll be able to see a certain amount from anywhere within the throng. Toilet and refreshment facilities are minimal, which is perhaps why so little drinking goes on among the crowd – for at least two hours you won't be able to leave the centre of the square. If you arrive **late in the day**, you might try making your way to Via Giovanni Dupré, behind the Palazzo Pubblico. From here, the police usually allow people into the centre of the square an hour or so before the race.

Tickets for grandstand/balcony seats cost from £80 to £200 and are sold out for months before the race. If you're interested in a seat for next year's event, contact *Palio Viaggi*, Piazza Gramsci 7 (☎ 0577/280.828).

Inevitably, **rooms** are extremely difficult to find at Palio time, and if you haven't booked, either reckon on staying up all night, or commuting in from a neighbouring town. If you're in Italy during Palio time, but can't reach Siena, get to a bar with a TV – the races are shown live and generally repeated on the evening news.

Off to the left of the courtyard there is separate access to the **Torre del Mangia** (daily from 10am, closing at 1.30pm Jan–March, 5pm March–April & Sept–Oct, 6pm May–June, 7pm July–Sept, 4pm Nov–Dec; L4000); climb up the 503 steps and you have fabulous and vertigo-inducing views across town and countryside. The tower takes its name from its first watchman – a spendthrift (*mangiaguadagni*) called Giovanni di Balduccio, commemorated by a statue in the courtyard. It was the last great project of the *comune* before the Black Death and exercised a highly civic function – its bell being rung to order the opening of the city gates at dawn, the break for lunch, the end of work at sunset and finally the closing of the city gates three hours later.

THE MUSEO CIVICO

The **Museo Civico** (March 15–Nov 15 & Dec 27–31 Mon–Sat 9.30am–7.45pm, Sun 9.30am–1.45pm; rest of year daily 9.30am–1.30pm; L6000) starts on the first floor of the Palazzo, with a rather miscellaneous picture gallery, whose nineteenth-century hunting scenes are enough to put you off *cinghiale* for the rest of a visit. You then wind round into the **Sala del Risorgimento**, painted with scenes commemorating Vittorio Emanuele, first king of Italy. These depict various battle campaigns, the king's coronation, and his earlier meeting with Garibaldi and his army on the road to Capua, where he refused Garibaldi governorship of the Neapolitan provinces – instead inflicting a decade of martial rule.

Medieval interest begins as you reach the **Sala dei Priori**, frescoed by Spinello Aretino in 1407 with episodes from the life of Pope Alexander III and in particular his conflict with Frederick Barbarossa, the German Holy Roman Emperor. The story is a complex one. The pope and emperor came into dispute following Barbarossa's destruction of Milan in 1162 – an event that caused the formation of a Lombard League of Italian states, supported by the Vatican and the Venetians. Barbarossa entered Rome in 1166, whereupon the pope fled to Venice (where he is depicted, disguised as a monk, but recognised by a French pilgrim). The scenes include a superbly realised naval conflict – in which the Venetians are shown capturing the emperor's son and the Germans desperately trying to rescue him – and the pope's eventual reconciliation with Barbarossa, in a procession led by the doge of Venice. For a fresco-by-fresco explanation, it's worth investing in the crackly telephone commentary.

Beyond, you progress to the palace chapel through the **Sala dei Cardinali**, graced by a beautiful *Madonna and Child* by Matteo di Giovanni, and the **Sala di Balia**, frescoed with classical scenes by Siena's Mannerist star, Beccafumi. The **Cappella del Consiglio** itself is fronted by a majestic wrought-iron screen by Jacopo della Quercia. The frescoes, *Stories from the Life of the Virgin*, with *Great Men of Antiquity* in the ante-chapel, are contemporary with those of the Sala dei Priori and were painted by Taddeo di Bartolo, the last major exponent of Siena's conservative Gothic style.

All of these works, though, are little more than a warm-up to the great **Sala del Mappamondo**. Taking its name from its now scarcely visible frescoed cosmology, the room was used for several centuries as the city's law court and contains some of the greatest of all Sienese frescoes, by **Simone Martini**.

On the west wall is Martini's fabulous *Maestà*, a painting of almost translucent colour, which was the *comune*'s first major commission for the palace. Its political dimension is apparent in the depiction of the Christ child holding a parchment inscribed with the city's motto of justice, and the inscription of two stanzas from Dante on the steps below the throne, warning that the Virgin will not intercede for those who betray her or oppress the poor. It is one of Martini's earliest known works, painted at the age of thirty in 1315, though he touched up parts of the picture, following damage from damp, six years later. The richly decorative style is archetypal Sienese Gothic and its arrangement makes a fascinating comparison with the *Maestà* by Duccio, with whom Martini perhaps trained, in the cathedral museum. Martini's great innovation was the use of a canopy and a frieze of medallions which frame and organise the figures – a sense of space and hint of perspective that suggest a knowledge of Giotto's work. Martini was to experiment further in this direction, perhaps with greater freedom, in his great cycle of the *Life of St Martin* in Assisi, painted a couple of years later.

The fresco on the opposite wall, the marvellous *Equestrian Portrait of Guidoriccio da Fogliano*, is a motif for medieval chivalric Siena, and was until recently also credited to Martini. Depicting the knight setting forth from his battle camp to besiege a walled hill town, it would, if it were by Simone, be accounted one of the earliest Italian portrait paintings. Art historians, however, have long puzzled over the anachronistic castles – much later in style than the painting's supposed date of 1328 – and in the mid-1980s further evidence was found when, during restoration, an earlier fresco was revealed underneath. The current state of the debate is confused, with a number of historians – led by the American Gordon Moran (whom the council for a while banned from the Palazzo Pubblico) – interpreting the *Guidoriccio* as a sixteenth-century fake, and others maintaining that it is a genuine Martini overpainted by subsequent restorers. The newly revealed fresco below the portrait, of two figures in front of a castle, is meanwhile variously attributed to Martini, Duccio and Pietro Lorenzetti.

The Palazzo Pubblico's most important and interesting frescoes are to be seen in the **Sale dei Nove** (Room of the Nine): Ambrogio Lorenzetti's *Allegories of Good and Bad Government*, commissioned in 1338 to remind the councillors of the effects of their duties. The walled city they depict is clearly Siena, along with its countryside and domains, and the paintings are full of details of medieval life: agriculture, craftwork, trade and building, even hawking and dancing. They form the first-known panorama in western art and show an innovative approach to the human figure – the beautiful, reclining Peace (Pax) in the *Good Government* hierarchy is based on a Roman sarcophagus still on display in the Palazzo Pubblico. An odd detail is that the "dancing maidens" in *Good Government* are probably young men – women dancing in public, according to the historian Jane Bridgeman, would have been too shocking in medieval Siena, and the figures' short hair and slit skirts were characteristic of professional male entertainers.

The moral theme of the frescoes is expressed in a complex iconography of allegorical virtues and figures. *Good Government*, painted on the more brightly lit walls (and better preserved), is dominated by a throned figure representing the *comune*, flanked by the Virtues and with Faith, Hope and Charity buzzing about his head. To the left, Justice (with Wisdom in the air above) dispenses rewards and punishments, while below her throne Concordia advises the Republic's councillors on their duties. *Bad Government* is ruled by the figure of Fear, whose scroll reads: "Because he looks for his own good in the world, he places justice beneath tyranny. So nobody walks this road without Fear: robbery thrives inside and outside the city gates". Ironically, within a decade of the frescoes' completion, Siena was engulfed by the Black Death – in which Lorenzetti and his family were among the victims – and the city was under tyrannical government. However, the paintings retained an impact on the citizenry – Saint Bernardino preached sermons on their themes.

The room adjoining the Sala dei Nove, the **Sala della Pace**, displays panel paintings from the thirteenth to fifteenth centuries, whose conservatism and strict formulaic composition points up the scale of Lorenzetti's achievement. Notable among them are Guido da Siena's *Madonna* (1260), for which Duccio repainted the Virgin's face, and a graphically violent *Massacre of the Innocents* by Matteo di Giovanni – one of four he completed in the city.

Upstairs, it is worth taking time for a visit to the rear **loggia**, where, you can crane your neck to see the current council chambers and examine the original panels of the **Fonte Gaia**. Their state of erosion makes it hard to appreciate that Jacopo della Quercia was rated by Vasari on a par with Donatello and Ghiberti, with whom he competed for the commission of the Florence Baptistery doors. Michelangelo, too, was an admirer, struck perhaps by the physicality evident here in the much-damaged *Expulsion of Adam and Eve*.

South of the Campo

Behind the Palazzo Pubblico the streets descend several levels to the **Piazza del Mercato**, now mainly a car park with a belvedere-like platform and a pleasant café-pizzeria at the end. You realise here how abruptly the town ends: buildings rise to the right and left for a few hundred metres along the ridges of the **Terzo di San Martino** and **Terzo di Città**, but in the centre the land drops away to a rural valley. These two southern ridges reveal a neighbourhood Siena surprisingly unbothered by tourism and terminate in churches founded by the medieval orders – the **Servites** in San Martino, the **Carmelites** and **Augustans** in Città. Each has an important museum too, respectively the state archives of the **Palazzo Piccolomini**, and the **Pinacoteca Nazionale**, Siena's main art gallery.

Terzo di San Martino

Marking the start of Banchi di Sotto, the main thoroughfare through Terzo di San Martino, is the **Loggia di Mercanzia**, designed as a tribune house for the merchants to do their deals. The structure was the result of extraordinary architectural indecision by the city authorities, the chronicles recording that "on one day they build in a certain way and on the following destroy and rebuild in a different manner". It was completed in 1421 in accordingly hesitant style, with Gothic niches for the saints carved by Vecchietta and Federighi, two of the city's leading Renaissance sculptors.

Following the Banchi di Sotto from here, you pass the more committed Renaissance buildings of the **Palazzo Piccolomini** and **Logge del Papa**, commissioned in the 1460s by Pope Pius II, the Sienese-born Aeneas Sylvius Piccolomini. Pius, whose life is depicted in the Duomo, was the city's great Renaissance patron and an indefatigable builder. This palace – one of three he built for his family in the city – was designed by Bernardo Rossellino, architect of Piccolomini's famous "new town" of Pienza (see p.356).

ARCHIVIO DI STATO

The Palazzo Piccolomini at Banchi di Sotto 52 now houses the **Archivio di Stato** (Mon–Fri 9am–1pm; free). Ask at the reception to be taken up to the **Sala di Congresso**, where the painted wooden covers of the *Tavolette di Biccherna*, the city's account books, and the tax records, the *Gabelle*, are displayed.

The paintings began with religious themes, but soon moved towards secular images of city life, providing a record of six centuries of Sienese history. The city is depicted frequently in the background, protected by the Virgin and mushrooming with towers – much as San Gimignano today. Early panels include several pictures of the *camerlingo* (a duty always filled by a Cistercian monk from San Galgano) doing the audits. Later ones move into specific events: victories over the Florentines; Pius's coronation as pope (1458); entrusting the city keys to the Virgin in the Duomo (1483); the demolition of the Spanish fortress (1552); the fall of Montalcino, the Sienese Republic's last stand (1559) and the entry to Siena of Cosimo I (1560); war with the Turks (1570); and subsequent Medicean events.

Some of the later panels were designed to be hung as pictures in the council offices, rather than mounted on the books; among the artists employed were Sano di Pietro and Ambrogio Lorenzetti, who painted the 1344 *Gabella* with a version of his *Good Government* fresco in the Palazzo Pubblico.

Also on view in the archives are various manuscript documents, among them the *comune*'s contract with Della Quercia for the Fonte Gaia and Charles V's granting of a permit to the university.

SOUTH TO THE PORTA ROMANA

Heading south along the **Via Salicotto** – which runs directly behind the Torre del Mangia, a couple of blocks from the Logge del Papa – you find yourself in the territory of the *Torre* (tower) *contrada*. They maintain a museum at no. 76 (daily except Thurs 10am–12.30pm; call custodian in advance ☎0577/222.555) and a fountain-square a few houses beyond. A famous sign on this street, posted in 1641, informs the citizens that the Florentine governor forbids prostitutes to practise in the neighbourhood.

Via Salicotto, or Via San Martino, will bring you into the *Valdimontone* (ram) *contrada*, whose museum, fountain and parish church are in Via di Valdimontone, alongside the massive brick church and campanile of **Santa Maria dei Servi**, the Servites' monastic base. The church (closed 12.30–3pm) is set in a quiet piazza, approached by a row of cypresses and shaded by a couple of spreading trees – good for a midday picnic or siesta.

The Renaissance-remodelled interior is most remarkable for two contrasting frescoes of the *Massacre of the Innocents*: a Gothic version by Pietro Lorenzetti, Ambrogio's brother, in the second chapel behind the high altar; and a Renaissance treatment by Matteo di Giovanni (1492) in the fifth chapel on the right. The popularity of this subject in the late fifteenth century may have been due to the much publicised massacre of Christian children by the Saracens at Otranto in 1480. This version is one of four in Siena by Matteo, and the most bizarre, with older children delighting in the gore from behind the background columns. Other paintings in the church, more in the city's restrained, decorative tradition, include fine altarpieces by Lippo Memmi – a pupil of Simone Martini – and Taddeo di Bartolo. Pietro Lorenzetti is further represented by frescoes of the *Life of the Baptist*, in the second chapel to the left of the high altar.

From Santa Maria dei Servi, you're just a hundred yards from the **Porta Romana**, the massively bastioned south gate of the city. The outer arch of this gate has a fragmentary fresco of the *Coronation of the Virgin*, begun by Taddeo di Bartolo and completed by Sano di Pietro. If you leave the city here, and turn left along the Via Girolamo Gigli, you could follow the walls north to the **Porta**

Pispini, another impressive example of defensive architecture and again flanked by a fresco of the Virgin, this time a Renaissance effort by Sodoma.

On the city side of the Porta Romana, the huge ex-convent of San Niccolò now houses the city's psychiatric hospital. Opposite is the little church of **Santuccio**, worth looking into for its seventeenth-century frescoes depicting the life of Saint Galgano (see p.342). In the adjacent sacristy, at Via Roma 71, are the premises of the **Società Esecutori di Pie Disposizioni** – the Society of Benevolent Works, formerly the Society of Flagellants. This medieval order, suppressed in the eighteenth century, and later refounded along more secular lines, maintains a small collection of artworks (Mon–Fri 9am–noon; ring for admission). It includes a triptych of the *Crucifixion, Flagellation and Burial of Christ* attributed to Duccio and a semicircular tablet, with wonderful Renaissance landscape, of *St Catherine of Siena leading the Pope back to Rome* (currently with the restorers).

Terzo di Città and the Pinacoteca Nazionale

Via di Città cuts across the top of the Campo through the oldest quarter of the city, the area around the cathedral. The street and its continuation, Via San Pietro, is fronted by some of Siena's finest private palazzi, including the Buonsignori, home to the Pinacoteca Nazionale, the city's main picture gallery.

The **Palazzo Chigi-Saracini** at Via di Città 82 is a Gothic beauty, with its curved facade and back courtyard. You can wander freely into the courtyard, though the palace itself is normally closed to the public. It houses the **Accademia Chigiana**, who sponsor music programmes throughout the year, and maintain a small art collection (open Mon–Fri by appointment, ☎0577/46.152), including works by Botticelli and Donatello. It was from this palace that the Sienese victory over the Florentines at Montaperti was announced, the town herald having watched the battle from the tower.

Almost opposite is a second **Palazzo Piccolomini**, this one built in 1460 by Rossellino, as a residence for Pius II's sister, Caterina. Known as the Piccolomini delle Papesse (of the she-popes), it is now headquarters of the Banca d'Italia.

THE PINACOTECA NAZIONALE

The **Pinacoteca Nazionale** (summer Mon 8.30am–2pm, Tues–Sat 8.30am–7pm, Sun 8.30am–1pm; winter Tues–Sat 8.30am–2pm, Sun 8.30am–1pm; L8000), housed appropriately in another fourteenth-century palace, is a roll of honour of Sienese Gothic painting, and if your interest has been spurred by the works by Martini in the Palazzo Pubblico or Duccio in the cathedral museum, a visit is the obvious next step. It's a fairly specialised branch of art history, perhaps, but the collection offers an unrivalled chance to assess the development of art in the city from the twelfth century through to late Renaissance Mannerism.

The main rooms are arranged in chronological order, starting on the second floor. On the **ground floor** are a handful of Renaissance works, best of which are Sodoma's frescoes from Sant'Agostino and panel of the *Deposition*, displaying his characteristic drama and delight in costume and landscape, and **Beccafumi's** *St Michael and the Fallen Angels* and *St Catherine Receiving the Stigmata*. Currently installed on the **first floor** is a reconstruction of the strange *Santuario del Romituzzo* – a chapel removed from Colle di Val d'Elsa, crowded with anatomical ex-voto objects placed to appeal for the relevant divine intercession.

Up on the **second floor, room 1** begins with the earliest known Sienese work, an altar frontal dated 1215 of *Christ Flanked by Angels*, with side panels depicting the discovery of the True Cross (see p.384 for this story). The figures are clearly Romanesque; the gold background – intricately patterned – was to be a standard motif of Sienese art over the next two centuries. The first identified Sienese painter, **Guido da Siena**, makes an appearance with the same subject in **room 2**, though the influences on his work – dated around 1280 – are distinctively Byzantine rather than Romanesque, incorporating studded jewels amid the gold. In some of his narrative panels – *Christ Entering Jerusalem, The Life of St Peter* and *St Clare Repelling a Saracen Attack* – his hand seems rather freer, though the colouring is limited to a few delicate shades.

Duccio di Buoninsegna (1260–1319), the dominant figure in early Sienese art, is represented with his school in **rooms 3 and 4**. Bernard Berenson considered Duccio the last great painter of antiquity, in contrast to Giotto, the first of the moderns. The painter's advances in composition are best assessed in his *Maestà*, in the cathedral museum. Here Duccio simply shows that he "fulfilled all that the medieval mind demanded of a painter", in the words of Berenson: his dual purpose being to explain Christianity to an illiterate audience and make a sacrifice (a rich artwork) to God. A rather more Gothic and expressive character is suggested by **Ugolino di Nerio**'s *Crucifixion* and *Madonna* in room 3.

Sienese art over the next century has its departures from Duccio – Lorenzetti's mastery of landscape and life in the *Good and Bad Government*, for example – but the patrons responsible for commissioning works generally wanted more of the same: decorative paintings, whose gold backgrounds made their subjects stand out in the gloom of medieval chapels. As well as specifying the required materials and composition, the Sienese patrons – bankers, guilds, religious orders – often named a particular painting as the style model.

The innovations of **Simone Martini** – the attention to framing and the introduction of a political dimension – are best seen in the Palazzo Pubblico. Here, he has just a single, highly conventional and beautiful *Madonna* in **room 6**. The works by the **Lorenzetti brothers**, Pietro and Ambrogio, in **rooms 7 and 8**, are, however, more rewarding. Pietro's include a marvellous *Risen Christ*, which could almost hold company with Masaccio, and the *Carmine Altarpiece*, whose predella has five skilful narrative scenes of the founding of the Carmelite order. Attributed to Ambrogio are two tiny panels, *City by the Sea* and *Castles by a Lake*, which the art historian Enzo Carli claims are the first ever "pure landscapes", without any religious purpose. They are thought to have been painted on a door, one above the other.

Moving through the fourteenth century, in **rooms 9 to 11** the major Sienese artists are **Bartolo di Fredi** (1353–1410) and his pupil **Taddeo di Bartolo** (1362–1422). Bartolo is best known for the New Testament frescoes in San Gimignano, whose mastery of narrative is reflected in his *Adoration of the Magi*. Taddeo, painter of the chapel in the Palazzo Pubblico, has archaic elements – reinserting huge areas of gold around a sketch of landscape – but makes strides in portraiture and renders one of the first pieces of dynamic action in the museum in his *Stoning of SS. Cosmas and Damian*.

These advances are taken a stage further in **Sassetta**'s *St Anthony Beaten by Devils* (no. 166), where Siena seems at last to be entering the mainstream of European Gothic art, and taking note of Florentine perspective. The influence of the patrons, however, is still prevalent in the mass of stereotyped images – gold again very much to the fore – by **Giovanni di Paolo** (1403–82), which fill most of **rooms 12 and 13**, and the exquisite Madonnas by **Sano di Pietro** (1406–81) and **Matteo di Giovanni** (1435–95) in **rooms 14 to 18**. It is astonishing to think that their Florentine contemporaries included Uccello and Leonardo.

The **third floor** of the museum – not always open – presents the self-contained **Collezione Spannocchi**, a miscellany of Italian, German and Flemish works, including a Dürer, a fine Lorenzo Lotto *Nativity*, Paris Bordone's perfect Renaissance *Annunciation*, and Sofonisba Anguissola's *Bernardo Campi Painting Sofonisba's Portrait* – the only painting in the museum by a woman artist. Anguissola, who is mentioned by Vasari as a child prodigy, painted at the height of Mannerism; this work is a neat little joke, the artist excelling in her portrait of Campi, but depicting *his* portrait of her as a flat, stereotyped image.

SANT'AGOSTINO AND A LOOP TO THE DUOMO

Keeping south from the Pinacoteca, you pass **Sant'Agostino**, closed for several years despite the presence of paintings by Perugino and Matteo di Giovanni. The church **piazza** is quite a pleasant space, with a kids' playground and usually a few football games in progress. Along with the Campo, this square was the site of vicious medieval football matches – *ballone*, as they called it – which were eventually displaced in the festival calendar by the Palio.

At no. 4 in the piazza is the **Accademia dei Fisiocritici** (Mon–Wed 9am–1pm & 3–6pm, Thurs 9am–1pm; free), housing museums of zoology, geology and mineralogy: all a bit pedestrian, though with a few oddities – like terracotta models of *funghi* – to entertain botanists. Continuing the theme, you could make your way across the piazza to the **Orto Botanico** (daily 8am–5pm, closes at noon on Sat; free), whose herbarium is stocked with every Tuscan species.

An interesting walk from Sant'Agostino is to loop along the **Via della Cerchia**, a route that takes you past some good neighbourhood restaurants (see p.316) to the church of **San Niccolò al Carmine**, in a predominantly student-populated section of the town. The church, a Renaissance rebuilding, contains a *Saint Michael* by Beccafumi, painted following the monks' rejection of his more intense Mannerist version in the Pinacoteca. If you follow the **Via del Fosso di San Ansano**, north of the Carmine square, you find yourself on a country lane, above terraced vineyards and allotments, before emerging at the *Selva* (wood) *contrada*'s square and church of **San Sebastiano**. Climb up the stepped Vicolo di San Girolamo from here and you come out at the Duomo.

Alternatively from Sant'Agostino, you could cut back to the Campo along **Via Giovanni Dupré**, where the *Onda* (wave) *contrada* have their base at no. 111. Their church is San Giuseppe, at the Sant'Agostino end of the street.

The Duomo and around

Few buildings reveal so much of a city's history and aspirations as Siena's **Duomo**. Complete to virtually its present size around 1215, it was subjected to constant plans for expansion throughout the city's years of medieval prosperity. A project at the beginning of the fourteenth century attempted to double its extent by building a baptistery on the slope below and using this as a foundation for a rebuilt nave, but the work ground to a halt as the walls gaped under the pressure.

For a while, the chapter pondered knocking down the whole building and starting from scratch to the principles of the day, but eventually they hit on a new scheme to re-orientate the cathedral instead, using the existing nave as a transept and building a **new nave** out towards the Campo. Again cracks appeared, and then in 1348 came the Black Death. With the population halved and funds suddenly cut off, the plan was abandoned once and for all. The extension still stands at the north end of the square – a vast structure that would have created the largest church in Italy outside Rome.

The other sides of the square continue the history of Sienese power, with the **Archbishop's Palace**, the **Palazzo del Magnifico** built for Petrucci in 1508, and the **Palazzo Granducale**, built later in the century for the Medici. The southwest side of the square, facing the cathedral facade, is occupied by the medieval **Ospedale di Santa Maria della Scala**, still in use as a hospital.

The Duomo

Despite all the grand abandoned plans, the Duomo, as its stands, is a delight (daily mid-March to mid-Sept 7.30am–7.30pm; mid-Sept to mid-March 10am–1pm & 2.30pm–dusk). Its style is an amazing conglomeration of Romanesque and Gothic, delineated by bands of black and white marble, an idea adapted from Pisa and Lucca – though here with much bolder and more extravagant effect. The lower part of the **facade** was in fact designed by the Pisan sculptor Giovanni Pisano, who from 1284 to 1296 created, with his workshop, much of its statuary – the philosophers, patriarchs and prophets, now removed to the cathedral museum and replaced by copies.

In the next century the **Campanile** was added, its windows multiplying at each level, as was the Gothic **rose window** above the doors. Thereafter work came to a complete halt, with the **mosaics** designed for the gables having to wait until the nineteenth century, when money was found to employ Venetian artists. Immediately above the central door, note Saint Bernardino's bronze monogram of Christ's name (see p.315).

THE PAVEMENT AND CHOIR STALLS

The facade's use of black and white decoration is echoed by the Duomo's great marble **pavement**, which begins with geometric patterns and a few scenes outside the church and takes off into a startling sequence of fifty-six figurative panels within. These were completed between 1349 and 1547, with virtually every artist who worked in the city trying his hand on a design. The earliest employ a simple *sgraffito* technique, which involved chiselling holes and lines in the marble then filling them in with pitch; later tableaux are considerably more ambitious, worked in multicoloured marble. Unfortunately the whole effect can only be seen from August 7 to August 22; the rest of the year most of the panels around the central octagon are rather unimaginatively kept under cardboard wraps.

The subjects chosen for the panels are a strange mix, incorporating biblical themes, secular commemorations and allegories. The most ordered part of the scheme are the ten *Sibyls* – mythic prophetesses who foretold the coming of Christ – on either side of the main aisle. Fashioned towards the end of the fifteenth century, when Sienese painters were still imprinting gold around their conventional Madonnas, they are totally Renaissance in spirit. Between them, in the central nave, are the much earlier *Sienese she-wolf enclosed by the republic's twelve cities* (a) and *Wheel of Fortune* (c), along with Pinturicchio's wilfully obscure *Allegory of Virtue* (b), a rocky island of serpents with a nude posed between a boat and the land.

Moving down the nave, the central hexagon is dominated by Domenico Beccafumi's *Stories from the Life of Elijah* (d). Beccafumi worked intermittently on the pavement from 1518 to 1547, also designing the vast friezes of *Moses Striking Water from a Rock and on Mount Sinai* (e – kept covered) and the *Sacrifice of Isaac* (f). To the left of the hexagon is a *Massacre of the Innocents* (g), almost inevitably the chosen subject of Matteo di Giovanni.

It's interesting also to note the **choir stalls**, in the context of the pavement. These use intarsia techniques of a superb standard and again were made between the mid-fourteenth and mid-sixteenth centuries.

THE PULPIT, SCULPTURES AND CHAPELS

The rest of the cathedral interior is equally arresting, with its zebra-stripe bands of marble, and the line of **pope's heads** – including several Sienese – set above the pillars. These stucco busts were added through the fifteenth and sixteenth centuries and many seem sculpted with an apparent eye to their perversity.

The greatest individual artistic treasure is the **pulpit**. This was completed by Nicola Pisano in 1268, soon after his pulpit for the Baptistery at Pisa, with help from his son Giovanni and Arnolfo di Cambio. The design of the panels duplicates those in Pisa, though they are executed with much greater detail and high relief. The carving's distance from the Byzantine world is perhaps best displayed by the statuette of the *Madonna*, whose breast is visible beneath the cloak for the first time in Italy, and by the *Last Judgement*, with its mastery of the human figure and organisation of space. Come equipped with plenty of coins.

Almost all the cathedral sculpture is of exceptional standard. Close by the pulpit in the north transept are Tino di Camaino's **Tomb of Cardinal Petroni** (1318), a prototype for Italian tomb architecture over the next century, and, in front, **Donatello's** bronze pavement **Tomb of Bishop Pecci** (1426). The Renaissance **High Altar** is flanked by superb candelabra-carrying angels by Beccafumi. In the **Piccolomini Altarpiece**, the young **Michelangelo** also makes an appearance. He was commissioned to carve the whole series of fifteen statues here but after completing saints Peter, Paul, Pius and Gregory in the lower niches he left for a more tempting contract in Florence – the *David*.

Further Renaissance sculptural highlights are to be seen in the two circular transept chapels. The **Cappella di San Giovanni Battista**, on the left, focuses on a bronze statue of the Baptist by Donatello, cast in 1457, a couple of years after his expressionist Mary Magdalene in Florence, whom the Baptist's stretched and emaciated face recalls. The **frescoes** in this chapel, with their delightful landscape detailing, are by **Pinturicchio**, of whom more opposite.

The **Cappella Chigi**, or Cappella del Voto, was the last major addition to the Duomo, the behest of Pope Alexander VII, another local boy, in 1659. It was designed by **Bernini** as a new setting for the *Madonna del Voto*, a thirteenth-century painting which commemorates the Sienese dedication of their city to the Virgin on the eve of the Battle of Montaperti. The style is pure Roman Baroque, with wild, semi-clad figures of Mary Magdalene and Saint Jerome, the latter holding his cross in ecstasy like some 1970s rock guitarist. Outside the chapel, the walls are covered in a mass of devotional objects – silver limbs and hearts, *contrada* scarves, even the odd Palio costume and crash helmet.

Note that you can buy a L7500 **combined ticket** for entry to the Libreria Piccolomini, the Museo dell'Opera del Duomo and the Oratorio di San Bernardino. It's valid for three days and is available at all three places.

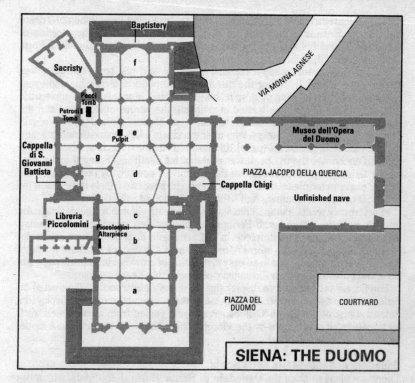

SIENA: THE DUOMO

LIBRERIA PICCOLOMINI

Midway along the nave, on the left, the entrance to the **Libreria Piccolomini** is signalled by Pinturicchio's brilliantly coloured fresco of the *Coronation of Pius II*. The library (daily summer 9am–7pm; winter 9am–5pm; L2000) is the one part of the Duomo that charges an admission fee – well worthwhile for the beautiful and evocative fresco cycle within.

The frescoes and library were commissioned by Francesco Piccolomini (who ruled for ten days as Pius III) to house the books of his uncle, **Aeneas Sylvius Piccolomini**, the pope **Pius II**. They do justice to the man whom Jacob Burckhardt adopted almost as a hero in his classic *The Civilisation of the Renaissance in Italy*. Pius, born at nearby Pienza in 1405, was the archetypal Renaissance man, writing poetry, a geography and the *Commentaries* – a deeply humanist work in which he enthuses over landscape, antiquity and architecture, and describes the languages, customs and industries encountered on his travels.

Pinturicchio's frescoes, painted with an equal love of nature and classical decor, and a keen sense of drama, commemorate the whole gamut of Pius's career. The cycle begins to the right of the window, with Aeneas's secular career as a diplomat: attending the council of Basle as secretary to an Italian bishop (panel 1); presenting himself as an envoy to James II of Scotland (panel 2); being crowned poet laureate by the Holy Roman Emperor, Frederick III (panel 3); and then representing Frederick on a visit to Pope Eugenius IV (panel 4). Aeneas subsequently returned to Italy and took orders, becoming first Bishop of Trieste and then of Siena, in which role he is depicted presiding over the meeting of Frederick III and his bride to be, Eleonora of Portugal, outside the city's Porta Camollia (panel 5).

In 1456 Aeneas was made a cardinal (panel 6) and just two years later was elected pope (panel 7), taking the title Pius II. In political terms, his eight-year rule was not a great papacy, despite his undoubted humanism and diplomatic skill, with much of the time wasted in crushing the barons of Romagna and the Marche. The crusade he called in 1456 at Mantua (panel 8) to regain Constantinople from the Turks – who took the city in 1453 – came to nothing, and the last picture of the series (panel 10) shows his death at Ancona, where he had come to encourage the troops. It was said that his death was brought on by grief for the failure to get the crusade off the ground, or possibly by poisoning by the troops, eager to terminate their pledge. Between these two panels is the event for which Siena most remembers him – the canonisation of Saint Catherine.

In art history terms, Pinturicchio stands as a relatively minor figure. Originally from Perugia, he worked with Perugino in the Sistine Chapel before beginning this, his acknowledged masterpiece, in 1502. His skills lie in the brilliant colouring, the naturalistic detail – the storm scene in Aeneas's departure for Basle is one of the first in western art – and in an easy disposition of crowds, ideal for the pageants here, and enhanced by their illusionistic placing within a series of loggias.

The library is now used to display the cathedral's **choirbooks**, illuminated by Sano di Pietro and other Sienese Gothics. At the centre of the room is displayed a Roman statue of the **Three Graces**, supposedly copied from a lost Greek work by Praxiteles. It was bought by the Piccolomini nephew and was used as a model by Pinturicchio and Raphael.

Ospedale di Santa Maria della Scala

There are plans to close the **Ospedale di Santa Maria della Scala**, which has seen hospital use for some eight hundred years, listing among its charitable workers both saints Catherine and Bernardino. It will be a shame, for the functioning building gives a sense of purpose to the cathedral square, which won't be matched by its intended use as a museum for archaeological and other collections.

At present, the hospital offers quite a range of artistic sights, though the most interesting – the fifteenth-century frescoes in its **Sala del Pellegrinaio** – are in a ward that's still in use and open only by appointment (Mon & Fri 8.30am–1pm; ☎0577/299.410). If you are staying a few days in the city, it is a visit well worth making. The frescoes, painted from 1440 to 1447, are very rare in depicting entirely secular scenes, including the building of the hospital, caring for the sick and feeding the poor. The best are those by Domenico di Bartolo, showing the influence of Masaccio's Brancacci Chapel frescoes in their mastery of the human figure, and perhaps recalling the Flemish painters in their naturalistic detailing of everyday life.

A number of the medieval confraternities maintained oratories in the basement vaults of the hospital, and one of these, the **Oratorio della Società Esecutori Pie Disposizioni**, at no. 1 in the piazza, can be visited by appointment (Mon–Sat 9am–noon; ☎0577/220.400 or 299.410). Its interest lies principally in its association with Saint Bernardino, who joined the order as a young man and was said to have received his monastic call in front of a fourteenth-century crucifix still on display. Terracotta statues of Bernardino and Catherine flank the cross.

At the centre of the hospital facade is the entrance to the **church of Santa Maria della Scala**, remodelled in the fifteenth century. It houses a marvellous bronze *Risen Christ* by Vecchietta, its features so gaunt the veins show through the skin. Vecchietta clearly understood and absorbed the new approach of Donatello, and several art historians consider this the finest Renaissance sculpture in the city. A brand-new **Museo Archeologico** should be open in the building immediately to the left of the hospital (Tues–Sat 9am–2pm & Sun 9am–1pm; L4000).

The Baptistery

The cathedral **Baptistery** (9am–1pm & 3–6pm; free) is unusual in being placed beneath the main building. It is an essential visit, containing one of the city's great Renaissance works – a hexagonal font with scenes illustrating the Baptist's life. To reach it, follow the flight of steps behind the Duomo, past the Cripta delle Statue museum – not worth the opportunistic entrance charge.

The cathedral chapter responsible for the baptistery **font** must have had a good sense of what was happening in Florence at the time for they managed to commission panels by **Ghiberti** (*Baptism of Christ* and *John in Prison*) and **Donatello** (*Herod's Feast*), as well as by the local sculptor **Jacopo della Quercia** (*The Angel Announcing the Baptist's Birth*). Donatello's scene, in particular, is a superb piece of drama, with Herod and his cronies recoiling at the appearance of the Baptist's head. Donatello was also responsible for two of the corner angels (the one with a chalice and the one with hands placed as if holding a football) and for two further angels on the tabernacle above (those dancing and playing trumpet). Once again, take plenty of coins for illumination.

In future years the baptistery may also offer some impressive **frescoes**, for its vaults were painted by **Vecchietta** in the mid-fifteenth century with scenes from the life of Christ. These were drastically repainted at the end of the last century, though, and restorers have only just started the process of trying to strip away the modern paint.

Museo dell'Opera del Duomo

After the Museo Civico, the best art in Siena is to be seen in the **Museo dell'Opera del Duomo** (daily 9am–7.30pm; L5000), which occupies the projected, re-orientated nave. An additional bonus to a visit is the chance to climb to the top of the **"new nave"**, an arguably better vantage point than the Torre di Mangia.

Downstairs, in the Galleria delle Statue, the statuary by **Giovanni Pisano** (1250–1314) seems a little bizarre when displayed at eye level: the huge, elongated, twisting figures are quite obviously adjusted to take account of the original viewing position. They are totally Gothic in conception, and for all their subject matter – philosophers from antiquity are represented alongside Old Testament prophets and other characters – show little of his father Nicola's experiment with classical forms on the cathedral pulpit. In marked contrast is Donatello's ochre-coloured *Madonna and Child*, a delicate piece in the centre of the room, alongside a bas relief by Jacopo della Quercia.

On the first floor a curator admits you to the **Sala di Duccio**, curtained and carefully lit to display the artist's celebrated **Maestà**. On its completion in 1311 this painting was taken in a ceremonial procession from Duccio's studio around the Campo and then to a special Mass in the Duomo; everything in the city was closed and virtually the entire population attended. This is one of the superlative works of Sienese art – its iconic, Byzantine spirituality accentuated by Duccio's flowing composition and a new attention to narrative detail in the panels of the predella and reverse of the altarpiece, both now displayed to its side.

The *Maestà* – the Virgin as Queen of Heaven – was a Sienese invention, designed as a "sacrifice" to the Virgin, the city's patroness, a quality emphasised by the lavish use of gold. Duccio's rendering of the theme was essentially the prototype for the next three centuries of Sienese painters; his achievement, as Bernard Berenson put it, was to add "the drama of light to that of movement and expression" and a realisation of the space in which action takes place.

This quality is best observed in the narrative panels, most of which have been gathered here after the altarpiece's dismemberment in the eighteenth century (only two panels are missing: one is in Washington, the other in London's National Gallery). One of the most effective is the *Betrayal of Judas*, where trees relieve the main group of figures – Christ is "pointed" by the central tree – and rows of lances break the golden sky. The *Descent from the Cross*, too, is a marvellously composed image.

In the room behind the Sala is a fascinating nineteenth-century drawing of the cathedral pavement, providing a unified view impossible on the spot. But for the art that followed Duccio, and some that preceded, you need to make your way upstairs. Here, past the **Sala di Tesoro**, featuring the head of Saint Galgano amid its reliquaries, you reach the **Sala della Madonna dagli Occhi Grossi**. The work that gives its name to this room is the cathedral's original, pre-Duccio altarpiece – a stark, haunting Byzantine icon (Madonna of the Big Eyes) in the centre of the room. Around it are grouped a fine array of panels, including works by Simone Martini, Pietro Lorenzetti and Sano di Pietro.

The **stairs to the new nave** – known as the **Scala del Falciatore** – are reached through a small door in the room beyond signed *Ingresso al Panorama*. Beyond, a balcony offers superb views over the city and surrounding hills: clamber the stairs of the narrow staircase midway up for still more angles on the panorama.

The Terzo di Camollia and beyond

The northern **Terzo di Camollia** is flanked, to west and east, by the churches of the most important medieval orders, the **Dominicans** and **Franciscans**, vast brick piles which rear above the city's outer ridges. Each has an important association with Siena's major saints, the former with **Catherine**, the latter with **Bernardino**. Bernardino's pilgrim trail also leads out of the city to the north, to the **Osservanza** monastery, his principal retreat.

The central part of the Camollia takes in the main thoroughfare of **Banchi di Sopra**, the base of the **Monte dei Paschi** – long the city's financial power. North from here, you move into a quiet residential quarter, all the more pleasant for its lack of specific sights or visitors. To the west, interestingly detached from the old city, is the **Fortress**.

San Domenico ... and Saint Catherine of Siena

The Dominicans founded their monastery in the city in 1125. Its church, **San Domenico**, is a vast, largely Gothic building, typical of the austerity of this militaristic order. The **Catherine association** is immediately asserted. On the right of the entrance is a kind of raised chapel, with a contemporary portrait of her by her friend Andrea Vanni; below are steps and a niche, where she received the stigmata. The saint's own chapel, on the south side of the church, has melodramatic frescoes of her in ecstasy, by Sodoma, and a reliquary containing her head.

Other notable chapels are the first of the right transept (a Matteo di Giovanni *Madonna*), the first of the left transept (a Sano di Pietro *Madonna* and a *St Barbara* and *Epiphany* by Matteo) and the fourth chapel of the right nave (with a detached fresco by Pietro Lorenzetti).

Saint Catherine's family house, where she lived as a Dominican tertiary – of the order but not resident – is a short distance away to the south. Known as the **Casa e Santuario di Santa Caterina** (daily 9am–12.30pm & 3.30–6pm; free), its entrance is on Via Benincasa, behind Via Santa Caterina. The building has been much adapted, with a Renaissance loggia and a series of oratories – one on the site of her cell. The paintings here are mostly unexceptional Baroque canvases but it is the life that is important: an extraordinary career that made her Italy's patron saint and the first ever canonised woman.

Born Caterina Benincasa on March 25, 1347 – Annunciation Day – she had her first visions aged five and took the veil at age sixteen, against strong family opposition. She spent three very strict years in silent contemplation, before experiencing a mystical "Night Obscure". Thereafter she went out into the turbulent, post-Black Death city, devoting herself to the poor and sick, and finally turning her hand to politics. She prevented Siena and Pisa joining Florence in rising against Pope Urban V, then absent in Avignon, and proceeded to bring him back to Rome. It was a fulfilment of the ultimate Dominican ideal – a union of the practical and mystical life. Catherine returned to Siena to a life of contemplation, visions and stigmata, though retaining a political role in her attempts to reconcile the later schism between the popes and anti-popes. She died in 1380 and was canonised by Pius II (as depicted in the cathedral) in 1460.

Close by the Santuario are the church of **Santa Caterina**, home of the *Oca* (goose) *contrada* – known as "the infamous ones" from their record number of Palio victories – and the best preserved of Siena's several fountains, the **Fonte Branda**. Aided by the fountain's reliable water supply, this part of the city was an area for tanneries into the present century. The fountain also features in Sienese folklore as the haunt of werewolves, who would throw themselves into the water at dawn to return to human form.

Monte dei Paschi di Siena

Between the two monastic churches lies the heart of business Siena, the **Piazza Salimbeni**, whose three interlocking palazzi have formed, since the fifteenth century, the head office of the **Monte dei Paschi di Siena**.

Banking was at the heart of medieval Sienese wealth, the town capitalising on its position on the "French road" between Rome and northwest Europe, and the main road between Rome and Florence and Bologna. Sienese banking families go back to the twelfth century and by the end of the thirteenth they were trading widely in France, Germany, Flanders, England and along the Danube, where they maintained networks of corresponding dealers. Activity declined after the Black Death but in the fifteenth century the Republic set up the *Monte* as a lending and charitable institution, in large part to combat the abuses of usury. It consolidated its role under Medici rule and slowly moved into more strictly banking activities. In the present century it merged with other Tuscan and Umbrian banks to become one of the key financial institutions in Italy.

There is some historical interest in the exteriors of the bank's palazzi: the **Spannocchi**, on the right, was the first great Renaissance palace built in Siena (1473) and the prototype for the Palazzo Strozzi in Florence, while the **Salimbeni**, in the centre, was a last flourish of Gothicism. However, to appreciate the role of the *Monte* in Siena you need to tour the building. The interest is twofold. In 1972, Pierluigi Spadolino undertook a **radical restructuring** of the buildings, encasing the interior medieval and Renaissance features within a superbly blended ultra-modern and hi-tech framework. This is a sight in itself and it provides a wonderful showcase for the bank's **art collection** – most of which is housed in the deconsecrated church of San Donato, linked by an underground passage with the main palazzi. The paintings here include some of the finest Gothic works in Siena, among them an exquisitely coloured *Madonna* by Giovanni di Paolo, a *Deposition* by Sano di Pietro, and a *Crucifixion* by Pietro Lorenzetti. Also displayed are a series of paintings depicting the Palio and its sixteenth-century bullfighting precedent in the Campo.

At certain times of year, the bank publicly exhibits its art collections, but you generally need to make an **appointment** a day in advance (☎0577/234.595 or 294.758). This is quite straightforward: ask for a tour of the *Raccolta della Sede Storica*. You will be shown the archives and major halls of the bank, as well as the paintings, and the visit ends with a trip up to the tower for a view over the Campo.

OFF PIAZZA SALIMBENI: THE BIBLIOTECA COMUNALE

The narrow medieval **Costa dell'Incrociata** leads west from Piazza Salimbeni into the Via della Sapienza, where at no. 1 is the **Biblioteca Comunale** (Mon–Fri 9am–8pm, Sat 9am–2pm; free). This is essentially a research library, though it has a small display of treasures – including Saint Catherine's letters, Sangallo's architectural notebook and an edition of Dante illuminated by Botticelli.

North to Porta Camollia – and the fortress

Heading north from the Piazza Salimbeni, Banchi di Sopra changes name to **Via Montanini** and then **Via di Camollia**, which run through the less monumental parts of the Terzo di Camollia, good for regular shopping and largely untouristed bars and restaurants.

Two churches are worth a brief look on this street. **Santa Maria delle Nevi** contains a famous altarpiece – *Our Lady of the Snows* – by Matteo di Giovanni (1477), while **San Bartolomeo** fronts one of the nicest *contrada* squares in the city, home of the *Istrici* (porcupine); the *contrada* has its museum at Via Camollia 89. At the end of the street is the Renaissance **Porta Camollia**, inscribed on its outer arch "Siena opens her heart to you wider than this gate". It was here that a vastly superior Florentine force was put to flight in 1526, following the traditional Sienese appeal to the Virgin.

A short distance east of Banchi di Sopra – reached by a circuitous network of alleys – is another of the city fountains, the **Fonte Nuova**. A further, highly picturesque fountain, the **Fonte Ovile**, is to be seen outside the Porta Ovile, a hundred metres or so beyond. Both were built at the end of the twelfth century. Near Fonte Nuova, in Via Vallerozzi, is the church of **San Rocco**, home of the *Lupa* (she-wolf) *contrada*; their museum is at no. 71.

Away to the west, behind Santo Stefano church, the gardens of **La Lizza** – taken over on Wednesdays by the town market – lead up to the walls of the **Forte di Santa Barbara** (free access). The fortress was built initially by Charles V after the siege of 1554–55, but subsequently torn down by the people, and had to be rebuilt by Cosimo I, who then moved his troops into the garrison. Its Medicean walls resemble the walls of Lucca, designed by the same architect. Occasional summer concerts are held within the fort, which is also a permanent home to the wine collections and bar of the *Enoteca Italiana* (see p.317).

San Francesco ... and Saint Bernardino

Saint Bernardino, born in the year of Catherine's death, began his preaching life at the monastic church of **San Francesco**, across the city to the east. A huge, hall-like structure, like that of the Dominicans, it has been heavily restored after damage by fire and subsequent use as a barracks. Its remaining artworks include fragmentary frescoes by the Lorenzetti brothers in the first and third chapels of the north transept (the latter depicting the *Martyrdom of Franciscans at Ceuta* in Morocco) and a *Madonna and Child* by Andrea Vanni in the south transept. The Renaissance **cloisters** now house the law departments of the university.

In the piazza to the right, adjoining the cloisters, is the **Oratorio di San Bernardino**, now opened after years of restoration (April–Nov Mon–Sat 10.30am–1.30pm & 3–5.30pm; Dec–April Mon–Sat 10.30am–1.30pm; L2000). The best artworks here are in the upper chapel: fourteen large frescoes by Sodoma, Beccafumi and Girolamo del Pacchia on the *Life of the Virgin*, painted between 1496 and 1518 when the former pair were Siena's leading painters. In the lower chapel are seventeenth-century scenes of the **saint's life**, which was taken up by incessant travel throughout Italy, preaching against usury, denouncing the political strife between the Italian city states and urging his audience to look for inspiration to the monogram of Christ. His actual political influence was fairly marginal but he was canonised within six years of his death in 1444, and remains one of the most famous of all Italian preachers. His dictum on rhetoric – "make it clear, short and to the point" – was rewarded in the 1980s with his adoption as the patron saint of advertising.

If your interest in the saint extends to a short pilgrimage, take bus #12 from Piazza Matteotti to Madonnina Rossa (10–15min), from where it's a short walk uphill to the monastery of **L'Osservanza** (daily 9am–1pm & 4–7pm). This was founded by Bernardino in 1423, in an attempt to restore the original Franciscan rule, by then corrupted in the cities. Much rebuilt since, the monastery has a small museum and a largely Renaissance church, whose features include an Andrea della Robbia *Annunciation* and a triptych by Sano di Pietro.

Eating, drinking, nightlife and events

Siena feels distinctly provincial after Florence. The main action of an evening is the **passeggiata** from Piazza Matteotti along Banchi di Sopra to the Campo – and there's not much in the way of nightlife to follow. For most visitors, though, the **Campo**, the city's universal gathering place, provides diversion enough, while the presence of the university ensures a bit of life in the bars, as well as a cluster of cheaper *trattorie* alongside the restaurants.

Restaurants

Siena used to have a poor reputation for **restaurants** but over the last few years things have looked up, with a range of imaginative *osterie* opening up and a general hike in standards. The only place you need surrender gastronomic ideals is for a meal out in the Campo: the posh restaurant here, *Il Campo*, isn't worth the money, leaving a choice of routine though reasonably priced pizzerias. For cheaper meals, you'll generally do best walking out a little from the centre, west towards San Niccolò al Carmine, or north towards the Porta Camollia.

Local specialities include *pici* (noodle-like pasta with toasted breadcrumbs), *salsicce secche* (dried sausages), *finocchiona* (minced pork flavoured with fennel), *capolocci* (spiced loin of pork), *pappa col pomodoro* (bread and tomato soup), *tortino di carciofi* (artichoke omelette) and *fagioli all'uccelletto* (bean and sausage stew). The city is also famous for a whole range of **cakes and biscuits**, including the ubiquitous *panforte*, a dense and delicious wedge of nuts, fruit and honey that originated with pilgrimage journeys, *cavallucci* (aniseed, nut and spice biscuits), *copate* (nougat wafers) and rich, almond *ricciarelli* biscuits.

UNDER L30,000

Mensa Universitaria, Via Sant'Agata 1 (daily noon–2pm & 6.45–9pm). The university canteen has full meals for L8000, pasta dishes for a lot less. It's a bit hidden away, on the continuation of Via G. Duprè, below the church of Sant'Agostino. Closed Aug.

Il Barbero, Piazza del Campo 80–81 (daily noon–2.30pm & 7–10pm). An excellent value if rather characterless self-service, bang on the Campo.

Buca di San Pietro, Vicolo di San Pietro 2. On a stepped alley leading to the Campo, this is a very popular place, though its atmosphere is often better than the food. Pizzas from L5000; full meals from L15,000. Also takeaway pizza. Closed Sun.

Ristorante Garibaldi, Via Giovanni Duprè 18. A cheap and filling restaurant sited below a *locanda*, just south of the Campo. Full meals from L16,000. Closed Sat.

La Nuova Grotta del Gallo Nero, Via del Porrione 65–67. Lively and inexpensive pizzeria and restaurant. Full meals – including some genuine specialities – from around L20,000. Stays open till 1am. Closed Mon.

Pizzeria Carlo e Franca, Via di Pantaneto 121b. Café-like place with generous pizza and pasta at very regular prices.

Pizzeria San Marco, Via San Marco 48 (closed Sun); **La Vecchia Osteria**, Via San Marco 8 (closed Tues); **La Mantellina**, Piana dei Mantellini 2 (closed Mon). Three local eateries in an untouristed part of the city behind San Niccolò al Carmine. From L17,000.

La Torre, Via Salicotto 7. Friendly place off the Campo that maintains a real local trattoria feel. All types of home-made pasta, excellent grills. No menu, so follow the advice of the waiters. Very popular, with many regulars, so call in earlier in the day to reserve one of the ten tables. L20,000. Closed Thurs.

Turiddo, Via Stalloreggi 62 (☎0577/282.121). Good homecooking, fine pizzas, and good views of the Duomo from a panoramic back terrace. On the southern continuation of Via di Città, south of the Duomo.

OVER L30,000

Cane e Gatto, Via Pagliaresi 6 (☎0577/220.751). Don't be put off by the lack of any menu: this friendly restaurant serves superb Tuscan *cucina nuova*, featuring seven courses on its *menù degustazione*. This will cost you around L50,000, but if you'd rather pay less, ask to take just a selection of dishes. Via Pagliaresi is southeast of the Campo, off Via di Pantaneto. Closed Thurs.

Osteria Castelvecchio, 65 Via di Castelvecchio (☎0577/49.586). Adventurous, health-conscious *osteria* which could be a good bet for vegetarians; it features a *menù bilogica* every Wednesday night. Sited off Via San Pietro, near the Pinacoteca Nazionale. Closed Tues.

Da Cice, Via S. Pietro 32 (☎0577/288.026). Excellent service and an interesting local menu.

Da Dino, Via Casato di Sopra 73–75 (☎0577/289.036). Imaginative variations on the Tuscan standards and an unusually wide selection of vegetable dishes, but far from being the best of Siena's better restaurants. Full meals from L30,000. Closed Fri.

Osteria Le Logge, Via del Porrione 33 (☎0577/48.013). The best restaurant in central Siena, in an old cabinet-lined *farmacia* by the Logge del Papa. Excellent pasta, some unusual *secondi*, and just about the nicest staff in Tuscany. L50,000 for a full meal. Closed Sun.

Mariotti da Mugolone, Via dei Pellegrini 8–12 (☎0577/283.235). On a good night you get perfectly cooked, classic Sienese dishes, but reports suggest that it's often off-form nowadays. L40,000. Closed Thurs.

Ai Marsali, Via del Castoro 3 (☎0577/47.154). One of the best places to splurge in Siena. Service can be shaky, but food is generally excellent; expect to pay around L40,000 – and be sure to book.

Il Medioevo, Via dei Rossi 40 (☎0577/280.315). A beautiful medieval building, near Piazza Tolomei, and Roman proprietor add a bit of style to this occasionally erratic restaurant. Superb cakes. L40,000 for the works. Closed Thurs.

Nello, Via del Porrione 28–30. Good quality Tuscan food and exceptionally friendly service. Around L40,000 per head.

Picnics, snacks and ice cream

It's an easy matter to put together your own picnic, allowing a very cheap meal in the Campo or other squares – Piazza Santa Maria dei Servi is a nice spot. There is **pizza by weight** just off the Campo at *Buca di San Pietro* (see opposite) and at the bar at Via delle Terme 10, and an extravagantly stocked **deli**, the *Pizzicheria Morbidi*, at Banchi di Sotto 27.

Nearby **bakeries** include the *Forno dei Galli* at Via dei Termini 45, with a fabulous selection of breads, *cantuccini* biscuits and pastas, and its own *panforte*, and the *Forno Indipendenza* at Piazza Indipendenza 27 – a block northwest of the Campo. The market building south of the Campo in Piazza del Mercato is also good for picnic provisions, while Wednesday mornings see a full-scale open-air **market** – with food and clothing stalls – sprawl across La Lizza, below the fortress.

Among the best **bars for snacks** are *Antico Sghenghero* at Via di Città 13, which has treats like *porcini* vol-au-vents and *tartufi* (truffle) rolls, and the main branch of *Nannini* at Banchi di Sopra 22–24, a constant call for locals with perhaps the largest range of sweet and savoury snacks. **Ice cream** is bought by most Sienese at one or other end of the *passeggiata* – either at the *Nannini Gelateria*, at the Piazza Matteotti end of Banchi di Sopra, or at *Gelateria Artigiani*, just off the Campo at the corner of Via di Città and Via dei Pellegrini.

Panforte is best bought fresh by the *etto* in any of the bakeries or the *pasticcerie* along Banchi di Sopra; the gift-packaged slabs aren't so good.

Bars

For a drink, there are pleasant, **neighbourhood bars** in most *contrade* – Via del Porrione, southeast of the Campo, has several, as does Via Camollia, north of Piazza Matteotti. In the **Campo**, *Bar Fonte Gaia* stays open later than most.

On a more sedate note, the **Enoteca** inside the Forte di Santa Barbara has a cellar exhibiting every single Italian wine, and a bar – at its best early evening – where you can order a glass of any wine costing under L13,000 a bottle, or any bottle from the range. At various times of year the Enoteca organises special *incontri* with particular wine regions. It also hosts occasional weekend **discos**.

For **live music**, there's *L'Officina* (every evening 7pm–2am) at Piazza del Sale 3a, at the north end of the Terzo di Camollia, which offers a hundred bottled beers and six on tap, along with *crostini* and *foccaccine* snacks. There are live bands on occasion, too, at the **disco-bar** *Al Cambio*, south of the Campo at Via di Pantaneto 48. And, lastly, if you want to watch the Sunday evening Italian league

football on TV, make your way to *Video Bar* at Via di Pantaneto 85, where you can have beer and pizza in front of the big screen.

Events

Posters for **city events** are to be seen around Piazza Matteotti or on the stepped alley leading out of Piazza del Mercato to Via di Salicotto. The day's **concerts, films and activities** are also advertised in the Siena supplement of *La Nazione* newspaper, and major cultural events are also detailed in the tourist office's free pamphlet. There are just three in-town **clubs** and dancefloors: *Al Cambio*, Via di Pantaneto 48; *Gallery*, Via di Pantaneto 13; and *L'Officina*, Piazza del Sale 3.

Classical music tastes are the most likely to be rewarded, as the *Monte dei Paschi* and *Accademia Chigiana* sponsor impressive concerts throughout the year. The most prestigious – often featuring a major opera production – are held in the period around the *Settimana Musicale Senese* (the third week of Aug). Details can be obtained from the tourist office or the Accademia Chigiana at Via di Città 89 (☎0577/46.152); tickets costing from L12,000 to L30,000 are available from *Viaggi SETI* at Piazza del Campo 56.

Other cultural events include **Siena Jazz**, a tuition fortnight in the last week of July and first week of August, which usually includes a few public sessions, and a range of concerts – mostly rock and jazz – in the communist party's summer **Festa dell'Unità**.

Listings

Banks and currency exchange Banks are concentrated along Banchi di Sopra, north of the Campo: the *Banca Toscana*, at the corner of Piazza Tolomei, is worth a visit for its building alone, and there's an automatic exchange machine and computer currency display in the window of the *Monte dei Paschi* at no. 92. The *Hotel Coop* opposite San Domenico, *Viaggi SETI* at Piazza del Campo 56, and the train station ticket office also operate cash and travellers' cheque exchange. The most central option is the new *Exact* in Via di Città; although its commission is high, it has the longest opening hours in the city (daily 8.30am–11pm).

Books and newspapers English-language books – novels plus a fair selection of books on Siena and Tuscany – are to be found at the *Libreria Senese*, Via di Città 94, *Feltrinelli*, Banchi di Sopra 66, and *Bassi*, Via di Città 6–8. *Bassi* also stocks British and American newspapers (the *Guardian* European edition and *International Herald Tribune* arrive in the afternoon) and magazines.

Bus enquiries *TRA–IN*, Piazza Gramsci (☎0577/204.111), or at Piazza San Domenico for out of town services.

Car and scooter rental Try *Autonoleggi Intercar Eurodrive* at Via San Marco 96 (☎0577/41.848), who hire both – they share office space with *Hertz*; *Avis*, Via Simone Martini 36 (☎0577/270.305); *Europe Car*, Viale Cavour 51 (☎0577/41.437).

Language courses The Sienese are reputed to speak the purest Italian in the country. To study here, contact the *Italian Language and Culture School for Foreigners*, Piazzetta Grassi 46 (☎0577/280.695).

Lost property Comune di Siena, Casato di Sotto 23 (Mon–Sat 9am–12.30pm).

Phones International calls can be made from the main SIP office at Via dei Termini 40 (Mon–Sat 8am–8.30pm, Sun 9am–12.45pm & 3–7.45pm). Alternatively, try *Bar Centrale* (open till midnight) at Via Cecco Angiolieri 37, a block north of the Campo; you pay at the bar after making your call.

Police *Questura*, Via del Castoro (immediately east of the Duomo).

Post office The main post office is on Piazza Matteotti (Mon–Fri 8.15am–7pm, Sat 8.15am–noon).

Swimming pool There's a *Piscina Comunale* on Piazza G. Amendola, to the north of the city, off Viale Vittorio Emanuele; take bus #5 from Piazza Matteotti.

Train enquiries ☎0577/280.115 (daily 7am–8.30pm).

Leaving Siena: buses and trains

Leaving Siena is easiest by **bus**. From the station by San Domenico, *Lazzi* and *TRA-IN* have connections throughout the province – half-hourly to Poggibonsi (for connections to San Gimignano buy a through ticket), and half a dozen times daily to Montalcino and Montepulciano. *Lazzi* services also run throughout the day to Florence, and regularly to Massa Maríttima, Volterra and Rome; for Rome buy tickets well in advance. For **Florence**, take a *diretto*, which arrives in an hour; those marked "Via Strove" take nearly three hours.

There's no shortage of information: you can make use of a computer display (with print-outs) in the bus office and there's a board by the church, detailing times and departure bays.

Trains are generally less convenient as they're slower – and getting to the station involves a connecting bus. However, Siena is linked with the Florence to Pisa line via Empoli, and is connected to Grosseto (and thence Rome) to the southwest. There's also a very pretty minor line southeast through Asciano and San Giovanni d'Asso – useful if you fancy a hike to the monastery of Monte Oliveto Maggiore (see p.345).

The *SETI* office on the Campo is the only place in the city apart from the train station where you can buy rail tickets in advance.

The road to San Gimignano

Heading west from Siena, most people have San Gimignano firmly in their sights. If you have time, the best route to follow is the N2 as far as the turreted fortress-hamlet of **Monteriggioni**, then turn west to **Colle di Val d'Elsa**, whose striking medieval upper town extends along a narrow ridge. From Colle, a scenic and minor road, which walkers might try paralleling across country, runs on via Bibbiano to San Gimignano.

Depending on **public transport**, you can stop easily enough at Colle, before catching another bus on to the industrial town of Poggibonsi – and a connection from there to San Gimignano; for Monteriggioni, you can catch a bus to the turning up to the village (and hail another one on from there to Colle or back to Siena). Most buses from Siena (or Florence) to San Gimignano involve a Poggibonsi connection, though there's a direct *TRA-IN* service in summer.

Note that the route north from Poggibonsi to Empoli – via Certaldo and Castelfiorentino – is covered on pages 184–88.

Monteriggioni

The perfectly preserved walls of **MONTERIGGIONI** declare their presence for miles ahead from the N2 or the Siena–Florence motorway. The citadel was a strategic target for any troops marching on Siena from the north and is immortalised in Dante's *Inferno*, in which he compares the towers to giants in an abyss. The verse greets you as you enter the village, which consists of just a couple of dozen houses, two restaurants, a bar and a communist party office. The houses give way to gardens as they near the ramparts, and an Olympic athlete could probably run the main street, from south to north gates, in under ten seconds.

All of which, of course, accounts for the charm of the place. The walls apart, there are no sights – just long views out over the Tuscan countryside. Of the **restaurants**, *Il Pozzo* (☎0577/304.127; closed Sun evening & Mon, Jan & Aug) is the better known, though pricey at around L40,000 for a full meal. *Il Castello*, opposite, is a fair bit cheaper. Both specialise in game and add liberal sprinklings of truffles and *porcini* to many dishes. Also on the main street is the *Fattoria Castello di Monteriggioni*, which sells a fine local Chianti, *vinsanto* and grappa. A brand-new four-star hotel has recently opened and its rooms – despite steep prices – are quickly snapped up: *Hotel Monterrigioni*, Via Maggio 4 (0577/305.009; [9]).

If you fancy the walk – or have transport – an excellent value **hotel-restaurant**, *La Casalta* (☎0577/301.002), is to be found 4km west at the little hamlet of Strove. Meals cost around L25–30,000; the ten rooms [5]. Midway to Strove is the outstanding Romanesque church and monastic remains of **Abbadia a Isola**, originally, as the name suggests, an abbey set on an island – amid marshes. Ask for the key from the caretaker in the house to the left of the church.

Colle di Val d'Elsa

COLLE DI VAL D'ELSA, despite plentiful bus connections to Siena and San Gimignano, is not much explored. Perhaps the lower town – a sprawl of light industry and new housing developments – puts visitors off. Paper-making, and then nail factories, have long made it a prosperous place. However, the walled upper town, Colle Alta, is a beauty, stretching along a ridge and with its one long street lined with medieval palazzi.

Buses stop in **Piazza Arnolfo**, the main piazza of the lower town, named from local boy Arnolfo di Cambio – architect of the Palazzo Vecchio in Florence. A block north is the city's major piece of modern architecture, a regional headquarters of the *Monte dei Paschi* bank, designed by **Michelucci**; mixing Portakabin-like offices with open girders, it's not one of his most captivating efforts.

Colle Alta

From Piazza Arnolfo, it's a steep ten-minute climb up to **Colle Alta**. Follow Via San Sebastiano and then the brick-paved **costa**, which will bring you out at the east tip of the town. If you drive up to Colle Alta, you're directed around a circuitous route to the west end of the ridge, by the Porta Nuova.

At the top of the *costa*, you've little choice but to follow **Via del Castello**, the centre of a three-street grid, past a scattering of tower-houses; Arnolfo was born in the one at no. 63, on the left at the beginning of the street. Midway along, the **Piazza del Duomo** opens out, flanked by the cathedral – its main treasure a Renaissance pulpit by Giuliano da Maiano – and three museums, all of which can be visited on the same L4000 ticket.

The **Museo d'Arte Sacra** (Oct–March Sat & Sun 10am–noon & 3.30–6.30pm; April–Sept Tues–Fri 4–6pm, Sat & Sun 10am–noon & 4.30–7.30pm) is the most interesting of these, housed in the old bishop's palace, which retains frescoes of hunting scenes by Bartolo di Fredi; it also has a fair collection of Sienese paintings gathered from local churches. Next door is the **Museo Civico** (same hours) with a miscellany of paintings and a photographic display on Arnolfo; across the street, the **Museo Archeologico** (same hours) is of passing interest only.

About a hundred metres beyond Piazza Duomo, alongside the Mannerist **Palazzo Campagna**, a bridge connects this medieval core to its fifteenth- and sixteenth-century expansions. Off to the north is an imposing Franciscan monastery, whose church has another Sano di Pietro altarpiece. Following the main road through this quarter you come to the *Hotel Arnolfo* in Piazza Santa Caterina. Off to the left of this square is an alleyway called **Vicolo della Fontanella**, with a **glass workshop** – Colle makes much of its money from glass factories in the lower town – and the *Enoteca della Fortuna*, a wine shop with a tiny restaurant upstairs (see below). At the end of the main road is the hugely bastioned **Porta Nuova**, constructed by Giuliano da Sangallo.

Practicalities

Colle's **tourist office** is at Via Campana 18 (☎0577/920.015). If the town's artistic attractions seem on the slight side, **food** provides a major spur to a couple of hours' exploration. In **Colle Alta**, the *Enoteca della Fortuna*, mentioned above, is a great little Tuscan restaurant – very reasonably priced at L16–20,000 (☎0577/923.102). If money is no object, there is the *Arnolfo*, adjoining the hotel, whose *cucina nuova* scores high in all the Italian foodie guides: the *menù gastronomica* runs to L70,000 and booking is essential (☎0577/920.549; closed Tues, first week of Aug & Jan 10–Feb 10).

Highly recommended in the **lower town** is *Antica Trattoria* at Piazza Arnolfo 23 (☎0577/923.747), worth the L40–45,000 for wonderful vegetable soufflés, cold meats in gorgonzola, and an obsessive grappa collection – some kept virtually frozen in the fridge. To round things off, call in at the main café in Piazza Arnolfo for an **ice cream**, reckoned by not a few Tuscans as the finest in the province.

The town has four **hotels**. On a budget, the choice is between the *Pensione Olimpia* at Via A. Diaz 5, five blocks south of Piazza Arnolfo (☎0577/921.662; [4]), and the *Hotel Nazionale* at Via Garibaldi 20, just west of the square (☎0577/920.039; [4]). More upmarket are *La Vecchia Cartiera*, Via Oberdan 5, again just off Piazza Arnolfo (☎0577/921.107; [6]), and the *Arnolfo*, the only hotel in Colle Alta (☎0577/922.020; [5]). An alternative choice is the *Hotel Villa Belvedere* (☎0577/920.966; [6]), an eighteenth-century villa 3km south of town on the Monteriggioni road, with tennis and riding facilities and a pool.

Colle has all the facilities you'd expect of a moderate-sized town, including a very useful **bike rental** agency, *Gippo Motorshop* at Via Roma 12 (☎0577/920.870), which does scooters and mountain bikes by the day or week. **Nightlife** is restricted to a single club, *H_2O* in Via Savalgna.

South of Colle

The roads south of Colle lead into the **Colline Metallífere** (Metal Hills), dotted with geothermal energy plants (the largest are out towards Larderello, see p.337) and their snaking pipelines. Other sights are few, though the countryside, as ever, is liberally sprinkled with Romanesque churches and inspiringly placed farmhouses and cypress groves.

Casole d'Elsa, Radicóndoli and Mensano

Heading for the abbey church of San Galgano (see p.342), there are buses down the N541 (direction Massa Maríttima). If you are driving, you might consider the very pretty rural route through **CASOLE D'ELSA** and **RADICÓNDOLI**, villages which look inviting from a distance, though yield little of substantial interest close to. Casole's fortress, the most imposing sight, is now occupied as council offices; the town's Collegiata has a Della Robbia altar. Both villages, however, have useful **hotels**: the *Gemini* at Strada Provinciale 4 in Casole (☎0577/948.622; [6]); *Verde Oasis* at Via Guido Rossa 18 in Radicóndoli (☎0577/790.760; [5]); and *La Sorgente* in Bagni delle Galleraie, a hamlet of Radicóndoli (☎0577/793.150; [5]). Casole also has *agriturismo* rooms to let, just north of the village, and a **restaurant**, *Il Merlo* (closed Tues), that serves reasonable traditional Tuscan food. Radicóndoli has the panoramically sited *Caffè-Bar-Trattoria-Pizzeria La Pergola*.

Another possible lunch stop is the hilltop hamlet of **MENSANO**, between the two villages, which has a tiny, family-run trattoria – up by the children's playground at the summit.

Poggibonsi

POGGIBONSI has little more than its transport links and its politics to recommend it. A serious industrial town, conspicuously ugly alongside its Tuscan neighbours, it is reputed as the home of Italy's reddest council. Prior to the last war it might have looked more like Colle, but bombing left little trace of its past other than the **Castello della Magione**, a little Romanesque complex, possibly with Templar origins, consisting of a chapel and pilgrim hospice. The unfinished **Medici fort** at the top of the town isn't worth the slog.

If transport connections aren't working in your favour, there are bars and cafés to pass the time, and – if things are desperate – a moderately priced **hotel**, the *Italia*, at Via Trento 36 (☎0577/936.142; [4]). Poggibonsi's best **restaurant**, *Palazzo al Piano*, Via Montenero 16 (☎0577/345.559; closed Mon & Tues), might perhaps tempt a longer stop; it's acclaimed for its fish dishes, costing around L45,000. A good, cheaper restaurant is *Il Sole* at Via Trento 5 (☎0577/936.283; closed Mon & July–Aug).

Note that in addition to its **bus** connections, Poggibonsi has a station on the Siena–Empoli **train line**.

San Gimignano

SAN GIMIGNANO – "delle Belle Torri" – is perhaps the best-known village in Italy. Its stunning skyline of towers, built in aristocratic rivalry by the feuding nobles of the twelfth and thirteenth centuries, evoke the appearance of medieval Tuscany more than any other sight. And its image as a "Medieval Manhattan" has for decades caught the tourist imagination, helped along by its convenience as a day trip from Florence or Siena.

The town is all that it's cracked up to be: quietly monumental, very well-preserved, enticingly rural and with a fine array of religious and secular frescoes. However, from May through to October, San Gimignano has very little life of its own – and a lot of day-trippers, with a preponderance of high-spending Germans. If you want to get any feel for the place, beyond the level of art treasures or quaintness, you really need to come well out of season. If you can't, then aim to spend the night here – in the evenings the town takes on a very different pace and atmosphere.

Some history
Founded by the omnipresent Etruscans, San Gimignano was quite a force to be reckoned with by the early Middle Ages. It was controlled by two great families – the Ardinghelli and the Salvucci – and its 15,000 population (twice the present number) prospered on agricultural holdings and its position on the pilgrim route to Rome. At its heyday, in the fourteenth century, the town's walls enclosed five monasteries, four hospitals, public baths and a brothel.

Feuds, however, had long wreaked havoc. The first Ardinghelli-Salvucci conflict erupted in 1246, and for the following century there were few years of peace. Guelph-Ghibelline loyalties provided further fuel, and whenever the town itself was united there were wars with Volterra, Poggibonsi and other nearby towns. The vendettas came to a halt only through the Black Death of 1348. It had a devastating effect both on the population and – as the pilgrim trade collapsed – on the economy. The Ardinghelli family, despite opposition from the Salvucci, applied to Florence for the town to become a part of that city's *comune*: an appeal that was accepted by only one vote – a reflection on San Gimignano's fractious reputation.

Subjection to Florence broke the power of the nobles and so San Gimignano was unaffected by the struggles between aristocracy and town council which racked other Tuscan towns. The tower houses, symbolic of real control elsewhere, posed little threat – and so were not torn down; today, fifteen (of an original seventy-two) survive. The town itself, further hit by plague in 1464 and 1631, passed into a rural backwater existence. Its only historical importance was an early adoption of Savonarola, who preached in the cathedral here well before his rise to fame in Florence.

At the turn of the last century, travellers spoke of San Gimignano as "miserably poor", a condition that was barely romanticised by E.M. Forster, who took the town (he calls it Monteriano) as the setting for his novel *Where Angels Fear to Tread*. San Gimignano's postwar history has been one of ever-increasing affluence, through tourism and the production of an old-established, but recently rejuvenated, white wine, *Vernaccia*. Recently, however, its *comune* has been thrown into a state of some crisis, after the discovery that leaking ancient drains have been undermining the foundations of several towers, causing large cracks to appear. A £1.5million restoration appeal is in progress.

Arrival, information and accommodation

Once up at the walled town, **orientation** is straightforward. Arriving by **bus**, you can get out either at **Piazzale Martiri di Monte Maggio**, just outside **Porta Giovanni**, the south gate, or by the northern gate, **Porta San Matteo**.

If you're **driving**, follow the road clockwise around the walls and you pass a couple of paying **car parks** – the simplest option for a short stay. Free parking is possible on the outskirts of town, but not really worth the effort in summer, unless you need a space for several days. To drive within the walls, you need to be issued with a permit from one of the hotels; the way in is through **Porta San Jacopo** at the northeast corner.

The **tourist office** on Piazza del Duomo is helpful, supplying full lists of hotels, rooms and apartments both inside and outside the walls. A crucial factor to enjoying San Gimignano is to get a room inside the walls – which from May to October means booking ahead, arriving early in the day, or chancing your luck. The town's four hotels are all expensive three-star joints but budget alternatives are to be found in a new youth hostel, a convent and dozens of privately let rooms.

To help in the search, try the **Cooperativa Turistiche**, just inside the Porta San Giovanni at Via S. Giovanni 125 (Mon–Sat 9.30am–12.30pm & 2.30–7.30pm, Sun 9.30am–12.30pm; ☎0577/940.809), or **Agenzia Munitravel**, Via San Matteo 74 (☎0577/940.827). Both arrange rooms in hotels and private houses, apartments and *agriturismo* lets.

GUESTHOUSES AND HOTELS

Il Pino, Via San Matteo (☎0577/940.414). Small guesthouse above a restaurant, just inside the Porta San Matteo. ④.

Le Vecchie Mura, Via Piandornella 15 (☎0577/940.270). More rooms above a restaurant, but more appetising than it sounds, with welcoming owners and spectacular views from some rooms. The street is first right off Via San Giovanni, coming in at Porta San Giovanni. ④.

Bel Soggiorno, Via San Giovanni 91 (☎0577/940.375). Similar quality – though beware of having to take full pension in summer. Sited twenty yards down the street from Porta San Giovanni. ⑥.

La Cisterna, Piazza della Cisterna 23 (☎0577/940.328). The oldest-established and most elegant hotel. ⑥.

Leon Bianco, Piazza della Cisterna (☎0577/941.294). Tasteful hotel in an old mansion in the main square. ⑥.

L'Antico Pozzo, Via San Matteo 87 (☎0577/942.014). Painted ceilings and very chi-chi decor, hence the highest prices in town. ⑦.

THE CONVENT, YOUTH HOSTEL AND CAMPSITE

Convento di Sant'Agostino, Piazza di Sant'Agostino (☎0577/940.383). Definite budget first choice: an active monastery which lets twenty or so cells for one or two people. When you arrive, ring the bell (unlabelled) by the huge doors to the left of the church. There are no rules or curfew: men and women can share rooms, married or not. To reach the convent, take the first turning left inside the Porta San Matteo. ③.

Ostello della Gioventù, Via delle Fonti 1 (☎0577/941.991). IYHF hostel, well positioned in the north of town. Reception open 7.30–9.30am and 5–11.30pm. ①.

Camping Il Boschetto (☎0577/940.352). The nearest campsite is 3km downhill from Piazzale Martiri di Monte Maggio at Santa Lucia, off the Volterra road. It has a bar and shop.

PRIVATE ROOMS

Within the walls, San Gimignano's **private rooms** are scattered around a dozen or so houses. They charge from around L50,000 for a double, a little less – reluctantly – for a single.

Cesarina Benucci, Via Diaccetto 23 (no phone).

Aladina Bettini, Via Berignano 51 (☎0577/940.431).

Pietro Boldrini, Via San Matteo 95 (☎0577/940.908).

Dina Conforti Totti, Via Mainardi 6 (☎0577/940.478).

Lida Gonnelli, Via Quercecchio 5 (☎0577/941.228).

Loris Maccianti, Via Piandornella 20 (☎0577/940.248).

Ivosca Marri Gattolin, Via San Piero 1 (☎0577/940.433).

Piero Marrucci, Via San Giovanni 70 (☎0577/940.978).

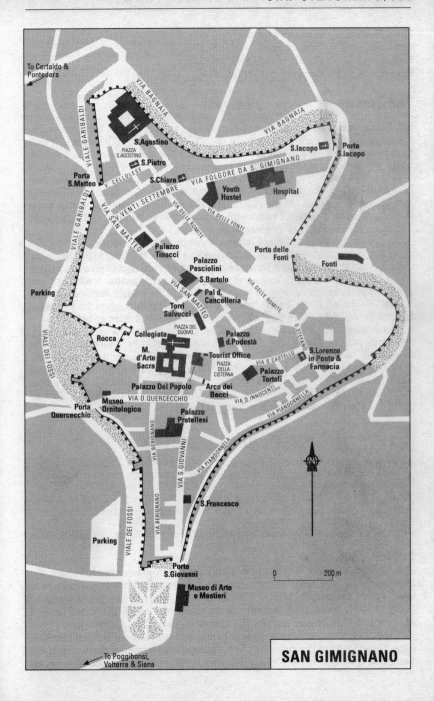

To Certaldo &
Pontedera

VIA BAGNAIA

VIA BAGNAIA

S.Agostino

PIAZZA
S.AGOSTINO

S.Pietro

V. CELLOLESE

VIALE GARIBALDI

Porta
S.Matteo

S.Chiara

S VENTI SETTEMBRE

VIA FOLGORE DA S. GIMIGNANO

S.Iacopo

Porta
S.Iacopo

Youth
Hostel

Hospital

VIA DELLE FONTI

VIA DELLE ROMITE

Porta delle
Fonti

Fonti

VIALE GARIBALDI

VIA SAN MATTEO

Palazzo
Tinacci

Palazzo
Pesciolini

S.Bartolo

VIA DELLE ROMITE

Parking

VIA SAN MATTEO

Pal d.
Cancelleria

Torri
Salvucci

VIALE DEI FOSSI

Rocca

Collegiata

PIAZZA DEL
DUOMO

Palazzo
d.Podestà

S. STEFANO

S.Lorenzo
in Ponte &
Farmacia

M.
d'Arte
Sacra

Tourist Office

PIAZZA
DELLA
CISTERNA

VIA D. CASTELLO

Palazzo
Tortoli

Palazzo Del Popolo

VIA D. QUERCECCHIO

Arco dei
Becci

VIA D. INNOCENTI

VIA PIANDORNELLA

Museo
Ornitologico

Porta
Quercecchio

Palazzo
Pratellesi

VIA BERIGNANO

VIA PIANDORNELLA

VIA S.GIOVANNI

N

VIALE DEI FOSSI

VIA BERIGNANO

S.Francesco

Parking

Porta
S.Giovanni

0   200 m

Museo di Arte
e Mestieri

To Poggibonsi,
Volterra & Siena

SAN GIMIGNANO

Marzi Mezzetti, Via Don Castaldi 5 (☎0577/940.589).
Graziano Nacci, Via Santo Stefano 6 (☎0577/940.730).
Nello Nencioni, Via Piandornella 20 (☎0577/940.546).
Rino Nencioni, Via Mainardi 6 (☎0577/940.137).

The Town

San Gimignano is not much more than a village: you could walk from one end to the other in fifteen minutes, or around the walls in an hour. It deserves at least a day, however, both for the frescoes in the churches and museums, and for the countryside – some of the loveliest in Tuscany.

From the south gate, **Porta San Giovanni**, the palazzo-lined **Via San Giovanni** leads to the town's interlocking main squares, the Piazza della Cisterna and Piazza del Duomo. On the right of the street, about a hundred metres up, is the former church of **San Francesco** – a Romanesque building converted now, like many of the palazzi, to a *Vernaccia* wine cellar.

You enter the **Piazza della Cisterna** through another majestic gateway, the **Arco dei Becci**, part of the original fortifications before the town expanded in the twelfth century. The square is flanked by an anarchic cluster of towers and palazzi, with a thirteenth-century cistern – still functioning – in the centre. It was here, and in other streets within these inner walls, that most of the leading families had their houses. To the left of the square, beside an arch leading through to the Piazza del Duomo, is one of the old Ardinghelli towers; a Salvucci rival rears up behind.

The more austere **Piazza del Duomo**, off to the left, introduces further towers and civic palazzi. Facing the Duomo (more properly the **Collegiata**, as San Gimignano no longer has a bishop), the crenellated **Palazzo del Popolo**, the town hall and home to the Museo Civico, stands to your left, the older **Palazzo del Podestà** behind you. The latter's Torre della Rognosa was once set as the maximum height – 160 feet – for any tower. Looking around the skyline, it would seem that the rule was not much respected.

> ### SAN GIMIGNANO MUSEUMS
>
> Note that a single **museum ticket** (greatly overpriced at L15,000) covers admission to the Museo Civico, Santa Fina chapel, and the Etruscan, sacred art and ornithological museums. Individual entry charges are L5000 per site, which constitutes perhaps the most blatant profiteering in the province. **Opening hours** for all of these are standard: April–Sept daily 9.30am–12.30pm & 3–6pm; Oct–March Tues–Sun 9.30am–12.30pm & 2.30–5.30pm.

The Collegiata

The Collegiata's plain facade could hardly provide a greater contrast with the interior, one of the most comprehensively frescoed churches in Tuscany. You need a good pocketful of L100 or L200 coins to do justice to the cycles, which fill every available space, their brilliant colours set off by Pisan Romanesque arcades of black and white striped marble. The church is closed from 12.30 to 3pm.

The principal cycles are scenes of the Old Testament (on the left wall) and the New Testament (on the right); in the lunettes above, scenes of the Creation are paralleled by those of the Nativity. Somewhat surprisingly, the **Old Testament** scenes, whose vision seems entirely medieval, were painted later. Created by Bartolo di Fredi in 1367, they reflect the influence of Lorenzetti's *Good and Bad Government* in Siena in their delight in genre detail, forming an essentially human narrative: *Abraham and Lot leading their flock towards Canaan*, for example, is a Tuscan farming scene, with appropriate landscape. They are also quirkily naturalistic – there are few odder frescoes than that of the *Drunkenness of Noah*, exposing himself in his stupor.

If your biblical knowledge breaks down, the cycle (which is read left to right, top to bottom) follows the story of the *Flood* with those of *Abraham and Lot* (their trip to Canaan), *Joseph* (his dream, being let down the well, having his brothers arrested and being recognised by them), *Moses* (changing a stick into a serpent before the Pharoah; the Red Sea; Mount Sinai) and *Job* (temptation; the devil killing his herds and destroying his house; thanking God; and being consoled by friends). The authorship of the **New Testament** scenes (begun 1333) is disputed, with some historians now attributing them to Lippo Memmi, a collaborator and brother-in-law of Simone Martini. Traditionally, the attribution is to Barna di Siena, another follower of Martini, possibly a pupil, who is supposed to have died in a fall from the scaffolding while at work here in the 1350s. Whatever, they mark quite a departure from Martini's style, with their interest in emotional expression. In *The Kiss of Judas* the focus of eyes is startlingly immediate, as is the absorption of all the figures in the action – Saint Peter thrusting into the foreground with his assault on the Roman soldier, while the other disciples gather their cloaks and flee. The same dramatic vision comes through in *Christ Carrying the Cross* and the dark dealings of *Judas Accepting the Pieces of Silver*.

An altogether more vicious sensibility pervades Taddeo di Bartolo's **Last Judgement** (1410), on the inner wall of the facade. This is one of the most gruesome depictions of a customarily lurid subject, with no-holds-barred delineations of the Seven Deadly Sins, including Bosch-like fantasies on lust and gluttony. Below is a **Saint Sebastian** – blithely unaffected by a casual and courtly display of archery. It was commissioned from Benozzo Gozzoli in gratitude at the end of an outbreak of plague in 1464; the inscription below reads "in praise of the most glorious athlete, Sebastian". Close by, on pedestals, are two fine wooden figures by **Jacopo della Quercia**, depicting the Annunciation.

THE CAPPELLA DI SANTA FINA

The chapels of the cathedral were remodelled in the mid-fifteenth century by Giuliano da Maiano, bringing San Gimignano into the Florentine Renaissance orbit. His masterpiece is the **Cappella di Santa Fina**, for which his brother Benedetto designed a shrine and Domenico Ghirlandaio was commissioned to produce a pair of frescoes.

Saint Fina, the subject of the frescoes and the frieze of the shrine, was born in San Gimignano in 1238, and struck by a dreadful and incurable disease at the age of ten. She gave herself immediately to God, repented her sins (the worst seems to have been accepting an orange from a boy), and spent the five years until her death – predicted in a vision of Saint Gregory (depicted in the lunette) – lying on a plank on the floor. On her expiration, the towers of San Gimignano allegedly sprouted with wall flowers. The interest of the chapel lies in Ghirlandaio's splendid colouring, portraiture and the background depiction of San Gimignano and its towers – into one of which an angel soars to ring the bells to herald the saint's fortunate relief from mortal life.

THE BAPTISTERY AND MINOR MUSEUMS
To the left of the Collegiata, an arch surmounted by a statue of Saint Gimignano leads into a courtyard. Straight ahead is the loggia to the baptistery, frescoed with an *Annunciation* by Ghirlandaio. Rather anonymous **Sacred Art** and **Etruscan museums** are housed in the old Rector's Palace off to the left of the court, which is a favourite for busking musicians in summer.

Palazzo del Popolo: the Museo Civico

A visit to the **Palazzo del Popolo** gives you the chance to climb the **Torre Grossa**, the highest surviving and best preserved of the towers – and the only one you can ascend. It's an impressively solid structure, with various vaults and a gallery of spectacular panoramic views.

The **Palazzo** is impressive, too, with its courtyard (decorated with the crests of various medieval magistrates), external loggia and halls. A few of these are still in use by the town council, but most have been given over to the **Museo Civico**. Within the courtyard itself are preserved several frescoes relating to justice, among them a Renaissance chiaroscuro by Sodoma depicting the magistrate Saint Ivo.

The first of the palazzo's public chambers, frescoed with hunting scenes, is known as the **Sala di Dante** – the poet visited as Florence's ambassador to the town in 1300, making a plea here for Guelph unity. Most of the paintings displayed are fourteenth-century works, Sienese in origin or inspiration in these years before San Gimignano passed into Florentine control and influence. The highlight in the Sala di Dante is Lippo Memmi's *Maestà* (1317), his finest work, closely modelled on that of Simone Martini in Siena.

Other notable works in the **Pinacoteca** – occupying the rooms following – include Madonnas by Gozzoli, Filippino Lippi and Pinturicchio, a further representation of Saint Fina, by Lorenzo di Niccolò Girini, and Taddeo di Bartolo's *San Gimignano and Stories from His Life*. The latter depicts the town's eponymous saint in his bishop's robes, holding the medieval town in his lap.

The most fascinating and enjoyable paintings, though, are the **frescoes of wedding scenes** hidden away in a small room off the stairs. Unique in their subject matter, they show a tournament where the wife rides on her husband's back, followed by the lovers taking a shared bath and climbing into bed. They were completed in the 1320s by Memmo di Filipuccio, who was then working as a more or less official painter for the *comune*, following a period helping Giotto on his frescoes in Assisi.

The Rocca

Just behind the Piazza del Duomo, a signposted lane leads to the **Rocca**, the old fortress, with its one surviving tower. It was built in 1353, to Florentine orders but at local expense, "in order to remove every cause of evil thinking from the inhabitants". A couple of centuries later, its purpose presumably fulfilled, it was dismantled by Cosimo I. Nowadays it encloses an orchard-like public garden, with figs, olives and a well in the middle. From the ramparts, there are superb views over the countryside.

A block south of the Rocca, a **Museo Ornithologico** has been created from the stuffed bird collections of some local worthy in the deconsecrated church near the Porta Quercecchio.

North to Sant'Agostino

Heading away from the central squares and Via San Giovanni, the crowds quickly thin away. Following the Via di Castello east of Piazza della Cisterna leads past Romanesque **San Lorenzo in Ponte**, one of the few other churches kept open – with dramatic fragments of a frescoed *Last Judgement* – and the attached **Farmacia Preindustriale**. This was part of a medieval hospital, supported by the town council, and has an interesting display of medicines and equipment, as well as the story of San Gimignano under plague, and its role on the pilgrims' road to Rome. (At the time of writing, San Lorenzo is undergoing restoration and the Farmacia Preindustriale displays are temporarily installed in the Museo Civico.) At the end of the street a rural lane winds down to the walls, a public well-house – the **Fonti** – and open countryside. North from Piazza del Duomo, **Via San Matteo** is one of the grandest and best preserved of the city streets, with quiet little alleyways again running down to the walls. Passing a couple of mighty tower houses, the street ends at the **Porta San Matteo**, just inside of which, in a corner of walls, is the **Convento di Sant'Agostino** (see p.324 for details about staying here).

SANT'AGOSTINO

After the Collegiata, **Sant'Agostino** is the most important church in San Gimignano, a large, hall-like thirteenth-century structure with an outstanding fresco cycle by Benozzo Gozzoli on the *Life of St Augustine*. Unfortunately, at the time of writing, this is completely covered over for restoration – when work is complete, you should find the building open from 8am to noon, then from about 3pm to dusk.

Lining the chapel to the right of the high altar, the frescoes provide a wonderful record of life in Renaissance Italy – and especially the city life of Florence, which forms a backdrop to many of the scenes.

The first panels depict the saint – who was born in what is now Tunisia in 354 – being taken to school by his parents and flogged by his teacher, studying grammar at Carthage university, and crossing the sea to Italy. The next move through his academic career: teaching philosophy and rhetoric in Rome and Milan – Gozzoli depicts the journey between the cities as a marvellously rich procession – and being received by the Emperor Theodosius. Then comes the turning point in his life, when he listens to the preaching of Saint Ambrose, and then, while reading Saint Paul's Epistles to the Romans, hears a child's voice extolling him "Tolle, lege" – take and read. After this, Augustine was baptised, returned to Tunisia to form a monastic community and was subsequently made Bishop of Hippo. He was one of the fathers of the Early Christian church, producing two of its fundamental great theological works – the *Commentaries* and the *City of God*. Gozzoli depicts just a few crucial scenes: Augustine meeting the child whose voice he had heard (and who now rebuked him for trying to penetrate the mysteries of the Trinity); the death of his mother, Saint Monica; blessing the people, as bishop; confuting a heretic; having a vision of Saint Jerome in Paradise; and his death.

Gozzoli started out with considerable promise, working as assistant to Fra' Angelico at the Vatican, then landing the contract for the Palazzo Medici chapel in Florence. These frescoes were painted late in life, after a frustrating, jobbing career spent on minor commissions around the Tuscan countryside. The wonderful narrative freshness of the cycle prompted Bernard Berenson to characterise him as "a Fra' Angelico who had forgotten heaven and become enamoured of the earth and the spring time".

Other frescoes in the church include a *Life of the Virgin* by Bartolo di Fredi, a *St Sebastian* by Sodoma, an *Altar of the True Cross* by a local Renaissance painter, Vincenzo Tamagni, and the remains of a *Madonna* by Lippo Memmi. Worth a look, too, are the Cappella di San Bartolomeo, designed by Benedetto da Maiano and frescoed by Sebastiano Mainardi, and the fifteenth-century cloister.

Food and other practicalities

San Gimignano isn't especially famous for its **food** – there are too many tourists and too few locals to ensure standards. However, the tables set out in summer on the car-less streets and squares and the local wines still make for a beguiling evening. At lunchtime, you might prefer to pick up some snacks from the bars or delicatessens and head out to the countryside – a matter of walking out from just about any of the gates.

Snack bars and restaurants

Recommendations below are in ascending order of price, starting with snack bars and pizzerias, and with a clutch of out-of-town treats at the end. As an after-meal treat, drop in on the award-winning *Gelateria di Piazza*, on Piazza della Cisterna – the jovial owner creates some of the best ice cream in Tuscany.

WITHIN THE WALLS

Rosticceria-Pizzeria Chiribi, off Via San Giovanni – first left inside the Porta San Giovanni (closed Mon). Very cheap snack bar that does *primi* and *secondi* at L4000, and small pizzas for L2500. Also take-out snacks.

Pizzeria da Nino, Via San Giovanni 38. More good-value pizza – either as a meal, or by weight to take out. Open all week.

Ristorante Pizzeria Paradiso, by Arco dei Becci on Via San Giovanni. Another inexpensive pizzeria but far from the best to found in Tuscany.

Le Vecchie Mura, Via Piandornella 15. Housed in an old vaulted stable within the structure of the city walls; good atmosphere; fair-value pizzas and set meals (L15–20,000). Follow sign off Via San Giovanni. Closed Mon.

La Mandragora, off Via San Giovanni. Modern, spacious decor and imaginative cooking. L18–25,000.

Ristorante Il Pino, Via San Matteo 102. Lovely interior, specialises in *antipasti* and dishes sprinkled with truffle. L20–30,000.

Ristorante La Stella, Via San Matteo 75. Touristy spot, but good value; pleasant and reputed restaurant that serves produce from its own farm. From L22,000. Closed Wed.

Ristorante Dorandò, Vicolo dell'Oro 2. Advertises itself as recreating Etruscan and Renaissance dishes – "each dish we present is a fragment of Tuscan history, an archaeological fragment". Don't be put off: the dishes are classic Tuscan cooking and the chef knows his business. L30,000. Closed Mon.

La Mangiatoia, Via Mainardi 5. Nice ambience and inspired if erratic food that belies its name (The Trough). L40,000. Closed Tues.

OUT OF TOWN

Casa al Chino, Larniano (☎0577/955.022). In a lovely, country setting 6km northwest of town. Excellent *antipasti* and *cinghiale* and home-produced *Vernaccia*. L20–30,000.

I Cinque Gigli at the *Hotel Pescille*, 4km down Castel San Gimignano road (☎0577/940.186). The best restaurant in the area: specialities include *antipasti saporosi*, soups, roast meats and *bollito*, with crêpes to finish. Full meals from L35,000. Closed Wed & Jan–Feb.

Da Pode, Sovestro (☎0577/941.653). Just outside town, on the Poggibonsi road. First-class local food – mainly game – served in a cool tiled rustic dining room. Closed Mon.

The market and festivals

If you're in town on Thursday or Saturday morning, a variety of fare – including rolls with *cinghiale* filling – are on offer at the open-air **market** in Piazza del Duomo. Clothes and crafts are on sale, too; the Saturday market, though, is very small. Market days aside, San Gimignano is very much on the quiet side, with little entertainment beyond the evening *passeggiata* along Via San Giovanni and Via San Matteo. **Festival** moments include a good effort at **Carnevale** (February), with floats and parades through town, and a small **summer cultural festival** (June–Oct), whose events include a series of classical concerts, theatre and films held in an open-air theatre in the Rocca.

Banks, phones and buses

There are several **banks** in the Piazza della Cisterna, including an automatic exchange machine. The tourist office changes currency, too, though not at the most advantageous rates. For international **phone calls**, the bar opposite the Collegiata has a cabin that you can use and pay after a call, and there's a SIP office at Via San Matteo 13.

Bus timetables are displayed in the Piazza del Duomo and **tickets** can be bought from the tourist office; virtually all major destinations (Florence, Siena, Volterra, Colle di Val d'Elsa) involve connections at Poggibonsi, which is also the nearest **train station**. Last buses back to Florence or Siena are usually around 8.30–9pm. Buses pick up passengers at the north gate, San Matteo, and by the southern gate, San Giovanni, in Piazzale Martiri di Monte Maggio.

Walks

San Gimignano's position, with the best of Tuscan countryside spread below, may well inspire the idea of walking. If you plan anything more than a ramble, it's worth calling in at the *Ufficio Tecnico* in the town hall to buy copies of the local *IGM* contour maps, available at about L5000 each.

A good **circular walk**, which would take most of the day, is to strike directly west into the hills to Poggio Attendi, follow the ridge south to San Donato, and loop back to San Gimignano via Montauto and Santa Lucia. Another possibility is to walk to **Colle di Val d'Elsa** (about 5hr): follow the Volterra road out of town, turn immediately left to Monteoliveto and Santa Lucia, and then make for the villages of Monti and Borgatello. With an early start, you could also walk to **Volterra** (6–7hr): make initially for San Donato, then cut across country past Castelvécchio (now a farm), the villa of Pignano and Monte Voltráio.

Volterra

Built on a high plateau enclosed by volcanic hills, **VOLTERRA** has a bleak, isolated appearance – a surprise after the pastoralism of the region around. However, its small, walled medieval core certainly merits a stop, with its cobbled and stone streets, dark stone palazzi and walled gateways. There are great views from the windswept heights, enjoyable walking, and one of the country's most important Etruscan museums.

The town lies at the heart of a mining region which yields alabaster (every other shop sells artefacts), as well as a variety of minerals. The mines – and the easily defended site – made it one of the largest Etruscan settlements, Velathri, and ensured its survival through the Roman and Dark Ages. In the Middle Ages, however, the mines proved Volterra's downfall as the Florentines began to cast a covetous eye on their wealth. Florence took control of the town from 1360, and in 1472 crushed all pretensions to independence with a terrible siege and pillage by Lorenzo de' Medici and the Duke of Urbino – one of the three principal crimes Lorenzo confessed to Savonarola on his deathbed.

Subsequently, Volterra was a Florentine fief, unable to keep pace with changing and expanding patterns of trade and sliding into provincial obscurity. Physically, the town also began to subside, its walls and houses slipping away to the west over the *Balze* (cliffs), which form a dramatic prospect from the Pisa road. Today, Volterra occupies less than a third of its ancient extent.

Arrival, information and accommodation

There is little more to Volterra than its old, walled centre, so orientation is straightforward. **Buses** arrive on the south side of the town at **Piazza Martiri della Libertà**, from where it's a five-minute walk to the central **Piazza dei Priori**, with the **Duomo** and **tourist office** (Via G. Turazza 2) around the corner. You can buy bus tickets and check the *TRA-IN* schedules at the tourist office.

Cars are best parked outside the north circuit of walls, by the Porta San Francesco or Porta Fiorentina, though if you're in luck you might find a space at

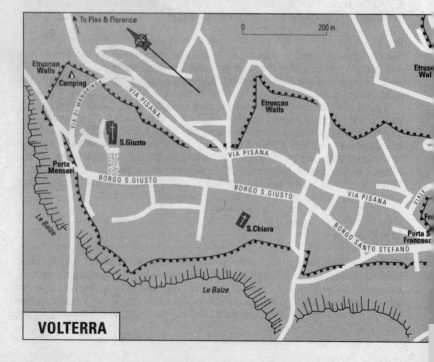

the Piazza Martiri della Libertà. The nearest **train station** is 9km west at Saline di Volterra (connecting bus); the rail line links to the busy coastal route between Pisa and Rome.

Volterra looks thin on **accommodation** if you judge by official hotel lists, but the local *Cooperativa Nuova SCAP* fill the gaps for most budgets, running a youth hostel, campsite and a couple of villa accommodations just outside the town. Apartments and *agriturismo* stays in and around Volterra are also on offer – ask at the tourist office or *Viaggi ATUV*, Piazza Martiri della Libertà (☎0588/85.019). As at San Gimignano you can stay in private rooms at a convent, too. All the town's accommodation is listed below, in ascending order of price.

HOTELS

Etruria, Via Matteotti 32 (☎0588/87.377). Best value of the hotels proper – and located on the main street, right in the centre. ④.

Nazionale, Via dei Marchesi 11 (☎0588/86.284). In the heart of town, this is the inn D.H. Lawrence stayed at when researching *Etruscan Places*. Now much modernised, with tiny rooms, all with bath. ⑤.

Sole, Via dei Cappuccini 10 (☎0588/84.000). Outside the town walls to the south, near the church of San Alessandro. Again, all rooms with bath. ⑤.

Villa Giardino, San Girolamo (☎0588/85.634); **Villa Domus Aeoli**, Borgo San Lazzero (☎0588/86.041). Respectively 500m and 1km out of town, these two *SCAP* villas are beautiful places to stay, with rooms (2–6 beds) at roughly three-star hotel prices. ⑤.

Villa Nencini, Borgo Santo Stefano 55 (☎0588/86.386). Attractive hotel, with a pool and garden, sited just outside Porta San Francesco. ⑤.

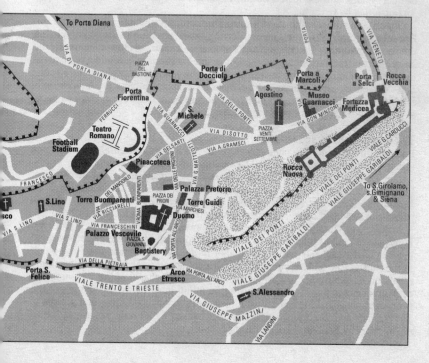

San Lino, Via San Lino 26 (☎0588/85.250). Volterra's grandest – a four-star hotel on the street leading in from Porta San Francesco. [6].

THE CONVENT, HOSTEL AND CAMPSITE

Convento Sant'Andrea, on the northeast outskirts of the town – follow the road out of Porta Marcoli (☎0588/86.028). There are beautiful views from the old cells, now let as private rooms – to both women and men, and couples. [2].

Ostello della Gioventù, Via Don Minzoni (☎0588/85.577). Housed in a converted mansion beyond the Etruscan museum, close to the Porta a Selci; open from 6pm, IYHF membership is not required, and the 11.30pm curfew is unlikely to prove a problem given Volterra nightlife. Very helpful staff. z[1].

Camping Le Balze, Via Mandringa (☎0588/87.880). Well equipped and positioned site, 1km from the city, outside Borgo San Giusto (follow signs for the *Balze*). Has a pool and tennis courts; riding can also be arranged. Open April–Sept.

The Town

The **Piazza dei Priori** is the heart of Volterra, enclosed by an almost totally medieval group of buildings. The town hall, or **Palazzo dei Priori**, is the eyecatcher. Built in the thirteenth century and said to be the oldest such palace in Italy, it may have served as the model for Florence's Palazzo Vecchio – though the influences are largely reversed on its facade, studded with Florentine medallions. The tower has been closed for the last few years – though if you find it open, pay and enter for spectacular views of the area. In the main building, you can take a look at the **council chamber** on the first floor, frescoed with a huge *Annunciation* by Orcagna.

Opposite the town hall is the **Palazzo Pretorio**, surmounted by the **Torre del Porcellino** (Piglet's Tower), named for the boar carved on its front; completing the ensemble are the Bishop's Palace and a pair of tower houses, the **Buomparenti**, at the junction of Via Roma and Via Ricciarelli. Modest relatives of those of San Gimignano, the towers are linked by a passageway above the street.

A **Museo di Arte Sacra** in the Bishop's Palace contains an Andrea della Robbia bust of Saint Linus – a Volterran who was Saint Peter's successor as pope; at present, however, it is also closed to visits.

The Duomo and its square

Backing directly onto the civic power centre, Volterra's cathedral square seems rather down-at-heel, with its partial facades and crumbling masonry.

The **Duomo** and **Baptistery** are essentially Romanesque, clad in bands of black and white marble – the style popularised in the twelfth century by Pisa. Behind the Baptistery (which is closed due to perilous condition), Della Robbia plaques of swaddled babies signal a building that was once a foundlings' hospital.

Inside the Duomo, striped marble Romanesque aisles and a coffered Renaissance ceiling lend a rather makeshift appearance. There are a few good touches of Romanesque carving – an altar to the left of the main door, the pulpit in the north aisle, and an outstanding thirteenth-century *Deposition*, disarmingly repainted in its original bright colours, in the south chapel of the transept. The cathedral's other major artworks are to be found in an oratory to the left of the main entrance. These are a pair of fifteenth-century painted terracotta groups of *The Nativity* and *The Epiphany*, the former backed by a lovely panoramic fresco of *The Magi* by Benozzo Gozzoli (bring coins).

The Pinacoteca

Paintings and sculpture gathered from Volterra's churches, including one that was swallowed up by the *Balze*, are displayed at the **Pinacoteca Comunale**, installed in the Palazzo Minucci-Solaini at Via dei Sarti 1, just off the Piazza dei Priori (daily summer 9.30am–6pm; winter 9am–1pm & 3–6.30pm; L6000 – but L3000 for students, teachers, writers and just about anyone interested in a visit). The collections that used to be displayed in the Palazzo dei Priori have all now been moved here.

The mansion is an interesting building in its own right, part frescoed and with a multi-level cloister; its designer may have been Antonio da Sangallo. The collections are arranged chronologically, and begin with a group of **statuary** from the lost church of San Giusto al Bostro, including a wonderful Romanesque capital carved from local alabaster, its mix of pagan and Christian emblems featuring a double-tailed mermaid and Daniel in the lion's den. The **painting** displays begin with largely Sienese works, by Taddeo di Bartolo and others, but by the fifteenth century Florence dominates the art scene – as it did the politics. Major Renaissance paintings from this period include a *Christ in Glory* with a marvellous imaginary landscape by Ghirlandaio, and a Signorelli *Annunciation*.

The museum's best work comes at the end – **Rosso Fiorentino**'s extraordinary *Descent from the Cross*, painted for the church of San Francesco in 1521. This is one of the masterpieces of Mannerism, its figures, without any central focus, creating an agitated, circular tension from sharp lines and blocks of discordant colour. The art historian Frederick Hartt sees in the painting "the dilemma of a lost generation" – it was painted in the decade that culminated in the Sack of Rome – and virtual blasphemy in the vision of a smiling Christ and gibbering Joseph of Arimathea (at the top).

The Rocca, Arco Etrusco and archaeological remains

South of Piazza dei Priori, **Via Marchesi** leads to a lush area of grass, trees and shade known as the **Parco Archeologico** (daily 10am–noon & 4–7pm; free). There's not much archaeology about the place – a few odd lumps of rock, said to be part of a Roman bathhouse – but it's a beautiful part of the town to lie around for a few hours, and there is a good value café-bar in one corner. Overlooking the park to the east is the **Rocca** – built by the Medici after their sacking of the town – and with its rounded bastions and central tower, one of the great examples of Italian military architecture. For the last century and a half it has been a prison, for lifers and hardcases.

The first turning left off Via Marchesi, **Via Porta dell'Arco**, runs downhill to the **Arco Etrusco**, an Etruscan gateway, third-century BC in origin, built in Cyclopean blocks of stone, with Roman and medieval surrounds; the three blackened and eroded lumps on its outer face are probably images of Etruscan gods. The gate was narrowly saved from German destruction in the last war, during the course of a ten-day battle between the partisans (Volterra was a stronghold) and Germans. A memorial commemorates the partisan losses.

If you turn north instead off Via Marchesi, and follow Via Matteotti and its continuation, Via Guarnacci, you reach the Porta Fiorentina. Just to the west of the gate, below the road, is an area of excavations including a **Roman theatre** (now restored for use in the summer theatre festival) and a **bath complex** with mosaic floors. Following the **Via Diana**, straight ahead from the gate, makes for a pleasant walk, leading past the cemetery to remains of the Etruscan Porta Diana. Out beyond here tracks lead through farmland that was once a vast **Etruscan necropolis** – wandering through, you'll spot various unmarked, underground tombs.

The Museo Guarnacci

Volterra's Etruscan legacy is represented most importantly at the **Museo Guarnacci**, Via Don Minzoni 15 (daily April–Sept 9am–1pm & 2.30–6pm; Oct–March 10am–2pm; L5000). One of Italy's major archaeological museums, it consists entirely of local finds, including some six hundred funerary urns.

Carved in alabaster, tufo and terracotta, the **urns** date from the fourth to first centuries BC – earlier tombs were lost as the cliffs fell to nothing. On their sides, bas-reliefs depict domestic events (often boar hunting) or Greek myths (usually a trip to the underworld); on the lid are a bust of the subject and symbolic flowers – one for a young person, two for middle-aged, three for elderly.

Unfortunately the display, grouped according to subject, is stultifyingly old-fashioned and uninstructive, and only a few pieces manage to stand out from the mass-produced ware. Most of the best are arranged on the top floor and date from the "golden age" of the third and second centuries BC. Among them is the much-reproduced **Gli Sposi**, a disturbing portrait scene of a supposed husband and wife – all piercing eyes and dreadful looks. On this floor, too, are a number of small bronze sculptures, including the extraordinary **Ombra della Sera** (Shadow of the Evening), an elongated nude which provided inspiration for Giacometti. The farmer who unearthed it displayed rather less reverence – he used it as a poker for a few years.

To the Balze

To reach the *Balze* – the famous eroded cliffs – follow the Via di San Lino northwest from the Piazza dei Priori. This passes the church of **San Francesco**, with fifteenth-century frescoes of the *Legend of the True Cross* (see p.384) by Cenni di Cenni, before leaving town through the **Porta San Francesco**. From here, follow Borgo Santo Stefano and its continuation, Borgo San Giusto, past the Baroque church and former abbey of **San Giusto** – its dilapidated but striking facade framed by an avenue of cypress trees.

At the **Balze** you gain a real sense of the extent of Etruscan Volterra, whose old town walls drop away into the chasms. Gashes in the slopes and the natural erosion of sand and clay are made more dramatic by alabaster mines, ancient and modern. Below are buried great tracts of the Etruscan and Roman city and landslips continue – as evidenced by the locked and ruined monastery ebbing away over the precipice.

Food and festivals

As a hunting centre, Volterra's gastronomic efforts are dominated by wild boar (*cinghiale*). You see stuffed heads of the unfortunate beasts throughout town, and the meat is packaged as salamis or hams, as well as roasted in the restaurants, along with *lepre* (hare) and *coniglio* (rabbit).

Restaurant recommendations below cover the best of a similarly priced bunch. **Cheaper options** include a self-service at Via Matteotti 19 and a few pizzerias – there's a good one opposite the *Ristorante Beppino* in Via delle Prigioni. Buying your own food, there's a good choice of shops on Via Matteotti and a **Saturday market** in the Piazza dei Priori.

Restaurants

Da Badò, Borgo San Lazzero 9. Excellent local trattoria, serving up delicious *crostini*, and Volterran game staples such as *pappardelle alla lepre*. Closed Wed & mid-July to mid-Sept. From L20,000.

Da Beppino, Via delle Prigioni 15. Reliable, old-established restaurant that's only a tad pricier than other lesser places on this street. Outside tables and lots of hunting dishes. From L24,000. Closed Wed.

Etruria, Piazza dei Priori 6 (☎0588/86.064). Best of the more expensive places: booking ahead is a good idea.

La Pace, Via Don Minzoni 55. Welcoming neighbourhood restaurant located near the youth hostel – excellent pasta dishes and no pressure to have full meals. If you do, count on around L15–18,000.

Osteria dei Poeti, Via Matteotti 55–57. One of the most popular restaurants in town – and they don't stint on portions. From L20,000. Closed Thurs.

Pozzo degli Etruschi, Via delle Prigioni 28–30. Busy place, offering the best *menù turistico* in town.

Taverna del Priore, Via Matteotti 19. Cheap, cheerful self-service *taverna*, always full of young crowds.

La Tavernetta, Via Guarnacci 14. Promotes itself as a *ristorante-spaghetteria*, so the emphasis as you'd expect is on pasta. L14,000 would provide a fair feed. Next door, at no. 16, is a *birreria* (open to midnight), where the youth hang out in this generally low-level-nightlife town.

Festivals

The major Volterran festival is a **crossbow contest** – a colourful spectacle held in the Piazza dei Priori in July or August. In July, too, there's a small **theatre festival**, and the last Monday of September sees the Piazza dei Priori play host to a **bird fair**.

South to Massa Maríttima

Most travellers take in Volterra from the Florence–San Gimignano–Siena route, heading back east, or striking north to Pisa. The road south (N439), **over to Massa Maríttima** (covered by *APT* buses), is much less explored – a very wild, mountainous route that is given an added surreal quality by the presence of *soffioni*, hot steam geysers from which boric acid is extracted. To the east of the road are the **Colline Metallifere** – the metal hills – mined by the Etruscans and still harbouring wolves: an odd thought, just fifty miles from Rome.

Pomarance, Larderello and Castelnuovo

Leaving Volterra, it's a highly scenic drive down to **POMARANCE**, itself a dull and largely modern centre. Just east is the great ruined bastion of the **Rocca di Silano** – a landmark for almost the whole extent of this route.

Billing itself as the "World Centre of Geothermal Energy", **LARDERELLO** signals the heart of *soffioni* country and takes its name from a nineteenth-century Frenchman who introduced the system for harnessing energy from the vapours. *ENEL*, the electricity company, have set up a small **Museo Storico** (Mon–Sat 8am–5pm, but call first – ☎0588/673.712) on the subject. Modernist buffs might also take a look at the **Michelucci church**, near the centre of town.

All around Larderello huge silver pipes run across the fields, with steam and smoke rising intermittently from chimneys amid the dark foliage. Settlements are few, presumably due to the strong whiffs of sulphur, and the only sizeable village past Larderello is **CASTELNUOVO DI VAL DI CECINA**, a neat little *borgo medievale*, with a single **hotel**, the *Albergo-Ristorante Castagno*, just out of town to the south. Beyond here, the road is hemmed in by woods and there's scarcely a farmhouse to be seen.

With transport, you could cut east along a tiny, winding road, south of Castelnuovo, through **MONTIERI** (with a **hotel-rifugio**) and on to San Galgano (see p.342).

travel details

Trains

From Siena to Empoli (hourly; 50min–1hr 20min; change for Florence and Pisa, respectively 25min and 30min); Asciano/Chiusi (12 daily; 35min/1hr 35min); Buonconvento/Grosseto (6 daily; 25min/1hr 20min).

From Saline di Volterra Cécina (8 daily; 35min; connections to Pisa/Rome).

Buses

From Siena *TRA-IN* and *Lazzi* departures from San Domenico include: Arezzo, Asciano, Buonconvento, Certaldo, Chianciano Terme, Chiusi, Colle di Val d'Elsa, Florence, Gaiole, Greve, Grosseto, Lucca, Massa Maríttima, Montalcino, Monte Amiata, Montepulciano, Monteriggioni, Monte San Savino, Pienza, Poggibonsi, Radda, Rome, San Gimignano (via Poggibonsi), San Quirico d'Orcia, Sinalunga, Vescovado and Volterra.

From Poggibonsi Innumerable connections to San Gimignano and Colle di Val d'Elsa, also to Volterra and Massa Maríttima.

From San Gimignano Regular departures to Poggibonsi, whence connections to Florence, Siena and Volterra.

From Volterra To San Gimignano (via Poggibonsi), Siena, Florence, Massa Maríttima and Livorno.

CHAPTER SEVEN

SOUTHERN TUSCANY

The region **south of Siena** is Tuscany at its best: an infinite gradation of hills, trees and cultivation that encompasses the *Crete Senese*, the vineyards of Montepulciano and Montalcino, the Monte Amiata uplands, and finally a landscape of sulphurous springs and castle-topped outcrops of tufa. The *crete*, especially, is fabulous: a sparsely populated region of pale clay hillsides, dotted with sheep, cypresses and the odd monumental-looking farmhouse.

The towns on the whole live up to this environment. **Montepulciano**, the most elegant and enjoyable, makes a superb base, with its independent hill-town life, acclaimed Vino Nobile wine and backdrop of Renaissance buildings. **Montalcino** too has wine attractions – its Brunello is regarded as Tuscany's finest vintage – and classic hill-town looks, while **Pienza** is a unique Renaissance monument, a new town created by the great humanist pope, Pius II. In the south of the region, the urban highlights are **Pitigliano**, isolated on an amazing crag, and nearby the forgotten, half-abandoned medieval town of **Sovana**.

Monasteries constitute a major attraction of the area, featuring some of the greatest houses of the medieval Italian orders: Cistercian **San Galgano** and **Abbadia San Salvatore**, Benedictine **Monte Oliveto Maggiore** and **Sant'Antimo**, and Vallambrosan **Torri**. All are tremendous buildings, encompassing the best that Tuscany came up with in Romanesque and Gothic church architecture.

Equally memorable sights are the extraordinary **sulphur springs** that erupt from the rocks, or are channelled into geothermal energy, punctuating the landscape with pillars of white smoke. Several of the springs have for centuries formed the nucleus of **spas**. The most interesting is **Bagno Vignoni**, which preserves its Medicean basin in the village square. Here, and at **Bagni di Petriolo**, **Bagni San Filippo** and – most spectacularly – **Saturnia**, you can immerse yourself in open-air rock pools below warm cascades.

ACCOMMODATION PRICES

Throughout this guide, accommodation is graded on a scale from ① to ⑨. Grades ① and ② apply to **hostel** accommodation, and indicate the lowest price a **single person** could expect to pay for one night in that establishment in high season. Grades ③ to ⑨ apply to **hotels**, and indicate the cost of the **cheapest double room in high season**. The price bands to which these codes refer are as follows:

① under L20,000 per person	④ L50–70,000 per double	⑦ L120–150,000 per double
② over L20,000 per person	⑤ L70–90,000 per double	⑧ L150–200,000 per double
③ under L50,000 per double	⑥ L90–120,000 per double	⑨ over L200,000 per double

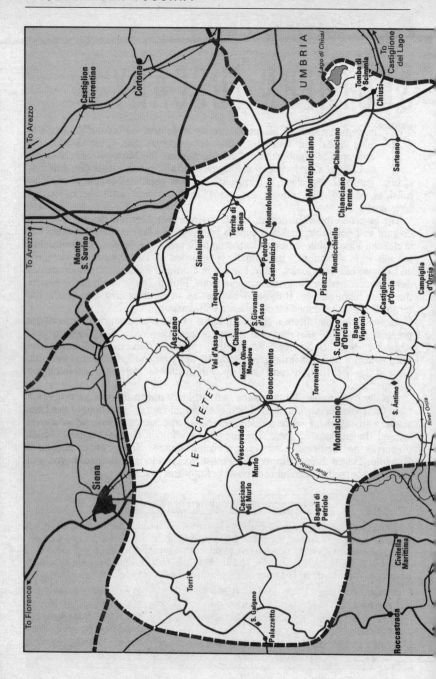

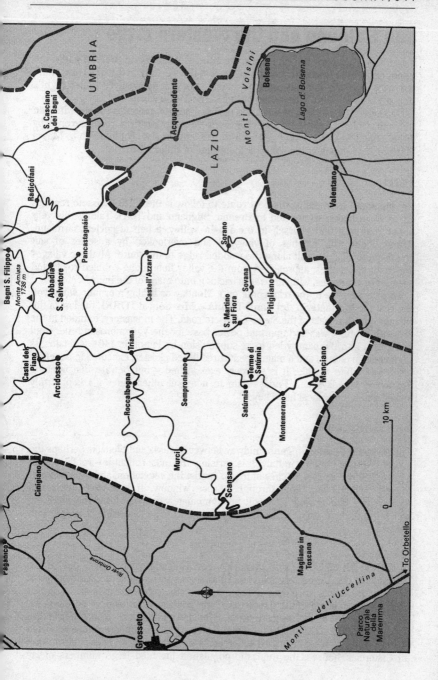

San Galgano and the western *crete*

If you have transport, the route past the abbeys of **Torri** and **San Galgano**, the sulphur spring of **Petriolo**, and the villages of the western *crete* makes one of the best trips out from Siena. It could be done in a day, or alternatively with a night's stop at Buonconvento, Montalcino or one of the Murlo villages.

Dependent on public transport, it's perhaps best to content yourself with San Galgano, which lies just off the N73 Siena–Massa Maríttima road, covered by three daily buses. You could get back to Siena in the day, continue on to Massa Maríttima, or stop near the abbey at the village of **Palazzetto**.

Torri

Driving south from Siena, the best route to follow is the N223 Grosseto road, as far as the junction signposted to Brenna, Stigliano and Torri. Taking this very minor road you find yourself in the **Rosia valley**, a belt of ancient farmland, strung about with patches of vineyard and overlooked by a series of soft cream-stone villages built along the wooded ridge to the south. All these villages are pastoral beauties, approached from the valley floor along cobbled roads and avenues of cypresses, with farmyards backing onto many of the houses.

To give purpose to the trip, come on a Monday or Friday morning, when you can visit the **Monasterio dei Santi Trinità e Mustiola** at **TORRI**, the last of the villages, just 2km east of the Siena–Grosseto road. The monastery, founded in the eleventh century, was an important power base for the Vallombrosan order until difficulties with the papacy led to its suppression by Pius II in 1464. It retains its Romanesque church and a magnificent three-tiered cloister, executed in panels of black and white marble. It is scarcely ever visited – but beware that opening hours are Mondays and Fridays 9am to noon; at other times it's kept firmly locked and nobody local has a key.

San Galgano

The **Abbazia di San Galgano**, midway between Massa and Siena, is perhaps the greatest Gothic building in Italy. It is certainly the most romantic – roofless, with a grass field for a nave, patches of fresco amidst the vegetation, and panoramas of the sky, clouds and hills through a rose window. If you have ever seen Tarkovsky's film *Nostalgia*, it will be immediately familiar from the finale, in which the director transformed the nave into a Russian landscape complete with a *dacha*.

The Abbey

In the twelfth and thirteenth centuries, San Galgano – which was one of the Cistercians' two largest foundations in Italy – was the leading monastic power in Tuscany. Its abbots ruled over disputes between the cities, and at Siena its monks oversaw the building of the duomo and held posts as *casalinghi*, or accountants, for the *comune*. The monks were a mix of Italians and French – from the principal house at Cîteaux – and through them the ideas of Gothic building were imported to Italy, along with sophisticated schemes for land drainage and agriculture. As at all Cistercian houses, the monastic population included large numbers of lay brothers, who dedicated themselves to manual labour, while the "Choir Monks" looked after the prayer and study.

The order built the **church** and **abbey** here between 1218 and 1288, at which time the complex must have looked like a small town, with its numerous workshops, dormitories and guest quarters. However, at the end of the century, during the wars between the Tuscan cities, the English *condottiere* Sir John Hawkwood sacked the abbey with his mercenary troops, and by 1397 the abbot was San Galgano's sole occupant. During the fifteenth century it recovered its numbers for a while, until the papacy made over its income to a particularly profligate cardinal. The monks left and the building gradually decayed – the campanile collapsing during a Mass attended by villagers.

The vast church, with its seventy-metre nave and shored-up aisles, now encloses little more than a stone altar. Birds hover about the glassless windows and capitals. Outside, there are brief runs of cloister and a few conventual buildings, which are being restored for use by a small community of Benedictine Olivetan nuns.

MONTE SIEPI AND THE SWORD IN THE STONE

The monastery commemorates **Saint Galgano Guidotti**, a noble from the nearby village of Chiusdino, who spent his youth in the usual saintly apprenticeship of dissipation and battles. Following a vision of Saint Michael, he then renounced his life as a knight and embarked on a career as a hermit. His conviction was fortified by a kind of reversed sword-in-the-stone miracle when, during a visit by his family and fellow knights to persuade him back into the world, he ran his sword into the rock beside his hut: it stuck fast, forming a crucifix. In 1181, at the age of thirty-three, Galgano died, and within four years was canonised.

The saint's hermitage was transformed into the circular **Cappella di Monte Siepi** – the building on the hill above the main abbey – between 1182 and 1185, with the **sword in the stone** still forming a centrepiece. The chapel was designed as a mausoleum but Galgano's body has been lost, though his head is preserved in the Siena cathedral museum. In the fourteenth century a Gothic side chapel was added to the original Romanesque chapel, and in the 1700s a rectory was attached, the three forming a rustic, farmhouse-like group. It is well worth the climb, as much for the views over the abbey as for the chapels themselves. The interior of the rotunda is interesting for its strange striped dome, which has an almost cosmological appearance; the side chapel has patches of frescoes by Ambrogio Lorenzetti, including a just about discernible image of Galgano offering the rock-embedded sword to Saint Michael.

Rooms

If you need to stay nearby, there is **accommodation** in the village of Palazzetto, 4km south on the Massa road, at the *Bar-Albergo Il Palazzetto* (☎0577/750.160; ④). The *Palazzetto* has a good restaurant, too, with meals in the L30,000 range, as well as bar snacks.

Bagni di Petriolo and into the *crete*

From San Galgano, you can cut across to the **N223 Siena–Grosseto road** by means of a minor road that leaves the N73 at the walled village of Monticiano. The road east of Monticiano is attractive, if unremarkable, twisting its way through wooded hills before finally emerging on the N223 about 20km south of Siena.

South from here, the N223 follows the River Merse before rearing into the hills by way of various viaducts. To reach **BAGNI DI PETRIOLO** you need to turn left after about 4km, then follow this road for 9km (no buses) down to a bridge beside the river – a tributary of the Ombrone – and a rough enclosure of huge medieval walls. Here, on the right, is a tiny thermal station (open summer only), offering treatment for visitors. On the left, below the bridge, the spa's **sulphur springs** continue to flow freely into a little rock pool, before mixing with the river. It's a wonderful, weird spot: leave your clothes well away from the sulphur, soak in the hot springwater, then wash off with a dip in the river – it's all very moody, especially if you arrive midweek, when you'll have the place to yourself.

The only buildings apart from the spa are a **pizzeria-restaurant**, *Il Murlino* (on the left of the road before the bridge, coming from Siena), whose food makes up for the bland surroundings, and a **hotel-restaurant**, *La Locanda di Petriolo*, currently in the throes of restoration.

The Murlo villages

With transport, you can follow a paved track off the Petriolo road, through the hills to **CASCIANO DI MURLO**; the track runs alongside a formidable estate that is fenced off to protect its woodland and shooting. Scarcely more than a hamlet, Casciano has a small **hotel**, the *Mirella* (☎0577/817.677; ⑤), a **riding centre**, and a **campsite**, *Le Soline* (☎0577/817.414), open year round, located at nearby Casafranci. A fine place to break your journey, or base yourself for a few days, Casciano is also easily reached from the N223 (it's 6km from the turning).

East from Casciano, a very high and beautiful road leads into the beginnings of the *crete*, its hills punctuated by an occasional lake and farmhouse on the approach to **VESCOVADO DI MURLO**. Vescovado, a largely modern village, is worth a stop for its **bar-restaurant**, the *Osteria Deo*, a thoroughly unpretentious place off the square which serves up vast portions of pasta, fish and roasts; it's frequented by the local priests – always a good sign. Vescovado also has a **hotel**, the *Murlo* (☎0577/814.033; ⑤), with the bonus of a swimming pool thrown in. There is also *agiturismo* accommodation at Palazzina (☎0577/817.776; ④), a farmhouse between Casciano and Vescovado.

Just a couple of kilometres south of Vescovado is **MURLO** – a tiny medieval *borgo* whose ring of houses forms its defensive walls, enclosing the town hall and church. The oldest settlement in the area, it commemorates its past as Etruscan Poggio Civitate in a new **Museo Etrusco**, housed in the village palazzo (Tues–Sun 9.30am–12.30pm & 2.30–5.30pm; L4000). Exhibits include sphinx statues, a large terracotta tomb frieze depicting hunting scenes, and odd bowls carved with warriors holding women – whose legs form the handles. To the south of Murlo, a track leads to an even smaller *borgo*, ten-house La Befa, which has a renowned **osteria** (closed Wed), set in rich mushroom territory; meals are around L20,000.

At Vescovado or Murlo, you're within easy striking distance of Buonconvento, and near enough to Asciano, Montalcino or Siena. The **Asciano road** is a superb scenic route, taking you into the heart of the *crete*, across very sparsely populated countryside. Just off the N2, which you need to join for a few kilometres before heading east to Asciano, there are **rooms** at the medieval hamlet of Lucignano d'Arbia.

Monte Oliveto and the central *crete*

The heartland of the *crete* is the area southeast of Siena, around the Benedictine monastery of **Monte Oliveto Maggiore** – arguably Tuscany's finest. This is reached easily enough by car via **Asciano** or **Buonconvento**, 9km distant, respectively to the north and west; **Montalcino**, too, is only 24km distant to the south. On **public transport**, you can get to Asciano or Buonconvento by train or bus from Siena, though you'll have to hitch (more promising from Buonconvento) or hike (prettier from Asciano) the rest of the way.

Buonconvento

BUONCONVENTO is the most obvious base if you are visiting Monte Oliveto Maggiore and travelling on south. The small town looks unremittingly industrial on the approach but once through the suburbs you come upon a perfect, walled medieval village. This old centre is characteristically Sienese, with its brick bastions, town hall and its works of art – most of which have been removed from the churches to the excellent and little-known **Museo d'Arte Sacra** at Via Soccini 17 (Tues & Thurs 10am–noon, Sat 10am–noon & 4–6pm, Sun 9am–1pm; L4000). Pride of place in the museum goes to a *Madonna and Child with Angels* by Matteo di Giovanni, whose knowing Mary must surely be a portrait.

Art attractions aside, Buonconvento makes an enjoyable stop, with a single **hotel-restaurant**, the *Albergo Roma* (☎0577/806.021; ④), inside the walls. The hotel is a bit basic but its food is fine. Across the way from the hotel, in the Palazzo del Popolo in Piazza Gramsci, there are regular weekend **dance** evenings – a great experience, with all the local farmers coming in for a waltz.

Alternative **accommodation** near Buonconvento is provided by the Pieve a Salti farm (☎0577/807.244; ④) at Pieve a Salti, part of the *agriturismo* scheme; it's both comfortable and welcoming, and the beautifully situated swimming pool has views over what seems like half of southern Tuscany. For details of other *agriturismo* lettings in the area contact *Azienda Agricola Bartalucci*, Pieve a Sprenna (☎0577/806.213).

Monte Oliveto Maggiore

The **Abbazia di Monte Oliveto Maggiore** is sited in one of the most beautiful tracts of Sienese countryside. Approaching from Buonconvento, you climb through forests of pine, oak and cypress, and then into the olive groves that enclose the monastery. From the east, coming through Asciano or San Giovanni d'Asso, the road passes through perhaps the wildest section of all the *crete*. It is all much as it must have appeared to Pope Pius II, who in 1463 eulogised the woods and gardens that the monks had created from the chalk hills, and the way the russet-coloured brick buildings merged with their setting. To his impressions, the main point to add is that the monastery preserves one of the most absorbing of all Renaissance fresco cycles, a *Life of St Benedict* painted by Sodoma and Signorelli.

The monastery had been founded a century and a half before Pius's visit by one Giovanni Tolomei. A Sienese noble, Giovanni was a major political force in Siena before renouncing his worldly goods after being struck blind and experiencing visions of the Virgin. Adopting the name Bernardo, he came with two companions to the *crete* and lived the life of a hermit. They soon drew a following in this heyday of monasticism, and within six years the pope recognised them as an order – the **Olivetans**, or White Benedictines. Attempting to re-establish the simplicity of the original Benedictine rule, these first Olivetans were a remarkable group, going out in pairs during the Black Death to nurse the sick and minister to the dying in all the Sienese towns. During the Feast of the Assumption in 1348, they all met up in Siena, miraculously with no casualties after their months of work – though Bernardo died later in the year, as did many of the brothers.

The remaining monks rebuilt the order and over the following two centuries Monte Oliveto Maggiore was transformed into one of the most powerful monasteries in the land. Pius II had a personal interest in his visit, as his relative Ambrogio Piccolomini was one of Bernardo's original companions. In 1536 the Emperor Charles V paid a call with an army of two thousand, whom the monks seem to have managed to entertain.

The monastery only really fell from influence with the nineteenth-century suppression of the Italian orders. After the last war, the Italian government allowed Olivetan monks to repopulate the monastery. They have largely restored the buildings and gardens, which they today maintain as a monument, supplementing their state income with an extremely advanced workshop for the restoration of ancient books. They also produce wine, honey, olive oil and a cure-all herb liquor, *Flora di Monte Oliveto*, for sale at the monastery shop.

The Monastery

Monte Oliveto is **open to visits** daily from 9.15am to 12.30pm and from 3.15 to 6.30pm (5.30pm in winter). At the gatehouse there is a good **café-restaurant**, and also a **hostel** – as is the Benedictine custom. This, however, has a minimum stay of ten days (most guests stay two to three months) and summer places are almost always taken; if you want to try your luck, phone ahead (☎0577/707.017). Otherwise the closest place to spend the night is the *agriturismo* option of the *Agricola Mocine* (☎0577/707.105; ④), situated in the hamlet of Chiusure, just over a kilometre to the east.

From the **gateway**, surmounted by a square watchtower and niches containing Della Robbia terracottas, an avenue of cypresses leads to the abbey. Off to the right signs direct you along a walk to the **Blessed Bernardo's grotto** – a chapel built on the site where Tolomei settled as a hermit. The **abbey** itself is a huge complex, though much of it remains off limits to visitors. The entrance leads past the giftshop to the **Chiostro Grande**, covered by the frescoes of the *Life of St Benedict*, the man traditionally regarded as the founder of Christian monasticism.

SODOMA AND SIGNORELLI'S LIFE OF SAINT BENEDICT

The Saint Benedict fresco cycle was begun by **Luca Signorelli**, a painter from Cortona who trained under Piero della Francesca before working for the papacy on the Sistine Chapel. He worked at Monte Oliveto in 1497, completing nine panels (in the middle of the series) before abandoning the work for a more stimulating commission at Orvieto Cathedral. Like much of his work elsewhere, the scenes show a passionate interest in human anatomy, with figures positioned to show off their muscular forms to maximum effect.

A few years after Signorelli's departure, Antonio Bazzi, known as **Il Sodoma**, took over, painting the remaining 27 scenes from 1505 to 1508. Sodoma was from

Milan and familiar with Leonardo's work, which he often emulates. How he took his nickname is unclear: Vasari suggests it was apt since "he was always surrounded by young men, in whose company he took great pleasure", though letters by Sodoma himself speak of three wives and thirty children. Whatever, the artist was a colourful figure, keeping an amazing menagerie of pets: "Badgers, apes, cat-a-mountains, dwarf asses, horses and barbs to run races, magpies, dwarf chickens, tortoises, Indian doves . . .".

Sodoma brought a sizeable contingent of these pets to Monte Oliveto, including a raven which imitated his voice, and they make odd appearances throughout his colourful, sensual frescoes – a badger is depicted at his feet in a self-portrait in the third panel. There's a notable eroticism, too, in many of the secular figures: especially the young men coming to join Benedict as monks, and the "evil women" seen tempting the monks in a panel towards the end of the series – originally nudes until protests from the abbot. If the panels strike you as of differing quality, you might give credence to Vasari's anecdote that Sodoma complained about the money he was being paid, which the abbot subsequently raised on condition that he took more care over the remaining work, the first three historical panels of the sequence.

The **cycle** begins on the east wall, on the right of the door into the church. Saint Benedict, who was born in Norcia in 480, is depicted in events recorded in Gregory the Great's *Dialogues*. In the early panels he is shown leaving home to study in Rome, before withdrawing to the life of a hermit, where he experiences various tribulations and temptations before agreeing to become abbot to a group of disciples. He was an indefatigable builder of monasteries and the next panels focus on this activity: the foundation of the twelve houses which formed the basis of the Benedictine order, and various miracles to help in their construction.

The mid-sequence of the cycle depicts various attempts by an evil priest, Florentius, to disrupt the saint's work: he tries first to poison Benedict and then sends in the temptresses, before God steps in and flattens his house (the first of Signorelli's panels). The following eight scenes painted by Signorelli depict aspects of monastic life, and Benedict's trial by – and reception of – Totila, king of the Goths, before Sodoma takes over again with the saint foretelling the destruction of Monte Cassino, the chief Benedictine house, by the Lombards. More scenes of monastic life follow, including the burial of a monk whom the earth would not accept, another monk's attempted escape (Benedict intercepts him with a serpent), and the release of a peasant persecuted by a Goth.

THE CHURCH, LIBRARY AND REFECTORY

The rest of the monastery is inevitably overshadowed by the frescoes. The main **church** – entered off the Chiostro Grande – was given a Baroque remodelling in the eighteenth century and some superb stained glass in the present one. Its main treasure is the **choir stalls**, inlaid by Giovanni di Verona and others from 1500 to 1520 with architectural, landscape and domestic scenes (including a nod to Sodoma's pets with a depiction of a cat in a window).

Back in the cloister, stairs lead up past a fresco of the Virgin by Sodoma to the **library**, a fine Renaissance arcade lavished with carving by Giovanni and associates. Sadly, it has had to be viewed from the door since the theft of sixteen codices in 1975. Also on view is the **refectory**, a vast room frescoed with allegorical and Old Testament figures, which gives some idea of Monte Oliveto's heyday.

Asciano

ASCIANO lies on a tiny branch rail line between Siena and Grosseto that takes you through marvellous *crete* countryside. The road approach, the N438 from Siena, is still more scenic, with scarcely a hamlet amid the hills; this is covered by bus only once daily (the same departure as for Chiusure).

The town itself is partially walled and shelters a couple of tiny provinical museums. In an oratory adjoining the Collegiata in Piazza Fratelli Bandiera is the **Museo d'Arte Sacra** (free; ring the bell or apply for admission at the Collegiata) with a dozen or so paintings by major Sienese painters, among them Ambrogio Lorenzetti, Sano di Pietro, Taddeo di Bartolo and Matteo di Giovanni. Close by, at Corso Matteotti 46, is a **Museo Archeologico** (mid–June to mid–Sept Tues–Sun 10am–12.30pm & 4.30–6.30pm; rest of year 10am–12.30pm; L3000), whose exhibits are mainly finds from local Etruscan tombs.

Asciano has a single, reasonably priced, three-star **hotel**, *Il Bersagliere*, Via Roma 39–41 (☎0577/718.629; ④). Local bars provide basic food, though the best **restaurant** in the vicinity is *La Pievina* (closed Mon & Tues), 5.5km north along the Siena road at the hamlet of the same name. If you fancy a swim, there is a **lake** 5km south of Asciano, a hundred metres or so down the beautiful road from Val d'Asso to Trequanda.

San Giovanni d'Asso and east to Sinalunga

Continuing on the train line from Asciano, the next stop – and another possible starting point to hike to Monte Oliveto – is **SAN GIOVANNI D'ASSO**, a quiet, rustic place which hints at a more significant medieval past by the presence of half a dozen churches – Romanesque San Pietro is the most interesting – and an imposing castle. In the fourteenth century, several Sienese bankers operated from the village.

East from San Giovanni, a fine but bus-less road rambles towards Sinalunga. The attraction lies primarily in the landscape – classic Tuscan miniatures – though the road is marked out by a series of good-looking hilltop villages, most of them endowed with a castle and a scattering of medieval churches. **CASTELMUZIO** was a favourite preaching ground for Bernardino of Siena, whose confraternity houses a small Museo d'Arte Sacra; the saint is also depicted in panels by Giovanni di Paolo and his pupil Matteo di Giovanni in the church of SS. Trinità e Bernardino. Close by is one of Tuscany's oldest churches – the eighth-century **Pieve di Santo Stefano** in **CENNANO** – while at neighbouring **PETROIO** is the best **castle** in the district, where Siena's magistrates were obliged to live for a period in the thirteenth century. A few kilometres to the northeast is the **Abbadia a Sicille**, built by the Templars as a hospice on the pilgrim road to Rome. **TREQUANDA**, a slightly larger village with a couple of restaurants and bars, also preserves a good section of its castle and, in the central square, Romanesque **San Pietro** has a fresco by Sodoma.

East of Trequanda you reach **SINALUNGA**, a modern, thriving centre with rail connections to Siena, Arezzo and Chiusi. It has one notable painting – an *Annunciation* by Benvenuto di Giovanni – in the church of **San Francesco**, sited beside the Franciscan convent at the top of an avenue of cypresses. The church should have another fine picture – a *Madonna* by Sano di Pietro – but that went missing in 1972 and has been replaced by a sad facsimile. Just out of town in the hamlet-suburb of Pieve is a pleasant **hotel**, the *Santorotto* (☎0577/679.012; ⑤). In Sinalunga itself, at Viale Matteotti 5, there's a friendly and idiosyncratic **restaurant** called *Kris* (☎0577/631.225; closed Mon), which specialises in fish dishes but becomes an Indian restaurant on Wednesday nights.

Other good value **hotels** in these parts are to be found 7km south at the next rail stop, Torrita di Siena: the *Belvedere* (☎0577/685.246; ④) and *La Stazione* (☎0577/685.158; ⑤). There is further accommodation at the spas of Rapolano Terme and Terme San Giovanni, north of Sinalunga on the Siena road. Both of these spas are modern upmarket establishments, of little interest for anyone not intent on taking their cures.

Montalcino and around

MONTALCINO is a classic Tuscan hill town, set within a full circuit of walls and watched over by a *rocca*. A quiet place, affluent in an unshowy way, it is scarcely changed in appearance since the sixteenth century. It looks tremendous from below, and once up at the town the rolling hills, vineyards, orchards, olive groves and ancient oaks look equally wonderful in turn.

Inhabited sporadically since Etruscan times, Montalcino was permanently settled around the year 1000 by fugitives from the Saracens. Their four family groups – the Borghetto, Pianello, Ruca and Travaglio – defined the four quarters or *contrade* of the town; the rival flags still hang outside the houses and they compete against each other in twice-yearly archery tournaments. The town's great moment came in 1557, when a group of Sienese exiles held out here for two years after Siena's capitulation to the Florentines, as a last bastion of the republic. This role is acknowledged at the Siena Palio, where the Montalcino contingent, under their medieval banner proclaiming "The Republic of Siena in Montalcino", still take place of honour.

In the following centuries, the town declined to a poor, malaria-stricken village. Although the malaria was sorted out in the last century, in the 1960s Montalcino was still the poorest locality in Siena. Its change in fortunes – it is now the second richest – is due principally to the revival and marketing of its wines, notably the **Brunello**, which is reckoned by many the finest in Italy. Production of high-quality honey and olive oil, and tourism, also play a part.

The Town

Once up at the town, you find yourself on a ring road around the walls. Buses loop around to the north to stop in the **Piazza Cavour**; those with cars should aim to park near the southern gate, **Porta Cervara**.

The heart of town, **Piazza del Popolo**, lies between the two, only a few minutes' walk from any of the gates in the walls. An odd little square, it is set beneath the elongated medieval tower of the **Palazzo Civico**, modelled on that of Siena. Inside the town hall there is an exhibition on the history and making of Brunello. Occupying other sides of the square are an elegant Renaissance double **loggia**, almost a reprimand in proportional architecture, and a wonderful nineteenth-century **café**, the *Fiaschetteria Italiana*. The café is the heart of town life and the focus, inevitably, of the *passeggiata* along Via Mazzini.

Following Via Mazzini's continuation, Via Matteotti, or Via Ricasoli, you emerge at the south end of town by the **Rocca** (May–Sept daily 9am–1pm & 2–

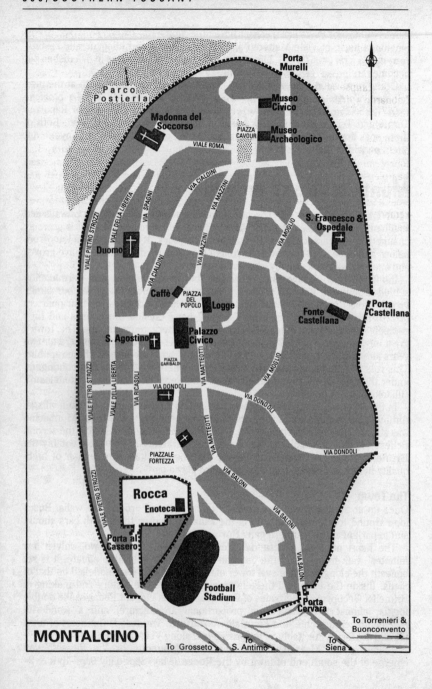

Parco
Postierla

Porta
Murelli

Museo
Civico

Madonna del
Soccorso

PIAZZA
CAVOUR

Museo
Archeologico

VIALE ROMA

VIA CIALDINI

VIA MAZZINI

VIA SPAGNI

VIALE DELLA LIBERTA

S. Francesco &
Ospedale

VIA MOGLIO

VIA PIETRO STROZZI

Duomo

VIA MAZZINI

VIA CIALDINI

Caffè

PIAZZA
DEL
POPOLO

Logge

Fonte
Castellana

Porta
Castellana

S. Agostino

Palazzo
Civico

PIAZZA
GARIBALDI

VIA MOGLIO

VIALE DELLA LIBERTA

VIA RICASOLI

VIA DONDOLI

VIA MATTEOTTI

VIA DONDOLI

VIA DONDOLI

VIA PIETRO STROZZI

PIAZZALE
FORTEZZA

VIA MATTEOTTI

VIA SALONI

Rocca
Enoteca

VIA SALONI

Porta al
Cassero

VIA SALONI

Football
Stadium

Porta
Cervara

MONTALCINO

To Grosseto

To
S. Antimo

To
Siena

To Torrenieri &
Buonconvento

8pm; Oct–April Tues–Sun 9am–1pm & 2–6pm; free). Impressively complete, this encloses a public park and plush **Enoteca** – a good place to sample some of the famed Brunello along with a snack of bread, cheese and salami. The *enoteca* also sells tickets giving access to the ramparts (L2000 or L4000 with Museo Civico) and a glimpse at the famous banner. The castle view is said to have inspired Leonardo's drawing of a bird's-eye view of the earth; the Val d'Órcia is easily made out and on a clear day you can even see Siena.

To the east of the Rocca, Viale Strozzi runs just inside the walls, past plots and orchards, to the distinctive Renaissance **Santuario della Madonna del Soccorso**. Of the town's other churches, Romanesque **Sant'Agostino** has fourteenth-century frescoes, possibly by Bartolo di Fredi, and **San Francesco** has pleasant cloisters, Della Robbia school terracottas and an annexe that was used as a medieval hospital. Nearby, facing the Porta Castellana, is a medieval washhouse, the **Fonte Castellane**. In the centre of town, the **Duomo** was remodelled in Neoclassical style in the eighteenth century by an architect called Fantastici; its interior, however, is uninteresting.

In the Palazzo Arcivescovile at Via Spagni 4 there's a **Museo Civico** and adjacent **Museo Archeologico** (summer Tues–Sun 9.30am–1pm & 3.30–7pm; winter same days 10am–1pm & 3–5pm; L4000 combined entry with Rocca's ramparts). The archaeological collections are a miscellany of Roman and Etruscan fragments; the Civico has a fair showing of fourteenth- and fifteenth-century Sienese artworks and some fine polychrome wooden sculptures.

Accommodation

Accommodation is severely limited and it's wise to book ahead at almost any time of year. There are just two central **hotels**: *Albergo Giardino*, Piazza Cavour (☎0577/848.257; ⑤), with a rather mixed bag of doubles, and *Albergo Il Giglio*, Via S. Saloni 49 (☎0577/848.167; ⑤). About 2km out at Belaria, on the Grosseto road, is the comfortable, but soullessly modern *Al Brunello* (☎0577/849.304; ⑤). **Private rooms** are less expensive and there's more choice. Try *Maccioni*, Piazza del Popolo 28 (☎0577/849.319), *Anna Affitacamare* at Via S. Saloni 31 (☎0577/848.666), or *Casali*, Via Spagni 3 (☎0577/848.083); all ④.

In summer you might find it easier to phone and book through the *Porposta* **accommodation bureau** at Costa del Municipio 8 (daily 9.30am–1pm & 3.30–7pm; ☎0577/849.321), which arranges private rooms and *agriturismo* lettings for a commission. The main **tourist office** is also at Costa del Municipio 8, with a smaller *pro loco* at Via G. Mazzini 42.

Wines and food

Sampling **Montalcino's wines** is easily done. Apart from the *enoteca* in the Rocca and the *Fiaschetteria Italiana* – which has a superb *cantina* at the back – there are half a dozen cheaper café-bars with good stocks. The *Caffè Cacciatore*, opposite the *Fiaschetteria*, is plain but doesn't impose too much surcharge on sitting outside. Further along Via Matteotti, there's the *Enoteca-Caffè di Mariccia*, with a breathtaking view from the back if you want to sit inside (and the town's only pay-after-the-call phone). For bottles to take away, try the *Enoteca Ars Bibendi* on Piazza del Popolo, which has a knowledgeable English-speaking owner. In addition to the classic Brunello and the less barrel-aged Rosso di Montalcino table wine, it's worth trying some of the white Moscadelletto di Montalcino, a dessert wine produced in small quantity and at its best chilled.

BRUNELLO VERSUS THE RUBBISH DUMP

The last couple of years have been unusually active for Montalcino politicians. In 1990 the Sienese provincial council announced the siting of a huge new plant for incinerating rubbish and fermenting recyclable waste at San Giovanni d'Asso – right on the edge of the Brunello vineyards. It soon became apparent that the fermentation would release gases into the environment and anything less than perfect control of the waste could lead to ecological disaster for the vineyards.

With Brunello sales alone valued at 130 billion lire (£60m) a year, local anxiety is easy to imagine – and the winemakers were soon joined by those with tourist interests, plus the local beekeepers and truffle businesses. A campaign led by local winemaker Franco Biondi Santi called in the Italian wine authorities, who predicted "a concrete risk of damage to the image and eventually the quality of one of the most prestigious Italian products". Protest marches were held, the town hall was occupied and half the Montalcino population signed a petition urging secession from the province. To date, however, the Sienese council – and their communist allies who control Montalcino council – have remained inflexible and in spring 1991 final planning approval was given to the scheme. The controversy continues.

The town's best budget **meals** are to be found at *Il Moro*, Via Mazzini 44, and the *Pizzeria-Enoteca S. Giorgio* on Via Saloni. A bit pricier but excellent is *Il Giardino d'Alberto* in Piazza Cavour, where the chef is the owner. Resist any temptation to try the swanky *La Cucina di Edgardo*, which makes a peculiarly ill-starred attempt at *cucina nuova*. For the region's gourmet experience, you need to head out of town – either to *Il Poggio Antico*, on the road to Buonconvento, or the *Fattoria dei Barbi* (see p.354).

Festivals

Festa della Madonna del Soccorso (May 8). A small palio – featuring the same horses that will appear later in the year at Siena – is held on the sports field below the fort.

Montalcino Teatro (third and fourth weeks of July). An international theatre festival, presenting works in progress in the churches, Rocca, eighteenth-century *Teatro degli Astrusi*, and sometimes in the *crete* around the town.

Torneo della Apertura della Caccia (second Sun in Aug). Tournament marking the start of the hunting season that is said to have fourteenth-century origins – inspiring some of the tales in the *Decameron*. Half the town dresses up in medieval costume for parades and archery competitions (on the sports field) between the *contrade*. Street banquets complete the day.

Festa dell'Unità (mid-Aug). Ten-day festival organised by the communist party in the pine wood above the town. Live music most nights, cheap food and wine – and usually a lot of fun.

Sagra del Tordo (last Sun in Oct). Similar events to the *Caccia* festival.

Montalcino's disco: Camigliano

One of the stranger features of northern Italy is the distance people are prepared to drive to a party, restaurant or disco. Montalcino is no exception, offering zilch in the way of its own nightlife. Instead, on Saturday nights in summer, the locals drive 14km southwest to an **open-air disco** at the village of Camigliano. It's quite an occasion, patronised by just about everyone from the surrounding farms and villages, as well as a fair section of foreign residents – immediately identifiable by their eccentric dancing. Music ranges from the latest Europop to traditional Italian songs and with an entrance fee of L5000 and large glasses of wine at L500 a time, it hardly breaks the bank. The only problem is that you need to drive: there's no local accommodation or transport.

Transport

TRA-IN **buses** run more or less hourly from Piazza Cavour and Viale P. Strozzi to Buonconvento and Siena, most of them via Torrenieri, and five times daily (Mon–Sat) to Monte Amiata, passing Sant'Antimo (see below). At Torrenieri you can also pick up one of six daily buses south to Arcidosso, five east to San Quírico and Montepulciano.

For **rail connections** to Siena or Grosseto, head either to Torrenieri or to Sant'Angelo, 9km south of Montalcino and connected by three buses daily.

Sant'Antimo

At the hamlet of Castelnuove dell'Abate, 10km south of Montalcino, is the **Abbazia di Sant'Antimo** (daily April–Sept 10.30am–12.30pm & 3–6pm; Oct–March 11am–12.30pm & 3–5pm; free), a glorious, isolated Benedictine monastery which stands good comparison with San Galgano, Monte Oliveto and San Salvatore. The abbey is today maintained by a small group of French Cistercians, who celebrate Mass several times daily in haunting Gregorian chant.

The monks' quarters aside, little remains of the monastic buildings – a ruined refectory and chapterhouse are used as barns. But the **Church** itself is in good repair and one of the outstanding examples of Italian Romanesque, perfectly proportioned and built in a soft, creamy stone that reflects the season's light. Built in the twelfth century, it has a rounded apse flanked by roofed side chapels, and inside, columns running around both apse and nave. Equally delightful are the details of the **carving and frescoes**. As so often with the Romanesque, these feature animals and have an earthy sense of humour. One of the alabaster capitals depicts *Daniel in the Lions' Den*, the hero aloof while his fellow prisoners are crushed and eaten by romping beasts. In the rarely opened **sacristy**, an array of primitive black-and-white frescoes include such details as a rat looking up attentively at Saint Benedict, and a pair of copulating pigs. Further·frescoes are to be found in some of the rooms built around the **women's gallery**, approached from the nave by a circular stairway, though all too often access is restricted.

There are occasional **buses** along the Sant'Antimo road, currently leaving Montalcino from Monday to Friday at 6am and 1.40pm, Saturday at 4.35pm, and returning Monday to Friday at 7.50am and 3.35pm, Saturday at 4.50pm. Alternatively, it's a pleasant country walk or feasible hitch. Additional rewards are offered by the *Bar-Trattoria Bassomondo* (closed Mon) across the road, which does wonderful *crostini*, *ribollita* and *pici*; it's around L25,000 a head.

Vineyards and villages around Montalcino

As Brunello is Italy's premier wine, it seems a shame not to get out to at least one of the **vineyards**. As well as those detailed overleaf, you can visit most others if you ask at the winegrowers' headquarters in the Palazzo del Popolo; the only period when visitors might not be welcome is at harvest time (Sept/Oct).

Fattoria dei Barbi

The **Fattoria dei Barbi** is 7km southeast of Montalcino, signposted off to the left just after the hamlet of La Croce on the Sant'Antimo road. Its *cantina* (Mon–Sat 9.30am–noon & 2–5.30pm, Sun 3–6pm) offers tasting facilities and a superb stock of vintages. Attached is a very fine **restaurant**, the *Taverna dei Barbi* (☎0577/848.277; closed Tues evening & Wed), run by an Englishwoman but serving up strictly local recipes – lots of *porcini*, *pici*, *papardelle* and delicious grilled pork, the *brasato al Brunello*, washed down, of course, with the Barbi's own wine. Count on around L35,000 for an extensive meal.

Villa Banfi, Castello di Poggio alle Mure and Sant'Angelo in Colle

With a third of its three thousand hectares devoted to vineyards, **Villa Banfi** is Montalcino's largest and most modern wine producer. It was taken over in the 1970s by an Italian-American wine-importing family, the Mariani, and has English-speaking guides available to show you round. The villa is located just outside the village of Sant'Angelo Scala, 18km southwest of Montalcino; it's served by occasional weekday buses from Montalcino (most convenient is the 2.40pm, returning at 6.05pm) and is on the Siena–Asciano–Grosseto rail line. By the station are a couple of **restaurants**: *Trattoria Casini*, which serves basic food at basic prices, and *Il Manideto*, which is fancy and expensive.

Five kilometres to the west of the station, inside the Banfi estate, is the **Castello di Poggio alle Mure**, a thirteenth-century castle built for the Salimbeni clan of Siena, though subsequently added to in a mish-mash of styles. Recently renovated, it has a small museum of Roman and Etruscan artefacts, and a display of traditional implements for wine-making. If the main gate is closed, ask at the *enoteca* alongside, or at the nearby post office. Visits are free.

At the halfway point on the road from Montalcino to Villa Banfi is the tiny walled village of **SANT'ANGELO IN COLLE**, set on a low hill. The Sienese used it as a military base against Montalcino in the mid-thirteenth century and as part of their frontier thereafter. It has some interesting frescoes inside the main church on the piazza and a couple of **bar-restaurants**. The one on the piazza, *Il Pozzo*, is recommended for its roasts – about L20,000 for two courses and wine; the other, in the tower, has fine views but no atmosphere.

The Val d'Órcia and Bagno Vignoni

The **Val d'Órcia** stretches from San Quírico d'Órcia down towards the border with Lazio and the lake of Bolsena. A gorgeous stretch of country, it is marked at intervals by fortresses built from the eighth century on, when the road through the valley, the **Via Francigena**, was a vital corridor north from Rome.

The major attraction along the initial section of the valley is the remarkable Medicean sulphur baths of **Bagno Vignoni**. With transport – or a taste for walking – you might strike off south from here to the region's medieval power base, the monastery of San Salvatore (see p.366). **Walkers** might also consider approaching Bagno Vignoni across country from Montalcino (a five-hour hike which would entail staying in Bagno Vignoni), or going on from Bagno Vignoni along the old track to Pienza; it's worth asking local tourist offices for maps, as some will provide photocopies of detailed walking maps.

San Quírico d'Órcia

A rambling, part-walled village, **SAN QUÍRICO D'ÓRCIA** stands at a cross-roads on the Siena to Bolsena road, overlooking the Órcia and Asso valleys. It's quiet and rather decayed, overlooked by the precarious ruins of a seventeenth-century palazzo, whose Baroque exterior frescoes are fading before your eyes. The main reason for stopping is to look around the exceptionally pretty Romanesque **Collegiata**, with its three portals sculpted with lions and other beasts; the south door may be the work of Giovanni Pisano. Inside the church is a delicate triptych of the *Virgin and Saints* by Sano di Pietro and a marvellous set of Renaissance inlaid choir stalls. There's a **tourist office** at Via Dante Aligheri 33 (June–Oct daily 10.30am–1pm & 3.30–7pm; ☎0577/897.211) and a *Pro Loco* at Piazza della Libertà 2 when the main office is shut.

San Quírico is a regular stop on the Siena–Buonconvento–Pienza–Montepulciano **bus** route and has a small **hotel**, *La Motel Patrizia* (☎0577/897.715; ④) on the Via Cassia, the main road. Steer clear of the *Palazzuolo*, the only other hotel, which is in the middle of a housing estate. If you want an isolated and peaceful place to stay, Ripa d'Órcia, 5km southwest of San Quírico at the end of a very minor road, has a perfect hotel-restaurant, *Castello Ripa d'Órcia* (☎0577/897.376; ⑤).

Bagno Vignoni

Six kilometres south of San Quírico, **BAGNO VIGNONI** is scarcely even a hamlet – just a handful of buildings around a central square. The square, however, is one of Tuscany's most memorable sights, occupied by an arcaded Renaissance **piscina**. This was built by the Medici, who, like Saint Catherine of Siena, took the sulphur cure here. The hot springs still bubble away in the bath (they formed an amazing set in Tarkovsky's film *Nostalgia*), though they are currently out of bounds for bathing; plans to restore the *piscina* and develop the spa as a resort have so far been thwarted by the Siena council.

You can, however, bathe in the sulphur springs where they emerge from the hillside below the village, or use the sulphur pool at the four-star *Posta Marcucci* **hotel**, a fifteenth-century summer house erected by Pius II on the side of the piazza. The *Posta Marcucci* (☎0577/887.112; ⑥) allows non-residents use of the pool for L15,000 a day. The village's other hotel, the three-star *Le Terme* (☎0577/887.150; ⑤), has a better restaurant. You can **rent bikes** from *Club Mountain Bike* in Piazza del Moretto.

Rocca, Castiglione and Vivo d'Órcia

The **Rocca d'Órcia**, three kilometres south of Bagno Vignoni, is visible almost the whole way from San Quírico: a dramatic pile of a castle, which from the eleventh to fourteenth centuries belonged, like almost every castle along this stretch of the Via Francigena, to the **Aldobrandeschi** family. Although Santa Fiora (see p.369) was the clan's base, this was their most important fortress, a strategic site allowing them to rob or extract tolls from all traffic along the route. After a change of ownership to the Salimbeni family, who built most of the present structure, the castle was only properly incorporated into the Sienese republic in 1418.

CASTIGLIONE D'ÓRCIA, the village below the *rocca*, is a fine-looking place, built amost entirely of stone, with an elaborately cobbled piazza and trio of medieval churches. In **Santo Stefano** are panels by Pietro Lorenzetti, Vecchietta and one attributed to Simone Martini – a hint of the wealth Castiglione must once have enjoyed. Moving south towards Monte Amiata, the hamlet of **VIVO D'ÓRCIA** is another medieval treat, with beautiful walks along by the river and the woods, where you come upon the Romanesque **Cappella dell'Ermicciolo**. There are **restaurants** at both villages: *Le Rocche* (closed Wed) in Castiglione; *Amiata* (closed Fri) and *La Flora* (closed Wed) in Vivo. Castiglione also has a bank and a couple of **agriturismo** centres, *I Lecci* (☎0577/887.287) and *La Querce* (☎0577/887.154); both offers rooms, meals and pony-trekking.

Bagni San Filippo and Radicófani

East of Vivo d'Orcia, just a few hundred metres off the N2, is the tiny spa of **BAGNI SAN FILIPPO**. Like Vignoni, this has an outdoor sulphur spring cascading its hot waters from the rocks, as well as an unostentatious modern spa building and pool. There is also a tiny chapel, **La Grotta del Santo**, commemorating the village saint, who took refuge here after being offered the papacy. Otherwise, San Filippo consists of just a handful of houses, a bar and a single **hotel-restaurant**, *Le Terme* (☎0577/872.982; ③); restaurant closed Thurs).

On the other side of the N2 from San Filippo, a road veers east into the hills to the **Rocca** of **RADICÓFANI**, which vies with the Rocca d'Órcia for the title of most imposing fortress in southern Tuscany. The castle is identified with one Ghino di Tacco, a fourteenth-century bandit who features in the writings of both Dante and Boccaccio – the *Decameron* tells of Tacco's imprisoning the Abbot of Cluny in this fortress, then curing him of indigestion. Views from the walls are stunning. Below the castle is a handsome little village, with an old Capuchin convent, a cluster of churches and the **Posta** – the "Great Duke's Inn", where centuries of Grand Tourists put up on their way to Rome. The village remains a handy place to stay, with two modest **hotels** – the *Eni* (☎0577/520.25; ③) and *La Torre* (☎0577/559.43; ③).

Pienza

PIENZA is as complete a Renaissance creation as any in Italy, conceived as a Utopian "New Town" by **Pope Pius II**, Aeneas Sylvius Piccolomini (see p.309). The site Pius chose was the village of Corsignano, where he was born into an exiled Sienese family in 1405. His architect was **Bernardo Rossellino**, who worked on all the major buildings here under the guidance of Leon Battista Alberti, the great theorist of Renaissance art, building and town planning.

The construction of Pienza began in 1459, just a year after Pius's election to the papacy. Rossellino's commission was to build a cathedral, papal palace and town hall, but Pius instructed the various cardinals who followed his court to build their own residences, too, and the project was really no less than a Vatican in miniature. Astonishingly, the cathedral, the papal and bishop's palaces, and the core of the town, were completed in just three years.

After consecration of the cathedral, Pius issued a papal bull rechristening the "city" Pienza, in his own honour, and stipulating that no detail of the cathedral or palaces should be changed. The wish was fulfilled rather more easily than he could have expected, for he died within two years, and of his successors only Pius III, his nephew, paid Pienza any regard. The city, intended to spread across the hill, never grew beyond a couple of blocks to either side of the main Corso and its population remained scarcely that of a village. Today, with a population of 2500, it still has an air of emptiness and folly: a natural stage set, which was in fact used by Zeffirelli for his film of *Romeo and Juliet*.

The Town

There is no difficulty finding your way about Pienza. Roads, buses and cars converge on the **Piazza Dante**, just outside the Porta al Murello, main entrance gate to the papal town.

From here the **Corso** leads to Rossellino's centrepiece, **Piazza Pio II**, enclosed by the Duomo, Palazzo Piccolomini, Bishop's Palace, Palazzo Pubblico, and a palace built by one of Pius's more ambitious Vatican followers – Cardinal Borgia, the future Pope Alexander VI. Apart from the town hall, based on the medieval Palazzo Vecchio in Florence, the ensemble is entirely Renaissance in conception.

The **Duomo** (closed 1–3pm) has one of the earliest Renaissance facades in Tuscany but the interior, on Pius's orders, took inspiration from the German hall-churches he had seen on his travels, and is essentially Gothic. The chapels – for once well-lit – house a series of Sienese altarpieces, commissioned by the pope and his architect from the major painters of the age: Giovanni di Paolo, Matteo di Giovanni, Vecchietta and Sano di Pietro. How long the building will remain standing is uncertain, as, to fit the cramped site, Rossellino had to build on sandstone with a substratum of clay. Before completion a crack appeared, and after an earthquake this century it has required progressively more buttressing and ties.

Pius's residence, the **Palazzo Piccolomini** was modelled on Alberti's Palazzo Rucellai in Florence, with an imaginative addition of a triple-tiered loggia at the back. Its cost was astronomical, Rossellino spending three times his allotted budget – a charge that he was liable to repay. Pius, however, accepted the bills, in his delight at the building and its views:

> *From the three porticoes which face the sun at mid-day the view extends to Amiata, that towering and densely wooded mountain. Thence the eye travels down into Val d'Órcia, passing over green pasturelands and hills clothed with long grass or rich corn in season, and many vineyards, and so up again to castles and villages set on precipitous rocks, and to the right as far as a place called Bagno di Vignoni, and leftwards to Monte Cetona, which is higher than Radicófani and is the portal of the winter sun.*

For this vista, you can walk into the courtyard at any time of day and through to the original "hanging garden" behind. The **apartments** (Tues–Sun 10am–12.30pm & 4–7pm, or 3–5pm in winter; L5000), occupied into this century by the Piccolomini family, include Pius II's bedroom, library and other rooms filled with weapons and medals.

Further mementoes of the pope – notably his embroidered cope – are to be seen, along with Sienese panels, across the piazza in the **Museo Civico** (Wed–Sun 10am–1pm & 4–7pm, or 2–5pm in winter; L3000), housed in the former palace of the cathedral canons.

From the original Corsignano, two earlier churches survive. **San Francesco**, adjacent to the Palazzo Piccolomini, has fourteenth-century frescoes, a cloister and a panoramic snack bar above the Piccolomini gardens, which is set to become an upmarket three-star hotel. Down below, ten minutes' walk to the west, is the Romanesque **Pieve** where Pius was baptised. An odd structure, with a cylindrical tower, it has a portal sculpted with knights, fish and mermaids.

Practicalities

There's not much life to Pienza, and it's perhaps best seen as a day trip from Montepulciano. *TRA-IN* **buses** cover the routes to Buonconvento/Siena (7 daily) and Montepulciano (9 daily); for details of times, call in at the **tourist office** (summer daily 10am–12.30pm & 3.30–6.30pm; winter closed Mon) inside the Palazzo Civico on Piazza Pio II.

If you want to stay, there are **rooms** at the *Ristorante dal Falco* (☎0578/ 748.551; ④) at Piazza Dante 7. Slightly more expensive, is the *Hotel Il Corsignano*, Via della Madonnina 11, west of the piazza (☎0578/748.501; ⑤).

Among **restaurants**, the best are the *Falco* (closed Fri), which offers superb *gnocchi* and *pecorino alla griglia* (hot cheese wrapped in *prosciutto*) at around L30,000 for a full meal, the slightly pricier *La Buca delle Fate*, Corso Il Rossellino 38 (closed Mon), and the newly opened and excellent *Latte di Luna* at the bottom of the main street , blessed with a small terrace for outdoor eating and an ancient well incorporated into the old interior. Alternatively, you can get good value beers and *crostini* at the *Birreria Sperone Nudo* in the middle of the town, and you're spoilt for choice for picnic food as the town, centre of a region producing *pecorino* sheep's cheese, seems to have gone overboard on *alimentari* and "natural food" shops.

Festivals include a **"Meeting with a Master of Art"** (Aug–Sept), when a contemporary Italian artist is featured in the Palazzo Civico, and the **Fiera del Calcio** (first Sun in Sept), which celebrates the local *pecorino* with a medieval market and fair in the main square.

East to Montepulciano: Monticchiello

The area around Pienza is enticing walking country. The track west to Bagno Vignoni is a fine two-hour walk. To the east, it's only around 11km along the old road through Monticchiello to Montepulciano. If you are dependent on buses, which have a lull in the morning along this route, it's certainly worth hiking at least one of these stretches.

MONTICCHIELLO is a minor attraction in itself: a walled village with a leaning watchtower and a **Pieve** (key in house next door) housing fourteenth-century Sienese frescoes and a *Madonna* by Pietro Lorenzetti. During the last week of July and the first week of August, the village puts on a **Teatro Povero**, featuring a play written and performed by the villagers to evoke the local folk and farming traditions – a kind of Tuscan *Archers*. It's a pleasantly informal occasion, enjoyed as much for the food at the *taverna* set up for the duration of the festival.

Montepulciano

The highest of the Tuscan hill towns, **MONTEPULCIANO** is built along a narrow tufa ridge, with a long main street and alleys that drop away to the walls. It's a stunningly good-looking town, full of vistas, odd squares and corners, and endowed with dozens of Renaissance palazzi and churches, which show the state of architecture fifty years after Rossellino's pioneering work at Pienza. Largely forgotten in subsequent centuries, the town is wealthy today from its wine industry, based on the famed **Vino Nobile**, and maintains a remarkably low-key tourist profile. As such, it is perhaps the best base in southern Tuscany, with Pienza, Chiusi and Bagno Vignoni all within easy reach using a mix of buses and walking.

Arrival and accommodation

Montepulciano is on the main **bus** routes between Siena and Chiusi, and is also served by a couple of buses from Florence daily. Its **train station** is on the Siena–Chiusi line, too, but only the *locali* stop and you'll need a (not always connecting) bus for the 10km trip into town. Regular buses also link with more frequent main line trains at Chiusi, not much further away. The buses stop in town at both the north and south gates, the **Porta al Prato** and **Porta di Farine**; the first is the main "bus station". If you're **driving**, follow the road around below the east circuit of walls and look for a parking space; don't be tempted by the area around the Porta al Prato or you'll be ticketed.

The Prato and Farine gates are equally convenient for exploring the town, though our account assumes a starting point at the Porta al Prato. Between the two gates runs the town's main street, the **Corso**, whose name is appended in turn to **Via Gracciano, Via di Voltaia** and **Via dell'Opio**.

Accommodation

Once again, accommodation is sparse and well worth booking ahead. If you can't get into any of our recommendations, try contacting the **tourist office** to check on the availability of private rooms or *agriturismo*; the main office is at Via Ricci 9 (Tues–Sun 10am–noon & 4–6pm; ☎0578/757.985 or 757.442), with a smaller one outside the Porta al Prato. Unless you have transport, don't settle for a room or hotel at the outlying station area (Montepulciano-Stazione/Acquaviva), or at Sant'Albino/Terme di Montepulciano (5km southeast). If you're really stuck, it's probably best to get the bus to the spa resort of Chianciano Terme, 9km southeast (see p.363).

GUESTHOUSES AND HOTELS

Ristorante Cittino, Vicolo della Via Nuova 2 (☎0578/757.335). Off Via di Voltaia nel Corso – so equidistant between the gates. Decent rooms above a restaurant. [4].

Meublè Il Riccio, Via Talosa 21 (☎0578/757.713). Well-kept guesthouse off Piazza Grande; get off at Porta di Farine. [4].

Duomo, Via San Donato 14 (☎0578/757.473). Comfortable rooms and a nice setting off the Piazza Grande, near Porta di Farine. [5].

La Terrazza, Via Piè al Sasso 16 (☎0578/757.440). Pleasant rooms in an ancient house close by the Duomo; get off at Porta di Farine. [5].

Marzocco, Piazza Savonarola (☎0578/757.262). The town's first choice hotel – an elegant nineteenth-century inn with a full-size billiards table, 50m up the Corso on the left from Porta al Prato. Very courteous owners. [5]

Il Borghetto, Via Borgo Buio (☎0578/757.335). Montepulciano's grandest – off Via Gracciano nel Corso, turning left after Piazza Michelozzo. [6].

The Town

Montepulciano's unusually consistent array of Renaissance palazzi and churches is a reflection of its remarkable development after 1511, when, following intermittent alliance with Siena, the town finally threw in its lot with Florence. In that year the Florentines sent **Antonio da Sangallo the Elder** to rebuild the town's gates and walls, which he did so impressively that the council took him on to work on the town hall and a series of churches. The local nobles meanwhile hired him, his nephew, and later the Modena-born architect, **Vignola** – a founding figure of

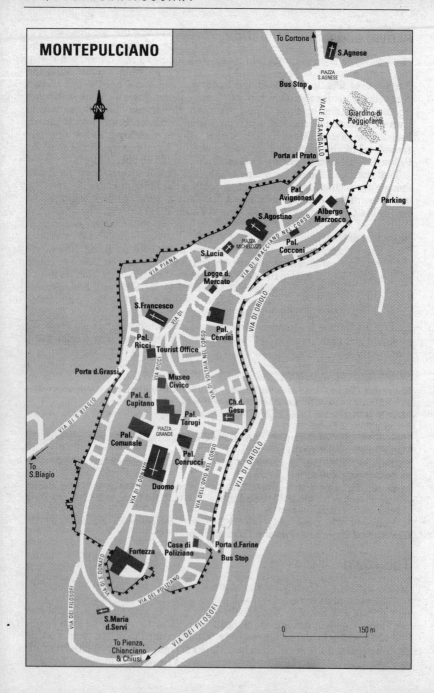

MONTEPULCIANO

To Cortona

S.Agnese

PIAZZA
S.AGNESE

Bus Stop

Giardino di
Poggiofanti

Porta al Prato

Pal.
Avignonesi

Parking

S.Agostino

Albergo
Marzocco

PIAZZA
MICHELOZZO

Pal.
Cocconi

S.Lucia

Logge d.
Mercato

VIA PIANA

VIA DI GRACCIANO NEL CORSO

S.Francesco

Pal.
Cervini

VIA DI ORIOLO

Pal.
Ricci

VIA DI

Tourist Office

Porta d.Grassi

VIA RICCI

Museo
Civico

VIA DI VOLTAIA NEL CORSO

Pal. d.
Capitano

Ch.d.
Gesu

Pal.
Tarugi

VIA DI S.BIAGIO

PIAZZA
GRANDE

Pal.
Comunale

Pal.
Conrucci

VIA DELL'ORIOLO NEL CORSO

VIA DI ORIOLO

To
S.Biagio

Duomo

VIA DI S.DONATO

Fortezza

Casa di
Poliziano

Porta d.Farine

Bus Stop

VIA DEL POLIZIANO

VIA DI S.DONATO

VIA DEI FILOSOFI

S.Maria
d.Servi

VIA DEI FILOSOFI

0   150 m

To Pienza,
Chianciano
& Chiusi

Baroque – to work on their own palazzi. The work of this trio, totally assured in its conception and execution, makes a fascinating comparison with Rossellino's work at Pienza.

The Corso: Porta al Prato to the Fortress

Sangallo's first commission was Montepulciano's main gate, the **Porta al Prato**, at the north end of town. Inside the gate the **Corso** begins, the palazzi immediately making clear the town's allegiance to Florence. In the first square, beside the *Albergo Marzocco*, is a stone column bearing the heraldic lion (*marzocco*) of Florence, while across the street further lion heads decorate the **Palazzo Avignonesi** (no. 91), probably the work of Vignola. Sangallo makes a second appearance with the **Palazzo Cocconi** (no. 70), opposite the **Palazzo Bucelli** (no. 73), whose base is inset with Roman and Etruscan reliefs.

Just beyond this crop of palazzi is the church of **Sant'Agostino**, designed by the earlier Medici protegé, Michelozzo – who also carved the relief above the door; within are good Sienese paintings by Lorenzo di Credi and Giovanni di Paolo, and a Crucifix attributed to Donatello. Across the street a medieval **tower house**, a rare survival in Montepulciano, is surmounted by a Commedia dell'Arte figure of a clown, the **Pulcinella**, who strikes out the hours on the town clock; most un-Tuscan, it is said to have been put up by an exiled bishop from Naples.

About a hundred metres further along you reach the Renaissance **Loggia di Mercato** and a fork in the roads. The Corso continues to the left past further palazzi, including Sangallo's **Palazzo Cervini**, occupied by the Banco Toscana, with its grand civic gesture of an external courtyard. Beyond this, you pass the church of **Gesù**, remodelled in Baroque style by Andrea Pozzo (as are many other churches in the town and region), before the road turns the corner and rambles outside the town walls. Just prior to the turn – at no. 5 – is the **Casa di Poliziano**, birthplace of the Renaissance humanist and poet Angelo Ambrogini, known as Poliziano, who translated many of the Greek classics under the patronage of Lorenzo de' Medici. (*Poliziani* is the name given to natives of Montepulciano.)

Via di Poliziano loops outside the walls to the **Santa Maria dei Servi**, another Baroque job by Pozzo, before re-entering town by the old **Fortezza**, now part-occupied by houses. At the end of Via di San Donato, the last stretch back into town, you find yourself in the cathedral and town hall square, Piazza Grande.

Santa Lucia, Via del Poggio and the Museo Civico

A quicker approach to Piazza Grande would be to head right at the Loggia di Mercato. A block to the north of here, a beautiful little piazza fronts the church of **Santa Lucia**, which has a fabulous *Madonna* by Signorelli in a chapel on the right, though it is rarely open. Turning instead to the south, Via del Poggio runs down to the church of San Francesco, then the imposing Via Ricci takes over for the last stretch to the Piazza Grande; it is flanked on one side by the Renaissance **Palazzo Ricci** (housing the tourist office), on the other by the Sienese-Gothic **Palazzo Neri-Orselli**.

The latter is home to the town's **Museo Civico** (Tues–Sun 10.30am–12.30pm, plus 4.30–7pm in summer; L5000), an extensive collection of small-town Gothic and Renaissance works. The most important panel is a *St Francis*, painted by his near-contemporary, Margaritone da Arezzo; the most enjoyable is Jacopo de Mino's lush *Coronation of the Virgin*.

The Piazza Grande

The **Piazza Grande**, the town's theatrical flourish of a main square, is built on the highest point of the ridge. Its most distinctive building is the **Palazzo Comunale**, a thirteenth-century Gothic palace to which Michelozzo added a tower and rustication in imitation of the Palazzo Vecchio in Florence. You can climb the tower for free (closed Sun), and on those fabled clear days the view supposedly stretches to Siena, 65km northwest.

Two of the palazzi on the square were designed by Sangallo. The **Palazzo Tarugi**, by the lion and griffon fountain, is a highly innovative building, with a public loggia cut through one corner; it originally had an extension on the top floor, though this has been bricked in. More tangible pleasures await at the **Palazzo Cantucci**, one of many buildings scattered about the town that serve as *cantine* for the **wine trade**, offering *degustazione* and sale of the Vino Nobile.

Sangallo and his contemporaries never got around to building a facade for the **Duomo** (closed 1–3.30pm), whose plain brick pales against the neighbouring palazzi. Its interior, however, is an elegant Renaissance design, and it is scattered with superb classical sculptures by Michelozzo. These pieces originally comprised a tomb for Bartolomeo Aragazzi, a local papal secretary, the core of which remains by the west door – but with the worthy forgotten, the statuary was distributed about the chapels, while the frieze was co-opted for the high altar. The finest of the church's paintings, Taddeo di Bartolo's iridescent altarpiece of the *Assumption*, belongs to an earlier age when Montepulciano was within Siena's orbit.

San Biagio

Antonio da Sangallo's greatest commission came in 1518, when he was invited to design the pilgrimage church of **San Biagio** on the hillside below the town. The model for this was his brother Giuliano's design for the facade of San Lorenzo in Florence, which was never built. The Montepulciano project was more ambitious – the only bigger church project of its time was Saint Peter's in Rome – and exercised Antonio until his death in 1534. To reach the church, follow Via San Biagio out from the Porta di Grassi; it's about half an hour's walk.

The church is one of the most harmonious Renaissance creations in Italy, constructed inside and out from a porous travertine, whose soft honey-coloured stone blends perfectly into its niche in the landscape. A deeply intellectualised building, its major architectural novelty was the use of freestanding towers (only one was completed) to flank the facade; within, it is spoilt a little by extraneous decoration – a Baroque trompe l'oeil covers the barrel vault – but is equally harmonious. It also has a superb acoustic.

Nearby, scarcely less perfect a building, is a **Canonica** (rectory), endowed by Sangallo with a graceful portico and double-tiered loggia.

Food, festivals and transport

The town has a fair spread of **restaurants**, all of them offering local wines. Best, perhaps, is the *Trattoria Diva* (☎0578/716.951; closed Tues), just inside the Porta al Prato on Via Gracciano nel Corso; it has superb home-made pasta and works out only around L35,000, unless you go for a vintage Vino Nobile from the co-owned *enoteca* next door. Alternatives include the next-door *Pulcino*, which has an excellent wine list and does a fine *ribollito*, the *Ristorante Il Cantuccio*, on an alley to the right of Via Gracciano nel Corso 67, and the *Rosticceria di Voltaia* at Via di Voltaia nel Corso 86 (closed Fri), with full meals around L25,000 and cheaper takeouts. The *Caffè Poliziano*, Via di Voltaia nel Corso 27–29, has a lovely Art Nouveau interior, serves wonderful cakes and snacks, and has live music on a Sunday night.

There's an open-air **market** (with especially good *porchetta*), held in the gardens outside the Porta al Prato, on Thursday mornings; this is also the site of the local **youth bar**, with table football and a jukebox through to midnight.

Festivals
Cantiere Internazionale d'Arte (July–Aug). A major international contemporary performing arts festival (especially music), founded by composer Hans Werner Henze in the 1970s. Look out for opera performed in the intimate *Teatro Poliziano*.
Bruscello (Aug 14–16). The Festival of Assumption is celebrated with a sequence of masked plays and light opera in the town squares.
Bravío delle Botti (last Sun in Aug). A barrel race through the streets, from Sant'Agnese to the Piazza Grande, between teams from each of the town's eight *contrade*. Costume processions precede the race and a street banquet follows. Also around this time is a festival to celebrate bringing in the Vino Nobile.

Transport
The main **transport** links are with Chiusi. *LFI* **buses** run more or less every half-hour (last at 9.10pm) to Chianciano Terme, Chiusi and Chiusi station. To the west, *TRA-IN* has seven buses daily on the circuit through Pienza, San Quírico d'Órcia, Torrenieri (change for Montalcino) and Buonconvento, with three continuing to Siena. All buses leave from outside Porta al Prato and Porta di Farine; buy tickets from bars or shops in town, not on the bus.

If you're making a **train** connection, take a bus to Chiusi; Montepulciano's own station, 10km northeast, is a stop only for *locali*.

East to Chianciano Terme and Chiusi

CHIANCIANO TERME, midway between Montepulciano and Chiusi, is one of Tuscany's major spas, as evidenced by the presence of some two hundred-odd hotels. Its particular specialities are liver and bladder complaints, handy if you've overworked the Vino Nobile, though the clinic-like spa buildings aren't the obvious image of a Tuscan holiday.

If you find yourself staying here, with Montepulciano full, you might want to wander up to the old hill town, **Chianciano Vecchio**, though there's little specific to see, save a Romanesque Collegiata and middling sacred art museum. The local tourist handouts fastidiously map out a series of "Medically Recommended Walks" in its *Chianciano . . . What a healthy liver!* pamphlet. Perhaps the most compelling is to the huge outdoor **municipal pool**.

Through Sarteano

If you have transport, a more enjoyable route to Chiusi is the minor road that runs south just before Montepulciano's own little spa at Sant'Albino. This follows a fine, scarcely populated stretch of the **Val d'Órcia** down through the estates of Castellúccio and **La Foce** – the latter the home for many years of the American writer Iris Origo, author of the classic *Merchant of Prato*. It was at La Foce that she hid partisans and allied troops during the German occupation of Italy after Mussolini's fall in 1943, events recorded in her autobiography *War in Val d'Órcia*. You turn north to reach Chiusi at **SARTEANO**, a pleasant village set below a castle and within patches of Etruscan wall; it has a Beccafumi *Annunciation* in the church of San Martino, and an excellent **restaurant**, *La Giara*, at Viale Europa 1.

Chiusi

CHIUSI, 14km southeast of Montepulciano, is a useful transport hub, with trains and buses west to Siena, south to Orvieto and Rome, and north to Montepulciano, Castiglione del Lago, Cortona and Arezzo. As a target in its own right, it is only really worth a special detour for Etruscan enthusiasts: the town – known to the Etruscans as Camars – has a reasonable archaeological museum and a half-dozen ancient tombs on its periphery, out towards Lago di Chiusi.

The museum and the duomo, Chiusi's other worthwhile site, are close by each other on Via Porsenna, a short walk up from the **bus stop** on the Viale Garibaldi; there's a **tourist office** at Via Porsenna 61 and a small kiosk at the **train station** which is 3km east at Chiusi Scalo, a regular stop for all the inter-town buses.

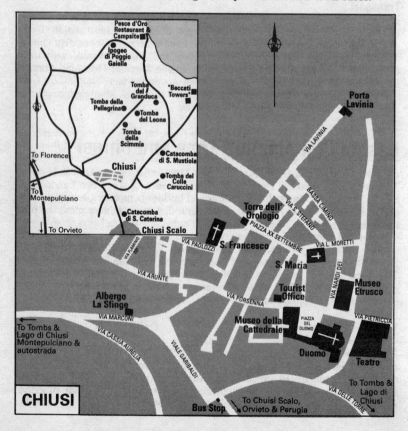

The Etruscan museum, tombs and Duomo

Chiusi's **Museo Etrusco** (Tues–Thurs 9am–2pm, Sat & Sun 9am–1pm; L5000) ought to be pretty good, for the region is littered with tombs. Many of the best exhibits, however, have been spirited away to Florence and Rome, and what remains is a modest collection: numerous sarcophagi, a few terracottas with traces of ancient paint, cabinets of pots (one with erotic dancing scenes), and the odd treasure – notably the *Gualandi Urn*. If you are interested in seeing the **tombs** themselves, ask one of the museum guards if they'll take you to the *Tomba della Pelegrina e Leone*, 3km north, for which they hold the keys. Other local tombs (including the more famous frescoed *Scimmia* and *Colle*) have been locked in recent years.

At the Romanesque **Duomo** there is further evidence of Chiusi's ancient past. The building itself consists almost entirely of Etruscan and Roman blocks, while the museum (L1500) gives access to **catacombs**, which were used by early Christians in the fifth century. The cathedral interior is a mass of what appears at first sight to be mosaic work, but is in reality mock-Byzantine paintwork, created in 1915.

Lago di Chiusi

Chiusi's **lake** lies 5km north of the town, reached along the road past the Etruscan tombs. The route is served only sporadically by bus (4 daily Mon–Fri) but for anyone driving, or planning to camp for a few days, it makes a fine detour. The buses run to the **restaurant-bar-campsite** *Pesce d'Oro* (☎0578/21.403), set amid trees by a small quay for rowing boats; the swimming is warm in summer. For food alone, you're best off at the lake's other signposted restaurant, *Da Gino* (closed Wed); they serve fine fish meals at around L25,000.

Practicalities

With time to kill in Chiusi, the best thing to do is **eat**. The *Osteria dei Bonci* on Via dei Bonci (an alley off Via Porsenna) is a pleasant bar-pizzeria, and there are excellent pizzas at *Il Capannino* in the same street, while the *Ristorante Zaira*, just up the road at Piazza Graviano, serves "Etruscan dishes" – boar, pigeon and the like – for L25,000 and up.

Should you want to stay, Chiusi has just one **hotel**, *Albergo La Sfinge* at Via Marconi 2 (☎0578/20.157; ④). Less expensive hotels are clustered down at Chiusi Scalo, an unattractive modern suburb that makes its living from a very large slaughterhouse and meat storage plant.

Monte Amiata

At 1738 metres, **Monte Amiata** is the highest point in southern Tuscany, a broad-based mountain visible for miles from the low hills of the Sienese *crete*. A circle of towns rings its lower slopes, some historical spots, others more modern, servicing **skiing** and **walking** activities.

The main centre and transport hub is **Abbadia San Salvatore**, worth a visit whether you intend to venture onto the mountain or not, with its great Romanesque abbey. The town is accessible by bus from Siena (2 daily), Buonconvento (6 daily), Chiusi (3 daily), Arcidosso and Santa Fiora (6 daily), Grosseto (6 daily), and Montepulciano (1 daily).

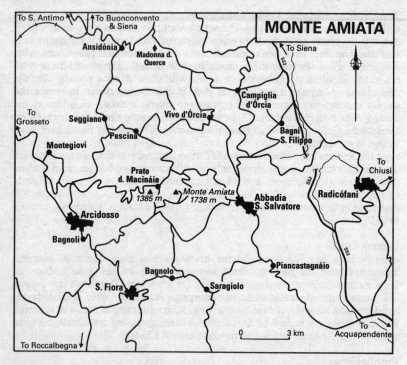

MONTE AMIATA

To S. Antimo
To Buonconvento & Siena
Ansidónia
Madonna d. Querce
To Siena
Campíglia d'Órcia
To Grosseto
Seggiano
Vivo d'Órcia
Pescína
Bagni S. Filippo
Montegiovi
To Chiusi
Prato d. Macináie
1385 m
Monte Amiata 1738 m
Abbadia S. Salvatore
Radicófani
Arcidosso
Bagnoli
Piancastagnáio
Bagnolo
S. Fiora
Saragiolo
To Roccalbegna
0   3 km
To Acquapendente

Abbadia San Salvatore

There's been a settlement on the site of **ABBADIA SAN SALVATORE** since prehistoric times, though its real significance dates from the eighth century when it became the controlling centre of the Via Francigena. Its importance only waned with the rise of the Aldobrandeschi in the eleventh century.

Today the town is an initially disorientating modern sprawl that hides a perfect and largely self-contained **medieval quarter**. Buses will drop you on the **Viale Roma**, immediately outside the old walls; if you arrive by car you'll have to negotiate a maze of tree-lined streets. The abbey itself is actually in the modern part of the town, and best reached with Viale Roma as the starting point. From the north end of the street, walk down Via Cavour, passing Via Mentana (with the **tourist office**) on the left, and take the next right, Via del Monastero.

The Abbey

Church tradition ascribes the foundation of the **Abbadia San Salvatore** to one King Rachis, a Lombard ruler visited by an apparition of Christ as he went to do battle with the Perugians. He became a monk, created the abbey and insisted that his wife and daughter join a nunnery. Archaeological evidence in the crypt – one of the building's most fascinating corners – suggests there was a building here as early as the sixth century.

The bulk of the present **church**, built in Amiata's distinctive brown trachite, is a Cistercian Romanesque building started in 1036. The **facade** is squeezed between two towers, its narrow frontage preparing you for a thin and immensely long **interior**. The single-naved basilica culminates in a raised chancel, framed by a series of broad and beautifully decorated arches. Little survives in the way of art, much having been removed to Florence when the abbey was owned by the Medici – a period when it remained monkless for 157 years; best of the remnants is a wooden **crucifix**, carved in the twelfth century though disquietingly modern-looking and easily passed by. The eccentric **frescoes** in the chancel, episodes from the *Life of King Rachis*, are by a seventeenth-century artist called Nasino.

The chief highlight is the **crypt** under the chancel, an astounding space of bare, crude stone supported by thirty-five strange fluted columns. Atop each pillar is a superbly carved lintel, whose motifs and figures show a Lombard and in some cases Byzantine hand.

Practicalities

Abbadia's **tourist office** is one of the best-hidden in Tuscany, upstairs at Via Mentana 97 (☎0577/778.608 or 779.013); look out for the Canon photocopier shop next door. As the tourism headquarters for the Amiata region, the office is well worth tracking down; there's little on display but they have a lot of information if you ask. For more information on **walking**, plus innovative and cheap tours, contact *Amiata Trekking*, Piazza Fratelli Cervi 21 (☎0577/777.751).

There are numerous **hotels** in the modern town. The cheapest central choice is the *Alessandra*, Via Trieste 10 (☎0577/778.171; ③), just off the junction with Viale Roma. The nearby *San Marco*, Via Matteotti 13 (☎0577/778.089; ④), is brand new and more expensive. More upmarket still is the *Italia*, Viale Roma 34 (☎0577/778.007; ⑤). The *San Marco* has a reasonable **restaurant**, or there are any number of cheap, if rather characterless, pizzerias.

The **bus terminal** is in front of the *Bar Centrale* in Viale Roma; there's a time-table fixed to the *Agenzia VAII*, Viale Roma 45, which is also the place to buy **tickets**. In addition to the two through services to Siena, there are six buses daily to Buonconvento (for train connections to Siena and Grosseto), three daily to Chiusi (trains to Rome, Florence and Siena), six daily to Arcidosso and Santa Fiora, two daily to Grosseto, one to Montepulciano (school days only) and two daily to Rome (via Orvieto).

The summit and slopes

The summit of **Monte Amiata** is accessible by road and in summer is packed out with car-driven parties, often ill-shod for the last few steps to the highest point. In July and August it has a three-times-daily bus from Abbadia San Salvatore; at other times, hitching should be possible. A number of the bars at the summit rent out mountain bikes to explore the lower slopes.

At the car park is what amounts to an alpine hamlet, with bars, a handful of hotels, and a short ski run – all in the shadow of an Eiffel Tower structure adapted in the form of a cross, erected in 1946 by Pope Pius XII. Alongside are a crop of radio masts and huts selling some of the trashiest trinkets conceivable. None of this detracts from the **views**, which stretch southeast to Bolsena and west to the sea, with the nearer towns neatly delineated in a circle below. The best viewpoint is from the so-called *Madonna delle Scout*, a statue covered in the pendants of innumerable scout troops.

Amiata walking: the Anello della Montagna

Away from the summit, the woods and pathways of Amiata's **lower slopes** make up one of the region's most beautiful natural enclaves, huge forests of beech and chestnut blanketing the area and providing refuge for deer and wild boar. The mountain's extravagant greenery, so at odds with much of the surrounding countryside, derives from its volcanic origins, eruptions having formed ridges of trachite, which is fertile when broken down and also porous, allowing surface water to filter away. When the water hits the impervious volcanic rock below, it flows out in a series of **springs**, a striking feature of Amiata, whose slopes frequently echo to the sound of running water.

The combination of Amiata's lush vegetation and crisp mountain air make it superb **walking** territory. The appearance of a new, detailed *Multigraphic* map has made hiking in the region a far more straightforward undertaking (*Carta dei Sentieri e Rifiugi Masiccio del Monte Amiata*; L9000), and considerable effort has gone into marking the **Anello della Montagna**, a path which circles the mountain between about 900 and 1300 metres. With a car you can join the path from virtually any of the roads which climb from the surrounding towns; large boards mark the departure points from the road, and detail the route to either side. It's also possible, however, to walk up from the towns on paths which radiate from the main circuit: the best departure point for this approach is Abbadia San Salvatore.

The Anello's total circuit is 29km, in theory walkable in a day, though the local council have broken it into ten basic sections. It's fairly practical to walk half the route, and then take a **bus** back from Santa Fiora or Arcidosso (each have six connections daily with Abbadia San Salvatore). The trail markings are clearly indicated on concrete posts in red, yellow and green, though they coincide with the older CAI markings of red and white stripes; either way, it's fairly hard to go wrong. It's also possible to walk at will from the road, though if you venture too far, the chances are you'll wind up lost.

Staying on the mountain

If you want to **stay** on the mountain, the best base is **Prato Macinie** (1385m), a tree-enclosed patch of meadow and the site of one of Amiata's ski lifts (there are fourteen in all, along with twelve pistes). It's not far from the summit, but far enough to be unspoilt and away from the commercialism. The hotel, *Le Macinaie* (☎0564/955.011; July & Aug; ④) fills up, so book ahead.

In a similarly pretty setting, the **Prato della Contessa** (1500m), two kilometres south on the summit road, has the four-star *Hotel Contessa* (☎0564/955.378; Jan, Feb, July & Aug; ⑥), while nearby there's *Lo Scoiattolo* (☎0564/955.660; Jan, Feb, July & Aug; ⑤). All of these hotels function as **restaurants**. The nearest **campsite** is at Castel del Piano (see p.370).

Villages around Monte Amiata

If you have transport, the ring of towns around Monte Amiata are worth a little exploration. None have outstanding features but all claim a rural setting and more or less medieval centres – usually built around an Aldobrandeschi castle. Most also have a good sprinkling of hotels.

DAVIDE LAZZERETTI OF MONTE LABBRO

Arcidosso-born **Davide Lazzeretti** (1834–78) is the most extraordinary figure Monte Amiata has thrown up: either a visionary prophet or a crazed communist born before his time, according to greatly divergent Italian points of view.

He was the founder of an ill-defined socio-religious sect, the **Jurisdavidic Church**, which as well as preaching Christianity under the banner "Long live the Republic, God and Liberty" agitated for justice and social reform amongst the peasant community which made up his following. Though promptly excommunicated, he continued to preach both in Italy and abroad, calling for a society based on co-operative principles and republican government. In time, his five thousand followers organised themselves into Italy's first co-operative, sharing land and animals, and building a huge temple to the movement on top of Monte Labbro, south of Arcidosso. Eventually Lazzeretti met the violent end of many a radical, shot – with the connivance of local landowners – by the *carabinieri* as he led an unauthorised religious procession through Arcidosso.

Repression soon dispersed the movement, which was anyway being undermined by a drift from the land to Amiata's mercury mines. Nonetheless, Lazzeretti is remembered today as a precursor of socialist and land reform movements still twenty years away at the time of his death. He is commemorated by sympathisers on the night of August 14, when a huge bonfire is lit at the largely ruined temple on Monte Labbro. Whether or not you want to pay your respects, the trip to the summit makes a fine walk or drive – there's a rough road virtually to the top.

Piancastagnaio

Five kilometres south of Abbadia San Salvatore, **PIANCASTAGNAIO** spreads across a mountain plateau, capped by one of the area's most impressive fortresses. It has a prettily situated Franciscan convent, too, plus a fine Romanesque church, the twelfth-century Santa Maria Assunta. Its five one-star hotels are all grouped along Viale Gramsci and Via Grossetana – the *Del Bosco*, Via Grossetana (☎0564/786.090; ④), has pleasant doubles. A rural alternative, similarly priced, is the *Piccolo Mondo* (☎0565/788.520; ④), 4km east on the minor road to Quaranta.

Santa Fiora

SANTA FIORA's craggy position drew an impressed observation from Dante as to its impregnability and its castle was the feudal seat of the Aldobrandeschi. The village has a couple of fine churches – the **Pieve di Santa Fiora e Lucilla**, housing some of the finest terracottas by Andrea della Robbia, and **Sant'Agostino**, with a fine painted wooden image of the Madonna and Child by Jacopo della Quercia – but perhaps the nicest feature is the **Peschiera**, a spring-fed lake surrounded by woodland. The road beyond passes evidence of Amiata's industrial side, tall chimneys signalling the thermal power plants and mercury mines that have kept the area's economic head above water.

The village has a **tourist office** at Piazza Garibaldi (☎0564/971.124) and a couple of **hotels**. The best option is the *Fiora*, Via Roma 8 (☎0564/977.043; ④); the *Eden* (☎0564/977.033; ④), Via Roma 1, is dour but slightly cheaper.

Arcidosso and Castel del Piano

To the north of the summit, **ARCIDOSSO** is one of the larger Amiata towns, dominated by a blunt Sienese tower, but of little other interest. Walkers, however, might find the local *Comunità Montana dell'Amiata* office of use and there are three small **hotels**: the *Gatto d'Oro*, Via dei Venti (☎0564/967.074; ④); *Giardino*, Via Risorgimento (☎0564/966.466; ④); and *Toscana*, Via Amiata (☎0564/967.488; ⑤).

More tempting on the horizon is **CASTEL DEL PIANO**, the main commercial town of this area. It doesn't really live up to the promise, though the old centre, as ever, warrants a quick wander, with its covered market, Palazzo Pretorio and Romanesque San Leonardo. It has a tourist office at Via Marconi 9 (☎0564/955.284) and a broad range of hotel choices, the best value being the *Poli*, Piazza Garibaldi (☎0564/955.287; ④). There is also a **campsite**, the *Amiata*, Via Roma 15 (☎0564/955.107; open all year).

Seggiano and Pescina

SEGGIANO is an old Etruscan centre, today distinguished principally by its Renaissance church of **Madonna della Carità**, set in an olive grove. Nearby, also in a beautiful setting, is a tiny fortified hamlet, Potentino.

Five very winding kilometres east of Seggiano is **PESCINA**, which deserves mention for its superlative **restaurant**, *Le Silene,* visited by punters from miles around (☎0564/950.922; ④); this doubles as a modest **hotel**.

South to Saturnia and Manciano

At around fourteen kilometres from Arcidosso, **TRIANA** stands on the junction of the roads west to Grosseto and south to Saturnia and Pitigliano. A perfect little fortified hamlet, it commands huge views from its castle. If you have a car, a rewarding detour off the road south is to follow the new highway to Grosseto as far as Roccalbegna. Relying on buses, this only really makes sense if you're making for Grosseto: two buses daily cover the route.

Roccalbegna

ROCCALBEGNA is one of the finest villages in southern Tuscany: aerial pictures of its perfect medieval streets decorate many local tourist offices, though the place is not on any obvious route and visitors are few. The village's single **hotel**, the *Albergo-Ristorante La Pietra*, Via XXIV Maggio (☎0564/989.019; ④), has very reasonable half-board.

The **Rocca** of the town's name is obvious from afar, perched on a crag that rises almost to a pyramid above the village. A superb walk to the top (522m) starts from the Piazza IV Novembre at the far end of the village: turn left up Salita Sasso (a yellow sign), go past the *Bar-Tabacchi* and it's then ten minutes up the winding lane and a final scramble to the fortifications. The views over the wild and rocky countryside are tremendous, though outflanked by the famed vista over the village's grid of streets. The local saying "se il sasso scrocca, addio la Rocca" (If the rock crumbles, it's goodbye to the village) seems incontrovertible from this point.

In the village, take a look at Romanesque **SS. Apostoli Pietro e Paolo**, with its *Madonna* accredited to Ambrogio Lorenzetti, and the small **art museum** (open on request) up Via Campana, the alley to the left.

South to Saturnia

Moving south to Saturnia, there are a couple of minor points of note. **PETRICCI**, 5km south of Triana, has a **hotel**, the *Ristorante-Albergo La Cerinella* (☎0564/984.015; [4]). Another 5km on you reach **SEMPRONIANO**, a crumbling half-forgotten village centred on another Aldobrandeschi castle. Its Romanesque church of **San Vincenzo** has a painting of a dragon supposedly slain locally and placed in the castle for public edification. On a minor road to the east is the virtually abandoned hamlet of **ROCCHETTE**, sited below a castle on a spur overlooking the Albegna valley.

Saturnia: Le Cascatelle

Word is spreading about the sulphurous hot springs at **SATURNIA**, as the virtually year-round crowds of battered Volkswagen campers testify. Nonetheless, they're not that easy to find. If all you want is a dip you should initially ignore the hill town and follow the road south towards Montemerano. A large **spa complex** – with fierce admission charges, a vast pool and a five-star hotel – is signposted to the left, and about two hundred metres on (as the road takes a sharp curve) a dirt track heads off straight, unsignposted but usually signalled by a cluster of cars and vans. Two minutes' walk from here brings you to the **cascatelle**, sulphur streams and springs which burst from the ground, forming natural rock-pool jacuzzis of warm water, in which you can lie around for hours submerged up to your neck. Entrance is unrestricted and free, and even on cold days there are invariably a few people ready to indulge. The heavy pedestrian traffic inevitably means there's a bit of litter, but apart from a small café, there's no commercialism at all.

The bubbling main pool is a bizarre sight, the water an intense turquoise, and all the more surreal if the weather is overcast and the steam rising overhead. The place also has something of a cult aspect, and it's not unusual for parties to come up at night from Rome. The only problem is the rumour that the water that ends up here has already been channelled through the resort's treatment centre: not a very nice thought, and perhaps enough to discourage bathing in the April to October spa season.

ACCESS AND ACCOMMODATION

There are two daily **buses** along the road between Santa Fiora and Manciano: be sure to get out at the springs (*Le Terme*) and not at Saturnia village; hitching should be reasonably easy, as there's usually someone heading for the springs.

If you intend to **stay** near the springs, you'll need a shower to wash off the sulphur smell, which is not too noticeable when bathing, but can linger for days. The nearest cheap **hotel** is the excellent two-star *Albergo-Ristorante Cascata* (☎0564/602.978; [5]), in an isolated spot 1km down from the falls on the road to Manciano (it's signposted left on a dirt road). The nearest **campsite**, *La Ciabatta*, is 4km down the same road at Montemerano.

All the other accommodation possibilities are in Saturnia proper, a fairly unassuming place. Camper vans are allowed to park overnight in the more modern of the main squares, and there are a couple of **hotels** – the *Saturnia*, Via Mazzini 4 (☎0564/601.007; [4]), and *Villa Clodia*, Via Italia 43 (☎0564/601.212; [4]), which is tucked away in one of the village's nicer quarters.

Montemerano and Manciano

Midway between Saturnia and Manciano is **MONTEMERANO**, a medieval hill village, with modern component below. The old town is cannily fortified on two levels, and though there's nothing very concrete to see, the balconies and interlocked alleys are hung with a more than usual abundance of geraniums and greenery. August offers the unappetising prospect of a tripe festival.

If you do want to **stay**, the smart three-star *Oliveto* (☎0564/602.849; ⑥) is the upmarket choice, located on the outskirts of the village, near the turn-off for Saturnia. A cheaper alternative is the one-star *Laudomia* (☎0564/620.213; ④) at Poderi di Montemerano, midway between Montemerano and Manciano. Functioning as a coaching inn for centuries, it has an attractive, antique-crammed **restaurant** to go with its handful of rooms. About two kilometres north of Montemerano is the *Acqua Viva* (☎0564/602.890; ⑦), a definite – if expensive – treat with rooms in two attractively converted buildings, surrounded by the hotel's own wine estate.

Manciano

MANCIANO, though hardly somewhere you'd make a special journey for, is an attractive market town, with a medieval quarter grouped around a Sienese fortress, and a plentiful supply of bars in which to soak up its small-town atmosphere.

As well as a supplies stop, Manciano is an important hub of the southern Tuscan **bus** network. *RAMA* buses leave from the bottom of Via Marsala, the street that leads from the roundabout up to the old town; you can get tickets from the tobacconist's at no. 57. Services include four daily to Grosseto (via Orbetello and Albinia), three to Saturnia, one to Scansano and five to Pitigliano. It's unlikely you'll want to stay in the town, but if stranded there are four **hotels**, most central of which is the *Rossi*, Via Gramsci 2 (☎0564/629.248; ④).

Pitigliano and around

PITIGLIANO, the largest town in Tuscany's deep south, is best approached along the road from Manciano, to the west. As you approach, it soars above on a spectacular outcrop of tufa, with medieval buildings perched above the valley floor, and its quarters linked by the arches of an immense aqueduct. **Etruscan tombs** – some converted to storage cellars for wine – honeycomb the cliffs, a feature repeated all over the surrounding area.

In the early Middle Ages the town belonged to the ubiquitous Aldobrandeschi, and then passed by marriage to the Roman counts of Orsini and ultimately to the Grand Duchy of Tuscany. Later, Pitigliano was best known for its thriving **Jewish community**, until its annihilation in the last war. It has today a slightly grim, occcasionally sinister, sort of grandeur, the result partly of its mighty fortress – dividing the upper town from the more modern lower suburb – partly of the tall alleys of the ghetto area. Seen on a sunny day, though, it is a gem of small-town Italy, seemingly populated entirely by old women knitting or lacemaking. Together with the villages of **Sorano** and **Sovana** it constitutes one of the most worthwhile and neglected visits in the province.

The Town

The only entry point to the medieval town is through **Piazza Petruccioli** – host to a car park, hotel and the main bus stop, and to a small belvedere that looks along the houses and cliffs on the town's southern edge. Immediately through the gate is the high-walled and rather claustrophobic Piazza Garibaldi, and beyond it the massive **aqueduct** and **fortress**, contemporary building projects completed in the sixteenth century under Antonio da Sangallo the Younger, along with a complex string of fortifications. Within the fortress is the Renaissance **Palazzo Orsini**, home to a small museum (Mon–Sat 9am–1pm & 3–6pm, Sun 9am–1pm; L3000) of rather motley odds and ends. Far more absorbing is the new **Museo della Civaltà Giubonnai**, located in a series of cellars beneath the fortress which were discovered by accident during a clean-up. Some of the labyrinth had remained unseen and untouched for 300 years; other parts had been filled with rubble during Sangallo's work on the foundations. The collection, growing all the time, centres on folk, domestic and agricultural ephemera of the Maremma. At present you need to make an appointment (☎0564/615.243) with the curator, but the hope is to fix regular hours and admission.

The fortress backs onto **Piazza della Repubblica**, the town's elongated and beautiful main square, its symmetry accentuated by a pair of fountains and immaculately pollarded ilex trees. Wander over to the balcony for a panorama taking in the river, trees, waterfalls and the faint outline of Monte Amiata away to the north.

Beyond lies the old town proper, a tight huddle of arches, alleys and medieval streets. It consists of three main streets, merging to one at the end of the town. Taking the left fork out of the square, Via Zuccarelli brings you to the ruins of the **synagogue** – its rusted gates are the only identifying sign, despite the claims of the local tourist pamphlet that restoration is under way. The Jewish community moved here in 1649, from nearby Castro, which Pope Innocent X had ordered to be destroyed. A couple of minutes' walk beyond, the road comes to an end by the Renaissance church of **San Rocco**, its door flanked by the arms of the Orsini family; inside are a few patches of fresco. Nearby, immediately outside the Porto Capisotto and the medieval ramparts, is a stretch of **Etruscan wall**.

Heading back to Piazza della Repubblica, Via G. Orsini brings you to Piazza Gregorio VII and the Baroque **Duomo**, with its butter-coloured stucco facade and giant campanile. The third street of the grid, **Via Roma**, best encapsulates the town's provincial feel, a collection of odd, half-empty shops giving off a smell of mothballs; here, as elsewhere, the main pleasure is exploring the arches and alleys that lead off the main street.

Practicalities

Pitigliano has a summer **tourist office** on Via Roma. The town doesn't exactly buzz with visitors, though, and with luck you should find room at its single **hotel**, the *Albergo Guastini* on Piazza Petruccioli (☎0564/616.065; [4]); the hotel is happier doing full-board deals, which is no problem, as the rates are reasonable and the food fair. An out-of-town alternative is the *Albergo Corano* (☎0564/616.112; [5]), a modern place with a pool; it's located just beyond the village of Madonna delle Grazie on the road to Manciano.

The best **restaurant** is a tiny wooden-beamed trattoria, *Del Corso*, on Via Roma. The town's one stab at **nightlife** is the *Birreria dell'Orso*, Piazza Gregorio

VII, good for beer and snacks, and with outside tables next to the duomo. The local **wine**, Bianco di Pitigliano, hard to find elsewhere, is sold at two good-value outlets on Via Santa Chiara (off Piazza Petruccioli) and celebrated in a September **wine festival**.

There's a reasonable **bus** service (pick-up and drop-off in Piazza Petruccioli), with three departures daily to Grosseto via Manciano, three to Orbetello (weekdays only), four to San Quírico. A school bus serves Sovana and Sorano at 1.30pm from Monday to Saturday.

Sovana

SOVANA's Etruscan tombs and pristine Romanesque architecture would place it firmly on the tour circuit if it were only closer to Siena or Florence. As it is, you can explore this breathtaking, part-abandoned medieval centre in virtual solitude – save at weekends, when Romans and, increasingly, northern Europeans flock to the place in force.

The town's monuments derive from its time as the capital of the **Aldobrandeschi**, a noble clan whose domain extended over much of southern Tuscany and northern Lazio; they were said to have a castle for every day of the year. Their golden age came with the birth in Sovana of a scion who in 1073 was to become Pope Gregory VII, a great reforming pontiff who also kept a favourable eye on family business. Decline set in during the fourteenth century, when Sovana's low-lying position made it vulnerable both to malaria and to Sienese attacks, which saw both population and power drift to nearby Pitigliano. Today, Sovana's residents number just one hundred and twenty-three.

The village

Sovana's main street, **Via di Mezzo**, is almost the sum of the place, a broad expanse of fishbone-patterned brick paving, laid in 1580 and recently restored to impressive effect. Guarding its start are the ruins of the Aldobrandeschi **castle**, which fell into greater disrepair with each of its subsequent owners – the Sienese, Orsini and Medici, who tried to repopulate the place in the sixteenth century by importing families of Albanians.

At its end, the street swells slightly to form the **Piazza del Pretorio**, a perfect medieval ensemble dominated on the left by **Santa Maria**, one of the most beautiful churches in southern Tuscany. Built in the thirteenth century to a Romanesque-Gothic plan, Santa Maria has a simple stone interior dominated by an exquisite **ciborio**, a unique piece of pre-Romanesque sculpture from the eighth or ninth century. Superbly preserved frescoes around the walls set the seal on a marvellous building.

Opposite the church is the low-arched **Loggia del Capitano**, whose stone coats of arms proclaim Medici possession, and whose arches conceal a nice bar with a handful of outdoor tables. Next to it is the **Palazzo Pretorio**, home to a small museum and gallery which traces the area's history, paying particular attention to local Etruscan tombs and discoveries. Particularly illuminating are the reconstructions of how tombs might originally have looked, well worth seeing if you intend to head out and explore the necropolis (see opposite). The nine stone banners here are those of the town's Sienese and Medici governors.

From the square a back lane to the left leads through gardens and olive groves to the huge **Duomo** (closed 1–3pm), whose exterior wall and superb portal bear some of the finest Lombard-Romanesque carvings in Tuscany. The church's nucleus went up in the eighth century, the date of many of the carvings, and was augmented in the tenth with the addition of an apse and crypt. The bare, triple-naved interior features some twelth-century carved capitals, reminiscent of the Benedictine work in Sant'Antimo. There are also traces of fresco, a fine Gothic font and a wonderful **crypt**, divided into five tiny naves by ancient columns. Access to the crypt has recently been restricted, and you can now only peer in rather than wander around.

Beyond the duomo you can walk down to an old town **gateway** and traces of Etruscan wall, or turn back to Piazza Pretorio along the village's modest residential street. It sports a couple of shops and little more.

The Etruscan tombs

All round Sovana, but especially on the road to Saturnia, **Etruscan tombs** riddle the countryside, many approached by original "sunken" Etruscan roads. Why these roads should be sunken still puzzles scholars: some believe the purpose was defensive, in that they would enable people to move unseen from town to town, others that they were used for moving livestock and were cut below ground level to prevent the animals from straying. The larger graves are well marked off the road by yellow signs. The necropolis as a whole, of which the marked tombs form a tiny part, extends for miles and rates in archeological (if not tourist) terms with the graves at Tarquinia and Cerveteri. Most of the tombs date from the seventh century BC and just about every type of Etruscan grave is present, including *colombari*, small niches cut into the rock to take cinerary urns. What the tombs lack in paintings they often make up for with elaborate carvings.

The key tombs are the **Tomba Ildebranda**, considered the best single tomb in Tuscany, the **Tomba della Sileno** and the **Tomba del Sireno**. If you take the road to Saturnia, tombs start to appear after the tunnel. You pass the Sireno on your left, followed by the Poggio Pesca and the Pola, a couple of minutes' uphill scramble from the road.

Rooms and food

Sovana is an evocative place to stay and has two good **hotels**. Opposite Santa Maria is the *Albergo-Ristorante Etrusca* (☎0564/616.183; [5]), a tiny place that's worth booking to be sure of a room. The *Etrusca*'s **restaurant** is first-rate, its beautifully elegant interior scattered with highly covetable antique furniture; expect to part with L35–40,000. Just off the piazza is the cheaper *Hotel Scilla* (☎0564/616.531; [4]), whose restaurant also has a beautiful setting, with a pergola draped in flowers and greenery. There's also a pizzeria, *La Tavernetta,* midway down Via di Mezzo.

Sorano

All the approaches to **SORANO** are extraordinary: from the south the route is lined with caves and tombs cut into the hillside; from the west, the road is cut into walls of tufa. The village, visible for miles on either approach, has a decidedly weird air, with only a fraction of the old houses still lived in. Parts of the tangled streets suggest a faded grandeur, others are desolate and derelict. Landslips are the main problem, several streets having been declared terminally uninhabitable after one big slide. Recent attempts to keep Sorano alive have included a policy of sponsoring ceramic workshops and various other arts and crafts businesses. The small **tourist office**, Piazza della Chiesa, makes a point of promoting these, and will also help if you want guidance around the wealth of Etruscan remnants in the valley.

The village itself is full of intriguing medieval corners, though has little in the way of specific sights. The old castle, the **Masso Leopoldino**, dominates the centre but offers no more than views from its aerial-ringed battlements. The more impressive fortress as you enter the town is the **Fortezza Orsini**, a blunt and perfectly preserved piece of Renaissance military engineering. Built over an old Aldobrandeschi fort in 1552, it was often besieged but never taken.

Nearby Sovana is perhaps a better overnight option, but if you need to stay Sorano has one **hotel**, the one-star *La Botte* (☎0564/638.633; ④).

San Quírico

From Sorano there are constant **views** over the wooded gorge of the River Lente, whose rushing waters echo through the streets. Down on the valley floor, tantalising tracks (known as *vie cave*) crisscross the countryside, linking clearly visible **rock tombs**, Roman wells and old watermill workings.

Five kilometres east of Sorano is the hamlet of **SAN QUÍRICO**, to the north of which you can explore the **Rupestre di Vitozza**, a series of two hundred tombs, grottoes and palaeo-Christian remains, and the remnants of Vitozza, San Quírico's medieval antecedent. The village has a salubrious two-star **hotel**, the *Agnelli* (☎0564/619.015; ④); the hotel **restaurant** has a great village atmosphere and serves up surprisingly good fish and seafood (bought in fresh daily). Prices are keen, making it extremely popular with locals, and there are pizzas too, if you don't want a full meal.

travel details

Trains

Siena–Chiusi (10 daily; 1hr 30min) via Asciano (35min) and Sinalunga (1hr).

Siena – Asciano – Sant'Angelo – Grosseto 3 daily.

Siena–Buonconvento–Grosseto 3 daily.

From Sinalunga to Monte San Savino and Arezzo (12 daily; 35min/1hr).

From Chiusi to Cortona and Arezzo (hourly; 20min/1hr); Rome (hourly; 40min).

Buses

From Torrenieri to Montalcino (15 daily; 20min); Buonconvento (6 daily; 25min); Arcidosso (6 daily; 40min); Grosseto (2 daily; 1hr 20min).

From Montalcino to Buonconvento (hourly – change for Siena; 35min).

From Montepulciano to Pienza, San Quírico, Torrenieri and Buonconvento (7 daily; 20min/40min/50min/1hr; four continue to Siena); Chianciano and Chiusi (every 30min; 25min/50min).

From Chiusi to Chianciano and Montepulciano (14 daily; 30min/45min).

From Abbadia San Salvatore to Siena (2 daily); Buonconvento (6 daily); Chiusi (3 daily); Arcidosso/Santa Fiora (6 daily); Grosseto (6 daily); Montepulciano (1 daily).

From Pitigliano to Grosseto via Manciano (3 daily); Orbetello (3 daily – weekdays only); San Quírico (4 daily); Viterbo (1 daily); Sovana and Sorano (1 daily Mon–Sat).

CHAPTER EIGHT

AREZZO PROVINCE

Upstream from Florence the Arno valley – the **Valdarno** – is a solidly industrialised district, with warehouses and manufacturing plants enclosing many of the small towns strung along the train line. Some of the villages up on the valley sides retain an appealing medieval square or a cluster of attractive buildings but there's no very compelling stop before you reach the provincial capital of the upper Arno region, **Arezzo**, one hour's train ride from Florence. This solidly bourgeois city has its share of architectural delights – including one of the most photogenic squares in central Italy – though the droves of foreign visitors who travel to Arezzo come to see one thing: the fresco cycle by **Piero della Francesca** in the church of San Francesco. These are not the only crowds to fill Arezzo's hotels, for Italians flock here in even greater numbers for antiques, traded each month on the Piazza Grande in quantities scarcely matched anywhere else in the country.

For visitors on the trail of the masterpieces of Tuscan art, there are two essential calls in the vicinity of Arezzo. The first is the modest hill town of **Monterchi**, where Della Francesca painted one of the most powerful images of the Renaissance, the pregnant *Madonna del Parto*. Two other magnificent works by the same artist are to be seen in his birthplace, **Sansepolcro**, almost on the Umbrian border to the east and one of the pleasantest Tuscan backwaters.

Art is far from being this province's sole attraction. In the **Casentino**, the stretch of the Arno valley between Arezzo and the source of the river to the north, small hill towns such as **Poppi** and **Bibbiena** stand above a terrain of vineyards and pastures, cradled by thickly wooded upland. The secluded peaks of the Casentino also harbour two of Italy's most influential monasteries, **Camáldoli** and the Franciscan sanctuary of **La Verna**, Tuscany's holiest pilgrimage site.

ACCOMMODATION PRICES

Throughout this guide, accommodation is graded on a scale from ① to ⑨. Grades ① and ② apply to **hostel** accommodation, and indicate the lowest price a **single person** could expect to pay for one night in that establishment in high season. Grades ③ to ⑨ apply to **hotels**, and indicate the cost of the **cheapest double room in high season**. The price bands to which these codes refer are as follows:

① under L20,000 per person
② over L20,000 per person
③ under L50,000 per double
④ L50–70,000 per double
⑤ L70–90,000 per double
⑥ L90–120,000 per double
⑦ L120–150,000 per double
⑧ L150–200,000 per double
⑨ over L200,000 per double

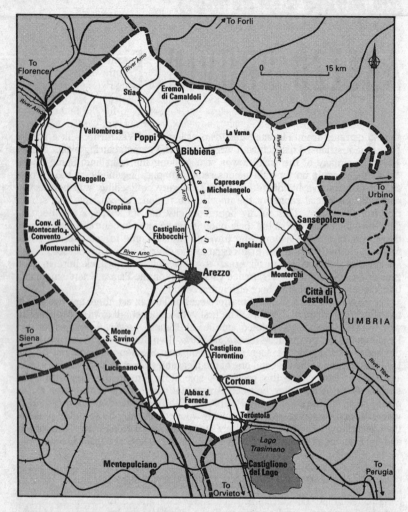

To the south of Arezzo stretches the agricultural plain of the **Valdichiana**, where the ancient hill town of **Cortona** is the major attraction, its steep streets forming a distinctive urban landscape and giving an unforgettable view over Lago Trasimeno and the hills to the west.

Trains on the Florence–Rome rail line run up the Arno valley, through Arezzo and on down the Valdichiana. For the Casentino, there's a private rail line which runs to the head of the valley – or will do, when long-term improvements are complete. Otherwise, Arezzo and Cortona are the centres of overlapping **bus** networks, which between them cover most of Arezzo province, though a car is essential if you want to get to some of the remoter sights and back on the same day, or to get the most out of the wilder reaches.

Florence to Arezzo

If you're travelling by public transport from Florence to Arezzo there's no choice of route, as buses and trains all follow the **Valdarno**, just about the most unattractive stretch of waterway in Tuscany. Moving around by car, the obvious choice is between the two major roads that run roughly parallel to the river: the Autostrada del Sole and the SS69. If you want to cover the kilometres quickly, take the former; if you want to see the few sights of Valdarno, go for the latter, but be warned that the tarmac is perpetually clogged with lorries rumbling in and out of the industrial estates that pepper this part of the region. There is a third alternative, in the shape of the road that skirts the upland region known as the **Pratomagno**. It's a fairly tiring drive, with a gear-change required every couple of hundred metres, but at least the passengers have the benefit of the view across to Chianti, and there's the odd Romanesque church along the way if the blind corners get a bit too much.

The Valdarno route

River, rail line and *autostrada* come together at the bottleneck known as Incisa Valdarno, 25km out of central Florence. Petrarch grew up here and some vestiges of the old town are preserved – but insufficient to make the place appealing. **FIGLINE VALDARNO**, 5km south, was the birthplace of another eminent Tuscan, Marsilio Ficino, court philosopher to Lorenzo il Magnifico. The old quarter around Piazza Ficino has a few handsome buildings and one interesting interior – the frescoed **Collegiata di Santa Maria**, which contains a fourteenth-century *Madonna* by the so-called Maestro di Figline.

SAN GIOVANNI VALDARNO, midway betwen Florence and Arezzo, is the most heavily industrialised but also the most rewarding town in the valley. The arcaded **Palazzo Comunale** is yet another design from Arnolfo di Cambio, who in the thirteenth century was put in charge of fortifying this Florentine town against the Aretines – the citizens of Arezzo. At the back of the palazzo, next to the church of Santa Maria della Grazia, the **Museo della Basilica di Santa Maria della Grazia** (Tues, Wed & Fri 5–7pm, Thurs, Sat & Sun 10am–noon & 5–7pm; free) houses a Fra' Angelico *Annunciation* painted for the Convento di Montecarlo, plus a lovely version of the same subject by his obscure contemporary, Jacopo del Sellaio. Also on show is a *Madonna and Child with Four Saints*, attributed to Masaccio, who was born at San Giovanni in 1401. The Gothic church of San Francesco, at right angles to Santa Maria, is blotched with frescoes as well.

In the Pliocene era the Valdarno was a vast lake, its shores patrolled by troops of prehistoric elephants. Fossil remnants of these colossal beasts are the pride of **MONTEVARCHI**, where they are installed in the **Museo Paleontologico** (Tues–Sat 9am–noon & 4–7pm, Sun 10am–noon; closed Aug; L3000; around 1500 other exhibits keep them company. In the centre of town, the sacristy of the **Collegiata di San Lorenzo** has been converted into a small Museo di Arte Sacra (opened by the sacristan), which has a little temple covered in ceramics by Andrea della Robbia. In the church there's a reliquary containing one of Tuscany's more desperate holy mementoes – water from a spring in a cave where the Holy Family are said to have rested on the flight from Egypt.

This might not seem reason enough to stop on the way to Arezzo; beyond Montevarchi, there's no reason at all, unless, that is, you have time to take a meandering diversion off the SS69 into the southeastern corner of the Chianti hills. If you do, you should arm yourself with a large-scale road map and follow the road to Mercatale, then take the turning for Bucine; from this road you can reach the fortified hilltop eyrie of **SAN LEOLINO**, which gives fabulous views. From there, head to **CENNINA**, where the castle ruins stare across the Arno towards the Pratomagno, then strike west for the highlight of this diversion, the completely unspoiled medieval village of **CIVITELLA**, with its magnificent ruined thirteenth-century castle. From here, it's just 8km to the autostrada, to the south-west of Arezzo.

The Pratomagno route

To maximise the pleasure of the wooded road above the east bank of the Arno, drive to Pontassieve and get onto the N70 towards the Passo della Consuma (see p.165). The first turning to the right rises to **VALLOMBROSA**, whose **abbey** is the mother foundation of the Vallombrosan order, established in 1038 by the Florentine Giovanni Gualberto (see p.92). When Giovanni was canonised in 1193 this abbey became extremely influential, and by the fifteenth century it was administering wide tracts of Tuscan territory. Much rebuilt since those days, it now resembles a fortified villa with its high perimeter wall and corner towers and impresses mainly by its location, pillowed against the fir-covered hills. Part of the complex is still occupied by monks, part by a forestry school; neither contingent welcomes visitors.

Milton stayed at Vallombrosa and in *Paradise Lost* he compared the throng of demons in hell to the "autumn leaves that strow the brooks/In Vallombrosa", which is a bit odd, given the preponderance of evergreens hereabouts. Though the forests have dwindled in the intervening centuries, they are still extensive, as you'll appreciate if you drive over the Pratomagno ridge to Poppi (see p.393) through Montemignaio – a beautiful route round the flank of Monte Secchieta. For a **walk** through the forests, as good a starting point as any is the tiny resort of Saltino, the next village after Vallombrosa along the road to Arezzo. From here paths lead up to the peak of Monte Secchieta, a winter ski resort; the view from the summit is amazing.

Beyond Saltino the terrain opens out, with terraces bordering the road as it snakes down to Reggello, a diffused and characterless place much praised by connoisseurs of Tuscan olive oil. A kilometre to the south, the church of **San Pietro a Cascia** has some columns that might appeal to Romanesque cognoscenti. More Romanesque architecture appears at **PIAN DI SCÒ**, 10km on, where there's an eleventh-century *pieve*, as well as superb *agriturismo* **accommodation** at *Fattoria Cavini*, in the neighbouring hamlet of Canova (May–Sept; ☎055/865.6623; ⑤).

CASTELFRANCO DI SOPRA, 2km further, was yet another town fortified by Arnolfo di Cambio but the street plan and one gate are virtually the only traces of his handiwork; its most attractive feature is a much-restored thirteenth-century *badìa* on the main road. Another 10km brings you to Loro Ciuffenna, where ranks of new apartments form an unflattering prelude to a small medieval quarter down by the Ciuffenna river; a Romanesque tower and bridge form the core. A short distance south of Loro Ciuffenna, tucked into the hills at Penna Alta, you'll find the best **restaurant** along this route, the family-run *Il Canto di Maggio* (☎055/970.5147); the splendid Tuscan menu works out at around L40,000 per head.

The most substantial cultural site comes a couple of kilometres on, in the hamlet of **GRÓPINA**, which is reached by taking a steep and sharp left turn just outside Loro. Here the parish church of **San Pietro** (daily 8am–noon & 3–7pm) has some of the finest Romanesque carving in Tuscany, dating from the early thirteenth century. The capitals depict knights, fighting animals and various standard motifs, but you'll have to travel a long way to find anything quite like the **pulpit**, with its knotted columns and rows of alarmed-looking figures with upraised arms.

The last place of any interest before Arezzo is Castiglion Fibocchi, whose central patch – now enclosed by light industry – is little changed since the Middle Ages; you'll get the measure of the place by driving through in low gear.

Arezzo

Maecenas, the wealthy patron of Horace and Virgil, was born in **AREZZO** and it's still a place with the moneyed touch. Its economy rests on the profits of its jewellers and goldsmiths, a clan so numerous that the city has the world's largest gold manufacturing plant. Topping up the coffers are the proceeds of Arezzo's antiques industry: in the vicinity of the Piazza Grande there are shops filled with the sort of furniture you put in a bank vault rather than in your house, and every month the **Fiera Antiquaria** (Antiques Fair) turns the piazza into a vast showroom.

Occupying a site that controls the major passes of the central Apennines, Arezzo was one of the most important settlements of the Etruscan federation. It maintained its pre-eminence under Roman rule, and was a prosperous independent republic in the Middle Ages, until, in 1289, its Ghibelline loyalties brought about a catastrophic clash with the Guelph Florentines at Campaldino. Arezzo temporarily recovered from this reversal under the leadership of Bishop Guido Tarlati, whose bellicosity earned him eventual excommunication. However, definitive subjugation came about in 1384, when Florence paid the ransom demanded from Arezzo by the conquering army of Louis d'Anjou. When the French departed, the city's paymaster was left in power.

Even as a mortgaged political power Arezzo continued to be a major cultural force, as it had been since the tenth century, when Guido d'Arezzo, the first theorist of musical notation, was born here. Petrarch (1304–74) later brought further prestige to the city, and in the sixteenth century Pietro Aretino and Giorgio Vasari, both Aretines, maintained its reputation. Yet it was an outsider who gave Arezzo its greatest monument – **Piero della Francesca**, whose frescoes for the church of San Francesco belong in the company of Masaccio's cycle in Florence and Michelangelo's in Rome.

Information and accommodation

The main **tourist office** is on the edge of the train station forecourt, on the right as you come out of the station (summer Mon–Sat 9am–1pm & 4–7pm, Sun 9am–1pm; winter Mon–Fri 9am–1pm & 3–6pm, Sat 9am–1pm; ☎0575/20.839); the helpful staff speak English and have masses of information on Arezzo and its province. The administrative office for regional tourism, at Piazza Risorgimento 116, second right off Via Guido Monaco (same hours; ☎0575/23.952), displays the latest information on Arezzo accommodation outside, so you can get the up-to-date essentials even if you roll into town in the evening.

Rooms are scarce at any time of year in Arezzo, and are almost impossible to come by on the first weekend of every month, owing to the antiques fair; in addition the town is booked solid at the end of August and beginning of September, when the *Concorso Polifonico Guido d'Arezzo* and the *Giostra del Saracino* follow in quick succession. Assured of regular bookings throughout the year, Arezzo's hoteliers seem to try that little bit less hard than many in the region.

HOTELS

Milano, Via Madonna del Prato 83 (☎0575/26.836). Best of the one-stars, if only because it's the most central. [4].

La Toscana, Via M. Perennio 56 (☎0575/21.692). On the main road coming in from the west; has more single rooms than any other one-star. [4].

Cecco, Corso Italia 215 (☎0575/20.986). Very central two-star, spacious if slightly institutional in feel. [5].

Astoria, Via Guido Monaco 54 (☎0575/24.361). Large two-star right by the main post office; has been known to negotiate its prices during slack periods. [5].

Continentale, Piazza Guido Monaco 7 (☎0575/20.251). Large old three-star right on the hub of the lower town. Excellent views from the roof terrace. [7].

HOSTEL

Ostello Villa Severi, Via Redi 13 (☎0575/29.047). Occupying an old villa some way out of the town – a 30-minute walk from the station, or take bus #4 from Piazza Guido Monaco. Reception open 8am–2pm & 5pm–midnight. [1].

The Town

There are two distinct parts to Arezzo: the **older quarter**, at the top of the hill, and the businesslike **lower town**. Most of the lower town remains hidden from day-trippers, as it spreads behind the **train station** and the adjacent **bus terminal**. From the station forecourt you go straight ahead for Via Guido Monaco, the traffic axis between the upper and lower town and a street which nobody walks along except to shop or to call at the main post office. The parallel **Corso Italia,** now pedestrianised, is the route to take up the hill, and the stretch immediately north of Via Francesco Crispi is also the place to hang out in the evenings; the *passeggiata* crowds – and the bars – thin out towards the top of the climb.

San Francesco – Piero della Francesca's church

Off to the left of the Corso, on Via Cavour, not far from its summit, stands the building everyone comes to Arezzo to see – the church of **San Francesco** (summer 8.30am–noon & 1.30–7pm; winter 8.30am–noon & 1.30–6.30pm). Built after 1322, the shabby brick basilica earned its renown in the early 1450s, when the Bacci family commissioned **Piero della Francesca** to continue the decoration of the choir. The project had been started by the recently deceased Bicci di Lorenzo, who had got no further than scenes of Heaven, Purgatory and Hell in the vault. For the wall paintings, Piero's patrons nominated a subject with rather fewer dramatic possibilities, but which suited the contemplative personality of this artist perfectly: it inspired a work that carries an emotional charge unsurpassed by any other fresco cycle.

The theme chosen was **The Legend of the True Cross**, a story in which the physical material of the Cross forms the link in the cycle of redemption that begins with humanity's original sin. Starting with the right wall, Piero painted the

series in narrative sequence, working continuously until about 1457 – the precise chronology isn't known. However, the episodes are not arranged in narrative sequence, the artist preferring to arrange them according to the precepts of symmetry: thus the two battle scenes face each other across the chapel, rather than coming where the story dictates. As is always the case with this mystical rationalist painter, smaller-scale symmetries are present in every part of the work: the retinue of the Queen of Sheba appears twice, in mirror-image arrangement, and the face of the queen is exactly the same as the face of the Empress Helena. This orderliness, combined with the pale light and the statuesque quality of the figures, create an atmosphere that's unique to Piero, a sense of each incident as a part of a greater plan.

Damp has badly damaged areas of the chapel and some bits have peeled away as a result of Piero's notoriously slow working procedures. For example, the cloak of Solomon in the scene showing his meeting with the Queen of Sheba was painted after the plaster had dried, and so has weathered far worse than the surrounding pigment. Most of the rest, however, is emerging in magnificent condition from the massive restoration that was planned for completion in 1992, the five-hundredth anniversary of Piero's death, but has dropped a little behind schedule.

The literary source for the cycle, the medieval *Golden Legend* by Jacopo de Voragine, is a very convoluted story; what follows is a simple key to the events depicted, the numbers referring to the plan below. The *Annunciation* and two *Prophets* on the window wall are not explicitly related to the legend, but the former is pictorially linked to the narrative by its cruciform plan and by the visual allusion of the beam above the Virgin's head.

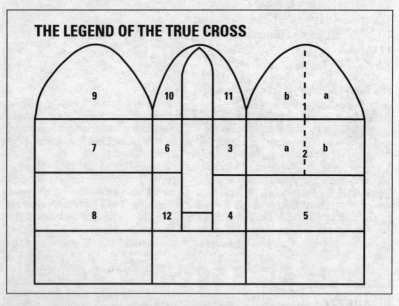

THE LEGEND OF THE TRUE CROSS

1a. Adam announces his death and implores Seth, his son, to seek the "oil of mercy" from the Angel of Eden.

1b. Instead the Angel gives Seth a sprig from the Tree of Knowledge, which is planted in the dead Adam's mouth.

2a. Solomon orders a bridge to be built from a beam fashioned from the tree that grew from Adam's grave. The Queen of Sheba, visiting Solomon, kneels in prayer before the bridge, sensing the holiness of the wood.

2b. The Queen of Sheba foresees that the beam will later be used to crucify a man, and that the death will bring disgrace to the Jews; she tells Solomon of her prophecy.

3. Solomon orders the beam to be buried.

4. The Emperor Constantine has a vision of the Cross, hearing a voice that declares "Under this sign shall you be victorious".

5. Constantine defeats the rival emperor Maxentius, and then is baptised. An interesting historical note is that the figure of Constantine – the first emperor to rule from Byzantium – is a portrait of the Byzantine Emperor John Paleologus, the last but one Byzantine emperor, who had been in Florence in 1439.

6. The Levite Judas, under torture, reveals to the servants of Saint Helena – mother of Constantine – the burial place of the three crosses from Golgotha.

7. The crosses are excavated; the true Cross is recognised when it brings about a man's resurrection. Arezzo – serving as Jerusalem – is shown in the background.

8. The Persian king Chosroes, who had stolen the Cross, is defeated by the Emperor Heraclius. On the right he kneels awaiting execution; behind him is visible the throne into which he had incorporated the Cross.

9. Heraclius returns the Cross to Jerusalem.

10. A prophet (by an assistant).

11. A prophet.

12. The Annunciation.

The Pieve di Santa Maria and Piazza Grande

A short distance to the west of San Francesco a huge Baroque tower signals the presence of the hulking **Badìa**, otherwise known as the church of SS. Flora and Lucilla. Inside, the main altarpiece by Giorgio Vasari is encased in a marble frame that looks like a monstrous sideboard. The generally inaccessible cloister refectory has a similarly heavy-footed example of Giorgio's output.

Further up the Corso from San Francesco stands one of the finest Romanesque structures in Tuscany, the twelfth-century **Pieve di Santa Maria**. Its arcaded facade, elaborate yet severe, belongs to a type associated more with Pisa and western Tuscany, and is doubly unusual in presenting its front to a fairly narrow street rather than to the town's main square. Dating from the 1210s, the carvings of the months over the portal are an especially lively group – though currently concealed by a long-term restoration. The campanile, known locally as "the tower of the hundred holes", was added in the fourteenth century.

The oldest section of the chalky grey **interior** is the raised sanctuary, where the altarpiece is Pietro Lorenzetti's *Madonna and Saints* polyptych, painted in 1320 and horribly restored. The unfamiliar saint on the far left, accompanying Matthew, the Baptist and John the Evangelist, is Saint Donatus, bishop of Arezzo in the fifth century and martyred in the pagan backlash following the Goths' invasion. His relics are contained in a beautiful fourteenth-century silver bust in the crypt.

The **Piazza Grande**, on the other side of the church, is a handsome if somewhat impractical public square, slanting down towards its fountain at a sweeping gradient. The *passeggiata* runs out of steam before reaching this altitude, and the piazza really comes alive for the *Fiera Antiquaria* and – more raucously – for September's *Giostra del Saraceno* (see p.387). A diverting assortment of buildings encloses the space, the wooden balconied apartments on the east side facing the apse of Santa Maria, the Baroque Palazzo dei Tribunali and the **Palazzetto della Fraternità dei Laici**, whose Gothic ground floor gives way to fifteenth-century upper storeys. The northern edge is formed by the arcades of **Vasari's loggia**, occupied by shops that in some instances still retain their original stone counters.

The Duomo and around

At the highest point of the town rises the large and unfussy **Duomo** (daily 7am–noon & 3–6.30pm), whose harmonious appearance belies the protracted process of its construction. Begun in the late thirteenth century, it was virtually finished by the start of the sixteenth, but the campanile comes from the last century and the facade from this.

The church's stained-glass windows, a rarity in Italy, were made around 1520 by Guillaume de Marcillat; they let in so little light that his other contributions to the interior – the paintings on the first three bays of the nave – are virtually impossible to see. Off the left aisle, separated from the nave by a huge screen, the Cappella della Madonna del Conforto has terracottas by the Della Robbia family, but the best of the building's artworks lie further down the aisle. Just beyond the organ is the **tomb of Bishop Guido Tarlati**, head of the *comune* of Arezzo during its resurgence in the early fourteenth century; the monument, plated with marble reliefs showing scenes from the militaristic bishop's career, was possibly designed by Giotto. The tiny fresco nestled against the right side of the tomb is **Piero della Francesca**'s *Magdalen*, his only work in Arezzo outside San Francesco. The small Museo Diocesano (Thurs–Sat 9am–noon; L5000), alongside the duomo, won't make anyone's day.

Arezzo's public park, the **Passeggio del Prato**, extends from the east end of the duomo; the **Fortezza Medicea**, at its far end, is a good place to take a picnic and gaze down over the town or across the vineyards towards the Casentino. Cosimo I's fortress here was demolished in the eighteenth century, leaving only the ramparts.

San Domenico, Vasari's house and the art museum

A short distance in the opposite direction from the duomo is the church of **San Domenico** (daily 7am–noon & 3–7pm), constructed mostly in the late thirteenth century but with a Gothic campanile. It's more striking inside: the high altar has a dolorous *Crucifix* by **Cimabue** (1260), painted when the artist would have been about twenty, while tatters of fifteenth- and sixteenth-century frescoes all round the church create the effect of a gigantic picture album.

From here signs point the way to the **Casa di Giorgio Vasari** (Tues–Sat 9am–7pm, Sun 9am–1pm; free), designed by the biographer-architect-painter. Born in Arezzo in 1511, Vasari was taught to paint by his distant relative Luca Signorelli, and went on to become court painter, architect and general artistic supremo to Cosimo I. His major contribution to western culture, however, is his *Lives of the Most Excellent Italian Architects, Painters and Sculptors*, the first attempt to relate artists' work to their social context, and a primary source for all histories of the Renaissance. Taking greater pleasure from the products of his imagination than later generations have managed to extract, Vasari frescoed much of his house with portraits and mythological characters, a decorative scheme that makes this one of the brashest domestic interiors in Tuscany. Portraits include his wife as the muse of conjugal love (in the "Chamber of Apollo") and Michelangelo and Andrea del Sarto (in the "Chamber of Fame"). Minor paintings are strewn all over the place, proof that Giorgio was far from the most inept painter of his day.

At the foot of the hill, in Via San Lorentino, the fifteenth-century Palazzo Bruni-Ciocchi houses the **Museo Statale d'Arte Medioevale e Moderna** (Tues–Sun 9am–7pm; L6000). Its collection of paintings by local artists and majolica pieces from the thirteenth to the eighteenth centuries, generously spread over three floors, requires severe editorial work from the visitor.

The Museo Archeologico

All the principal sights are in the upper part of Arezzo, with the exception of the **Museo Archeologico** (Tues–Sat 9am–7pm; L6000), which occupies part of an abandoned monastery built into the wall of the town's Roman amphitheatre, to the right of the station. The desultory remains of the amphitheatre are part of the museum, but more impressive are the marvellously coloured **coralline vases**; produced here in the first century BC, they show why Arezzo's glassblowers achieved their reputation as consummate craftsmen throughout the Roman world. If you're here out of high season you may not be able to see them, though – the erratic opening hours of this museum reflect the low consumer demand, and it's often shut for days at a time in winter.

Food and festivals

Though there's no cut-price gourmet experience to be had in Arezzo, the town's restaurants more than atone for its hotels, offering menus to suit every budget, at a generally reliable standard. The restaurants below are listed in ascending order of price. Nightlife goes on in bars around piazzas Guido Monaco, Grande and San Domenico.

Snacks and ice cream

Penny's Pub, Piazza San Agostino 13. Good selection of sandwiches and snacks; open till 1am.

Yogurt House, Via Madonna del Prato 89. Gelateria specialising in delicious yoghurt-based ice cream, desserts and drinks.

Restaurants

Olga & Albano, Via Francesco Crispi 34. Excellent wood-oven pizzas – evenings only except during antique fair. Closed Mon.

Bikos, Via Garibaldi 150. A popular night-time spot with reasonably priced pizzas and pasta dishes and a touch of live music, usually jazz (Oct–May). Open 7pm–2am.

Da Guido, Via Madonna del Prato 85. Very basic local trattoria, with no written menu. Closed Sun.

La Scaletta, Piazza del Popolo 11. Down the steps to the side of the main post office, dishing up set meals from L25,000. Closed Mon.

Otello, Piazza Risorgimento 16. Opposite the regional tourist office, close to the *Milano* hotel. Bright and trendy joint, with generally good if unambitious food. Closed Mon.

Il Saraceno, Via Mazzini 6. Set menus of Aretine specialities from L20,000; pizzas too. Closed Wed & mid-July.

Osteria Agania, Via Mazzini 10. Excellent local dishes, at around L25,000 per head, drawing much of its clientele from the antiques dealers. Closed Mon.

La Buca di San Francesco, Via S. Francesco 1. Tourist-oriented place next to San Francesco, but food at around L25,000 per head. Closed Mon evening & all Tues.

Lancia d'Oro, Piazza Grande 19. Occupies the best site in town, underneath Vasari's loggia; you can eat very well here for L30,000. Closed Mon.

Le Tastevin, Via di Cenci. Highly recommended by Arentines for local, home-made food at about L30–35,000.

Festivals

Arezzo's premier folkloric event is the **Giostra del Saraceno**, held in the Piazza Grande on the first Sunday in September. The day starts off with various costumed processions; in the afternoon the action switches to the jousting arena in the piazza. The piazza is the junction of the four quarters of the city and the sides of the square are decked with flags to mark their affiliations. Each quarter is represented by a pair of knights on horseback, who do battle against a wooden effigy of a Saracen king. In one hand the effigy holds a shield marked with squares numbered with the points scored when the riders hit that part of it; in the other it has a cat-of-three-tails which swings round when the shield is hit, necessitating nifty evasive action from the rider. A golden lance is awarded to the highest-scoring rider. In recent years this event has become so popular that reduced versions of the show have been staged in the summer; check at the tourist office for the latest information on dates and ticket availability.

The musical tradition that began with Guido d'Arezzo is kept alive chiefly through the international choral competition that bears his name: the **Concorso Polifonico Guido d'Arezzo**, held in the last week of August. The less ambitious **Pomeriggi Musicali** is a season of early-evening free concerts held in various churches, museums and libraries; on average there's one concert a week from mid-January to June. In late June the **Arezzo Wave** rock festival hits the Fortezza Medicea; with this and the other festivals, posters all over town give details of the offices and shops where tickets are being issued.

The **Fiera Antiquaria** takes over the Piazza Grande on the Saturday before the first Sunday of each month. The most expensive stuff is laid out by the Vasari loggia, with cheaper pieces lower down the square and in the side streets. The Roman numberplates in the car parks give an idea of what sort of league this market is playing in; nothing – not even the old postcards – could be described as a bargain.

To Sansepolcro – the Piero trail

Arezzo is the springboard for one of Tuscany's most rewarding art itineraries – the Piero della Francesca trail, whose other stops lie east of the city at **Monterchi** and **Sansepolcro**, the artist's birthplace. There's no train link between Arezzo and Sansepolcro, the rail approach to Sansepolcro being the private Terni–Perugia line. The *SITA* and *Baschetti* **bus** companies run seventeen services a day to Sansepolcro, nearly all of which continue to Città di Castello (see p.426); unfortunately, only a couple stop at Monterchi, and they are at useless times of the day. The nearest regular stop to the village is Le Ville, 2km to the west, from where the buses veer away through Anghiari – a pleasant enough place, but best seen by car. If you don't have your own transport, hitching is a viable alternative, as this is a busy stretch of road.

Monterchi – the Madonna del Parto

The farming village of **MONTERCHI** is 25km east of Arezzo, and for the last few kilometres of the journey the roadsides bear signs for the **Madonna del Parto**, which must be the only painting in Tuscany to be treated as though it were a town. The sole representation of the pregnant Madonna in Renaissance art, the fresco was painted for a cemetery chapel that stands on the outskirts of Monterchi, and remained hidden under plaster for centuries before its rediscovery in 1889 – by which time the *St Lucy* and the *Pietà* that Piero also painted here had both been lost. The Madonna was removed to Sansepolcro after an earthquake damaged the chapel in 1917 but at the insistence of the local *comune* it was brought back here within five years. During World War II they became so worried that some misfortune might befall the fresco that a false wall was constructed to protect it, and since then the Madonna has received the attentions of a number of restorers.

Most of the church has been knocked down to create more burial space, leaving the whitewashed transept as a small audience chamber for one of Italy's most revered images. However, at the time of writing the Madonna has been moved into an elementary school on Via Reglia, in the village, where she forms the centrepiece of an exhibition about the fresco and its restoration (9am–1pm & 2.30–7.30pm; L5000). She may or may not return to the orginal chapel.

Despite the recent restoration, the colours of the *Madonna del Parto* lack the freshness of the Arezzo cycle, but even bleached to black and white this would be an overwhelming picture. Two attendant angels draw back the flap of a small pavilion to reveal the pregnant Virgin, who places her hand on the upper curve of her belly, her eyes downcast as if preoccupied with a foreknowledge of the full course of the child's life. No other artist of the Renaissance produced anything comparable to its beautiful gravity.

Anghiari – and Michelangelo's birthplace

Most buses from Arezzo to Sansepolcro call at **ANGHIARI**, an agricultural hill town set amid fields of sunflowers and tobacco plants, all thriving on EC subsidies. The battle here between Florence and the Milanese army of Filippo Maria Visconti in 1440 was the subject of perhaps the most famous lost artwork of the Renaissance, Leonardo da Vinci's fresco in Florence's Palazzo Vecchio. Anghiari's diminutive historic centre of narrow streets, stepped alleyways and tunnels commands a fine view across the upper Tiber towards Sansepolcro, but its main draw is the *Da Alighiero* **restaurant** at Via Garibaldi 8 (closed Thurs). An excellent meal here should set you back about L35,000.

Michelangelo, effectively Leonardo's competitor in the decoration of the Palazzo Vecchio, was born 17km north of Anghiari in the place that now carries the name **CAPRESE MICHELANGELO** – it was just plain Caprese before the town's chief magistrate and his wife produced their prodigious son. The ancient village is perched high on a cliff overlooking the car park, bus stop (regular services from Anghiari) and the only **hotel**, the *Buca di Michelangelo* (☎0575/793.921; ④). A stepped path rises from here through cypresses and allotments to the arched gateway. The castle and Michelangelo's supposed birthplace, the Casa del Podestà, have been converted into a **Museo Michelangelo** (daily 9.30am–12.30pm & 3.30–5.30pm; free), where a few bits of Renaissance furniture and a load of plaster casts create the undernourishing experience that's par for the course with these shrines to the mighty.

On the plus side, there are some excellent **walks** in the surrounding hills. The best starts a short distance to the north of Caprese: follow the plunging road to Lama (2km), then take the turning for nearby Fragaiolo; from here a waymarked trail rises to La Verna (see p.392), a solid half-day's trek.

Sansepolcro

The *SITA* bus from Arezzo takes an hour to get to **SANSEPOLCRO**, an unassuming place which makes its way in the world as a manufacturer of lace and, more lucratively, pasta. If the historic district within the industrialised zones were a bit more substantial it could make a lot more money out of tourism; as it is, thousands of people come here each year to see **Piero della Francesca**'s *Madonna della Misericordia* and *Resurrection*, then leave a couple of hours later. There really isn't much more to the place than these pictures, but it's a relaxing, friendly town, and has a couple of fine restaurants to complete the day.

Born here at some time around 1420, Piero spent much of his life in the isolation of what was then the village of Borgo San Sepolcro, a three-year sojourn in Florence being probably his longest continuous absence. Patrons in Ferrara, Rome and Urbino called upon his services, even though his creative process was so painstaking that on one occasion his father had to apologise to a client for Piero's slowness. He returned to Sansepolcro in the 1470s, having abandoned painting as his eyesight failed. Most of his last twenty years were devoted to working on his treatises *On Perspective in Painting* and *On the Five Regular Bodies*, in which he propounded the geometrical rules that determine all accurate representation of the world, and extolled the human form as the exemplar of perfect proportion.

The Museo Civico

The **Museo Civico** is at Via Niccolò Aggiunti 65 (daily 9.30am–1pm & 2.30–6pm; L5000), in the road that emerges from the town walls right by the bus station. The museum starts badly, with a room full of clerical trappings, but then come two panels by Matteo di Giovanni that used to flank Della Francesca's *Baptism* (now in London's National Gallery) and a painted standard by Signorelli, who was one of his pupils.

A couple of minor Della Francesca paintings are hung by the entrance to the main room, but the eye immediately latches onto the **Madonna della Misericordia**, his earliest known painting and the epitome of his graceful solemnity. It was created in the 1440s, soon after he had been made a member of Sansepolcro's governing council, a position he was to hold for the rest of his life. Tiny panels surround the central image of the Madonna, a conventional and antiquated format that was specified by his patrons, the charitable Compagnia della Misericordia. There's no conventional fragility about this Madonna, though: compassionate and all-capable, she protects her worshippers with a cape as solid as a wall. The hooded man at her feet is wearing the uniform of the Misericordia, a sinister garb still worn by members of the modern Misericordia when bearing a body to a funeral.

The **Resurrection**, opposite, was painted for the adjoining town hall, probably in the early 1450s, and moved here in the sixteenth century. Aldous Huxley once dubbed this "the greatest painting in the world", a piece of hyperbole that might well have saved the painting from obliteration. In 1944 the British Eighth Army was ordered to bombard Sansepolcro, but an officer recalled Huxley's article and delayed the assault in the hope that the Germans would withdraw – which they did.

Much of the picture's power comes from its unique emphasis on the Resurrection as a physical event: implacable and muscular, Christ steps onto the edge of the tomb – banner in hand – as if it were the rampart of a conquered city. One of the soldiers in the foreground places his hand on his eyes, a gesture that might be read as simple weariness or as the despair of the vanquished heathen. The strange landscape in the background – with leafless trees on one side and reborn foliage on the other – was the starting point for Kenneth Clark's description, which pinpoints a pre-Christian strand to the painting's significance: "This country god, who rises in the grey light while humanity is asleep, has been worshipped ever since man first knew that the seed is not dead in the winter earth, but will force its way upwards through an iron crust."

After this, everything else in the gallery seems trivial, though it's difficult not to get hooked by Pontormo's sadistic *Martyrdom of St Quentin*, giving a new meaning to the word "fingernails". In the basement there's a tedious collection of carved bits from old Sansepolcro houses, and on the top floor an equally dull fresco show.

The rest of the town

Lesser art treasures are to be found round the corner from the Museo Civico in the Romanesque-Gothic **Duomo**, where the chapel to the left of the chancel houses a mighty tenth-century *Volto Santo*, depicting Christ as a robed patriarch. The crown and gown with which this crucifix is dressed for November's Feast of the Redeemer are usually on show in the Museo Civico.

The church of **San Lorenzo** – down in the southwest corner of the *centro storico* – has a *Deposition* by the Mannerist Rosso Fiorentino, painted within half a century of Della Francesca's last works but seeming to belong to another world.

Practicalities

The last **bus** back to Arezzo leaves at 7.25pm. If you decide to stay, there is usually space in the town's half-dozen **hotels**. Cheapest is the *Orfeo*, near the bus terminal at Viale Diaz 12 (☎0575/742.061; ③). First recommendation, though, is the three-star *Fiorentino*, Via Pacioli 60 (☎0575/740.350; ④), a homely hotel with a wonderful **restaurant** (closed Fri) – meals here are excellent value at around L35,000, and the proprietors are the most welcoming people imaginable. Another restaurant in the same price range is the *Ventura*, Via Aggiunti 30 (closed Sat & Aug), renowned for its *antipasti*. Pizzerias and bars are clustered in Viale Diaz.

Just about the only time you'll have difficulty in finding a room is the second Sunday in September, the date of the **Palio della Balestra**, the return leg of the crossbow competition against the archers of Gubbio. The shoot-out is preceded by some very flashy flag-hurling, whose practitioners – clad in costumes inspired by Piero's paintings – show off their skills at various other times of the year as well. For details call in at the **tourist office** in Via della Fonte, two minutes' walk from the museum (daily April–Oct 10.30am–1pm & 4–7pm; Nov–March 10am–1pm & 4–6pm).

North of Arezzo: the Casentino

North of Arezzo, beyond the city's textile factories, lies the lush upper valley of the Arno, a thoroughly agricultural area known as the **Casentino**, whose unshowy little towns see few tourists. From Bibbiena to Pratovecchio the valley is a broad green dish, ruffled by low hills and bracketed by the peaks of the Pratomagno on one side and on the other by the ridge between the Arno and the Tiber. Thick woodland of oak, beech and pine covers much of the upper slopes, the remnant of the forest that used to coat much of the Casentino. During the Medici centuries the timber from here supplied the shipyards of Pisa, Livorno and Genoa, as well as the building sites of Tuscany.

Florence did not always have territorial rights in this region. From the eleventh century the northern part of the Casentino was ruled by the **Guidi** dynasty of Poppi, who kept control from a string of castles whose ruins still litter the hills. In the Middle Ages Arezzo, landlord of the southern Casentino, brawled constantly with Florence for possession of this lucrative valley. After Florence's victory over Arezzo at Campaldino (see p.394), the traditionally Ghibelline Guidi counts recognised the authority of the Guelph city, and were in return allowed to maintain their power base here, though within a century or so the Florentines had ousted them completely. The seclusion of the higher ground fostered a strong **monastic** tradition as well, and the communities at **Camáldoli** and at **La Verna** continue to be important centres for their respective orders.

By **public transport**, the best target for a day trip from Arezzo is **Poppi**, which is connected to the city by bus and by the private *LFI* **train** line which shares the state *FS* station in Arezzo. To strike into the hills, to the monasteries of La Verna and Camáldoli, really requires a car; buses do run through Bibbiena to La Verna and through Poppi to Camáldoli, but they are too infrequent to make a round trip feasible.

Bibbiena

The chief commercial town of the Casentino is **BIBBIENA**, a place swathed with straggling development, much of it connected with tobacco production. In the fairly attractive innermost quarter, the main sight is the church of **San Lorenzo**, a fifteenth-century building that contains a fair quantity of terracotta from the Della Robbia workshops. Up the top end of town, close to Piazza Tarlati – its name a sign of its links with Arezzo (see p.381) – the oddly shaped church of **SS. Ippolito e Donato** has a fine altarpiece by Bicci di Lorenzo. Once you've seen these, there's no reason to hang around.

La Verna

In 1213 a pious member of the Guidi clan, Count Orlando, donated to **Saint Francis** a plot of land at **LA VERNA**, 23km east of Bibbiena. It was at this hermitage, on September 14, 1224, that Francis received the **stigmata** from a vision of the crucified Christ, a badge of sanctity never previously bestowed.

Francis's mountaintop sanctuary grew into a monastic village, whose ten chapels are connected by a network of corridors, cloisters, dormitories and stone pathways. Thousands of pilgrims come here annually, some of them staying in the guesthouse adjoining the monks' quarters, most coming to pay an hour's homage at the site of the miracle. A few visitors make the climb to see the magnificent ceramics by **Andrea della Robbia**, but unlike at the basilica at Assisi, the secular sightseers don't obscure the purpose of the place. The sanctuary is open every day from 6am to 8.30pm, though in winter the road can be heavy going.

Relics of the saint – his walking stick, belt, drinking glass – are displayed in the fifteenth-century **Basilica**, where there's a glorious *Ascension* by Della Robbia, whose other masterpieces are the focal points of the **Chiesa delle Stimmate** and the **Cappella di Santa Maria degli Angeli**. Halfway along the corridor leading to the Stimmate (stigmata) chapel – a walkway painted with modern scenes of the story of Francis – a small door opens into a gash in the crag, where Francis used to sleep. (According to Franciscan orthodoxy, the rocks at La Verna were split apart at the moment of Christ's death.) The route also passes the marginally more comfortable cell in which Saint Anthony of Padua stayed in 1230. The **Sasso Spicco**, reached by a flight of steps near the corridor, was Francis's place of meditation.

A path through the forest above the sanctuary leads to the summit of **La Penna** (1283m), from where there's a panorama of the Casentino meadows in one direction and the savage serrations of the Apennines in the other. The drive from La Verna to Sansepolcro is a fabulous descent into the upper Tiber valley; but the valley itself is a mess of light industry and quarries.

Poppi

POPPI, 6km to the north of Bibbiena and plainly visible from there, is sited high above the bus and train terminals. If you emerge at these, in the modern lower suburb of Ponte a Poppi, follow Via Dante Alighieri, a cobbled short cut which leads to the upper town in ten minutes' walk.

The old town is not much more than a couple of squares and an arcaded main street, Via Cavour, but it is lent a monumental aspect by the Casentino's chief landmark, the **Castello dei Conti Guidi** (daily 9.30am–12.30pm & 3.30–7.30pm; L5000). Built for the Guidi lords in the thirteenth century, its design is based closely on Florence's Palazzo Vecchio and it's likely that Arnolfo di Cambio was the architect here as well. The courtyard, with its wooden landings and beautiful staircases, is the most attractive bit of architecture in the Casentino; much of the interior is occupied by a massive library but the parts that are open to the public contain a superb array of arms and some well-preserved medieval frescoes.

At its lower end, Via Cavour climaxes at the magnificent twelfth-century **Badìa di San Fedele**; its very dark interior – locked most of the time – contains a beguiling thirteenth-century painting of the *Madonna and Child*.

Opposite the *castello* is the town's one **hotel**, the small two-star *Pension Casentino* (☎0575/529.090; ④), with a bar, but no restaurant. Finally, just outside Ponte a Poppi is the **Primo Parco Zoo** (daily summer 8am–8pm; winter 8am–5pm; L6000 adults, L4500 children), the first zoo devoted entirely to European species.

Camáldoli

Just over 15km northeast of Poppi is **CAMÁLDOLI**, where in 1012 Saint Romauldo (aka Rumbold) founded an especially ascetic order of the Benedictines. Notwithstanding the severity of the order, this sylvan retreat became a favourite with non-monastic penitents, so much so that a second site was opened up to accommodate visitors and to administer the woodlands that Romauldo had been granted. This lower complex has been much rebuilt and the only point of interest is its sixteenth-century pharmacy, which now sells herbal products.

On summer weekends lots of people come out here for a postprandial shop followed by a stroll through the forest up to the **Eremo**, the more fundamentalist wing of the monastery – which is around one thousand feet higher up the mountain. These days both men and women can visit, but no one is allowed near the actual living quarters.

If you really want to get into the thick of the Camaldolese forest, head for the summer resort of Badia Prataglia, 10km east, where there are some fine walks.

North of Poppi

A short distance north of Poppi, where the road splits, is the site of the crucial **Battle of Campaldino**, where in 1289 the Florentine Guelphs defeated the Arezzo Ghibellines to establish Florence's pre-eminence in the power struggles of Tuscany. Nearly two thousand men died in the battle – one who survived the carnage was Dante, then twenty-four years old. A column right on the junction marks the battle site.

The right-hand fork follows the rail line to **PRATOVECCHIO**, on the northern rim of Casentino. The birthplace of Paolo Uccello, it retains some old arcaded streets, but the major attractions are outside the town, up a narrow little road to the southwest. **Pieve di Romena**, though patched up a few times since its foundation in the twelfth century, is a wonderfully preserved Romanesque church, with splendid capitals and a beehive-shaped sacristy. An inscription on the first column to the right identifies the sculptor as the parish priest, Albericus; on the second pillar on the left another line states that the work was completed during a famine in 1152. Close by are the still intimidating ruins of the **Castello di Romena**, built by the Guidi counts and once the mightiest castle in the Casentino. Dante was a guest here and in the *Inferno* he mentions one of its former tenants, Adamo da Brescia, whose counterfeit coins wreaked such havoc with the local economy that the enraged Florentines roasted him alive.

The *LFI* rail line finishes two kilometres on at the wool-producing town of **STIA**, the nearest town to the source of the Arno, which rises to the north on Monte Falterona. Winters can be arduous here, and the steep roofs give Stia an alpine feel. The porticoed Piazza Tanucci is the heart of the medieval town, where the Romanesque interior of **Santa Maria della Assunta** features a *Madonna* by Andrea della Robbia and a triptych by Lorenzo di Bicci. Stia has a couple of reasonably low-price **hotels**: the *Falterona*, Piazza Tanucci 7 (☎0575/58.797; ③), and *La Buca*, Via Fiorentina 2 (☎0575/58.797; ③). There's also a good **restaurant** on the piazza, the *Filetto* (closed Sat, June & Oct), costing no more than L25,000 per head.

At Stia the road divides: to the west of Monte Falterona one branch passes another Guidi fortress and the frescoed church of Santa Maria delle Grazie on its way to the Sieve valley (see p.165); the other, to the east, crosses the Passo la Calla then drops down into Emilia-Romagna.

South of Arezzo: the Valdichiana

Travelling south from Arezzo you enter the **Valdichiana**, prosperous cattle country that produces the much-prized Florentine *bistecca*. As with the Maremma, this former swampland was first drained by the Etruscans, whose good work was allowed to unravel in medieval times, when the encroaching marshes drove the farmers of the region back up to the hill towns. Only in the last century, with the reclamation schemes of the Lorraine dukes of Tuscany, did the Valdichiana become fertile again. It's an underwhelming landscape but its flatness does at least mean that the towns on its flanks – of which **Cortona** is the most inspiring – have very long sight-lines.

In contrast to the Casentino, public transport is very good. Frequent Rome-bound **trains** from Florence and Arezzo run down the valley, most of them stopping at Camucia or Teróntola (often both), access points for Cortona. **Buses** from Arezzo serve the intervening villages, and other bus services from Cortona cover the routes across the valley.

Castiglion Fiorentino and Montecchio Vesponi

Looming high above the road 17km south of Arezzo are the walls and massive tower of **CASTIGLION FIORENTINO** – known as Castiglion Aretino until Arezzo became a Florentine holding in 1384. The fortified old town is so far above the train station that it makes more sense to visit by bus; the half-hourly bus from Arezzo to Cortona bowls through here thirty minutes into its one-hour journey, stopping right outside the walls in Piazza Matteotti.

From here the Corso Italia rises to the navel of the *centro storico*, the elegant Piazza del Municipio. There's a tiny **tourist office** in the corner of the square, and a modest **Pinacoteca** in its Palazzo Comunale (Tues–Sun 10am–1pm & 2–5pm; L2000), starring a Signorelli *Virgin with St Anne*. Opposite the palazzo is Castiglion's distinguishing feature, a **loggia** – supposedly by Vasari – which forms a picture-frame for the hills to the east. Look down to the right through the loggia and you'll see the rooftops of the two churches worth a call – the **Collegiata**, for a *Holy Family* by Lorenzo di Credi, and the adjoining **Pieve**, for Signorelli's fresco of the *Deposition*.

Four kilometres south from here, the eleventh-century castle of **Montecchio Vesponi** jabs up from the horizon. Commanding a great sweep of valley, this was the base of the *condottiere* Sir John Hawkwood – he of the fresco in Florence's Duomo. It is now a private residence, open for guided tours on Mondays, on the hour from 9am to noon; you'll need your own transport to get to it.

Cortona

From the valley floor a five-kilometre road winds up through terraces of vines and olives to the hill town of **CORTONA**, whose heights survey a vast domain: the Valdichiana stretching westward, with Lago Trasimeno visible over the low hills to the south. A scattering of Etruscan tombs aside, it is the medieval period that dominates the steep streets of Cortona – limitations of space have confined almost all later development to the lower suburb of Camucia, which is where the approach road begins. Even without its art treasures, this would be a good place to rest up, with pleasant hotels, excellent restaurants, and an amazing view at night, with the villages of southern Tuscany glistening like ships' lights on dark sea.

According to folklore, Cortona was founded by Dardanus, later to establish the city of Troy and to give his name to the Dardanelles. Whatever its precise origins, there was already a sizeable Umbrian settlement here when the **Etruscans** took over in the eighth century BC. About four hundred years later it passed to the Romans and remained a significant Roman centre until its destruction by the Goths. By the eleventh century it had become a free *comune*, constantly at logger-heads with Perugia and Arezzo; in 1258 the Aretines destroyed Cortona, but the town soon revived under the patronage of Siena. It changed hands yet again at the start of the fifteenth century, when it was appropriated by the Kingdom of Naples and then sold off to the Florentines, who never let go.

Cortona is easily visited as a day trip from Arezzo. There are hourly *LFI* **buses** between the two towns, and stopping **trains** from Arezzo call at Camucia-Cortona station (6km), from where a shuttle runs up to the centre of the old town. The fast Florence–Rome trains stop at Teróntola, 10km south, which is also served by a shuttle; Teróntola is the station to get off at if you are approaching from Umbria.

The Town

The bus terminus is in **Piazza Garibaldi**, from where the only level street in town, **Via Nazionale**, leads into Piazza della Repubblica, the first of three interconnected squares. This one is the most sociable – the town's best restaurants are all within seconds of the piazza, and the tall staircase of the squat, castellated **Palazzo del Comune** is the grandstand from which the *ragazzi* appraise the world as it goes by.

THE MUSEO DELL'ACCADEMIA ETRUSCA

One flank of the Palazzo del Comune forms a side of **Piazza Signorelli**, named after the artist Luca Signorelli, Cortona's most famous son – as is the decorously peeling nineteenth-century theatre. Opposite the theatre the crudely powerful Palazzo Casali, its facade like a rockface with windows, houses the **Museo dell'Accademia Etrusca** (summer Tues–Sun 10am–1pm & 4–7pm; winter same days 9am–1pm & 3–5pm; L5000). Notwithstanding the name, just three rooms are given over to the Etruscans, though one is an enormous hall with unengrossing paintings round the walls and Etruscan stuff in smart new cabinets in the middle. The major exhibit – honoured with its own bijou temple – is an Etruscan bronze lamp from the fifth century BC, its circumference decorated with alternating male and female squatting figures.

Elsewhere there are ranks of Etruscan figurines and masses of domestic odds and ends which evidently don't even interest the curators, as they can't be bothered labelling anything. The painter **Gino Severini**, another native of Cortona, gets a room to himself at the end. An acolyte of the Futurist firebrand Filippo Marinetti, Severini seems to have lacked any convictions of his own, being content to jog along through semi-Cubist prints, conventional portraits and sub-Schwitters collages.

THE MUSEO DIOCESANO

Piazza Signorelli links with Piazza del Duomo, where you might not realise that the cathedral is in front of you, as all you see on entering the square is the well-scrubbed arcade along its flank. Built in the sixteenth century, the **Duomo** is now in such a state that its facade has been buttressed with brick; the interior is fresh but rather vacant.

The couple of churches that used to face the duomo have been knocked together to house the **Museo Diocesano** (Tues–Sun summer 9am–1pm & 3–6.30pm; winter 9am–1pm & 3–5pm; L5000), a tiny collection of Renaissance art plus a fine Roman sarcophagus, carved with fighting centaurs. Inevitably Luca Signorelli features strongly, his anatomical drawing and perspective slightly out of kilter in a way that's endearing or irritating according to taste. Sassetta and Pietro Lorenzetti are also on show, but neither bears up to **Fra' Angelico**, represented by a *Madonna, Child and Saints* and an exquisite *Annunciation*. Painted during Fra' Angelico's ten years at Cortona's monastery of San Domenico, the latter has a courtly Adam and Eve being expelled from Eden in the background, the bruised sky contrasting with the dazzle of the angel's wings.

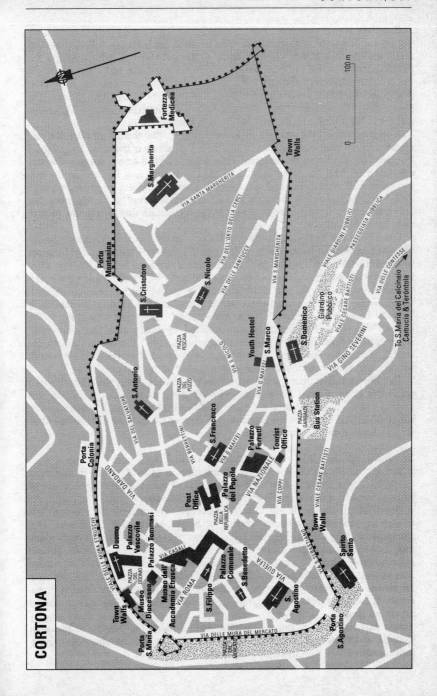

CORTONA

Fortezza Medicea

Town Walls

100 m

S.Margherita

VIA SANTA MARGHERITA

Porta Montanina

S.Cristoforo

S.Nicolo

VIA DELL'ORTO DELLA CRETI

VIA DELLE SANTUCCE

VIA S.MARGHERITA

Giardino Pubblico

VIALE GIARDINI PUBBLICI

PASSEGGIATA PUBBLICA

VIA DELLE COMTESSE

To S.Maria del Calcinaio
Camucia & Terontola

VIALE CESARE BATTISTI

S.Domenico

PIAZZA PESCAIA

Youth Hostel

S.Marco

VIA G.MAFFEI

VIA GINO SEVERINI

S.Antonio

VIA DEL SALVATORE

PIAZZA DEL POZZO

VIA S.NICOLO

PIAZZA GARIBALDI

Bus Station

Porta Colonia

VIA DARDANO

VIA BERRETTINI

S.Francesco

VIA G.MAFFEI

Palazzo Ferretti

Tourist Office

VIA NAZIONALE

Post Office

Palazzo del Popolo

PIAZZA DELLA REPUBBLICA

VIA COPPI

VIALE CESARE BATTISTI

Town Walls

VIA SEBASTIANI

Dioromo

Palazzo Vescovile

Palazzo Tommasi

VIA CASALI

Spirito Santo

Town Walls

Museo Diocesano

Museo dell' Accademia Etrusca

VIA ROMA

S.Filippo

Palazzo Comunale

S.Benedetto

VIA GUELFA

S. Agostino

Porta S.Agostino

Porta S.Maria

VIALE DELLE MURA ETRUSCHE

PIAZZA DEL DUOMO

VIA DELLE MURA DEL MERCATO

PIAZZA DELLE MURA DEL MERCATO

THE UPPER TOWN

To get the full taste of Cortona take Via Santucci from Piazza della Repubblica and then clamber along Via Berrettini, at the near end of which stands the Gothic-Baroque hybrid of **San Francesco**. Crusty outside and dusty within, it has a Byzantine ivory reliquary for a piece of the True Cross on the high altar. Above the third altar on the left hangs an *Annunciation* by the man the street is named after, Pietro Berrettini, otherwise known as Pietro da Cortona. This is his last work, left unfinished; the best of him is in Rome.

A further work by Signorelli is to be found in the church of **San Nicolò**, reached by veering right across Piazza della Pescaia then going up the stepped Via San Nicolò. It's an unassuming little church with a gravel forecourt like a country hotel, and has to be opened by the caretaker – ring the bell on the left-hand side wall. Signorelli's high altarpiece is a standard which he painted on both sides: a characteristically awkward *Entombment* on the front and a *Madonna and Saints* on the back – revealed by a neat hydraulic system that swivels the picture away from the wall.

From Piazza della Pescaia, a steep path leads to the mock-Romanesque **Santa Margherita**. Rebuilt in the nineteenth century, it contains the tomb of **Margaret of Cortona**, the town's patron saint. The daughter of a local farmer, she spent her long years of widowhood helping the poor and sick of Cortona, founding a hospital that stood close to the site of this church. So intense was her relationship with the Almighty that the townspeople would pack into the Franciscan church at Mass to observe her delirious behaviour – "she became ashen pale, her pulse ceased, she froze, her throat was so affected by hoarseness that she could scarcely be understood when she returned to her senses". Her tomb, with marble angels lifting the lid of her sarcophagus, was created in the mid-fourteenth century, and is now mounted on the wall to the left of the chancel.

The **Fortezza Medicea**, at the summit of the town, is often shut, but the area around is good ground for a picnic, looking down over ruined Etruscan and Roman walls towards Trasimeno. You could descend to Piazza Garibaldi by the stepped Via Crucis, where the Stations of the Cross are marked with booths sheltering unsubtle mosaics by Severini.

SAN DOMENICO AND SANTA MARIA DEL CALCINAIO

A last church to check out is **San Domenico**, a minute's walk from Piazza Garibaldi, where the high altar's *Coronation of the Virgin* polyptych by Lorenzo di Niccolò Gerini is proudly spotlit even during daylight hours.

Below the piazza, the middle distance is occupied by the perfectly proportioned though crumbling Renaissance church of **Santa Maria del Calcinaio**. The masterpiece of Giorgio di Martini, it was begun in 1484 to enshrine a miraculous image of the Virgin that a lime burner had unearthed here. Another Tuscan church of this vintage – Santa Maria delle Carceri in Prato – was built for similar reasons, but the the number of pilgrims who flocked to Cortona made it impossible for the architect to employ the fashionable central-plan design used in Prato. Hence this highly refined compromise – classical detailing on a Gothic-sized cruciform church.

Just past the church, signs direct you further down the hill to the Etruscan **Tanella di Pitagora** – a well-preserved fourth-century BC chamber tomb, fancifully identified with the Greek mathematician.

Practicalities

The **tourist office** at Via Nazionale 70–72 (Mon–Fri 8am–1pm & 3–6pm, Sat 8am–1pm; ☎0575/630.557) can provide leaflets and help out with accommodation. There are half a dozen **hotels** in the town proper, only two of which could be described as budget options: the one-star *Athens*, Via S. Antonio 12 (☎0575/630.508; ③), and comfortable two-star *Italia*, Via Ghibellina 5 (☎0575/630.254; ④). After that, only the tiny three-star *Sabrina*, Via Roma 37 (☎0575/630.397; ⑤), offers any chance of a modestly priced double room; the others are in the most expensive range. There are a few one- and two-stars down at Camucia and Teróntola, but there really is no point coming to Cortona and then spending the night down in the valley. However, Cortona does have an IYHF **youth hostel**, the *Ostello San Marco*, situated in the heart of the town at Via Maffei 57 (☎0575/601.392; open March 1–Oct 15; ①); it's a clean and spacious hostel in an old monastery, with fantastic views from the dormitories, and friendly management.

For **meals**, Cortona is a town where you can treat your stomach without ruining your finances. Best of the restaurants is probably *La Loggetta* (closed Mon), which occupies the best site in town, overlooking Piazza della Repubblica at Piazza Pescheria 3; a memorable evening will cost around L45,000. The *Trattoria Grotta di San Francesco* (closed Tues), just off the piazza at Piazzetta Baldelli 3, is less self-conscious, almost as good, and about L15,000 cheaper. The *Tonino* in Piazza Garibaldi (closed Tues) specialises in *antipasti*: a large selection of *antipasti* and a pasta dish costs L40,000, or the tourist menu is L20,000, both accompanied by a panoramic view from the terrace. Another great view is from the popular and reasonably priced pizzeria *La Casina dei Tigli*, in the public gardens below Piazza Garibaldi.

For summer evenings, a favourite night-time hang-out is the piano bar of the *Teatro Signorelli*, with live **music** from Friday to Sunday. For other entertainment the public gardens below Piazza Garibaldi have an open-air **cinema**; the only summer **disco** is *Tuchulcha*, in Piazza Garibaldi (Fri, Sat & Sun).

Lastly, a Saturday **market** is held in the Piazza della Repubblica, and on Mondays a huge agricultural fair and general market takes place in Camucia.

Monte San Savino and around

On the opposite side of the Valdichiana from Cortona stands **MONTE SAN SAVINO**, now a market town, once a contentious border post between the territories of Florence, Siena and Arezzo – it was completely razed in 1325 on the orders of Bishop Tarlati of Arezzo. The town retains a slightly decrepit mix of medieval and Renaissance monuments, but it is not one of Tuscany's more seductive hill towns. Should you be determined to explore every facet of Tuscan life, however, there are regular trains from Arezzo to the station in the lower town, from where there's the usual bus shuttle; buses from Cortona also periodically cross the valley.

The town was the birthplace of **Andrea Sansovino**, now best remembered as the mentor of Jacopo Sansovino, a crucial figure in Venice's artistic history. Terracotta was one of his preferred media – the town remains a major producer of majolica – and some of Andrea's best ceramic work is in the church of **Santa Chiara**, which stands in the northern Piazza Gamurrini, the square nearest the place where the buses stop. The altarpiece of *SS. Lawrence, Roch and Sebastian* was his first major work, while the tabernacle to the left of the high altar was a collaboration with Andrea della Robbia.

Virtually next door to the church stands the fourteenth-century Sienese castle known as the **Cassero**, which houses a small tourist office and stages the odd art exhibition. Also on the square is a monument to Monte San Savino's one-time governor, Mattias de' Medici; it allegedly cost so much that Mattias forbade any more such ruinous projects.

Continuing down the narrow main street from Piazza Gamurrini you'll pass the **Loggia dei Mercanti**, a collaboration between Sansovino and Antonio da Sangallo the Elder – architect of the Palazzo Comunale, across the way. Beyond the Palazzo Pretorio lies the small central square, Piazza di Monte, on both of whose churches Sansovino left his mark. He designed the now disintegrating portal of **San Giovanni**, and added the cloister to the fourteenth-century Sant'Agostino. Inside are some fifteenth-century frescoes and a typically unrestrained altarpiece from Vasari, who evidently ferreted his way into every cranny of the region.

Lucignano

Eight kilometres south of Monte San Savino and served by six buses a day is the trim little town of **LUCIGNANO**. It is laid out as a concentric pattern of four ellipses, though the density of the centre and its gradients make it difficult to discern the arrangement on the ground. Nucleus of the pattern is the **Collegiata**, an unexceptional church given a touch of panache by the circular staircase leading to its door – like a terrace for a diminutive amphitheatre.

Round the back, the **Museo Comunale** (summer Tues–Sun 9.30am–1pm & 3–7.30pm; winter 9.30am–1pm & 3–6.30pm; L5000) contains the most arresting artefact on this side of the Valdichiana, an amazing fourteenth-century reliquary made in Arezzo. Thirteenth- and fourteenth-century frescoes, some of them by Bartolo di Fredi, decorate the adjacent striped church of **San Francesco**. And that's about it, apart from the inevitable Medici fortress on the hill to the north, with its smart new dovecot.

Accommodation is at *Da Totò*, right by the Collegiata at Piazza del Tribunale 6 (☎0575/836.988; ④); the hotel **restaurant** is good value, at around L25,000 per head (closed Tues). For a quick bite, there's the *Tavernetta* pizzeria-restaurant at Via Roma 15 – signposted, but you'll pass it anyway.

Farneta

If you're driving back to Cortona, the quickest route takes you past the ancient Benedictine **Abbazia di Farneta**, which stands close to the Val di Chiana exit from the autostrada. Built largely with stone plundered from a nearby Roman temple to Bacchus, this beautiful building has been restored virtually single-handedly by the local priest, who since the late 1930s has stripped the abbey of its eighteenth-century accretions. He has also excavated the remarkable **crypt**, dating from the ninth and tenth centuries – an operation that yielded numerous archeological discoveries. A few minor finds are on show in the priest's house, but repeated attempted robberies have made it necessary to transfer the more precious pieces – such as an eighth-century Lombard carving of the Crucifixion – to the museum in Cortona.

travel details

Trains

From Arezzo to Florence (hourly; 1hr); Rome (hourly; 1hr 40min), most calling at Camucia-Cortona (20min) and Teróntola (25min); Chiusi (hourly; 1hr), 7 calling at Orvieto (1hr 20min); Assisi (2 daily; 1hr 35min); Monte San Savino (12 daily; 25min); Perugia/Foligno (every 2hr; 1hr 15min/1hr 50min); Terni (1 daily; 2hr 35min); Verona/Trento/Bolzano (5 daily; 5hr 15min/7hr/7hr 30min); Venice/Udine (5 daily; 5hr 10min/7hr). Plus *LFI* services to Bibbiena & Poppi (hourly; 50 & 57min).

Buses

From Arezzo to Sansepolcro (17 daily; 1hr), some via Monterchi, most via Anghiari – and most continuing to Città di Castello (1hr 30min); Bibbiena & La Verna (1 daily – change at Bibbiena for Poppi & Camáldoli); Cortona (hourly; 1hr); Siena (5 daily Mon–Fri).

From Cortona to Arezzo (hourly; 50min); Castiglion del Lago (7 daily; 1hr); Chianciano, changing for Montepulciano (4 daily; 1hr).

PART THREE

UMBRIA

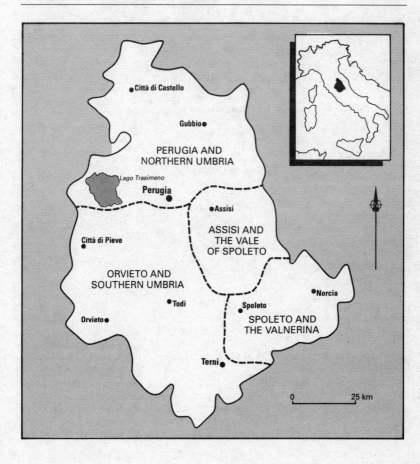

Città di Castello

Gubbio

PERUGIA AND NORTHERN UMBRIA

Lago Trasimeno

Perugia

Assisi

ASSISI AND THE VALE OF SPOLETO

Città di Pieve

ORVIETO AND SOUTHERN UMBRIA

Norcia

Todi

Spoleto

SPOLETO AND THE VALNERINA

Orvieto

Terni

0   25 km

CHAPTER NINE

PERUGIA AND NORTHERN UMBRIA

Perugia, most people's first taste of Umbria, is a distinctly uncharacteristic introduction to the region. The home of Buitoni pasta and Perugino chocolate, it is a thriving, industrial city, living on a wholly different plane from its bucolic, hill-town neighbours, with its summer **jazz festival**, universities and spread of cultural events. If you've come to Umbria for the rural experience, you may be tempted to pass straight through. However, its medieval core, hidden within the ring roads, demands at least a day's exploration: the city's town hall, the **Palazzo dei Priori**, is justifiably hyped as one of the greatest public palaces in Italy, and the **Galleria Nazionale** boasts the best collection of Umbrian art, to name just the two highlights. If actually staying in Perugia doesn't appeal, its sights can easily enough be taken in on day trips from Assisi or Spoleto.

West of Perugia is the placid **Lago Trasimeno**, not that spectacular scenically but a magnet for campers and a chance to put your feet up on a beach. The best town, if you want to save a long trawl round its shores, is **Castiglione del Lago**, with the more brash **Passignano** the main camping and after-hours resort.

Head north from Perugia and you'll find a rather bleak region centred on the upper reaches of the **Tiber valley**. Routes follow the river's lacklustre course, useful mainly for onward forays into Tuscany and the Marche – in particular to Sansepolcro or Urbino for the paintings of Piero della Francesca. **Città di Castello** is the only worthwhile Umbrian port of call, a plain-bound town whose extensive art gallery rates second to that of Perugia.

East of the Tiber, potholed minor roads climb through swathes of barren country to **Gubbio**, one of Italy's medieval gems, and pushed by the hype as the Umbrian Siena. Plenty in the town merits the claim, not least its overbearing civic palace, the **Palazzo dei Consoli**, in the same league as Perugia's Palazzo dei Priori; its annual festive blowout, the **Corsa dei Ceri**; and a honeycomb of old streets riddled with enough interest fully to warrant a day trip. Moving east, you come up against the first of the Apennines, their slopes home to a couple of half-forgotten hill towns, **Gualdo Tadino** and **Nocera Umbra**. The mountains behind, Monte Cucco in particular, are the places to enjoy some of the region's best **walking**, with the well-equipped village of **Costacciaro** the obvious base.

Getting around

Perugia is the transport hub for the region, with trains to most of the major Umbrian towns, complemented by fast new roads and an extensive if complicated bus network. Coming from Tuscany, there are regular trains from Teróntola on the main Florence to Rome line, and a dual-carriageway spur from the *Autostrada del Sole*. If you've wound up in Sansepolcro, you could also ride the private *FCU* railway through Città di Castello.

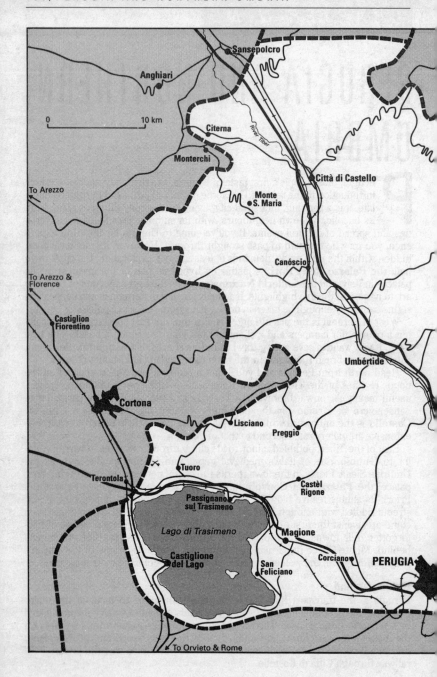

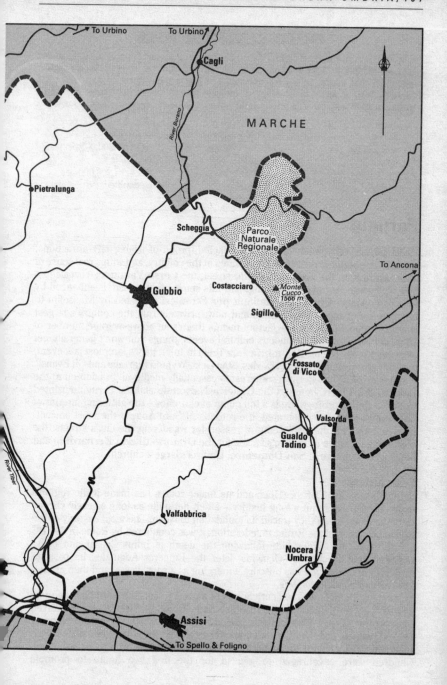

To Urbino

To Urbino

Cagli

River Burano

MARCHE

Pietralunga

To Ancona

Scheggia

Parco
Naturale
Regionale

Gubbio

Costacciaro

Monte
Cucco
1566 m

Sigillo

**Fossato
di Vico**

Valsorda

River Tiber

**Gualdo
Tadino**

Valfabbrica

**Nocera
Umbra**

Assisi

To Spello & Foligno

ACCOMMODATION PRICES

Throughout this guide, accommodation is graded on a scale from ① to ⑨. Grades ① and ② apply to **hostel** accommodation, and indicate the lowest price a **single person** could expect to pay for one night in that establishment in high season. Grades ③ to ⑨ apply to **hotels**, and indicate the cost of the **cheapest double room in high season.** The price bands to which these codes refer are as follows:

① under L20,000 per person

② over L20,000 per person

③ under L50,000 per double

④ L50–70,000 per double

⑤ L70–90,000 per double

⑥ L90–120,000 per double

⑦ L120–150,000 per double

⑧ L150–200,000 per double

⑨ over L200,000 per double

Perugia

PERUGIA is very much the regional capital, proud of its big city attractions, home to one of the largest state universities in the country, and with a real sense of style. A drink on the great *passeggiata* street, the **Corso Vannucci**, reveals just how well some Perugians are doing, and this sense of dynamism is enhanced by the cosmopolitan **Università Italiana per Stranieri** – created by Mussolini to improve the image of Italy abroad and now, privately run, the country's largest language school. All of these factors means there's an above-average number of films, concerts and miscellaneous cultural events, things you won't generally get elsewhere in the region. At **Umbria Jazz** (held in July), Italy's foremost jazz event, past stars have included Miles Davies, Stan Getz, Wynton Marsalis and Gil Evans.

In terms of sights, Perugia's interest is essentially medieval. In addition to the **Palazzo dei Priori**, home to the **Galleria Nazionale** and the Perugino-painted **Collegio del Cambio**, there is a full quota of churches – the glittering interior of **San Pietro** the most celebrated, the rotonda of **Sant'Angelo** the most ancient. Idiosyncratic one-offs give plenty of reason for wandering the city's streets, the best being Agostino di Duccio's facade for the **Oratorio di San Bernardino** and the Gothic sculpture of **San Domenico**, Umbria's largest church.

Some history

Perugia's command of the Tiber and its major routes has made it the region's main player throughout a long history – albeit not quite as long as early chroniclers made out when they traced its foundation to Noah. The most easterly of the twelve key cities of the Etruscan federation, it was conquered by Rome in 309 BC before taking the wrong side following the death of Julius Caesar and being besieged and wrecked by Octavius, later the Emperor Augustus. Its passage through the Dark Ages was obscure, emerging as a papal vassal and then around 1140 an independent *comune*.

Medieval Perugia was evidently a hell of a place to be: "the town had the most warlike people of Italy," wrote the historian Sismondi, "who always preferred Mars to the Muse." Male citizens played a game in which two teams, wearing beaked helmets and thickly padded in clothes stuffed with deer hair, stoned each other mercilessly until the majority of the other side were dead or wounded. Children were encouraged to join in for the first two hours to promote "application and aggression". In 1265 Perugia was also the birthplace of the **Flagellants**, who within ten years had half of Europe whipping itself into a frenzy, before the movement was declared heretical. In addition to some hearty scourging, they took to the streets on moonlit nights, wailing, singing dirges and clattering human bones together – all as expiation for the wrongs of the world.

Using its economic muscle, and numerous short-lived alliances, the city built up a huge power base, the zenith of its influence coming with the conquest of Siena in 1358. Around this time the *Priori* (members of the ten leading guilds), noble families and papal agents began vying for control, plunging Perugia into a period when, according to one chronicler, "perfect pandemonium reigned in and about the city". Individual *condottieri* rose briefly from the chaos, the key figures being Biondo Michelotti – stabbed to death in 1398, after five years in power – and the oddly named Braccio Fortebraccio (Arm the Strong Arm), whose eight years of rule brought short-lived stability. The Oddi nobility ran the town until 1488, when the demented but colourful **Baglioni** took over.

The story of the Baglioni is the stuff of great soap opera – madly complicated vendettas, mass slayings, lions kept as pets, incestuous marriages, hearts torn out of bodies and then eaten, and any number of people murdered on their wedding nights. After one episode which required one hundred murders, the bloodied cathedral had to be washed down with wine and reconsecrated. One Baglioni, Malatesta IV, assigned the defence of Florence in 1530, simply sold his services to the enemy, earning the title of the "world's greatest traitor".

When the last Baglioni, the wimpish Ridolpho, bungled an assassination of the papal legate, it was a cue for the papacy to step in. Pope Paul III, one of the more powerful and peculiar pontiffs, razed the Baglioni palaces in 1538, then entered the city demanding that all its nuns line up and kiss his feet. The walkabout, he said, left him "very greatly edified". Thus refreshed, he built the Rocca Paolina, a huge fortress that guaranteed church supremacy for three centuries. During the nineteenth-century Unification the city's liberation from the papacy was particularly bloodthirsty, with numerous citizens massacred by a detachment of Swiss Guards sent to bolster church control.

Arrival, information and accommodation

The centre of medieval Perugia revolves around the pedestrian thoroughfare of **Corso Vannucci**, capped at its northern end by the **Piazza IV Novembre**, and at its southern extreme by **Piazza Italia**. Once off the Corso, be prepared for **steep climbs** between Perugia's many levels. Hi-tech lifts and escalators help out only occasionally.

Points of arrival

Arriving on the state **train** network you'll find yourself well away from the centre at **Piazza V. Veneto**: from here it's a fifteen-minute ride on bus #26, #27, #29 or #32–36 to Piazza Italia. City bus tickets (valid for 40 or 70min) are available from a small booth in the forecourt or a machine by the entrance: forty-minute tickets cost L1000.

If you're coming on the private *FCU* lines from Todi or Terni to the south, or from Città di Castello or Sansepolcro to the north, you'll arrive at the much more central **Stazione Sant'Anna**, near the **bus terminal** at **Piazza dei Partigiani**. If you're arriving by **car**, the best bet is to follow the signs for Piazza dei Partigiani,

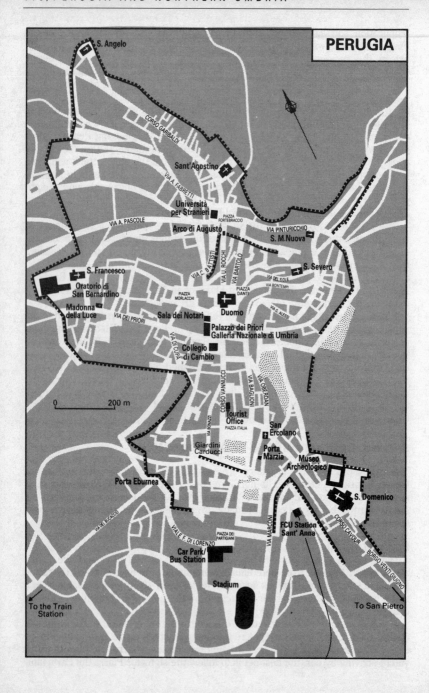

PERUGIA

S. Angelo

CORSO GARIBALDI

Sant'Agostino

VIA A. FABRETTI

Università
per Stranieri
PIAZZA
FORTEBRACCIO

VIA A. PASCOLE

Arco di Augusto

VIA PINTURICCHIO

S. M. Nuova

VIA C. BATTISTI
VIA U. ROCCHI
VIA BARTOLO

S. Severo

VIA DEL SOLE
VIA BONTEMPI

S. Francesco

Oratorio di
San Bernardino

PIAZZA
MORLACCHI

PIAZZA
DANTI

Madonna
della Luce

VIA DEI PRIORI

Duomo

VIA G. ALESSI

Sala dei Notari

Palazzo dei Priori
Galleria Nazionale di Umbria

VIA DI CUPA

Collegio
di Cambio

0   200 m

CORSO VANNUCCI
VIA BONAZZI
VIA BAGLIONI
VIA OBERDAN

Tourist
Office
PIAZZA ITALIA

San
Ercolano

Giardini
Carducci

Porta
Marzia

Museo
Archeologico

Porta Eburnea

VIA DEI BACCOLO

S. Domenico

VALE F. DI LORENZO

PIAZZA DEI
PARTIGIANI

VIA MARCONI

FCU Station
Sant' Anna

CORSO CAVOUR

BORGO VENTIGUGNO

Car Park/
Bus Station

Stadium

To the Train
Station

To San Pietro

where there's a large and convenient covered car park. From here you can jump on one of the signed *scala mobile* (escalators) through the weird subterranean Via Baglioni Sotteranea to Piazza Italia. If you're driving in from the north, however, you may well find the car park in **Via Sant'Antonio** more convenient.

Information

The **tourist office** at Piazza IV Novembre 3 (Mon–Sat 8.30am–1.30pm & 4–7pm, Sun 9am–1pm; ☎075/572.3327) is good for advice on city events and helpful in finding accommodation. The regional office is at Via Mazzini 21 (Mon–Fri 9am–1pm & 3–7pm; ☎075/572.5341), and there's a small summer-only office at the train station (daily 8.30am–1.30pm). At the station and in Piazza Italia you'll see some hi-tech *Digiplan* machines, primed to provide tourist information (in Italian) on computer print-out – great in theory and almost invariably broken.

Accommodation

Perugia has plenty of **accommodation** in all price ranges, though reservations are in order during the July jazz festival – when prices are also raised. Unlike most Tuscan cities, **prices** are otherwise pretty standard year-round, with no real "low season". Recommendations below are the most central.

HOTELS

Anna, Via dei Priori 48 (☎075/66.304). Inexpensive central one-star. ③.

Etruria, Via della Luna 21 (☎075/572.3730). Just off the Corso. ④.

Piccolo Hotel, Via Bonazzi 25 (☎075/572.2987). Functional place, but in an excellent position immediately off the Corso on its west side, four alleys south of Via dei Priori. ④.

Pensione Paola, Via della Canapina 5 (☎075/572.3816). Very popular one-star place, so be sure to call in advance. It's tricky to find: follow signs for the *Umbria* from the Corso (see below), go down the steps in the passageway, turn right and follow the second set of steps towards the car park. ④.

Aurora, Viale Indipendenza 21 (☎075/572.4819). On a busy street immediately south of Piazza Italia. Simple and clean, with very helpful staff. ⑤.

Rosalba, Via del Circo 7 (☎075/572.285). One-star hotel right on the edge of Piazza IV Novembre. ⑤.

Signa, Via del Grillo 9 (☎075/572.4180). Large two-star in small alley in the southeast of the city, 200m beyond the church of San Domenico. ⑤.

Umbria, Via Boncampi 37 (☎075/572.1203). Comfortable two-star. ⑤.

Palace Hotel Bellavista, Piazza Italia 12 (☎075/572.0741). Quiet three-star; the most reasonably priced of the hotels at the southern end of Corso Vannucci. ⑥.

YOUTH HOSTEL AND STUDENT ROOMS

Centro Internazionale Accoglienza per Giovani, Via Bontempi 13 (☎075/572.2880). Non-IYHF hostel just two minutes from the Duomo; there's a midnight curfew and the place is shut 9.30am–4pm; single-sex dorms at L12,000 per night. ①.

CTGS Student Centre, Via del Roscetto 21 (☎075/61.695). Arranges rooms for students in summer. More trouble than it's worth unless you're planning a long stay.

Corso Vannucci and Piazza IV Novembre

Medieval Perugia hinges around the **Corso Vannucci**, one of the country's greatest people-watching streets, packed from dawn through to the early hours with a parade of Umbria's style-makers and style-followers. Named after the city's most celebrated artist, Pietro Vannucci, better known simply as Perugino, the street has the most atmospheric café in the city – the *Pasticceria Sandri* at no. 32 – and one of the better places for coffee and lunchtime snacks – the *Café del Cambio* at no. 29.

The Corso strikes off from **Piazza Italia** towards the austere **Piazza IV Novembre**, site of a Roman reservoir before being filled to provide a focus to the medieval town. On opposite sides of it are the city's two traditional power centres: the **Palazzo dei Priori**, still the home of the council, and the **Duomo**. At the centre is perhaps the most graceful fountain in Italy, the **Fontana Maggiore**.

FONTANA MAGGIORE

The **Fontana Maggiore** has an excellent pedigree: designed in 1277 by Fra' Bevignate, the monk who had a hand in the shaping of Orvieto's cathedral, and sculpted by the father and son team Nicola and Giovanni **Pisano**, possibly with help from Arnolfo di Cambio. It was installed to receive the water from the town's new aqueduct, though as the chronicler Bonazzi observed, "beasts, barrels and unwashed pots and unclean hands were forbidden the use of the water, and indeed it was guarded with such jealous care that it seemed as though the people of Perugia had built their fountain for the sake of beauty only".

The sculptures and bas-reliefs on the two basins – now decidedly the worse for wear – show episodes from the Old Testament, classical myth, Aesop's fables and the months of the year. By some canny calculation none of them line up directly, encouraging you to walk around the fountain chasing a point of repose that never comes. The saints and nymphs on the upper basin are later additions.

The Palazzo dei Priori

The far end of the Corso is dominated by the gaunt mass of the **Palazzo dei Priori**, with its majestic Gothic doorway, rows of trefoil windows (from which convicted criminals were thrown to their deaths) and businesslike Guelph crenellations. Impressive through sheer bulk alone, it derives a certain beauty from the harmony set up by the buildings around it.

Orientation within the palazzo can be confusing, as several worthwhile sights are dotted around its rambling precincts, which were built over a 130-year period from the end of the thirteenth century.

THE SALA DEI NOTARI

The **Sala dei Notari** (daily 9am–1pm & 3–6pm; free), the lawyers' meeting hall, is entered by the fan-shaped steps opposite the Duomo. It's an obvious point of reference, its doorway topped by a bronze Guelph lion and Perugian griffon; once thought to be Roman, these were actually made in 1274 and are thus among the first pieces of large-scale casting in medieval Italy. According to tradition, the chains below were snatched from the gate and gallows of Siena during a raid in 1358.

The Sala is one of the oldest parts of the palazzo, dating from the late 1290s – about the same time as the civic palaces in Florence and Siena were being raised. Its celebrated frescoes, however, were substantially repainted in the last century, contriving little more than flashes of colour, fancy flags and swirls.

THE SALA DEL COLLEGIO DELLA MERCANZIA AND COLLEGIO DEL CAMBIO

Hidden behind an inconspicuous door further down the Corso side of the palazzo, the **Sala del Collegio della Mercanzia** (May–Oct Tues–Sat 9am–12.30pm & 3–

6pm, Sun 9am–12.30pm; Nov–April Tues–Sat 8am–2pm, Sun 9am–12.30pm; L2000) was the seat of the merchants' guild. At first glance it amounts to little, but at close quarters the single small room reveals its intricately inlaid wooden panelling, fifteenth-century work, considered some of Italy's finest.

You need a separate L4000 ticket to get into the **Collegio del Cambio** a few doors down (same hours). Once the town's money exchange, its walls are covered with frescoes by **Perugino** that are considered the artist's masterpieces. The commission was awarded by the bankers' guild in 1496, about the same time as Perugino was approached to fresco part of the duomo in Orvieto, an undertaking eventually executed by Luca Signorelli. The city's bankers were determined to have paintings commensurate with their own sense of self-importance. To this end they probably paid Perugino – then at the peak of his powers – more than was on offer in Orvieto, but also determined to tie the painter to the theme of their choice.

Francesco Maturanzio, a leading humanist theorist, was brought in as consultant, and it was he who proposed the fusion of classical and Christian culture, painting Christian icons alongside figures of classical myth. Though not an unusual Renaissance conceit, the vigour and uncompromising way in which the themes are yoked together make the paintings a distinctly curious juxtaposition. The thesis intended to suggest that human perfection, expressed by classical art, was obtainable through Christ's example, and that there was unity in variety.

Whatever the metaphysical intent, the frescoes certainly succeed aesthetically, unified by Perugino's melancholy tone, idealised and soft-focus figures and mellow landscapes. The paintings cover virtually all the walls and ceiling vaults of the single room, part of which – probably the prophets and sibyls on the right-hand wall (behind the ticket desk) – were painted by Perugino's pupil Raphael, then only about thirteen years old. Up on the door-side wall there's a famous but unremarkable self-portrait of the master, looking on with sour-faced disapproval, ironically the only element to disturb the frescoes' beautiful evenness of tone.

The ceiling vaults illustrate the main gods of the classical world: Apollo on his chariot at the centre; Saturn, Jupiter and Mars above the Corso wall; Mercury, Venus and Diana towards the window. Right of the window are portraits of famous Greeks and Romans, real and mythical, with the allegorical figures of Prudence and Justice joined by Cato (symbol of Wisdom), and with Socrates and Trajan, among others, below. The end wall, farthest from the entrance, introduces the Christian strand, with a *Nativity* and the *Transfiguration*, both blackened by smoke from the room's former oil lamps. The right-hand wall shows God amongst the angels, with sibyls above and men below: Isaac, Moses, Daniel (possibly a portrait of Raphael), David, Jeremiah and Solomon.

THE GALLERIA NAZIONALE

The **Galleria Nazionale di Umbria** (Tues–Sat 9am–2pm & 3–6.30pm, Sun 9am–1pm; L8000), on the fourth floor of the palace complex, is the region's main repository of Umbrian art. Its entrance is through the opulently carved doorway on the Corso; having pushed past harassed Perugians on their way to do battle with council bureaucracy, you might well find the small lift isn't working, in which case you have to clamber up the stairs that the local nobles once rode their horses up. At time of writing restoration work is still ongoing but, although the main gallery is closed, more rooms are gradually being opened. For the time being this makes a nonsense of the entrance fee; when the dust settles, however, the gallery should be returned to its status as one of central Italy's best – a 33-room romp through both the history of Umbrian painting and the schools which influenced it.

The entire chronology of the **Umbrian art** canon is traced, from its Byzantine-influenced roots, its parallel development with the Sienese in the thirteenth and fourteenth centuries, through to its late fifteenth-century golden age when Perugia became the main focus of its endeavour. After the works of Perugino and Pinturicchio, this era's principal artists, several rooms explore more mainstream Umbrians, largely Perugino imitators, or artists who worked in a late-Renaissance vein and fall outside the confines of the Umbrian school.

Some of the gallery's finest moments, however, have nothing to do with indigenous painters. This is particularly true of early rooms, where the **Sienese** largely hold sway. Amongst a welter of anonymous works, the first room's highlight is a small *Madonna and Angels* by **Duccio** (1308), its static beauty the obvious model for many of the Umbrian works that follow. Alongside is a large Crucifixion by the so-called **Maestro di San Francesco**, one of the gallery's earliest pieces, and painted by the anonymous hand believed to be responsible for some of the superlative frescoes in the nave of the Lower Church in Assisi's Basilica di San Francesco. Other named Sienese masters include Bartolomeo da Siena, Domenico di Bartolo and Taddeo di Bartolo, the last-named responsible here for three altarpieces, including a *Pentecost* which displays a radical compositional approach obviously at odds with the more conservative Umbrians to come.

Dozens of anonymous **early fifteenth-century Umbrian works** follow, amounting in many cases to no more than a surfeit of the religious iconography that fills Umbrian paintings without the redeeming dulcet qualities of the Sienese. The better of the Umbrians are Matteo da Gualdo and Nicolò Alunno, the latter represented by a *gonfalone*, or painted banner, later to be the special preserve of Perugian painters.

In acknowledging the increasing influence of Tuscan painters on Umbrians as the fifteenth century progressed, the gallery almost allows a pair of paintings by outsiders to steal the show. Given the luxury of a room to themselves are a huge triptych by **Fra' Angelico**, *Madonna and Child with Angels and Saints*, and a *Madonna and Child with Saints* by **Piero della Francesca**. Angelico's painting, radiant with his gorgeous swathes of blue, was painted in 1437 for Perugia's church of San Domenico. Piero's work, executed around 1460 at about the time of his Arezzo cycle, is full of eccentric compositional nuances, particularly in the small *Annunciation* hinged to the top of the main painting, in which a mannered succession of arches around the Virgin recedes into a blank wall.

Heralded by a bevy of Perugian contemporaries, **Perugino** marks the apotheosis of the Umbrian school. His immense output is encapsulated here by about a dozen works, though many are often out on loan or under restoration. The two finest pieces, painted around 1475, are a *Pietà* and *Adoration of the Magi*. The second-ranked Umbrian, and Perugino's occasional collaborator, **Pinturicchio**, is not so well covered, with little here to compare with the frescoes of Spello's Santa Maria Maggiore or the works in Siena's Piccolomini library. Subsequent rooms contain perfectly good works by followers of Perugino; the names to look out for particularly are Sinibaldo Ibi, Giannicola di Paolo and Eusebio di San Giorgio, all fluent interpreters of Perugino's merging of Umbrian and Florentine traditions.

Towards the end of the sequence of rooms is the palazzo's **chapel**; decorated by Bonfigli with episodes from the life of Saint Ercolano (Perugia's patron), it gives a detailed picture of aspects of fifteenth-century Perugia – walls, towers and monuments – that have now largely vanished. The rest of the gallery ploughs a remorseless course through sevententh- to nineteenth-century Umbrian offerings, most large gloomy canvases.

The Duomo

Piazza IV Novembre is backed by the plain-faced **Duomo**, only recently reopened after earthquake damage inflicted in 1983. There's been a church on this site for a thousand years, but the cornerstone for the present building was laid late in the Middle Ages, in 1345, and soon interrupted by the Black Death. Most of the building was completed late in the following century and even then the facade, which is in the lovely pink stone of most local towns, was left unfinished. Taking a pragmatic approach to the problem, the Perugians pinched the marble facing intended for Arezzo's cathedral, though a subsequent hammering from Arezzo brought about its shame-faced return.

The most interesting face of the cathedral is the one fronting the piazza. To the right of the portal is a bronze statue of Pope Julius III, and to the left an unfinished **pulpit** built for the roving Saint Bernardino of Siena, who was something of a hit with the Perugians. It was here that he preached the original Bonfire of the Vanities, urging women to burn their wigs and everyone else to give up books, fine clothes and general good times. To the left are remains of the Loggia Fortebraccio, taken from the house of the city's one-time ruler.

The Baroque **interior** is imposing enough, though short on artworks. Its great relic, as a change from pieces of the True Cross, is the Virgin's "wedding ring", housed in the Cappella del Sant'Anello (first chapel on the left). An unwieldy piece of agate, said to change colour according to the character of the person wearing it, it was stolen by the Perugians from Chiusi in 1473 and encased in a series of fifteen boxes, fitted like Russian dolls; it's brought out for public edification once a year on July 30. Embedded in the wall nearby are fragments of an altar by Agostino di Duccio (1473); next to them is a lovely painting by Berto di Giovanni showing 1520s Perugia in the background, with a small lunette above by Giannicola di Paolo.

In the right aisle, the first chapel contains a *Deposition* painted in 1569 by Barocci, apparently under the influence of poison administered by a jealous rival. More toxin-related mementoes are contained in the transepts, where urns hold the ashes of Pope Martin IV, who died in the city after eating too many eels, and Urban IV, who was was reputedly poisoned with *aquetta*, an imaginative little brew made by rubbing arsenic into pork fat and distilling the resultant ooze.

The most conspicuous piece of art, though, is the *Madonna delle Grazie* by Giannicola di Paolo, on the third pillar of the right nave. Easily recognised by its tinselly votive offerings, it's supposed to have miraculous powers, and mothers still bring their newly baptised children to kneel before it.

MUSEO DELL'OPERA DEL DUOMO

Through the cathedral sacristy (or if it's closed, through a courtyard to the left of the entrance) are the cloisters and **Museo dell'Opera del Duomo** (daily 8am–noon & 3.30–6pm; free, but "temporarily" closed at time of writing), a rich little treasury with some fine examples of the miniatures for which medieval Perugia was renowned, and a *Madonna and Saints* by Luca Signorelli.

West and east of the Corso

For a feel of medieval Perugia, the most rewarding streets are to the west of the Corso, in particular **Via dei Priori**, entered through the archway in the Palazzo dei Priori. East of the Corso there are a couple of extra diversions in the fine medieval quarter around **Piazza Danti**, the small square behind the Duomo.

West: Via dei Priori to San Francesco

The steeply sloping **Via dei Priori** was a conduit for rivers of blood, medieval chroniclers claimed, and the side streets too have associations with Perugia's gory past. In **Via della Gabbia**, part way down, there once hung a large iron cage used to imprison thieves and sometimes even clergy. A journal written in 1492 records the fate of the priest Angelo di Ferolo – "it was very cold and there was much snow, and he remained there until the first day of February both night and day and that same day he was brought out dead." You can still make out long spikes on some of the lower walls of the street, used as hooks for the heads of executed criminals.

A little further along Via dei Priori are the church of **SS. Stefano e Valentino**, an atmospheric building with fragments of frescoes, and the unmissable **Torre degli Sciri**, one of the few medieval towers – reputed to have numbered 700 – to have survived Perugia's violent historical passage. Off to the right near here, Via della Cupa leads off towards Via Deliziosa and signs for the **Casa di Perugino** – not really worth the detour.

Towards the end of Via dei Priori comes the **Madonna della Luce**, a chapel dominated by an altarpiece by Caporali, a follower of Perugino. It takes its name – Madonna of the Light – from an incident in 1513, when a young barber swore so profusely on losing at cards that a Madonna in a wayside shrine closed her eyes in horror, and kept them closed for four days. The miracle caused celebrations, processions and the building of this new church.

Bearing right beyond the Madonna della Luce brings you to a patch of grass, frequented by students from the art school next door, and conveniently placed for admiring Agostino di Duccio's colourful **Oratorio di San Bernardino**. Its richly embellished facade is far and away the best piece of sculpture in the city – an odd but appealing mix of bas-reliefs and coloured marble, commissioned in 1461 by the city's magistrates in gratitude to Saint Bernardino for trying to bring peace to Perugia. The detail of the carving warrants a close look, especially the lower frieze depicting the Bonfire of the Vanities – a pile of Perugian wigs, books and hosiery elicited by the saint's preaching. The church interior is rarely open.

To the right of the Oratorio is what's left of **San Francesco**, Bernardino's lodging in the city, and in its time Perugia's most sumptuous church. Started just four years after Francis' death in 1226, it's been laid low by earthquakes and landslips, though the curiously jumbled facade is still just about standing and the interior is often used as a concert hall.

East: around Piazza Danti

Piazza Danti is a pleasant little square, the scene of a weekend flower and terracotta market and site of an **Etruscan well**, entered at no. 18 (Tues–Sun 9am–1pm). Close by, and the chief sight of this district, is the church of **San Severo** (April–Sept Tues–Sun 10.30am–6pm; Oct–March same days 10am–12.30pm &

2.30–4.30pm). It's a little difficult to find: take Via Bontempi off the square, then the tiny Via Raffaello curving left, and the church is straight ahead. Legend claims it was built on the site of a pagan temple to the sun – the spot is east-facing and the town's highest point – which gave its name to the Porta Sole district of the Etruscan city. There would have been five such districts, spreading down from the temple to five corresponding gates in the outer wall. Most of the church is a Baroque rehash, grafted onto a building that dates from 1007, though one chapel was spared – the one that contains one of **Raphael's** first complete works, a *Holy Trinity and Saints*, painted shortly before he settled in Florence in 1505. The lower panels, depicting *Six Saints*, were painted in 1521 by Perugino, then in his dotage, a year after the death of his erstwhile pupil.

Return to Via Bontempi, turn left downhill, and you'll come to **Santa Maria Nuova**, a sprawling and much knocked-about church recently returned to its Gothic form. Its main point of interest is the *gonfalone* in the second chapel on the right; created in 1472 by Bonfigli, a local lad who specialised in such things, it features a view of Perugia under attack from divine thunderbolts.

In the area above here, the **Porta Sole** proper, there once stood the palace of Cardinal Montemaggiore of Cluny, the city's papal governor from 1372. Though his residence was described by contemporaries as the most beautiful in Italy, he was hated by the locals as "that French Vandal, that most iniquitous Nero" – perhaps because he removed bits of the Duomo to aid its construction. Within three years a revolt and siege had sent him scurrying; the palace was reduced to rubble by a vast catapult, the so-called *cacciaprete* – the priest-hunter.

The northern quarters

The **northern quarters** of the *centro storico* focus on **Piazza Fortebraccio**, ten minutes' walk downhill from Piazza IV Novembre, or a similar distance from San Francesco along Via A. Pascoli. The first route follows Perugia's oldest street, the 2500-year-old **Via Ulisse Rocchi**; the latter passes the modern university buildings and goes under the famous raised walkway, the **Via del Aquadotto**, pictures of which dominate Perugia's tourist handouts.

Piazza Fortebraccio and Sant'Agostino

Above **Piazza Fortebraccio** is the massive patched-up gateway of the **Arco di Augusto**, whose lowest section is one of the few remaining monuments to Etruscan Perugia. It dates from the second century BC, when it was the city's main entrance. The upper arch and bulwarks were added by the Romans when they recaptured the city in 40 BC; under the arch you can still see the letters spelling out its new name, Augusta Perusia – the first part immodestly large, the latter considerably smaller. The top-storey loggia is a sixteenth-century addition.

On the western side of the square, housed in the Palazzo Gallenga, is the **Università Italiana per Stranieri**. The bar downstairs here is a friendly, cosmopolitan meeting ground, but don't expect much joy from the ironically titled information desk in the foyer. Posters around the place give details of concerts and English films, especially frequent in the April to December term times.

A short walk north from Piazza Fortebraccio, along Corso Garibaldi, brings you out at the half-defunct church of **Sant'Agostino**, originally Romanesque, now botched Baroque, and filled with wistful signs explaining what paintings used to hang in the church before they were spirited to France by light-fingered Napoleonic troops. The missing pictures have been replaced with what someone presumably considers "modern art". The church, however, is not entirely ruined: there's a beautiful **choir**, probably based on drawings by Perugino, and a couple of patches of fresco on the left-hand wall, giving a tantalising idea of what the place must once have been. Adjoining is the fifteenth-century **Oratorio di Sant'Agostino**, its ludicrously ornate ceiling looking as if it's about to erupt in an explosion of gilt, stucco and chubby plaster cherubs.

Sant'Angelo

At the end of Corso Garibaldi, tucked into the northern corner of the walls, is the circular **Sant'Angelo**, founded in the fifth century and thus one of the oldest churches in Umbria. It was possibly built on the site of a Roman temple: its two rings of pillars are undoubtedly from an earlier building and there was once a third set – removed to build the church of San Pietro (see opposite).

In a touch of decorative subtlety, all the columns of the inner ring are made from a different type of stone, but otherwise the church is beautifully plain, its Baroque additions having been recently stripped away. The setting, too, is delightful, a grassy and tranquil retreat, the shade of the walls and cypresses outside providing a favourite siesta spot.

Piazza Italia and south along Corso Cavour

Perugia's other highlights are grouped together on the southern side of town along **Corso Cavour**, the busy main road out of town towards Assisi, which leads off from the nineteenth-century **Piazza Italia**.

The piazza itself has a couple of curiosities nearby. Just to the east is the strange octagonal church of **Sant'Ercolano** (now a war memorial and rarely open), raised on the spot where the head of Perugia's first bishop miraculously reattached itself after the Goths had chopped it off. A little to the south of this is the **Porta Marzia** (Tues–Sun 8am–2pm), a superb Etruscan archway which forms an entrance to **Via Baglioni Sotterranea**, a submerged medieval street that is one of the city's most extraordinary sights. Its houses now form part of the foundations for the piazza, but were once part of the **Rocca Paolina**, a colossal sixteenth-century papal fortress designed by Sangallo. Taking in ten churches and four hundred houses, the Rocca was connected by tunnels to strategic points throughout the city. At Unification the fort was pulled down, using dynamite and bare hands, by what appears to have been every man, woman and child in the city – and even then the process took thirty years. Trollope, watching the demolition, wrote that "few buildings have been laden with a heavier amount of long-accumulated hatred".

San Domenico

The unmissable landmark on Corso Cavour is **San Domenico**, Umbria's biggest church. Its unfinished exterior has an attractively melancholy air, with pigeons nesting and grass growing on the pinkish marble, but the Romanesque interior collapsed in the sixteenth century and the vast, cold Baroque replacement is like an EC warehouse waiting for a food-mountain.

Like Sant'Agostino, however, it's full of hints of past beauties. In the fourth chapel on the right is a superb **carved arch** by Agostino di Duccio (1459), spoilt only by nineteenth-century frescoes and a doll-like Madonna. To the right of the altar is the **tomb of Benedict XI**, another pope who died in Perugia – this time from eating poisoned figs – after ruling just eight months in 1304. He left to posterity one of the greatest Gothic carvings of its kind in Italy, an elegant and well-preserved piece by one of the period's leading sculptors – Giovanni Pisano, Lorenzo Maitini or Arnolfo di Cambio, nobody knows which. Certainly it's modelled on the tomb of Cardinal de Braye in Orvieto, one of Arnolfo's most influential works (see p.533). Some of the marble work is missing, picked out by troops when a Napoleonic cavalry regiment was billeted in the church. Nearby are extensive patches of fresco, another good choir, and – a welcome splash of colour – some impressive **stained-glass windows**, the largest in Italy after Milan cathedral.

Housed in the church's unfinished cloisters is the **Museo Archeologico Nazionale dell'Umbria** (Mon–Sat 9am–1.30pm & 2.30–6.30pm, Sun 9am–1pm; L4000). Before being wrecked by Augustus, Perugia was a big-shot in the Etruscan federation, which is why this museum has one of the most extensive Etruscan collections around. The site that produced the bulk of the exhibits is the small **Ipogeo dei Volumni**, 7km east of the city (Tues–Sat 9am–5pm, Sun 9am–1pm; L4000; bus or train to Ponte San Giovanni) – a trip that only the keenest Etruscophiles will find rewarding. In the museum there are also sizeable sections devoted to prehistory and Roman finds.

San Pietro

Further down Corso Cavour, through the double-arched **Porta San Pietro** (1147), is the tenth-century basilica of **San Pietro**, the city's first cathedral and still the most beautiful and idiosyncratic of its churches. Advertised by a rocket-shaped bell tower, it's tangled up in a group of buildings belonging to the university's agricultural department; the none-too-obvious entrance is through a doorway in the far left-hand corner of the first courtyard off the road.

The interior comes as quite a shock. Few churches even in Italy are so sumptuously decorated, every inch of space being covered in gilt, paint or marble, yet the effect is not overwhelming and in the candle-lit gloom it actually feels like a sacred place. That so much of the Romanesque building survives is due to events at Unification, when the church's Benedictine monks sided with the townspeople in their revolt against papal control. Loyalty to the cause of liberation was not forgotten, and when the religious houses were broken up a year later, San Pietro was allowed to keep its patrimony.

The finest single component of the interior is the extraordinary **choir**, which has been called the greatest in Italy; in fact, all the woodwork here is superb – look out also for the intricately gilded side-pulpits. As for the **paintings**, there's a *Pietà* by Perugino between the first and second altars on the left, while the eleven frescoes around the upper walls are by a disciple of Veronese. The baffling fresco on the rear wall is a genealogical tree of the Benedictines, collecting together the most eminent members of the Order. The best pictures of all are the paintings by Perugino and Caravaggio, plus a possible Raphael, gathered in the **sacristy**; you'll probably have to get the sacristan to let you in.

Eating, drinking and entertainment

Perugia is strong on events, with films, theatre and concerts packing a page or so each day in the local supplement of *La Nazione* newspaper. It's a bit less rewarding, though, in its cuisine. While fast-food and snack bars abound for the student market, good restaurants are surprisingly hard to find. Selections below cover just about everything of quality, and are ranged in order of price.

Restaurants

Fratelli Brizi, Via Fabreti 75. Cheap, reliable pizzeria near the Università per Stranieri, and very busy in term time.

Trattoria Cavour, Via Cavour 28. Another good choice for basic and cheap meals.

Dal mi Cocco, Corso Garibaldi 12. Set five-course menus which change daily; excellent value at around L25,000. Closed Mon.

Falchetto, Via Bartolo 20. Excellent restaurant in a fine medieval setting just off Piazza Danti; reasonably priced if you stick to the basics. L25–30,000. Closed Mon.

Trattoria Ubu Re, Via Baldeschi 17 (☎075/65.461). Manageably priced, nouvelle-ish Umbrian dishes; a touch too pretentious for some tastes. Closed Mon & Jan.

La Taverna, Via delle Streghe (☎075/61.028). Serious restaurant with a mixture of traditional regional and one-off inventive dishes – and ultra heavyweight desserts. Big portions for about L40,000. Closed Mon & July 15–31.

La Lanterna, Via Ulisse Rocchi 6 (☎075/66.064). Beautifully prepared regional dishes; around L45,000 per head. Closed Wed.

Osteria del Bartolo, Via Bartolo 30 (☎075/61.461). Elegant and expensive, but the city's top restaurant of the moment, featuring exotic dishes as well as daily specials that stick to Umbrian staples. L60,000. Closed Tues, Jan 7–18 & July 25–Aug 7.

Cafés, bars and gelaterie

Bar Etrusca, Via Ulisse Rocchi. Close to the Arco di Augusto; popular with foreign students.

Bar Morlacchi, Piazza Morlacchi 6. Smart but student-oriented bar; get to it along Via delle Volte from Piazza IV Novembre.

Café del Cambio, Corso Vannucci 29. The trendiest café, with reasonable snacks and an efficient lunchtime service; there's a snappy restaurant downstairs too.

Enoteca Provinciale, Via Ulisse Rocchi 16. Close to the Duomo, this wineshop-cum-bar is the best place to indulge in the local wines.

Gelateria 2000, Via L. Bonazzi 3. Perugia's finest ice cream.

Pasticceria Sandri, Corso Vannucci 32. The most atmospheric café in Perugia – turn-of-the-century Viennese style with lots of brass, wood panels and frescoed ceilings. Worth at least one pricey *cappuccino* just for the streetlife.

La Terrazza, Piazza Matteotti and Piazza Grimana. Two bar-pizzeria outlets under the same management that are regular student hang-outs.

Markets

There is a permanent **covered food market** – the Mercato Coperto – off Piazza Matteotti (Mon–Sat 7.30am–1pm). An open-air general market operates on the **Scala di Sant'Ercolano**, near the church of the same name, on Tuesdays and Saturdays (8am–1pm).

Events

Tickets for the July **Umbria Jazz** festival are sold at the tourist office and the *Negozio Ceccherini* at Piazza della Repubblica 65; for an advance programme, phone the festival office (☎075/62.432). Most concerts cost between L10,000 and

L30,000, but some are free. Other key events include open air-theatre, *Teatro in Piazza*, in July and August, and a September festival of **classical music**, the *Sagra Musicale*, held in various venues around the city.

Listings

Books and newspapers *Libreria Filosofi*, Via dei Filosofi 18–20, has the best selection of English-language titles. For English newspapers, try the stands along the Corso.

Bus enquiries *ASP*, Piazza dei Partigiani (☎075/573.1707) or Pian di Massiano (☎075/751.145).

Car rental *Paoletti*, Piazza Danti 28 (☎075/572.1705); *La Ditta Pero*, Via Bontempi 6 (☎075/572.2819).

Exchange facilities Foreign exchange is handled by most of the banks on Corso Vannucci and at the *CIT* office in the corner of Piazza IV Novembre.

First aid ☎075/61.341.

Hospital Via Bonacci Brunamonti (☎075/60.81).

Maps *Eliografica*, Via delle Streghe, can supply hiking maps for the province.

Post office The main branch is on Piazza Matteotti (Mon–Fri 10am–5.30pm, Sat 10am–2pm).

Student travel *CTGS Student Centre*, Via del Roscetto 21 (☎075/572.0284 or 7050).

Study courses For details and prospectuses contact the Università Italiana per Stranieri, Palazzo Gallenga, Piazza Fortebraccio 4 (☎075/64.344). Summer painting and sculpture courses are run by the Accademia di Belle Arti, Piazza San Francesco al Prato 5 (☎075/29.106).

Scooter hire *Easy Bike*, Via Marconi.

Telephones Booths at the post office are open until 11.45pm; the SIP offices in Via Marconi, Corso Cavour and Corso Vannucci are open 8.30am–10pm.

Train enquiries *FS* state railways, Piazza V. Veneto (☎075/500.1091); *FCU* private line, Stazione Sant'Anna (☎075/29.121).

Lago Trasimeno

The most tempting option around Perugia – whose surroundings are generally pretty bleak – is **Lago Trasimeno**. An ideal spot to hole up for a few days and get in some swimming (if you don't mind murky water), it is the biggest stretch of water on the Italian peninsula and the fourth largest in Italy overall – after Garda, Maggiore and Como – though currently in danger of drying up completely. With modern demands on water from agriculture and increased silting, the lake's greatest depth now reaches no more than seven metres – hence bath-like warm water in the summer. Because the tourist and fishing industries are the area's economic bread and butter, it's also clean; large banks of weed drift in during the summer, but they are taken care of by the council, who simply dump them on the shore.

The main drawback to Trasimeno is its popularity. In high season the water is scattered with speed boats, yachts and windsurfers by the hundred. If you're after relative seclusion, steer clear of the northern shore – recently opened up by Perugia's motorway spur – and head instead for the stretches south of Magione and Castiglione. Be warned, also, that **unofficial camping** is not as easy as it looks, because the best spots have been grabbed by commercial sites and much of the remaining shoreline is marshy.

Passignano

The lake's most accessible point is **PASSIGNANO**, a newish town strung out along the northern shore and served by hourly **trains** from Perugia and Teróntola (near Cortona). Popular with Italians whose idea of a day out is to spend most of it in a car, the town in summer is often one big traffic jam, Sundays being especially bad. In the evenings, though, it's an enjoyable place as people come flooding in from the surrounding campsites, livening up the bars, discos and fish restaurants. The waterfront strip is the chief focus, and there's plenty going on in the web of streets behind as well. Bar two dull Renaissance churches, there's nothing to see in the old centre – so you can skip the town in the daytime unless it's to mingle with posturing teenagers.

Passignano's **tourist office** is at Via Roma 36 (June–Sept Mon–Sat 9am–noon & 4–7pm, Sun 9am–noon; Oct–May Mon–Fri 9am–noon & 3–6pm, Sat 9am–noon; ☎075/827.635). There are dozens of **hotels**, most in the upper bracket – the best value are the one-star *Aviazione*, Via Roma 54 (☎075/827.162; [4]), *Del Pescatore*, Via San Bernardino 5 (☎075/827.165; [4]), and *Florida*, Via II Giugno 2 (☎075/827.228; [4]), or the more upmarket *Trasimeno*, Via Roma 16a (☎075/829.355; [5]). You can also find **rooms** for rent at Via A. Costi 1 (☎075/827.503; [3]) and Via Fratelli Rossi 18 (☎075/827.504; [3]). The two main **campsites** are the three-star *Kursaal*, Via Europa 41 (April–Sept; ☎075/827.182), and the two-star *Europa* (April–Sept; ☎075/827.403), the latter in the nearby hamlet of San Donato. The **restaurant** of the *Aviazione* hotel is the best in town, specialising in lake fish and truffle-spiced dishes.

HANNIBAL AND THE BATTLE OF LAGO TRASIMENO

On the coast west of Passignano, between Sanguineto (the Place of Blood) and Ossaia (the Place of Bones), is the spot where the Romans suffered their traumatic defeat at the hands of **Hannibal** in 217 BC. The Carthaginian leader was headed for Rome, having already crossed the Alps and won a sweeping victory at Placentia – though by this stage only one of the famous elephants was still alive. He was met by the Romans under the Consul **Flaminius**, close to an amphitheatre of hills – a location, said the historian Livy, that was "formed by Nature for an ambush".

Things might have gone better for Flaminius if he'd heeded the omens that piled up on the morning of battle. First he fell off his horse, next the legionary standards had to be dug from the mud, then – and this really should have raised suspicions – the sacred chickens refused their breakfast. Poultry accompanied all Roman armies in the field, their behaviour or the look of their innards at moments of crisis being interpreted as communications of the will of the gods. With the chickens against him Flaminius didn't stand a chance. Hannibal lured him into a masterful ambush, with the only escape a muddy retreat into the lake. Sixteen thousand Romans – two entire legions – were killed, including the hapless commander, run through with a lance. The attack was so sudden that many Romans didn't even have time to draw their swords. The slaughter lasted for three hours. Hannibal, for his part, is thought to have lost just 1500 men.

Hannibal's sappers had orders to bury the dead where they fell, and recently 113 mass graves – deep stone-lined pits with lids – have been discovered. Scientific dating of the remains tallies exactly with the date of the battle.

Tuoro and Castel Rigone

The shady, rambling village of **TUORO**, four kilometres west of Passignano, and three kilometres' walk from the Trasimeno battlefield, is a quiet little place giving road access into the desolate, beautiful mountains north of the lake – the best of the scenery within easy reach of Perugia. In summer you can also take boats across to Isola Maggiore (see p.424) and to main towns on the lake's shore – details are available from *SPNT*, on the waterfront at Pontile di Tuoro, Punta Navaccia.

The office is also home to a seasonal **tourist office** (June–Aug daily 9am–1pm & 4–7pm; ☎075/827.157), which has information on two new itineraries around the battlefield: the *Interno* (8km) takes you through the Valle della Battaglia itself, whilst the *Esterno* (16km) concentrates more on the area's scenery. Both routes start at the Tuoro exit from the Perugia N75 road immediately southwest of the village and finish in Tuoro itself.

· Accommodation is tricky, though, as there's only one **hotel**, the eight-roomed *Volante Inn*, Via Sette Martiri 52 (☎075/826.107; ④), and a couple of places renting **rooms**: at Via Roma 47 (☎075/826.191; ④), and Via A. Gramsci 18 (☎075/ 826.670; ④). Otherwise there is a three-star **campsite**, the *Punta Navaccia* (April–Sept; ☎075/826.357).

CASTEL RIGONE, 8km north of Tuoro, is the outstanding village in the mountains, with superb views and a small, geranium-strewn medieval centre. Most of the incumbents are pensioners, here for the bracing climate and fresh air. There are two smart, rather staid **hotels**, the better of which is the obvious *Relais La Fattoria*, Via Rigone 1 (☎075/845.322; ⑦). Cheaper and more rustic is the **agriturismo** *Locanda del Galluzzo* (☎075/845.352; ④) in the hamlet of Trecine, 2km west of Castel Rigone. Each of the hotels has a cavernous **restaurant**, the only places for a bite to eat. A little outside the village is the Renaissance church of **Madonna dei Miracoli**, somewhat out of place in the overall medieval context.

Castiglione del Lago

CASTIGLIONE DEL LAGO cuts a fine silhouette from other points on the lake, jutting into the water on a fortified promontory. In the event it doesn't quite live up to its distant promise, but is a friendly, unpretentious place that can hold anyone's attention for a couple of days – longer if all you want to do is crash out on a beach, albeit a modest one. It's easy to reach by road and rail, though as a lot of the fast trains on the Rome–Florence line no longer stop here, you'll probably end up taking a *locale* either from Chiusi or Teróntola.

There's little in the town to make a point of seeing, though the largely sixteenth-century **castle** is well preserved, particularly its strange fortified passageway. The ramparts offer good views of the lake, and there's a central stage for outdoor summer events. You might also hunt down the church of **Santa Maria Maddalena** at the western end of the main Via V. Emanuele, where there's a fine *Madonna and Child* by Eusebio di San Giorgio, a follower of Perugino.

Small **beaches** are dotted around the promontory, with the best swimming at the modest public beach on its southern side.

Practicalities

The main **tourist office** for the Trasimeno region is in Castiglione's main square, at Piazza Mazzini 10 (June–Sept Mon–Sat 8.30am–1.30pm & 3–7.30pm, Sun 8am–1pm; Oct–May Mon–Fri 8.30am–1.30pm & 3–7pm, Sat 8am–1.30pm; ☎075/952.184); they have on their books around fifteen *agriturismo* choices in the surrounding countryside, a lot of reasonable if characterless **rooms** in private houses, and apartments to rent on a weekly basis, usually a cheaper option if you can get a party together. Amongst the **hotels**, the top-priced places are the three-star *Duca della Corgna*, Via B. Buozzi 143 (☎075/953.238; ⑤), and *La Torre*, Via V. Emanuele 50 (☎075/951.666; ⑤). Slightly less expensive than these are the *Trasimeno*, Via Roma 174 (☎075/965.2494; ⑤), and the two-star *Miralago*, Piazza Mazzini 6 (☎075/953.063; ⑤), a more atmospheric establishment, chiefly because it commands good views of the lake. The modern *Fazzouli*, Piazza Marconi 11 (☎075/951.119; ④), is the town's budget hotel, and also has three- and four-person apartments for rent.

Most of the **campsites** are off the main road some way south of the town. The *Lido Trasimeno* (April–Sept ☎075/954.120) on the shore north of the castle has good facilities (swimming, windsurfing school, sailing) but it's next to a training school for police Alsatians. Best **eating**, apart from the summer-only restaurants on the promenade, is the excellent *La Cantina*, Via V. Emanuele 89a. The lively market is on Wednesdays.

Isola Maggiore

In summer, regular boats from the lakeshore jetty make the trip out to **Isola Maggiore**, one of the lake's three islands, a fun ride if you don't mind the crowds. The crossing takes twenty minutes, and there are connecting boats to Tuoro and Passignano, as well as to lesser resorts on the lake's southern and eastern shores. (For times of sailings call ☎075/827.157.)

Once over, there's a single village – known for its lace – and a pretty walk round the island perimeter. The island is famed for a visit by Saint Francis, a forty-day sojourn during which he consumed just half a loaf of bread; a chapel marks the point of his disembarkation, and there's a small Franciscan monastery on the southeast shore. The best outing, though, is to the church of **San Archangelo**; sited at the island's highest point, it's decorated with frescoes and has a *Crucifixion* painted by Bartolomeo Caporali in 1460.

The village's single two-star **hotel** is *Da Sauro*, Via G. Guglielmi 1 (075/826.168; ⑤); be sure to book ahead, whether it's for a room or for a table in the adjoining and equally popular **fish restaurant**. Alternatively, once everyone's gone home you might discreetly pitch a tent.

South of the lake: Panicale

The low hills to the south of Trasimeno make a good scenic backdrop. If you have a car you might take a detour to **PANICALE**, 5km south of the shore, which offers picture-postcard views of the lake, plus two easily missed Perugino paintings in the church of **San Sebastiano**, off Piazza Vittoria. Apart from a tiny medieval core, there's little else to the place, though during the April *festa* some miraculous plumbing fills the fountains with wine – well worth investigation. The village is a quiet place for a stopover, and also breaks your journey if you're walk-

WALKS AROUND LAGO TRASIMENO

There's some good **walking** locally, with treks possible up Monte Castiglione on the mule track from the Passo di Gosparani (7km north of Tuoro); up Monte Acuto from Galera or Monteacuto (15km northeast on the Umbértide road); or up Monte Murlo from Preggio, a hill village 6km north of Castel Rigone, and worth a visit in its own right. If you feel less adventurous, twelve new **walking trails** have been marked around the lake from centres such as Magione, Panicale, Passignano and Castiglione del Lago. Ask at tourist offices for the map-brochure *Itinerari Turistici del Trasimeno* (free). Trail 3, for example, links Castel Rigone to Tuoro (30km; 9–10hr or two days) via Passignano, mostly via the high ridges above the lake; Trail 2 (26km; 8–9hr or two days) follows a lower route between Tuoro and Passignano, continuing east to Magione. Trail 4 is an easy 18km (6hrs) from Tuoro to Castiglione del Lago. You could, in theory, link several trails and effect a full circuit of the lake. Paths are mainly cross-country and have been designed to take in historic churches and buildings en route; longer routes, of course, can easily be split into manageable one-day walks.

ing some of Trasimeno's marked trails. There are just two hotels, the three-star *Le Grotte di Boldrino*, Via V. Ceppari 43 (☎075/837.161; ⑥), and one-star *Masolino*, Via Roma (☎075/837.151; ④).

On the map, the **main road** below Panicale from Perugia to Città della Pieve (the SS220) looks a good touring proposition; in fact it's a laborious route, spotted by light industry and the odd factory chimney. The only point of interest is the **Santuario di Mongiovino**, a Renaissance temple high above the road, 7km south of Panicale, and roughly equidistant from Perugia and Città della Pieve. It looks a good deal more impressive from afar than it does close to.

The Upper Tiber

Rome's great and famously polluted river, the **Tiber** (Tevere), actually spends most of its life in Umbria, rising just to the north of the province. In its unexciting upper reaches, north of Perugia, you're faced with the problem that its most attractive areas – the fine countryside and walking territory above the valley – are out of reach without a car, bike or lucky hitch.

The *Ferrovie Centrale Umbra* (Central Umbrian Railway) and fast SS3, however, connect Perugia with **Umbértide** and **Città di Castello**, the area's only sizeable towns. At Umbértide there's the option of striking east across the mountains to Gubbio, while at Città di Castello you have the choice of moving east to Urbino (in the Marche) or following the Tiber along the trail of Piero della Francesca's unsettling masterpieces at Sansepolcro, Arezzo and Monterchi (all of theses are covered in Chapter Eight).

Santa Maria di Valdiponte

Highlight of the area immediately north of Perugia is the abbey of **Santa Maria di Valdiponte** at Montelabate, on the east side of the valley 16km from Perugia. This monastic foundation once controlled twenty castles in the area, and similar abbeys administered great swathes of the land between Gubbio and the Tiber. Built between the twelfth and fourteenth centuries, the church itself is of rather less interest than the **cloisters**, which are medieval perfection, and the various artistic treasures scattered around the complex – including frescoes by such as Fiorenzo di Lorenzo and Bartolomeo Caporali.

Umbértide and around

Bombed to the edge of oblivion in the last war, **UMBÉRTIDE** is now a lightly industrial town relieved by a tiny and captivating medieval centre. Artistic attractions are limited to the **Palazzo Comunale** – the best Baroque conversion in Umbria – and a *Deposition* by Luca Signorelli in the church of **Santa Croce**.

You'd only want to use this place as a way-station. There are a couple of **hotels** on the main road, the cheaper being the two-star *Moderno*, Via Nazionale 186 (☎075/941.3759; ⑤); rather better is the central *Capponi*, Piazza XXV Aprile 19 (☎075/941.2662; ④), whose **restaurant** is the standard place to eat.

The castle of **Civitella Ranieri** rises invitingly just to the northeast of Umbértide, but it's privately owned, so don't bother with the steep climb for a closer look. More worthwhile is the hill village of **MONTONE**, 6km north, which harbours a collection of minor Umbrian paintings in the church of San Francesco. The village also has a **hotel**, the two-star *Fortebraccio*, Via dei Magistrati 11 (☎075/930.6215; ④), and there's another, the two-star *Adamo* (☎075/930.6146; ④), in the hamlet of Corlo, midway along the road from Umbértide. If you're heading east to Gubbio – the most likely reason to be passing through – you might stop off at **CAMPO REGGIANO**, 11km east of Umbértide, for a look at its tiny eleventh-century church and crypt of San Bartolomeo.

Monte Corona (693m), 6km south of Umbértide, is topped by the **Badìa di San Salvatore**, a twelfth-century monastery – which again looks good from the outside, but was ravaged by a sixteenth-century interior conversion.

Walking in the Upper Tiber

With thousands of hectares of natural woodland and abandoned pasture, the desolate countryside on each flank of the Upper Tiber teems with protected wildlife, including many rare species of birds, deer, wild boar and even wolves – now pushing further up the Italian peninsula every year. Freelance exploration is easy, especially if you have transport, but for detailed information on **walking** in the region, contact the *CAI* branch in Città di Castello, at Via della Tina 14 (☎075/855.6788).

The area's only **hotel** is the three-star *Candeleto* (☎075/936.183; ⑤) in the village of Candeleto close to Pietralunga; there's a campsite nearby, *La Pineta* (June–Sept; ☎075/936.180). Cheaper than the *Candeleto*, and more in keeping with the region's rural tone, are the **agriturist** bed and breakfasts near Pietralunga – Claudio Capaccioni, Via Fornelli 6, Castelguelfo (☎075/933.061; ③) or *La Cerva* in the hamlet of San Salvatore (☎075/946.0283; ⑤).

Città di Castello

Umbria's northernmost town, **CITTÀ DI CASTELLO**, is a plain-bound spot with a more than passable *centro storico* spoilt by the industry on its outskirts – mainly tobacco processing plants, the town being one of Italy's leading producers. Once an important Roman trading centre – the grid-iron of streets is their main legacy – Città di Castello reached its peak around 1500, when the enlightened despotism of the Vitelli nobles brought leading artists here, the young Raphael and Signorelli among them. Nemesis arrived in the form of Cesare Borgia, who invited the head of the Vitellis to a banquet, had him strangled, and took the town for the papacy. The church's seventh-century nickname for the place was *castrum felicitas* (Castle of Happiness), though quite why is hard to fathom. Today there's nothing overly cheerful about the place, unless you've drunk sufficient quantities of the local Colli Altotiberini wines. The only real pull is its **Pinacoteca**, arguably the best in the province after Perugia.

Access is by direct **train** on the private *FCU* line from Perugia or Terni to the south, or from Sansepolcro to the north; the station is outside the walls to the southeast. You could alternatively take a main line *FS* train to Arezzo and pick up an *ACT* bus to Città di Castello, whose **bus station** is in Piazza Garibaldi, on the east edge of the *centro storico*.

The Pinacoteca

The **Pinacoteca**, to the south of the walled town at Via della Cannoniera 22 (Tues–Sun 10am–noon & 3–6pm; L5000), is housed in one of the town's more prepossessing buildings, a palazzo designed by Sangallo the Younger in 1520 and decorated with *sgraffito* by Vasari on the garden facade. Inside, the painted stairwells and period furniture complement the paintings. Not all the palazzo's guests had time to appreciate the high-class fittings; Laura, one of the Vitelli women, was wont to throw her rejected lovers to their deaths from the windows.

Most of the gallery's rooms – many of them splendidly frescoed – have something of interest, with the highlights provided by Lorenzo Ghiberti's golden reliquary, *The Martyrdom of Saint Sebastian* by Luca Signorelli, and a damaged standard by Raphael. Raphael spent about five years in Umbria and the region once had many works by him, several of them in Città di Castello. Today the only pieces in Umbria entirely by him are the standard here and the panel in Perugia's San Severo church – the others were removed to the Louvre by Napoleon. A marvellous *Maestà* by the anonymous Maestro di Città di Castello has been backwards and forwards to Florence for restoration since 1969, so may or may not be on show. Other lesser works include Sienese and later Venetian paintings, as well as ceramics from the Della Robbias and a varied sculpture collection.

The rest of the town

Elsewhere, many of Città di Castello's older buildings have lost their medieval aspect to later facades – Neoclassical in the case of the **Palazzo del Podestà**, Baroque for the **Duomo**, though it has hung onto its Romanesque campanile. Only the **Palazzo Comunale** has held onto its rough stone exterior; its design is attributed to Angelo da Orvieto, the architect responsible for Gubbio's more impressive palaces.

The most interesting visit is to the **Museo del Duomo** (daily 10am–1pm & 3–5.30pm; L5000), where pride of place goes to the *Tesoro di Canoscio*, a hoard of palaeo-Christian silverware, probably originating in Constantinople. The nine plates and eleven spoons, some beautifully engraved, date from the sixth century and were dug up near the town in 1935. Other lesser points of interest, if you have time to kill, include the **Torre Civico**, seat of the town's medieval prison (Mon–Sat 10am–1pm & 3.30–6pm; L5000), and a handful of minor churches: **San Domenico** (fragments of early fresco), **San Francesco** (a lovely inlaid choir) and **Santa Maria delle Grazie** (a minor fresco by Ottaviano Nelli).

Practicalities

Città di Castello's **tourist office** at Via Raffaele de Cesare 2b (☎075/855.4817; daily 9am–1pm & 4–7pm) deals with the whole Upper Tiber region and so is a useful stop if you're thinking of spending any time locally. The town's top-of-the-range **hotel** is the central four-star *Tiferno*, Piazza R. Sanzio 13 (☎075/885.0331; [7]). Two modern alternatives are the three-star *Le Mure*, Via Borgo Farinario (☎075/852.1070; [6]), and the two-star *Umbria*, Via dei Galanti 4 (☎075/855.4925; [5]). There's also a pleasant, rural **campsite** at La Montesca, 1km west of town on the minor road to Monte San Marina – the *Montesca* (May–Sept; ☎075/855.8566).

The best **restaurants** are that of the *Tiferno* and *Il Bersaglio*, Via V. E. Orlando 14 (closed Wed & Nov; ☎075/855.5534), where meals including the local speciality, the white truffle, cost around L40,000. Budget choices include the *Collesi* in Via San Florido, a family-run place with home-made pasta (closed Sat); the pizzeria *Adriano Due*, Piazza Che Guevara (closed Wed); *Pizzeria da Fez*, Via Mario Angeloni; and the unpretentious *Trattoria Lea*, Via San Florido 28 (closed Mon).

The tourist office can provide details of the town's internationally renowned **Festival of Chamber Music**, held in August and September. An equally well-known **Mercato del Tartufo** – a truffle show and market – is held every November. On the third weekend of every month there's also a **flea market**, the *Fiera del Rigattiere*, held in Piazza Matteotti.

Around Città di Castello

Beyond Città di Castello you have a choice of three routes: striking east towards Urbino and the Marche or pressing on into Tuscany, either by heading north towards Sansepolcro or west towards Arezzo. All are accessible by train or bus from Città di Castello, though only drivers are likely to want to stop en route.

Garavelle

A couple of kilometres south of Città di Castello, in the hamlet of **GARAVELLE**, is one of Umbria's best **folk museums** (daily 9.30am–noon & 3.30–6pm; free). Situated in Via Marchese Cappelletti, this is basically an eighteenth-century farmhouse, preserved with all the accoutrements of daily life – pots, pans, furniture and so forth, plus a range of exhibits covering rural activities from wine-making, weaving and carpentry through to the blacksmith's forge. Totally out of context, the museum also has a **model railway collection** (Mon–Fri 3–5pm).

The Sansepolcro route

North along the Sansepolcro road, a kilometre east of **LAMA**, you can see faint remains believed to have been a villa owned by Pliny. Five kilometres beyond, **SAN GIUSTINO** is a more or less modern settlement, save for the **Castello Bufalani**, a thirteenth-century castle partly converted by Vasari into a splendid villa. Visits are at the discretion of the owners; enquire at the tourist office in Città di Castello. By quirk of fate, **COSPAIA**, a huddle of houses on the hill outside, was a tiny independent republic until 1826, though today has no visible reminders of such past glories.

West towards Arezzo

Head west on the SS221 out of Città di Castello and you hit **CITERNA**, a perfect fortified village whose powerful position attracted attention as late as 1944, when the Germans destroyed its strategically important castle. The local church, **San Francesco**, built in 1316 and revamped in 1508, has a modest assortment of frescoes. The village also has a good **hotel**, the ten-room *Sabaria*, Via della Pineta (☎075/859.2118; [5]). As a rustic alternative, there are three **bed and breakfast** options in farms in the countryside nearby: F. Parigi, Petralta (☎075/857.0228 – horse-riding available); Giancarlo Signorelli, Rovereto (☎075/857.0276); and Massimina Pieracci, Ranzola (☎075/850.2187).

From Citerna it's an extremely short hop into Tuscany to see Piero della Francesca's *Madonna del Parto* at Monterchi (see p.388).

Gubbio

High, remote **GUBBIO** has the most medieval appearance of the northern Umbrian towns – indeed it is so well preserved that the tourist authorities promote it as the Umbrian Siena. It's not quite that, but the streets are all rosy-pink stone and the countryside around is gorgeous – the forest-covered mountains of the Apennines rearing up behind and the waters of the Camignano gorge tumbling into the town itself. A broad and largely unspoilt plain stretches out in front of the town, the whole natural ensemble – especially on grey, windswept days – maintaining Gubbio's tough mountain outpost atmosphere.

Some history

Local folklore insists that Gubbio was one of the first five towns built after the Great Flood, and it is certainly of very ancient foundation, beginning life under the Umbrians, before passing into Etruscan hands – the easternmost limit of their expansion. Romans followed, too, leaving a sprinkling of monuments and the grid-iron of streets in the lower town; subsequently, the focus of Gubbio moved from the plain to the hillside in the wake of barbarian attacks.

In the medieval period, Gubbio maintained a strategic importance as the pivotal town between Rome and Ravenna, its *comune* achieving a status that rivalled Perugia. The population grew to 50,000, twice its present size, giving the town a considerable cultural impulse. Umbria's first school of painting developed here, as did a ceramic tradition which continues to the present day – the market in pricey ceramics being the town's only serious pandering to its sightseers. From about 1350 the papacy and Gabrielli nobility jostled for power, though it was the Montefeltro dukes of Urbino who wrested eventual control, ruling virtually unbroken from 1383 until 1508. Gubbio remained in the Duchy of Urbino until 1624, then became part of the Papal States, perhaps one reason why it still feels a town apart, not properly a part of either Tuscany, Umbria or the Marche.

Arrival, information and accommodation

Gubbio is easiest approached by **bus** from Città di Castello or Perugia (*ASP*) on the lovely cross-country SS298 road. The nearest train station is at Fossato di Vico, 19km south on the Rome–Foligno–Ancona line; there are ten connecting shuttle buses to Gubbio from Monday to Saturday, six on Sundays.

By whatever means you arrive, you'll find yourself outside the medieval heart of the old town – probably in the **Piazza Quaranta Martiri**, site of the **bus terminal** and main **car park**. Dominating the old town's skyline above is the colossal bulk of the **Palazzo dei Consoli**, while on the east edge of town a second landmark is the **Basilica di Sant'Ubaldo**, connected by a funicular. There's a **tourist office** at Piazza Odersi 6, off the central Corso Garibaldi (Mon–Sat 8.30am–1.30pm & 3–6pm, Sun 9.30am–12.30pm; ☎075/922.0693). Apart from banks, currency exchange is available at the post office, Via Carioli 11 (Mon–Sat 8.30am–6pm), while telephones are to be found at Via della Repubblica 13 (Mon–Sat 8am–9pm, Sun 9.30am–12.30pm).

Accommodation

You shouldn't have any problem finding a place to stay in Gubbio, though the place gets busy, and many of the **hotels** cater to well-heeled Italians. If you don't mind being out of town, inquire at the tourist office about the twenty or so **agriturismo** options dotted around the countryside close to Gubbio – there's some magnificent accommodation in Vallingegno, 14km south of Gubbio, including apartments in a converted abbey. The places listed below are as usual in ascending order of price.

HOTELS

Galletti, Via Piccardi 1 (☎075/927.4247). The only one-star; overlooking the river; has a good restaurant with a picturesque terrace. ④.

Grotta dell'Angelo, Via Gioia 47 (☎075/927.1747). Reliable two-star, again with a good restaurant. ⑤.

Della Rocca, Monte Ingino (☎075/927.3286). A little out-of-town hotel; to get there from the centre, take the funicular or walk up to Monte Ingino and follow the signs from the Basilica. ⑤.

Dei Consoli, Via dei Consoli 59 (☎075/927.3335). One of the best locations – in an atmospheric street – so try to book ahead. Closed Jan & Feb. ⑤.

Gattapone, Via G. Ansidei 6 (☎075/927.2489). Central hotel off Via della Repubblica, with a quiet garden. ⑤.

Bosone, Via XX Settembre 22 (☎075/927.0668). A modest touch of luxury. ⑦.

Park Hotel ai Cappuccini, Via Tifernate (☎075/9234). Major league hedonism, in an elegantly converted fourteenth-century monastery. ⑨.

CAMPSITES

Città di Gubbio (☎075/927.2037). Large site in a good setting, in Ortoguidone, 1.5km south of town, off the Perugia road. Open all year.

Villa Ortoguidone (☎075/927.2037). The only four-star campsite in Umbria, but with only 14 pitches you will be lucky to get a space. Close to the *Città di Gubbio* site. Open April–Sept.

The Town

The obvious place to start a tour of the town is **Piazza Quaranta Martiri**, named after forty citizens shot by the Nazis in 1944 as a reprisal for partisan attacks in the surrounding hills. In the square, slightly stranded from the medieval heart of town, is the town's finest church, Gothic **San Francesco**, possibly designed by Fra' Bevignate, the brains behind Perugia's Fontana Maggiore. Within the newly restored interior is an engaging cycle of frescoes painted by the local Ottaviano Nelli in the 1510s. Lined along the left-hand apse, the seventeen panels show

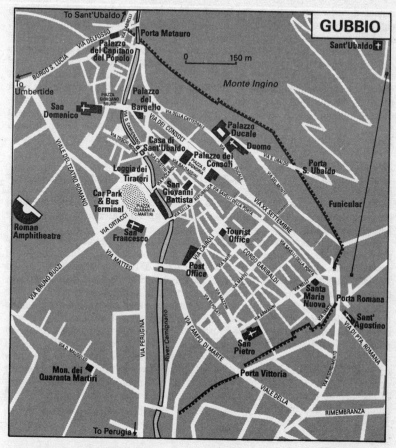

Scenes from the Life of the Virgin Mary. A small chapel nearby is claimed to be the room in which Saint Francis slept when he visited Gubbio and tamed the wolf which had been terrorising the town. Take a look, too, at the simple cloisters beyond, still clinging to a few fourteenth-century frescoes.

Opposite the church is the distinctive fourteenth-century **Tiratoio**, a weavers' loggia that's the country's best surviving example of this now rare type of building. Wool was stretched out in the shade of its arches to dry and shrink evenly away from the heat of the sun. Behind it is the church of **San Giovanni Battista**, restored to its thirteenth-century state, and distinguished by an enormous door and elongated tower.

The Palazzo dei Consoli

Heading into the medieval town, along Via della Repubblica, centre-stage is taken by the austere **Palazzo dei Consoli**, a superb building whose crenellated outline and 300-foot campanile dominate the countryside for miles around. The plain facade is disturbed only by a three-window motif that's unique to Gubbio and repeated elsewhere in the town, by a lovely doorway, and by a hole at the top right-hand corner – made to hold the cage, or *gogna* (from *vergogna* or "shame"), in which criminals were incarcerated.

An overbearing gesture of civic pride, the palace took the place of the previous civic headquarters in Via Ducale, which had been embarrassingly overshadowed by the duomo. Work started in 1321, probably to the plans of local architect Gattapone, and took a couple of hundred years to finish. In the process, vast tracts of the medieval town were levelled, most of the space going to accommodate the huge **Piazza della Signoria**, a windswept belvedere with excellent views, and a suitable setting for this colossal building and for the lesser **Palazzo Pretorio** opposite, built to the same design.

THE MUSEO CIVICO

The cavernous **Salone dell'Arengo**, where the council officers discussed their business, now accommodates a **Museo Civico** (daily 9am–1pm & 3–5pm; L4000). Much of this consists of coins and sculptures scattered like a medieval jumble sale, but it also includes Umbria's most important archaeological find, the **Eugubine Tablets**.

Discovered in 1444 by an illiterate shepherd, who was later conned into swapping the priceless treasure for a worthless piece of land, the tablets consist of seven bronze slabs, four of which date from about 200 BC, and three from around 100 BC. They are the most significant extant record of the **Umbrian language**, believed to have been a vernacular tongue without standard written characters. The bastardised Latin and Etruscan of their texts aimed at producing a phonetic transliteration of the dialect using the main languages of the day. Gubbio was close to the shrine of the so-called Apennine Jove, a major pagan deity visited by pilgrims from all over Italy, and it's thought the tablets were the work of Roman and Etruscan priests taking advantage of the established order to impose new religious cults in a region where their languages weren't understood. The text comprises a prayer divided into stanzas, a list of Gubbio's enemies, and a series of instructions for conducting services and the art of divination from sacrificed animals and the flight of birds. Most importantly, they suggest Romans, Etruscans and Umbrians achieved some sort of co-existence, refuting a long-held belief that succeeding civilisations wiped out their predecessors.

THE PINACOTECA

The museum ticket also gets you into the **Pinacoteca**, housed in five wonderful medieval rooms on the second floor of the palace. Though the paintings aren't anything special, they trace the development of the Gubbian School, one of central Italy's earliest. Sienese artists are also represented and there's a lovely *Crucifix* by the Maestro di San Francesco (best known for his work in the Basilica di San Francesco in Assisi). The gallery's star painting, the *Madonna del Melograno* (Madonna of the Pomegranate), was stolen in the 1980s.

The Duomo, Palazzo Ducale and around

A couple of streets north of the Palazzo dei Consoli, the town's rather plain Gothic **Duomo** is redeemed by a fine **interior**. Immediately noticeable is the strange arched ceiling, a Gubbian speciality known as "wagon vaulting", in which the ten arches are gracefully curved, apparently to emulate the meeting of hands in prayer. There are some fine twelfth-century stained-glass windows, a glitzy

Baroque chapel and a wealth of frescoes and panel paintings, some good, some indifferent. Look for the panels by Eusebio di San Giorgio (first niche on the left), the altarpiece alongside by Timoteo Vito, and the work by Sinibaldo Ibi next door. The small **Museo Capitolare** adjoining the church is worth a look, too, if only for the florid Flemish cope presented to the cathedral by local boy Pope Marcellus II; extravagantly embroidered, it shows seven scenes from the Passion.

Opposite the duomo – and overshadowing it – is the **Palazzo Ducale** (Tues–Sun 9am–2pm; L4000), built in 1470 over a Lombard palace by the Montefeltro dukes as a scaled-down copy of their palace in Urbino. The courtyard is particularly good, but most of the interior has been closed for years. According to the powers that be, it is to be opened imminently.

Around the corner into Via Ducale is one of Umbria's oddest novelties, the **Botte dei Canoncini**, a house-sized wine barrel with a 40,000-litre capacity, made in the sixteenth century.

The funicular and Basilica di Sant'Ubaldo

A path near the duomo zigzags uphill to the **Basilica di Sant'Ubaldo**, but the fun way up (providing you're not acrophobic) is to take the **funicular** from Porta Romana over on the east side of town. En route to the Porta, you can take in Ottaviano Nelli's masterpiece, the *Madonna del Belvedere*, at **Santa Maria Nuova** (if the church is shut, try the custodian at Via Dante 66). Just outside the walls, **Sant'Agostino** has Nelli frescoes of *Scenes from the Life of St Augustine* and panel paintings by him on the second and fifth altars.

Once atop Monte Ingino, the views and a bar are the main attractions. Even better vistas are at hand if you climb up to the **Rocca**. The **Basilica** itself is not of great interest, though it's revered for the body of the town's patron saint, Ubaldo, whose missing three fingers were hacked off by his manservant as a religious keepsake. Amid the interior, you can't miss the big wooden pillars, or *ceri* (candles), featured in Gubbio's annual *Corsa dei Ceri* (see p.434).

Via dei Consoli and the Anfiteatro

Wandering around the old town you'll soon come across Gubbio's **Porte della Morte**, the "doors of death" – narrow, bricked-up doorways wedged into the facades of medieval town houses. An historical conundrum found only in Gubbio, Assisi and southern France, the party line has it they were cut to carry a coffin out of the house and then, having been tainted by death, sealed up. A nice theory, and very Italian, but to judge by the constricted stairways behind the doors, their purpose was probably defensive – the main door could be barricaded, leaving the more easily defended passageway as the only entrance. Gubbio's best examples are in **Via dei Consoli**.

There are dozens of other picturesque odds and ends around Gubbio's streets, which lend themselves to a slow ramble. The **Bargello** – the medieval police station – in Via dei Consoli is worth tracking down and gives you a chance to survey the adjoining **Fontana dei Matti** (Fountain of the Mad), undistinguished but for the tradition that anyone walking round it three times will wind up deranged. There is usually someone wondering whether to give it a go. Two other impressive medieval buildings, both up the road from the fountain, are the fifteenth-century **Palazzo Beni** and the **Palazzo del Capitano del Popolo**.

Following the walls back round, anticlockwise, to the Piazza Quaranta Martiri, you might make a detour to the **Anfiteatro Romano**. Built in the first century, it's tame by Colosseum standards, though at 112 metres in diameter still one of the largest in the Roman world. It retains its seats and much of the lower arcades – the setting for a summer festival of Shakespeare and classical drama. Current excavations are uncovering more remains. Close by is a Roman **mausoleum**, easily reached from Piazza del Mercato; a blockhouse affair, nine metres high, no one is really sure for whom it was intended.

Food and festivals

Gubbio offers some of Umbria's best small-town cooking. A workaday **restaurant** is the *Bargello*, Via dei Consoli 37 (closed Mon), a friendly pizzeria in a pleasant street. Similarly good and homely is the *San Francesco e il Lupo*, Via Carioli 24, for pizzas or full meals. The *Grotta dell'Angelo* (closed Tues), annexed to the hotel, has a wonderful cave of a dining room (the *grotta* of its name), with excellent if basic meals for under L20,000.

Well known and more pricey – with meals around L50,000 and up – are the *Taverna del Lupo*, Via Ansidei 21 (☎075/927.4368; closed Mon & Jan), and the *Maestro Giorgio*, Via M. Giorgio 2 (☎075/927.5740; closed Mon & Feb 4–28), sited in the converted workshop of one of Gubbio's medieval master ceramicists. The *Bosone Garden* restaurant, attached to the *Bosone* hotel, opposite the *Maestro Giorgio*, has an interesting menu (around L40,000) and an excellent view – perhaps the nicest spot for outdoors eating in Gubbio.

The Corsa dei Ceri and Palio della Balestra

Held each year on May 15, the **Corsa dei Ceri** is little known outside Italy but second only to Siena's Palio in its exuberance and bizarre pageantry. The rules and rigmarole of the 900-year-old ceremony are mind-boggling, but in essence it's a race from Piazza della Signoria to the Basilica between three teams of ten men, each team carrying a *cero* on a wooden stretcher and each *cero* bearing the image of a different saint. The *cero* of Ubaldo always wins, but the other teams have to ensure they're in the Basilica before the doors are shut by the leaders. There's hours of ritual at each end, vast crowds, and plenty of drinking.

A scholarly debate rages over the origins, which are variously cited as intrinsically religious, or a secular feast commemorating the day in 1155 when Ubaldo talked Barbarossa out of flattening Gubbio, or a hangover from some pagan fertility rite. These days the church claims it as its own, though judging by the very phallic *ceri* and the roar that goes up when they're raised to the vertical, there's something more than Christian jubilation going on.

Gubbio's other excuse for a blowout is the **Palio della Balestra**, a crossbow tournament held at the end of May against Sansepolcro. Participants and onlookers alike don medieval garb, and do wonders for trade in the fake crossbows that festoon the town's souvenir shops.

Gualdo Tadino

The main centre to the east of Gubbio is **GUALDO TADINO**, a hill town with an even stronger feel of the outpost to it. Sprawling over the lower slopes of the Apennines, it has a rather bleak medieval centre, with little of substance to see, but it's quiet and atmospheric, and makes a good base for exploring the beautiful **Monte Cucco** region (see below). The town makes its money from **ceramics** and hosts a big summer exhibition of the craft.

The Town

The **Duomo**, in the central Piazza Martiri, has a facade similar to the one in Todi and a fine carved doorway – but an interior that was done to death in the last century. A meatier sight is the small **Pinacoteca** in the church of **San Francesco** on the same square. Most of the exhibits are by the local painter **Matteo da Gualdo** (1435–1503), active in churches as far south as Spoleto. Nineteenth-century critics lampooned him for his "incorrect drawing", but his brilliant colouring has brought him back into favour. However, Matteo's paintings in the apse are eclipsed by a sublime polyptych by **Nicolò Alunno**, whom Berenson described as "the first painter in whom the emotional, now passionate and violent, now mystic and ecstatic temperament of Saint Francis's countrymen was revealed". If you find the Pinacoteca closed, ask at the nearby **tourist office** at Via Calai 39.

There's another bright Matteo triptych in **Santa Maria**, in Piazza XX Settembre, close by. And if the paintings of Matteo really appeal, it's worth driving to the hill village of San Pellegrino, 10km to the northwest just off the Gubbio road (SS219), where the church has several of his works.

Practicalities

Gualdo is an easy trip by **bus** from both Gubbio and Città di Castello, and there are three connections daily from Foligno (Mon–Sat); **trains** from Assisi, Foligno or Spoleto are frequent, and there's a **shuttle bus** from the train station to the old centre.

The cheapest **hotel** is the one-star *Centro Sociale Verde Soggiorno*, Via D. Bosco 50 (☎075/916.263; ④). Otherwise try *Dal Bottaio*, Via Casimiri 17 (075/ 913.230; ④), or two-star *Gigiotto*, Via Morone 5 (☎075/912.283; ④); this also has the town's most venerable **restaurant** (closed Wed & Nov).

Alternative accommodation lies in the hamlet of Boschetto, 7km south, at the five-roomed, one-star *Da Anna* (☎075/810.171; ③). The nearest **campsite** is in the mountains at Valsorda (see below).

Parco Regionale del Monte Cucco

Some of Umbria's best upland scenery is to be found in the mountains east and north of Gualdo on the border with the Marche, much of it protected by the **Parco Regionale del Monte Cucco**. Where this area really scores is in its organised trails and backup for outdoor activities of every kind; if you want to don walking boots without too much fuss, this is the area to do it. Most importantly, and unusually for Italy, good **maps** are also available: it's worth investing in the 1:50,000 *Kompass* sheet "Assisi-Camerino" (no. 665), which covers the area around Gualdo, and in the special trail map issued in Costacciaro, the main centre inside the park.

Access is easy, with buses from Gualdo to Valsorda and from Perugia, Gualdo, Gubbio and Assisi to Costacciaro.

Valsorda

The southernmost base for exploration of the park is the resort of **Valsorda** (1000m), 8km northeast of Gualdo on the southern extremity of the park. Regular buses run from Gualdo to the village, which is a launching pad for easy hill walks and a reasonably scenic, if developed, spot in its own right.

You can tackle the straightforward trek up **Serra Santa** (1421m), on a track of motorway proportions carved out by pilgrims over the years. From the summit you could then drop into the spectacular **Valle del Fonno** gorge and follow it down to Gualdo. Paths follow the main ridge from Valsorda north and south, and it's feasible to walk all the way to Nocera Umbra (described opposite).

Valsorda has only one **hotel**: the three-star *Stella* (☎075/913.282; ⑥) which also doubles as a restaurant. There's also a **campsite**, the forty-pitch, one-star *Valsorda* (June–Sept; ☎075/913.261).

Costacciaro

To get closer to the heart of the mountains you head north from Gualdo past Fossato di Vico, a hill town whose eleventh-century Romanesque gem, **San Pietro**, contains some fine Nelli frescoes. Beyond Fossato the road passes through Sigillo and then **COSTACCIARO**, centre for all the park's outdoor pursuits and access point for the **Grotta di Monte Cucco**, at 922 metres the fifth-deepest cave system in the world. The cave was explored as early as 1889, but has only recently been opened up by the hundreds of cavers that flock here from all over Europe; over 40km of galleries have now been charted. Above, the huge, bare-sloped Monte Cucco (1566m) is the main playground for **walkers**.

Costacciaro activities

The best place to go if you want to get seriously wet or muddy, or just tag along with a tour party, is the **Centro Nazionale di Speleologia**, Corso Mazzini 9 (June–Sept daily, Oct–May Sat & Sun only; ☎075/917.0236). One of the country's most energetic and organised outdoor centres, it offers sorties for enthusiasts and guidance for visiting experts – public access is restricted to a metal ladder that runs forty metres down into a large cavern.

For **walkers**, the centre's main offering is a good 1:16,000 **map** which charts the area's thirty **marked trails**. The straightforward ascent of Monte Cucco (4-hr round trip) begins from the **Val di Ranco**, a valley which cuts east into the mountains from Costacciaro: follow trail 1 to the summit, via Pian delle Macinare, and trail 2 for the descent (both with yellow and red trail markings).

As well as the lowdown on caving, the centre also supplies information and gear to **hang-gliders**, Monte Cucco being one of Italy's leading centres for the sport. The centre **hires equipment** for other activities too – the area has modest ski runs and a few limestone walls for climbers at Le Lecce and the Fossa Secca.

Park accommodation

There are plenty of **accommodation** possibilities in and around Costacciaro, the best of them the *Monte Cucco da Tobia* in the Val di Ranco (☎075/917.7194; ④), a fabled mountaineers' and cavers' hangout. Also convenient for walkers is the one-star *Cappelloni*, Val di Ranco (May–Sept; ☎075/917.7131; ③). The park centre has **hostel** accommodation (June–Sept daily; Oct–May Sat & Sun; ①), and there's a **youth hostel**, the *Ostello Centro di Volo Libero* (☎075/870.9124; ②), a hang-gliders' hangout, at Villa Scirca, 3km north of Sigillo. Sigillo itself has a few rooms in the *pensione* above the *Pizzeria Dal Lepre*, Via Livio Fazi 21–23 (☎075/917.7733; ④).

The nearest **campsite** is at Fornace, 3km north of Costacciaro – *Rio Verde* (Easter–Sept; ☎075/917.0307). Freelance camping is prohibited within the *parco regionale*, but elsewhere you'll have few problems finding a discreet pitch for a tent.

Nocera Umbra

Sitting on a spur above the Topino valley 15km south of Gualdo, **NOCERA UMBRA** is in some ways a carbon copy of its neighbours, with wooded hills as a backdrop and a new town on the valley floor detracting from an excellent medieval quarter above. It's best known for its bottled **mineral waters**, processed in a large plant by the station, but the nearby spa facilities and the mountains to the east are now beginning to bring the visitors in.

As in Gualdo, the town's main attraction is a small **art gallery**, housed in the church of San Francesco on Piazza Caprera (July & Aug 9.30am–12.30pm & 4–5pm; rest of year call ☎0742/81.246). Saint Francis was probably in Nocera as early as 1215 and by 1221 had been asked to form a convent here; it was ransacked by Frederick II in 1248 and replaced by the present church in 1336. It now houses several pieces by Matteo da Gualdo, a *Madonna and Child* by the Sienese Segna di Bonaventura, a large thirteenth-century *Crucifix* and – the high spot – another polyptych by Alunno, encased in a glorious frame. Archaeological bits and pieces round the place off.

The **Duomo** in Via San Rinaldo is the only other thing to see – and there's not much to it, the interior having been gutted in the eighteenth century.

Practicalities

Highly accessible from Gualdo, Nocera could just as easily be seen from Assisi or from Foligno, 20km to the southwest, both with good **bus** and **rail** links to the town. The station, however, is a long way from the town it's meant to serve, though there are regular connecting buses to the old centre.

For **accommodation**, it's a choice between the central *Europa*, Largo Bisleri 9 (☎0742/818.874; ⑤), the huge *Casa Soggiorno Bagni di Nocera* spa hotel in Bagni di Nocera (☎0742/819.332; ④), or the San Paolo **convent**, Via S. Paolo 13 (☎0742/818.814; ④). There's a **campsite** 1000 metres up on Monte Alago to the east of Nocera, the *Pian delle Stelle* (all year; ☎0742/818.241); to reach it go north on the SS3 and after 1km take the second minor road right (not the Bagnara road) towards the *Rifugio M. Alago*. Another all-year site is *La Valle* (☎0742/810.329), 6km north of Nocera at Colle.

For **food** in town there's little but the standard pizzerias, though in the nearby hamlet of Costa *Il Castello di Malatesta* draws punters from some distance (☎075/810.267; closed Wed); meals are around L30,000.

Bagni di Nocera and the hills

To sample the spa life, take the road to **BAGNI DI NOCERA**, 4km east, where the Sorgente Angelica spring (open June–Oct) has been famous since the seventeenth century. People came from as far away as Portugal and the Middle East to enjoy its supposedly miraculous cures; these days the spa is a modern and characterless complex, partly redeemed by its natural surroundings.

If you have transport, the villages and hilly countryside to the east repay aimless exploration. The main local outing is to **Monte Pennino** (1571m), a minor winter resort, accessible on a road that reaches virtually to the summit.

To the west is a quieter pocket of countryside, a good way to meander towards Assisi, with the well-preserved castle at **Rocca di Posignano** a spot to head for if you want a focus to your itinerary.

travel details

Trains

From Perugia to Foligno (hourly; 40min) via Assisi (25min) and Spello (35min); Teróntola (hourly; 40min) via Passignano (30min), with connections at Teróntola for Rome (6 daily; 2hr), Florence (6 daily; 2hr 15min) and Siena (6 daily; 3hr 30min – changing again at Chiusi); Sansepolcro (hourly; 1hr 40min) via Città di Castello (50min); Terni (hourly; 1hr 50min), via Deruta (30min) and Todi (50min).

From Fossato di Vico (for Gubbio) to Foligno (10 daily; 50min) via Nocera Umbra (20min); Rome (10 daily; 2hr 40min), via Spoleto (1hr 15min), Terni (1hr 30min) and Orte (1hr 55min); Gualdo Tadino (5 daily, 10min).

From Città di Castello to Sansepolcro (hourly; 50min); Perugia (hourly; 50min).

Buses

From Perugia to Assisi (12 daily); Todi (12 daily); Passingnano (12 daily); Chiusi (5 daily); Rome (2 daily); and regular services to Orvieto, Siena and Urbino.

From Gubbio to Fossato di Vico (to connect with trains), continuing to Gualdo Tadino and Nocera Umbra (10 daily); Perugia (10 daily); also services to Città di Castello, Umbértide, Arezzo and Florence.

From Città di Castello to Perugia, Sansepolcro, Umbértide, Gubbio and Arezzo.

CHAPTER TEN

ASSISI AND THE VALE OF SPOLETO

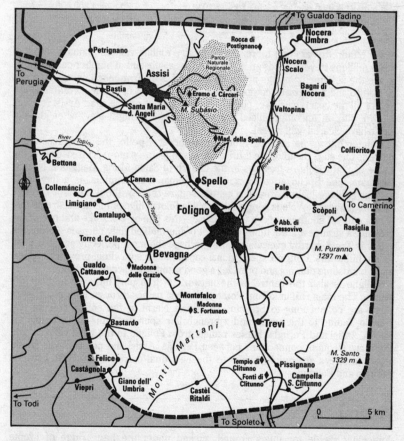

T he **Vale of Spoleto**, the broad plain between Perugia and Spoleto, is Umbria's historic and spiritual heartland: a beautiful sweep of countryside that has a majestic focus in **Assisi**. Birthplace of Saint Francis, Italy's premier saint, this hill town has been a site of pilgrimage for the last

ACCOMMODATION PRICES

Throughout this guide, accommodation is graded on a scale from ① to ⑨. Grades ① and ② apply to **hostel** accommodation, and indicate the lowest price a **single person** could expect to pay for one night in that establishment in high season. Grades ③ to ⑨ apply to **hotels**, and indicate the cost of the **cheapest double room in high season.** The price bands to which these codes refer are as follows:

- ① under L20,000 per person
- ② over L20,000 per person
- ③ under L50,000 per double
- ④ L50–70,000 per double
- ⑤ L70–90,000 per double
- ⑥ L90–120,000 per double
- ⑦ L120–150,000 per double
- ⑧ L150–200,000 per double
- ⑨ over L200,000 per double

seven hundred years and more, attracting five million visitors annually. Most of these millions travel here as an act of faith, but a substantial number come simply to see the sublime paintings in the **Basilica di San Francesco**, where frescoes by **Giotto** and **Lorenzetti** comprise one of the greatest monuments of Italian art. Yet for all the coach parties of pilgrims, both religious and secular, Assisi remains a town with an uncompromised identity – as an overnight stay, when the car parks have cleared, will reveal.

Quieter hill towns are just around the corner. **Spello**, the most accessible, remains one step ahead of the tourist boom and features more art treasures in the shape of Pinturicchio's frescoes in the church of Santa Maria Maggiore. Nearby **Bevagna**, like Spello an outpost on the Roman Via Flaminia, is a tiny, wall-enclosed village locked around a central square that's without equal in Umbria. Lording it over the Vale is **Montefalco**, a windblown hive of medieval streets that is home to yet another superb fresco cycle – this one by Gozzoli – and one of the province's strangest attractions, a quartet of mummified holy corpses. Across the valley is **Trevi**, hardly ever visited, but perhaps the most perfectly situated of all Italian hill towns. **Foligno**, the regional capital, has a sprawling, provincial appeal and a handsome duomo, and provides a good standby for accommodation.

Foligno is also the centre of the network of transport links throughout the region. The main **rail** link from Rome to Ancona passes through Foligno, whence there are connections to Spoleto, Terni and Narni to the south, Nocera and Gualdo Tadino to the north, and a branch line spur that runs to Terόntola via Spello, Assisi and Perugia. **Buses** radiate from Foligno to the local villages, and there are frequent connections between Perugia, Assisi and points to the south. **Road** journeys are quick thanks to the new dual carriageway (SS3) between Perugia and Foligno.

Assisi

Enticingly visible for miles around, tucked under the huge ridge of Monte Subasio, **ASSISI** would be an irresistible target even without the Franciscan sideshow. At close quarters the tacky tourist paraphernalia and mountains of religious kitsch are offset by tranquil backstreets, geranium-filled window boxes, and buildings in the muted, pinkish stone that distinguishes all the Vale's towns.

With sufficient enthusiasm you can see almost all the sights in a day, but the town changes for the better come evening, and it's worth trying to stay at least a night.

Assisi's history is not all tied to the Franciscan masthead. Founded by the Umbrians – in contrast to Perugia's Etruscan heritage – the town later achieved prominence as a Roman *municipium*. Thereafter invaders passed it over, attracted by the richer pickings of Perugia, but in the end it fell under the control of that city's monstrous Baglioni family. These were men, said one Franciscan historian, "who did not shudder to murder men, cook their flesh, and give it to the relations of the slain to eat in their prison dungeons". Plague, famine and eventually Church control turned the town into a moribund backwater. Only Francis's elevation to the status of national saint in 1939 managed to reverse its economic decline.

Arrival, information and accommodation

Getting in and out of Assisi is easy. There are hourly **trains** from Foligno (via Spello) and from Teróntola (via Perugia) to Assisi station, at Santa Maria degli Angeli, 8km from the old town. Half-hourly buses run from the station to **Piazza Matteotti**, some by way of Largo Properzio, east of the Basilica di Santa Chiara – from where there's an unreliable escalator to the gateway at Porta Nuova. Both spots are less than five minutes' walk from the heart of the medieval town, **Piazza del Comune**. From Piazza del Comune, the main street leads west along the ridge of the town to the Basilica di San Francesco.

The main **bus terminal** and a massive underground **car park** are in **Piazza Matteotti**, in the east of the town above the Duomo. A board in the piazza's north-west corner, on the junction of Via del Comune Vecchio, has a full schedule for bus departures, and there's a flashy electronic display next to the ticket and information office, *ASP Agenzia* (daily 7.30am–9.30pm). Long-distance *SULGA* buses to Rome and Florence leave from Piazza San Pietro, at the other end of town.

Parking in central Assisi is virtually impossible, traffic being restricted chiefly to service vehicles. It's best to leave cars in Piazza Matteotti or in Piazza Unità d'Italia (the latter is closer to the Basilica); if you don't mind a long walk to the Basilica, park up by the Rocca, where there are hundreds of free spaces. Orange **minibuses** provide connecting services around the town, though in practice you'll find distances are short and that it's easiest to walk. Minibus tickets are sold at shops and newsagents with an *ASP* or *Comune di Assisi* ticket flash on display.

Information
The **tourist office** is at Piazza del Comune 12 (Mon–Sat 8.30am–1pm & 3.30–6.30pm, Sun 9am–1pm; ☎075/812.534); clearly overworked, the staff do their best to help with finding accommodation and provide some useful maps and pamphlets. Note that the bus and train timetable on the wall outside doesn't show all the bus connections available; for full details check the board in Piazza Matteotti.

Accommodation
There are getting on for a hundred **hotels** in Assisi, along with a large stock of **private rooms** and **pilgrim hostels** (*Case Religiose di Ospitalità*). At most times of year this is just about adequate for the number of visitors, though advance booking is still highly advisable. It is essential if you plan to visit over Easter or during the *Festa di San Francesco* (Oct 3–4) or *Calendimaggio* (May 21–22).

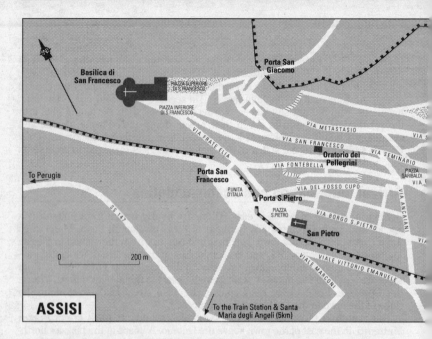

Listings below detail a selection of the best (and generally most central) hotels, hostels and rooms. The **tourist office** can provide full lists of all lodgings, including over fifty rooms for rent, and will make reservations for you, too. For a full list of rooms ask for the special leaflet *Esercizi Extralberghieri:* note that you can get good deals on weekly rates for most private lodgings. Try to insist on a central location, avoiding the concentrations of cheaper rooms and hotels in Santa Maria degli Angeli or the grim little village of Bastia, 4km out. Accommodation is listed below in ascending order of price.

HOTELS

Italia, Vicolo della Fortezza 2 (☎075/812.625). The most central one-star hotel, in an alley off the north side of Piazza del Comune. Open March–Oct. ③.

Anfiteatro Romano, Via Anfiteatro Romano 4 (☎075/813.025). Good-value hotel, in one of the most pleasant parts of town. ④.

La Rocca, Via di P. Perlici 27 (☎075/816.467). Beyond the Duomo at the very end of Via di P. Perlici; quiet and with fine views from some rooms. ④.

Sole, Corso Mazzini 35 (☎075/812.373). Big, functional hotel in a convenient position one minute's walk from the Basilica di Santa Chiara. Also has an annex at Corso Mazzini 20, so a good chance of finding space when other spots are full. ④.

Berti, Piazza San Pietro 29 (☎075/813.466). Located in a quiet piazza, and handy for the Basilica. ⑤.

Garibaldi, Piazza Garibaldi 1 (☎075/812.624). Recently restored hotel housed in an imposing palazzo – just downhill from Piazza del Comune in one of Assisi's quieter corners. ⑤.

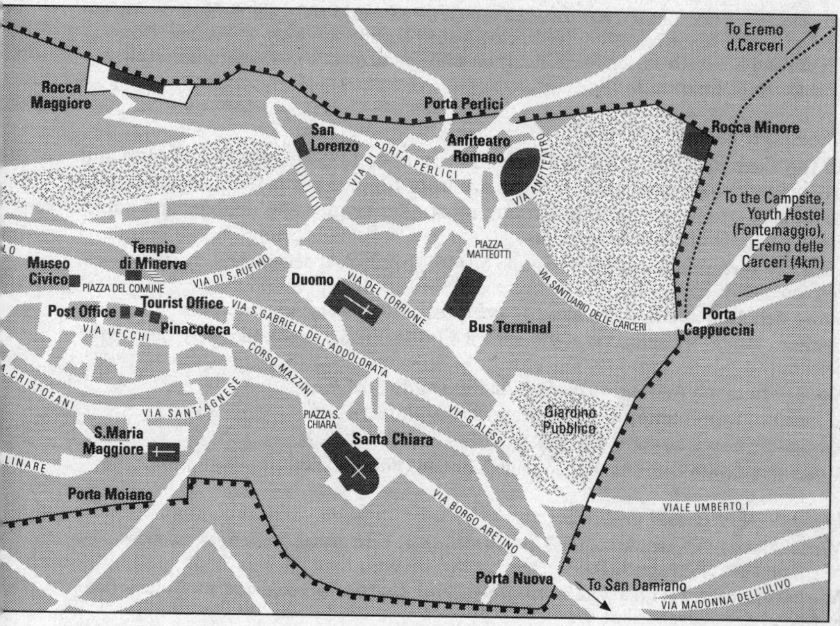

Ideale per Turisti, Piazza Matteotti 1 (☎075/813.570). Follow signs south from Piazza Matteotti a short way outside the walls to reach this rather isolated but very reasonable two-star hotel. ⑤.

Pallotta, Via San Rufino 6 (☎075/812.307). Seven-roomed place in a good location between the Duomo and Piazza del Comune. ⑤.

Posta Panoramica, Via San Paolo 17–19 (☎075/812.558). Central location west of the Duomo – on the street parallel to Via San Francesco. ⑤.

Properzio, Via San Francesco 38b (☎075/813.188). Simple, 11-roomed hotel handily placed on the main street between Piazza del Comune and the Basilica. ⑤.

San Pietro, Piazza San Pietro 5 (☎075/812.452). Large but rather perfunctory three-star hotel by the gate south of the Basilica. ⑤.

Umbra, Vicolo degli Archi 6 (☎075/812.240). Good upmarket choice, almost immediately off the southern edge of Piazza del Comune. ⑤.

Del Viaggiatore, Via Sant'Antonio 14 (☎075/816.297). Small, personal hotel above a decent restaurant; south of the Duomo. ⑤.

Porta Nuova, Viale Umberto I 21 (☎075/812.405). Basic three-star standby south of Piazza Matteotti in a quiet area above Basilica di Santa Chiara. ⑥.

Dei Priori, Corso Mazzini 15 (☎075/812.237). Three-star, 34-room hotel, slightly east of Piazza del Comune. ⑥.

San Francesco, Via San Francesco 48 (☎075/812.281). Conveniently situated three-star hotel just a minute's walk from the Basilica; 45 rooms so there's a good chance of finding space. ⑥.

Fontebella, Via Fontebella 25 (☎075/812.456). Most elegant and intimate of Assisi's smart hotels: try for a room on the top two floors for views over the rooftops and the Vale of Spoleto. ⑧.

Subasio, Via Frate Elia 2 (☎075/812.206). Full of old-world style, the Subasio is Assisi's hotel of choice if you're feeling flush: past guests include the likes of Marlene Dietrich, Chaplin and Elizabeth Taylor. Surprisingly unstuffy for all that; rooms vary considerably, but the majority have views. ⑧.

PILGRIM HOSTELS

All the *Case Religiose di Ospitalità* below are open to both women and men and are located in the town proper. Costs are from L15,000 per person, depending on how many people are sharing a room; most offer singles and doubles and sometimes a couple of dormitory rooms.

Casa del Terziario, Piazza del Vescovado 5 (☎075/812.366). A definite first choice for location and rooms.

Suore dell'Atonement, Via G. Alessi 10 (☎075/812.542). Run by American nuns.

Instituto Beata Angelina, Via Merry del Val 4 (☎075/812.511). A location very close to the Basilica.

Monastero Santa Andrea, Vicolo Sant'Andrea (☎075/812.274).

Monastero San Coletta, Borgo San Pietro 3 (☎075/812.345).

Monastero San Giuseppe, Via Sant'Apollinare 1 (☎075/812.332).

Monastero Santo Quirico, Via Giovanni di Borino (☎075/812.688).

ROOMS IN PRIVATE HOUSES

Maria Alunni, Via dell'Acquario 3 (☎075/813.182). Charming proprietress; spotless, airy rooms and lots of greenery. ③.

Mariella Bacchi, Via Frate Elia 6 (☎075/806.5200). One double room near the *Subasio* hotel just 100m east of the Basilica. ③.

Il Duomo, Vicolo San Lorenzo 2 (☎075/812.742). The best private lodgings in town, located in a tiny flower-decked medieval alley; walk up Via P. Perlici from the Duomo and Vicolo San Lorenzo is second on the left. ③.

Marco Gambacorta, Via Sermei 9 (☎075/812.783). Six double rooms in the small lane immediately north of the Basilica di Santa Chiara off Via Santa Chiara. ③.

Giustina Lanfaloni, Borgo San Pietro 13 (☎075/813.356). A hundred metres up from San Pietro on the right. Out of the way and a good chance of space. ③.

Annalisa Martini, Via San Gregorio 6 (☎075/813.536). Six rooms in the second alley on the left off Via Portica after leaving Piazza del Comune. ③.

Maria Fortini, Via Villamena 19 (☎075/812.715). Just off Piazza Matteotti on a street leading to Porta Perlici. ④.

Bernardo Pampanini, Piazza Matteotti 2 (☎075/813.020). Three doubles in one of the less medieval corners of Assisi, but still convenient for all the sights. ④.

YOUTH HOSTELS

Ostello di Fontemaggio, Strada Eremo delle Carceri 8, at the hamlet of Fontemaggio, 3km down the road to the Eremo delle Carceri (☎075/813.636 or 812.317). Clean, ten-bed, single-sex dorms; ①. Or a choice of 15 one-star hotel rooms; ④.

Ostello della Pace, Via San Pietro Campagna (☎075/816.767). New hostel located on the road that leads west out of town from Porta San Pietro and Viale G. Marconi. ②.

CAMPSITES

Fontemaggio, Strada Eremo delle Carceri 8 (☎075/813.636). 244-pitch site alongside the youth hostel at Fontemaggio and under the same management (see above). Open all year, with full services and adjoining supermarket.

Internazionale Assisi, Via S. Giovanni Campiglione 110 (☎075/813.710). Not such a pleasant setting, 3km west of Assisi on the SS147 to Bastia. Open all year.

The Basilica di San Francesco

The **Basilica di San Francesco** ranks second only to Saint Peter's in Rome as a point of Catholic pilgrimage, and its cycle of paintings by Giotto has long been considered one of the turning points in western art, moving from the Byzantine world of iconic saints and Madonnas to one of humanist narrative.

The building also has an extraordinary history. It was conceived, shortly after Francis's death, by the man who had taken over the running of the order a decade or so earlier, one **Elias of Cortona**. Elias, one of the saint's earliest disciples, served as Vicar General of the Franciscans through to 1239, presiding over a series of bitter disputes and schisms, until eventually being displaced from the leadership and excommunicated. In the early years of the post-Francis order, however, he was firmly in control and running things very much his way, capitalising on the popular appeal of the saint to build the Franciscans into the most powerful force possible, and raising all the necessary money to make the founder's Basilica one of the great Christian shrines. To the horror of the more ascetic and zealous followers of the saint – with whom Francis himself had allied in his last years – Elias set about a massive fundraising project, selling indulgences across Europe.

The "fundamentalist" wing argued that the indulgences were a corruption and the proposed magnificence at odds with Francis's maxim that "small churches should be built, for they ought not to raise great churches for the sake of preaching to the people or for any other reason, for they will show greater humility and give a better example by going to preach in other churches". They pointed out, too, that Francis's choice of burial site was intended as a gesture of humility – he had picked one of the most despised spots of medieval Assisi, known as the Colle del Inferno, or Infernal Hill, where criminals were taken for execution. It was to little avail. The burial site was rechristened "Hill of Paradise" and a building more ambitious than any in Italy was begun.

While construction of the Basilica proceeded, the political background became increasingly murky and tangled, the strangest twist coming on the day of Francis's canonisation. Elias by this time had fallen out with the papacy, who were organising the ceremony, and as the saint's hearse proceeded through the streets of Assisi he and a posse burst on to the scene and seized the body. Ignoring the anger of the crowd and the indignation of the papal entourage, they hurried the coffin into the Lower Church and bolted the doors behind them. Prompted perhaps by the fear that his master's remains would be stolen or desecrated – medieval relics had enormous financial and spiritual value – Elias had decided to bury Francis in a secret, Pharaoh-like tomb deep within the Basilica.

The episode gave rise to a myth, retailed by Vasari, that a vast hidden church had been built below the Basilica, far greater in beauty and grandeur than the churches above. Inside this vast, sealed chamber it was believed the body of the "almost alive saint" hovered above the altar awaiting his call to Heaven. The tomb actually remained undiscovered, or at least unreached, until a two-month search in 1818.

The construction of the Basilica is in two tiers, with one church placed on top of the other. This audacious idea posed enormous practical engineering problems, which were solved by the use of massive arched buttressing that effectively propped up the western end of the town. One of the wonders of early medieval architecture, its originator is unknown, all the original drawings having been burnt in a raid by the Perugians. Most historians presume it to have been the work of Lombard masons, who would have drawn for inspiration on the Gothic models of southern France. As one of the earliest examples of Italian Gothic, the Basilica exerted great architectural influence, its single-naved Upper Church setting a precedent for countless Franciscan churches around the country.

Admission to both parts of the Basilica is free. Both are open daily from 6.30am to 7.30pm (except Nov–March when both may close noon–2pm), though the Upper Church may close or have restricted opening on Sundays; both close on holy days. If possible, visit early or late in the day: the crowds at other times make it hard to get a view of the frescoes. It's also worth taking a couple of minutes to wander the **cloisters**, entered from the Lower Church. One final point – the custodians of the Basilica enforce their dress code extremely vigorously, so don't turn up with arms and legs exposed.

SAINT FRANCIS OF ASSISI

Saint Francis is the most extraordinary figure that the Italian church has produced, a revolutionary spirit who took Christianity back to basics. The impact that he had upon the evolution of the Catholic church stands without parallel, and everything he accomplished in his short life was achieved by nothing more persuasive than the power of preaching and personal example. Dante placed him alongside another Messianic figure, John the Baptist, and his appeal has remained undiminished – Mussolini, of all people, called him "il piu santo dei santi" (the most saintly of the saints).

The events of his life, though doubtless encrusted with myth, are well chronicled. He was born in Assisi in 1182, the son of a wealthy merchant and a Provençal woman – which is why he replaced his baptismal name, Giovanni, with Francesco (Little Frenchman). The Occitan literature of Provence, with its troubadour songs and courtly love poems, was later to be the making of Francis as a poet and speaker. One of the earliest writers in the vernacular, Francis laid the foundation of a great Franciscan literary tradition – his *Fioretti* and famous *Canticle to the Sun* ("brother sun . . . sister moon") stand comparison with the best of medieval verse.

In line with the standard early life of most saints, his formative years were full of drinking and womanising; he was, says one chronicler, "the first instigator of evil, and behind none in foolishness". Illness and imprisonment in a Perugian jail instilled the first seeds of contemplation. Abstinence and solitary wanderings soon followed. The call from God, the culmination of several visions, came in Assisi in 1209, when the crucifix in San Damiano bowed to him and told him to repair God's Church. Francis took the injunction literally, sold his father's stock of cloth and gave the money to Damiano's priest, who refused it.

Francis subsequently renounced his inheritance in the Piazza del Comune: before a large crowd and his outraged father, he stripped naked in a symbolic rejection of wealth and worldly shackles. Adopting the peasant's grey sackcloth (the brown Franciscan habit came later), he began to beg, preach and mix with lepers, a deliberate embodiment of Christ's invocation to the Apostles "to heal the sick, and carry neither purse, nor scrip [money], nor shoes". His message was disarmingly simple – throw out the materialistic trappings of daily life, and return to a love of God rooted in poverty, chastity and obedience. Furthermore, learn to see in the beauty and profusion of the natural world the all-pervasive hand of the Divine – a keystone of humanist thought, and a departure from the doom-laden strictures of the Dark Ages.

The Lower Church

The sombre **Lower Church** – down the steps to the left – is the place to begin if you want to follow the architectural and artistic chronology of the shrine. Its convoluted floor plan and low-lit vaults were intended to create a mood of calm and meditative introspection. The low-level natural light has recently been augmented by fairly discreet spotlighting, a modernisation that has inevitably altered the atmosphere of the chapel, but at last makes it possible to study the frescoes and intricate decoration that cover every available surface, so densely that they really need several visits to take it all in.

The highlights span a century of continuous artistic development. Somewhat stilted early works by Byzantine-influenced artists line the walls of the main nave, several of them credited to the mysterious **Maestro di San Francesco**, the anonymous hand which crops up elsewhere in Umbria. Telling the story of Saint

In time he gathered his own twelve apostles and, after some difficulty, obtained permission from Pope Innocent III to found an order that espoused no dogma and maintained no rule. Francis himself never became a priest. In 1212 he created a second order for women, the Poor Clares, and continued the vast peregrinations that took him as far as the Holy Land with the armies of the Crusades. (The Italian equivalent of "shanks's pony" is "il cavallo di San Francesco" – Saint Francis's horse.) In Egypt he confronted the Sultan, Melek el-Kamel, offering to undergo a trial by fire to prove his faith. On another occasion, in the Lazio village of Greccio, he produced the first ever Christmas crib: a real-life tableau, complete with cows and sheep, it was perhaps the most striking example of the earthy Franciscan style.

In 1224 Francis received the stigmata on the mountaintop at La Verna (see p.392). Two years later, nursing his exhausted body, he died on the mud floor of his hovel in Assisi, having scorned the offer of the bishop's palace. His canonisation followed swiftly, in 1228 in a service conducted by Pope Gregory. His eulogistic tribute, delivered in a mournful and booming voice, was broken intermittently by uncontrollable sobs. Accolade followed accolade, as he compared the saint to "a full moon, a rising sun . . . the morning star hovering above dawn mists". A subdeacon read an extended list of Francis's miracles, while a learned cardinal – "not without copious weeping" – provided a running commentary on his deeds, the pope listening, with "rivers of tears punctuated by deep-drawn wails". Priests and the attendant entourage wept so piteously that "their vestments were in great part wet and the ground was drenched with their tears".

Almost immediately after his death the first schism arose in the Franciscan order over the building of the grandiose Basilica for the saint's mausoleum (see main text). A split in the order was inevitable, though. Francis's message and movement had few sympathisers in the wealthy and morally bankrupt papacy of the time, and while his popularity had obliged the Vatican to applaud while he was alive, the papacy quickly moved in to quash the purist elements and encourage the more "moderate" wings. Gradually it shaped the movement to its own designs, institutionalising Francis's message in the process.

For all the subsequent history, however, Francis's achievement as the first man to fracture the rigid orthodoxy of the hierarchical Church is beyond question. Moreover, the Franciscans have not lost their ideological edge, and their views on the primacy of poverty are thought by many to be out of favour with the current pope.

Francis, they are faded and in places have been obliterated by the chapels opened up to accommodate the rising number of pilgrims. Alongside these painters are Roman artists like **Cavallini**, who with **Cimabue** pioneered the development of fresco. After them came **Giotto**, and after him the masters of the Sienese School, **Simone Martini** and **Pietro Lorenzetti**.

CIMABUE

Cenno di Pepo, popularly known as **Cimabue** (c.1240–1302), was the first great named artist to work on the Basilica. Vasari's *Lives of the Artists* opens with an account of him, in which he is described as the father of Italian painting, and an obsessional perfectionist, often destroying work with which he was not completely happy. He probably painted in the transepts of the Upper Church between 1270 and 1280, and in the Lower Church some time later.

His major work in the Lower Church is in the **right transept**, the over-restored *Madonna, Child and Angels with St Francis*. Ruskin described this painting as the noblest depiction of the Virgin in Christendom. It includes the famous portrait of Saint Francis, which you'll already have seen plastered all over the town. To the saint's left, on the side wall, is another much-duplicated portrait, believed to be Saint Clare, founder of the women's wing of the Franciscans (see p.456). The painting shows a clear attempt at the depiction of emotion, the use of light and shade to add verisimilitude to figures, and the creation of a coherent three-dimensional sense of space – all first steps on the path trodden later with more certainty by Giotto and the Sienese.

GIOTTO

The question of **Giotto**'s involvement in the Basilica has been at the centre of one of Italy's greatest art history controversies. Informed opinion earlier this century decided that Giotto had never painted in Assisi at all. Some still hold this view, though the modern consensus is that Giotto was responsible for the bulk of the paintings in the Upper Church, which he executed from about 1295.

Authorship in the Lower Church is more dubious, and credit for the allegorical frescoes in the **vaults over the altar** – some of the church's most beautiful and complex – has been taken from Giotto and given to nameless assistants. The same goes for the *Life of Mary Magdalene* cycle in the **Cappella della Maddalena**, the third chapel on the right. In the hothouse atmosphere of the Basilica during its decoration, however, cross-fertilisation and joint efforts must have been commonplace – so definitive judgements are all but impossible.

SIMONE MARTINI

Simone Martini's frescoes in the **Cappella di San Martino**, the first chapel on the left as you enter the nave, are more certainly attributed. He worked here in the mid-1310s, shortly after painting the great *Maestà* in Siena, and was given completely free rein – every detail, even the floor and stained glass, came under his control.

The panels on the underside of the arch as you enter the chapel were probably painted in 1317. They show eight saints, and were painted to honour Saint Louis of Toulouse, who had just been sanctified – he is the red-robed figure in the upper left panel, flanked by saints Francis, Anthony and Clare.

In the interior chapel, a far more distinct and insular space than much of the Lower Church, is a complete fresco cycle of the life of **Saint Martin of Tours**. The father of monasticism in France, Martin was venerated as far afield as Ireland

and Africa; here, however, he is featured partly as a sop to the Franciscan friar who commissioned the chapel, who had been made cardinal with the title of San Martino ai Monti. The ten-panel cycle starts on the left-hand wall and moves clockwise around the chapel, the lowest four panels on both walls representing scenes from the secular part of Martin's life, the remaining four wall frescoes and two painted ceiling vaults treating the period after his conversion.

Martin was born in 315 in what is now Hungary and brought up in Italy at Pavi. The key event of his conversion – and the first depicted in the cycle – came as a young officer at Amiens, when he gave half his cloak to a beggar, a figure he was later led to recognise as Christ. To the right is the *Dream of St Martin*, in which Christ and angels appear to the saint, a panel which mingles secular and sacred iconography amid a panoply of courtly emblems. This trait is continued in the next panel on the right-hand wall, *St Martin is Knighted*, which is an out and out evocation of life at court without religious iconography of any kind. To its right is the scene where *St Martin Renounces his Weapons* – "I am Christ's soldier; I am not allowed to fight." Here too, Martini seems to reserve his finest painting for the background: the tents, spears, lances and costumes of the Roman camp and the Emperor Julian.

The narrative moves to the second tier back on the left-hand wall, starting with the *Meditation*, with the saint moved to distraction by contemplation of the Divine, and unmoved by the acolytes trying to direct his attention to the Mass. On its right is the *Miraculous Mass*, an unusual subject portrayed here for the first time. Martin has again given a cloak to a beggar, and is about to celebrate Mass when angels appear to present him with a beautifully embroidered piece of material. Across on the right-hand wall is the *Miracle of the Resurrected Child*, another episode never before depicted in Italian art, in which Martin, transported by artistic licence to Siena (the city's Palazzo Pubblico is in the background) raises a child from the dead before its mother and an expectant crowd. Both this and the next fresco, the *Miracle of Fire*, are damaged, though the sense of the scene is clear – a tongue of flame is forced down the throat of the Emperor Valentinian for refusing to give Martin an audience.

The uppermost level describes two self-explanatory scenes, the saint's death and burial, both distinguished by the exquisite detail of the saint's robes, and by the architectural details which correspond to the moods of the episodes: severe, bare-walled and geometrical around the scene of death, and more ornate in the Gothic chapel that hosts the funeral.

PIETRO LORENZETTI

Simone's Sienese contemporary, **Pietro Lorenzetti** is represented by a beautiful series of works in the **transept** and **chapel left of the main altar**. Recent criticism sees the *Six Stories of the Passion*, on the ceiling of the left-hand transept, as his earliest surviving works, probably painted on a visit to Assisi in about 1314. Restrained, static pieces, they betray the influence of Duccio, an impulse shrugged off when the artist returned to the Basilica in the years 1324–25 and 1327–28. By this time he had absorbed the lessons of Giotto, bringing them to bear on the *Passion of Christ* in the left transept, a cycle he had probably started on his visit ten years earlier.

The frescoes portraying scenes leading up to Christ's crucifixion are comparatively weak. The *Last Supper*, however, in which Christ and the Apostles are crowded into a curious hexagonal loggia, reveals a treatment of light and shadow hardly matched during the trecento. The moon and stars light the sky, while to

BASILICA DI SAN FRANCESCO, ASSISI

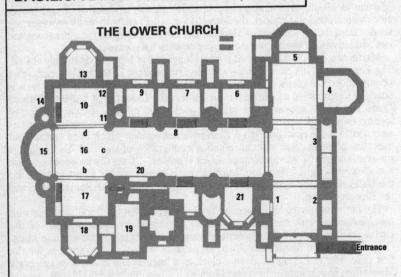

THE LOWER CHURCH

1. Cappella di San Sebastiano.
2. Pulpit (1459).
3. Tomb of Filippo di Courtenay.
4. Tomb of Blascio Fernandez.
5. Tomb of Cardinal Albornoz (by Gattapone).
   Frescoes (1368) by Andrea da Bologna.
6. Life of San Stefano by Dono Doni (1575).
7. Cappella di San Antonio di Padua. Frescoes (1610)
   by Cesare Sermei da Orvieto.
8. Stairway to the crypt and the Tomb of St. Francis.
9. Frescoes by Giotto or School of Giotto.
10. Right Transept: frescoes by Giotto, Cimabue and
    followers.
11. Portrait of St. Francis (Cimabue ?).
12. Five Saints (Martini ?) incl. Portrait of St. Clare
    (fourth left).
13. Cappella di San Nicola; scenes from the Life of
    St. Nicola by followers of Giotto.
14. Entrance to cloisters, Tesoro and the Upper
    Church.
15. Choir (1471).
16. Vaults of the High Altar by Giotto and/or
    followers of Giotto:
    a. Apotheosis - St. Francis Enthroned.
    b. Allegory of Obedience.
    c. Allegory of Poverty.
    d. Allegory of Chastity.

17. Left transept: frescoes by Pietro Lorenzetti
    (assisted by Ambrogio Lorenzetti?).
18. Cappella di S.G. Battista (1288) Madonna and
    Child with SS. Francis and John by Pietro
    Lorenzetti.
19. Sacristy. Relics of St. Francis and Madonna
    and Child (Umbrian anon).
20. Pulpit Niche Coronation of the Virgin by
    Puccio Capanna d' Assisi.
21. Cappella di San Martino. Scenes from the Life of
    St. Martin (1322) by Simone Martini.

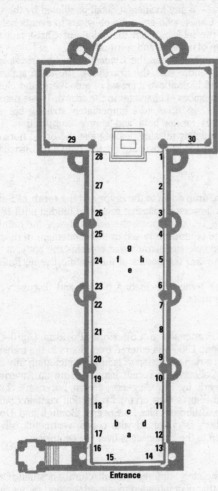

1. Homage in Piazza del Comune.
2. Francis offers cloak to a poor man.
3. The dream of the weapons.
4. Francis's calling in San Damiano.
5. Francis before his father in the Assisi.
6. Francis appears to Innocent III in a dream.
7. Innocent III approves the Franciscan Order.
8. Francis appears to his companions in a flaming chariot.
9. Brother Leone sees the celestial throne destined for St. Francis.
10. Francis chases the Devils from Arezzo.
11. Francis proposes trial by fire before the Sultan.
12. The ecstasy of Francis.
13. The Christmas crib at Greccio.
14. Francis causes a fountain to flow.
15. The sermon to the birds.
16. Francis predicts the death of a man.
17. Francis preaches before Pope Onorio III.
18. Francis appears to the Franciscan friars at Arles.
19. Francis receives the stigmata.
20. The death and funeral of Francis.
21. Francis appears to Brother Augustin and the Bishop of Assisi.
22. The truth of the stigmata confirmed.
23. St. Clare mourns at San Damiano.
24. The Canonization of St. Francis.
25. Francis appears to Pope Gregory IX.
26. The recovery of a man from a mortal wound.
27. The triumph of a woman after confession.
28. Pietro d' Alife, accused of heresy, released from prison.
29. Crucifixion by Cimabue (1277), and Five Apocalyptic Scenes.
30. Crucifixion and Life of St. Peter by Cimabue.

Entrance

THE UPPER CHURCH

a. St. Jerome - (by Filippo Rusuti?).
b. St. Ambrose ("   "   ").
c. St. Gregory ("   "   ").
d. St. Augustine("   "   ").
e. St. Francis   - by Jacopo Torriti (1290).
f. Virgin Mary   ("   "   "   ").
g. Christ   ("   "   "   ").
h. John the Baptist ("   "   "   ").

the left is a kitchen illuminated by light from a fire, in which servants unconcernedly scrape food into a dog's bowl – a fine incidental detail paralleled by the two chattering servants to the left of Christ, who are quite oblivious to events before them. The only illumination at the table is from the haloes of Christ and the Apostles, a deliberate juxtapostion of material and spiritual light.

Three other panels stand out in the cycle: the *Entombment, Crucifixion* and *Deposition.* Dominating almost an entire wall, the *Crucifixion* shows an amazing sense of drama, with Christ raised high above a crowd of onlookers, and closer study reveals carefully observed nuances of character in the crowd. These natural touches recur in the faces of the *Deposition,* less immediately striking but still amongst Lorenzetti's masterpieces for its bold and simple composition. The upper portion of the Cross is completely missing, leaving just the broad horizontal and huge amounts of vacant space, all focusing on the figure of Christ, his limbs bent with rigor mortis.

THE TOMB

Before leaving the Lower Church, drop down to the **crypt** and the **tomb of Saint Francis** and four of his closest followers, a spot that remained hidden until 1818. The present tomb, rebuilt in the 1920s, respects the saint's desire for humble burial, replacing a more elaborate tabernacle raised in the excitement of discovery. Above the main altar is the simple stone coffin that contains the body; at the four corners of the central canopy are the bodies of the beatific Leone, Rufino, Masseo and Angelo.

There's a short account of the tomb's fascinating history and discovery (in English) tacked to the bare stone walls.

THE TREASURY MUSEUM

The **Tesoro Basilica di San Francesco e Collezione Perkins** (April–Oct Mon–Sat 9.30am–12.30pm & 2–6pm; L3000) is entered from doors in the transept behind the main altar. It contains a rich collection of paintings, including fifty-five masterpieces from the Perkins Collection, a recent bequest from an American philanthropist which includes work by Fra' Angelico, Pietro Lorenzetti, Luca Signorelli and Masolino. The museum's own original collection contains paintings by Gozzoli and little-known Umbrians like Lo Spagna, Bonfigli and Dono Doni. The remainder of the gallery is crammed with copes, vestments, silverware, tapestries and the like, given to the Franciscans over the centuries.

The Upper Church

The **Upper Church** is a completely different architectural, aesthetic and emotional experience, its airy Gothic plan intended to stir celebration rather than contemplation. In fact it feels less a church than a gallery for **Giotto**'s dazzling frescoes on the **Life of St Francis**.

GIOTTO'S LIFE OF ST FRANCIS

Giotto's cycle starts from the far right-hand side of the nave. Although a consensus has not been achieved by critics over the date of the frescoes, most believe they are early works, painted with assistants some time around 1296, when he was aged just 29. The style and peripheral narrative content of the last four frescoes of the twenty-eight has led to their being attributed to the so-called **Maestro di Santa Cecilia**, who may also have overpainted parts of the first panel.

Giotto was by far the most important artist to work in the Basilica. Dante immediately recognised his supremacy and in a famous passage (actually intended to illustrate the hollowness of earthly glory) wrote: "Cimabue thought to lord it over painting's field / And now his fame is obscured and the cry is Giotto". It seems that he actually got the commission on the prompting of Cimabue, and that some test pieces in the Lower Church persuaded the friars that Giotto was equal to the task of decorating the upper part of the Basilica.

Like many writers and artists of the age, Giotto was a member of the Franciscan Tertiaries – a lay order which had occupied much of the saint's last years. His frescoes reveal a profound sympathy for the spirit of Saint Francis and show an almost total rejection of the artistic language of the Byzantines, whose remote icons were highly inappropriate for Francis's very human message. The cycles are full of the natural beauty that moved the saint to such profound joy, and the figures are mobile and expressive – aspects of Giotto's art typified by the famous panel showing *The Sermon to the Birds*. More than any other, this fresco crystallises the essence of Franciscan humility, with the flock addressed as an indivisible part of God's creation and attending to the saint as a creature distinct from them solely by virtue of the power of speech.

Giotto's narrative genius cuts straight to the heart of the matter, as seen in the very first panel, *The Homage in Piazza del Comune*, in which the universality of Francis's appeal is evoked in a single act of tribute. Moreover, the frescoes display a wealth of everyday detail that made them accessible to the ordinary people of his age, just as Dante's poetry was accessible to anyone with a command of the vernacular. Thus the first people to look at *Francis Offering his Cloak to a Poor Man* would have recognised the world in which it is set as the one they themselves inhabited – the backdrop includes a detailed view of Assisi from the Porta Nuova, along with the Benedictine abbey on Monte Subasio, now vanished. This attention to the tone and substance of the real world, to its textures and solidity, makes the art of Giotto as revolutionary as was Francis's message to the medieval church.

THE CHOIR AND THE OTHER FRESCOES
The **choir** is a second focal point after the Giotto frescoes. Its hundred and five inlaid stalls – completed in the fifteenth century – are of immense intricacy and delicacy, most of them depicting famous Franciscans or episodes from their lives. The central throne is a papal seat, the only one in the country outside Saint Peter's in Rome.

Behind the throne, and in the left transept, are frescoes by Giotto's probable master, **Cimabue**. These are now almost ruined from the oxidation of badly chosen pigments, though the transept's *Crucifixion* remains an impressive composition, its dynamism an obvious departure from static Byzantine order. Giotto and Duccio may have helped on the painting as pupils.

Running around the church immediately above Giotto's Franciscan panels is another much damaged though virtually complete cycle depicting *Scenes from the Old and New Testaments*. Vasari believed these scenes were by Cimabue, though today they are attributed to artists of the Roman school – **Torriti**, **Rusuti** and **Cavallini** – who were working in the church around the same time. Before coming to Assisi all three had worked primarily in mosaic, a traditional Byzantine medium, but in the Basilica they turned to fresco, moving, like Cimabue, with cautious innovation towards a freer interpretation of old themes. The *Four Doctors of the Church* (in the vaults), especially, shows a narrative sense absent in earlier art: cloaks are left thrown over chairs, books lie open as if half-read. The Doctors, moreover, are depicted as characters in their own right, distinct individuals rather than the symbolic representatives of artistic convention.

Via San Francesco to the Piazza del Comune

East from the Basilica, the trinket-lined **Via San Francesco** heads off along the ridge of medieval Assisi towards the Piazza del Comune. To each side steep and often stepped alleyways lead down to city gates and peripheral churches, of which **San Pietro** most rewards the effort.

San Pietro

Wonderfully restored to its Romanesque-Gothic state, **San Pietro** is a peaceful antidote to the crowds of the Basilica above it. Grass and benches outside offer fine views over the Vale of Spoleto and of the fine, two-tiered facade – pink below, creamy-white above – with its three huge rose windows.

Originally Benedictine, the church dates from the thirteenth century, though it may have been founded as long ago as the second century. The bare interior, mainly Romanesque, also shows the first hints of Gothic in its gently pointed arches and in the ceiling, supported by strange curved vaulting.

Via San Francesco

Along **Via San Francesco** itself there are several minor sights. The first of them, on the left at no. 14, is Assisi's finest medieval town house, the headquarters of the masons' guild, known as the **Casa dei Maestri Comacini**, as a disproportionate number of the Basilica's builders hailed from Como. At no. 11 is the **Oratorio dei Pellegrini** (daily 9am–noon & 3–8pm; free), an exquisite fifteenth-century building that served as a hospice for visiting pilgrims. The interior is covered in frescoes, some by Matteo da Gualdo, with faded samples outside under the wooden-eaved exterior. If people are at prayer here, you may have to content yourself with a glimpse of the paintings through the glass door.

A short way beyond the hospice on the right is the arched portico of **Monte Frumentario**, a thirteenth-century hospital adjoining the **Fontano di Corletta**, whose inscription warns that the penalty for washing your smalls in the water was one *scudo* and the surrender of your laundry.

The **Museo Civico** (daily Easter–Nov 4 9.30am–1pm & 3–6pm; L2500), almost at the end of the street, is a nondescript affair, housed in the crypt of the defunct church of San Nicolò. Bar a few busts in the first section (visible from the street), the show is extremely dull. A passage from the museum runs under the Piazza del Comune, where excavations are in progress to uncover the Roman forum without disrupting the piazza above; at present it's hard to make any sense of the underground maze.

Piazza del Comune

Built on the site of the Roman forum, the **Piazza del Comune** is a stunning medieval square, lined with plenty of pricey bars from which to watch your fellow pilgrims. The **tourist office** is here, as are the **post office** and the SIP telephones, housed in a frescoed medieval hall complete with vaulted ceilings.

The piazza is dominated by the **Tempio di Minerva**, six Corinthian columns and a pediment from a Roman temple – a perfectly preserved and now dazzlingly restored facade from the first century. It was the only thing Goethe wanted to see in Assisi, and he went overboard for it – "the first complete classical monument I have seen . . . so perfect in design . . . I cannot describe the sensations which this work aroused in me, but I know they are going to bear fruit for ever." He didn't bother with the Basilica, calling it a "Babylonian pile". While the temple is great from the outside, the interior is a seventeenth-century conversion of no interest whatever.

On the other side of the piazza, the much-restored **Palazzo Comunale** contains the town's **Pinacoteca** (Tues–Sun 9am–noon & 4–7pm; L2500), whose collection seems very small beer in the light of the riches in the churches. Artists represented – mainly Umbrian – include followers of Giotto, Ottaviano Nelli, Nicolò Alunno and the anonymous L'Ingegno (The Genius).

The Duomo, Santa Chiara and the Rocca

East of the Piazza del Comune, the Franciscan trail continues, with important stops at the **Duomo** and **Santa Chiara**. Up in the northeast corner of the walls a sweep of park leads to the **Rocca** – the best-preserved castle in Umbria, with fine views over the city.

The Duomo

The typically three-tiered Umbrian facade of the **Duomo** is a captivating sight as you emerge from the narrow streets. Its Romanesque **portal**, though dirty and worn, is a superb piece of carving, guarded by two red marble lions and framed by lilies, leaves, faces, penguins, winged crocodiles and a pair of griffons. Look for the child being suckled in the lunette, and its two dour, stony-faced parents. Alongside is a huge, stolid **campanile**, managing somehow to fit into the overall scheme of the church. A small museum, the **Cripta della Basilica Ugoniana** (daily 9.30am–noon & 2.30–6.30pm; L1000), down steps to the right contains fragments of the earlier churches that occupied the site.

Inside, the main point of interest is the **font** used to baptise Saint Francis, Saint Clare and the future Emperor Frederick II, born prematurely in a nearby village. It's at the near end of the church on the right, fronted by Romanesque statues of a lion and winged cow. There are a couple of offbeat sights, too: a terra-cotta Virgin (left of the altar) which burst into tears in 1494, and a stone knelt on by an angel attending Francis's baptism – he left the imprint of his knee on it. The **Museo Capitolare della Cattedrale** (daily Easter–Nov 4 9.30am–noon & 2.30–6pm; L1000), midway down the right aisle, features a fine triptych by Alunno, showing scenes from the life of Saint Rufino, Assisi's martyred first bishop.

The Basilica di Santa Chiara

South of the Duomo, though easiest reached from the Piazza del Comune, is the **Basilica di Santa Chiara** (daily 7am–noon & 2pm–dusk; free), the burial place of Saint Clare, Saint Francis's devoted follower. The church was consecrated in 1265, twelve years after her death, on the site formerly occupied by the church of San Giorgio, where Saint Francis had gone to school and where his body had lain during construction of the Basilica.

The church is a virtual facsimile of the Basilica di San Francesco, with its simple facade and opulent rose window. Its engineering, however, wasn't up to the same standards, and the strange buttresses were added in 1351 to prevent collapse.

The **interior** is dark and bare. A seventeenth-century German bishop called Spader, afraid that the nuns might be corrupted by contact with worldly tourists, had its cycle of frescoes obliterated. Only a few patches of earlier Sienese frescoes from the original San Giorgio have survived, in a couple of chapels off the right aisle – one of which contains the Byzantine **crucifix** that bowed its head to Francis along with various clothes and oddments that belonged to Clare and Francis. The **body of Clare** herself, now back from a session with a Roman saint-restorer, rests in the Baroque horror of the **crypt**.

The Rocca

The seductive medieval **streets** leading up from the Duomo to the Rocca are the quietest in Assisi, partly because of their distance from tourist targets, but perhaps as much due to their fierce gradients. They have another attraction, too, in that this is where you'll find the cheapest bars and snacks.

Rising above the town, the **Rocca Maggiore** (summer daily 9am–8pm; winter officially daily 10am–4pm but usually on the whim of the caretaker; L3000) dates back to Charlemagne, who is supposed to have raised the first defensive walls here after sacking the town. The structure you see today, though, owes most to one Cardinal Albornoz, who arrived to assert papal authority in 1367, repairing an earlier castle that had been ravaged by repeated skirmishes with Perugia. Church governors cruelly dispensed justice by hanging criminals from the battlements or by throwing them out of a castle window into the ravine. The fortress is well worth the climb, with its looming towers, turrets and parapets, and the green surrounds provide ideal picnic territory. You'll also be rewarded with all-embracing views taking in Assisi, Perugia and the Vale of Spoleto across to Montefalco and the Monti Martani.

Outside the walls: San Damiano and the monasteries

After a visit to Santa Chiara, the Franciscan trail leads south to **San Damiano** and, for the energetic, to a couple of sites further outside town – the **Eremo delle Carceri** (4km east) and **Santa Maria degli Angeli** in the new town around the station (8km).

San Damiano

To reach **San Damiano** (daily 10am–6pm; free), walk down the Borgo Aretino from Santa Chiara and then follow the signs through the car park and olive grove – a very steep downhill walk of about fifteen minutes.

It was in this church in 1205 that Francis received his calling to make repairs, and where he brought Saint Clare and her followers, "pouring the sweetness of Christ into her ears". Clare herself remained here to her death, though the nuns left seven years after their mistress's departure. After installing the Poor Clares, Francis came here just once, towards the end of his life, when – sick and half-blind – he composed the "Canticle to the Sun". His body, however, rested here briefly after death, fulfilling a promise to Clare that she might see him once more.

Owned by Lord Lothian until 1983, the church now belongs to the Friars Minor, who have kept it in much the same state as it was centuries ago – a condition laid down by Lothian when he made his bequest. Alone amongst the spots in Assisi with Franciscan associations, this one preserves something of an ideal that is recognisably Franciscan – rural and peaceful in its groves of olives, cypresses and wild flowers, with the pastoral Vale of Spoleto stretching away below.

Signs point the way round the complex, starting outside with a fresco depicting Saint Roch – the saint invoked against infectious diseases – proudly displaying a black plague sore. The little **balcony** above the main entrance is the point from which Clare, holding aloft the Sacrament, turned back an entire Saracen army that was pursuing Assisi's Guelphs.

Inside, the nave of the church – which was a Benedictine foundation at least as early as 1030 – is simple and smoke-darkened, with a beautifully decrepit wooden choir and lectern. On the right-hand side is the small window where San Damiano's priest threw the money that Francis offered him to repair the church. Nearby you can see the tiny hole where the saint hid "for a month" from the wrath of his father. Beyond some stairs leading to a terrace and small garden is a vestibule with a woodwormed choir and two frescoes, one a lovely *Madonna and Child* by an unknown Giottesque artist.

Up the stairs you reach the **oratorio**, and then a small **dormitory**, with a cross and flowers marking the spot where Clare died. A door to the right leads to the **cloisters**, where you may catch a glimpse of the refectory, still equipped with its original table and oak benches.

The Eremo delle Carceri

All over Assisi you'll see pictures of the **Eremo delle Carceri** (daily 8am–dusk; free), an active monastery situated in oak woods about 4km east of the town. It can be reached by road but the best approach is to walk: a footpath, a very steep climb for the first kilometre, runs all the way from the Porta Cappuccini (outside the gate turn left along the track of cypresses, and then follow the marked path up and to the right behind the Rocca Minore). The monastery is only closed for religious festivals; admission is free, but a gratuity is expected as the monks – who act as guides – live only off the alms they receive.

The hermitage was an early place of retreat for Francis and his followers: the saint caused the well in the courtyard to flow (as depicted by Giotto) and a cell known as the **Oratorio Primitivo** has been identified as that occupied by Francis. There's also a chapel containing various unlikely relics – Francis's pillow and a piece of the Golden Gate through which Jesus passed into Jerusalem. The hermitage once owned a lock of the Virgin's hair, too, and some earth from the mound which God used to create Adam, though these treasures have sadly disappeared.

On the other side of the church is a dry river bed, once a torrent until Francis told it to hush because it was spoiling his prayers. It fills up today only when some public calamity is at hand. One of the walls here was built over the so-called *buco del diavolo*, a crevice into which Francis cast a devil by the power of prayer. The old holm oak, kept upright by iron stakes, is said to have shaded the saint, and to have been a spot where birds collected to hear his sermons.

Santa Maria degli Angeli

Difficult to miss from almost any point in the Vale of Spoleto, the huge domed basilica of **Santa Maria degli Angeli** rises from the new town clustered around Assisi station – an area to which it has given its name. A majestically uninspiring pile, it was built between 1569 and 1684, then rebuilt after an earthquake in 1832.

The basilica's function is to shelter the **Porzuincola** (Little Portion), the hut-cum-chapel that Francis made the centre of the earliest Franciscan movement. Stranded like a doll's house in the church's austere Baroque bowels, it has been embellished with dreadful nineteenth-century frescoes on the outside, but inside there are features claimed to be those of Francis's rough-stone hovel, as well as good fourteenth-century frescoes on the life of the saint.

Bits of the old monastery have been excavated under the main altar, site of the saint's death and of Clare's abrupt conversion. Buried in the chapel is Brother Cataneii, one of the earliest Franciscans. He performed so many miracles from beyond the grave, and attracted so many expectant crowds as a result, that Francis implored him in prayer, "now that we are infected with all these people of the world, I enjoin thee by obedience to make an end of thy miracles and allow us to recover in peace"; the miracles stopped.

In the garden you can see descendants of the **rose bushes** into which Francis threw himself whilst grappling with some immense nocturnal temptation. The thorns obligingly dropped off after contact with his saintly flesh. They now bloom, thornless, every May, their leaves stained with the blood shed that night.

Pilgrims flock to the basilica on August 1–2 for the **Pardon of Saint Francis**, a visit which guarantees automatic absolution. The pardon recalls a vision of Christ that Francis experienced, when he was asked what might be best for the human soul. Francis replied forgiveness for all who crossed the threshold of his chapel. The already vast numbers of pilgrims were swelled in the 1920s by the supposed movement of the eight-metre-high bronze Madonna on the facade.

Eating

Multilingual tourist menus proliferate in the town's **restaurants** and prices can be steep; for cheaper and more authentic outlets make for peripheral districts away from the Basilica and Piazza del Comune. Listings below are in ascending order of price.

Restaurants

I Monaci, Via Fontebella. Entrance in a stepped alley off north side of Via Fontebella, a few steps down from Piazza Garibaldi. Large, friendly medieval spot for pastas and pizzas from a wood-fired oven; one of the rare places where pizzas are available at lunchtime.

Il Pozzo Romano, Via Sant'Agnese 10. Down-to-earth trattoria near Santa Chiara; good for pizzas. Closed Thurs.

Palotta, Via San Rufino 4. Near some sticky tourist traps, but a reasonable, unpretentious and welcoming trattoria; arrive before 12.30pm to be sure of getting a place for lunch. Closed Tues.

Ristorante La Rocca, Via di Porta Perlici 27. Annexed to the hotel, this is a cheap, high-quality locals' place with good food and no frills. About L20,000.

Buca di San Francesco, Via Brizi 1 (☎075/812.204). The reputation as the best in town is belied by erratic quality, though when it delivers the cooking is outstanding. As a bonus there's a half-covered outside terrace for summer eating. From L25,000. Closed Mon & July 1–28.

La Fortezza, Vicolo della Fortezza 2 (☎075/812.418). Invariably busy but friendly restaurant, with a high reputation, great food, medieval setting and reasonable prices. Essential to reserve in summer; L20–30,000. Closed Thurs & Feb.

Medioevo, Via dell'Arco dei Priori 4 (☎075/813.068). Just south off the Piazza del Comune, this medieval vaulted dining room is highly recommended for a real splurge – L30–50,000. Closed Wed, Jan & July 1–21.

ASSISI FESTIVAL CALENDAR

Easter week. Processions and festivities thoughout the week.

Calendimaggio (week after 1st Tues in May). Procession to celebrate Saint Francis's vision of Lady Poverty.

Festa della Voto (June 22). Procession in medieval costume to celebrate the town's salvation.

Perdono (Aug 1–2). Pilgrimage to the church of Santa Maria degli Angeli.

Palio della Balestra (Aug 11). Medieval tournament.

Francis's return to Assisi (first Sunday of Sept). Festival held most years to celebrate the saint's final return home.

Festa di San Francesco (Oct 3–4). The big event – a major pilgrimage that draws crowds of pilgrims and ecclesiastics from all over Italy and beyond.

Festa del Corpus Domini (Nov). Another major procession, through flower-strewn streets.

Listings

Car rental *Nicola Corridoni* on Via Frate Elia (☎075/812.983) rents cars with or without a driver.

Exchange Slickest facilities at the *Cassa di Risparmio* in Piazza del Comune, though you'll probably find fewer queues and less paperwork at the small *cambio* in front of the Basilica di Santa Chiara. You can also change money at the post office at Via San Paolo 2, and at the railway station ticket office.

Police Piazza Matteotti 3b (☎075/812.239).

Post office Piazza del Comune 10 (Mon–Sat 8am–6.30pm; Sun 8am–1pm).

Telephones SIP, Piazza del Comune 11 (daily 8am–10pm), for international phonecalls.

Travel agent *Stoppini*, Corso Mazzini 31 (☎075/812.597), sells train tickets.

Spello

Ranged on broad terraces above the Vale of Spoleto, **SPELLO** offers an easily accessible taste of small-town Umbria and a major art attraction in its superlative frescoes by **Pinturicchio** in the church of Santa Maria Maggiore. It also boasts a few reminders of its Roman past, when as **Hispellum** it was a retirement home for pensioned-off legionnaires and an important staging post on the Via Flaminia. The main core of the town is, as ever, medieval, evoking a typically Umbrian career, racked by internal rivalry, pestered by other cities – usually Assisi – and eventually dragged into near oblivion by the Church. Today, despite its proximity to Assisi and Spoleto, it remains quiet and rural, though new hotels and chintzy shops seem to presage an imminent tourist boom.

The Town

Buses stop just outside the **Porta Consolare**, one of five Roman gates in the Augustan-era walls that more or less enclose the town. The gate is in a sorry state, propped up by scaffolding and with a small tree growing from its crumbling upper reaches, but it still gives some idea of the glory that was Rome, and retains three original **statues**, figures that local folklore claims depict a family killed by eating poisonous mushrooms. Inside the gate begins the single main street, **Via Cavour**, which bends and climbs steeply to the town proper. A couple of minutes' walk will bring you to Santa Maria Maggiore.

Santa Maria Maggiore

The church of **Santa Maria Maggiore** presents an unpromising facade – a twelfth-century design remodelled five centuries later to dull effect. However, once inside there is immediate fascination in the **Pinturicchio** paintings covering the Cappella Baglioni, on the left as you enter. Depicting New Testament stories, they rank with the artist's masterpieces in Siena's Piccolomini library and Rome's Sistine Chapel and Borgia apartments. The frescoes were executed in 1501 – possibly with the help of Umbrian painters G.B. Caporali and Eusebio di San Giorgio – and are now glowing from restoration work in 1978 which brought out Pinturicchio's colourfully decorative detail to stunning effect. The left-hand wall shows the *Annunciation* (with a self-portrait beneath a shelf in the lower right-hand corner), the right-hand wall the *Dispute in the Temple*, the rear wall the *Adoration of the Shepherds* and the *Coming of the Magi*. The ceiling vaults, less narrative in scope, contain four sibyls. Sadly the paintings are behind glass, and you need L1000 notes to illuminate the spectacle. The barrier also means you can't get a proper look at the chapel's fifteenth-century **ceramic pavement**, a faded testimony to the skill of Deruta's medieval craftsmen (see p.526).

Elsewhere in the church are a couple of minor paintings by Pinturicchio: in the chapel to the left of the apse is a faintly etched angel, and beyond that a *Madonna and Child*. The chapel to the right of the apse has been adapted as a small **museum**, though after recent thefts it's likely to be out of bounds.

The rest of the town

A short distance uphill lies the town's other main church, **San Andrea**, a simple thirteenth-century facade hiding a darkly atmospheric interior. Most surfaces are inexpertly painted, though the overall effect is superb, and there is another

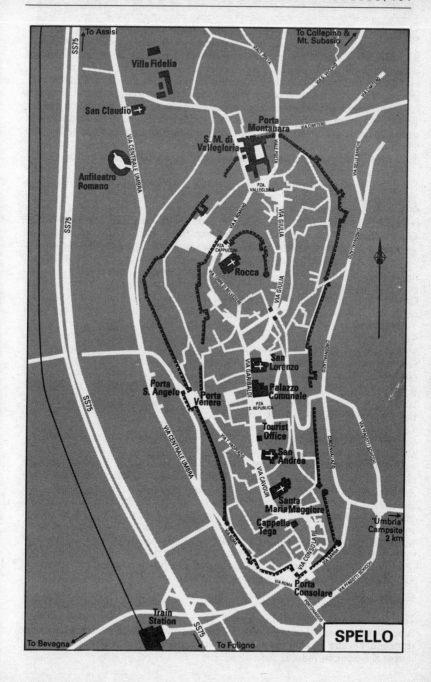

To Assisi

Villa Fidelia

San Claudio

VIA CENTRALE UMBRA

SS75

Anfiteatro Romano

To Collepino & Mt. Subasio

VALE PORTA

VIA S. VECCHIO

VIA CIMITERO

Porta Montanara

VIA CIMITERO

S. M. di Valleglioria

VALE PORTA

VIA DELLE RANCHE

PZA. VALLEGLORIA

VIA ROMANO

VIA GIULIA

VIA VIALE DI EREMITA

PZA. CAPPUCCINI

Rocca

VIA GIULIA

CIRCONVALLAZIO

San Lorenzo

VIA GARIBALDI

Palazzo Comunale

Porta S. Angelo

Porta Venere

PZA. D. REPUBLICA

Tourist Office

San Andrea

VIA T. PINZACCO

VIA CAVOUR

CIRCONVALLAZIO

VIA PIAGGETTI SCHIOCHI

Santa Maria Maggiore

Cappella Tega

'Umbria' Campsite 2 km

VIA ROMA

VIA CONSOLA RE

PZA. SANTA

Porta Consolare

VIA ROMA

PORTONACCIO

VIA PIAGGETTI SCHIOCHI

SS75

VIA CENTRALE UMBRA

Train Station

To Bevagna

SS75

To Foligno

SPELLO

outstanding **Pinturicchio** – a *Madonna and Child* in the right transept, executed with Eusebio di San Giorgio. The *Resurrection* on the pulpit is also attributed to Pinturicchio, whilst the eye-catching hanging crucifix is by an unknown fourteenth-century Umbrian follower of Giotto.

A diversion from San Andrea along Via Torri di Properzio (left off Via Cavour) brings you to the best remnant of Roman Spello, the perfectly preserved if forlorn **Porta Venere**, named after a long-vanished temple to Venus. Spello was a major religious centre, and Constantine is said to have built one of Umbria's largest shrines to the goddess in the vicinity. The imposing twin towers flanking the gate might be Roman or medieval – no one's sure.

Further up the main street, the main **Piazza della Repubblica** is part grotesque twentieth-century, part medieval, with its arched **Palazzo Comunale** boasting a couple of fourteenth-century frescoes by local painters. A few doors beyond, still on the main street, **San Lorenzo** rates as one of Umbria's more successful Baroque conversions. A mongrel of a church, its succession of architects left a variety of decorative effects, some laughable, like the obviously fake marbles, others more persuasive – as with the *baldacchino*, a bronze canopy copied from Bernini's piece for Saint Peter's in Rome. The most bizarre sight is the minutely realistic statue of Saint Peter Martyr, midway down the west wall, complete with trickle of blood from the cleaver planted in his forehead.

The highest point of the town, reached through the arch at the top of the main street, is occupied by the **belvedere** and **Rocca** – the latter giving the only view you need of the paltry and overgrown remains of the first-century AD Roman **amphitheatre** to the west.

If you do trek out to the amphitheatre, you could make the trip more worthwhile by continuing to the half-collapsed twelfth-century church of **San Claudio**, which has a strange Romanesque asymmetry inside and out. It was raised from the ashes of an old Roman building on the same site. A ten-minute walk beyond the church is the little-known **Villa Fidelia** with a beautiful **garden** and miscellaneous collection of paintings, sculptures, old furniture and costumes (Thurs, Sat & Sun 10am–1pm & 4–7pm; L3000).

The Monte Subasio trail

A stiffer but wonderful **walk** starts beyond the Rocca at the Porta Montanara. This route is worth climbing just for twenty minutes or so for superb views of the Vale of Spoleto, though if you follow it the whole way you can reach Assisi (allow a full day for this) via the top of Monte Subasio and the Eremo delle Carceri.

To get onto the route, take the second right turn after the gate (signposted for Collepino), walk past the olive oil works and after 100 metres take the track left at the fountain. The path is marked by the *Club Alpino Italiano* – look for trail no. 50 and red spot markings which run all the way to Assisi. Detailed walking maps of the area are available from the newsagents' to the right of San Lorenzo near the top of Via Garibaldi. If you're driving, be sure to follow the well-signed part-gravel road over Monte Subasio to Assisi for superlative views.

Practicalities

Spello is an alternative base for Assisi, with a good range of accommodation, fair restaurants and a small **tourist office** at Piazza Matteotti 3 (Mon–Sat 9.30am–1pm & 3–6pm; ☎0742/651.408).

Accommodation

Convento Santa Maria Maddalena, Via Cavour 1 (☎0742/651.156). Very pleasant and low-cost rooms almost immediately oppposite Santa Maria Maggiore. ③.

Portonaccio, Via Centrale Umbra 46 (☎075/651.313). If you baulk at the prices in Spello's central hotels and don't mind being outside the walls make for this big place on the main road roundabout about 100m south of Porta Consolare. ④.

Il Cacciatore, Via Giulia 42 (☎0742/651.141). Excellent value and friendly two-star hotel, with fine views from some rooms. It's worth staying here just for the superlative panoramic terrace. ⑤.

Alta Villa, Via Mancinelli 1 (☎0742/653.315). Very comfortable, if rather gaudily luxurious hotel, five minutes' walk from the old town (follow the signs from the corner of Piazza S.M. di Vallegloria). ⑥.

La Bastiglia, Via dei Mollini 17 (☎0742/651.277). Small but smart rooms all command a fine view. ⑥.

Julia, Via S. Angelo 22 (☎0742/651.174). Rather over-priced for what it offers, sited close by Santa Maria Maggiore. ⑥.

Del Teatro, Via Giulia 24 (☎075/301.140). Stung by competition from the *Alta Villa* and *Bocci*, the owners of the *Cacciatore* have opened this new and superbly appointed intimate three-star hotel down the road. ⑥.

Palazzo Bocci, Via Cavour 17 (☎075/301.021). Brand-new, tasteful and immensely smart hotel in a converted, frescoed palazzo just up from Santa Maria Maggiore. First choice if you're doing Umbria in style. ⑨.

CAMPING

Camping Umbria (☎0742/651.772). The nearest campsite, 2km east of town at Chiona. Open April to mid-Oct.

Eating

Spello's best **restaurant**, set in a vaulted medieval town house, is *La Cantina*, Via Cavour 2 (closed Wed), a friendly local place serving plenty of regional specialities – and wonderful fresh pasta. *Il Molino* at Piazza Matteotti 6–7 (closed Tues) is flashier and more expensive, with an equally pleasing medieval setting and some good food if you avoid the occasional unfortunate pretension to Italian *nouvelle cuisine*. *Il Cacciatore*, Via Giulia 42 (closed Mon), has middling food and service, but a great terrace for summer eating. You should be able to have a full meal in any of the three spots for under L35,000.

Another important gastronomic stop is the *Bar-Gelateria Ennio*, just outside the Porta Santa Maria Maggiore, which serves up **ice cream** and sorbets just a wafer away from perfection.

Foligno and around

Sooner or later you're almost bound to find yourself in **FOLIGNO**, one of the largest Umbrian towns and a nodal point for trains and buses. A largely modern place, ringed with factories and concrete sprawl, its star turns were bombed out of existence in the war. What remains is a not unpleasant provincial town, though with nothing that would merit a special visit. However, the residue of its medieval heritage is conveniently concentrated in the central **Piazza della Repubblica**, so a quick look is feasible as you're passing through or changing trains. The town is also a good **accommodation** standby if surrounding towns are fully booked.

Both the **train and bus stations** are just outside the Viale, which follow the circuit of the old walls. From either it's a ten-minute walk into the Piazza della Repubblica. The **tourist office** is across the square from the bus station in Piazzale Alunno. If you are headed to Montefalco (see p.468), there are infrequent buses, or you could try hitching from the Porta Todi, round Via N. Sauro from Piazzale Alunno.

The Town

The **Duomo** is the main eye-catcher on Piazza della Repubblica, the twelfth-century Palazzo Comunale opposite having been ruined by a Neoclassical facade at the beginning of this century. Unusually, the church boasts two facades, the south frontage containing one of the most impressive **portals** in the region – a riot of carving full of zodiac signs, intricate patterning and enough bizarre animals to fill a zoo. Check out two curious details – a likeness of Frederick II on the left (one of only two in Italy) and a Muslim star and crescent near the apex of the arch. The other facade is only a little less appealing, though its mosaics are a nineteenth-century afterthought. The interior holds little joy; a panel by Nicolò Alunno in the sacristy is the only feature worth seeking out.

To the duomo's right, at the western end of the piazza, is the **Palazzo Trinci**, the much-altered home of the Trinci, Foligno's medieval big shots. Between 1305 and 1339 they rode a wave of expansion which saw their influence spread over broad swathes of Umbria. Before this the town had suffered repeated thumpings from Saracens, Goths and Barbarossa, eventually becoming a bastion of imperial power – an allegiance which put it in almost constant conflict with Perugia. When the family's power waned the town continued to thrive, and it was in Foligno that the first book was printed in Italian – three hundred copies of Dante's *Divine Comedy*. The palazzo itself is in the last throes of a restoration project that has been under way for donkey's years. Now visible are a fine courtyard and frescoed staircase, though opening dates for the **Pinacoteca Comunale** on the second floor are still not fixed. Its high points are a frescoed chapel by Ottaviano Nelli, an *Annunciation* attributed to Gozzoli and a painted passageway known as the *Hall of the Planets and Liberal Arts*.

The only other monument which hints at Foligno's former glory is **Santa Maria Infraportas**, a church of pagan origins in which Saint Peter is said to have celebrated Mass. The oldest part of the current eighth-century church is the **Cappella dell'Assunta** off the left nave; the Byzantine mural behind its altar is the town's most precious piece of art.

Practicalities

If Assisi's and Spello's hotels are full, you may have cause to use Foligno's accommodation options. None is especially cheap, though they are more likely to have space, and there's a youth hostel for stand-by.

Accommodation

Ostello Fulginium, Piazza San Giacomo 11 (☎0742/352.882). An official IYHF hostel, with showers and breakfast included. To reach it take bus #1 from the train station and ask to be dropped at the *ostello*. ②.

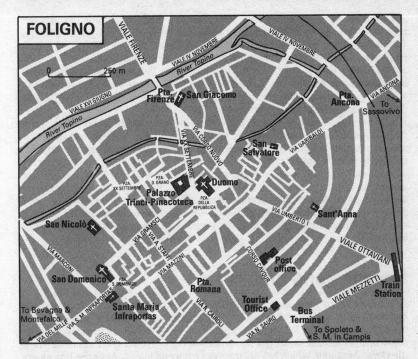

Roma, Viale Mezzetti 10 (☎0742/350.472). Handily placed for the train and bus stations. ④.
Belvedere, Via F. Ottaviani 23 (☎0742/353.990). Just north of the train station. ⑤.
Villa Roncalli, Viale Roma 25 (☎0742/391.091). Best of the upmarket places. ⑥.
Italia, Piazza Matteotti 12 (☎0742/352.258). A large and functional place, very centrally located immediately south of Piazza della Repubblica. ⑦.
Umbria, Via Cesare Battisti 1 (☎0742/352.821). Similar, but convenient for the train station; usually comes up with a room. ⑦.

Food

Cheap **pizzerias** are numerous, and any walk around the streets will uncover one to suit. If you want to treat yourself, the local favourite is the **restaurant** of the *Villa Roncalli* hotel (closed Mon & Aug 1–10); expect to pay about L50,000 a head. For meals at around half this price, head for the *Da Remo*, Via Cesare Battisti 49.

East of Foligno

Visible from afar from the Vale of Spoleto, the Benedictine **Abbazia di Sassovivo**, 6km east of Foligno, is one of the oldest monasteries in Umbria, dating from 1070. Set in wooded countryside, it also claims the region's finest medieval **cloisters**, with 128 variegated columns and 58 arches all decorated with mosaics and coloured marbles. The church is dull, however, save for its eleventh-century crypt.

To the north of the abbey, the SS77 road to Camerino threads through the beautiful **Menotre valley**, a region of small, lost villages and virgin hill country. To explore properly, you'll need transport or the will to hike. With the latter in mind, the *Kompass* "Assisi-Camerino" **map** (no. 665) is invaluable.

PALE, 8km east of Foligno, is the first village you'll come to in the Menotre. It has a castle and a stalactite-crammed cave, the **Grotta di Pale**. Paths from the village cover the 4km to the summit of the craggy **Sasso di Pale** (958m), also accessible from Santa Lucia, 1km on from Pale.

The only place of any real size in the valley is **COLFIORITO**, 25km from Foligno. Once an important Iron Age site, controlling one of the lowest Apennine passes into the Marche, it sits at the heart of some extraordinary countryside, mostly marsh and upland plain – rather like the Valnerina – surrounded by fields of grass and mountain peaks. Green and cool in summer, the town has become something of a vacation retreat and is well served by **hotels**, though it has to be said that none is especially prepossessing. The best bet is the two-star *Lieta Sosta*, Via Adriatica 230 (☎0742/681.321; ④), which also has a smaller one-star annexe. Another, similarly priced, is the *Valico*, Via Casette di Cupigliolo (☎0742/681.140; ④).

Bevagna and around

BEVAGNA, 8km southwest of Foligno, is even more serene and handsome a backwater than Spello, with a windswept central piazza of austere perfection and two of Umbria's finest Romanesque churches. An Umbrian and then an Etruscan settlement, it became under the Romans a staging post on the Via Flaminia – now the Corso Matteotti, which bisects the town from end to end. After the Roman era it was sacked by just about everybody – Barbarossa, Frederick II, Foligno's Trinci family and, inevitably, by Perugia's Baglioni. Today it has scarcely spread beyond its medieval walls, unscarred by the urban blight of most nearby hill towns.

Irregular **buses** run from Foligno, Montefalco, Perugia and Assisi, and it's a straightforward hitch across the plain from Foligno.

The Town
On whatever bearing you start to wander the village, the backstreets sooner or later converge on the pedestrianised main square, **Piazza Silvestri**, vast and open after the shadowed streets of its surroundings. Every member of this unimprovable arrangement is thoroughly medieval, with the sole exception of the nineteenth-century fountain, and even that blends in perfectly.

Two churches face each other across the square, both untouched and creaking with age. The smaller, deconsecrated **San Silvestro**, is a magnificent squat example of early Umbrian Romanesque; its exterior bears a plaque with the date of construction – 1195 – and the name of the builder, Binello, who was also responsible for San Michele opposite, but of whom nothing else is known. Pieces of Roman remains are woven into the facade, whose upper half is faced in pink Subasio stone and boasts the stump of an unfinished tower. The **interior** – which tends to be open when the rest of the town is shut – is superbly ancient in look and feel, with a raised presbytery and sunken crypt. Look out for the capitals of the blunt columns in the nave, which are of an Egyptian order (rather than Doric,

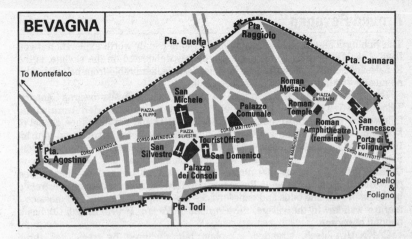

Ionic or Corinthian), and were perhaps copied from a Roman temple to distant deities.

The second church, **San Michele**, appears and feels more recent, perhaps due to its rose window, punched through in the eighteenth century. It is in fact Silvestro's contemporary and is built to a similar interior plan; its capitals are similarly eccentric, as are the surreal **gargoyles** over the main doorway. The square's third component is the twelfth-century **Palazzo dei Consoli**, distinguished by a broad stone staircase and an interior converted into a theatre in 1886. To its left is **San Domenico**, rectangular and workaday, its Baroque interior relieved only by fragments of fresco and two early wooden sculptures. The church's prime position was a gift from the *comune* to the Dominicans for help in rebuilding the town after one of its sackings.

If you really want to exhaust Bevagna's tourist offerings, the church of **San Francesco** claims to have the stone from which Saint Francis preached his famous sermon to the birds, a discourse that according to the local claim occurred on the road between Bevagna and Cannara (perhaps Francis spoke to several flocks of Umbrian birds, for the spot is commemorated too at Assisi's Eremo delle Carceri). Of even vaguer interest is the small **Pinacoteca** (daily 9am–2pm; L2000) at Via Porta Guelfa 2, where you can see a fragmentary mosaic from the town's Roman baths.

Practicalities

The small **tourist office** in Piazza Silvestri provides a good map and leaflet on the town, with English translations. No official **accommodation** is listed, though it is possible to stay at the Benedictine Santa Maria del Monte **convent** at Corso Matteotti 15 (☎0742/360.133; ④). Food is excellent, but the nuns are happiest if you attend Mass.

Restaurant choice is otherwise limited to the cheap and cheerful *Da Nina*, Piazza Garibaldi (closed Tues). The **bar** just off the piazza is good for ice cream and snacks and has perhaps Umbria's most miserable service and most oddball clientele.

Around Bevagna

The rich agricultural plain surrounding Bevagna is only worth exploration if you have a car. In the hills above the town, clearly delineated on the skyline, is the Renaissance church of **Santa Maria delle Grazie**, admirable from below, but by no means worth the journey for a closer look.

The most rewarding trip is to take the minor road northwest towards Cannara. Two kilometres out is the restored but very pretty **Convento dell'Annunziata**, followed by the one-horse hamlet of **CANTALUPO** and the tiny stone chapel of Madonna della Pia. Take a minor left turn one kilometre beyond and you hit **LIMIGIANO**, a classic fortified hamlet centred on a thirteenth-century church, San Michele. At the crossroads for Cannara, a left turn leads to **COLLEMANCIO**, where 300 metres north of the village are the unexcavated ruins of Urbinum Hortense, a Roman or possibly Etruscan settlement destroyed by Totila in 545. The odds and ends – traces of a temple, pavement and mosaics – merit a wander. In the village, the *Pensione Il Rientro* (☎075/72.420; [5]) has a handful of **rooms**.

CANNARA itself, stranded mid-plain but sheltered by trees, has three churches, each with significant paintings by major Umbrian artists: San Giovanni has frescoes by Lo Spagna, while San Matteo and San Francesco have works by Nicolò Alunno. The Palazzo Comunale in Piazza Umberto houses a small art gallery.

Montefalco

As you'd expect from its name – the Falcon's Mount – **MONTEFALCO** commands the Vale of Spoleto. The local tag of "la ringhiera dell'Umbria" (the balcony of Umbria) may be a touch hyperbolic but the views are nonetheless majestic and once past the modern suburbs you enter one of the finest hill towns in the area, a maze of tiny, cobbled streets, with an artistic heritage – including frescoes by Gozzoli and Perugino – out of all proportion to its size.

The town was the birthplace of eight saints, good going even by Italian standards, but its historical interest lies mainly in a brief interlude in the fourteenth century, when the town became a refuge to Spoleto's papal governors, left vulnerable by the defection of the popes to Avignon. Their munificent presence resulted in the rich decoration of local churches and the commissioning of Lorenzo Maitini, who was later to work on the Duomo in Orvieto, to strengthen the town **walls** (still impressively intact) and to build a fortress for the exiled rulers. Power thereafter devolved to Foligno's Trinci family, to the rapacious Baglioni and eventually to the Church – cue for several centuries of quiet decline.

The Town

The five buses daily from Foligno's Porta Romana (Mon–Sat), and one daily from Perugia (Mon–Sat) drop you at the foot of Via Umberto, the main offshoot of **Piazza del Comune**, the town's main square. The main attraction, the ex-church of **San Francesco** and its museum, is a stone's throw away from the square, while the rest of the town is little more than five minutes' walk from end to end. The only outlying site, **San Fortunato**, is about fifteen minutes' walk away.

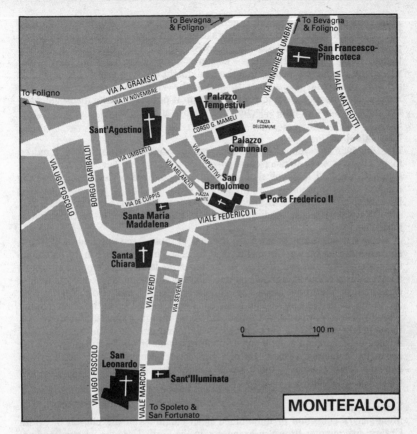

To Bevagna & Foligno

To Bevagna & Foligno

San Francesco-Pinacoteca

VIA A. GRAMSCI

VIA IV NOVEMBRE

VIA RINGHIERA UMBRA

VIALE MATTEOTTI

To Foligno

Palazzo Tempestivi

CORSO G. MAMELI

PIAZZA DELCOMUNE

Sant'Agostino

VIA UMBERTO

Palazzo Comunale

VIA UGO FOSCOLO

BORGO GARIBALDI

VIA TEMPESTIVI

VIA MELANZIO

VIA DE CUPPIS

San Bartolomeo

PIAZZA DANTE

Porta Frederico II

Santa Maria Maddalena

VIALE FEDERICO II

Santa Chiara

VIA VERDI

VIA SEVERINI

0   100 m

VIA UGO FOSCOLO

San Leonardo

VIALE MARCONI

Sant'Illuminata

To Spoleto & San Fortunato

MONTEFALCO

San Francesco

The cavernous church of **San Francesco** (June–Aug Tues–Sat 10am–1pm & 4–7pm; Sept–May same days 10am–1pm & 2–5pm; L6000) hosts one of the great Renaissance fresco cycles, a series of panels on the *Life of St Francis* by **Benozzo Gozzoli**. Gozzoli, a pupil of Fra' Angelico, has a comparatively lowly place in the pantheon of Florentine artists, but this delightful cycle – which duplicates in its subjects many of Giotto's panels in Assisi – is marvellously bold in its colouring and utterly in control of its narrative. It is also of great social interest for its closely observed townscapes: Arezzo is depicted, as is Montefalco – visited by Saint Francis after his sermon to the birds outside Bevagna. The panels completely fill the apse, with twenty medallions around them depicting famous Franciscans; underneath the main window appear Petrarch, Dante and Giotto, members of the lay Tertiary Order. Further work by Gozzoli fills the walls and vaults to the right.

Elsewhere are displayed paintings by many of the leading lights of the Umbrian Renaissance – **Perugino**, **Nicolò Alunno**, **Tiberio d'Assisi** – and some fascinating little-known characters. Works originally commissioned for San

Francesco remain in situ, with others housed in the excellent adjacent **Museo Civico di San Francesco** (same hours & ticket as church). Look out for the two panels showing the *Madonna del Soccorso*. The story – common in Umbria though rarely painted elsewhere – concerns a young mother who, tired of her whingeing child, cries "would that the devil might take you away"; the devil duly appears, prompting the mother to invoke the Virgin to save her infant. The museum also operates as a **tourist information point** with town maps and walking tours, as well as a wide selection of art books and magazines.

Sant'Agostino

The Augustinians' monastery and church of **Sant'Agostino** is two hundred metres away from the Franciscans' power base, across the Piazza del Comune. A simple Gothic hall, it is typical of the order, designed with a view to minimise the fripperies and maximise the preaching space. It has a few frescoes that have survived the damp – including a *Coronation of the Virgin* by Caporali (1522) – but its main interest, lending a distinctly spooky air, lies in its collection of mummies.

Midway down the right nave are the first of these – the tiny bodies of **Beata Illuminata** and **Beata Chiarella**, clad in dusty muslin which only half-hides their bones, skin and yellow faces. At the top of the left-hand side of the church is another dusty cadaver, propped on one elbow and looking very comfortable in a glass-fronted wardrobe. Known as the **Beato Pellegrino** (Holy Pilgrim), he apparently came to venerate Illuminata and Beata, fell asleep in the church in the position he's in now, and was found dead next morning against a confessional. Immediately placed in a sepulchre, he was found outside it the next day, and refused to stay put on several subsequent occasions. His body and clothes didn't decay for a hundred years. Despite this impressive behaviour, nothing was known of the character, so there was no sainthood, and he was plonked for posterity in his wardrobe.

Santa Chiara

Montefalco's collection of mummified flesh continues in the church of **Santa Chiara**, five minutes from San Francesco in Via Verdi. Here the wizened body of Saint Clare of Montefalco languishes in a see-through casket high up on the altar. The saint – not to be confused with her more famous namesake at Assisi – has a small **fresco cycle** on her life in a chapel inside the convent (ring the bell on the door to the right of the casket and ask one of the nuns to unlock it). Born in Montefalco in 1290, she became a nun at the age of six and embarked on a series of miracles connected with the Passion of Christ. The frescoes were restored in 1932, as a small plaque beside them declares, as well as extolling the virtues of fascism.

If you're lucky, the nuns might show you around the rest of the adjoining **convent**. On show is a small crucifix enshrining three of the saint's gallstones (representing the Trinity) as well as the remains of her heart and the scissors with which the relic was hacked out of her, all of which are kept in a cupboard under her body – which is cleverly shared by the main church and this private chapel. The story of Clare's cardiac organ relates that Christ appeared to her, saying the burden of the Cross was becoming too heavy for him; Clare replied she would help by carrying it within, and when she was opened up a cross-shaped

SAGRANTINO

Montefalco's **wines** have always been prized within Umbria but have recently started to achieve wider fame. Their reputation rests not so much on the serviceable *Rosso di Montefalco* as on two powerful reds of mysterious origin, the extraordinary **Sagrantino** and **Sagrantino Passito**. Both are made from the Sagrantino grape, a variety found nowhere else in Europe. Why it should be unique to a tiny area of central Italy is a mystery: it appears in records in the last century, but experts claim a far more ancient pedigree, some saying it was imported by the Saracens, others that it was introduced by Syrian monks in the seventh century, or perhaps came from Piedmont or Catalonia. Its name may derive from its sacramental use by Franciscan communities who used to cultivate this grape.

Sagrantino is a dry red, usually made with up to five percent of the common Trebbiano Toscano. Sagrantino Passito is similar, with the important difference that it uses semi-dried or *passito* grapes to produce that rarest of drinks – a sweet red dessert wine. Both varieties, in the words of Italian wine guru Burton Anderson, have a remarkable "dark purple-garnet colour, rich, berry-like scent, and warm, rich full flavour". The Sagrantino, he adds, has "voluptuous body" and "staggering strength", qualities to which even the least educated palate will be able to attest after a couple of glasses. **Adanti** are the leading producers of both varieties, their singular *Rosso d'Arquata*, in Anderson's words, "one of central Italy's most original and enjoyable red wines". Any of the many producers in the tiny DOC area, however, should come up trumps, especially Antonelli, Benincasa, Caprai, Rocca di Fabbri and Paolo Bea – the last are producers of what Anderson describes as a "titanic" Sagrantino Passito. The *alimentari* in Montefalco's main Piazza del Comune contains a superb selection of all the area's wines.

piece of tissue was duly found on her heart. Other sights include a miraculous tree that grew from a staff planted by Christ, who appeared again to Clare in the shrubbery. The nuns think it's the sole wild specimen of its species in all of Europe; the berries are used to make rosaries, and are said to have powerful medicinal properties.

Sant'Illuminata and San Fortunato

Down the street from Santa Chiara's seat of miracles is the tiny church of **Sant'Illuminata**, worth a visit for its triple-arched Renaissance **portico** and comprehensively frescoed **interior**. The standard of painting isn't always terribly high – most are by the obscure local man Melanzio – but the overall effect is captivating.

Keep on heading out of town from here, down the avenue of horse chestnuts, then turn left at the T-junction, and a fifteen-minute trudge brings you out at the **Monastero di San Fortunato**, set amongst ilex woods. It has noted frescoes by Tiberio d'Assisi – one of Perugino's leading disciples – in its Cappella delle Rose, to the left of the main courtyard. Gozzoli painted the very faded angels over the door of the main church and the dark fresco of Saint Fortunato inside, over the remains of Fortunato himself, whose bones are laid out in a macabre skull and crossbones arrangement. He died in 390 and proved rather more corruptible than Sant'Agostino's holy personages.

Practicalities

Practicalities are straightforward in Montefalco, with everything within a few minutes' walk of everything else. There is no proper tourist office, though the ticket desk at the San Francesco museum has some information on the town, as well as a detailed resumé of the gallery's contents.

There's just a couple of hotels within the town walls. The cheaper is the small and cosy *Ringhiera Umbra*, Via Umberto 1 (☎0742/79.166; ④), which also has a restaurant downstairs. Fifty metres away at the end of the side street is the two-star *Santa Chiara*, Via de Cuppis 18 (☎0742/79.114; ④), whose main reason for a stay is the owner's Aladdin's Cave of kitsch and memorabilia – one of the town's sights in its own right. Just opened is the *Villa Pambuffetti*, Via Vittoria 3 (☎0742/378.823; ⑨), a fantastic villa-hotel with park and pool, 100m out of town on the road west towards Montefalco. Prices are high, but if you're honeymooning, or want one night of credit card madness in Umbria, this is the place – though make sure you're in the main villa, not the gate-house.

For something grander than the *Ringhiera*'s **restaurant**, try the *Coccorone* on the corner of Largo Tempestivi and Via Fabbri (☎0742/79.535; closed Wed), where the chances are you'll have one of Umbria's better meals – great pastas and *crespelli* (rolled pancakes), and superlative *tiramisù*; for total culinary immersion go for the set *menu degustazione* at L35,000. To find it, follow the offputting yellow signs for the "Tipical Ristorant". There's not much else in the way of life, though you might while away an hour in the **bar** off the main square – quite a nice place when it's not full of noisy kids.

Over the last couple of years Montefalco has been tidied up considerably, and the tell-tale signs of tourism are manifest in places hawking local produce. The best of these is the old shop on Piazza del Comune, which has a well-priced stock of truffles, local oils and leading **wines** (see box above).

Trevi

Heading south from Foligno across the plain of Spoleto, few people give **TREVI** more than an admiring glance from the train or highway. From across the valley, the town looks merely enticing, but at closer range Trevi has the most stupendous appearance of any town in Umbria – its medieval houses perched on a pyramidal hill and encircled by miles and miles of olive groves. Because so few bother to make the steep detour, the town's atmosphere is that of a pleasant, ordinary, provincial town still apparently stuck somewhere in the 1950s.

If you are coming by **train**, from Foligno or Spoleto, make sure you don't catch an express, which won't stop at Trevi station. From the station be sure to jump on the connecting bus for the four-kilometre haul into town. The buses will drop you near Piazza Mazzini, off which, in Via Roma, is a **tourist office**. Cars can be parked in Piazza Garibaldi, outside the town walls to the east.

The Town

As with most Umbrian hill towns, the pleasure of Trevi lies in tramping the medieval streets, here obsessively well-kept and characterised by complicated patterns of cobblestones. The **Pinacoteca** in the Palazzo Comunale on Piazza

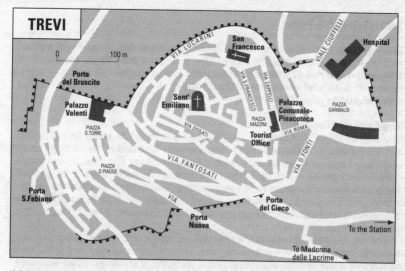

Mazzini offers artistic diversions in the form of a *Madonna* by Pinturicchio, a ragbag of Umbrian works, and the usual accompaniment of sculptures, ceramics and Roman remains. However, don't count on finding it open – hours are highly variable and often you'll have to negotiate entry in the council offices alongside the gallery. Further bits of Roman Trevi are embedded in the inner of two sets of medieval **walls**, raised when Trevi paraded as a minor independent *comune*.

The highest point of the town is **Sant'Emiliano**, comely twelfth-century Romanesque on the outside, Baroque horror-show within. Another of Umbria's many martyrs and saints, Emiliano was an Armenian missionary cut off in his prime in 302. The only early survivors of the butchery of the building are an *Altar of the Sacrament* and frescoes by Melanzio, who was active in many villages hereabouts at the start of the sixteenth century.

Most noteworthy of the peripheral churches is the **Madonna delle Lacrime**, on the approach road from the station, home to a late *Epiphany* by Perugino. The conventual church of **San Martino**, a kilometre downhill from Piazza Garibaldi, along Via Augusto Ciufelli, has the best of the rest, featuring (along with the chapel next door) paintings by Lo Spagna, Tiberio d'Assisi and Pier Antonio Mezzastris.

Practicalities

Trevi has just one **hotel**, the *Cochetto*, Via Dogali 13 (☎0742/78.229; ⑤); downstairs is a good **restaurant** (closed Tues). Alternative accommodation is offered by the **convent** of San Martino at Via Ciufelli 4 (☎0742/78.297; see above for directions; ④). You can also rent **private rooms** at Via Lucharini 35 (☎0742/780.343; ③), with weekly rates available.

Four kilometres south, in the hamlet of Pigge, the *Pescatore*, Via Chiesa Tonda 5 (☎0742/78.483; ④), has rooms and another restaurant. In Bovara, between Trevi and Pigge, bed and breakfast *agriturismo* accommodation, with swimming pool, is available at *Casa Giulia*, Via Corciano 1 (☎0742/78.257; ⑥).

South of Trevi

Moving south from Trevi, the Vale of Spoleto becomes increasingly pockmarked with new houses and small factories. This makes its main sight, the **Fonti di Clitunno** – a series of springs revered since Roman times – all the more unexpected. It is located above the fortified hamlet of **Campello**, an out-of-the-way accommodation possibility.

The Fonti di Clitunno

The sacred **Fonti di Clitunno** has provided inspiration to poets from Virgil to Byron. Originally dedicated to the oracular god **Clitunnus**, the springs were often used as a party venue by the likes of Caligula and Claudius, even though their major curative effect is allegedly that of removing any appetite for alcohol. Earthquakes over the years have upset many of the underground sources, so the waters aren't as plentiful as they once were, but they still flow as limpid as they did when Byron extolled "the sweetest wave of the most living crystal . . . the purest god of gentle waters".

There's a certain amount of commercialised fuss around the entrance but the springs, streams and willow-shaded lake beyond are languidly romantic, with faint traffic noise and the occasional coach party the only intrusions on weekdays – at weekends the racket is more intense. The site closes for lunch, but opens again until dusk, with a small admission charge to get in.

The Tempietto di Clitunno

A few hundred metres north of the Fonti is the so-called **Tempietto di Clitunno**, looking like a miniature classical temple, but actually an eighth-century Christian church cobbled together with columns from the ruins of Roman temples and villas, all long vanished. Scholars until recently were fooled into thinking it a genuine piece of Roman antiquity, though Goethe was one notable dissenter from the party line. The track which runs below the facade is the remains of the original Via Flaminia.

The entrance is to the side; if it's shut, try ringing the bell on the gate. Inside are some faded **frescoes** said to be the oldest in Umbria; dated to the eighth century, these Byzantine fragments represent Christ, Saint Peter and Saint Paul.

Campello and around

Though its position above the Fonti di Clitunno is impressive enough, the main attraction of the small fortified hamlet of **CAMPELLO** is its accommodation. For **hotel** rooms try either the *Fontanelle*, Via d'Elci 1 (☎0743/521.091; ⑤), or the *Ravale*, Ravale Campello, close to the Fonti at Via Virgilio (☎0743/521.320; ⑤); both have **restaurants** and reasonable rooms.

Equipped with a car or bike, there are superb **mountain excursions** on the roads northeast of Campello. Minor roads follow deep-cut valleys via **PETTINO** and Spina into marvellous countryside, the hills on either side rising to over 1400 metres at Monte Maggiore and Monte Brunnette. Pettino also boasts an excellent rustic **restaurant**, the *Trattoria Pettino* (closed Tues).

travel details

Trains

From Assisi to Perugia (hourly; 25min) and on to Teróntola (1hr) for connections for Rome, Florence and Arezzo; Foligno (hourly; 15min) via Spello (10min), with connections south from Foligno to Spoleto, Terni and Rome, and north to Fossato di Vico (for Gubbio) and the Marche.

From Foligno to Teróntola via Spello, Assisi, Perugia and halts en route (hourly); to Rome via Spoleto, Terni, Narni and Orte (10 daily); Ancona via Nocera Umbra (10 daily; 15min), Fossato di Vico (40min), Fabriano, Jesi and Falconara.

Buses

From Assisi to Perugia (8 daily); Foligno, via Spello (4 daily); Bastia and Capodacqua (7 daily); Cannara (4 daily); Gualdo Tadino (1 daily); Rome (1 daily); Florence (1 daily); Gubbio (2 weekly); Todi and Orvieto (1 weekly – Fri); Cascia and the Valnerina (1 weekly – Wed).

From Foligno to Assisi, Spoleto (via the Fonti di Clitunno and Trevi), Nocera Umbra, Gualdo Tadino, Gubbio, Montefalco, Spello and Bevagna.

CHAPTER ELEVEN

SPOLETO AND THE VALNERINA

Eastern Umbria is in many ways the most enjoyable part of the region. The area offers superb walking amid some of the wildest scenery anywhere in central Italy, and in its main city and transport hub, **Spoleto**, you have the most stimulating base in Umbria. The walking is at its best in the extreme east, where the savage **Monti Sibillini** look down over the **Piano Grande**, a vast highland plateau which in spring becomes a breathtakingly beautiful expanse of wild flowers. There is sporadic access to these areas from both Spoleto and **Norcia**, the earthquake-prone birthplace of Saint Benedict, founder of western monasticism. Equally beautiful, and a little easier to reach, are the villages of the **Valnerina**, an upland valley enclosed by high mountain walls immediately east of Spoleto.

Spoleto should feature on any Umbrian itinerary – particularly if you have the chance to catch its summer **Festival dei Due Mondi**, a contemporary arts jamboree which carries considerable international clout. The festival has had a trickle-down effect on the rest of Spoleto's year, too, providing a full programme of exhibitions and concerts. This is a hill town which, for all its medieval and Roman sights, is not overwhelmed by its past.

Access to Spoleto is straightforward, as the town lies on the Rome–Ancona rail line, with links to Terni and Narni to the south, and to Foligno, Assisi and Perugia to the north. Buses provide feasible links for the main villages of the Valnerina, and for the trailheads of the Monti Sibillini and Piano Grande, though to get the most from the countryside really requires transport of your own – or, better still, some determined hiking.

ACCOMMODATION PRICES

Throughout this guide, accommodation is graded on a scale from ① to ⑨. Grades ① and ② apply to **hostel** accommodation, and indicate the lowest price a **single person** could expect to pay for one night in that establishment in high season. Grades ③ to ⑨ apply to **hotels**, and indicate the cost of the **cheapest double room in high season**. The price bands to which these codes refer are as follows:

- ① under L20,000 per person
- ② over L20,000 per person
- ③ under L50,000 per double
- ④ L50–70,000 per double
- ⑤ L70–90,000 per double
- ⑥ L90–120,000 per double
- ⑦ L120–150,000 per double
- ⑧ L150–200,000 per double
- ⑨ over L200,000 per double

Spoleto

Even without the summer festival, **SPOLETO** would still demand a visit. One of the most graceful of all Italian hill towns, it maintains a superb assembly of Romanesque monuments, a seductively medieval appearance and a real sense of a life of its own. Its road and transport links make it the natural base for exploring eastern Umbria, and it's a possible base for visits further afield – Assisi, for example, is an easy day trip. The one drawback to the place is its ever-increasing popularity. During the height of the summer festival, accommodation is tight and prices inflated.

The city's ancient grandeur is attested by a series of well-preserved **Roman walls**. Cicero described Spoletium, founded in 241 BC, as Rome's most renowned colony and it was strong enough to turn away Hannibal in 217 BC after his victory at Trasimeno (see p.422). Strategically sited between Rome and Ravenna, the town prospered as the focus of the Western Empire shifted from one to the other, though its real prominence was to come after 576 AD when it was established first as a Lombard and later as a Frankish dukedom. The autonomous **Duchy of Spoleto** eventually stretched almost to Rome, dominating the greater part of central Italy.

The fall from grace came in the shape of Barbarossa, who flattened the city in 1155 during an Italian sojourn to restore his imperial authority. Decline and deliverance into the hands of the Church followed a century later, the humdrum years that ensued being relieved in 1499 when the nineteen-year-old Lucrezia Borgia was appointed governor by her father, Pope Alexander VI. Thereafter it was downhill towards obscurity until the arrival of the festival thirty years ago.

Arrival, information and accommodation

Transport to Spoleto is straightforward. Regular fast **trains** on the Rome–Ancona line stop at the town, and there are local links with Terni, Orte and Foligno; city buses run from the station to Piazza della Libertà in the old Upper Town. Most **inter-town buses** terminate in Piazza Garibaldi, again in the Lower Town though across the River Tessino; an exception are the Norcia buses, which operate from outside the train station.

The major architectural attractions are to be found in the medieval **Upper Town**, though the largely modern **Lower Town** also has a few key sights. The whole is a relatively compact area and getting around is easy enough on foot. For help on accommodation – and to pick up details of cultural events and a handy pamphlet on walking in the region – the **tourist office** at Piazza della Libertà 7 (daily 9/10am–1pm & 4.30–7.30pm; ☎0743/220.311 or 220.435) is a useful first stop. Opposite is the main **post office**, at Piazza della Libertà 12 (Mon–Sat 8am–12.30pm & 3–7.30pm) which has a foreign exchange facility.

Accommodation

Rooms are hard to come by when the festival's in full swing – turning up without a booking, the best you can hope for is a room in the Lower Town, very much a second choice, but more likely to have space. If there's absolutely nothing going, your best bet is to head for Foligno, or to ask for the tourist office's *Affitacamere* list of fifteen or so private rooms.

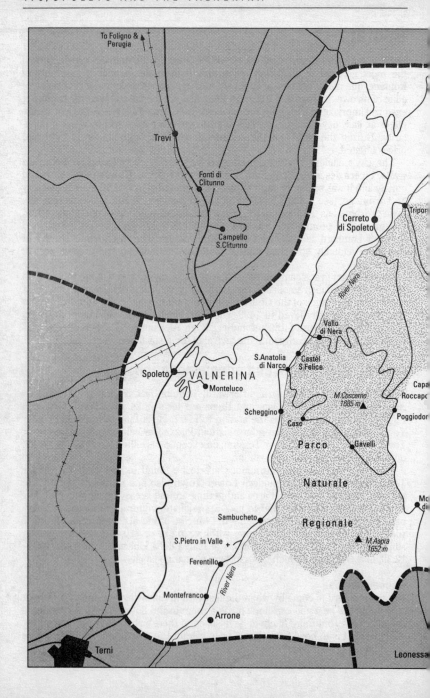

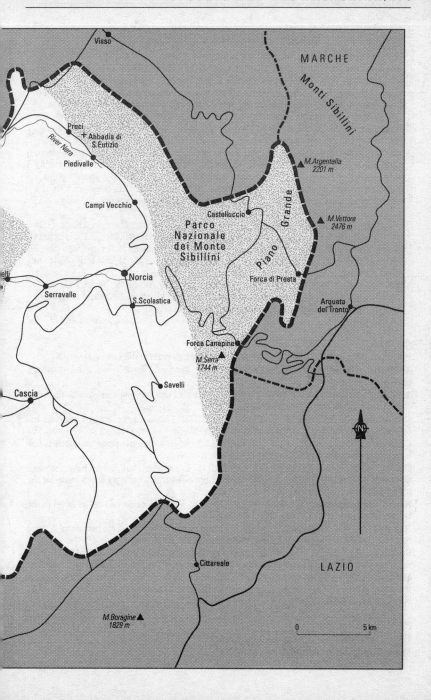

MARCHE

Monti Sibillini

Visso

Preci

Abbadia di
S.Eutizio

River Nera

Piedivalle

Campi Vecchio

M.Argentella
2201 m

Parco
Nazionale
dei Monte
Sibillini

Castelluccio

Piano Grande

M.Vettore
2476 m

Norcia

Forca di Presta

elli

Serravalle

S.Scolastica

Arquata
del Tronto

Forca Canapine

M.Serra
1744 m

Savelli

Cascia

N

Cittareale

LAZIO

M.Boragine
1829 m

0   5 km

THE FESTIVAL DEI DUE MONDI

The **Festival dei Due Mondi** – the Festival of the Two Worlds – is an Italo-American co-venture, tied to a sister festival in Charleston, West Virginia. Now established as Italy's leading international arts festival, it came to Spoleto in 1958, when composer Giancarlo Menotti and his advisers chose the town over the thirty other contenders on account of its scenery, small venues and general good vibes.

The festival is staged annually for two weeks from late June, encompassing music, dance and theatre, performed by top Italian and international companies. Tickets for the premier events can be expensive and elusive, but the festival generates an Edinburgh-type fringe, and the organisers have recently looked to more avant-garde acts to recover the edge of the festival's early days – so count on seeing some wacky shows on the programme. Cultural ripples continue to spread outside the main season: organ and classical music recitals in local churches precede the festival from April to June, and an opera season – mixing classics and the weird and wonderful – runs from August to September.

Tickets and information are issued from the **tourist office** in Piazza della Libertà and the **festival box office** at Piazza del Duomo 9 (☎0743/28.120); tickets can also be obtained from travel agents in many larger Italian cities – prices range from L15,000 to L250,000. Details of future line-ups are available from the Festival Press Agency, Via del Duomo 7 (☎0743/32.141). All the larger Italian newspapers print pull-outs, reviews and timetables during and in the run-up to the festival.

Be warned that the festival attracts big crowds and hiked-up hotel and restaurant prices. If at all possible, it's best to book **rooms** well ahead.

HOTELS
Fracassa, Via Focaroli 15 (☎0743/221.177). Good budget hotel in the Lower Town. ③.

Anfiteatro, Via dell'Anfiteatro 14 (☎0743/49.853). Another Lower Town hotel – though slightly dingier rooms. ④.

Aurora, Via dell'Apollinare 4 (☎0743/220.315). Excellent and very popular place at the heart of the Upper Town, just off Piazza della Libertà. ④.

Dell'Angelo, Via Arco del Druso 25 (☎0743/222.385). Pleasant *pensione* in a very central Upper Town location; only seven double rooms (no singles) so reservations are essential. ⑤.

Charleston, Piazza Collicola 10 (☎0743/220.052). Slightly fancier place in another fine Upper Town location, by the church of San Domenico. ⑤.

Clarici, Piazza della Vittoria 32 (☎0743/223.311). Reasonable, but rather basic, modern three-star hotel set just outside the walls of the Upper Town off a busy piazza en route for the train station. ⑤.

Nuovo Clitunno, Piazza Sordini 6 (☎0743/223.340). The best value mid-range hotel in the Upper Town, just west of Piazza della Libertà. ⑤.

Il Panciolle, Via del Duomo 3 (☎0743/45.598). Seven newly fitted rooms above a good restaurant in a quietish but convenient part of the Upper Town. A good bet. ⑤.

Paradiso, Monteluco 19 (☎0743/223.082). One to think about in the wooded hills above Spoleto if you don't fancy in-town options or their alternatives on the main road to Terni. ⑤.

Gattapone, Via del Ponte (☎0743/223.447). Hotels do not come any better than this. Spend a fortune or a honeymoon to enjoy views over the gorge and Ponte delle Torri in one of central Italy's best hotels. ⑨.

PRIVATE ROOMS
Delia Ferracchiato, Via Focaroli 12 (no phone). ②.

Maria Conti, Vicolo Leoncilli 8 (☎0743/49.976). ③.

Irene Ferracchiato, Via Mura Ciclopiche (no phone). ③.
Clara Schiarelli, Via Guido da Spoleto (☎0743/49.976). ③.
Iole Tomassoni, Via Cavallotti 9 (☎0743/220.441). ③.
Marcella Venanzi, Vicolo II 1, Corso Mazzini (☎0743/44.050). ③.

CAMPSITES
Camping Monteluco (☎0743/220.358). The closest campsite to town, just behind the church of San Pietro; very pleasant but tiny. Open April–Sept.
Il Girasole (☎0743/51.335). In the quiet village of Petrognano, served by hourly buses from the station, this is a bigger and flashier affair, with swimming pool and tennis courts. Open all year.

The Lower Town

Spoleto's art-festival credentials are immediately established by a grotesque monumental sculpture by Alexander Calder outside the train station. A relic of the 1962 festival, it serves as a gateway to the Lower Town, a quarter much rebuilt after bomb damage in the last war, but retaining a trio of Romanesque churches and some Roman fragments. If that doesn't appeal, catch the city bus from the station to Piazza della Libertà, heart of the old town, tempting from this distance with its skyline of spires and tiled roofs and splashes of craggy country-side; the fifteen-minute walk is an enjoyable one, too, once beyond the new concrete of Viale Trento e Trieste.

San Salvatore and San Ponziano

One of Italy's oldest churches, **San Salvatore** lies on the edge of the Lower Town, half-hidden in the cemetery, whose glimpse of the Italian way of death provides a faintly bizarre attraction in itself. Little has changed in the church since it was built by monks from the Eastern Mediterranean in the fourth or fifth century, on a site probably chosen for its proximity to Christian and Neolithic. catacombs. Conceived when the only models for religious buildings were Roman temples, the end result has a distinctly pagan feel, its dusty, gloomy **interior** (daily 7am–6/7pm) evoking an almost eerie antiquity, an atmosphere best enjoyed at dusk. The walls are bare, the floors covered in fallen stone, the crumbling Corinthian columns are wedged awkwardly alongside one another and the arches in the nave have been filled in to prevent total collapse. The apse, ringed round with Roman friezes and capitals, is a later addition that gives the church's upper half a crowded and lopsided appearance.

By contrast with San Salvatore's shattered facade, just a couple of minutes away is twelfth-century **San Ponziano**, dedicated to Spoleto's patron saint, with a Romanesque frontage which promises much but delivers little inside. A walk past and admiring glance are all the place merits, unless you can tempt the caretaker out of his house to show you the **tenth-century crypt**, a fascinating structure of odd, triangular columns believed to be *metae* (turning posts) from a Roman *circo* (race-track), backed by well-preserved patches of Byzantine fresco.

San Gregorio and the Anfiteatro Romano

Across the river in Piazza Garibaldi, **San Gregorio** dates from 1069 at the latest, but parts look as if they were built yesterday, a result of restoration after years of fire, flood and earthquake damage. Its narrow, porticoed **facade** incorporates a

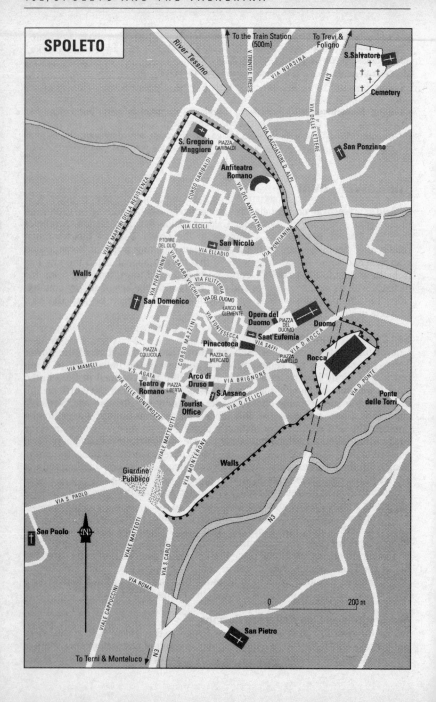

SPOLETO

River Tessino

To the Train Station
(500m)
V. TRENTO E TRIESTE

VIA NURSINA

To Trevi &
Foligno

S.Salvatore

Cemetery

N3

VIA DELLE LETTERE

CORSO GARIBALDI

S. Gregorio
Maggiore

PIAZZA
GARIBALDI

San Ponziano

VIA CACCIAGUERRA D. ALPI

Anfiteatro
Romano

VIA DEL ANFITEATRO

VIALE MARTIRI DELLA RESISTENZA

VIA CECILI

Walls

P.TORRE
DEL OLIO

San Nicolò

VIA ELLADIO

VIA PONZIANINA

VIA PIERLEONE

VIA SALARA VECCHIA

VIA FILITTERIA

San Domenico

VIA DEL DUOMO

LARGO M.
CLEMENTE

Opera del
Duomo

PIAZZA
DEL
DUOMO

Duomo

VIA FONTESECCA

Sant'Eufemia

VIA SAFFI

CORSO MAZZINI

Pinacoteca

VIA D. ROCCA

PIAZZA
COLLICOLA

PIAZZA D.
MERCATO

PIAZZA
CAMPELLO

Rocca

VIA MAMELI

VIA BRIGNONE

VIA D. PONTE

V.S. AGATA

Teatro
Romano

PIAZZA
LIBERTA

Arco di
Druso

Ponte
delle Torri

VIALE DELLE MONTEROZZE

S.Ansano

VIA D. FELICI

Tourist
Office

VIALE MATTEOTTI

Walls

Giardino
Pubblico

VIA MONTEFIORE

VIA S. PAOLO

N3

San Paolo

N

VIALE MATTEOTTI

VIALE CAPPUCCINI

VIA S. CARLO

VIA ROMA

0   200 m

To Terni & Monteluco

N3

San Pietro

patchwork of fragments filched from Roman remains. The pragmatic mix of materials is most obvious in the tower, its lower half built of massive Roman blocks, the upper of more refined fifteenth-century workmanship. The similarly patchworked **portico** was a sixteenth-century afterthought, added when the church was heightened to imitate the duomo in the Upper Town. The **interior** commands most interest, its walls stripped back to their Romanesque state, with substantial frescoes interrupted by a series of intimidating stone confessionals. The frescoes are local fourteenth-century efforts, the best of them in the presbytery, which is raised several metres above the nave, allowing for a **crypt** supported by dozens of tiny, mismatched pillars.

Tradition has it that somewhere under the church are the bones of ten thousand Christian martyrs killed by the Romans in the amphitheatre close by; the chapel alongside the portico, the Cappella degli Innocenti, is the favoured candidate for their resting place. Parts of the **amphitheatre** itself are still visible in the barracks up the road, on Via dell'Anfiteatro. No one seems to mind if you walk straight into the complex, which was formerly a monastery; bear right from the main gateway for the most substantial remains. When the Romans passed on, the huge arena was cannibalised for its stone, first by Totila and then by Cardinal Albornoz for the castle in the Upper Town. What remained was adapted as a medieval shopping arcade, and later bricked up in the courtyard you see today.

The ever-ingenious Romans constructed special gutters to drain blood from the arena into the Tessino river, which ran crimson as a result. The liberal flow of Christian blood is said to have suggested the name for the Roman bridge under nearby Piazza Garibaldi – the **Ponte Sanguinaria**. It formed part of the improvements to the Via Flaminia ordered by the Emperor Augustus, remaining in use until the fourteenth century. Much is supposedly intact below the piazza, and travel guides unfailingly suggest you can see it by climbing down the steps from the piazza; having actually been shut for years, Spoleto's council have recently tried to open it on a regular basis (daily 10am–1pm & 3–5pm), though don't be surprised to find that all you can see is a glimpse of a single arch through closed railings.

The Upper Town

There's really no single, central piazza in Spoleto, but the place to head first in the Upper Town is **Piazza della Libertà**, terminus for a few local bus services and home to the tourist office. With few obvious reference points, orientation is difficult in the jumble of levels and twisting, narrow streets around, though distances are short and everything worthwhile is a short walk from the square. Shops, banks and services are concentrated in **Corso Mazzini**, which runs north from Piazza della Libertà, and in **Corso Garibaldi**, which drops down to Piazza Garibaldi.

Around Piazza della Libertà

For an introduction to Spoleto's much-touted Roman heritage, you only have to cross Piazza della Libertà from the tourist office. Here you are confronted by the much-restored first-century **Roman theatre** (daily 9am–1.30pm & 3–7pm; free), complete enough, if overshadowed by the gaudily painted buildings on all sides. The worst of these offenders, the church and convent of Sant'Agata, absorbed much of the stage area in the Middle Ages and now houses a restoration centre and a very modest, two-roomed, **archaeological collection** of busts and stone fragments (same hours). The theatre stage, such as it is, is used for festival and other performances throughout the summer. Its past includes a grisly episode in 1319 when four hundred Guelph supporters were rounded up by the Spoletans and dumped on the stage with their throats cut; the corpses were then pushed into a pile and burnt.

Cutting into the adjoining Piazza della Fontana are further Roman remains. The **Arco di Druso**, straddling the entrance to the Piazza del Mercato – the old forum – is the only one of innumerable arches scattered around town not embedded in a wall. It was raised in 23 AD by the Spoletan senate to commemorate victories in Germany by Drusus, son of Tiberius and heir to the Empire until an early death ushered in Caligula. The **walls** hereabouts, and in Via dei Felici, are the city's oldest, built in the sixth century BC by the mysterious Umbrians.

To the right of the arch is what's described as a Roman **temple**, though you'll need a vivid imagination to see it as anything other than a ditch. However, it's worth nipping into the church of **San Ansano**, to the right of the arch, for the **crypt of Saint Isaac**, entered by the glass door on the left of the high altar. As well as containing more persuasive fragments of the temple than lie outside, the crude stone walls are decorated with recently restored frescoes that may date from the sixth century, a time when the spot was home to refugee Christian monks. The main structure dates from the twelfth century.

Nowhere do you get a better sense of Spoleto's market-town roots than in the homely **Piazza del Mercato**, which again is host to festival sculptures. In the square, old women wash fruit and vegetables in a fountain (its crown embellished with a highly eccentric clock), the men drink in the bars and swap stall-holders' gossip, and tourists make barely a dent in the overall proceedings. The *alimentari* on all sides are a cornucopia of picnic provisions, with a bias towards truffles and sticky liqueurs, notably the grim *Amaro di Tartufo*, often on special offer in the bargain bin. The piazza's open **market** runs from Monday to Saturday, 8.30am to 1pm, but there's almost more going on late in the evening when the outdoor tables of the main bar here are the best place for in-town summer drinking.

The Duomo

It's a short walk from Piazza del Mercato to the **Duomo**, whose restrained and elegant facade is one of the loveliest in Umbria. The careful balance of Romanesque and Renaissance elements is framed by a gently sloping piazza and hanging gardens, with the broad background of sky and open countryside setting the seal on the beautifully unified whole.

The building was consecrated in 1198, having been commissioned by Pope Innocent III to replace a seventh-century church flattened by Barbarossa. The **campanile** borrowed much of its stone from Roman ruins, a hotch-potch technique continued in the rest of the building. Architectural details unusual in Italy add interest for the technically minded, most notably the flying buttresses tucked out of sight on the side walls – climb to the park to the right for the best view. Strange, too, are the eight rose windows, clustered around a restored thirteenth-century mosaic of *Christ, the Virgin and St John*. In the Renaissance years, the arched portico with a superb carved doorway was added to the facade.

Less successful transformations were commissioned for the interior, where Pope Urban VIII's architect, Luigi Arrigucci, applied great dollops of Baroque midway through the seventeenth century. His improvements, however, are eclipsed by the building's original **marble floor**, and by magnificent **frescoes** on the *Life of the Virgin*, painted in 1467 by **Filippo Lippi** and his assistants Fra' Diamanti and Pier Matteo. The newly-restored cycle fills the domed apse, starting from the left wall with the *Annunciation* and *The Passage of the Virgin* (showing the three painters to the right), and concluding with the *Nativity*. Above spreads the most glittering scene of all, the *Coronation of the Virgin*.

Filippo Lippi died shortly after the cycle's completion, the rumour being that he was poisoned for seducing the daughter of a local noble family. The Spoletan cathedral authorities, not too bothered by such moral laxity, were delighted to have someone famous to put in their cathedral, being, as Vasari put it, "poorly provided with . . . distinguished men". Thus they refused to send the dead artist back to Lorenzo de' Medici, his patron, who had loaned Filippo to Spoleto, reputedly to stop his Florentine philandering. Interred in a **tomb** designed by his son Filippino, the corpse disappeared during restoration two centuries later, according to local legend spirited away by descendants of the compromised girl – a sort of vendetta beyond the grave. The empty tomb is in the right transept.

Take a look, too, at the **Cappelle Erioli** at the beginning of the right nave, adorned by Pinturicchio's faded *Madonna and Child* with Lago Trasimeno in the background, and with cruder frescoes in the adjoining chapel by the Sicilian Jacopo Santori. Minor titbits elsewhere in the cathedral include a bronze of Urban VIII by Bernini, too high above the main door to get a good look at, and an **icon** presented by Barbarossa in 1185 to make amends for having wrecked the town thirty years earlier, housed in the chapel below the organ loft. If lucky you might also be able to see the ninth-century **crypt** of San Primiano.

The Museo Civico

Spoleto's museums are minor and motley affairs, and the dread hand of restoration means they may be out of bounds for the foreseeable future. One that may be accessible is the **Museo Civico** at Piazza del Duomo 3 (10am–noon & 3–5pm; closed Tues; L3000), housed in the vaulted guard hall of an unfinished medieval palazzo and reached by the small lane left off the piazza as you face the duomo. Amidst a less than absorbing collection of cannonballs, sarcophagi, chimney-pieces and other bits and bobs, only the **Lex Spoletina** merits a special mention, a pair of Roman inscriptions which forbade the chopping down of trees in the sacred woods of Monteluco.

The injunction must have worked, because the forests, home to second-century hermits and later to saints Francis and Bernardino, are still there, cloaking the hills 8km east of the town. If you want to roam through the woods, take bus #9 from Piazza della Libertà or, if you're feeling strong, walk from the Ponte delle Torri; maps of the route are available from the tourist office.

Sant'Eufemia

The town's most celebrated **church** is twelfth-century **Sant'Eufemia**, above and to the left of the piazza in Via Aurelio Saffi. It's unique in Umbria for its *matroneum*, high-arched galleries above the aisles which served the purpose of segregating the women of the congregation. The entrance is easily missed, as the church is inside a courtyard off the street, and is all too often locked.

The church was built in honour of a local bishop, San Giovanni, martyred by the Goths and reputedly buried here in 980, on a site within both the precincts of the old Benedictine monastery and the archbishop's palace. Excavations have revealed that it also lies over the Lombards' eighth-century ducal palace, and Roman remains have been found, too. Good use was obviously made of materials from these previous buildings, one or two of the mismatched columns being carved with distinctive Lombard motifs. Like San Salvatore in the Lower Town, Sant'Eufemia is redolent with age and dank solemnity, its walls bare but for the odd patch of fresco and the only frills a stone chair and simple **altar**, both brought from the duomo in the thirteenth century. A new museum has opened in the same courtyard as the church, the **Museo Diocesano d'Arte Sacra** (July–Aug daily 10am–12.30pm & 4.30–7.30pm; other times on request; free), reached through the arch and up the stairs to the left of the facade. Its seven rooms trace faith and history in the Spoletan diocese from Roman times to the nineteenth century, its highlight being a painting from Mannerist star, Domenico Beccafumi.

The Pinacoteca

Spoleto's **Pinacoteca** is stuck away in the farthest reaches of the Palazzo del Municipio, usually accessed off the east side of Piazza del Mercato on Via del Municipio (10am–1pm & 3–5pm; closed Mon). Restoration work however may mean you have to enter by climbing the stairs of the council offices themselves, signed off Via A. Saffi almost opposite the courtyard entrance to Sant'Eufemia. The L5000 ticket for the gallery also gives entry to the remains of a Roman house in nearby Via Visiale (same hours; usually seen with the gallery's guide), the missable Galleria Comunale d'Arte Moderna on Corso Mazzini, and the chapel of SS. Giovanni e Paolo (see p.488).

After buying your ticket from a policeman in a very officious office to the right of the Via del Municipio entrance, you then have to wait for someone to show you around the gallery on the upper floor. The process may change when the collection is moved to the Rocca; timing of the move depends on completion of the castle's restoration, which could be any time this side of the millennium. The gallery's half-dozen rooms are sumptuously decorated (hence the guide), and worth seeing in their own right. Many of the paintings are outstanding, the highlights being the Umbrian works in the last two rooms – look out for an *Adoration of the Magi* by Perugino and the canvases by Lo Spagna, one of his local followers.

The Rocca and Ponte delle Torri

If you do nothing else in Spoleto, take the short walk out to the Ponte delle Torri, the town's picture-postcard favourite. It's best taken in as part of a circular walk around the base of the Rocca, or on the longer trek to San Pietro (see opposite). The **Rocca** itself is a perfectly endowed castle, with a half-dozen towers, neatly delineated crenellations and sheer walls. It was built as one of a chain of fortresses with which the tireless Cardinal Albornoz tried to re-establish Church authority in central Italy in the years preceding the Great Schism. Later it became part fortress, part holiday home, with several popes staying over, most notably Julius II, sometimes accompanied by Michelangelo. The fort's main latter-day function has been as a high-security prison, testimony to the skill of its medieval builders; Slavic and Italian political prisoners were held here during the war, while more recent inmates included members of the Red Brigades and Pope John Paul II's would-be assassin, Ali Agha. Since its demise as a prison, almost a decade of restoration has kept the Rocca closed, but opening is reputedly imminent. When the builders move out the entrance will be from Piazza Campello, near the Pinacoteca.

Within minutes of leaving the shady gardens of Piazza Campello you suddenly find yourself in open countryside, with a dramatic view across the Tessino gorge and south to the mountains of Castelmonte. There's an informal little bar about a hundred metres before the Ponte to help you enjoy the view.

This is also a good point to look down on a fine stretch of the town's **walls** and the **Ponte delle Torri**, an astonishing piece of medieval engineering with a 240-metre span supported by ten 80-metre-high arches. Designed by the Gubbian architect Gattapone – the man responsible for Gubbio's Palazzo dei Consoli – it was planned initially as an aqueduct to bring water from Monteluco, replacing a Roman causeway whose design Gattapone borrowed and enlarged upon. In time it became part of the town's defences, providing an escape from the castle when Spoleto was under siege. The remains of what used to be a covered passageway connecting the two are still visible straggling down the hillside.

San Pietro
Across the bridge, a left turn takes you to Monteluco via ilex woods and the mildly diverting **San Giuliano**, a twelfth-century church incorporating fragments of a sixth-century antecedent. If the idea of another church doesn't appeal, you can easily double back to town from here on the circular Via della Rocca. Views back to the bridge are best on this loop, and you could scramble partway down into the gorge for time out from the crowds.

Taking the right fork on the far side of the bridge leads in a couple of kilometres to the church of **San Pietro** – a pleasant, shaded walk that again offers good glimpses of Spoleto. The church's facade is visible from the bridge, and as you draw close reveals a series of twelfth-century **sculptures** that – with Maitini's bas-reliefs in Orvieto – constitute the finest Romanesque carving in Umbria. Partly Lombard in their inspiration, they draw variously on the Gospels and medieval legend for their complicated narrative and symbolic purpose. Much of the allegory is elusive, but reasonably self-explanatory panels include a *Wolf disguised as a Friar* before a fleeing ram – a dig at dodgy monastic morals – and, particularly juicy, the *Death of a Sinner* (left series, second from the top). Here the Archangel Michael abandons the sinner to a couple of demons who bind and torture the unfortunate before bringing in the burning oil to finish him off. Compare this with the panel above, the *Death of a Just Man*, where Saint Peter frees the man of his chains while Michael holds his soul in his scales; the Devil, lashed by the keys of Saint Peter, tries to tip the scales in his favour and holds a scroll that laments *doleo quia ante erat meus* (I mourn because he was mine before).

Best combined with a San Pietro excursion is a visit to the least-visited of all Spoleto's churches, **San Paolo inter Vineas**, stranded south of the town centre off Viale Giacomo Matteotti. Mentioned as early as the sixth century by St Gregory the Great, it was rebuilt in the tenth century and has now been restored to its beautifully simple twelfth-century state. It preserves frescoes of the Creation and prophets painted before the consecration of the present structure, which makes them among the oldest in the region. If the church is shut ring for admission at the old people's home next door (daily 9am–2pm).

San Domenico to San Nicolò
Among Spoleto's lesser churches, the massive monastic **San Domenico**, on the town's western margins, warrants a diversion for its colourful pink and white marble banding. Inside – in an interior of stripped-down Baroque – there are some fragments of fresco fossilised in new yellow plaster, the outstanding picture

being a large, early fifteenth-century **fresco** on the southern right-hand wall, *The Triumph of St Thomas Aquinas*. At the back of the church to the right of the presbytery is a small room of crude early frescoes; the Cappella dei Montevecchio in the left transept enshrines the umpteenth Nail of the Cross.

Close by in Via Filitteria, and nearing the end of a long renovation, the tiny chapel of **SS. Giovanni e Paolo**, consecrated in 1174, has an impressive thirteenth-century fresco outside, and has an interior covered in superb **frescoes** dating from the twelfth century onwards (daily 10am–1pm & 3–5pm; combined ticket – see p.486).

During even half-hearted wandering you'll probably come across **San Nicolò**, a couple of minutes north of SS. Giovanni e Paolo, impressively Gothic from the outside, but long deconsecrated and now a setting for third-rate exhibitions and jumble sales. In previous incarnations it was also a truffle market and workshop for repairing steam engines. Alongside is what must have been a beautiful **cloister**, now half-restored to its original state.

Food and drink

As you'd expect from its festival and cultural aspirations, Spoleto is a town that takes its food pretty seriously. **Restaurants** below are in ascending order of price. For a **picnic**, stock up at the market and food shops in the Piazza del Mercato. The best **bar** in town is the *Vincenzo*, on Corso Mazzini – you'll see the big names there during the festival.

RESTAURANTS

Piazza del Mercato, nos 10 and 29. A couple of nameless and cheap eating places, both catering mainly to Spoleto's workmen and market traders. L14,000.

Pizzeria dell'Angelo, Via Arco del Druso 25. Busy trattoria-pizzeria downstairs from the hotel. L18,000 for meals; pizzas for much less.

Trattoria del Teatro, Via Giustolo 9. A good, basic trattoria of white-washed, part pine-clad walls between Corso Mazzini and San Domenico.

Barcaccia, off Via Fontesecca. Located in a nook behind the Piazza Mercato fountain, this little trattoria does a roaring trade during the festival, when it stays open all day to feed the hungry musicians.

Il Grottino, Via Macello Vecchio. Very quiet place, off Corso Mazzini; moderately priced, large portions.

Il Panciolle, Largo Muzio Clemente. Although this restaurant has moved round the lime tree-filled piazza from its former idyllic setting and ritzed up its interior, it still has a great outside terrace at the back and remains an excellent choice for a reasonably priced, if never over-exciting, meal of Umbrian specialities like *strangozzi* and truffle dishes. Also known for its selection of cheeses. L15–30,000.

Trattoria San Giuliano, near San Giuliano church. Excellent views over the town and well-prepared Umbrian staples. L25–30,000.

Pentagramma, Via Martani 4 (☎0743/223.141). Owned by relatives of *Sabatini*'s chef-patron, this medieval vaulted dining-room with its out-of-place red-chequered tablecloths specialises in excellent Spoletan staples. Middling to upper price bracket, but a relaxed, un-Italian bistro atmosphere. Located immediately off Piazza della Libertà. L20–40,000.

Sabatini, Corso Mazzini 54. Best choice in the Upper Town; simple elegant interior and garden for summer eating; interesting, if occasionally over-elaborate variations of local dishes: just avoid cheese risotto, the house speciality. L20–40,000.

The Valnerina

The **Valnerina** has a stark, wild sort of beauty, all the more dramatic after the pastoral hill country to the west. The "little valley of the Nera", it constitutes a self-contained area of high mountains, steep wooded valleys, upland villages and vast stretches of barren nothingness. Deserted farms bear witness to a century of continuous emigration, and wolves still roam the summit ridges, soon to be protected by a long-awaited *Parco Regionale*. Few parts of Tuscany or Umbria are so genuine a "forgotten corner".

Access to the heart of the region can be tricky without your own transport but there are six **bus** services daily from Spoleto to Norcia, with stops at most villages along the way. In many cases you'll find a bus waiting at key junctions to connect with more distant towns and villages. **Piedipaterno** and **Borgo Cerreto** are the main intersections, where you can pick up connections south towards Terni. Because access to the Valnerina's lower reaches is more straightforward from the south, that region is dealt with in Chapter Twelve.

Spoleto to San Felice

Just before the Norcia road drops to the valley and the junction with the main SS209, the beautiful and tortuous **SS395** meets the minor road north to Geppa and Montefiorello, a superb switchback that rejoins the main road at Borgo Cerreto, 15km on. If you have time for a leisurely exploration of the Valnerina, this is definitely a diversion to go for.

A kilometre south of the junction of the SS395 and SS209 is the twelfth-century church of **San Felice**, its facade bearing only the bare essentials – arched doorway, rose window and two pairs of narrow windows. Lumpen red and white marble slabs floor the lovely interior, which is distinguished by a raised sanctuary, an ancient sarcophagus in the crypt, and fifteenth-century frescoes of Christ and the Magi. From here another minor road, to Monteleone di Spoleto, strikes southeast, offering great **views** and cutting across the main mountain ridge. Off-road walks from here to nearby summits are straightforward, the best target being **Monte Coscerno** (1685m), home to Umbria's two pairs of **golden eagles**.

San Anatolia di Narco

Three kilometres south of San Felice is the village of **SAN ANATOLIA DI NARCO**, continually inhabited since the eighth century BC and a typical Umbrian composite of castle, walls and medieval streets.

Until the 1960s a train service between Spoleto and Norcia ran this way, by all accounts one of the most beautiful lines in Italy. There are tentative and almost certainly foredoomed plans to reopen it; in the meantime you can use the line's route as a **footpath**, a trek which has recently become popular. The best stretch is between Spoleto and San Anatolia di Narco (see box over the page), a fairly level walk which takes about six hours – and requires a torch for the two-kilometre tunnel midway. The most enjoyable arrangement is to take an early bus from Spoleto and return on foot from San Anatolia, using the itinerary described below.

Alternatively you could overnight in the **hotel** in San Anatolia, the *Tre Valli*, Via della Stazione 10 (☎0743/613.118; ④).

THE WALK FROM SAN ANATOLIA TO SPOLETO

Leave San Anatolia on the road north over the river and pick up the track over the old railway bridge, opposite the bar-hotel *Tre Valli*. Follow the former course of the railway to the first tunnel. Turn right onto the track 20m before the tunnel, following it down for 200m; just before the stream-bed cut left to the top of a small vineyard. Take the steep track left at the junction of the woods and a field, and follow it to the intersection with the railway. Then either follow the old railway track and tunnels, or follow the track that cuts twice across the line's hairpins to emerge at a viaduct. Towards the end of the climb (1hr 45min) you come to open patches of green – fine for camping – with marvellous views of the Valnerina and mountains of Coscerno and Bacugno. Then walk through the main tunnel (2km – torch essential) and beyond it a longish stretch surfaced with gravel. Two viaducts follow, then some scrub (this part is private property) and then the first views of and descent towards the Vale of Spoleto. After another broad patch of green, the line becomes road once more, leaving an hour's walk to Spoleto itself. As an alternative to the road, 100m after the last viaduct, drop down left (through a hedge) to another road, turn left for 25m and turn right (sign for Villa San Giovanni). Turn left again and Spoleto appears; follow the old aqueduct and the red signs in the valley bottom to the Ponte delle Torri.

For full details of this and **other local walks**, ask for the special pamphlet from the tourist office in Spoleto or contact the *Club Alpino Italiano* at Via Piancini 4 (☎0744/28.233).

Scheggino, Triponzo and the Corno valley

Three kilometres south of San Anatolia and again laid out below a castle, **SCHEGGINO** is one of the most enchanting spots in the region. Much of this charm derives from a lattice of tiny canals below the medieval streets, themselves as captivating – especially in the evening – as any in Umbria. A further fine incentive for stopping is an excellent **hotel-restaurant**, the *Albergo-Trattoria del Ponte*, Via di Borgo 17 (☎075/61.131; [4]; restaurant closed Mon & Sept 1–15). Make a point of sampling one of the local specialities – trout, crayfish and truffles, the first two plucked from the ice-clear river, the last harvested by the local Urbani family, the top operators in the Italian truffle world. The only **campsite** for miles around is the *Valnerina* at nearby Valcasana (June 1–Sept 30; ☎0743/61.257) reached by taking the road east for a kilometre past the trout farm just outside Scheggino. There's a great outdoor public swimming pool on the left, midway between the village and campsite (June–Aug only).

You can continue south from Scheggino to Terni, but a better itinerary would be to return to San Anatolia and head north to **TRIPONZO** (Three Bridges), an ancient hamlet whose prominent marking on the map belies its size – just a shop and a couple of houses. Nonetheless, it was mentioned by Virgil, who talked of the Nera's creamy waters, an allusion to the **sulphurous springs** that feed into the river here.

Forsaking the Nera valley at Triponzo, the SS396 heads off north along the deep **Corno valley to Norcia**, the scenery becoming increasingly wild amid steep, bare mountains cut by tempting deserted side valleys. On the road, there are **hotels** at the hamlet of Biselli – two-star *Dei Cacciatori* (☎0743/818.126; [5]) – and a couple of kilometres further on at the larger village of Serravalle, which has a good three-star, the *Italia* (☎0743/818.120; [5]).

Preci, the Abbazia di San Eutizio and on to Norcia

If you stay with the **Nera valley**, the next point beyond Triponzo is the fortified village of **PRECI** – 12km north – which has a **hotel** with a swimming pool, the *Agli Scacchi* (☎0743/99.224; [4]). Nearby at Castelvecchio is a beautifully sited and top-grade **campsite**, the *Collaccio* (April–Oct; ☎0743/99.430), with friendly, English-speaking owner, swimming pool, and a chance to indulge in horse-riding, cycling, tennis and hang-gliding. There are also wooden chalets for rent, sleeping 4–6 people ([5] per chalet), and bunk rooms ([1]) or farmhouse rooms ([5]).

Two kilometres south, signposted off the Norcia road at Piedivalle, is the **Abbazia di San Eutizio**, a rambling monastic complex which was one of the cradles of the Benedictine movement. Initially a cemetery for hermits who had lived in the hills, it became a community that eventually controlled over one hundred churches and local castles. Its Romanesque church, built in 1190, has a fourteenth-century apse and gallery and, inside, a *Crucifixion* by Nicola da Siena (1461). The altar houses the sepulchre of Saint Eutizio, one of the early hermits, who was known for his missionary zeal and for his ability to induce rain; when there is a drought, locals still parade his tunic round the fields. Crawling through the specially constructed tunnel below the altar is also supposed to guarantee relief from all manner of back ailments. Steps behind the abbey church lead to the caves of the earliest monks – according to Gregory the Great it was in conversation with Eutizio and a fellow hermit in these grottoes that Benedict discovered his religious vocation.

The fifteen-kilometre stretch of road south from the Abbazia runs through delightful and pastoral country, the Castoriana valley, past the medieval hamlets of Piedivalle and Campi Vecchio. Just outside the former, on the roadside, is the church of **San Salvatore**, studded with frescoes and Roman fragments; at the latter, clearly visible high above the valley to the north, is the superb church of **Sant'Andrea**, whose portico frames one of the loveliest views in the area. The key to the church is kept by the old woman in the first house to the left: with a little prompting she should regale you with stories of the cholera pit beneath the

THE SURGEONS OF PRECI

Preci was once famous for its thirty families of **surgeons**, who from the twelfth to the mid-eighteenth century handed down their medical knowledge and hearsay from generation to generation. Over the years their patients included such luminaries as Pope Sixtus V, Sultan Mehmed the Conqueror and Elizabeth I of England. Their most notorious sideline was the castration of young boys foolish enough to show operatic potential, a spin-off that developed from the technique of using castration to prevent death from hernia – an area of expertise that the Preci surgeons picked up from their work on pigs.

The methods employed by the surgeons were entirely empirical: if something didn't work and the patient died, another approach was tried the next time. Their only classroom was the operating table, more often than not the kitchen table of the patient concerned. Crude anaesthetics in the shape of a jug of rum or strong wine were administered to induce unconsciousness, with boiling vinegar used as a post-operative antiseptic. Though some of Preci's surgeons gained a reputation for their skill in extracting kidney stones, most of the doctors were quacks, and when the papacy introduced more stringent licensing of medical practitioners the end of the tradition was swift. Not one of Preci's sawbones was granted a licence.

church, and the evil princess buried under the inverted Roman inscription on the facade, as well as showing you the beautifully kept interior. Beyond Sant'Angelo, 4km south of Piedivalle, the road climbs to 1008m at Forca d'Ancarano, a pass which affords spectacular views over surrounding mountains before the precipitous drop down to Norcia.

From Preci **an alternative route** to Norcia runs through Visso (in the Marche), then onwards by the desolate and stunning road over the Passo di Gualdo (1496m) and through Castelluccio.

Norcia

Noted on the one hand as the birthplace of Saint Benedict – founder of Western monasticism – and on the other as one of the country's great culinary capitals, small, walled and stolid **NORCIA** is the only place of substance in eastern Umbria. Its air of shadowy desolation and low, sturdy houses are a world away, though, from the bucolic towns to the west, a contrast explained by the constant threat of earthquakes. Thick-walled and heavily buttressed, Norcia's buildings have been compulsorily stunted since 1859, when a law forbade the raising of houses over 12.5 metres high. The last tremor, a particularly violent one, was in 1979; outside the town you'll see ranks of temporary housing, ready for the next quake.

Ancient Norcia was the northernmost town of the Sabines, contemporaries of the Umbrians, before becoming a minor Roman *municipio*. After the attention of sixth-century barbarians, recovery took a long time to come – and when it did, **earthquakes** periodically discouraged long-term development. For five centuries before Unification, though, the town was effectively a frontier post between the Papal States and the Kingdom of Naples, making a safe haven for bandits and refugees from opposing sides. Papal reaction was to build the **Castellina** in 1554, a huge, blunt fortress that dominates the town centre. Thereafter Norcia and the surrounding countryside was drained by emigration, a trend that continues today.

The Town

Buses drop you at the **Porta Romana**, from where it's a straight walk on Corso Sertorio to the central **Piazza San Benedetto**, a large, open area with something of a High Noon atmosphere, presided over by a statue of Benedict. Buses leave on the opposite side of town, just outside Porta Ascolana.

The square's most arresting sight is the church of **San Benedetto**, built, according to legend, over the house where Benedict and his sister, Saint Scholastica, were born; it's more likely to have been the site of a Roman temple, as the square itself was the site of the forum. Despite repeated post-earthquake reconstructions, the facade – sole survivor from the 1389 original – remains an attractive, two-tiered affair, with Gothic portal, rose window, and thirteenth-century campanile to the rear. During Norcia's blast-furnace summers the newer arched gallery to the right provides welcome shade, and it has a drinking fountain too. Notice also the unusual old stone measures, used for selling or distributing wine and olive oil. Little remains of interest within, though it's worth going down into the **crypt** and searching the north transept for Filippo Napoletano's *St Benedict and Totila*, the town's major painting. Stone fragments of a late-Roman edifice are clearly visible here, in the most suggestive part of the church.

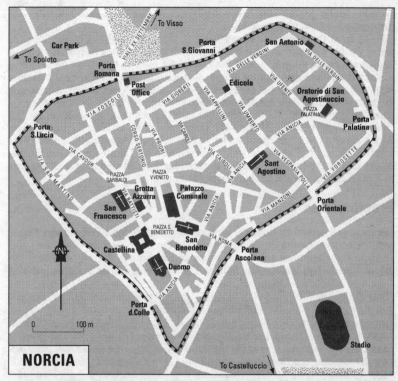

NORCIA

Across the square is the unmissable **Castellina**, an extraordinarily gaunt affair with no concessions to architectural subtlety. It was built for Pope Julius III by the usually sophisticated Vignola and now houses the town's **Museo Civico** (though at the time of writing the museum is shut indefinitely). Most of the five rooms are taken up with sculptures, the highlight being a rare thirteenth-century *Deposition*. Adjacent is the uninteresting sixteenth-century **Duomo**, its less than dominating position a result of comparative modernity, its forlorn interior the legacy of countless earthquakes. Completing the piazza's ensemble is the now superbly restored **Palazzo Comunale**, oddly but beautifully multicoloured, and based around a 1492 portico and later additions which blend delightfully to create the town's most distinctive building.

The piazza's other main component is its **food shops**. Anything that can be done to a pig, food-wise, the Norcians apparently do, and better than anyone else – which is why you'll see butchers in other parts of Italy are called *Un Norcino*. Sausages, salami, hams and wild boar, reputedly the country's best, are all in abundance, as are less appetising non-porcine delicacies such as mountain ram and sausage-filled sacs claiming to be mules' testicles. Local mountain cheeses are excellent too – two years old and never in a fridge – and if finances stretch you could indulge in the area's rare **black truffle**. The season runs from January to April, but all year you can sample the foul truffle digestif called *Amaro di*

Tartufo, truffle *grappa*, and even truffle ice cream. The bar opposite San Benedetto is a good place to indulge.

Away from the square, head northeast to the **Edicola** (literally the "kiosk"), one of the town's more unusual buildings. Built in 1354 by Vanni Tuzi, it's a small arched structure, decorated with bas-reliefs and open to the street on all sides. Beyond the Edicola is a quarter of town that fell into disrepair during the Middle Ages and was taken over by shepherds from Castelluccio (see p.496). Adopting it as their own, they built small houses – complete with stalls for their sheep – amidst a jumble of streets that contrasts with the central grid. Look out for the church of **Sant'Antonio Abate** – the shepherds' saint, invoked to protect their flocks. Among the other churches be sure to see **Sant'Agostino**, half-filled with surprisingly accomplished and well-preserved frescoes (located in Via Anicia, two blocks east of the Edicola), and the tremendous wooden ceiling of the **Oratorio di Sant'Agostinccio** just behind Piazza Palatina.

Practicalities

Norcia is well served by **buses** from Spoleto, Terni, Perugia, Foligno and Assisi, and can be the base for some good trips into the Piano Grande (see p.496) and north to the Castoriana valley and abbey of San Eutizio. A new road over the mountains into the Marche also looks set to open up the area though squabbles

---

TRUFFLES

Though disconcertingly turd-like in appearance, weight for weight **truffles** are the world's costliest foodstuff. In 1993 the lowliest variety was fetching L350,000 (about £150) per kilo in Norcia, one of the handful of places in Europe where they grow in abundance, and the most expensive variety was retailing at a staggering L4.5 million (£2000). They have been prized for their reputed aphrodisiac qualities and earthy, aromatic flavour since Roman times, when they were believed to have been formed by lightning striking the earth.

Truffles are subterranean fungi of the class *Ascomycetes*, part of the *Tuber* genus, a species that's believed to be some 100 million years old. Unable to carry out photosynthesis, they live symbiotically with certain forest plants, and the conditions necessary for their growth are extremely subtle and specific, something which has made commercial production something of an agricultural Holy Grail. They thrive best in calcareous soils, amid oak and hazel woods, but altitude and climate are also critical factors in distribution.

Anything from the size of peas to the size of footballs, they attain their final dimensions in only two or three days, generally in the spring, but then take up to eight months to mature. It is only when they are ripe that they give off their distinctive smell and can be tracked from above ground. Once mature, they remain in good condition for only ten days, and if not harvested within this time they become poisonous. Truffles in a single bed, however, might mature at varying times over a period of four or five months, allowing the skilled hunter a steady supply.

Scent is the key to finding truffles, though the old hands can recognise likely areas by distinctive patches of bare, stony ground. Truffles exude countless volatile compounds, including one that closely resembles the musky sexual **pheromones** of the wild boar – it is thought the fungi give off almost twice the amount of this scent as the testicles of the male boar. One explanation for this is that they exude

between regional councils over who's to pay for drainage of the major tunnel – which lies under the Umbria–Marche border – has kept the completed multi-billion lire project closed since 1989. Lack of funds has closed Norcia's tourist office and at present the only source of town maps (no other information) is a hole-in-the-wall left of the dry cleaner's behind the Palazzo Comunale. In the southeast corner of Piazza San Benedetto there's a *tabacchaio* that sells walking maps and guides – handy if you're going on into the Sibillini.

You should have few problems with **hotel** rooms, first choice on a budget being the one-star *Monastero San Antonio*, Via delle Vergini 13 (☎0743/816.657; [4]), located just east of Porta San Giovanni. Of the slightly more upmarket options, *Da Benito*, Via Marconi 5 (☎0743/816.670; [4]), is pleasant enough, but if you can afford the extra get a room at the far superior *Grotta Azzurra*, Via Alfieri 12 (☎0743/816.513; [6]), the town's best, busiest and friendliest hotel (it's also extremely central, immediately off the main square – and right alongside *Da Benito*). Recently opened under the same management as the *Grotta Azzurra* is the *Salicone*, immediately outside the town walls at Porta Romana, an astoundingly smart four-star hotel – soon to have some of the best sports facilities in central Italy – with extremely competitive rates for a place of this quality (phone and price as for *Grotta Azzurra*). The nearest **campsite** is just outside the hamlet of Scheggino (see p.490), though a short walk out of town to the east offers scope for freelance pitching.

the chemical to attract wild pigs, which then eat the fungus and thereby help disperse its spores. Thus sows were once used as truffle trackers, but they have long been displaced by dogs, as sows were prone to sexual frenzies when close to the truffle hoard. So valuable are the finds that it's not unusual for people to hunt at night equipped with a torch and trowel, searching a spot where dogs have sniffed out their prey earlier in the day.

Every aspect of truffle exploitation is **controlled by law**, from hunting and final sale to the ownership of land rights and the precise definition of varieties, but in practice most people moonlight (literally), with only those working for large producers such as *Urbani* in Scheggino (the world's largest) being obliged to obey the bureaucratic niceties. Old-timers say this free-for-all, a relatively recent phenomenon, is ruining the business as new-comers ravage old beds for short-term gain, thereby destroying yields not only for a season, but for years to come.

There are countless **types of truffle**. Nine are edible, though only six are well known and commercialised. Four are considered a delicacy, and of these two are found in quantity around Norcia and Spoleto. Varieties mature at different depths and at different times of the year, so that April and May are the only times of the year when fresh truffles are not available. Umbria's most common type is the **tartufo nero**, gathered from a few centimetres below the ground between mid-November and mid-March. More prized is the **tartufo pregiato**, available over the same period. Rarer are the two summer and autumn **scorzone** varieties.

You'll find shops all over Norcia selling truffle paste, truffles under oil (to preserve them), and truffle-flavoured oils, cheeses, liqueurs, pâtés – even truffle chocolate. For the real thing, however, head for the *Grotta Azzurra*'s tremendous restaurant, a temple to Umbrian cuisine, and treat yourself to either *risotto al tartufo* or *tagliolini al tartufo*, the latter the classic way to tackle a truffle. If finances allow, indulge in their award-winning marriage of truffle and steak, *Filetto del Cavatore* (Fillet of the Truffle-Hunter).

You'd be foolish not to try local specialities in the **restaurants**, the best known of which is the *Trattoria del Francese*, Via Riguardati 16 (☎0743/816.290; closed Fri), which in the event turns out to have a rather tatty trattoria atmosphere. Far better is to make for the medieval dining halls of the *Grotta Azzurra*, complete with huge fire, suits of armour and tapestries, where you can sample Castelluccio lentils, truffles, mountain mushrooms, cheeses and hams, and probably enjoy one of the finer meals you'll eat in Umbria.

The Piano Grande and the Monti Sibillini

The mountainous landscape east of Norcia is one of the most distinctive in all Italy, with its centrepiece the eerie **Piano Grande** – an upland prairie devoid of any feature save sheep, hang-gliders and the odd bedraggled haystack. Surrounded on all sides by the sheer and barren mountains of the **Monti Sibillini**, the Piano Grande forms a colossal amphitheatre that's often swathed in a dense, early morning mist. Gazing down on this intimidating wilderness from the remote hamlet of **Castelluccio**, it's easy to imagine the hazards for the unsuspecting traveller in past centuries. Papal rulers actually forbade crossing the plain during winter, and even today the bells of Castelluccio toll on gloomy days to guide shepherds across its desolation. If it looks familiar, you've probably seen Zeffirelli's glutinous Franciscan epic, *Brother Sun, Sister Moon*, for which it was a key set. Recently the plain achieved a more modest fame as the world's largest football pitch, when it hosted a match between two teams of a hundred players each; the home side went down by twelve goals to one.

Spring is the best period to visit the *piano*, when it blazes with an extraordinary profusion of **wild flowers**, one month radiant with buttercups, the next with poppies and narcissi. Woven into the floral carpet are rare Alpine flora, including the *Carex buxbaumi*, an Ice-Age relic discovered in 1971 and believed to be unique. On the mountains around you find tulips, fritillaries and peonies as well as further rarities like Apennine edelweiss (found elsewhere only in parts of the Abruzzo), the Martagon lily, Bear's grape, Apennine potentilla and the Alpine buckthorn – though you don't need to be an expert to enjoy the startling general spectacle.

Throughout the area you'll come across so-called *marcite* – strips of cultivated land irrigated by a tracery of canals of a type found only in Umbria and Lombardy. They're different because the water in them emerges from limestone springs at a constant 10°C, creating an artificially mild climate that allows for several annual crops of hay.

Castelluccio

At 1452m, **CASTELLUCCIO** is one of Italy's highest settlements, and the only habitation for many miles around: an isolated farming settlement, served by **bus** twice a day for only half the week, from Norcia's Porta Ascolana (Mon–Thurs 6.25am & 1.30pm). As well as its appeal as a belvedere onto the grasslands and a trailhead for mountain walks, the village has started to attract attention from hang-gliders, drawn by the Sibillini's treeless slopes. There's likely to be at least one camper parked in the windblown square.

So far, though, the place has made few concessions to tourism and the feel is of an uncompromising and bleak working village. The almost incestuously inter-related population has dropped from 700 in 1951 to around 150 today; most of the remaining inhabitants are migrant shepherds, many of them Sardinians or Yugoslavs, who spend the winter months down in Norcia. The most immediately noticeable thing in the village is its **graffiti**, daubed in thick white paint on huge walls; this forms a kind of social document for the community, the pieces – often malicious and some going back generations – recording stories and myths about local people. Wander up to the parish church, currently being restored, which has a a marvellous fresco cycle describing the life of San Antonio Abate, patron saint of shepherds and their flocks. On the arch outside the church to the right as you look down to the Piano Grande notice also the Fascist plaque, of a type long ago removed from other, less remote towns and villages in Italy, which salutes the "refounder of the Italian Empire".

Practicalities

It's well worth calling ahead for a room. There is only one **hotel** as such, the newly expanded and smartened-up two-star, *Sibilla* (☎0743/870.113; ④), an Alpine-looking building in the village centre with just eleven double rooms. The only alternative are rooms offered in a rather chilly modern annexe behind the *Taverna di Castelluccio* (☎0743/870.158; ④). The *Taverna* itself is a friendly place, with excellent **food**; it's well worth trying the tiny lentils for which the village is famous. The *Sibilla* also has a reasonable, though less appealingly rustic, restaurant annexe. Castelluccio's shops have only the most basic supplies, though fruit and bread vans visit regularly – except in winter, when the place is frequently cut off by snow.

   Camping anywhere in the hills around is no problem, there being plenty of grassy flat ground a stone's throw from the village. Further afield, be sure to take huge amounts of water, as the limestone hills have no surface source. There is a summer **campsite**, *Monte Prata* (☎0743/9828), in the small ski-lift area on the road north of Castelluccio at Schianceto. You could also stay at the smartly refurbished *Forca Canapine* (☎0743/816.508; ④), a huge pink building on the Norcia to Arquata road on the pass at the southern edge of the Piano Grande (8km from Castelluccio) – also an excellent base for walks. A similar distance north of the village on the Visso road, and similarly well-sited for hiking, is the lonely *La Fiorita* (☎0737/98.148; ④).

   For **hang-gliding** information contact the *Scuola di Volo* just north of the village. For **walking information** – and maps and books on the area – the *Bar del Capitano*, on the southern edge of the village, with a great belvedere over the Piano Grande, is handy, as is the *Hotel Sibilla*.

Walking in the Sibillini

The **Monti Sibillini** are the only really wild mountains of Tuscany and Umbria, and the most precious natural environment for many hundreds of miles. The most northerly of the big Apennine massifs, they run north to south for about forty kilometres, their summit ridge marking both the Umbrian border and the watershed between the Adriatic and Tyrrhenian seas. In **Monte Vettore** (2476m) they have the third highest point on the peninsula, a massive, barren mountain that rises above the Piano Grande with majestic grandeur. The Sibillini have recently been designated a **national park**, a status that sadly exists more on paper than on the ground, with no binding laws to stop hunting or building.

According to local tradition, the mountains were home to one of the three ancient **sibyls** – the wise women with oracular powers who were supposed to have foretold the coming of Christ. Later misogynist versions of the sibyl myth transformed them into temptresses possessed by the devil – those lured to the sibyls' caves were doomed to remain trapped there until the Day of Judgement – which perhaps explains why these mountains have a reputation for necromancy and devil worship. By happy coincidence the code for the *Kompass* map to the area is 666, the devil's number.

Hiking in the Sibillini is superb, whether you fancy casual day hikes or more demanding backpack ventures. Unlike the Alps or Abruzzo there are few marked paths – these are not yet well-known mountains – and you're unlikely to meet many people other than shepherds. However, the *Club Alpino Italiano* (*CAI*) have discreetly tagged a few trails, with a view to ultimately creating a continuous path on the summit ridge.

Among **maps**, the 1:50,000 *Kompass: Sibillini* is adequate and widely available, though locally you should be able to pick up the better 1:25,000 *Montevettore* produced by *Universo* and the *Unione Italiana Sport Popolare*; the latest stretches of the *CAI* path are recorded in a supplement that comes with the *Universo* map. **Paths** marked on maps do generally exist – not always the case with *Kompass* maps – but in good weather the hills are so open (bar a few glorious beech woods) that you can wander pretty much at will, at least on the western, Umbrian side of the mountains. This is less true on the eastern flanks (in the Marche) which are dotted with dangerous crags and screes. However, around Castelluccio and the western ramparts the worst you'll have to contend with are some of the steepest grass slopes you'll ever come across.

For enthusiasts or emergencies there are several **mountain huts** (marked on maps), none with services, and often in a poor state.

The hikes

Castelluccio is undoubtedly the best base for **day hikes**, with trails leaving from the village in all directions. **Monte Vettore** via Forca di Presta (8km east of Castelluccio on the road to the Marche) is the obvious big target, returning along the ridge via Quarto San Lorenzo and Forca Viola. This is a pretty tough full day's outing, which you could take at a more leisurely pace by starting at the summer-only **refuge** at Forca di Presta (☎0743/99.278 or 99.165; always call in advance). Sited at 1500m, the *rifugio* is a source of basic food, maps and information.

Another good walk from Forca di Presta or Castelluccio, mainly downhill through woods, takes you to **ARQUATA DEL TRONTO**, in the Marche, a small-ish place with two **hotels**, the best of which is *Ca' Martina* (☎0743/99.261; ④). A third rewarding hike is to strike across country from Castelluccio to Norcia, a route comfortably accomplished in a day.

For a quick and easy glimpse of the scenery north of Castelluccio follow the *strada bianca* (gravel road), for about twenty minutes, past the *Scuola di Volo*, round the corner into the Valle Canatra and on to the Fonte Valle Canatra. It's an all but level stroll which you could prolong by following the obvious cart track to the head of the lovely pastoral valley and the open plains under Monte delle Rose (1881m). Another excellent, straightforward and not overly demanding walk is to leave Castelluccio on the obvious upper *strada bianca* west and then follow the rough road and clear path along the ridges of the Piano Grande's western rim (Colle Tosto, Monte Vetica etc), and overnight at Forca Canapine.

A more ambitious and longer hiking route is to cross over the ridge east of Castelluccio into the Marche, where the best-known walk runs to the **Lago di Pilato**, an idyllic spot under Monte Vettore. This is supposedly the burial place of Pontius Pilate, the story being that Pilate's body was dispatched from Rome on a cart pulled by two oxen, who traipsed through wild country and then plunged into the lake, disappearing without trace. The legend has made the lake the heart of the mountains' supposed necromantic practices; Norcians used to sacrifice animals here, and humans too, so it is said, to placate the demons and protect themselves from storms and bad weather. When the area was part of the Papal States a wall was built by the church to prevent access to the lake, and stones inscribed with occult symbols have been found on the shores. Recently, the lake has all but dried up, putting in danger an endemic crustacean (*chirecephalus marchesonii*) which used to stain the water red, a colouring anciently attributed to the blood of Pilate.

From Lago di Pilato, another superb trail runs under the main ridge along the Valle del Aso to the hamlet of **FOCE**, where there are **beds** at the *Rifugio della Montagna* (☎0743/960.327; ④). The combined trek from Castelluccio to the lake and then to Foce makes a perfect day's walk.

East of Foce, **MONTEMONACO** in the Marche makes another good Sibillini walking base. A nice medieval village in itself, it provides a starting point for walks up Monte Sibilla (2173m) and the spectacular yet easy hike in the **Gola del Infernaccio** (Hell's Canyon). This is a huge gorge complete with cliffs and crashing river, which opens out into a broader upland where an upper track takes you to the **Eremo di San Leonardo**, home to the Capuchin hermit and eccentric, Pietro Lavini (who has become something of a tourist attraction). Cheapest of the village's **hotels** is the *Orsa Maggiore*, Via Roma (☎0736/960.128; ④); the *Rifugio Monte Sibilla*, handier for the mountains, is eight kilometres from the village.

Cascia and around

CASCIA, 18km south of Norcia, figures large on the map but is disappointing in actuality, only recommendable to pilgrims in search of **Saint Rita**. Her presence – and the stupendously ugly twentieth-century **Basilica** – dominate both the new and the earthquake-damaged hill town, which was abandoned for a time in the eighteenth century. Little-known elsewhere, Rita has a massive cult following in Italy, especially amongst women, for whom she is a semi-official patron saint. Thousands come annually to venerate her shrine.

The Basilica di Santa Rita and the town

Rita's Basilica in the old town is a monument to religious vulgarity probably without equal – a piece of fascist architectural brutalism that attempts to place Byzantine and Romanesque elements in a modern context, and in doing so produces a fantasy in white marble that looks like it belongs in Disneyland. Rita's exhumed and mummified body lies behind grilles on the left, northern side of the basilica, surrounded in half-gloom by flickering candles and votive offerings, whose appeals for the saint's miraculous salvaging of impossible situations include the pennants of several Italian football teams.

SAINT RITA

Rita experienced – and came through – virtually all a woman can suffer, which is the main reason for her appeal, and also why she's sometimes known as the "saint of the impossible". Apparently you can invoke Saint Rita when an ordinary miracle isn't enough. Born in 1381, a poor child of aged parents, she was pushed into a forced marriage at fifteen and endured eighteen years of mistreatment from an alcoholic husband. Having weaned himself from the bottle and repented his past, the husband died in a brawl a few weeks later. Rita's children, wretched wasters at the best of times, both died attempting to avenge their father.

Beaten, widowed and childless, Rita sensibly thought it about time she became a nun. Her knowledge of the marital bed, however, made this impossible; only a relaxation of convent rules allowed her to become an Augustinian, a development held up as one of her "impossible" miracles. No sooner had she joined than she developed a sore in the middle of her forehead, an excrescence so foul-smelling that none of the nuns would come near her. This was supposedly developed when a thorn fell from a crown of thorns as she was praying to a statue of Christ and was regarded by her companions as a kind of stigmata. The smell abated only once – to allow her to join her companions in a week's visit to Rome to meet the pope; on their return the odour resurfaced as virulent as ever.

Rita died in 1457, but the process of her beatification was laborious, hampered by doubts as to the veracity of her miracles, by the fact she was a woman – and worse, a woman with a past – and doubtless by the size of her grassroots support, a groundswell the papacy feared beyond their control. Hence the proclamation of her beatification came only in 1628, and her elevation to sainthood as late as 1900, and then only in the wake of a huge public campaign.

The interior is smothered in extravagant stonework – all bearing the robust, strong-lined bludgeoning of fascist masonry – and the vaulted ceiling and cupola glow with garish painting-by-numbers frescoes. The altar is surrounded by what appears to be gold barbed wire and is surmounted by a large golden egg. Visitors are taken in groups to Rita's original Augustinian monastery, which is now annexed to the building, for a view of the cell in which she died, a vine which grew from her walking stick, and a rose – which Rita coaxed into life out of season – transplanted from her garden in Roccaporena (see opposite).

Cascia's other remaining sights are few, and many are still under restoration following a catastrophic earthquake in 1979. The most important is the small **Pinacoteca** in the church of **Sant'Antonio Abate**, which contains fifteenth-century Umbrian frescoes on the *Life of St Anthony* and a depiction of *The Passion* by Nicola da Siena. A new gallery, collecting together the best of the town's paintings, is due to open in the Palazzo Santa above Piazza Garibaldi. In the Upper Town, **San Francesco**, rebuilt almost completely in 1925, houses a fourteenth-century Gothic choir and a *Madonna and Child* by Nicola da Siena – in a niche left of the entrance. Nearby **Santa Maria** is the town's oldest church, a large airy space, still with a medieval atmosphere of sorts, but with only a few fragments of early fresco.

Practicalities

The **tourist offices**, in the central square at Piazza Garibaldi 1 (☎0743/71.147; Mon–Sat 9am–1pm & 4–6pm) and at Via G. Da Chiavano 2 (☎0743/71.401; Mon–Fri 9am–1pm & 4–6pm), are the main offices for eastern Umbria, including the

Valnerina, Norcia and the Piano Grande, and so can be worth a visit for maps and pamphlets.

Amongst the huge, pilgrim-oriented **hotels**, the best for general purposes is the two-star *Centrale*, Piazza Garibaldi 16 (☎0743/76.736; ④); a little more upmarket is the three-star *Cursula*, Via Cavour 3 (☎0743/76.206; ⑤), which has Cascia's best **restaurant**. If you have a car, a far preferable alternative is to drive 6km south into the mountains to Onelli, where you can stay at the tiny *Belvedere* (April–Oct; ☎0743/76.172; ③).

Roccaporena and the Corno valley

Cascia's countryside is considerably more rewarding than the town. If you want a quick taste – and to stay on the Saint Rita trail – the trip to **ROCCAPORENA**, the saint's birthplace, admirably fits the bill. The best way to get here is to take the marked and well-worn **Sentiero-Passeggiata di Santa Rita**, a perfectly level path that contours above the Corno gorge for 6km between Cascia and the village. The track can be picked up in the centre of town through the forecourt of the *Delle Rose* hotel, or about 200m down on the left, up steps off the road from the centre of Cascia to Roccaporena. After 5km cut down to cross the river on a wooden bridge, just after a ruined house and the point where a large and obvious pipe crosses the river. The last kilometre is on the road.

The village of Roccaporena, six kilometres west of Cascia, sits at the bend of a deep-sided, heavily wooded valley, dominated by a soaring vegetation-shrouded crag, the **Scoglio di Santa Rita**. Perched on the needle-point summit is a tiny chapel, exhausting to reach but with magnificent views. In the village, a small but often pilgrim-thronged place, the parish church of **San Montano** has the graves of Rita's family, and is the spot where she concluded her unfortunate marriage.

More people make the pilgrimage to the site of the saint's garden, an unlikely spot for horticulture, given its barren, cliff-edge location. It's easily found by following signs for the **Orto di Santa Rita** towards the cross on the valley side opposite the Scoglio. The spot is marked by a modern bronze statue of the saint, on and around which are hundreds of invocations, scrawled on scraps of paper. There's just one place to **stay**, the *Casa del Pellegrino* (☎0743/71.205; ④), an institutional but spotless and comfortable pilgrims' hotel (look out for the luminous crucifixes above the beds). It also has a cheap, Fifties-era canteen-like restaurant, the only place in the village to eat.

The Corno valley and Monteleone

There are plenty of opportunities for **walks** into the hills from Roccaporena, and particularly along the wooded arm of the **Corno valley** that makes a dog's leg turn to the south. To pick up paths simply follow the gravel road beyond the *Casa del Pellegrino*, which climbs quickly, becoming a cart track after a couple of kilometres. One kilometre east into the valley, it's worth making a brief detour to the hamlet of Capanne, for its views and small fifteenth-century church. An hour's walk northwest from there, over upland, leads to the lonely **Madonna delle Stelle**, a restored monastery which you can also reach – more easily – from the Borgo Cerreto to Monteleone road.

MONTELEONE itself, on the only road south into Lazio, is the only place of any size for miles around. Surrounded by grand hill country, it's a fine, if in parts earthquake-battered, medieval village, noted for wood-carving and delicacies such as olives, wine and truffles. The main sight is the church of **San Francesco**, graced with an exceptional Gothic door, and scattered with artistic and archaeological fragments excavated from a massive Neolithic necropolis nearby.

travel details

Trains

From Spoleto to Foligno via Trevi (15 daily; 20min; connections for Spello, Assisi, Perugia and Teróntola); Perugia direct (1 daily; 45min); Nocera Umbra (8 daily; 40min); Fossato di Vico (12 daily; 1hr); Terni (15 daily; 30min); Narni (10 daily; 40min); Orte (9 daily; 55min; connections to Rome and Florence).

Buses

From Spoleto to Foligno via Trevi and Fonti di Clitunno (7 daily); Montefalco (2 daily); Norcia and the Valnerina (6 daily; change at Piedipaterno for San Anatolia and Monteleone — 3 daily); Perugia (2 daily, early morning); Rome (1 daily); Urbino (1 daily).

From Norcia to Spoleto (6 daily) and frequent services to Cascia. One weekly to Castellucio. Daily services to Foligno, Perugia, Rome and Terni.

From Cascia to Foligno, Monteleone, Norcia, Perugia, Rieti, Roccaporena, Rome, Spoleto and Terni.

CHAPTER TWELVE

ORVIETO AND SOUTHERN UMBRIA

Southern Umbria features two of the province's most illustrious hill towns – **Orvieto** and **Todi**. Each has become a little too popular for its own good, but they are essential visits, the former for Italy's richest Gothic cathedral, the latter for its atmosphere and stunning high-altitude location. Often bypassed in the rush to these star attractions are a number of smaller but perhaps more enjoyable centres, notably **Narni** – occupying a promontory above the River Nera – and **Amelia**, whose encircling **walls** are among the most redoubtable in the country.

Terni, the main transport focus and the province's largest supply centre after Perugia, is the area's low spot, a grim industrial city whose most valuable role is as the southern gateway to the **Valnerina**. Buses up to the valley's historical highlight, the **Abbazia di San Pietro in Valle**, pass close to the most celebrated landscape attraction in this part of Umbria, the **Cascate delle Marmore** – a partly artificial waterfall that is nonetheless an impressive spectacle.

Umbria's main **rail line** goes through Terni, from where northbound trains head through Spoleto and southbound services via Narni to connect with the Rome–Florence route at Orte; northbound services from here will take you to Orvieto. The most enjoyable ride is provided by the *Ferrovia Centrale Umbra* (*FCU*), a private **single-track line** that runs from Terni to Perugia, and then on to Città di Castello and Sansepolcro. Using spartan two-carriage trains, this fills the gaps left by the state network, rattling through lovely countryside to provide access to Todi, and to minor halts like **Deruta**, heart of the region's ceramic tradi-

ACCOMMODATION PRICES

Throughout this guide, accommodation is graded on a scale from ① to ⑨. Grades ① and ② apply to **hostel** accommodation, and indicate the lowest price a **single person** could expect to pay for one night in that establishment in high season. Grades ③ to ⑨ apply to **hotels**, and indicate the cost of the **cheapest double room in high season**. The price bands to which these codes refer are as follows:

① under L20,000 per person	④ L50–70,000 per double	⑦ L120–150,000 per double
② over L20,000 per person	⑤ L70–90,000 per double	⑧ L150–200,000 per double
③ under L50,000 per double	⑥ L90–120,000 per double	⑨ over L200,000 per double

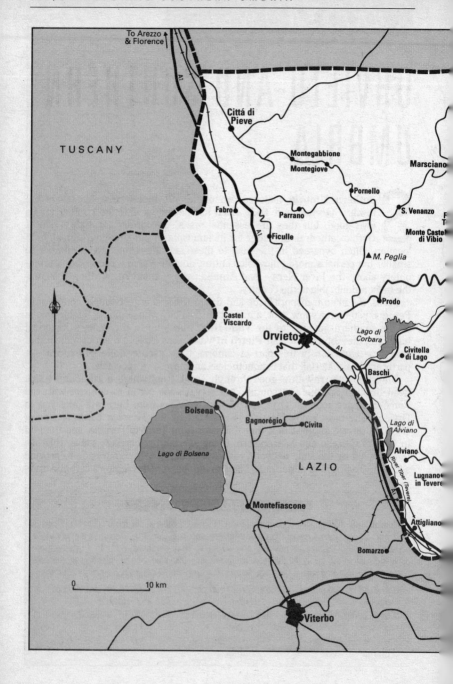

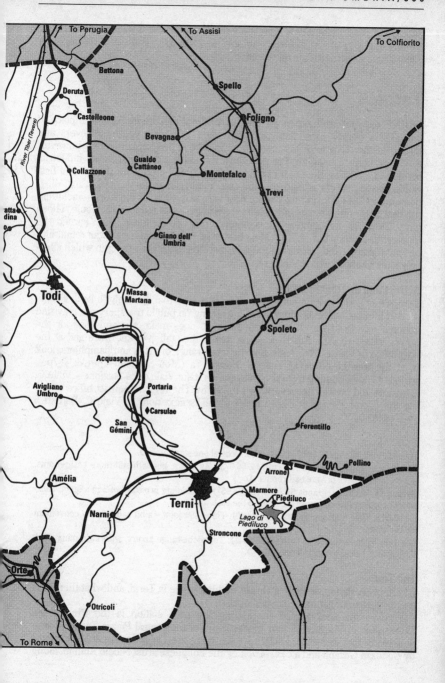

tion. Good **road** links follow almost identical routes, and if you're hitching, the big junction with the A1 at **Orte** – an obvious gateway in and out of the region – offers great opportunities in all directions.

Terni

TERNI, the southernmost major town in Umbria, was the unlikely birthplace of one of the world's most famous saints, Saint Valentine, patron of lovers and bishop of the town until his martyrdom in 273. A less romantic city, however, would be hard to imagine. Pre-war Terni formed the cradle of Italy's industrial revolution, claiming the country's first steel mill and producing the world's first viable plastic, and its armaments and steel industries made it a target for Allied bombing in 1944. During over a hundred air raids, most of the town – including the best part of its Roman and medieval heritage – was reduced to rubble. These days Terni is no longer the manufacturing powerhouse that earned its nineteenth-century tag as the "Manchester of Italy", though postwar rebuilding has put the arms and chemical industries back on their feet – the gun which allegedly shot Kennedy was made here.

Arrival and accommodation

Terni's function as a communications centre means that it's likely to have a walk-on part in most Umbrian itineraries, but relying on public transport you may find yourself having to stay here – and the town does make a useful base for the Lower Valnerina. You can **change money** at the station ticket office and at the post office in Via del Plebiscito. For the usual range of maps and pamphlets, look in at the **tourist office** at Viale C. Battisti 7a (Mon–Sat 9am–1pm & 4–7pm; ☎0744/43.047); coming from the train station, take Viale della Stazione – Viale C. Battisti is 300 metres up, seventh on the right. The regional tourist office covering the Lower Valnerina, Narni and Otricoli is next door at Viale C. Battisti 5 (☎0744/43.047).

HOTELS
Brenta, Viale Brenta 12 (☎0744/283.007). Central one-star hotel. ④.
Del Teatro, Corso Vecchio 124 (☎0744/56.073). As above, but with still more basic rooms, none of which have private bathrooms. ④.
Brenta II, Via Montegrappa 51 (☎0744/273.957). A middling two-star hotel in a quiet, backwater neighbourhood, across the river to the east. ⑤.
De Paris, Viale Stazione 52 (☎0744/58.040). Three-star joint – a bit soulless but convenient for the station. ⑤.
Garden, Viale Bramante 4 (☎0744/300.041). Top-of-the-range luxury, with swimming pool, flower-filled balconies and all the frills. ⑦.

The Town

By Umbrian standards there's almost nothing to see in Terni, and what there is is usually lost amongst modern buildings.

Perhaps the best reason for leaving the train station is the **Pinacoteca Comunale**, in Via Fratini, four blocks south of the central Piazza Tacito (Tues–Sun 10am–1pm & 4–7pm; L3000). Its star turns are *The Marriage of St Catherine* by Benozzo Gozzoli and a *Crucifixion* by the Folignese artist Nicolò Alunno, along

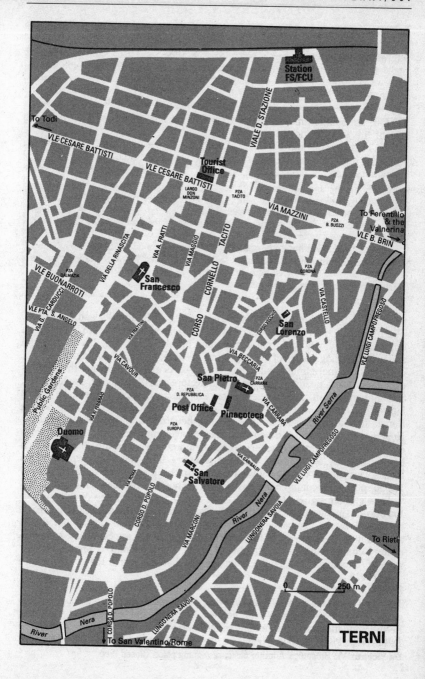

TERNI

SAINT VALENTINE

Terni's tourist literature treads carefully around the subject of **Saint Valentine**, talking of his "delicate tradition" – delicate, that is, because there are doubts about whether he ever existed and exactly whose body it is that pilgrims venerate in the Basilica di San Valentino, two kilometres south of Terni. The uncertain identity of the corpse, however, didn't stop someone stealing the saint's head as a love-token in 1986; it was found three years later, wrapped in newspaper, under a park bench.

According to the delicate tradition, Valentine was elected first bishop of Terni in the year 197 and attempted to bring converts to Christianity – then still outlawed – by encouraging the religious marriage of young people. It's also said that star-crossed lovers would turn to him for advice, drawn by his open-mindedness and his custom of giving them flowers from his garden. His most famous success was the union of Sabino and Serapia, two lovers – he pagan, she Christian – barred from marriage by their lack of shared faith. Valentine comforted them with the assurance that their souls would never be separated and, when the young Serapia died, converted Sabino and thus achieved the reunion of the lovers when Sabino died soon after.

Evidence of Valentine's other qualifications for sainthood is scarce, though after his martyrdom in Rome, his head is said to have rolled fifty-eight miles from its place of execution. Oddly enough, his following in Italy is considerably less than in the unromantic Anglo-Saxon countries.

with works by a triumvirate of moderns – Chagall, Kandinsky and Jean Mirò. There's also a two-room showing devoted to Orneore Metelli (1872–1938), an impoverished shoemaker from Terni who chronicled his daily life in colourful and naive paintings. Most of his output has been bought up by the Japanese.

If you have more time to kill, the greenest parts of a grey city are the gardens of its southwest quadrant around San Salvatore and the Roman amphitheatre. **San Salvatore**, off the shapeless sprawl of Piazza Europa, is the town's most interesting church, featuring a rotunda that was long believed to have been a Roman temple to the sun, but has recently been dated to the eleventh century. Nonetheless, excavations have revealed extensive remains from Roman buildings on the site. The portico dates from the twelfth century, and the chapel – which has frescoes by an unknown Umbrian painter – from two centuries later. Two blocks west are the remains of the **Roman amphitheatre**, built in 32 AD to hold 10,000 spectators; comprehensively ruined, it's home to the town's bowls club.

Terni's other sights are minor league attractions, led by the church of **San Francesco**, just north of San Salvatore. Started on a Romanesque plan in 1265, it is defined by its campanile, a fourteenth-century addition picked out on its corners in vivid ceramics. In the centre, off Via Cavour, are **Sant'Alò**, a twelfth-century church built by the Knights of Malta, and the **Palazzo Spada**, the last work of Antonio da Sangallo the Younger, who died in Terni in 1546.

Food

The town puts on a rather better showing in its restaurants, with a couple of top-grade gastronomic venues and numerous cheap and serviceable trattorias. Recommendations are in ascending order of price.

Tacito, Piazza Tacito. Good local trattoria on the square south of the station. Closed Fri.

Da Vicenzo, Via Biblioteca. Another basic, easy-going place. Closed Wed.

Lu Pilottu, Strada delle Grazie (☎0744/274.412). Busy enough to make booking a good idea, this restaurant is reached by following Via Montegrappa south out of town. Food is an Umbrian and pan-Italian mix; outside tables in summer; from L20,000. Closed Mon & Aug.

Erba Dolce, Via Castello 2 (☎0744/418.297). Refined Umbrian specialities, a welter of desserts and a full selection of regional wines; L30,000 and up. Closed Tues & Aug.

La Fontanella, Via Plinio il Giovane 3 (☎0744/55.246). Terni's best-known restaurant is geared largely to expense accounts but features sublime cooking, blending Umbrian and international cuisine. The setting is enjoyable, too, particularly the outside terrace. Around L45,000. Closed Sun.

Festivals

As far as festivals go, the best times to be in Terni are **May Day** – celebrated with unusual vigour and a parade of floats by this committed communist town – and **Saint Valentine's Day**, February 14, marked by a festival and market. Classical music buffs might want to see the June **International Piano Festival**, a high-class event that was won a couple of years back by Ivo Pogorelich, just about the most glamorous and controversial figure on the concert circuit.

Leaving Terni: transport

Terni is a major **rail** junction, with trains running on the state network (information ☎0744/401.283) to Rome (connections at Orte for Orvieto, Florence and the north), to Spoleto and Foligno (connections for Assisi, Spello and Perugia), and to Rieti in the south (connections for the east coast and the Abruzzo). There's also the private *FCU* line (information ☎0744/415.2970), which shares the *FS* station, with hourly trains to Todi, Perugia, Città di Castello, Sansepolcro and stations en route.

Buses are run by *ACT* and leave from the forecourt near the train station. Services run to numerous local villages, and to Narni, Todi, the Cascate delle Marmore, Piediluco, Arrone, Ferentillo, Triponzo, Spoleto, Orvieto, Viterbo and Scheggino.

The Lower Valnerina

Terni is the ideal point of entry for the **Lower Valnerina**, driving or taking a bus along the glorious SS209, which follows the valley into its upper reaches (see p.489). Buses from Terni go as far as Triponzo (see p.490), via Piedipaterno, where you could link up with bus connections on to Norcia or Spoleto. The lower valley's highlight is undoubtedly the **Abbazia di San Pietro** in Valle, 18km north of the city, but on the way you'll pass a number of fine natural diversions, like the **Marmore waterfalls** and **Lago di Piediluco**.

The Cascate delle Marmore

The first stop of interest in the valley comes just six kilometres southeast of Terni at the **Cascate delle Marmore** (access by train or buses from Terni's Piazza Dante), which at 165 metres are among the highest waterfalls in Europe. They were created by the Romans in 271 BC, when they diverted the River Velino into the Nera during drainage of marshlands to the south. Further channels were cut in 1400 and 1785, both with the intention of draining Rieti's plain without flooding Terni, though the falls' major boost came with the damming of Lago di Piediluco in the 1930s to satisfy industrial demand for hydroelectric power. Terni's power-station complex is the largest hydroelectric plant in Italy.

Pictures of the falls in full spate adorn most Umbrian tourist offices, but what they don't tell you is that the water can be diverted through turbines at the flick of a switch, leaving a none-too-spectacular trickle. The times when the water flows are notoriously variable, but evenings are usually the best option, especially during July and August when there's an impressive *son et lumière*. (Current flow times are: May–Aug Sat 5–9pm, Sun 10am–1pm & 3–11pm, plus July 15–Aug 11 Mon–Fri 5–6.30pm; Sept–Oct & March 16–April, Sat 6–9pm and Sun 10am–noon & 3–9pm; Nov–March 15 Sun 3–6pm.)

There are two **observations** points: the belvedere in Marmore village, and the SS209 road down below. A steep and frequently muddy path connects the two, starting a hundred metres downstream of the falls, and there are **swimming pools** at the bottom of the cascade when the water's turned off. The green and luxuriant setting, tumbling water and acres of gleaming marble add up to a spectacular show – shame about the factories around the corner.

Marmore has a single **hotel**, the *Velino*, Via Pilastri 1 (☎0744/67.425; ④), and a **campsite** (June–Sept; ☎0744/67.198).

Lago di Piediluco and Piediluco village

Surrounded by steep, thickly wooded hills, **Lago di Piediluco** is rather like a miniature alpine lake: its waters are dark and deep, a bit on the cold side for swimming and in places unsafe, though the fringes are edged with beaches. Piediluco **train station** is sited on the southwest edge of the lake, three kilometres from Marmore and a kilometre or so from Piediluco village on the north shore. The station is a perfect access point if you want to put up a tent on the southern, less-visited shore or to walk the scenic minor road (no vehicle access) to Monte Caperno – reached by walking through the quarry by the station.

At **Monte Caperno** there's a quay for boats to and from Piediluco village, and a famous **echo** that's constantly being tried out. It reproduces with perfect clarity phrases up to four seconds in length – the stock Italian test phrase being lines from the mystic poet Jacopone da Todi (see p.522): "Per te, amor, conumone languendo e vo stridendo, per te abbracciare" (I'm pining for you my darling, and I'm looking forward to embracing you).

PIEDILUCO village is a major sailing and canoeing centre, always crowded at weekends with people escaping from Terni. **Accommodation** can be tight. Head first for the two-star *Lido*, Piazza Bonanni 2 (☎0744/368.354; ④), and if this is full, try the smart three-star *Casalago*, Mazzalvetta 3 (☎0744/368.421; ⑤), overlooking the lake. The *Casa dell'Amicizia*, Strada Panoramica 7 (☎0744/368.088; ⑤), is a new, intimate three-star hotel. The **campsite**, *Lago di Piediluco* (May 10–Sept 30; ☎0744/69.195), is large and often busy. For cheap **agriturist** bed and breakfast call Rosa Virili, *La Ciriola*, Valle Spolentina 18, Piediluco (☎0744/368.179; ③).

Nearby Labro, whose medieval houses look attractive from a distance, is owned lock, stock and barrel by Belgians and operates only as a holiday village.

Arrone and Montefranco

Desolate and sparsely populated these days, the Valnerina was once the hub of communications between the Kingdom of Naples and the Dukedom of Spoleto, and later a bone of contention between the Church and the Holy Roman Empire – which explains the liberal sprinkling of castles.

Moving north up the valley, **ARRONE** and **MONTEFRANCO** are the first of several fortress villages. Montefranco has the better of the views, but portions of its medieval centre are in ruins, and there's little cheer either in the shape of food and drink, or from its inhabitants. Across the valley Arrone sits atop a rocky pinnacle, crowned by an inviting little tower. The village's alleys again lack the sparkle of their distant promise, though the church of **Santa Maria Assunta** in the central Piazza Garibaldi contains recently uncovered sixteenth-century frescoes.

With transport you could make the wonderful scenic drive from Arrone to **POLINO**, a twelve-kilometre succession of hairpins through dense forest to Umbria's smallest *comune* – just a couple of hundred people, a tiny castle and one nameless trattoria. Press on and you reach **COLLE BERTONE** (1232m), a minor winter resort in good walking country. There's a small **hotel** here, perched idyllically at 1241m, *La Baita* (☎0744/789.132; [5]).

Other local **accommodation** is scarce. Near Arrone on the main road, look for the *Rossi*, Isola 7, Castel del Lago (☎0744/788.372; [5]); its **restaurant** (closed Fri) is one of the best around. At Racognano, on the SS209 near Montefranco, there's the ritzier *Fonteghia* (☎0744/388.621; [6]), also with a restaurant. A cheaper place to eat is the *Rema* on the Polino road from Arrone.

Ferentillo and its mummies

FERENTILLO is rapidly becoming the **free-climbing** capital of Italy, its crags swarming at weekends as new and more difficult routes are pioneered. A new **hostel** is under construction to accommodate the influx. The village itself sprawls across two rocky hillsides, guarded by twin fourteenth-century towers, and merits a stop for one of Umbria's more grotesque menages – the Ferentillo **mummies**.

These are to be found propped up in the crypt of **San Stefano**, in the Precetto quarter, on the east side of the Nera. Now behind glass – a precaution taken in the wake of the recent theft of a head – the corpses were simply dumped in the crypt and preserved by accident, apparently dried by their bed of sandy soil and a desiccating wind from the south-facing windows. The characters are a curious mix: two French soldiers hanged during the Napoleonic wars; a bearded dwarf; a mother who died in childbirth (the child on show alongside her); a papal soldier, bolt upright with his gun, housed in the case of a grandfather clock; a lawyer shot in a local feud over a farm; a farmer whose gun backfired in the same feud and blasted a hole in his stomach; and a hapless Chinese couple who came to Italy in 1880 for their honeymoon and died of cholera. To round things off there's a pile of leering skulls with a mummified owl perched in their midst.

San Pietro in Valle

Six kilometres up the valley from Ferentillo, at an abrupt turn to the left, is a more highbrow distraction, the **Abbazia di San Pietro in Valle** (daily summer 10am–noon & 2–5pm; free; if closed ring at the custodian's house, signed on the left midway up the 2-km approach road), one of central Italy's finest abbeys and one of Umbria's few memorials to the Lombards' Dukedom of Spoleto. Founded by Duke Faroaldo II, who retired to the monastic life after being deposed by his son in 720, the abbey was amongst the most powerful religious houses in the region, controlling vast tracts of land and dominating the lives of thousands of people. Set high on the hillside near a thickly wooded cleft, privy to the most sublime views, the first impression it makes is of a dull blockhouse affair, with nothing to hint at the splendour of the art within.

The highlight of the complex is the **church**, much of which survives from an eighth-century plan, including the transept, the three apses and parts of the rough mosaic pavement behind the main altar. The altar cloth, remarkably, has also come down from the same era, and still displays an inscription by Hildercius, one of the dukes of Spoleto. The breathtaking, if often badly faded, **frescoes** which cover the body of the main church were painted in 1190 and are currently approaching the end of long restoration. They are amongst the first attempts to move away from the stylised influence of Byzantine painting, an influence that nonetheless was to prevail until the advent of Cimabue and Giotto a century later. Most of these precocious pictures are Biblical scenes, those on the left-hand wall from the Old Testament, those on the right-hand from the New. Particularly eye-catching episodes show God separating Light from Darkness (high up at the start of the left wall) and a view of Noah, eyes closed in a transport of ecstasy, sweeping off a storm-torn cloak.

The church's **altar**, beautifully set off by the rose-coloured stone, rich Romanesque architecture and the surrounding frescoes, is a rare example of Lombard sculpture, carved with what look like Celtic figures and motifs. To each side are well-preserved Roman sarcophagi, the right-hand specimen – reputedly Faroaldo's tomb – especially appealing, backed by gorgeously coloured frescoes. Three further carved sarcophagi lie elsewhere in the church, along with odd stone fragments around the walls, including a bas-relief of a monk, brought from Syria by refugee Christians in the seventh century. Look out also for the low cylindrical Etruscan altar to the right of the main door as you leave.

A doorway from the apse leads to the twelfth-century **campanile**, similar to the Lombard-influenced towers common in Rome and Lazio, and distinguished by fragments and reliefs salvaged from the original eighth-century church. Alongside is a faultless two-tiered **cloister** decked out with a profusion of flower-filled pots, sheltering a Roman sacrificial altar, one of several Roman oddments. Down to the left of the abbey entrance is an atmospheric **restaurant**, with medieval ambience and high prices (closed Wed).

Before leaving the abbey, look across the valley to the ruins of **Umbriano**, claimed to be the first city of Umbria. A couple of kilometres distant, with no road access, it makes a pleasant hike up an obvious track from the south of Colleponte below.

The nearest **accommodation** is at Sambucheto, the hamlet at the foot of the approach road, where the nine-roomed *Ninfa del Nera* sits on the busy main road at Via del Monastero 3 (☎0744/780.172; ④); it also has a **restaurant**.

Narni

Half an hour by train either from Terni or from Orte (including a spectacular trip through a tree-filled gorge), **NARNI** is an intimate and unspoilt hill town, jutting into the Nera valley on a majestic spur crowned by another of Cardinal Albornoz's formidable citadels. The fortress draws an admiring glance before you see the welter of steel and chemical works around Narni Scalo, the new town that's grown up around the station – thankfully almost invisible from the medieval core. Narni's stage-set medievalism is even more complete than Perugia's or Assisi's, its quiet piazzas, Romanesque churches and labyrinth of ancient streets and stepped passageways forming one of Italy's most congenial townscapes. There are also vestiges from the time when Narni was a Roman colony established in 299 BC – one of the first in Umbria – and a linchpin in the capital's defences, standing close to the Tiber valley and the undefended road to the capital.

Buses run from the forecourt at **Narni Scalo station**, with tickets available on the bus or from the newsagent's kiosk in the station. You may have to wait for a connection, but don't be tempted into the long and very tedious walk.

The Town

The circuitous bus route from Narni Scalo to the medieval town allows a good view of the Roman **Ponte di Augusto**, a solitary arch in the middle of the river, remnant of a bridge which in its day spanned 130 metres, a product of Augustan renovations. The buses terminate at **Piazza Garibaldi**, the town's social hub. From here, Via Mazzini leads to the heart of the old town through an arch in the city walls, following the course of the Via Flaminia, whose construction in 220 BC cemented Narni's importance.

The Duomo

The **Duomo**, fronting Via Mazzini's first bend, was rebuilt in 1145 and is now an intriguing mix of accretions from most centuries since. Its facade is small and unassuming, cramped by surrounding buildings and the Lombard-influenced portico which dates from 1492 (with later additions).

Inside, an extravagant Baroque altar is overshadowed by gold-leafed **pulpits** and an intricate **screen** – mainly fifteenth-century, though incorporating fragments of Romanesque and palaeo-Christian reliefs. The Cosmati pavement is also attractive, while elsewhere parts of the original church show through, chiefly in the patches of fresco – best in the apse behind the choir – and in the cellar-like chapel on the right, the **Cappella San Giovenale**. An important piece of early Christian architecture, it dates from 558; its crude, age-blackened walls contain a **ninth-century mosaic** of Christ, the oldest in the region.

Piazza del Popolo and along Via Mazzini

The Via Mazzini continues through a vibrant residential centre and into the **Piazza del Popolo**. Pride of place in this perfect little civic square goes to the fourteenth-century **Palazzo dei Priori**, distinguished by a fountain and a loggia designed by the Gubbian architect Gattapone; its exterior pulpit was built for the peripatetic Saint Bernardino. Behind the palazzo the narrowest and steepest of Narni's alleys descend to the tatty, water-stained church of **Sant'Agostino**, with a few medieval faded frescoes amid half-hearted Baroque.

The somewhat eccentric building opposite the Palazzo dei Priori is the **Palazzo del Podestà**, cobbled together by amalgamating three town houses and adding some token decoration. The thirteenth-century sculptures above the main door are worth a glance, and if you can get into the Sala di Consiglio (admission on request downstairs) you'll see an *Annunciation* by Benozzo Gozzoli and Ghirlandaio's *Coronation of the Virgin*. The latter is the town's pride and joy and it was so admired by the authorities of Todi and Trevi that they commissioned cheaper copies by the local artist Lo Spagna. All the town's paintings, however, are currently being shuffled around several locations, with the Palazzo Erioli earmarked as their final resting place.

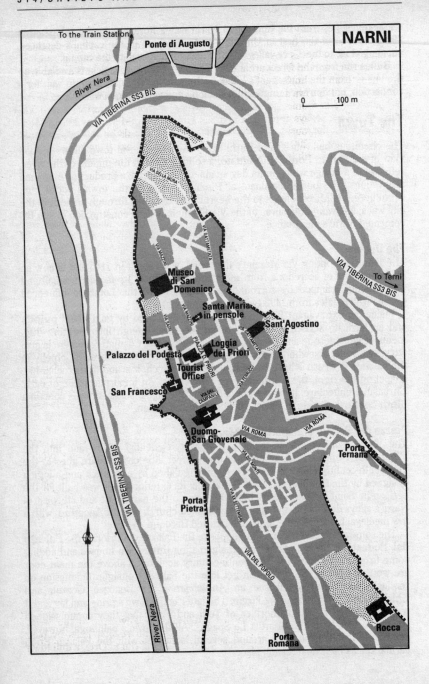

NARNI

To the Train Station

Ponte di Augusto

River Nera

VIA TIBERINA SS3 BIS

0   100 m

VIA DELLA MURA

VIA BATAMEATA

VIA VOLZINI

Museo di San Domenico

Santa Maria in pensole

VIA VOLZINI

VIA SGH

Sant'Agostino

VIA BATAMEATA

Palazzo del Podestà

PIAZZA PRIORI

Loggia dei Priori

Tourist Office

VIA GLUCO

San Francesco

VIA DEL CAMPANILE

Duomo-San Giovenale

VIA ROMA

VIA ROMA

Porta Ternana

VIA DEL MONTE

Porta Pietra

PIAZZA SETTIMARE

Rocca

VIA DEL POPOLO

Porta Romana

VIA TIBERINA SS3 BIS

To Terni

N

Beyond the piazza, Via Mazzini passes the inconspicuous church of **Santa Maria in Pensole**, on the right after fifty metres. An utterly simple basilica, unchanged since it was built in 1175, it has an enchanting triple-arched portico and a beautiful carved frieze around the square doorways. Inside, the church is plain save for a few simple carvings and capitals.

The bulk of the town's paintings have been removed to the **Pinacoteca** in the ex-church of San Domenico, a forlorn building a short way further down Via Mazzini. It's not always open (official times Mon–Fri 9am–1pm plus 3–6pm Mon, Wed & Fri) but the tourist office in Piazza del Popolo should be able to stir somebody with a key. The main works are by Benozzo Gozzoli and Fiorenzo di Lorenzo, together with frescoes and statuary salvaged from surrounding villages.

The Rocca

A massive affair lording it over the town and surrounding country, the **Rocca** is reached from Piazza Garibaldi by Via del Monte, a street that threads through the *terziere di Mezule*, one of the three areas into which the medieval town was divided. Currently being restored, the castle was commissioned by Cardinal Albornoz in the 1370s and is attributed to Gattapone (responsible for Spoleto's fortress and Ponte delle Torri); it is a link in the chain of fortresses by which Albornoz sought to reassert papal authority across Umbria.

Practicalities

The **tourist office** is at Piazza del Popolo 18 (Mon–Sat 9am–1pm & 4–6pm). Narni shows refreshingly little interest in tourism but if you can find a room it makes a superb spot to go to ground for a couple of days. The cheaper of the two old-town **hotels** is the three-star *Minareto*, Via dei Capuccini Nuovi 32 (✆0744/726.343; ⑥), but if you're prepared to pay the extra you're better off plumping for the old-world finery of the four-star *Dei Priori*, Vicolo del Comune 4 (✆0744/726.843; ⑦). The alternatives are four hotels in Narni Scalo, all ④ or over: two are in Via Tuderete (the best, the *Fina*, at no. 419; ✆0744/733.648; ⑥; and the cheaper *Ponte d'Augusto* at no. 303; ✆0744/750.635; ④), the other two on the approach road to the station. There's an out-of-town **campsite** at Monte del Sole, on the road to Borgheria (April–Oct; ✆0744/796.336). Virtually the only proper **restaurant** is the classy *La Loggia*, Vicolo del Comune (✆0744/722.744; closed Mon and second half of July). **Pizzerias** and bars are gathered on Piazza Garibaldi, and there are good snacks at *Il Forno* bakery off Piazza del Popolo.

Buses for the train station and out-of-town destinations like Terni, Amelia and Orvieto leave from Piazza Garibaldi; the *ATC* office for information and tickets is at no. 27. Train links are frequent to both Terni and Orte (where you can pick up connections to Orvieto on the Rome–Florence line). The **post office** is at Via Vittorio Emanuele 40 and has a foreign exchange facility.

Around Narni

Narni's outlying villages – **Amelia** and **Lugnano in Teverina** to the west, **Otrícoli** to the south – make pleasant excursions, with regular links by bus. Following the Nera valley to the southwest, road and rail run to Orte, a dull town of note only for its rail junction.

Amelia

AMELIA, perched on top of a sugarloaf hill, is a delightful town, enclosed by some of the oldest and mightiest **walls** in Italy. Formed from vast polygonal blocks joined without mortar, they are up to seven metres wide and twenty high. Parts are known to have belonged to an Umbrian acropolis of the fifth century BC, and the Romans took advantage of the fortifications when they used the town as a staging post on the Via Amerina, one of nine military roads linking Etruria to the Via Flaminia. Thereafter the town within the walls was all but destroyed by Totila, and later history followed a predictable course through rule by the nobility and slow decline.

The Town

Access to the town is through one of its four original gates: the main entry is the **Porta Romana**, with the **tourist office**, Via Orvieto 1 (Mon–Fri 9am–1pm & 4–6pm; ☎0744/981.453), located to its left. A minibus shuttle runs between here and the centre. Immediately inside the Porta Romana stands the church of **San Francesco**, where Agostino di Duccio's tombs of Matteo and Elisabetta Geraldini are placed near the altar – two of six tombs in the Cappella di Sant'Antonio. It's also worth nipping next door to look at the **cloister** of the ex-Collegio Boccarini.

From San Francesco, the spiralling street draws you to the town's summit, site of a panoramic cathedral square. The most striking feature of the **Duomo**, a Romanesque church ruined by Baroque superfluities and nineteenth-century frescoes, is a twelve-sided tower, dated 1050 and claimed by some to symbolise the Apostles, by others to represent the signs of the zodiac. Inside, the church boasts two standards won from the Turks at the Battle of Lepanto (either side of the entrance to the second chapel on the right), bas-reliefs by Agostino di Duccio and a column against which Saint Fermina, the local patron saint, is said to have been martyred (first on the right).

Art is otherwise thin on the ground – a collection of Roman statuary in the courtyard of the Palazzo Comunale's **Municipio** is one diversion, and you might investigate the recently uncovered frescoes in Sant'Agostino's sacristy, thought to date back to the year 1000, showing four saints, red star motifs and floral decoration. Amelia's attraction otherwise is the typically Umbrian mix of views, medieval streets and close-at-hand countryside. You could walk the short distance to **Monte San Salvatore**, worthwhile for its views and a tiny ninth-century chapel, or head for the nearby rural church of **Madonna delle Cinque Fonti**, supposed site of a Saint Francis sermon.

Practicalities

Buses run from the village to Terni, Orte, and Orvieto, together with the lesser centres of Lugnano in Teverina, Attigliano and Avigliano. On the main approach road to the town, close to the tourist office, is one of two local **hotels**, the *Scoglio dell'Aquilone*, Via Orvieto 23 (☎0744/982.445; ⑥). The other is the *Anita*, Via Roma 31 on the Narni road (☎0744/982.146; ⑤). Another option is the one-star, seven-roomed *Amerino*, Via Amerina 54 (☎0744/989.667; ④), at Fórnole, midway to Narni.

For **food** try *Le Colonne*, Via Roma 191, the restaurant in the *Anita* or *La Tavernetta* pizzeria in the old centre on Via della Repubblica.. If you want to give your wallet a dusting down, *La Gabelletta* (☎0744/982.159; closed Mon & July

15–30) at Gabelletta, 3.5km northeast on the Foce road, is a highly rated restaurant whose local speciality is a tooth-rotting combination of white figs, chopped nuts and chocolate. Expect to pay up to L40,000 for the full works.

Lugnano in Teverina

The run along the back roads to Orvieto from Amelia (possible by bus) is a treat, offering plenty of oak forests and the chance to catch one of Umbria's Romanesque highlights, the twelfth-century **Santa Maria Assunta** in **LUGNANO IN TEVERINA**. Fronted by an exotic portico, the church has finely carved twin pulpits and has somehow hung onto a triptych by Nicolò Alunno in the apse; the crypt features a fine sculpted screen and Cosmati marble work.

The village has a single **hotel**, the central *La Rocca*, Via Cavour 60 (☎0744/902.129; ④); food in the attached **restaurant** is also good. Additionally, there's fairly cheap **agriturist** farm accommodation in Giove, a crumbling hamlet to the south; contact Signore Cardillo, *Le Fossate* (☎0744/992.606; ④).

From Lugnano it's well worth crossing the Lazian border to **BOMARZO**, just 17km south. Ten minutes' walk from the village is the **Parco dei Mostri** (daily dawn–dusk; L7000), a sixteenth-century theme park of fantasy and horror devised by the hunch-backed Duke of Orsino. It has become one of the area's primary tourist attractions.

Otrícoli

OTRÍCOLI, 15km south of Narni, is almost the last town in Umbria and a reasonable enough representative of its hill towns. However, its medieval streets are eclipsed by the remains of **Otriculum**, a collection of Roman ruins within easy walking distance. To reach them, get on the main road that bypasses the village, head downhill for two hundred metres, and take the signposted track that strikes off right towards the Tiber.

Unusually the settlement has no walls, having served more as a pleasure garden than a defensive site; it was built as a sort of holiday village for Rome's hoi polloi, who cruised in by boat on the Tiber. The colony is still largely unexcavated and draped in clinging undergrowth; the best of the visible remains are a partly buried amphitheatre, a succession of twin-level arches and the rambling ruins of some small villas, cisterns and bath-houses.

Turner stopped off here to paint the scene (a work now in the Tate Gallery) and in the sixteenth century Montaigne described the spot as "infinitely pleasant". It may not stay that way for much longer. So far no more than a trickle of tourists visit but plans to make this an archaeological park mean it's headed for the big time. In the meantime you can find **rooms** up in Otrícoli at the one-star *Pensione Umbria*, Via Roma 18–20 (☎0744/719.112; ③).

Towards Todi – Carsulae and around

Moving north from Narni on the new SS3bis dual carriageway, or on the parallel *FCU* railway or road from Terni, the principal attraction is **Carsulae**, the largest **Roman site** in Umbria.

The hills east and west of these routes contain a number of typical Umbrian villages, of which the most substantial is **CESI**, 12km northwest of Terni and known as the *la ringhiera della valle Ternana* (the balcony of the Terni valley). In addition to a handful of churches and a ruined fort, it offers a fine walk to the church of Sant'Erasmo and on to the summit of Monte Torre Maggiore.

Carsulae

The building of the Via Flaminia from Rome to Ancona confirmed this region's importance as the crossroads of Italy, and colonies along its route were to evolve into modern-day Narni, Terni, Spoleto and Spello. Some settlements, however, such as **CARSULAE**, 15km from Terni, were abandoned after earthquakes and civil war. In its day, this particular pile of stones was known as the Pompeii of central Italy, and its beauty praised by both Tacitus and Pliny the Younger. To get there, take the first junction for San Gemini Fonte on the main Todi to Terni road (ie before the tunnel heading south), and then just before that village (not before plain San Gemini) take the dusty signposted track to the ruins.

The unenclosed site is today dominated by a church, **San Damiano**, made from materials filched from the ruins; other precious marbles went to build local houses. Behind the church you can follow a long stretch of the original **Via Flaminia** (complete with grooves made by chariots) to a substantial arched gateway, built by Trajan; beyond the arch, on the left, is a large square Roman tomb.

Walking back on the Flaminia, the site of the **Basilica Forense**, the law courts, is off to the left; behind it (across the modern lane) rise the remnants of the **amphitheatre**, built in the hollow of a natural depression. Behind the arena is a **theatre**, its orchestra still impressively intact, and to its rear a spread of ruins still awaiting excavation. Back across the site, behind San Damiano and the Flaminia, is the **forum**, composed of numerous low walls and the vague outlines of baths, well, and two temples.

North to Todi

PORTARIA, 3km north of Carsulae, is an inviting-looking village, clearly visible from the SS3bis, straggling along the cliffs on the eastern side of the valley. If you have your own transport it's worth driving up for bird's-eye views over the valley.

To the west, **SAN GEMINI** and **ACQUASPARTA** are both spa towns, each with passable medieval centres but plenty of modern building. In San Gemini, there's **accommodation** at the *Antica Carsulae*, Viale Fonte 8 (☎0744/630.163; ④), and the adjacent *Alla Fonte* (☎0744/630.025; ④).

The high, wooded hills west of Acquasparta shelter a handful of windblown hamlets. All are within about fifteen kilometres of Acquasparta, and only readily seen in a car. Montenero has the best of the many **castles** in the area, and virtually every other village boasts a **Romanesque church**; the best are Santa Maria at Quadrelli, and San Martino and Santa Vittoriana in Dunrobba. In Avigliano, 3km southwest of Dunrobba, there's a **hotel**, the one-star *La Laterna*, Via Matteotti 13 (☎0744/933.104; ④).

Driving round the hills, though rewarding, is a slow business; if you're going west there's no petrol almost until you reach Orvieto.

Todi

TODI is one of the emerging Umbrian hill towns, still at heart an agricultural centre but an increasingly favoured retreat for Rome's arts and media types. Imminent gentrification is manifest in a scattering of estate agents and in the revamped and decidedly high-profile **Todi Festival** – ten days of music, ballet and other arts at the beginning of September. The town has its sights, too, with an impressive **Piazza del Popolo** and the churches of **San Fortunato** and **Santa Maria della Consolazione**, though what lingers most in the memory is its position, a stunning and daunting prospect from below.

Todi's history is one of the region's longest, Iron Age remains suggesting some three thousand years of continual habitation. Tradition has it the Umbrian town was built where an eagle dropped a tablecloth snatched from a local family – hence the eagle and cloth in the town's insignia. More certain is the Etruscan heritage, and coins bearing the name **Tutare** suggest a town of some independence during pre-Roman rule. The name means "border", and Tutare was probably one of several outposts used by the Etruscans to defend their frontier along the Tiber. Necropolises all round Todi have yielded some of the finest Etruscan treasures, most of them – including a famous bronze statue of Mars – shipped off to Rome. Ancient Roman rule came and went, leaving little except a second set of walls to add to those of the Etruscans.

The town's heyday was the thirteenth century, when as a free *comune* it managed to annex Amelia and Terni, and to build a third set of walls and a crop of civic palaces. The Atti were the leading noble family, overseeing – in tandem with the Church's representatives – a period of decline interrupted only by a flicker of sixteenth-century prosperity that produced more palaces and Todi's great Renaissance church of Santa Maria della Consolazione.

Transport

Access to Todi by public transport can be a headache. By **train** you can approach from Terni or Perugia on the *FCU* line, but the town's two **stations** are both in the middle of nowhere and connecting buses often involve a half-hour wait. **Ponte Naia**, 5km distant, is marginally closer, and has a more reliable bus shuttle to the old town; the other station is **Ponte Rio**, 6km northeast of the town.

A more convenient way to visit the town is by **bus** from Perugia – there are eight daily, the last bus back leaving at 5pm. They stop at the **terminus** for long-haul buses in Piazzale della Consolazione next to Santa Maria della Consolazione; orange **minibuses** run from the terminus up to the centre; if you fancy the walk follow the marked footpath that strikes off Viale della Consolazione, twenty metres beyond the corner on the right. Buy tickets for the minibuses and long-haul buses from the unlikely looking stall that sells nuts and miscellaneous nibbles.

Buses **back to Ponte Naia** station leave from Piazza Jacopone – between Piazza del Popolo and San Fortunato – fifteen minutes before each train departure. Some inter-town buses also leave from Piazza Jacopone. Tickets and information are issued from the fruit shop in the piazza next to the *Ristorante Jacopone*. If you're arriving by car you'll be hard pressed to navigate Todi's narrow streets and one-way system, never mind find a parking place in the centre. The best plan is to leave your car outside the walls at Porta Perugina, Piazzale della Consolazione or Porta Romana.

The Town

All the main sights in Todi are within a few minutes' walk of each other. If you take a minibus up from the terminus you'll find yourself at the central **Piazza del Popolo**; walking up via the footpath leaves you in the municipal gardens, near the church of **San Fortunato**. Shuttle buses from the station drop passengers in front of San Fortunato.

The Piazza del Popolo

The **Piazza del Popolo** is often described as the most perfect medieval piazza in Italy – and with full justice, even if the cars detract slightly from the overall effect. Flanked by a range of palazzi and a superb duomo, it's enough to take the breath away, however many other Italian hill towns you've seen. Originally the site of the Roman forum, it is built above a surviving complex of Roman cisterns.

The **Duomo**, atop a broad flight of steps, is a merging of the last of the Romanesque and the first of the Gothic forms filtering in from France in the early fourteenth century. Construction started at the beginning of the twelfth century, on the site of a Roman temple to Apollo, and continued intermittently until the seventeenth. The square, three-tiered **facade** – in the throes of restoration – is inspired simplicity, with just a sumptuous rose window and ornately carved doorway to embellish the pink weathered marble – the classic example of a form found all over Umbria. The exterior sides of the church are more complicated and it's worth walking down adjoining side streets for glimpses of arches, windows and bulging buttresses.

Inside there's some impressive nineteenth-century stained glass in the arched right-hand aisle, a lovely font, an exquisite fourteenth-century *Madonna and Child,* and a good altarpiece by Perugino's follower Giannicolo di Paolo. Nothing, however, matches the **choir**, carved with incredible delicacy and precision in the sixteenth century; a nice touch are the panels at floor level near the front which depict the tools used to carve the piece – though you may have to run the gauntlet of church attendants to get a close look. On the rear west wall, a truly dreadful sixteenth-century copy of Michelangelo's *Last Judgement* defaces the back wall. Underground, there's a mildly interesting crypt-cum-passageway, scattered with Roman and possibly Etruscan fragments.

The piazza's other key buildings are a trio of thirteenth-century **public palaces**, squared off near the duomo in provocative fashion – the *comune*'s aim being to put one over on the Church. The **Palazzo del Capitano**, built around 1290, and the adjoining **Palazzo del Popolo**, dating from 1213 (one of Italy's earliest civic palaces), are the most prominent, thanks mainly to their external staircase, which looks like the scene of a thousand B-movie sword fights. Several films have in fact been shot in Todi, which offers the twin attractions of scenographic authenticity and proximity to Cinecittà, Italy's major film studios across the border in Lazio. Most notable was the doomed *Cleopatra*, which explains the yellowing photographs of a pouting Elizabeth Taylor in many of the local bars.

The Palazzo del Capitano houses a small **Pinacoteca**, closed for "reordering" since 1977 and showing no sign of reopening. It's hard to know why because it only has a couple of dozen paintings, chief among which is a Lo Spagna copy of Ghirlandaio's *Coronation of the Virgin*. More of a loss is the similarly *in restauro* **Etrusco-Romano** museum in the same building, by all accounts a small but interesting collection. Changing exhibitions elsewhere give you a chance to see

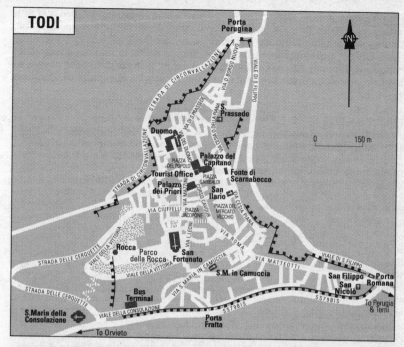

some of the palaces' interior spaces. The **Palazzo dei Priori**, built between 1293 and 1337, recently restored and functioning, was the seat of Todi's various rulers and is now the town hall; if you can look like you're on council business you should be able to look inside.

The best place to enjoy the piazza's streetlife is from the **bar** down on its right-hand side, a locals' local in contrast to the flashy newcomer midway down the piazza – though the latter does a good line in sandwiches.

San Fortunato

The single most celebrated site after the piazza is the enormous **San Fortunato**, set above some half-hearted gardens. Its disproportionate size is testimony to Todi's medieval wealth, and the messy-looking and squat facade – an amalgam of Romanesque and Gothic – reflects the time it took to build (1292–1462). Lorenzo Maitani was commissioned to decorate the facade in the manner of his work on Orvieto's Duomo, and the story goes that the burghers of that town, unable to stomach the prospect of a rival church, took out a contract on him. If true, it was money spent too late, because his florid **doorway** stands good comparison with that in Orvieto, all arched swirls and carved craziness. The angel among the figures flanking the portico is outstanding, and has been attributed to the Sienese sculptor, Jacopo della Quercia.

The light, airy **interior**, recently highlighted by cleaning and several controversial coats of whitewash, marks the pinnacle of the Umbrian Gothic tradition of large vaulted churches. The style was based on the smaller "barn" churches

common in Tuscany, distinguished – as here – by a single, low-pitched roof with
naves and aisles of equal height. (San Domenico in Perugia is another, less
successful example.) Notice the grey stone brackets, added to correct the
increasingly alarming lean of the supporting pilasters. It features an excellent
choir, heavier and with more hints of the Baroque than the one in the duomo, as
well as a few scant patches of fresco – the scenes by **Masolino di Panicale**

JACOPONE DI TODI

Fra' Jacomo dei Benedetti, known to all as **Jacopone**, was among Italy's leading
medieval poets, a trenchant critic of the papacy, and the author of what was to
become one of Christendom's most famous carols, the *Stabat Mater Dolorosa*. For
much of his life, however, he displayed an eccentricity perhaps unequalled by any
of Italy's plethora of crazed medieval mystics. Born in Todi in 1228, he pursued the
life of decadence that seems the birthright of all those ultimately destined for
sainthood. He gambled, was extravagant, feasted, cavorted in fine clothes, and
rarely levered himself from bed before midday. After training as a lawyer in
Bologna, however, he returned to Todi a respectable attorney. Aged about 38 he
married **Vanna**, a young, rich and deeply devout member of the Umbrian
aristocracy. A year after the marriage, however, Vanna was attending a local public
festival when the platform on which she was sitting gave way. Injured, she was
carried from the scene by Jacopone, who, tearing away her fine clothes, found she
had been wearing a hair shirt beneath her *haute couture*. Seconds later she died in
his arms.

Jacopone was inconsolable, shocked at both Vanna's death and his ignorance of
her deep devotion. The experience became the catalyst for his own conversion. He
sold his house, gave his wealth to the poor, distanced himself from family and
friends and tramped Todi's streets dressed in rags, often spending days on all fours.
He appeared at a niece's wedding dressed in tar and feathers. He added soil and
wormwood to his food, to make it repugnant, and demanded to be given the most
menial tasks. Applying to join the Franciscans, who had recently been established
in Todi by Francis himself, he was rejected because his behaviour was deemed too
extreme even by the Franciscans' exacting standards – it was to be many years
before they allowed him into their community.

Spurned, he wandered Umbria's countryside for a decade, remaining deliber-
ately cold, hungry, thirsty and dirty to atone for his sins. He also began to compose
the poems and *laude* (hymns) for which he was to become famous, writing 211 in
all and becoming, in the words of one modern authority, "the most popular and the
most inspired of the poets of the Franciscan tradition".

He also achieved considerable fame for his outspoken criticism of the papacy.
Boniface VIII, one of the most vice-ridden of popes, was a regular visitor to Todi,
where he had a reserved stall in the cathedral. One of his favourite tricks was to
have the tongues of heretics nailed to doors. Jacopone bravely – if tactlessly – said
of him: "Blasphemous tongue, that has poisoned the world,/There is no kind of
ugly sin/In which you have not become infamous." He was quickly imprisoned for
his eloquence, lucky to escape with his life, remaining incarcerated for five years in
the papal dungeons of Palestrina, near Rome. Only the election of Pope Benedict XI
in 1303 secured his release. Returning to Todi he joined a Franciscan convent at
Collazzone, north of Todi, where he contrived to die on Christmas Day, 1306. Todi
remembers him with a piazza and the vast mausoleum in the crypt of San
Fortunato.

(1432) in the fourth chapel on the right are good if battered examples of this painter's work. Finally, take a look at the last chapel on the right, the **Cappella del Sacramento** (an amazing concentration of lovers' graffiti), at the mausoleum of Jacopone in the crypt (see box opposite), and at the **cloisters**, outside and to the right of the church.

Santa Maria della Consolazione

Many architectural cognoscenti rate **Santa Maria della Consolazione** (closed daily 1–3pm) as one of the best Renaissance churches in Italy. Completed in 1607, the project was initiated a century earlier by Cola da Caprarola, possibly using one of Bramante's drafts from Saint Peter's in Rome: the church's use of alternating types of window in the cupola – "rhythmic bays" – are a Bramante trademark. Over the years, virtually every leading architect of the day had his say, including Sangallo, Peruzzi and Vignola. Eventually it came to conform to most of the precepts articulated by Alberti, the great theoretician of Renaissance architecture: a Greek-cross floor plan (purity of form and proportion), isolation in an open piazza, a white or near-white finish (purity again), high windows (cutting off from earthly contact), and a preference for statuary over painting (again of greater "purity" than painting).

Time can be spent equally enjoyably taking a siesta in the nearby **Giardino Pubblico**, full of shady nooks and narrow pathways, and a cut above the normal town plot. On this western edge of town, there's also a kids' playground and a very small **Rocca** – of Albornoz vintage – both far less noteworthy than the views, which are extensive but often obscured by haze. A zigzag path cuts up from Viale della Consolazione, but the gardens are best tackled via the stony track to the right of San Fortunato.

The rest of the town

For a reminder of ancient Todi, take a look at the so-called **nicchioni** (niches) in Piazza del Mercato Vecchio; sited just below the Piazza del Popolo, they constitute more or less all that's left of the Roman colony. The town's proud of them, but they don't amount to much: four slightly overgrown arches, which perhaps formed the wall of an Augustan basilica.

Two minutes' walk down the lane from the lowest corner of the piazza brings you to **San Ilario** (also known as San Carlo), an ancient Lombard chapel well off the beaten track, and all too often locked to protect a set of frescoes by Lo Spagna. Just beyond the church, adjoining a crumbling, flower-strewn arbour, is the **Fonte Scarnabecco** (1241), an unusual arched fountain that was Todi's life-blood and social meeting place before piped water.

Last-call churches include **San Filippo**, dull except for frescoed panels on the right-hand wall, and the more interesting **San Nicolò**, distinguished by a striking wooden ceiling, three imposing Gothic arches and two small Umbrian frescoes on the left-hand wall. Both are immediately inside the medieval walls at Porta Romana. You might also drop in on thirteenth-century **Santa Maria in Camuccia**, two minutes off Via Roma, recently robbed of – but later re-united with – a priceless wooden Madonna. Two beautifully fluted Roman columns flanking the entrance are the most substantial parts of a large collection of Roman pieces dug up from under the church; for a look at the minor pieces, chat up the resident priest – the stuff is in his quarters.

Practicalities

Todi is still not really geared up to deal with visitors and the town's **tourist office** (daily 9am–1pm & 4–7pm; closed Sun afternoon in winter; ☎075/894.2626 or 3456) seems a little surprised that anyone should want information. The office also houses **telephone booths** and bus timetables. It's located under the arcade of the Palazzo del Popolo at Piazza del Popolo 38. The tourist office for the surrounding area is at Piazza Umberto I 6 (☎075/894.2686 or 3395). The **post office** is in Piazza Garibaldi (Mon–Fri 8.30am–6.30pm, Sat 8am–noon); for currency **exchange** there's a convenient bank opposite the tourist office.

Accommodation

All Todi's **hotels** are outside the walls, the most central and least expensive being the *Zodiaco*, Via del Crocefisso 23 (☎075/894.2625; ③), one minute east of Porta Romana. Ten minutes' walk straight down the main road from Porta Romana brings you to the *Tuder*, Via Maestà dei Lombardi 13 (☎075/894.2184; ⑤), a functional place in an uninspiring spot. A short distance beyond it is the better located but rather posh *Villa Luisa*, Via A. Cortesi 147 (☎075/894.8571; ⑥). If you can afford its high prices the prime choice is the converted convent, *Bramante*, Via Orvietana 48 (☎075/894.8381; ⑧), 100m past Santa Maria della Consolazione. Todi does, however, have three sets of **rooms** for rent within the walls: Elisa Mariotti, Via del Forno 12 (☎075/894.2809; ④); Serenella Proietti, Via del Monte 17 (075/894.3231; ④); and the luxurious *San Lorenzo*, San Lorenzo 3 (☎075/894.4555; ⑥). The monastery of SS. Annunziata, Via San Biagio 2 (☎075/894.2268; ③), will also take women, families and couples, and the Convento di Montesanto, Viale Montesanto (☎075/894.8886; ③), occasionally accepts guests, but in both cases be certain to confirm availability.

With a car or bike you might use the **agriturismo** accommodation in nearby hamlets. Bed and breakfast, swimming and horse riding are offered at the idyllically situated *La Palazzetta*, c/o Patrizia Caracciolo, in Aspoli, 8km west of Todi in the hills (☎075/885.3219; March–Dec; ⑥), and at *Agricola Todini* in Collevalenza (☎075/887.231; ④), 11km southeast of Todi on the Massa Martana road.

Restaurants

The town's most enjoyable restaurant for lunch is the *Umbra*, behind the tourist office; prices are high – up to L35,000 – and service can be slapdash, but the panorama from the outside terrace makes it all worthwhile; in season arrive early or book to be sure of an outside table (☎075/894.390).

Cheaper alternatives include the friendly, old-fashioned *Cavour* at Corso Cavour 21 (closed Wed) and the basic *Pizzeria-Rosticceria* off Corso Cavour in Piazza B. d'Alviano, a hundred metres from Piazza del Popolo (closed Mon after 8pm).

Along the Tiber valley

North of Todi, the **Tiber valley** broadens out to a plain, edged with low hills and dotted with light industry. It's not an area where you'll want to spend a lot of time – and most people tear through on the new dual carriageway or crawl along on the *FCU* railway. A few of the castles, villages and Romanesque churches, however, are worthwhile if you're in no hurry to get to Perugia.

The west bank

Off to the west of the valley, the spectacularly sited **MONTE CASTELLO DI VIBIO** is a possible first halt, 12km from Todi, off the N397. This eagle's nest of a village dominates the countryside almost more than Todi and its castle was one of a reputed 365 fortresses that formed a defensive screen around the town. There's little to see, save extraordinary **views** and the usual maze of medieval alleyways.

Below Monte Castello the walled village of **FRATTA TODINA** is guarded by another castle, strengthened in the fifteenth century by the local warlord Braccio Fortebraccio (see p.409) as a garrison for his troops. Near the centre of the village is a Franciscan monastery, which features in many of the stories and legends of the order. Moving north, **MARSCIANO** is the region's main town – modern and without interest. **CERQUETO** has Perugino frescoes of *St Sebastian* in its parish church – and there are other damaged works attributed to the artist at the edge of the village in the Maestà di Santa Lucia. Impressive castle remains are to be seen a kilometre away at Sant'Elena.

The east bank

The most substantial village on the east flank of the valley is **GIANO DELL'UMBRIA**, 23km from Todi along a looping detour off the N316. Two buses daily (Mon–Sat) come here from Foligno, one more on school days. A perfect fortified hamlet, it is ringed by olive groves and pastoral countryside. Take the road south of the village and after about a kilometre you'll come to the only **campsite** in the region, the *Pineta di Giano*, Colle del Gallo, Montecerreto (April–Sept; ☎0742/90.178). It has a swimming pool and a beautiful site, backed by the tree-covered slopes of the Monti Martani. Several **paths** run up to the summit ridge, which in May and June has exceptional carpets of **wild flowers**, and magnificent views as far as Todi all year. Opposite the campsite is an eccentric **hotel-restaurant**, the *Park Montecerreto* (☎0742/90.186; [5]), noted for its Thursday evening fish specials, for which people come from miles around. If the hotel's full, ask the owner about renting **rooms** in the village – though don't expect much in the way of luxury. There's an excellent little-known restaurant, *Il Buongustaio*, immediately within Giano's walls at the village's southern entrance.

North of Giano, the intriguingly named Bastardo is a modern mess with nothing to recommend it. **GUALDO CATTANEO**, just beyond, is by contrast an enticing medieval hill village, whose single **hotel**, the *Marinangeli*, Piazza Umberto I 17 (☎0742/91.412; [3]), would make an enjoyable base. Virtually every hamlet within a ten-kilometre radius of here has a **castle**, those at Barattano, Cisterna, Pozzo and Sargano being particularly outstanding. Some hamlets have a castle and Romanesque church, as at Marcellano, with its frescoed twelfth-century church of **Sant'Angelo**, and Grutti, whose name derives from the nearby grottoes of early Christians.

Slightly north are two further short-stop villages. **COLLAZZONE** has the usual hilltown tally – good views and medieval streets – with scenic roads around through olives and oak forest. The parish church in **CASTELLEONE**, over towards Deruta, has frescoes by Matteo da Gualdo, a fifteenth-century Umbrian more usually active further north. There's also a well-known **hotel**, housed in a somewhat sham castle – the three-star *Nel Castello* (☎075/971.1302; [6]); it has only nine rooms, so book ahead.

ROMANESQUE CHURCHES EAST OF THE TIBER

With a car you might try to take in some of the hill villages east of the Tiber – almost any you choose will be quiet and boast a **Romanesque church**. Most of these are built over the graves of early monks and martyrs, the Tiber and Naia valleys having been amongst the earliest to be colonised by Christians fleeing Roman persecution.

This area and the region south towards Terni thus formed the springboard of Umbria's monastic tradition. Perhaps the most rewarding churches are those you come on by accident, in crumbling hamlets or in the midst of the ilex woods that blanket surrounding hills. If you prefer to plan a visit, the following are outstanding: Viepri, Villa di San Faustino, Santa Maria in Partano, San Teranzano and the Abbazia di San Fidenzio.

Madonna dei Bagni

The church of **Madonna dei Bagni**, 2km south of Deruta, is the one sight on the main SS3bis that's definitely worth a detour. Its walls are covered with hundreds of votive tiles left by pilgrims over the last three centuries, yielding a unique insight into the peculiarities of religious belief and the changes in daily life. The most entertaining are those offered as thanks for escapes from dangerous and not so dangerous corners – fire, flood, famine, a fall from a cow, a bite from a donkey. They also represent an offbeat record of the area's thriving ceramic tradition. Sadly, a hundred tiles were stolen in 1980, so opening times are curtailed as a result. The best time to try is on Saturday morning, when it's not unknown for coach parties to show up; otherwise ask at the tourist office in Deruta.

Deruta

DERUTA is best known for its **ceramics** and seems to be devoted entirely to the craft. Some of the stuff is mass-produced trash and some so big that you'd need a trailer to get them home – most, though, are handmade, hand-painted, portable and by general consent among Italy's best. The Romans worked the local clay, but it was the discovery of distinctive blue and yellow glazes in the fifteenth century, allied with the Moorish-influenced designs of southern Spain, that put the town firmly on the map. Some fifty workshops traded as far afield as Britain, and pieces from Deruta's sixteenth-century heyday have found their way into the world's major museums. Designs these days are mainly copies, with little original work; if you're serious about this sort of thing, avoid the roadside stalls and head for the workshops of the new town for the best selection and prices.

The **old town** on the hill isn't particularly compelling, apart from the **Museo Regionale della Ceramica** (Mon–Sat 9am–1pm; L3000), alongside the **tourist office** on the main Piazza dei Consoli. The museum features a varied ceramic collection, with a few works by contemporary craftspeople, and a sixteenth-century **tiled floor** lifted wholesale from the church of San Francesco. It also contains a tiny art gallery whose high spots are a work by Fiorenzo di Lorenzo and two paintings by Nicolò Alunno. San Francesco itself is the only other mild distraction in the town, largely ruined in the eighteenth century and distinguished only by the tiniest fragments of fourteenth-century fresco.

Torgiano

TORGIANO, 8km north of Deruta, is the last worthwhile stop before Perugia. Though a fairly dull town, it is home to Umbria's finest wines, all of them produced by **Giorgio Lungarotti**, one of the new breed of Italian producers. A self-made man and now something of a national celebrity, he's put together an unexpectedly interesting **wine museum** in a fine palazzo on Via Garibaldi (daily 9am–noon & 3–7pm; L6000). A varied and comprehensive look at every aspect of viticulture, the collections include oddments of medieval machinery.

You can buy the cheaper Torgiano wines in most Italian supermarkets, but the **Rubesco Riserva** rates as one of Italy's very finest wines. Also look out for Torre di Giano, Chardonnay and Castel Grifone, all widely available in the town.

Orvieto

ORVIETO sits on a table-top of volcanic tufa whose sheer sides fall 325 metres to the vine-covered valley floor – a cliff-edged remnant of the four volcanoes whose eruptions also bequeathed the soils that produce Orvieto's fine wines. Out on a limb from the rest of Umbria, the town is perfectly placed between Rome and Florence to serve as an historical picnic for tour operators, and tourists flood here in their millions, drawn by the **Duomo** – one of the greatest Gothic buildings in the country and home of some amazing frescoes by Signorelli (still under restorative wraps at the time of writing). Once these have been admired, Orvieto is not especially exhilarating, though the *centro storico*, the views and the renowned white **wine** are enough to justify a night's stop.

The city is one of the most ancient in Italy, thanks to its irresistible site. Bronze and Iron Age tribes were present before it became **Volsinium**, a leading member of the twelve-strong Etruscan federation. In 264 BC the Romans displaced the Etruscans to present-day Bolsena – the place they abandoned becoming known as **Urbs Vetus** (the old city), thus Orvieto. Its medieval influence was considerable, the independent *comune* challenging Florence and eventually claiming land from Monte Amiata in the north to the coast at Orbetello. Power and prestige remained high until the usual internecine squabbling, the Black Death of 1348 sounding the town's effective death knell. It passed to the Church for good a hundred years later and became something of a papal home from home – thirty-two popes in all were to stay in the city.

Arrival and accommodation

Fast **trains** on the Rome–Florence line tend to bypass Orvieto, so you may well have to change to a slower *locale* at Orte or Chiusi. Orvieto's **station** is in the grim new town of Orvieto Scalo, a twisting three-kilometre drive from the old centre. The #1 bus makes the trip every fifteen minutes to Piazza XXIX Marzo, a short way north of the Duomo; tickets are on sale from the revamped station bar – buy one for the return trip, too, as outlets are few. As a fun alternative, you could take the newly restored nineteenth-century **funicular** from the far side of the station forecourt. Its end-point is Piazza Cahen, from where minibus A runs to Piazza del Duomo; bus tickets are valid for the ride. Cars aren't prohibited in the old town, but finding a parking space is a tall order. There are car parks in Piazza

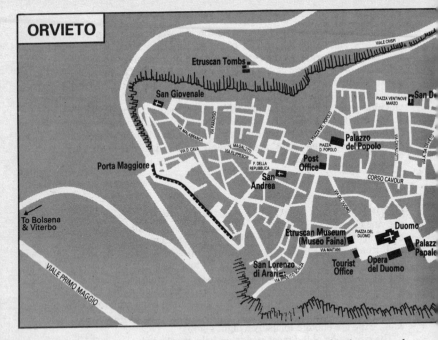

Cahen and off Via Poma, but you may be best off parking in the big free car park on the east side of the station and taking the bus or funicular to the old town.

Accommodation

The **tourist office** at Piazza del Duomo 24 (Mon–Fri 8am–2pm & 4–7pm, Sat 10am–1pm & 3–8pm, Sun 9am–7pm; ☎0763/41.772 or 42.562) operates a free **accommodation service**; in addition to the hotels, it has details of a few private rooms and a dozen or so bed and breakfast **agriturist** options in hamlets scattered around the town. Usually, hotels are pretty easy to find in the centre of town. If you run into problems there are a dozen or so cheap, modern but characterless places in Orvieto Scalo. All but one of the local **campsites** are some way out.

HOTELS

Corso, Corso Cavour 343 (☎0763/42.020). Best hotel near Piazza Cahen. ④.

Posta, Via Signorelli 18 (☎0763/41.909). First choice amongst the cheaper central hotels, two minutes from the Duomo, with a garden and cool, quiet and pleasant rooms. ④.

Duomo, Via Maurizio 7 (☎0763/41.887). An excellent central option. ⑤.

Grand Hotel Reale, Piazza del Popolo 25 (☎0763/41.247). Slightly less expensive three-star than the neighbouring *Italia*, with a few cheaper rooms without private bathrooms. ⑥.

Virgilio, Piazza del Duomo 5–6 (☎0763/41.882). Perfect position, though only a handful of the thirteen rooms actually have views of the Duomo. ⑥.

Grand Hotel Italia, Piazza del Popolo 13 (☎0763/42.065). The biggest central hotel, with 45 rooms, and thus likely to have space in an emergency. ⑦.

Maitani, Via Maitani 5 (☎0763/42.011). The best and most central of Orvieto's quartet of four-star hotels if you're splashing out – and with 40 rooms there's a good chance of space. ⑧.

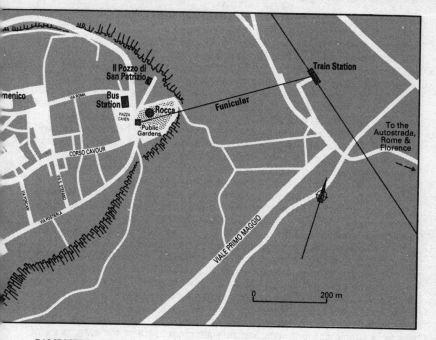

CAMPSITES

Agricampeggio Sossogna, Rocca Ripasena 61 (☎0763/43.141). Small site in Orvieto, with limited tenting space. Open July to mid-Oct.

Orvieto (☎0744/950.240). Smart three-star site on the Lago di Corbara shore, reached by the SS448 Todi road; it's a couple of kilometres' walk from the *Scacco Matto* (see below). Open all year.

Scacco Matto (☎0744/950.163). Basic one-star 48-pitch site; take the bus for Civitella del Lago (two daily) or Narni (six daily; alight at Baschi). Open all year.

The Duomo

The historian Jacob Burckhardt described Orvieto's **Duomo** as "the greatest and richest polychrome monument in the world"; Pope Leo XIII called it the "Golden Lily of Italian cathedrals", adding that on the Day of Judgement it would float to Heaven carried by its own beauty. Though the cathedral's overall effect might be a bit rich for some tastes, it rates – with Assisi's Basilica di San Francesco – as one of the two essential sights in Umbria.

The construction of the Duomo

Church tradition holds that the Duomo was built to celebrate the **Miracle of Bolsena**, which occurred in 1263. The protagonist, a young Bavarian priest, was on a pilgrimage to Rome to shake off his disbelief in transubstantiation – the idea that the body and blood of Christ are physically present in the Eucharist. While he celebrated Mass in a church near Lago di Bolsena, blood started to drip from the Host onto the *corporale*, the white linen cloth that covers the altar, "each stain severally assuming the form of a human head with features like the Volto Santo, the face of the Saviour". The linen was whisked off to Pope Urban IV, who was holed up in Orvieto to escape the literal and political heat in Rome. He proclaimed a miracle and a year later Thomas Aquinas, then teaching in Orvieto's San Domenico, drew up a papal bull instigating the feast of **Corpus Domini**.

The cornerstone for the building was not in fact put in place for another thirty years (on November 13, 1290) and Aquinas's bull makes no specific mention of Bolsena, so it's likely that the raising of the Duomo was as much a shrewd piece of political pragmatism as a celebration of a miracle. The papacy at the time was in retreat and the Umbrian towns – not least Orvieto – at the height of their civic expansion. Thus it's likely that the building of an awe-inspiring cathedral, in one of the region's most powerful towns, was a piece of political muscle-flexing to remind errant citizens – on the crest of lay expansion – of the papacy's enduring power.

Perhaps the most miraculous event was that the Duomo was built at all. Medieval Orvieto was so violent that at times the population considered abandoning the city for good. Dante wrote that its family feuds were worse than those between Verona's Montecchi and Cappelli – the inspiration for Shakespeare's murderous Montagues and Capulets in *Romeo and Juliet*. In addition to civic strife, the building was also dogged by a committee approach to design, the plans being modified continually to accommodate changes in architectural taste. At least the site posed no problems: the city's highest point was previously home to an Etruscan temple and Orvieto's first cathedral, Santa Maria Prisca. Even today the cathedral continues to dominate the skyline for miles around.

The architect of the building is unknown, though it seems possible that it was Arnolfo di Cambio, designer of Florence's Duomo. At Orvieto the plan initially was for a simple and orthodox Romanesque church, but in the early years of work a local architect's extravagant departures into the Gothic brought the structure close to collapse, leading to the call-up of the Sienese master, **Lorenzo Maitani**. In the course of three decades he guided the construction at its most crucial stage and produced the magnificent carvings on the facade. Though building dragged on for over three hundred years, exhausting 33 architects, 152 sculptors, 68 painters and 90 mosaicists, the final product is a surprisingly unified example of the transitional Romanesque-Gothic style.

The facade

The monumental facade is just the right side of overkill: a riot of columns, spires, bas-reliefs, sculptures, dazzling colour, colossal doorways and hundreds of capricious details held together by four enormous fluted pillars. Many have compared it to a painted triptych in an elaborate frame. Fifty-two metres high and recently cleaned and overhauled, it is a stunning spectacle from the piazza, particularly at sunset or under floodlights.

The four pillars at the base are among the highlights of fourteenth-century Italian **sculpture**. The work of Maitani and his pupils, they depict episodes from the **Old and New Testaments** in staggering detail: lashings of plague, famine, martyrdom, grotesque mutilation and murder – Cain slaying Abel is particularly strong. They were created to point an accusing finger at Orvieto's moral slackers, as the extraordinary final panel makes clear, with the damned packed off to eternal fire, brimstone and the company of an awful lot of snakes.

Maitani was also responsible for the four large bronzes of the Evangelists across the first tier, and for the angels over the beautiful central **doorway**. The mosaics, the facade's showiest aspect, are mostly eighteenth- and nineteenth-century additions, replacements for originals nabbed by Rome. Only the four examples in the corner of Orcagna's huge **rose window** (1359) have any vintage, dating from 1388. The central bronze doors, by Emilio Greco, were made as recently as 1965, and in the best traditions of the Duomo were added after much talk and controversy.

The interior

At first little holds your attention in the **interior** (daily 7am–1pm & 2.30–7pm), save a few snatches of fresco in the scalloped side niches and the work immediately on your left as you enter, a newly restored *Madonna and Child* by Gentile da Fabriano, with a very sickly Jesus. However, in the right transept – the Cappella Nuova – are **Luca Signorelli**'s superlative paintings of the **Last Judgement** (1499–1504), one of Italy's great fresco cycles and a profound influence on Michelangelo's version in the Sistine Chapel, painted forty years later. At the time of writing the frescoes are completely covered for restoration.

Several painters tackled the chapel before Signorelli. Fra' Angelico made a start in 1447, completing two of the ceiling vaults, *The Prophets* and *The Saviour in Glory*, with the assistance of Benozzo Gozzoli. Fra' Angelico was then called to Rome, then the murder of a local grandee, Arigo Monaldeschi, brought work on the Duomo to one of its periodic halts. Perugino popped up forty years later and for reasons unknown disappeared – never to return – after working for five days. Signorelli saved the day, graciously restoring Fra' Angelico's work and completing the vaults to his original plan.

Work then started in earnest on the walls, all but the lowest of which are crowded with passionate and beautifully observed muscular figures, creating an effect that's both realistic and almost grotesquely fantastic. There are seven main episodes, the most dramatic being the *Last Judgement*, the *Preaching of the Antichrist* (an unusual theme), *Hell* and the *Resurrection of the Dead*. A mass of monstrous lechery and writhing flesh fills the *Hell* panel, in which the Antichrist stands alongside the painter's unfaithful girlfriend – immortalised as a prostitute in hell. Signorelli, suitably clad in black, has painted himself with Fra' Angelico in the lower left-hand corner of the *Preaching of the Antichrist*. Both seem unperturbed by the garrotting taking place nearby. The outstanding medallions on the lower parts of the walls are also by Signorelli and include portraits of Homer, Dante, Ovid, Virgil, Horace, Lucan and Empedocles, together with episodes from classical myth and Dante's *Divine Comedy*.

All this overshadows the opposite transept's **Cappella del Corporale**, which contains the sacred *corporale* of the Miracle of Bolsena, locked away in a massive, jewel-encrusted casket designed in 1358 as a copy of the facade. On the chapel walls are extensive **frescoes** (1357–64) by a local artist, Ugolino di Prete Ilario, depicting episodes from the *Miracle of Bolsena* (right-hand wall) and various *Miracles of the Sacrament* (opposite). The chapel also houses the freestanding *Madonna dei Raccomandati* (1339) by the Sienese painter Lippo Memmi, currently removed for restoration.

The entire **apse** is covered in frescoes by Ugolino (again under restoration), many of which were touched up by Pinturicchio, who was eventually kicked off the job for "consuming too much gold, too much azure, and too much wine". They describe episodes from the *Life of the Virgin*.

The rest of the town

Nothing in Orvieto is on a par with the Duomo, though the piazza has a couple of worthwhile sights and some of the peripheral parts of town provide attractions that justify the walk – **San Giovenale** and the strange **Pozzo di San Patrizio** in particular. Trying to arrange a logical itinerary is difficult, but random wandering brings its own rewards.

Around the piazza – and the Etruscan tombs

On the right of the Duomo is the **Museo dell'Opera del Duomo** (Tues–Sun 9am–1pm & 2–5pm; but closed at time of writing), previously one of the most chaotic museums in Italy though the restoration that's been under way for several years will probably tidy things up. Amidst a meaningless assembly of stone fragments, moth-eaten vestments, dusty pottery and woodwormy sculptures, however, one or two items manage to stand out. They include some fine paintings by Maitani – five parts of a polyptych from San Domenico and a marvellous *Madonna, Child and Angels*. Also outstanding are sculptures by Andrea Pisano and Arnolfo di Cambio, and a font filled with Escher-like fishes. Housed below the museum is the new **Museo Archeologico Nazionale** (Mon–Sat 9am–1.30pm & 3–7pm, Sun 9am–1pm; free), as yet largely empty, save for four rooms which contain Greek vases (fourth century BC), two painted tombs with their original murals, and other Etruscan artefacts excavated from Orvieto's own Cannicella and Crocifisso del Tufo tombs (see below). Close by in Palazzo Soliano, Piazza del Duomo, is the **Museo Emilio Greco** (Tues–Sun April–Sept 10.30am–1pm & 3–7pm; Oct–March 10.30am–1pm & 2–6pm; L5000 or L10,000 with *biglietto cumulativo* which includes entry to Pozzo di San Patrizio): a collection of bronzes and other work by the contemporary sculptor responsible for the Duomo's doors.

Opposite the Duomo, the **Museo Etrusco** (or **Museo Claudio Faina**, Tues–Sun 9am–1pm & 3–6.30pm; L3000) has a collection of vases and fragments excavated from local tombs. Nothing's been done to cheer up a display that would be dull at the best of times, though a bust known as *Larth Cupures Aranthia* and a fourth-century sarcophagus are mildly interesting. Worth the admission price alone is the superb **view** of the Duomo from the upper floor (where much-needed restoration is belatedly under way).

If Etruscan remains appeal, their sixth-century BC tombs, the **Crocifisso del Tufo**, are well worth a look (daily 8am–dusk; free); walk down the town's approach road from Piazza Cahen to the small car park on the left and follow the signs. There are rows of massive and sombre stone graves (more are being excavated), though none have the grandeur or the paintings of the more famous necropolises in Tarquinia or Cerveteri. Still visible, however, are Etruscan inscriptions above the tomb entrances – thought to refer to the name of the erstwhile occupants. More interesting still are guided tours (English or Italian) which visit the **Grotte della Rupe**, the honeycomb of caves and tunnels, in the crag below the town, used since Etruscan times (see p.534). Trips leave at 10am and 4pm in the summer (10am & 3pm Oct–March) from the tourist office, costing L10,000 per person.

The churches

The tiny Romanesque **San Lorenzo di Arari**, a short walk west of the Duomo, was built in 1291 on the site of a church destroyed by monks from nearby San

Francesco because the sound of its bells got on their nerves. Four restored frescoes on the left of the nave describe traumatic scenes from the *Life of St Lawrence*, including execution by roasting. An Etruscan sacrificial slab rather oddly serves as the altar from which the church derives its name, *arari* meaning "altar".

From nearby Piazzale Cacciatore there's a good **walk** around the city's southern **walls** along Via Ripa Medici, with views over to a prominent outcrop of rock in the mid-distance, part of the old volcanic crater.

Ten minutes or so brings you to the ancient **San Giovenale**, set amid rustic surroundings on the western tip of Orvieto's plateau. New studies have established the previously accepted date of its foundation – 1004 – as the date of its first restoration. It's not much to look at from outside, but the musty **interior** is a distinctive hybrid of a church, the thirteenth-century Gothic transept, with its two pointed arches, standing rather oddly a metre above the rounded Romanesque nave. Beautiful thirteenth- and fifteenth-century **frescoes** cover all available surfaces: they include a *Tree of Life* to the right of the main door and the macabre *Calendar of Funeral Anniversaries* partly covered by the side entrance.

From the church back to the centre of town, Via Malabranca and Via Filippeschi are the best-preserved of the medieval streets. En route, **San Andrea**, in Piazza della Repubblica, is worth a look for its twelve-sided campanile, odd patches of fresco and pieces of Roman and Etruscan city in the crypt.

San Domenico, a convenient stop before taking the bus back to the station, stands next to the town's fascist-era barracks – far and away the ugliest building in the town. Half of the church, built between 1233 and 1264, was sliced off during the construction of the barracks. The principal artwork is the *Tomb of Cardinal de Braye*, a pioneering work by **Arnolfo di Cambio** on the left as you enter. This defined the format of wall tombs for the next century, showing the deceased lying on a coffin below the Madonna and Child, within an elaborate architectural framework.

The Pozzo di San Patrizio and Rocca

Orvieto's novelty act is the huge cylindrical well known as the **Pozzo di San Patrizio**, signposted to the left of the funicular terminus in Piazza Cahen (daily April–Sept 9.30am–7pm; Oct–March 10am–6pm; L6000). Pope Clement VII commissioned it, from Antonio da Sangallo the Younger, two years after the Sack of Rome, which he'd been forced to flee disguised as a greengrocer. An attack on Orvieto was expected from the imperial troops and the well was designed to guarantee the town's water supply during siege; the attack never materialised, which was fortunate, as it took ten years of digging to hit water. Incidentally, whilst in Orvieto Clement took the fateful decision not to annul Henry VIII's marriage to Catherine of Aragon.

The well is a virtuosic piece of engineering, thirteen metres wide and sixty-two deep, and takes its name from a supposed resemblance to the Irish cave where Saint Patrick died at the ripe old age of 133. Water was brought to the surface by donkeys on two broad 248-step staircases, cannily designed in a double helix so that they never intersect. Half the well is carved from solid tufa, half is brick-lined, and all is lit by 72 strange windows cut from the spirals into the central shaft. Skinflints in Italy are said to have pockets as deep as the Pozzo di San Patrizio.

The direct recipient of the water from the *pozzo* was the nearby **Rocca**, built in 1364 by Cardinal Albornoz. Views from the ruins are wonderful, and they are close to the small **public gardens**, one of Orvieto's few patches of green and home to the prominent remains of an Etruscan temple, the Tempio del Belvedere. The castle itself was built over the only strata of travertine in the town, a robust piece of rock that escapes the landslips which strike the tufa with increasing regularity. Defoliation, the collapse of ancient sewers, the lowering of the water table and the intensification of traffic culminated in disastrous slips during 1977 and 1979, finally prompting the injection of vast funds from the European Community. Miles of tunnels and caves dating back to the Etruscans still honeycomb the rock, a labyrinth once used for quarrying, burials and the fermenting of wine. The subterranean conditions were said to be responsible for the excellence of Orvieto's wine; modern methods now make a drier product, better selling but less exalted than the traditional semi-sweet *abboccato*.

Practicalities

The **tourist office** at Piazza del Duomo 24 (Mon–Fri 8am–2pm & 4–7pm, Sat 10am–1pm & 3–8pm, Sun 9am–7pm; ☎0763/41.772 or 42.562) supplies exhaustive listings for the town and province. Among points of practical use, the main **post office** is in Via Cesare Nebbia, off Corso Cavour; there is a bank of **telephones** in the station bar, and in *Bar Valentino*, Corso Cavour 127–129; and for **exchange**, the *Ufficio Cambio Valuta* at Via del Duomo 58 (daily May–Sept 9am–10pm; Oct–April 10am–1pm & 4–7pm; ☎0763/42.297) is far quicker than the banks. There is also an exchange facility at the main post office.

Eating and drinking

Orvieto's tourist traffic has inflated prices in the town's many **restaurants**, and it has fewer genuine culinary high spots than neighbouring towns. One or two backstreet eateries, however, should keep you under budget; the cheaper **pizzerias** are mostly clustered together at the bottom of Corso Cavour. Recommendations below are in ascending order of price.

CRAMST or *Al San Francesco*, Via Maitani 15. Walk fifty metres up Via Maitani from Piazza del Duomo, take the first left, and follow the big signs to the tree-shaded piazza. Very popular with locals, this is a co-operatively run 450-seat canteen affair, offering a choice between a restaurant and self-service trattoria; L10,000 and under. Closed Sun.

La Bottega del Buon Vino, Via della Cava 26. An *enoteca*/bar annexed to the tiny *Sciarra* restaurant, a cheap and reliable choice for basic Italian staples; meals under L15,000. It boasts a few outside tables on a steep street, and an Etruscan well of which the owner is immensely proud. This is also a better place to sample Orvieto wine than the expensive bars around the Duomo. Closed Tues.

La Grotta, Via Signorelli 5. Just off Via del Duomo and opposite the hotel *Posta*, this is a good-value and friendly trattoria, offering standard Italian fare for under L20,000. Closed Mon.

Da Anna, Piazza Scalza 2. Small, homely place off Piazza del Popolo, with usual pastas plus pizzas in the evening. Again around L20,000 for meals. Closed Fri.

Le Grotte del Funaro, Via Ripa di Serancia 41. On the southern edge of the old town and distinguished by its underground setting – in one of the caves dug into the rock. Best for solid lunchtime Umbrian specialities and pizza as it turns into a dubious piano bar-restaurant in the evening; up to L35,000. Closed Mon.

Maurizio, Via del Duomo 78. The smart-looking, modern interior may be off-putting, but the food here is good if you're prepared to pay more than just the basics.

Trattoria Etrusca, Via Maitani 10 (☎0763/44.016). A serious restaurant with surprisingly fair prices and a medieval vaulted dining room, featuring top-notch Umbrian specialities and excellent service. Be sure to go downstairs to see the wine cellars, carved out of solid tufa. Full meals run up to L35,000. Closed Mon & Jan 20–Feb 20.

Around Orvieto

The environs of Orvieto are not the most compelling in Umbria. However, if you have transport and time to spare, **Monte Péglia** might make you dally en route to Todi or Perugia, as might the **Lago di Corbara** on the way to Todi, and **Città della Pieve** if you're heading to Montepulciano.

West of Orvieto: Cìvita

The road to Lago di Bolsena – which lies across the border in Lazio – gives some of the best **views** of Orvieto: it's where the postcard shots are taken from and where Turner set up his easel for a landscape now in the Tate Gallery. In itself, the wooded pocket of countryside around Castel Giorgio is pretty enough, but only worth bothering with if you're in a car. Further afield, however, straddling the Lazio border, lies an almost lunar landscape, scarred with deeply eroded canyons, some wooded but most just bare, wasted slopes.

At the heart of this district lies the tiny, crag-top **CÌVITA**, known as "la città che muore" – the city which is dying – due to the crumbling of the rock below it. People have been emigrating from these disintegrating dwellings since the sixteenth century, leaving a population today of around seven – though apparently an Italian computer company have just bought up the place wholesale. The only access is via a precarious bridge from the nearby village of Bagnoregio, 15km southwest of Orvieto.

Monte Péglia

Monte Péglia is the name for the triangular expanse of wild, sparse land that rises between the Chiani valley and the Tiber, to the northeast of Orvieto. With its hilltop hamlets, olive groves, vines, herds of white oxen and miles of deserted roads and tracks, this is the archetype of pastoral lowland Umbria. Villages marked on the maps often turn out to be no more than scattered farms, many of them abandoned.

The only realistic way of tackling this remoteness is with your own transport, and you'll get the best quick taste of the area on the circuitous and beautifully deserted SS79bis from Orvieto Scalo to Todi. Superb initial views peter out as the road climbs through hairpins into densely wooded hill country – though, haze allowing, there are occasional glimpses as far as Perugia. The picturesque castle at Prodo is perhaps the best vantage point.

The best of the scenery is north of this road and something of a **wildlife** haven. The summit of **Monte Péglia** itself (837m) is disfigured by a radio mast, but there is a bar on the road up to it, plus a couple of **hotels** beyond the summit, along the run towards San Venanzo. Best budget option for miles is on this stretch – the *CTG Umbria* (☎075/870.9124; ③), a hostel in all but name, open from mid-June to the end of September. Otherwise try the two-star *L'Incontro*, just north of Monte Péglia in Ospedaletto (☎075/870.9111; ⑤), or the nearby one-star *Tullioloa*, Colle Spaccato 32 (☎075/870.9147; ④).

Lago di Corbara

The new SS448 to Todi is almost as scenic a route as that through Monte Péglia, passing medieval Baschi and running along the flattish southern shore of **Lago di Corbara**, before taking off into an unexpectedly dramatic **gorge** for the rest of the route onto Todi. Close to the lake's southern tip, enclosed on three sides by water, there's the *Villa Bellago* (☎0744/950.521; ⑦), a beautiful hotel-resort set in a twenty-acre estate; it has just twelve rooms, occupying converted nineteenth-century farm buildings. Beyond, midway down the shore, is the *Vissani* **restaurant** (☎0744/950.396; closed Wed), rated by virtually every Italian gastronomic guide as one of the finest in Italy; you'll need around L130,000 to dispose of, per person.

Further east, the lakeside scenery improves considerably, the strange purple-red rocks of the gorge contrasting with the forested slopes. The road's fairly quiet, with plenty of **camping** and picnic opportunities as the valley flattens out towards Todi.

Città della Pieve

CITTÀ DELLA PIEVE is the sort of place that can easily be seen in an hour, despite the vague enticement of the distant view. Travelling by rail, it's perhaps not worth the long haul up from the train station, unless you happen to coincide with the April *festa*, when the town's fountains run with wine, or you're a committed fan of **Perugino**, the town's most illustrious son.

Straggling along its ridge, the town, founded by the Etruscans, consists of tiny, red-brick houses (there is no local building stone) and narrow streets, one of which, Via della Baciadonna, claims to be the narrowest in Italy – the width of a woman's kiss, the name suggests. The **Duomo** has a couple of late works which show Perugino in his worst light. However, in nearby **Santa Maria dei Bianchi** (daily 10.30am–12.30pm & 3.30pm–dusk), on Via Vannucci, the main street , is one of his masterpieces – *The Adoration of the Magi*, which was painted in just 29 days in 1504. Other lesser pieces are to be found in **San Pietro, San Antonio Abate** and **Santa Maria dei Servi** – yellow tourist signs point the way. Unhappily for Città, Napoleon removed cartloads of the town's other Peruginos to the Louvre.

The town makes a peaceful enough stop and has two two-star **hotels**: the 34-room *Barzanti*, Via S. Lucia 53 (☎0578/298.010; ⑤), with tennis courts and swimming pool; and the smaller *Vannucci*, Via I. Vanni 1 (☎0578/298.063; ⑤). A **tourist office** at Piazza Matteotti 4 is sporadically open.

travel details

Trains

From Terni to Narni (12 daily; 15min) and Orte (40min; connections to Rome, Orvieto, Chiusi, Arezzo and Florence); Spoleto (12 daily; 20min), Foligno (40min; connections for Assisi and Perugia), Nocera Umbra (1hr) and towns in the Marche (Fabriano, Ancona). Frequent trains on the *FCU* line to Todi, Deruta and Perugia, with connections to Teróntola and Foligno (on the *FS* network) and Città di Castello and Sansepolcro (on the *FCU* line).

From Orvieto to Rome (7 daily; 1hr 30min); Florence (7 daily; 1hr 30min); Chiusi (7 daily; 40min; connections for Siena, 1hr 30min); Arezzo (7 daily; 1hr 20min); Orte (12 daily; 40min; connections to Narni, Terni, Spoleto and Foligno).

Stopping trains to Orte for Attigliano (for Bomarzo), and to Chiusi for Città della Pieve and all stations en route.

Buses

From Terni to Orte, Todi, Rieti (via Marmore, Piediluco and Colli sul Vellino), Narni, Amelia, Arrone, Pollino and Scheggino (via Ferentillo and Ceselli).

From Narni Frequent buses to Terni and Amelia. Fewer services to Orvieto, Calvi dell'Umbria, Moricone and Otricoli.

From Amelia to Narni, Terni, Lugnano in Teverina (and Attigliano), Avigliano (connecting bus for Todi via Dunarobba).

From Todi to Orvieto (1 daily, early morning); Perugia and Deruta (3 daily); Terni (8 daily); Pesciano (4 daily); Marsciano (2 daily).

From Orvieto to Narni, Amelia and Terni (6 daily); Perugia (1 daily, early morning); Todi (1 daily, 1.30pm).

PART FOUR

THE

CONTEXTS

THE HISTORICAL BACKGROUND: TUSCANY

A comprehensive history of Tuscany in its medieval and Renaissance heyday would consist in large part of a mosaic of more or less independent histories, as each of the region's cities has a complex story to tell. In an overview such as this, fidelity to the entanglements of central Italy's past is impossible. Instead, within a broad account of the main trends in the evolution of Tuscany, we have concentrated on the city that emerged as the dominant force – Florence. The brief reviews of the other major towns – Siena, Pisa, Arezzo, Prato, Pistoia and so on – are supplemented by background given in the appropriate sections of the guide. Similarly, crucial episodes in the history of Florence and its culture – for instance, the ascendancy of Savonarola – are covered in greater detail in the chapter on that city.

ETRUSCANS AND ROMANS

The name of the province of Tuscany derives from the **Etruscans**, the most powerful civilisation of pre-Roman Italy. There's no scholarly consensus on the origins of this people, with some experts insisting that they migrated into Italy from Anatolia at the start of the ninth

century BC, and others maintaining that they were an indigenous tribe. All that's known for certain is that the Etruscans were spread thoughout central Italy from the eighth century BC, and that the centre of gravity of their domain was in the southern part of the modern province, roughly along a line drawn from Orbetello to Lago Trasimeno. Their principal settlements in Tuscany were Roselle, Vetulonia, Populonia, Volterra, Chiusi, Cortona, Arezzo and – most northerly of them all – Fiesole.

It seems that the Etruscans absorbed elements of those cultures with whom they came into contact – thus their trade with Greek settlements produced some classically influenced art that can be seen at its best in Florence's archaeological museum and in Cortona. The Etruscan language has still not been fully deciphered (a massive translation programme is under way in Perugia), so at the moment their wall paintings and terracotta funerary sculptures are the main source of information about them, and this information is open to widely differing interpretations. Some people have inferred an almost neurotic fear of death from the evidence of their burial sites and monuments, while others – most notably D.H. Lawrence – have on the contrary intuited an irrepressible and uncomplicated vitality.

There may have been an Etruscan settlement where Florence now stands, but it would have been subservient to their base in the hill town of Fiesole. The substantial development of Tuscany's chief city began with the **Roman** colony of **Florentia**, established by Julius Caesar in 59 BC as a settlement for army veterans – by which time Romans had either subsumed or exterminated most Etruscan towns. Expansion of Florentia itself was rapid, with a steady traffic of trading vessels along the Arno providing the basis of accelerated growth in the second and third centuries AD.

This rise under the empire was paralleled by the growth of **Siena**, **Pisa** and **Lucca**, establishing an economic primacy in the north of Tuscany that has endured to the present. According to legend Siena was founded by the sons of Remus, supposedly fleeing their uncle Romulus, while the port at Pisa was developed by the Romans in the second century BC. Lucca was even more important, and it was here that Julius Caesar, Crassus and Pompey established their triumvirate in 56 BC.

BARBARIANS AND MARGRAVES

Under the comparative tranquillity of the Roman colonial regime, **Christianity** began to spread through the region. Lucca claims to have been the first Christian city in Tuscany – evangelised by a disciple of Saint Peter – though Pisa's church of San Pietro a Grado is said to have been founded by Peter himself. In Florence, the church of San Lorenzo and the martyr's shrine at San Miniato were both established in the fourth century.

This period of calm was shattered in the fifth century by the invasions of the **Goths** from the north, though the scale of the destruction in this first barbarian wave was nothing compared to the havoc of the following century. After the fall of Rome, the empire had split in two, with the western half ruled from Ravenna and the eastern from Constantinople (Byzantium). By the 490s Ravenna was occupied by the Ostrogoths, and forty years later the Byzantine emperor Justinian launched a campaign to repossess the Italian peninsula.

The ensuing mayhem between the Byzantine armies of Belisarius and Narsus and the fast-moving Goths was probably the most destructive phase of central Italian history, with virtually all major settlements ravaged by one side or the other – and sometimes both. In 552 Florence fell to the hordes of the Gothic king **Totila**, whose depredations so weakened the province that less than twenty years later the **Lombards** were able to storm in, subjugating Florence to the duchy whose capital was in Pavia, though its dukes preferred to rule from Lucca.

By the end of the eighth century Charlemagne's **Franks** had taken control of much of Italy, with the administration being overseen by imperial **margraves**, again based in Lucca. These proxy rulers developed into some of the most powerful figures in the Holy Roman Empire and were instrumental in spreading Christianity even further, founding numerous religious houses. Willa, widow of the margrave Uberto, established the Badìa in Florence in 978, the first monastic foundation in the centre of the city; her son Ugo, margrave in turn, is buried in the Badìa's church.

The hold of the central authority of the Holy Roman Empire was often tenuous, with feudal grievances making the region all but ungoverna-ble, and it was under the imperial margraves that the notion of an autonomous Tuscan entity began to emerge. In 1027 the position of margrave was passed to the **Canossa** family, who took the title of the Counts of Tuscia, as Tuscany was then called. The most influential figure produced by this dynasty was **Matilda**, daughter of the first Canossa margrave. When her father died she was abducted by the German emperor Henry III, and on her release and return to her home territory she began to take the side of the papacy in its protracted disputes with the empire. The culmination of her anti-imperialist policy came in 1077, when she obliged the emperor Henry IV to wait in the snow outside the gates of Canossa before making obeisance to Pope Gregory VII. Later friction between the papacy, empire and Tuscan cities was assured when Matilda bequeathed all her lands to the pope, with the crucial excep-tions of Florence, Siena and Lucca.

GUELPHS AND GHIBELLINES

Though Lucca had been the titular base of the imperial margraves, Ugo and his successors had shown a degree of favouritism towards **Florence** and over the next three hundred years Florence gained pre-eminence among the cities of Tuscany, becoming especially impor-tant as a religious centre. In 1078 Countess Matilda supervised the construction of new fortifications for Florence, and in the year of her death – 1115 – granted it the status of an independent city. The new *comune* of Florence was essentially governed by a council of one hundred men, the great majority drawn from the rising merchant class. In 1125 the city's increasing dominance of the region was confirmed when it crushed the rival city of Fiesole. Fifty years later, as the population boomed with the rise of the textile industry, new walls were built around what was now one of the largest cities in Europe.

Not that the other mercantile centres of Tuscany were completely eclipsed, as their magnificent heritage of medieval buildings makes plain. **Pisa** in the tenth and eleventh centuries had become one of the peninsula's wealthiest ports and its shipping lines played a vital part in bringing the cultural influences of France, Byzantium and the Muslim world into Italy. Twelfth-century **Siena**, though racked by conflicts between the bishops and the secular authorities and between the nobility and the merchant class, was booming thanks to its cloth industries and its exploitation of a local silver mine – foundation of a banking empire that was to see the city rivalling the bankers of Venice and Florence on the international markets.

Throughout and beyond the thirteenth century Tuscany was torn by conflict between the **Ghibelline** faction and the **Guelphs**. The names of these two political alignments derive from **Welf** – the family name of the emperor Otto IV – and **Waiblingen** – the name of a castle owned by their implacable rivals, the Hohenstaufen. Though there's no clear documentation, it seems that the terms Guelph and Ghibelline entered the Italian vocabulary at the end of the twelfth century, when supporters of Otto IV battled for control of the central peninsula with the future Frederick II, nephew of Otto and grandson of the Hohenstaufen emperor Barbarossa (1152–90). Within the first few years of Frederick II's reign (1212–50), the labels Guelph and Ghibelline had changed their meaning – the latter still referred to the allies of the Hohenstaufen, but the Guelph party was defined chiefly by its loyalty to the papacy, thus reviving the battle lines drawn up during the reign of Matilda.

To muddy the waters yet further, when Charles of Anjou conquered Naples in 1266, alliance with the anti-imperial French became another component of Guelphism, and a loose Guelph alliance soon stretched from Paris to Naples, substantially funded by the bankers of Tuscany.

Ghibelline/Guelph divisions approximately corresponded to a split between the feudal **nobility** and the rising **business classes**, but this is only the broadest of generalisations. By the beginning of the thirteenth century the major cities of Tuscany were becoming increasingly self-sufficient and inter-city strife was soon a commonplace of medieval life. In this climate, affiliations with the empire and the papacy were often struck on the basis that "my enemy's enemy is my friend", and allegiances changed at baffling speed – if, for instance, the Guelphs gained the ascendancy in a particular town, its neighbours might switch to the Ghibelline camp to maintain their rivalry. Nonetheless, certain patterns did emerge from the confusion: Florence and Lucca were generally Guelph strongholds, while Pisa, Arezzo,

Prato, Pistoia and Siena tended to side with the empire.

As a final complicating factor, this was also the great age of **mercenary** armies, whose loyalties changed even quicker than those of the towns that paid for their services. Thus **Sir John Hawkwood** – whose White Company was the most fearsome band of hoodlums on the peninsula – is known today through the monument to him in Florence's Duomo, but early in his career was employed by Ghibelline Pisa to fight the Florentines. He was then taken on by Pope Gregory XI, whom he deserted on the grounds of underpayment, and in the end was granted a pension of 1200 florins a year by Florence, basically as a form of protection money. Even then he was often absent fighting for other cities whenever a fat purse was waved in his direction.

MEDIEVAL FLORENCE BEFORE THE MEDICI

In this period of superpower manoeuvring and shifting economic structures, city governments in Tuscany were volatile. The administration of Siena, for example, was carried out by various combinations of councils and governors and in 1368 its constitution was redrawn no fewer than four times. However, Florence provides perhaps the best illustration of the turbulence of Tuscan politics in the late Middle Ages.

In 1207 the city's governing council was replaced by the ***Podestà***, an executive official who was traditionally a non-Florentine, in a semi-autocratic form of government that was common throughout the region. It was around this time, too, that the first ***Arti*** (Guilds) were formed to promote the interests of the traders and bankers, a constituency of ever-increasing power. Then in 1215 Florence was riven by a feud that was typical of the internecine violence of central Italy at this period. On Easter Sunday one **Buondelmonte de' Buondelmonti**, on his way to his wedding, was stabbed to death at the foot of the Ponte Vecchio by a member of the Amidei clan, in revenge for breaking his engagement to a young woman of that family. The prosecution of the murderers and their allies polarised the city into those who supported the *comune* – which regarded itself as the protector of the commercial city against imperial ambitions – and the followers of the Amidei, who seem to have politicised their personal grievances by aligning themselves against the *comune* and with the emperor.

These Ghibellines eventually enlisted the help of Emperor Frederick II to oust the Guelphs in 1248, but within two years they had been displaced by the Guelph-backed regime of the *Primo Popolo*, a quasi-democratic government drawn from the mercantile class. The *Primo Popolo* was in turn displaced in 1260, when the Florentine army marched on Siena to demand the surrender of some exiles who were hiding out in the city. Though greatly outnumbered, the Sienese army and its Ghibelline allies overwhelmed the aggressors at **Montaperti**, after which the Sienese were prevented from razing Florence only by the intervention of Farinata degli Uberti, head of the Ghibelline exiles.

By the 1280s the balance had again moved back in favour of Florence, where the Guelphs were back in control – after the intervention of Charles of Anjou – through the *Secondo Popolo*, a regime run by the *Arti Maggiori* (Great Guilds). It was this second bourgeois administration that definitively shifted the fulcrum of power in Florence towards its bankers, merchants and manufacturers – whereas in Siena, the second richest city in Tuscany, the feudal families retained a stranglehold for far longer. Agitation from the landed nobility of the countryside around Florence had been a constant fact of life until the *Secondo Popolo*, which in 1293 passed a programme of political reforms known as the *Ordinamenti della Giustizia*, excluding the nobility from government and investing power in the *Signoria*, a council drawn from the *Arti Maggiori*.

Strife between the virulently anti-imperial "Black" and more conciliatory "White" factions within the Guelph camp marked the start of the fourteenth century in Florence, with many of the Whites – Dante among them – being exiled in 1302. Worse disarray was to come. In 1325 the army of Lucca under **Castruccio Castracani** defeated the Florentines and was about to overwhelm the city when the death of their leader took the momentum out of the campaign. Then in 1339 the Bardi and Peruzzi banks – Florence's largest – both collapsed, mainly owing to the bad debts of Edward III of England. The ultimate catastrophe came in 1348, when the **Black Death** destroyed as many as half the city's population.

However, even though the epidemic hit Florence so badly that it was generally referred to as the Florentine Plague, its effects were equally devastating throughout the region and thus did nothing to reverse the economic – and thus political – supremacy of the city. Florence had subsumed Pistoia in 1329 and gained Prato in the 1350s. In 1406 it took control of Pisa and thus gained a long-coveted sea port, and five years later Cortona became part of its territory. From this time on, despite the survival of Sienese independence into the sixteenth century, the history of Tuscany increasingly becomes the history of Florence.

THE EARLY MEDICI

A crucial episode in the liberation of Florence from the influence of the papacy was the so-called **War of the Eight Saints** in 1375–78, which brought Florence into direct territorial conflict with Pope Gregory XI. This not only signalled the dissolution of the old Guelph alliance, but had immense repercussions for the internal politics of Florence. The increased taxation and other economic hardships of the war provoked an uprising of the industrial day-labourers, the **Ciompi**, on whom the wool and cloth factories depended. Their short-lived revolt resulted in the formation of three new guilds and direct representation for the workers for the first time. However, the prospect of increased proletarian presence in the machinery of state provoked a consolidation of the city's oligarchs and in 1382 an alliance of the city's Guelph party and the *Popolo Grasso* (the wealthiest merchants) took control of the *Signoria* away from the guilds, a situation that lasted for four decades.

Not all of Florence's most prosperous citizens aligned themselves with the *Popolo Grasso*, and the foremost of the well-off mavericks were the **Medici**, a family from the agricultural Mugello region whose fortune had been made by the banking prowess of Giovanni Bicci de' Medici. The political rise of his son, **Cosimo de' Medici**, was to some extent due to his family's sympathies with the *Popolo Minuto*, as the members of the disenfranchised lesser guilds were known. With the increase in public discontent at the autocratic rule of the Signoria – where the Albizzi clan were the dominant force – Cosimo came to be seen as the figurehead of the more democratically inclined sector of the upper class. In 1431 the authorities imprisoned him in the tower of the Palazzo Vecchio and two years later, as Florence became embroiled in a futile and domestically unpopular war against Lucca, they sent him into exile. He was away for only a year. In 1434, after a session of the *parlamento* – a general council called in times of emergency – it was decided to invite him to return. Having secured the military support of the Sforza family of Milan, Cosimo became the pre-eminent figure in the city's political life, a position he maintained for more than three decades.

Cosimo il Vecchio – as he came to be known – rarely held office himself, preferring to exercise power through backstage manipulation and adroit investment. His extreme generosity to charities and religious foundations in Florence was no doubt motivated in part by genuine piety, but clearly did no harm as a public relations exercise – even if it didn't impress the contemporary who recorded that his munificence was due to the fact that "he knew his money had not been over-well acquired".

Dante, Boccaccio and Giotto in the first half of the fourteenth century had established the **literary and artistic ascendancy** of Florence, laying the foundations of Italian humanism with their emphasis on the importance of the vernacular and the dignity of humanity. Florence's reputation as the most innovative cultural centre in Europe was strengthened during the fifteenth century, to a large extent through Medici patronage. Cosimo commissioned work from Donatello, Michelozzo and a host of other Florentine artists, and took advantage of the 1439 Council of Florence – a conference of the Catholic and Eastern churches – to foster scholars who were familiar with the literatures of the ancient world. His grandson **Lorenzo il Magnifico** (who succeeded Piero il Gottoso – the Gouty) continued this literary patronage, promoting the study of the classics in the Platonic academy that used to meet at the Medici villas. Other Medici were to fund projects by Botticelli, Michelangelo, Pontormo – in fact, most of the seminal figures of the Florentine Renaissance.

Lorenzo il Magnifico's status as the *de facto* ruler of Florence was even more secure than that of Cosimo il Vecchio, but it did meet one stiff challenge. While many of Florence's financial dynasties were content to advise and support the Medici, others – notably the mighty Strozzi clan – were resentful of the power now wielded by their fellow businessmen. In 1478 one of these disgruntled families, the Pazzi, conspired with Pope Sixtus IV, who had been riled by Lorenzo's attempt to break the papal monopoly of alum mining. This **Pazzi Conspiracy** resulted in an assault on Lorenzo and his brother Giuliano during Mass in the Duomo; Lorenzo was badly injured and Giuliano murdered, an outcome that only increased the esteem in which Lorenzo was held. Now that the plot had failed, Sixtus joined forces with the ferocious King Ferrante of Naples to launch a war on Florence, and excommunicated Lorenzo into the bargain. Taking his life in his hands, Lorenzo left Florence to persuade Ferrante to leave the alliance, a mission he somehow accomplished successfully, to the jubilation of the city.

THE WARS OF ITALY

Before Lorenzo's death in 1492 the Medici bank failed, and in 1494 Lorenzo's son Piero was obliged to flee following his surrender to the invading French army of Charles VIII. This invasion was the commencement of a bloody half-century dominated by the so-called **Wars of Italy**.

After the departure of Charles's troops, Florence for a while was virtually under the control of the inspirational monk **Girolamo Savonarola**, but his career was brief. He was executed as a heretic in 1498, after which the city continued to function as a more democratic republic than that of the Medici. In 1512, however, following Florence's defeat by the Spanish and papal armies, the Medici returned, in the person of the vicious **Giuliano, Duke of Nemours**.

Giuliano's successors – his equally unattractive nephew **Lorenzo, Duke of Urbino**, and **Giulio**, illegitimate son of Lorenzo il Magnifico's brother – were in effect just the mouthpieces of Giovanni de' Medici (the Duke of Nemours' brother), who in 1519 became **Pope Leo X**. Similarly, when Giulio became **Pope Clement VII**, he was really the absentee ruler of Florence, where the family presence was maintained by the ghastly Ippolito (illegitimate son of the Duke of Nemours) and **Alessandro** (illegitimate son of the Duke of Urbino).

The Medici were again evicted from Florence in the wake of Charles V's pillage of Rome in 1527, Pope Clement's humiliation by the imperial army providing the spur to eject his deeply unpopular relatives. Three years later the pendulum swung the other way – after a siege by the combined papal and imperial forces, Florence capitulated and was obliged to receive Alessandro, who was proclaimed **Duke of Florence**, the first Medici to bear the title of ruler. Though the sadistic Alessandro lost no opportunity to exploit the immunity that came from his title, in the wider scheme of Italian politics he was a less powerful figure than his ancestors. Tuscany was becoming just one more piece in the vast jigsaw of the Habsburg empire, a superpower far more interventionist than the medieval empire of Frederick II could ever have been.

THE LATER MEDICI

After the assassination of Alessandro in 1537, power passed to another **Cosimo**, not a direct heir but rather a descendant of Cosimo il Vecchio's brother. The Emperor Charles V, now related to the Medici through the marriage of his daughter to Alessandro, gave his assent to the succession of this seemingly pliable young man – indeed, without Habsburg consent it would not have happened. Yet it turned out that Cosimo had the clear intention of maintaining Florence's role as the regional power-broker, and he proved immensely skilful at judging just how far he could push the city's autonomy without provoking the imperial policy makers.

Having finally extinguished the subversive threat of the Strozzi faction at the battle of **Montemurlo**, Cosimo went on to buy the territory of Siena from the Habsburgs in 1557, giving Florence control of all of Tuscany with the solitary exception of Lucca. Two years later Florentine hegemony in Tuscany was confirmed in the Treaty of Cateau-Cambrésis, the final act in the Wars of Italy. Soon after, though, the new Habsburg emperor, Philip II, installed a military outpost in the Orbetello area to keep Tuscany under scrutiny.

Imperial and papal approval of Cosimo's rule was sealed in 1570, when he was allowed to take the title **Cosimo I, Grand-Duke of Tuscany**. In European terms Tuscany was a second-rank power, but by comparison with other states on the peninsula it was in a very comfortable position, and during Cosimo's reign there would have been little perception that Florence was drifting inexorably towards the margins of European politics. It was Cosimo who built the Uffizi, extended and overhauled the Palazzo Vecchio, installed the Medici in the Palazzo Pitti, had the magnificent Ponte Santa Trìnita constructed across the Arno and commissioned much of the public sculpture around the Piazza della Signoria.

Cosimo's descendants were to remain in power until 1737, and aspects of their rule continued the city's intellectual tradition – the Medici were among Galileo's strongest supporters, for example. Yet it was a story of almost continual if initially gentle economic decline, as bad harvests and recurrent epidemics worsened the gloom created by the shift of European trading patterns in favour of northern Europe. The half-century reign of **Ferdinando II** had scarcely begun when the market for Florence's woollen goods collapsed in the 1630s, and the city's banks simultaneously went into a terminal slump. The last two male Medici, the insanely pious **Cosimo III** and the drunken pederast **Gian Gastone** – who was seen in public only once, vomiting from the window of the state coach – were fitting symbols of the moribund Florentine state.

TO THE PRESENT

Under the terms of a treaty signed by Gian Gastone's sister, Anna Maria de' Medici, Florence passed in 1737 to the **House of Lorraine**, cousins of the Austrian Habsburgs. The first Lorraine prince, the future Francis I of Austria, was a more enlightened ruler than the last Medici had been and his successors presided over a placid and generally untroubled region, doing much to improve the condition of Tuscany's agricultural land and rationalise its production methods. Austrian rule lasted until the coming of the French in 1799, an interlude that ended with the fall of **Napoleon**, who had made his sister – Elisa Baciocchi – Grand Duchess of Tuscany.

After this, the Lorraine dynasty was brought back, remaining in residence until the last of the line, **Leopold II**, consented to his own deposition in 1859. Absorbed into the united Italian state in the following year, Florence became the **capital of the Kingdom of Italy** in 1861, a position it held until 1871.

Italy's unpopular entry into World War I cost thousands of Tuscan lives, and the economic disruption that followed was exploited by the regime of Benito **Mussolini**. The corporate fascist state of the 1920s did effect various improvements in the infrastructure of the region, but Mussolini's alliance with Hitler's Germany was to prove a calamity. In 1943, as the Allied landing at Monte Cassino was followed by a campaign to sweep the occupying German forces out of the peninsula, Tuscany became a battlefield between the Nazis and the **partisans**. The districts around Monte Amiata and the Val d'Órcia sheltered particularly strong partisan groups, and many of the province's hill towns had their resistance cells, as numerous well-tended war memorials testify.

Yet, as elsewhere in Italy, the loyalties of Tuscany were split, as is well illustrated by the case of Florence, an ideological centre for the resistance but also home to some of Italy's most ardent Nazi collaborators. Wartime Florence in fact produced one of the strangest paradoxes of the time: a fascist sympathiser in charge of the British Institute and a German consul who did so much to protect suspected partisans that he was granted the freedom of the city after the war.

Although most of the major monuments of Tuscany survived the war — sometimes as a result of pacts between the two sides — there was inevitably widespread destruction. Grosseto, Pisa and Livorno were badly damaged by Allied bombing raids, while Florence was wrecked by the retreating German army, who bombed all the bridges except the Ponte Vecchio and blew up much of the medieval city near the banks of the Arno.

POSTWAR TUSCANY

Tuscany is a prosperous, conservative region that tends to return **Christian Democrat** (DC) members of parliament. On a local level, however, **communist** support is high, the party's record in the war and subsequent work on land reform maintaining a loyal following. Excluded from national government by the machinations of the DC, the communist party has projected itself as the grassroots opposition to the centralisation and corruption of Roman politics. It's a strategy that has been particularly successful in Tuscany, which has clung onto an image of itself as a state within the state. Since the 1970s the town halls of the region have been governed predominantly by communist-led coalitions, forming the heartland of the so-called "red belt" of central Italy.

Despite migration from the land in the 1950s and 1960s, the economy of Tuscany has been adroitly managed. The labour-intensive vineyards, olive groves and farms continue to provide a dependable source of income, boosted by industrial development in the Arno valley and around Livorno and Piombino. Production of textiles, leather goods and jewellery have brought money into Prato, Florence and Arezzo, but **tourism** plays an uncomfortably large and ever-increasing part in balancing the books of these and other historic centres.

The problem is worst in Florence, where the latest and most ambitious attempt to break the city's ever-increasing dependence on its visitors is the so-called **Firenze Nuova**, a development to the northwest of the city, on the way to Prato. Underwritten by Fiat and La Fondiaria (the insurance and property wing of the Montedison conglomerate), the scheme is touted as a fully viable city, where people will work, live and play, leaving Florence to develop as a cultural and small-scale commercial city. The doubters, however, see it as a cynical exercise by the two giant companies, one of which owns much of the land that Firenze Nuova is to be raised on, while the other plans to build a car plant out there. At the moment speculation about the impact of Firenze Nuove appears premature — the construction work seems to be progressing in fits and starts, and there is little chance of Florence's twin being completed within the fifteen-year timetable drawn up for it.

DESCENDANTS OF COSIMO IL VECCHIO

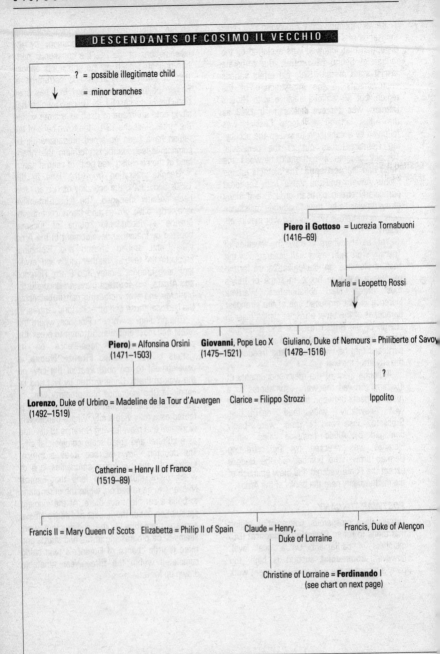

- ⋯⋯⋯ ? = possible illegitimate child
- ↓ = minor branches

Piero il Gottoso = Lucrezia Tornabuoni
(1416–69)

Maria = Leopetto Rossi

Piero) = Alfonsina Orsini   Giovanni, Pope Leo X   Giuliano, Duke of Nemours = Philiberte of Savoy
(1471–1503)   (1475–1521)   (1478–1516)

                                                                                            ?

Lorenzo, Duke of Urbino = Madeline de la Tour d'Auvergen   Clarice = Filippo Strozzi   Ippolito
(1492–1519)

Catherine = Henry II of France
(1519–89)

Francis II = Mary Queen of Scots   Elizabetta = Philip II of Spain   Claude = Henry,   Francis, Duke of Alençon
                                                                          Duke of Lorraine

                                                                   Christine of Lorraine = Ferdinando I
                                                                   (see chart on next page)

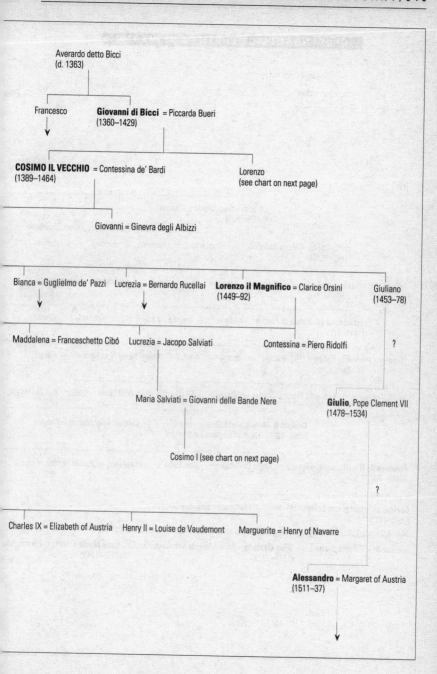

DESCENDANTS OF LORENZO DE'MEDICI

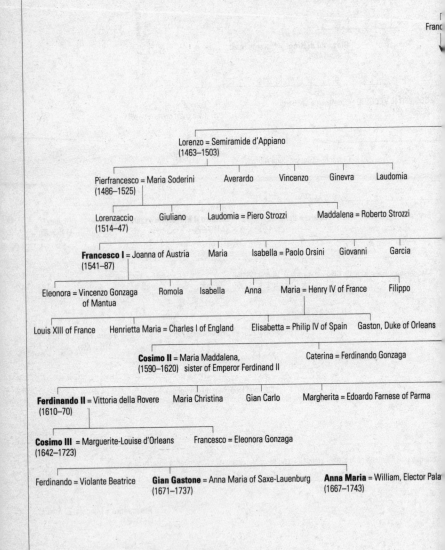

Franc

Lorenzo = Semiramide d'Appiano
(1463–1503)

Pierfrancesco = Maria Soderini   Averardo   Vincenzo   Ginevra   Laudomia
(1486–1525)

Lorenzaccio   Giuliano   Laudomia = Piero Strozzi   Maddalena = Roberto Strozzi
(1514–47)

Francesco I = Joanna of Austria   Maria   Isabella = Paolo Orsini   Giovanni   Garcia
(1541–87)

Eleonora = Vincenzo Gonzaga   Romola   Isabella   Anna   Maria = Henry IV of France   Filippo
of Mantua

Louis XIII of France   Henrietta Maria = Charles I of England   Elisabetta = Philip IV of Spain   Gaston, Duke of Orleans

Cosimo II = Maria Maddalena,   Caterina = Ferdinando Gonzaga
(1590–1620)   sister of Emperor Ferdinand II

Ferdinando II = Vittoria della Rovere   Maria Christina   Gian Carlo   Margherita = Edoardo Farnese of Parma
(1610–70)

Cosimo III = Marguerite-Louise d'Orleans   Francesco = Eleonora Gonzaga
(1642–1723)

Ferdinando = Violante Beatrice   **Gian Gastone** = Anna Maria of Saxe-Lauenburg   **Anna Maria** = William, Elector Pala
(1671–1737)   (1667–1743)

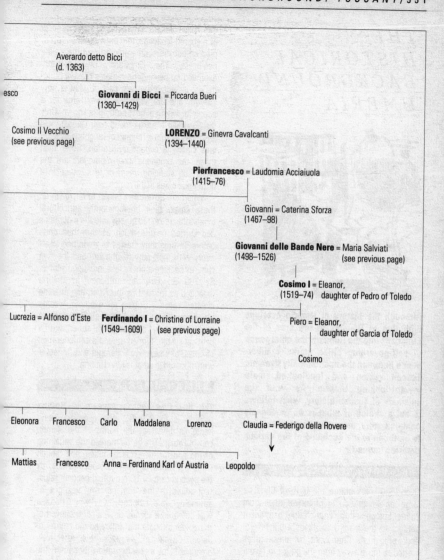

Averardo detto Bicci
(d. 1363)

...esco

Giovanni di Bicci = Piccarda Bueri
(1360–1429)

Cosimo Il Vecchio
(see previous page)

LORENZO = Ginevra Cavalcanti
(1394–1440)

Pierfrancesco = Laudomia Acciaiuola
(1415–76)

Giovanni = Caterina Sforza
(1467–98)

Giovanni delle Bande Nere = Maria Salviati
(1498–1526)   (see previous page)

Cosimo I = Eleanor,
(1519–74)   daughter of Pedro of Toledo

Lucrezia = Alfonso d'Este   Ferdinando I = Christine of Lorraine
              (1549–1609)   (see previous page)

Piero = Eleanor,
       daughter of Garcia of Toledo

Cosimo

Eleonora   Francesco   Carlo   Maddalena   Lorenzo   Claudia = Federigo della Rovere

Mattias   Francesco   Anna = Ferdinand Karl of Austria   Leopoldo

THE HISTORICAL BACKGROUND: UMBRIA

Although the history of Umbria overlaps with that of Tuscany in the eras of the Etruscans and the Romans, the emergence of self-governing cities marks a divergence between the economically dynamic Tuscan region and landlocked, more inward-looking Umbria. As with the summary of Tuscan history, what follows is but a sketch of what is an immensely complex story, more details of which are to be found in the accounts of the various Umbrian towns.

PRE-ROMAN UMBRIA

Over 1500 years before the birth of Christ, a large-scale migration of primitive tribes from central Europe and the East brought permanent settlers to the marshy lowlands around Terni and Perugia. As time went by, these tribes started to move away from the plains in favour of the uplands around Norcia, giving rise to the first of the **hill towns** that were eventually to dominate the entire region.

By the eighth century BC these peoples were absorbed by the larger and more sophisticated tribes that followed them from the north. These gradually formed themselves into three distinct groups: the Samnites, the Latins (who later became the Romans), and the **Umbrians**. All three had common cultural roots, spoke dialects of a shared language, and between them occupied all but the southernmost tip of the Italian peninsula. The Umbrians' own territory extended far beyond the region's present boundaries, including the best part of what is now Tuscany and the Marche – a vast area for a people of whom almost nothing is known. Only the Eugubine Marbles found near Gubbio yield any clues as to the religion or language of what was clearly a cogent civilisation. Other than these, the Umbrians' only memorials are the walls still standing, more or less intact, in a dozen-odd cities in the region.

When the **Etruscans** began to encroach on these cities, their predominantly agricultural inhabitants retreated quietly into the mountains and carried on life much as they had done before. In time they started to trade and inter-marry with their new neighbours and the two cultures became more or less indistinguishable. By 700 BC Etruscan influence in Umbria extended as far east as the Tiber, and in some isolated cases – Gubbio for example – some way beyond it. All aspects of their life point to a sophisticated and ordered social set-up, with a political system formed around a confederation of cities, of which two – Perugia and Orvieto – were situated in what is now Umbria.

ROMAN UMBRIA

The first time Umbria appears in **Roman** records is in 309 BC, the occasion being Perugia's defeat at the hands of the Roman consul Fabius. The battle marked the beginning of the end for the Etruscan cities, and though some continued to cling to independence, by the second century BC most had become reluctant allies of the Romans. Any vestiges of autonomy were stripped away when Perugia was defeated a second time, a consequence of the power struggle that followed the murder of Julius Caesar in 44 BC. This effectively amounted to a confrontation between the consul Mark Antony, his brother Lucius, and **Octavius**, Caesar's great-nephew. In 40 BC the dispute reached crisis point, and while Antony was preoccupied with Cleopatra in Egypt, Octavius succeeded in harrying Lucius from Rome. Lucius, unhappily for the citizens of Perugia, decided to take refuge within the city's walls – an action that resulted in the city's destruction at the hands of Octavius.

Octavius went on to proclaim himself the **Emperor Augustus**, and with this proclamation the Imperial Age began. Under his rule, Umbria continued to enjoy a period of prosperity that had begun with the opening of the **Via Flaminia** in 220 BC. The new road linked Rome to the Adriatic coast and to the cities of the north, and gave Umbria immense strategic importance. It superseded the Tiber as the focal point of the region and brought in its wake a massive increase in trade and prosperity: colonies were built from scratch or on the sites of Umbrian and Etruscan settlements, land was drained and roads constructed. Umbria – named as such for the first time – became a unified and thriving province.

EARLY CHRISTIANITY AND THE BARBARIAN INVASIONS

Christianity spread quickly in Umbria, thanks mainly to Roman lines of communication. By the first century AD towns such as Spoleto and Foligno had become bishoprics, and within 200 years most towns had Christian communities. As religious practice increasingly adhered to the monastic pattern established in the eastern Mediterranean, however, it was in Umbria's remote countryside, rather than its cities, that Christianity found its most enduring home. The first recorded **monastery** was founded at Monteluco, near Spoleto, by Julian, a Syrian from Antioch. From such beginnings was born the extraordinary religious and monastic tradition in Umbria that was to culminate with Saint Francis, nearly a millennium later.

Saint Benedict, the most significant of Umbria's early saints, was born in Norcia in 480 AD, within a few years of the deposition of the last Roman Emperor, and at the very moment that the first Barbarian invaders from the north were turning towards Italy. The order he founded and the rule he drew up to guide its members were of incalculable importance in ensuring the survival of Western culture in the tumult that followed the fall of Rome. The rule aimed to move men to a perfect love of God through a combination of prayer, study and work, thus ensuring that countless monks were quietly working, studying and preserving aspects of learning that might otherwise have vanished for good.

As the **Goths** and **Huns** plundered the country, Umbria succumbed to the consequences of plague and famine. The only order in these desperate times came from the clergy, who began to take over the civic functions formerly carried out by the Roman state. Bishops took it upon themselves to become generals, frequently instigating resistance to the invaders. While on the face of things their achievements seemed negligible, in that virtually every Umbrian city was razed to the ground, they won increasing respect for themselves and the Church they represented.

After the death of their leader, **Totila**, at Gualdo Tadino, the Goths were replaced by the **Lombards**, who by 571 had established three principalities in Italy, the central one of which contained most of Umbria and had Spoleto as its capital. This **Dukedom of Spoleto** was to achieve great importance throughout central Italy, despite being cut off from the Lombard kingdom centred on Pavia to the north by a narrow corridor of territory controlled by the Byzantines – a ribbon of land running from the Adriatic to Rome, including Narni, Amelia, Terni and Perugia. This buffer-state remained a thorn in the Lombards' side for 300 years, though in Umbria it had the effect of guaranteeing the Dukedom of Spoleto considerable independence of action, a habit that in the coming years would be a hard one to break. The Lombards generally adopted the manners and customs of the local people, establishing an order which brought a short-lived increase in artistic and commercial initiative. Acknowledging the increasing growth of Christianity, they built monasteries alongside those of the Benedictines.

In 754 the growing power of the **papacy** as a force in Italian politics was illustrated by Pope Stephen III's appeal to the **Franks** to rid Italy of the Lombards. The Franks took up the invitation, first under Pepin the Short, and then under his more famous son, **Charlemagne**. By 800 the Lombards and Byzantines had both been driven out of the country.

BETWEEN THE EMPIRE AND THE PAPACY

The papacy received great tracts of land from Charlemagne, who in return demanded that Pope Leo III crown him emperor of the new **Holy Roman Empire**. Peace reigned while Charlemagne lived, but the harmony between papacy and empire disappeared within a few years of his death. The divisions amongst his successors and their preoccupations in northern Europe again left much of Italy prey to invasion and conflict. The papacy was no healthier, weakened by the rival claims of powerful families; with no central authority, it was not long before the whole country reverted once more to chaos.

The anarchy of the next few years set the tone of events for centuries to come. Many towns and old Roman centres, such as Carsulae (near Todi), unsuited to the rigours of constant invasion and siege, were either abandoned or destroyed, to be replaced by **fortified villas and castles**, for which the region's hilly terrain was ideal. Around these fortresses developed independent and self-sufficient communities, creating a pattern of isolated, independent and ambitious hill towns, each with an eye on the territory of its neighbour.

Throughout this whole period Italy was the scene of a complicated, confused and constantly shifting conflict between the parties of the empire and the papacy, the **Guelphs** and **Ghibellines** (see p.506). As elsewhere, Umbrian towns frequently switched their allegiances, exacting new measures of independence from whoever ruled them at the time, in exchange for promises of loyalty. Yet of all its cities, only Perugia ever really came to merit attention on a national scale. It had become a free *comune* in 1139, owing its wealth to trade links with Rome and the burgeoning economic power of Florence, and was soon the prime mover in any machinations that affected the region as a whole.

Occasionally, however, the Umbrians were distracted from their squabbles by events taking place in the world at large. In 1152, for example, the truce between the empire and the papacy produced by the Concordat of Worms was shattered by the election of a new and ambitious emperor: Frederick Hohenstaufen. His determination to reassert the power of the empire in Italy spelt doom for the Umbrian cities, who soon had cause to fear the man better known by his Italian nickname of **Barbarossa**. As he marched south, some towns, such as Assisi, took his side while others, such as Perugia, tried to stand up to him; the majority – of which Spoleto was the most notable example – were partly or completely destroyed.

Like Charlemagne before him, Barbarossa was unable to ensure the survival of the authority he had imposed on the empire. After his death Pope Innocent III set about exploiting the anti-imperialist feeling aroused in Italy by the ferocity of his campaigns, and to ally it with the collective guilt at the capture of Jerusalem by the infidel Saladin in 1187, hoping thereby to resurrect papal fortunes. When he came to Umbria, however, he met with little success, cities such as Perugia and Spoleto being quite happy to accept new powers of autonomy, but turning obstructive when papal governors were sent to oversee them.

MEDIEVAL COMMUNES AND WAR LORDS

In 1308 the papacy moved to Avignon, and the outlook for the Church grew even more bleak from 1387 until 1417, when Europe was divided in its support for rival popes in Rome and France. The power vacuum which resulted from this **Great Schism** was the single most important factor in allowing the development of democratic communes in central Italy. At the same time, the influence of the older noble families was eclipsed by the emergence of a mercantile class, brought to prominence by the increase and diversification of trade. With the influx of new money and new men, secular building took place on an unprecedented scale, giving the rapidly expanding cities the appearances that they have largely retained to the present day.

Liberal and sophisticated **constitutions** were drawn up to administer the new towns, of which **Spoleto**'s, instituted at the end of the thirteenth century, serves as a typical example. Originally civic issues were decided by a show of hands in the *arringo*, a general assembly of all adult males convoked in the central piazza. By 1296, when a new constitution was drawn up, the size of the population had made such an arrangement impracticable, and the role of the *arringo* was reduced to a body that could express opinions, but no longer take decisions. The legislative function was taken over by a General Council elected from the twelve parishes that made up Spoleto's administrative districts. Final executive and judicial power lay with the *Podestà*, a kind of troubleshooter elected for a year and often brought in from outside the city – as in Tuscany. He was answerable to the **Capitano del Popolo**, a police chief and appeals judge who was also responsible for the day-to-day running of the administration. Below him were a host of elected minor officials, all of whom were, in the manner of contemporary Italian bureaucracy, constrained by rigid job specifications.

The theory was reasonable, but the practice was often rather different. First, the cities spent so much time arguing with their neighbours that their administrations were obliged to be almost constantly prepared for war. Second, towns were plagued by continual dissent from within as Guelphs and Ghibellines fought each other, most of them citing their allegiances to distant authority merely as an excuse to wipe out local rivals and seize power. Citizens soon came to realise that a strong executive was the only means to combat such disorder, and began to accept the domination of forceful individuals, usually the heads of the strongest **noble families** of the moment, or the person who could muster the largest private army – in most cases one and the same man.

At about the same time, other powerful individuals began to figure in Umbria's affairs: the **condottieri**, or itinerant private soldiers hired to fight battles on behalf of their citizens. Most of them were English or French refugees from the Hundred Years' War, or German and Swiss stragglers from the imperial armies. Some were astute enough to form themselves into efficient bands and soon found in Umbria a healthy market for their services. The cities were losers in every way in these contracts, wasting money on unreliable allies while property was destroyed and land plundered. Added to this, there was the everyday chaos produced by warring noble families, whose disputes were often settled in bloodshed worthy of Jacobean tragedy. Taking into account the normal range of calamities, such as plague and famine, which could strike the medieval world at any time, life in Umbria should have been intolerable.

But against this background of violence and suffering, the artistic and intellectual life of the region went from strength to strength. The same subtle changes being wrought throughout northern Italy that were to culminate in the **Renaissance** were also taking place in Umbria. In religion, Saint Francis had almost single-handedly revitalised man's relations to the divine. In painting, Cimabue, Giotto and their followers had introduced a naturalism that left behind the stilted beauty of the Byzantines. A university was founded in Perugia as early as 1308, and the first edition of Dante's *Divine Comedy* was printed not in Florence, but in Foligno.

PAPAL CONSOLIDATION AND THE RISORGIMENTO

Gradually the infighting exhausted the cities, and the **papacy** – which out of choice or necessity had largely stood back from the centuries of bloody disorder – seized the opportunity to exert its power. One by one the cities fell: Spoleto in 1354 to the crusading Cardinal Albornoz; Foligno in 1439, when the ruling Trinci family surrendered to soldiers of Pope Euginius V; Spello in 1535, after 150 years of despotic rule; and Gubbio in 1624, handed over to Urban VIII by the last of the ruling Montefeltro.

The old civic administrations were replaced by papal governors and for the two centuries before Unification Umbria slumbered under the **rule of the Church**. Although order was restored, peace and papal rule were no guarantee of prosperity. The isolation that had once served the region so well now began to tell against it. Absentee landlords – amongst whom the papacy figured large – collected rents but took little interest in land management, so that the soil deteriorated and with it the agriculture on which Umbria depended. Such industry as existed was agriculture-based and so shared in its stagnation, and in any case it was cut off from the prosperous markets to the north by poor communications. To anyone surveying the Umbrian scene at the end of the eighteenth century it would have seemed as if very little had changed in almost 500 years.

Matters improved somewhat in the upheaval that followed the French Revolution and the rule of **Napoleon**, when the French organised the region into two districts and tried to encourage economic growth. In the more liberal atmosphere of the times, a more free-thinking class of merchants emerged, which the return of papal rule after Napoleon's death could do little to repress. By the time of the battle for the unification of Italy, this spirit had found broader and more popular support, and Umbria welcomed Garibaldi's troops into Perugia on September 11, 1860.

Unfortunately, when trade barriers between the regions were abolished the Umbrian economy was subjected to the rigours of free competition, with which it was ill-equipped to deal. Traditional craft and agricultural industries crumbled in the face of industrialisation in the north. Private wealth remained idle, or was invested in the north, while the state failed to make the improvements to the region's infrastructure that might have halted the agricultural decline.

UMBRIA IN THE TWENTIETH CENTURY

In the first years of the twentieth century the Italian economy as a whole was on an upswing, and for a while things began to look up for Umbria as well, with light industry appearing in the region for the first time. But this flicker of prosperity came to an abrupt end when the small **Banca di Perugia**, which had been largely responsible for funding the new investments, was swallowed by the Banca Commerciale, which preferred to invest in the more profitable and less risky ventures in the north.

Where the capital went, the people went too. Although in 1911 half the region's population was illiterate, they did not need education to know that their future lay outside Umbria. Thousands **emigrated** to America or to the new factories of Turin and Germany, leaving a population at home who increasingly saw socialism as the answer to the region's ills. By 1919, Umbria's scattered left-wing parties commanded 48 percent of the vote and had established control of many local and regional councils. Hopes of reform, however, were quickly dashed by the rise of Mussolini, even if the preparations for war did put some energy into the regional economy.

World War II left Umbria relatively unscathed until the German retreat up the peninsula, when the key strategic corridors — between Lago Trasimeno, Perugia and Orvieto — made it the seat of bitter fighting. Resistance groups were active in the hills above the main valleys, with the area around Gubbio seeing particularly intense partisan activity.

Postwar emigration rates were higher than ever. Only when central government devolved more power to the regions did Umbria begin to prosper. Political control by now was in the hands of the **Communist Party**, which carefully directed funds at co-operative ventures and projects appropriate to the region's special needs, with transport, agriculture and latterly tourism as the main priorities. Road and rail links at last provided an economic lifeline to Rome and the north.

Finally, and perhaps most importantly, the last twenty years have seen the birth of what can only be described as a new pride and enthusiasm in Umbria. There is still poverty and there are still problems but there is also a powerful sense of vigour and community which seems determined to overcome them. It is a spirit that even the most casual visitor cannot fail to notice, manifestly obvious in the region's extraordinary range of cultural events, the diversity and skill of its craftspeople, the Umbrians' own obvious pride in their countryside and their heritage, and a host of more minor signs that at last point to progress.

T

A

S

T

S

A DIRECTORY OF ARTISTS AND ARCHITECTS

Agostino di Duccio (1418–81). Born in Florence, Agostino served as a mercenary before turning to sculpture. Having possibly studied with Jacopo della Quercia, he carved the altarpiece for Modena cathedral then returned to Florence in 1442. His masterpiece is the Tempio Malatestiano in Rimini, on which Alberti and Piero della Francesca also worked. The best example in this region of his marble relief work, with its emphasis on linear grace, is the Oratory of San Bernardino in Perugia. He returned to Florence briefly in the 1460s, a period during which he spoiled the marble block that was to become Michelangelo's *David*.

Alberti, Leon Battista (1404–72). Born illegitimately to a Florentine exile, probably in Genoa, Alberti was educated in Padua and Bologna. One of the most complete personifications of the Renaissance ideal of universal genius, he was above all a writer and theorist: his *De Re Aedificatoria* (1452) was the first architectural treatise of the Renaissance, and he also wrote a tract on the art of painting, *Della Pittura*, dedicated to his friend Brunelleschi. His theory of harmonic proportions in musical and visual forms was first put into practice in the facade of Santa Maria Novella in Florence, while his archaeological interest in classical architecture found expression in the same city's Palazzo Rucellai, his first independent project. Even more closely linked to his researches into the styles of antiquity is the miniature temple built for the Rucellai family in the church of San Pancrazio. His other buildings are in Mantua and Rimini.

Albertinelli, Mariotto (1474–1515). A colleague of Fra' Bartolommeo in the workshop in San Marco, Albertinelli abandoned painting to be an innkeeper. His best work is the Uffizi *Visitation*.

Alunno, Nicolò (1430–1502). The greatest of the purely Umbrian painters before Perugino, Alunno was probably the pupil of the Venetian Carlo Crivelli, whose bright colouring and precise contours are a feature of his work. Emotionally more intense than Perugino, he usually rejects the conventional dulcet pastoralism of Umbrian art for a bleaker landscape like that around Gubbio and Foligno.

Ammannati, Bartolomeo (1511–92). A Florentine sculptor-architect, much indebted to Michelangelo, Ammannati is best known for his additions and amendments to the Palazzo Pitti and for the graceful Ponte San Trìnita (though in all likelihood this was largely designed by Michelangelo). He created the fountain in the Piazza della Signoria, with some assistance from his pupil Giambologna, and the Bargello contains some of his pieces made for the Bóboli gardens.

Andrea del Sarto (1486–1530). The dominant artist in Florence at the time of Michelangelo and Raphael's ascendancy in Rome. His strengths are not those associated with Florentine draughtsmanship, being more Venetian in his emphasis on delicacy of colour and the primacy of light. He made his name with frescoes for two Florentine churches in the San Marco district – the Scalzo and Santissima Annunziata. For a period in the 1510s he was in France, and the received wisdom is that his talent did not develop after that. However, two of his other major works in Florence date from after his return – the *Last Supper* in San Salvi and the *Madonna del Sacco* in the cloister of the Annunziata. His major easel painting is the *Madonna of the Harpies* in the Uffizi.

Arnolfo di Cambio (c.1245–1302). Pupil of Nicola Pisano, with whom he worked on sculptural projects in Bologna, Siena and Perugia before going to Rome in 1277. The most important of his independent sculptures are the pieces in Florence's Museo dell'Opera del Duomo and the *Tomb of Cardinal de Braye* in San Domenico in Orvieto. The latter defined the format of wall tombs for the next century, showing the deceased lying on a coffin below the Madonna and Child, set within an elaborate architectural framework. However, Arnolfo is best known as the architect of Florence's Duomo and Palazzo Vecchio, and various fortifications in central Tuscany, including the fortress at Poppi.

Bandinelli, Baccio (1493–1560). Born in Florence, Bandinelli trained as a goldsmith, sculptor and painter. He perceived himself as an equal talent to Michelangelo and to Cellini, his most vocal critic. Despite manifest shortcomings as a sculptor, he was given prestigious commissions by Cosimo I, the most conspicuous of which is the *Hercules and Cacus* outside the Palazzo Vecchio. Other pieces by him are in the Bargello.

Beccafumi, Domenico (1484/6–1551). The last great Sienese painter, Beccafumi was in Rome during the painting of the Sistine chapel ceiling and Raphael's *Stanze*. He returned to Siena in 1513, when his work showed tendencies that were to become prevalent in Mannerist art – contorted poses, strong lighting, vivid artificial colouration. His decorative skill is especially evident in his illusionist frescoes in the Palazzo Pubblico and the pavement of the Duomo.

Benedetto da Maiano (1442–97). Florentine sculptor, best known for his portrait busts in the Bargello and the pulpit in Santa Croce.

Botticelli, Sandro (c.1445–1510). Possibly a pupil of Filippo Lippi, Botticelli was certainly influenced by the Pollaiuolo brothers, whose paintings of the *Virtues* he completed. The mythological paintings for which he is celebrated – including the *Birth of Venus* and *Primavera* – are distinguished by their emphasis on line rather than mass, and by their complicated symbolic meaning, a reflection on his involvement with the neoplatonist philosophers whom the Medici gathered about them. In the last decade of his life his lucid, slightly archaic style suffered from comparison with the more radical paintings of Michelangelo and Leonardo da Vinci, and his devotional pictures

became almost clumsily didactic – a result, perhaps, of his involvement with Savonarola and his followers.

Bronzino, Agnolo (1503–72). The adopted son of Pontormo, Bronzino became the court painter to Cosimo I. He frescoed parts of the Palazzo Vecchio for Eleanor of Toledo, but his reputation rests on his glacially elegant portraits, whose surface brilliance makes no discrimination between the faces of the subjects and their apparel.

Brunelleschi, Filippo (1377–1446). Trained as a sculptor and goldsmith, Brunelleschi abandoned this career after his failure in the competition for the Florence Baptistery doors. The main product of this period is his contribution to the *St James* altarpiece in Pistoia. He then devoted himself to the study of the building techniques of the classical era, travelling to Rome with Donatello in 1402. In 1417 he submitted his design for the dome of Florence's Duomo, and all his subsequent work was in that city – San Lorenzo, the Spedale degli Innocenti, Cappella Pazzi (Santa Croce) and Santa Spirito. Unlike the other great architect of this period, Alberti, his work is based on no theoretical premise, but rather on an empiricist's admiration for the buildings of Rome. And unlike Alberti he oversaw every stage of construction, even devising machinery that would permit the raising of the innovative structures he had planned.

Buontalenti, Bernardo (c.1536–1608). Florentine architect, who began as a military architect to the papacy. Much of his later output was for the court of the Medici – the grotto of the Bóboli gardens, the gardens of the villa at Pratolino and tableaux for court spectaculars. Less frivolous work included the Fortezza del Belvedere, the facade of Santa Trìnita, the villa Artimino and the fortifications at Livorno.

Castagno, Andrea (c.1421–57). The early years of Castagno's life are mysterious, and the exact year of his birth is not known. Around 1440 he painted the portraits of some executed rebels in the Bargello, a job that earned him the nickname "Andrea of the Hanged Men". In 1442 he was working in Venice, but a couple of years later he was back in Florence, creating stained glass for the Duomo and frescoes for Sant'Apollonia. His taut sinewy style is to a large extent derived from the sculpture of his contemporary Donatello, an affinity that is especially clear in his frescoes for Santissima Annunziata. Other major works in Florence include the series of *Famous Men and Women* in the Uffizi and the portrait of *Niccolò da Tolentino* in the Duomo – his last piece.

Cellini, Benvenuto (1500–71). Cellini began his career in Rome, where he fought in the siege of the city by the imperial army in 1527. His sculpture is greatly influenced by Michelangelo, as is evident in his most famous large-scale piece, the *Perseus* in the Loggia della Signoria. His other masterpiece in Florence is the heroic *Bust of Cosimo I* in the Bargello. Cellini was an even more accomplished goldsmith and jeweller, creating some exquisite pieces for Francis I, by whom he was employed in the 1530s and 1540s. He also wrote a racy *Autobiography*, a fascinating insight into the artistic world of sixteenth-century Italy and France.

Cimabue (c.1240–1302). Though celebrated by Dante as the foremost painter of the generation before Giotto, very little is known about Cimabue – in fact, the only work that is definitely by him is the mosaic in Pisa's Duomo. He is generally given credit for the softening of the hieratic Byzantine style of religious art, a tendency carried further by his putative pupil, Giotto. Some works can be attributed to him with more confidence than others – the short-list would include *The Madonna of St Francis* in the lower church at Assisi, the *Passion* cycle in the upper church, the *Maestà* in the Uffizi and the crucifixes in Santa Croce (Florence) and San Domenico (Arezzo).

Civitali, Matteo (1436–1501). Probably self-taught sculptor from Lucca, where all his important work is to be found.

Daddi, Bernardo (c.1290–1349). A pupil of Giotto, Daddi combined the solidity of his master's style with the more decorative aspects of the Sienese style. His work can be seen in the Uffizi and Santa Croce in Florence.

Desiderio da Settignano (c.1428–64). Desiderio continued the low relief technique pioneered by Donatello in the panel for the Orsanmichele *St George*, and carved the tomb of Carlo Marsuppini in Santa Croce, Florence. Better known for his exquisite busts of women and children – a good selection of which are on show in the Bargello.

Donatello (c.1386–1466). A pupil of Ghiberti, Donatello assisted in the casting of the first set of Florence Baptistery doors in 1403, then worked for Nanni di Banco on the Duomo. His early marble *David* (Bargello) is still Gothic in its form, but a new departure is evident in his heroic *St Mark* for Orsanmichele (1411) – possibly produced after a study of the sculpture of ancient Rome. Four years later he began the intense series of prophets for the Campanile, and at the same time produced the *St George* for Orsanmichele – the epitome of early Renaissance humanism, featuring a relief that is the very first application of rigorous perspective in western art.

In the mid-1520s Donatello started a partnership with Michelozzo, with whom he created the tomb of Pope John XXIII in the Florence Baptistery, a refinement of the genre initiated by Arnolfo di Cambio. He went to Rome in 1431, possibly with Brunelleschi, and it was probably on his return that he made the classical bronze *David* (Bargello), one of the first nude statues of the Renaissance period. Also at this time he made the *cantoria* to be placed opposite the one already made by Luca della Robbia, the pulpit for Prato cathedral (with Michelozzo) and the decorations for the old sacristy in Florence's church of San Lorenzo – the parish church of his great patrons, the Medici.

After a period in Padua – where he created the first bronze equestrian statue since Roman times – he returned to Florence, where his last works show an extraordinary harshness and angularity. The main sculptures from this period are the *Judith and Holofernes* (Palazzo Vecchio), the *Magdalene* (Museo dell'Opera del Duomo) and the two bronze pulpits for San Lorenzo.

Duccio di Buoninsegna (c.1255–c.1318). Though occupying much the same pivotal position in the history of Sienese art as Giotto does in Florentine art, Duccio was a less revolutionary figure, refining the stately Byzantine tradition rather than subverting its conventions. One of his earliest works was ordered by Florence's church of Santa Maria Novella – the *Maestà* now in the Uffizi – but the bulk of his output is in his home city. Despite frequent ructions with the civic authorities, for refusing to do military service among other transgressions, in 1308 he received his most prestigious assignment, the painting of a *Maestà* for Siena's Duomo. The polyptych no longer exists in its original form, but most of the panels are now in Siena's Museo dell'Opera del Duomo. This iconic image of the Madonna, with its rich use of gold and decorative colour, was to profoundly influence such painters as the Lorenzettis and Simone Martini, while the small scenes on the back of the panels reveal a less frequently acknowledged mastery of narrative painting.

Fra' Angelico (1387/1400–55). Born in Vicchio, Fra' Angelico joined the Dominican order in Fiesole, near his home town and later entered their monasteries in Cortona and Foligno. His first authenticated painting dates from the mid-1420s, but the first one that can be definitely dated is a *Madonna* he produced for the linen guild of Florence in 1433. Three years later the Dominicans took over the San Marco monastery in Florence, and soon after he embarked on the series of frescoes and altarpieces now displayed in the museum there. In the mid-1440s he was called to Rome to work on the Vatican, after which he worked at Orvieto, served for three years as prior of the monastery in Fiesole, and returned to Rome around 1452, where he died. For all their sophistication of technique, Fra' Angelico's paintings, with their atmosphere of tranquil piety, seem to belong to a less complex world than that inhabited by Donatello, his contemporary. His altarpieces of the *Madonna and Saints* – a genre known as *sacre conversazione* – were, however, extremely influential compositions.

Fra' Bartolommeo (c.1474–1517). Fra' Bartolommeo's earliest known work is the Raphael-influenced *Last Judgement* painted for the San Marco monastery in Florence in 1499. The following year he became a monk there, then in 1504 became head of the workshop, a post previously occupied by Fra' Angelico. In 1514 he was in Rome, but according to Vasari was discouraged by Raphael's fame. The works he later produced in Florence had an influence on High Renaissance art, with their repression of elaborate backgrounds and anecdotal detail, concentrating instead on expression and gesture.

Francesco di Giorgio Martini (1439–1501/2). Sienese painter, sculptor and architect, whose treatise on architectural theory was circulated widely in manuscript form – Leonardo had a copy. Employed for a long period by Federico da Montefeltro – also a patron of Piero della Francesca – he probably designed the loggia for the Palazzo Ducale in Urbino and the church of San Bernardino. The church of Santa Maria degli Angeli in Siena and the Palazzo Ducale in Gubbio might be by him; the one Tuscan building that was certainly designed by him is Santa Maria del Calcinaio in Cortona, one of the finest early Renaissance structures in Italy.

Gaddi, Taddeo (d.1366). According to tradition, Taddeo Gaddi worked with Giotto for 24 years, and throughout his life barely wavered from the precepts of his master's style. His first major independent work is the cycle for the Cappella Baroncelli in Santa Croce, Florence. Other works by him are in Florence's Uffizi, Accademia, Bargello and Museo Horne.

Agnolo Gaddi (d.1396), Taddeo's son, continued his father's Giottoesque style; his major projects were for Santa Croce in Florence and the duomo of Prato.

Gentile da Fabriano (c.1370–1427). Chief exponent of the International Gothic style in Italy, Gentile da Fabriano came to Florence in 1422, when he painted the gorgeous *Adoration of the Magi* now in the Uffizi. In 1425 he went on to Siena and Orvieto, where the intellectual climate was perhaps more conducive than that in the Florence of Masaccio; he finished his career in Rome.

Ghiberti, Lorenzo (1378–1455). Trained as a goldsmith, painter and sculptor, Ghiberti concentrated on the last discipline almost exclusively after winning the competition to design the doors for Florence's Baptistery. His first set of doors are to a large extent derived from Andrea Pisano's earlier Gothic panels for the building, yet his workshop was a virtual academy for the seminal figures of the early Florentine Renaissance – Donatello and Uccello among them. The commission took around twenty years to complete, during which time he also worked on the Siena Baptistery and the church of Orsanmichele in Florence, where his *Baptist* and *St Matthew* show the influence of classical statuary. This classicism reached its peak in the second set of doors for Florence's Baptistery (the *Gates of Paradise*) – taking the innovations of Donatello's low relief carving to a new pitch of perfection. The panels occupied much of the rest of his life but in his final years he wrote his *Commentarii*, the main source of information on fourteenth-century art in Florence and Siena, and the first autobiography by an artist.

Ghirlandaio, Domenico (1449–94). The most accomplished fresco artist of his generation, Ghirlandaio was the teacher of Michelangelo. After a short period working on the Sistine Chapel with Botticelli, he came back to Florence, where his cycles in Santa Trìnita and Santa Maria Novella provide some of the most absorbing documentary images of the time, being filled with contemporary portraits and vivid anecdotal details.

Giambologna (1529–1608). Born in northern France, Giambologna – Jean de Boulogne – arrived in Italy in the mid-1550s, becoming the most influential Florentine sculptor after Michelangelo's death. Having helped Ammannati on the fountain for the Piazza della Signoria, he went on to produce a succession of pieces that typify the Mannerist predilection for sculptures with multiple viewpoints – such as the *Rape of the Sabines* (Loggia della Signoria) and the *Mercury* (Bargello). His workshop also turned out scores of reduced bronze copies of his larger works – the Bargello has an extensive collection.

Giotto di Bondone (1266–1337). It was with Giotto's great fresco cycles that religious art shifted from being a straightforward act of devotion to the dramatic presentation of incident. His unerring eye for the significant gesture, his ability to encapsulate moments of extreme emotion and his technical command of figure modelling and spatial depth brought him early recognition as the greatest artist of his generation – and even as late as the sixteenth century artists were studying his frescoes for their solutions to certain compositional problems. Yet, as with Cimabue, the precise attribution of work is problematic. In all probability his first major cycle was the *Life of St Francis* in the upper church at Assisi, though the extent to which his assistants carried out his designs is still disputed. The Arena chapel in Padua is certainly by him, as are large parts of the Bardi and Peruzzi chapels in Santa Croce in Florence. Of his attributed panel paintings, the Uffizi *Maestà* is the only one universally accepted.

Gozzoli, Benozzo (1421–97). Though a pupil of Fra' Angelico, Gozzoli was one of the more worldly artists of the fifteenth century, with a fondness for pageantry that is seen to most impressive effect in the frescoes in Florence's Palazzo Medici-Ricardi. His celebrated cycle in Pisa's Camposanto was all but destroyed in the last war; his other surviving fresco cycles include the *Life of St Francis* in Montefalco and the *Life of St Augustine* in San Gimignano.

Guido da Siena (active mid-thirteenth century). Guido was the founder of the Sienese school of painters, but his life is one of the most problematic areas of Siena's art history. A signed painting by him in the Palazzo Pubblico is dated 1221, but some experts think that the date may have been altered, and that the work is from the 1260s or 1270s – a period when other pictures associated with him are known to have been painted.

Leonardo da Vinci (1452–1519). Leonardo trained as a painter under Verrocchio, the legend being that his precocious talent caused his master to abandon painting in favour of sculpture. Drawings of landscapes and drapery have survived from the 1470s, but the first completed picture is the *Annunciation* in the Uffizi. The sketch of the *Adoration of the Magi*, also in the Uffizi, dates from 1481, at which time there was no precedent for its fusion of geometric form and dynamic action. Two years later he was in the employment of Lodovico Sforza of Milan, remaining there for sixteen years. During this second phase of his career he produced the *Lady with the Ermine* (Kraków), the fresco of the *Last Supper* and – probably – the two versions of *The Virgin of the Rocks*, the fullest demonstrations to date of his so-called *sfumato*, a blurring of tones from light to dark. Innumerable scientific studies and military projects engaged him at this time, and he also made a massive clay model for an equestrian statue of Francesco Sforza – never completed, like so many of his schemes.

When the French took Milan in 1499 Leonardo returned to Florence, where he devoted much of his time to anatomical researches. It was during this second Florentine period that he was commissioned to paint a fresco of the *Battle of Anghiari* in the main hall of the Palazzo Ducale, where his detested rival Michelangelo was also set to work. Only a fragment of the fresco was completed, and the innovative technique that Leonardo had employed resulted in its speedy disintegration. His cartoons for the *Madonna and Child with St Anne* (Louvre and National Gallery, London) also date from this period, as does the most famous of all his paintings, the Louvre's *Mona Lisa*, the portrait of the wife of a Florentine merchant. In 1506 he went back to Milan, thence to Rome and finally, in 1517, to France. Again, military and scientific work occupied much of this last period – the only painting to have survived is the *St John*, also in the Louvre.

Lippi, Filippo (c.1406–69). In 1421 Filippo Lippi was placed in the monastery of the Carmine in Florence, just at the time Masaccio was beginning work on the Cappella Brancacci there. His early works all bear the stamp of Masaccio, but by the 1530s he was becoming interested in the representation of movement and a more luxuriant surface detail. The frescoes in the cathedral at Prato, executed in the 1550s, show his highly personal, almost hedonistic vision, as do his panel paintings of wistful Madonnas in patrician interiors or soft landscapes – many of them executed for the Medici. His last work, the *Life of the Virgin* fresco cycle in Spoleto, was probably largely executed by assistants.

Filippino Lippi (1457/8–1504) completed his father's work in Spoleto – aged about twelve – then travelled to Florence, where his first major commission was the completion of Masaccio's frescoes in Santa Maria del Carmine (c.1484). At around this time he also painted the *Vision of St Bernard* for the Badia, which shows an affinity with Botticelli, with whom he is known to have worked. His later researches in Rome led him to develop a self-consciously antique style – seen at its most ambitious in Santa Maria Novella.

Lippo Memmi (d.1357). Brother-in-law of Simone Martini, Lippo Memmi was his assistant on the Uffizi *Annunciation*. His major work is the *Maestà* in the Palazzo Pubblico in San Gimignano, and he may also have been responsible for the dramatic New Testament frescoes in the Collegiata of the same town.

Lorenzetti, Ambrogio (active 1319–47). Though Sienese, Ambrogio spent part of the 1320s and 1330s in Florence, where he would have witnessed the decoration of Santa Croce by Giotto and his pupils. He's best known for the *Allegory of Good and Bad Government* in the Palazzo Pubblico, which shows painting being used for a secular, didactic purpose for the first time, and is one of the first instances of a landscape being used as an integral part of a composition rather than as a mere backdrop. The Uffizi *Presentation of the Virgin* highlights the difference between Ambrogio's inventive complexity and the comparative simplicity of his brother's style (see below). There's a fine altarpiece by him in Massa Maríttima as well.

Lorenzetti, Pietro (active 1306–48). Brother of Ambrogio, Pietro Lorenzetti was possibly a pupil of Duccio's in Siena. His first authenticated work is the altarpiece in Arezzo's Pieve di Santa Maria (1320); others include frescoes in Assisi's lower church, in which the impact of Giotto is particularly noticeable, and the *Birth of the Virgin* in Siena's Museo dell'Opera del Duomo, one of the best demonstrations of his skill as a narrative painter. It's probable that both the Lorenzettis died during the Black Death.

Lorenzo Monaco (1372–1425). A Sienese artist, Lorenzo Monaco joined the Camaldolese monastery in Florence, for which he painted the *Coronation of the Virgin*, now in the Uffizi. This and his other earlier works are fairly conventional Sienese-style altarpieces, with two-dimensional figures on gold backgrounds. However, his late *Adoration of the Magi* (Uffizi), with its fastidious detailing and landscape backdrop, anticipates the arrival of Gentile da Fabriano and fully fledged International Gothic.

Lo Spagna (1450–1528). Possibly of Spanish origin – hence the name – Lo Spagna spent much of his life in Umbria. Like many of his contemporaries he came under the influence of Raphael, who spent at least five of his formative years in the region.

Maitini, Lorenzo (c.1270–1330). Sienese architect and sculptor, Maitini was the only local artist to challenge the supremacy of the Pisani. In 1310 he was made supervisor of Orvieto's Duomo, for which he designed the Biblical panels of the facade – though it's not certain how much of the carving was actually by Maitini. Virtually nothing else about him is known.

Martini, Simone (c.1284–1344). The most important Sienese painter, Simone Martini was a pupil of Duccio but equally influenced by Giovanni Pisano's sculpture and the carvings of French Gothic artists. He began his career by painting a fresco counterpart of Duccio's *Maestà* in the city's Palazzo Pubblico (1315). Soon after he was employed by Robert of Anjou, the King of Naples, and there developed a sinuous, graceful and courtly style. In the late 1320s he was back in Siena, where he probably produced the portrait of *Guidoriccio da Fogliano* – though some experts doubt its authenticity. At some point he went to Assisi, where he painted a cycle of *The Life of St Martin* in the lower church. In 1333 he produced a sumptuous *Annunciation* for the Siena duomo; now in the Uffizi, this is the quintessential fourteenth-century Sienese painting, with its immaculately crafted gold surfaces and emphasis on fluid outline and bright colouration. In 1340 Martini travelled to the papal court of Avignon, where he spent the rest of his life. It was at Avignon that he formed a friendship with Petrarch, for whom he illustrated a magnificent copy of Virgil's poetry.

Masaccio (1401–28). Born just outside Florence, Masaccio entered the city's painters' guild in 1422. His first large commission was an altarpiece for the Carmelites of Pisa (the central panel is now in the National Gallery in London), which shows a massive grandeur at odds with the International Gothic style then being promulgated in Florence by Gentile da Fabriano. His masterpieces – the *Trinity* fresco in Santa Maria Novella and the fresco cycle in Santa Maria del Carmine – were produced in the last three years of his life, the latter being painted in collaboration with Masolino. With the architecture of Brunelleschi and the sculpture of Donatello, the Carmine frescoes are the most important achievements of the early Renaissance.

Maso di Banco (active 1340s). Maso was perhaps the most inventive of Giotto's acolytes, and his reputation depends chiefly on the cycle of the *Life of St Sylvester* in Santa Croce, Florence.

Masolino da Panicale (1383–1447). Masolino was employed in Ghiberti's workshop for the production of the first set of Baptistery doors, and the semi-Gothic early style of Ghiberti conditioned much of his subsequent work. His other great influence was the younger Masaccio, with whom he worked on the Brancacci chapel.

Michelangelo Buonarroti (1475–1564). Though a titanic figure of Renaissance Italy, Michelangelo was in many ways the antithesis of Renaissance aesthetics, which had previously emphasised order, proportion and the continuity of tradition. He was born in Caprese, in eastern Tuscany, but his family soon moved to Florence, where he became a pupil of Ghirlandaio. Through Ghirlandaio he came into contact with the Medici, making his first stone reliefs for Lorenzo de' Medici. After the expulsion of the Medici he went to Rome in 1496, where he carved the *Bacchus* now in the Bargello. At his time he also created the *Pietà* for St Peter's, a work that secured his reputation as the most skilled sculptor of his day. He came back to Florence for four years in 1501, during which period he carved the *David* and the *St Matthew* (both in the Accademia) and painted the *Doni Tondo*, one of his very few forays into what he regarded as the menial art of easel painting.

Shortly before leaving Florence again, he was employed to paint a fresco of the *Battle of Cáscina* in the Palazzo Vecchio. Only the cartoon was finished, but this became the single most influential work of art in the city, with its exclusive emphasis on the nude form and its use of twisting figures – a recurrent motif in later Mannerist art. Work was suspended in 1505 when Michelangelo was called to Rome by Pope Julius II, who wanted the artist to create his monumental tomb. The project was never finished, like many of Michelangelo's schemes, and cost him forty years of intermittent labour. The *Slaves* in the Accademia were intended for one version of the tomb.

In 1508 Michelangelo began his other superhuman project, the decoration of the Sistine Chapel ceiling. In 1516 he was back in Florence, when he began the new sacristy of San Lorenzo for the Medici pope, Leo X. Work was interrupted frequently, building really only beginning in 1523, when he was also asked to build a library alongside the church – the Biblioteca Laurenziana. In the San Lorenzo project, as in his designs for the Campidoglio and St Peter's in Rome, Michelangelo created a vocabulary that was to provide the basis of

Mannerist design – employing paradoxical details like brackets that support nothing, and emphasising the building as a dynamic rather than a static ensemble (eg tapering window frames, columns that shrink into the wall rather than stand out from it). The sacristy contains a large array of sculptures but again the work represents just a portion of that planned.

The Medici were again expelled from Florence in 1527, and Michelangelo stayed in the city to supervise the defences when it was besieged by the Medici and Charles V in 1530. He left Florence for ever four years later, and spent his last thirty years in Rome, the period that produced the *Last Judgement* in the Sistine Chapel. Florence has one work from this final, tortured phase of Michelangelo's long career, the *Pietà* (now in the Museo dell'Opera del Duomo) that he intended for his own tomb.

Michelozzo di Bartolommeo (1396–1472). Born in Florence, Michelozzo worked in Ghiberti's studio and collaborated with Donatello before turning exclusively to architecture. His main patrons were the Medici, for whom he altered the villa at Careggi and built the Palazzo Medici, which set a prototype for patrician mansions in the city, with its rusticated lower storey, smooth upper facade, overhanging cornice and inner courtyard. He later designed the Villa Medici at Fiesole for the family, and for Cosimo de' Medici he added the light and airy library to the monastery of San Marco. In the Alberti-influenced tribune for the church of Santissima Annunziata, Michelozzo produced the first centrally planned church design to be built in the Renaissance period.

Mino da Fiesole (1429–84). Florentine sculptor, perhaps a pupil of Desiderio da Settignano, Mino is known chiefly for his tombs and portrait busts; there are examples of the former in Fiesole's Duomo and the Badìa in Florence, and of the latter in the Bargello.

Nanni di Banco (c.1384–1421). A Florentine sculptor who began his career as an assistant to his father on the Florence Duomo, Nanni was an exact contemporary of Donatello, with whom he shared some early commissions – Donatello's first *David* was ordered at the same time as an *Isaiah* from Nanni. The finest works produced in his short life are his niche sculptures at Orsanmichele (especially the *Four Saints*) and the relief above the Duomo's Porta della Mandorla.

Nelli, Ottaviano (active 1400–44). The artist that brought the International Gothic style to Umbria; his intricate and glittering paintings can be seen in Foligno, Assisi and Gubbio.

Odersi, or Oderigi (1240–99). The founder of the Umbrian school, little is known of Odersi except that he was a friend of Giotto and worked mainly in Gubbio. A handful of his miniatures survive, though Dante called him "l'onor d'Agobbio" (the pride of Gubbio) and stuck him in Purgatory as punishment for an obsession with art that left him no time for anything else.

Orcagna, Andrea (c.1308–68). Architect-sculptor-painter, Orcagna was a dominant figure in the period following the death of Giotto, whose emphasis on spatial depth he rejected – as shown in his only authenticated panel painting, the Strozzi altarpiece in Santa Maria Novella. Damaged frescoes can be seen in Santa Croce and Santo Spirito, but Florence's principal work by Orcagna is the massive tabernacle in Orsanmichele. Orcagna's brothers, **Nardo** and **Jacopo di Cione** were the most influential painters in Florence at the close of the fourteenth century – the frescoes in the Strozzi chapel are by Nardo.

Perugino (1445/50–1523). Born Pietro di Cristoforo Vannucci in Città della Pieve, Perugino was the greatest Umbrian artist. Possibly a pupil of Piero della Francesca, he later trained in Florence in the workshop of Andrea Verrocchio, studying alongside Leonardo da Vinci. By 1480 his reputation was such that he was invited to paint in the Sistine Chapel, filling the east wall with his distinctive gently melancholic figures; today only one of Perugino's original three panels remains. In 1500 he executed his greatest work in Umbria, a fresco cycle commissioned by the bankers' guild of Perugia for their Collegio di Cambio. This was probably the first occasion on which he was assisted by his pupil Raphael – and the moment his own career began to wane. Vasari claimed that he was "a man of little or no religion, who could never bring himself to believe in the immortality of the soul" and the production-line altarpieces that his workshop later turned out were often lacking in genuine passion. Yet he was still amongst the most influential of the Renaissance painters, the catalyst for Raphael and mentor for a host of Umbrian artists. In Tuscany he is best seen in the Uffizi and in the church of Santa Maria Maddalena dei Pazzi.

Piero della Francesca (1410/20–92). Piero was born in Borgo Sansepolcro, on the border of Tuscany and Umbria. In the late 1430s he was in Florence, working with Domenico Veneziano, and his later work shows the influence of such Florentine contemporaries as Castagno and Uccello, as well as the impact of Masaccio's frescoes. The exact chronology of his career is contentious, but much of his working life was spent in his native town, for which he produced the *Madonna della Misericordia* and the *Resurrection*, both now in the local Museo Civico. Other patrons included Sigismondo Malatesta of Rimini and Federico da Montefeltro of Urbino — of whom there's a portrait by Piero in the Uffizi. In the 1450s he was in Arezzo, working on the fresco cycle in the church of San Francesco, the only frescoes in Tuscany that can bear comparison with the Masaccio cycle in Florence. He seems to have stopped painting completely in the early 1470s, perhaps to concentrate on his vastly influential treatises on perspective and geometry, but more likely because of failing eyesight.

Piero di Cosimo (c.1462–1521). One of the more enigmatic figures of the High Renaissance, Piero di Cosimo shared Leonardo's scholarly interest in the natural world but turned his knowledge to the production of allusive mythological paintings. There are pictures by him at the Uffizi, Palazzo Pitti, Museo degli Innocenti and Museo Horne.

Pietro da Cortona (1596–1669). Painter-architect, born Pietro Berrettini, who with Bernini was the guiding force of Roman Baroque. The style was introduced to Florence by Pietro's ceiling frescoes in the Palazzo Pitti. His last painting is in his home town.

Pinturicchio (1454–1513). Born Bernardino di Betto in Perugia, Pinturicchio was taught by Perugino, with whom he collaborated on the painting of the Sistine Chapel. His rich palette earned him his nickname, as well as Vasari's condemnation for superficiality. Most of his work is in Rome but his last commission, one of his most ambitious projects, was his *Life of Pius II* for the Libreria Piccolimini in Siena.

Pisano, Andrea (c.1290–1348). Nothing is known of Andrea Pisano's life until 1330, when he was given the commission to make a new set of doors for the Florence Baptistery. He then succeeded Giotto as master mason of the

Campanile; the set of reliefs he produced for it are the only other works definitely by him (now in the Museo dell'Opera del Duomo). In 1347 he became the supervisor of Orvieto's Duomo, a job later held by his sculptor son, **Nino**.

Pisano, Nicola (c.1220–84). Born somewhere in the southern Italian kingdom of the emperor Frederick II, Nicola Pisano was the first great classicising sculptor in pre-Renaissance Italy; the pulpit in Pisa's Baptistery (1260), his first masterpiece, shows clearly the influence of Roman figures. Five years later he produced the pulpit for the Duomo in Siena, with the assistance of his son **Giovanni** (c.1248–1314) and Arnolfo di Cambio. Father and son again worked together on the Fonte Gaia in Perugia, which was Nicola's last major project. Giovanni's more turbulent Gothic-influenced style is seen in two other pulpits, for San Andrea in Pistoia and for the Pisa Duomo. The Museo dell'Opera del Duomo in Siena has some fine large-scale figures by Giovanni, while its counterpart in Pisa contains a large collection of work by both the Pisani.

Pollaiuolo, Antonio del (c.1432–98) and **Piero del** (c.1441–96). Though their Florence workshop turned out engravings, jewellery and embroideries, the Pollaiuolo brothers were known mainly for their advances in oil-painting technique and for their anatomical researches, which bore fruit in paintings and small-scale bronze sculptures. The influences of Donatello and Castagno (Piero's teacher) are evident in their dramatic, often violent work, which is especially well represented in the Bargello. The Uffizi's collection of paintings suggests that Antonio was by far the more skilled artist.

Pontormo, Jacopo (1494–1556). Born near Empoli, Pontormo studied under Andrea del Sarto in Florence in the early 1510s. His friendship with Rosso Fiorentino was crucial in the evolution of the hyper-refined Mannerist aesthetic. His early independent works include the frescoes in the atrium of Santissima Annunziata in Florence, where his work shows an edgy quality quite unlike that of his master, who also frescoed this part of the church. In the 1520s he was hired by the Medici to decorate part of their villa at Poggio a Caiano, after which he executed a *Passion* cycle for the Certosa, to the south of the city. His masterpiece in Florence is the *Deposition* in Santa Felìcita (1525) — unprecedented in its lurid colour scheme but showing some indebtedness to Michelangelo's figures. The major project of his later years, a fresco cycle in San Lorenzo, Florence, has been totally destroyed. Other pieces by him are to be seen in the Uffizi and at Carmignano and Sansepolcro.

Quercia, Jacopo della (1374–1438). A Sienese contemporary of Donatello and Ghiberti, Della Quercia entered the competition for the Florence Baptistery doors which Ghiberti won in 1401. The first known work by him is the tomb of Ilaria del Carretto in Lucca's Duomo. His next major commission was a fountain for Siena's main square, a piece now reassembled in the loggia of the Palazzo Pubblico; before that was finished (1419) he had begun work on a set of reliefs for Siena's Baptistery, a project to which Ghiberti and Donatello also contributed. From 1425 he expended much of his energy on reliefs for San Petronio in Bologna – so much so, that the Sienese authorities ordered him to return some of the money he had been paid for the Baptistery job.

Raphael (1483–1520). With Leonardo and Michelangelo, Raphael Sanzio forms the triumvirate whose works define the essence of the High Renaissance. Born in Urbino, he joined Perugino's workshop some time around 1494 and within five years was receiving commissions independently of his master. From 1505 to 1508 he was in Florence, where he absorbed the compositional and tonal innovations of Leonardo; many of the pictures he produced at that time are now in the Palazzo Pitti. From Florence he went to Rome, where Pope Julius II set him to work on the papal apartments (the *Stanze*). Michelangelo's Sistine ceiling was largely instrumental in modulating Raphael's style from its earlier lyrical grace into something more monumental, but all the works from this more rugged later period are in Rome.

Robbia, Luca della (1400–82). Luca began as a sculptor in conventional materials, his earliest achievement being the marble *cantoria* (choir gallery) now in the Museo dell'Opera del Duomo in Florence, typifying the cheerful tone of most of his work. Thirty years later he made the sacristy doors for this city's Duomo, but by then he had devised a technique for applying durable potter's glaze to clay sculpture and most of his energies were given to the art of glazed terracotta. His distinctive blue, white and yellow compositions are seen at their best in the Pazzi chapel in Santa Croce, the Bargello, and at Impruneta, just outside Florence.

Andrea della Robbia (1435–1525) continued the lucrative terracotta business started by his uncle, Luca. His best work is at the Spedale degli Innocenti in Florence and at the monastery of La Verna.

Giovanni della Robbia (1469–1529), son of Andrea, best known for the frieze of the Ceppo in Pistoia.

Rossellino, Bernardo (1409–64). An architect-sculptor, Rossellino worked with Alberti and carried out his plans for the Palazzo Rucellai in Florence. His major architectural commission was Pius II's new town of Pienza. As a sculptor he's best known for the monument to Leonardo Bruni in Santa Croce – a derivative of Donatello's tomb of John XXIII in the Baptistery. His brother and pupil **Antonio** (1427–79) produced the tomb of the Cardinal of Portugal in Florence's San Miniato al Monte, and a number of excellent portrait busts (Bargello).

Rosso Fiorentino (1494–1540). Like Pontormo, Rosso Fiorentino was a pupil of Andrea del Sarto, but went on to develop a far more aggressive, acidic style than his colleague and friend. His early *Deposition* in Volterra (1521) and the roughly contemporaneous *Moses Defending the Daughters of Jethro* (Uffizi) are typical of his extreme foreshortening and tense deployment of figures. After a period in Rome and Venice, he eventually went to France, where with Primaticcio he developed the distinctive Mannerist art of the Fontainbleau school.

Sangallo, Antonio da, the Elder (1455–1534). A Florence-born architect, Antonio da Sangallo the Elder produced just one major building, but one of the most influential of his period – San Biagio in Montepulciano, based on Bramante's plan for St Peter's in Rome.

His nephew, **Antonio the Younger** (1485–1546), was also born in Florence but did most of his work in Rome, where he began his career as assistant first to Bramante then to Peruzzi. He went on to design the Palazzo Farnese, the most spectacular Roman palace of its time. In Tuscany his most important building is the Fortezza da Basso in Florence.

Giuliano da Sangallo (1445–1516), sculptor, architect and military engineer, was the brother of Antonio the Elder. A follower of Brunelleschi, he produced a number of buildings in and around Florence – the Villa Medici at Poggio a Caiano, Santa Maria delle Carceri in Prato (the first Renaissance church to have a Greek-cross plan) and the Palazzo Strozzi, the most ambitious palace of the century.

Sassetta (c.1392–1450). Sassetta was basically a conventional Sienese painter, though his work does show the influence of International Gothic. Works by him are on show in Siena, Assisi and the Uffizi.

Signorelli, Luca (1450–1523). Though a pupil of Piero della Francesca, Signorelli is more indebted to the muscular drama of the Pollaiuolo brothers and the gestural vocabulary developed by Donatello. In the early 1480s he was probably working on the Sistine Chapel with Perugino and Botticelli, but his most important commission came in 1499, when he was hired to complete the cycle begun by Fra' Angelico in Orvieto's Duomo. The emphasis on the nude figure in his *Last Judgement* was to greatly affect Michelangelo. Shortly after finishing this cycle he went to Rome but the competition from Raphael and Michelangelo drove him back to his native Cortona, where he set up a highly proficient workshop. Works are to be seen in Cortona, Arezzo, Monte Oliveto, Perugia, Sansepolcro and in the Uffizi and Museo Horne in Florence.

Sodoma (1477–1549). Born Giovanni Antonio Bazzi, Sodoma arrived in Siena in 1501, having become familiar with the work of Leonardo da Vinci during a four-year spell in Milan. His major work was begun four years later, a cycle of 31 frescoes at Monte Oliveto. He later won contracts to work in Rome, though the work he commenced in the Vatican was handed over to Raphael.

Spinello Aretino (active 1370s–1410). Probably born in Arezzo, Spinello studied in Florence, possibly under Agnolo Gaddi. He harks back to the monumental aspects of Giotto's style – thus, paradoxically paving the way for the most radical painter of the next generation, Masaccio. His main works are in Florence's church of San Miniato al Monte and Santa Caterina d'Antella, just to the south of the city.

Uccello, Paolo (1396–1475). After training in Ghiberti's workshop, Uccello went to Venice, where he worked on mosaics for the Basilica di San Marco. He returned to Florence in 1431 and five years later was contracted to paint the commemorative portrait of *Sir John Hawkwood* in the Duomo. This trompe l'oeil painting is the first evidence of his interest in the problems of perspective and foreshortening, a subject that was later to obsess him. After an interlude in Padua, he painted the frescoes for the cloister of Santa Maria Novella (c.1445), in which his systematic but non-naturalistic use of perspective is seen at its most extreme. In the following decade he painted the three-scene sequence of the *Battle of San Romano* (Louvre, London National Gallery and Uffizi) for the Medici – his most ambitious non-fresco paintings, and similarly notable for their strange use of foreshortening.

Vasari, Giorgio (1511–74). Born in Arezzo, Vasari trained with Luca Signorelli and Andrea del Sarto. He became the leading artistic impresario of his day, working for the papacy in Rome and for the Medici in Florence, where he supervised (and partly executed) the redecoration of the Palazzo Vecchio. His own house in Arezzo is perhaps the most impressive display of his limited pictorial talents. He also designed the Uffizi gallery and oversaw a number of other architectural projects, including the completion of the massive Madonna dell'Umiltà in Pistoia. He is now chiefly famous for his Tuscan-biased *Lives of the Most Excellent Painters, Sculptors and Architects*, which charted the rebirth of the fine arts with Giotto and the process of refinement that culminated with Michelangelo.

Veneziano, Domenico (1404–61). Despite the name, Domenico Veneziano was probably born in Florence, though his preoccupation with the way in which colour alters in different light conditions is more of a Venetian concern. From 1439 to 1445 he was working on a fresco cycle in Florence with Piero della Francesca, a work that has now perished. Only a dozen surviving works can be attributed to him with any degree of certainty and only two signed pieces by him are left – one of them is the central panel of the so-called *St Lucy Altar* in the Uffizi.

Verrocchio, Andrea del (c.1435–88). A Florentine painter, sculptor and goldsmith, Verrocchio was possibly a pupil of Donatello's and certainly his successor as the city's leading sculptor. A highly accomplished if sometimes over-facile craftsman, he ran one of Florence's busiest workshops, whose employees included the young Leonardo da Vinci. In Florence his work can be seen in the Uffizi, Bargello, San Lorenzo, Santo Spirito, Orsanmichele and Museo dell'Opera del Duomo.

BOOKS

Most of the books recommended below are currently in print, and those that aren't shouldn't be too difficult to track down in secondhand stores. Wherever a book is in print, the UK publisher is given first in each listing, followed by the publisher in the US, unless the title is available in one country only, in which case we have specified the country concerned. If the same publisher produces the book in the UK and US, the publisher is simply named once.

TRAVEL BOOKS AND JOURNALS

Michael Adams, *Umbria* (Bellew in UK). Account by a former *Guardian* correspondent, excellent on the Roman and medieval periods, but – reissued from the 1964 original – badly dated on more modern matters.

Hilaire Belloc, *Path to Rome* (Penguin/ Regnery Gateway). Entertaining account of a turn-of-the-century walk from France to Rome, via Florence and a fair swathe of Tuscany.

Charles Dickens, *Pictures from Italy* (Granville/Ecco). The classic mid-nineteenth-century Grand Tour, recording the sights of Emilia, Tuscany, Rome and Naples in measured and incisive prose.

Wolfgang Goethe, *Italian Journey* (Penguin). Revealing for what it says about the tastes of the time – Roman antiquities taking precedence over the Renaissance.

Edward Hutton, *Florence; Country Walks About Florence; The Valley of the Arno; A Wayfarer in Unknown Tuscany; Siena and Southern Tuscany; Cities of Umbria; Assisi and Umbria Revisited; The Cosmati* (all out of print). A Tuscan resident from the 1930s to 1960s,

Hutton was nothing if not prolific. Some of his prose adds a new shade to purple, but his books, between them, cover almost every inch of Tuscany and Umbria and are packed with assiduous background on the art and history.

Henry James, *Italian Hours* (Century/Ecco). Urbane travel pieces from the young James; perceptive about particular monuments and works of art; superb on the different atmospheres of Italy.

Jonathan Keates, *Tuscany* (George Philip in UK); *Umbria* (George Philip, in UK). Keates's contemporary rambles around the provinces read at times as if he was writing in the same age as Hutton (whose purple prose he also rivals). Nonetheless, both books are strong on stories, reliable on art and beautifully illustrated – though the photos, remarkably, feature not a living soul amid the monuments.

D.H. Lawrence, *Etruscan Places* (Olive Press in UK); also included in *D.H. Lawrence in Italy* (Penguin). Published posthumously, these are Lawrence's musings on Etruscan art and civilization – which he considered pretty ideal ("ripe with the phallic knowledge", etc).

Mary McCarthy, *The Stones of Florence* (Penguin/Harvest). Written in the mid-1960s, *Stones* is a mix of high-class reporting on the contemporary city and anecdotal detail on its history – one of the few accounts that doesn't read as if it's been written in a library.

H.V. Morton, *A Traveller in Italy* (Methuen in UK). Morton's leisurely and amiable books were written in the 1930s, long before modern tourism got into its stride and their nostalgic charm has a lot to do with their enduring popularity. But they are also packed with learned details and marvellously evocative descriptions.

Iris Origo, *War in the Val d'Órcia* (Century/ Godine). A stirring account of Origo's activities in the last war, hiding partisans and Allied troops on her estate near Montepulciano. In her biography *Images and Shadows* (John Murray, out of print), Origo expands on her Tuscan residence, with some intriguing insights into peasant life in the 1930s.

Tobias Smollett, *Travels through France and Italy* (Oxford University Press in UK). One of the funniest travel journals ever written – the apotheosis of Little Englandism, calling on an unmatched vocabulary of disgust at all things foreign.

Matthew Spender, *Within Tuscany* (Penguin). Recollections of twenty years of living in Tuscany – on the whole, refreshingly free of the condescension that besets most "Brits abroad" memoirs.

ANTHOLOGIES

Francis King, *A Literary Companion to Florence* (John Murray).

Harold Acton, *Florence: A Traveller's Companion* (Constable in UK).

HISTORY AND SOCIETY

GENERAL

Harry Hearder, *Italy: A Short History* (Cambridge University Press). The best one-volume survey of the country from prehistory to the present.

Giuliano Procacci, *History of the Italian People* (Penguin/Harper & Row). A comprehensive if undigestibly dense history of the peninsula, charting the development of Italy as a nation state and giving a context for the story of Tuscany and Umbria.

MEDIEVAL

Iris Origo, *The Merchant of Prato* (Penguin/Godine). Based on the massive documentation of Datini's business empire, this is a wonderfully lively recreation of domestic life in four-teenth-century Tuscany.

Daniel Waley, *The Italian City Republics* (Longman in UK). Excellent general account, which gives much prominence to Florence and its Tuscan rivals.

FLORENCE AND THE RENAISSANCE

Harold Acton, *The Last Medici* (Cardinal in UK). Elegant biography of the least elegant member of the dynasty, the perpetually wine-sodden Gian Gastone.

Gene A. Brucker, *Renaissance Florence* (Univ of California). Concentrating on the years 1380–1450, this brilliant study of Florence at its cultural zenith uses masses of archival material to fill in the social, economic and political background to its artistic achievements.

Jacob Burckhardt, *Civilization of the Renaissance in Italy* (Penguin). Nineteenth-century classic of Renaissance scholarship – a book that did more than any other to form our image of the period.

Eric Cochrane, *Florence in the Forgotten Centuries 1527–1800* (University of Chicago Press). Massively erudite account of the twilight centuries of Florence; intimidating in its detail, it's unrivalled in its coverage of the years when the city's scientists were more famous than its painters.

J.R. Hale, *Florence and the Medici* (Thames & Hudson in UK). Scholarly yet lively, this covers the full span of the Medici story from the foundation of the family fortune to the calamitous eighteenth century. Vivid in its recreation of the various personalities involved, it also presents a fascinating picture of the evolution of the mechanics of power in the Florentine state.

Denys Hays, *The Italian Renaissance in its Historical Background* (Cambridge University Press). The best brief coverage of a formidably complex subject.

Christopher Hibbert, *The Rise and Fall of the Medici* (Penguin/Morrow). More anecdotal than Hale's book, this is a gripping read, chock full of heroic successes and squalid failures.

Christopher Hibbert, *Florence: The Biography of a City* (Viking/Norton). Yet another excellent Hibbert production, packed with illuminating anecdotes and fascinating illustrations – unlike most books on the city, it's as interesting on the political history as on the artistic achievements, and doesn't grind to a standstill with the fall of the Medici.

Mary Hollingsworth, *Patronage in Renaissance Italy* (John Murray in UK). The first comprehensive English-language study of the relationship between artist and patron in *quattrocento* Italy's city-states. A salutary corrective to the mythology of self-inspired Renaissance genius.

George Holmes, *Florence, Rome and the Origins of the Renaissance* (Oxford University Press). Magnificent portrait of the world of Dante and Giotto, with especially compelling sections on the impact of Saint Francis and the role of the papacy in the the political and cultural life of central Italy.

Mark Phillips, *The Memoir of Marco Parenti* (Heinemann/University of Princeton). The journal of a Florentine patrician, evoking the backroom politics and financial wheeler-dealing of fifteenth-century Florence.

SIENA, ASSISI AND PERUGIA

Edmund G. Gardner, *The Story of Siena*;
Margaret Symonds & L. Duff Gordon, *The Story of Perugia* and *The Story of Assisi* (published in Dent's "Medieval Towns" series in the 1920s – now staples of secondhand bookshops). Pocket encyclopedias with lots of anecdote and historical detail you won't find elsewhere.

Judith Hook, *Siena: A City and its History* (Hamish Hamilton, out of print – but available in Siena). This superb study of the city and its art concentrates on the medieval heyday but also takes the story through to the present, and includes a good analytical section on the Palio.

Daniel Waley, *Siena and the Sienese in the Thirteenth Century* (Cambridge University Press). Thorough socio-economic study.

CONTEMPORARY ITALY

Luigi Barzini, *The Italians* (Penguin/ Atheneum). Published in 1964, Barzini's study left no stone unturned in the quest to pinpoint what exactly makes Italians. Packed with historical excursions, much remains valid.

Peter Nichols, *Italia, Italia* (Little, Brown in US). Excellent survey of Italian life, written in the 1970s by the long-term *Times* correspondent.

Frederic Spotts & Theodor Wieser, *Italy: A Difficult Democracy: A Survey of Italian Politics* (Cambridge University Press). Authoritative and highly readable account of religion, social history and economics in postwar Italy.

William Ward, *Getting it Right in Italy* (Bloomsbury). A "manual" for living in and understanding contemporary Italy, Ward's array of statistics and stories make a totally compelling read.

ART AND ARCHITECTURE

Harold Acton, *The Villas of Tuscany* (Thames & Hudson in UK). Huge and lavishly illustrated tome, with good architectural and historical background on most of the major Tuscan villas – many of them the homes of Sir Harold and his chums.

Frederick Antal, *Florentine Painting and its Social Background* (Harvard University Press). Very authoritative – and often very dull – study of patronage in early Renaissance Florence.

Charles Avery, *Florentine Renaissance Sculpture* (John Murray). Serviceable introduction to the milieu of Donatello and Michelangelo.

Michael Baxandall, *Painting and Experience in Fifteenth-Century Italy* (Oxford University Press). Invaluable analysis, concentrating on the way in which the art of the period would have been perceived at the time.

Keith Christiansen, *Painting in Renaissance Siena* (Abrams/Metropolitan Museum). Definitive study of the city's art.

Vincent Cronin, *The Florentine Renaissance* and *The Flowering of the Renaissance* (both Pimlico in UK). Concise and gripping narrative of Italian art's golden years – the first volume covers the fifteenth century, the second switches the focus to sixteenth-century Rome and Venice.

J.R. Hale (ed.), *Concise Encyclopaedia of the Italian Renaissance* (Thames & Hudson in UK). Exemplary reference book, many of whose summaries are as informative as essays twice their length; covers individual artists, movements, cities, philosophical concepts, the lot.

Frederick Hartt, *History of Italian Renaissance Art* (Thames & Hudson/Abrams). If one book on this vast subject can be said to be indispensable, this is it. The price might seem daunting, but in view of its comprehensiveness and the range of its illustrations, it's actually a bargain.

Michael Levey, *Early Renaissance* (Penguin). Precise and fluently written account, and well illustrated; probably the best introduction to the subject. Levey's *High Renaissance* (Penguin) continues the story in the same style.

Anthony McIntyre, *Medieval Tuscany and Umbria* (Viking/Chronicle). Excellent survey of the architecture of the period, ranging from vernacular buildings to the great cathedrals.

Anna Maria Massinelli and Filippo Tuena, *Treasures of the Medici* (Thames & Hudson/ Vendome). Illustrated inventory of the Medici family's collection of jewellery, vases and other *objets d'art*, published to celebrate the five-hundredth anniversary of the death of Lorenzo il Magnifico, perhaps the clan's most compulsive collector. Not the first book to buy for your Florentine library, but definitive in its field.

Peter Murray, *The Architecture of the Italian Renaissance* (Thames & Hudson/Schocken).

Begins with Romanesque buildings and finishes with Palladio – useful both as a gazetteer of the main monuments and as a synopsis of the underlying concepts.

John Shearman, *Mannerism* (Penguin). The self-conscious art of sixteenth-century Mannerism is one of the most complex topics of Renaissance studies; Shearman's brief discussion analyses the main currents, yet never oversimplifies nor becomes pedantic.

Giorgio Vasari, *Lives of the Artists* (Penguin, 2 vols). Abridgement of the sixteenth-century artist's classic work on his predecessors and contemporaries. Includes essays on Giotto, Brunelleschi, Leonardo and Michelangelo. The first real work of art history, and still among the most penetrating books you can read on Italian Renaissance art.

INDIVIDUAL ARTISTS

The Complete Paintings series: Botticelli, Leonardo da Vinci, Piero della Francesca (Penguin). Paperback picture books, reproducing every painting in black and white, plus several colour plates. Also gives detailed analysis of dates, authenticity and a host of other art-historical issues.

James A. Ackerman, *The Architecture of Michelangelo* (Penguin/Univ of Chicago). If you come out of the Sagrestia Nuova in Florence wondering why people make such a fuss about Michelangelo's buildings, Ackerman's book will make you see it with fresh eyes.

Umberto Baldini and Ornella Casazza, *The Brancacci Chapel* (Thames & Hudson/Abrams). Written by the chief restorers of the Brancacci cycle of frescoes by Masaccio, Masolino and Filippino Lippi, this luscious book is illustrated with magnificent life-size reproductions of the freshly cleaned masterpieces. One to request for your birthday.

Bonnie Bennett and David Wilkins, *Donatello* (Phaidon/Moyer Bell). Worthy homage to one of the most influential figures in the history of western art.

Kenneth Clark, *Leonardo da Vinci* (Penguin). Rather old-fashioned in its reverential connoisseurship, but still highly recommended.

Kenneth Clark, *Piero della Francesca* (Phaidon, out of print). First full-length study of the painter in English and still a standard reference, though superseded by more recent scholarship.

Bruce Cole, *Giotto and Florentine Painting 1280–1375* (Harper Row/HarperCollins. Excellent introduction to the art of Giotto and his immediate successors.

Carlo Ginzburg, *The Enigma of Piero* (Verso). Art history as detective story, on a quest to decipher Piero's *Baptism*, the Arezzo cycle and the *Flagellation*.

Ludwig Goldscheider, *Michelangelo: Paintings, Sculpture, Architecture* (Phaidon, out of print). Virtually all monochrome reproductions, but a good pictorial survey of Michelangelo's output, covering everything except the drawings.

William Hood, *Fra Angelico at San Marco* (Yale University Press). Maintaining this imprint's reputation for elegantly produced, scholarly yet accessible art books, Hood's socio-aesthetic study of the panel paintings and frescoes of Fra' Angelico is unsurpassed in its scope. A book to read after you've made your first acquaintance with the pictures.

Marilyn Aronberg Lavin, *Piero della Francesca* (Thames & Hudson/Abrams). Despite looking like a book for browsing, the commentaries on the paintings are immensely informative and astute. The best English-language introduction to this most elusive and demanding of artists.

John Pope-Hennessy, *The Piero della Francesca Trail* (Thames & Hudson). This is basically a brief chronological survey of the artist's career, serviceable as a beginner's guide but nowhere near as stimulating as the Lavin book (see above) and its patrician tone gets a bit wearing.

John White, *Duccio* (Thames & Hudson in UK). The only study of the Sienese master available in English, concentrating on his art in the context of medieval workshop practices.

LITERATURE

Dante Alighieri, *The Divine Comedy* (Oxford University Press, 3 vols). No work in any other language bears comparison with Dante's poetic exegesis of the moral scheme of God's creation – in late medieval Italy it was venerated both as a book of almost scriptural authority and as the ultimate refinement of the vernacular Tuscan language. Numerous translations have been attempted – the Oxford University Press edition is clear, and has the original text facing the English version. One of the better translations, Laurence Binyon's, is printed in full in the *Portable Dante* (Penguin).

Ludovico Ariosto, *Orlando Furioso* (Penguin, 2 vols). Italy's chivalric epic, set in Charlemagne's Europe; has its exciting moments, but most readers would be grateful for a rather more abridged version.

Giovanni Boccaccio, *The Decameron* (Penguin). Set in the plague-racked Florence of 1348, Boccaccio's assembly of one hundred short stories is a fascinating social record as well as a constantly diverting and often smutty comedy.

Benvenuto Cellini, *Autobiography* (Penguin). Shamelessly egocentric record of the travails and triumphs of the sculptor and goldsmith's career; one of the freshest literary productions of its time.

Niccolo Machiavelli, *The Prince* (Penguin). A treatise on statecraft which actually did less to form the political thought of Italy than it did to form foreigners' perceptions of the country; yet there was far more to Machiavelli than the *realpolitik* of *The Prince*, as is shown by the selection of writings included in Penguin's anthology *The Portable Machiavelli*.

Petrarch (Francesco Petrarca), *Selections from the Canzoniere* (Oxford University Press). Often described as the first modern poet, by virtue of his preoccupation with worldly fame and secular love, Petrarch wrote some of the Italian language's greatest lyrics. This slim selection at least hints at what is lost in translation.

Leonardo da Vinci, *Notebooks* (Oxford University Press). Miscellany of speculation and observation from the universal genius of Renaissance Italy; essential to any understanding of the man.

TUSCANY AND UMBRIA IN ENGLISH FICTION

Michael Dibdin, *Rat King* (Faber/Bantam). Crime time in Perugia.

Timothy Holme, *The Assisi Murders* (Futura/Walker). Dark doings in Umbria.

George Eliot, *Romola* (Penguin). Ponderous tale of fifteenth-century Florence; researched to the hilt, but will probably remain the great unread Eliot novel.

E.M. Forster, *Where Angels Fear to Tread* and *Room with a View* (Penguin/Vintage). The settings are, respectively, San Gimignano and Florence, the milieu uptight Edwardian English society in Forster's two perfectly formed Italian novels.

Magdalen Nabb, *Death in Springtime*, *Death in Autumn*, and many other titles (Collins in UK). Florence is the locale for many of Nabb's brilliant thrillers, based on a good knowledge of the city's low life . . . and the Sardinian shepherds who dabble in a spot of kidnapping in the hills.

Michael Ondaatje, The English Patient (Picador/Knopf). At the close of World War II, a badly burned English aviator sees out his days in a wrecked Tuscan villa, attended by a cast of characters who come from widely differing backgrounds yet all think and speak in high-flown lyrical language. Some find Ondaatje's prose hypnotic, others think this is one of the most portentous and overpraised novels of recent years.

FLORA AND FAUNA

Heinzel, Fitter & Parslow, *The Birds of Britain and Europe* (Collins in UK). Best-known general guide, with plentiful maps and illustrations.

Higgins & Riley, *Field Guide to the Butterflies of Britain and Europe* (Collins in UK). Amply illustrated and detailed handbook.

Oleg Polunin & Antony Huxley, *Flowers of the Mediterranean* (Hogarth Press). Excellent guide, with colour pictures, line drawings and concise reference list as aids to identification.

Thomas Schauer, *Field Guide to the Wild Flowers of Britain and Europe* (Collins in UK). Comprehensive handbook with good drawings and detailed descriptions.

Christopher Grey Wilson & Marjorie Blamey, *Alpine Flowers of Britain and Europe* (Collins in UK). Full account of mountain flora, particularly useful as a handbook for the Monti Sibillini, Orecchiella and Alpi Apuane.

HIKING GUIDES

Stefano Ardito, *A Piedi in Umbria* (Edizione Iter). In the same series as the above titles, written by the doyen of Italian backpackers.

Antonio Arrighi and Roberto Pratesi, *A Piedi in Toscana* (Edizione Iter, 2 vols). Useful route guides for walkers, with basic maps. Widely available in Italy.

WINE AND FOOD

Burton Anderson, *Vino* (Papermac/Little, Brown). The definitive book on Italian wines, detailing production methods, grape varieties, climates and geology, and written in a light-hearted and readable style.

Burton Anderson, *The Pocket Guide to Italian Wines* (Mitchell Beazley/Simon & Schuster. Excellent handbook for selecting rarer or vintage wines on the spot.

Burton Anderson and others, *Chianti* (Edizioni Grafica Comense). Comprehensive handbook to the wines, producers, and restaurants of the region.

Leslie Forbes, *A Table in Tuscany* (Penguin/Chronicle). Regional recipes presented in the format of a facsimile manuscript, illustrated with colourful drawings.

Marcella Hazan, *Classic Italian Cookbook* (Papermac/Ballantine). Marcella features a fair number of Tuscan recipes and issues the kind of instructions that inspire total confidence.

Pino Luongo, *A Tuscan in the Kitchen* (Headline/Clarkson Potter). Serious recipes.

Elizabeth Romer, *The Tuscan Year: Life and Food in an Italian Valley* (Weidenfeld/North Point). Mix of recipes and background on countryside traditions.

Janet Ross and Michael Waterfield, *Leaves from our Tuscan Kitchen* (Penguin in UK). Classic vegetarian recipes, first published in 1899.

LANGUAGE

The ability to speak English confers prestige in Italy, and there's often no shortage of people willing to show off their knowledge, particularly in the main cities and resorts. However, in more remote areas you may find no one speaks English at all.

PRONUNCIATION

Wherever you are, it's a good idea to master at least a little Italian, a task made easier by the fact that your halting efforts will often be rewarded by smiles and genuine surprise. In any case, it's one of the easiest European languages to learn, especially if you already have a smattering of French or Spanish, both of which are extremely similar grammatically.

Easiest of all is the **pronunciation**, since every word is spoken exactly as it's written, and usually enunciated with exaggerated, open-mouthed clarity. The only difficulties you're likely to encounter are the few **consonants** that are different from English:

c before e or i is pronounced as in **ch**urch, while **ch** before the same vowel is hard, as in **c**at.

sci or **sce** are pronouced as in **sh**eet and **sh**elter respectively. The same goes with **g** – soft before e or i, as in **g**eranium; hard when followed by h, as in **g**arlic.

gn has the ni sound of our on**i**on.

gl in Italian is softened to something like li in English, as in stal**li**on.

h is not aspirated, as in **h**onour.

When **speaking** to strangers, the third person is the polite form (ie *Lei* instead of *Tu* for "you"); using the second person is a mark of disrespect or stupidity. It's also worth remembering that Italians don't use "please" and "thank you" half as much as we do: it's all implied in the tone, though if you're in any doubt, err on the polite side.

All Italian words are **stressed** on the penultimate syllable unless an **accent** (´ or `) denotes otherwise, although accents are often left out in practice. Note that the ending -*ia* or -*ie* counts as two syllables, hence *trattoria* is stressed on the *i*. Generally, in the text we've put accents in whenever it isn't immediately obvious how a word should be pronounced – though you shouldn't assume that this is how you'll see the words written in Italian. For example, in *Maríttima*, the accent is on the first i, but on Italian maps it's often written Marittima.

ITALIAN WORDS AND PHRASES

NUMBERS

1	uno	9	nove	17	diciassette	50	cinquanta	200	duecento
2	due	10	dieci	18	diciotto	60	sessanta	500	cinquecento
3	tre	11	undici	19	diciannove	70	settanta	1000	mille
4	quattro	12	dodici	20	venti	80	ottanta	5000	cinquemila
5	cinque	13	tredici	21	ventuno	90	novanta	10,000	diecimila
6	sei	14	quattordici	22	ventidue	100	cento	50,000	cinquanta mila
7	sette	15	quindici	30	trenta	101	centuno		
8	otto	16	sedici	40	quaranta	110	centodieci		

BASICS

Good morning	Buon giorno	Tomorrow	Domani
Good afternoon/ evening	Buona sera	Day after tomorrow	Dopodomani
		Yesterday	Ieri
Good night	Buona notte	Now	Adesso
Hello/goodbye	Ciao (informal; to strangers use phrases above)	Later	Più tardi
		Wait a minute!	Aspetta!
Goodbye	Arrivederci (formal)	In the morning	di mattina
Yes	Si	In the afternoon	nel pomeriggio
No	No	In the evening	di sera
Please	Per favore	Here (there)	Qui/La
Thank you (very much)	Grázie (molte/mille grazie)	Good/bad	Buono/Cattivo
		Big/small	Grande/Píccolo
You're welcome	Prego	Cheap/expensive	Económico/Caro
Alright/that's OK	Va bene	Early/late	Presto/Ritardo
How are you?	Come stai/sta? (informal/formal)	Hot/cold	Caldo/Freddo
		Near/far	Vicino/Lontano
I'm fine	Bene	Quickly/slowly	Velocemente/ Lentamente
Do you speak English?	Parla inglese?		
I don't understand	Non ho capito	Slowly/quietly	Piano
I don't know	Non lo so	With/without	Con/Senza
Excuse me	Mi scusi/Prego	More/less	Più/Meno
Excuse me (in a crowd)	Permesso	Enough, no more	Basta
I'm sorry	Mi dispiace	Mr . . .	Signor . . .
I'm here on holiday	Sono qui in vacanza	Mrs . . .	Signora . . .
I'm English/Scottish/ Welsh/Irish	Sono inglese/scozzese/ gallese/irlandese	Miss . . .	Signorina . . .
I live in . . .	Abito a . . .	(il Signor, la Signora, la Signorina when speaking about someone else)	
Today	Oggi		

DRIVING

Left/right	Sinistro/Destro	No entry	Senso vietato
Go straight ahead	Sempre diritto	Slow down	Rallentare
Turn to the right/left	Gira a destra/sinistra	Road closed/up	Strada chiusa/guasta
Parking	Parcheggio	No through road	Vietato il transito
No parking	Divieto di sosta/Sosta vietata	No overtaking	Vietato il sorpasso
		Crossroads	Incrocio
One-way street	Senso único	Speed limit	Limite di Velocità

SOME SIGNS

Entrance/exit	Entrata/Uscita	To let	Affítasi
Free entrance	Ingresso líbero	Platform	Binario
Gentlemen/ladies	Signori/Signore	Cash desk	Cassa
WC	Gabinetto	Go/walk	Avanti
Vacant/engaged	Libero/Occupato	Stop/halt	Alt
Open/closed	Aperto/Chiuso	Customs	Dogana
Arrivals/departures	Arrivi/Partenze	Do not touch	Non toccare
Closed for restoration	Chiuso per restauro	Danger	Perícolo
Closed for holidays	Chiuso per ferie	Beware	Attenzione
Pull/push	Tirare/Spingere	First aid	Pronto soccorso
Out of order	Guasto	Ring the bell	Suonare il campanello
Drinking water	Acqua potabile	No smoking	Vietato fumare

ACCOMMODATION

Hotel	*Albergo*
Is there a hotel nearby?	*C'è un albergo qui vicino?*
Do you have a room . . .	*Ha una camera . . .*
for one/two/three people	*per una/due/tre person(a/e)*
for one/two/three nights	*per una/due/tre nott(e/i)*
for one/two weeks	*per una/due settiman(a/e)*
with a double bed	*con un letto matrimoniale*
with a shower/bath	*con una doccia/un bagno*
with a balcony	*con una terrazza*
hot/cold water	*acqua calda/freddo*
How much is it?	*Quanto costa?*
It's expensive	*È caro*
Is breakfast included?	*È compresa la prima colazione?*
Do you have anything cheaper?	*Ha niente che costa di meno?*
Full/half board	*Pensione completa/ mezza pensione*
Can I see the room?	*Posso vedere la camera?*
I'll take it	*La prendo*
I'd like to book a room	*Vorrei prenotare una camera*
I have a booking	*Ho una prenotazione*
Can we camp here?	*Possiamo fare il campeggio qui?*
Is there a campsite nearby?	*C'è un camping qui vicino?*
Tent	*Tenda*
Cabin	*Cabina*
Youth hostel	*Ostello per la gioventù*

QUESTIONS AND DIRECTIONS

Where? (where is/are . . .?)	*Dove? (Dov'è/Dove sono)*
When?	*Quando?*
What? (what is it?)	*Cosa? (Cos'è?)*
How much/many?	*Quanto/Quanti?*
Why?	*Perchè?*
It is/there is (is it/is there . . .?)	*È/C'è (È/C'è . . .?)*
What time is it?	*Che ora è/Che ore sono?*
How do I get to . . .?	*Come arrivo a . . .?*
How far is it to . . .?	*Cuant'è lontano a . . .?*
Can you give me a lift to . . .?	*Mi può dare un passaggio a . . .?*
Can you tell me when to get off?	*Mi può dire scendere alla fermata giusta?*
What time does it open?	*A che ora apre?*
What time does it close?	*A che ora chiude?*
How much does it cost (. . . do they cost?)	*Quanto costa? (Quanto costano?)*
What's it called in Italian?	*Comè si chiama in italiano?*

TRAVELLING

English	Italian	English	Italian
Aeroplane	*Aeroplano*	Bicycle	*Bicicletta*
Bus	*Autobus/pullman*	Ferry	*Traghetto*
Train	*Treno*	Ship	*Nave*
Car	*Macchina*	Hydrofoil	*Aliscafo*
Taxi	*Taxi*	Hitchhiking	*Autostop*
On foot	*A piedi*		
Bus station	*Autostazione*		
Railway station	*Stazione ferroviaria*		
Ferry terminal	*Stazione maríttima*		
Port	*Porto*		

A ticket to . . .	*Un biglietto a . . .*
One-way/return	*Solo andata/andata e ritorno*
Can I book a seat?	*Posso prenotare un posto?*
What time does it leave?	*A che ora parte?*
When is the next bus/train/ferry to . . .?	*Quando parte il prossimo pullman/treno/traghetto per . . .?*
Do I have to change?	*Devo cambiare?*
Where does it leave from?	*Da dove parte?*
What platform does it leave from?	*Da quale binario parte?*
How many kilometres is it?	*Quanti chilometri sono?*
How long does it take?	*Quanto ci vuole?*
What number bus is it to . . .?	*Que número di autobus per . . .?*
Where's the road to . . .?	*Dov'è la strada a . . .?*
Next stop please	*La pro'ssima fermata, per favore*

GLOSSARY OF ARTISTIC AND ARCHITECTURAL TERMS

AMBO A kind of simple pulpit, popular in Italian medieval churches.

ANFITEATRO Amphitheatre.

APSE Semicircular recess at the altar, usually eastern, end of a church.

ARCHITRAVE The lowest part of the entablature.

ATRIUM Inner courtyard.

BADÌA Abbey.

BALDACCHINO A canopy on columns, usually placed over the altar in a church.

BALUARDO Bastion.

BASILICA Originally a Roman administrative building, adapted for early churches; distinguished by lack of transepts.

BATTISTERO Baptistery.

BELVEDERE A terrace or lookout point.

BORGO Medieval suburb or hamlet.

CALDARIUM The steam room of a Roman bath.

CAMPANILE Bell tower, sometimes detached, usually of a church.

CAMPO Square.

CAMPOSANTO Cemetery.

CANTORIA Choir loft.

CAPITAL Top of a column.

CAPPELLA Chapel.

CASTELLO Castle.

CENACOLO Last Supper.

CHANCEL Part of a church containing the altar.

CHIESA Church.

CHIOSTRO Cloister.

CIBORIUM Another word for baldacchino.

COLLEGIATA Church just below the hierarchy of a cathedral.

CONTRADA Ancient quarter of a town.

CORTILE Galleried courtyard or cloister.

CORNICE The top section of a classical facade.

COSMATI WORK Decorative mosaic work on marble, usually highly coloured, found in early Christian Italian churches, especially in Rome. Derives from the name Cosma, a common name among families of marble workers at the time.

CRYPT Burial place in a church, usually under the choir.

CUPOLA Dome.

CYCLOPEAN WALLS Fortifications built of huge, rough stone blocks.

DECUMANUS MAXIMUS The main street of a Roman town. The second cross-street was known as the *Decumanus Inferiore*.

DIPTYCH Twin-panelled painting.

DUOMO/CATTEDRALE Cathedral.

ENTABLATURE The section above the capital on a classical building, below the cornice.

EX-VOTO Artefact designed in thanksgiving to a saint. The adjective is *ex-votive*.

FONTE Fountainhouse.

FORTEZZA Fortress.

FRESCO Wall-painting technique in which the artist applies paint to wet plaster for a more permanent finish.

GONFALONI Painted flags or standards.

INTARSIA Inlaid stone or wood.

LOGGIA Roofed gallery or balcony.

LUNETTE Semicircular space in vault or ceiling.

MAESTÀ Madonna and Child enthroned.

MATRONEUM Women's gallery in early church.

MUNICIPIO Town hall.

NARTHEX Vestibule of a church.

NAVE Central space in a church, usually flanked by aisles.

PALAZZO Palace, mansion, or block of flats.

PALAZZO DEL PODESTÀ Magistrate's palace.

PALAZZO DEL POPOLO, PALAZZO PUBBLICO, PALAZZO COMUNALE Town hall.

PANTOCRATOR An image of Christ, usually portrayed in the act of blessing.

PIANO NOBILE Main floor of a palace, usually the first.

PIETÀ Image of the Virgin mourning the dead Christ.

PIETRA DURE Hard or semiprecious stones used for decorative inlay.

PIEVE Parish church.

PINACOTECA Picture gallery.

POLYPTYCH Painting on several joined panels.

PORTA Gate.

PORTICO Covered entrance to a building.

PREDELLA Small panel below the main scenes of an altarpiece.

PUTTI Cherubs.

RELIQUARY Receptacle for a saint's relics, usually bones. Often highly decorated.

ROCCA Castle.

SALA DEI PRIORI Council chamber.

SANTUARIO Sanctuary or chancel.

SGRAFFITO Decorative technique whereby a layer of plaster is scratched to form a pattern.

SINOPIA Sketch for a fresco, applied to the wall.

STUCCO Plaster made from water, lime, sand and powdered marble, used for decorative work.

TEATRO Theatre

TEMPIO Temple.

THERMAE Baths, usually elaborate buildings in Roman villas.

TONDO Round painting or relief.

TORRE Tower.

TROMPE L'OEIL Work of art that deceives the viewer by tricks of perspective.

TRIPTYCH Painting on three joined panels.

GLOSSARY OF ITALIAN WORDS AND ACRONYMS

ITALIAN WORDS

ALISCAFO Hydrofoil.
ALTO Upper.
AUTSTAZIONE Bus station.
AUTOSTRADA Motorway.
BAGNO Bath or spa.
BASSO (or SCALO) Lower.
BIBLIOTECA Library.
CENTRO Centre.
CENTRO STORICO Historic centre.
COMUNE An administrative area; also the local council or town hall.
CORSO Avenue or boulevard.
ENTRATA Entrance.
FESTA Festival, holiday.
FIUME River.
GIARDINO Garden; GIARDINO BOTANICO (or ORTO BOTANICO), botanical garden.
GOLFO Gulf.
LAGO Lake.
LUNGOMARE Seafront road or promenade.
MARE Sea.
MERCATO Market.
MUSEO Museum.
OSPEDALE Hospital.
PAESE Place, area, or village.
PALIO Horse race (most famously in Siena).
PARCO Park.
PASSEGGIATA The customary early evening walk – sometimes applied to a promenade.

PIANO Plain.
PIAZZA Square.
QUESTURA Main police station.
SENSO UNICO One-way street.
SOTTOPASSAGIO Subway.
SPIAGGIA Beach.
STAZIONE Station.
STRADA Road.
TRAGHETTO Ferry.
USCITA Exit.
VIA Road (always used with name, eg Via Roma).

ACRONYMS

AAST Azienda Autonoma di Soggiorno e Turismo.
ACI Automobile Club d'Italia.
APT Azienda Provinciale di Turismo.
CAI Club Alpino Italiano.
DC Democrazia Cristiana; the Christian Democrat party.
EPT Ente Provinciale di Turismo (provincial tourist office); see also *APT* and *AAST*.
FS Italian State Railways.
IVA Imposta Valore Aggiunto (VAT).
MSI Movimento Sociale Italiano; the Italian Fascist party.
PDI Partito Democratica della Sinistra; new name for the Italian communist party.
PSI Partito Socialista Italiano; the Italian Socialist party.
RAI The Italian state TV and radio network.
SIP Italian state telephone company.
SS Strada Statale; equivalent to a British "A" road, eg SS18.
TCI Touring Club d'Italia; map and guide publishers.

INDEX

HELP US UPDATE

We've gone to a lot of effort to ensure that this second edition of *The Rough Guide to Tuscany and Umbria* is up-to-date and accurate. However, Italian information changes frequently: works are closed for restoration for years then suddenly emerge in glory, museums shift round their displays and opening hours, restaurants and hotels fluctuate in their prices and standards. If you feel there are places we've under-praised or overrated, omitted or ought to omit, please let us know. All suggestions, comments or corrections are much appreciated and we'll send a copy of the next edition (or any other *Rough Guide* if you prefer) for the best letters.

Please mark letters "Rough Guide Tuscany and Umbria update" and send them to:
Rough Guides, 1 Mercer Street, London WC2H 9QJ
or Rough Guides, 375 Hudson Street, Fourth Floor, New York, NY10014.

THANKS

Thanks to all the readers who sent us their comments on and revisions to the first edition of this guide: Scott Ferguson, Ann Johnston, Dymphna Halpin, Claire Roberts, Steven C. Erwin, Andrew Morgan, Russell Edwards, K. Edwards, John Gill, Kevin Francis, Alan Stewart, Daniel Mack and Lorraine Ellis, T. Elliott, A. M. Young, R. Dunham, Chantal Ashwell, D. Piggott, E. Bin, Diana Grandi, Kathryn Graham, Caroline Boucher, Jo Rosenfelder, Geoffrey Sheridan, Sebastian Olden-Jørgensen, Roy Coad, Peter Crane, J. F. Peter, Richard Gregg, David Schofield, Susan M. Reid, Ellen Fox, Robin Stelfox, Seán MacCann, Ilana Karber, Simon Jordan, Abigail Kirby-Harris, Ann Maidman, Nicolette Berkley, Diana Lloyd, Mark Ellwood, Liz Miller, Monica Haughey, Ros Ward, Emile Bruls, Alice S. Kao, Mollie Bickerstaff, Shelley N. Nott, Chris Higgins, Julian M. Davies, Judith Stark, Martyn Wild, Sam Howison, Ian R. Godwin, Sarah White, Simon Gallagher and Sharon Alefounder, Christine Hughes, Myrtle Hirsh, the Reverend Canon B. R. Pearson, Catherine Lütken, Sam Davenport and Matthew Sheehan, Derek and Brenda Ashardt, Colin Greaves, Dave Giles, Dr Rosemary Martin, and Don Sante Felici.

DIRECT ORDERS IN THE UK

Title	ISBN	Price
Amsterdam	1858280869	£7.99
Andalucia	185828094X	£8.99
Australia	1858280354	£12.99
Barcelona & Catalunya	1858281067	£8.99
Berlin	1858280338	£8.99
Brazil	1858281024	£9.99
Brittany & Normandy	1858281261	£8.99
Bulgaria	1858280478	£8.99
California	1858280907	£9.99
Canada	185828130X	£10.99
Classical Music on CD	185828113X	£12.99
Corsica	1858280893	£8.99
Crete	1858281326	£8.99
Cyprus	185828032X	£8.99
Czech & Slovak Republics	185828029X	£8.99
Egypt	1858280753	£10.99
England	1858280788	£9.99
Europe	185828077X	£14.99
Florida	1858280109	£8.99
France	1858280508	£9.99
Germany	1858281288	£11.99
Greece	1858281318	£9.99
Greek Islands	1858281636	£8.99
Guatemala & Belize	1858280451	£9.99
Holland, Belgium & Luxembourg	1858280877	£9.99
Hong Kong & Macau	1858280664	£8.99
Hungary	1858281237	£8.99
India	1858281040	£13.99
Ireland	1858280958	£9.99
Italy	1858280311	£12.99
Kenya	1858280435	£9.99
London	1858291172	£8.99
Mediterranean Wildlife	0747100993	£7.95
Malaysia, Singapore & Brunei	1858281032	£9.99
Morocco	1858280400	£9.99
Nepal	185828046X	£8.99
New York	1858280583	£8.99
Nothing Ventured	0747102082	£7.99
Pacific Northwest	1858280923	£9.99
Paris	1858281253	£7.99
Poland	1858280346	£9.99
Portugal	1858280842	£9.99
Prague	185828015X	£7.99
Provence & the Côte d'Azur	1858280230	£8.99
Pyrenees	1858280931	£8.99
St Petersburg	1858281334	£8.99
San Francisco	1858280826	£8.99
Scandinavia	1858280397	£10.99
Scotland	1858280834	£8.99
Sicily	1858280370	£8.99
Spain	1858280818	£9.99
Thailand	1858280168	£8.99
Tunisia	1858280656	£8.99
Turkey	1858280885	£9.99
Tuscany & Umbria	1858280915	£8.99
USA	185828080X	£12.99
Venice	1858280362	£8.99
Wales	1858280966	£8.99
West Africa	1858280141	£12.99
More Women Travel	1858280982	£9.99
World Music	1858280176	£14.99
Zimbabwe & Botswana	1858280419	£10.99

Rough Guide Phrasebooks

Title	ISBN	Price
Czech	1858281482	£3.50
French	185828144X	£3.50
German	1858281466	£3.50
Greek	1858281458	£3.50
Italian	1858281431	£3.50
Spanish	1858281474	£3.50

Rough Guides are available from all good bookstores, but can be obtained directly in the UK* from Penguin by contacting:

Penguin Direct, Penguin Books Ltd, Bath Road, Harmondsworth, West Drayton, Middlesex UB7 0DA; or telephone our credit line on 0181-899 4036 (9am–5pm) and ask for Penguin Direct. Visa, Access and Amex accepted. Delivery will normally be within 14 working days. Penguin Direct ordering facilities are only available in the UK.

The availability and published prices quoted are correct at the time of going to press but are subject to alteration without prior notice.

* For USA and international orders, see separate price list

DIRECT ORDERS IN THE USA

Title	ISBN	Price
Amsterdam	1858280869	$13.59
Andalucia	185828094X	$14.95
Australia	1858280354	$18.95
Barcelona & Catalunya	1858281067	$17.99
Berlin	1858280338	$13.99
Brazil	1858281024	$15.95
Brittany & Normandy	1858281261	$14.95
Bulgaria	1858280478	$14.99
California	1858280907	$14.95
Canada	185828130X	$14.95
Classical Music on CD	185828113X	$19.95
Corsica	1858280893	$14.95
Crete	1858281326	$14.95
Cyprus	185828032X	$13.99
Czech & Slovak Republics	185828029X	$14.95
Egypt	1858280753	$17.95
England	1858280788	$16.95
Europe	185828077X	$18.95
Florida	1858280109	$14.95
France	1858281245	$16.95
Germany	1858281288	$17.95
Greece	1858281318	$16.95
Greek Islands	1858281636	$14.95
Guatemala & Belize	1858280451	$14.95
Holland, Belgium & Luxembourg	1858280877	$15.95
Hong Kong & Macau	1858280664	$13.95
Hungary	1858281237	$14.95
India	1858281040	$22.95
Ireland	1858280958	$16.95
Italy	1858280311	$17.95
Kenya	1858280435	$15.95
London	1858291172	$12.95
Mediterranean Wildlife	0747100993	$15.95
Malaysia, Singapore & Brunei	1858281032	$16.95
Morocco	1858280400	$16.95
Nepal	185828046X	$13.95
New York	1858280583	$13.95
Nothing Ventured	0747102082	$19.95
Pacific Northwest	1858280923	$14.95
Paris	1858281253	$12.95
Poland	1858280346	$16.95
Portugal	1858280842	$15.95
Prague	1858281229	$14.95
Provence & the Côte d'Azur	1858280230	$14.95
Pyrenees	1858280931	$15.95
St Petersburg	1858281334	$14.95
San Francisco	1858280826	$13.95
Scandinavia	1858280397	$16.99
Scotland	1858280834	$14.95
Sicily	1858280370	$14.99
Spain	1858280818	$16.95
Thailand	1858280168	$15.95
Tunisia	1858280656	$15.95
Turkey	1858280885	$16.95
Tuscany & Umbria	1858280915	$15.95
USA	185828080X	$18.95
Venice	1858280362	$13.99
Wales	1858280966	$14.95
West Africa	1858280141	$24.95
More Women Travel	1858280982	$14.95
World Music	1858280176	$19.95
Zimbabwe & Botswana	1858280419	$16.95

Rough Guide Phrasebooks

Title	ISBN	Price
Czech	1858281482	$5.00
French	185828144X	$5.00
German	1858281466	$5.00
Greek	1858281458	$5.00
Italian	1858281431	$5.00
Spanish	1858281474	$5.00

You are
A STUDENT

You **travel**
THE WORLD

You **want**
TO SAVE MONEY

Here's
how

The International Student Identity Card

Available at Student Travel Offices Worldwide.

Entitles you to discounts and special services worldwide.